2005 | WORLD DEVELOPMENT INDICATORS

D1397960

This volume is a product of the staff of the Development Data Group of the World Bank's Development Economics Vice Presidency, and the judgments herein do not necessarily reflect the views of the World Bank's Board of Executive Directors or the countries they represent.

The World Bank does not guarantee the accuracy of the data included in this publication and accepts no responsibility whatsoever for any consequence of their use. The boundaries, colors, denominations, and other information shown on any map in this volume do not imply on the part of the World Bank any judgment on the legal status of any territory or the endorsement or acceptance of such boundaries. This publication uses the Robinson projection for maps, which represents both area and shape reasonably well for most of the earth's surface. Nevertheless, some distortions of area, shape, distance, and direction remain.

Photo credits: Front cover, from top to bottom and left to right, Penny Tweddie/Getty Images, Photodisc, Photodisc, Fredrik Nauman/Panos Pictures; back cover, Steven Harris/World Bank; page xxvi, Edwin Huffman/World Bank; page 2, Julio Pantoja/World Bank; page 6, Ami Vitale/World Bank; page 8, Curt Carnemark/World Bank; page 10, Tran Thi Hoa/World Bank; pages 12, 14, 16, and 18, Curt Carnemark/World Bank.

If you have questions or comments about this product, please contact:

Development Data Center
The World Bank
1818 H Street NW, Room MC2-812, Washington, DC 20433, USA
Hotline: 800 590 1906 or 202 473 7824; fax 202 522 1498
Email: data@worldbank.org
Web site: www.worldbank.org or www.worldbank.org/data

ISBN 0-8213-6071-X

2005 | WORLD DEVELOPMENT INDICATORS

The World Bank

FOREWORD

The World Bank is committed to achieving the Millennium Development Goal of halving global poverty by 2015. As the international community measures its progress toward that goal, it must have solid and credible statistics that show where we are advancing and where we are falling behind. This year's *World Development Indicators* gives policymakers that set of statistics—as a tool it can use in the fight against global poverty.

Since 1978 these World Development Indicators have drawn the world's attention to the successes, failures, and continuing challenges of development. In 1997 *World Development Indicators* was launched in this new format, accompanied by a CD-ROM. It is now widely available on the World Wide Web. I am proud to have overseen this evolution and to have been able to reach out to so many people with timely and reliable information about our mutual effort to fight poverty in all its forms.

Much has changed in the past decade. Global output has increased by 25 percent since 1995, and developing countries are leading the way, growing by more than 35 percent. Global population has also increased, from 5.7 billion in 1995 to 6.3 billion in 2004, most of it in developing countries. Although population growth has been slowing, another 1 billion people will be added to the world's population by 2014. This is one of the great challenges ahead—expanding our economies and social systems to meet the needs of more than 7 billion people, efficiently and equitably.

Achieving all the Millennium Development Goals will require more than economic growth. Those goals are about meeting the most basic needs of people for education, health care, and clean air and water—and empowering people to make choices for themselves and their children. The statistics in *World Development Indicators* offer evidence of progress toward the Millennium Development Goals. Since 1990 infant mortality rates in low-income countries have fallen from 95 deaths per 1,000 to to 80—still too high, but evidence that further progress can be made. More people have access to water and sanitation services, especially in rural areas. And more girls are attending school, with more than 66 percent of them now completing primary school, up from 57 percent a decade ago.

But we must not be complacent. Progress in some places has been offset by setbacks in others. Inequality within countries is worsening. Disease, armed conflict, and natural disasters have also taken their toll. We know there will be many obstacles ahead. But we must not shrink from the challenge or look the other way. What has been accomplished is evidence of how much more can be accomplished, if we persevere.

James D. Wolfensohn
President
The World Bank Group

ACKNOWLEDGMENTS

This book and its companion volumes, *The Little Data Book* and *The Little Green Data Book,* are prepared by a team coordinated by M. H. Saeed Ordoubadi. Team members are Mehdi Akhlaghi, Augusto Clavijo, David Cieslikowski, Mahyar Eshragh-Tabary, Richard Fix, Amy Heyman, Masako Hiraga, Raymond Muhula, Murat Omur, Sulekha Patel, Juan Carlos Rodriguez, Eric Swanson, K. M. Vijayalakshmi, Vivienne Wang, and Estela Zamora, working closely with other teams in the Development Economics Vice Presidency's Development Data Group. The CD-ROM development team included Azita Amjadi, Ramgopal Erabelly, Saurabh Gupta, Reza Farivari, and William Prince. The work was carried out under the management of Shaida Badiee.

The choice of indicators and text content was shaped through close consultation with and substantial contributions from staff in the World Bank's five thematic networks—Environmentally and Socially Sustainable Development, Human Development, Poverty Reduction and Economic Management, Private Sector Development and Infrastructure—and staff of the International Finance Corporation and the Multilateral Investment Guarantee Agency. Most important, the team received substantial help, guidance, and data from external partners. For individual acknowledgments of contributions to the book's content, please see the *Credits* section. For a listing of our key partners, see the *Partners* section.

Communications Development Incorporated provided overall design direction, editing, and layout, led by Meta de Coquereaumont and Bruce Ross-Larson. The editing and production team consisted of Joseph Costello, Christopher Trott, Timothy Walker, and Elaine Wilson. Communications Development's London partner, Grundy & Northedge, provided art direction and design. Staff from External Affairs oversaw publication and dissemination of the book.

PREFACE

The annual publication of *World Development Indicators* is the culmination of a process that involves many people and many organizations, starting with national statistical offices and continuing to the international agencies that compile global databases. Some are highly specialized. Others have a broad mandate with large responsibilities. All need to work together to produce consistent and timely data. We are grateful to our many partners who help us bring this book to you.

Efforts to improve and expand the scope of national and international statistics are ongoing. This year's *World Development Indicators* reports on initiatives to improve the measurement of gender statistics, urban and housing indicators, business conditions and the investment climate, and migration and remittance flows. Agreement has been reached on proceeding with revisions to the 1993 System of National Accounts. And the latest round of data collection for the International Comparison Program was launched in February 2005. This will be the biggest global effort ever undertaken to collect comparable price data from countries. New estimates of purchasing power parities will appear in 2006.

While these initiatives will lead to improvements in specific data sets, it is widely recognized that sustainable improvement in development statistics requires continuing investment in national and international statistical systems. The Marrakech Action Plan for Statistics, agreed last year at the Second Roundtable on Managing for Results, sets out an ambitious agenda for the development of statistics, based on investment in national strategies, and for better coordination of activities at the international level.

Good progress is being made in implementing the Marrakech plan. More than 40 developing countries are now using a strategic development plan for developing their statistical system, and more than 30 more have proposals to do so. PARIS21, the international partnership in statistics for development, has produced knowledge resources to help countries develop better statistical systems. The World Bank has implemented a multicountry lending program, STATCAP, to provide financing for statistical capacity building. International agencies have formed the International Household Survey Network to provide wide access to information from household surveys conducted by countries and agencies. And because benchmark demographic data collected through censuses is so important, the United Nations has convened an interagency group to prepare for the 2010 round of censuses.

Improvements in global statistics require the combined efforts of many partners. A good example is the work of the UN's interagency and expert group on the Millennium Development Goals. By bringing together the many agencies responsible for compiling indicators used to monitor progress toward the Goals, the group has created an important forum for identifying statistical gaps, harmonizing work, and disseminating reliable indicators. The results of their activities are visible in the report on the Goals in the *World view* section and throughout the rest of this book.

Of course much work remains to be done. As always, we invite your comments and suggestions. You can find out more about our work at www.worldbank.org/data. Or you can send email to data@worldbank.org.

Shaida Badiee, Director
Development Data Group

TABLE OF CONTENTS

FRONT

 ## 1. WORLD VIEW

2. PEOPLE

3. ENVIRONMENT

TABLE OF CONTENTS

 ## 4. ECONOMY

 ## 5. STATES AND MARKETS

6. GLOBAL LINKS

BACK

PARTNERS

Defining, gathering, and disseminating international statistics is a collective effort of many people and organizations. The indicators presented in World Development Indicators are the fruit of decades of work at many levels, from the field workers who administer censuses and household surveys to the committees and working parties of the national and international statistical agencies that develop the nomenclature, classifications, and standards fundamental to an international statistical system. Nongovernmental organizations and the private sector have also made important contributions, both in gathering primary data and in organizing and publishing their results. And academic researchers have played a crucial role in developing statistical methods and carrying on a continuing dialogue about the quality and interpretation of statistical indicators. All these contributors have a strong belief that available, accurate data will improve the quality of public and private decisionmaking.

The organizations listed here have made World Development Indicators possible by sharing their data and their expertise with us. More important, their collaboration contributes to the World Bank's efforts, and to those of many others, to improve the quality of life of the world's people. We acknowledge our debt and gratitude to all who have helped to build a base of comprehensive, quantitative information about the world and its people.

For easy reference, this section includes Web addresses for organizations that maintain Web sites. The addresses shown were active on March 1, 2005. Information about the World Bank is also provided.

International and government agencies

Carbon Dioxide Information Analysis Center

The Carbon Dioxide Information Analysis Center (CDIAC) is the primary global climate change data and information analysis center of the U.S. Department of Energy. The CDIAC's scope includes anything that would potentially be of value to those concerned with the greenhouse effect and global climate change, including concentrations of carbon dioxide and other radiatively active gases in the atmosphere; the role of the terrestrial biosphere and the oceans in the biogeochemical cycles of greenhouse gases; emissions of carbon dioxide to the atmosphere; long-term climate trends; the effects of elevated carbon dioxide on vegetation; and the vulnerability of coastal areas to rising sea levels.

For information, contact the CDIAC, Oak Ridge National Laboratory, PO Box 2008, Oak Ridge, TN 37831-6335, USA; telephone: 865 574 0390; fax: 865 574 2232; email: cdiac@ornl.gov; Web site: http://cdiac.esd.ornl.gov.

Deutsche Gesellschaft für Technische Zusammenarbeit

The Deutsche Gesellschaft für Technische Zusammenarbeit (GTZ) GmbH is a German government-owned corporation for international cooperation with worldwide operations. GTZ's aim is to positively shape political, economic, ecological, and social development in partner countries, thereby improving people's living conditions and prospects.

The organization has more than 10,000 employees in some 130 countries of Africa, Asia, Latin America, and Eastern Europe.

For publications, contact Deutsche Gesellschaft für Technische Zusammenarbeit (GTZ) GmbH Corporate Communications, Dag-Hammarskjöld-Weg 1-5, 65760 Eschborn, Germany; telephone: 49 0 6196 79 1174; fax: 49 0 6196 79 6196; email: presse@gtz.de; Web site: www.gtz.de/.

Food and Agriculture Organization

The Food and Agriculture Organization (FAO), a specialized agency of the United Nations, was founded in October 1945 with a mandate to raise nutrition levels and living standards, to increase agricultural productivity, and to better the condition of rural populations. The organization provides direct development assistance; collects, analyzes, and disseminates information; offers policy and planning advice to governments; and serves as an international forum for debate on food and agricultural issues.

Statistical publications of the FAO include the *Production Yearbook, Trade Yearbook,* and *Fertilizer Yearbook.* The FAO makes much of its data available online through its FAOSTAT and AQUASTAT systems.

FAO publications can be ordered from national sales agents or directly from the FAO Sales and Marketing Group, Viale delle Terme di Caracalla, 00100 Rome, Italy; telephone: 39 06 5705 5727; fax: 39 06 5705 3360; email: Publications-sales@fao.org; Web site: www.fao.org/.

International Civil Aviation Organization

The International Civil Aviation Organization (ICAO), a specialized agency of the United Nations, was founded on December 7, 1944. It is responsible for establishing international standards and recommended practices and procedures for the technical, economic, and legal aspects of international civil aviation operations. ICAO's strategic objectives include enhancing global aviation safety and security and the efficiency of aviation operations, minimizing the adverse effect of global civil aviation on the environment, maintaining the continuity of aviation operations, and strengthening laws governing international civil aviation.

To obtain ICAO publications, contact the ICAO, Document Sales Unit, 999 University Street, Montreal, Quebec H3C 5H7, Canada; telephone: 514 954 8219; fax: 514 954 6077; email: sales@icao.int; Web site: www.icao.int/.

International Labour Organization

The International Labour Organization (ILO), a specialized agency of the United Nations, seeks the promotion of social justice and internationally recognized human and labor rights. Founded in 1919, it is the only surviving major creation of the Treaty of Versailles, which brought the League of Nations into being. It became the first specialized agency of the United Nations in 1946. Unique within the United Nations system, the ILO's tripartite structure has workers and employers participating as equal partners with governments in the work of its governing organs.

As part of its mandate, the ILO maintains an extensive statistical publication program. The *Yearbook of Labour Statistics* is its most comprehensive collection of labor force data.

Publications can be ordered from sales agents and major booksellers throughout the world and ILO offices in many countries or from ILO Publications, 4 route des Morillons, CH-1211 Geneva 22, Switzerland; telephone: 41 22 799 6111; fax: 41 22 798 8685; email: publns@ilo.org; Web site: www.ilo.org/.

International Monetary Fund

The International Monetary Fund (IMF) was established at a conference in Bretton Woods, New Hampshire, United States, on July 1–22, 1944. (The conference also established the World Bank.) The IMF came into official existence on December 27, 1945, and commenced financial operations on March 1, 1947. It currently has 184 member countries.

The statutory purposes of the IMF are to promote international monetary cooperation, facilitate the expansion and balanced growth of international trade, promote exchange rate stability, help to establish a multilateral payments system, make the general resources of the IMF temporarily available to its members under adequate safeguards, and shorten the duration and lessen the degree of disequilibrium in the international balance of payments of members.

The IMF maintains an extensive program for developing and compiling international statistics and is responsible for collecting and reporting statistics on international financial transactions and the balance of payments. In April 1996 it undertook an important initiative to improve the quality of international statistics, establishing the Special Data Dissemination Standard (SDDS) to guide members that have, or seek, access to international capital markets in providing economic and financial data to the public. In 1997 the IMF established the General Data Dissemination System (GDDS) to guide countries in providing the public with comprehensive, timely, accessible, and reliable economic, financial, and sociodemographic data. Building on this work, the IMF established the Data Quality Assessment Framework (DQAF) to assess data quality in subject areas such as debt and poverty. The DQAF comprises dimensions of data quality such as methodological soundness, accuracy, serviceability, and accessibility. In 1999 work began on Reports on the Observance of Standards and Codes (ROSC), which summarize the extent to which countries observe certain internationally recognized standards and codes in areas including data, monetary and financial policy transparency, fiscal transparency, banking supervision, securities, insurance, payments systems, corporate governance, accounting, auditing, and insolvency and creditor rights.

The IMF's major statistical publications include *International Financial Statistics, Balance of Payments Statistics Yearbook, Government Finance Statistics Yearbook,* and *Direction of Trade Statistics Yearbook.*

For more information on IMF statistical publications, contact the International Monetary Fund, Publications Services, Catalog Orders, 700 19th Street NW, Washington, DC 20431, USA; telephone: 202 623 7430; fax: 202 623 7201; telex: RCA 248331 IMF UR; email: publications@imf.org; Web site: www.imf.org/; SDDS and GDDS bulletin board: http://dsbb.imf.org/.

International Telecommunication Union

Founded in Paris in 1865 as the International Telegraph Union, the International Telecommunication Union (ITU) took its current name in 1934 and became a specialized agency of the United Nations in 1947. The ITU is unique among international organizations in that it was founded on the principle of cooperation between governments and the private sector. With a membership encompassing telecommunication policymakers and regulators, network operators, equipment manufacturers, hardware and software developers, regional standards-making organizations, and financing institutions, ITU's activities, policies, and strategic direction are determined and shaped by the industry it serves.

The ITU's standardization activities, which have already helped foster the growth of new technologies such as mobile telephony and the Internet, are now being put to use in defining the building blocks of the emerging global information infrastructure and in designing advanced multimedia systems that deftly handle a mix of voice, data, audio, and video signals. ITU's continuing role in managing the radio-frequency spectrum ensures that radio-based systems such as cellular phones and pagers, aircraft and maritime navigation systems, scientific research stations, satellite communication systems, and radio and television broadcasting continue to function smoothly and provide reliable wireless services to the world's inhabitants. And ITU's increasingly important role as a catalyst for forging development partnerships between government and private industry is helping bring about rapid improvements in telecommunication infrastructure in the world's developing economies.

The ITU's main statistical publications are the *ITU Yearbook of Statistics* and the *World Telecommunication Development Report.*

Publications can be ordered from ITU Sales and Marketing Service, Web site: www.itu.int/ITU-D/ict/publications/index.htm; telephone: 41 22 730 6141 (English), 41 22 730 6142 (French), and 41 22 730 6143 (Spanish); fax: 41 22 730 5194; email: sales@itu.int; telex: 421 000 uit ch; telegram: ITU GENEVE; Web site: www.itu.int/.

National Science Foundation

The National Science Foundation (NSF) is an independent U.S. government agency whose mission is to promote the progress of science; to advance the national health, prosperity, and welfare; and to secure the national defense. It is responsible for promoting science and engineering through almost 20,000 research and education projects. In addition, the NSF fosters the exchange of scientific information among scientists and engineers in the United States and other countries, supports programs to strengthen scientific and engineering research potential, and evaluates the impact of research on industrial development and general welfare.

As part of its mandate, the NSF biennially publishes *Science and Engineering Indicators,* which tracks national and international trends in science and engineering research and education.

Electronic copies of NSF documents can be obtained from the NSF's online document system (www.nsf.gov/publications/ods/). NSF publications are also available in print. To request print publications fill out the web-based order form (www.nsf.gov/publications/orderpub.jsp) or send a letter with the publication numbers to NSF Publications, National Science Foundation, Suite P-60, Arlington, VA 22230, USA. For more information, contact the National Science Foundation, 4201 Wilson Boulevard, Arlington, VA 22230, USA; telephone: 703 292 5111; Web site: www.nsf.gov/.

Organisation for Economic Co-operation and Development

The Organisation for Economic Co-operation and Development (OECD) was set up in 1948 as the Organisation for European Economic Co-operation (OEEC) to administer Marshall Plan funding in Europe. The OECD includes 30 member countries sharing a commitment to democratic government and the market economy. With active relationships with some 70 other countries, NGOs, and civil society, it has a global reach. It is best known for its publications and statistics, which cover economic and social issues from macroeconomics to trade, education, development, and science and innovation.

The Development Assistance Committee (DAC, www.oecd.org/dac) is one of the principal bodies through which the OECD deals with issues related to cooperation with developing countries. The DAC is a key forum of major bilateral donors, who work together to increase the effectiveness of their common efforts to support sustainable development. The DAC concentrates on two key areas: the contribution of international development to the capacity of developing countries to participate in the global economy and the capacity of people to overcome poverty and participate fully in their societies.

The OECD's statistical publications cover 25 topics, including development, environment, labor, national accounts, productivity, science and technology, and transport.

OECD publications are available through distributors in 40 countries; OECD Centers in Germany, Japan, Mexico, and the United States; OECD's fulfillment contractor, Extenza-Turpin; and the OECD Online Bookshop (www.oecdbookshop.org/oecd/index.asp), for ordering books and CD-ROMs and downloading PDFs. Faculty and students at institutions subscribing to the OECD online service, SourceOECD, can access publications online at http://new.sourceoecd.org. National libraries are also depositories for OECD publications.

Stockholm International Peace Research Institute

The Stockholm International Peace Research Institute (SIPRI) was established by the Swedish Parliament as an independent foundation in July 1966. SIPRI conducts research on questions of conflict and cooperation of importance for international peace and security, with the aim of contributing to an understanding of the conditions for peaceful solutions to international conflicts and for a stable peace.

SIPRI's research work is disseminated through books and reports as well as through symposia and seminars. SIPRI's main publication, *SIPRI Yearbook,* serves as a single authoritative and independent source on armaments and arms control, armed conflicts and conflict resolution, security arrangements, and disarmament. *SIPRI Yearbook* provides an overview of developments in international security, weapons and technology, military expenditure, the arms trade and arms production, and armed conflicts, along with efforts to control conventional, nuclear, chemical, and biological armaments.

For more information on SIPRI publications contact SIPRI at Signalistgatan 9, SE-169 70 Solna, Sweden; telephone: 46 8 655 97 00; fax: 46 8 655 97 33; email: sipri@sipri.org; for book orders: http://first.sipri.org/non_first/book_order.php; Web site: www.sipri.org/.

United Nations

The United Nations officially came into existence on October 24, 1945, and currently has 191 member states. The purposes of the United Nations, as set forth in the Charter, are to maintain international peace and security; to develop friendly relations among nations; to cooperate in solving international economic, social, cultural, and humanitarian problems and in promoting respect for human rights and fundamental freedoms; and to be a center for harmonizing the actions of nations in attaining these ends.

The United Nations and its specialized agencies maintain a number of programs for the collection of international statistics, some of which are described elsewhere in this book. At United Nations headquarters the Statistics Division provides a wide range of statistical outputs and services for producers and users of statistics worldwide.

The Statistics Division publishes statistics on international trade, national accounts, demography and population, gender, industry, energy, environment, human settlements, and disability. Its major statistical publications include the *International Trade Statistics Yearbook, Yearbook of National Accounts,* and *Monthly Bulletin of Statistics,* along with general statistics compendiums such as the *Statistical Yearbook* and *World Statistics Pocketbook.*

For publications, contact United Nations Publications, Room DC2-853, Department I004, 2 UN Plaza, New York, NY 10017, USA; telephone: 212 963 8302 or 800 253 9646 (toll free); fax: 212 963 3489; email: publications@un.org; Web site: www.un.org/.

United Nations Centre for Human Settlements, Global Urban Observatory

The Urban Indicators Programme of the United Nations Centre for Human Settlements (UN-HABITAT) was established to address the urgent global need to improve the urban knowledge base by helping countries and cities design, collect, and apply policy-oriented indicators related to development at the city level.

In 1997 the Urban Indicators Programme was integrated into the Global Urban Observatory, the principal United Nations program for monitoring urban conditions and trends and for tracking progress in implementing the goals of the Habitat Agenda. With the Urban Indicators and Best Practices programs, the Global Urban Observatory is establishing a worldwide information, assessment, and capacity building network to help governments, local authorities, the private sector, and nongovernmental and other civil society organizations.

Contact the Co-ordinator, Global Urban Observatory and Statistics, Urban Secretariat, UN-HABITAT, PO Box 30030, Nairobi, Kenya; telephone: 254 20 623119; fax: 254 20 623080; email: habitat.publications@unhabitat.org or guo@unhabitat.org ; Web site: www.unhabitat.org/.

United Nations Children's Fund

The United Nations Children's Fund (UNICEF), the only organization of the United Nations dedicated exclusively to children, works with other United Nations bodies and with governments and nongovernmental organizations to improve children's lives in more than 140 developing countries through community-based services in primary health care, basic education, and safe water and sanitation.

UNICEF's major publications include *The State of the World's Children* and *The Progress of Nations.*

For information on UNICEF publications contact the Chief, EPS, Division of Communication, UNICEF, 3 United Nations Plaza, New York, NY 10017, USA; telephone: 212 326 7000; fax: 212 303 7985; email: pubdoc@unicef.org; Web site: www.unicef.org/ and www.un.org/Publications.

United Nations Conference on Trade and Development

The United Nations Conference on Trade and Development (UNCTAD) is the principal organ of the United Nations General Assembly in the field of trade and development. It was established as a permanent intergovernmental body in 1964 in Geneva with a view to accelerating economic growth and development, particularly in developing countries. UNCTAD discharges its mandate through policy analysis; intergovernmental deliberations, consensus building, and negotiation; monitoring, implementation, and follow-up; and technical cooperation.

UNCTAD produces a number of publications containing trade and economic statistics, including the *Handbook of International Trade and Development Statistics.*

For information, contact UNCTAD, Palais des Nations, 8-14, Avenue de la Paix, 1211 Geneva 10, Switzerland; telephone: 41 22 907 1234; fax: 41 22 907 0043; email: info@unctad.org; Web site: www.unctad.org/.

United Nations Educational, Scientific, and Cultural Organization, Institute for Statistics

The United Nations Educational, Scientific, and Cultural Organization (UNESCO) is a specialized agency of the United Nations established in 1945 to promote "collaboration among nations through education, science, and culture in order to further universal respect for justice, for the rule of law, and for the human rights and fundamental freedoms . . . for the peoples of the world, without distinction of race, sex, language, or religion."

The UNESCO Institute for Statistics' principal statistical publications are the *Global Education Digest* and regional statistical reports, as well as the on-line database.

For publications, contact the UNESCO Institute for Statistics, C.P. 6128, Succursale Centre-ville, Montreal, Quebec, H3C 3J7, Canada; telephone: 514 343 6880; fax: 514 343 6882; email: uis@unesco.org; Web site: www.unesco.org/; and for the Institute for Statistics: www.uis.unesco.org/.

United Nations Environment Programme

The mandate of the United Nations Environment Programme (UNEP) is to provide leadership and encourage partnership in caring for the environment by inspiring, informing, and enabling nations and people to improve their quality of life without compromising that of future generations.

UNEP publications include *Global Environment Outlook* and *Our Planet* (a bimonthly magazine).

For information, contact the UNEP, PO Box 30552, Nairobi, Kenya; telephone: 254 20 621234; fax: 254 20 624489/90; email: eisinfo@unep.org; Web site: www.unep.org/.

United Nations Industrial Development Organization

The United Nations Industrial Development Organization (UNIDO) was established in 1966 to act as the central coordinating body for industrial activities and to promote industrial development and cooperation at the global, regional, national, and sectoral levels. In 1985 UNIDO became the 16th specialized agency of the United Nations, with a mandate to help develop scientific and technological plans and programs for industrialization in the public, cooperative, and private sectors.

UNIDO's databases and information services include the Industrial Statistics Database (INDSTAT), Commodity Balance Statistics Database (COMBAL), Industrial Development Abstracts (IDA), and the International Referral System on Sources of Information. Among its publications is the *International Yearbook of Industrial Statistics.*

For information, contact UNIDO Public Information Section, Vienna International Centre, PO Box 300, A-1400 Vienna, Austria; telephone: 43 1 26026 5031; fax: 43 1 21346 5031 or 26026 6843; email: publications@unido.org; Web site: www.unido.org/.

World Bank Group

The World Bank Group is made up of five organizations: the International Bank for Reconstruction and Development (IBRD), the International Development Association (IDA), the International Finance Corporation (IFC), the Multilateral Investment Guarantee Agency (MIGA), and the International Centre for Settlement of Investment Disputes (ICSID). Established in 1944 at a conference of world leaders in Bretton Woods, New Hampshire, United States, the World Bank is the world's largest source of development assistance. In fiscal 2004 the World Bank provided $20.1 billion in development assistance and worked in almost 100 developing countries on 245 projects, bringing finance and technical expertise to help reduce poverty in those countries.

The World Bank Group's mission is to fight poverty and improve the living standards of people in the developing world. It is a development bank, providing loans, policy advice, technical assistance, and knowledge sharing services to low- and middle-income countries to reduce poverty. The Bank promotes growth to create jobs and to empower poor people to take advantage of these opportunities. It uses its financial resources, trained staff, and extensive knowledge base to help each developing country onto a path of stable, sustainable, and equitable growth in the fight against poverty. The World Bank Group has 184 member countries.

For information about the World Bank, visit its Web site at www.worldbank.org/. For more information about development data, contact the Development Data Group, World Bank, 1818 H Street NW, Washington, DC 20433, USA; telephone: 800 590 1906 or 202 473 7824; fax: 202 522 1498; email: data@worldbank.org; Web site: www.worldbank.org/data.

World Health Organization

The constitution of the World Health Organization (WHO) was adopted on July 22, 1946, by the International Health Conference, convened in New York by the Economic and Social Council of the United Nations. The objective of the WHO, a specialized agency of the United Nations, is the attainment by all people of the highest possible level of health.

The WHO carries out a wide range of functions, including coordinating international health work; helping governments strengthen health services; providing technical assistance and emergency aid; working for the prevention and control of disease; promoting improved nutrition, housing, sanitation, recreation, and economic and working conditions; promoting and coordinating biomedical and health services research; promoting improved standards of teaching and training in health and medical professions; establishing international standards for biological, pharmaceutical, and similar products; and standardizing diagnostic procedures.

The WHO publishes the *World Health Statistics Annual* and many other technical and statistical publications.

For publications, contact the World Health Organization, Marketing and Dissemination, CH-1211 Geneva 27, Switzerland; telephone: 41 22 791 2476; fax: 41 22 791 4857; email: pubrights@who.int; Web site: www.who.int/.

World Intellectual Property Organization

The World Intellectual Property Organization (WIPO) is an international organization dedicated to helping to ensure that the rights of creators and owners of intellectual property are protected worldwide and that inventors and authors are thus recognized and rewarded for their ingenuity. This international protection acts as a spur to human creativity, pushing forward the boundaries of science and technology and enriching the world of literature and the arts. By providing a stable environment for the marketing of intellectual property products, WIPO also oils the wheels of international trade.

WIPO's main tasks include harmonizing national intellectual property legislation and procedures, providing services for international applications for industrial property rights, exchanging intellectual property information, providing legal and technical assistance to developing and other countries facilitating the resolution of private intellectual property disputes, and marshalling information technology as a tool for storing, accessing, and using valuable intellectual property information.

A substantial part of its activities and resources is devoted to development cooperation with developing countries.

Publications may be ordered from the online bookshop at www.wipo.int/ebookshop; for further information, contact the World Intellectual Property Organization, 34, chemin des Colombettes, CH-1211 Geneva 20, Switzerland; telephone: 41 22 338 9111; fax: 41 22 740 1812; email: ebookshop@wipo.int; Web site: www.wipo.int/.

World Tourism Organization

The World Tourism Organization is an intergovernmental body entrusted by the United Nations with promoting and developing tourism. It serves as a global forum for tourism policy issues and a source of tourism know-how. The organization began as the International Union of Official Tourist Publicity Organizations, set up in 1925 in The Hague. Renamed the World Tourism Organization, it held its first general assembly in Madrid in May 1975. Its membership includes 141 countries, seven territories, and some 350 Affiliate Members representing the private sector, educational institutions, tourism associations, and local tourism authorities.

The World Tourism Organization publishes the *Yearbook of Tourism Statistics, Compendium of Tourism Statistics,* and *Travel and Tourism Barometer* (triannual).

For information, contact the World Tourism Organization, Calle Capitán Haya, 42, 28020 Madrid, Spain; telephone: 34 91 567 8100; fax: 34 91 571 3733; email: infoshop@world-tourism.org; Web site: www. world-tourism.org/.

World Trade Organization

The World Trade Organization (WTO), established on January 1, 1995, is the successor to the General Agreement on Tariffs and Trade (GATT). The WTO has 144 member countries and is the only international organization dealing with the global rules of trade between nations. Its main function is to ensure that trade flows as smoothly, predictably, and freely as possible. It does this by administering trade agreements, acting as a forum for trade negotiations, settling trade disputes, reviewing national trade policies, assisting developing countries in trade policy issues—through technical assistance and training programs—and cooperating with other international organizations. At the heart of the system—known as the multilateral trading system—are WTO's agreements, negotiated and signed by a large majority of the world's trading nations and ratified by their parliaments.

The WTO's *International Trade Statistics* is its main statistical publication, providing comprehensive, comparable, and up-to-date statistics on trade.

For publications, contact the World Trade Organization, Publications Services, Centre William Rappard, rue de Lausanne 154, CH-1211, Geneva 21, Switzerland; telephone: 41 22 739 5208 or 5308; fax: 41 22 739 5792; email: publications@wto.org; Web site: www.wto.org/.

Private and nongovernmental organizations

Containerisation International

Containerisation International Yearbook is one of the most authoritative reference books on the container industry. It has more than 850 pages of data, including detailed information on more than 560 container ports in more than 150 countries and a review section that features two-year rankings for 350 ports. The information can be accessed on the Containerisation International Web site, which also provides a comprehensive online daily business news and information service for the container industry.

For more information, contact Informa UK at 69-77 Paul Street, London, EC2A 4LQ, UK; telephone: 44 20 7017 5531; fax: 44 20 7017 4782; email: webtechhelp@informa.com; Web site: www.ci-online.co.uk/.

International Institute for Strategic Studies

The International Institute for Strategic Studies (IISS), founded in 1958, initially focused on nuclear deterrence and arms control. Later, it began to cover more comprehensively political and military issues in all continents. The IISS provides information and analysis on strategic trends and facilitates contacts between government leaders, business people, and analysts that could lead to better public policy in international security and international relations. IISS's staff and governing boards are international and its network of some 3,000 individual members and 500 corporate and institutional members draws from more than 100 countries.

The IISS is a primary source of accurate, objective information on international strategic issues. It publishes The Military Balance, an annual assessment of the military capabilities and defense economics covering 170 countries.

Publications may be obtained through Taylor and Francis Journals (www.tandf.co.uk/journals/). For information, contact the London office at Arundel House, 13–15 Arundel Street, Temple Place, London WC2R 3DX, UK; telephone: 44 0 20 7379 7676; fax: 44 0 20 7836 3108; email: iiss@iiss.org; Web site: www.iiss.org/, or the Washington, D.C., office at 1747 Pennsylvania Ave NW, 7th Floor, Washington DC 20006, USA; telephone: 202 659 1490; fax: 202 296 1134; email: taylor@iiss.org.

International Road Federation

The International Road Federation (IRF) is a nongovernmental, not-for-profit organization with public and private sector members in some 70 countries. The IRF's mission is to encourage and promote development and maintenance of better and safer roads and road networks. It helps put in place technological solutions and management practices that provide maximum economic and social returns from national road investments.

The IRF believes that rationally planned, efficiently managed and well-maintained road networks offer high levels of user safety and have a significant impact on sustainable economic growth, prosperity, social well-being, and human development.

The IRF has a major role to play in all aspects of road policy and development worldwide. For governments and financial institutions, the IRF provides a wide base of expertise for planning road development strategy and policy. For its members, the IRF is a business network, a link to external institutions and agencies and a business card of introduction to government officials and decisionmakers. For the community of road professionals, the IRF is a source of support and information for national road associations, advocacy groups, companies, and institutions dedicated to the development of road infrastructure.

The IRF publishes *World Road Statistics.*

Contact the Geneva office at chemin de Blandonnet 2, CH-1214 Vernier, Geneva, Switzerland; telephone: 41 22 306 0260; fax: 41 22 306 0270; or the Washington, DC, office at 1010 Massachusetts Avenue NW, Suite 410, Washington, DC 20001, USA; telephone: 202 371 5544; fax: 202 371 5565; email: info@irfnet.com; Web site: www.irfnet.org/.

Netcraft

Netcraft is an Internet services company based in Bath, United Kingdom. Netcraft's work includes the provision of network security services and research data and analysis of the Internet. It is an authority on the market share of Web servers, operating systems, hosting providers, Internet service providers, encrypted transactions, electronic commerce, scripting languages, and content technologies on the Internet.

For information, visit www.netcraft.com/.

PricewaterhouseCoopers

Drawing on the talents of 122,000 people in 144 countries, PricewaterhouseCoopers provides industry-focused assurance, tax, and advisory services for public and private clients in corporate accountability, risk management, structuring and mergers and acquisitions, and performance and process improvement.

PricewaterhouseCoopers publishes *Corporate Taxes: Worldwide Summaries* and *Individual Taxes: Worldwide Summaries.*

For information, contact PricewaterhouseCoopers, 300 Madison Avenue, New York, NY 10017, USA; telephone: 646 471 4000; telecopier/rightfax: 813 286 6000; Web site: www.pwcglobal.com/.

Standard & Poor's Emerging Markets Data Base

Standard & Poor's Emerging Markets Data Base (EMDB) is the world's leading source for information and indices on stock markets in developing countries. The EMDB was the first database to track emerging stock markets. It currently covers 53 markets and more than 2,000 stocks. Drawing a sample of stocks in each EMDB market, Standard & Poor's calculates indices to serve as benchmarks that are consistent across national boundaries. Standard & Poor's calculates one index, the S&P/IFCG (Global) index, that reflects the perspective of local investors and those interested in broad trends in emerging markets and another, the S&P/IFCI (Investable) index, that provides a broad, neutral, and historically consistent benchmark for the growing emerging market investment community.

For information on subscription rates, contact S&P Emerging Markets Data Base, 55 Water Street, 42nd Floor, New York, NY, 10041-0003; Telephone: 212 438 2046; Fax: 212 438 3429; Email: indexservices@sandp.com; Web site: www.standardandpoors.com/.

World Conservation Monitoring Centre

WORLD CONSERVATION
MONITORING CENTRE

The World Conservation Monitoring Centre (WCMC) provides information on the conservation and sustainable use of the world's living resources and helps others to develop information systems of their own. It works in close collaboration with a wide range of people and organizations to increase access to the information needed for wise management of the world's living resources.

Committed to the principle of data exchange with other centers and noncommercial users, the WCMC, whenever possible, places the data it manages in the public domain.

For information, contact the World Conservation Monitoring Centre, 219 Huntington Road, Cambridge CB3 0DL, UK; telephone: 44 12 2327 7314; fax: 44 12 2327 7136; email: info@unep-wcmc.org; Web site: www.unep-wcmc.org/.

World Information Technology and Services Alliance

The World Information Technology and Services Alliance (WITSA) is a consortium of leading information technology industry associations in 65 countries, representing more than 15,000 information technology companies. As the global voice of the information technology industry, WITSA is dedicated to advocating policies that advance the industry's growth and development; facilitating international trade and investment in information technology products and services; strengthening WITSA's national industry associations; and providing members with a broad network of contacts. WITSA also hosts the World Congress on Information Technology and other worldwide events.

WITSA's publication, *Digital Planet 2004: The Global Information Economy,* uses data provided by Global Insight covering the world's 70 largest information and communications technology buying countries and regions.

For information, contact WITSA, 1401 Wilson Boulevard, Suite 1100, Arlington, VA 22209, USA; telephone: 703 284 5333; fax: 703 525 2279; email: ahalvorsen@itaa.org; Web site: www.witsa.org/.

World Resources Institute

The World Resources Institute is an independent center for policy research and technical assistance on global environmental and development issues. The institute provides—and helps other institutions provide—objective information and practical proposals for policy and institutional change that will foster environmentally sound, socially equitable development. The institute's current areas of work include trade, forests, energy, economics, technology, biodiversity, human health, climate change, sustainable agriculture, resource and environmental information, and national strategies for environmental and resource management.

For information, contact the World Resources Institute, Suite 800, 10 G Street NE, Washington, DC 20002, USA; telephone: 202 729 7600; fax: 202 729 7610; email: front@wri.org; Web site: www.wri.org/.

USERS GUIDE

Tables

The tables are numbered by section and display the identifying icon of the section. Countries and economies are listed alphabetically (except for Hong Kong, China, which appears after China). Data are shown for 152 economies with populations of more than 1 million, as well as for Taiwan, China, in selected tables. Table 1.6 presents selected indicators for 56 other economies—small economies with populations between 30,000 and 1 million and smaller economies if they are members of the International Bank for Reconstruction and Development (IBRD) or, as it is commonly known, the World Bank. The term *country,* used interchangeably with *economy,* does not imply political independence, but refers to any territory for which authorities report separate social or economic statistics. When available, aggregate measures for income and regional groups appear at the end of each table.

Indicators are shown for the most recent year or period for which data are available and, in most tables, for an earlier year or period (usually 1990 in this edition). Time-series data are available on the *World Development Indicators* CD-ROM and in *WDI Online.*

Known deviations from standard definitions or breaks in comparability over time or across countries are either footnoted in the tables or noted in *About the data.* When available data are deemed to be too weak to provide reliable measures of levels and trends or do not adequately adhere to international standards, the data are not shown.

Aggregate measures for income groups

The aggregate measures for income groups include 208 economies (the economies listed in the main tables plus those in table 1.6) wherever data are available. To maintain consistency in the aggregate measures over time and between tables, missing data are imputed where possible. The aggregates are totals (designated by a *t* if the aggregates include gap-filled estimates for missing data and by an *s,* for simple totals, where they do not), median values (*m*), weighted averages (*w*), or simple averages (*u*). Gap filling of amounts not allocated to countries may

result in discrepancies between subgroup aggregates and overall totals. For further discussion of aggregation methods, see *Statistical methods.*

Aggregate measures for regions

The aggregate measures for regions include only low- and middle-income economies (note that these measures include developing economies with populations of less than 1 million, including those listed in table 1.6).

The country composition of regions is based on the World Bank's analytical regions and may differ from common geographic usage. For regional classifications, see the map on the inside back cover and the list on the back cover flap. For further discussion of aggregation methods, see *Statistical methods.*

Statistics

Data are shown for economies as they were constituted in 2003, and historical data are revised to reflect current political arrangements. Exceptions are noted throughout the tables.

Additional information about the data is provided in *Primary data documentation.* That section summarizes national and international efforts to improve basic data collection and gives information on primary sources, census years, fiscal years, and other background. *Statistical methods* provides technical information on some of the general calculations and formulas used throughout the book.

Data consistency and reliability

Considerable effort has been made to standardize the data, but full comparability cannot be assured, and care must be taken in interpreting the indicators. Many factors affect data availability, comparability, and reliability: statistical systems in many developing economies are still weak; statistical methods, coverage, practices, and definitions differ widely; and cross-country and intertemporal comparisons involve complex technical and conceptual problems that cannot be unequivocally resolved. Data coverage may not be complete because of special circumstances or for economies experiencing problems (such as those stemming from

conflicts) affecting the collection and reporting of data. For these reasons, although data are drawn from the sources thought to be most authoritative, they should be construed only as indicating trends and characterizing major differences among economies rather than offering precise quantitative measures of those differences. Discrepancies in data presented in different editions of *World Development Indicators* reflect updates by countries as well as revisions to historical series and changes in methodology. Thus readers are advised not to compare data series between editions of *World Development Indicators* or between different World Bank publications. Consistent time-series data for 1960–2003 are available on the *World Development Indicators* CD-ROM and in *WDI Online.*

Except where otherwise noted, growth rates are in real terms. (See *Statistical methods* for information on the methods used to calculate growth rates.) Data for some economic indicators for some economies are presented in fiscal years rather than calendar years; see *Primary data documentation.* All dollar figures are current U.S. dollars unless otherwise stated. The methods used for converting national currencies are described in *Statistical methods.*

Country notes

China. On July 1, 1997, China resumed its exercise of sovereignty over Hong Kong, and on December 20, 1999, it resumed its exercise of sovereignty over Macao. Unless otherwise noted, data for China do not include data for Hong Kong, China; Taiwan, China; or Macao, China.

Democratic Republic of Congo. Data for the Democratic Republic of Congo (Congo, Dem. Rep., in the table listings) refer to the former Zaire. (The Republic of Congo is referred to as Congo, Rep., in the table listings.)

Czech Republic and Slovak Republic. Data are shown whenever possible for the individual countries formed from the former Czechoslovakia—the Czech Republic and the Slovak Republic.

Eritrea. Data are shown for Eritrea whenever possible, but in most cases before 1992 Eritrea is included in the data for Ethiopia.

Germany. Data for Germany refer to the unified Germany unless otherwise noted.

Serbia and Montenegro. On February 4, 2003, the Federal Republic of Yugoslavia changed its name to Serbia and Montenegro.

Timor-Leste. On May 20, 2002, Timor-Leste became an independent country. Data for Indonesia include Timor-Leste through 1999 unless otherwise noted.

Union of Soviet Socialist Republics. In 1991 the Union of Soviet Socialist Republics came to an end. Available data are shown for the individual countries now existing on its former territory (Armenia, Azerbaijan, Belarus, Estonia, Georgia, Kazakhstan, Kyrgyz Republic, Latvia, Lithuania, Moldova, Russian Federation, Tajikistan, Turkmenistan, Ukraine, and Uzbekistan). External debt data presented for the Russian Federation prior to 1992 are for the former Soviet Union. The debt of the former Soviet Union is included in the Russian Federation data after 1992 on the assumption that 100 percent of all outstanding external debt as of December 1991 has become a liability of the Russian Federation. Beginning in 1993 the data for the Russian Federation have been revised to include obligations to members of the former Council for Mutual Economic Assistance and other countries in the form of trade-related credits amounting to $15.4 billion as of the end of 1996.

República Bolivariana de Venezuela. In December 1999 the official name of Venezuela was changed to República Bolivariana de Venezuela (Venezuela, RB, in the table listings).

Republic of Yemen. Data for the Republic of Yemen refer to that country from 1990 onward; data for previous years refer to aggregated data for the former People's Democratic Republic of Yemen and the former Yemen Arab Republic unless otherwise noted.

Changes in the System of National Accounts

World Development Indicators uses terminology in line with the 1993 United Nations System of National Accounts (SNA). For example, in the 1993 SNA *gross national income* (GNI) replaces *gross national product* (GNP). See *About the data* for tables 1.1 and 4.9.

Most economies continue to compile their national accounts according to the 1968 SNA, but more and more are adopting the 1993 SNA. Economies that use the 1993 SNA are identified in *Primary data documentation*. A few low-income economies still use concepts from older SNA guidelines, including valuations such as factor cost, in describing major economic aggregates.

Classification of economies

For operational and analytical purposes the World Bank's main criterion for classifying economies is GNI per capita. Every economy is classified as low income, middle income (subdivided into lower middle and upper middle), or high income. For income classifications see the map on the inside front cover and the list on the front cover flap. Low- and middle-income economies are sometimes referred to as developing economies. The use of the term is convenient; it is not intended to imply that all economies in the group are experiencing similar development or that other economies have reached a preferred or final stage of development. Note that classification by income does not necessarily reflect development status. Because GNI per capita changes over time, the country composition of income groups may change from one edition of *World Development Indicators* to the next. Once the classification is fixed for an edition, based on GNI per capita in the most recent year for which data are available (2003 in this edition), all historical data presented are based on the same country grouping.

Low-income economies are those with a GNI per capita of $765 or less in 2003. Middle-income economies are those with a GNI per capita of more than $765 but less than $9,386. Lower-middle-income and upper-middle-income economies are separated at a GNI per capita of $3,035. High-income economies are those with a GNI per capita of $9,386 or more. The 12 participating member countries of the European Monetary Union (EMU) are presented as a subgroup under high-income economies.

Symbols

..

means that data are not available or that aggregates cannot be calculated because of missing data in the years shown.

0 or 0.0

means zero or less than half the unit shown.

/

in dates, as in 1990/91, means that the period of time, usually 12 months, straddles two calendar years and refers to a crop year, a survey year, an academic year, or a fiscal year.

$

means current U.S. dollars unless otherwise noted.

>

means more than.

<

means less than.

Data presentation conventions

- A blank means not applicable or, for an aggregate, not analytically meaningful.
- A billion is 1,000 million.
- A trillion is 1,000 billion.
- Figures in italics refer to years or periods other than those specified.
- Data for years that are more than three years from the range shown are footnoted.

The cutoff date for data is February 1, 2005.

1 | WORLD VIEW

Five years ago the Millennium Declaration recorded the commitment of the members of the United Nations to eliminate poverty and to build a secure and peaceful world conducive to human development. The Millennium Development Goals embody that commitment and set quantified targets for reducing poverty, educating all children, improving the status of women, combating disease and reducing premature deaths, ensuring environmental sustainability, and establishing an effective partnership between rich countries and developing countries. The Goals have become widely accepted as a framework for measuring development progress. Their benchmarks and targets, looking back to 1990 and forward to 2015, provide yardsticks for measuring results. Taking the Goals seriously has helped to concentrate the attention of politicians, development professionals, and ordinary citizens on the need to work together and to use scarce resources more effectively.

Since the articulation of the Millennium Development Goals, *World Development Indicators* has reported on progress toward each goal. This year's edition provides a more comprehensive survey of the main targets and indicators. Although the presentation here is based largely on regional averages, it is important to remember that the goals are commitments by countries. We cannot claim complete success as long as some countries lag behind. Nor is progress within countries uniform. Some important disparities are illustrated by examples of the differences between poor and rich and between urban and rural populations.

One third of the way toward the target date of 2015, there is evidence of progress but many challenges lie ahead. Global prospects for achieving the income poverty goal are good, thanks to strong economic growth in China, India, and other countries in Asia. But malnutrition persists even in rapidly growing economies, and millions of people are hungry.

Many countries have achieved the goal of universal primary education and, with primary school enrollment rates rising, many more will by 2015. But progress has been slow in parts of Africa and Asia, and more than 100 million children remain out of school.

The first target year of the gender equality goal has already arrived. Although more girls are attending school and in some places they outnumber boys, full equality of enrollments in primary and secondary school has not been universally achieved.

Progress toward the health goals has been slow. Only 33 countries are on track to reach the child mortality goal. Effective strategies for reducing maternal mortality are well known but hard to implement. HIV/AIDS continues to spread, and malaria and tuberculosis still afflict millions.

Most regions are on track to meet the drinking water target, but only Latin America and East Asia are on track to reach the sanitation target. Poor sanitation and contaminated drinking water remain major sources of disease. Slum populations continue to grow, and the indicators for the natural environment show that the world has not yet found the path to sustainable development.

Finally, building a global partnership for development between developed and developing countries and with the full and effective support of the international institutions remains a work in progress. With a decade to go achieving the Millennium Development Goals remains a huge challenge, one requiring additional resources and sustained effort.

- **Halve, between 1990 and 2015, the proportion of people living on less than $1 a day**

- **Halve, between 1990 and 2015, the proportion of people who suffer from hunger**

Reducing poverty and hunger

POVERTY AND HUNGER

Poverty exists everywhere, but it is most cruel and debilitating in developing countries, where more than one person in five subsists on less than $1 day. There has been progress. Since 1990 extreme poverty in developing countries has fallen from 28 percent to 21 percent. Over the same time population grew 15 percent to 5 billion people, leaving 1.1 billion people in extreme poverty. If economic growth rates in developing countries are sustained, global poverty will fall to 10 percent—a striking success.

But hundreds of millions of people will still be trapped in poverty, especially in Sub-Saharan Africa and South Asia and wherever poor health and lack of education deprive people of productive employment; environmental resources have been depleted or spoiled; and corruption, conflict, and misgovernance waste public resources and discourage private investment. Even as the first target of the Millennium Development Goals appears in sight, the effort to eliminate poverty must be renewed.

Poverty rates are falling, but progress has been uneven

Share of people living on less than $1 or $2 a day (%)

While accelerating growth in India has put South Asia on track to meet the goal, Sub-Saharan Africa lags behind. In some countries poverty rates exceed 70 percent.

Sub-Saharan Africa

44.6 · 46.4 · 38.4 · 22.3

South Asia

41.3 · 31.3 · 20.7 · 12.8

East Asia has experienced a sustained period of economic growth, led by China, while Latin America and the Caribbean has stagnated, with little poverty reduction.

East Asia & Pacific

29.6 · 14.9 · 14.8 · 0.9

Latin America & Caribbean

28.4 · 24.5 · 19.6 · 11.3 · 9.5 · 6.9 · 5.7

The transition economies of Europe and Central Asia saw poverty rates rise in the 1990s and then fall. There and in the Middle East and North Africa consumption of $2 a day may be a more realistic limit of extreme poverty.

Europe & Central Asia

4.9 · 0.5 · 19.7 · 3.6 · 5.2 · 0.4 · 0.3

Middle East & North Africa

21.4 · 23.2 · 11.9 · 2.3 · 2.4 · 0.9 · 1.2

Poverty rate at $1 a day —— Actual ····· Projected —— Goal
Poverty rate at $2 a day —— Actual ····· Projected

Source: World Bank staff estimates.

China leads the way

Proportion of people living on less than $1 a day (%)

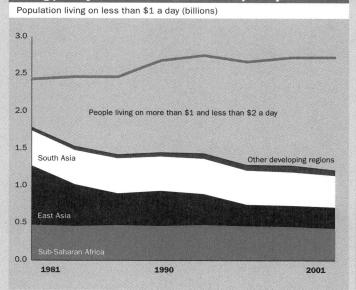

China

All developing countries

All developing countries, excluding China

1981   1990   2001

Source: World Bank staff estimates.

The global poverty rate began to fall rapidly in the 1980s due in large part to China's rapid economic growth. In 1981 China was among the poorest countries, with more than 60 percent of its population living on less than $1 a day. China's poverty was cut in half by 1990 and in half again by 2001. Excluding China, the poverty rate in developing countries has been falling by about half a percentage point a year, but many economies stagnated in the 1990s and in those places poverty increased.

Rising poverty in Africa—and between the poverty lines

Population living on less than $1 a day (billions)

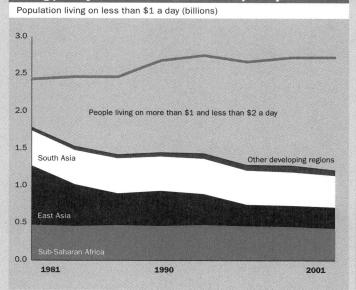

People living on more than $1 and less than $2 a day

South Asia   Other developing regions

East Asia

Sub-Saharan Africa

1981   1990   2001

Source: World Bank staff estimates.

In contrast to East Asia, the number of extremely poor people in Sub-Saharan Africa has almost doubled since 1981 to 313 million people in 2001. This is a terrible human tragedy and represents the greatest challenge to development.

And globally, even as poverty rates fell and the number of people living on less than $1 a day diminished, the number living on less than $2 a day increased from 2.4 billion in 1981 to 2.7 billion in 2001. The 1.6 billion people in the middle, between the $1 and $2 a day poverty lines, are still very poor and remain vulnerable to economic slowdowns. Success in reaching the first Millennium Development Goal will make the needs of this group even greater.

Fewer people in extreme poverty

People living on less than $1 a day (millions)

1981—1.5 billion poor
In 1981 more than half of the people in extreme poverty lived in East Asia and over a quarter in South Asia.

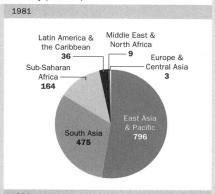

1981

Latin America & the Caribbean **36**
Middle East & North Africa **9**
Sub-Saharan Africa **164**
Europe & Central Asia **3**
South Asia **475**
East Asia & Pacific **796**

1990—1.2 billion poor
By 1990 there were 260 million fewer people worldwide living in extreme poverty—and more than 300 million fewer in East Asia. Had poverty rates not fallen, population growth alone would have added 288 million more poor people.

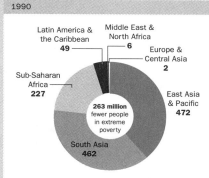

1990

Latin America & the Caribbean **49**
Middle East & North Africa **6**
Europe & Central Asia **2**
Sub-Saharan Africa **227**
East Asia & Pacific **472**
South Asia **462**
263 million fewer people in extreme poverty

2001—1.1 billion poor
In 2001 there were 100 million fewer people living in poverty than in 1990 and almost 400 million fewer than in 1981. But in Sub-Saharan Africa the number of people in extreme poverty rose to almost 320 million, and they now make up over a quarter of the global total.

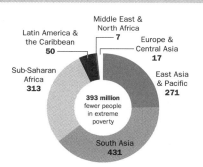

2001

Latin America & the Caribbean **50**
Middle East & North Africa **7**
Europe & Central Asia **17**
Sub-Saharan Africa **313**
East Asia & Pacific **271**
South Asia **431**
393 million fewer people in extreme poverty

2015—0.6 billion poor
With sustained growth, many more people could climb out of poverty. Based on current trends, 90 percent of those still in extreme poverty in 2015 would be living in South Asia and Sub-Saharan Africa.

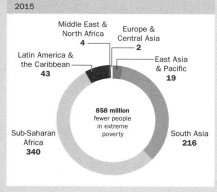

2015

Middle East & North Africa **4**
Europe & Central Asia **2**
Latin America & the Caribbean **43**
East Asia & Pacific **19**
Sub-Saharan Africa **340**
South Asia **216**
858 million fewer people in extreme poverty

Source: World Bank staff estimates.

POVERTY AND HUNGER

Africa's poor get poorer

Average daily income of the extreme poor (1993 PPP$)

As people living in extreme poverty increased in number in Africa, they also became poorer. The average daily income or consumption of those living on less than $1 a day fell from 64 cents in 1981 to 60 cents in 2001. In the rest of the developing world it increased from 72 cents to 83 cents. Because Africa's 313 million poor people have such low incomes, relatively higher rates of economic growth will be required to lift them above the poverty line. In Sub-Saharan Africa the median share of income or consumption going to the poorest 20 percent of the population is 4.9 percent, almost 2 percentage points less than in other developing regions. Only in Latin America and the Caribbean do the poorest 20 percent fare worse.

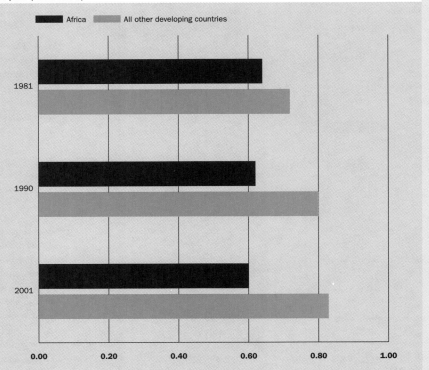

■ Africa   ■ All other developing countries

Source: World Bank staff estimates.

Which countries are on track to reach the MDG target?

$1 a day poverty rate, 2001 (%)

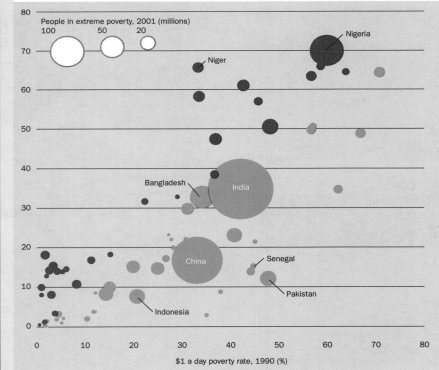

People in extreme poverty, 2001 (millions)
100   50   20

$1 a day poverty rate, 1990 (%)

■ Poverty has decreased, but not on track
■ On track to achieve Millennium Development Goal
■ Poverty has increased

Since 1990 rates of extreme poverty have declined in many countries. The majority of the extremely poor population lives in countries that are on track to achieve the Millennium Development Goal target. This includes countries with large populations such as China, India, Pakistan, and Indonesia, where many people have climbed out of poverty. In other countries, such as Bangladesh, poverty rates have been declining but not fast enough to be cut in half by 2015. And there are many more countries where poverty rates have increased since 1990. In Sub-Saharan Africa only a handful of countries such as Senegal are on track to reach the target. Reversing the trend will require higher rates of economic growth and benefits reaching the poor—a daunting task on top of the burdens of disease, famine, and armed conflict.

Source: World Bank staff estimates.

Starting life at a disadvantage

Malnutrition prevalence (% of children under age five)

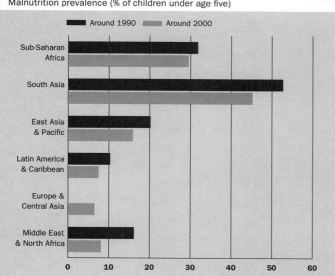

Source: World Bank staff estimates.

Malnutrition in children often begins at birth, when poorly nourished mothers give birth to underweight babies. Malnourished children develop more slowly, enter school later, and perform less well. The proportion of severely underweight children is falling, but fewer than 40 percent of the 77 countries with adequate data to monitor trends are on track to reach the Millennium Development Goal target. Faster progress is possible. Programs to encourage breastfeeding and to improve the diets of pregnant and lactating mothers help. So do appropriate care and feeding of sick children, oral rehydration therapy, control of parasitic diseases, and programs to treat vitamin A deficiency.

Hunger rising in Africa

Prevalence of undernourishment (%)

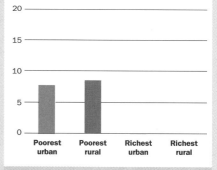

Source: World Bank staff estimates based on Food and Agriculture Organization data.

Hunger, measured by undernourishment, means consuming too little food to maintain normal levels of activity. Rates of undernourishment have been falling in most regions, but too slowly to reach the Millennium Development Goal target, and in many regions the number of hungry people continues to grow. By 2002 only East Asia and Pacific and Latin America and the Caribbean had fewer undernourished people than 10 years earlier. Countries that reduced hunger had higher economic growth, especially in agriculture and in rural areas. They have also had lower population growth and lower rates of HIV infection.

Poor and malnourished

Proportion of children under age five severely underweight, by family wealth quintile and location (%)

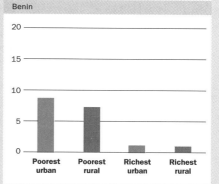

Poverty, more than location, determines who is malnourished in some countries. In Benin, a poor country, but far from the poorest, malnutrition is more common among the urban poor.

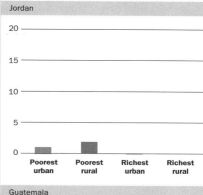

In Jordan, whose GNI per capita is four times higher than Benin's (on a purchasing power parity basis), malnutrition is a rare occurrence, but somewhat more frequent in rural areas.

Income distribution also matters. Guatemala, with an average income similar to Jordan's, has much higher rates of malnutrition among the poorest 20 percent of its population, and the rural poor are the worst off.

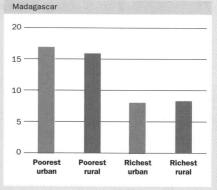

Madagascar, one of the poorest countries in the world, has significant malnutrition, even among the children of the richest 20 percent of its population.

Source: World Bank staff estimates based on Demographic and Health Survey data.

2 GOAL

- **Ensure that by 2015 children everywhere, boys and girls alike, will be able to complete a full course of primary schooling**

EDUCATION

Educating all children

Education is the foundation of democratic societies and globally competitive economies. It is the basis for reducing poverty and inequality, improving health, enabling the use of new technologies, and creating and spreading knowledge. In an increasingly complex, knowledge-dependent world, primary education, as the gateway to higher levels of education, must be the first priority.

Since 1990 the world has called for all children to be able to complete primary school, but more than 100 million primary school age children remain out of school.

To reach the target of universal primary education by 2015, school systems with low completion rates will need to start now to train teachers, build classrooms, and improve the quality of education. Most important, they will have to remove barriers to attendance such as fees and lack of transportation, and address parents' concern for the safety of their children.

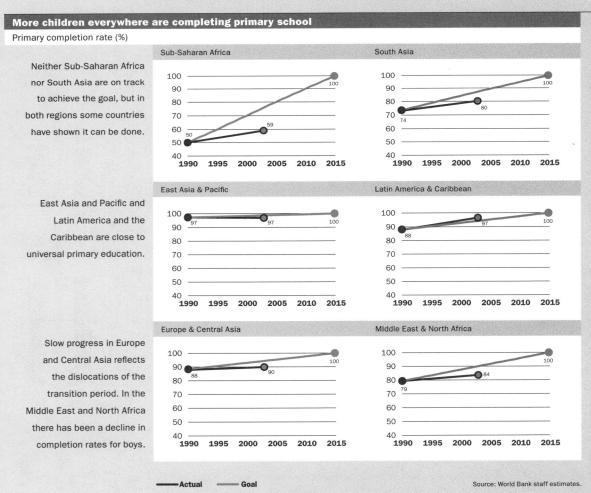

More children everywhere are completing primary school

Primary completion rate (%)

Neither Sub-Saharan Africa nor South Asia are on track to achieve the goal, but in both regions some countries have shown it can be done.

Sub-Saharan Africa — 1990: 50, ~2003: 59, 2015 goal: 100

South Asia — 1990: 74, ~2003: 80, 2015 goal: 100

East Asia and Pacific and Latin America and the Caribbean are close to universal primary education.

East Asia & Pacific — 1990: 97, ~2003: 97, 2015 goal: 100

Latin America & Caribbean — 1990: 88, ~2003: 97, 2015 goal: 100

Slow progress in Europe and Central Asia reflects the dislocations of the transition period. In the Middle East and North Africa there has been a decline in completion rates for boys.

Europe & Central Asia — 1990: 88, ~2003: 90, 2015 goal: 100

Middle East & North Africa — 1990: 79, ~2003: 84, 2015 goal: 100

— Actual   — Goal

Source: World Bank staff estimates.

Education for all means girls and boys

Primary completion rate, most recent year (% of relevant age group)

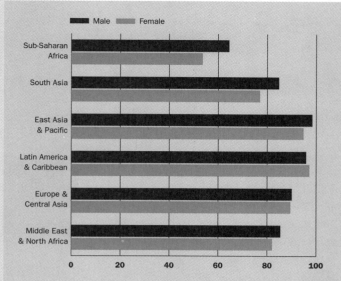

Source: World Bank staff estimates.

Except in Latin America and the Caribbean, girls are less likely than boys to complete primary school. Some never enroll, and others drop out because their families need their labor. This disadvantages them permanently. Parents may also be concerned about the safety of girls, especially when schools are far from home.

Inefficient schools slow progress

Net and gross enrollment ratios, primary school, 2001 (% of relevant age group)

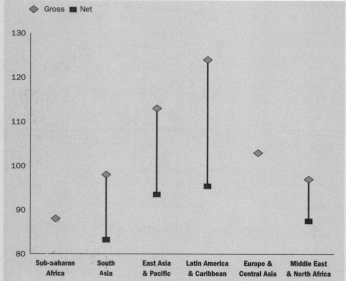

Source: World Bank staff estimates.

Large differences between gross enrollment (all ages) rates and net enrollment (age appropriate) rates occur when children delay entering school or frequently repeat grades. Excessive repetition raises the cost of schooling and discourages students from continuing. Sub-Saharan Africa and Europe and Central Asia lack sufficient data to measure regional net enrollment rates.

Rich and poor: an attendance gap

Share of 15- to 19-year-olds completing each grade or higher, by family wealth quintile (%)

In Egypt school attendance of the poorest 20 percent of the population lags from 30 to 45 percentage points behind that of the richest.

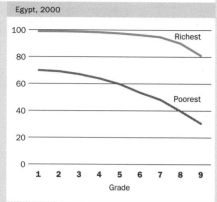

In India, as in Egypt, most children from rich families enroll and stay in school. But many poor children never enroll, and those who do stay only a few years.

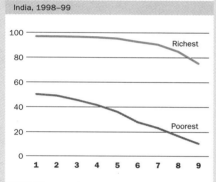

In a very poor country even children from the richest families may not attend primary school. In Niger few children, rich or poor, stay in school past the primary stage.

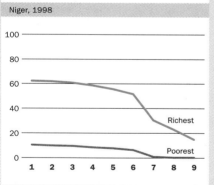

Enrolling all children in school is the starting point. Keeping them in school is the next step. In Peru many children from poor families soon leave school.

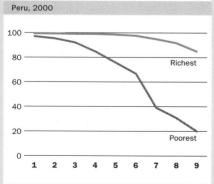

Source: World Bank staff estimates.

3 GOAL

- **Eliminate gender disparity in primary and secondary education, preferably by 2005, and at all levels by 2015.**

GENDER EQUALITY

Empowering women

Gender inequality keeps women at a disadvantage throughout their lives and stifles the development prospects of their societies. Illiterate and poorly educated mothers are less able to care for their children. Low education levels and responsibilities for household work prevent women from finding productive employment or participating in public decisionmaking.

When a country educates both its boys and its girls, economic productivity tends to rise, maternal and infant mortality rates usually fall, fertility rates decline, and the health and education prospects of the next generation improve.

What does it take to improve girls' enrollments? Mainly overcoming the social and economic obstacles that stop parents from sending their daughters to school. For many poor families the economic value of girls' work at home exceeds the perceived returns to schooling. Improving the quality and affordability of schools is a first step.

More girls in school, but the 2005 target will be missed

Ratio of girls to boys in primary and secondary education (%)

The differences between boys' and girls' schooling are greatest in regions with the lowest primary school completion rates and the lowest average incomes.

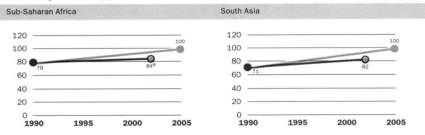

East Asia and Pacific has almost achieved the 2005 target. In some Latin American countries girls' enrollments exceed boys'.

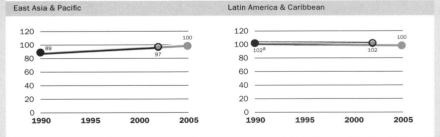

In Europe and Central Asia a strong tradition of educating girls needs to be sustained. In the Middle East and North Africa more girls are overcoming a bias against educating them.

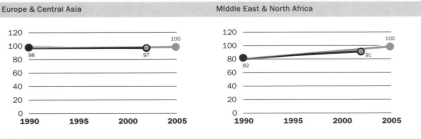

a. Based on 40 percent of the eligible population.

Source: World Bank staff estimates.

— Actual   — Goal

More women working for wages

Share of women in wage employment in the nonagricultural sector (%)

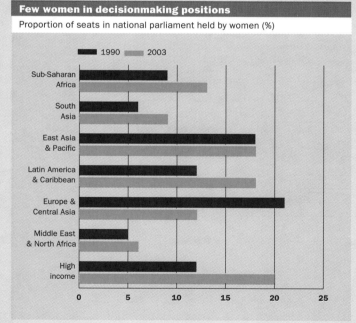

Source: World Bank staff estimates.

Although women's participation in the labor force has increased in almost every region, their share of wage employment in the nonagricultural sector has changed little. Women typically occupy low-paid, low-status jobs or work in family enterprises. Wage employment in modern sectors of the economy offers greater security and access to other social and economic benefits. But even in the same sector, women usually earn less than men.

Few women in decisionmaking positions

Proportion of seats in national parliament held by women (%)

■ 1990   ■ 2003

Sub-Saharan Africa
South Asia
East Asia & Pacific
Latin America & Caribbean
Europe & Central Asia
Middle East & North Africa
High income

Source: World Bank staff estimates.

Around the world women are underrepresented in parliaments and other high-level decisionmaking bodies. Women's presence in public life has been rising, but in 2004 women still occupied only 16 percent of the seats in national parliaments. Women's representation at the ministerial and executive levels of government is even lower.

Some countries have formal limitations on women's voting rights and election. In others, women have only recently acquired rights to participate in elections. In some places political parties have quota systems for women's representation in their governing bodies, and a few countries have quotas for women's representation in parliaments.

Income and tradition determine girls' opportunities for schooling

Ratio of girls' to boys' gross participation rates, by family wealth quintile (%)

■ Poorest   ■ Richest

In a poor country with low enrollment rates, girls are much less likely than boys to attend school.

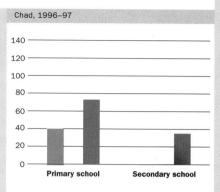

In Colombia, as in much of South America, girls' enrollment rates have caught up with boys', especially at the secondary level.

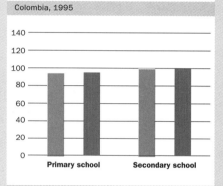

Girls are overrepresented in primary school in Tanzania, but poor girls are unlikely to reach the secondary level.

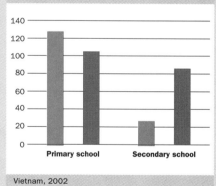

Although girls' enrollment rates lag behind boys', there is no clear difference between rich and poor families.

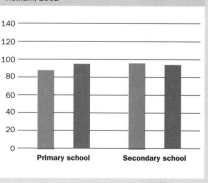

Source: World Bank staff estimates from Demographic and Health Survey data.

4
GOAL

- **Reduce by two thirds, between 1990 and 2015, the under-five mortality rate.**

CHILD MORTALITY

Saving children

Every year almost 11 million children in developing countries die before the age of five, most from causes that are readily preventable in rich countries: acute respiratory infections, diarrhea, measles, and malaria. Rapid improvements before 1990 gave hope that mortality rates for infants and children under five could be cut by two-thirds in the following 25 years. But progress slowed almost everywhere in the 1990s.

Only two regions, Latin America and the Caribbean and Europe and Central Asia, may be on track to achieve the target.

Progress has been particularly slow in Sub-Saharan Africa, where civil disturbances and the HIV/AIDS epidemic have driven up rates of infant and child mortality. By the most recent data available, only 33 countries are making enough progress to reduce under-five mortality rates to one-third of their 1990 level and save the lives of millions of children.

Improving the odds for children

Under-five mortality rate (deaths per 1,000)

The gap between goal and reality is greatest in Sub-Saharan Africa, but millions of children are also at risk in populous South Asia.

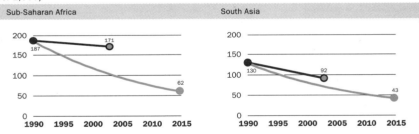

The pace of mortality reduction in East Asia and Pacific is slowing. The regional average in Latin America and the Caribbean disguises wide variations.

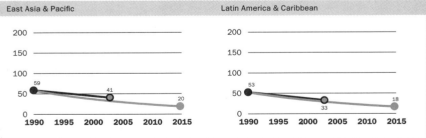

Although Europe and Central Asia appears to be on track, questions remain about the quality and comparability of data over time.

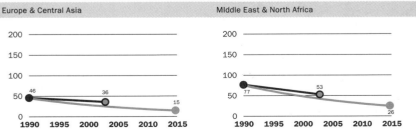

Source: World Bank staff estimates.

To reduce child deaths, infants must survive

Infant mortality rate (deaths per 1,000 live births)

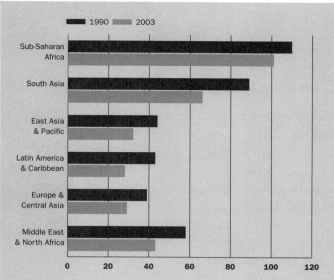

Legend: ■ 1990 ▨ 2003

Categories (top to bottom): Sub-Saharan Africa, South Asia, East Asia & Pacific, Latin America & Caribbean, Europe & Central Asia, Middle East & North Africa

X-axis: 0, 20, 40, 60, 80, 100, 120

Source: World Bank staff estimates.

A large proportion of child deaths occur among children in their first year, many of them among newborns. Inequalities within and across countries mean that a disproportionate burden of infant deaths is borne by the poorest people within the poorest countries. Greater efforts are needed so that health care and other public services reach poor mothers and children.

Many children's deaths are preventable

Causes of deaths, children under age five, developing countries, 2000–03

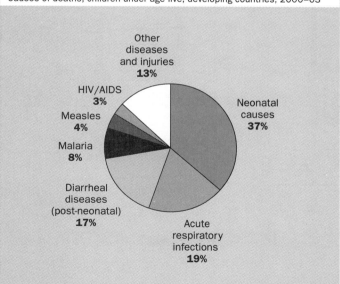

- Other diseases and injuries 13%
- HIV/AIDS 3%
- Measles 4%
- Malaria 8%
- Diarrheal diseases (post-neonatal) 17%
- Acute respiratory infections 19%
- Neonatal causes 37%

Source: World Health Organization.

Five diseases—pneumonia, diarrhea, malaria, measles, and HIV/AIDS—account for more than half of all deaths of children under age five. Antibiotics, immunization, and oral rehydration therapy for diarrhea could save the lives of many of these children. So would access to safe water and improved sanitation facilities. Good nutrition is also needed, because malnutrition increases the risk of dying from many of these diseases.

Unequal risks

Under-five mortality rate, by family wealth quintile and location (deaths per 1,000)

Mortality rates are generally higher in rural areas, where modern health care is less available. Higher mortality rates among the urban poor in Egypt are an exception.

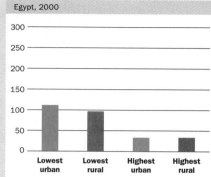

Egypt, 2000

Y-axis: 0, 50, 100, 150, 200, 250, 300
Categories: Lowest urban, Lowest rural, Highest urban, Highest rural

In India and many other countries mortality rates are 3 or 4 times as high in the poorest population quintile as in the richest.

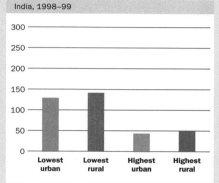

India, 1998–99

Y-axis: 0, 50, 100, 150, 200, 250, 300
Categories: Lowest urban, Lowest rural, Highest urban, Highest rural

Indonesia has reduced under-five mortality rates from 91 to 41 since 1990, but large differences remain between rich and poor.

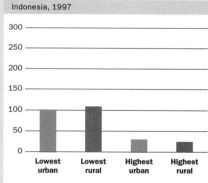

Indonesia, 1997

Y-axis: 0, 50, 100, 150, 200, 250, 300
Categories: Lowest urban, Lowest rural, Highest urban, Highest rural

Even among the more wealthy in Mali in 1995–96, 15 percent of children were expected to die before age five. There has been little improvement since.

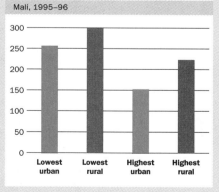

Mali, 1995–96

Y-axis: 0, 50, 100, 150, 200, 250, 300
Categories: Lowest urban, Lowest rural, Highest urban, Highest rural

Source: World Bank staff estimates based on Demographic and Health Survey data.

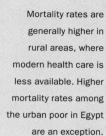

5
GOAL

- **Reduce by three-quarters, between 1990 and 2015, the maternal mortality ratio**

Caring for mothers

MATERNAL MORTALITY

More than 500,000 women die each year in childbirth, most of them in developing countries. What makes maternal mortality such a compelling problem is that it strikes young women experiencing a natural function of life. They die because they are poor. Malnourished. Weakened by disease. Exposed to multiple pregnancies. And they die because they lack access to trained health care workers and modern medical facilities.

Death in childbirth is a rare event in rich countries, where there are typically fewer than 15 maternal deaths for every 100,000 live births. But in the poorest countries of Africa and Asia the ratio may be 100 times higher. And because women in poor countries have more children, their lifetime risk of maternal death may be more than 200 times greater than for women in Western Europe and North America.

Mothers at risk in Africa and South Asia

Left axis (line): total fertility rate (births per woman); right axis (bar): maternal mortality ratio (deaths per 100,000 live births)

Maternal mortality ratios are still unacceptably high in many developing countries as a result of high fertility rates and a high risk of dying each time a woman becomes pregnant.

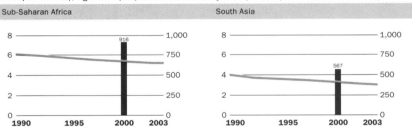

Sub-Saharan Africa — 916 (2000)

South Asia — 567 (2000)

Some developing countries have improved maternal health significantly through better services in hospitals and increased numbers of trained birth attendants and midwives.

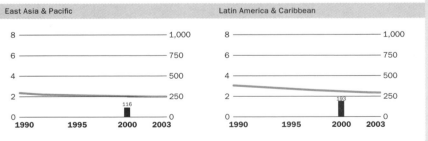

East Asia & Pacific — 116 (2000)

Latin America & Caribbean — 193 (2000)

Still others not only improved maternal health, but significantly lowered fertility rates directly through use of contraceptives and indirectly through increased female education.

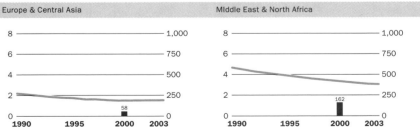

Europe & Central Asia — 58 (2000)

Middle East & North Africa — 162 (2000)

Source: World Bank staff estimates.

Mothers die because of inadequate health care

Causes of maternal death, 2000 (%)

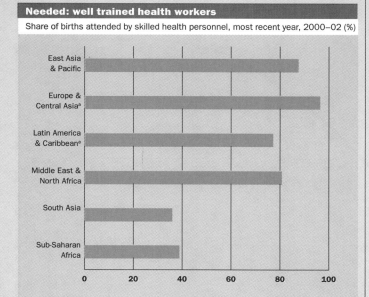

a. Includes anemia, malaria, and heart disease.
b. Includes ectopic pregnancy, embolism, and anesthesia-related deaths.
Source: AbouZahr 2003.

Maternal deaths are difficult to measure because they are relatively rare events and because reporting systems are least adequate in the countries with the highest levels of mortality. Deaths may go unreported or their connection to pregnancy or childbirth may go unnoted. When a maternal death is reported, the cause of death may not be known. Recent estimates of major obstetric complications based on aggregate data suggest that severe bleeding after delivery is the leading cause of maternal deaths. As with many complications of childbirth, skilled personnel and modern medical facilities are needed to treat such cases and save the lives of mothers.

Needed: well trained health workers

Share of births attended by skilled health personnel, most recent year, 2000–02 (%)

a. Available data represent 40 percent of the population.

Source: World Bank staff estimates from data compiled by WHO and UNICEF.

Women are most in need of skilled care during and immediately after delivery, when most maternal deaths occur. The single most critical intervention is to ensure that a competent health worker with midwifery skills is present at every birth and that transport is available to a referral facility.

Apart from Sub-Saharan Africa and South Asia, delivery care has improved significantly in developing regions, though not all countries have shared equally in such improvements. About half the births in developing countries are not assisted by a skilled health worker.

Poor and rural women are least well served

Share of births attended by skilled health personnel, by family wealth quintile and location (%)

Health care during childbirth varies considerably. Births to women in the richest quintile are six times more likely on average to be attended by a trained professional such as a doctor, nurse, or midwife.

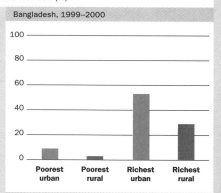

Urban-rural differences are greatest when overall use of health care professionals is low, as in Bangladesh, Cambodia, and Guatemala, where 40 percent or fewer births are attended by skilled personnel.

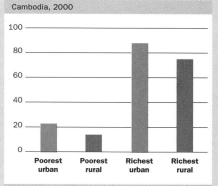

Urban women are more likely to have access to doctors, nurses, and medically trained midwives and to hospital facilities equipped to deal with obstetric emergencies.

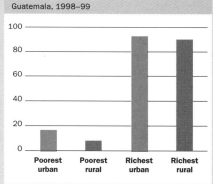

Poor quality services and limited access are major causes of maternal illness and death. Investment in infrastructure (roads, communication facilities) is needed, along with more skilled health workers.

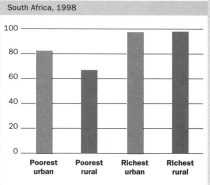

Source: World Bank staff estimates based on Demographic and Health Survey data.

- Have halted by 2015 and begun to reverse the spread of HIV/AIDS.

- Have halted by 2015 and begun to reverse the incidence of malaria and other major diseases.

Combating disease

Epidemic diseases exact a huge toll in human suffering and lost opportunities for development. Poverty, armed conflict, and natural disasters contribute to the spread of disease and are made worse by it.

In Africa the spread of HIV/AIDS has reversed decades of improvements in life expectancy and left millions of children orphaned. It is draining the supply of teachers and eroding the quality of education.

There are 300–500 million cases of malaria each year, leading to more than 1 million deaths. Nearly all the cases (almost 90 percent) occur in Sub-Saharan Africa, and most deaths from malaria are among children younger than five years old.

Tuberculosis kills some 2 million people a year, most of them 15–45 years old. The disease is spreading more rapidly because of the emergence of drug-resistant strains of tuberculosis; the spread of HIV/AIDS, which reduces resistance to tuberculosis; and the growing number of refugees and displaced people.

While Sub-Saharan Africa struggles, HIV/AIDS spreads in other regions

Adult (ages 15–49) HIV prevalence rate (%)

HIV has infected more than 60 million people worldwide. Each day 14,000 people are newly infected, more than half of them under age 25. At the end of 2004, 37 million adults and 2 million children were living with HIV/AIDS—more than 95 percent of them in developing countries and 70 percent in Sub-Saharan Africa.

The proportion of adults living with HIV/AIDS in Sub-Saharan Africa has stabilized—not because the epidemic has been halted, but because the death rate now equals the rate of new cases. While prevalence rates are lower in other regions, the numbers are growing. There were almost a million new cases in South and East Asia, where more than 7 million people now live with HIV/AIDS.

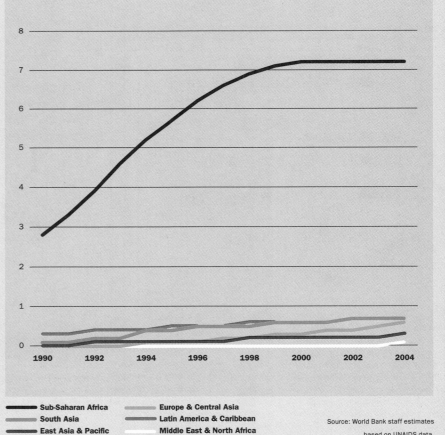

Sub-Saharan Africa
South Asia
East Asia & Pacific
Europe & Central Asia
Latin America & Caribbean
Middle East & North Africa

Source: World Bank staff estimates based on UNAIDS data.

The risk to women is growing

Ratio of female to male HIV prevalence rates, ages 15–24, 2001

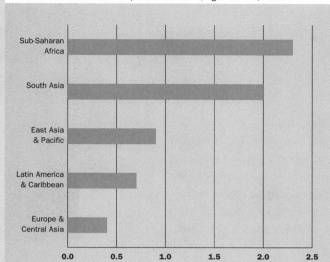

Source: World Bank staff estimates.

For social and physiological reasons, women and girls are more vulnerable to HIV infection than are men and boys. Women make up slightly less than half of adults living with HIV/AIDS, but where the epidemic is spreading, prevalence rates are rising fastest among young women. In parts of Sub-Saharan Africa young women are more than three times as likely as young men to be infected. This points to a failure to provide women with the knowledge and services needed to avoid infections.

In Africa AIDS is leaving millions of children orphaned

Children losing both parents (millions)

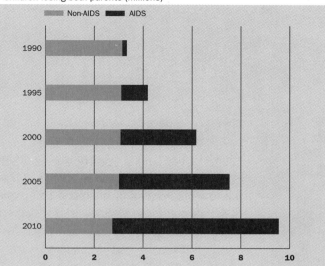

Source: UNAIDS.

AIDS is an increasing cause of death in young children, but it is also leaving millions of children orphaned. By the end of 2003, 15 million children worldwide, 12 million in Sub-Saharan Africa, had lost one or both parents to AIDS.

In Sub-Saharan Africa, where the epidemic is most widespread, the number of children who have lost both parents is increasing rapidly. These children are particularly vulnerable to disease and neglect, creating an unprecedented social problem.

The risk of tuberculosis grows for the most vulnerable

Incidence of tuberculosis (per 100,000 people)

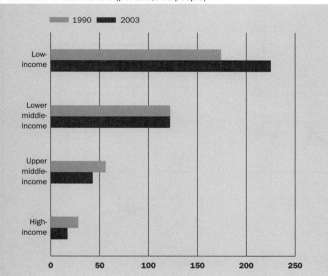

Source: World Bank staff estimates.

Each year there are 8 million new cases of tuberculosis—3 million in South and East Asia, 2 million in Sub-Saharan Africa, and more than a quarter million in countries of the former Soviet Union.

The disease has spread fastest in poor countries with ineffective health systems. Poorly managed tuberculosis programs allow drug-resistant strains to spread. The World Health Organization has developed a treatment strategy—DOTS—that emphasizes positive diagnosis followed by a course of treatment and follow-up care. DOTS has proven successful, but many cases of tuberculosis still go undetected or untreated.

Young children bear the burden of malaria

Malaria deaths by age and location, 2000 (per 100,000)

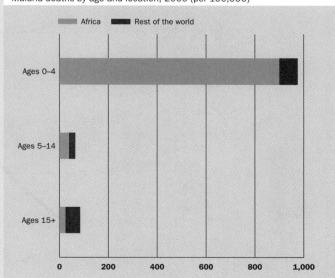

Source: WHO and UNICEF 2003.

Malaria is a disease of poverty and a cause of poverty. About 90 percent of malaria deaths occur in Sub-Saharan Africa, where a million people die each year, most of them children under five and most poor. In Zambia malaria prevalence is almost three times higher among the poorest 20 percent as among the wealthiest.

Malaria has slowed economic growth in Africa by an estimated 1.3 percent a year (World Bank 2001). Insecticide-treated bednets are effective in preventing new infections but are not widely available. With the emergence of drug-resistant strains, new means of treatment and prevention are urgently needed.

7 GOAL

- Integrate the principles of sustainable development into country policies and programs and reverse the loss of environmental resources.

- Reduce by half the proportion of people without sustainable access to safe drinking water.

- Achieve significant improvement in the lives of at least 100 million slum dwellers by 2020.

Using resources wisely

ENVIRONMENT

Sustainable development can be ensured only by protecting the environment and using its resources wisely. Poor people, often dependent on environmental resources for their livelihood, are the most affected by environmental degradation and natural disasters (fires, storms, earthquakes) whose effects are worsened by environmental mismanagement.

Most countries have adopted principles of sustainable development and agreed to international accords on protecting the environment. But good intentions are not enough. Around the world land is being degraded. Forests are being lost, fisheries overused, and plant and animal species are becoming extinct. And carbon emissions are leading to climate change.

Rich countries are major consumers of products from the environment. Thus rich countries and poor countries alike have a stake in using environmental resources wisely.

People need safe, reliable supplies of water

Population without access to an improved water source (%)

In Sub-Saharan Africa 300 million people lack access to improved water sources. South Asia has made excellent progress, but contamination of water sources poses new risks.

Sub-Saharan Africa
51 — 42 — 26

South Asia
30 — 16 — 15

In East Asia rapid urbanization is posing a challenge for the provision of water and other public utilities. With faster progress here and in other regions, the world as a whole will achieve the target.

East Asia & Pacific
29 — 22 — 15

Latin America & Caribbean
18 — 11 — 9

Data are lacking for Europe and Central Asia in the early 1990s. In the Middle East and North Africa, Egypt, Tunisia, and Morocco have made the fastest progress.

Europe & Central Asia
8.7

Middle East & North Africa
13 — 12 — 6

——— Actual ——— Goal

Source: World Bank staff estimates.

Many still lack adequate sanitation

Share of population with access to improved sanitation, 2002 (%)

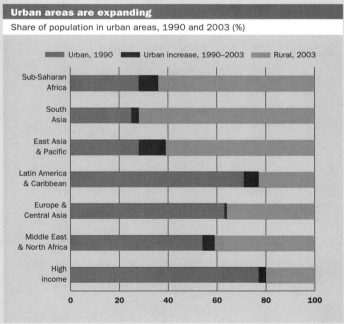

Source: World Bank staff estimates.

Lack of clean water and basic sanitation is the main reason diseases transmitted by feces are so common in developing countries. While water systems are improving quickly, sanitation systems lag behind. A basic sanitation system provides disposal facilities that can effectively prevent human, animal, and insect contact with excreta. It does not, however, ensure treatment of effluents to remove harmful substances before they are released into the environment.

Urban areas are expanding

Share of population in urban areas, 1990 and 2003 (%)

Source: World Bank staff estimates.

Almost half the world's people live in urban areas, and the number is increasing rapidly. While the movement of people to cities may reduce immediate pressure on the rural environment, it increases people's exposure to environmental hazards. UN-HABITAT estimates that nearly 1 billion people live in slums, where they lack basic services, live in overcrowded and substandard housing, and are exposed to unhealthy living conditions in hazardous locations.

More environmental challenges ahead

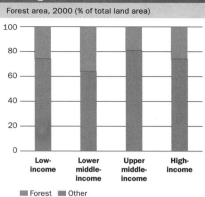

Forest area, 2000 (% of total land area)

Almost a third of Earth's land area is forested, but almost 1 million square kilometers of forest were lost from 1990 to 2000. The largest losses were in low-income economies, which felled 7 percent of their forests.

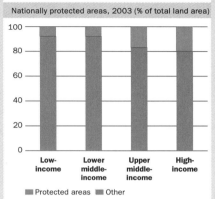

Nationally protected areas, 2003 (% of total land area)

Protected areas and natural reserves can help to preserve habitat for plants and animals. Some of the most important regions of biodiversity are in developing countries, especially those on or near the equator.

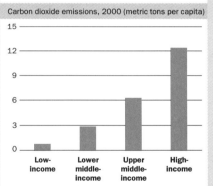

Carbon dioxide emissions, 2000 (metric tons per capita)

Emissions of carbon dioxide, a greenhouse gas that contributes to global climate change, have increased in most developing regions. But high-income economies remain the largest emitters of carbon dioxide.

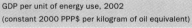

GDP per unit of energy use, 2002 (constant 2000 PPP$ per kilogram of oil equivalent)

More efficient use of energy can decrease the emissions of carbon dioxide and other pollutants. High-income economies are the most energy efficient on average, but developing economies are catching up.

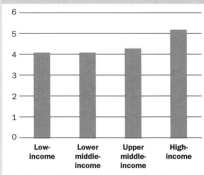

Source: World Bank staff estimates.

DEVELOPMENT PARTNERSHIP

8
GOAL

- **Develop further an open trading and financial system that is rule-based, predictable, and nondiscriminatory.**
- **Address the special needs of the least developed countries.**
- **Address the special needs of landlocked and small island developing states.**
- **Deal comprehensively with**

developing countries' debt problems to make debt sustainable in the long term.
- **Develop decent and productive work for youth.**
- **Provide access to affordable essential drugs in developing countries.**
- **Make available the benefits of new technologies—especially information and communications technologies.**

Working together

The eighth and final goal complements the others. In partnership, wealthy countries work with developing countries to create an environment in which rapid, sustainable development is possible. Important steps toward global partnership were taken at international meetings in 2001 in Doha, which launched a new "development round" of trade negotiations, and in 2002 at the conference on financing for development in Monterrey, Mexico, where high-income and developing countries reached consensus on mutual responsibilities for achieving the Millennium Development Goals. The consensus calls for developing countries to improve governance and policies aimed at increasing economic growth and reducing poverty and for high-income countries to provide more and better aid and greater access to their markets.

Goal 8 also reminds us that the development challenges differ for large countries and small countries. And that developing countries need access to new technologies to increase productivity and improve people's lives.

Many sources and many patterns of financing
Selected net financial flows, 2003 (US$ billions)

Aid is not the only source of development finance or, for many countries, the most important. Remittances and private voluntary transfers meet some of their need. But the extremely poor countries of Africa and Asia require substantial increases in aid to reach their development goals.

Rapidly growing economies need and attract large flows of private direct and portfolio investment. East Asian exporters have also recorded large trade surpluses. Latin America and the Caribbean receives high levels of remittances from people living and working abroad.

Many countries in the Middle East and North Africa generate substantial trade surpluses, which provide a source of public and private finance. Although countries in all regions borrow from multilateral institutions like the World Bank, some are repaying more than they borrow.

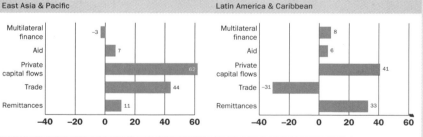

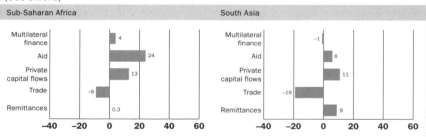

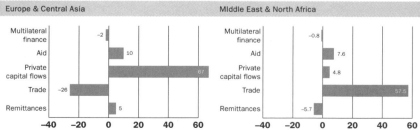

Source: World Bank staff estimates.

Official development assistance is rising, but still too little

Left axis (bars): Official development assistance (2002 US$ billions)
Right axis (line): Official development assistance as share of donors' GNI (%)

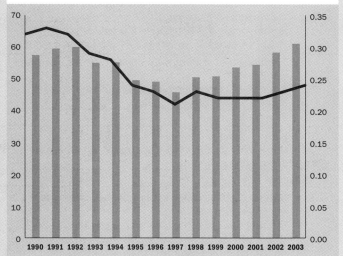

Source: OECD Development Assistance Committee.

Official development assistance (ODA) is the aid provided by the richest countries to the poorest. Through much of the 1990s ODA levels fell while ODA as a proportion of donors' GNI fell even faster. Many donors pledged to provide at least 0.7 percent of GNI, but the average remains below .25 percent. As much as a third of aid goes to middle-income countries, not to the neediest. Since 2002 donors have pledged to increase aid by $20 billion a year in 2006 and to provide more than $100 billion a year by 2010.

Debt service is falling, but more relief is needed

Ratio of external debt service to exports of goods and services (%)

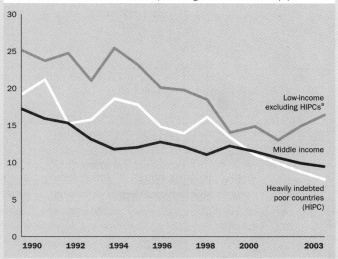

a. Includes a one-time balloon payment on an Indian bond in 2003.
Source: World Bank staff estimates.

Low-income countries paid $28 billion in debt service on public debt in 2003. Middle-income countries paid $177 billion. Developing country export earnings, needed to acquire the currencies to pay their creditors, have been rising while debt service has grown more slowly, reducing debt burdens for many countries. But for extremely poor countries debt service represents a crucial loss of potential development resources. Since 1998 the HIPC initiative has provided $54 billion in debt relief for heavily indebted poor countries.

Tariffs remain high on poor countries' exports

Average tariffs imposed by high-income countries on developing country imports (%)

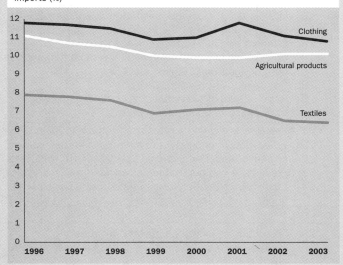

Source: International Trade Centre, World Trade Organization, and United Nations Conference on Trade and Development.

Creating opportunities for developing countries to sell their products in wealthier markets is an important complement to aid. Tariffs have been falling. Many high-income countries have offered special concessions, allowing selected exports of poor countries to enter duty-free. The recent dropping of quotas on textiles has created new opportunities for efficient producers. But tariffs charged by high-income countries on goods important to developing countries, such as textiles and agricultural products, remain high. Subsidies of $350 billion a year to agricultural producers in OECD countries are another barrier to developing country exports. Global trade is not yet a level playing field.

New technologies are spreading quickly

Information and communications technology users in low- and middle-income economies (per 1,000 people)

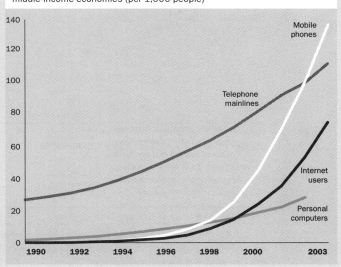

Source: World Bank staff estimates and data from the International Telecommunication Union.

New technologies bring new opportunities to developing countries. Mobile phones have helped to eliminate the bottlenecks of fixed, mainline phone service. Personal computers are more widely available, and the Internet, unknown 15 years ago, is expanding rapidly. These are examples of integrating technologies, which reduce barriers of time, space, and culture.

Developing countries also need access to new medicines to reduce the terrible burden of disease. Bringing these and other life-saving technologies to poor people will require willing cooperation between the public and private sectors.

Goals, targets, and indicators

Goals and targets from the Millennium Declaration	**Indicators for monitoring progress**

Goal 1	**Eradicate extreme poverty and hunger**		
Target 1	Halve, between 1990 and 2015, the proportion of people whose income is less than $1 a day	1 1a 2 3	Proportion of population below $1 (PPP) a day [a] Poverty headcount ratio (percentage of population below the national poverty line) Poverty gap ratio [incidence x depth of poverty] Share of poorest quintile in national consumption
Target 2	Halve, between 1990 and 2015, the proportion of people who suffer from hunger	4 5	Prevalence of underweight children under five years of age Proportion of population below minimum level of dietary energy consumption

Goal 2	**Achieve universal primary education**		
Target 3	Ensure that, by 2015, children everywhere, boys and girls alike, will be able to complete a full course of primary schooling	6 7 8	Net enrollment ratio in primary education Proportion of pupils starting grade 1 who reach grade 5 [b] Literacy rate of 15- to 24-year-olds

Goal 3	**Promote gender equality and empower women**		
Target 4	Eliminate gender disparity in primary and secondary education, preferably by 2005, and in all levels of education no later than 2015	9 10 11 12	Ratios of girls to boys in primary, secondary, and tertiary education Ratio of literate women to men ages 15–24 Share of women in wage employment in the nonagricultural sector Proportion of seats held by women in national parliaments

Goal 4	**Reduce child mortality**		
Target 5	Reduce by two-thirds, between 1990 and 2015, the under-five mortality rate	13 14 15	Under-five mortality rate Infant mortality rate Proportion of one-year-old children immunized against measles

Goal 5	**Improve maternal health**		
Target 6	Reduce by three-quarters, between 1990 and 2015, the maternal mortality ratio	16 17	Maternal mortality ratio Proportion of births attended by skilled health personnel

Goal 6	**Combat HIV/AIDS, malaria, and other diseases**		
Target 7	Have halted by 2015 and begun to reverse the spread of HIV/AIDS	18 19 19a 19b 19c 20	HIV prevalence among pregnant women ages 15–24 Condom use rate of the contraceptive prevalence rate [c] Condom use at last high-risk sex Percentage of 15- to 24-year-olds with comprehensive correct knowledge of HIV/AIDS [d] Contraceptive prevalence rate Ratio of school attendance of orphans to school attendance of nonorphans ages 10–14
Target 8	Have halted by 2015 and begun to reverse the incidence of malaria and other major diseases	21 22 23 24	Prevalence and death rates associated with malaria Proportion of population in malaria-risk areas using effective malaria prevention and treatment measures [e] Prevalence and death rates associated with tuberculosis Proportion of tuberculosis cases detected and cured under directly observed treatment, short course (DOTS)

Goal 7	**Ensure environmental sustainability**		
Target 9	Integrate the principles of sustainable development into country policies and programs and reverse the loss of environmental resources	25 26 27 28 29	Proportion of land area covered by forest Ratio of area protected to maintain biological diversity to surface area Energy use (kilograms of oil equivalent) per $1 GDP (PPP) Carbon dioxide emissions per capita and consumption of ozone-depleting chlorofluorocarbons (ODP tons) Proportion of population using solid fuels
Target 10	Halve, by 2015, the proportion of people without sustainable access to safe drinking water and basic sanitation	30 31	Proportion of population with sustainable access to an improved water source, urban and rural Proportion of population with access to improved sanitation, urban and rural

Goals and targets from the Millennium Declaration | Indicators for monitoring progress

Goals and targets from the Millennium Declaration	Indicators for monitoring progress
Target 11 By 2020, to have achieved a significant improvement in the lives of at least 100 million slum dwellers	32 Proportion of households with access to secure tenure
Goal 8 **Develop a global partnership for development**	
Target 12 Develop further an open, rule-based, predictable, nondiscriminatory trading and financial system Includes a commitment to good governance, development and poverty reduction—both nationally and internationally	Some of the indicators listed below are monitored separately for the least developed countries (LDCs), Africa, landlocked countries and small island developing states. **Official development assistance (ODA)** 33 Net ODA, total and to the least developed countries, as a percentage of OECD/DAC donors' gross national income 34 Proportion of total bilateral, sector-allocable ODA of OECD/DAC donors to basic social services (basic education, primary health care, nutrition, safe water and sanitation)
Target 13 Address the special needs of the least developed countries Includes tariff and quota free access for the least developed countries' exports; enhanced programme of debt relief for heavily indebted poor countries (HIPC) and cancellation of official bilateral debt; and more generous ODA for countries committed to poverty reduction	35 Proportion of bilateral official development assistance of OECD/DAC donors that is untied 36 ODA received in landlocked countries as a proportion of their gross national incomes 37 ODA received in small island developing states as proportion of their gross national incomes
Target 14 Address the special needs of landlocked countries and small island developing states (through the Programme of Action for the Sustainable Development of Small Island Developing States and the outcome of the 22nd special session of the General Assembly)	**Market access** 38 Proportion of total developed country imports (by value and excluding arms) from developing countries and from the least developed countries, admitted free of duty 39 Average tariffs imposed by developed countries on agricultural products and textiles and clothing from developing countries 40 Agricultural support estimate for OECD countries as a percentage of their gross domestic product 41 Proportion of ODA provided to help build trade capacity
Target 15 Deal comprehensively with the debt problems of developing countries through national and international measures in order to make debt sustainable in the long term	**Debt sustainability** 42 Total number of countries that have reached their HIPC decision points and number that have reached their HIPC completion points (cumulative) 43 Debt relief committed under HIPC Debt Initiative 44 Debt service as a percentage of exports of goods and services
Target 16 In cooperation with developing countries, develop and implement strategies for decent and productive work for youth	45 Unemployment rate of 15- to 24-year-olds, male and female and total [f]
Target 17 In cooperation with pharmaceutical companies, provide access to affordable essential drugs in developing countries	46 Proportion of population with access to affordable essential drugs on a sustainable basis
Target 18 In cooperation with the private sector, make available the benefits of new technologies, especially information and communications	47 Telephone lines and cellular subscribers per 100 people 48a Personal computers in use per 100 people 48b Internet users per 100 people

Note: Goals, targets, and indicators effective September 8, 2003.
a. For monitoring country poverty trends, indicators based on national poverty lines should be used, where available. b. An alternative indicator under development is "primary completion rate." c. Among contraceptive methods, only condoms are effective in preventing HIV transmission. Since the condom use rate is only measured among women in union, it is supplemented by an indicator on condom use in high-risk situations (indicator 19a) and an indicator on HIV/AIDS knowledge (indicator 19b). Indicator 19c (contraceptive prevalence rate) is also useful in tracking progress in other health, gender, and poverty goals. d. This indicator is defined as the percentage of 15- to 24-year-olds who correctly identify the two major ways of preventing the sexual transmission of HIV (using condoms and limiting sex to one faithful, uninfected partner), who reject the two most common local misconceptions about HIV transmission, and who know that a healthy-looking person can transmit HIV. However, since there are currently not a sufficient number of surveys to be able to calculate the indicator as defined above, UNICEF, in collaboration with UNAIDS and WHO, produced two proxy indicators that represent two components of the actual indicator. They are the percentage of women and men ages 15–24 who know that a person can protect herself from HIV infection by "consistent use of condom," and the percentage of women and men ages 15–24 who know a healthy-looking person can transmit HIV. e. Prevention to be measured by the percentage of children under age five sleeping under insecticide-treated bednets; treatment to be measured by percentage of children under age five who are appropriately treated. f. An improved measure of the target for future years is under development by the International Labour Organization.

1.1 Size of the economy

	Population	Surface area	Population density	Gross national income		Gross national income per capita		PPP gross national income[a]			Gross domestic product	
	millions	thousand sq. km	people per sq. km	$ billions	Rank	$	Rank	$ billions	Per capita $	Rank	% growth	Per capita % growth
	2003	**2003**	**2003**	**2003**[b]	**2003**	**2003**[b]	**2003**	**2003**	**2003**	**2003**	**2002–03**	**2002–03**
Afghanistan	..	652	..	..	..	..[c]	..	..	..	..	..	..
Albania	3	29	116	5.5	115	1,740	120	15	4,710	126	6.0	5.4
Algeria	32	2,382	13	61.6	49	1,930	112	189[d]	5,930[d]	103	6.8	5.1
Angola	14	1,247	11	10.0	93	740	148	26[d]	1,910[d]	162	4.5	1.4
Argentina	37	2,780	13	140.1	30	3,810	84	420	11,410	66	8.8	8.0
Armenia	3	30	108	2.9	143	950	139	12	3,790	134	13.9	14.4
Australia	20	7,741	3	436.5	14	21,950	27	572	28,780	15	3.8	2.7
Austria	8	84	98	216.9	20	26,810	16	241	29,740	12	0.7	0.5
Azerbaijan	8	87	100	6.7	104	820	145	28	3,390	139	11.2	10.4
Bangladesh	138	144	1,061	55.0	51	400	173	258	1,870	163	5.3	3.4
Belarus	10	208	48	15.8	79	1,600	121	60	6,050	102	6.8	7.3
Belgium	10	31	343	267.3	18	25,760	20	300	28,920	14	1.1	0.7
Benin	7	113	61	3.0	141	440	170	7	1,110	184	4.8	2.2
Bolivia	9	1,099	8	7.9	99	900	142	22	2,490	151	2.5	0.5
Bosnia and Herzegovina	4	51	81	6.4	109	1,530	122	26	6,250	101	2.7	2.0
Botswana	2	582	3	6.1	112	3,530	86	14	8,370	83	5.4	4.8
Brazil	177	8,515	21	479.5	13	2,720	95	1,326	7,510	86	–0.2	–1.4
Bulgaria	8	111	71	16.6	76	2,130	107	59	7,540	85	4.3	4.9
Burkina Faso	12	274	44	3.6	135	300	183	14[d]	1,170[d]	183	6.5	4.1
Burundi	7	28	281	0.6	186	90	207	5[d]	630[d]	205	–1.2	–3.1
Cambodia	13	181	76	4.1	126	300	183	27[d]	2,000[d]	160	5.2	3.3
Cameroon	16	475	35	10.1	92	630	154	32	1,990	161	4.7	2.6
Canada	32	9,971	3	773.9	8	24,470	24	950	30,040	11	2.0	1.1
Central African Republic	4	623	6	1.0	172	260	190	4[d]	1,080[d]	185	–7.3	–8.8
Chad	9	1,284	7	2.1	151	240	192	9	1,080	185	11.3	8.2
Chile	16	757	21	68.7	46	4,360	76	155	9,810	77	3.3	2.1
China	1,288	9,598[e]	138	1,416.8	6	1,100	134	6,410[f]	4,980[f]	119	9.3	8.6
Hong Kong, China	7	..	6,541	176.2	26	25,860	19	195	28,680	16	3.2	2.8
Colombia	45	1,139	43	80.5	42	1,810	118	286[d]	6,410[d]	97	3.9	2.2
Congo, Dem. Rep.	53	2,345	23	5.4	117	100	206	35[d]	660[d]	204	5.6	2.5
Congo, Rep.	4	342	11	2.4	147	650	153	3	730	200	2.7	–0.1
Costa Rica	4	51	78	17.2	75	4,300	77	37[d]	9,140[d]	79	6.5	4.8
Côte d'Ivoire	17	322	53	11.1	86	660	152	24	1,400	180	–3.8	–5.6
Croatia	4	57	79	23.9	64	5,370	71	47	10,610	73	4.3	4.2
Cuba	11	111	103	..	..	..[g]	..	..	..	..	..	..
Czech Republic	10	79	132	72.9	45	7,150	63	159	15,600	56	3.1	3.1
Denmark	5	43	127	180.9	25	33,570	8	167	31,050	8	0.4	0.2
Dominican Republic	9	49	181	18.6	72	2,130	107	55[d]	6,310[d]	99	–0.4	–1.8
Ecuador	13	284	47	23.8	66	1,830	117	45	3,440	137	2.7	1.1
Egypt, Arab Rep.	68	1,001	68	93.9	38	1,390	126	266	3,940	132	3.2	1.4
El Salvador	7	21	315	15.3	82	2,340	100	32[d]	4,910[d]	122	1.8	0.0
Eritrea	4	118	43	0.9	175	190	198	4[d]	1,020[d]	190	3.0	0.8
Estonia	1	45	32	7.3	101	5,380	70	17	12,680	63	5.1	5.5
Ethiopia	69	1,104	69	6.4	108	90	207	48[d]	710[d]	201	–3.7	–5.6
Finland	5	338	17	141.0	29	27,060	13	143	27,460	24	1.9	1.6
France	60	552	109	1,521.6[h]	5	24,730[h]	23	1,652	27,640	22	0.5	0.0
Gabon	1	268	5	4.5	124	3,340	89	7	5,500	110	2.8	0.6
Gambia, The	1	11	142	0.4	191	270	189	2[d]	1,740[d]	169	6.7	4.3
Georgia	5	70	74	3.9	130	770	147	13[d]	2,610[d]	148	11.1	12.2
Germany	83	357	237	2,085.5	3	25,270	22	2,279	27,610	23	–0.1	–0.1
Ghana	21	239	91	6.5	107	320	181	45[d]	2,190[d]	155	5.2	3.3
Greece	11	132	86	146.0	28	13,230	45	220	19,900	40	4.3	4.0
Guatemala	12	109	114	23.5	67	1,910	114	50[d]	4,090[d]	130	2.1	–0.5
Guinea	8	246	32	3.4	138	430	171	16	2,080	158	1.2	–0.9
Guinea-Bissau	1	36	53	0.2	203	140	202	1[d]	680[d]	202	0.6	–2.3
Haiti	8	28	306	3.3	139	400	173	15[d]	1,730[d]	170	0.4	–1.4

	Population	Surface area	Population density	Gross national income		Gross national income per capita		PPP gross national income[a]			Gross domestic product	
	millions	thousand sq. km	people per sq. km	$ billions	Rank	$	Rank	$ billions	Per capita $	Rank	% growth	Per capita % growth
	2003	**2003**	**2003**	**2003**[b]	**2003**	**2003**[b]	**2003**	**2003**	**2003**	**2003**	**2002–03**	**2002–03**
Honduras	7	112	62	6.8	103	970	137	18[d]	2,590[d]	149	3.0	0.5
Hungary	10	93	110	64.3	47	6,350	67	140	13,840	58	3.0	3.4
India	1,064	3,287	358	570.8	12	540	159	3,062[d]	2,880[d]	146	8.6	7.1
Indonesia	215	1,905	119	173.5	27	810	146	689	3,210	142	4.1	2.7
Iran, Islamic Rep.	66	1,648	41	133.2	32	2,010	110	465	7,000	90	6.6	5.2
Iraq	25	438	56	..	..	..[g]	..	..	..	..	..	..
Ireland	4	70	58	107.9	36	27,010	14	123	30,910	9	3.7	2.0
Israel	7	22	308	108.6	35	16,240	38	130	19,440	44	1.3	−0.6
Italy	58	301	196	1,243.2	7	21,570	28	1,546	26,830	25	0.3	0.3
Jamaica	3	11	244	7.9	100	2,980	92	10	3,790	134	2.3	1.4
Japan	128	378	350	4,360.8	2	34,180	7	3,629	28,450	19	2.7	2.5
Jordan	5	89	60	9.8	95	1,850	116	23	4,290	129	3.2	0.5
Kazakhstan	15	2,725	6	26.5	62	1,780	119	93	6,280	100	9.2	9.2
Kenya	32	580	56	12.8	84	400	173	33	1,030	189	1.8	0.0
Korea, Dem. Rep.	23	121	188	..	..	..[c]	..	..	..	..	..	..
Korea, Rep.	48	99	485	576.4	11	12,030	49	862	18,000	47	3.1	2.5
Kuwait	2	18	134	43.0	56	17,960	34	47[d]	19,480[d]	43	9.9	7.1
Kyrgyz Republic	5	200	26	1.7	156	340	179	9	1,690	175	6.7	5.7
Lao PDR	6	237	25	1.9	152	340	179	10	1,730	170	5.0	2.6
Latvia	2	65	37	10.2	91	4,400	75	24	10,210	75	7.5	8.2
Lebanon	4	10	440	18.2	73	4,040	81	22	4,840	124	2.7	1.4
Lesotho	2	30	59	1.1	169	610	156	6[d]	3,100[d]	144	3.3	2.4
Liberia	3	111	35	0.4	193	110	205	..	..	203	−29.5	−31.1
Libya	6	1,760	3	..	..	..[i]	..	..	..	..	..	..
Lithuania	3	65	55	15.6	80	4,500	74	39	11,390	67	9.0	9.4
Macedonia, FYR	2	26	81	4.1	128	1,980	111	14	6,750	93	3.2	2.7
Madagascar	17	587	29	4.9	121	290	187	13	800	199	9.8	6.8
Malawi	11	118	117	1.8	155	160	200	6	590	207	4.4	2.3
Malaysia	25	330	75	96.1	37	3,880	82	222	8,970	81	5.3	3.3
Mali	12	1,240	10	3.4	137	290	187	11	960	192	6.0	3.5
Mauritania	3	1,026	3	1.1	167	400	173	5[d]	1,870[d]	163	4.9	2.6
Mauritius	1	2	602	5.0	119	4,100	78	14	11,280	68	3.2	2.2
Mexico	102	1,958	54	637.2	10	6,230	68	919	8,980	80	1.3	−0.2
Moldova	4	34	129	2.1	150	590	157	7	1,760	167	6.3	6.7
Mongolia	2	1,567	2	1.2	164	480	165	5	1,820	165	5.6	4.3
Morocco	30	447	67	39.4	57	1,310	128	119	3,940	132	5.2	3.6
Mozambique	19	802	24	3.9	131	210	195	20[d]	1,060[d]	187	7.1	5.1
Myanmar	49	677	75	..	..	..[c]	..	..	..	..	..	..
Namibia	2	824	2	3.9	132	1,930	112	13[d]	6,660[d]	95	3.7	2.2
Nepal	25	147	172	5.9	113	240	192	35	1,420	179	3.1	0.8
Netherlands	16	42	479	425.6	15	26,230	18	463	28,560	18	−0.9	−1.4
New Zealand	4	271	15	62.2	48	15,530	40	86	21,350	36	3.6	1.8
Nicaragua	5	130	45	4.1	127	740	148	17	3,180	143	2.3	−0.3
Niger	12	1,267	9	2.4	148	200	197	10[d]	830[d]	195	5.3	2.3
Nigeria	136	924	150	47.5	53	350	178	123[d]	900[d]	193	10.7	8.0
Norway	5	324	15	198.0	23	43,400	3	173	37,910	3	0.4	−0.1
Oman	3	310	8	..	..	..[i]	..	..	..	..	..	..
Pakistan	148	796	193	77.6	44	520	161	303	2,040	159	5.1	2.6
Panama	3	76	40	12.1	85	4,060	79	19[d]	6,420[d]	96	4.1	2.5
Papua New Guinea	6	463	12	2.8	144	500	163	12[d]	2,250[d]	153	2.7	0.4
Paraguay	6	407	14	6.3	110	1,110	132	26[d]	4,690[d]	127	2.6	0.1
Peru	27	1,285	21	58.2	50	2,140	106	138	5,080	117	3.8	2.2
Philippines	82	300	273	87.8	41	1,080	135	379	4,640	128	4.5	2.5
Poland	38	313	125	201.7	22	5,280	72	428	11,210	69	3.7	3.8
Portugal	10	92	114	123.3	34	11,800	51	185	17,710	50	−1.2	−1.9
Puerto Rico	4	9	440	..	..	..[j]	..	..	..	..	..	..

	Population	Surface area	Population density	Gross national income		Gross national income per capita		PPP gross national income[a]			Gross domestic product	
	millions	thousand sq. km	people per sq. km	$ billions	Rank	$	Rank	$ billions	Per capita $	Rank	% growth	Per capita % growth
	2003	**2003**	**2003**	**2003[b]**	**2003**	**2003[b]**	**2003**	**2003**	**2003**	**2003**	**2002–03**	**2002–03**
Romania	22	238	95	49.0	52	2,260	102	155	7,140	88	4.9	5.2
Russian Federation	143	17,075	8	374.8	16	2,610	97	1,284	8,950	82	7.3	7.8
Rwanda	8	26	340	1.8	154	220	194	11[d]	1,290[d]	182	3.2	0.3
Saudi Arabia	23	2,150	10	208.1	21	9,240	56	298[d]	13,230[d]	61	7.2	4.1
Senegal	10	197	53	5.6	114	540	159	17[d]	1,620[d]	177	6.5	4.0
Serbia and Montenegro	8	102	79	15.8	78	1,910[k]	114	..	..	121	3.0	3.7
Sierra Leone	5	72	75	0.8	177	150	201	3	530	208	6.6	4.6
Singapore	4	1	6,343	90.2	39	21,230	29	103	24,180	30	1.1	−1.0
Slovak Republic	5	49	110	26.6	61	4,940	73	72	13,440	59	4.2	4.0
Slovenia	2	20	99	23.8	65	11,920	50	38	19,100	45	2.5	2.5
Somalia	10	638	15	..	..	..[c]	..	..	..	..	..	..
South Africa	46	1,219	38	126.0	33	2,750	94	464[d]	10,130[d]	76	1.9	0.8
Spain	41	506	82	700.5	9	17,040	36	910	22,150	34	2.4	2.0
Sri Lanka	19	66	298	17.8	74	930	140	72	3,740	136	5.9	4.7
Sudan	34	2,506	14	15.4	81	460	167	59[d]	1,760[d]	167	6.0	3.6
Swaziland	1	17	64	1.5	160	1,350	127	5	4,850	123	2.2	0.6
Sweden	9	450	22	258.9	19	28,910	11	239	26,710	26	1.6	1.2
Switzerland	7	41	186	299.0	17	40,680	4	237	32,220	7	−0.4	−1.2
Syrian Arab Republic	17	185	95	20.2	71	1,160	130	60	3,430	138	2.5	0.1
Tajikistan	6	143	45	1.3	162	210	195	7	1,040	188	10.2	9.5
Tanzania	36	945	41	10.7[l]	89	300[l]	183	22	620	206	7.1	5.0
Thailand	62	513	121	135.9	31	2,190	105	462	7,450	87	6.9	6.2
Togo	5	57	89	1.5	159	310	182	8[d]	1,640[d]	176	2.7	0.5
Trinidad and Tobago	1	5	256	10.2	90	7,790	60	14	10,390	74	13.2	12.4
Tunisia	10	164	64	22.2	68	2,240	103	68	6,850	92	5.6	4.4
Turkey	71	775	92	197.8	24	2,800	93	475	6,710	94	5.8	4.2
Turkmenistan	5	488	10	5.4	116	1,120	131	29	5,860	106	16.9	15.2
Uganda	25	241	128	6.2	111	250	191	36[d]	1,430[d]	178	4.7	1.9
Ukraine	48	604	83	46.7	54	970	137	262	5,430	112	9.4	10.2
United Arab Emirates	4	84	48	..	..	..[j]	..	..	..	..	..	..
United Kingdom	59	243	246	1,680.1	4	28,320	12	1,643	27,690	21	2.2	2.0
United States	291	9,629	32	11,012.6	1	37,870	5	10,978	37,750	4	3.1	2.2
Uruguay	3	176	19	12.9	83	3,820	83	27	7,980	84	2.5	1.9
Uzbekistan	26	447	62	10.8	88	420	172	44	1,720	172	4.4	3.1
Venezuela, RB	26	912	29	89.7	40	3,490	87	122	4,750	125	−9.4	−11.0
Vietnam	81	332	250	38.8	58	480	165	202	2,490	151	7.2	6.1
West Bank and Gaza	3	6	541	3.7	133	1,110	132	..	..	140	−1.7	−5.6
Yemen, Rep.	19	528	36	9.9	94	520	161	16	820	196	3.8	0.7
Zambia	10	753	14	4.0	129	380	177	9	850	194	5.1	3.5
Zimbabwe	13	391	34	..	..	..[c]	..	..	..	..	..	..
World	**6,273 s**	**133,942 s**	**48 w**	**34,577 t**		**5,510 w**		**51,401 t**	**8,190 w**		**2.8 w**	**1.6 w**
Low income	2,312	31,551	76	1,021		440		4,877	2,110		6.9	5.0
Middle income	2,989	69,921	43	5,756		1,930		17,926	6,000		4.9	4.0
Lower middle income	2,655	57,002	47	3,944		1,490		14,615	5,500		5.7	4.8
Upper middle income	333	12,919	26	1,812		5,440		3,327	9,990		3.3	2.1
Low & middle income	5,300	101,473	53	6,777		1,280		22,793	4,300		5.2	3.9
East Asia & Pacific	1,855	16,302	117	1,988		1,070		8,542	4,610		8.1	7.2
Europe & Central Asia	472	24,207	20	1,217		2,580		3,555	7,530		5.8	5.7
Latin America & Carib.	533	20,418	27	1,747		3,280		3,801	7,130		1.6	0.1
Middle East & N. Africa	312	11,141	28	744		2,390		1,826	5,860		5.7	3.7
South Asia	1,425	5,140	298	733		510		3,761	2,640		7.5	5.7
Sub-Saharan Africa	705	24,265	30	351		500		1,236	1,750		3.9	1.6
High income	972	32,469	31	27,806		28,600		28,753	29,580		2.2	1.7
Europe EMU	307	2,507	126	6,999		22,810		8,087	26,350		0.5	0.3

a. PPP is purchasing power parity; see *Definitions*. b. Calculated using the *World Bank Atlas* method. c. Estimated to be low income ($765 or less). d. The estimate is based on regression; others are extrapolated from the latest International Comparison Program benchmark estimates. e. Includes Taiwan, China; Macao, China; and Hong Kong, China. f. Estimate based on bilateral comparison between China and the United States (Ruoen and Kai 1995). g. Estimated to be lower middle income ($766–$3,035). h. GNI and GNI per capita estimates include the French overseas departments of French Guiana, Guadeloupe, Martinique, and Réunion. i. Estimated to be upper middle income ($3,036–$9,385). j. Estimated to be high income ($9,386 or more). k. Excludes data for Kosovo. l. Data refer to mainland Tanzania only.

About the data

Population, land area, income, output, and growth in output are basic measures of the size of an economy. They also provide a broad indication of actual and potential resources. Population, land area, income (as measured by gross national income, GNI) and output (as measured by gross domestic product, GDP) are therefore used throughout *World Development Indicators* to normalize other indicators.

Population estimates are generally based on extrapolations from the most recent national census. For further discussion of the measurement of population and population growth, see *About the data* for table 2.1 and *Statistical methods*.

The surface area of an economy includes inland bodies of water and some coastal waterways. Surface area thus differs from land area, which excludes bodies of water, and from gross area, which may include offshore territorial waters. Land area is particularly important for understanding an economy's agricultural capacity and the environmental effects of human activity. (For measures of land area and data on rural population density, land use, and agricultural productivity, see tables 3.1–3.3.) Innovations in satellite mapping and computer databases have resulted in more precise measurements of land and water areas.

GNI (or gross national product in the terminology of the 1968 United Nations System of National Accounts) measures the total domestic and foreign value added claimed by residents. GNI comprises GDP plus net receipts of primary income (compensation of employees and property income) from nonresident sources. The World Bank uses GNI per capita in U.S. dollars to classify countries for analytical purposes and to determine borrowing eligibility. For definitions of the income groups in *World Development Indicators,* see *Users guide.* For discussion of the usefulness of national income and output as measures of productivity or welfare, see *About the data* for tables 4.1 and 4.2.

When calculating GNI in U.S. dollars from GNI reported in national currencies, the World Bank follows its *Atlas* conversion method, using a three-year average of exchange rates to smooth the effects of transitory exchange rate fluctuations. (For further discussion of the *Atlas* method, see *Statistical methods.*) Note that GDP and GDP per capita growth rates are calculated from data in constant prices and national currency units, not from the *Atlas* estimates.

Because exchange rates do not always reflect international differences in relative prices, this table also converts GNI and GNI per capita estimates into international dollars using purchasing power parity (PPP) rates. PPP rates provide a standard measure allowing comparison of real price levels between countries, just as conventional price indexes allow comparison of real values over time. The PPP conversion factors used here are derived from price surveys covering 118 countries conducted by the International Comparison Program. For Organisation for Economic Co-operation and Development (OECD) countries data come from the most recent round of surveys, completed in 2000; the rest are either from the 1996 or the 1993 survey or earlier round and extrapolated to the 1996 benchmark. Estimates for countries not included in the surveys are derived from statistical models using available data.

All economies shown in *World Development Indicators* are ranked by size, including those that appear in table 1.6. The ranks are shown only in table 1.1. (*World Bank Atlas* includes a table comparing the GNI per capita rankings based on the *Atlas* method with those based on the PPP method for all economies with available data.) No rank is shown for economies for which numerical estimates of GNI per capita are not published. Economies with missing data are included in the ranking at their approximate level, so that the relative order of other economies remains consistent. Where available, rankings for small economies are shown in *World Bank Atlas.*

Definitions

• **Population** is based on the de facto definition of population, which counts all residents regardless of legal status or citizenship—except for refugees not permanently settled in the country of asylum, who are generally considered part of the population of their country of origin. The values shown are midyear estimates for 2003. See also table 2.1. • **Surface area** is a country's total area, including areas under inland bodies of water and some coastal waterways. • **Population density** is midyear population divided by land area in square kilometers. • **Gross national income** (GNI) is the sum of value added by all resident producers plus any product taxes (less subsidies) not included in the valuation of output plus net receipts of primary income (compensation of employees and property income) from abroad. Data are in current U.S. dollars converted using the *World Bank Atlas* method (see *Statistical methods*). • **GNI per capita** is gross national income divided by midyear population. GNI per capita in U.S. dollars is converted using the *World Bank Atlas* method. • **PPP GNI** is gross national income converted to international dollars using purchasing power parity rates. An international dollar has the same purchasing power over GNI as a U.S. dollar has in the United States. • **Gross domestic product** (GDP) is the sum of value added by all resident producers plus any product taxes (less subsidies) not included in the valuation of output. Growth is calculated from constant price GDP data in local currency. • **GDP per capita** is gross domestic product divided by midyear population.

1.1a

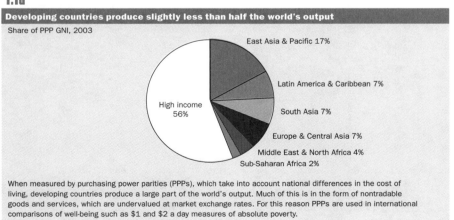

Developing countries produce slightly less than half the world's output

Share of PPP GNI, 2003

High income 56%
East Asia & Pacific 17%
Latin America & Caribbean 7%
South Asia 7%
Europe & Central Asia 7%
Middle East & North Africa 4%
Sub-Saharan Africa 2%

When measured by purchasing power parities (PPPs), which take into account national differences in the cost of living, developing countries produce a large part of the world's output. Much of this is in the form of nontradable goods and services, which are undervalued at market exchange rates. For this reason PPPs are used in international comparisons of well-being such as $1 and $2 a day measures of absolute poverty.

Source: World Bank staff estimates.

Data sources

Population estimates are prepared by World Bank staff from a variety of sources (see *Data sources* for table 2.1). The data on surface and land area are from the Food and Agriculture Organization (see *Data sources* for table 3.1). GNI, GNI per capita, GDP growth, and GDP per capita growth are estimated by World Bank staff based on national accounts data collected by World Bank staff during economic missions or reported by national statistical offices to other international organizations such as the OECD. Purchasing power parity conversion factors are estimates by World Bank staff based on data collected by the International Comparison Program.

1.2 Millennium Development Goals: eradicating poverty and improving lives

	Eradicate extreme poverty and hunger			Achieve universal primary education		Promote gender equality		Reduce child mortality		Improve maternal health		
	Share of poorest quintile in national consumption or income %	Prevalence of child malnutrition Underweight % of children under age 5		Primary completion rate %		Ratio of female to male enrollments in primary and secondary school[a] %		Under-five mortality rate per 1,000		Maternal mortality ratio per 100,000 live births Modeled estimates	Births attended by skilled health staff % of total	
	1990–2003[b,c]	1989–94[b]	2000–03[b]	1988/89–1993/94[d]	2000/01–2003/04[b]	1990/91	2002/03	1990	2003	2000	1990–92[b]	2000–03[b]
Afghanistan	..	..	..	23	..	..	52	260	257	1,900	..	14
Albania	9.1	..	14	..	101	96	102	45	21	55	..	94
Algeria	7.0	9	6	80	96	83	99	69	41	140	77	92
Angola	..	20	31	39	..	..	..	260	260	1,700	..	45
Argentina	3.1	2	..	100	103	..	103	28	20	82	96	99
Armenia	6.7	..	3	91	110	..	101	60	33	55	..	97
Australia	5.9	..	..	..	..	101	99	10	6	8	100	..
Austria	8.1	..	..	..	101	95	97	10	6	4	..	..
Azerbaijan	7.4	..	7	..	106	100	97	105	91	94	..	84
Bangladesh	9.0	68	52	46	73	77	107	144	69	380	..	14
Belarus	8.4	..	..	94	99	..	102	17	17	35	..	100
Belgium	8.3	..	..	..	..	101	107	9	5	10	..	..
Benin	..	35	23	22	51	48	66	185	154	850	..	66
Bolivia	4.0	15	..	71	101	90	98	120	66	420	..	65
Bosnia and Herzegovina	9.5	..	4	..	..	..	..	22	17	31	97	100
Botswana	2.2	..	13	91	91	109	102	58	112	100	..	99
Brazil	2.4	7	..	97	112	..	103	60	35	260	72	..
Bulgaria	6.7	..	..	90	97	99	98	19	17	32	..	..
Burkina Faso	4.5	33	38	19	29	61	72	210	207	1,000	..	..
Burundi	5.1	38	45	47	31	82	79	190	190	1,000	..	25
Cambodia	6.9	..	45	..	81	73	85	115	140	450	..	32
Cameroon	5.6	15	..	56	70	83	85	139	166	730	58	60
Canada	7.0	..	..	..	..	99	100	8	7	6	..	..
Central African Republic	2.0	..	..	27	..	60	..	180	180	1,100	..	44
Chad	..	..	28	19	25	41	59	203	200	1,100	..	16
Chile	3.3	1	1	..	104	101	100	19	9	31	..	100
China	4.7	17	10	105	98	87	97	49	37	56	..	97
Hong Kong, China	5.3	..	..	102	101	103	100	..	5	..	..	..
Colombia	2.7	10	7	71	88	114	104	36	21	130	82	86
Congo, Dem. Rep.	..	..	31	47	32	..	..	205	205	990	..	61
Congo, Rep.	..	24	..	54	59	85	87	110	108	510	..	..
Costa Rica	4.2	2	..	72	94	100	101	17	10	43	98	98
Côte d'Ivoire	5.2	24	..	46	51	66	..	157	192	690	..	63
Croatia	8.3	1	..	83	96	102	101	13	7	8	..	..
Cuba	..	..	4	94	94	106	97	13	8	33	..	100
Czech Republic	10.3	1	..	..	106	98	101	13	5	9	..	..
Denmark	8.3	..	..	98	107	101	103	9	6	5	..	..
Dominican Republic	5.1	10	5	62	93	..	108	65	35	150	93	98
Ecuador	3.3	17	..	92	100	..	100	57	27	130	..	..
Egypt, Arab Rep.	8.6	10	9	..	91	81	93	104	39	84	41	69
El Salvador	2.9	11	10	59	89	101	96	60	36	150	..	69
Eritrea	..	41	40	19	40	..	76	147	85	630	..	28
Estonia	6.1	..	..	95	104	104	99	17	9	63	..	..
Ethiopia	9.1	48	47	22	39	68	69	204	169	850	..	6
Finland	9.6	..	..	97	101	109	106	7	4	6	..	..
France	7.2	..	..	104	98	102	100	9	6	17	..	..
Gabon	..	..	12	67	74	..	..	92	91	420	..	86
Gambia, The	4.8	..	17	45	68	64	90	154	123	540	44	55
Georgia	6.4	..	..	81	82	98	100	47	45	32	..	..
Germany	8.5	..	..	101	101	99	99	9	5	8	..	..
Ghana	5.6	27	22	61	62	77	91	125	95	540	..	..
Greece	7.1	..	..	100	..	99	101	11	5	9	..	..
Guatemala	2.6	33	23	..	66	..	93	82	47	240	..	41
Guinea	6.4	..	..	17	41	44	69	240	160	740	31	..
Guinea-Bissau	5.2	..	25	..	28	..	..	253	204	1,100	..	35
Haiti	..	27	17	29	..	95	..	150	118	680	..	24

Millennium Development Goals: eradicating poverty and improving lives | 1.2

	Eradicate extreme poverty and hunger			Achieve universal primary education		Promote gender equality		Reduce child mortality		Improve maternal health		
	Share of poorest quintile in national consumption or income % 1990–2003[b,c]	Prevalence of child malnutrition Underweight % of children under age 5 1989–94[b]	2000–03[b]	Primary completion rate % 1988/89–1993/94[d]	2000/01–2003/04[b]	Ratio of female to male enrollments in primary and secondary school[a] % 1990/91	2002/03	Under-five mortality rate per 1,000 1990	2003	Maternal mortality ratio per 100,000 live births Modeled estimates 2000	Births attended by skilled health staff % of total 1990–92[b]	2000–03[b]
Honduras	2.7	18	17	65	79	..	..	59	41	110	45	56
Hungary	9.5	2	..	82	102	100	100	17	7	16	..	..
India	8.9	53	..	78	81	70	80	123	87	540	..	43
Indonesia	8.4	40	27	93	95	93	98	91	41	230	32	68
Iran, Islamic Rep.	5.1	..	..	101	107	85	96	72	39	76	..	90
Iraq	..	12	16	62	56	78	80	50	125	250	..	72
Ireland	7.1	..	..	..	..	104	104	9	7	5	..	..
Israel	6.9	..	..	..	..	105	99	12	6	17	..	..
Italy	6.5	..	..	104	101	100	97	9	6	5	..	..
Jamaica	6.7	5	..	89	85	102	101	20	20	87	..	..
Japan	10.6	..	..	101	..	101	100	6	5	10	100	..
Jordan	7.6	6	4	104	98	101	101	40	28	41	87	100
Kazakhstan	7.8	..	..	..	110	102	100	63	73	210	..	..
Kenya	6.0	23	20	86	73	92	94	97	123	1,000	..	41
Korea, Dem. Rep.	..	..	28	..	..	..	..	55	55	67	..	97
Korea, Rep.	7.9	..	..	98	97	99	100	9	5	20	98	..
Kuwait	..	..	..	53	96	97	104	16	9	5	..	..
Kyrgyz Republic	7.7	..	6	..	93	..	100	80	68	110	..	..
Lao PDR	7.6	40	40	46	74	75	83	163	91	650	..	19
Latvia	7.3	..	..	73	101	100	100	18	12	42	..	..
Lebanon	..	..	..	..	68	..	102	37	31	150	..	..
Lesotho	1.5	21	18	67	67	124	105	104	110	550	..	60
Liberia	..	..	27	..	21	..	..	235	235	760	..	51
Libya	..	..	..	..	..	..	103	42	16	97	..	..
Lithuania	7.9	..	..	89	102	..	99	14	11	13	..	..
Macedonia, FYR	8.4	..	..	99	100	99	99	33	11	23	..	98
Madagascar	4.9	45	33	35	47	98	..	168	126	550	57	46
Malawi	4.9	28	25	36	71	81	92	241	178	1,800	55	61
Malaysia	4.4	22	..	88	92	102	104	21	7	41	..	97
Mali	4.6	31	33	12	40	58	71	250	220	1,200	..	41
Mauritania	6.2	48	32	33	43	67	94	162	107	1,000	40	57
Mauritius	..	..	..	102	105	100	101	25	18	24	..	..
Mexico	3.1	17	..	88	99	98	102	46	28	83	..	..
Moldova	6.8	..	..	95	83	105	102	37	32	36	..	..
Mongolia	5.6	12	13	..	108	109	110	104	68	110	..	99
Morocco	6.5	10	..	47	75	70	88	85	39	220	31	..
Mozambique	6.5	..	..	28	52	73	79	242	147	1,000	..	48
Myanmar	..	31	..	..	73	96	99	130	107	360	..	..
Namibia	1.4	26	24	77	92	111	104	86	65	300	68	78
Nepal	7.6	..	48	55	78	57	83	145	82	740	7	11
Netherlands	7.6	..	..	..	98	97	98	9	6	16	..	..
New Zealand	6.4	..	..	98	96	100	103	11	6	7	..	..
Nicaragua	5.6	11	10	44	75	112	104	68	38	230	..	67
Niger	2.6	43	40	18	26	56	69	320	262	1,600	15	16
Nigeria	4.4	39	29	63	82	78	..	235	198	800	31	35
Norway	9.6	..	..	..	..	102	101	9	5	16	..	..
Oman	..	24	..	73	73	89	97	30	12	87	..	95
Pakistan	8.8	40	35	..	..	..	71	138	98	500	19	23
Panama	2.4	6	..	86	98	99	100	34	24	160	..	..
Papua New Guinea	4.5	..	..	51	53	79	88	101	93	300	..	..
Paraguay	2.2	4	..	66	93	98	98	37	29	170	67	..
Peru	2.9	11	7	..	102	..	97	80	34	410	..	59
Philippines	5.4	30	..	87	95	100	102	63	36	200	..	60
Poland	7.6	..	..	96	98	101	98	19	7	13	..	..
Portugal	5.8	..	..	98	..	103	102	15	5	5	..	..
Puerto Rico	..	..	..	..	..	..	..	..	11	25	..	..

| | Eradicate extreme poverty and hunger | | | Achieve universal primary education | | Promote gender equality | | Reduce child mortality | | Improve maternal health | | |
| | Share of poorest quintile in national consumption or income % | Prevalence of child malnutrition Underweight % of children under age 5 | | Primary completion rate % | | Ratio of female to male enrollments in primary and secondary school[a] % | | Under-five mortality rate per 1,000 | | Maternal mortality ratio per 100,000 live births Modeled estimates | Births attended by skilled health staff % of total | |
	1990–2003[b,c]	1989–94[b]	2000–03[b]	1988/89–1993/94[d]	2000/01–2003/04[b]	1990/91	2002/03	1990	2003	2000	1990–92[b]	2000–03[b]
Romania	7.9	6	3	96	89	99	100	32	20	49	..	..
Russian Federation	8.2	4	6	95	93	104	100	21	21	67	..	99
Rwanda	..	29	24	44	37	96	95	173	203	1,400	26	31
Saudi Arabia	..	..	..	57	61	84	93	44	26	23	..	..
Senegal	6.4	22	23	45	48	68	87	148	137	690	..	41
Serbia and Montenegro	..	..	2	71	96	103	101	26	14	11	..	99
Sierra Leone	..	29	27	..	56	67	70	302	284	2,000	..	42
Singapore	5.0	..	3	..	..	95	..	8	5	30	..	..
Slovak Republic	8.8	..	..	96	99	..	101	15	8	3	..	..
Slovenia	9.1	..	..	97	95	..	100	9	4	17	100	..
Somalia	..	..	26	..	..	..	..	225	225	1,100	..	..
South Africa	3.5	..	..	81	99	103	100	60	66	230	..	..
Spain	7.5	..	..	..	..	104	103	9	4	4	..	..
Sri Lanka	8.3	38	..	103	113	102	103	32	15	92	..	87
Sudan	..	34	41	44	49	77	86	120	93	590	69	..
Swaziland	2.7	..	10	69	75	96	94	110	153	370	..	70
Sweden	9.1	..	..	96	101	102	112	7	4	2	..	100
Switzerland	6.9	..	..	..	99	97	96	9	6	7	..	..
Syrian Arab Republic	..	12	7	99	88	85	93	44	18	160	..	..
Tajikistan	7.9	..	..	100	100	..	88	119	95	100	..	71
Tanzania	6.8	29	..	46	58	96	..	163	165	1,500	44	..
Thailand	6.1	19	..	..	86	95	95	40	26	44	..	69
Togo	..	25	..	40	78	59	..	152	140	570	..	49
Trinidad and Tobago	5.5	7	6	100	91	101	102	24	20	160	..	96
Tunisia	6.0	10	4	75	101	86	100	52	24	120	..	90
Turkey	6.1	10	..	..	95	81	85	78	39	70	..	..
Turkmenistan	6.1	..	12	..	..	..	..	97	102	31	..	97
Uganda	5.9	23	23	..	63	77	96	160	140	880	..	39
Ukraine	8.8	..	3	56	59	..	99	22	20	35	..	..
United Arab Emirates	..	..	..	107	71	106	100	14	8	54	..	..
United Kingdom	6.1	..	..	..	..	98	116	10	7	13	..	..
United States	5.4	1	..	..	..	100	100	11	8	17	..	..
Uruguay	4.8	4	..	95	92	..	105	24	14	27	..	..
Uzbekistan	9.2	..	8	..	103	94	98	79	69	24	..	96
Venezuela, RB	3.0	5	4	81	90	105	104	27	21	96	..	94
Vietnam	7.5	45	34	..	95	..	93	53	23	130	..	85
West Bank and Gaza	..	..	..	..	106	..	..	53	24	..	..	..
Yemen, Rep.	7.4	39	..	..	66	..	61	142	113	570	16	..
Zambia	3.3	25	28	..	69	..	91	180	182	750	51	43
Zimbabwe	4.6	16	..	96	81	96	95	80	126	1,100	..	..
World	.. w	.. w	.. w	.. w		87 w	93 w	95 w	86 w	407 w	.. w	.. w
Low income	..	..		65	71	74	84	149	123	689	..	..
Middle income	..		11	93	95	91	98	55	37	115	..	..
Lower middle income	..		11	94	95	90	97	57	39	121	..	..
Upper middle income	..		..	87	93	99	102	34	22	67	..	..
Low & middle income	..		..	81	84	84	91	103	87	444	..	..
East Asia & Pacific	..	19	15	97	97	89	97	59	41	116	..	91
Europe & Central Asia	..		..	88	90	98	97	46	36	58	..	..
Latin America & Carib.	..		..	88	96	..	102	53	33	193	..	..
Middle East & N. Africa	..		..	79	84	82	94	77	53	162	..	..
South Asia	..	53	..	74	80	71	83	130	92	567	..	43
Sub-Saharan Africa	..		..	50	59	79	..	187	171	916	..	..
High income	..		..	..	..	100	101	10	7	13	..	..
Europe EMU	..		..	..	..	100	100	9	6	9	..	..

a. Break in series between 1997 and 1998 due to change from International Standard Classification of Education 1976 (ISCED76) to ISCED97. b. Data are for the most recent year available. c. See table 2.7 for survey year and whether share is based on income or consumption expenditure. d. Data are for 1990 or closest year.

Millennium Development Goals: eradicating poverty and improving lives

1.2

About the data

This table and the following two present indicators for 17 of the 18 targets specified by the Millennium Development Goals. Each of the eight goals comprises one or more targets, and each target has associated with it several indicators for monitoring progress toward the target. Most of the targets are set as a value of a specific indicator to be attained by a certain date. In some cases the target value is set relative to a level in 1990. In others it is set at an absolute level. Some of the targets for goals 7 and 8 have not yet been quantified.

The indicators in this table relate to goals 1–5. Goal 1 has two targets between 1990 and 2015: to reduce by half the proportion of people whose income is less than $1 a day and to reduce by half the proportion of people who suffer from hunger. Estimates of poverty rates can be found in table 2.5. The indicator shown here, the share of the poorest quintile in national consumption, is a distributional measure. Countries with less equal distributions of consumption (or income) will have a higher rate of poverty for a given average income. No single indicator captures the concept of suffering from hunger. Child malnutrition is a symptom of inadequate food supply, lack of essential nutrients, illnesses that deplete these nutrients, and undernourished mothers who give birth to underweight children.

Progress toward achieving universal primary education is measured by primary school completion rates. Before *World Development Indicators 2003*, progress was measured by net enrollment ratios. But official enrollments sometimes differ significantly from actual attendance, and even school systems with high average enrollment ratios may have poor completion rates. Estimates of primary school completion rates have been calculated by World Bank staff using data provided by the United Nations Educational, Scientific, and Cultural Organization (UNESCO) and national sources.

Eliminating gender disparities in education would help to increase the status and capabilities of women. The ratio of girls' to boys' enrollments in primary and secondary school provides an imperfect measure of the relative accessibility of schooling for girls. With a target date of 2005, this is the first of the goals to fall due. The targets for reducing under-five and maternal mortality are among the most challenging. Although estimates of under-five mortality rates are available at regular intervals for most countries, maternal mortality is difficult to measure, in part because it is relatively rare.

Most of the 48 indicators relating to the Millennium Development Goals can be found in *World Development Indicators*. Table 1.2a shows where to find the

indicators for the first five goals. For more information about data collection methods and limitations, see *About the data* for the tables listed there. For information about the indicators for goals 6, 7, and 8, see *About the data* for tables 1.3 and 1.4.

Definitions

• **Share of poorest quintile in national consumption or income** is the share of consumption or, in some cases, income that accrues to the poorest 20 percent of the population. • **Prevalence of child malnutrition** is the percentage of children under age five whose weight for age is more than two standard deviations below the median for the international reference population ages 0–59 months. The reference population, adopted by the World Health Organization in 1983, is based on children from the United States, who are assumed to be well nourished. • **Primary completion rate** is the number of students successfully completing (or graduating from) the last year of primary school in a given year, divided by the number of children of official graduation age in the population. • **Ratio of female to male enrollments in primary and secondary school** is the ratio of female students enrolled in primary and secondary school to male students. • **Under-five mortality rate** is the probability that a newborn baby will die before reaching age five, if subject to current age-specific mortality rates. The probability is expressed as a rate per 1,000. • **Maternal mortality ratio** is the number of women who die from pregnancy-related causes during pregnancy and childbirth, per 100,000 live births. The data shown here have been collected in various years and adjusted to a common 2000 base year. The values are modeled estimates (see *About the data* for table 2.17). • **Births attended by skilled health staff** are the percentage of deliveries attended by personnel trained to give the necessary supervision, care, and advice to women during pregnancy, labor, and the postpartum period; to conduct deliveries on their own; and to care for newborns.

1.2a

Location of indicators for Millennium Development Goals 1–5

Goal 1. Eradicate extreme poverty and hunger	Table
1. Proportion of population below $1 a day	2.5
2. Poverty gap ratio	2.5
3. Share of poorest quintile in national consumption	1.2, 2.7
4. Prevalence of underweight in children under five	1.2, 2.17
5. Proportion of population below minimum level of dietary energy consumption	2.17
Goal 2. Achieve universal primary education	
6. Net enrollment ratio	2.11
7. Proportion of pupils starting grade 1 who reach grade 5	2.12
8. Literacy rate of 15- to 24-year-olds	2.13
Goal 3. Promote gender equality and empower women	
9. Ratio of girls to boys in primary, secondary, and tertiary education	1.2*
10. Ratio of literate females to males among 15- to 24-year-olds	2.13*
11. Share of women in wage employment in the nonagricultural sector	1.5
12. Proportion of seats held by women in national parliament	1.5
Goal 4. Reduce child mortality	
13. Under-five mortality rate	1.2, 2.19
14. Infant mortality rate	2.19
15. Proportion of one-year-old children immunized against measles	2.15
Goal 4. Improve maternal health	
16. Maternal mortality ratio	1.2, 2.16
17. Proportion of births attended by skilled health personnel	1.2, 2.16

* Table shows information on related indicators.

Data sources

The indicators here and throughout this book have been compiled by World Bank staff from primary and secondary sources. Efforts have been made to harmonize these data series with those published by the United Nations Millennium Development Goals Web site (www.un.org/millenniumgoals), but some differences in timing, sources, and definitions remain.

1.3 Millennium Development Goals: protecting our common environment

	Combat HIV/AIDS and other diseases		Ensure environmental sustainability						Develop a global partnership for development	
	HIV prevalence % of adults 2003	Incidence of tuberculosis per 100,000 people 2003	Carbon dioxide emissions per capita metric tons 1990	2000	Access to an improved water source % of population 1990	2002	Access to improved sanitation facilities % of population 1990	2002	Unemployment % ages 15–24 2002	Fixed-line and mobile phone subscribers per 1,000 people[a] 2003
Afghanistan	..	333	0.1	0.0	..	13	..	8	..	12
Albania	..	23	2.2	0.9	97	97	..	89	..	441
Algeria	0.1	53	3.2	2.9	95	87	88	92	..	115
Angola	3.9	259	0.5	0.5	32	50	30	30	..	15
Argentina	0.7	44	3.4	3.9	94	..	82	..	32	396
Armenia		70	1.1	1.1	..	92	..	84	..	178
Australia	0.1	6	15.6	18.0	100	100	100	100	12	1,262
Austria	0.3	14	7.4	7.6	100	100	100	100	5	1,360
Azerbaijan	<0.1	76	6.4	3.6	66	77	..	55	..	242
Bangladesh	..	246	0.1	0.2	71	75	23	48	11	16
Belarus	..	53	9.3	5.9	100	100	..	..	..	424
Belgium	0.2	14	10.1	10.0	..	..	..	..	16	1,282
Benin	1.9	87	0.1	0.3	60	68	11	32	..	43
Bolivia	0.1	225	0.8	1.3	72	85	33	45	9	224
Bosnia and Herzegovina	<0.1	55	..	4.8	98	98	..	93	..	519
Botswana	37.3	633	1.7	2.3	93	95	38	41	..	372
Brazil	0.7	62	1.4	1.8	83	89	70	75	18	486
Bulgaria	0.1	43	8.6	5.3	100	100	100	100	38	847
Burkina Faso	1.8[b]	163	0.1	0.1	39	51	13	12	..	24
Burundi	6.0	346	0.0	0.0	69	79	44	36	..	12
Cambodia	2.6	508	0.0	0.0	..	34	..	16	..	38
Cameroon	5.5[c]	180	0.1	0.4	50	63	21	48	..	50
Canada	0.3	6	15.4	14.2	100	100	100	100	14	1,046
Central African Republic	13.5	325	0.1	0.1	48	75	23	27	..	5
Chad	4.8	225	0.0	0.0	20	34	6	8	..	6
Chile	0.3	16	2.7	3.9	90	95	85	92	19	732
China	0.1	102	2.1	2.2	70	77	23	44	3	424
Hong Kong, China	0.1	77	4.6	5.0	..	..	..	..	11	1,638
Colombia	0.7	52	1.6	1.4	92	92	82	86	36	321
Congo, Dem. Rep.	4.2	369	0.1	0.1	43	46	18	29	..	11
Congo, Rep.	4.9	380	0.8	0.5	..	46	..	9	..	96
Costa Rica	0.6	15	1.0	1.4	..	97	..	92	13	362
Côte d'Ivoire	7.0	396	1.0	0.7	69	84	31	40	..	91
Croatia	<0.1	43	3.8	4.5	..	..	..	..	37	952
Cuba	0.1	11	3.0	2.8	..	91	98	98	..	52
Czech Republic	0.1	12	13.4	11.6	..	..	..	..	16	1,325
Denmark	0.2	8	9.9	8.4	100	100	..	..	7	1,553
Dominican Republic	1.7	96	1.3	3.0	86	93	48	57	23	387
Ecuador	0.3	138	1.6	2.0	69	86	56	72	15	312
Egypt, Arab Rep.	<0.1	28	1.4	2.2	94	98	54	68	..	212
El Salvador	0.7	57	0.5	1.1	67	82	51	63	11	292
Eritrea	2.7	271	..	0.1	40	57	8	9	..	9
Estonia	1.1	50	16.2	11.7	..	..	..	..	22	1,119
Ethiopia	4.4	356	0.1	0.1	25	22	4	6	..	8
Finland	0.1	9	10.6	10.3	100	100	100	100	21	1,402
France	0.4	12	6.3	6.2	..	..	..	..	20	1,262
Gabon	8.1	233	7.0	2.8	..	87	..	36	..	253
Gambia, The	1.2	233	0.2	0.2	..	82	..	53	..	101
Georgia	0.1	83	2.8	1.2	..	76	..	83	20	240
Germany	0.1	8	11.1	9.6	100	100	..	..	10	1,442
Ghana	3.1	210	0.2	0.3	54	79	43	58	..	49
Greece	0.2	20	7.1	8.2	..	..	..	..	26	1,356
Guatemala	1.1	74	0.6	0.9	77	95	50	61	..	202
Guinea	3.2	236	0.2	0.2	42	51	17	13	..	18
Guinea-Bissau	..	198	0.8	0.2	..	59	..	34	..	9
Haiti	5.6	323	0.2	0.2	53	71	15	34	..	55

	Combat HIV/AIDS and other diseases		Ensure environmental sustainability						Develop a global partnership for development	
	HIV prevalence % of adults 2003	Incidence of tuberculosis per 100,000 people 2003	Carbon dioxide emissions per capita metric tons 1990	2000	Access to an improved water source % of population 1990	2002	Access to improved sanitation facilities % of population 1990	2002	Unemployment % ages 15–24 2002	Fixed-line and mobile phone subscribers per 1,000 people[a] 2003
Honduras	1.8	81	0.5	0.7	83	90	49	68	6	97
Hungary	0.1	29	5.6	5.4	99	99	..	95	13	1,117
India	0.9	168	0.8	1.1	68	86	12	30	..	71
Indonesia	0.1	285	0.9	1.3	71	78	46	52	..	127
Iran, Islamic Rep.	0.1	28	3.9	4.9	91	93	83	84	..	271
Iraq	<0.1	157	2.7	3.3	83	81	81	80	..	29
Ireland	0.1	12	8.5	11.1	..	..	..	..	8	1,371
Israel	0.1	9	7.4	10.0	100	100	..	..	19	1,419
Italy	0.5	7	7.0	7.4	..	..	..	..	26	1,502
Jamaica	1.2	8	3.3	4.2	92	93	75	80	..	704
Japan	<0.1	31	8.7	9.3	100	100	100	100	10	1,151
Jordan	<0.1	5	3.2	3.2	98	91	..	93	..	356
Kazakhstan	0.2	145	15.3	8.1	86	86	72	72	..	195
Kenya	6.7[b]	610	0.2	0.3	45	62	42	48	..	61
Korea, Dem. Rep.	..	178	12.3	8.5	100	100	..	59	..	21
Korea, Rep.	<0.1	87	5.6	9.1	..	92	..	..	8	1,239
Kuwait	..	27	19.9	21.9	..	..	..	..	..	776
Kyrgyz Republic	0.1	124	2.4	0.9	..	76	..	60	..	103
Lao PDR	0.1	157	0.1	0.1	..	43	..	24	..	32
Latvia	0.6	75	4.8	2.5	..	..	..	..	21	811
Lebanon	0.1	12	2.5	3.5	100	100	..	98	..	426
Lesotho	28.9	733	..	..	..	76	37	37	..	56
Liberia	5.9	250	0.2	0.1	56	62	38	26	..	3
Libya	0.3	21	8.8	10.9	71	72	97	97	..	159
Lithuania	0.1	70	5.8	3.4	..	..	..	..	29	869
Macedonia, FYR	<0.1	31	5.5	5.5	..	..	..	..	..	448
Madagascar	1.7	216	0.1	0.1	40	45	12	33	..	21
Malawi	14.2	442	0.1	0.1	41	67	36	46	..	21
Malaysia	0.4	106	3.0	6.2	..	95	96	..	..	624
Mali	1.7[d]	288	0.0	0.1	34	48	36	45	..	10
Mauritania	0.6	287	1.3	1.2	41	56	28	42	..	141
Mauritius	..	64	1.1	2.4	100	100	99	99	..	552
Mexico	0.3	33	3.7	4.3	80	91	66	77	5	449
Moldova	0.2	139	4.8	1.5	..	92	..	68	..	351
Mongolia	<0.1	194	4.7	3.1	62	62	..	59	..	186
Morocco	0.1	112	1.0	1.3	75	80	57	61	..	284
Mozambique	12.2	457	0.1	0.1	..	42	..	27	..	19
Myanmar	1.2	171	0.1	0.2	48	80	21	73	..	8
Namibia	21.3	722	0.0	1.0	58	80	24	30	11	182
Nepal	0.5	211	0.0	0.1	69	84	12	27	..	18
Netherlands	0.2	8	10.0	8.7	100	100	100	100	6	1,382
New Zealand	0.1	11	6.8	8.3	97	..	..	..	11	1,097
Nicaragua	0.2	63	0.7	0.7	69	81	47	66	20	123
Niger	1.2	157	0.1	0.1	40	46	7	12	..	3
Nigeria	5.4	293	0.9	0.3	49	60	39	38	..	32
Norway	0.1	6	7.5	11.1	100	100	..	..	11	1,622
Oman	0.1	11	7.1	8.2	77	79	83	89	..	255
Pakistan	0.1	181	0.6	0.8	83	90	38	54	13	44
Panama	0.9	48	1.3	2.2	..	91	..	72	29	390
Papua New Guinea	0.6	235	0.6	0.5	39	39	45	45	..	14
Paraguay	0.5	70	0.5	0.7	62	83	58	78	14	345
Peru	0.5	188	1.0	1.1	74	81	52	62	15	173
Philippines	<0.1	296	0.7	1.0	87	85	54	73	19	311
Poland	0.1	31	9.1	7.8	..	..	..	..	44	770
Portugal	0.4	45	4.3	5.8	..	..	..	..	12	1,310
Puerto Rico	..	6	3.3	2.3	..	..	..	..	21	662

Millennium Development Goals: protecting our common environment

	Combat HIV/AIDS and other diseases		Ensure environmental sustainability						Develop a global partnership for development	
	HIV prevalence % of adults 2003	Incidence of tuberculosis per 100,000 people 2003	Carbon dioxide emissions per capita metric tons 1990		Access to an improved water source % of population 1990		Access to improved sanitation facilities % of population 1990		Unemployment % ages 15–24 2002	Fixed-line and mobile phone subscribers per 1,000 people[a] 2003
			1990	2000	1990	2002	1990	2002	2002	2003
Romania	<0.1	149	6.7	3.8	..	57	..	51	18	524
Russian Federation	1.1	112	13.3	9.9	94	96	87	87	..	362
Rwanda	5.1	374	0.1	0.1	58	73	37	41	..	16
Saudi Arabia	..	40	11.3	18.1	90	..	..	..	..	477
Senegal	0.8	245	0.4	0.4	66	72	35	52	..	78
Serbia and Montenegro	0.2	35	..	3.7	93	93	87	87	..	581
Sierra Leone	..	427	0.1	0.1	..	57	..	39	..	18
Singapore	0.2	41	13.8	14.7	..	..	..	..	5	1,303
Slovak Republic	<0.1	24	8.4	6.6	100	100	100	100	37	925
Slovenia	<0.1	18	6.2	7.3	..	..	..	..	16	1,278
Somalia	..	411	0.0	..	..	29	..	25	..	13
South Africa	15.6[e]	536	8.3	7.4	83	87	63	67	44	410
Spain	0.7	27	5.5	7.0	..	..	..	..	22	1,343
Sri Lanka	<0.1	60	0.2	0.6	68	78	70	91	24	122
Sudan	2.3	220	0.1	0.2	64	69	33	34	..	47
Swaziland	38.8	1,083	0.6	0.4	..	52	..	52	..	129
Sweden	0.1	4	5.7	5.3	100	100	100	100	13	1,625
Switzerland	0.4	7	6.4	5.4	100	100	100	100	6	1,534
Syrian Arab Republic	<0.1	42	3.0	3.3	79	79	76	77	..	147
Tajikistan	<0.1	168	3.7	0.6	..	58	..	53	..	45
Tanzania	8.8	371	0.1	0.1	38	73	47	46	..	29
Thailand	1.5	142	1.7	3.3	81	85	80	99	7	499
Togo	4.1	351	0.2	0.4	49	51	37	34	..	56
Trinidad and Tobago	3.2	9	13.9	20.5	92	91	100	100	..	528
Tunisia	<0.1	22	1.6	1.9	77	82	75	80	..	310
Turkey	..	26	2.6	3.3	81	93	84	83	20	662
Turkmenistan	<0.1	67	7.2	7.5	..	71	..	62	..	79
Uganda	4.1	411	0.0	0.1	44	56	43	41	..	33
Ukraine	1.4	92	11.5	6.9	..	98	99	99	24	300
United Arab Emirates	..	18	34.3	18.1	..	..	100	100	..	1,017
United Kingdom	0.2	12	9.9	9.6	..	..	..	..	11	1,431
United States	0.6	5	19.3	19.8	100	100	100	100	12	1,164
Uruguay	0.3	28	1.3	1.6	..	98	..	94	34	472
Uzbekistan	0.1	115	5.3	4.8	89	89	58	57	..	80
Venezuela, RB	0.7	42	5.8	6.5	..	83	..	68	23	384
Vietnam	0.4	178	0.3	0.7	72	73	22	41	..	88
West Bank and Gaza	..	24	..	..	..	..	..	..	..	220
Yemen, Rep.	0.1	93	0.7	0.5	69	69	21	30	..	49
Zambia	15.6[f]	656	0.3	0.2	50	55	41	45	..	29
Zimbabwe	24.6	659	1.6	1.2	77	83	49	57	..	58
World	**1.1 w**	**140 w**	**3.9 w**	**3.8 w**	**75 w**	**82 w**	**43 w**	**54 w**		**406 w**
Low income	2.1	225	0.8	0.8	64	75	20	36		56
Middle income	0.7	114	3.6	3.2	77	83	48	61		403
Lower middle income	0.7	122	3.4	2.9	77	82	46	60		381
Upper middle income	0.6	43	5.2	6.3	..	..	..	..		594
Low & middle income	1.2	162	2.4	2.2	72	79	37	50		249
East Asia & Pacific	0.2	143	1.9	2.1	71	78	30	49		357
Europe & Central Asia	0.7	82	10.2	6.7	..	91	86	82		438
Latin America & Carib.	0.7	66	2.2	2.7	82	89	68	74		416
Middle East & N. Africa	0.1	55	3.3	4.2	87	88	69	75		237
South Asia	0.8	179	0.7	0.9	70	84	17	35		61
Sub-Saharan Africa	7.2	353	0.9	0.7	49	58	32	36		62
High income	0.4	17	11.8	12.4	..	99	..	..		1,268
Europe EMU	0.3	13	6.9	7.9	..	..	..	..		1,386

a. Data are from the International Telecommunication Union's (ITU) *World Telecommunication Development Report* database. Please cite the ITU for third-party use of these data.
b. Survey data, 2003. c. Survey data, 2004. d. Survey data, 2001. e. Survey data, 2002. f. Survey data 2001/02.

About the data

The Millennium Development Goals address issues of common concern to people of all nations. Diseases and environmental degradation do not respect national boundaries. Epidemic diseases, wherever they persist, pose a threat to people everywhere. And damage done to the environment in one location may affect the well-being of plants, animals, and human beings in distant locations.

The indicators in the table relate to goals 6 and 7 and the targets of goal 8 that address youth employment and access to new technologies. For the other targets of goal 8, see table 1.4.

Measuring the prevalence or incidence of a disease can be difficult. Much of the developing world lacks reporting systems needed for monitoring the course of a disease. Estimates are often derived from surveys and reports from sentinel sites that must be extrapolated to the general population. Tracking diseases such as HIV/AIDS, which has a long latency between contraction of the virus and the appearance of outward symptoms, or malaria, which has periods of dormancy, can be particularly difficult. For some of the most serious illnesses international organizations have formed coalitions such as the Joint United Nations Programme on HIV/AIDS (UNAIDS) and the Roll Back Malaria campaign to gather information and coordinate global efforts to treat victims and prevent the spread of disease.

Antenatal care clinics are a key site for monitoring sexually transmitted diseases such as HIV and syphilis. The prevalence of HIV in young people provides an indicator of the spread of the epidemic. Prevalence rates in the older population can be affected by life-prolonging treatment. The table shows the estimated prevalence among adults ages 15–49. The incidence of tuberculosis is based on data on case notifications and estimates of the proportion of cases detected in the population.

Carbon dioxide emissions are the primary source of greenhouse gases, which are believed to contribute to global warming.

Access to reliable supplies of safe drinking water and sanitary disposal of excreta are two of the most important means of improving human health and protecting the environment. There is no widespread program for testing the quality of water. The indicator shown here measures the proportion of households with access to an improved source, such as piped water or protected wells. Improved sanitation facilities prevent human, animal, and insect contact with excreta but do not include treatment to render sewage outflows innocuous.

The eighth goal—to develop a global partnership for development—takes note of the need for decent and productive work for youth. Labor market information, such as unemployment rates, is still generally unavailable for most low- and middle-income economies. Fixed telephone lines and mobile phones are among the telecommunications technologies that are changing the way the global economy works. For more information on goal 8, see table 1.4.

Definitions

- **Prevalence of HIV** is the percentage of people ages 15–49 who are infected with HIV. • **Incidence of tuberculosis** is the estimated number of new tuberculosis cases (pulmonary, smear positive, extrapulmonary). • **Carbon dioxide emissions** are those stemming from the burning of fossil fuels and the manufacture of cement. They include carbon dioxide produced during consumption of solid, liquid, and gas fuels and gas flaring. • **Access to an improved water source** refers to the percentage of the population with reasonable access to an adequate amount of water from an improved source, such as a household connection, public standpipe, borehole, protected well or spring, or rainwater collection. Unimproved sources include vendors, tanker trucks, and unprotected wells and springs. Reasonable access is defined as the availability of at least 20 liters a person a day from a source within 1 kilometer of the dwelling. • **Access to improved sanitation facilities** refers to the percentage of the population with access to at least adequate excreta disposal facilities (private or shared but not public) that can effectively prevent human, animal, and insect contact with excreta. Improved facilities range from simple but protected pit latrines to flush toilets with a sewerage connection. To be effective, facilities must be correctly constructed and properly maintained. • **Unemployment** refers to the share of the labor force without work but available for and seeking employment. Definitions of labor force and unemployment differ by country. • **Fixed-line and mobile phone subscribers** are telephone mainlines connecting a customer's equipment to the public switched telephone network, and users of portable telephones subscribing to an automatic public mobile telephone service using cellular technology that provides access to the public switched telephone network.

1.3a

Location of indicators for Millennium Development Goals 6–7	
Goal 6. Combat HIV/AIDS, malaria, and other diseases	**Table**
18. HIV prevalence among 15- to 24-year-old pregnant women	1.3*
19. Knowledge and use of methods to prevent HIV transmission	—
20. School attendance of orphans and nonorphans	—
21. Prevalence and death rates associated with malaria	—
22. Proportion of population in malaria-risk areas using effective malaria prevention and treatment measures	2.15*
23. Tuberculosis prevalence and death rates	1.3*, 2.18*
24. Proportion of tuberculosis cases detected and cured under directly observed treatment, short course	2.15
Goal 7. Ensure environmental sustainability	
25. Proportion of land area covered by forest	3.4
26. Ratio of area protected to maintain biological diversity to surface area	3.4
27. Energy use (kilograms of oil equivalent) per $1 of GDP (PPP)	3.8
28. Carbon dioxide emissions per capita and consumption of ozone-depleting chlorofluorocarbons	3.8*
29. Proportion of population using solid fuels	3.7*
30. Proportion of poluation with sustainable access to an improved water souce	2.15, 3.5
31. Proportion of urban population with access to improved sanitation	2.15
32. Proportion of population with access to secure tenure	3.11

— No data are available in the World Development Indicators database.
* Table shows information on related indicators.

Data sources

The indicators here and throughout this book have been compiled by World Bank staff from primary and secondary sources. Efforts have been made to harmonize these data series with those published on the United Nations Millennium Development Goals Web site (http://www.un.org/millenniumgoals), but some differences in timing, sources, and definitions remain.

1.4 Millennium Development Goals: overcoming obstacles

Development Assistance Committee members

	Official development assistances (ODA) by donor		Least developed countries' access to high-income markets								Support to agriculture
	Net % of donor GNI	For basic social services[a] % of total sector-allocable ODA	Goods (excluding arms) admitted free of tariffs %		Average tariff on exports of least developed countries						% of GDP
					Agricultural products %		Textiles %		Clothing %		
	2003	2002–03	1997	2003	1997	2003	1997	2003	1997	2003	2003
Australia	0.25	18.1	96.6	99.9	0.2	0.2	10.0	0.2	28.3	0.9	0.3
Canada	0.24	27.8	65.9	97.2	0.5	0.2	11.4	0.3	21.8	1.5	0.9
European Union			97.3	96.4	3.2	2.7	0.0	0.2	0.0	1.0	1.3
Austria	0.20	7.1									
Belgium	0.60	19.4									
Denmark	0.84	14.3									
Finland	0.35	13.4									
France	0.41	10.3									
Germany	0.28	11.5									
Greece	0.21	18.4									
Ireland	0.39	30.6									
Italy	0.17	20.0									
Luxembourg	0.81	*22.7*									
Netherlands	0.80	19.9									
Portugal	0.22	2.9									
Spain	0.23	12.4									
Sweden	0.79	17.0									
United Kingdom	0.34	28.9									
Japan	0.20	5.0	67.8	91.8	13.4	12.6	2.0	0.4	0.0	0.0	1.3
New Zealand	0.23	14.8									0.4
Norway	0.92	20.2									1.5
Switzerland	0.39	14.3	72.8	99.2	8.9	6.1	0.0	0.0	0.0	0.0	2.0
United States	0.15	23.4	22.5	56.1	5.1	3.6	7.4	6.4	15.3	14.2	0.9

Heavily indebted poor countries (HIPCs)

	HIPC decision point[b]	HIPC completion point[c]	Estimated total nominal debt service relief[d] $ millions		HIPC decision point[b]	HIPC completion point[c]	Estimated total nominal debt service relief[d] $ millions
Benin	Jul. 2000	Mar. 2003	460	Madagascar	Dec. 2000	Oct. 2004	1,873
Bolivia	Feb. 2000	Jun. 2001	2,060	Malawi	Dec. 2000	Floating	1,000
Burkina Faso	Jul. 2000	Apr. 2002	930	Mali	Sep. 2000	Mar. 2003	895
Cameroon	Oct. 2000	Floating	2,800	Mauritania	Feb. 2000	Jun. 2002	1,100
Chad	May 2001	Floating	260	Mozambique	Apr. 2000	Sep. 2001	4,300
Congo, Dem. Republic	Jul. 2003	Floating	10,389	Nicaragua	Dec. 2000	Jan. 2004	4,500
Côte d'Ivoire	Mar. 1998	..	800	Niger	Dec. 2000	Apr.2004	1,200
Ethiopia	Nov. 2001	Apr. 2004	3,275	Rwanda	Dec. 2000	Floating	800
Gambia, the	Dec. 2000	Floating	90	São Tomé & Principe	Dec. 2000	Floating	200
Ghana	Feb. 2002	Jun 04	3,500	Senegal	Jun. 2000	Apr. 2004	850
Guinea	Dec. 2000	Floating	800	Sierra Leone	Mar. 2002	Floating	950
Guinea-Bissau	Dec. 2000	Floating	790	Tanzania	Apr. 2000	Nov. 2001	3,000
Guyana	Nov. 2000	Dec. 2003	1,354	Uganda	Feb. 2000	May 2000	1,950
Honduras	Jul. 2000	Floating	900	Zambia	Dec. 2000	Floating	3,850

a. Includes basic health, education, nutrition, and water and sanitation services. b. Except for Côte d'Ivoire the date refers to the HIPC enhanced initiative. The following countries reached their decision point under the original HIPC framework: Bolivia in September 1997, Burkina Faso in September 1997, Côte d'Ivoire in March 1998, Guyana in December 1997, Mali in September 1998, Mozambique in April 1998, and Uganda in April 1997. c. The date refers to the HIPC enhanced framework. The following countries also reached completion points under the original framework: Bolivia in September 1998, Burkina Faso in July 2000, Guyana in May 1999, Mali in September 2000, Mozambique in July 1999, and Uganda in April 1998. d. Includes estimated total nominal debt service relief under original and enhanced HIPC, as well as topping-up of HIPC debt relief at completion point for Burkina Faso, Ethiopia, and Niger.

About the data

Achieving the Millennium Development Goals will require an open, rule-based global economy in which all countries, rich and poor, participate. Many poor countries, lacking the resources to finance their development, burdened by unsustainable levels of debt, and unable to compete in the global marketplace, need assistance from rich countries. For goal 8—develop a global partnership for development—many of the indicators therefore monitor the actions of members of the Development Assistance Committee (DAC) of the Organisation for Economic Co-operation and Development (OECD).

Official development assistance (ODA) has declined in recent years as a share of donor countries' gross national income (GNI). The poorest countries will need additional assistance to achieve the Millennium Development Goals. Recent estimates suggest that $30–$60 billion more a year would allow most of them to achieve the goals, if the aid goes to countries with good policies. Donor countries have pledged to increase ODA by $20 billion by 2006 and to a total of more than $100 billion by 2010.

One of the most important actions that high-income economies can take to help is to reduce barriers to the exports of low- and middle-income economies. The European Union has announced a program to eliminate tariffs on developing country exports of "everything but arms," and the United States has launched a special program of concessions to exports from Sub-Saharan Africa.

The average tariffs in the table were calculated by the World Trade Organization (WTO). They reflect the tariff schedules applied by high-income OECD members to exports of countries designated "least developed countries" (LDCs) by the United Nations. Agricultural commodities, textiles, and clothing are three of the most important categories of goods exported by developing economies. Although average tariffs have been falling, averages may disguise high tariffs targeted at specific goods (see table 6.6 for estimates of the share of tariff lines with "international peaks" in each country's tariff schedule). The averages in the table include ad valorem duties and ad valorem equivalents of non-ad valorem duties.

Subsidies to agricultural producers and exporters in OECD countries are another form of barrier to developing economies' exports. The table shows the value of total support to agriculture as a share of the economy's gross domestic product (GDP). Agricultural subsidies in OECD economies are estimated at $350 billion in 2003.

The Debt Initiative for Heavily Indebted Poor Countries (HIPCs) is the first comprehensive approach to reducing the external debt of the world's poorest, most heavily indebted countries. It represents an important step forward in placing debt relief within an overall framework of poverty reduction. While the initiative yielded significant early progress, multilateral organizations, bilateral creditors, HIPC governments, and civil society have engaged in an intensive dialogue about its strengths and weaknesses. A major review in 1999 led to an enhancement of the original framework.

Definitions

- **Net official development assistance** (ODA) comprises grants and loans (net of repayments of principal) that meet the DAC definition of ODA and are made to countries and territories in part I of the DAC list of recipient countries. • **ODA for basic social services** is aid reported by DAC donors for basic health, education, nutrition, and water and sanitation services. • **Goods admitted free of tariffs** refer to the value of exports of goods (excluding arms) from least developed countries admitted without tariff, as a share of total exports from LDCs. • **Average tariff** is the simple mean tariff, the unweighted average of the effectively applied rates for all products subject to tariffs. • **Agricultural products** comprise plant and animal products, including tree crops but excluding timber and fish products. • **Textiles and clothing** include natural and synthetic fibers and fabrics and articles of clothing made from them. • **Support to agriculture** is the annual monetary value of all gross transfers from taxpayers and consumers arising from policy measures that support agriculture, net of the associated budgetary receipts, regardless of their objectives and impacts on farm production and income, or consumption of farm products. • **HIPC decision point** is the date at which a heavily indebted poor country with an established track record of good performance under adjustment programs supported by the International Monetary Fund and the World Bank commits to undertake additional reforms and to develop and implement a poverty reduction strategy. • **HIPC completion point** is the date at which the country successfully completes the key structural reforms agreed on at the decision point, including developing and implementing its poverty reduction strategy. The country then receives the bulk of debt relief under the HIPC Debt Initiative without further policy conditions. • **Estimated total nominal debt service relief** is the amount of debt service relief, calculated at the decision point, that will allow the country to achieve debt sustainability at the completion point.

1.4a

Location of indicators for Millennium Development Goal 8

Goal 8. Develop a global partnership for development	Table
33. Net ODA as a percentage of DAC donors' gross national income	6.9
34. Proportion of ODA for basic social services	1.4
35. Proportion of ODA that is untied	6.9
36. Proportion of ODA received in landlocked countries as a percentage of GNI	—
37. Proportion of ODA received in small island developing states as a percentage of GNI	—
38. Proportion of total developed country imports (by value, excluding arms) from developing countries admitted free of duty	1.4
39. Average tariffs imposed by developed countries on agricultural products and textiles and clothing from developing countries	6.6*
40. Agricultural support estimate for OECD countries as a percentage of GDP	1.4
41. Proportion of ODA provided to help build trade capacity	—
42. Number of countries reaching HIPC decision and completion points	1.4
43. Debt relief committed under new HIPC initiative	1.4
44. Debt services as a percentage of exports of goods and services	4.17
45. Unemployment rate of 15- to 24-year-olds	2.4*, 2.8*
46. Proportion of population with access to affordable, essential drugs on a sustainable basis	—
47. Telephone lines and cellular subscribers per 100 people	1.3, 5.10
48a. Personal computers in use per 100 people	5.11
48b. Internet users per 100 people	5.11

— No data are available in the World Development Indicators database.
* Table shows information on related indicators.

Data sources

The indicators here, and where they appear throughout the rest of the book, have been compiled by World Bank staff from primary and secondary sources. The WTO, in collaboration with the UN Conference on Trade and Development and the International Trade Centre, provided the estimates of goods admitted free of tariffs and average tariffs. Subsidies to agriculture are compiled by the OECD.

1.5 Women in development

	Female population	Life expectancy at birth		Pregnant women receiving prenatal care	Teenage mothers	Women's paid work in non-agricultural sector	Women's paid work in agricultural sector	Unpaid family workers		Women in parliaments	
								Male % of male employment	Female % of female employment		
	% of total	Male years	Female years	%	% of women ages 15–19	% of total	% of total	2000–03[a]	2000–03[a]	% of total seats	
	2003	2003	2003	1995–2003[a]	1995–2003[a]	2002	2000–03[a]			1990	2004
Afghanistan	..	..	..	37	..	..	..	..	..	4	..
Albania	48.9	72	77	95	..	40.2	..	..	..	29	6
Algeria	49.4	70	72	81	..	*14.2*	..	..	..	2	6
Angola	50.6	45	48	66	..	..	..	..	..	15	16
Argentina	51.0	71	78	..	..	45.9	22.0	0.7	1.8	6	31
Armenia	51.5	71	79	92	6	..	..	1.1	0.8	36	5
Australia	50.1	77	83	..	..	48.9	31.3	0.4	0.7	6	25
Austria	51.5	76	82	..	..	44.1	47.0	1.4	3.7	12	34
Azerbaijan	50.9	..	..	69	..	48.4	46.8	..	..	..	11
Bangladesh	49.7	62	63	40	35	25.0	46.4	10.1	73.2	10	2
Belarus	53.1	62	74	100	..	55.8	..	..	..	..	10
Belgium	50.9	75	81	..	..	45.2	29.8	..	..	9	35
Benin	50.8	51	55	81	22	..	..	..	..	3	7
Bolivia	50.2	62	66	83	14	37.3	30.2	5.2	11.1	9	19
Bosnia and Herzegovina	50.5	71	77	99	..	..	..	..	..	..	17
Botswana	50.2	38	38	97	..	44.8	..	16.9	17.4	5	17
Brazil	50.7	65	73	86	18	46.6	31.9	..	..	5	9
Bulgaria	51.4	69	76	..	..	51.3	..	..	..	21	26
Burkina Faso	50.4	42	43	73	25	14.0	..	..	..	..	12
Burundi	50.9	41	42	78	..	..	..	..	..	..	18
Cambodia	51.4	53	56	38	8	53.2	..	31.6	53.3	..	10
Cameroon	50.3	47	49	75	31	..	..	..	..	14	9
Canada	50.5	76	83	..	..	48.7	26.8	0.1	0.3	13	21
Central African Republic	51.3	41	42	62	36	..	..	..	..	4	7
Chad	50.6	47	50	42	39	..	..	..	..	..	6
Chile	50.5	73	80	..	..	36.5	11.6	..	..	..	13
China	48.4	69	73	90	..	39.3	..	..	..	21	20
Hong Kong, China	50.9	78	83	..	..	45.9	32.3	..	..	..	..
Colombia	50.6	69	75	91	19	49.2	13.5	5.1	7.1	5	12
Congo, Dem. Rep.	50.4	45	46	68	..	..	..	..	..	5	8
Congo, Rep.	50.6	50	54	..	..	..	..	..	..	14	9
Costa Rica	50.1	76	81	70	..	39.6	8.5	2.5	3.6	11	35
Côte d'Ivoire	49.0	45	46	88	31	19.6	..	..	..	6	9
Croatia	51.9	70	78	..	..	45.7	45.1	2.4	7.8	..	18
Cuba	50.0	75	79	100	..	37.7	..	..	..	34	36
Czech Republic	51.2	72	79	..	..	46.7	..	0.2	1.1	..	17
Denmark	50.5	75	80	..	..	49.0	24.8	..	..	31	38
Dominican Republic	49.3	64	70	99	21	34.9	..	..	..	8	17
Ecuador	49.8	69	74	69	..	40.0	21.6	4.4	10.2	5	16
Egypt, Arab Rep.	49.1	68	71	69	9	20.3	20.8	8.2	26.0	4	2
El Salvador	50.9	67	74	76	..	31.1	5.6	..	..	12	11
Eritrea	50.4	50	52	70	23	..	..	..	..	..	22
Estonia	53.5	65	77	..	..	51.5	30.7	0.8	0.9	..	19
Ethiopia	49.8	41	43	27	16	..	..	..	..	..	8
Finland	51.2	75	82	..	..	50.7	32.8	0.6	0.4	32	38
France	51.4	76	83	..	..	47.0	..	..	..	7	12
Gabon	50.3	52	54	94	33	..	..	..	..	13	9
Gambia, The	50.5	52	55	91	..	..	..	..	..	8	13
Georgia	52.3	69	78	95	..	46.5	49.5	23.2	40.2	..	7
Germany	50.8	76	81	..	..	45.9	35.0	0.5	2.1	..	32
Ghana	50.2	54	55	92	14	..	..	..	..	..	9
Greece	50.7	75	81	..	..	40.5	43.8	4.2	14.7	7	9
Guatemala	49.6	63	69	84	22	39.2	..	..	..	7	8
Guinea	49.7	46	47	71	37	..	..	..	..	..	19
Guinea-Bissau	50.6	44	47	62	..	..	..	..	..	20	*8*
Haiti	50.9	50	54	79	18	..	..	..	..	..	4

Women in development | 1.5

	Female population	Life expectancy at birth		Pregnant women receiving prenatal care	Teenage mothers	Women's paid work in non-agricultural sector	Women's paid work in agricultural sector	Unpaid family workers		Women in parliaments	
								Male	Female		
	% of total	years		%	% of women ages 15–19	% of total	% of total	% of male employment	% of female employment	% of total seats	
	2003	Male 2003	Female 2003	1995–2003[a]	1995–2003[a]	2002	2000–03[a]	2000–03[a]	2000–03[a]	1990	2004
Honduras	49.7	63	69	83	..	50.2	..	..	..	10	6
Hungary	52.2	69	77	..	..	46.7	..	0.4	1.0	21	10
India	48.4	63	64	60	21	17.5	..	..	..	5	9
Indonesia	50.1	65	69	92	12	29.7	..	..	..	12	8
Iran, Islamic Rep.	49.8	68	71	77	..	..	..	..	..	2	4
Iraq	49.2	62	64	77	..	..	..	..	..	11	8
Ireland	50.3	75	80	..	..	47.6	10.4	0.8	1.5	8	13
Israel	50.3	77	81	..	..	48.7	..	0.2	0.7	7	15
Italy	51.5	77	83	..	..	40.9	31.6	3.0	6.0	13	12
Jamaica	50.7	74	78	99	..	47.2	20.5	..	..	5	12
Japan	51.1	78	85	..	..	40.6	42.9	1.6	10.1	1	7
Jordan	48.4	71	74	99	6	21.9	..	..	..	..	6
Kazakhstan	51.6	56	67	91	7	48.1	47.1	..	..	..	10
Kenya	49.8	45	46	88	21	37.6	..	..	..	1	7
Korea, Dem. Rep.	49.8	61	65	..	..	..	..	..	..	21	20
Korea, Rep.	49.7	71	78	..	..	39.7	48.3	1.8	19.5	2	6
Kuwait	39.1	75	79	95	..	19.7	..	..	..	..	0
Kyrgyz Republic	51.1	61	69	97	9	45.4	..	..	..	..	10
Lao PDR	50.0	54	56	27	..	..	..	..	..	6	23
Latvia	54.1	66	76	..	..	53.4	37.1	4.2	4.9	..	21
Lebanon	50.7	69	73	87	..	..	..	..	..	..	2
Lesotho	52.6	36	38	85	..	..	..	..	..	..	12
Liberia	49.7	46	48	85	..	..	..	..	..	..	8
Libya	48.4	70	75	81	..	..	..	..	..	..	..
Lithuania	52.9	66	78	..	..	50.3	39.6	2.8	3.5	..	11
Macedonia, FYR	50.1	71	76	100	..	41.8	40.3	..	..	..	18
Madagascar	50.1	54	57	73	36	..	50.1	..	..	7	4
Malawi	50.7	37	38	94	33	12.2	..	..	..	10	9
Malaysia	49.4	71	76	..	..	34.6	26.5	..	..	5	11
Mali	50.9	40	42	57	40	..	..	..	..	..	10
Mauritania	50.7	49	53	64	16	..	..	..	..	..	4
Mauritius	50.5	69	76	..	..	38.2	..	..	..	7	6
Mexico	51.4	71	77	86	..	37.1	11.9	6.8	12.5	12	23
Moldova	52.3	63	71	99	..	53.7	49.8	4.7	10.7	..	13
Mongolia	50.3	64	68	97	..	47.4	..	..	..	25	11
Morocco	50.0	67	71	68	..	25.8	19.6	..	..	..	11
Mozambique	51.3	40	42	76	40	..	..	..	..	16	30
Myanmar	50.4	55	60	76	..	..	..	..	..	..	..
Namibia	50.9	41	40	91	..	50.0	44.8	..	..	7	26
Nepal	48.7	60	60	28	21	..	..	..	..	6	6
Netherlands	50.5	76	81	..	..	45.0	29.5	0.2	1.1	21	37
New Zealand	51.0	77	81	..	..	50.6	29.6	0.6	1.2	14	28
Nicaragua	50.2	67	71	86	27	..	..	..	..	15	21
Niger	49.7	46	47	41	43	..	..	..	..	5	1
Nigeria	50.6	44	45	58	22	..	..	..	..	..	7
Norway	50.4	77	82	..	..	48.9	27.5	0.2	0.5	36	36
Oman	47.5	73	76	100	..	25.2	19.1	..	..	..	..
Pakistan	48.3	63	65	43	..	8.2	21.1	16.7	50.1	10	22
Panama	49.6	73	77	72	..	43.5	6.0	..	..	8	10
Papua New Guinea	48.6	56	58	78	..	..	..	..	..	..	1
Paraguay	49.5	69	73	89	..	40.5	..	..	..	6	10
Peru	49.7	68	72	84	13	35.0	33.2	4.7	11.5	6	18
Philippines	49.6	68	72	88	7	40.7	28.2	..	..	9	18
Poland	51.4	71	79	..	..	47.5	44.1	4.0	6.8	14	20
Portugal	51.9	73	80	..	..	46.5	51.6	1.1	3.2	8	19
Puerto Rico	51.9	72	82	..	..	40.1	4.3	0.2	1.0	..	..

	Female population	Life expectancy at birth		Pregnant women receiving prenatal care	Teenage mothers	Women's paid work in non-agricultural sector	Women's paid work in agricultural sector	Unpaid family workers		Women in parliaments	
		years						Male % of male employment	Female % of female employment		
	% of total 2003	Male 2003	Female 2003	% 1995–2003[a]	% of women ages 15–19 1995–2003[a]	% of total 2002	% of total 2000–03[a]	2000–03[a]	2000–03[a]	% of total seats 1990	2004
Romania	51.2	66	74	..	..	45.2	48.2	10.4	29.1	34	11
Russian Federation	53.3	60	72	..	..	49.6	..	..	..	..	10
Rwanda	52.4	39	40	92	7	..	..	..	..	17	49
Saudi Arabia	46.0	72	75	90	..	14.0	1.8	..	..	..	0
Senegal	50.3	51	54	77	22	..	..	..	..	13	19
Serbia and Montenegro	50.2	70	75	..	..	..	..	..	..	..	8
Sierra Leone	50.9	36	39	68	..	..	..	..	..	..	15
Singapore	48.8	*76*	*80*	..	..	46.7	..	0.3	1.7	5	16
Slovak Republic	51.4	69	78	..	..	52.0	..	0.1	0.2	..	19
Slovenia	51.3	72	80	..	..	47.9	46.1	3.8	7.0	..	12
Somalia	50.4	46	49	32	..	..	..	..	..	4	..
South Africa	50.8	45	46	94	16	..	..	0.7	1.4	3	30
Spain	51.1	76	84	..	..	39.9	27.9	1.0	3.3	15	28
Sri Lanka	50.6	72	76	98	..	44.6	..	..	..	5	4
Sudan	49.7	57	60	60	..	14.7	..	..	..	..	10
Swaziland	51.6	42	43	87	..	29.3	..	..	..	4	11
Sweden	50.3	78	82	..	..	50.9	23.9	0.3	0.4	38	45
Switzerland	50.3	78	83	..	..	47.2	..	..	..	14	25
Syrian Arab Republic	49.5	68	73	71	..	18.4	35.3	..	..	9	12
Tajikistan	50.2	63	69	71	..	50.4	..	..	..	..	13
Tanzania	50.3	42	43	49	25	..	51.8	..	..	..	21
Thailand	50.8	67	72	92	..	46.1	42.5	16.4	39.8	3	9
Togo	50.4	49	51	73	19	..	..	..	..	5	7
Trinidad and Tobago	50.4	70	74	92	..	40.8	11.1	1.0	0.6	17	19
Tunisia	49.5	71	75	92	..	..	..	..	..	4	12
Turkey	50.2	66	71	68	10	20.6	48.9	10.2	51.3	1	4
Turkmenistan	50.5	61	68	98	4	..	..	..	..	26	26
Uganda	50.0	43	44	92	31	..	..	..	..	12	25
Ukraine	53.5	63	74	..	..	53.2	43.6	0.8	1.7	..	5
United Arab Emirates	35.0	74	77	97	..	12.7	0.1	..	..	..	0
United Kingdom	50.8	75	80	..	..	50.4	22.8	0.2	0.5	6	18
United States	51.0	75	80	..	..	48.6	25.7	0.1	0.1	7	14
Uruguay	51.5	72	79	94	..	45.8	12.0	..	..	6	12
Uzbekistan	50.3	64	70	97	10	41.8	..	..	..	..	7
Venezuela, RB	49.7	71	77	90	..	41.8	7.2	..	..	10	10
Vietnam	50.5	68	72	86	6	..	..	..	..	18	27
West Bank and Gaza	49.3	71	75	..	..	..	37.0	6.0	27.3	..	..
Yemen, Rep.	49.0	57	58	45	16	5.8	..	..	..	4	0
Zambia	49.9	36	37	93	32	..	..	..	..	7	12
Zimbabwe	50.3	39	38	93	21	20.6	..	..	..	11	10
World	**49.7 w**	**65 w**	**69 w**			**36.6 w**				**13 w**	**15 w**
Low income	49.2	57	59			19.9				11	12
Middle income	49.7	67	72			39.9				14	14
Lower middle income	49.6	67	72			39.7				15	14
Upper middle income	50.6	71	77			41.6				12	16
Low & middle income	49.5	63	66			34.4				13	14
East Asia & Pacific	49.0	68	71			38.7				18	17
Europe & Central Asia	52.0	64	73			45.7				21	12
Latin America & Carib.	50.6	68	74			42.9				12	19
Middle East & N. Africa	49.2	67	70			..				5	6
South Asia	48.6	62	64			18.3				6	9
Sub-Saharan Africa	50.3	45	46			..				9	13
High income	50.8	76	81			45.8				12	21
Europe EMU	51.1	76	82			44.4				12	22

a. Data are for the most recent year available.

About the data

Despite much progress in recent decades, gender inequalities remain pervasive in many dimensions of life—worldwide. But while disparities exist throughout the world, they are most prevalent in poor developing countries. Gender inequalities in the allocation of such resources as education, health care, nutrition, and political voice matter because of the strong association with well-being, productivity, and economic growth. This pattern of inequality begins at an early age, with boys routinely receiving a larger share of education and health spending than do girls, for example.

Because of biological differences girls are expected to experience lower infant and child mortality rates and to have a longer life expectancy than boys. This biological advantage, however, may be overshadowed by gender inequalities in nutrition and medical interventions, and by inadequate care during pregnancy and delivery, so that female rates of illness and death sometimes exceed male rates, particularly during early childhood and the reproductive years. In high-income countries women tend to outlive men by four to eight years on average, while in low-income countries the difference is narrower—about two to three years. The difference in child mortality rates (table 2.19) is another good indicator of female social disadvantage because nutrition and medical interventions are particularly important for the 1–5 age group. Female child mortality rates that are as high as or higher than male child mortality rates might be indicative of discrimination against girls.

Having a child during the teenage years limits girls' opportunities for better education, jobs, and income and increases the likelihood of divorce and separation. Pregnancy is more likely to be unintended during the teenage years, and births are more likely to be premature and are associated with greater risks of complications during delivery and of death.

In many countries maternal mortality (tables 1:2 and 2.16) is a leading cause of death among women of reproductive age. Most maternal deaths result from preventable causes—hemorrhage, infection, and complications from unsafe abortions. Prenatal care is essential for recognizing, diagnosing, and promptly treating complications that arise during pregnancy. In high-income countries most women have access to health care during pregnancy, but in developing countries an estimated 8 million women suffer pregnancy-related complications every year, and over half a million die (WHO 2004). This is reflected in the differences in maternal mortality ratios between high- and low-income countries.

Women's wage work is important for economic growth and the well-being of families. But restricted access to education and vocational training, heavy workloads at home and in nonpaid domestic and market activities, and labor market discrimination often limit women's participation in paid economic activities, lower their productivity, and reduce their wages. When women are in salaried employment, they tend to be concentrated in the nonagricultural sector. However, in many developing countries women are a large part of agricultural employment, often as unpaid family workers.

Among people who are unsalaried, women are more likely than men to be unpaid family workers, while men are more likely than women to be self-employed or employers.

There are several reasons for this. Few women have access to credit markets, capital, land, training, and education, which may be required to start up a business. Cultural norms may prevent women from working on their own or from supervising other workers. Also, women may face time constraints due to their traditional family responsibilities. Because of biases and misclassification substantial numbers of employed women may be underestimated or reported as unpaid family workers even when they work in association or equally with their husbands in the family enterprise.

Women are vastly underrepresented in decision-making positions in government, although there is some evidence of recent improvement. Gender parity in parliamentary representation is still far from being realized. In 2004 women represented 16 percent of parliamentarians worldwide, compared with 9 percent in 1987. Without representation at this level, it is difficult for women to influence policy.

For information on other aspects of gender, see tables 1.2 (Millennium Development Goals: eradicating poverty and improving lives), 2.3 (employment by economic activity), 2.4 (unemployment), 2.12 (education efficiency), 2.13 (education outcomes), 2.16 (reproductive health), 2.18 (health risk factors and future challenges), and 2.19 (mortality).

Definitions

• **Female population** is the percentage of the population that is female. • **Life expectancy at birth** is the number of years a newborn infant would live if prevailing patterns of mortality at the time of its birth were to stay the same throughout its life. • **Teenage mothers** are the percentage of women ages 15–19 who already have children or are currently pregnant. • **Pregnant women** receiving prenatal care are the percentage of women attended at least once during pregnancy by skilled health personnel for reasons related to pregnancy. • **Women's paid work in nonagricultural sector** refer to women wage employees in the nonagricultural sector as a percentage of total nonagricultural employment. • **Women's paid work in agricultural sector** refer to women wage employees in the agricultural sector as a percentage of total agricultural employment.• **Unpaid family workers** are those who work without pay in a market-oriented establishment or activity operated by a related person living in the same household. • **Women in parliaments** are the percentage of parliamentary seats in a single or lower chamber occupied by women.

Data sources

The data on female population and life expectancy are from the World Bank's population database. The data on pregnant women receiving prenatal care are from United Nations Children's Fund's (UNICEF) *State of the World's Children 2005.* The data on teenage mothers are from Demographic and Health Surveys by Macro International. The data on labor force and employment are from the ILO's *Key Indicators of the Labour Market,* third edition and LaborSta. The data on women in parliaments are from the Inter Parliamentary Union.

	Population	Surface area	Population density	Gross national income				Gross domestic product		Life expectancy at birth	Adult literacy rate	Carbon dioxide emissions
						PPP[a]					%	
					Per capita		Per capita		Per capita		ages 15	thousand
	thousands	thousand sq. km	people per sq. km	$ millions	$	$ millions	$	% growth	% growth	years	and older	metric tons
	2003	2003	2003	2003[b]	2003	2003	2003	2002–03	2002–03	2003	2003	2000
American Samoa	57	0.2	285	..	..[c]	..	..	..	..	73	..	286
Andorra	66	0.5	141	..	..[d]	..	..	..	..	..	..	..
Antigua and Barbuda	79	0.4	179	719	9,160	765	9,730	3.2	0.4	..	..	352
Aruba	99	0.2	521	..	..[d]	..	..	..	..	..	..	1,924
Bahamas, The	317	13.9	32	*4,684*	*14,920*	*5,068*	*16,140*	0.7	−0.6	70	..	1,795
Bahrain	712	0.7	1,002	*7,569*	*10,850*	*11,291*	*16,180*	5.1	3.0	74	88	19,500
Barbados	271	0.4	630	2,507	9,260	4,076	15,060	1.6	0.9	75	100	1,176
Belize	274	23.0	12	923	3,370	1,729	6,320	9.4	6.0	72	..	780
Bermuda	64	0.1	1,290	..	..[d]	..	..	..	..	..	..	462
Bhutan	874	47.0	19	554	630	..	..	6.7	3.9	63	..	396
Brunei	356	5.8	68	..	..[d]	..	..	..	..	76	..	*4,668*
Cape Verde	470	4.0	117	675	1,440	2,409[e]	5,130[e]	5.0	2.4	70	76	139
Cayman Islands	42	0.3	162	..	..[d]	..	..	..	..	..	..	286
Channel Islands	149	0.2	745	..	..[d]	..	..	..	..	78	..	..
Comoros	600	2.2	269	269	450	1,030[e]	1,720[e]	2.5	0.1	63	56	81
Cyprus	770	9.3	83	*9,373*	*12,320*	15,094[e]	19,600[e]	4.0	3.3	79	97	6,423
Djibouti	705	23.2	30	643	910	1,509[e]	2,140[e]	3.5	1.8	..	..	385
Dominica	71	0.8	95	237	3,330	358	5,020	−0.7	−0.8	76	..	103
Equatorial Guinea	494	28.1	18	*327*	*700*	2,398[e]	5,100[e]	14.7	11.9	44	..	205
Faeroe Islands	47	1.4	34	..	..[d]	..	..	..	..	..	..	649
Fiji	835	18.3	46	1,871	2,240	4,716	5,650	5.0	3.3	68	..	725
French Polynesia	243	4.0	67	..	..[d]	..	..	..	..	73	..	542
Greenland	56	410.5	0	..	..[d]	..	..	..	..	*69*	..	557
Grenada	105	0.3	309	388	3,710	736	7,030	2.5	4.6	73	..	213
Guam	162	0.6	294	..	..[d]	..	..	..	..	75	..	4,071
Guyana	769	215.0	4	689	900	3,061[e]	3,980[e]	−0.6	−1.1	63	..	1,598
Iceland	289	103.0	3	8,932	30,910	8,835	30,570	4.0	3.7	81	..	2,158
Isle of Man	74	0.6	129	..	..[d]	..	..	..	..	..	..	..

About the data

The table shows data for 56 economies with populations from 30,000 to 1 million and smaller economies if they are members of the World Bank. Where data on gross national income (GNI) per capita are not available, an estimated range is given. For more information on the calculation of GNI (or gross national product in the 1968 System of National Accounts) and purchasing power parity (PPP) conversion factors, see *About the data* for table 1.1. Since 2000 this table has excluded France's overseas departments—French Guiana, Guadeloupe, Martinique, and Réunion—for which GNI and other economic measures are now included in the French national accounts.

Definitions

• **Population** is based on the de facto definition of population, which counts all residents regardless of legal status or citizenship—except for refugees not permanently settled in the country of asylum, who are generally considered part of the population of their country of origin. The values shown are midyear estimates for 2003. See also table 2.1. • **Surface area** is a country's total area, including areas under inland bodies of water and some coastal waterways. • **Population density** is midyear population divided by land area in square kilometers. • **Gross national income** (GNI) is the sum of value added by all resident producers plus any product taxes (less subsidies) not included in the valuation of output plus net receipts of primary income (compensation of employees and property income) from abroad. Data are in current U.S. dollars converted using the *World Bank Atlas* method (see *Statistical methods*). • **GNI per capita** is gross national income divided by midyear population. GNI per capita in U.S. dollars is converted using the *World Bank Atlas* method. • **PPP GNI** is gross national income converted to international dollars using purchasing power parity rates. An international dollar has the same purchasing power over GNI as a U.S. dollar has in the United States. • **Gross domestic product**

Key indicators for other economies

	Population	Surface area	Population density	Gross national income				Gross domestic product		Life expectancy at birth	Adult literacy rate	Carbon dioxide emissions
						PPPa					%	
	thousands 2003	thousand sq. km 2003	people per sq. km 2003	$ millions 2003b	Per capita $ 2003	$ millions 2003	Per capita $ 2003	% growth 2002–03	Per capita % growth 2002–03	years 2003	ages 15 and older 2003	thousand metric tons 2000
Kiribati	96	0.7	132	83	860	..	..	1.4	0.7	63	..	26
Liechtenstein	33	0.2	206	..	..d	..	..	..	..	..	..	..
Luxembourg	448	2.6	173	20,492	45,740	24,862	55,500	2.1	1.1	78	..	8,482
Macao, China	444	0.0	21,143	6,335f	14,600f	9,634e	21,950e	10.1	8.9	..	91	1,634
Maldives	293	0.3	977	690	2,350	..	..	9.2	6.8	66	97	498
Malta	399	0.3	1,247	4,302	10,780	7,095	17,780	1.5	−2.2	78	93	2,814
Marshall Islands	53	0.2	290	142	2,710	..	..	2.0	2.0	67	..	..
Mayotte	166	0.4	444	..	..c	..	..	..	..	..	..	..
Micronesia, Fed. Sts.	125	0.7	178	258	2,070	..	..	2.4	0.6	67	..	..
Monaco	33	0.0	16,923	..	..d	..	..	..	..	..	..	..
Netherlands Antilles	220	0.8	275	..	..d	..	..	..	..	76	97	9,929
New Caledonia	225	18.6	12	..	..d	..	..	..	..	75	..	1,667
Northern Mariana Islands	76	0.5	159	..	..c	..	..	..	..	76	..	..
Palau	20	0.5	43	130	6,500	..	..	1.5	..	68	..	242
Qatar	624	11.0	57	..	..d	..	..	..	..	73	..	40,685
Samoa	178	2.8	63	257	1,440	1,029e	5,780e	3.1	2.5	70	99	139
São Tomé and Principe	157	1.0	164	48	300	..	..	4.5	2.4	63	..	88
Seychelles	84	0.5	186	626	7,490	..	..	−5.1	−6.4	73	92	227
Solomon Islands	457	28.9	16	255	560	783e	1,710e	5.1	2.0	62	..	165
San Marino	28	0.1	463	653	..d	..	..	..	..	..	..	..
St. Kitts and Nevis	47	0.4	130	309	6,630	502	10,740	0.0	0.0	72	..	103
St. Lucia	161	0.6	263	650	4,050	852	5,310	1.7	0.8	74	..	322
St. Vincent & Grenadines	109	0.4	280	361	3,310	640	5,870	4.0	4.0	71	..	161
Suriname	438	163.3	3	998	2,280	..	..	3.0	4.0	69	..	2,118
Timor-Leste	877	14.9	59	372	460	..	..	−2.0	−7.0	..	..	..
Tonga	102	0.8	141	152	1,490	701e	6,910e	2.5	2.1	70	..	121
Vanuatu	210	12.2	17	248	1,180	610e	2,900e	2.0	−0.2	67	..	81
Virgin Islands (U.S.)	112	0.3	329	..	..d	..	..	..	..	78	..	13,106

a. PPP is purchasing power parity; see *Definitions*. b. Calculated using the *World Bank Atlas* method. c. Estimated to be upper middle income ($3,036–$9,385). d. Estimated to be high income ($9,386 or more). e. The estimate is based on regression; others are extrapolated from the latest International Comparison Program benchmark estimates. f. Refers to GDP and GDP per capita.

(GDP) is the sum of value added by all resident producers plus any product taxes (less subsidies) not included in the valuation of output. Growth is calculated from constant price GDP data in local currency. • **Life expectancy at birth** is the number of years a newborn infant would live if prevailing patterns of mortality at the time of its birth were to stay the same throughout its life. • **Adult literacy rate** is the percentage of adults ages 15 and older who can, with understanding, read and write a short, simple statement about their everyday life. • **Carbon dioxide emissions** are those stemming from the burning of fossil fuels and the manufacture of cement. They include carbon dioxide produced during consumption of solid, liquid, and gas fuels and gas flaring.

Data sources

The indicators here and throughout the book were compiled by World Bank Group staff from primary and secondary sources. More information about the indicators and their sources can be found in the *About the data*, *Definitions*, and *Data sources* entries that accompany each table in subsequent sections.

2 | PEOPLE

This section examines the progress of countries in reducing poverty in its income and non-income dimensions and in improving the welfare of their people. Evidence confirms that expanding economic opportunities for poor people—through pro-poor growth policies—raises their incomes. The key to expanding their economic opportunities is to help them build up their assets. Human capabilities such as health and education are of intrinsic value and also have powerful effects on material well-being. Broad access to such basic infrastructure as clean water and adequate sanitation is also important to the material prospects of poor people. And a range of public interventions, such as old-age pensions and unemployment insurance, can reduce their vulnerabilities.

The challenge for governments: formidable. The tables in this section track the progress of countries in reducing poverty and improving human capital. The expanded table on poverty (table 2.5) shows the poverty levels prevailing in countries and the longer term trends for regional and income groups. Other tables provide information on population size and growth, labor force participation, and employment by economic activity. Information is also available on the vulnerabilities in populations and government efforts to alleviate those vulnerabilities. The tables also provide information on improvements in education and health and some clues to remaining and emerging challenges. Together, the tables identify a country's accomplishments and the tasks that still lie ahead.

The third Millennium Development Goal: Promote gender equality and empower women
Gender issues are highly relevant to achieving all the Millennium Development Goals, from reducing poverty and hunger to protecting the environment. Because the Goals are mutually reinforcing, progress toward gender equality will advance other Goals, while success in achieving other Goals will positively affect gender equality. The target for the third Goal is to achieve gender parity in primary and secondary education, preferably by 2005 but no later than 2015, and in tertiary education by 2015. The indicator for monitoring progress toward this target is the ratio of female to male gross enrollment rates in primary, secondary, and tertiary education.

What do the statistics tell us about gender and equality? The 2005 milestone year for this goal is already upon us, so we need to map countries' progress. But a three-year delay in the production of education statistics and a lack of baseline and recent data in many countries make it impossible to assess with certainty how many countries will have achieved gender equality in education. The most recent data refer to the school period 2002/03. So conclusions about where countries stand in 2005 are based on the progress between 1990 and 2002 and on hypotheses of what would happen if progress continued at the same rate.

The data show that the prospects for achieving gender equality in education vary considerably between educational levels and regions. There has been more progress in gender equality in primary school enrollments than in secondary and tertiary enrollments (figure 2a). Still, more than

Progress toward gender parity in primary, secondary, and tertiary education is uneven across regions

Share of countries in each region, around 2002 (%)

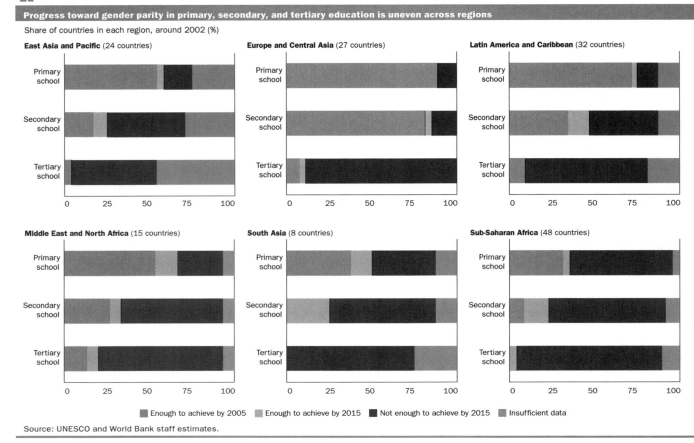

East Asia and Pacific (24 countries)

Europe and Central Asia (27 countries)

Latin America and Caribbean (32 countries)

Middle East and North Africa (15 countries)

South Asia (8 countries)

Sub-Saharan Africa (48 countries)

■ Enough to achieve by 2005   ▨ Enough to achieve by 2015   ■ Not enough to achieve by 2015   ▨ Insufficient data

Source: UNESCO and World Bank staff estimates.

a third of developing countries will not achieve gender parity in primary school enrollments this year, and most of them risk not meeting the target in 2015 if they do not take immediate action to increase girls' school attendance. The risk is greatest for Sub-Saharan Africa and South Asia, the regions reporting the slowest progress in closing the gender gap in primary schooling.

Fewer than 30 percent of developing countries have made enough progress in the last 15 years to achieve gender parity in secondary enrollments by 2005, and only 40 percent are expected to achieve this target by 2015 without stronger efforts to increase boys' and girls' enrollment in secondary education (figure 2b). Countries in South Asia and Sub-Saharan Africa are seriously off track. And on current trends only 9 percent of developing countries are making enough progress to achieve gender equality in tertiary education by 2015.

Even though the first target for the third Millennium Development Goal has not been met globally, in the two regions with the deepest educational inequality an impressive number of countries have achieved it for primary education. In Sub-Saharan Africa they include Botswana, Mauritius, Namibia, Seychelles, Tanzania, and Uganda, and in South Asia, Sri Lanka. Several other countries are working to increase intake rates to make school accessible to previously unenrolled

Achieving equal access to education for boys and girls leads to progress toward the goal

Female to male enrollment ratio, around 2002 (%)

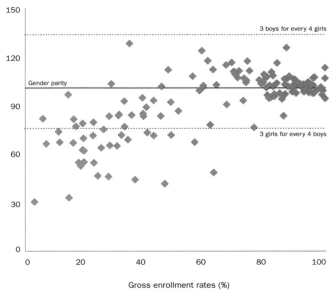

Gross enrollment rates (%)

Source: UNESCO.

2c

Population estimates and enrollment rates

Population estimates are generally based on extrapolations from the most recent census—and are the product of demographic modeling. Extrapolations are uncertain because the present demographic situation is not known perfectly, and future trends of births, deaths, and net migration, even in the very short term, are subject to unpredictable influences.

Errors in projecting population totals are generally accompanied by errors in the sizes of particular age groups. Projections of younger and older age groups tend to be unreliable because of age-heaping and underenumeration of children, particularly of girls and women in countries where gender inequality remains pervasive.

How does this affect enrollment rates? Used as a denominator, population estimates bias enrollment rates, with the extent and direction of the bias often unknown. Efforts are made to adjust for the bias, but as noted above, models may miss important demographic events. Three other conceptual and technical issues relating to population that affect enrollment rates, especially their international comparability, are de facto versus de jure enumeration, completeness of coverage, and availability and recency of population data.

populations. But a lack of recent data on enrollments makes it difficult to monitor whether these actions are working.

Equally difficult is to assess accurately where individual countries stand in relation to the target, because measuring the dynamics of education and gender is highly complex. Several technical and conceptual factors are responsible for this. First, the data for gender equality in education come from two sources: enrollment data from school censuses reported by education ministries and national agencies, and estimates of the school age population based commonly on population censuses and population estimates and projections. The reliability of enrollment data collected through school censuses is suspect in some countries because of overreporting, perhaps linked to financial incentives or other factors. And the lack of reliable population estimates biases enrollment rates, with the extent and direction of the bias unclear (box 2c).

Second, the indicator is only an approximation of gender differences in school enrollment among school-age children. As such, it can overestimate or underestimate the extent of gender inequalities, but the size of the error is difficult to assess. Two factors, in particular, affect the accuracy of the ratio of female to male gross enrollment rates as a measure of gender inequality:

- *Underreporting of private education by officials underestimates enrollment rates.* This may affect the ratio of girls to boys enrolled in school if girls and boys have different probabilities of attending a private school. A recent study in Pakistan suggests that this may be the case in countries where the determinants of school attendance differ for girls and boys (Alderman, Orazem, and Paterno 2001).

- *Repetition rates are generally higher for boys than for girls.* A high pattern of male repetition is likely to underestimate actual progress in gender parity.

Third, the indicator does not reflect how many of the girls and boys who should be in school are actually attending school. Improvements in the gender ratio can result from an increase in girls' school attendance or a decrease in boys'. In Cambodia, for example, the ratio of girls to boys in secondary school increased from 0.43 in 1990 to 0.60 in 2001. The improvement was the result not of an increase in girls' gross enrollment—it fell from 19 percent to 17 percent—but of a marked decrease in boy's enrollment, which fell from 45 percent to 27 percent.

This analysis demonstrates the urgency to take action on two fronts as countries endeavor to achieve this target by 2015.

What needs to be done

Promoting gender equality in education requires addressing the conditions that prevent girls and boys from attending school. Evidence shows that scholarships, lower fees, and subsidies in the form of food and cash transfers conditional on school attendance increase girls' and boys' enrollment rates. They also reduce the probability of dropping out of school and close gender gaps in school attainment. In countries where girls are less likely than boys to attend school, these subsidies have a larger effect on girls' attendance than on boys', even when girls are not targeted. Subsidies are even more effective in reducing gender disparities in schooling when they are directed to girls. For example, the Female Secondary School Assistance Program in Bangladesh paid tuition and stipends directly into

2d

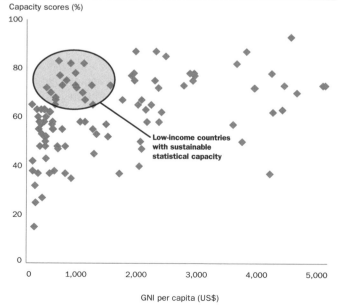

Sustainable statistical capacity is possible in low-income countries

Capacity scores (%)

Low-income countries with sustainable statistical capacity

GNI per capita (US$)

Source: World Bank.

a national bank for all girls attending school for at least 75 percent of the school year. An assessment of the pilot phase shows that girls' secondary enrollment in the program area rose from 27 percent to 44 percent in five years—more than double the national average increase (World Bank 2001).

Equally important is the need for countries to implement standardized concepts and methodologies of data collection. This is likely to place a stress on poor countries with weak administrative systems. Generally, statistical capacity is low in low-income countries, but several low-income countries have sustainable statistical capacity, including Albania, Armenia, India, Nicaragua, and Senegal (figure 2d).

Building capacity for monitoring progress
Countries acknowledge the role of reliable and timely data, both for analyzing, evaluating, and monitoring the effectiveness of current and longer term policies and for reporting to the international development community on country progress on international initiatives such as the Millennium Development Goals. A sophisticated international statistical system has been developed over the years by the international community. This system relies considerably on data originated in national statistical systems, many of which are institutionally weak and undervalued.

Managing for results and monitoring the Millennium Development Goals generate demand that may result in trapping these systems in a vicious spiral of underperformance, domestic underfunding, and conflicting donor agendas. An effective and efficient national statistical system, providing the data needed to support better policies and to monitor progress, needs to be put in place before further demands are made by the international community.

Key gender performance indicators

The third Millennium Development Goal recognizes that promoting gender equality and empowering women involves more than gender parity in education enrollments. Three additional indicators are proposed to obtain a more rounded assessment:

- Ratio of literate women to men 15 to 24 years old.
- Share of women in wage employment in the nonagricultural sector.
- Proportion of seats held by women in national parliaments.

No targets were set for these indicators, and progress has been slow, especially in women's participation in nonagricultural employment and in parliament (table 1.5).

All the Goal 3 indicators still fail to capture many important dimensions of gender equality and women's empowerment. Working women have less social protection and fewer employment rights than do men. In some countries as many as 40 percent of women have been victims of physical violence by an intimate partner. More than 500,000 women die each year in pregnancy and childbirth. And rates of HIV/AIDS infection among women are rapidly increasing. To eliminate other gender inequalities in society, women must enjoy equal rights with men, equal economic opportunities, use of productive assets, freedom from domestic drudgery, equal representation in decisionmaking bodies (including those at the local level), and freedom from threats of violence and coercion (UN Millennium Project 2005).

There is, therefore, strong support in the international development community for supplementing the four indicators. The UN Millennium Project Task Force on Education and Gender Equality identified seven strategic priorities for empowering women and redressing gender differences and proposed 12 indicators to monitor progress (see table).

Measuring and monitoring these proposed indicators will pose an additional challenge for both countries and the specialized UN agencies. Countries need to develop capacity within line ministries to collect and analyze the recommended data and to set up or expand coordination mechanisms across ministries. UN specialized agencies need to work with bilateral and multilateral partners to develop improved methodologies and systems for the national production of these statistics.

Proposed indicators to monitor progress in achieving the third Millennium Development Goal

Goal and proposed indicators	Data source
Ensure universal primary education and strengthen opportunities for postprimary education	United Nations Educational, Scientific and Cultural Organization
• Ratio of female to male gross enrollment rates in primary, secondary, and tertiary education*	
• Ratio of female to male completion rates in primary, secondary, and tertiary education	
Guarantee sexual and reproductive health and rights	Specialized household surveys—Demographic and Health Surveys (DHS), Multiple Indicator Cluster Surveys—and United Nations Population Fund
• Proportion of contraceptive demand satisfied	
• Adolescent fertility rate	
Invest in infrastructure to reduce women's and girls' time burden	Time-use surveys and certain household surveys such as Living Standards Measurement Study (LSMS) surveys
• Hours per day (or year) women and men spend fetching water and collecting fuel	
Guarantee women's and girls' property rights and inheritance	Land registry and certain household surveys such as LSMS
• Land ownership by male, female, and jointly held	UN-HABITAT project, housing titles registry, and certain household surveys such as LSMS
• Housing title, disaggregated by male, female, and jointly held	
Eliminate gender inequality in employment	International Labour Organization (ILO), Women in Informal Employment: Globalizing and Organizing (WIEGO), and labor force and household surveys such as LSMS
• Share of women in employment, both wage and self-employed, by type	ILO, labor force surveys, and certain household surveys
• Gender gaps in earnings in wage and self-employment	
Increase women's share of seats in national parliaments and local government bodies	Inter-Parliamentary Union
• Percentage of seats held by women in national parliament*	
• Percentage of seats held by women in local government bodies	
Combat violence against women	United Cities and Local Governments, DHS, World Health Organization multicountry study on women's health and domestic violence, and other national surveys with similar methodologies
• Prevalence of domestic violence	

* Current Millennium Development Goal indicators.
Source: UN Millennium Project 2005.

	Total population			Average annual population growth rate		Population age composition			Dependency ratio		Crude death rate	Crude birth rate
							%		dependents as proportion of working-age population		per 1,000 people	per 1,000 people
						Ages 0–14	Ages 15–64	Ages 65+	Young	Old		
		millions		%								
	1990	2003	2015	1990–2003	2003–15	2003	2003	2003	2003	2003	2003	2003
Afghanistan	17.7	..	..	..	..	..	..	..	..	..	..	..
Albania	3.3	3.2	3.5	−0.3	0.8	27.3	65.4	7.3	0.4	0.1	6	17
Algeria	25.0	31.8	38.3	1.9	1.5	33.9	62.0	4.1	0.5	0.1	5	22
Angola	9.3	13.5	18.9	2.8	2.8	47.6	49.4	2.9	1.0	0.1	19	50
Argentina	32.3	36.8	42.9	1.0	1.3	27.0	63.2	9.8	0.4	0.2	8	18
Armenia	3.5	3.1	3.0	−1.1	−0.1	20.5	69.3	10.2	0.3	0.1	8	9
Australia	17.1	19.9	21.9	1.2	0.8	20.0	67.5	12.5	0.3	0.2	7	13
Austria	7.7	8.1	8.1	0.4	−0.0	16.2	67.8	16.0	0.2	0.2	10	10
Azerbaijan	7.2	8.2	9.0	1.1	0.7	27.0	65.5	7.5	0.4	0.1	7	16
Bangladesh	110.0	138.1	166.0	1.7	1.5	35.5	61.2	3.4	0.6	0.1	8	28
Belarus	10.2	9.9	9.3	−0.2	−0.5	16.8	69.1	14.0	0.2	0.2	14	9
Belgium	10.0	10.4	10.5	0.3	0.1	17.0	66.3	16.8	0.3	0.3	10	11
Benin	4.7	6.7	9.0	2.7	2.4	45.0	52.4	2.7	0.9	0.1	13	38
Bolivia	6.7	8.8	10.8	2.1	1.7	38.4	57.3	4.4	0.7	0.1	8	29
Bosnia and Herzegovina	4.5	4.1	4.2	−0.6	0.2	17.2	71.9	10.9	0.2	0.2	8	12
Botswana	1.3	1.7	1.8	2.3	0.4	41.5	56.2	2.3	0.7	0.0	23	29
Brazil	148.0	176.6	201.0	1.4	1.1	27.5	67.1	5.4	0.4	0.1	7	19
Bulgaria	8.7	7.8	7.2	−0.8	−0.7	14.4	69.2	16.4	0.2	0.2	14	8
Burkina Faso	8.9	12.1	15.6	2.4	2.1	46.9	50.4	2.7	0.9	0.1	19	43
Burundi	5.5	7.2	8.8	2.1	1.7	45.3	52.1	2.5	0.9	0.1	20	38
Cambodia	9.6	13.4	16.4	2.6	1.7	41.0	55.8	3.2	0.7	0.1	12	29
Cameroon	11.7	16.1	19.7	2.5	1.7	41.1	55.2	3.7	0.7	0.1	16	35
Canada	27.8	31.6	33.5	1.0	0.5	18.2	69.0	12.8	0.3	0.2	7	11
Central African Republic	2.9	3.9	4.6	2.1	1.5	41.8	54.7	3.5	0.8	0.1	20	35
Chad	5.8	8.6	12.1	3.0	2.8	48.0	49.2	2.8	1.0	0.1	16	45
Chile	13.1	15.8	17.8	1.4	1.0	26.9	65.7	7.4	0.4	0.1	5	17
China	1,135.2	1,288.4	1,389.5	1.0	0.6	23.6	69.1	7.3	0.3	0.1	8	15
Hong Kong, China	5.7	6.8	7.0	1.4	0.2	15.8	72.6	11.6	0.2	0.2	5	7
Colombia	35.0	44.6	51.8	1.9	1.2	31.8	63.5	4.8	0.5	0.1	6	22
Congo, Dem. Rep.	37.4	53.2	75.2	2.7	2.9	47.9	49.5	2.6	1.0	0.1	18	45
Congo, Rep.	2.5	3.8	5.2	3.2	2.8	46.9	50.1	3.1	0.9	0.1	14	44
Costa Rica	3.1	4.0	4.7	2.1	1.4	29.8	64.4	5.8	0.5	0.1	4	17
Côte d'Ivoire	11.8	16.8	20.2	2.7	1.5	41.5	55.9	2.6	0.7	0.1	17	37
Croatia	4.8	4.4	4.3	−0.6	−0.3	16.2	68.1	15.8	0.2	0.2	12	10
Cuba	10.6	11.3	11.7	0.5	0.3	20.3	69.2	10.4	0.3	0.2	8	13
Czech Republic	10.4	10.2	9.9	−0.1	−0.3	15.5	70.6	13.9	0.2	0.2	11	9
Denmark	5.1	5.4	5.4	0.4	0.1	18.6	66.5	14.9	0.3	0.2	11	12
Dominican Republic	7.1	8.7	10.1	1.6	1.2	32.0	63.5	4.5	0.5	0.1	7	22
Ecuador	10.3	13.0	15.3	1.8	1.4	32.7	62.4	4.9	0.5	0.1	6	23
Egypt, Arab Rep.	52.4	67.6	80.9	1.9	1.5	33.5	62.2	4.3	0.5	0.1	6	24
El Salvador	5.1	6.5	7.9	1.9	1.5	34.7	60.3	5.0	0.6	0.1	6	25
Eritrea	3.1	4.4	5.6	2.6	2.0	44.3	53.0	2.7	0.8	0.1	13	37
Estonia	1.6	1.4	1.3	−1.1	−0.5	16.1	68.6	15.2	0.2	0.2	13	10
Ethiopia	51.2	68.6	87.3	2.3	2.0	45.4	51.8	2.8	0.9	0.1	20	40
Finland	5.0	5.2	5.3	0.3	0.1	17.6	67.0	15.3	0.3	0.2	9	11
France	56.7	59.8	61.8	0.4	0.3	18.6	65.3	16.1	0.3	0.2	9	13
Gabon	1.0	1.3	1.7	2.6	2.2	40.4	54.0	5.5	0.7	0.1	15	35
Gambia, The	0.9	1.4	1.8	3.3	1.9	40.5	56.2	3.2	0.7	0.1	14	36
Georgia	5.5	5.1	4.7	−0.5	−0.7	18.4	67.3	14.3	0.3	0.2	10	8
Germany	79.4	82.5	80.6	0.3	−0.2	14.9	67.8	17.3	0.2	0.3	10	9
Ghana	15.3	20.7	25.8	2.3	1.9	41.9	53.7	4.4	0.8	0.1	13	31
Greece	10.2	11.0	11.0	0.6	−0.0	14.7	66.7	18.7	0.2	0.3	9	9
Guatemala	8.8	12.3	16.3	2.6	2.3	42.5	54.1	3.5	0.8	0.1	7	33
Guinea	5.8	7.9	9.8	2.4	1.8	43.6	53.8	2.5	0.8	0.1	17	38
Guinea-Bissau	1.0	1.5	2.0	2.9	2.6	44.4	52.1	3.4	0.9	0.1	20	49
Haiti	6.5	8.4	10.3	2.0	1.6	39.0	57.5	3.5	0.7	0.1	14	32

	Total population			Average annual population growth rate		Population age composition			Dependency ratio		Crude death rate	Crude birth rate
							%		dependents as proportion of working-age population		per 1,000 people	per 1,000 people
		millions		%		Ages 0–14	Ages 15–64	Ages 65+	Young	Old		
	1990	2003	2015	1990–2003	2003–15	2003	2003	2003	2003	2003	2003	2003
Honduras	4.9	7.0	8.9	2.8	2.0	40.8	55.9	3.3	0.7	0.1	6	30
Hungary	10.4	10.1	9.6	−0.2	−0.5	16.3	69.0	14.7	0.2	0.2	13	10
India	849.5	1,064.4	1,231.6	1.7	1.2	32.4	62.5	5.1	0.5	0.1	8	24
Indonesia	178.2	214.7	246.8	1.4	1.2	29.7	65.4	4.9	0.5	0.1	7	21
Iran, Islamic Rep.	54.4	66.4	77.5	1.5	1.3	29.5	65.8	4.7	0.4	0.1	6	18
Iraq	18.1	24.7	31.1	2.4	1.9	39.4	57.6	3.1	0.7	0.1	8	29
Ireland	3.5	4.0	4.4	1.0	0.8	21.3	67.5	11.2	0.3	0.2	7	16
Israel	4.7	6.7	7.9	2.8	1.4	27.4	63.0	9.7	0.4	0.2	6	20
Italy	56.7	57.6	55.1	0.1	−0.4	14.0	67.0	19.0	0.2	0.3	10	9
Jamaica	2.4	2.6	3.0	0.8	1.0	29.7	63.5	6.9	0.5	0.1	6	19
Japan	123.5	127.6	124.8	0.2	−0.2	14.2	67.2	18.6	0.2	0.3	8	9
Jordan	3.2	5.3	6.8	4.0	2.1	37.4	59.4	3.2	0.6	0.1	4	28
Kazakhstan	16.3	14.9	15.5	−0.7	0.3	24.5	67.4	8.1	0.4	0.1	10	15
Kenya	23.4	31.9	37.5	2.4	1.3	42.1	55.2	2.7	0.8	0.1	17	34
Korea, Dem. Rep.	20.0	22.6	24.0	1.0	0.5	25.7	67.7	6.6	0.4	0.1	11	17
Korea, Rep.	42.9	47.9	50.0	0.9	0.4	20.7	71.7	7.6	0.3	0.1	7	12
Kuwait	2.1	2.4	3.0	0.9	1.9	24.8	73.3	1.9	0.3	0.0	3	20
Kyrgyz Republic	4.4	5.1	5.8	1.0	1.1	31.7	62.2	6.1	0.5	0.1	8	19
Lao PDR	4.1	5.7	7.3	2.4	2.1	41.8	54.7	3.5	0.8	0.1	12	35
Latvia	2.7	2.3	2.1	−1.1	−0.7	15.1	69.3	15.5	0.2	0.2	14	9
Lebanon	3.6	4.5	5.2	1.6	1.2	30.3	63.8	5.9	0.5	0.1	6	19
Lesotho	1.6	1.8	2.0	1.0	0.9	41.4	53.4	5.1	0.8	0.1	24	33
Liberia	2.4	3.4	4.4	2.5	2.2	44.1	53.1	2.8	0.8	0.1	20	43
Libya	4.3	5.6	6.9	2.0	1.7	32.5	63.8	3.7	0.5	0.1	4	27
Lithuania	3.7	3.5	3.3	−0.5	−0.4	17.7	68.2	14.2	0.3	0.2	12	9
Macedonia, FYR	1.9	2.1	2.2	0.6	0.5	21.5	67.8	10.7	0.3	0.2	9	14
Madagascar	11.6	16.9	22.5	2.9	2.4	44.1	52.9	3.0	0.8	0.1	12	38
Malawi	8.5	11.0	13.6	2.0	1.8	44.9	51.8	3.4	0.9	0.1	25	44
Malaysia	18.2	24.8	29.6	2.4	1.5	33.0	62.6	4.4	0.5	0.1	5	21
Mali	8.5	11.7	15.6	2.5	2.4	47.2	50.1	2.8	0.9	0.1	23	48
Mauritania	2.0	2.8	3.6	2.6	1.9	42.6	54.3	3.1	0.8	0.1	15	34
Mauritius	1.1	1.2	1.4	1.1	0.9	25.0	68.6	6.4	0.4	0.1	7	16
Mexico	83.2	102.3	120.6	1.6	1.4	32.3	62.5	5.2	0.5	0.1	5	19
Moldova	4.4	4.2	4.1	−0.2	−0.2	20.4	68.6	11.1	0.3	0.2	13	11
Mongolia	2.1	2.5	2.9	1.3	1.3	31.7	64.2	4.1	0.5	0.1	6	22
Morocco	24.0	30.1	35.4	1.7	1.4	32.9	62.7	4.4	0.5	0.1	6	22
Mozambique	14.2	18.8	22.7	2.2	1.6	42.3	54.1	3.6	0.8	0.1	21	40
Myanmar	40.5	49.4	55.7	1.5	1.0	31.9	63.6	4.5	0.5	0.1	12	23
Namibia	1.4	2.0	2.3	2.8	1.1	41.9	54.3	3.8	0.8	0.1	21	35
Nepal	18.1	24.7	31.1	2.4	1.9	40.1	56.1	3.8	0.7	0.1	10	31
Netherlands	15.0	16.2	16.6	0.6	0.2	18.3	67.7	14.0	0.3	0.2	9	12
New Zealand	3.4	4.0	4.5	1.2	0.9	21.9	66.4	11.7	0.3	0.2	7	14
Nicaragua	3.8	5.5	7.0	2.8	2.0	40.9	56.0	3.1	0.7	0.1	5	29
Niger	7.7	11.8	16.3	3.3	2.7	48.9	48.8	2.3	1.0	0.1	20	48
Nigeria	96.2	136.5	173.8	2.7	2.0	44.1	53.3	2.6	0.8	0.1	18	43
Norway	4.2	4.6	4.7	0.6	0.3	19.7	65.4	14.9	0.3	0.2	9	12
Oman	1.6	2.6	3.4	3.6	2.2	41.3	55.9	2.8	0.7	0.1	3	26
Pakistan	108.0	148.4	192.8	2.4	2.2	40.1	56.6	3.4	0.7	0.1	8	32
Panama	2.4	3.0	3.5	1.7	1.2	30.0	64.2	5.8	0.5	0.1	5	20
Papua New Guinea	4.0	5.5	6.9	2.5	1.8	40.9	56.6	2.5	0.7	0.1	10	33
Paraguay	4.2	5.6	7.2	2.4	2.0	38.4	58.1	3.5	0.7	0.1	5	30
Peru	21.6	27.1	31.6	1.8	1.3	33.0	62.2	4.9	0.5	0.1	6	22
Philippines	61.0	81.5	98.2	2.2	1.6	36.0	60.0	4.0	0.6	0.1	6	26
Poland	38.1	38.2	37.9	0.0	−0.1	17.6	69.9	12.5	0.3	0.2	9	9
Portugal	9.9	10.4	10.5	0.4	0.0	17.3	67.6	15.2	0.3	0.2	10	11
Puerto Rico	3.5	3.9	4.2	0.7	0.7	23.4	66.3	10.3	0.4	0.2	8	15

	Total population			Average annual population growth rate		Population age composition			Dependency ratio		Crude death rate	Crude birth rate
							%		dependents as proportion of working-age population			
						Ages 0–14	Ages 15–64	Ages 65+	Young	Old	per 1,000 people	per 1,000 people
	millions			%								
	1990	2003	2015	1990–2003	2003–15	2003	2003	2003	2003	2003	2003	2003
Romania	23.2	21.7	21.1	−0.5	−0.3	16.7	69.5	13.9	0.2	0.2	12	10
Russian Federation	148.3	143.4	134.5	−0.3	−0.5	16.3	70.4	13.2	0.2	0.2	15	10
Rwanda	6.9	8.4	10.1	1.5	1.5	45.7	51.3	3.0	0.9	0.1	22	43
Saudi Arabia	15.8	22.5	30.8	2.7	2.6	40.2	56.9	2.9	0.7	0.1	4	31
Senegal	7.3	10.2	13.0	2.6	2.0	43.6	53.7	2.7	0.8	0.1	13	35
Serbia and Montenegro	10.5[a]	8.1	10.7	0.1[b]	2.3	19.6	66.4	14.0	0.3	0.2	14	11
Sierra Leone	4.0	5.3	6.7	2.2	1.9	43.6	53.8	2.6	0.8	0.1	25	44
Singapore	3.1	4.3	4.8	2.6	1.1	20.7	71.7	7.6	0.3	0.1	5	11
Slovak Republic	5.3	5.4	5.3	0.2	−0.1	18.2	70.4	11.4	0.3	0.2	10	10
Slovenia	2.0	2.0	2.0	−0.0	−0.1	15.0	70.4	14.6	0.2	0.2	10	9
Somalia	7.2	9.6	14.0	2.3	3.1	47.8	49.8	2.4	1.0	0.1	18	50
South Africa	35.2	45.8	47.2	2.0	0.3	32.0	63.6	4.4	0.5	0.1	20	25
Spain	38.8	41.1	41.5	0.4	0.1	15.0	68.0	17.1	0.2	0.3	9	10
Sri Lanka	16.3	19.2	21.5	1.3	0.9	25.1	68.2	6.7	0.4	0.1	6	19
Sudan	24.9	33.5	42.6	2.3	2.0	39.5	56.9	3.6	0.7	0.1	10	33
Swaziland	0.8	1.1	1.3	2.8	1.1	42.1	55.1	2.8	0.8	0.1	19	35
Sweden	8.6	9.0	9.0	0.3	0.1	17.5	65.0	17.5	0.3	0.3	10	11
Switzerland	6.7	7.4	7.6	0.7	0.2	16.6	67.8	15.6	0.2	0.2	9	10
Syrian Arab Republic	12.1	17.4	22.0	2.8	1.9	38.2	58.7	3.1	0.7	0.1	4	29
Tajikistan	5.3	6.3	7.2	1.3	1.1	36.5	58.8	4.6	0.6	0.1	7	23
Tanzania	25.5	35.9	43.9	2.6	1.7	44.7	52.9	2.4	0.8	0.1	18	38
Thailand	55.6	62.0	66.3	0.8	0.6	22.9	70.5	6.6	0.3	0.1	8	15
Togo	3.5	4.9	6.2	2.6	2.0	43.2	53.6	3.2	0.8	0.1	15	35
Trinidad and Tobago	1.2	1.3	1.4	0.6	0.8	23.7	69.8	6.5	0.3	0.1	7	16
Tunisia	8.2	9.9	11.5	1.5	1.3	27.5	66.5	6.1	0.4	0.1	6	17
Turkey	56.2	70.7	81.2	1.8	1.2	28.3	65.8	5.9	0.4	0.1	7	21
Turkmenistan	3.7	4.9	5.7	2.2	1.3	33.8	61.7	4.5	0.5	0.1	8	22
Uganda	17.4	25.3	35.9	2.9	2.9	49.8	48.4	1.8	1.0	0.0	18	44
Ukraine	51.9	48.4	44.7	−0.5	−0.7	16.0	68.9	15.1	0.2	0.2	15	9
United Arab Emirates	1.8	4.0	3.7	6.3	−0.7	24.8	72.1	3.1	0.3	0.0	4	17
United Kingdom	57.6	59.3	60.0	0.2	0.1	18.2	65.7	16.1	0.3	0.2	10	12
United States	249.6	290.8	318.0	1.2	0.7	21.0	66.6	12.4	0.3	0.2	9	14
Uruguay	3.1	3.4	3.6	0.7	0.6	24.4	63.0	12.6	0.4	0.2	9	16
Uzbekistan	20.5	25.6	30.1	1.7	1.3	33.3	61.9	4.9	0.5	0.1	6	20
Venezuela, RB	19.8	25.7	30.4	2.0	1.4	32.2	63.1	4.7	0.5	0.1	5	23
Vietnam	66.2	81.3	92.4	1.6	1.1	30.6	64.1	5.3	0.5	0.1	6	18
West Bank and Gaza	2.0	3.4	4.9	4.1	3.1	45.1	51.8	3.1	0.9	0.1	4	34
Yemen, Rep.	11.9	19.2	27.3	3.7	2.9	45.2	52.1	2.6	0.9	0.1	10	41
Zambia	7.8	10.4	12.9	2.2	1.8	46.8	50.5	2.7	0.9	0.1	23	38
Zimbabwe	10.2	13.1	14.1	1.9	0.6	43.4	53.5	3.1	0.8	0.1	22	29
World	**5,253.4 s**	**6,272.5 s**	**7,100.9 s**	**1.4 w**	**1.0 w**	**28.9 w**	**64.0 w**	**7.1 w**	**0.5 w**	**0.1 w**	**9 w**	**21 w**
Low income	1,777.6	2,311.9	2,794.9	2.0	1.6	36.9	59.0	4.2	0.6	0.1	11	30
Middle income	2,588.7	2,988.6	3,299.0	1.1	0.8	26.2	66.8	7.0	0.4	0.1	8	17
Lower middle income	2,305.8	2,655.5	2,918.3	1.1	0.8	25.9	67.2	6.9	0.4	0.1	8	17
Upper middle income	282.9	333.1	380.6	1.3	1.1	28.5	64.1	7.4	0.4	0.1	7	18
Low & middle income	4,366.2	5,300.5	6,093.9	1.5	1.2	30.8	63.4	5.8	0.5	0.1	9	23
East Asia & Pacific	1,597.1	1,854.6	2,039.7	1.2	0.8	25.8	67.6	6.6	0.4	0.1	8	17
Europe & Central Asia	466.2	472.2	477.3	0.1	0.1	20.4	68.2	11.4	0.3	0.2	12	13
Latin America & Carib.	434.9	532.7	620.2	1.6	1.3	30.5	63.9	5.6	0.5	0.1	6	21
Middle East & N. Africa	237.1	311.6	382.7	2.1	1.7	34.6	61.4	4.0	0.6	0.1	5	22
South Asia	1,120.4	1,424.7	1,683.3	1.8	1.4	33.8	61.5	4.7	0.5	0.1	9	26
Sub-Saharan Africa	510.4	704.5	890.8	2.5	2.0	43.7	53.3	3.0	0.8	0.1	18	39
High income	887.2	972.1	1,007.0	0.7	0.3	18.2	67.3	14.5	0.3	0.2	9	12
Europe EMU	293.3	306.9	305.9	0.3	0.0	15.8	67.4	16.8	0.2	0.3	10	10

a. Includes population of Kosovo until 2001. b. Data are for 1990 to 2001.

About the data

Population estimates are usually based on national population censuses, but the frequency and quality of these vary by country. Most countries conduct a complete enumeration no more than once a decade. Pre- and post-census estimates are interpolations or extrapolations based on demographic models. Errors and undercounting occur even in high-income countries; in developing countries such errors may be substantial because of limits in the transport, communications, and other resources required to conduct a full census.

The quality and reliability of official demographic data are also affected by the public trust in the government, the government's commitment to full and accurate enumeration, the confidentiality and protection against misuse accorded to census data, and the independence of census agencies from undue political influence. Moreover, the international comparability of population indicators is limited by differences in the concepts, definitions, data collection procedures, and estimation methods used by national statistical agencies and other organizations that collect population data.

Of the 152 economies listed in the table, 118 (about 78 percent) conducted a census between 1995 and 2004. The currentness of a census, along with the availability of complementary data from surveys or registration systems, is one of many objective ways to judge the quality of demographic data. In some European countries registration systems offer complete information on population in the absence of a census. See *Primary data documentation* for the most recent census or survey year and for the completeness of registration.

Current population estimates for developing countries that lack recent census-based data, and pre- and post-census estimates for countries with census data, are provided by national statistical offices, the United Nations Population Division, and other agencies. The standard estimation method requires fertility, mortality, and net migration data, which are often collected from sample surveys, some of which may be small or limited in coverage. The population estimates are the product of demographic modeling and so are susceptible to biases and errors because of shortcomings in the model as well as in the data. Population projections are made using the cohort component method.

The growth rate of the total population conceals the fact that different age groups may grow at very different rates. In many developing countries the population under 15 was earlier growing rapidly but is now starting to shrink. Previously high fertility rates and declining mortality rates are now reflected in the larger share of the working-age population.

Dependency ratios take into account the variations in the proportions of children, elderly people, and working-age people in the population. Separate calculations of young-age and old-age dependency suggest the burden of dependency that the working-age population must bear in relation to children and the elderly. But dependency ratios show the age composition of a population, not economic dependency. Some children and elderly people are part of the labor force, and many working-age people are not.

The vital rates shown in the table are based on data derived from birth and death registration systems, censuses, and sample surveys conducted by national statistical offices, United Nations agencies, and other organizations. The estimates for 2003 for many countries are based on extrapolations of levels and trends measured in earlier years.

Vital registers are the preferred source of these data, but in many developing countries systems for registering births and deaths do not exist or are incomplete because of deficiencies in the coverage of events or of geographic areas. Many developing countries carry out special household surveys that estimate vital rates by asking respondents about births and deaths in the recent past. Estimates derived in this way are subject to sampling errors as well as errors due to inaccurate recall by the respondents.

The United Nations Statistics Division monitors the completeness of vital registration systems. The share of countries with at least 90 percent complete vital registration increased from 45 percent in 1988 to 55 percent in 2002. Still, some of the most populous developing countries—China, India, Indonesia, Brazil, Pakistan, Bangladesh, Nigeria—do not have complete vital registration systems. Fewer than 30 percent of births and 40 percent of deaths worldwide are thought to be registered and reported.

International migration is the only other factor besides birth and death rates that directly determines a country's population growth. From 1990 to 2000 the number of migrants in high-income countries increased by 23 million. About 175 million people currently live outside their home country, accounting for about 3 percent of the world's population. Estimating international migration is difficult. At any time many people are located outside their home country as tourists, workers, or refugees or for other reasons. Standards relating to the duration and purpose of international moves that qualify as migration vary, and accurate estimates require information on flows into and out of countries that is difficult to collect.

Definitions

• **Total population** of an economy includes all residents regardless of legal status or citizenship—except for refugees not permanently settled in the country of asylum, who are generally considered part of the population of their country of origin. The values shown are midyear estimates for 1990 and 2003 and projections for 2015. • **Average annual population growth rate** is the exponential change for the period indicated. See *Statistical methods* for more information. • **Population age composition** refers to the percentage of the total population that is in specific age groups. • **Dependency ratio** is the ratio of dependents—people younger than 15 or older than 64—to the working-age population—those ages 15–64. • **Crude death rate** and **crude birth rate** are the number of deaths and the number of live births occurring during the year, per 1,000 population estimated at midyear. Subtracting the crude death rate from the crude birth rate provides the rate of natural increase, which is equal to the population growth rate in the absence of migration.

Data sources

The World Bank's population estimates are produced by its Human Development Network and Development Data Group in consultation with its operational staff and country offices. Important inputs to the World Bank's demographic work come from the following sources: census reports and other statistical publications from national statistical offices; Demographic and Health Surveys conducted by national agencies, Macro International, and the U.S. Centers for Disease Control and Prevention; United Nations Statistics Division, *Population and Vital Statistics Report* (quarterly); United Nations Population Division, *World Population Prospects: The 2002 Revision;* Eurostat, *Demographic Statistics* (various years); Centro Latinoamericano de Demografía, Boletín Demográfico (various years); and U.S. Bureau of the Census, International Database.

	Labor force participation rate				Labor force				
	% ages 15–64				Total millions		Average annual growth rate %	Female % of labor force	
	Male		Female						
	1990	**2003**	**1990**	**2003**	**1990**	**2003**	**1990–2003**	**1990**	**2003**
Afghanistan	87.9	..	48.1	..	7.2	..	..	34.0	..
Albania	86.2	85.3	63.2	65.7	1.6	1.6	0.2	40.2	41.5
Algeria	79.5	80.1	20.1	35.1	7.0	11.7	3.9	21.1	29.9
Angola	91.0	89.9	76.1	74.6	4.4	6.1	2.5	46.5	46.2
Argentina	85.5	84.3	33.7	45.4	12.1	15.4	1.8	28.5	35.1
Armenia	79.5	78.1	69.1	71.2	1.7	1.6	-0.4	47.8	48.9
Australia	84.7	82.3	61.9	67.3	8.5	10.1	1.4	41.3	44.3
Austria	80.2	78.1	55.2	56.6	3.6	3.7	0.4	40.7	41.6
Azerbaijan	77.7	77.9	56.4	61.4	3.0	3.9	2.0	43.3	44.6
Bangladesh	89.4	88.6	67.3	68.4	53.6	70.8	2.1	41.1	43.2
Belarus	82.1	81.1	72.6	73.4	5.3	5.4	0.1	48.8	49.0
Belgium	72.4	71.8	47.8	51.8	4.0	4.3	0.4	39.4	41.3
Benin	85.3	82.3	78.6	75.2	2.1	3.1	2.8	48.2	48.1
Bolivia	84.1	83.5	46.3	49.7	2.7	3.7	2.5	36.9	38.1
Bosnia and Herzegovina	79.0	77.8	47.4	49.1	2.0	1.9	-0.2	37.6	38.2
Botswana	84.6	82.6	68.2	65.0	0.5	0.8	2.6	47.4	44.4
Brazil	89.0	87.1	47.6	46.9	65.5	82.3	1.8	34.8	35.5
Bulgaria	77.7	77.3	72.2	70.6	4.4	4.1	-0.7	48.0	47.7
Burkina Faso	91.7	88.7	79.3	77.2	4.5	5.7	1.8	48.8	47.9
Burundi	94.4	93.4	86.5	85.0	3.0	3.8	2.0	49.0	48.6
Cambodia	86.3	84.3	85.2	83.9	4.6	6.7	2.8	53.5	51.9
Cameroon	87.8	85.6	48.5	51.7	4.7	6.7	2.8	36.9	38.3
Canada	84.9	82.4	68.2	72.0	14.7	17.0	1.1	44.0	46.2
Central African Republic	88.8	86.0	70.3	67.3	1.4	1.8	1.9	47.1	46.4
Chad	89.8	88.6	69.3	70.5	2.7	3.9	2.8	44.2	45.1
Chile	82.1	81.8	35.0	44.7	5.0	6.6	2.2	29.9	35.1
China	89.6	88.8	79.9	79.2	670.7	772.9	1.1	45.0	45.0
Hong Kong, China	86.2	85.6	54.7	57.7	2.9	3.7	1.9	36.8	39.5
Colombia	83.1	83.3	45.2	52.6	13.9	19.7	2.7	36.0	39.7
Congo, Dem. Rep.	86.1	84.3	64.1	62.2	15.9	21.5	2.3	43.9	43.3
Congo, Rep.	84.5	83.1	58.4	58.7	1.0	1.5	2.9	43.2	43.2
Costa Rica	87.2	83.9	35.5	41.4	1.2	1.6	2.7	28.1	32.6
Côte d'Ivoire	90.1	87.4	44.2	45.6	4.6	6.9	3.2	31.4	33.2
Croatia	76.8	75.4	56.4	60.2	2.2	2.1	-0.5	42.7	44.7
Cuba	82.7	84.9	47.3	57.8	4.8	5.7	1.3	36.0	40.1
Czech Republic	82.2	82.3	74.1	74.0	5.5	5.7	0.3	47.4	47.0
Denmark	87.3	84.0	77.5	76.5	2.9	2.9	0.0	46.1	46.7
Dominican Republic	86.3	86.1	35.5	44.2	2.8	3.9	2.6	27.1	32.0
Ecuador	85.9	85.6	28.9	36.3	3.6	5.3	2.9	24.7	29.2
Egypt, Arab Rep.	83.4	82.3	32.0	38.9	18.3	26.7	2.9	27.1	31.4
El Salvador	87.9	85.3	39.1	51.2	1.9	2.8	2.9	31.3	38.5
Eritrea	87.7	86.5	77.6	76.4	1.6	2.2	2.5	47.5	47.4
Estonia	83.1	81.6	75.7	74.0	0.9	0.8	-0.9	49.4	49.4
Ethiopia	86.5	85.2	59.4	58.5	23.1	30.1	2.0	42.0	41.4
Finland	79.4	75.1	72.4	71.4	2.6	2.6	0.0	47.2	48.2
France	74.6	74.9	57.0	62.4	24.7	27.0	0.7	43.4	45.5
Gabon	87.1	85.1	66.4	66.9	0.5	0.6	2.0	44.2	44.5
Gambia, The	91.7	90.8	69.8	70.6	0.5	0.7	3.4	44.7	45.0
Georgia	80.2	79.5	63.6	67.0	2.7	2.6	-0.1	46.1	46.9
Germany	83.0	80.6	61.2	62.9	39.9	40.5	0.1	41.8	42.6
Ghana	82.5	82.3	82.4	80.8	7.1	10.3	2.9	50.9	50.1
Greece	77.8	78.3	42.5	49.2	4.2	4.8	1.1	35.4	38.3
Guatemala	91.0	86.8	29.0	40.8	3.0	4.6	3.3	23.4	31.3
Guinea	88.9	87.1	81.6	79.6	2.9	3.9	2.4	47.4	47.1
Guinea-Bissau	91.2	91.2	59.6	59.3	0.5	0.7	2.7	40.2	40.7
Haiti	82.8	80.9	59.2	57.5	2.7	3.7	2.3	43.3	43.4

Labor force structure | 2.2

	Labor force participation rate				Labor force				
	% ages 15–64				Total		Average annual growth rate	Female	
	Male		Female		millions		%	% of labor force	
	1990	2003	1990	2003	1990	2003	1990–2003	1990	2003
Honduras	88.5	83.1	34.9	44.3	1.7	2.6	3.4	27.7	34.5
Hungary	78.4	77.9	59.3	61.0	4.7	4.8	0.2	44.0	44.6
India	87.9	86.6	42.4	45.2	360.6	473.3	2.1	31.2	32.6
Indonesia	84.4	84.7	52.1	59.5	78.3	106.6	2.4	38.1	41.2
Iran, Islamic Rep.	83.1	80.2	22.2	33.8	16.5	24.6	3.1	20.3	29.4
Iraq	76.3	76.3	15.1	20.9	4.6	7.0	3.2	16.3	20.9
Ireland	79.7	79.7	38.3	45.5	1.3	1.7	2.1	31.6	35.9
Israel	79.5	78.9	48.9	58.0	1.8	2.9	3.6	37.9	42.2
Italy	78.3	78.4	45.0	50.4	24.4	25.4	0.3	36.7	39.0
Jamaica	83.4	81.6	72.1	73.0	1.1	1.3	1.3	47.0	47.6
Japan	84.2	84.9	56.2	62.9	64.1	68.1	0.5	39.8	41.8
Jordan	75.9	79.7	17.8	30.3	0.8	1.7	6.0	17.1	25.5
Kazakhstan	81.7	80.0	68.0	69.1	7.7	7.5	-0.2	46.2	47.3
Kenya	90.8	88.9	76.5	76.7	11.1	16.6	3.1	46.3	46.2
Korea, Dem. Rep.	82.2	82.7	65.3	64.8	10.3	11.6	0.9	43.5	43.3
Korea, Rep.	77.4	79.9	51.1	59.7	19.6	25.0	1.8	39.3	40.7
Kuwait	85.6	79.6	38.9	42.9	0.9	1.1	1.4	22.8	23.9
Kyrgyz Republic	78.0	77.9	65.0	68.0	1.8	2.3	1.8	46.2	47.3
Lao PDR	91.2	90.0	76.9	77.9	2.0	2.9	2.6	46.6	46.7
Latvia	83.5	82.4	75.6	74.6	1.5	1.3	-0.9	49.6	49.6
Lebanon	77.6	80.9	26.5	33.8	1.1	1.7	3.0	26.6	30.1
Lesotho	86.8	85.3	48.1	49.9	0.7	0.8	1.2	36.2	38.2
Liberia	82.5	82.5	55.5	55.3	0.9	1.3	3.0	39.5	39.5
Libya	82.4	78.1	21.4	27.9	1.3	1.9	3.2	18.4	24.7
Lithuania	81.7	81.4	70.6	71.1	1.9	1.8	-0.3	48.0	48.0
Macedonia, FYR	77.8	75.9	52.6	57.3	0.8	1.0	1.0	40.1	42.6
Madagascar	90.4	89.3	71.6	70.6	5.7	8.1	2.8	44.7	44.5
Malawi	88.3	86.2	80.1	78.0	4.2	5.3	1.7	49.5	48.7
Malaysia	84.0	81.4	46.4	51.9	7.4	10.7	2.9	35.0	38.4
Mali	90.8	89.3	75.0	73.2	4.3	5.6	2.1	46.4	46.0
Mauritania	88.7	87.3	66.5	65.0	0.9	1.3	2.5	44.3	43.8
Mauritius	84.9	83.5	37.2	42.2	0.4	0.5	1.7	30.3	33.4
Mexico	85.1	85.3	35.5	43.2	30.7	43.6	2.7	30.0	34.4
Moldova	81.5	79.5	70.4	69.9	2.1	2.2	0.3	48.6	48.5
Mongolia	87.5	86.2	75.6	77.6	1.0	1.3	2.4	46.3	45.8
Morocco	83.3	82.3	40.5	44.6	8.9	12.2	2.4	34.5	35.2
Mozambique	91.5	90.1	84.3	83.1	7.5	9.8	2.0	48.4	49.0
Myanmar	90.1	89.3	68.5	68.5	20.9	27.0	2.0	43.3	43.6
Namibia	83.5	81.8	55.9	56.4	0.6	0.8	2.6	41.6	41.7
Nepal	89.1	86.5	57.4	58.4	8.8	11.7	2.2	38.5	39.5
Netherlands	80.1	77.7	52.9	56.4	6.9	7.5	0.6	39.0	41.2
New Zealand	82.7	81.5	62.6	68.3	1.7	2.0	1.5	43.0	46.1
Nicaragua	88.3	83.8	42.0	51.6	1.4	2.2	3.5	32.1	38.2
Niger	94.2	92.4	71.9	70.8	3.6	5.4	3.1	43.3	43.4
Nigeria	88.1	85.6	48.1	49.4	38.0	54.5	2.8	34.6	36.5
Norway	81.2	80.6	68.9	73.8	2.1	2.4	0.8	44.9	46.8
Oman	83.6	77.9	13.4	23.3	0.5	0.8	4.0	10.7	20.1
Pakistan	87.9	85.6	29.5	39.3	39.4	55.7	2.7	23.6	30.3
Panama	82.7	81.0	41.4	47.9	0.9	1.3	2.4	32.4	36.6
Papua New Guinea	89.2	86.9	68.6	69.2	1.9	2.7	2.6	41.2	42.6
Paraguay	89.5	87.5	35.6	39.9	1.5	2.2	2.8	27.9	30.7
Peru	81.1	81.7	30.6	38.3	7.3	10.7	2.9	27.5	31.8
Philippines	83.0	82.6	48.1	52.0	24.0	34.6	2.8	36.5	38.3
Poland	80.1	77.7	65.1	66.2	18.7	20.0	0.5	45.5	46.5
Portugal	82.8	82.2	58.7	63.7	4.8	5.3	0.7	42.7	44.1
Puerto Rico	73.1	73.9	35.3	42.8	1.2	1.5	1.6	34.0	38.3

	Labor force participation rate				Labor force				
	% ages 15–64				Total		Average annual growth rate	Female	
	Male		Female		millions		%	% of labor force	
	1990	2003	1990	2003	1990	2003	1990–2003	1990	2003
Romania	76.7	76.8	60.5	61.2	10.6	10.5	-0.1	44.3	44.8
Russian Federation	81.6	79.8	71.7	72.3	77.2	78.4	0.1	48.4	49.1
Rwanda	94.6	94.4	86.2	85.1	3.6	4.6	1.7	48.9	50.2
Saudi Arabia	85.9	78.8	15.7	25.2	5.0	6.9	2.5	11.4	20.2
Senegal	87.8	86.6	62.9	63.6	3.3	4.6	2.6	42.4	43.2
Serbia and Montenegro	77.0	76.4	54.9	58.9	4.9[a]	3.9	0.4[b]	41.7	43.1
Sierra Leone	85.8	84.3	43.9	47.2	1.5	2.0	2.1	35.5	37.2
Singapore	83.8	81.7	54.4	54.5	1.6	2.1	2.3	38.9	38.6
Slovak Republic	82.5	82.0	74.1	74.0	2.7	3.0	0.8	47.7	47.6
Slovenia	77.1	75.5	65.8	66.0	1.0	1.0	0.0	46.3	46.4
Somalia	88.3	87.0	65.4	64.4	3.1	4.1	2.0	43.3	43.4
South Africa	82.9	82.0	49.2	50.3	13.7	19.1	2.6	37.5	38.4
Spain	79.0	79.8	41.5	48.8	15.8	18.2	1.1	34.6	37.8
Sri Lanka	83.7	82.6	42.8	47.8	6.8	8.8	2.0	31.4	36.1
Sudan	86.8	86.2	31.2	37.1	9.4	13.4	2.7	27.1	30.3
Swaziland	83.8	82.3	41.3	44.7	0.3	0.4	3.1	34.0	36.4
Sweden	84.9	83.5	80.6	80.9	4.6	4.9	0.4	47.7	48.0
Switzerland	90.9	89.9	60.7	65.1	3.6	3.9	0.7	39.2	40.7
Syrian Arab Republic	80.7	80.7	24.5	31.7	3.4	5.8	4.1	24.4	27.9
Tajikistan	77.6	77.3	56.2	64.1	1.9	2.7	2.6	42.2	45.5
Tanzania	89.1	88.1	84.6	82.4	13.1	18.6	2.7	49.7	48.9
Thailand	89.5	89.7	78.5	77.7	31.9	37.0	1.1	47.2	47.0
Togo	88.1	87.2	54.4	54.9	1.4	2.1	2.7	39.9	40.0
Trinidad and Tobago	82.3	81.3	43.0	50.1	0.5	0.6	2.0	34.0	38.4
Tunisia	83.0	83.0	34.5	41.3	2.9	4.2	2.9	29.1	32.7
Turkey	85.6	84.6	45.0	54.0	24.3	33.7	2.5	34.6	38.9
Turkmenistan	81.2	80.4	64.2	67.3	1.5	2.2	2.9	44.7	46.0
Uganda	92.7	90.8	82.8	80.9	8.8	12.3	2.5	47.6	47.1
Ukraine	79.7	78.7	69.8	69.8	26.0	25.2	-0.3	48.9	48.8
United Arab Emirates	91.9	88.2	30.1	34.6	0.9	2.1	6.4	10.7	14.5
United Kingdom	86.2	83.1	63.8	67.2	28.6	29.8	0.3	42.4	44.1
United States	82.6	80.7	66.5	70.2	125.8	149.4	1.3	44.3	46.6
Uruguay	83.7	82.3	52.4	59.6	1.4	1.5	0.9	39.3	42.6
Uzbekistan	77.9	78.1	64.2	68.2	8.1	11.6	2.8	45.6	46.8
Venezuela, RB	83.9	83.0	40.0	47.8	7.4	10.8	3.0	31.3	35.7
Vietnam	88.1	83.5	81.0	77.3	33.6	43.3	1.9	48.3	48.6
West Bank and Gaza	67.4	72.0	6.5	11.1	0.4	0.7	5.0	..	12.8
Yemen, Rep.	82.8	83.5	29.4	32.2	3.6	5.8	3.7	29.7	28.9
Zambia	88.4	87.4	67.2	66.2	3.4	4.4	2.1	43.7	43.0
Zimbabwe	86.7	85.2	67.1	65.7	4.6	5.9	1.8	44.0	44.0
World	**86.1 w**	**85.2 w**	**59.2 w**	**60.9 w**	**2,483.7 t**	**3,062.5 t**	**1.6 w**	**39.9 w**	**40.8 w**
Low income	87.5	86.3	51.8	54.6	775.8	1,040.0	2.3	36.4	37.6
Middle income	86.6	85.8	64.7	65.1	1,287.4	1,549.4	1.4	41.5	42.2
Lower middle income	87.0	86.2	67.2	67.2	1,173.5	1,404.2	1.4	42.2	42.7
Upper middle income	83.3	82.4	44.8	49.4	114.0	145.2	1.9	34.8	37.7
Low & middle income	87.0	86.0	59.3	60.4	2,063.3	2,589.4	1.7	39.6	40.4
East Asia & Pacific	88.6	87.9	75.0	75.0	887.4	1,058.3	1.4	44.2	44.6
Europe & Central Asia	80.9	79.9	65.4	66.8	225.8	241.8	0.5	45.7	46.6
Latin America & Carib.	86.2	85.4	41.4	46.3	173.6	232.8	2.3	32.5	35.7
Middle East & N. Africa	82.0	80.8	26.3	34.5	74.2	111.6	3.1	23.8	29.2
South Asia	88.0	86.7	43.9	47.3	476.7	632.6	2.2	31.9	33.8
Sub-Saharan Africa	88.1	86.6	62.2	62.3	225.6	312.3	2.5	42.0	42.1
High income	81.9	80.9	58.9	63.7	420.4	473.1	0.9	41.5	43.3
Europe EMU	79.1	78.5	52.8	57.1	132.3	141.1	0.5	39.9	41.5

a. Includes population of Kosovo until 2001. b Data are for 1990 to 2001.

The labor force is the supply of labor available for the production of goods and services in an economy. It includes people who are currently employed and people who are unemployed but seeking work as well as first-time job-seekers. Not everyone who works is included, however. Unpaid workers, family workers, and students are among those usually omitted, and in some countries members of the military are not counted. The size of the labor force tends to vary during the year as seasonal workers enter and leave it.

Data on the labor force are compiled by the International Labour Organization (ILO) from labor force surveys, censuses, establishment censuses and surveys, and various types of administrative records such as employment exchange registers and unemployment insurance schemes. For some countries a combination of sources is used. While the resulting statistics may provide rough estimates of the labor force, they are not comparable across countries because of the noncomparability of the original data and the different ways the original sources may be combined.

For international comparisons the most comprehensive source is labor force surveys. Despite the ILO's efforts to encourage the use of international standards, labor force data are not fully comparable because of differences among countries, and sometimes within countries, in both concepts and methodologies. The single most important contributor to data comparability is the nature of the data source. Labor force data obtained from population censuses are often based on a limited number of questions on the economic characteristics of individuals, with little scope to probe. The resulting data are often contrary to labor force survey data, which themselves may vary from economy to economy, depending on their scope and coverage. Establishment censuses and surveys on the other hand only provide data on the employed population, leaving out unemployed workers, workers in small establishments, and workers in the informal sector (ILO, *Key Indicators of the Labour Market 2001–2002*).

The reference period of the census or survey is another important source of differences: in some countries data refer to people's status on the day of the census or survey or during a specific period before the inquiry date, while in others the data are recorded without reference to any period. In developing countries, where the household is often the basic unit of production and all members contribute to output, but some at low intensity or irregular intervals, the estimated labor force may be significantly smaller than the numbers actually working.

The labor force estimates in the table were calculated by World Bank staff by applying labor force participation rates from the ILO database to World Bank population estimates to create a series consistent with these population estimates. This procedure sometimes results in estimates of labor force size that differ slightly from those in the ILO's *Yearbook of Labour Statistics*. The labor force participation rate of the population ages 15–64 provides an indication of the relative size of the supply of labor. But in many developing countries children under 15 work full or part time. And in some high-income countries many workers postpone retirement past age 65. As a result, labor force participation rates calculated in this way may systematically over- or under-estimate actual rates. The largest gap between men and women in labor force participation is observed in the Middle East and North Africa, where low participation of women in the work force also brings down the overall labor force participation rate.

In general, estimates of women in the labor force are lower than those of men and are not comparable internationally, reflecting the fact that for women, demographic, social, legal, and cultural trends and norms determine whether their activities are regarded as economic. In many countries large numbers of women work on farms or in other family enterprises without pay, while others work in or near their homes, mixing work and family activities during the day. Countries differ in the criteria used to determine the extent to which such workers are to be counted as part of the labor force. In most economies the gap between male and female labor force participation rates has been narrowing since 1980.

• **Labor force participation rate** is the proportion of the population ages 15–64 that is economically active: all people who supply labor for the production of goods and services during a specified period.
• **Total labor force** comprises people who meet the ILO definition of the economically active population. It includes both the employed and the unemployed. While national practices vary in the treatment of such groups as the armed forces and seasonal or part-time workers, the labor force generally includes the armed forces, the unemployed, and first-time job-seekers, but excludes homemakers and other unpaid caregivers and workers in the informal sector. • **Average annual growth rate of the labor force** is calculated using the exponential endpoint method (see *Statistical methods* for more information). • **Females as a percentage of the labor force** show the extent to which women are active in the labor force.

The labor force participation rates are from the ILO database *Estimates and Projections of the Economically Active Population, 1950–2010, Fourth edition*. The ILO publishes estimates of the economically active population in its *Yearbook of Labour Statistics*.

| | Agriculture[a] | | | | Industry[a] | | | | Services[a] | | | |
| | Male % of male employment | | Female % of female employment | | Male % of male employment | | Female % of female employment | | Male % of male employment | | Female % of female employment | |
	1990–92[b]	2000–02[b]	1990–92[b]	2000–02[b]	1990–92[b]	2000–02[b]	1990–92[b]	2000–02[b]	1990–92[b]	2000–02[b]	1990–92[b]	2000–02[b]
Afghanistan	63	..	85	..	10	..	13	..	28	..	3	..
Albania	..	..	..	..	..	..	..	..	..	..	..	..
Algeria	18	..	57	..	38	..	7	..	45	..	36	..
Angola	65	..	86	..	14	..	2	..	21	..	13	..
Argentina	0[c]	1	0[c]	0[c]	40	30	18	12	59	69	81	87
Armenia	..	..	..	..	..	..	..	..	..	..	..	..
Australia	6	6	4	3	32	30	12	10	62	64	85	87
Austria	..	5	..	6	..	43	..	14	..	52	..	80
Azerbaijan	..	37	..	43	..	14	..	7	..	49	..	50
Bangladesh	54	53	85	77	16	11	9	9	26	30	2	12
Belarus	..	..	..	..	..	..	..	..	..	..	..	..
Belgium	3	..	2	..	38	..	13	..	57	..	84	..
Benin	62	..	65	..	12	..	4	..	27	..	30	..
Bolivia	3	6	1	3	42	39	17	14	55	55	82	82
Bosnia and Herzegovina	9	..	16	..	54	..	37	..	37	..	48	..
Botswana	..	22	..	17	..	26	..	14	..	51	..	67
Brazil	31	24	25	16	27	27	10	10	43	49	65	74
Bulgaria	..	..	..	..	..	..	..	..	..	..	..	..
Burkina Faso	91	..	94	..	2	..	2	..	7	..	5	..
Burundi	..	..	..	..	..	..	..	..	..	..	..	..
Cambodia	..	..	..	..	..	..	..	..	..	..	..	..
Cameroon	62	..	83	..	12	..	3	..	26	..	14	..
Canada	6	4	3	2	31	33	11	11	63	64	86	87
Central African Republic	74	..	87	..	6	..	0	..	20	..	13	..
Chad	77	..	91	..	7	..	1	..	16	..	8	..
Chile	24	18	6	5	32	29	15	13	45	53	79	83
China	..	..	..	..	..	..	..	..	..	..	..	..
Hong Kong, China	1	0[c]	0[c]	0[c]	37	27	27	10	63	73	73	90
Colombia	2	33	1	7	35	19	25	17	63	48	74	76
Congo, Dem. Rep.	58	..	81	..	20	..	5	..	23	..	14	..
Congo, Rep.	33	..	69	..	23	..	4	..	44	..	27	..
Costa Rica	32	22	5	4	27	27	25	15	41	51	69	80
Côte d'Ivoire	54	..	72	..	12	..	6	..	34	..	22	..
Croatia	..	16	..	15	..	37	..	21	..	47	..	63
Cuba	24	..	8	..	36	..	21	..	41	..	71	..
Czech Republic	9	6	7	3	55	50	33	28	36	44	61	68
Denmark	..	5	..	2	..	36	..	14	..	59	..	85
Dominican Republic	26	21	3	2	23	26	21	17	52	53	76	81
Ecuador	10	10	2	4	29	30	17	16	62	60	81	79
Egypt, Arab Rep.	35	27	52	39	25	25	10	7	41	48	37	54
El Salvador	48	34	15	4	23	25	23	22	29	42	63	74
Eritrea	77	..	85	..	8	..	2	..	16	..	13	..
Estonia	23	10	13	4	42	42	30	23	36	48	57	73
Ethiopia	..	..	..	..	..	..	..	..	..	..	..	..
Finland	12	7	6	4	39	40	15	14	49	53	78	82
France	2	2	1	1	40	34	17	13	58	64	83	86
Gabon	46	..	59	..	21	..	10	..	33	..	32	..
Gambia, The	74	..	92	..	12	..	2	..	14	..	6	..
Georgia	..	53	..	53	..	12	..	6	..	35	..	41
Germany	4	3	4	2	51	44	24	18	45	52	72	80
Ghana	66	..	59	..	10	..	10	..	23	..	32	..
Greece	20	15	26	18	32	30	17	12	48	56	56	70
Guatemala	..	50	..	18	..	18	..	23	..	27	..	56
Guinea	83	..	92	..	3	..	1	..	15	..	7	..
Guinea-Bissau	78	..	96	..	3	..	1	..	19	..	3	..
Haiti	..	..	..	..	..	..	..	..	..	..	..	..

	Agriculture[a]				Industry[a]				Services[a]			
	Male % of male employment		Female % of female employment		Male % of male employment		Female % of female employment		Male % of male employment		Female % of female employment	
	1990–92[b]	2000–02[b]	1990–92[b]	2000–02[b]	1990–92[b]	2000–02[b]	1990–92[b]	2000–02[b]	1990–92[b]	2000–02[b]	1990–92[b]	2000–02[b]
Honduras	53	..	6	..	18	..	25	..	29	..	69	..
Hungary	15	9	8	4	42	42	29	26	44	49	64	71
India	..	..	..	..	..	..	..	..	..	..	..	..
Indonesia	54	..	57	..	15	..	13	..	31	..	31	..
Iran, Islamic Rep.	..	..	..	..	..	..	..	..	..	..	..	..
Iraq	12	..	39	..	19	..	9	..	69	..	52	..
Ireland	19	11	3	2	33	39	18	14	48	50	78	83
Israel	5	3	2	1	38	34	15	12	57	62	83	86
Italy	8	6	9	5	38	39	22	20	54	55	70	75
Jamaica	36	..	16	..	25	..	12	..	39	..	72	..
Japan	6	5	7	5	40	37	27	21	54	57	65	73
Jordan	..	..	..	..	..	..	..	..	..	..	..	..
Kazakhstan	..	..	..	..	..	..	..	..	..	..	..	..
Kenya	19	..	20	..	23	..	9	..	58	..	71	..
Korea, Dem. Rep.	35	..	42	..	38	..	23	..	27	..	35	..
Korea, Rep.	14	9	18	12	40	34	28	19	46	57	54	70
Kuwait	1	..	1	..	32	..	2	..	67	..	98	..
Kyrgyz Republic	..	..	..	..	..	..	..	..	..	..	..	..
Lao PDR	76	..	81	..	7	..	5	..	17	..	14	..
Latvia	25	18	14	12	37	35	26	16	38	47	59	72
Lebanon	6	..	10	..	34	..	22	..	60	..	68	..
Lesotho	29	..	59	..	41	..	5	..	30	..	36	..
Liberia	65	..	84	..	9	..	1	..	26	..	16	..
Libya	7	..	28	..	27	..	5	..	66	..	68	..
Lithuania	..	20	..	12	..	34	..	21	..	45	..	67
Macedonia, FYR	..	..	..	..	..	..	..	..	..	..	..	..
Madagascar	70	..	88	..	10	..	3	..	20	..	9	..
Malawi	..	..	..	..	..	..	..	..	..	..	..	..
Malaysia	23	21	20	14	31	34	32	29	46	45	48	57
Mali	83	..	89	..	2	..	2	..	15	..	9	..
Mauritania	49	..	63	..	16	..	4	..	35	..	34	..
Mauritius	17	..	11	..	32	..	64	..	48	..	24	..
Mexico	33	24	10	6	25	28	18	22	43	48	72	72
Moldova	..	52	..	50	..	18	..	10	..	31	..	40
Mongolia	..	..	..	..	..	..	..	..	..	..	..	..
Morocco	4	..	3	..	33	..	46	..	63	..	51	..
Mozambique	70	..	96	..	15	..	1	..	15	..	3	..
Myanmar	..	..	..	..	..	..	..	..	..	..	..	..
Namibia	46	33	67	29	21	17	12	7	33	49	21	63
Nepal	..	..	..	..	..	..	..	..	..	..	..	..
Netherlands	..	4	..	2	..	31	..	9	..	64	..	86
New Zealand	13	12	8	6	31	32	13	12	56	56	80	82
Nicaragua	..	..	..	..	..	..	..	..	..	..	..	..
Niger	..	..	..	..	..	..	..	..	..	..	..	..
Nigeria	..	..	..	..	..	..	..	..	..	..	..	..
Norway	8	6	3	2	35	33	10	9	57	58	86	88
Oman	48	..	19	..	23	..	35	..	30	..	46	..
Pakistan	45	44	69	73	20	20	15	9	35	36	16	18
Panama	35	29	3	6	20	20	11	10	45	51	85	85
Papua New Guinea	72	..	89	..	9	..	3	..	19	..	8	..
Paraguay	3	39	0[c]	20	33	21	19	10	64	40	80	69
Peru	1	11	0[c]	6	30	24	13	10	69	65	87	84
Philippines	53	45	32	25	17	18	14	12	29	37	55	63
Poland	..	19	..	19	..	40	..	18	..	40	..	63
Portugal	11	12	13	14	40	44	24	23	49	44	63	63
Puerto Rico	5	3	0[c]	0[c]	27	27	19	14	67	69	80	86

| | Agriculture[a] | | | | Industry[a] | | | | Services[a] | | | |
| | Male % of male employment | | Female % of female employment | | Male % of male employment | | Female % of female employment | | Male % of male employment | | Female % of female employment | |
	1990–92[b]	2000–02[b]	1990–92[b]	2000–02[b]	1990–92[b]	2000–02[b]	1990–92[b]	2000–02[b]	1990–92[b]	2000–02[b]	1990–92[b]	2000–02[b]
Romania	29	40	38	45	44	30	30	22	28	30	33	33
Russian Federation	..	..	..	..	..	..	..	..	..	..	..	..
Rwanda	86	..	98	..	6	..	1	..	8	..	2	..
Saudi Arabia	20	..	12	..	21	..	6	..	59	..	82	..
Senegal	70	..	86	..	10	..	4	..	20	..	11	..
Serbia and Montenegro	..	..	..	..	..	..	..	..	..	..	..	..
Sierra Leone	60	..	81	..	22	..	4	..	18	..	16	..
Singapore	1	0[c]	0[c]	0[c]	36	31	32	18	63	69	68	81
Slovak Republic	..	8	..	4	..	48	..	26	..	44	..	71
Slovenia	..	10	..	10	..	46	..	29	..	43	..	61
Somalia	66	..	87	..	13	..	2	..	21	..	11	..
South Africa	..	..	..	..	..	..	..	..	..	..	..	..
Spain	11	8	8	5	41	42	16	15	48	51	76	81
Sri Lanka	..	..	..	..	..	..	..	..	..	..	..	..
Sudan	64	..	84	..	10	..	5	..	26	..	11	..
Swaziland	..	..	..	..	..	..	..	..	..	..	..	..
Sweden	5	3	2	1	40	36	12	11	55	61	86	88
Switzerland	5	5	4	3	39	36	16	13	56	59	80	84
Syrian Arab Republic	..	..	..	..	..	..	..	..	..	..	..	..
Tajikistan	..	..	..	..	..	..	..	..	..	..	..	..
Tanzania	78	..	90	..	7	..	1	..	15	..	8	..
Thailand	60	50	62	48	18	20	13	17	22	30	25	35
Togo	66	..	65	..	12	..	7	..	22	..	29	..
Trinidad and Tobago	15	..	6	..	34	..	14	..	51	..	80	..
Tunisia	..	..	..	..	..	..	..	..	..	..	..	..
Turkey	33	24	72	56	26	28	11	15	41	48	17	29
Turkmenistan	..	..	..	..	..	..	..	..	..	..	..	..
Uganda	91	..	91	..	4	..	6	..	5	..	3	..
Ukraine	..	22	..	17	..	39	..	22	..	33	..	55
United Arab Emirates	9	9	0	0[c]	30	36	3	14	61	55	97	86
United Kingdom	1	2	1	1	34	36	15	11	45	62	75	88
United States	4	3	1	1	33	32	14	12	62	65	85	87
Uruguay	7	6	1	2	36	32	21	14	57	62	78	85
Uzbekistan	..	..	..	..	..	..	..	..	..	..	..	..
Venezuela, RB	17	15	2	2	32	28	16	12	52	57	82	86
Vietnam	..	..	..	..	..	..	..	..	..	..	..	..
West Bank and Gaza	20	9	20	26	43	32	30	11	37	58	50	62
Yemen, Rep.	50	..	88	..	22	..	6	..	29	..	7	..
Zambia	68	..	83	..	13	..	3	..	19	..	14	..
Zimbabwe	..	..	..	..	..	..	..	..	..	..	..	..
World	.. w	.. w	.. w	.. w	.. w	.. w	.. w	.. w	.. w	.. w	.. w	.. w
Low income	..	..	..	..	..	..	..	..	..	..	..	..
Middle income	..	..	..	..	..	..	..	..	..	..	..	..
Lower middle income	..	..	..	..	..	..	..	..	..	..	..	..
Upper middle income	22	17	8	8	32	32	22	19	46	51	70	73
Low & middle income	..	..	..	..	..	..	..	..	..	..	..	..
East Asia & Pacific	..	..	..	..	..	..	..	..	..	..	..	..
Europe & Central Asia	..	..	..	..	..	..	..	..	..	..	..	..
Latin America & Carib.	23	21	13	9	29	27	15	14	48	52	71	76
Middle East & N. Africa	23	..	39	..	27	..	19	..	50	..	41	..
South Asia	..	..	..	..	..	..	..	..	..	..	..	..
Sub-Saharan Africa	..	..	..	..	..	..	..	..	..	..	..	..
High income	6	4	4	3	38	35	19	15	55	60	76	82
Europe EMU	7	5	6	4	43	40	20	16	51	55	74	80

a. Data may not add up to 100 because of the workers not classified by sectors. b. Data are for the most recent year available. c. Less than 0.5.

Employment by economic activity | 2.3

The International Labour Organization (ILO) classifies economic activity on the basis of the International Standard Industrial Classification (ISIC) of All Economic Activities. Because this classification is based on where work is performed (industry) rather than on what type of work is performed (occupation), all of an enterprise's employees are classified under the same industry, regardless of their trade or occupation. The categories should add up to 100 percent. Where they do not, the differences arise because of workers who cannot be classified by economic activity.

Data on employment are drawn from labor force surveys, household surveys, establishment censuses and surveys, administrative records of social insurance schemes, and official national estimates. The concept of employment generally refers to people above a certain age who worked, or who held a job, during a reference period. Employment data include both full-time and part-time workers.

There are, however, many differences in how countries define and measure employment status, particularly for students, part-time workers, members of the armed forces, and household or contributing family workers. Where the armed forces are included, they are allocated to the service sector, causing that sector to be somewhat overstated relative to the service sector in economies where they are excluded. Where data are obtained from establishment surveys, they cover only employees; thus self-employed and contributing family workers are excluded. In such cases the employment share of the agricultural sector is severely underreported.

Countries also take very different approaches to the treatment of unemployed people. In most countries unemployed people with previous job experience are classified according to their last job. But in some countries the unemployed and people seeking their first job are not classifiable by economic activity. Because of these differences, the size and distribution of employment by economic activity may not be fully comparable across countries.

The ILO's *Yearbook of Labour Statistics* and its database *Key Indicators of the Labour Market* report data by major divisions of the ISIC revision 2 or ISIC revision 3. In this table the reported divisions or categories are aggregated into three broad groups: agriculture, industry, and services. Classification into such broad groups may obscure fundamental shifts within countries' industrial patterns. Most economies report economic activity according to the ISIC revision 2, although a group of economies moved to ISIC revision 3. The use of one classification or another should not have a significant impact on the information for the three broad sectors presented in this table.

The distribution of economic wealth within the world remains strongly correlated with employment by economic activity. The wealthier economies are those with the largest share of total employment in services, whereas the poorer economies are largely agriculture-based.

The distribution of economic activity by gender reveals some interesting patterns. Industry accounts for a larger share of male employment than female employment worldwide, whereas a higher proportion of women work in the services sector. Employment in agriculture is also male-dominated, although not as much as industry. Segregating one sex in a narrow range of occupations significantly reduces economic efficiency by reducing labor market flexibility and thus the economy's ability to adapt to change. This segregation is particularly harmful for women, who have a much narrower range of labor market choices and lower levels of pay than men. But it is also detrimental to men when job losses are concentrated in industries dominated by men and job growth is centered in service occupations, where women often dominate, as has been the recent experience in many countries.

There are several explanations for the rising importance of service jobs for women. Many service jobs—such as nursing and social and clerical work—are considered "feminine" because of a perceived similarity to women's traditional roles. Women often do not receive the training needed to take advantage of changing employment opportunities. And the greater availability of part-time work in service industries may lure more women, although it is not clear whether this is a cause or an effect.

• **Agriculture** corresponds to division 1 (ISIC revision 2) or tabulation categories A and B (ISIC revision 3) and includes hunting, forestry, and fishing. • **Industry** corresponds to divisions 2–5 (ISIC revision 2) or tabulation categories C–F (ISIC revision 3) and includes mining and quarrying (including oil production), manufacturing, construction, and public utilities (electricity, gas, and water). • **Services** correspond to divisions 6–9 (ISIC revision 2) or tabulation categories G–P (ISIC revision 3) and include wholesale and retail trade and restaurants and hotels; transport, storage, and communications; financing, insurance, real estate, and business services; and community, social, and personal services.

The employment data are from the ILO database *Key Indicators of the Labour Market,* third edition.

2.4 Unemployment

	Unemployment						Long-term unemployment			Unemployment by level of educational attainment		
	Male % of male labor force		Female % of female labor force		Total % of total labor force		% of total unemployment			% of total unemployment		
										Primary 1999–2001[a]	Secondary 1999–2001[a]	Tertiary 1999–2001[a]
	1990–92[a]	2000–02[a]	1990–92[a]	2000–02[a]	1990–92[a]	2000–02[a]	Male 2000–02[a]	Female 2000–02[a]	Total 2000–02[a]			
Afghanistan	..	..	..	..	..	..	..	..	..	..	..	..
Albania	24.8	13.6	28.3	19.1	26.5	15.8	..	..	..			
Algeria	24.2	..	20.3	..	23.0	27.3	..	..	..			
Angola	..	..	..	..	..	..	..	..	..			
Argentina	6.4	20.2	7.0	18.8	6.7	19.6	..	..	..			
Armenia	1.3	6.1	2.4	13.1	1.8	9.4	72.2	70.8	71.6	..	..	..
Australia	11.3	6.2	9.5	5.8	10.5	6.0	25.9	17.1	22.1	54.3	31.5	14.0
Austria	3.5	4.1	3.8	3.9	3.7	4.0	25.8	24.2	25.1	36.0	57.6	6.4
Azerbaijan	0.1	1.2	0.2	1.5	0.2	1.3	..	..	..	4.5	35.4	60.1
Bangladesh	2.0	3.2	1.9	3.3	1.9	3.3	..	..	..	54.3	22.7	8.4
Belarus	0.2	2.3	0.8	3.5	0.5	3.0	..	..	..	7.9	15.3	76.9
Belgium	5.7	6.2	10.7	7.8	7.7	6.9	45.8	53.3	49.4	50.0	34.9	15.1
Benin	..	..	..	..	..	..	..	..	..	..	..	..
Bolivia	5.5	4.5	5.6	6.2	5.5	5.2	..	..	..	60.2	32.5	4.4
Bosnia and Herzegovina	..	..	..	..	..	..	..	..	..	..	..	..
Botswana	..	14.7	..	17.2	..	15.8	..	..	..			
Brazil	5.6	7.5	8.0	11.9	6.5	9.4	..	..	..	26.1	20.2	2.5
Bulgaria	..	18.3	..	16.9	15.3	17.6	..	..	..	36.7	53.0	10.3
Burkina Faso	..	..	..	..	..	..	..	..	..	46.8	19.3	5.6
Burundi	..	..	..	..	..	..	..	..	..	..	..	..
Cambodia	..	1.5	..	2.2	..	1.8	..	..	..			
Cameroon	..	..	..	..	..	..	..	..	..	..	..	..
Canada	12.0	8.1	10.1	7.1	11.2	7.7	9.9	8.4	9.3	30.7	30.3	39.0
Central African Republic	..	..	..	..	..	..	..	..	..	..	..	..
Chad	..	..	..	..	..	..	..	..	..	..	..	..
Chile	4.1	7.5	5.6	8.5	4.4	7.8	..	..	..	22.7	54.9	21.6
China	..	..	..	..	2.3	4.0	..	..	..	..	..	..
Hong Kong, China	2.0	8.4	1.9	6.0	2.0	7.3	..	..	..	..	..	..
Colombia	6.5	11.6	12.6	19.1	9.2	14.7	..	..	..	22.8	57.2	17.2
Congo, Dem. Rep.	..	..	..	..	..	..	..	..	..	..	..	..
Congo, Rep.	..	..	..	..	..	..	..	..	..	..	..	..
Costa Rica	3.5	5.6	5.4	7.9	4.1	6.4	8.9	13.3	10.9	71.6	15.2	10.0
Côte d'Ivoire	..	..	..	..	..	..	..	..	..	..	..	..
Croatia	..	13.4	..	16.6	15.3	14.8	..	..	56.4	19.1	71.3	9.1
Cuba	..	..	..	..	4.6	3.3	..	..	..	..	..	..
Czech Republic	2.2	5.9	3.0	9.0	2.6	7.3	50.2	51.0	50.6	27.3	69.1	3.6
Denmark	8.3	4.2	9.9	4.3	9.0	4.3	17.1	22.1	19.5	35.1	44.9	20.0
Dominican Republic	11.7	9.4	34.9	26.0	20.3	15.6	2.2	1.3	1.6	..	..	..
Ecuador	6.0	6.0	13.2	14.0	8.9	9.3	..	..	..	26.8	50.8	20.2
Egypt, Arab Rep.	6.4	5.1	17.0	22.7	9.0	9.0	..	..	..	..	..	..
El Salvador	8.4	8.1	7.2	3.5	7.9	6.2	..	..	..	..	..	..
Eritrea	..	..	..	..	..	..	..	..	..	..	..	..
Estonia	3.9	10.8	3.5	9.7	3.7	10.3	..	..	..	19.3	62.7	18.1
Ethiopia	..	..	..	..	..	..	..	..	..	26.9	61.3	8.1
Finland	13.7	9.0	9.7	9.1	11.8	9.0	30.0	22.6	26.2	38.2	45.8	16.0
France	7.9	7.9	12.7	10.1	10.0	8.9	30.2	33.1	31.7	..	..	..
Gabon	..	..	..	..	..	..	..	..	..	..	..	..
Gambia, The	..	..	..	..	..	..	..	..	..	..	..	..
Georgia	..	13.7	..	10.7	..	12.3	..	..	..	5.5	33.1	61.4
Germany	5.3	8.7	8.4	8.3	6.6	8.6	44.9	48.7	46.6	26.8	60.4	12.8
Ghana	..	..	..	..	..	..	..	..	..	..	..	..
Greece	4.9	6.2	12.9	14.6	7.8	9.6	47.1	55.7	52.4	35.1	49.4	14.5
Guatemala	2.6	1.6	4.6	2.3	3.2	1.8	..	..	..	..	..	..
Guinea	..	..	..	..	..	..	..	..	..	..	..	..
Guinea-Bissau	..	..	..	..	..	..	..	..	..	..	..	..
Haiti	..	..	..	..	..	..	..	..	..	..	..	..

	Unemployment						Long-term unemployment			Unemployment by level of educational attainment		
	Male % of male labor force		Female % of female labor force		Total % of total labor force		% of total unemployment			% of total unemployment		
							Male	Female	Total	Primary	Secondary	Tertiary
	1990–92[a]	2000–02[a]	1990–92[a]	2000–02[a]	1990–92[a]	2000–02[a]	2000–02[a]	2000–02[a]	2000–02[a]	1999–2001[a]	1999–2001[a]	1999–2001[a]
Honduras	3.2	3.4	3.0	4.7	3.1	3.8	..	..	..	..	..	..
Hungary	11.0	6.1	8.7	5.4	9.9	5.8	47.1	41.7	44.8	35.4	60.5	4.1
India	..	..	..	..	..	..	..	..	..	29.0	40.3	30.7
Indonesia	..	..	..	..	..	9.1	..	..	..	46.0	36.6	6.7
Iran, Islamic Rep.	..	8.2	..	4.1	..	12.3	..	..	..	..	..	..
Iraq	..	..	..	..	..	..	..	..	..	..	..	..
Ireland	15.2	4.6	15.2	3.7	15.2	4.2	35.9	18.2	29.4	60.8	20.8	16.1
Israel	9.2	10.1	13.9	10.6	11.2	10.3	..	..	..	20.7	44.2	34.1
Italy	8.1	6.9	17.3	12.2	11.6	9.0	58.0	61.6	59.9	49.1	41.9	7.2
Jamaica	9.4	..	22.2	..	15.4	..	24.4	36.2	31.7	..	..	..
Japan	2.1	5.6	2.2	5.1	2.2	5.4	34.8	21.6	29.7	21.5	53.4	24.8
Jordan	..	11.8	..	20.7	..	13.2	..	..	..	..	..	..
Kazakhstan	..	..	..	..	0.4	2.6	..	..	..	7.2	52.5	40.3
Kenya	..	..	..	..	..	..	..	..	..	..	..	..
Korea, Dem. Rep.	..	..	..	..	..	..	..	..	..	..	..	..
Korea, Rep.	2.8	3.5	2.1	2.5	2.5	3.1	3.1	1.2	2.5	26.1	51.0	22.9
Kuwait	..	0.8	..	0.6	..	0.8	..	..	..	..	11.9	2.7
Kyrgyz Republic	..	..	..	..	..	..	..	..	..	33.4	55.7	10.9
Lao PDR	..	..	..	..	..	..	..	..	..	..	..	..
Latvia	1.8	12.9	2.8	11.0	2.3	12.0	..	..	..	24.6	67.0	8.2
Lebanon	..	..	..	..	..	..	..	..	..	..	..	..
Lesotho	..	..	..	..	..	..	..	..	..	..	..	..
Liberia	..	..	..	..	..	..	..	..	..	..	..	..
Libya	..	..	..	..	..	..	..	..	..	..	..	..
Lithuania	4.3	14.6	2.8	12.9	3.5	13.8	..	..	57.8	15.4	55.8	28.8
Macedonia, FYR	22.1	31.7	32.5	32.3	26.3	31.9	..	..	..	..	..	..
Madagascar	..	..	..	..	..	..	..	..	..	29.3	47.7	..
Malawi	..	..	..	..	..	..	..	..	..	..	..	..
Malaysia	..	..	..	..	3.7	3.8	..	..	..	..	..	..
Mali	..	..	..	..	..	..	..	..	..	..	..	..
Mauritania	..	..	..	..	..	..	..	..	..	..	..	..
Mauritius	..	..	..	..	..	..	..	..	..	35.5	63.9	..
Mexico	2.7	2.4	4.0	2.4	3.1	2.4	1.0	0.3	0.7	51.5	23.9	22.2
Moldova	..	8.1	..	5.5	0.7	6.8	..	..	..	..	..	..
Mongolia	..	..	..	..	..	3.4	..	..	..	..	..	..
Morocco	13.0	11.6	25.3	12.5	16.0	11.6	..	..	..	..	..	..
Mozambique	..	..	..	..	..	..	..	..	..	..	..	..
Myanmar	..	..	..	..	..	..	..	..	..	..	..	..
Namibia	20.0	28.3	19.0	39.0	19.0	33.8	..	..	..	..	..	..
Nepal	..	..	..	..	..	..	..	..	..	..	..	..
Netherlands	4.2	2.8	7.2	3.6	5.4	3.1	21.5	20.7	21.1	49.5	35.9	13.2
New Zealand	10.9	5.0	9.6	5.3	10.3	5.2	14.9	10.0	12.6	0.5	44.5	19.2
Nicaragua	11.3	..	19.4	..	14.4	12.2	..	..	..	56.3	23.4	14.7
Niger	..	..	..	..	..	..	..	..	..	..	..	..
Nigeria	..	..	..	..	..	..	..	..	..	..	..	..
Norway	6.6	4.1	5.1	3.7	5.9	3.9	8.1	3.7	6.2	25.0	50.0	22.6
Oman	..	..	..	..	..	..	..	..	..	..	..	..
Pakistan	4.3	6.1	14.2	17.3	5.8	7.8	..	..	..	..	..	..
Panama	10.8	10.5	22.3	18.2	14.7	13.2	24.0	35.7	29.3	47.0	35.5	11.3
Papua New Guinea	..	..	..	..	..	..	..	..	..	..	..	..
Paraguay	6.4	..	3.8	..	5.3	..	..	..	..	..	..	..
Peru	7.5	7.5	12.5	10.0	9.4	8.7	..	..	..	15.8	54.9	28.3
Philippines	7.9	9.4	9.8	10.3	8.6	9.8	..	..	..	..	..	..
Poland	12.2	19.1	14.7	20.9	13.3	19.9	45.1	52.0	48.4	19.1	76.8	4.2
Portugal	3.5	4.2	5.0	6.1	4.1	5.1	31.9	31.4	31.6	73.3	13.6	8.1
Puerto Rico	19.0	13.2	12.8	10.9	16.6	12.3	..	..	..	..	..	..

	Unemployment						Long-term unemployment			Unemployment by level of educational attainment		
	Male % of male labor force		Female % of female labor force		Total % of total labor force		% of total unemployment			% of total unemployment		
							Male	Female	Total	Primary	Secondary	Tertiary
	1990–92[a]	2000–02[a]	1990–92[a]	2000–02[a]	1990–92[a]	2000–02[a]	2000–02[a]	2000–02[a]	2000–02[a]	1999–2001[a]	1999–2001[a]	1999–2001[a]
Romania	6.2	8.9	10.3	7.7	8.2	8.4	..	..	..	20.6	72.7	5.5
Russian Federation	5.2	9.9	5.2	8.8	5.2	8.6	..	..	..	16.8	41.6	41.6
Rwanda	0.6	..	0.2	..	0.3	..	..	..	..	60.7	24.1	5.9
Saudi Arabia	..	3.9	..	9.1	..	4.6	..	..	..	..	..	..
Senegal	..	..	..	..	..	..	..	..	..	..	..	..
Serbia and Montenegro	..	12.4	..	15.8	..	13.8	..	..	..	..	..	..
Sierra Leone	..	..	..	..	..	..	..	..	..	..	..	..
Singapore	2.7	5.4	2.6	5.0	2.7	5.2	..	..	..	25.5	26.9	32.0
Slovak Republic	11.1	18.6	11.7	18.7	11.4	18.6	..	..	..	19.8	77.1	3.0
Slovenia	..	5.7	..	6.3	..	5.9	58.6	61.4	59.9	33.3	63.2	5.3
Somalia	..	..	..	..	..	..	..	..	..	..	..	..
South Africa	..	26.1	..	33.3	..	29.5	..	..	..	..	..	..
Spain	13.9	8.0	25.8	16.4	18.1	11.4	31.6	41.8	37.5	57.1	19.7	22.2
Sri Lanka	10.6	8.7	21.0	12.8	14.1	8.7	..	..	..	41.0	..	56.1
Sudan	..	..	..	..	..	..	..	..	..	..	..	..
Swaziland	..	..	..	..	..	..	..	..	..	..	..	..
Sweden	6.7	5.6	4.6	4.7	5.7	5.2	23.0	18.1	20.9	28.6	56.6	13.1
Switzerland	2.3	2.8	3.5	3.1	2.8	2.9	19.0	23.9	21.3	43.0	43.0	14.0
Syrian Arab Republic	5.2	8.3	14.0	24.1	6.8	11.7	..	..	..	..	..	..
Tajikistan	0.4	..	0.4	..	0.4	..	..	..	..	..	..	..
Tanzania	2.7	..	3.6	..	3.2	..	..	..	..	..	..	..
Thailand	1.3	2.7	1.5	2.5	1.4	2.6	..	..	..	70.6	7.2	19.2
Togo	..	..	..	..	..	..	..	..	..	..	..	..
Trinidad and Tobago	17.0	8.6	23.9	14.4	19.6	10.8	20.3	34.7	27.6	38.2	60.7	0.8
Tunisia	..	..	..	..	..	15.6	..	..	..	..	..	..
Turkey	8.6	10.9	7.6	9.9	8.3	10.6	26.4	34.5	28.5	60.1	29.0	8.4
Turkmenistan	..	..	..	..	..	..	..	..	..	..	..	..
Uganda	1.2	..	0.7	..	0.9	..	..	..	..	..	..	..
Ukraine	..	10.3	..	10.0	..	10.2	..	..	..	8.6	27.3	64.1
United Arab Emirates	..	2.2	..	2.6	..	2.3	..	..	..	..	..	..
United Kingdom	11.5	5.6	7.3	4.4	9.7	5.1	26.4	17.0	22.8	33.7	44.4	12.7
United States	7.9	5.9	7.0	5.6	7.5	5.8	8.9	8.1	8.5	20.3	35.3	44.4
Uruguay	6.9	11.5	11.9	19.7	9.0	18.6	..	..	..	50.7	21.2	27.8
Uzbekistan	0.2	..	0.3	..	0.2	..	..	..	..	..	..	..
Venezuela, RB	8.1	14.3	6.8	18.1	7.7	15.8	..	..	..	57.9	24.0	14.4
Vietnam	..	..	..	..	..	..	..	..	..	..	..	..
West Bank and Gaza	..	33.5	..	17.1	..	31.3	..	..	..	..	..	..
Yemen, Rep.	..	..	..	..	..	..	..	..	..	..	..	..
Zambia	11.7	..	13.7	..	12.4	..	..	..	..	..	..	..
Zimbabwe	..	..	..	..	..	..	..	..	..	16.4	81.8	0.8
World	.. w	.. w	.. w	.. w	.. w	.. w	.. w	.. w	.. w	30.0 w	40.2 w	25.2 w
Low income	..	..	..	..	..	..	..	..	..	29.0	40.6	30.4
Middle income	..	..	..	..	4.6	6.4	..	..	..	28.6	39.4	21.3
Lower middle income	..	..	..	..	4.3	6.0	..	..	..	27.3	..	23.4
Upper middle income	6.2	10.3	7.3	10.8	6.6	10.1	..	..	..	34.8	52.6	11.3
Low & middle income	..	..	..	..	..	..	..	..	..	28.8	40.0	25.8
East Asia & Pacific	..	..	..	..	2.5	4.7	..	..	..	..	..	..
Europe & Central Asia	6.4	11.0	6.8	10.6	6.6	10.3	..	..	..	21.3	45.8	32.6
Latin America & Carib.	5.6	7.8	8.3	11.0	6.6	9.0	..	..	..	31.3	28.3	9.6
Middle East & N. Africa	..	11.3	..	15.5	..	13.5	..	..	..	..	..	..
South Asia	..	..	..	..	..	..	..	..	..	29.3	40.3	31.0
Sub-Saharan Africa	..	..	..	..	..	..	..	..	..	..	..	..
High income	7.0	6.3	8.3	6.8	7.5	6.5	24.7	22.8	24.1	31.1	41.8	25.9
Europe EMU	7.5	7.3	13.3	10.2	9.8	8.5	40.7	44.6	42.8	42.1	43.7	13.3

a. Data are for the most recent year available.

Unemployment and total employment in an economy are the broadest indicators of economic activity as reflected by the labor market. The International Labour Organization (ILO) defines the unemployed as members of the economically active population who are without work but available for and seeking work, including people who have lost their jobs and those who have voluntarily left work. Some unemployment is unavoidable in all economies. At any time some workers are temporarily unemployed—between jobs as employers look for the right workers and workers search for better jobs. Such unemployment, often called frictional unemployment, results from the normal operation of labor markets.

Changes in unemployment over time may reflect changes in the demand for and supply of labor, but they may also reflect changes in reporting practices. Ironically, low unemployment rates can often disguise substantial poverty in a country, while high unemployment rates can occur in countries with a high level of economic development and low incidence of poverty. In countries without unemployment or welfare benefits, people eke out a living in the informal sector. In countries with well-developed safety nets, workers can afford to wait for suitable or desirable jobs. But high and sustained unemployment indicates serious inefficiencies in the allocation of resources.

The ILO definition of unemployment notwithstanding, reference periods, the criteria for those considered to be seeking work, and the treatment of people temporarily laid off and those seeking work for the first time vary across countries. In many developing countries it is especially difficult to measure employment and unemployment in agriculture. The timing of a survey, for example, can maximize the effects of seasonal unemployment in agriculture. And informal sector employment is difficult to quantify where informal activities are not registered and tracked.

Data on unemployment are drawn from labor force sample surveys and general household sample surveys, censuses, and other administrative records such as social insurance statistics, employment office statistics, and official estimates, which are usually based on information drawn from one or more of the above sources. Labor force surveys generally yield the most comprehensive data because they include groups not covered in other unemployment statistics, particularly people seeking work for the first time. These surveys generally use a definition of unemployment that follows the international recommendations more closely than that used by other

sources and therefore generate statistics that are more comparable internationally.

In contrast, the quality and completeness of data from employment offices and social insurance programs vary widely. Where employment offices work closely with social insurance schemes and registration with such offices is a prerequisite for receipt of unemployment benefits, the two sets of unemployment estimates tend to be comparable. Where registration is voluntary and where employment offices function only in more populous areas, employment office statistics do not give a reliable indication of unemployment. Most commonly excluded from both these sources are discouraged workers who have given up their job search because they believe that no employment opportunities exist or do not register as unemployed after their benefits have been exhausted. Thus measured unemployment may be higher in countries that offer more or longer unemployment benefits.

Women tend to be excluded from the unemployment count for various reasons. Women suffer more from discrimination and from structural, social, and cultural barriers that impede them from actively seeking work. Also, women are often responsible for the care of children and the elderly or for other household affairs. They may not be available for work during the short reference period, as they need to make arrangement before starting work. Furthermore, women are considered to be employed when they are working part-time or in temporary jobs in the informal sector, despite the instability of these jobs and that they may be actively looking for more secure employment.

Long-term unemployment is measured in terms of duration, that is, the length of time that an unemployed person has been without work and looking for a job. The underlying assumption is that shorter periods of joblessness are of less concern, especially when the unemployed are covered by unemployment benefits or similar forms of welfare support. The length of time a person has been unemployed is difficult to measure, because the ability to recall the length of that time diminishes as the period of joblessness extends. Women's long-term unemployment is likely to be lower in countries where women constitute a large share of the unpaid family workforce. Women in such countries have more access than men to nonmarket work and are more likely to drop out of the labor force and not be counted as unemployed.

Unemployment by level of educational attainment provide insights into the relationship between the

educational attainment of workers and unemployment. Besides the limitations to comparability raised for measuring unemployment, the different ways of classifying the level of education across countries may also cause inconsistency. The level of education is supposed to be classified according to International Standard Classification of Education 1997 (ISCED97). For more information on ISCED97, see *About the data* for table 2.11.

• **Unemployment** refers to the share of the labor force without work but available for and seeking employment. Definitions of labor force and unemployment differ by country (see *About the data*). • **Long-term unemployment** refers to the number of people with continuous periods of unemployment extending for a year or longer, expressed as a percentage of the total unemployed. • **Unemployment by level of educational attainment** shows the unemployed by level of educational attainment, as a percentage of the total unemployed. The levels of educational attainment accord with the International Standard Classification of Education 1997 of the United Nations Educational, Cultural, and Scientific Organization (UNESCO).

Data sources

The unemployment data are from the ILO database *Key Indicators of the Labour Market,* third edition.

	National poverty line								International poverty line				
		Population below the poverty line				Population below the poverty line				Population below $1 a day	Poverty gap at $1 a day	Population below $2 a day	Poverty gap at $2 a day
	Survey year	Rural %	Urban %	National %	Survey year	Rural %	Urban %	National %	Survey year	%	%	%	%
Afghanistan	..	..	..	..		..	..	..		..	..	..	..
Albania	2002	29.6	19.8	25.4		..	..	..	2002[a]	<2	<0.5	11.8	2.0
Algeria	1995	30.3	14.7	22.6	1998	16.6	7.3	12.2	1995[a]	<2	<0.5	15.1	3.8
Angola	..	..	..	..		..	..	..		..	..	..	..
Argentina	1995	..	28.4		1998		29.9		2001[b]	3.3	0.5	14.3	4.7
Armenia	1998–99	50.8	58.3	55.1	2001	48.7	51.9	50.9	1998[a]	12.8	3.3	49.0	17.3
Australia	..	..	..	..		..	..	..		..	..	..	..
Austria	..	..	..	..		..	..	..		..	..	..	..
Azerbaijan	1995	..	..	68.1	2001	42.0	55.0	49.0	2001[a]	3.7	<1	9.1	3.5
Bangladesh	1995–96	55.2	29.4	51.0	2000	53.0	36.6	49.8	2000[a]	36.0	8.1	82.8	36.3
Belarus	2000	..	..	41.9					2000[a]	<2	<0.5	<2	0.1
Belgium	..	..	..	..		..	..	..		..	..	..	..
Benin	1995	25.2	28.5	26.5	1999	33.0	23.3	29.0		..	..	..	..
Bolivia	1997	77.3	53.8	63.2	1999	81.7	50.6	62.7	1999[a]	14.4	5.4	34.3	14.9
Bosnia and Herzegovina	2001–02	19.9	13.8	19.5		..	..	..		..	..	..	..
Botswana	..	..	..	..		..	..	..	1993[a]	23.5	7.7	50.1	22.8
Brazil	1996	54.0	15.4	23.9	1998	51.4	14.7	22.0	2001[b]	8.2	2.1	22.4	8.8
Bulgaria	1997	..	..	36.0	2001	..	..	12.8	2001[a]	4.7	1.4	16.2	5.7
Burkina Faso	1994	51.0	10.4	44.5	1998	51.0	16.5	45.3	1998[a]	44.9	14.4	81.0	40.6
Burundi	1990	36.0	43.0	36.4		..	..	..	1998[a]	58.4	24.9	89.2	51.3
Cambodia	1997	40.1	21.1	36.1	1999	40.1	13.9	35.9	1997[a]	34.1	9.7	77.7	34.5
Cameroon	1996	59.6	41.4	53.3	2001	49.9	22.1	40.2	2001[a]	17.1	4.1	50.6	19.3
Canada	..	..	..	..		..	..	..		..	..	..	..
Central African Republic	..	..	..	..		..	..	..	1993[a]	66.6	38.1	84.0	58.4
Chad	1995–96	67.0	63.0	64.0		..	..	..		..	..	..	..
Chile	1996	..	..	19.9	1998	..	..	17.0	2000[b]	<2	<0.5	9.6	2.5
China	1996	7.9	<2	6.0	1998	4.6	<2	4.6	2001[a]	16.6	3.9	46.7	18.4
Hong Kong, China	..	..	..	..		..	..	..		..	..	..	..
Colombia	1995	79.0	48.0	60.0	1999	79.0	55.0	64.0	1999[b]	8.2	2.2	22.6	8.8
Congo, Dem. Rep.	..	..	..	..		..	..	..		..	..	..	..
Congo, Rep.	..	..	..	..		..	..	..		..	..	..	..
Costa Rica	1992	25.5	19.2	22.0		..	..	..	2000[b]	2.0	0.7	9.5	3.0
Côte d'Ivoire	..	..	..			..	..	..	2002[a]	10.8	1.9	38.4	13.6
Croatia	..	..	..	..		..	..	..	2001[a]	<2	<0.5	<2	<0.5
Cuba	..	..	..	..		..	..	..		..	..	..	..
Czech Republic	..	..	..	..		..	..	..	1996[b]	<2	<0.5	<2	<0.5
Denmark	..	..	..	..		..	..	..		..	..	..	..
Dominican Republic	1992	49.0	19.3	33.9	1998	42.1	20.5	28.6	1998[b]	<2	<0.5	<2	<0.5
Ecuador	1994	47.0	25.0	35.0		..	..	..	1998[b]	17.7	7.1	40.8	17.7
Egypt, Arab Rep.	1995–96	23.3	22.5	22.9	1999–2000	..	..	16.7	1999–2000[a]	3.1	<0.5	43.9	11.3
El Salvador	1992	55.7	43.1	48.3		..	..	..	2000[b]	31.1	14.1	58.0	29.7
Eritrea	1993–94	..	..	53.0		..	..	..		..	..	..	..
Estonia	1995	14.7	6.8	8.9		..	..	..	1998[a]	<2	<0.5	5.2	0.8
Ethiopia	1995–96	47.0	33.3	45.5	1999–2000	45.0	37.0	44.2	1999–2000[a]	26.3	5.7	80.7	31.8
Finland	..	..	..	..		..	..	..		..	..	..	..
France	..	..	..	..		..	..	..		..	..	..	..
Gabon	..	..	..	..		..	..	..		..	..	..	..
Gambia, The	1992	..	..	64.0	1998	61.0	48.0	57.6	1998[a]	59.3	28.8	82.9	51.1
Georgia	1997	9.9	12.1	11.1		..	..	..	2001[a]	2.7	0.9	15.7	4.6
Germany	..	..	..	..		..	..	..		..	..	..	..
Ghana	1992	..	..	50.0	1998–99	49.9	18.6	39.5	1998–99[a]	44.8	17.3	78.5	40.8
Greece	..	..	..	..		..	..	..		..	..	..	..
Guatemala	1989	71.9	33.7	57.9	2000	74.5	27.1	56.2	2000[b]	16.0	4.6	37.4	16.0
Guinea	1994	..	..	40.0		..	..	..		..	..	..	..
Guinea-Bissau	..	..	..	..		..	..	..		..	..	..	..
Haiti	1987	..	..	65.0	1995	66.0				..	..	..	..

Poverty | 2.5

	National poverty line							International poverty line				
		Population below the poverty line				Population below the poverty line			Population below $1 a day	Poverty gap at $1 a day	Population below $2 a day	Poverty gap at $2 a day
	Survey year	Rural %	Urban %	National %	Survey year	Rural %	Urban %	National %	Survey year	%	%	%	%
Honduras	1992	46.0	56.0	50.0	1993	51.0	57.0	53.0	1999[b]	20.7	7.5	44.0	20.2
Hungary	1993	..	..	14.5	1997	..	..	17.3	2002[a]	<2	<0.5	<2	<0.5
India	1993–94	37.3	32.4	36.0	1999–2000	30.2	24.7	28.6	1999–2000[a]	34.7	8.2	79.9	35.3
Indonesia	1996	..	..	15.7	1999			27.1	2002[a]	7.5	0.9	52.4	15.7
Iran, Islamic Rep.		..	..	..		..	..	..	1998[a]	<2	<0.5	7.3	1.5
Iraq		..	..	..		..	..	..		..	..	..	..
Ireland		..	..	..		..	..	..		..	..	..	..
Israel		..	..	..		..	..	..		..	..	..	..
Italy		..	..	..		..	..	..		..	..	..	..
Jamaica	1995	37.0	18.7	27.5	2000	25.1	12.8	18.7	2000[a]	<2	<0.5	13.3	2.7
Japan													
Jordan	1991	..	..	15.0	1997	..	..	11.7	1997[a]	<2	<0.5	7.4	1.4
Kazakhstan	1996	39.0	30.0	34.6					2003[a]	<2	<.5	24.9	6.3
Kenya	1994	47.0	29.0	40.0	1997	53.0	49.0	52.0	1997[a]	22.8	5.9	58.3	23.9
Korea, Dem. Rep.		..	..	..		..	..	..		..	..	..	..
Korea, Rep.		..	..	..		..	..	..	1998[b]	<2	<0.5	<2	<0.5
Kuwait		..	..	..		..	..	..		..	..	..	..
Kyrgyz Republic	2000	56.4	43.9	52.0	2001	51.0	41.2	47.6	2002[a]	<2	<0.5	24.7	5.8
Lao PDR	1993	48.7	33.1	45.0	1997–98	41.0	26.9	38.6	1997–98[a]	26.3	6.3	73.2	29.6
Latvia		..	..	..		..	..	..	1998[a]	<2	<0.5	8.3	2.0
Lebanon		..	..	..		..	..	..		..	..	..	..
Lesotho		..	..	..		..	..	..	1995[a]	36.4	19.0	56.1	33.1
Liberia		..	..	..		..	..	..		..	..	..	..
Libya		..	..	..		..	..	..		..	..	..	..
Lithuania		..	..	..		..	..	..	2000[a]	<2	<0.5	6.9	1.5
Macedonia, FYR		..	..	..		..	..	..	1998[a]	<2	<0.5	4.0	0.6
Madagascar	1997	76.0	63.2	73.3	1999	76.7	52.1	71.3	2001[a]	61.0	27.9	85.1	51.8
Malawi	1990–91	..	..	54.0	1997–98	66.5	54.9	65.3	1997–98[a]	41.7	14.8	76.1	38.3
Malaysia	1989	..	..	15.5					1997[b]	<2	<0.5	9.3	2.0
Mali	1998	75.9	30.1	63.8					1994[a]	72.3	37.4	90.6	60.5
Mauritania	1996	65.5	30.1	50.0	2000	61.2	25.4	46.3	2000[a]	25.9	7.6	63.1	26.8
Mauritius		..	..	..		..	..	..		..	..	..	..
Mexico	1988	..	..	10.1					2000[a]	9.9	3.7	26.3	10.9
Moldova	1997	26.7	19.3	23.3					2001[a]	22.0	5.8	63.7	25.1
Mongolia	1995	33.1	38.5	36.3	1998	32.6	39.4	35.6	1998[a]	27.0	8.1	74.9	30.6
Morocco	1990–91	18.0	7.6	13.1	1998–99	27.2	12.0	19.0	1999[a]	<2	<0.5	14.3	3.1
Mozambique	1996–97	71.3	62.0	69.4		..	..	..	1996[a]	37.9	12.0	78.4	36.8
Myanmar		..	..	..		..	..	..		..	..	..	..
Namibia		..	..	..		..	..	..	1993[b]	34.9	14.0	55.8	30.4
Nepal	1995–96	44.0	23.0	42.0		..	..	..	1995–96[a]	37.7	9.7	82.5	37.5
Netherlands		..	..	..		..	..	..		..	..	..	..
New Zealand		..	..	..		..	..	..		..	..	..	..
Nicaragua	1993	76.1	31.9	50.3	1998	68.5	30.5	47.9	2001[a]	45.1	16.7	79.9	41.2
Niger	1989–93	66.0	52.0	63.0		..	..	..	1995[a]	61.4	33.9	85.3	54.8
Nigeria	1985	49.5	31.7	43.0	1992–93	36.4	30.4	34.1	1997[a]	70.2	34.9	90.8	59.0
Norway		..	..	..		..	..	..		..	..	..	..
Oman		..	..	..		..	..	..		..	..	..	..
Pakistan	1993	33.4	17.2	28.6	1998–99	35.9	24.2	32.6	1998–99[a]	13.4	2.4	65.6	22.0
Panama	1997	64.9	15.3	37.3		..	..	..	2000[b]	7.2	2.3	17.6	7.4
Papua New Guinea	1996	41.3	16.1	37.5		..	..	..		..	..	..	..
Paraguay	1991	28.5	19.7	21.8		..	..	..	2002[b]	16.4	7.4	33.2	16.2
Peru	1994	67.0	46.1	53.5	1997	64.7	40.4	49.0	2000[b]	18.1	9.1	37.7	18.5
Philippines	1994	53.1	28.0	40.6	1997	50.7	21.5	36.8	2000[a]	14.6	2.7	46.4	17.2
Poland	1993	..	..	23.8		..	..	..	2001[a]	<2	<0.5	<2	<0.5
Portugal		..	..	..		..	..	..	1994[b]	<2	<0.5	<0.5	<0.5
Puerto Rico		..	..	..		..	..	..		..	..	..	..

| | National poverty line | | | | | | | | International poverty line | | | | |
| | Population below the poverty line | | | | Population below the poverty line | | | | Population below $1 a day | Poverty gap at $1 a day | Population below $2 a day | Poverty gap at $2 a day |
	Survey year	Rural %	Urban %	National %	Survey year	Rural %	Urban %	National %	Survey year	%	%	%	%
Romania	1994	27.9	20.4	21.5	..	..	..	..	2002[a]	<2	0.5	14.0	3.4
Russian Federation	1994	..	..	30.9	..	..	..	..	2002[a]	<2	<0.5	7.5	1.3
Rwanda	1993	..	..	51.2	1999–2000	65.7	14.3	60.3	1999–2000[a]	51.7	20.0	83.7	45.5
Saudi Arabia	..	..	..	..	..	..	..	..	..	..	..	..	..
Senegal	1992	40.4	23.7	33.4	..	..	..	..	1995[a]	26.3	7.0	67.8	28.2
Serbia and Montenegro	..	..	..	..	..	..	..	..	..	..	..	..	..
Sierra Leone	1989	76.0	53.0	82.8	2003–04	79.0	56.4	70.2	1989[a]	57.0	39.5	74.5	51.8
Singapore	..	..	..	..	..	..	..	..	..	..	..	..	..
Slovak Republic	..	..	..	..	..	..	..	..	1996[b]	<2	<0.5	2.9	0.8
Slovenia	..	..	..	..	..	..	..	..	1998[a]	<2	<0.5	<2	<0.5
Somalia	..	..	..	..	..	..	..	..	..	..	..	..	..
South Africa	..	..	..	..	..	..	..	..	2000[a]	10.7	1.7	34.1	12.6
Spain	..	..	..	..	..	..	..	..	..	..	..	..	..
Sri Lanka	1990–91	22.0	15.0	20.0	1995–96	27.0	15.0	25.0	1999–2000[a]	7.6	1.5	50.7	15.2
Sudan	..	..	..	..	..	..	..	..	..	..	..	..	..
Swaziland	1995	..	..	40.0	..	..	..	..	..	..	..	..	..
Sweden	..	..	..	..	..	..	..	..	..	..	..	..	..
Switzerland	..	..	..	..	..	..	..	..	..	..	..	..	..
Syrian Arab Republic	..	..	..	..	..	..	..	..	..	..	..	..	..
Tajikistan	..	..	..	..	..	..	..	..	2003[a]	7.4	1.3	42.8	13.0
Tanzania	1991	40.8	31.2	38.6	2000–01	38.7	29.5	35.7	1993[a]	19.9	4.8	59.7	23.0
Thailand	1990	..	..	18.0	1992	15.5	10.2	13.1	2000[a]	<2	<0.5	32.5	9.0
Togo	1987–89	..	..	32.3	..	..	..	..	..	..	..	..	..
Trinidad and Tobago	1992	20.0	24.0	21.0	..	..	..	..	1992[b]	12.4	3.5	39.0	14.6
Tunisia	1990	13.1	3.5	7.4	1995	13.9	3.6	7.6	2000[a]	<2	<0.5	6.6	1.3
Turkey	..	..	..	..	..	..	..	..	2000[a]	<2	<0.5	10.3	2.5
Turkmenistan	..	..	..	..	..	..	..	..	1998[a]	12.1	2.6	44.0	15.4
Uganda	1993	..	..	55.0	1997	..	..	44.0	..	..	..	..	..
Ukraine	1995	..	..	31.7	..	..	..	..	1999[b]	2.9	0.6	45.7	16.3
United Arab Emirates	..	..	..	..	..	..	..	..	..	..	..	..	..
United Kingdom	..	..	..	..	..	..	..	..	..	..	..	..	..
United States	..	..	..	..	..	..	..	..	..	..	..	..	..
Uruguay	..	..	..	..	..	..	..	..	2000[b]	<2	<0.5	3.9	0.8
Uzbekistan	2000	30.5	22.5	27.5	..	..	..	..	2000[a]	21.8	5.4	77.5	28.9
Venezuela, RB	1989	..	..	31.3	..	..	..	..	1998[b]	15.0	6.9	32.0	15.2
Vietnam	1998	45.5	9.2	37.4	2002	35.6	6.6	28.9	..	..	..	..	..
West Bank and Gaza	..	..	..	..	..	..	..	..	..	..	..	..	..
Yemen, Rep.	1998	45.0	30.8	41.8	..	..	..	..	1998[a]	15.7	4.5	45.2	15.0
Zambia	1996	82.8	46.0	69.2	1998	83.1	56.0	72.9	1998[a]	63.7	32.7	87.4	55.4
Zimbabwe	1990–91	35.8	3.4	25.8	1995–96	48.0	7.9	34.9	1995–96[a]	56.1	24.2	83.0	48.2

a. Expenditure base. b. Income base.

2.5a

Regional poverty estimates

People living on less than $1 a day (millions)

Region	1981	1984	1987	1990	1993	1996	1999	2001
East Asia & Pacific	796	562	426	472	415	287	282	271
China	634	425	308	375	334	212	223	212
Europe & Central Asia	3	2	2	2	17	20	30	17
Latin America & Caribbean	36	46	45	49	52	52	54	50
Middle East & North Africa	9	8	7	6	4	5	8	7
South Asia	475	460	473	462	476	461	429	431
Sub-Saharan Africa	164	198	219	227	242	271	294	313
Total	**1,482**	**1,277**	**1,171**	**1,218**	**1,208**	**1,097**	**1,096**	**1,089**
Excluding China	848	852	863	844	873	886	873	877

Share of people living on less than $1 a day (%)

Region	1981	1984	1987	1990	1993	1996	1999	2001
East Asia & Pacific	57.7	38.9	28.0	29.6	24.9	16.6	15.7	14.9
China	63.8	41.0	28.5	33.0	28.4	17.4	17.8	16.6
Europe & Central Asia	0.7	0.5	0.4	0.5	3.7	4.3	6.3	3.6
Latin America & Caribbean	9.7	11.8	10.9	11.3	11.3	10.7	10.5	9.5
Middle East & North Africa	5.1	3.8	3.2	2.3	1.6	2.0	2.6	2.4
South Asia	51.5	46.8	45.0	41.3	40.1	36.6	32.2	31.3
Sub-Saharan Africa	41.6	46.3	46.8	44.6	44.0	45.6	45.7	46.4
Total	**40.4**	**32.8**	**28.4**	**27.9**	**26.3**	**22.8**	**21.8**	**21.1**
Excluding China	31.7	29.8	28.4	26.1	25.6	24.6	23.1	22.5

People living on less than $2 a day (millions)

Region	1981	1984	1987	1990	1993	1996	1999	2001
East Asia & Pacific	1,170	1,109	1,028	1,116	1,079	922	900	864
China	876	814	731	825	803	650	627	594
Europe & Central Asia	20	18	15	23	81	98	113	93
Latin America & Caribbean	99	119	115	125	136	117	127	128
Middle East & North Africa	52	50	53	51	52	61	70	70
South Asia	821	859	911	958	1,005	1,029	1,039	1,064
Sub-Saharan Africa	288	326	355	382	410	447	489	516
Total	**2,450**	**2,480**	**2,478**	**2,654**	**2,764**	**2,674**	**2,739**	**2,735**
Excluding China	1,574	1,666	1,747	1,829	1,961	2,024	2,111	2,142

Share of people living on less than $2 a day (%)

Region	1981	1984	1987	1990	1993	1996	1999	2001
East Asia & Pacific	84.8	76.6	67.7	69.9	64.8	53.3	50.3	47.4
China	88.1	78.5	67.4	72.6	68.1	53.4	50.1	46.7
Europe & Central Asia	4.7	4.1	3.3	4.9	17.2	20.7	23.8	19.7
Latin America & Caribbean	26.9	30.4	27.8	28.4	29.5	24.1	25.1	24.5
Middle East & North Africa	28.9	25.2	24.2	21.4	20.2	22.3	24.3	23.2
South Asia	89.1	87.2	86.7	85.5	84.5	81.7	78.1	77.2
Sub-Saharan Africa	73.3	76.1	76.1	75.0	74.6	75.1	76.1	76.6
Total	**66.7**	**63.7**	**60.1**	**60.8**	**60.2**	**55.5**	**54.4**	**52.9**
Excluding China	58.8	58.4	57.5	56.6	57.4	56.3	55.8	54.9

The World Bank produced its first global poverty estimates for *World Development Report 1990* for developing countries using household survey data for 22 countries (Ravallion, Datt, and van de Walle 1991). Incorporating survey data collected during the last 15 years, the database has expanded considerably and now includes 440 surveys representing almost 100 developing countries. Some 1.1 million randomly sampled households were interviewed in these surveys, representing 93 percent of the population of developing countries. The surveys asked detailed questions on sources of income and how it was spent, and on other household characteristics such as the number of people sharing that income. Most interviews were conducted by staff of government statistics offices. Along with improvements in data coverage and quality, the underlying methodology has also improved, resulting in better and more comprehensive estimates.

Data availability. Since 1979 there has been considerable expansion in the number of countries that field such surveys, the frequency of the surveys, and the quality of their data (table 6.5a). The number of data sets rose dramatically from a mere 13 between 1979 and 1981 to 100 between 1997 and 1999. The drop to 41 available surveys after 1999 reflects the lag between the time data are collected and the time they become available for analysis, not a reduction in data collection. Data coverage is improving in all regions, but Sub-Saharan Africa continues to lag, with only 28 countries out of 48 having at least one data set available.

Data quality. The problems of estimating poverty and comparing poverty rates do not end with data availability. Several other issues, some related to data quality, also arise in measuring household living standards from survey data. One relates to the choice of income or consumption as a welfare indicator. Income is generally more difficult to measure accurately, and consumption comes closer to the notion of standard of living. And income can vary over time even if the standard of living does not. But consumption data are not always available. Another issue is that household surveys can differ widely, for example, in the number of consumer goods they identify. And even similar surveys may not be strictly comparable because of differences in timing or the quality and training of survey enumerators.

Comparisons of countries at different levels of development also pose a potential problem because of differences in the relative importance of consumption of nonmarket goods. The local market value of all consumption in kind (including own production, particularly important in underdeveloped rural economies) should be included in total consumption expenditure. Similarly, imputed profit from the production of nonmarket goods should be included in income. This is not always done, though such omissions were a far bigger problem in surveys before the 1980s. Most survey data now include valuations for consumption or income from own production. Nonetheless, valuation methods vary. For example, some surveys use the price in the nearest market, while others use the average farmgate selling price.

Whenever possible, the table uses consumption data for deciding who is poor and income surveys only when consumption data are unavailable. In recent editions there has been a change in how income surveys are used. In the past, average household income was adjusted to accord with consumption and income data from national accounts. But in testing this approach using data for some 20 countries for which income and consumption expenditure data were both available from the same surveys, income was found to yield a higher mean than consumption but also higher inequality. When poverty measures based on consumption and income were compared, these two effects roughly cancelled each other out: statistically, there was no significant difference. So recent editions use income data to estimate poverty directly, without adjusting average income measures.

International poverty lines. International comparisons of poverty estimates entail both conceptual and practical problems. Countries have different definitions of poverty, and consistent comparisons between countries can be difficult. Local poverty lines tend to have higher purchasing power in rich countries, where more generous standards are used, than in poor countries. Is it reasonable to treat two people with the same standard of living—in terms of their command over commodities—differently because one happens to live in a better-off country?

Poverty measures based on an international poverty line attempt to hold the real value of the poverty line constant across countries, as is done when making comparisons over time. The commonly used $1 a day standard, measured in 1985 international prices and adjusted to local currency using purchasing power parities (PPPs), was chosen for the World Bank's *World Development Report 1990: Poverty* because it is typical of the poverty lines in low-income countries. PPP exchange rates, such as those from the Penn World Tables or the World Bank, are used because they take into account the local prices of goods and services not traded internationally. But PPP rates were designed for comparing aggregates from national accounts, not for making international poverty comparisons. As a result, there is no certainty that an international poverty line measures the same degree of need or deprivation across countries.

Early editions of *World Development Indicators* used PPPs from the Penn World Tables. Recent editions use 1993 consumption PPP estimates produced by the World Bank. Recalculated in 1993 PPP terms, the original international poverty line of $1 a day in 1985 PPP terms is now about $1.08 a day.

2.5b

Coverage of survey data by developing country region, 1978–81 to 2000–01								
	1979–81	1982–84	1985–87	1988–90	1991–93	1994–96	1997–99	2000–01	Number of countries
East Asia	3	4	7	6	11	11	16	7	9
China	2	1	4	1	5	6	6	2	1
Eastern Europe and Central Asia	0	0	5	18	18	24	30	17	26
Latin America and Caribbean	6	2	11	23	16	26	28	12	22
Middle East and North Africa	0	1	3	5	2	4	5	1	7
South Asia	2	5	7	9	6	11	5	1	5
India	2	2	4	6	4	6	4	0	1
Sub-Saharan Africa	2	1	8	6	20	18	12	5	28
Total	**13**	**13**	**41**	**67**	**73**	**94**	**100**	**43**	**97**

Source: Computed from *PovcalNet*, February 2005.

Any revisions in the PPP of a country to incorporate better price indexes can produce dramatically different poverty lines in local currency.

Issues also arise when comparing poverty measures within countries. For example, the cost of living is typically higher in urban than in rural areas. One reason is that food staples tend to be more expensive in urban areas. So the urban monetary poverty line should be higher than the rural poverty line. But it is not always clear that the difference between urban and rural poverty lines found in practice reflects only differences in the cost of living. In some countries the urban poverty line in common use has a higher real value—meaning that it allows the purchase of more commodities for consumption—than does the rural poverty line. Sometimes the difference has been so large as to imply that the incidence of poverty is greater in urban than in rural areas, even though the reverse is found when adjustments are made only for differences in the cost of living. As with international comparisons, when the real value of the poverty line varies it is not clear how meaningful such urban-rural comparisons are.

By combining all this information, a team in the World Bank's Development Research Group calculates the number of people living below various international poverty lines, as well as other poverty and inequality measures that are published in *World Development Indicators*. The database is updated annually as new survey data become available, and a major reassessment of progress against poverty is made about every three years.

Do it yourself: PovcalNet. Recently this research team developed *PovcalNet,* an interactive web-based computational tool that allows users to replicate the calculations by the World Bank's researchers in estimating the extent of absolute poverty in the world. *PovcalNet* is self-contained and powered by reliable built-in software that performs the relevant calculations from a primary database. The underlying software can also be downloaded from the site and used with distributional data of various formats. The *PovcalNet* primary database consists of distributional data calculated directly from household survey data. Detailed information for each of these is also available from the site.

Estimation from distributional data requires an interpolation method. The method chosen was Lorenz curves with flexible functional forms, which have proved reliable in past work. The Lorenz curve can be graphed as the cumulative percentages of total consumption or income against the cumulative number of people, starting with the poorest individual. The empirical Lorenz curves estimated by *PovcalNet* are weighted by household size, so they are based on percentiles of population, not households.

PovcalNet also allows users to calculate poverty measures under different assumptions. For example, instead of $1 a day, users can specify a different poverty line, say $1.50 or $3. Users can also specify different PPP rates and aggregate the estimates using alternative country groupings (for example, UN country groupings or groupings based on average incomes) or a selected set of individual countries. *PovcalNet* is available online at http://iresearch. worldbank.org/povcalnet/.

Definitions

• **Survey year** is the year in which the underlying data were collected. • **Rural poverty rate** is the percentage of the rural population living below the national rural poverty line. • **Urban poverty rate** is the percentage of the urban population living below the national urban poverty line. • **National poverty rate** is the percentage of the population living below the national poverty line. National estimates are based on population-weighted subgroup estimates from household surveys. • **Population below $1 a day** and **population below $2 a day** are the percentages of the population living on less than $1.08 a day and $2.15 a day at 1993 international prices. As a result of revisions in PPP exchange rates, poverty rates for individual countries cannot be compared with poverty rates reported in earlier editions. • **Poverty gap** is the mean shortfall from the poverty line (counting the nonpoor as having zero shortfall), expressed as a percentage of the poverty line. This measure reflects the depth of poverty as well as its incidence.

Data sources

The poverty measures are prepared by the World Bank's Development Research Group. The national poverty lines are based on the Bank's country poverty assessments. The international poverty lines are based on nationally representative primary household surveys conducted by national statistical offices or by private agencies under the supervision of government or international agencies and obtained from government statistical offices and World Bank Group country departments. The World Bank Group has prepared an annual review of its poverty work since 1993. For details on data sources and methods used in deriving the Bank's latest estimates, see Chen and Ravallion (2004), "How Have the World's Poorest Fared Since the Early 1980s?"

2.6 Social indicators of poverty

	Survey year	Prevalence of child malnutrition		Under-five mortality rate		Child immunization rate		Contraceptive prevalence		Births attended by skilled health staff[a]	
		Underweight % of children under age 5		per 1,000		Measles % of children ages 12–23 months[b]		% of women ages 15–49		% of total	
		Poorest quintile	Richest quintile	Poorest quintile	Richest quintile	Poorest quintile	Richest quintile	Poorest quintile	Richest quintile	Poorest quintile	Richest quintile
Armenia	2000	3	2	61	30	68	74[c]	16	29	93	100
Bangladesh	2000	60	29	140	72	59	86	37	50	4	42
Benin	1996	37	19	208	110	49	80	1	9	34	98
Bolivia	1998	14	3	147	32	58	85	7	46	20	98
Brazil	1996	12	3	99	33	78	90	56	77	72	99
Burkina Faso	1998–99	38	26	239	155	33	69	2	16	18	75
Cambodia	2000	52	34	155	64	44	82	13	25	15	81
Cameroon	1998	33	9	199	87	37	78	1	17	28	89
Central African Republic	1994–95	37	20	193	98	31	80	1	9	14	82
Chad	1996–97	50	29	171	172	12	39	0[d]	5	3	47
Colombia	2000	9	3	39	20	74	85	54	66	64	99
Comores	1996	36	18	129	87[c]	51	86	7	19	26	85
Côte d'Ivoire	1994	31	13	190	97	31	79	1	13	17	84
Egypt, Arab Rep.	2000	7	2	98	34	95	99	43	61	31	94
Eritrea	1995	51	25	152	104	37	92	0[d]	19	5	74
Ethiopia	2000	49	37	159	147	18	52	3	23	1	25
Gabon	2000	19	8	93	55	34	71	6	18	67	97
Ghana	1998	33	12	139	52	61	87	8	18	18	86
Guatemala	1998	34	10	78	39	80	91	5	60	9	92
Guinea	1999	29	17	230	133	33	73	1	9	12	82
Haiti	2000	24	8	164	109	43	63	17	24	4	70
India	1999	61	26	141	46	28	81	29	55	16	84
Indonesia	1997	..	..	109	29	59	85	46	57	21	89
Jordan	1997	9	3	42	25	90	93	28	47	91	99
Kazakhstan	1999	5	6	82	45	74	76[c]	49	55	99	99
Kenya	1998	32	10	136	61	64	89	13	50	23	80
Kyrgyz Republic	1997	13	8	96	49	82	81	44	54	96	100
Madagascar	1997	45	32	195	101	32	79	2	24	30	89
Malawi	2000	33	13	231	149	80	90	20	40	43	83
Mali	2001	39	17	248	148	40	77	4	18	21	86
Mauritania	2000–01	37	18	98	78	42	86	0[d]	17	15	93
Morocco	1992	17	2	112	39	62	95	18	48	5	78
Mozambique	1997	37	14	278	145	33	94	1	17	18	82
Namibia	1992	36	13	110	76	69	79	5	57	51	91
Nepal	2001	57	31	130	68	61	83	24	55	4	45
Nicaragua	2001	16	3	64	19	76	94	50	71	78	99
Niger	1998	52	37	282	184	23	66	1	18	4	63
Nigeria	1990	40	22	240	120	35	70	1	12	12	70
Pakistan	1990	54	26	125	74	28	75	1	23	5	55
Paraguay	1990	6	1	57	20	48	69	21	46	41	98
Peru	2000	15	1	93	18	81	92	37	58	21	99
Philippines	1998	..	..	80	29	68	92	20	29	21	92
Rwanda	2000	27	14	246	154	84	89	2	15	17	60
Senegal	1997	..	..	181	70	..	..	1	24	20	86
South Africa	1998	..	..	87	22	74	85	34	70	68	98
Tanzania	1999	32	22	160	135	63	89	6	32	29	83
Togo	1998	32	12	168	97	35	63	3	13	25	91
Turkey	1998	17	3	85	33	64	89	24	48	53	98
Uganda	2000–01	27	12	192	106	49	65	11	41	20	77
Uzbekistan	1996	25	13	70	50	96	93	46	52	92	100
Vietnam	1997	..	..	63	23	64	88	47	56	49	99
Yemen, Rep.	1997	56	30	163	73	16	73	1	24	7	50
Zambia	2001	33	20	192	92	81	88	11	53	20	91
Zimbabwe	1999	18	6	100	62	80	86	41	67	57	94

a. Based on births in the five years before the survey. b. Refers to children who were immunized before 12 months or, in some cases, at any time before the survey (12–23 months). c. The data contain large sampling errors because of the small number of cases. d. Less than 0.5.

About the data

The data in the table describe the health status and use of health services by individuals in different socioeconomic groups within countries. The data are from Demographic and Health Surveys conducted by Macro International with the support of the U.S. Agency for International Development. These large-scale household sample surveys, conducted periodically in developing countries, collect information on a large number of health, nutrition, and population measures as well as on respondents' social, demographic, and economic characteristics using a standard set of questionnaires. The data presented here draw on responses to individual and household questionnaires.

The table defines socioeconomic status in terms of a household's assets, including ownership of consumer items, features of the household's dwelling, and other characteristics related to wealth. Each household asset on which information was collected was assigned a weight generated through principal component analysis. The resulting scores were standardized in relation to a standard normal distribution with a mean of zero and a standard deviation of one. The standardized scores were then used to create break points defining wealth quintiles, expressed as quintiles of individuals in the population rather than quintiles of individuals at risk with respect to any one health indicator.

The choice of the asset index for defining socioeconomic status was based on pragmatic rather than conceptual considerations: Demographic and Health Surveys do not provide income or consumption data but do have detailed information on households' ownership of consumer goods and access to a variety of goods and services. Like income or consumption, the asset index defines disparities in primarily economic terms. It therefore excludes other possibilities of disparities among groups, such as those based on gender, education, ethnic background, or other facets of social exclusion. To that extent the index provides only a partial view of the multidimensional concepts of poverty, inequality, and inequity.

Creating one index that includes all asset indicators limits the types of analysis that can be performed. In particular, the use of a unified index does not permit a disaggregated analysis to examine which asset indicators have a more or less important association with health status or use of health services. In addition, some asset indicators may reflect household wealth better in some countries than in others—or reflect different degrees of wealth in different countries. Taking such information into account and creating country-specific asset indexes with country-specific choices of asset indicators might produce a more effective and accurate index for each country. The asset index used in the table does not have this flexibility.

The analysis has been carried out for 54 countries, with the results issued in country reports. The table shows the estimates for the poorest and richest quintiles only; the full set of estimates for more than 70 indicators is available in the country reports (see *Data sources*).

Definitions

• **Survey year** is the year in which the underlying data were collected. • **Prevalence of child malnutrition** is the percentage of children whose weight for age is more than two standard deviations below the median reference standard for their age as established by the World Health Organization, the U.S. Centers for Disease Control and Prevention, and the U.S. National Center for Health Statistics. The figures in the table are based on children under age three, four, or five years of age, depending on the country. • **Under-five mortality rate** is the probability that a newborn baby will die before reaching age five, if subject to current age-specific mortality rates. The probability is expressed as a rate per 1,000. Data in the table are based on births in the 10 years preceding the survey and may therefore differ from the estimates in table 2.19. • **Child immunization rate** is the percentage of children ages 12–23 months at the time of the survey who received a dose of measles vaccine by 12 months at any time before the interview date. These data may differ from those in table 2.15. • **Contraceptive prevalence** is the percentage of women who are practicing, or whose sexual partners are practicing, any modern method of contraception. It is usually measured for married women ages 15–49. • **Births attended by skilled health staff** are the percentage of deliveries attended by personnel trained to give the necessary supervision, care, and advice to women during pregnancy, labor, and the postpartum period; to conduct deliveries on their own; and to care for newborns. Skilled health staff include doctors, nurses, or trained midwives, but exclude trained or untrained traditional birth attendants. Data in the tables are based on births in the five years preceding the survey and may therefore differ from the estimates in table 2.16.

Data sources

The data are from an analysis of Demographic and Health Surveys by the World Bank and Macro International. Country reports are available at http://www.worldbank.org/poverty/health/home/index.htm.

	Survey year	Gini index	Percentage share of income or consumption						
			Lowest 10%	Lowest 20%	Second 20%	Third 20%	Fourth 20%	Highest 20%	Highest 10%
Afghanistan		..	..	..	..	..	..	..	..
Albania	2002[a, b]	28.2	3.8	9.1	13.5	17.3	22.8	37.4	22.4
Algeria	1995[a, b]	35.3	2.8	7.0	11.6	16.1	22.7	42.6	26.8
Angola		..	..	..	..	..	..	..	..
Argentina[e]	2001[c, d]	52.2	1.0	3.1	7.2	12.3	21.0	56.4	38.9
Armenia	1998[a, b]	37.9	2.6	6.7	11.3	15.4	21.6	45.1	29.7
Australia	1994[c, d]	35.2	2.0	5.9	12.0	17.2	23.6	41.3	25.4
Austria	1997[c, d]	30.0	3.1	8.1	13.2	17.3	22.9	38.5	23.5
Azerbaijan	2001[a, b]	36.5	3.1	7.4	11.5	15.3	21.2	44.5	29.5
Bangladesh	2000[a, b]	31.8	3.9	9.0	12.5	15.9	21.2	41.3	26.7
Belarus	2000[a, b]	30.4	3.5	8.4	13.0	17.0	22.5	39.1	24.1
Belgium	1996[c, d]	25.0	2.9	8.3	14.1	17.7	22.7	37.3	22.6
Benin		..	..	..	..	..	..	..	..
Bolivia	1999[a, b]	44.7	1.3	4.0	9.2	14.8	22.9	49.1	32.0
Bosnia and Herzegovina	2001[a, b]	26.2	3.9	9.5	14.2	17.9	22.6	35.8	21.4
Botswana	1993[a, b]	63.0	0.7	2.2	4.9	8.2	14.4	70.3	56.6
Brazil	2001[c, d]	59.3	0.7	2.4	5.9	10.4	18.1	63.2	46.9
Bulgaria	2001[c, d]	31.9	2.4	6.7	13.1	17.9	23.4	38.9	23.7
Burkina Faso	1998[a, b]	48.2	1.8	4.5	7.4	10.6	16.7	60.7	46.3
Burundi	1998[a, b]	33.3	1.7	5.1	10.3	15.1	21.5	48.0	32.8
Cambodia	1997[a, b]	40.4	2.9	6.9	10.7	14.7	20.1	47.6	33.8
Cameroon	2001[a, b]	44.6	2.3	5.6	9.3	13.7	20.4	50.9	35.4
Canada	1998[c, d]	33.1	2.5	7.0	12.7	17.0	22.9	40.4	25.0
Central African Republic	1993[a, b]	61.3	0.7	2.0	4.9	9.6	18.5	65.0	47.7
Chad		..	..	..	..	..	..	..	..
Chile	2000[c, d]	57.1	1.2	3.3	6.6	10.5	17.4	62.2	47.0
China	2001[a, b]	44.7	1.8	4.7	9.0	14.2	22.1	50.0	33.1
Hong Kong, China	1996[c, d]	43.4	2.0	5.3	9.4	13.9	20.7	50.7	34.9
Colombia	1999[c, d]	57.6	0.80	2.70	6.59	10.83	18.03	61.85	46.46
Congo, Dem. Rep.		..	..	..	..	..	..	..	..
Congo, Rep.		..	..	..	..	..	..	..	..
Costa Rica	2000[c, d]	46.5	1.4	4.2	8.9	13.7	21.7	51.5	34.8
Côte d'Ivoire	2002[a, b]	44.6	2.0	5.2	9.1	13.7	21.3	50.7	34.0
Croatia	2001[a, b]	29.0	3.4	8.3	12.8	16.8	22.6	39.6	24.5
Cuba		..	..	..	..	..	..	..	..
Czech Republic	1996[c, d]	25.4	4.3	10.3	14.5	17.7	21.7	35.9	22.4
Denmark	1997[c, d]	24.7	2.6	8.3	14.7	18.2	22.9	35.8	21.3
Dominican Republic	1998[c, d]	47.4	2.1	5.1	8.6	13.0	20.0	53.3	37.9
Ecuador	1998[a, b]	43.7	0.9	3.3	7.5	11.7	19.4	58.0	41.6
Egypt, Arab Rep.	1999–2000[a, b]	34.4	3.7	8.6	12.1	15.4	20.4	43.6	29.5
El Salvador	2000[c, d]	53.2	0.9	2.9	7.4	12.4	20.2	57.1	40.6
Eritrea		..	..	..	..	..	..	..	..
Estonia	2000[c, d]	37.2	1.9	6.1	12.1	15.9	22.0	44.0	28.5
Ethiopia	1999–2000[a, b]	30.0	3.9	9.1	13.2	16.8	21.5	39.4	25.5
Finland	2000[c, d]	26.9	4.0	9.6	14.1	17.5	22.1	36.7	22.6
France	1995[c, d]	32.7	2.8	7.2	12.6	17.2	22.8	40.2	25.1
Gabon		..	..	..	..	..	..	..	..
Gambia, The	1998[a, b]	47.5	1.8	4.8	8.7	12.8	20.3	53.4	37.0
Georgia	2001[a, b]	36.9	2.3	6.4	11.4	16.1	22.6	43.6	27.9
Germany	2000[c, d]	28.3	3.2	8.5	13.7	17.8	23.1	36.9	22.1
Ghana	1998–99[a, b]	40.8	2.1	5.6	10.1	14.9	22.9	46.6	30.0
Greece	1998[c, d]	35.4	2.9	7.1	11.4	15.8	22.0	43.6	28.5
Guatemala	2000[c, d]	59.9	0.9	2.6	5.9	9.8	17.6	64.1	48.3
Guinea	1994[a, b]	40.3	2.6	6.4	10.4	14.8	21.2	47.2	32.0
Guinea-Bissau	1993[a, b]	47.0	2.1	5.2	8.8	13.1	19.4	53.4	39.3
Haiti		..	..	..	..	..	..	..	..

	Survey year	Gini index	Percentage share of income or consumption						
			Lowest 10%	Lowest 20%	Second 20%	Third 20%	Fourth 20%	Highest 20%	Highest 10%
Honduras	1999[c, d]	55.0	0.9	2.7	6.7	11.8	19.9	58.9	42.2
Hungary	2002[a, b]	26.9	4.0	9.5	13.9	17.6	22.4	36.5	22.2
India	1999–00[a, b]	32.5	3.9	8.9	12.3	16.0	21.2	43.3	28.5
Indonesia	2002[a, b]	34.3	3.6	8.4	11.9	15.4	21.0	43.3	28.5
Iran, Islamic Rep.	1998[a, b]	43.0	2.0	5.1	9.4	14.1	21.5	49.9	33.7
Iraq	..	..	..	..	..	..	..	..	..
Ireland	1996[c, d]	35.9	2.8	7.1	11.8	15.8	22.0	43.3	27.6
Israel	1997[c, d]	35.5	2.4	6.9	11.4	16.3	22.9	44.3	28.2
Italy	2000[c, d]	36.0	2.3	6.5	12.0	16.8	22.8	42.0	26.8
Jamaica	2000[a, b]	37.9	2.7	6.7	10.7	15.0	21.7	46.0	30.3
Japan	1993[c, d]	24.9	4.8	10.6	14.2	17.6	22.0	35.7	21.7
Jordan	1997[a, b]	36.4	3.3	7.6	11.4	15.5	21.1	44.4	29.8
Kazakhstan	2003[a, b]	32.3	3.2	7.8	12.1	16.8	23.3	40.0	24.4
Kenya	1997[a, b]	42.5	2.5	6.0	9.8	14.3	20.8	49.1	33.9
Korea, Dem. Rep.	..	..	..	..	..	..	..	..	..
Korea, Rep.	1998[c, d]	31.6	2.9	7.9	13.6	18.0	23.1	37.5	22.5
Kuwait	..	..	..	..	..	..	..	..	..
Kyrgyz Republic	2002[a, b]	34.8	3.2	7.7	11.8	15.7	21.8	43.0	27.9
Lao PDR	1997[a, b]	37.0	3.2	7.6	11.4	15.3	20.8	45.0	30.6
Latvia	1998[c, d]	33.6	2.8	7.3	12.3	16.7	22.5	41.1	26.1
Lebanon	..	..	..	..	..	..	..	..	..
Lesotho	1995[a, b]	63.2	0.5	1.5	4.3	8.9	18.8	66.5	48.3
Liberia	..	..	..	..	..	..	..	..	..
Libya	..	..	..	..	..	..	..	..	..
Lithuania	2000[a, b]	31.9	3.2	7.9	12.7	16.9	22.6	40.0	24.9
Macedonia, FYR	1998[a, b]	28.2	3.3	8.4	14.0	17.7	23.1	36.7	22.1
Madagascar	2001[a, b]	47.5	1.9	4.9	8.5	12.7	20.4	53.5	36.6
Malawi	1997[a, b]	50.3	1.9	4.9	8.5	12.3	18.3	56.1	42.2
Malaysia	1997[c, d]	49.2	1.7	4.4	8.1	12.9	20.3	54.3	38.4
Mali	1994[a, b]	50.5	1.8	4.6	8.0	11.9	19.3	56.2	40.4
Mauritania	2000[a, b]	39.0	2.5	6.2	10.6	15.2	22.3	45.7	29.5
Mauritius	..	..	..	..	..	..	..	..	..
Mexico	2000[a, b]	54.6	1.0	3.1	7.2	11.7	19.0	59.1	43.1
Moldova	2002[a, b]	36.9	2.7	6.8	11.2	15.6	22.3	44.1	28.4
Mongolia	1998[a, b]	30.3	2.1	5.6	10.0	13.8	19.4	51.2	37.0
Morocco	1998–99[a, b]	39.5	2.6	6.5	10.6	14.8	21.3	46.6	30.9
Mozambique	1996–97[a, b]	39.6	2.5	6.5	10.8	15.1	21.1	46.5	31.7
Myanmar	..	..	..	..	..	..	..	..	..
Namibia	1993[c, d]	70.7	0.5	1.4	3.0	5.4	11.5	78.7	64.5
Nepal	1995–96[a, b]	36.7	3.2	7.6	11.5	15.1	21.0	44.8	29.8
Netherlands	1999[c, d]	30.9	2.5	7.6	13.2	17.2	23.3	38.7	22.9
New Zealand	1997[c, d]	36.2	2.2	6.4	11.4	15.8	22.6	43.8	27.8
Nicaragua	2001[a, b]	43.1	2.2	5.6	9.8	14.2	21.1	49.3	33.8
Niger	1995[a, b]	50.5	0.8	2.6	7.1	13.9	23.1	53.3	35.4
Nigeria	1996–97[a, b]	50.6	1.6	4.4	8.2	12.5	19.3	55.7	40.8
Norway	2000[c, d]	25.8	3.9	9.6	14.0	17.2	22.0	37.2	23.4
Oman	..	..	..	..	..	..	..	..	..
Pakistan	1998–99[a, b]	33.0	3.7	8.8	12.5	15.9	20.6	42.3	28.3
Panama	2000[c, d]	56.4	0.7	2.4	6.5	11.2	19.6	60.3	43.3
Papua New Guinea	1996[a, b]	50.9	1.7	4.5	7.9	11.9	19.2	56.5	40.5
Paraguay	2002[c, d]	57.8	0.6	2.2	6.3	11.3	18.8	61.3	45.4
Peru	2000[c, d]	49.8	0.7	2.9	8.3	14.1	21.5	53.2	37.2
Philippines	2000[a, b]	46.1	2.2	5.4	8.8	13.1	20.5	52.3	36.3
Poland	2002[a, b]	34.1	3.1	7.6	12.0	16.2	22.3	41.9	26.7
Portugal	1997[c, d]	38.5	2.0	5.8	11.0	15.5	21.9	45.9	29.8
Puerto Rico	..	..	..	..	..	..	..	..	..

2.7 Distribution of income or consumption

	Survey year	Gini index	Percentage share of income or consumption						
			Lowest 10%	Lowest 20%	Second 20%	Third 20%	Fourth 20%	Highest 20%	Highest 10%
Romania	2002[a, b]	30.3	3.2	7.9	12.3	16.5	22.3	41.0	26.1
Russian Federation	2002[a, b]	31.0	3.3	8.2	12.7	16.9	23.0	39.3	23.8
Rwanda	1983–85[a, b]	28.9	4.2	9.7	13.2	16.5	21.6	39.1	24.2
Saudi Arabia		..	..	..	..	..	..	..	..
Senegal	1995[a, b]	41.3	2.6	6.4	10.3	14.5	20.6	48.2	33.5
Serbia and Montenegro		..	..	..	..	..	..	..	..
Sierra Leone	1989[a, b]	62.9	0.5	1.1	2.0	9.8	23.7	63.4	43.6
Singapore	1998[c, d]	42.5	1.9	5.0	9.4	14.6	22.0	49.0	32.8
Slovak Republic	1996[c, d]	25.8	3.1	8.8	14.9	18.7	22.8	34.8	20.9
Slovenia	1998–99[c, d]	28.4	3.6	9.1	14.2	18.1	22.9	35.7	21.4
Somalia		..	..	..	..	..	..	..	..
South Africa	2000[a, b]	57.8	1.4	3.5	6.3	10.0	18.0	62.2	44.7
Spain	1990[c, d]	32.5	2.8	7.5	12.6	17.0	22.6	40.3	25.2
Sri Lanka	1999–2000[a, b]	33.2	3.4	8.3	12.5	16.0	21.0	42.2	27.8
Sudan		..	..	..	..	..	..	..	..
Swaziland	1994[c, d]	60.9	1.0	2.7	5.8	10.0	17.1	64.4	50.2
Sweden	2000[c, d]	25.0	3.6	9.1	14.0	17.6	22.7	36.6	22.2
Switzerland	1992[c, d]	33.1	2.6	6.9	12.7	17.3	22.9	40.3	25.2
Syrian Arab Republic		..	..	..	..	..	..	..	..
Tajikistan	2003[a, b]	32.6	3.3	7.9	12.3	16.5	22.4	40.8	25.6
Tanzania	1993[a, b]	38.2	2.8	6.8	11.0	15.1	21.6	45.5	30.1
Thailand	2000[a, b]	43.2	2.5	6.1	9.5	13.5	20.9	50.0	33.8
Togo		..	..	..	..	..	..	..	..
Trinidad and Tobago	1992[c, d]	40.3	2.1	5.5	10.3	15.5	22.7	45.9	29.9
Tunisia	2000[a, b]	39.8	2.3	6.0	10.3	14.8	21.7	47.3	31.5
Turkey	2000[a, b]	40.0	2.3	6.1	10.6	14.9	21.8	46.7	30.7
Turkmenistan	1998[a, b]	40.8	2.6	6.1	10.2	14.7	21.5	47.5	31.7
Uganda	1999[a, b]	43.0	2.3	5.9	10.0	14.0	20.3	49.7	34.9
Ukraine	1999[a, b]	29.0	3.7	8.8	13.3	17.4	22.7	37.8	23.2
United Arab Emirates		..	..	..	..	..	..	..	..
United Kingdom	1999[c, d]	36.0	2.1	6.1	11.4	16.0	22.5	44.0	28.5
United States	2000[c, d]	40.8	1.9	5.4	10.7	15.7	22.4	45.8	29.9
Uruguay[e]	2000[c, d]	44.6	1.8	4.8	9.3	14.2	21.6	50.1	33.5
Uzbekistan	2000[a, b]	26.8	3.6	9.2	14.1	17.9	22.6	36.3	22.0
Venezuela, RB	1998[c, d]	49.1	0.6	3.0	8.4	13.7	21.6	53.4	36.3
Vietnam	2002[a, b]	37.0	3.2	7.5	11.2	14.8	21.1	45.4	29.9
West Bank and Gaza		..	..	..	..	..	..	..	..
Yemen, Rep.	1998[a, b]	33.4	3.0	7.4	12.2	16.7	22.5	41.2	25.9
Zambia	1998[a, b]	52.6	1.0	3.3	7.6	12.5	20.0	56.6	41.0
Zimbabwe	1995[a, b]	56.8	1.8	4.6	8.1	12.2	19.3	55.7	40.3

a. Refers to expenditure shares by percentiles of population. b. Ranked by per capita expenditure. c. Refers to income shares by percentiles of population. d. Ranked by per capita income. e. Urban data.

About the data

Inequality in the distribution of income is reflected in the percentage shares of income or consumption accruing to segments of the population ranked by income or consumption levels. The segments ranked lowest by personal income receive the smallest shares of total income. The Gini index provides a convenient summary measure of the degree of inequality.

Data on personal or household income or consumption come from nationally representative household surveys. The data in the table refer to different years between 1983–85 and 2003. Footnotes to the survey year indicate whether the rankings are based on per capita income or consumption. Each distribution is based on percentiles of population—rather than of households—with households ranked by income or expenditure per person.

Where the original data from the household survey were available, they have been used to directly calculate the income (or consumption) shares by quintile. Otherwise shares have been estimated from the best available grouped data.

The distribution data have been adjusted for household size, providing a more consistent measure of per capita income or consumption. No adjustment has been made for spatial differences in cost of living within countries, because the data needed for such calculations are generally unavailable. For further details on the estimation method for low- and middle-income economies, see Ravallion and Chen (1996).

Because the underlying household surveys differ in method and type of data collected, the distribution data are not strictly comparable across countries. These problems are diminishing as survey methods improve and become more standardized, but achieving strict comparability is still impossible (see *About the data* for table 2.5).

Two sources of noncomparability should be noted in particular. First, the surveys can differ in many respects, including whether they use income or consumption expenditure as the living standard indicator. The distribution of income is typically more unequal than the distribution of consumption. In addition, the definitions of income used usually differ among surveys. Consumption is usually a much better welfare indicator, particularly in developing countries. Second, households differ in size (number of members) and in the extent of income sharing among members. And individuals differ in age and consumption needs. Differences among countries in these respects may bias comparisons of distribution.

World Bank staff have made an effort to ensure that the data are as comparable as possible. Wherever possible, consumption has been used rather than income. Income distribution and Gini indexes for high-income countries are calculated directly from the Luxembourg Income Study database, using an estimation method consistent with that applied for developing countries.

Definitions

• **Survey year** is the year in which the underlying data were collected. • **Gini index** measures the extent to which the distribution of income (or, in some cases, consumption expenditure) among individuals or households within an economy deviates from a perfectly equal distribution. A Lorenz curve plots the cumulative percentages of total income received against the cumulative number of recipients, starting with the poorest individual or household. The Gini index measures the area between the Lorenz curve and a hypothetical line of absolute equality, expressed as a percentage of the maximum area under the line. Thus a Gini index of 0 represents perfect equality, while an index of 100 implies perfect inequality. • **Percentage share of income or consumption** is the share that accrues to subgroups of population indicated by deciles or quintiles. Percentage shares by quintile may not sum to 100 because of rounding.

Data sources

The data on distribution are compiled by the World Bank's Development Research Group using primary household survey data obtained from government statistical agencies and World Bank country departments. The data for high-income economies are from the Luxembourg Income Study database.

2.8 | Assessing vulnerability

	Urban informal sector employment		Youth unemployment		Children in the labor force		Female-headed households		Pension contributors			Private health expenditure
	% of urban employment		Male % of male labor force ages 15–24	Female % of female labor force ages 15–24	% ages 10–14					% of labor force	% of working-age population	% of total
	Male 1995–2002[a]	Female 1995–2002[a]	1995–2003[a]	1995–2003[a]	1990	2003	Year	% of total	Year			2002
Afghanistan	..	..	..	..	26	24	..		..	..	..	60.8
Albania	..	..	..	..	2	0	..		1995	32.0	31.0	30.7
Algeria	..	..	..	..	3	0	..		1997	31.0	23.0	26.0
Angola	..	..	..	..	28	26	..		..	..	..	58.1
Argentina	..	..	31	33	7	2	..		1995	53.0	39.0	49.8
Armenia	..	..	..	..	0	0	2000	29	2002	64.4	48.3	75.9
Australia	..	..	13	12	0	0	..		..	..	..	32.1
Austria	..	..	5	6	0	0	..		1993	95.8	76.6	30.1
Azerbaijan	..	..	..	..	0	0	..		1996	52.0	46.0	77.9
Bangladesh	..	..	11	10	32	27	1999–2000	9	1993	3.5	2.6	74.8
Belarus	..	..	..	..	0	0	..		1992	97.0	94.0	26.1
Belgium	..	..	16	15	0	0	..		1995	86.2	65.9	28.8
Benin	50	41	..	..	29	26	2001	21	1996	4.8	..	55.6
Bolivia	..	..	7	10	17	10	1998	19	1999	14.8	13.3	40.2
Bosnia and Herzegovina	..	..	..	..	0	0	..		..	..	..	50.2
Botswana	..	..	38	47	19	13	..		..	..	..	38.1
Brazil	27	27	15	22	18	13	1996	20	1996	36.0	31.0	54.1
Bulgaria	..	..	42	35	0	0	..		1994	64.0	63.0	39.1
Burkina Faso	..	..	..	..	59	39	1998–99	7	1993	3.1	3.0	54.1
Burundi	..	..	..	..	49	48	..		1993	3.3	3.0	78.5
Cambodia	..	..	..	..	26	23	2000	25	..	..	..	82.9
Cameroon	..	..	..	..	28	22	1998	22	1993	13.7	11.5	73.8
Canada	..	..	15	12	0	0	..		1992	91.9	80.2	30.1
Central African Republic	..	..	..	..	34	27	1994–95	21	..	..	..	58.4
Chad	..	..	..	..	40	36	1996–97	22	1990	1.1	1.0	58.1
Chile	..	..	17	22	0	0	..		2001	54.8	34.9	54.9
China	..	..	..	..	15	6	..		1994	17.6	17.4	66.3
Hong Kong, China	..	..	14	9	0	0	..		..	..	..	..
Colombia	..	..	32	41	7	6	2000	28	1999	35.0	29.3	17.1
Congo, Dem. Rep.	..	..	..	..	31	28	..		..	..	..	71.3
Congo, Rep.	..	..	..	..	27	25	..		1992	5.8	5.6	29.7
Costa Rica	..	..	12	16	7	3	..		1998	50.6	38.5	34.6
Côte d'Ivoire	..	..	..	..	22	18	1998–99	14	1997	9.3	9.1	77.6
Croatia	..	..	35	40	0	0	..		2001	67.0	57.0	18.6
Cuba	..	..	..	..	0	0	..		..	..	..	13.5
Czech Republic	..	..	15	17	0	0	..		1995	85.0	67.2	8.6
Denmark	..	..	9	5	0	0	..		1993	89.6	88.0	17.1
Dominican Republic	..	..	16	34	19	11	1999	33	2001	26.8	17.7	63.6
Ecuador	..	..	11	20	7	4	..		2002	23.2	14.9	64.0
Egypt, Arab Rep.	..	..	14	37	13	8	2000	12	1994	50.0	34.2	63.4
El Salvador	..	..	14	10	17	10	..		1996	26.2	25.0	55.3
Eritrea	..	..	..	..	41	38	1995	31	..	..	..	36.3
Estonia	..	..	19	26	0	0	..		1995	76.0	67.0	23.7
Ethiopia	39	65	..	..	43	40	2000	24	..	..	..	55.1
Finland	..	..	21	20	0	0	..		1993	90.3	83.6	24.3
France	..	..	18	23	0	0	..		1993	88.4	74.6	24.0
Gabon	..	..	..	..	23	11	2000	26	1995	15.0	14.0	58.7
Gambia, The	..	..	..	..	40	32	..		..	..	..	55.4
Georgia	21	7	20	20	0	0	..		2000	41.7	40.2	72.9
Germany	..	..	11	8	0	0	..		1995	94.2	82.3	21.5
Ghana	..	..	..	..	15	11	1998	37	1993	7.2	9.0	59.0
Greece	..	..	19	34	0	0	..		1996	88.0	73.0	47.1
Guatemala	..	..	..	..	18	13	1998–99	20	1999	22.8	19.3	52.5
Guinea	..	..	..	..	37	29	1999	13	1993	1.5	1.8	84.5
Guinea-Bissau	..	..	..	..	40	36	..		..	..	..	51.8
Haiti	..	..	..	..	28	21	2000	43	..	..	..	60.6

Assessing vulnerability | 2.8

	Urban informal sector employment		Youth unemployment		Children in the labor force		Female-headed households		Pension contributors			Private health expenditure
	% of urban employment		Male % of male labor force ages 15–24	Female % of female labor force ages 15–24	% ages 10–14					% of labor force	% of working-age population	% of total
	Male 1995–2002a	Female 1995–2002a	1995–2003a	1995–2003a	1990	2003	Year	% of total	Year			2002
Honduras	..	..	7	8	10	5		..	1999	20.6	17.7	48.8
Hungary	..	..	13	12	0	0		..	1996	77.0	65.0	29.8
India	54	41	..	..	17	11	1998–99	10	1992	10.6	7.9	78.7
Indonesia	..	..	12	15	11	7	1997	12	1995	8.0	7.0	64.0
Iran, Islamic Rep.	..	..	..	..	7	2		..	2000	30.0	15.9	52.2
Iraq	..	..	..	..	4	2		..	..	..	..	83.1
Ireland	..	..	9	7	0	0		..	1992	79.3	64.7	24.8
Israel	..	..	19	18	0	0		..	1992	82.0	63.0	34.3
Italy	..	..	23	31	0	0		..	1997	87.0	68.0	24.4
Jamaica	..	..	24	46	0	0		..	1999	44.4	45.8	42.6
Japan	..	..	11	9	0	0		..	1994	97.5	92.3	18.3
Jordan	..	..	..	..	1	0	1997	10	1995	40.0	25.0	53.9
Kazakhstan	..	..	..	..	0	0	1999	33	2001	38.0	28.3	46.8
Kenya	..	..	..	..	43	38	1998	32	1995	18.0	24.0	56.0
Korea, Dem. Rep.	..	..	..	..	0	0		..	..	..	..	23.4
Korea, Rep.	..	..	10	7	0	0		..	1996	58.0	43.0	47.1
Kuwait	..	..	..	..	0	0		..	..	..	..	24.8
Kyrgyz Republic	33	25	..	..	0	0	1997	26	1997	44.0	42.0	48.8
Lao PDR	..	..	..	..	29	24		..	..	..	..	49.1
Latvia	..	..	20	21	0	0		..	1995	60.5	52.3	35.9
Lebanon	..	..	..	..	0	0		..	..	..	..	69.9
Lesotho	..	..	38	59	23	20		..	..	..	..	15.1
Liberia	..	..	..	..	22	13		..	..	..	..	32.0
Libya	..	..	..	..	0	0		..	..	..	..	52.8
Lithuania	50	27	31	26	0	0		..	2002	77.0	60.0	31.4
Macedonia, FYR	..	..	..	..	0	0		..	1995	49.0	47.0	15.3
Madagascar	..	..	..	..	38	33	1997	22	1993	5.4	4.8	45.0
Malawi	..	..	..	..	39	29	2000	27		..	..	58.9
Malaysia	..	..	..	..	4	2		..	1993	48.7	37.8	46.2
Mali	..	..	..	..	58	49	2001	11	1990	2.5	2.0	49.2
Mauritania	..	..	..	..	26	21	2000–01	29	1995	5.0	4.0	25.8
Mauritius	..	..	..	..	4	1		..	1995	60.0	57.0	23.1
Mexico	18	22	5	6	9	6		..	1997	30.0	31.0	55.1
Moldova	..	..	..	..	0	0		..	..	..	..	41.8
Mongolia	..	..	..	..	2	1		..	2002	61.4	49.1	29.6
Morocco	..	..	16	15	11	0	1992	16	2000	17.3	11.3	67.2
Mozambique	..	..	..	..	35	32	1997	27	1995	2.0	2.1	29.0
Myanmar	..	..	..	..	26	22		..	..	..	..	81.5
Namibia	..	..	33	41	26	15	1992	31	..	..	..	29.9
Nepal	60	76	..	..	48	40	2001	16	..	..	..	72.8
Netherlands	..	..	6	6	0	0		..	1993	91.7	75.4	34.4
New Zealand	..	..	12	11	0	0		..	..	..	..	22.1
Nicaragua	..	..	20	20	16	9	1997–98	31	1999	14.3	13.3	50.9
Niger	..	..	..	..	47	43	1998	13	1992	1.3	1.5	49.2
Nigeria	..	..	..	..	28	23	1999	17	1993	1.3	1.3	74.4
Norway	..	..	12	11	0	0		..	1993	94.0	85.8	16.5
Oman	..	..	..	..	1	0		..	..	..	..	18.4
Pakistan	64	61	11	29	20	14	1991	7	1993	3.5	2.1	65.1
Panama	..	..	25	37	5	2		..	1998	51.6	40.7	28.3
Papua New Guinea	..	..	..	..	22	16		..	..	..	..	11.4
Paraguay	..	..	12	17	10	5	1990	17	2001	18.0	12.0	61.9
Peru	..	..	13	14	3	2	2000	19	2001	31.0	19.0	50.1
Philippines	16	19	17	23	11	4	1998	14	1996	28.3	13.6	61.0
Poland	..	..	44	44	0	0		..	1996	68.0	64.0	27.6
Portugal	..	..	10	14	2	1		..	1996	84.3	80.0	29.3
Puerto Rico	..	..	23	16	0	0		..	..	..	..	..

| | Urban informal sector employment | | Youth unemployment | | Children in the labor force | | Female-headed households | | Pension contributors | | | Private health expenditure |
| | % of urban employment | | Male % of male labor force ages 15–24 | Female % of female labor force ages 15–24 | % ages 10–14 | | | | | % of labor force | % of working-age population | % of total |
	Male 1995–2002[a]	Female 1995–2002[a]	1995–2003[a]	1995–2003[a]	1990	2003	Year	% of total	Year			2002
Romania	..	..	18	17	0	0		..	1994	55.0	48.0	34.1
Russian Federation	10	9	24	26	0	0		..		..	..	44.2
Rwanda	..	..	..	..	42	41	2000	36	1993	9.3	13.3	42.8
Saudi Arabia	..	..	..	..	0	0		..		..	..	22.9
Senegal	..	..	..	..	35	25	1997	18	1998	4.3	4.7	54.8
Serbia and Montenegro	..	..	..	..	0	0		..		..	..	37.2
Sierra Leone	..	..	..	..	17	13		..		..	..	39.7
Singapore	..	..	4	6	0	0		..	1995	73.0	56.0	69.1
Slovak Republic	..	..	39	36	0	0		..	1996	73.0	72.0	10.6
Slovenia	..	..	15	18	0	0		..	1995	86.0	68.7	25.1
Somalia	..	..	..	..	35	30		..		..	..	55.4
South Africa	16	28	42	47	0	0	1998	42		..	..	59.4
Spain	..	..	18	27	0	0		..	1994	85.3	61.4	28.7
Sri Lanka	..	..	20	31	3	1		..	1992	28.8	20.8	51.3
Sudan	..	..	..	..	31	26		..	1995	12.1	12.0	79.3
Swaziland	..	..	42	48	15	11		..		..	..	40.5
Sweden	..	..	14	12	0	0		..	1994	91.1	88.9	14.7
Switzerland	..	..	7	4	0	0		..	1994	98.1	96.8	42.1
Syrian Arab Republic	..	..	..	..	9	2		..		..	..	54.2
Tajikistan	..	..	..	..	0	0		..		..	..	72.3
Tanzania	60	85	..	..	42	35	1999	23	1996	2.0	2.0	45.2
Thailand	..	..	7	6	20	10	1999	..	1999	18.0	17.0	30.3
Togo	..	..	..	..	30	26	1998	24	1997	15.9	15.0	26.5
Trinidad and Tobago	..	..	22	31	0	0		..		..	..	62.7
Tunisia	..	..	..	..	0	0		..	2000	40.0	23.0	50.1
Turkey	10	6	21	18	16	6	1998	10	1997	37.1	27.4	34.2
Turkmenistan	..	..	..	..	0	0	2000	27		..	..	29.3
Uganda	..	..	..	..	47	43	2000–01	28	1994	8.2	..	72.1
Ukraine	5	5	23	25	0	0		..	1995	69.8	66.1	28.9
United Arab Emirates	..	..	6	6	0	0		..		..	..	26.6
United Kingdom	..	..	13	9	0	0		..	1994	89.7	84.5	16.6
United States	..	..	13	11	0	0		..	1993	94.0	91.9	55.1
Uruguay	..	..	29	42	3	1		..	1995	82.0	78.0	71.0
Uzbekistan	..	..	..	..	0	0	1996	22		..	..	54.5
Venezuela, RB	..	..	20	28	2	0		..	1999	23.6	18.2	53.1
Vietnam	..	..	..	..	13	4	1997	25	1998	8.4	10.0	70.8
West Bank and Gaza	..	..	..	..	1	0		..		..	..	..
Yemen, Rep.	..	..	..	..	22	18	1997	9		..	..	72.8
Zambia	..	..	..	..	17	15	2001–02	23	1994	10.2	7.9	47.1
Zimbabwe	..	..	17	11	32	26	1999	33	1995	12.0	10.0	48.4
World	.. w	.. w			15 w	10 w						**40.0 w**
Low income	..	..			23	18						72.2
Middle income	..	..			11	5						50.6
Lower middle income	..	..			12	5						54.6
Upper middle income	17	22			5	3						42.4
Low & middle income	..	..			17	12						53.8
East Asia & Pacific	..	..			15	6						62.2
Europe & Central Asia	22	24			3	1						34.4
Latin America & Carib.	13	19			11	8						52.2
Middle East & N. Africa	..	..			8	4						42.9
South Asia	..	..			19	14						76.0
Sub-Saharan Africa	..	..			32	28						59.5
High income	14	13			0	0						36.7
Europe EMU	16	20			0	0						25.4

a. Data are for the most recent year available.

About the data

As traditionally defined and measured, poverty is a static concept, and vulnerability a dynamic one. Vulnerability reflects a household's resilience in the face of shocks and the likelihood that a shock will lead to a decline in well-being. Thus it depends primarily on the household's asset endowment and insurance mechanisms. Because poor people have fewer assets and less diversified sources of income than the better-off, fluctuations in income affect them more.

Poor households face many risks, and vulnerability is thus multidimensional. The indicators in the table focus on individual risks—informal sector employment, youth unemployment, child labor, female-headed household, income insecurity in old age, private health expenditure—and the extent to which publicly provided services may be capable of mitigating some of these risks. Poor people face labor market risks, often having to take up precarious, low-quality jobs in the informal sector and to increase their household's labor market participation through their children. Income security is a prime concern for the elderly. And affordable access to health care is a primary concern for all poor people, for whom illness and injury have both direct and opportunity costs.

For informal sector employment, the data are from labor force and special informal sector surveys, various household surveys, surveys of household industries or economic activities, surveys of small and micro enterprises, and official estimates. The international comparability of the data is affected by differences among countries in definitions and coverage and in the treatment of domestic workers and those who have a secondary job in the informal sector. The data in the table are based on national definitions of urban areas established by countries. For details on these definitions, see the notes in *Data sources*.

Youth unemployment is an important policy issue for many economies. Experiencing unemployment may permanently impair a young person's productive potential and future employment opportunities. In this table unemployment among youth ages 15–24 is presented, but the lower age limit for young people in a country could be determined by the minimum age for leaving school, so age groups could differ across countries. Also since this age group is likely to include school leavers, the level of youth unemployment varies significantly over the year as a result of different school opening and closing dates. The youth unemployment rate shares similar limitations on comparability to the general unemployment rate. For further information, see *About the data* for table 2.4.

Reliable estimates of child labor are difficult to obtain. In many countries child labor is officially presumed not to exist and so is not included in surveys or in official data. Underreporting also occurs because data exclude children engaged in agricultural or household activities with their families. Available statistics suggest that more boys than girls work. But the number of girls working is often underestimated because surveys exclude girls working as unregistered domestic help or doing full-time household work to enable their parents to work outside the home.

The data on female-headed household are from recent Demographic and Health Surveys. The definition and concept of the female-headed household differ greatly across economies, making cross-country comparison difficult. In some cases it is assumed that a woman cannot be the head of any household in which an adult male is present, because of sex-biased stereotype. Users need to be cautious when interpreting the data.

The data on pension contributors come from national sources, the International Labour Organization, and International Monetary Fund country reports. Coverage by pension schemes may be broad or even universal where eligibility is determined by citizenship, residency, or income status. In contribution-related schemes, however, eligibility is usually restricted to individuals who have made contributions for a minimum number of years. Definitional issues—relating to the labor force, for example—may arise in comparing coverage by contribution-related schemes over time and across countries (for country-specific information, see Palacios and Pallares-Miralles 2000). Coverage of the share of the labor force covered by a pension scheme may be overstated in countries that do not attempt to count informal sector workers as part of the labor force.

The expenditure on health in a country can be divided into two main categories by source of funding: public and private. Public health expenditure consists of spending by central and local governments, including social health insurance funds. Private health expenditure includes private insurance, direct out-of-pocket payments by households, spending by nonprofit institutions serving households, and direct payments by private corporations. In countries where the share of out-of-pocket spending is large, poor households may be particularly vulnerable to the impoverishing effects of health care needs.

Definitions

• **Urban informal sector employment** is broadly characterized as employment in urban areas in units that produce goods or services on a small scale with the primary objective of generating employment and income for those concerned. These units typically operate at a low level of organization, with little or no division between labor and capital as factors of production. Labor relations are based on casual employment, kinship, or social relationships rather than contractual arrangements. • **Youth unemployment** refers to the share of the labor force ages 15–24 without work but available for and seeking employment. Definitions of labor force and unemployment may differ by country (see *About the data*). • **Children in the labor force** refer to the share of children ages 10–14 active in the labor force. • **Female-headed households** refer to the percentage of households with a female head. • **Pension contributors** refer to the share of the labor force or working-age population (here defined as ages 15–64) covered by a pension scheme. • **Private health expenditure** includes direct (out-of-pocket) spending by households, private insurance, spending by nonprofit institutions serving households (other than social insurance), and direct service payments by private corporations.

Data sources

The data on urban informal sector employment and youth unemployment are from the International Labour Organization (ILO) database *Key Indicators of the Labour Market*, third edition. The child labor force participation rates are from the ILO database *Estimates and Projections of the Economically Active Population, 1950–2010, Fourth edition*. The data on female-headed household are from Demographic and Health Surveys by Macro International. The data on pension contributors are drawn from Robert Palacios and Montserrat Pallares-Miralles's "International Patterns of Pension Provision" (2000), and updates. For further updates, notes, and sources, go to "Knowledge and information" on the World Bank's Web site on pensions (http://www.worldbank.org/pensions). The data on private health expenditure for developing countries are largely from the World Health Organization's *World Health Report 2004* and updates, from household surveys, and from World Bank poverty assessments and sector studies. The data on private health expenditure for member countries of the Organisation for Economic Co-operation and Development (OECD) are from the OECD.

	Public expenditure on pensions				Public expenditure on health	Public expenditure on education	
	Year	% of GDP	Year	Average pension % of per capita income	% of GDP 2002	% of GDP 2002/03	Per student % of GDP per capita 2002/03
Afghanistan		..		..	3.1	..	..
Albania	1995	5.1	1995	36.4	2.4	..	..
Algeria	1997	2.1	1991	75.0	3.2	..	..
Angola		..		..	2.1	2.8	..
Argentina	1994	6.2		..	4.5	4.6	14.5
Armenia	2002	2.5	1996	18.7	1.3	3.2	14.5
Australia	1997	5.9	1989	37.3	6.5	4.9	17.4
Austria	1995	14.9	1993	69.3	5.4	5.8	30.4
Azerbaijan	1996	2.5	1996	51.4	0.8	3.2	10.9
Bangladesh	1992	0.0			0.8	2.4	11.6
Belarus	1997	7.7	1995	31.2	4.7	6.0	..
Belgium	1997	12.9			6.5	..	..
Benin	1993	0.4	1993	189.7	2.1	3.3	..
Bolivia	2000	4.5			4.2	6.3	17.7
Bosnia and Herzegovina		..		..	4.6	..	..
Botswana		..		..	3.7	2.2	7.3
Brazil	1997	9.8		..	3.6	4.3	13.8
Bulgaria	1996	7.3	1995	39.3	4.4	3.5	18.6
Burkina Faso	1992	0.3	1992	207.3	2.0	..	..
Burundi	1991	0.2	1991	57.4	0.6	3.9	25.1
Cambodia		..		..	2.1	1.8	..
Cameroon	1993	0.4			1.2	3.8	..
Canada	1997	5.4	1994	54.3	6.7	5.2	..
Central African Republic	1990	0.3			1.6	..	..
Chad	1997	0.1			2.7	..	..
Chile	2001	2.9	1993	56.1	2.6	4.2	16.0
China	1996	2.7		..	2.0	..	..
Hong Kong, China		..		..	..	4.1	22.9
Colombia	1994	1.1	1989	72.2	6.7	5.2	18.1
Congo, Dem. Rep.		..		..	1.1	..	..
Congo, Rep.	1992	0.9		..	1.5	3.2	14.5
Costa Rica	1997	4.2	1993	76.1	6.1	5.1	21.2
Côte d'Ivoire	1997	0.3			1.4	4.6	..
Croatia	2001	13.2			5.9	4.5	24.8
Cuba	1992	12.6		..	6.5	9.0	41.4
Czech Republic	1999	9.8	1996	37.0	6.4	4.2	19.6
Denmark	1997	8.8	1994	46.7	7.3	8.5	38.3
Dominican Republic	2000	0.8	2000	42.0	2.2	2.3	..
Ecuador	2002	1.4	2002	55.3	1.7	1.0	..
Egypt, Arab Rep.	1994	2.5	1994	45.0	1.8	..	..
El Salvador	1997	1.3		..	3.6	2.9	9.9
Eritrea	2001	0.3		..	3.2	4.1	25.7
Estonia	2002	6.7	1995	56.7	3.9	5.5	22.8
Ethiopia	1993	0.9		..	2.6	4.6	..
Finland	1997	12.1	1994	57.4	5.5	6.2	26.2
France	1997	13.4		..	7.4	5.7	25.2
Gabon		..		..	1.8	3.9	..
Gambia, The		..		..	3.3	2.8	..
Georgia	2000	2.7	1996	12.6	1.0	2.2	..
Germany	1997	12.1	1995	62.8	8.6	4.6	23.4
Ghana	1996	1.1		..	2.3	..	..
Greece	1993	11.9	1990	85.6	5.0	3.9	19.6
Guatemala	1995	0.7	1995	27.6	2.3	..	..
Guinea		..		..	0.9	1.8	..
Guinea-Bissau		..		..	3.0	..	..
Haiti		..		..	3.0	..	..

Enhancing security | 2.9

	Public expenditure on pensions				Public expenditure on health	Public expenditure on education	
	Year	% of GDP	Year	Average pension % of per capita income	% of GDP **2002**	% of GDP **2002/03**	Per student % of GDP per capita **2002/03**
Honduras	1994	0.6		..	3.2	..	..
Hungary	1996	9.7	1996	33.6	5.5	5.1	22.1
India		..		..	1.3	4.1	20.9
Indonesia		..		..	1.2	1.3	6.0
Iran, Islamic Rep.	1994	1.5		..	2.9	4.9	13.9
Iraq		..		..	0.3	..	..
Ireland	1997	4.6	1993	77.9	5.5	4.3	16.9
Israel	1996	5.9	1992	48.1	6.0	7.3	22.8
Italy	1997	17.6		..	6.4	5.0	27.9
Jamaica	1996	..	1989	25.9	3.4	6.1	22.2
Japan	1997	6.9	1989	33.9	6.5	3.6	20.4
Jordan	1995	4.2	1995	144.0	4.3	..	..
Kazakhstan	2001	3.8	2001	23.0	1.9	3.0	10.9
Kenya	1993	0.5		..	2.2	7.0	..
Korea, Dem. Rep.		..		..	3.5	..	..
Korea, Rep.	1997	1.3		..	2.6	4.3	13.5
Kuwait	1990	3.5		..	2.9	..	..
Kyrgyz Republic	1997	6.4	2001	45.0	2.2	3.1	9.4
Lao PDR		..		..	1.5	2.8	11.0
Latvia	1995	10.2	1994	47.6	3.3	5.5	22.4
Lebanon		..		..	3.5	2.7	..
Lesotho		..		..	5.3	10.4	35.6
Liberia		..		..	1.4	..	..
Libya		..		..	1.6	..	..
Lithuania	2002	7.1	1995	21.3	4.3	5.9	..
Macedonia, FYR	1998	8.7	1996	91.6	5.8	..	..
Madagascar	1990	0.2		..	1.2	2.9	..
Malawi		..		..	4.0	6.0	..
Malaysia	1999	6.5		..	2.0	7.9	30.4
Mali	1991	0.4		..	2.3	..	..
Mauritania	1992	0.2		..	2.9	..	..
Mauritius	1999	4.4		..	2.2	4.7	13.1
Mexico	2000	0.3[a]		..	2.7	5.2	17.2
Moldova	1996	7.5		..	4.1	4.9	23.1
Mongolia	2002	5.8		..	4.6	9.0	29.0
Morocco	1994	1.8	1994	118.0	1.5	6.5	31.4
Mozambique	1996	0.0		..	4.1	..	..
Myanmar		..		..	0.4	..	..
Namibia		..		..	4.7	7.2	24.8
Nepal		..		..	1.4	3.4	12.6
Netherlands	1997	11.1	1989	48.5	5.8	5.0	23.1
New Zealand	1997	6.5		..	6.6	6.7	23.6
Nicaragua	1996	2.5		..	3.9	3.1	11.7
Niger	1992	0.1		..	2.0	2.3	26.3
Nigeria	1991	0.1	1991	40.5	1.2	..	..
Norway	1997	8.2	1994	49.9	8.0	7.0	26.4
Oman		..		..	2.8	4.6	17.5
Pakistan	1993	0.9		..	1.1	1.8	..
Panama	1996	4.3		..	6.4	4.5	15.5
Papua New Guinea		..		..	3.8	2.3	..
Paraguay	2000	0.8[b]		..	3.2	4.8	15.9
Peru	2000	2.6		..	2.2	2.9	9.3
Philippines	1993	1.0		..	1.1	3.2	11.3
Poland	1997	15.5	1995	61.2	4.4	5.6	18.5
Portugal	1997	10.0	1989	44.6	6.6	5.9	27.5
Puerto Rico		..		..	..	..	..

	Public expenditure on pensions				Public expenditure on health	Public expenditure on education	
	Year	% of GDP	Year	Average pension % of per capita income	% of GDP 2002	% of GDP 2002/03	Per student % of GDP per capita 2002/03
Romania	1996	5.1	1994	34.1	4.2	*3.3*	..
Russian Federation	1996	5.7	1995	18.3	3.5	*3.1*	..
Rwanda		..		..	3.1	*2.8*	*12.8*
Saudi Arabia		..		..	3.3	..	..
Senegal	1998	1.5	1997	85.0[b]	2.3	*3.2*	..
Serbia and Montenegro		..		..	5.1	*3.3*	..
Sierra Leone		..		..	1.7	*3.7*	*22.3*
Singapore	1996	1.4		..	1.3	..	..
Slovak Republic	1994	9.1	1994	44.5	5.3	*4.0*	*17.1*
Slovenia	1996	13.6	1996	49.3	6.2	..	..
Somalia		..		..	*1.2*	..	..
South Africa		..		..	3.5	*5.3*	*17.5*
Spain	1997	10.9	1995	54.1	5.4	*4.4*	*22.0*
Sri Lanka	1996	2.4		..	1.8	..	..
Sudan		..		..	1.0	..	..
Swaziland		..		..	3.6	*7.1*	*18.6*
Sweden	1997	11.1	1994	78.0	7.8	*7.3*	*28.7*
Switzerland	1997	13.4	1993	44.4	6.5	*5.5*	*29.5*
Syrian Arab Republic	1991	0.5		..	2.3	..	..
Tajikistan	1996	3.0		..	0.9	*2.8*	*8.7*
Tanzania		..		..	2.7	..	..
Thailand		..		..	3.1	*5.2*	*17.1*
Togo	1997	0.6	1993	178.8	5.1	*2.6*	..
Trinidad and Tobago	1996	0.6		..	1.4	*4.3*	*19.0*
Tunisia	2000	4.2	1991	89.5	2.9	*6.8*	*23.9*
Turkey	1997	4.5	1993	56.0	4.3	*3.7*	*16.4*
Turkmenistan	1996	2.3		..	3.0	..	..
Uganda	1997	0.8		..	2.1	..	..
Ukraine	1996	8.6	1995	30.9	3.3	*5.4*	*21.7*
United Arab Emirates		..		..	2.3	*1.6*	*7.1*
United Kingdom	1997	10.3		..	6.4	*4.7*	*16.8*
United States	1997	7.5	1989	33.0	6.6	*5.7*	*24.7*
Uruguay	1996	15.0	1996	64.1	2.9	*3.2*	*12.4*
Uzbekistan	1995	5.3	1995	45.8	2.5	..	..
Venezuela, RB	2001	2.7		..	2.3	..	..
Vietnam	1998	1.6		..	1.5	..	..
West Bank and Gaza		..		..	..	..	..
Yemen, Rep.	1994	0.1		..	1.0	*9.5*	..
Zambia	1993	0.1		..	3.1	*2.0*	*11.0*
Zimbabwe		..		..	4.4	*4.7*	*17.7*
World					**5.8 w**	**4.4 m**	**.. m**
Low income					1.5	*3.2*	..
Middle income					3.0	*4.3*	..
Lower middle income					2.7	*3.5*	..
Upper middle income					3.4	*4.5*	*18.2*
Low & middle income					2.7	*4.0*	..
East Asia & Pacific					1.9	*3.2*	..
Europe & Central Asia					4.2	*3.8*	..
Latin America & Carib.					3.3	*4.3*	..
Middle East & N. Africa					2.7	..	..
South Asia					1.3	*3.1*	..
Sub-Saharan Africa					2.6	*3.3*	..
High income					6.6	*5.5*	*25.7*
Europe EMU					7.0	*5.0*	*25.7*

a. Refers only to the scheme for civil servants. b. Refers to system covering private sector workers.

About the data

Enhancing security for poor people means reducing their vulnerability to such risks as ill health, providing them the means to manage risk themselves, and strengthening market or public institutions for managing risk. The tools include microfinance programs, old age assistance and pensions, and public provision of basic health care and education.

Public interventions and institutions can provide services directly to poor people, although whether these work well for the poor is debated. State action is often ineffective, in part because governments can influence only a few of the many sources of well-being and in part because of difficulties in delivering goods and services. The effectiveness of public provision is further constrained by the fiscal resources at governments' disposal and the fact that state institutions may not be responsive to the needs of poor people.

The data on public pension spending are from national sources and cover all government expenditures, including the administrative costs of pension programs. They cover noncontributory pensions or social assistance targeted to the elderly and disabled and spending by social insurance schemes for which contributions had previously been made. The pattern of spending in a country is correlated with its demographic structure—spending increases as the population ages.

The lack of consistent national health accounting systems in most developing countries makes cross-country comparisons of health spending difficult. Compiling estimates of public health expenditures is complicated in countries where state or provincial and local governments are involved in financing and

delivering health care because the data on public spending often are not aggregated. The data in the table are the product of an effort to collect all available information on health expenditures from national and local government budgets, national accounts, household surveys, insurance publications, international donors, and existing tabulations.

The data on education spending in the table refer solely to public spending—government spending on public education plus subsidies for private education. The data generally exclude foreign aid for education. They may also exclude spending by religious schools, which play a significant role in many developing countries. Data for some countries and for some years refer to spending by the ministry of education only (excluding education expenditures by other ministries and departments and local authorities). The share of gross domestic product (GDP) devoted to education can be interpreted as reflecting a country's effort in education. It often bears a weak relationship to the output of the education system as reflected in educational attainment. The pattern in this relationship suggests wide variations across countries in the efficiency with which the government's resources are translated into education outcomes. Data for education expenditure are reported for school years.

Definitions

• **Public expenditure on pensions** includes all government expenditures on cash transfers to the elderly, the disabled, and survivors and the administrative costs of these programs. • **Average pension** is estimated by dividing total pension expenditure by the number of pensioners. • **Public expenditure on health** consists of recurrent and capital spending from government (central and local) budgets, external borrowings and grants (including donations from international agencies and nongovernmental organizations), and social (or compulsory) health insurance funds. • **Public expenditure on education** consists of public spending on public education plus subsidies to private education at the primary, secondary, and tertiary levels.

2.9a

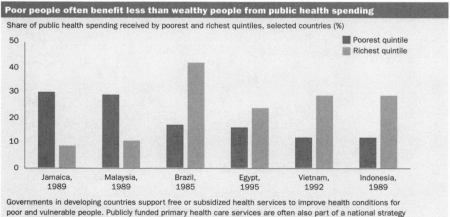

Poor people often benefit less than wealthy people from public health spending

Share of public health spending received by poorest and richest quintiles, selected countries (%)

■ Poorest quintile
■ Richest quintile

Jamaica, 1989 · Malaysia, 1989 · Brazil, 1985 · Egypt, 1995 · Vietnam, 1992 · Indonesia, 1989

Governments in developing countries support free or subsidized health services to improve health conditions for poor and vulnerable people. Publicly funded primary health care services are often also part of a national strategy to reduce poverty. In many countries, however, poor people are not benefiting as much as better-off groups.

Source: Carr 2004.

Data sources

The data on pension spending are drawn from Robert Palacios and Montserrat Pallares-Miralles's "International Patterns of Pension Provision" (2000) and updates. For further updates, notes, and sources, go to "Knowledge and information" on the World Bank's Web site on pensions (http://www.worldbank.org/pensions). The estimates of health expenditure come from the World Health Organization's *World Health Report 2004* and updates, from the Organisation for Economic Co-operation and Development for its member countries, and from countries' national health accounts, supplemented by World Bank country and sector studies. The data on education expenditure are from the UNESCO Institute for Statistics.

	Public expenditure per student[a]						Public expenditure on education	Trained teachers in primary education	Primary pupil-teacher ratio
			% of GDP per capita				% of total government expenditure	% of total	pupils per teacher
	Primary		Secondary		Tertiary				
	1990/91	2002/03	1998/99	2002/03	1998/99	2002/03	2002/03	2002/03	2002/03
Afghanistan	..	..	..	..	..	..	..	..	61
Albania	..	..	..	..	..	..	..	..	22
Algeria	..	11.1	..	16.8	..	..	..	97.9	28
Angola	32.1	..	..	..	..	..	..	..	..
Argentina	..	12.4	13.6	15.8	20.2	17.8	13.7	67.0	18
Armenia	..	9.6	..	11.6	..	35.5	..	..	12
Australia	..	16.6	14.5	15.1	26.9	25.4	13.3	..	..
Austria	18.1	23.8	30.0	28.1	52.8	49.6	11.1	..	13
Azerbaijan	..	7.3	14.9	12.9	16.6	12.6	20.7	99.6	15
Bangladesh	..	8.9	13.2	14.1	49.4	35.5	15.5	66.9	56
Belarus	..	..	..	..	..	..	..	97.7	16
Belgium	15.9	18.7	..	23.6	..	..	..	..	12
Benin	..	9.7	14.0	17.4	126.5	..	..	62.3	62
Bolivia	..	15.5	13.9	12.8	51.4	44.0	19.7	74.1	24
Bosnia and Herzegovina	..	..	..	..	..	..	..	..	..
Botswana	..	6.1	..	5.7	..	90.5	25.6	89.5	27
Brazil	..	11.3	..	10.9	84.9	58.6	12.0	91.9	23
Bulgaria	22.1	16.9	16.7	19.1	14.1	19.7	..	..	17
Burkina Faso	..	..	..	..	..	..	..	86.8	45
Burundi	13.6	12.5	..	63.5	..	545.5	13.0	..	50
Cambodia	..	5.9	..	..	..	..	15.3	96.0	56
Cameroon	..	..	18.5	..	70.7	..	17.3	68.1	57
Canada	..	..	..	..	49.0	48.2	12.7	..	17
Central African Republic	10.6	..	..	..	..	..	..	..	..
Chad	..	..	25.6	..	..	..	..	..	68
Chile	..	15.8	14.8	15.6	22.5	17.7	18.7	92.5	33
China	..	..	10.5	..	61.6	..	..	96.8	20
Hong Kong, China	..	13.5	..	19.3	..	70.3	21.9	..	20
Colombia	..	15.9	14.9	17.9	38.1	30.4	15.6	..	27
Congo, Dem. Rep.	..	..	..	..	..	..	..	..	..
Congo, Rep.	..	8.1	..	17.0	..	220.8	12.6	57.1	65
Costa Rica	..	16.2	..	22.9	..	50.6	22.4	88.2	23
Côte d'Ivoire	..	14.6	32.1	..	138.8	..	21.5	100.0	42
Croatia	..	48.7	..	11.3	..	31.4	10.0	100.0	18
Cuba	18.1	32.3	36.7	40.9	78.2	90.0	18.7	100.0	11
Czech Republic	..	11.8	21.3	21.6	..	29.0	9.6	..	17
Denmark	..	24.4	38.2	35.5	60.5	74.2	15.4	..	10
Dominican Republic	..	8.9	..	3.5	..	..	12.4	58.5	39
Ecuador	..	3.0	11.7	6.3	..	..	8.0	69.9	24
Egypt, Arab Rep.	..	..	..	..	..	..	..	99.9	22
El Salvador	..	10.0	8.1	9.4	10.4	10.7	20.0	..	26
Eritrea	..	11.8	..	35.7	..	445.1	..	80.5	47
Estonia	..	20.1	22.5	24.8	30.3	23.9	..	..	14
Ethiopia	29.6	..	..	..	..	..	13.8	69.3	65
Finland	19.9	17.8	..	26.3	..	37.5	12.7	..	16
France	11.8	17.8	..	28.7	..	29.3	11.4	..	19
Gabon	..	4.7	13.9	..	52.4	..	..	95.3	49
Gambia, The	13.2	11.9	..	13.6	..	..	8.9	73.1	38
Georgia	..	..	..	..	..	..	11.8	97.4	14
Germany	..	16.9	20.8	21.8	40.7	41.2	9.5	..	14
Ghana	6.4	..	..	..	..	..	..	62.9	31
Greece	8.0	14.5	15.9	22.4	29.4	24.7	..	..	13
Guatemala	..	6.7	..	3.6	..	..	..	100.0	30
Guinea	..	9.2	..	..	..	..	25.6	..	45
Guinea-Bissau	..	..	..	..	..	..	..	..	..
Haiti	9.9	..	..	..	..	..	..	..	..

	Public expenditure per student[a]						Public expenditure on education	Trained teachers in primary education	Primary pupil-teacher ratio
	Primary		% of GDP per capita Secondary		Tertiary		% of total government expenditure	% of total	pupils per teacher
	1990/91	2002/03	1998/99	2002/03	1998/99	2002/03	2002/03	2002/03	2002/03
Honduras	..	..	..	..	..	..	..	..	34
Hungary	20.3	20.3	18.5	19.7	32.3	31.3	14.1	..	10
India	..	12.4	..	20.9	..	86.4	12.7	..	41
Indonesia	..	3.7	..	7.2	..	20.8	9.8	93.5	21
Iran, Islamic Rep.	..	11.3	..	12.1	..	33.5	17.7	98.4	24
Iraq	..	..	..	..	..	..	..	..	19
Ireland	11.2	12.0	18.0	17.9	27.9	27.2	13.5	..	19
Israel	11.3	21.7	22.2	22.2	31.7	27.0	..	..	12
Italy	15.1	24.7	28.6	30.9	24.6	25.3	10.3	..	11
Jamaica	9.8	15.1	..	23.5	..	66.9	12.3	79.5	34
Japan	..	21.5	20.5	20.9	14.8	17.1	10.5	..	20
Jordan	..	15.0	15.8	18.0	..	..	..	..	..
Kazakhstan	..	8.1	..	12.7	..	10.2	..	..	19
Kenya	..	..	..	..	..	..	22.1	..	34
Korea, Dem. Rep.	..	..	..	..	..	..	..	..	..
Korea, Rep.	11.6	16.6	14.9	21.1	7.0	7.3	13.1	..	31
Kuwait	..	16.1	..	19.9	..	..	..	100.0	13
Kyrgyz Republic	..	6.1	17.0	10.2	34.3	14.0	18.6	52.0	24
Lao PDR	..	7.9	10.3	10.2	..	76.2	11.0	77.5	31
Latvia	..	22.0	24.3	24.1	29.4	18.4	..	..	14
Lebanon	..	..	..	..	..	19.0	12.3	14.0	17
Lesotho	..	23.8	68.2	55.8	1,233.7	692.4	18.4	72.6	47
Liberia	..	..	..	..	..	..	..	..	..
Libya	..	..	..	..	..	..	..	..	..
Lithuania	..	..	..	..	..	31.4	..	..	16
Macedonia, FYR	..	..	..	..	..	..	..	..	21
Madagascar	..	8.2	26.0	..	155.9	181.7	..	..	52
Malawi	..	..	..	..	..	..	..	51.2	62
Malaysia	..	17.0	..	27.6	..	114.0	20.0	..	20
Mali	..	..	61.1	..	262.8	..	..	..	57
Mauritania	..	..	47.2	..	103.8	..	..	..	41
Mauritius	10.1	9.0	..	14.0	..	48.7	13.3	100.0	25
Mexico	3.5	13.8	17.0	18.4	44.3	35.0	24.3	..	27
Moldova	..	18.1	..	26.6	..	19.7	21.4	..	19
Mongolia	..	38.3	..	19.5	43.9	36.4	..	92.9	31
Morocco	..	18.9	49.5	48.3	100.5	94.6	26.4	..	28
Mozambique	10.5	..	..	..	..	..	..	59.6	67
Myanmar	..	..	..	..	..	..	..	65.0	33
Namibia	..	21.0	36.3	25.2	157.2	93.5	..	36.0	22
Nepal	..	12.0	12.7	10.1	..	68.7	14.9	16.2	36
Netherlands	12.2	16.6	21.7	22.7	46.4	40.8	10.7	..	..
New Zealand	16.5	18.9	23.9	21.8	40.9	37.5	..	..	18
Nicaragua	..	8.9	..	5.2	..	62.4	15.0	74.2	35
Niger	..	15.5	..	52.8	..	304.5	..	71.7	42
Nigeria	..	..	..	..	..	..	..	..	42
Norway	32.8	27.1	19.4	17.2	46.6	42.2	16.2	..	..
Oman	11.0	17.7	22.4	18.4	..	50.2	..	99.8	21
Pakistan	..	..	..	..	..	..	7.8	..	40
Panama	11.5	10.4	19.8	15.9	..	32.7	7.7	75.3	24
Papua New Guinea	..	12.4	18.7	19.2	44.6	..	17.5	100.0	35
Paraguay	..	13.0	..	15.4	..	47.1	9.7	..	..
Peru	..	7.0	10.7	9.2	..	21.3	23.5	78.2	29
Philippines	..	11.6	..	9.3	..	13.8	14.0	..	35
Poland	..	34.4	..	11.6	31.5	21.6	12.2	..	11
Portugal	15.3	23.3	..	31.5	..	27.5	12.7	..	11
Puerto Rico	..	..	..	..	..	..	..	..	..

	Public expenditure per student[a]						Public expenditure on education	Trained teachers in primary education	Primary pupil-teacher ratio
	Primary		Secondary % of GDP per capita		Tertiary		% of total government expenditure	% of total	pupils per teacher
	1990/91	2002/03	1998/99	2002/03	1998/99	2002/03	2002/03	2002/03	2002/03
Romania	..	..	..	..	..	30.3	..	..	17
Russian Federation	..	..	..	..	..	..	11.5	..	17
Rwanda	..	6.9	..	22.0	..	575.0	..	81.2	60
Saudi Arabia	..	32.6	..	31.4	84.0	..	..	93.3	12
Senegal	..	..	32.8	..	244.3	..	..	100.0	49
Serbia and Montenegro	..	..	10.1	..	36.9	..	..	100.0	20
Sierra Leone	..	16.8	..	8.2	..	615.2	..	78.9	37
Singapore	..	..	..	..	..	..	..	..	..
Slovak Republic	..	11.4	..	16.7	..	29.4	7.5	..	19
Slovenia	..	..	..	..	..	..	..	..	12
Somalia	..	..	..	..	..	..	..	..	..
South Africa	21.1	14.3	20.6	17.7	62.5	53.2	18.5	67.9	35
Spain	12.1	18.9	25.9	24.3	20.2	22.4	11.3	..	14
Sri Lanka	..	..	..	..	..	..	..	..	23
Sudan	..	..	..	..	..	..	..	..	29
Swaziland	..	11.2	26.5	28.9	393.7	245.9	..	90.6	31
Sweden	46.2	22.5	28.1	26.2	53.3	47.4	12.8	..	11
Switzerland	34.4	23.2	28.5	28.1	50.0	53.8	15.1	..	14
Syrian Arab Republic	..	13.8	..	24.2	..	..	..	88.0	24
Tajikistan	..	6.8	..	8.7	..	21.5	17.8	82.0	22
Tanzania	..	..	..	..	..	..	..	100.0	53
Thailand	13.0	16.5	..	11.7	..	33.0	28.3	..	19
Togo	8.3	5.7	21.1	..	247.1	..	13.6	80.5	35
Trinidad and Tobago	9.0	16.1	11.6	18.1	112.8	70.6	13.4	83.3	19
Tunisia	..	15.8	29.2	25.7	96.2	68.0	17.4	94.1	22
Turkey	9.4	11.6	..	13.8	..	48.5	..	..	..
Turkmenistan	..	..	..	..	..	..	..	..	..
Uganda	..	..	..	..	..	..	..	80.5	53
Ukraine	..	11.9	..	17.3	25.7	39.3	20.3	99.7	19
United Arab Emirates	..	6.9	12.0	8.6	..	1.6	22.5	..	15
United Kingdom	14.8	15.1	15.7	16.2	26.1	23.2	11.4	..	17
United States	..	21.2	..	24.5	28.6	31.7	17.1	..	15
Uruguay	8.2	11.0	..	10.9	..	22.5	12.8	..	21
Uzbekistan	..	..	..	..	..	..	..	..	..
Venezuela, RB	..	..	..	..	..	..	..	..	..
Vietnam	..	..	..	..	..	..	..	87.0	25
West Bank and Gaza	..	..	..	..	..	..	..	..	..
Yemen, Rep.	..	..	..	..	..	..	32.8	..	..
Zambia	..	7.1	..	19.3	..	163.8	..	100.0	43
Zimbabwe	20.5	16.2	..	24.2	..	201.3	..	95.3	39
World	.. m	14.4 m	.. m	18.4 m	.. m	36.4 m	.. m	.. m	24 m
Low income	..	10.7	..	19.2	..	163.8	..	..	43
Middle income	..	11.6	..	13.8	..	37.4	..	..	21
Lower middle income	..	13.0	..	16.3	..	32.8	..	..	23
Upper middle income	..	16.0	18.5	18.1	..	31.3	13.3	..	19
Low & middle income	..	11.9	..	17.0	..	39.3	..	..	33
East Asia & Pacific	..	12.0	..	..	..	..	16.1	91.5	32
Europe & Central Asia	..	11.9	17.7	15.3	30.3	26.4	..	..	17
Latin America & Carib.	..	12.4	13.9	15.4	..	39.5	13.4	78.2	25
Middle East & N. Africa	..	15.4	..	21.3	..	50.2	..	95.7	23
South Asia	..	12.0	..	14.1	..	68.7	12.9	..	40
Sub-Saharan Africa	..	11.2	..	20.7	..	220.8	..	..	45
High income	15.1	18.7	21.3	22.4	31.7	30.5	13.1	..	14
Europe EMU	13.6	17.8	21.7	24.3	29.4	28.4	11.1	..	14

a. Medians are computed based on data in the table.

Data on education are compiled by the UNESCO Institute for Statistics from official responses to surveys and from reports provided by education authorities in each country. Such data are used for monitoring, policymaking, and resource allocation. For a variety of reasons, however, education statistics generally fail to provide a complete and accurate picture of a country's education system. Statistics often lag by two to three years, though an effort is being made to shorten the delay. Moreover, coverage and data collection methods vary across countries and over time within countries, so the results of comparisons should be interpreted with caution.

The data on education spending in the table refer solely to public spending—government spending on public education plus subsidies for private education. The data generally exclude foreign aid for education. They may also exclude spending by religious schools, which play a significant role in many developing countries. Data for some countries and for some years refer to spending by the ministry of education only (excluding education expenditures by other ministries and departments and local authorities).

Many developing countries have sought to supplement public funds for education. Some countries have adopted tuition fees to recover part of the cost of providing education services or to encourage development of private schools. Charging fees raises difficult questions relating to equity, efficiency, access, and taxation, however, and some governments have used scholarships, vouchers, and other methods of public finance to counter criticism. Data for a few countries include private spending, although national practices vary with respect to whether parents or schools pay for books, uniforms, and other supplies. For greater detail, see the country- and indicator-specific notes in the source.

The share of public expenditure devoted to education allows an assessment of the priority a government assigns to education relative to other public investments. It also reflects a government's commitment to investing in human capital development However, returns on investment to education cannot be understood by simply comparing current education indicators with national income. It takes a long time before currently enrolled children can productively contribute to the national economy (Hanushek 2002).

The share of trained teachers in primary schools measures the quality of the teaching staff. It does not take account of competencies acquired by teachers through their professional experience or self-instruction, or of such factors as work experience,

teaching methods and materials, or classroom conditions, all of which may affect the quality of teaching. Since the training teachers receive varies greatly, care should be taken in comparing across countries.

The comparability of pupil-teacher ratios across countries is affected by the definition of teachers and by differences in class size by grade and in the number of hours taught. Moreover, the underlying enrollment levels are subject to a variety of reporting errors (for further discussion of enrollment data, see *About the data* for table 2.11). While the pupil-teacher ratio is often used to compare the quality of schooling across countries, it is often weakly related to the value added of schooling systems (Behrman and Rosenzweig 1994)

In 1998, UNESCO introduced new International Standard Classification of Education (ISCED) 1997. Thus the time-series data for the years through 1997 are not consistent with those for 1998 and later. Any time-series analysis should therefore be undertaken with extreme caution.

• **Public expenditure per student** is public current spending on education divided by the number of students by level, as a percentage of gross domestic product (GDP) per capita. • **Public expenditure on education** is current and capital public expenditure on education expressed as a percentage of total government expenditure. • **Trained teachers in primary education** are the percentage of primary school teachers who have received the minimum organized teacher training (pre-service or in service) required for teaching. • **Primary pupil-teacher ratio** is the number of pupils enrolled in primary school divided by the number of primary school teachers (regardless of their teaching assignment).

Data sources

The data are from the UNESCO Institute for Statistics, which compiles international data on education in cooperation with national commissions and national statistical services.

2.11 Participation in education

	Gross enrollment ratio							Net enrollment ratio			
	% of relevant age group							% of relevant age group			
	Preprimary	Primary		Secondary[a]		Tertiary[a]		Primary		Secondary[a]	
	2002/03	1990/91	2002/03	1990/91	2002/03	1990/91	2002/03	1990/91	2002/03	1990/91	2002/03
Afghanistan	..	29	..	10	..	2	..	27	..	..	..
Albania	44	100	107	78	78	7	15	95	97	..	74
Algeria	4	101	109	61	80	12	21	93	95	54	67
Angola	..	92	101	12	19	1	1	58	..	..	..
Argentina	61	106	120	71	100	..	56	94	..	..	81
Armenia	32	..	99	..	86	..	28	..	94	..	84
Australia	102	108	104	82	154	36	74	99	97	79	88
Austria	84	101	103	102	99	33	48	88	90	..	89
Azerbaijan	25	111	92	88	83	24	16	100	80	..	76
Bangladesh	21	80	96	20	47	4	6	71	85	19	44
Belarus	102	96	102	95	91	51	62	86	94	..	85
Belgium	114	100	105	102	157	38	60	96	100	87	95
Benin	5	59	109	12	28	3	..	45	..	..	20
Bolivia	47	95	115	37	86	22	39	91	95	29	71
Bosnia and Herzegovina	..	..	..	..	..	..	..	..	..	..	..
Botswana	..	103	103	38	73	3	5	85	81	29	54
Brazil	67	105	148	38	108	11	18	86	97	15	72
Bulgaria	70	98	99	75	94	32	38	86	90	63	87
Burkina Faso	1	33	46	7	11	1	1	26	36	..	9
Burundi	1	71	77	5	11	1	2	53	57	..	9
Cambodia	7	83	124	29	25	1	3	67	93	..	18
Cameroon	15	99	108	27	31	3	5	74	..	..	..
Canada	65	104	101	101	105	93	58	98	100	89	98
Central African Republic	3	66	66	11	..	2	..	53	..	..	..
Chad	..	55	78	7	15	..	..	36	63	..	10
Chile	49	100	100	73	89	..	42	88	86	55	79
China	36	125	116	49	67	3	13	97	95	..	..
Hong Kong, China	73	102	108	80	78	..	26	..	98	..	72
Colombia	37	102	110	50	71	13	24	68	87	..	54
Congo, Dem. Rep.	1	71	..	..	..	2	..	54	..	..	..
Congo, Rep.	4	117	80	46	32	5	4	79	54	..	..
Costa Rica	41	102	108	43	56	26	20	87	90	37	50
Côte d'Ivoire	3	65	78	21	..	..	..	46	61	..	21
Croatia	45	80	97	69	90	22	39	74	89	57	87
Cuba	115	98	98	89	93	21	34	92	93	69	86
Czech Republic	96	96	104	91	96	17	34	87	88	..	89
Denmark	90	98	105	109	129	36	63	98	100	87	93
Dominican Republic	34	95	124	..	59	..	34	58	92	..	36
Ecuador	74	116	117	55	59	20	..	98	100	..	50
Egypt, Arab Rep.	13	91	97	71	88	17	..	84	90	..	81
El Salvador	49	81	113	26	59	17	17	73	90	..	49
Eritrea	6	21	63	..	28	..	2	16	45	..	22
Estonia	106	111	101	98	96	27	64	99	96	..	87
Ethiopia	2	32	66	14	19	1	2	23	47	..	15
Finland	55	99	102	116	126	48	86	98	100	93	94
France	114	108	105	98	108	40	54	100	100	..	93
Gabon	14	142	132	..	51	..	..	86	78	..	..
Gambia, The	18	61	85	18	34	..	..	48	79	..	33
Georgia	43	97	90	95	80	37	38	97	89	..	61
Germany	101	101	100	98	100	32	49	84	..	..	88
Ghana	45	72	79	35	39	1	3	52	63	..	33
Greece	68	98	99	94	96	36	68	95	97	83	85
Guatemala	27	78	106	..	43	..	9	64	87	..	30
Guinea	..	34	81	9	24	1	..	25	65	..	21
Guinea-Bissau	..	50	..	..	..	..	..	38	..	..	..
Haiti	..	48	..	21	..	..	..	22	..	..	..

	Gross enrollment ratio							Net enrollment ratio			
	Preprimary	Primary		Secondary[a]		Tertiary[a]		Primary		Secondary[a]	
	% of relevant age group							% of relevant age group			
	2002/03	1990/91	2002/03	1990/91	2002/03	1990/91	2002/03	1990/91	2002/03	1990/91	2002/03
Honduras	21	109	106	..	..	9	15	90	87	..	..
Hungary	79	95	101	79	104	14	44	91	91	75	92
India	30	99	99	44	50	6	11	..	83	..	..
Indonesia	20	114	111	45	58	9	15	97	92	39	..
Iran, Islamic Rep.	31	109	92	57	78	10	21	92	87	..	..
Iraq	4	116	110	49	43	..	14	100	..	..	..
Ireland	6	102	105	100	105	31	50	90	95	80	82
Israel	108	98	113	88	94	36	58	92	100	..	89
Italy	98	104	101	83	98	32	53	100	99	..	91
Jamaica	87	101	101	65	84	7	17	96	95	64	75
Japan	84	100	101	97	103	31	49	100	100	97	100
Jordan	31	101	99	63	87	24	31	94	91	..	81
Kazakhstan	29	88	102	97	92	42	45	88	91	..	87
Kenya	48	94	92	24	33	2	3	74	66	..	25
Korea, Dem. Rep.	..	..	..	..	..	..	..	..	..	..	..
Korea, Rep.	83	105	104	90	90	39	85	100	100	86	87
Kuwait	70	60	94	43	89	..	..	49	83	..	77
Kyrgyz Republic	11	..	101	100	92	15	42	..	89	..	..
Lao PDR	8	103	116	24	44	..	5	63	85	..	35
Latvia	60	97	96	91	95	26	69	92	88	..	88
Lebanon	75	113	103	..	79	..	44	78	91	..	..
Lesotho	30	112	126	25	35	1	3	73	86	..	22
Liberia	..	..	..	..	..	..	..	..	..	..	..
Libya	8	105	114	86	105	15	58	96	..	..	..
Lithuania	55	94	101	92	101	34	64	..	94	..	93
Macedonia, FYR	28	99	99	56	84	17	27	94	92	..	81
Madagascar	10	94	120	18	..	3	2	65	79	..	..
Malawi	..	68	140	8	33	1	..	50	..	..	29
Malaysia	89	94	95	56	70	7	27	94	95	..	69
Mali	2	25	58	7	20	1	2	20	44	5	..
Mauritania	2	50	88	13	23	3	3	35	68	..	16
Mauritius	87	109	105	53	81	3	15	95	90	..	71
Mexico	76	114	110	53	76	15	21	99	99	45	60
Moldova	47	93	86	80	73	36	30	89	79	..	69
Mongolia	34	97	101	82	84	14	37	90	79	..	77
Morocco	56	65	110	36	45	11	11	57	90	..	36
Mozambique	..	64	103	7	16	..	..	45	55	..	12
Myanmar	..	109	92	22	39	4	12	98	84	..	35
Namibia	28	124	105	39	62	..	7	83	78	..	44
Nepal	12	114	119	33	61	5	5	81	70	..	..
Netherlands	98	102	108	120	122	39	57	95	99	84	90
New Zealand	88	106	102	89	118	40	74	100	100	85	93
Nicaragua	28	94	108	40	61	8	18	72	85	..	39
Niger	1	28	44	6	7	1	1	24	38	6	6
Nigeria	12	92	119	25	..	..	8	60	..	..	..
Norway	81	100	101	103	113	42	74	100	100	88	95
Oman	5	85	81	45	80	4	7	69	72	..	69
Pakistan	47	..	68	25	23	3	3	..	59	..	..
Panama	56	106	112	61	71	21	43	92	100	50	63
Papua New Guinea	55	66	69	12	26	..	..	66	69	..	24
Paraguay	30	105	112	31	64	8	19	93	92	26	50
Peru	60	119	120	67	89	31	32	88	100	..	69
Philippines	33	109	112	71	82	28	31	96	93	..	56
Poland	49	98	100	81	101	22	60	97	98	76	91
Portugal	70	123	116	67	115	24	53	100	100	..	85
Puerto Rico	..	..	..	..	..	..	..	..	..	..	..

	Gross enrollment ratio							Net enrollment ratio			
				% of relevant age group						% of relevant age group	
	Preprimary	Primary		Secondary[a]		Tertiary[a]		Primary		Secondary[a]	
	2002/03	1990/91	2002/03	1990/91	2002/03	1990/91	2002/03	1990/91	2002/03	1990/91	2002/03
Romania	76	91	98	92	84	10	30	81	88	..	80
Russian Federation	92	109	114	93	92	53	70	99	..	..	..
Rwanda	3	71	122	8	16	..	3	67	87	7	..
Saudi Arabia	5	73	67	44	67	10	25	59	54	31	53
Senegal	3	58	80	16	19	3	..	47	58	..	..
Serbia and Montenegro	44	72	98	63	89	..	36	69	..	62	83
Sierra Leone	4	50	79	17	26	1	2	41	..	..	..
Singapore	..	104	..	68	..	18	..	96	..	..	..
Slovak Republic	83	..	101	..	89	..	32	..	87	..	87
Slovenia	73	108	103	91	108	25	66	..	93	..	93
Somalia	..	..	..	..	..	..	..	..	..	..	..
South Africa	32	107	106	66	88	12	15	88	89	..	66
Spain	106	109	107	104	116	37	59	100	100	..	94
Sri Lanka	..	113	112	77	86	5	..	90	..	..	..
Sudan	27	52	60	22	35	3	..	43	..	..	..
Swaziland	..	98	98	41	45	4	5	77	75	..	32
Sweden	75	100	110	90	146	32	76	100	100	85	99
Switzerland	97	90	107	99	98	25	44	84	99	80	87
Syrian Arab Republic	11	102	115	49	48	18	..	92	98	43	43
Tajikistan	10	91	110	102	86	23	16	77	..	..	79
Tanzania	14	67	84	5	..	0[b]	1	50	69	..	..
Thailand	86	98	98	31	83	..	37	76	86	..	..
Togo	3	110	121	23	..	3	..	75	91	18	..
Trinidad and Tobago	66	97	100	80	82	7	9	91	91	..	70
Tunisia	20	114	112	44	79	9	23	94	97	..	68
Turkey	7	99	94	48	76	13	25	89	88	42	..
Turkmenistan	..	..	..	..	..	22	..	..	..	..	..
Uganda	4	69	141	12	17	1	3	53	..	..	14
Ukraine	76	89	93	93	97	48	62	80	84	..	85
United Arab Emirates	75	111	97	65	79	7	35	99	83	58	71
United Kingdom	83	107	100	88	178	30	64	98	100	81	96
United States	61	103	98	92	93	72	81	97	93	85	85
Uruguay	63	109	108	81	101	31	37	92	90	..	72
Uzbekistan	28	81	103	99	95	31	16	78	..	..	..
Venezuela, RB	53	96	104	35	70	29	40	88	91	19	59
Vietnam	45	107	101	32	72	2	12	90	94	..	65
West Bank and Gaza	..	..	..	..	..	..	..	..	..	..	..
Yemen, Rep.	1	65	83	..	47	..	..	52	72	..	..
Zambia	..	94	82	20	28	2	2	79	68	..	23
Zimbabwe	36	104	94	47	40	5	4	86	80	..	38
World	**36** w	**101** w	**103** w	**55** w	**71** w	**16** w	**26** w	**84** w	**87** w	**..** w	**..** w
Low income	21	87	94	35	46	5	10	..	77	..	..
Middle income	40	112	112	56	74	13	22	92	93	..	..
Lower middle income	38	114	114	55	74	12	21	93	93	..	..
Upper middle income	60	102	103	63	81	17	36	91	91	50	68
Low & middle income	31	100	103	47	63	10	18	82	86	..	..
East Asia & Pacific	36	119	113	47	66	5	15	96	93	..	..
Europe & Central Asia	49	98	101	85	89	36	49	90	..	..	..
Latin America & Carib.	61	104	123	49	87	16	25	86	95	29	64
Middle East & N. Africa	19	95	97	56	65	13	..	83	87	..	..
South Asia	28	95	97	40	49	6	11	..	83	..	..
Sub-Saharan Africa	15	73	95	22	..	3	..	53	..	..	..
High income	79	103	101	94	107	47	66	97	96	87	90
Europe EMU	99	105	104	97	108	35	56	95	99	..	91

a. Break in series between 1997 and 1998 due to change from International Standard Classification of Education (ISCED) 1976 to ISCED97. b. Less than 0.5.

About the data

School enrollment data are reported to the United Nations Educational, Scientific and Cultural Organization (UNESCO) Institute for Statistics by national education authorities. Enrollment ratios help to monitor two important issues for universal primary education: whether the Millennium Development Goal that implies achieving a net primary enrollment ratio of 100 percent is on track, and whether an education system has sufficient capacity to meet the needs of universal primary education, as indicated in part by its gross enrollment ratios.

Enrollment ratios, while a useful measure of participation in education, also have significant limitations. They are based on data collected during annual school surveys, which are typically conducted at the beginning of the school year. They do not reflect actual rates of attendance or dropouts during the school year. And school administrators may report exaggerated enrollments, especially if there is a financial incentive to do so. Often the number of teachers paid by the government is related to the number of pupils enrolled.

Also as international indicators, the gross and net primary enrollment ratios have an inherent weakness: the length of primary education differs significantly across countries, although the International Standard Classification of Education (ISCED) tries to eliminate the difference. A short duration for primary education tends to increase the ratio, and a long duration to decrease it (in part because there are more dropouts among older children).

Overage or underage enrollments frequently occur, particularly when parents prefer, for cultural or economic reasons, to have children start school at other than the official age. Children's age at enrollment may be inaccurately estimated or misstated, especially in communities where registration of births is not strictly enforced. Parents who want to enroll their underage children in primary school may do so by overstating the age of the children. And in some education systems ages for children repeating a grade may be deliberately or inadvertently underreported.

Other problems affecting cross-country comparisons of enrollment data stem from errors in estimates of school-age populations. Age-gender structures from censuses or vital registration systems, the primary sources of data on school-age populations, are commonly subject to underenumeration (especially of young children) aimed at circumventing laws or regulations; errors are also introduced when parents round up children's ages. While census data are often adjusted for age bias, adjustments are rarely made for inadequate vital registration systems. Compounding these problems, pre- and post-census estimates of school-age children are interpolations or projections based on models that may miss important demographic events (see the discussion of demographic data in *About the data* for table 2.1).

In using enrollment data, it is also important to consider repetition rates. These rates are quite high in some developing countries, leading to a substantial number of overage children enrolled in each grade and raising the gross enrollment ratio. A common error that may also distort enrollment ratios is the lack of distinction between new entrants and repeaters, which, other things equal, leads to underreporting of repeaters and overestimation of dropouts.

Thus gross enrollment ratios indicate the capacity of each level of the education system, but a high ratio does not necessarily mean a successful education system. The net enrollment ratio excludes overage students in an attempt to capture more accurately the system's coverage and internal efficiency. It does not solve the problem completely, however, because some children fall outside the official school age because of late or early entry rather than because of grade repetition. The difference between gross and net enrollment ratios shows the incidence of overage and underage enrollments.

Definitions

• **Gross enrollment ratio** is the ratio of total enrollment, regardless of age, to the population of the age group that officially corresponds to the level of education shown. • **Net enrollment ratio** is the ratio of children of official school age (as defined by the national education system) who are enrolled in school to the population of the corresponding official school age. Based on the International Standard Classification of Education 1997 (ISCED97). • **Preprimary education** refers to the initial stage of organized instruction, designed primarily to introduce very young children to a school-type environment. • **Primary education** provides children with basic reading, writing, and mathematics skills along with an elementary understanding of such subjects as history, geography, natural science, social science, art, and music. • **Secondary education** completes the provision of basic education that began at the primary level and aims at laying the foundations for lifelong learning and human development by offering more subject- or skill-oriented instruction using more specialized teachers. • **Tertiary education,** whether or not leading to an advanced research qualification, normally requires, as a minimum condition of admission, the successful completion of education at the secondary level.

2.11a

Access to education remains elusive, especially for poor children

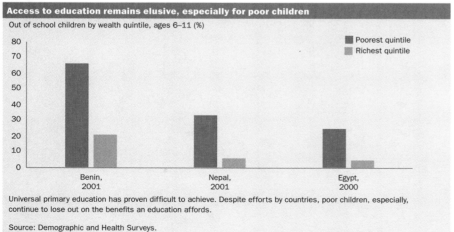

Out of school children by wealth quintile, ages 6–11 (%)

Universal primary education has proven difficult to achieve. Despite efforts by countries, poor children, especially, continue to lose out on the benefits an education affords.

Source: Demographic and Health Surveys.

Data sources

The data are from the UNESCO Institute for Statistics.

	Gross intake rate in grade 1		Share of cohort reaching grade 5				Primary completion rate					
	% of relevant age group		% of grade 1 students				% of relevant age group					
							Total		Male		Female	
	Male	Female	Male		Female		1988/89–	2000/01–	1988/89–	2000/01–	1988/89–	2000/01–
	2002/03	2002/03	1990/91	2001/02	1990/91	2001/02	1993/94[a]	2003/04[b]	1993/94[a]	2003/04[b]	1993/94[a]	2003/04[b]
Afghanistan	..	..	..	..	..	..	23	..	34	..	12	..
Albania	103	101	..	..	..	..	..	101	..	102	..	100
Algeria	97	95	95	96	94	97	80	96	87	96	74	95
Angola	82	71	..	..	..	..	39	..	..	..	..	..
Argentina	112	112	..	91	..	95	100	103	103	101	96	105
Armenia	98	97	..	..	..	..	91	110	87	112	96	108
Australia	..	..	99	..	100	..	..	..	..	..	..	..
Austria	108	105	..	..	..	..	..	101	..	101	..	101
Azerbaijan	90	87	..	..	..	..	..	106	..	107	..	104
Bangladesh	115	116	..	49	..	59	46	73	..	71	..	76
Belarus	104	102	..	..	..	..	94	99	94	99	94	98
Belgium	..	..	90	..	92	..	..	..	..	..	..	..
Benin	128	102	54	70	56	66	22	51	30	65	14	37
Bolivia	121	121	..	85	..	84	71	101	78	103	64	99
Bosnia and Herzegovina	..	..	..	..	..	..	..	..	..	..	..	..
Botswana	114	110	93	85	100	90	91	91	82	87	99	96
Brazil	130	119	..	..	..	..	97	112	96	112	97	111
Bulgaria	98	98	91	..	90	..	90	97	89	98	92	96
Burkina Faso	61	45	71	68	68	71	19	29	24	34	14	24
Burundi	93	80	65	66	58	70	47	31	50	36	43	26
Cambodia	138	126	..	60	..	62	..	81	..	85	..	76
Cameroon	107	93	..	65	..	65	56	70	60	76	52	64
Canada	..	..	95	..	98	..	..	..	..	..	..	..
Central African Republic	76	53	24	..	22	..	27	..	36	..	19	..
Chad	105	77	56	67	41	51	19	25	31	34	7	16
Chile	94	93	98	100	100	100	..	104	..	105	..	103
China	98	99	..	100	..	96	105	98	111	100	99	95
Hong Kong, China	105	103	..	..	..	..	102	101	..	..	..	..
Colombia	132	126	..	66	..	73	71	88	60	86	82	90
Congo, Dem. Rep.	..	..	58	..	50	..	47	32	59	35	35	30
Congo, Rep.	57	54	56	65	65	67	54	59	60	62	48	56
Costa Rica	105	105	81	90	84	93	72	94	70	94	73	95
Côte d'Ivoire	82	75	75	73	70	65	46	51	58	61	34	40
Croatia	100	98	..	..	..	..	83	96	84	95	83	96
Cuba	93	92	..	98	..	98	94	94	95	95	93	94
Czech Republic	102	101	..	96	..	97	..	106	..	106	..	106
Denmark	103	103	94	100	94	100	98	107	98	106	97	107
Dominican Republic	146	135	..	65	..	74	62	93	..	90	..	97
Ecuador	138	137	..	74	..	75	92	100	91	99	93	100
Egypt, Arab Rep.	96	94	..	99	..	99	..	91	..	92	..	90
El Salvador	137	132	..	67	..	71	59	89	57	88	61	89
Eritrea	65	55	..	90	..	82	19	40	22	47	17	33
Estonia	94	95	..	98	..	99	95	104	94	105	95	103
Ethiopia	92	74	16	62	23	54	22	39	26	49	17	29
Finland	100	99	100	100	100	100	97	101	98	101	97	101
France	..	..	69	98	95	97	104	98	..	99	..	98
Gabon	96	96	..	..	..	..	67	74	64	72	71	76
Gambia, The	85	89	..	..	..	..	45	68	57	76	34	60
Georgia	96	92	..	..	..	..	81	82	82	82	81	82
Germany	98	97	..	..	..	..	101	101	100	101	101	101
Ghana	89	86	81	62	79	65	61	62	70	64	53	60
Greece	104	97	100	..	100	..	100	..	101	..	100	..
Guatemala	125	124	..	67	..	64	..	66	..	70	..	63
Guinea	86	76	64	85	48	73	17	41	25	51	9	31
Guinea-Bissau	..	..	..	41	..	34	..	28	..	36	..	20
Haiti	..	..	..	..	..	..	29	..	31	..	28	..

Education efficiency and completion

	Gross intake rate in grade 1		Share of cohort reaching grade 5				Primary completion rate					
	% of relevant age group		% of grade 1 students				Total		Male		Female	
	Male	Female	Male		Female							
	2002/03	2002/03	1990/91	2001/02	1990/91	2001/02	1988/89–1993/94[a]	2000/01–2003/04[b]	1988/89–1993/94[a]	2000/01–2003/04[b]	1988/89–1993/94[a]	2000/01–2003/04[b]
Honduras	139	139	..	..	..	..	65	79	67	74	62	85
Hungary	97	96	77	..	98	..	82	102	81	102	83	101
India	132	110	..	60	..	64	78	81	88	85	67	77
Indonesia	119	113	34	87	78	92	93	95	93	94	93	96
Iran, Islamic Rep.	89	101	91	94	89	94	101	107	107	110	93	104
Iraq	..	..	..	67	..	63	62	56	68	62	56	50
Ireland	105	106	99	98	100	100	..	..	..	..	..	..
Israel	..	..	..	..	..	..	..	..	..	..	..	..
Italy	94	93	..	96	..	97	104	101	104	101	104	101
Jamaica	99	99	..	88	..	93	89	85	86	85	93	85
Japan	..	..	100	..	100	..	101	..	101	..	102	..
Jordan	103	103	..	98	..	97	104	98	103	98	104	99
Kazakhstan	103	102	..	..	..	..	..	110	..	110	..	110
Kenya	97	95	68	61	72	57	86	73	87	76	85	69
Korea, Dem. Rep.	..	..	..	..	..	..	..	..	..	..	..	..
Korea, Rep.	104	103	99	99	100	99	98	97	98	96	98	97
Kuwait	92	93	..	..	..	..	53	96	54	96	52	96
Kyrgyz Republic	110	105	..	..	..	..	..	93	..	94	..	91
Lao PDR	131	117	..	64	..	65	46	74	51	78	41	69
Latvia	90	90	..	..	..	..	73	101	73	101	73	100
Lebanon	101	101	..	90	..	94	..	68	..	66	..	70
Lesotho	134	124	57	66	82	81	67	67	48	57	87	77
Liberia	..	..	..	..	..	..	..	21	..	33	..	10
Libya	..	..	..	..	..	..	..	..	..	..	..	..
Lithuania	93	92	..	..	..	..	89	102	89	103	88	101
Macedonia, FYR	97	98	..	..	..	..	99	100	99	99	99	102
Madagascar	119	116	22	52	21	53	35	47	34	46	35	48
Malawi	..	..	71	50	57	39	36	71	40	73	31	69
Malaysia	93	93	98	..	98	..	88	92	88	93	88	92
Mali	63	53	71	78	67	70	12	40	14	49	9	32
Mauritania	103	103	76	61	75	60	33	43	40	45	26	41
Mauritius	92	94	98	98	98	100	102	105	103	105	102	105
Mexico	109	110	..	90	..	91	88	99	88	99	89	100
Moldova	91	90	..	..	..	..	95	83	95	83	95	82
Mongolia	115	115	..	..	..	..	..	108	..	106	..	111
Morocco	106	101	75	82	76	80	47	75	56	78	38	72
Mozambique	120	110	37	53	28	45	28	52	34	59	22	45
Myanmar	119	121	..	64	..	66	..	73	..	73	..	73
Namibia	98	97	63	92	65	93	77	92	70	90	85	94
Nepal	121	111	..	63	..	67	55	78	71	84	38	72
Netherlands	98	97	..	100	..	100	..	98	..	99	..	98
New Zealand	..	..	91	..	93	..	98	96	99	97	98	95
Nicaragua	142	134	12	62	37	67	44	75	39	70	49	79
Niger	68	50	61	70	65	67	18	26	23	31	13	20
Nigeria	..	..	63	..	67	..	63	82	71	92	54	73
Norway	..	..	99	..	100	..	..	..	..	..	..	..
Oman	72	70	97	98	96	98	73	73	77	76	69	71
Pakistan	108	79	..	..	..	..	..	..	..	..	..	..
Panama	124	120	..	89	..	91	86	98	86	97	87	98
Papua New Guinea	92	83	60	51	58	49	51	53	53	58	49	46
Paraguay	114	112	69	76	72	78	66	93	66	92	66	93
Peru	116	116	..	86	..	86	..	102	..	97	..	98
Philippines	137	127	..	76	..	83	87	95	86	97	89	94
Poland	97	98	89	..	96	..	96	98	94	98	97	99
Portugal	..	..	..	..	..	..	98	..	97	..	98	..
Puerto Rico	..	..	..	..	..	..	..	..	..	..	..	..

2.12 Education efficiency and completion

	Gross intake rate in grade 1		Share of cohort reaching grade 5				Primary completion rate					
	% of relevant age group		% of grade 1 students				% of relevant age group					
							Total		Male		Female	
	Male	Female	Male		Female		1988/89–	2000/01–	1988/89–	2000/01–	1988/89–	2000/01–
	2002/03	2002/03	1990/91	2001/02	1990/91	2001/02	1993/94[a]	2003/04[b]	1993/94[a]	2003/04[b]	1993/94[a]	2003/04[b]
Romania	108	106	..	..	..	..	96	89	97	90	96	89
Russian Federation	..	..	..	..	..	..	95	93	94	94	95	93
Rwanda	166	167	61	45	59	48	44	37	44	38	44	36
Saudi Arabia	67	66	82	92	84	91	57	61	61	62	52	61
Senegal	95	94	..	70	..	65	45	48	55	53	35	43
Serbia and Montenegro	98	99	..	..	..	..	71	96	..	97	..	96
Sierra Leone	..	..	..	..	..	..	..	56	..	67	..	45
Singapore	..	..	100	..	100	..	..	..	..	..	..	..
Slovak Republic	94	94	..	..	..	..	96	99	96	99	96	98
Slovenia	106	106	..	..	..	..	97	95	..	95	..	94
Somalia	..	..	..	..	..	..	..	..	..	..	..	..
South Africa	118	114	72	80	79	94	81	99	76	96	85	102
Spain	..	..	..	..	..	..	..	..	..	..	..	..
Sri Lanka	106	106	94	..	95	..	103	113	103	118	103	108
Sudan	69	61	90	81	99	88	44	49	48	53	39	45
Swaziland	97	92	74	77	78	69	69	75	66	73	72	77
Sweden	98	99	100	..	100	..	96	101	96	102	96	101
Switzerland	92	95	80	100	79	99	..	99	..	98	..	100
Syrian Arab Republic	126	123	97	91	95	92	99	88	104	90	93	85
Tajikistan	121	117	..	..	..	..	100	100	101	103	98	98
Tanzania	149	142	77	76	81	80	46	58	47	58	46	57
Thailand	..	..	..	92	..	96	..	86	..	86	..	87
Togo	110	99	52	73	42	64	40	78	55	92	26	63
Trinidad and Tobago	95	96	..	98	..	100	100	91	97	91	102	91
Tunisia	98	99	94	95	77	96	75	101	79	101	70	102
Turkey	..	..	98	..	97	..	..	95	..	103	..	88
Turkmenistan	..	..	..	..	..	..	..	..	..	..	..	..
Uganda	187	192	..	63	..	64	..	63	..	69	..	58
Ukraine	106	105	..	..	..	..	56	59	56	59	56	59
United Arab Emirates	108	108	80	93	80	93	107	71	104	71	111	72
United Kingdom	..	..	..	..	..	..	..	..	..	..	..	..
United States	..	..	..	..	..	..	..	..	..	..	..	..
Uruguay	104	104	93	87	96	90	95	92	92	90	97	93
Uzbekistan	105	105	..	..	..	..	..	103	..	103	..	102
Venezuela, RB	102	99	82	81	90	87	81	90	76	88	86	92
Vietnam	103	97	..	90	..	88	..	95	..	96	..	95
West Bank and Gaza	..	..	..	..	..	..	..	106	..	106	..	107
Yemen, Rep.	115	90	..	80	..	71	..	66	..	82	..	48
Zambia	86	86	..	79	..	75	..	69	..	74	..	64
Zimbabwe	114	111	..	..	..	..	96	81	99	83	93	78
World	**113** w	**104** w	**..** w	**..** w	**..** w	**..** w	**..** w	**..** w	**..** w	**..** w	**..** w	**..** w
Low income	119	103	..	63	..	66	65	71	75	76	57	66
Middle income	107	105	..	93	..	92	93	95	93	96	92	94
Lower middle income	108	106	..	94	..	92	94	95	94	97	93	94
Upper middle income	101	101	..	90	..	93	87	93	87	93	88	94
Low & middle income	113	104	..	80	..	81	81	84	86	87	78	81
East Asia & Pacific	106	104	..	94	..	92	97	97	97	98	97	95
Europe & Central Asia	..	..	..	..	..	..	88	90	88	90	89	90
Latin America & Carib.	122	117	..	..	..	..	88	96	87	96	90	97
Middle East & N. Africa	98	94	..	92	..	93	79	84	83	85	73	82
South Asia	129	110	..	61	..	65	74	80	88	85	67	77
Sub-Saharan Africa	..	..	..	..	..	..	50	59	55	65	45	54
High income	..	..	..	..	..	..	..	..	..	..	..	..
Europe EMU	..	..	..	..	..	..	..	..	..	..	..	..

a. Data are for 1990 or closest year. b. Data are for the most recent year available.

About the data

Indicators of students' progress through school are estimated by the United Nations Educational, Scientific and Cultural Organization (UNESCO) Institute for Statistics and the World Bank. These indicators measure an education system's success in extending coverage to all students, maintaining the flow of students from one grade to the next, and, ultimately, imparting a particular level of education.

Gross intake rate indicates the general level of access to primary education. It also indicates the capacity of the education system to provide access to primary education. Low gross intake rates in grade 1 reflect the fact that many children do not enter primary school even though school attendance, at least through the primary level, is mandatory in all countries. Because the gross intake rate includes all new entrants regardless of age, it can be more than 100 percent. Once enrolled, students drop out for a variety of reasons, including low quality of schooling, discouragement over poor performance, and the direct and indirect costs of schooling. Students' progress to higher grades may also be limited by the availability of teachers, classrooms, and educational materials.

The share of cohort reaching grade 5 (cohort survival rate) is estimated as the proportion of an entering cohort of grade 1 students that eventually reaches grade 5. It measures the holding power and internal efficiency of an education system. Cohort survival rates approaching 100 percent indicate a high level of retention and a low level of dropout.

Cohort survival rates are typically estimated from data on enrollment and repetition by grade for two consecutive years, in a procedure called the reconstructed cohort method. This method makes three simplifying assumptions: dropouts never return to school; promotion, repetition, and dropout rates remain constant over the entire period in which the cohort is enrolled in school; and the same rates apply to all pupils enrolled in a given grade, regardless of whether they previously repeated a grade (Fredricksen 1993). Given these assumptions, cross-country comparisons should be made with caution, because other flows—caused by new entrants, reentrants, grade skipping, migration, or school transfers during the school year—are not considered.

The UNESCO Institute for Statistics measures the share of cohort reaching grade 5 because research suggests that five to six years of schooling is a critical threshold for the achievement of sustainable basic literacy and numeracy skills. But the indicator only indirectly reflects the quality of schooling, and a high rate does not guarantee these learning outcomes. Measuring actual learning outcomes requires setting curriculum standards and measuring students' learning progress against those standards through standardized assessments or tests.

The primary completion rate reflects the primary cycle as defined by the International Standard Classification of Education (ISCED), ranging from three or four years of primary education (in a very small number of countries) to five or six years (in most countries) and seven (in a small number of countries).

The World Bank and the UNESCO Institute for Statistics are working jointly on developing the primary completion rate indicator. This indicator is increasingly used as a core indicator of an education system's performance. It reflects both the coverage of the education system and the educational attainment of students. It is vital as a key measure of educational outcome at the primary level and of progress on the Millennium Development Goals and the Education for All initiative. However, because curricula and standards for school completion vary across countries, a high rate of primary completion does not necessarily mean high levels of student learning.

The data in the table are for the proxy primary completion rate, calculated by subtracting the number of students who repeat the final primary grade from the number of students in that grade and dividing the result by the number of children of official graduation age in the population. Data limitations preclude adjusting this number for students who drop out during the final year of primary school. Thus proxy rates should be taken as an upper-bound estimate of the actual primary completion rate.

The numerator may include late entrants and over-age children who have repeated one or more grades of primary school but are now graduating as well as children who entered school early. The denominator is the number of children of official graduation age, which could cause the primary completion rate to exceed 100 percent. There are other data limitations that contribute to completion rates exceeding 100 percent, such as the use of estimates for the population, the conduct of school and population surveys at different times of year, and other discrepancies in the numbers used in the calculation.

Definitions

• **Gross intake rate in grade 1** is the number of new entrants in the first grade of primary education regardless of age, expressed as a percentage of the population of the official primary school entrance age. • **Share of cohort reaching grade 5** is the percentage of children enrolled in the first grade of primary school who eventually reach grade 5. The estimate is based on the reconstructed cohort method (see *About the data*). • **Primary completion rate** is the percentage of students completing the last year of primary school. It is calculated by taking the total number of students in the last grade of primary school, minus the number of repeaters in that grade, divided by the total number of children of official graduation age.

Data sources

Data on gross intake rate and share of cohort reaching grade 5 are from the UNESCO Institute for Statistics. The data on the primary completion rate are compiled by staff in the Development Data Group of the World Bank, in collaboration with the Education Anchor of the Human Development Network of the World Bank and the UNESCO Institute for Statistics.

	Adult literacy rate				Youth literacy rate				Expected years of schooling	
	% ages 15 and older				% ages 15–24					
	Male		Female		Male		Female		Male	Female
	1990	**2002**	**1990**	**2002**	**1990**	**2002**	**1990**	**2002**	**2002/03**[a]	**2002/03**[a]
Afghanistan	..	..	..	..	..	..	..	..	..	..
Albania	87	*99*[b]	67	*98*[b]	97	*99*[b]	92	*99*[b]	*11*	*12*
Algeria	64	78	41	60	86	94	68	86	..	..
Angola	..	..	..	..	..	..	..	..	..	..
Argentina	96	97	96	97	98	98	98	99	*15*	*17*
Armenia	99	*100*[b]	96	*99*[b]	100	*100*[b]	99	*100*[b]	11	11
Australia	..	..	..	..	..	..	..	..	*19*	*20*
Austria	..	..	..	..	..	..	..	..	*14*	*15*
Azerbaijan	..	..	..	..	..	..	..	..	11	10
Bangladesh	44	50	24	31	51	58	33	41	8	9
Belarus	100	100	99	100	100	100	100	100	14	15
Belgium	..	..	..	..	..	..	..	..	*18*	*20*
Benin	38	55	15	26	57	73	25	38	..	..
Bolivia	87	*93*[b]	70	*81*[b]	96	*99*[b]	89	*96*[b]	..	..
Bosnia and Herzegovina	..	98	..	91	..	*100*	..	*100*	..	..
Botswana	66	76	70	82	79	85	87	93	11	11
Brazil	83	*86*[b]	81	*87*[b]	91	*93*[b]	93	*96*[b]	*14*	*15*
Bulgaria	98	99	96	98	100	100	99	100	*12*	*13*
Burkina Faso	25	..	8	..	36	..	14	..	4	3
Burundi	48	58	27	44	58	67	45	65	6	5
Cambodia	78	81	49	59	81	85	66	76	10	8
Cameroon	69	*77*[c]	48	*60*[c]	86	*92*	76	*88*	10	8
Canada	..	..	..	..	..	..	..	..	16	16
Central African Republic	47	*65*[c]	21	*33*[c]	66	*70*[c]	39	*47*[c]	..	..
Chad	37	55	19	38	58	76	38	64	..	..
Chile	94	*96*[b]	94	*96*[b]	98	*99*[b]	98	*99*[b]	14	13
China	87	*95*[b]	69	*87*[b]	97	*99*[b]	93	*99*[b]	..	..
Hong Kong, China	..	..	..	..	..	..	..	..	*14*	*14*
Colombia	89	92	88	92	94	97	96	98	11	11
Congo, Dem. Rep.	..	..	..	..	..	..	..	..	..	..
Congo, Rep.	77	89	58	77	95	98	90	97	..	..
Costa Rica	94	96	94	96	97	98	98	99	11	11
Côte d'Ivoire	51	..	26	..	65	*70*[c]	40	*52*[c]	..	..
Croatia	99	*99*[b]	95	*97*[b]	100	*100*[b]	100	*100*[b]	13	13
Cuba	95	97	95	97	99	100	99	100	13	13
Czech Republic	..	..	..	..	..	..	..	..	*14*	*15*
Denmark	..	..	..	..	..	..	..	..	*16*	*17*
Dominican Republic	80	84	79	84	87	91	88	92	12	14
Ecuador	90	*92*[b]	85	*90*[b]	96	*96*[b]	95	*96*[b]	..	..
Egypt, Arab Rep.	60	..	34	..	71	..	51	..	..	..
El Salvador	76	82	69	77	85	90	83	88	11	11
Eritrea	..	..	..	..	..	..	..	..	*6*	*4*
Estonia	100	*100*[b]	100	*100*[b]	100	*100*[b]	100	*100*[b]	*14*	*17*
Ethiopia	37	49	20	34	52	63	34	52	*6*	*4*
Finland	..	..	..	..	..	..	..	..	*17*	*19*
France	..	..	..	..	..	..	..	..	*15*	*16*
Gabon	..	..	..	..	..	..	..	..	..	..
Gambia, The	..	..	..	..	..	..	..	..	..	..
Georgia	..	..	..	..	..	..	..	..	11	11
Germany	..	..	..	..	..	..	..	..	*16*	*16*
Ghana	70	82	47	66	88	94	75	90	8	7
Greece	98	99	92	96	99	100	100	100	*15*	*15*
Guatemala	69	77	53	62	80	86	66	74	9	9
Guinea	..	..	..	..	..	..	..	..	..	..
Guinea-Bissau	..	..	..	..	..	..	..	..	..	..
Haiti	43	54	37	50	56	66	54	67	..	..

Education outcomes **2.13**

	Adult literacy rate				Youth literacy rate				Expected years of schooling	
	% ages 15 and older				% ages 15–24					
	Male		Female		Male		Female		Male	Female
	1990	2002	1990	2002	1990	2002	1990	2002	2002/03[a]	2002/03[a]
Honduras	69	80[b]	67	80[b]	78	87[b]	81	91[b]	..	..
Hungary	99	99	99	99	100	100	100	100	15	16
India	62	68	36	45	73	80	54	65	10	8
Indonesia	87	92	73	83	97	99	93	98	11	11
Iran, Islamic Rep.	72	84[c]	54	70[c]	92	96	81	92	12	11
Iraq	..	..	..	..	..	..	..	..	..	..
Ireland	..	..	..	..	..	..	..	..	16	17
Israel	95	97	88	93	99	100	98	99	15	16
Italy	98	99	97	98	100	100	100	100	15	16
Jamaica	78	84	86	91	87	91	95	98	11	12
Japan	..	..	..	..	..	..	..	..	15	14
Jordan	90	96	72	86	98	99	95	100	13	13
Kazakhstan	99	100	98	99	100	100	100	100	13	14
Kenya	81	90	61	79	93	96	87	95	8	8
Korea, Dem. Rep.	..	..	..	..	..	..	..	..	..	..
Korea, Rep.	..	..	..	..	..	..	..	..	16	15
Kuwait	79	85	73	81	88	92	87	94	..	..
Kyrgyz Republic	..	..	..	..	..	..	..	..	12	13
Lao PDR	70	77	43	55	79	86	61	73	10	8
Latvia	100	100[b]	100	100[b]	100	100[b]	100	100[b]	14	16
Lebanon	..	..	..	..	..	..	..	..	13	13
Lesotho	65	74[c]	89	90[c]	77	83	97	99	11	11
Liberia	55	72	23	39	75	86	39	55	..	..
Libya	83	92	51	71	99	100	83	94	16	17
Lithuania	100	100[b]	99	100[b]	100	100[b]	100	100[b]	15	16
Macedonia, FYR	..	..	..	..	..	..	..	..	12	12
Madagascar	..	..	..	..	..	..	..	..	..	..
Malawi	69	76	36	49	76	82	51	63	..	..
Malaysia	87	92[b]	74	85[b]	95	97[b]	94	97[b]	12	13
Mali	28	27[b]	10	12[b]	38	32[b]	17	17[b]	..	..
Mauritania	46	51	24	31	56	57	36	42	7	7
Mauritius	85	88[b]	75	81[b]	91	94[b]	91	95[b]	13	12
Mexico	91	93[b]	84	89[b]	96	97[b]	94	96[b]	12	12
Moldova	99	100	96	99	100	100	100	100	10	10
Mongolia	98	98[b]	97	98[b]	99	97[b]	99	98[b]	10	12
Morocco	53	63	25	38	68	77	42	61	11	9
Mozambique	49	62	18	31	66	77	32	49	..	..
Myanmar	87	89	74	81	90	92	86	91	7	7
Namibia	77	84	72	83	86	91	89	94	12	12
Nepal	47	62	14	26	67	78	27	46	11	9
Netherlands	..	..	..	..	..	..	..	..	16	16
New Zealand	..	..	..	..	..	..	..	..	17	19
Nicaragua	63	77[c]	63	77[c]	68	84[c]	69	89[c]	10	11
Niger	18	25	5	9	25	34	9	15	3	2
Nigeria	59	74	38	59	81	91	66	87	..	..
Norway	..	..	..	..	..	..	..	..	16	18
Oman	67	82	38	65	95	100	75	97	11	10
Pakistan	49	..	20	..	63	..	31	..	6	5
Panama	90	93	88	92	96	97	95	97	13	14
Papua New Guinea	..	..	..	..	..	..	..	..	..	..
Paraguay	92	93[c]	88	90[c]	96	96[c]	95	96[c]	12	12
Peru	92	91[c]	79	80[c]	97	98[c]	92	96[c]	14	14
Philippines	92	93[b]	91	93[b]	97	94[b]	97	96[b]	12	12
Poland	..	..	..	..	..	..	..	..	15	16
Portugal	91	95	84	91	99	100	100	100	16	17
Puerto Rico	92	94	91	94	95	97	97	98	..	..

2.13 Education outcomes

	Adult literacy rate				Youth literacy rate				Expected years of schooling	
	% ages 15 and older				% ages 15–24					
	Male		Female		Male		Female		Male	Female
	1990	2002	1990	2002	1990	2002	1990	2002	2002/03[a]	2002/03[a]
Romania	99	98[b]	96	96[b]	99	98[b]	99	98[b]	12	13
Russian Federation	100	100	99	99	100	100	100	100	13	14
Rwanda	63	75	44	63	78	86	67	84	9	8
Saudi Arabia	76	84	50	69	91	95	79	92	10	9
Senegal	38	49	19	30	50	61	30	44	..	..
Serbia and Montenegro	..	..	..	..	..	..	..	..	13	13
Sierra Leone	..	..	..	..	..	..	..	..	8	6
Singapore	94	97[b]	83	89[b]	99	99[b]	99	100[b]	..	..
Slovak Republic	..	100[b]	..	100[b]	..	100[b]	..	100[b]	13	14
Slovenia	100	100	100	100	100	100	100	100	15	17
Somalia	..	..	..	..	..	..	..	..	..	..
South Africa	82	87	80	85	89	92	88	92	13	13
Spain	98	99	95	97	100	100	100	100	15	16
Sri Lanka	93	95	85	90	96	97	94	97	..	..
Sudan	60	71	32	49	76	84	54	74	..	..
Swaziland	74	82	70	80	85	90	85	92	10	10
Sweden	..	..	..	..	..	..	..	..	17	21
Switzerland	..	..	..	..	..	..	..	..	16	15
Syrian Arab Republic	82	91	48	74	92	97	67	93	..	..
Tajikistan	99	100[b]	97	99[b]	100	100[b]	100	100[b]	12	10
Tanzania	76	85	51	69	89	94	77	89	..	..
Thailand	95	95[b]	89	91[b]	99	98[b]	98	98[b]	13	12
Togo	60	74	29	45	79	88	48	67	..	..
Trinidad and Tobago	98	99	96	98	100	100	100	100	12	12
Tunisia	72	83	47	63	93	98	75	91	13	13
Turkey	89	94[b]	66	79[b]	97	98[b]	88	93[b]	12	10
Turkmenistan	..	..	..	..	..	..	..	..	..	..
Uganda	69	79	43	59	80	86	60	74	12	11
Ukraine	100	100	99	100	100	100	100	100	13	14
United Arab Emirates	71	76	71	81	82	88	89	95	11	13
United Kingdom	..	..	..	..	..	..	..	..	20	23
United States	..	..	..	..	..	..	..	..	15	16
Uruguay	96	97	97	98	98	99	99	99	13	15
Uzbekistan	99	100	98	99	100	100	100	100	12	11
Venezuela, RB	90	94	88	93	95	98	97	99	12	12
Vietnam	94	..	87	..	94	..	94	..	11	10
West Bank and Gaza	..	..	..	..	..	..	..	..	..	..
Yemen, Rep.	55	69	13	29	74	84	25	51	..	..
Zambia	79	86	59	74	86	91	76	87	7	7
Zimbabwe	87	94	75	86	97	99	91	96	10	9
World	**74** w	**80** w	**63** w	**73** w	**87** w	**90** w	**79** w	**86** w	**..** w	**..** w
Low income	60	68	38	48	73	79	55	66	10	8
Middle income	85	89	75	87	96	97	92	97	..	..
Lower middle income	84	88	74	86	96	97	92	97	..	..
Upper middle income	88	90	86	90	96	97	95	97	13	13
Low & middle income	73	79	62	73	87	89	78	85	..	..
East Asia & Pacific	88	90	72	86	97	98	93	98	..	..
Europe & Central Asia	98	98	94	96	99	99	98	99	12	12
Latin America & Carib.	83	86	83	88	93	94	93	95	13	14
Middle East & N. Africa	71	82	40	61	82	92	64	82	..	..
South Asia	64	73	34	44	70	77	50	62	10	8
Sub-Saharan Africa	59	71	40	58	75	84	60	77	..	..
High income	..	..	..	..	..	..	..	..	16	17
Europe EMU	..	..	..	..	..	..	..	..	16	16

a. Data are provisional for OECD and World Education Indicators countries. b. National estimates based on census data. c. National estimates based on survey data.

Many governments collect and publish statistics that indicate how their education systems are working and developing—statistics on enrollment and on such efficiency indicators as repetition rates, pupil-teacher ratios, and cohort progression through school.

Basic student outcomes include achievements in reading and mathematics judged against established standards. In many countries national learning assessments are enabling ministries of education to monitor progress in these outcomes. Internationally, the United Nations Educational, Scientific, and Cultural Organization (UNESCO) Institute for Statistics has established literacy as an outcome indicator based on an internationally agreed definition.

The literacy rate is defined as the percentage of people who can, with understanding, both read and write a short, simple statement about their everyday life. In practice, literacy is difficult to measure. To estimate literacy using such a definition requires census or survey measurements under controlled conditions. Many countries estimate the number of literate people from self-reported data. Some use educational attainment data as a proxy but apply different lengths of school attendance or level of completion. Because definition and methodologies of data collection differ across countries, data need to be used with caution.

The reported literacy data are compiled by the UNESCO Institute for Statistics based on national censuses and household survey data. The estimation methodology can be reviewed at www.uis. unesco.org. The national estimates are received from countries and are based on national censuses or household surveys during 1995–2004.

Literacy statistics for most countries cover the population ages 15 and older, by five-year age groups, but some include younger ages or are confined to age ranges that tend to inflate literacy rates. As an alternative, the UNESCO Institute for Statistics has proposed the narrower age range of 15–24, which better captures the ability of participants in the formal education system. The youth literacy rate reported in the table measures the accumulated outcomes of primary education over the previous 10 years or so by indicating the proportion of people who have passed through the primary education system without acquiring basic literacy and numeracy skills (or never entered the system). Reasons for this may include difficulties in attending school or dropping out before reaching grade 5 (see *About the data* for table 2.12) and thereby failing to achieve basic learning competencies.

Expected years of schooling is an estimate of the total years of schooling that a typical child at the age of school entry will receive, including years spent on repetition, given the current patterns of enrollment across cycles of education. It may also be interpreted as an indicator of the total education resources, measured in school years, that a child will acquire over his or her "lifetime" in school—or as an indicator of an education system's overall level of development.

Because the calculation of this indicator assumes that the probability of a child's being enrolled in school at any future age is equal to the current enrollment ratio for that age, it does not account for changes and trends in future enrollment ratios. The expected number of years and the expected number of grades completed are not necessarily consistent, because the first includes years spent in repetition. Comparability across countries and over time may be affected by differences in the length of the school year or changes in policies on automatic promotions and grade repetition.

• **Adult literacy rate** is the percentage of people ages 15 and older who can, with understanding, both read and write a short, simple statement about their everyday life. • **Youth literacy rate** is the literacy rate among people ages 15–24. • **Expected years of schooling** are the average number of years of formal schooling that children are expected to receive, including university education and years spent in repetition. They reflect the underlying age-specific enrollment ratios for primary, secondary, and tertiary education.

2.13a

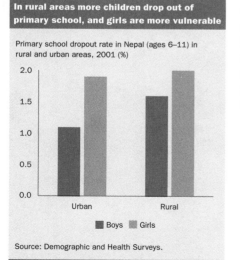

In rural areas more children drop out of primary school, and girls are more vulnerable

Primary school dropout rate in Nepal (ages 6–11) in rural and urban areas, 2001 (%)

Source: Demographic and Health Surveys.

Health: expenditure, services, and use

	Health expenditure					Health expenditure per capita	Physicians		Hospital beds	
	Total % of GDP	Public % of GDP	 % of total	Out of pocket % of private	External resources % of total	$	per 1,000 people		per 1,000 people	
	2002	2002	2002	2002	2002	2002	1990	2004	1990	1995–2002[a]
Afghanistan	8.0	3.1	39.2	80.0	42.6	14	0.1	0.2	0.2	..
Albania	3.4	2.4	69.3	98.9	6.8	52	1.4	1.4	4.0	3.3
Algeria	4.3	3.2	74.0	76.6	0.1	77	0.9	0.8	2.5	2.1
Angola	5.0	2.1	41.9	100.0	7.9	38	0.0[b]	0.1	1.3	..
Argentina	8.9	4.5	50.2	62.4	0.3	238	2.7	3.0	4.6	3.3
Armenia	5.5	1.3	24.1	82.3	19.6	42	3.9	3.5	9.1	4.3
Australia	9.5	6.5	67.9	61.4	0.0	1,995	2.3	2.5	9.2	7.9
Austria	7.7	5.4	69.9	58.0	0.0	1,969	2.2	3.2	10.1	8.6
Azerbaijan	3.7	0.8	22.1	100.0	4.0	27	3.9	3.5	10.1	8.5
Bangladesh	3.1	0.8	25.2	85.9	13.5	11	0.2	0.2	0.3	..
Belarus	6.4	4.7	73.9	79.7	0.1	93	3.6	4.5	13.2	12.6
Belgium	9.1	6.5	71.2	86.3	0.0	2,159	3.3	4.2	8.0	7.3
Benin	4.7	2.1	44.4	90.3	65.9	20	0.1	0.1	0.8	..
Bolivia	7.0	4.2	59.8	81.3	7.0	63	0.4	0.7	1.3	1.7
Bosnia and Herzegovina	9.2	4.6	49.8	100.0	1.8	130	1.6	1.3	4.5	3.2
Botswana	6.0	3.7	61.9	30.8	3.8	171	0.2	0.3	1.6	..
Brazil	7.9	3.6	45.9	64.2	0.5	206	1.4	2.1	3.3	3.1
Bulgaria	7.3	4.4	60.9	98.9	1.4	143	3.2	3.4	9.8	7.2
Burkina Faso	4.3	2.0	45.9	98.9	5.8	11	0.0[b]	0.0[b]	0.3	1.4
Burundi	3.0	0.6	21.5	100.0	16.2	3	0.1	0.1	0.7	..
Cambodia	12.0	2.1	17.1	85.2	4.9	32	0.1	0.2	2.1	..
Cameroon	4.6	1.2	26.2	93.7	6.4	31	0.1	0.1	2.6	..
Canada	9.6	6.7	69.9	50.3	0.0	2,222	2.1	2.1	6.3	3.9
Central African Republic	3.9	1.6	41.6	95.4	17.0	11	0.0[b]	0.0[b]	0.9	..
Chad	6.5	2.7	41.9	96.5	27.9	14	0.0[b]	0.0[b]	0.7	..
Chile	5.8	2.6	45.1	48.7	0.0	246	1.1	1.1	3.2	2.7
China	5.8	2.0	33.7	96.3	0.1	63	1.5	1.6	2.6	2.5
Hong Kong, China	..	..	..	..	..	..	..	..	..	..
Colombia	8.1	6.7	82.9	57.0	0.0	151	1.1	1.4	1.4	1.5
Congo, Dem. Rep.	4.0	1.1	28.7	100.0	28.4	4	0.1	0.1	1.4	..
Congo, Rep.	2.2	1.5	70.3	100.0	2.2	18	0.3	0.3	3.3	..
Costa Rica	9.3	6.1	65.4	99.0	1.3	383	1.3	1.7	2.5	1.7
Côte d'Ivoire	6.2	1.4	22.4	94.6	2.2	44	0.1	0.1	0.8	..
Croatia	7.3	5.9	81.4	100.0	1.1	369	2.1	2.4	7.4	6.0
Cuba	7.5	6.5	86.5	75.2	0.2	197	3.6	5.9	5.4	5.1
Czech Republic	7.0	6.4	91.4	100.0	0.0	504	2.8	3.4	11.3	8.8
Denmark	8.8	7.3	82.9	89.8	0.0	2,835	3.1	3.7	5.6	4.5
Dominican Republic	6.1	**2.2**	36.4	88.2	1.4	154	1.5	1.9	1.9	1.5
Ecuador	4.8	1.7	36.0	88.4	0.9	91	1.5	1.5	1.6	1.6
Egypt, Arab Rep.	4.9	1.8	36.6	92.0	1.6	59	0.8	2.1	2.1	2.1
El Salvador	8.0	3.6	44.7	93.9	0.7	178	0.8	1.3	1.5	1.6
Eritrea	5.1	3.2	63.7	100.0	49.2	8	..	0.0[b]	..	..
Estonia	5.1	3.9	76.3	83.9	0.0	263	3.5	3.2	11.6	6.7
Ethiopia	5.7	2.6	44.9	65.9	29.5	5	0.0[b]	0.0[b]	0.2	..
Finland	7.3	5.5	75.7	82.2	0.0	1,852	2.4	3.1	12.5	7.5
France	9.7	7.4	76.0	40.9	0.0	2,348	2.6	3.3	9.7	8.2
Gabon	4.3	1.8	41.3	100.0	2.8	159	0.5	0.3	3.2	..
Gambia, The	7.3	3.3	44.6	64.3	40.6	18	..	0.0[b]	0.6	..
Georgia	3.8	1.0	27.1	98.7	12.6	25	4.9	3.9	9.8	4.3
Germany	10.9	8.6	78.5	48.2	0.0	2,631	3.1	3.6	10.4	9.1
Ghana	5.6	2.3	41.0	100.0	18.5	17	0.0[b]	0.1	1.5	..
Greece	9.5	5.0	52.9	66.9	..	1,198	3.4	4.4	5.1	4.9
Guatemala	4.8	2.3	47.5	86.2	4.4	93	0.8	0.9	1.1	1.0
Guinea	5.8	0.9	15.5	99.5	9.5	22	0.1	0.1	0.6	..
Guinea-Bissau	6.3	3.0	48.2	100.0	35.9	9	..	0.2	1.5	..
Haiti	7.6	3.0	39.4	69.5	15.6	29	0.1	0.3	0.8	0.7

	Health expenditure				Health expenditure per capita	Physicians		Hospital beds	
	Total % of GDP	Public		Out of pocket % of private	External resources % of total	$	per 1,000 people		per 1,000 people	
		% of GDP	% of total							
	2002	**2002**	**2002**	**2002**	**2002**	**2002**	**1990**	**2004**	**1990**	**1995–2002[a]**
Honduras	6.2	3.2	51.2	85.4	8.0	60	0.7	0.8	1.0	1.1
Hungary	7.8	5.5	70.2	88.2	0.0	496	2.9	3.2	10.1	8.2
India	6.1	1.3	21.3	98.5	1.0	30	*0.5*	0.5	*0.8*	..
Indonesia	3.2	1.2	36.0	76.1	1.8	26	0.1	0.2	0.7	..
Iran, Islamic Rep.	6.0	2.9	47.8	96.4	0.3	104	*0.3*	1.0	1.4	1.6
Iraq	1.5	0.3	16.9	100.0	0.6	11	0.6	0.5	1.7	1.5
Ireland	7.3	5.5	75.2	53.0	0.0	2,255	1.6	2.4	10.5	9.7
Israel	9.1	6.0	65.7	87.8	3.9	1,496	3.2	3.9	6.2	6.2
Italy	8.5	6.4	75.6	83.3	0.0	1,737	4.7	6.1	7.2	4.9
Jamaica	6.0	3.4	57.4	61.8	4.1	180	0.6	0.9	2.2	2.1
Japan	7.9	6.5	81.7	89.8	0.0	2,476	1.7	2.0	16.0	16.5
Jordan	9.3	4.3	46.1	74.3	5.2	165	*1.3*	2.0	1.8	1.8
Kazakhstan	3.5	1.9	53.2	100.0	0.6	56	4.0	3.3	13.7	7.0
Kenya	4.9	2.2	44.0	80.0	16.4	19	0.0[b]	0.1	1.6	..
Korea, Dem. Rep.	4.6	3.5	76.6	100.0	59.0	0[c]	..	3.0	..	..
Korea, Rep.	5.0	2.6	52.9	82.3	0.0	577	0.8	1.8	3.1	6.1
Kuwait	3.8	2.9	75.2	94.3	0.0	547	0.2	1.5	*3.0*	2.8
Kyrgyz Republic	4.3	2.2	51.2	100.0	14.0	14	3.4	2.7	12.0	5.5
Lao PDR	2.9	1.5	50.9	80.0	9.6	10	0.2	0.6	2.6	..
Latvia	5.1	3.3	64.1	99.0	0.5	203	4.1	2.9	14.1	8.2
Lebanon	11.5	3.5	30.1	80.0	0.5	568	*1.3*	3.3	1.7	2.7
Lesotho	6.2	5.3	84.9	7.0	20.8	25	0.0[b]	0.1	..	..
Liberia	2.1	1.4	68.0	95.7	40.8	4	..	0.0[b]	..	..
Libya	3.3	1.6	47.2	100.0	0.0	121	1.1	1.3	4.2	4.3
Lithuania	6.3	4.3	68.6	80.9	0.6	255	4.0	4.0	12.5	9.2
Macedonia, FYR	6.8	5.8	84.7	100.0	0.9	124	2.2	2.2	5.9	4.8
Madagascar	2.1	1.2	55.0	88.8	32.2	5	0.1	0.1	0.9	0.4
Malawi	9.8	4.0	41.1	42.6	37.6	14	0.0[b]	0.0[b]	1.6	1.3
Malaysia	3.8	2.0	53.8	92.8	0.0	149	0.4	0.7	2.1	2.0
Mali	4.5	2.3	50.8	88.8	18.2	12	0.1	0.0[b]	..	0.2
Mauritania	3.9	2.9	74.2	100.0	3.3	14	0.1	0.1	0.7	..
Mauritius	2.9	2.2	76.9	100.0	1.8	113	0.8	0.9	*2.9*	..
Mexico	6.1	2.7	44.9	94.6	0.8	379	1.1	1.7	0.8	1.1
Moldova	7.0	4.1	58.2	100.0	2.8	27	3.6	2.7	13.1	5.9
Mongolia	6.6	4.6	70.4	74.0	0.7	27	2.5	2.7	*11.5*	..
Morocco	4.6	1.5	32.8	74.0	1.9	55	*0.2*	0.5	1.3	1.0
Mozambique	5.8	4.1	71.0	36.5	39.3	11	0.0[b]	0.0[b]	0.9	..
Myanmar	2.2	0.4	18.5	99.7	1.0	315	0.1	0.3	0.6	..
Namibia	6.7	4.7	70.1	20.5	5.2	99	*0.2*	0.3	..	..
Nepal	5.2	1.4	27.2	92.2	9.0	12	0.1	0.1	0.2	0.2
Netherlands	8.8	5.8	65.6	24.5	0.0	2,298	2.5	3.3	11.5	10.8
New Zealand	8.5	6.6	77.9	72.6	0.0	1,255	1.9	2.2	8.5	6.2
Nicaragua	7.9	3.9	49.1	96.0	9.3	60	0.7	1.6	1.8	1.5
Niger	4.0	2.0	50.8	94.6	37.7	7	0.0[b]	0.0[b]	..	0.1
Nigeria	4.7	1.2	25.6	90.4	6.1	19	*0.2*	0.3	1.7	..
Norway	9.6	8.0	83.5	97.2	0.0	4,033	*2.6*	3.6	*16.4*	14.6
Oman	3.4	2.8	81.6	51.4	0.0	246	0.6	1.3	2.1	2.2
Pakistan	3.2	1.1	34.9	98.3	1.8	13	0.5	0.7	0.6	..
Panama	8.9	6.4	71.7	81.8	0.9	355	1.6	1.7	2.5	2.2
Papua New Guinea	4.3	3.8	88.6	83.3	34.3	22	0.1	0.1	4.0	..
Paraguay	8.4	3.2	38.1	88.6	2.1	82	0.6	1.2	0.9	1.3
Peru	4.4	2.2	49.9	79.4	4.6	93	1.1	1.2	1.4	1.5
Philippines	2.9	1.1	39.0	77.8	2.8	28	0.1	1.2	1.4	..
Poland	6.1	4.4	72.4	100.0	0.0	303	2.1	2.2	5.7	4.9
Portugal	9.3	6.6	70.5	95.7	0.0	1,092	2.8	3.2	4.6	4.0
Puerto Rico	..	..	..	..	..	..	..	..	..	3.3

	Health expenditure					Health expenditure per capita	Physicians		Hospital beds	
	Total % of GDP	Public		Out of pocket % of private	External resources % of total	$	per 1,000 people		per 1,000 people	
		% of GDP	% of total							
	2002	**2002**	**2002**	**2002**	**2002**	**2002**	**1990**	**2004**	**1990**	**1995–2002**[a]
Romania	6.3	4.2	65.9	88.7	0.8	128	1.8	1.9	8.9	7.5
Russian Federation	6.2	3.5	55.8	63.6	0.2	150	4.1	4.2	13.1	10.8
Rwanda	5.5	3.1	57.2	65.2	32.8	11	0.0[b]	0.0[b]	1.7	..
Saudi Arabia	4.3	3.3	77.1	30.1	0.0	345	1.4	1.4	2.5	2.3
Senegal	5.1	2.3	45.2	96.5	16.9	27	0.1	0.1	0.7	0.4
Serbia and Montenegro	8.1	5.1	62.8	100.0	0.3	120	2.0	..	5.9	5.3
Sierra Leone	2.9	1.7	60.3	100.0	16.5	6	..	0.1	..	..
Singapore	4.3	1.3	30.9	97.3	0.0	898	1.3	1.4	3.6	..
Slovak Republic	5.9	5.3	89.4	100.0	0.0	265	2.9	3.3	7.4	7.8
Slovenia	8.3	6.2	74.9	40.9	0.1	922	2.0	2.2	6.0	5.2
Somalia	*2.6*	*1.2*	*44.6*	*100.0*	0.0	*6*	..	0.0[b]	0.8	..
South Africa	8.7	3.5	40.6	20.9	0.3	206	*0.6*	0.7	..	..
Spain	7.6	5.4	71.3	82.5	0.0	1,192	2.3	3.2	4.3	4.1
Sri Lanka	3.7	1.8	48.7	95.1	1.9	32	*0.1*	0.4	2.7	..
Sudan	4.9	1.0	20.7	99.5	2.6	19	..	0.2	1.1	..
Swaziland	6.0	3.6	59.5	41.7	3.5	66	0.1	0.2	..	..
Sweden	9.2	7.8	85.3	100.0	0.0	2,489	2.9	3.0	12.4	3.6
Switzerland	11.2	6.5	57.9	74.8	0.0	4,219	3.0	3.5	*19.9*	17.9
Syrian Arab Republic	5.1	2.3	45.8	100.0	0.2	58	0.8	1.4	1.1	1.4
Tajikistan	3.3	0.9	27.7	100.0	14.9	6	2.6	2.2	10.7	6.4
Tanzania	4.9	2.7	54.8	82.5	26.9	13	..	0.0[b]	1.0	..
Thailand	4.4	3.1	69.7	75.8	0.2	90	0.2	0.3	1.6	2.0
Togo	6.9	5.1	73.5	100.0	24.0	91	*0.1*	0.1	1.5	..
Trinidad and Tobago	3.7	1.4	37.3	85.8	6.6	264	0.7	0.8	4.0	5.1
Tunisia	5.8	2.9	49.9	83.0	0.7	126	0.5	0.7	1.9	1.7
Turkey	6.5	4.3	65.8	88.0	0.0	172	0.9	1.2	2.1	2.6
Turkmenistan	4.3	3.0	70.7	100.0	0.7	79	3.6	3.2	11.5	7.1
Uganda	7.4	2.1	27.9	52.3	28.8	18	0.0[b]	0.0[b]	*0.9*	..
Ukraine	4.7	3.3	71.1	95.5	3.6	40	4.3	3.0	13.0	8.7
United Arab Emirates	3.1	2.3	73.4	65.2	0.0	802	0.8	2.0	2.6	2.6
United Kingdom	7.7	6.4	83.4	55.9	0.0	2,031	1.4	1.7	5.9	4.1
United States	14.6	6.6	44.9	25.4	0.0	5,274	2.4	5.5	4.9	3.6
Uruguay	10.0	2.9	29.0	25.0	0.6	361	3.7	3.7	4.5	4.4
Uzbekistan	5.5	2.5	45.5	100.0	5.0	21	3.4	2.9	12.5	5.3
Venezuela, RB	4.9	2.3	46.9	87.2	0.1	184	1.6	1.9	2.7	1.5
Vietnam	5.2	1.5	29.2	87.6	1.8	23	0.4	0.5	3.8	1.7
West Bank and Gaza	..	..	..	..	..	..	..	0.8	..	1.2
Yemen, Rep.	3.7	1.0	27.2	85.8	3.0	23	0.0[b]	0.2	0.8	0.6
Zambia	5.8	3.1	52.9	75.3	18.6	20	0.1	0.1	..	..
Zimbabwe	8.5	4.4	51.6	47.3	2.5	118	0.1	0.1	0.5	..
World	**10.0 w**	**5.8 w**	**60.0 w**	**44.3 w**	**0.1 w**	**524 w**	**1.6 w**	**1.5 w**	**4.0 w**	**.. w**
Low income	5.5	1.5	27.8	95.8	3.9	29	..	0.4	..	..
Middle income	6.0	3.0	49.4	82.7	0.5	109	1.6	1.7	3.6	3.7
Lower middle income	6.0	2.7	45.4	82.1	0.6	84	1.6	1.6	3.5	3.8
Upper middle income	6.0	3.4	57.6	84.1	0.5	310	1.7	1.8	3.8	3.4
Low & middle income	5.9	2.7	46.2	85.7	1.1	75	1.3	1.1	3.1	..
East Asia & Pacific	5.2	1.9	37.8	94.8	0.5	63	1.2	1.3	2.3	2.5
Europe & Central Asia	6.3	4.2	65.6	82.1	0.4	152	3.2	3.1	10.1	8.9
Latin America & Carib.	6.8	3.3	47.8	77.3	0.8	218	1.4	1.8	2.4	2.2
Middle East & N. Africa	5.0	2.7	57.1	80.7	0.7	99	..	1.2	1.8	..
South Asia	5.5	1.3	24.0	97.7	2.1	26	*0.4*	0.5	..	..
Sub-Saharan Africa	6.3	2.6	40.5	56.0	7.2	32	..	0.1	1.2	..
High income	11.1	6.6	63.3	36.6	0.0	3,039	2.4	3.8	7.9	7.4
Europe EMU	9.4	7.0	74.6	57.5	0.0	2,043	3.1	4.0	8.5	8.0

a. Data are for the most recent year available. b. Less than 0.05. c. Less than 0.5.

National health accounts track financial flows in the health sector, including public and private expenditures, by source of funding. In contrast with high-income countries, few developing countries have health accounts that are methodologically consistent with national accounting approaches. The difficulties in creating national health accounts go beyond data collection. To establish a national health accounting system, a country needs to define the boundaries of the health care system and to define a taxonomy of health care delivery institutions. The accounting system should be comprehensive and standardized, providing not only accurate measures of financial flows but also information on the equity and efficiency of health financing to inform health policy.

The absence of consistent national health accounting systems in most developing countries makes cross-country comparisons of health spending difficult. Compiling estimates of public health expenditures is complicated in countries where state or provincial and local governments are involved in financing and delivering health care, because the data on public spending often are not aggregated. There are a number of potential data sources related to external resources for health, including government expenditure accounts, government records on external assistance, routine surveys of external financing assistance, and special surveys. Survey data are the major source of information about out of pocket expenditure on health. The data in the table are the product of an effort by the World Health Organization (WHO), the Organisation for Economic Co-operation and Development (OECD), and the World Bank to collect all available information on health expenditures from national and local government budgets, national accounts, household surveys, insurance publications, international donors, and existing tabulations.

Indicators on health services (physicians and hospital beds per 1,000 people) and health care utilization (inpatient admission rates, average length of stay, and outpatient visits) come from a variety of sources (see *Data sources*). Data are lacking for many countries, and for others comparability is limited by differences in definitions. In estimates of health personnel, for example, some countries incorrectly include retired physicians (because deletions to physician rosters are made only periodically) or those working outside the health sector. There is no universally accepted definition of hospital beds. Moreover, figures on physicians and hospital beds are indicators of availability, not of quality or use. They do not show how well trained the physicians are or how well equipped the hospitals or medical centers are. And physicians and hospital beds tend to be concentrated in urban areas, so these indicators give only a partial view of health services available to the entire population.

• **Total health expenditure** is the sum of public and private health expenditure. It covers the provision of health services (preventive and curative), family planning activities, nutrition activities, and emergency aid designated for health but does not include provision of water and sanitation. • **Public health expenditure** consists of recurrent and capital spending from government (central and local) budgets, external borrowings and grants (including donations from international agencies and nongovernmental organizations), and social (or compulsory) health insurance funds. • **Out of pocket expenditure** is any direct outlay by households, including gratuities and in-kind payments, to health practitioners and suppliers of pharmaceuticals, therapeutic appliances, and other goods and services whose primary intent is to contribute to the restoration or enhancement of the health status of individuals or population groups. It is a part of private health expenditure. • **External resources for health** are funds or services in kind that are provided by entities not part of the country in question. The resources may come from international organizations, other countries through bilateral arrangements, or foreign nongovernmental organizations. These resources are part of total health expenditure. • **Physicians** are graduates of any faculty or school of medicine who are working in the country in any medical field (practice, teaching, research). • **Hospital beds** include inpatient beds available in public, private, general, and specialized hospitals and rehabilitation centers. In most cases beds for both acute and chronic care are included.

2.14a

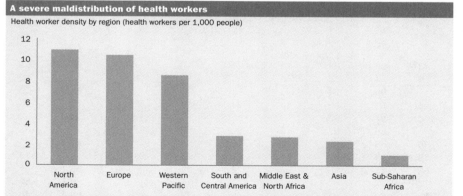

A severe maldistribution of health workers

Health worker density by region (health workers per 1,000 people)

Asia, with about 50 percent of the world's population, has about 30 percent of the world's global stock of health workers. North America and Europe have about 20 percent of the poluation, but over half the doctors and nurses. Average density is about 11 per 1,000 people in Europe and North America and 1 per 1,000 in Africa.

Note: Health workers include physicians, nurses, midwives, dentists, and pharmacists. Data are displayed by WHO regions.

Source: Joint Learning Initiative 2004.

The estimates of health expenditure come mostly from the WHO's *World Health Report 2004* and updates and from the OECD for its member countries, supplemented by World Bank poverty assessments and country and sector studies. Data are also drawn from World Bank public expenditure reviews, the International Monetary Fund's *Government Finance Statistics* database, and other studies. The data on private expenditure in developing countries are drawn largely from household surveys conducted by governments or by statistical or international organizations. The data on physicians and hospital beds are from the WHO, OECD, and TransMONEE, supplemented by country data.

	Access to an improved water source		Access to improved sanitation facilities		Child immunization rate		Children with ARI taken to a health provider	Children with diarrhea	Children with diarrhea who received ORS packet	Children sleeping under treated bednets[b]	Tuberculosis treatment success rate	DOTS detection rate
	% of population		% of population		% of children ages 12–23 months[a]		% of children under age 5	% of children under age 5	% of children with diarrhea	% of children under age 5	% of registered cases	% of estimated cases
	1990	2002	1990	2002	Measles 2003	DPT 2003	1998–2003[c]	1998–2003[c]	1998–2003[c]	1999–2003[c]	2002	2003
Afghanistan	..	13	..	8	50	54	..	..	..	..	87	18
Albania	97	97	..	89	93	97	83	7	35	..	90	29
Algeria	95	87	88	92	84	87	..	20	18	..	89	113
Angola	32	50	30	30	62	46	..	..	..	2.3	74	118
Argentina	94	..	82	..	97	88	..	..	..	..	58	65
Armenia	..	92	..	84	94	94	26	8	33	..	79	43
Australia	100	100	100	100	93	92	..	..	..	..	78	10
Austria	100	100	100	100	79	84	..	..	..	..	64	41
Azerbaijan	66	77	..	55	98	97	36	22	10	1.4	84	28
Bangladesh	71	75	23	48	77	85	27	6	61	..	84	33
Belarus	100	100	..	..	99	86	..	..	..	..	..	44
Belgium	..	..	..	..	75	90	..	..	..	..	69	57
Benin	60	68	11	32	83	88	35	13	23	7.4	80	94
Bolivia	72	85	33	45	64	81	47	25	30	..	84	71
Bosnia and Herzegovina	98	98	..	93	84	87	80	9	13	..	95	48
Botswana	93	95	38	41	90	97	14	7	49	..	71	68
Brazil	83	89	70	75	99	96	..	..	..	..	75	18
Bulgaria	100	100	100	100	96	96	..	..	..	..	86	81
Burkina Faso	39	51	13	12	76	84	22	..	..	..	64	18
Burundi	69	79	44	36	75	74	..	..	..	1.3	79	30
Cambodia	..	34	..	16	65	69	..	19	18	..	92	60
Cameroon	50	63	21	48	61	73	34	19	22	1.3	71	86
Canada	100	100	100	100	95	91	..	..	..	..	81	76
Central African Republic	48	75	23	27	35	40	..	..	..	1.5	61	6
Chad	20	34	6	8	61	47	22	31	16	0.6	72	11
Chile	90	95	85	92	99	99	..	..	..	..	86	114
China	70	77	23	44	84	90	..	..	..	..	93	43
Hong Kong, China	..	..	..	..	..	..	..	..	..	..	79	58
Colombia	92	92	82	86	92	91	51	14	36	0.7	84	7
Congo, Dem. Rep.	43	46	18	29	54	49	..	..	..	0.7	78	63
Congo, Rep.	..	46	..	9	50	50	..	..	..	..	71	57
Costa Rica	..	97	..	92	89	88	..	..	..	..	85	117
Côte d'Ivoire	69	84	31	40	56	54	38	20	16	1.1	67	39
Croatia	..	..	..	..	95	94	..	..	..	..	..	..
Cuba	..	91	98	98	99	71	..	..	..	..	92	93
Czech Republic	..	..	..	..	99	97	..	..	..	..	73	63
Denmark	100	100	..	..	96	96	..	..	..	..	77	75
Dominican Republic	86	93	48	57	79	65	68	20	28	..	78	65
Ecuador	69	86	56	72	99	89	39	20	29	..	84	37
Egypt, Arab Rep.	94	98	54	68	98	98	66	7	34	..	88	56
El Salvador	67	82	51	63	99	88	54	20	47	..	88	53
Eritrea	40	57	8	9	84	83	..	..	..	4.2	82	18
Estonia	..	..	..	..	95	94	..	..	..	..	67	69
Ethiopia	25	22	4	6	52	56	16	24	13	..	76	36
Finland	100	100	100	100	97	98	..	..	..	..	..	..
France	..	..	..	..	86	97	..	..	..	..	..	..
Gabon	..	87	..	36	55	38	48	16	25	..	47	93
Gambia, The	..	82	..	53	90	90	64	22	33	14.7	74	70
Georgia	..	76	..	83	73	76	99	6	25	..	65	52
Germany	100	100	..	..	92	89	..	..	..	..	69	55
Ghana	54	79	43	58	80	80	26	18	29	..	60	40
Greece	..	..	..	..	88	88	..	..	..	..	..	..
Guatemala	77	95	50	61	75	83	37	13	30	1.2	84	44
Guinea	42	51	17	13	52	45	39	21	35	..	72	51
Guinea-Bissau	..	59	..	34	61	77	64	32	39	7.4	48	55
Haiti	53	71	15	34	53	43	51	26	35	..	78	46

Disease prevention: coverage and quality

	Access to an improved water source (% of population)		Access to improved sanitation facilities (% of population)		Child immunization rate (% of children ages 12–23 months[a])		Children with ARI taken to a health provider (% of children under age 5)	Children with diarrhea (% of children under age 5)	Children with diarrhea who received ORS packet (% of children under age 5 with diarrhea)	Children sleeping under treated bednets[b] (% of children under age 5)	Tuberculosis treatment success rate (% of registered cases)	DOTS detection rate (% of estimated cases)
	1990	2002	1990	2002	Measles 2003	DPT 2003	1998–2003[c]	1998–2003[c]	1998–2003[c]	1999–2003[c]	2002	2003
Honduras	83	90	49	68	95	92	..	..	..	..	87	78
Hungary	99	99	..	95	99	99	..	..	..	..	55	41
India	68	86	12	30	67	70	64	19	27	..	87	47
Indonesia	71	78	46	52	72	70	..	..	..	0.1	86	33
Iran, Islamic Rep.	91	93	83	84	99	99	..	..	..	..	85	59
Iraq	83	81	81	80	90	81	..	..	..	..	91	20
Ireland	..	..	..	..	78	85	..	..	..	..	..	..
Israel	100	100	..	..	95	97	..	..	..	..	79	55
Italy	..	..	..	..	83	96	..	..	..	..	79	79
Jamaica	92	93	75	80	78	81	..	..	..	..	49	90
Japan	100	100	100	100	99	97	..	..	..	..	76	40
Jordan	98	91	..	93	96	97	..	..	..	..	89	89
Kazakhstan	86	86	72	72	99	99	48	13	32	..	78	86
Kenya	45	62	42	48	72	73	57	17	37	4.3	79	46
Korea, Dem. Rep.	100	100	..	59	95	68	..	..	81	..	88	91
Korea, Rep.	..	92	..	..	96	97	..	..	..	..	83	23
Kuwait	..	..	..	..	97	99	..	..	..	..	55	67
Kyrgyz Republic	..	76	..	60	99	98	..	..	..	..	82	57
Lao PDR	..	43	..	24	42	50	36	6	34	..	78	47
Latvia	..	..	..	..	99	98	..	..	..	..	76	83
Lebanon	100	100	..	98	96	92	74	19	44	..	91	67
Lesotho	..	76	37	37	70	79	..	..	..	..	71	70
Liberia	56	62	38	26	53	38	..	..	..	..	..	..
Libya	71	72	97	97	91	93	..	..	..	..	61	147
Lithuania	..	..	..	..	98	94	..	..	..	..	72	85
Macedonia, FYR	..	..	..	..	96	96	..	..	..	..	79	49
Madagascar	40	45	12	33	55	55	29	13	22	0.2	74	77
Malawi	41	67	36	46	77	84	27	18	48	2.9	72	35
Malaysia	..	95	96	..	92	96	..	..	..	..	76	69
Mali	34	48	36	45	68	69	..	19	12	8.4	50	18
Mauritania	41	56	28	42	71	76	41	18	23	..	..	..
Mauritius	100	100	99	99	94	92	..	..	..	..	92	28
Mexico	80	91	66	77	96	98	..	..	..	..	84	81
Moldova	..	92	..	68	96	98	78	4	8	..	61	39
Mongolia	62	62	..	59	98	98	78	8	56	..	87	68
Morocco	75	80	57	61	90	91	..	..	..	..	89	83
Mozambique	..	42	..	27	77	72	..	..	..	..	78	45
Myanmar	48	80	21	73	75	77	..	..	..	..	81	73
Namibia	58	80	24	30	70	82	..	..	..	3.4	62	86
Nepal	69	84	12	27	75	78	26	..	..	..	86	60
Netherlands	100	100	100	100	96	98	..	..	..	..	68	50
New Zealand	97	..	..	..	85	90	..	..	..	..	60	57
Nicaragua	69	81	47	66	93	86	58	14	56	..	82	91
Niger	40	46	7	12	64	52	27	40	14	5.8	..	54
Nigeria	49	60	39	38	35	25	50	15	34	1.0	79	18
Norway	100	100	..	..	84	90	..	..	..	..	80	46
Oman	77	79	83	89	98	99	..	..	..	..	92	81
Pakistan	83	90	38	54	61	67	..	..	..	..	77	17
Panama	..	91	..	72	83	86	..	..	..	..	73	92
Papua New Guinea	39	39	45	45	49	54	..	..	..	..	53	15
Paraguay	62	83	58	78	91	77	..	..	..	..	92	18
Peru	74	81	52	62	95	89	58	15	22	..	92	81
Philippines	87	85	54	73	80	79	64	7	43	..	88	68
Poland	..	..	..	..	97	99	..	..	..	..	86	56
Portugal	..	..	..	..	96	99	..	..	..	..	82	87
Puerto Rico	..	..	..	..	..	..	..	..	..	..	62	59

2.15 | Disease prevention: coverage and quality

	Access to an improved water source		Access to improved sanitation facilities		Child immunization rate		Children with ARI taken to a health provider	Children with diarrhea	Children with diarrhea who received ORS packet	Children sleeping under treated bednets[b]	Tuberculosis treatment success rate	DOTS detection rate
	% of population		% of population		% of children ages 12–23 months[a]		% of children under age 5	% of children under age 5	% of children under age 5 with diarrhea	% of children under age 5	% of registered cases	% of estimated cases
	1990	2002	1990	2002	Measles 2003	DPT 2003	1998–2003[c]	1998–2003[c]	1998–2003[c]	1999–2003[c]	2002	2003
Romania	..	57	..	51	97	97	..	..	..	..	76	38
Russian Federation	94	96	87	87	96	98	..	..	..	..	67	9
Rwanda	58	73	37	41	90	96	16	17	14	5.0	58	27
Saudi Arabia	90	..	..	..	96	95	..	..	..	..	76	38
Senegal	66	72	35	52	60	73	27	..	..	1.7	66	60
Serbia and Montenegro	93	93	87	87	87	89	97	9	23	..	91	37
Sierra Leone	..	57	..	39	73	70	50	25	42	1.5	81	33
Singapore	..	..	..	..	88	92	..	..	..	..	87	44
Slovak Republic	100	100	100	100	99	99	..	..	..	..	85	34
Slovenia	..	..	..	..	94	92	..	..	..	..	85	70
Somalia	..	29	..	25	40	40	..	23	30	0.3	89	29
South Africa	83	87	63	67	83	94	..	13	51	..	68	118
Spain	..	..	..	..	97	98	..	..	..	..	..	..
Sri Lanka	68	78	70	91	99	99	..	..	..	..	81	70
Sudan	64	69	33	34	57	50	..	..	..	0.4	78	34
Swaziland	..	52	..	52	94	95	..	..	..	0.1	47	35
Sweden	100	100	100	100	94	98	..	..	..	..	73	62
Switzerland	100	100	100	100	82	95	..	..	..	..	..	..
Syrian Arab Republic	79	79	76	77	98	99	..	..	..	..	87	45
Tajikistan	..	58	..	53	89	82	51	21	35	1.9	79	2
Tanzania	38	73	47	46	97	95	68	12	55	2.1	80	43
Thailand	81	85	80	99	94	96	..	..	..	..	74	72
Togo	49	51	37	34	58	64	26	31	17	2.0	68	17
Trinidad and Tobago	92	91	100	100	88	91	..	..	..	..	..	..
Tunisia	77	82	75	80	90	95	..	6	32	..	92	91
Turkey	81	93	84	83	75	68	..	30	14	..	..	..
Turkmenistan	..	71	..	62	97	98	51	3	47	..	77	49
Uganda	44	56	43	41	82	81	67	20	34	0.2	60	44
Ukraine	..	98	99	99	99	97	..	..	..	..	..	..
United Arab Emirates	..	..	100	100	94	94	..	..	..	..	79	32
United Kingdom	..	..	..	..	80	91	..	..	..	..	..	..
United States	100	100	100	100	93	96	..	..	..	..	..	89
Uruguay	..	98	..	94	95	91	..	..	..	..	82	80
Uzbekistan	89	89	58	57	99	98	..	5	32	..	80	20
Venezuela, RB	..	83	..	68	82	68	..	..	..	..	82	80
Vietnam	72	73	22	41	93	99	60	11	11	15.8	92	86
West Bank and Gaza	..	..	..	..	..	..	..	..	..	..	100	4
Yemen, Rep.	69	69	21	30	66	66	..	..	..	..	82	43
Zambia	50	55	41	45	84	80	69	21	53	6.5	83	65
Zimbabwe	77	83	49	57	80	80	50	14	..	..	67	42
World	**75 w**	**82 w**	**43 w**	**54 w**	**77 w**	**78 w**						
Low income	64	75	20	36	65	67						
Middle income	77	83	48	61	87	89						
Lower middle income	77	82	46	60	86	88						
Upper middle income	..	..	..	..	94	91						
Low & middle income	72	79	37	50	76	77						
East Asia & Pacific	71	78	30	49	82	86						
Europe & Central Asia	..	91	86	82	92	90						
Latin America & Carib.	82	89	68	74	93	89						
Middle East & N. Africa	87	88	69	75	92	92						
South Asia	70	84	17	35	67	71						
Sub-Saharan Africa	49	58	32	36	61	59						
High income	..	99	..	..	92	95						
Europe EMU	..	..	..	..	89	94						

a. Refers to children who were immunized before 12 months, or in some cases, at any time before the survey (12–23 months). b. For malaria prevention only. c. Data are for the most recent year available.

About the data

The indicators in the table are based on data provided to the World Health Organization (WHO) by member states as part of their efforts to monitor and evaluate progress in implementing national health strategies. Because reliable, observation-based statistical data for these indicators do not exist in some developing countries, some of the data are estimated.

People's health is influenced by the environment in which they live. Lack of clean water and basic sanitation is the main reason diseases transmitted by feces are so common in developing countries. The data on access to an improved water source measure the share of the population with ready access to water for domestic purposes. The data are based on surveys and estimates provided by governments to the Joint Monitoring Programme of the WHO and United Nations Children's Fund (UNICEF). The coverage rates for water and sanitation are based on information from service users on the facilities their households actually use rather than on information from service providers, who may include nonfunctioning systems. Access to drinking water from an improved source does not ensure that the water is safe or adequate, as these characteristics are not tested at the time of the surveys.

Governments in developing countries usually finance immunization against measles and diphtheria, pertussis (whooping cough), and tetanus (DPT) as part of the basic public health package. In many developing countries, lack of precise information on the size of the cohort of one-year-old children makes immunization coverage difficult to estimate from program statistics. The data shown here are based on an assessment of national immunization coverage

rates by the WHO and UNICEF. The assessment considered both administrative data from service providers and household survey data on children's immunization histories. Based on the data available, consideration of potential biases, and contributions of local experts, the most likely true level of immunization coverage was determined for each year.

Acute respiratory infection (ARI) continues to be a leading cause of mortality among young children, killing about 2 million children under age five in developing countries in 2000. An estimated 60 percent of these deaths can be prevented by the selective use of antibiotics by appropriate health care providers. Data are drawn mostly from household health surveys in which mothers report on number of episodes and treatment for ARI.

Since 1990 diarrhea-related deaths among children have declined tremendously. Most diarrhea-related deaths are due to dehydration, and many of these deaths can be prevented with the use of oral rehydration salts (ORS) at home. However, recommendations for the use of oral rehydration therapy (ORT) have changed over time based on scientific progress in the management of diarrhea, together with considerations of treatment feasibility. Because definitions of ORT adopted and promoted by countries have changed over time, it is difficult to accurately compare use rates among countries. Until the current recommended method for home management of diarrhea is adopted and applied in all countries, the data should be used with caution. Also, the prevalence of diarrhea may vary by season. Since country surveys are administered at different times, that contributes to further problems in comparability of the data between countries.

Insecticide-treated bednets, if properly used and maintained, are one of the most important malaria preventive strategies to limit human-mosquito contact. Studies have emphasized that mortality rates could be reduced by about 25–30 percent if every child under five in malaria-risk areas such as Africa slept under a treated bednet every night.

Data on the success rate of tuberculosis treatment are provided for countries that have implemented the recommended control strategy: directly observed treatment, short course (DOTS). Countries that have not adopted DOTS or have only recently done so are omitted because of lack of data or poor comparability or reliability of reported results. The treatment success rate for tuberculosis provides a useful indicator of the quality of health services. A low rate or no success suggests that infectious patients may not be receiving adequate treatment. An essential complement to the tuberculosis treatment success rate is the DOTS detection rate, which indicates whether there is adequate coverage by the recommended case detection and treatment strategy. A country with a high treatment success rate may still face big challenges if its DOTS detection rate remains low.

Definitions

- **Access to an improved water source** refers to the percentage of the population with reasonable access to an adequate amount of water from an improved source, such as a household connection, public standpipe, borehole, protected well or spring, or rainwater collection. Unimproved sources include vendors, tanker trucks, and unprotected wells and springs. Reasonable access is defined as the availability of at least 20 liters a person a day from a source within 1 kilometer of the dwelling. • **Access to improved sanitation facilities** refers to the percentage of the population with at least adequate access to excreta disposal facilities that can effectively prevent human, animal, and insect contact with excreta. Improved facilities range from simple but protected pit latrines to flush toilets with a sewerage connection. To be effective, facilities must be correctly constructed and properly maintained. • **Child immunization rate** is the percentage of children ages 12–23 months who received vaccinations before 12 months or at any time before the survey for four diseases—measles and diphtheria, pertussis (whooping cough), and tetanus (DPT). A child is considered adequately immunized against measles after receiving one dose of vaccine and against DPT after receiving three doses. • **Children with acute respiratory infection (ARI) who are taken to a health provider** refer to the percentage of children under age five with ARI in the last two weeks who were taken to an appropriate health provider, including hospital, health center, dispensary, village health worker, clinic, and private physician. • **Children with diarrhea** refer to the percentage of children under age five who had diarrhea in the two weeks prior to the survey. • **Children with diarrhea who received oral rehydration salts (ORS) packet** refer to the percentage of children under age five with diarrhea in the two weeks prior to the survey who received an ORS packet. • **Children sleeping under treated bednets** refer to the percentage of children under age five who slept under an insecticide-impregnated bednet to prevent malaria. • **Tuberculosis treatment success rate** is the percentage of new, registered smear-positive (infectious) cases that were cured or in which a full course of treatment was completed. • **DOTS detection rate** is the percentage of estimated new infectious tuberculosis cases detected under the directly observed treatment, short course case detection and treatment strategy.

Data sources

Data are drawn from a variety of sources, including WHO and UNICEF estimates of national immunization coverage, the WHO's *Global Tuberculosis Control Report 2004;* UNICEF's *State of the World's Children 2005* and Childinfo; Demographic and Health Surveys by Macro International; and the WHO and UNICEF's *Meeting the MDG Drinking Water and Sanitation Target* (www.unicef.org/wes/mdgreport).

2.15a

Children with acute respiratory infection have better access to health care in urban areas

Share of children with acute respiratory infection consulting a health provider, by urban and rural residence, 1990–2000 (%)

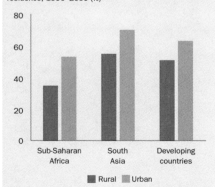

Children with acute respiratory infection have a better chance of receiving health care in urban areas than in rural areas because of greater access to health care providers and facilities.

Source: Childinfo.

	Total fertility rate		Adolescent fertility rate	Women at risk of unintended pregnancy	Contraceptive prevalence rate	Tetanus vaccinations	Births attended by skilled health staff		Maternal mortality ratio	
			births per 1,000 women ages 15–19	% of married women ages 15–49	% of women ages 15–49	% of pregnant women	% of total		per 100,000 live births National estimates	Modeled estimates
	births per woman									
	1990	**2003**	**2003**	**1990–2003[a]**	**1995–2003[a]**	**2003**	**1990–92[a]**	**2000–03[a]**	**1985–2003[a]**	**2000**
Afghanistan	6.9	..	..	..	10	40	..	14	1,600	1,900
Albania	3.0	2.2	15	..	75	..	..	94	20	55
Algeria	4.5	2.7	18	..	57	..	77	92	140	140
Angola	7.2	7.0	220	..	6	72	..	45	..	1,700
Argentina	2.9	2.4	54	..	..	..	96	99	46	82
Armenia	2.6	1.1	35	12	61	..	..	97	22	55
Australia	1.9	1.8	18	..	..	..	100	..	..	8
Austria	1.5	1.4	22	..	51	..	..	..	..	4
Azerbaijan	2.7	2.1	44	..	55	..	..	84	25	94
Bangladesh	4.1	2.9	119	15	54	89	..	14	380	380
Belarus	1.9	1.3	21	..	50	..	..	100	18	35
Belgium	1.6	1.6	11	..	..	..	..	..	..	10
Benin	6.6	5.2	101	27	19	56	..	66	500	850
Bolivia	4.8	3.7	70	26	58	..	..	65	390	420
Bosnia and Herzegovina	1.7	1.3	23	..	48	..	97	100	10	31
Botswana	5.1	3.7	66	..	48	..	..	99	330	100
Brazil	2.7	2.1	68	7	77	..	72	..	75	260
Bulgaria	1.8	1.2	49	..	42	..	..	..	15	32
Burkina Faso	7.0	6.2	132	26	14	50	..	..	480	1,000
Burundi	6.8	5.7	50	..	16	46	..	25	..	1,000
Cambodia	5.6	3.9	57	30	24	43	..	32	440	450
Cameroon	6.0	4.6	123	20	26	65	58	60	430	730
Canada	1.8	1.5	20	..	..	..	..	..	..	6
Central African Republic	5.5	4.6	122	16	28	63	..	44	1,100	1,100
Chad	7.1	6.2	178	10	8	43	..	16	830	1,100
Chile	2.6	2.2	43	..	..	..	..	100	17	31
China	2.1	1.9	15	..	87	..	..	97	50	56
Hong Kong, China	1.3	1.0	6	..	..	..	..	..	..	..
Colombia	3.1	2.5	70	6	77	..	82	86	78	130
Congo, Dem. Rep.	6.7	6.7	222	..	31	48	..	61	950	990
Congo, Rep.	6.3	6.3	143	..	..	59	..	..	..	510
Costa Rica	3.2	2.3	62	..	..	..	98	98	29	43
Côte d'Ivoire	6.2	4.5	116	28	15	80	..	63	600	690
Croatia	1.6	1.4	18	..	..	..	..	..	2	8
Cuba	1.7	1.6	67	..	73	..	..	100	34	33
Czech Republic	1.9	1.2	23	..	72	..	..	..	3	9
Denmark	1.7	1.8	8	..	..	..	..	..	10	5
Dominican Republic	3.4	2.6	81	12	70	..	93	98	180	150
Ecuador	3.7	2.7	62	..	66	..	..	..	80	130
Egypt, Arab Rep.	4.0	3.1	45	11	60	71	41	69	84	84
El Salvador	3.8	2.8	82	..	67	..	..	69	170	150
Eritrea	6.5	4.8	98	28	8	55	..	28	1,000	630
Estonia	2.0	1.4	28	..	..	..	..	..	46	63
Ethiopia	6.9	5.6	133	36	8	24	..	6	870	850
Finland	1.8	1.8	10	..	..	..	..	..	6	6
France	1.8	1.9	10	..	..	..	..	..	10	17
Gabon	5.1	4.0	154	28	33	54	..	86	520	420
Gambia, The	5.9	4.8	136	..	18	..	44	55	730	540
Georgia	2.2	1.1	27	..	41	..	..	..	67	32
Germany	1.5	1.3	14	..	..	..	..	..	8	8
Ghana	5.5	4.4	73	23	25	70	..	..	210[b]	540
Greece	1.4	1.3	17	..	..	..	..	..	1	9
Guatemala	5.3	4.3	97	23	40	..	..	41	150	240
Guinea	5.9	5.0	149	24	6	74	31	..	530	740
Guinea-Bissau	7.1	6.6	210	..	8	66	..	35	910	1,100
Haiti	5.4	4.2	69	40	28	52	..	24	520	680

	Total fertility rate		Adolescent fertility rate	Women at risk of unintended pregnancy	Contraceptive prevalence rate	Tetanus vaccinations	Births attended by skilled health staff		Maternal mortality ratio	
	births per woman		births per 1,000 women ages 15–19	% of married women ages 15–49	% of women ages 15–49	% of pregnant women	% of total		per 100,000 live births National estimates	Modeled estimates
	1990	2003	2003	1990–2003[a]	1995–2003[a]	2003	1990–92[a]	2000–03[a]	1985–2003[a]	2000
Honduras	5.2	4.0	103	..	62	..	45	56	110	110
Hungary	1.8	1.3	27	..	..	..	..	..	5	16
India	3.8	2.9	98	16	47	78	..	43	540	540
Indonesia	3.1	2.4	48	9	60	51	32	68	310	230
Iran, Islamic Rep.	4.7	2.0	25	..	74	..	..	90	37	76
Iraq	5.9	4.0	35	..	44	70	..	72	290	250
Ireland	2.1	2.0	15	..	..	..	..	..	6	5
Israel	2.8	2.7	23	..	..	..	..	..	5	17
Italy	1.3	1.3	8	..	60	..	..	..	7	5
Jamaica	2.9	2.3	81	..	65	..	..	..	110	87
Japan	1.5	1.3	4	..	..	..	100	..	8	10
Jordan	5.4	3.5	31	14	56	..	87	100	41	41
Kazakhstan	2.7	1.8	35	9	66	..	..	..	50	210
Kenya	5.6	4.8	94	24	38	66	..	41	590	1,000
Korea, Dem. Rep.	2.4	2.1	2	..	..	..	..	97	110	67
Korea, Rep.	1.8	1.5	4	..	81	..	98	..	20	20
Kuwait	3.4	2.5	30	..	50	..	..	..	5	5
Kyrgyz Republic	3.7	2.4	30	12	60	..	..	..	44	110
Lao PDR	6.0	4.8	89	..	32	36	..	19	530	650
Latvia	2.0	1.3	32	..	48	..	..	..	25	42
Lebanon	3.2	2.2	25	..	63	..	..	..	100[b]	150
Lesotho	5.1	4.3	76	..	30	..	..	60	..	550
Liberia	6.8	5.8	192	..	10	56	..	51	580	760
Libya	4.7	3.3	32	..	45	..	..	..	77	97
Lithuania	2.0	1.3	33	..	47	..	..	..	13	13
Macedonia, FYR	2.1	1.8	31	..	..	..	..	98	11	23
Madagascar	6.2	5.2	153	26	17	55	57	46	490	550
Malawi	7.0	6.0	136	30	31	70	55	61	1,100	1,800
Malaysia	3.8	2.8	26	..	..	..	..	97	50	41
Mali	..	6.4	173	29	8	32	..	41	580	1,200
Mauritania	6.0	4.6	110	32	8	41	40	57	750	1,000
Mauritius	2.3	2.0	39	..	26	..	..	..	21	24
Mexico	3.3	2.2	57	..	70	..	..	..	63	83
Moldova	2.4	1.4	44	..	62	..	..	..	44	36
Mongolia	4.0	2.4	43	..	67	..	..	99	110	110
Morocco	4.0	2.7	42	20	63	..	31	..	230	220
Mozambique	6.3	5.0	150	23	17	57	..	48	1,100	1,000
Myanmar	3.8	2.8	30	..	33	77	..	..	230	360
Namibia	5.4	4.8	100	22	44	85	68	78	270	300
Nepal	5.3	4.1	109	28	39	69	7	11	540	740
Netherlands	1.6	1.8	5	..	75	..	..	..	7	16
New Zealand	2.2	1.9	30	..	75	..	..	..	15	7
Nicaragua	4.8	3.4	114	15	69	..	..	67	97	230
Niger	7.6	7.1	201	17	14	36	15	16	590	1,600
Nigeria	6.5	5.6	122	17	13	51	31	35	..	800
Norway	1.9	1.8	10	..	..	..	..	..	6	16
Oman	7.4	4.0	53	..	32	..	..	95	23	87
Pakistan	5.8	4.5	60	32	28	57	19	23	530	500
Panama	3.0	2.4	67	..	..	..	..	..	70	160
Papua New Guinea	5.6	4.3	66	..	26	34	..	..	370[b]	300
Paraguay	4.6	3.8	71	15	57	..	67	..	180	170
Peru	3.7	2.7	58	10	69	..	..	59	190	410
Philippines	4.1	3.2	33	19	49	70	..	60	170	200
Poland	2.0	1.2	16	..	..	..	..	..	4	13
Portugal	1.4	1.4	23	..	..	..	..	..	8	5
Puerto Rico	2.2	1.9	64	..	78	..	..	..	..	25

	Total fertility rate		Adolescent fertility rate	Women at risk of unintended pregnancy	Contraceptive prevalence rate	Tetanus vaccinations	Births attended by skilled health staff		Maternal mortality ratio	
	births per woman		births per 1,000 women ages 15–19	% of married women ages 15–49	% of women ages 15–49	% of pregnant women	% of total		per 100,000 live births National estimates	Modeled estimates
	1990	2003	2003	1990–2003ᵃ	1995–2003ᵃ	2003	1990–92ᵃ	2000–03ᵃ	1985–2003ᵃ	2000
Romania	1.8	1.3	40	..	64		..	..	34	49
Russian Federation	1.9	1.3	46	..	..	..	..	99	37	67
Rwanda	7.1	5.7	52	36	13	76	26	31	1,100	1,400
Saudi Arabia	6.6	5.3	89	..	21	..	..	..	..	23
Senegal	6.2	4.9	87	35	11	75	..	41	560	690
Serbia and Montenegro	2.1	1.7	32	..	58	..	..	99	7	11
Sierra Leone	6.5	5.6	178	..	..	62	..	42	1,800	2,000
Singapore	1.9	1.4	8	..	..	..	..	..	6	30
Slovak Republic	2.1	1.2	23	..	..	..	..	..	16	3
Slovenia	1.5	1.2	9	..	..	..	100	..	17	17
Somalia	7.3	6.9	201	..	..	60	..	..	..	1,100
South Africa	3.3	2.8	42	15	62	52	..	..	150	230
Spain	1.3	1.3	9	..	81	..	..	..	6	4
Sri Lanka	2.5	2.0	29	..	70	..	..	87	92	92
Sudan	5.4	4.4	55	..	7	35	69	..	550	590
Swaziland	5.3	4.2	97	..	28	..	..	70	230	370
Sweden	2.1	1.7	9	..	..	..	..	100	5	2
Switzerland	1.6	1.4	5	..	82	..	..	..	5	7
Syrian Arab Republic	5.3	3.4	39	..	48	..	..	..	65	160
Tajikistan	5.1	2.9	25	..	34	..	..	71	45	100
Tanzania	6.3	5.0	112	22	25	83	44	..	530	1,500
Thailand	2.3	1.8	72	..	72	..	..	69	36	44
Togo	6.6	4.9	80	32	26	47	..	49	480	570
Trinidad and Tobago	2.4	1.8	42	..	38	..	..	96	45	160
Tunisia	3.5	2.0	15	..	66	..	..	90	69	120
Turkey	3.0	2.4	51	10	64	37	..	..	130ᵇ	70
Turkmenistan	4.2	2.7	18	10	62	..	..	97	9	31
Uganda	7.0	6.0	201	35	23	48	..	39	510	880
Ukraine	1.8	1.2	31	..	72	..	..	..	22	35
United Arab Emirates	4.1	3.0	61	..	28	..	..	..	3	54
United Kingdom	1.8	1.6	28	..	..	..	..	..	7	13
United States	2.1	2.0	46	..	64	..	..	..	8	17
Uruguay	2.5	2.2	63	..	..	..	..	..	26	27
Uzbekistan	4.1	2.3	36	14	68	..	..	96	34	24
Venezuela, RB	3.4	2.7	85	..	77	..	..	94	60	96
Vietnam	3.6	1.9	28	7	79	79	..	85	95	130
West Bank and Gaza	6.3	4.9	80	..	42	..	..	..	..	..
Yemen, Rep.	7.5	6.0	95	39	23	31	16	..	350	570
Zambia	6.3	5.0	156	27	34	60	51	43	730	750
Zimbabwe	4.8	3.6	81	13	54	60	..	..	700	1,100
World	**3.1 w**	**2.6 w**	**63 w**		**60 w**		**.. w**	**57 w**		**407 w**
Low income	4.7	3.7	102		39		..	38		689
Middle income	2.6	2.1	36		75		..	87		115
Lower middle income	2.6	2.1	34		76		..	86		121
Upper middle income	3.1	2.3	51		..		..	..		67
Low & middle income	3.4	2.8	67		59		..	57		444
East Asia & Pacific	2.4	2.1	24		79		..	87		116
Europe & Central Asia	2.3	1.6	38		..		97	..		58
Latin America & Carib.	3.1	2.4	67		71		..	..		193
Middle East & N. Africa	4.8	3.1	41		56		..	80		162
South Asia	4.1	3.1	97		45		..	36		567
Sub-Saharan Africa	6.1	5.2	127		22		..	39		916
High income	1.8	1.6	24		..		..	..		13
Europe EMU	1.5	1.5	11		..		..	..		9

a. Data are for most recent year available. b. Data refer to period other than specified, differ from the standard defination, or refer to only part of a country.

About the data

Reproductive health is a state of physical and mental well-being in relation to the reproductive system and its functions and processes. Means of achieving reproductive health include education and services during pregnancy and childbirth, provision of safe and effective contraception, and prevention and treatment of sexually transmitted diseases. Complications of pregnancy and childbirth are the leading cause of death and disability among women of reproductive age in developing countries. Reproductive health services will need to expand rapidly over the next two decades, when the number of women and men of reproductive age is projected to increase by 500 million.

Total and adolescent fertility rates are based on data on registered live births from vital registration systems or, in the absence of such systems, from censuses or sample surveys. As long as the surveys are fairly recent, the estimated rates are generally considered reliable measures of fertility in the recent past. Where no empirical information on age-specific fertility rates is available, a model is used to estimate the share of births to adolescents. For countries without vital registration systems, fertility rates are generally based on extrapolations from trends observed in censuses or surveys from earlier years.

An increasing number of couples in the developing world want to limit or postpone childbearing but are not using effective contraceptive methods. These couples face the risk of unintended pregnancy, shown in the table as the percentage of married women of reproductive age who do not want to become pregnant but are not using contraception (Bulatao 1998). Information on this indicator is collected through surveys and excludes women not exposed to the risk of unintended pregnancy because of menopause, infertility, or postpartum anovulation. Common reasons for not using contraception are lack of knowledge about contraceptive methods and concerns about possible health side-effects.

Contraceptive prevalence reflects all methods—ineffective traditional methods as well as highly effective modern methods. Contraceptive prevalence rates are obtained mainly from Demographic and Health Surveys and contraceptive prevalence surveys (see *Primary data documentation* for the most recent survey year). Unmarried women are often excluded from such surveys, which may bias the estimates.

Neonatal tetanus is an important cause of infant mortality in some developing countries. It can be prevented through immunization of the mother during pregnancy. Recommended doses for full protection are generally two tetanus shots during the first pregnancy and one booster shot during each subsequent pregnancy, with five doses considered adequate for lifetime protection. Information on tetanus shots during pregnancy is collected through surveys in which pregnant respondents are asked to show antenatal cards on which tetanus shots have been recorded. Because not all women have antenatal cards, respondents are also asked about their receipt of these injections. Poor recall may result in a downward bias in estimates of the share of births protected. But in settings where receiving injections is common, respondents may erroneously report having received tetanus shots.

The share of births attended by skilled health staff is an indicator of a health system's ability to provide adequate care for pregnant women. Good antenatal and postnatal care improve maternal health and reduce maternal and infant mortality. But data may not reflect such improvements because health information systems are often weak, maternal deaths are underreported, and rates of maternal mortality are difficult to measure.

Maternal mortality ratios are generally of unknown reliability, as are many other cause-specific mortality indicators. Household surveys such as the Demographic and Health Surveys attempt to measure maternal mortality by asking respondents about survivorship of sisters. The main disadvantage of this method is that the estimates of maternal mortality that it produces pertain to 12 years or so before the survey, making them unsuitable for monitoring recent changes or observing the impact of interventions. In addition, measurement of maternal mortality is subject to many types of errors. Even in high-income countries with vital registration systems, misclassification of maternal deaths has been found to lead to serious underestimation.

The maternal mortality ratios shown in the table as national estimates are based on national surveys, vital registration, or surveillance or are derived from community and hospital records. For countries with national data reported maternal mortality was adjusted by a factor of under- or over-estimation. For countries with no national data modeled estimates are used, based on an exercise by the World Health Organization (WHO), United Nations Children's Fund (UNICEF), and United Nations Population Fund (UNFPA). In this exercise, maternal mortality was estimated with a regression model using information on fertility, birth attendants, and GDP. Neither set of ratios can be assumed to provide an accurate estimate of maternal mortality for any of the countries in the table.

Definitions

• **Total fertility rate** is the number of children that would be born to a woman if she were to live to the end of her childbearing years and bear children in accordance with current age-specific fertility rates. • **Adolescent fertility rate** is the number of births per 1,000 women ages 15–19. • **Women at risk of unintended pregnancy** are fertile, married women of reproductive age who do not want to become pregnant and are not using contraception. • **Contraceptive prevalence rate** is the percentage of women who are practicing, or whose sexual partners are practicing, any form of contraception. It is usually measured for married women ages 15–49 only. • **Tetanus vaccinations** refer to the percentage of pregnant women who receive two tetanus toxoid injections during their first pregnancy and one booster shot during each subsequent pregnancy, with five doses considered adequate for a lifetime. • **Births attended by skilled health staff** are the percentage of deliveries attended by personnel trained to give the necessary supervision, care, and advice to women during pregnancy, labor, and the postpartum period; to conduct deliveries on their own; and to care for newborns. • **Maternal mortality ratio** is the number of women who die from pregnancy-related causes during pregnancy and childbirth, per 100,000 live births.

Data sources

The data on reproductive health come from Demographic and Health Surveys by Macro International, the WHO's *Coverage of Maternity Care* (1997) and other WHO sources, UNICEF's *State of the World's Children 2005* and Childinfo; and national statistical offices. Modeled estimates for maternal mortality ratios are from Carla AbouZahr and Tessa Wardlaw's "Maternal Mortality in 2000: Estimates Developed by WHO, UNICEF, and UNFPA" (2003).

	Prevalence of undernourishment		Prevalence of child malnutrition		Prevalence of overweight	Low-birthweight babies	Exclusive breastfeeding	Consumption of iodized salt	Vitamin A supplementation
	% of population		% of children under age 5		% of children under age 5	% of births	% of children under 6 months	% of households	% of children 6–59 months
	1990–92	2000–02	Underweight 1995–2003[a]	Stunting 1995–2003[a]	1995–2003[a]	1995–2003[a]	1995–2003[a]	1997–2003[a]	2002
Afghanistan	..	..	49.3	47.6	4.0	..	..	1	84
Albania	5[b]	6	13.6	35.1	22.4	3	6	62	..
Algeria	5	5	6.0	18.0	10.1	7	13	69	..
Angola	58	40	30.5	45.2	0.5	12	11	35	88
Argentina	<3	<3	5.4	12.4	9.2	7	..	..	..
Armenia	52[b]	34	2.6	12.9	10.4	7	30	84	..
Australia	..	..	0.0	0.0	5.2	7	..	..	..
Austria	..	..	..	..	..	7	..	..	..
Azerbaijan	34[b]	15	6.8	13.3	2.6	11	7	26	..
Bangladesh	35	30	52.2	48.5	0.6	30	46	70	84
Belarus	<3[b]	<3	..	..	..	5	..	..	..
Belgium	..	..	..	..	..	8	..	..	..
Benin	20	15	22.9	30.7	1.8	16	38	72	85
Bolivia	28	21	7.6	26.8	6.5	9	54	90	50
Bosnia and Herzegovina	9[b]	8	4.1	9.7	13.2	4	6	77	..
Botswana	23	32	12.5	23.1	6.9	10	34	66	85
Brazil	12	9	5.7	10.5	4.9	10	..	88	..
Bulgaria	8[b]	11	..	..	..	10	..	..	..
Burkina Faso	21	19	37.7	38.7	1.0	19	6	..	97
Burundi	48	68	45.1	56.8	0.7	16	62	96	89
Cambodia	43	33	45.2	44.6	2.0	11	12	14	34
Cameroon	33	25	22.2	29.3	5.0	11	12	61	86
Canada	..	..	..	..	..	6	..	..	..
Central African Republic	50	43	23.2	28.4	0.8	14	17	86	90
Chad	58	34	28.0	29.1	1.5	17	10	58	85
Chile	8	4	0.8	1.5	8.0	5	63	100	..
China	16	11	10.0	14.2	2.6	6	67[c]	93	..
Hong Kong, China	..	..	..	..	..	5	..	..	..
Colombia	17	13	6.7	13.5	3.7	9	26	92	..
Congo, Dem. Rep.	32	71	31.0	38.1	3.9	12	24	72	62
Congo, Rep.	54	37	..	..	..	..	4[c]	..	86
Costa Rica	6	4	5.1	6.1	6.2	7	..	..	..
Côte d'Ivoire	18	14	21.2	25.1	2.5	17	10	31	97
Croatia	16[b]	7	0.6	0.8	5.9	6	23	90	..
Cuba	8	3	3.9	4.6	..	6	41	83	..
Czech Republic	<3[b]	<3	..	..	..	7	..	..	..
Denmark	..	..	..	..	..	5	..	..	..
Dominican Republic	27	25	5.3	8.9	6.5	11	10	18	31
Ecuador	8	4	14.3	26.4	..	16	35	99	50
Egypt, Arab Rep.	4	3	8.6	15.6	8.6	12	30	56	..
El Salvador	12	11	10.3	18.9	2.6	13	16	..	..
Eritrea	..	73	39.6	37.6	0.7	21	52	68	51
Estonia	9[b]	5	..	..	..	4	..	..	..
Ethiopia	..	46	47.2	51.5	1.2	15	55	28	16
Finland	..	..	..	..	..	4	..	..	..
France	..	..	..	..	..	7	..	..	..
Gabon	10	6	11.9	20.7	3.7	14	6	15	87
Gambia, The	22	27	17.2	19.2	1.5	17	26	8	91
Georgia	39[b]	27	3.1	11.7	12.7	6	18[c]	68	..
Germany	..	..	..	..	..	7	..	..	..
Ghana	37	13	22.1	29.9	2.9	11	31	50	99
Greece	..	..	..	..	..	8	..	..	..
Guatemala	16	24	22.7	49.3	5.4	13	51	67	33
Guinea	39	26	23.2	26.1	2.7	12	11	68	95
Guinea-Bissau	..	..	25.0	30.5	3.3	22	37	2	80
Haiti	65	47	17.2	22.7	2.0	21	24	11	..

	Prevalence of undernourishment		Prevalence of child malnutrition		Prevalence of overweight	Low-birthweight babies	Exclusive breastfeeding	Consumption of iodized salt	Vitamin A supplemen-tation
	% of population		% of children under age 5		% of children under age 5	% of births	% of children under 6 months	% of households	% of children 6–59 months
	1990–92	2000–02	Underweight 1995–2003[a]	Stunting 1995–2003[a]	1995–2003[a]	1995–2003[a]	1995–2003[a]	1997–2003[a]	2002
Honduras	23	22	16.6	29.2	2.2	14	35	80	61
Hungary	<3[b]	<3	..	..	..	9	..	..	..
India	25	21	46.7	44.9	2.2	30	37[c]	50	27
Indonesia	9	6	27.3	42.2	4.0	9	40	73	82
Iran, Islamic Rep.	4	4	10.9	15.4	4.3	10	44	94	..
Iraq	..	..	15.9	22.1	..	15	12	40	..
Ireland	..	..	..	..	..	6	..	..	..
Israel	..	..	..	..	..	8	..	..	..
Italy	..	..	..	..	..	6	..	..	..
Jamaica	14	10	3.8	4.4	3.8	9	..	100	..
Japan	..	..	..	..	..	8	..	..	..
Jordan	4	7	4.4	8.5	2.8	10	27	88	..
Kazakhstan	<3[b]	13	4.2	9.7	3.0	8	36	20	..
Kenya	44	33	19.9	30.3	3.7	11	13	91	91
Korea, Dem. Rep.	18	36	27.9	45.2	..	7	70	..	99
Korea, Rep.	<3	<3	..	..	..	4	..	..	..
Kuwait	23	5	1.7	3.2	5.7	7	12[c]	..	..
Kyrgyz Republic	21[b]	6	5.8	24.8	6.3	7	24	27	..
Lao PDR	29	22	40.0	40.7	..	14	23	75	58
Latvia	3[b]	4	..	..	..	5	..	..	..
Lebanon	<3	3	3.0	12.2	..	6	27[c]	87	..
Lesotho	17	12	17.9	45.5	..	14	15	69	..
Liberia	34	46	26.5	39.5	2.3	..	35	..	40
Libya	<3	<3	4.7	15.1	..	7	..	..	..
Lithuania	4[b]	..	..	..	..	4	..	..	..
Macedonia, FYR	15[b]	11	5.9	6.9	4.9	5	37	80	..
Madagascar	35	37	33.1	48.6	2.0	14	41	52	95
Malawi	50	33	25.4	49.0	4.3	16	44	49	86
Malaysia	3	<3	19.0	15.6	3.3	10	29[c]	..	..
Mali	29	29	33.2	38.2	1.5	23	25	74	68
Mauritania	15	10	31.8	34.5	..	9	20	2	89
Mauritius	6	6	14.9	9.7	4.0	13	..	..	..
Mexico	5	5	7.5	17.7	5.3	9	..	90	..
Moldova	5[b]	11	..	..	..	5	..	33	..
Mongolia	34	28	12.7	24.6	4.8	11	51	45	84
Morocco	6	7	9.0	23.1	..	4	66[c]	41	..
Mozambique	66	47	26.1	35.9	3.4	14	30	..	71
Myanmar	10	6	28.2	41.6	7.7	15	11	48	92
Namibia	35	22	24.0	23.6	2.2	14	19	63	96
Nepal	20	17	48.3	50.5	0.2	21	68	63	83
Netherlands	..	..	..	..	..	..	..	..	..
New Zealand	..	..	..	..	..	6	..	83	..
Nicaragua	30	27	9.6	20.2	4.7	12	31	97	..
Niger	41	34	40.1	39.7	0.8	17	1	15	77
Nigeria	13	9	28.7	38.3	3.6	14	17	97	79
Norway	..	..	..	..	..	5	..	..	..
Oman	..	..	17.8	10.4	1.0	8	..	61	97
Pakistan	24	20	35.0	36.8	2.1	25	16[c]	17	95
Panama	21	26	8.1	18.2	4.2	10	25[c]	95	..
Papua New Guinea	..	..	..	..	..	11	59[c]	..	..
Paraguay	18	14	..	..	..	9	7[c]	83	..
Peru	42	13	7.1	25.4	7.6	11	71	93	6
Philippines	26	22	31.8	32.1	1.0	20	34	24	86
Poland	<3[b]	<3	..	..	..	6	..	..	..
Portugal	..	..	..	..	..	8	..	..	..
Puerto Rico	..	..	..	..	..	14	..	..	..

	Prevalence of undernourishment (% of population)		Prevalence of child malnutrition (% of children under age 5)		Prevalence of overweight (% of children under age 5)	Low-birthweight babies (% of births)	Exclusive breastfeeding (% of children under 6 months)	Consumption of iodized salt (% of households)	Vitamin A supplementation (% of children 6–59 months)
	1990–92	2000–02	Underweight 1995–2003[a]	Stunting 1995–2003[a]	1995–2003[a]	1995–2003[a]	1995–2003[a]	1997–2003[a]	2002
Romania	<3[b]	<3	3.2	10.1	5.5	9	..	53	..
Russian Federation	4[b]	4	5.5	10.6	..	6	..	35	..
Rwanda	44	37	24.3	42.6	4.0	9	84	90	36
Saudi Arabia	4	3	..	..	..	11	31[c]	..	..
Senegal	23	24	22.7	25.4	2.2	18	24[c]	16	83
Serbia and Montenegro	5[b]	11	1.9	5.1	12.9	4	11[c]	73	..
Sierra Leone	46	50	27.2	33.8	..	..	4	23	87
Singapore	..	..	3.4	2.2	2.2	8	..	..	..
Slovak Republic	4[b]	5	..	..	..	7	..	..	..
Slovenia	3[b]	<3	..	..	..	6	..	..	..
Somalia	..	..	25.8	23.3	..	..	9	..	60
South Africa	..	..	11.5	24.9	6.2	15	7	62	..
Spain	..	..	..	..	..	6	..	..	..
Sri Lanka	28	22	32.9	20.4	..	22	84	88	..
Sudan	32	27	40.7	43.3	3.4	31	16	1	93
Swaziland	14	19	10.3	30.2	..	9	24	59	68
Sweden	..	..	..	..	..	4	..	..	..
Switzerland	..	..	..	..	..	6	..	..	..
Syrian Arab Republic	5	4	6.9	18.8	..	6	81[c]	40	..
Tajikistan	21[b]	61	..	36.2	..	15	14	28	..
Tanzania	37	44	29.4	43.8	1.7	13	32	67	94
Thailand	28	20	17.6	13.4	2.8	9	4[c]	67	..
Togo	33	26	25.1	21.7	1.5	15	18	67	95
Trinidad and Tobago	13	12	5.9	3.6	..	23	2	1	..
Tunisia	<3	<3	4.0	12.3	4.5	7	46	97	..
Turkey	<3	3	8.3	16.0	2.2	16	7	64	..
Turkmenistan	13[b]	9	12.0	22.3	..	6	13	75	..
Uganda	24	19	22.9	39.1	2.6	12	63	95	46
Ukraine	<3[b]	3	3.2	15.9	20.1	5	22	32	..
United Arab Emirates	4	<3	7.0	..	..	15	34[c]	..	..
United Kingdom	..	..	..	..	..	8	..	..	..
United States	..	..	..	..	..	8	..	..	..
Uruguay	6	4	..	..	..	8	..	..	..
Uzbekistan	8[b]	26	7.9	21.1	14.4	7	19	19	79
Venezuela, RB	11	17	4.4	12.8	3.2	7	7[c]	90	..
Vietnam	31	19	33.8	36.5	2.7	9	15	83	55
West Bank and Gaza	..	..	4.1	7.3	2.3	6	..	..	..
Yemen, Rep.	34	36	46.1	51.7	4.3	32	18	39	49
Zambia	48	49	28.1	46.8	3.0	12	40	77	80
Zimbabwe	45	44	13.0	26.5	7.0	11	33	93	78
World	**20 w**	**16 w**	**.. w**	**.. w**		**16 w**		**67 w**	**.. w**
Low income	27	25	43.7	43.1		22		53	56
Middle income	14	10	11.1	27.1		9		79	..
Lower middle income	15	10	11.2	14.8		9		78	..
Upper middle income	..	..	..	..		8		..	..
Low & middle income	20	17	..	..		17		67	..
East Asia & Pacific	17	12	14.7	17.0		8		84	..
Europe & Central Asia	..	8	..	..		9		43	..
Latin America & Carib.	14	11	9.1	19.1		10		86	..
Middle East & N. Africa	6	6	14.5	..		13		64	..
South Asia	26	22	48.4	46.1		29		48	44
Sub-Saharan Africa	31	32	..	..		15		64	72
High income	..	..	..	..		7		..	..
Europe EMU	..	..	..	..		7		..	..

a. Data are for the most recent year available. b. Data are for 1993–95. c. Refers to exclusive breastfeeding for less than four months.

Data on undernourishment are produced by the Food and Agriculture Organization (FAO) based on the calories available from local food production, trade, and stocks; the number of calories needed by different age and gender groups; the proportion of the population represented by each age group; and a coefficient of distribution to take account of inequality in access to food (FAO 2000). From a policy and program standpoint, however, this measure has its limits. First, food insecurity exists even where food availability is not a problem because of inadequate access of poor households to food. Second, food insecurity is an individual or household phenomenon, and the average food available to each person, even corrected for possible effects of low income, is not a good predictor of food insecurity among the population. And third, nutrition security is determined not only by food security but also by the quality of care of mothers and children and the quality of the household's health environment (Smith and Haddad 2000).

Estimates of child malnutrition, based on weight for age (underweight) and height for age (stunting), are from national survey data. The proportion of children who are underweight is the most common indicator of malnutrition. Being underweight, even mildly, increases the risk of death and inhibits cognitive development in children. Moreover, it perpetuates the problem from one generation to the next, as malnourished women are more likely to have low-birthweight babies. Height for age reflects linear growth achieved pre- and postnatally, and a deficit indicates long-term, cumulative effects of inadequacies of health, diet, or care. It is often argued that stunting is a proxy for multifaceted deprivation and is a better indicator of long term changes in malnutrition.

Estimates of children who are overweight are also from national survey data. Overweight in children has become a growing concern in developing countries. Researchers show an association between obesity in childhood and a high prevalence of diabetes, respiratory disease, high blood pressure, and psychosocial and orthopedic disorders (de Onis and Blossner 2000). The survey data were analyzed in a standardized way by the World Health Organization (WHO) to allow comparisons across countries.

Low birthweight, which is associated with maternal malnutrition, raises the risk of infant mortality and stunts growth in infancy and childhood. There is also emerging evidence that low-birthweight babies are more prone to noncommunicable diseases such as diabetes and cardiovascular heart diseases. Estimates of low-birthweight infants are drawn mostly from hospital records and household surveys. Many births in developing countries take place at home, and these births are seldom recorded. A hospital birth may indicate higher income and therefore better nutrition, or it could indicate a higher-risk birth, possibly skewing the data on birthweights downward. The data should therefore be treated with caution.

It is estimated that improved breastfeeding practice can save some 1.5 million children a year. Breast milk alone contains all the nutrients, antibodies, hormones, and antioxidants an infant needs to thrive. It protects babies from diarrhea and acute respiratory infections, stimulates their immune systems and response to vaccination, and according to some studies, confers cognitive benefits as well. The data on breastfeeding are derived from national surveys.

Iodine deficiency is the single most important cause of preventable mental retardation, and it contributes significantly to the risk of stillbirth and miscarriage. Iodized salt is the best source of iodine, and a global campaign to iodize edible salt is significantly reducing the risks (UNICEF, *The State of the World's Children 1999*).

Vitamin A is essential for the functioning of the immune system. A child deficient in vitamin A faces a 25 percent greater risk of dying from a range of childhood ailments such as measles, malaria, and diarrhea. Improving the vitamin A status of pregnant women helps reduce anemia, improves their resistance to infection, and may reduce their risk of dying during pregnancy and childbirth. Giving vitamin A to new mothers who are breastfeeding helps to protect their children during the first months of life. Food fortification with vitamin A is being introduced in many developing countries.

• **Prevalence of undernourishment** is the percentage of the population that is undernourished. • **Prevalence of child malnutrition** is the percentage of children under age five whose weight for age (underweight) or height for age (stunting) is more than two standard deviations below the median for the international reference population ages 0–59 months. For children up to two years old height is measured by recumbent length. For older children height is measured by stature while standing. The reference population, adopted by the WHO in 1983, is based on children from the United States, who are assumed to be well nourished. • **Prevalence of overweight** is the percentage of children under age five whose weight for height is more than two standard deviations above the median for the international reference population of the corresponding age, established by the U.S. National Center for Health Statistics and the WHO. • **Low-birthweight babies** are newborns weighing less than 2,500 grams, with the measurement taken within the first hours of life, before significant postnatal weight loss has occurred. • **Exclusive breastfeeding** refers to the percentage of children less than 6 months old who are fed breast milk alone (no other liquids). • **Consumption of iodized salt** refers to the percentage of households that use edible salt fortified with iodine. • **Vitamin A supplementation** refers to the percentage of children ages 6–59 months old who received at least one high-dose vitamin A capsule in the previous six months.

Data sources

Data are drawn from a variety of sources, including the FAO's *State of Food Insecurity in the World 2004;* the WHO's *World Health Report 2004;* and the United Nations Children's Fund's (UNICEF) *State of the World's Children 2005.*

	Prevalence of smoking		Incidence of tuberculosis	Prevalence of diabetes	Mortality caused by road traffic injury	Prevalence of HIV			
	% of adults		per 100,000 people	% of population ages 20–79	per 100,000 people	Total % of population ages 15–49		Female % of population with HIV	
	Male 1998–2002[a]	Female 1998–2002[a]	2003	2001	1994–2001[a]	2001	2003	2001	2003
Afghanistan	..	..	333	..	..	..	..	..	..
Albania	60	18	23	5.0	11.1	..	..	..	..
Algeria	44	7	53	..	..	<0.1	0.1	11.8	15.6
Angola	..	..	259	..	..	3.7	3.9	55.0	59.1
Argentina	..	..	44	5.5	9.9	0.7	0.7	19.2	20.0
Armenia	68	3	70	..	5.6	0.1		35.0	36.0
Australia	21	18	6	6.1	9.3	0.1	0.1	6.7	7.1
Austria	..	..	14	3.8	10.1	0.2	0.3	22.2	22.0
Azerbaijan	30	1	76	7.1	6.9	..	<0.1	..	..
Bangladesh	48	21	246	4.1	..	..	..	..	..
Belarus	53	9	53	..	14.3	..	..	..	..
Belgium	28	20	14	4.1	13.9	0.2	0.2	35.8	35.0
Benin	..	..	87	..	..	1.9	1.9	57.6	56.5
Bolivia	..	..	225	4.4	..	0.1	0.1	27.5	27.1
Bosnia and Herzegovina	..	..	55	..	..	..	<0.1	..	..
Botswana	..	..	633	..	..	38.0	37.3	57.6	57.6
Brazil	35	27	62	4.5	25.6	0.6	0.7	37.1	36.9
Bulgaria	..	..	43	4.1	10.2	..	0.1	..	..
Burkina Faso	..	..	163	..	..	4.2	1.8[b]	56.0	55.6
Burundi	..	..	346	..	..	6.2	6.0	54.5	59.1
Cambodia	67	10	508	1.8	..	2.7	2.6	30.0	30.0
Cameroon	..	..	180	0.8	..	7.0	5.5[c]	56.0	55.8
Canada	24	20	6	5.0	9.3	0.3	0.3	25.0	23.6
Central African Republic	..	..	325	0.9	..	13.5	13.5	56.5	54.2
Chad	..	..	225	3.4	..	4.9	4.8	57.1	55.6
Chile	44	34	16	5.2	10.7	0.3	0.3	32.0	33.5
China	53	4	102	3.0	19.0	0.1	0.1	20.0	22.9
Hong Kong, China	25	4	77	12.1	..	0.1	0.1	30.8	34.6
Colombia	27	11	52	4.2	24.2	0.5	0.7	33.3	34.4
Congo, Dem. Rep.	..	6	369	1.6	..	4.2	4.2	56.8	57.0
Congo, Rep.	..	..	380	0.9	..	5.3	4.9	56.3	56.3
Costa Rica	29	10	15	3.8	20.1	0.6	0.6	31.8	33.3
Côte d'Ivoire	..	..	396	0.8	..	6.7	7.0	56.3	56.6
Croatia	34	27	43	5.6	11.4	..	<0.1	..	..
Cuba	..	..	11	11.5	13.9	0.1	0.1	31.3	33.3
Czech Republic	36	22	12	7.3	8.7	<0.1	0.1	35.7	32.0
Denmark	32	29	8	6.1	9.5	0.2	0.2	17.4	18.0
Dominican Republic	..	..	96	6.6	41.1	1.8	1.7	26.4	27.1
Ecuador	..	..	138	4.0	16.9	0.3	0.3	32.6	34.0
Egypt, Arab Rep.	40	18	28	6.1	7.5	<0.1	<0.1	10.9	13.3
El Salvador	42	15	57	3.6	41.7	0.6	0.7	32.1	34.3
Eritrea	..	..	271	1.0	..	2.8	2.7	56.4	56.4
Estonia	44	20	50	6.0	14.8	0.7	1.1	32.0	33.8
Ethiopia	..	..	356	1.0	..	4.1	4.4	55.8	55.0
Finland	27	20	9	5.5	7.7	0.1	0.1	..	..
France	33	21	12	4.0	12.1	0.4	0.4	27.3	26.7
Gabon	..	..	233	1.1	..	6.9	8.1	56.8	57.8
Gambia, The	..	..	233	0.3	..	1.2	1.2	55.6	57.1
Georgia	60	15	83	7.3	6.2	<0.1	0.1	..	33.3
Germany	39	31	8	4.2	8.8	0.1	0.1	19.8	22.1
Ghana	..	..	210	0.4	..	3.1	3.1	54.8	56.3
Greece	47	29	20	5.9	19.0	0.2	0.2	20.5	20.0
Guatemala	..	..	74	3.2	..	1.1	1.1	41.5	41.9
Guinea	59	47	236	1.0	..	2.8	3.2	59.0	55.4
Guinea-Bissau	..	..	198	..	..	..	..	..	..
Haiti	..	..	323	5.4	..	5.5	5.6	58.3	57.7

	Prevalence of smoking		Incidence of tuberculosis	Prevalence of diabetes	Mortality caused by road traffic injury	Prevalence of HIV			
	% of adults		per 100,000 people	% of population ages 20–79	per 100,000 people	Total % of population ages 15–49		Female % of population with HIV	
	Male 1998–2002[a]	Female 1998–2002[a]	2003	2001	1994–2001[a]	2001	2003	2001	2003
Honduras	..	..	81	3.1	..	1.6	1.8	56.3	55.9
Hungary	53	30	29	5.6	11.5	..	0.1	..	..
India	29	3	168	8.0	..	0.8	0.9	39.5	38.0
Indonesia	69	3	285	4.5	..	0.1	0.1	12.1	13.6
Iran, Islamic Rep.	22	2	28	3.5	..	0.1	0.1	10.6	12.3
Iraq	..	..	157	3.9	..	..	<0.1	..	..
Ireland	32	31	12	3.2	10.1	0.1	0.1	31.8	30.8
Israel	39	22	9	7.2	5.9	..	0.1	..	..
Italy	31	22	7	7.1	12.1	0.5	0.5	32.3	32.1
Jamaica	..	..	8	11.1	..	0.8	1.2	51.4	47.6
Japan	47	12	31	7.4	7.4	<0.1	<0.1	22.5	24.2
Jordan	48	10	5	7.0	..	<0.1	<0.1	..	..
Kazakhstan	..	..	145	1.4	..	0.1	0.2	34.0	33.5
Kenya	67	32	610	1.0	..	8.0	6.7[b]	62.5	65.5
Korea, Dem. Rep.	..	..	178	..	..	..	..	..	..
Korea, Rep.	..	..	87	6.1	21.9	<0.1	<0.1	10.7	10.8
Kuwait	..	..	27	7.0	23.7	..	..	..	..
Kyrgyz Republic	60	16	124	3.1	12.9	<0.1	0.1	..	..
Lao PDR	..	..	157	..	..	<0.1	0.1	..	..
Latvia	49	13	75	..	22.7	0.5	0.6	32.2	33.3
Lebanon	46	35	12	6.9	..	0.1	0.1	..	..
Lesotho	..	..	733	..	..	29.6	28.9	56.7	56.7
Liberia	..	..	250	..	..	5.1	5.9	56.3	56.3
Libya	..	..	21	3.1	..	..	0.3	..	..
Lithuania	51	16	70	3.2	19.3	0.1	0.1	..	..
Macedonia, FYR	..	..	31	5.1	5.1	<0.1	<0.1	..	..
Madagascar	..	..	216	1.0	..	1.3	1.7	56.1	58.5
Malawi	..	..	442	..	..	14.3	14.2	57.1	56.8
Malaysia	..	..	106	6.3	..	0.4	0.4	15.4	16.7
Mali	..	..	288	0.3	..	1.9	1.7[d]	54.2	59.2
Mauritania	..	..	287	..	..	0.5	0.6	55.9	57.3
Mauritius	42	3	64	12.1	14.7	..	..	..	..
Mexico	51	18	33	14.2	11.8	0.3	0.3	32.7	33.1
Moldova	46	18	139	..	14.1	..	0.2	..	..
Mongolia	68	26	194	..	..	<0.1	<0.1	..	..
Morocco	35	2	112	2.4	..	..	0.1	..	..
Mozambique	..	..	457	1.2	..	12.1	12.2	58.2	55.8
Myanmar	43	22	171	..	..	1.0	1.2	28.9	30.3
Namibia	..	..	722	..	..	21.3	21.3	52.6	55.0
Nepal	40	24	211	6.8	..	0.4	0.5	20.7	26.7
Netherlands	32	25	8	3.6	6.7	0.2	0.2	19.4	20.0
New Zealand	25	25	11	4.0	13.7	0.1	0.1	..	..
Nicaragua	..	..	63	3.6	20.1	0.2	0.2	32.7	33.9
Niger	..	..	157	..	..	1.1	1.2	56.9	56.3
Nigeria	..	..	293	0.4	..	5.5	5.4	58.1	57.6
Norway	31	32	6	3.8	7.7	0.1	0.1	..	..
Oman	..	..	11	..	..	0.1	0.1	..	..
Pakistan	..	..	181	9.2	..	0.1	0.1	6.9	12.2
Panama	20	6	48	4.1	16.4	0.7	0.9	37.3	41.3
Papua New Guinea	..	..	235	11.7	..	0.4	0.6	29.0	30.0
Paraguay	..	..	70	3.7	..	0.4	0.5	27.0	26.0
Peru	53	18	188	4.3	17.6	0.4	0.5	31.4	33.8
Philippines	51	8	296	3.1	..	<0.1	<0.1	20.9	22.5
Poland	42	23	31	7.3	13.3	..	0.1	..	..
Portugal	..	..	45	5.4	12.1	0.4	0.4	20.0	19.5
Puerto Rico	17	10	6	11.3	..	..	..	..	..

2.18 | Health: risk factors and future challenges

	Prevalence of smoking		Incidence of tuberculosis	Prevalence of diabetes	Mortality caused by road traffic injury	Prevalence of HIV			
	% of adults		per 100,000 people	% of population ages 20–79	per 100,000 people	Total % of population ages 15–49		Female % of population with HIV	
	Male 1998–2002[a]	Female 1998–2002[a]	2003	2001	1994–2001[a]	2001	2003	2001	2003
Romania	..	..	149	2.1	16.8	..	<0.1	..	..
Russian Federation	64	9	112	7.4	19.4	0.7	1.1	32.1	33.7
Rwanda	..	..	374	..	..	5.1	5.1	54.5	56.5
Saudi Arabia	19	8	40	12.3	..	..	..	..	..
Senegal	..	..	245	0.8	..	0.8	0.8	55.3	56.1
Serbia and Montenegro	..	..	35	5.5	..	0.2	0.2	20.0	20.0
Sierra Leone	..	..	427	..	..	..	..	..	..
Singapore	24	4	41	11.3	5.2	0.2	0.2	23.5	24.4
Slovak Republic	41	15	24	8.6	12.9	..	<0.1	..	..
Slovenia	28	20	18	8.0	13.4	<0.1	<0.1	..	..
Somalia	..	..	411	..	..	..	..	..	..
South Africa	44	12	536	3.4	..	20.9	15.6[e]	56.3	56.9
Spain	39	25	27	5.6	13.7	0.6	0.7	20.0	20.8
Sri Lanka	26	2	60	2.0	..	<0.1	<0.1	..	17.1
Sudan	24	2	220	3.4	..	1.9	2.3	56.7	57.9
Swaziland	..	..	1,083	..	..	38.2	38.8	57.9	55.0
Sweden	17	20	4	6.4	5.7	0.1	0.1	27.3	25.7
Switzerland	27	24	7	3.7	..	0.4	0.4	30.0	30.0
Syrian Arab Republic	51	10	42	6.3	..	..	<0.1	..	..
Tajikistan	..	..	168	..	5.6	..	<0.1	..	..
Tanzania	23	1	371	1.0	..	9.0	8.8	58.6	56.0
Thailand	39	2	142	2.0	21.0	1.7	1.5	32.3	35.7
Togo	..	..	351	0.3	..	4.3	4.1	56.4	56.3
Trinidad and Tobago	..	..	9	14.1	11.1	3.0	3.2	50.0	50.0
Tunisia	..	..	22	2.8	..	<0.1	<0.1	..	..
Turkey	51	11	26	7.4	..	..	..	..	..
Turkmenistan	..	..	67	..	10.3	..	<0.1	..	..
Uganda	..	..	411	0.8	..	5.1	4.1	59.6	60.0
Ukraine	57	10	92	3.5	10.8	1.2	1.4	32.0	33.3
United Arab Emirates	..	..	18	8.7	..	..	..	..	..
United Kingdom	28	26	12	3.5	5.6	0.2	0.2	28.2	29.8
United States	26	21	5	8.0	15.0	0.6	0.6	20.2	25.5
Uruguay	62	39	28	6.7	10.0	0.3	0.3	32.7	32.8
Uzbekistan	..	..	115	..	9.8	<0.1	0.1	33.3	33.6
Venezuela, RB	..	..	42	4.5	23.1	0.6	0.7	32.4	32.0
Vietnam	51	4	178	..	..	0.3	0.4	27.3	32.5
West Bank and Gaza	..	..	24	..	..	..	..	..	..
Yemen, Rep.	77	29	93	..	..	..	0.1	..	..
Zambia	..	..	656	1.0	..	16.7	15.6[f]	56.3	56.6
Zimbabwe	..	..	659	1.0	..	24.9	24.6	56.3	58.1
World	.. w	.. w	**140 w**	**5.2 w**	.. w	**1.1 w**	**1.1 w**	**29.1 w**	**30.5 w**
Low income	..	..	225	6.0	..	2.1	2.1	41.2	41.1
Middle income	..	..	114	4.4	18.3	0.7	0.7	23.6	25.6
Lower middle income	..	..	122	3.8	19.1	0.7	0.7	23.1	25.2
Upper middle income	..	..	43	8.9	13.0	0.7	0.6	29.3	29.8
Low & middle income	..	..	162	5.0	..	1.2	1.2	30.7	31.8
East Asia & Pacific	53	4	143	3.2	19.1	0.2	0.2	20.1	22.9
Europe & Central Asia	..	..	82	6.2	14.6	..	0.7	..	..
Latin America & Carib.	..	..	66	6.6	20.0	0.6	0.7	34.0	34.4
Middle East & N. Africa	..	..	55	5.1	..	..	0.1	..	..
South Asia	29	3	179	7.6	..	0.7	0.8	35.7	34.7
Sub-Saharan Africa	..	..	353	1.3	..	7.3	7.2	57.1	57.3
High income	..	..	17	6.4	11.9	0.3	0.4	22.0	24.2
Europe EMU	..	..	13	5.0	11.3	0.3	0.3	24.5	25.0

a. Data are for the most recent year available. b. Survey data, 2003. c. Survey data, 2004. d. Survey data, 2001. e. Survey data, 2002. f. Survey data, 2001/02.

The limited availability of data on health status is a major constraint in assessing the health situation in developing countries. Surveillance data are lacking for many major public health concerns. Estimates of prevalence and incidence are available for some diseases but are often unreliable and incomplete. National health authorities differ widely in their capacity and willingness to collect or report information. To compensate for the paucity of data and ensure reasonable reliability and international comparability, the World Health Organization (WHO) prepares estimates in accordance with epidemiological models and statistical standards.

Smoking is the most common form of tobacco use in many countries, and the prevalence of smoking is therefore a good measure of the extent of the tobacco epidemic (Corrao and others 2000). While the prevalence of smoking has been declining in some high-income countries, it has been increasing in many developing countries. Tobacco use causes heart and other vascular diseases and cancers of the lung and other organs. Given the long delay between starting to smoke and the onset of disease, the health impact of smoking in developing countries will increase rapidly in the next few decades. Because the data present a one-time estimate, with no information on the intensity or duration of smoking, and because the definition of adult varies across countries, the data should be interpreted with caution.

Tuberculosis is one of the main causes of death from a single infectious agent among adults in developing countries. In high-income countries tuberculosis has reemerged largely as a result of cases among immigrants. The estimates of tuberculosis incidence in the table are based on a new approach in which reported cases are adjusted using the ratio of case notifications to the estimated share of cases detected by panels of 80 epidemiologists convened by the WHO.

Diabetes, an important cause of ill health and a risk factor for other diseases in developed countries, is spreading rapidly in developing countries. While diabetes is most common among the elderly, prevalence rates are rising among younger and productive populations in developing countries. Economic development has led to the greater adoption of Western lifestyles and diet in developing countries, resulting in a substantial increase in diabetes. In 2001 some 177 million people worldwide had diabetes, an increase from 135 million in 1995. Without effective prevention and control programs, diabetes will likely continue to increase. Data are based on sample surveys.

Data for mortality caused by road traffic injury are collected by the WHO based on vital registries. There is considerable difference in completeness of the vital registry data. In some countries the vital registry system covers only part of the country. In some, not all deaths are registered. In addition, mortality from different causes is difficult to measure. For countries with incomplete vital registry systems, the WHO has used demographic techniques to estimate deaths.

Adult HIV prevalence rates reflect the rate of HIV infection in each country's population. Low national prevalence rates can be very misleading, however. They often disguise serious epidemics that are initially concentrated in certain localities or among specific population groups and threaten to spill over into the wider population. In many parts of the developing world most new infections occur in young adults, with young women especially vulnerable. The estimates of HIV prevalence are based on extrapolations from data collected through surveys and from surveillance of small, nonrepresentative groups.

Estimates from recent Demographic and Health Surveys (DHS) that have collected data on HIV/AIDS differ from those of the Joint United Nations Programme on HIV/AIDS (UNAIDS) and the WHO, which are based on surveillance systems that focus on pregnant women who attend sentinel antenatal clinics. There are reasons to be cautious about comparing the two sets of estimates. DHS is a household survey that uses a representative sample from the whole population, whereas surveillance data from antenatal clinics is limited to pregnant women. Representative household surveys also frequently provide better coverage of rural populations. However, the fact that some respondents refuse to participate or are absent from the household adds considerable uncertainty to survey-based HIV estimates, because the possible association of absence or refusal with higher HIV prevalence is unknown. UNAIDS and the WHO estimates are generally based on surveillance systems that focus on pregnant women who attend sentinel antenatal clinics. UNAIDS and the WHO use a methodology to estimate HIV prevalence for the adult population (ages 15–49) that assumes that prevalence among pregnant women is a good approximation of prevalence among men and women. However, this assumption might not apply to all countries or over time. There are also other potential biases associated with the use of antenatal clinic data, such as differences among women who attend antenatal clinics and those who do not.

• **Prevalence of smoking** is the percentage of men and women who smoke cigarettes. The age range varies among countries but in most is 18 and older or 15 and older. • **Incidence of tuberculosis** is the estimated number of new tuberculosis cases (pulmonary, smear positive, extrapulmonary). • **Prevalence of diabetes** refers to the percentage of people ages 20–79 who have type 1 or type 2 diabetes. • **Mortality caused by road traffic injury** refers to the number of deaths per 100,000 people caused by road traffic injury. • **Prevalence of HIV** is the percentage of people who are infected with HIV.

The data are drawn from a variety of sources, including the WHO's *World Health Report 2004, Tobacco Control Country Profiles 2003, Global Tuberculosis Control Report 2004,* and *World Report on Road Traffic Injury Prevention;* the International Diabetes Federation's e-Atlas; and UNAIDS and the WHO's *2004 Report on the Global AIDS Epidemic.*

Mortality

	Life expectancy at birth		Infant mortality rate		Under-five mortality rate		Child mortality rate		Adult mortality rate		Survival to age 65	
	years		per 1,000 live births		per 1,000		per 1,000		per 1,000		% of cohort	
							Male	Female	Male	Female	Male	Female
	1990	2003	1990	2003	1990	2003	1997–2003[a]	1997–2003[a]	2000–03[a]	2000–03[a]	2003	2003
Afghanistan	42	..	168	..	260	..	..	..	..	..	..	..
Albania	72	74	37	18	45	21	..	..	209	95	77	85
Algeria	67	71	54	35	69	41	..	..	155	119	74	79
Angola	45	47	154	154	260	260	..	..	492	386	34	39
Argentina	72	74	25	17	28	20	..	..	184	92	75	87
Armenia	72	75	52	30	60	33	5	3	223	106	71	84
Australia	77	80	8	5	10	6	..	..	100	52	85	92
Austria	76	79	8	5	10	6	..	..	122	58	83	92
Azerbaijan	71	65	84	75	105	91	..	..	261	150	59	72
Bangladesh	55	62	96	46	144	69	28	38	262	252	59	62
Belarus	71	68	14	13	17	17	..	..	381	133	55	81
Belgium	76	78	8	4	9	5	..	..	126	65	82	91
Benin	52	53	111	91	185	154	72	79	384	328	43	50
Bolivia	58	64	85	53	120	66	26	29	264	219	61	69
Bosnia and Herzegovina	71	74	18	14	22	17	..	..	200	93	75	86
Botswana	57	38	45	82	58	112	..	..	703	669	13	18
Brazil	66	69	50	33	60	35	..	..	259	136	62	79
Bulgaria	72	72	15	12	19	17	..	..	239	103	69	84
Burkina Faso	45	43	118	107	210	207	131	128	559	507	28	32
Burundi	44	42	114	114	190	190	..	..	648	603	25	28
Cambodia	50	54	80	97	115	140	34	30	373	264	42	49
Cameroon	54	48	85	95	139	166	69	75	488	440	35	40
Canada	77	79	7	5	8	7	..	..	101	57	84	92
Central African Republic	48	42	115	115	180	180	..	..	620	573	24	29
Chad	46	48	117	117	203	200	106	99	449	361	39	44
Chile	74	76	17	8	19	9	..	..	151	67	79	89
China	69	71	38	30	49	37	..	..	161	110	73	79
Hong Kong, China	78	80	6	4	..	5	..	..	97	50	85	92
Colombia	68	72	30	18	36	21	4	3	238	115	71	84
Congo, Dem. Rep.	52	45	129	129	205	205	..	..	571	493	32	36
Congo, Rep.	51	52	83	81	110	108	..	..	475	406	36	45
Costa Rica	77	79	15	8	17	10	..	..	131	78	82	90
Côte d'Ivoire	50	45	103	117	157	192	83	58	553	494	31	34
Croatia	72	74	12	6	13	7	..	..	150	110	71	87
Cuba	75	77	11	7	13	8	..	..	143	94	81	88
Czech Republic	71	75	11	4	13	5	..	..	160	75	76	88
Denmark	75	77	8	4	9	6	..	..	125	78	80	88
Dominican Republic	66	67	50	29	65	35	13	8	234	146	63	76
Ecuador	68	71	43	24	57	27	..	..	199	120	70	81
Egypt, Arab Rep.	63	69	76	33	104	39	15	16	210	147	70	76
El Salvador	66	70	46	32	60	36	..	..	250	148	69	81
Eritrea	49	51	85	45	147	85	55	50	493	441	37	43
Estonia	69	71	12	8	17	9	..	..	316	114	60	85
Ethiopia	45	42	131	112	204	169	83	86	594	535	26	31
Finland	75	78	6	3	7	4	..	..	133	61	80	91
France	77	79	7	4	9	6	..	..	136	59	83	92
Gabon	52	53	60	60	92	91	32	33	380	330	46	51
Gambia, The	49	53	103	90	154	123	..	..	373	320	41	47
Georgia	72	73	43	41	47	45	..	..	250	133	72	87
Germany	75	78	7	4	9	5	..	..	122	59	82	91
Ghana	57	54	78	59	125	95	53	51	379	326	48	52
Greece	77	78	10	4	11	5	..	..	114	47	83	91
Guatemala	61	66	60	35	82	47	15	18	286	182	59	72
Guinea	44	46	145	104	240	160	101	98	432	366	32	33
Guinea-Bissau	42	46	153	126	253	204	..	..	495	427	34	39
Haiti	53	52	102	76	150	118	52	54	524	373	38	48

	Life expectancy at birth		Infant mortality rate		Under-five mortality rate		Child mortality rate		Adult mortality rate		Survival to age 65	
							per 1,000		per 1,000		% of cohort	
	years		per 1,000 live births		per 1,000		Male	Female	Male	Female	Male	Female
	1990	2003	1990	2003	1990	2003	1997–2003[a]	1997–2003[a]	2000–03[a]	2000–03[a]	2003	2003
Honduras	65	66	44	32	59	41	..	..	221	157	59	73
Hungary	69	73	15	8	17	7	..	..	295	123	67	85
India	59	63	84	63	123	87	25	37	250	191	62	65
Indonesia	62	67	60	31	91	41	19	20	227	175	64	72
Iran, Islamic Rep.	65	69	54	33	72	39	..	..	170	139	72	76
Iraq	61	63	40	102	50	125	..	..	258	208	64	68
Ireland	75	78	8	5	9	7	..	..	108	62	80	89
Israel	76	79	10	5	12	6	..	..	99	56	84	90
Italy	77	80	8	4	9	6	..	..	100	50	82	91
Jamaica	73	76	17	17	20	20	..	..	169	127	81	87
Japan	79	82	5	3	6	5	..	..	98	44	86	94
Jordan	68	72	33	23	40	28	5	5	199	144	75	81
Kazakhstan	68	61	53	63	63	73	11	6	366	201	48	71
Kenya	57	45	63	79	97	123	36	38	578	529	28	32
Korea, Dem. Rep.	66	63	42	42	55	55	..	..	238	192	55	63
Korea, Rep.	70	74	8	5	9	5	..	..	186	71	73	87
Kuwait	75	77	14	8	16	9	..	..	100	68	82	88
Kyrgyz Republic	68	65	68	59	80	68	10	11	335	299	57	76
Lao PDR	50	55	120	82	163	91	..	..	355	299	45	51
Latvia	69	71	14	10	18	12	..	..	326	119	61	85
Lebanon	68	71	32	27	37	31	..	..	192	136	71	79
Lesotho	58	37	74	79	104	110	..	..	667	630	15	19
Liberia	45	47	157	157	235	235	..	..	448	385	33	37
Libya	68	73	34	13	42	16	..	..	210	157	73	83
Lithuania	71	72	12	8	14	11	..	..	311	109	67	87
Macedonia, FYR	72	74	32	10	33	11	..	..	160	89	75	85
Madagascar	53	56	103	78	168	126	75	68	385	322	49	55
Malawi	45	38	146	112	241	178	101	102	701	653	19	23
Malaysia	71	73	16	7	21	7	..	..	202	113	72	83
Mali	45	41	140	122	250	220	132	125	518	446	25	29
Mauritania	49	51	112	77	162	107	38	38	357	302	43	49
Mauritius	69	72	21	16	25	18	..	..	228	109	71	85
Mexico	71	74	37	23	46	28	..	..	180	101	75	86
Moldova	68	67	30	26	37	32	..	..	325	165	59	76
Mongolia	63	66	74	56	104	68	..	..	280	199	66	72
Morocco	63	69	66	36	85	39	..	..	174	113	68	76
Mozambique	43	41	146	101	242	147	85	82	674	612	25	30
Myanmar	55	57	91	76	130	107	..	..	343	245	47	58
Namibia	58	40	60	48	86	65	..	..	695	661	21	25
Nepal	54	60	100	61	145	82	28	40	314	314	58	57
Netherlands	77	78	7	5	9	6	..	..	94	66	84	90
New Zealand	75	79	10	5	11	6	..	..	99	65	83	90
Nicaragua	64	69	52	30	68	38	12	11	225	161	67	77
Niger	42	46	191	154	320	262	184	202	473	308	30	37
Nigeria	49	45	115	98	235	198	66	69	443	393	32	36
Norway	77	79	7	3	9	5	..	..	99	59	84	91
Oman	69	74	25	10	30	12	..	..	187	135	79	85
Pakistan	59	64	96	74	138	98	..	..	221	198	65	71
Panama	72	75	27	18	34	24	..	..	145	93	79	86
Papua New Guinea	55	57	74	69	101	93	..	..	359	329	49	53
Paraguay	68	71	30	25	37	29	..	..	173	129	70	80
Peru	66	70	60	26	80	34	19	17	190	139	69	79
Philippines	66	70	45	27	63	36	21	19	249	142	70	78
Poland	71	75	16	6	19	7	..	..	207	81	72	87
Portugal	74	76	13	4	15	5	..	..	164	66	78	89
Puerto Rico	75	77	14	9	..	11	..	..	148	55	77	91

Mortality

	Life expectancy at birth		Infant mortality rate		Under-five mortality rate		Child mortality rate		Adult mortality rate		Survival to age 65	
	years		per 1,000 live births		per 1,000		per 1,000 Male Female		per 1,000 Male Female		% of cohort Male Female	
	1990	2003	1990	2003	1990	2003	1997–2003[a]	1997–2003[a]	2000–03[a]	2000–03[a]	2003	2003
Romania	70	70	27	18	32	20	..	..	260	117	65	81
Russian Federation	69	66	21	16	21	21	..	..	420	149	49	77
Rwanda	40	40	103	118	173	203	105	97	667	599	23	25
Saudi Arabia	69	73	34	22	44	26	..	..	181	116	76	83
Senegal	50	52	90	78	148	137	76	74	355	303	38	47
Serbia and Montenegro	72	73	23	12	26	14	..	..	180	100	73	83
Sierra Leone	35	37	175	166	302	284	..	..	587	531	25	29
Singapore	74	78	7	3	8	5	..	..	114	61	83	90
Slovak Republic	71	73	14	7	15	8	..	..	204	82	70	86
Slovenia	73	76	8	4	9	4	..	..	170	76	77	89
Somalia	42	47	133	133	225	225	..	..	516	452	38	45
South Africa	62	46	45	53	60	66	18	13	621	583	26	33
Spain	77	80	8	4	9	4	..	..	119	48	83	93
Sri Lanka	70	74	26	13	32	15	..	..	244	124	77	85
Sudan	52	59	74	63	120	93	..	..	341	291	53	58
Swaziland	57	43	78	105	110	153	..	..	642	602	25	29
Sweden	78	80	6	3	7	4	..	..	87	55	86	92
Switzerland	77	80	7	4	9	6	..	..	92	52	85	93
Syrian Arab Republic	66	70	35	16	44	18	..	..	170	132	69	79
Tajikistan	69	66	92	76	119	95	..	..	293	204	62	75
Tanzania	50	43	102	104	163	165	61	58	569	520	27	30
Thailand	69	69	34	23	40	26	..	..	245	150	67	78
Togo	50	50	88	78	152	140	73	65	460	406	38	43
Trinidad and Tobago	71	72	21	17	24	20	..	..	209	133	74	82
Tunisia	70	73	41	19	52	24	..	..	169	99	76	83
Turkey	66	69	64	33	78	39	10	13	218	120	69	79
Turkmenistan	66	64	80	79	97	102	19	17	280	156	57	73
Uganda	47	43	93	81	160	140	78	70	617	567	25	28
Ukraine	70	68	18	15	22	20	..	..	365	135	57	81
United Arab Emirates	74	75	12	7	14	8	..	..	143	93	80	86
United Kingdom	76	78	8	5	10	7	..	..	106	65	82	90
United States	75	77	9	7	11	8	..	..	140	82	81	90
Uruguay	73	75	20	12	24	14	..	..	185	89	74	88
Uzbekistan	69	67	65	57	79	69	..	..	282	176	63	77
Venezuela, RB	71	74	23	18	27	21	..	..	178	99	75	86
Vietnam	65	70	38	19	53	23	10	13	203	139	68	78
West Bank and Gaza	69	73	42	20	53	24	..	..	154	97	74	84
Yemen, Rep.	52	58	98	82	142	113	33	36	278	226	50	53
Zambia	49	36	101	102	180	182	89	74	725	687	16	21
Zimbabwe	56	39	53	78	80	126	35	31	650	612	18	20
World	65 w	67 w	64 w	57 w	95 w	86 w	.. w	.. w	235 w	166 w	66 w	73 w
Low income	56	58	95	80	149	123	..	..	319	268	54	58
Middle income	68	70	42	30	55	37	..	..	211	128	69	78
Lower middle income	67	69	44	31	57	39	..	..	213	131	68	78
Upper middle income	71	74	27	18	34	22	..	..	196	103	74	85
Low & middle income	63	65	69	59	103	87	..	..	256	186	62	70
East Asia & Pacific	67	70	44	32	59	41	..	..	179	122	70	77
Europe & Central Asia	69	68	39	29	46	36	..	..	317	136	60	80
Latin America & Carib.	68	71	43	28	53	33	..	..	222	125	69	82
Middle East & N. Africa	64	69	58	43	77	53	..	..	193	144	70	76
South Asia	58	63	89	66	130	92	25	37	252	202	61	65
Sub-Saharan Africa	50	46	110	101	187	171	..	..	519	461	32	36
High income	76	78	8	5	10	7	..	..	127	65	82	91
Europe EMU	76	79	8	4	9	6	..	..	122	58	82	91

a. Data are for the most recent year available.

About the data

Mortality rates for different age groups—infants, children, or adults—and overall indicators of mortality—life expectancy at birth or survival to a given age—are important indicators of health status in a country. Because data on the incidence and prevalence of diseases (morbidity data) are frequently unavailable, mortality rates are often used to identify vulnerable populations. And they are among the indicators most frequently used to compare levels of socioeconomic development across countries.

The main sources of mortality data are vital registration systems and direct or indirect estimates based on sample surveys or censuses. A "complete" vital registration system—one covering at least 90 percent of vital events in the population—is the best source of age-specific mortality data. But such systems are fairly uncommon in developing countries. Thus estimates must be obtained from sample surveys or derived by applying indirect estimation techniques to registration, census, or survey data. Survey data are subject to recall error, and surveys estimating infant deaths require large samples because households in which a birth or an infant death has occurred during a given year cannot ordinarily be preselected for sampling. Indirect estimates rely on estimated actuarial "life" tables that may be inappropriate for the population concerned. Because life expectancy at birth is constructed using infant mortality data and model life tables, similar reliability issues arise for this indicator.

Life expectancy at birth and age-specific mortality rates are generally estimates based on vital registration or the most recent census or survey available (see *Primary data documentation*). Extrapolations based on outdated surveys may not be reliable for monitoring changes in health status or for comparative analytical work.

To produce harmonized estimates of infant and under-five mortality rates that make use of all available information in a transparent way, the United Nations Children's Fund (UNICEF) and the World Bank developed and adopted a methodology that fits a regression line to the relationship between mortality rates and their reference dates using weighted least squares. (For further discussion of methodology for childhood mortality estimates, see Hill and others 1999.)

Infant and child mortality rates are higher for boys than for girls in countries in which parental gender preferences are insignificant. Child mortality captures the effect of gender discrimination better than does infant mortality, as malnutrition and medical interventions are more important in this age group. Where female child mortality is higher, as in some countries in South Asia, girls probably have unequal access to resources.

Adult mortality rates have increased in many countries in Sub-Saharan Africa and Europe and Central Asia. In Sub-Saharan Africa the increase stems from AIDS-related mortality and affects both men and women. In Europe and Central Asia the causes are more diverse and affect men more. They include a high prevalence of smoking, a high-fat diet, excessive alcohol use, and stressful conditions related to the economic transition.

The percentage of a cohort surviving to age 65 reflects both child and adult mortality rates. Like life expectancy, it is a synthetic measure based on current age-specific mortality rates and used in the construction of life tables. It shows that even in countries where mortality is high, a certain share of the current birth cohort will live well beyond the life expectancy at birth, while in low-mortality countries close to 90 percent will reach at least age 65.

Definitions

• **Life expectancy at birth** is the number of years a newborn infant would live if prevailing patterns of mortality at the time of its birth were to stay the same throughout its life. • **Infant mortality rate** is the number of infants dying before reaching one year of age, per 1,000 live births in a given year. • **Under-five mortality rate** is the probability that a newborn baby will die before reaching age five, if subject to current age-specific mortality rates. The probability is expressed as a rate per 1,000. • **Child mortality rate** is the probability of dying between the ages of one and five, if subject to current age-specific mortality rates. The probability is expressed as a rate per 1,000. • **Adult mortality rate** is the probability of dying between the ages of 15 and 60—that is, the probability of a 15-year-old dying before reaching age 60—if subject to current age-specific mortality rates between ages 15 and 60. • **Survival to age 65** refers to the percentage of a cohort of newborn infants that would survive to age 65, if subject to current age-specific mortality rates.

2.19a

Inequalities in health and use of health services in Burkina Faso, 1998

	Urban	Rural
Under-five mortality (per 1,000)	129.1	234.7
Severe underweight (% of children under age 5)	4.5	12.8
Medical treatment for fever (% of relevant population)	35.0	11.9

Note: Inequality in health outcomes extends to rural populations. Most rural areas lack infrastructure, services, and trained personnel. Services are often difficult to reach, and travel costs may be prohibitive.

Source: Demographic and Health Survey.

Data sources

The data are from the United Nations Statistics Division's *Population and Vital Statistics Report*, publications and other releases from national statistical offices, Demographic and Health Surveys from national sources and Macro International, and UNICEF's *State of the World's Children 2005.*

3 | ENVIRONMENT

Another 2 billion people will be added to the global population over the next 25 years, most of them in poorer countries, generating huge new demands for goods and services and affordable shelter and housing and requiring faster economic growth and higher energy use. It is widely recognized that faster economic growth is the key to meeting the Millennium Development Goals by 2015. But if growth is not achieved in an environmentally sustainable way, its effect on poverty and human well-being will be disastrous.

Economic development has led to dramatic improvements in the quality of life in developing countries, producing gains unparalleled in human history. But the gains have been unevenly distributed, and a large part of the world's population remains desperately poor. Natural resources—land, water, and air—are being degraded at alarming rates in many countries. And environmental factors such as indoor and outdoor air pollution, waterborne diseases, and exposure to toxic chemicals threaten the health of millions of people. These concerns can be addressed by achieving the Millennium Development Goals.

A healthy environment is an integral part of meeting the Millennium Development Goals, which call for integrating principles of sustainable development into country policies and programs and reversing environmental losses. The environmental Goal sets a target of halving by 2015 the proportion of people without sustainable access to safe drinking water and basic sanitation. It also calls for achieving a significant improvement in the lives of at least 100 million slum dwellers by 2020, bringing to fore the inadequacy of shelters and housing conditions in many poor countries (see table 3.a for selected indicators of housing conditions). All this requires measuring and monitoring the state of the environment and its changes—with better data on access to safe water and sanitation and a minimum set of indicators to monitor the conditions of shelters and housing. It also requires measuring and monitoring the links between economic growth and environmental change.

Many such indicators are presented here. But despite greater awareness of the importance of environmental issues and efforts to improve environmental data, information on many aspects of the environment remains sparse. Data are often uneven in quality, cover different periods, and are sometimes out of date. The lack of adequate data hampers efforts to measure the state of the environment and to design sound policies. Many environmental indicators are not meaningful at the national level. Climate change has impacts that go beyond national boundaries. Environmental factors such as air and water pollution may have relevance only to the locality where they are measured. So global, regional, or city indicators (tables 3.11 and 3.13) are often more meaningful than national aggregates.

Indicators of economic growth and environmental change

Human activity and economic growth affect the natural environment. In a chapter dedicated to environmental protection, the 2000 Millennium Declaration explicitly referenced climate change, desertification, biodiversity, and forest and water management and established a set of indicators to monitor the state of natural resources and to measure environmental change. Most of these indicators are covered in the tables in this section.

Forest coverage and protected areas. Forests are shrinking, and with them the diversity of the plants and animals they support. With growth and development, forests are being converted to agricultural land and urban areas. At the beginning of the 20th century the Earth had some 5 billion hectares of forested area. Now it has less than 4 billion hectares. The loss has been concentrated in developing countries, driven by the growing demand for timber and agricultural land, exacerbated by weak monitoring institutions. Low-income countries lost some 60 million hectares—about 7 percent of their forest—in the 1990s. By contrast, high-income countries reforested about 8 million hectares of forest in the same period (table 3.4).

Closely linked to changes in land use is biodiversity, another important dimension of environmental sustainability. Many countries have designated a share of their land as protected areas (table 3.4). But even where protected areas have expanded and environmental regulations are respected, losses of biologically diverse areas cannot be reversed. About 12 percent of the world's nearly 10,000 bird species are vulnerable or in immediate danger of extinction, 24 percent of 4,800 mammal species, and 30 percent of fish species.

Energy use and carbon dioxide emissions. Energy, especially electricity, is important in raising people's standard of living. High-income countries use more than five times as much energy per capita as developing countries, and with only 15 percent of the world's population they use more than half of its energy (table 3.7). Energy use and electricity generation also have environmental consequences. Generating energy from fossil fuels produces emissions of carbon dioxide, the main greenhouse gas contributing to global warming. Anthropogenic (human-caused) carbon dioxide emissions result primarily from fossil fuel combustion and cement manufacturing, with high-income countries contributing half (figure 3a and table 3.8). Among countries in all income groups, per capita emissions vary widely (from 22 tons in Kuwait and 20 tons in the United States to 0.016 tons in Chad). How energy is generated largely determines the environmental damage. Burning coal releases twice as much carbon dioxide as burning an equivalent amount of natural gas (see *About the data* for table 3.8, and table 3.9 for the sources of generating electricity).

Access to safe water and sanitation. While water supply and access to safe drinking water receive considerable attention at the international level, sanitation problems are seldom mentioned. Yet water supply issues are closely linked to sanitation. Evidence suggests that sanitation is at least as

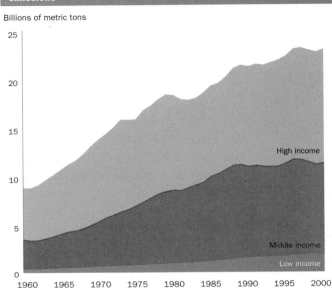

3a

High-income countries account for half the world's carbon dioxide emissions

Billions of metric tons

Source: Carbon Dioxide Information Analysis Center data.

important as water supply in preventing diseases, and many of the health benefits from access to water cannot be realized without improved access to sanitation. Lack of access to adequate water and sanitation has enormous health and economic costs for households, with consequences for national economies and the environment. It contributes to illness and death, especially in children. Every year 2.2 million children under age five die from diarrhea—closely linked to inadequate access to safe water and sanitation. In addition, almost half the people in developing countries suffer from diseases caused directly or indirectly by inadequate sanitation and consumption of contaminated water. In addition to diarrhea, these include intestinal infections, trachoma blindness, cholera, and schistosomiasis. Improving access is crucial for reducing illness and death among children under age five. World Bank estimates suggest that achieving the water target would save the lives of 400,000 children a year, while halving the proportion of people without access to sanitation would save the lives of 550,000 children a year.

Improvement in the lives of slum dwellers. The Cities without Slums Initiative was endorsed at the Millennium Summit, which included in the Millennium Declaration the goal of improving the lives of 100 million slum dwellers (target 11; see section 1). This initiative focuses on upgrading unhealthy and often threatening urban slums and squatter settlements by improving basic municipal services over the next 20 years. Improving slum dwellers' lives includes better housing; more secure tenure; greater access to water, sanitation, and waste management services and cleaner fuels; reduced urban air

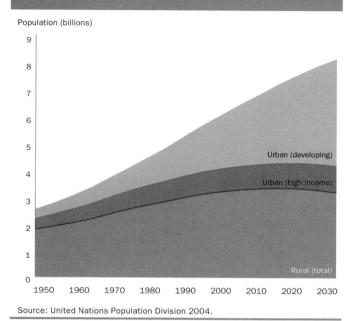

Most future urban growth will be absorbed by developing economies

Population (billions)

Urban (developing)

Urban (high income)

Rural (total)

1950 1960 1970 1980 1990 2000 2010 2020 2030

Source: United Nations Population Division 2004.

Expanding cities serve many needs—with many consequences. Urbanization can yield important social benefits, improving access to public services such as education, health care, and cultural facilities (table 3.11). It can also lead to adverse environmental effects that require policy responses. Greater urbanization usually means greater pollution, which can overwhelm the natural capacities of air and water to absorb pollutants. The costs of controlling pollution can be enormous. And pollution exposes people to severe health hazards. Several major urban air pollutants—lead, sulfur dioxide, suspended particulate matter—are known to harm human health (table 3.13). A big source of urban air pollution is motor vehicles, whose numbers are strongly linked to rising income. The number of passenger cars increased from 16 cars per 1,000 people in 1990 to 27 in 2002 in developing countries and from 400 cars per 1,000 people to 440 in high-income countries, with New Zealand having the highest number, at 613, up from 438 in 1990 (table 3.12).

While there is no evidence of a population threshold beyond which cities generate more negative than positive effects for their inhabitants, the rapid pace of population growth and enormous size of the population in many cities have overwhelmed the capacity of municipal authorities to respond. Millions of people in cities in developing countries cannot meet their basic needs for shelter, water, food, health, and education.

pollution; and easier access to safe transport services. In developing countries an estimated 38 percent of urban residents live in slums. As the urban population increases, the number of people living in slums will likely rise, increasing the challenges of providing services. The plight of slum dwellers has brought forward the more general issue of housing conditions, particularly in cities and urban areas.

Rapid urbanization and higher demand for shelter
The world is becoming increasingly urban. Urban areas are home to 48 percent of the world's population—two of five people in low- and middle-income countries and almost four of five in high-income countries. Most of Latin America is as urbanized as Europe, with 77 percent of the population living in urban areas. Asia is urbanizing rapidly. Even such traditionally rural countries as China, India, and Indonesia now have hundreds of millions of people living in urban areas, with both the number of people and the share of the population in cities growing rapidly (table 3.10).

In 1950 only 18 percent of people in developing countries lived in cities. In 2005 the proportion exceeded 40 percent, and by 2030 it is forecast to be 56 percent. Most future urban growth will be absorbed by urban centers in developing countries, which have a high average annual urban population growth rate of 2.2 percent, in contrast with the less than 1 percent rate in high-income economies.

Demand for housing and emergence of the slums. Ever since there have been cities, there has been demand for housing and shelter and there have been poor living quarters. But only since the sixteenth century have there been slums—places that are "squalid, overcrowded, and wretched."

The unmet demand for affordable housing, along with urban poverty, has led to the emergence of slums in many poor countries. Slums have been the only large-scale solution to housing for low-income people. In cities, where competition for land and profits is intense, slums are the only type of housing that is affordable and accessible to most poor people.

In 2001, 924 million people, or 31.6 percent of the world's urban population, lived in slums (UN-HABITAT 2003). The majority were in developing economies, accounting for 43 percent of the urban population, with Sub-Saharan Africa having the largest proportion of the urban population living in slums (72 percent). The expected growth rate of the urban labor force far outpaces the rate of creation of formal sector urban jobs, so in all likelihood the majority of new urban residents will eke out a living in the informal economy and many will end up living in slums.

Improving shelter requires a better understanding of the mechanisms governing housing availability. That requires better data and better policy-oriented analysis so that housing policy can be formulated in a more global comparative perspective and the accomplishments and lessons learned in one country can be drawn on by others. This comparative perspective can help countries chart their paths, formulate realistic development objectives, and measure their achievements over time and compare them with other countries in similar circumstances.

Housing is viewed increasingly as a commodity with an exchange value, rather than as a good to be produced and allocated outside the marketplace. It is also viewed as a commodity driven by market forces—especially supply and demand—that have a powerful influence across all parts of the market despite the existence of apparently distinctive submarkets. Housing demand and supply are both affected by the regulatory, institutional, and policy environment. Housing policies and outcomes in turn affect such broader socioeconomic conditions as the infant mortality rate, inflation, household saving, manufacturing wage and productivity levels, capital formation, and the government budget deficit. A good understanding of housing condition thus requires an extensive set of indicators within a reasonable framework.

Data deficiencies and a lack of serious quantitative analysis hamper decisionmakers in making informed choices on desirable policies to improve housing. As a result, costly policy failures have impeded development of the housing sector and frustrated broader development objectives. There is a strong demand for quantitative indicators that can measure housing conditions on a regular basis, so that decisionmakers can determine whether conditions are improving or worsening or whether broad housing policy goals are being attained—which are not possible now. Nor is it possible to determine how a particular country compares with other countries, whether its performance is above or below expected norms given its circumstances, or which policies lead to better outcomes and so are worthy of emulation.

The Millennium Development Goals have identified improving housing conditions as an integral part of the global development agenda. The United Nations Human Settlements Programme (UN-HABITAT) is charged with monitoring target 11 for improving the lives of slum dwellers and has proposed four measures of housing deprivation as proxies for the number of households living in slum conditions:

- Individuals lacking access to an improved water supply.
- Individuals lacking access to improved sanitation.

- Individuals living in overcrowded conditions.
- Individuals living in nondurable structures.

Data on these indicators are collected in national censuses using similar definitions and in household surveys such as Demographic and Health Surveys, Multiple Indicator Cluster Surveys, and Living Standards Measurement Study surveys. They are reported for the first time in *World Development Indicators* in the new table 3.a. In conjunction with data in tables 1.3, 3.5, and 3.10 on water and sanitation, they allow for the monitoring of most aspects of target 11 on a global scale. Table 3.a was constructed using available census data and will later incorporate household survey data as well.

Because published census tables do not provide data on the distribution of housing deprivations, it is not possible to tell how many households suffer from how many of the four housing deprivations—only the total number of households that suffer from any one housing deprivation. A recent investigation by UN-HABITAT's Monitoring System Branch of the distribution of housing deprivations in 20 Sub–Saharan African countries suggests that—even in the worst of circumstances—very few households suffer from all four basic shelter deprivations. The average number was 1.7. On average, 47 percent of slum dwellings in these countries had only one shelter deprivation, 33 percent had two, 17 percent had three, and only 2 percent had four.

Table 3.a focuses attention on urban areas, where housing conditions are typically most severe. Not all compiled indicators are presented in the table because of space limitations. More indicators for many more countries will be available in the online version of *World Development Indicators,* including data on housing deficits. Beyond the qualitative dimensions of available shelter, it also measures the quantitative housing deficit—the share of households in excess of available dwelling units—considering that a well-functioning housing sector should have a separate dwelling unit for each household. Quantitative housing deficits in most countries—even very poor ones—are relatively small, suggesting that the housing problem is still largely a qualitative rather than a quantitative one. Shelter is still being produced in adequate quantities in most countries. Though much of it is substandard, in some places it has improved over time. The data in table 3a will allow, for the first time, the monitoring of both quantitative and qualitative dimensions of the housing sector over time on a global scale, adding an important dimension to the mission of *World Development Indicators* to monitor all the key dimensions of development.

3.a

Urban housing conditions

	Census year	Household size (People)		Overcrowding — People living in overcrowded dwellings[a] %		Dwelling structure — Buildings with durable structure % of total		Home ownership — Privately owned dwellings % of total		Multiunit dwellings — Households in multiunit housing % of total		Vacancy rate — Unoccupied dwellings % of total	
		National	Urban	National	Urban	National	Urban	National	Urban	National	Urban	National	Urban
Armenia	2001	4.1	4.0	35	38	93	92	91	90				
Bahrain	1991	5.9	5.8	16				51		28		3	
Bangladesh	2001	4.8	4.8			21[b]	42[b]	88[b]	61[b]				
Belize	2000	4.6	4.4			45	54	63	53	4	5		
Bolivia	2001	4.2	4.3	35		38	54	58	49	3[b]	5[b]	6	4
Botswana	2001	4.2	3.9	54	47	88		61	47	1			
Brazil	2000	3.8	3.7					74	75				
Bulgaria	2001	2.7	2.7			79	89	98	98			23	17
Cameroon	1987	5.2	5.1	67	77	77	76						
Cape Verde	2000	4.6	3.8[b]	55[b]	60[b]	78[b]	88[b]	72[b]	60[b]	2[b]	5[b]		
Central African Republic	1988	5.2	5.8	31	28	77		85	74				
Chad	1993	5.1	5.1			3	1	85	47				
Chile	2002	3.4	3.5			53	59	47	45	13	15	11	10
Costa Rica	2000	4.0		3		68		65		2	2	9	6
Czech Republic	2001	2.4						52		56		12	
Ecuador	2001			25		59	73	58[b]	53[b]	9	14	12	7
El Salvador	1992			56		57	71	62	60	3	5	11	11
Equatorial Guinea	1993	7.5	7.0	29				75	55	14	26		
Ethiopia	1994	4.8	4.7	10			23		47			..	
Fiji	1996	5.8	5.6			56	72	78	62				
Ghana	2000	5.1	5.1			45		57		56		5	
India	2001	5.4	5.3	77	71	56	81	87	67			6	9
Iran, Islamic Rep.	1996	4.8	4.6			72	76	73	67				
Iraq	1997	7.7	7.2			88	96	70	66	4	6	13	15
Jamaica	2001	4.4				56[b]		60[b]		1[b]		72	
Jordan	1994	6.2	6.1			97	77	68	63	57	66	20	19
Kenya	1990	4.6	3.4			35	72	72	25			39	17
Lithuania	2001	2.6	2.5	17						71		8	
Macedonia, FYR	2002	3.6	3.6[b]			95[b]	95[b]	48[b]				7[b]	3[b]
Madagascar	1993	4.9	4.8	64	57			81	59				
Malawi	1987	4.3	4.3			48	85	86	48				
Mauritius	2000	3.9	3.8			91	94	87	81			7	6
Mexico	2000	4.4		27[b]		78		76					
Mozambique	1997	4.4	4.9	37	7	6	14	92	83	1	4	0	
Nicaragua	1995					46		77		0		8	
Pakistan	1998	6.8	6.8			58	86	81					
Panama	2000	4.1		25[b]		66	88[b]	68	60[b]	10[b]	17[b]	14	
Paraguay	2002	4.6	4.5	38[b]	38[b]	38[b]	38[b]	78	73	1[b]	2[b]	6[b]	6[b]
Peru	1993					32	46					7	3
Philippines	1990	5.3	5.3			62		83	76	6	12	4	4
Romania	1992	3.1	3.1			58		87	77	42	74	6	4
Rwanda	1991	4.8				75	64	92	55	19	25		
Slovenia	1991	3.1						66		35		9	
Solomon Islands	1999	6.3	6.9	50		23		85	43	1	3		
Sri Lanka	2001	3.8				91[b]	92[b]	65[b]	54[b]	1	13[b]	13	1[b]
Sudan	1993	5.8	6.0					79	58	0[b]	1[b]		
Tanzania	2002	4.9	4.5[b]	33[b]	7[b]			82[b]	43[b]				
Thailand	2000	3.8				93	93	83	76	3			
Trinidad and Tobago	2000	3.7		9[b]		58[b]		64[b]		15[b]			
Tunisia	1994	5.1	5.2					79[b]	89[b]	6[b]	10[b]	10[b]	12[b]
Uganda	2002	4.8	4.0[b]			21[b]		80[b]	24[b]	0[b]	2[b]		
Uruguay	1996	3.3	3.4[b]	22[b]				50[b]	50[b]			13[b]	13[b]
Venezuela. RB	2001	4.4						66		14		16	
Vietnam	1999	4.6	4.5			77	89	73	77				
Yemen	1994	6.7	6.8	52[b]	6[b]			88[b]	68[b]	3[b]	11[b]		
Zimbabwe	1992	4.8	4.2					57	30	4	10		

Note: This table is still a work in progress; coverage and quality are being enhanced.
a. More than two people per room. b. Data are from previous census.

3.1 Rural environment and land use

	Rural population			Rural population density	Land area	Land use					
	% of total		average annual % growth	people per sq. km of arable land	thousands of sq. km	Arable land		% of land area Permanent cropland		Other land	
	1990	2003	1990–2003	2002	2002	1990	2002	1990	2002	1990	2002
Afghanistan	82	77	3.3	273	652	12.1	12.1	0.2	0.2	87.6	87.6
Albania	64	56	–1.3	307	27	21.1	21.1	4.6	4.4	74.3	74.5
Algeria	49	41	0.6	171	2,382	3.0	3.2	0.2	0.3	96.8	96.5
Angola	72	64	1.9	282	1,247	2.3	2.4	0.4	0.2	97.3	97.4
Argentina	13	11	–0.3	12	2,737	10.6	12.3	0.4	0.5	89.0	87.2
Armenia	33	33	–1.2	202	28	17.7	17.6	2.7	2.3	79.7	80.1
Australia	15	8	–3.5	3	7,682	6.2	6.3	0.0	0.0	93.7	93.7
Austria	33	32	0.2	188	83	17.2	16.8	1.0	0.9	81.8	82.3
Azerbaijan	46	48	1.4	220	83	18.1	21.6	3.5	2.7	78.5	75.7
Bangladesh	80	73	1.0	1,249	130	70.2	61.6	2.3	3.1	27.5	35.2
Belarus	34	30	–1.1	54	207	29.3	27.0	0.9	0.6	69.8	72.4
Belgiuma	4	3	–2.4	36	33	23.3	24.9	0.5	0.7	76.2	74.4
Benin	66	55	1.5	144	111	14.6	23.1	0.9	2.4	84.5	74.6
Bolivia	44	36	0.5	109	1,084	1.9	2.7	0.1	0.2	97.9	97.1
Bosnia and Herzegovina	61	56	–1.2	231	51	16.6	19.5	2.9	1.9	80.5	78.7
Botswana	58	50	1.2	232	567	0.7	0.7	0.0	0.0	99.3	99.3
Brazil	25	17	–1.6	53	8,459	6.0	7.0	0.8	0.9	93.2	92.1
Bulgaria	34	32	–1.1	76	111	34.9	30.3	2.7	2.1	62.4	67.6
Burkina Faso	86	82	2.0	225	274	12.9	15.9	0.2	0.2	86.9	83.9
Burundi	94	90	1.8	648	26	36.2	38.4	14.0	14.2	49.8	47.4
Cambodia	87	81	2.0	292	177	20.9	21.0	0.6	0.6	78.5	78.4
Cameroon	60	49	0.9	131	465	12.8	12.8	2.6	2.6	84.6	84.6
Canada	23	21	0.0	14	9,221	5.0	5.0	0.0	0.0	95.0	95.0
Central African Republic	63	57	1.5	114	623	3.1	3.1	0.1	0.2	96.8	96.8
Chad	79	75	2.6	175	1,259	2.6	2.9	0.0	0.0	97.4	97.1
Chile	17	13	–0.3	108	749	3.7	2.6	0.3	0.4	95.9	96.9
Chinab	73	61	–0.3	559	9,327	13.3	15.3	0.8	1.2	85.9	83.5
Hong Kong, China	0	0	..	..	1	..	..	..	..	..	..
Colombia	31	24	–0.3	459	1,039	3.2	2.2	1.6	1.5	95.2	96.3
Congo, Dem. Rep.	..	..	..	..	2,267	2.9	3.0	0.5	0.5	96.5	96.6
Congo, Rep.	44	33	0.8	642	342	0.5	0.6	0.1	0.1	99.4	99.3
Costa Rica	46	39	0.9	700	51	5.1	4.4	4.9	5.9	90.0	89.7
Côte d'Ivoire	60	55	2.1	296	318	7.6	9.7	11.0	11.9	81.4	78.3
Croatia	46	41	–1.4	126	56	21.7	26.1	2.0	2.3	76.3	71.6
Cuba	26	24	–0.2	103	110	29.6	24.3	7.4	10.2	63.0	65.5
Czech Republic	25	25	–0.1	84	77	..	39.7	..	3.1	..	57.2
Denmark	15	15	0.2	35	42	60.4	53.6	0.2	0.2	39.3	46.2
Dominican Republic	42	33	–0.2	263	48	21.7	22.7	9.3	10.3	69.0	67.0
Ecuador	45	36	0.1	286	277	5.8	5.9	4.8	4.9	89.4	89.2
Egypt, Arab Rep.	56	57	2.0	1,309	995	2.3	2.9	0.4	0.5	97.3	96.6
El Salvador	51	36	–0.7	365	21	26.5	31.9	12.5	12.1	60.9	56.1
Eritrea	84	80	2.2	691	101	..	5.0	..	0.0	..	95.0
Estonia	29	30	–0.7	68	42	26.7	14.5	0.4	0.4	72.9	85.1
Ethiopia	87	83	1.9	567	1,000	..	9.9	..	0.7	..	89.3
Finland	39	41	0.8	97	305	7.4	7.2	0.0	0.0	92.5	92.7
France	26	24	–0.2	78	550	32.7	33.5	2.2	2.1	65.1	64.4
Gabon	32	16	–2.5	69	258	1.1	1.3	0.6	0.7	98.2	98.1
Gambia, The	75	67	2.4	378	10	18.2	25.0	0.5	0.5	81.3	74.5
Georgia	45	43	–0.8	280	69	11.4	11.5	4.8	3.8	83.8	84.7
Germany	15	12	–1.3	85	349	34.3	33.8	1.3	0.6	64.4	65.6
Ghana	66	63	1.9	307	228	11.9	18.4	6.6	9.4	81.5	72.2
Greece	41	39	0.2	160	129	22.5	21.1	8.3	8.8	69.2	70.2
Guatemala	62	59	2.3	526	108	12.0	12.5	4.5	5.0	83.5	82.4
Guinea	77	71	1.9	616	246	3.0	3.7	2.0	2.6	95.0	93.7
Guinea-Bissau	76	66	1.8	322	28	10.7	10.7	4.2	8.8	85.2	80.5
Haiti	71	62	1.1	669	28	28.3	28.3	11.6	11.6	60.1	60.1

	Rural population			Rural population density	Land area	Land use					
	% of total		average annual % growth	people per sq. km of arable land	thousands of sq. km	Arable land		% of land area Permanent cropland		Other land	
	1990	2003	1990–2003	2002	2002	1990	2002	1990	2002	1990	2002
Honduras	58	44	0.7	289	112	13.1	9.5	3.2	3.2	83.7	87.2
Hungary	38	35	−0.9	77	92	54.7	50.1	2.5	2.1	42.7	47.8
India	74	72	1.4	466	2,973	54.9	54.4	2.1	2.8	43.0	42.8
Indonesia	69	56	−0.2	588	1,812	11.2	11.3	6.5	7.3	82.4	81.4
Iran, Islamic Rep.	44	34	−0.4	151	1,636	9.3	9.2	0.8	1.3	89.9	89.6
Iraq	30	32	2.9	137	437	12.1	13.1	0.7	0.8	87.2	86.1
Ireland	43	40	0.5	142	69	15.1	16.3	0.0	0.0	84.8	83.7
Israel	10	8	1.2	157	22	15.8	15.6	4.1	4.0	80.1	80.5
Italy	33	33	0.0	228	294	30.6	28.2	10.1	9.4	59.3	62.4
Jamaica	49	42	−0.3	647	11	11.0	16.1	9.2	10.2	79.8	73.8
Japan	23	21	−0.4	603	365	13.1	12.1	1.3	0.9	85.6	86.9
Jordan	28	21	1.8	369	89	3.3	3.3	1.0	1.2	95.7	95.5
Kazakhstan	43	44	−0.5	30	2,700	13.0	8.0	0.1	0.1	87.0	92.0
Kenya	76	64	1.0	441	569	7.4	8.1	0.9	1.0	91.7	90.9
Korea, Dem. Rep.	42	39	0.4	352	120	19.0	20.8	1.5	1.7	79.5	77.6
Korea, Rep.	26	16	−2.7	481	99	19.8	17.1	1.6	2.0	78.6	81.0
Kuwait	5	4	−1.4	689	18	0.2	0.7	0.1	0.1	99.7	99.2
Kyrgyz Republic	62	66	1.4	244	192	6.5	7.0	0.4	0.3	93.1	92.6
Lao PDR	85	79	1.9	480	231	3.5	4.0	0.3	0.4	96.3	95.7
Latvia	30	40	1.1	50	62	27.2	29.5	0.4	0.5	72.4	70.0
Lebanon	16	9	−2.4	253	10	17.9	16.6	11.9	14.0	70.2	69.4
Lesotho	80	70	0.0	379	30	10.4	10.9	0.1	0.1	89.4	89.0
Liberia	58	53	1.9	467	96	4.2	3.9	2.2	2.3	93.6	93.8
Libya	18	12	−1.5	35	1,760	1.0	1.0	0.2	0.2	98.8	98.8
Lithuania	32	31	−0.8	37	63	47.8	46.7	0.9	0.9	51.3	52.3
Macedonia, FYR	42	40	0.2	146	25	23.8	22.3	2.2	1.8	74.0	75.9
Madagascar	76	69	2.0	386	582	4.7	5.1	1.0	1.0	94.3	93.9
Malawi	88	84	1.6	395	94	19.3	24.4	1.2	1.5	79.5	74.1
Malaysia	50	41	0.7	557	329	5.2	5.5	16.0	17.6	78.9	76.9
Mali	76	68	1.6	167	1,220	1.7	3.8	0.0	0.0	98.3	96.1
Mauritania	56	38	−0.3	226	1,025	0.4	0.5	0.0	0.0	99.6	99.5
Mauritius	60	58	0.9	702	2	49.3	49.3	3.0	3.0	47.8	47.8
Mexico	28	25	0.8	102	1,909	12.6	13.0	1.0	1.3	86.4	85.7
Moldova	53	58	0.5	134	33	52.8	56.1	14.2	9.1	33.0	34.8
Mongolia	43	43	1.3	88	1,567	0.9	0.8	0.0	0.0	99.1	99.2
Morocco	52	43	0.3	153	446	19.5	18.8	1.6	2.0	78.8	79.2
Mozambique	79	64	0.6	288	784	4.4	5.4	0.3	0.3	95.3	94.3
Myanmar	75	71	1.0	353	658	14.5	15.0	0.8	1.1	84.7	83.9
Namibia	73	68	2.1	166	823	0.8	1.0	0.0	0.0	99.2	99.0
Nepal	91	87	2.0	659	143	16.0	22.4	0.5	0.7	83.6	77.0
Netherlands	11	10	−0.2	182	34	25.9	27.0	0.9	1.0	73.2	72.0
New Zealand	15	14	0.4	37	268	9.4	5.6	5.1	7.0	85.6	87.4
Nicaragua	47	43	2.0	120	121	10.7	15.9	1.6	1.9	87.7	82.2
Niger	84	78	2.7	200	1,267	2.8	3.5	0.0	0.0	97.2	96.4
Nigeria	65	53	1.2	239	911	32.4	33.2	2.8	3.1	64.8	63.8
Norway	28	24	−0.5	129	306	2.8	2.8	..	..	..	..
Oman	38	22	−0.4	1,534	310	0.1	0.1	0.1	0.1	99.7	99.7
Pakistan	69	66	2.0	447	771	26.6	27.8	0.6	0.9	72.8	71.3
Panama	46	43	1.1	231	74	6.7	7.4	2.1	2.0	91.2	90.7
Papua New Guinea	85	82	2.2	2,007	453	0.4	0.5	1.3	1.4	98.3	98.1
Paraguay	51	42	0.8	78	397	5.3	7.6	0.2	0.2	94.5	92.2
Peru	31	26	0.4	192	1,280	2.7	2.9	0.3	0.5	96.9	96.6
Philippines	51	39	0.1	559	298	18.4	19.1	14.8	16.8	66.9	64.1
Poland	39	37	−0.4	102	306	47.3	45.5	1.1	1.0	51.6	53.6
Portugal	53	32	−3.5	173	92	25.6	21.7	8.5	7.8	65.8	70.4
Puerto Rico	29	24	−0.7	2,662	9	7.3	3.9	5.6	5.5	87.0	90.5

	Rural population			Rural population density	Land area	Land use					
	% of total		average annual % growth	people per sq. km of arable land	thousands of sq. km	Arable land		Permanent cropland		Other land	
								% of land area			
	1990	2003	1990–2003	2002	2002	1990	2002	1990	2002	1990	2002
Romania	46	44	−0.8	103	230	41.0	40.9	2.6	2.2	56.4	56.9
Russian Federation	27	27	−0.1	32	16,889	7.8	7.3	0.1	0.1	92.1	92.6
Rwanda	95	93	1.4	684	25	35.7	45.2	12.4	10.9	52.0	43.9
Saudi Arabia	22	12	−1.6	79	2,150	1.6	1.7	0.0	0.1	98.4	98.2
Senegal	60	50	1.2	208	193	12.1	12.8	0.1	0.2	87.8	87.0
Serbia and Montenegro	49	48	−2.2	116	102	27.5	..	2.8	..	69.7	..
Sierra Leone	70	61	1.2	607	72	6.8	7.5	0.8	0.9	92.5	91.6
Singapore	0	0	..	0	1	1.5	1.5	1.5	1.5	97.0	97.0
Slovak Republic	44	42	−0.1	..	49	..	..	..	..	..	..
Slovenia	50	51	0.2	603	20	9.9	8.3	1.8	1.5	88.3	90.2
Somalia	76	71	1.8	638	627	1.6	1.7	0.0	0.0	98.3	98.3
South Africa	51	41	0.3	128	1,214	11.1	12.1	0.7	0.8	88.2	87.1
Spain	25	22	−0.5	65	499	30.7	27.5	9.7	10.0	59.6	62.5
Sri Lanka	79	76	1.0	1,588	65	13.5	14.2	15.9	15.5	70.6	70.4
Sudan	73	61	0.9	125	2,376	5.5	6.8	0.1	0.2	94.4	93.0
Swaziland	76	73	2.4	446	17	10.5	10.3	0.7	0.7	88.8	89.0
Sweden	17	17	0.2	56	412	6.9	6.5	0.0	0.0	93.1	93.5
Switzerland	40	32	−1.0	579	40	9.9	10.3	0.5	0.6	89.6	89.1
Syrian Arab Republic	51	47	2.2	177	184	26.6	25.0	4.0	4.5	69.4	70.5
Tajikistan	68	72	1.8	488	141	6.1	6.6	0.9	0.9	93.0	92.5
Tanzania	78	65	1.2	578	884	4.0	4.5	1.0	1.2	95.0	94.2
Thailand	81	80	0.7	310	511	34.2	31.1	6.1	6.9	59.7	62.1
Togo	71	65	1.9	124	54	38.6	46.1	1.7	2.2	59.7	51.6
Trinidad and Tobago	31	25	−1.1	437	5	14.4	14.6	9.0	9.2	76.6	76.2
Tunisia	42	33	−0.5	117	155	18.7	17.8	12.5	13.8	68.8	68.4
Turkey	39	33	0.5	90	770	32.0	33.7	3.9	3.4	64.0	62.9
Turkmenistan	55	55	2.1	142	470	2.9	3.9	0.1	0.1	97.0	95.9
Uganda	89	85	2.5	410	197	25.4	25.9	9.4	10.7	65.2	63.5
Ukraine	33	32	−0.8	48	579	57.6	56.2	1.9	1.6	40.5	42.3
United Arab Emirates	20	12	2.5	621	84	0.4	0.9	0.2	2.3	99.3	96.8
United Kingdom	11	10	−0.2	107	241	27.5	23.9	0.3	0.2	72.2	75.9
United States	25	22	0.3	37	9,159	20.3	19.2	0.2	0.2	79.5	80.6
Uruguay	11	7	−2.4	20	175	7.2	7.4	0.3	0.2	92.5	92.3
Uzbekistan	60	63	2.1	357	414	10.8	10.8	0.9	0.8	88.3	88.3
Venezuela, RB	16	12	0.0	130	882	3.2	2.8	0.9	0.9	95.9	96.3
Vietnam	80	75	1.1	901	325	16.4	20.6	3.2	6.7	80.4	72.7
West Bank and Gaza	..	..	..	..	6	..	..	..	..	..	..
Yemen, Rep.	77	74	3.4	903	528	2.9	2.9	0.2	0.2	96.9	96.8
Zambia	61	60	2.1	117	743	7.1	7.1	0.0	0.0	92.9	92.9
Zimbabwe	72	63	0.9	255	387	7.5	8.3	0.3	0.3	92.2	91.3
World	**56 w**	**51 w**	**0.7 w**	**477 w**	**130,331 s**	**10.7 w**	**10.8 w**	**0.9 w**	**1.0 w**	**88.4 w**	**88.2 w**
Low income	74	70	1.5	509	30,456	12.2	12.6	1.0	1.2	86.9	86.2
Middle income	56	47	−0.1	480	68,844	9.5	9.6	1.0	1.1	89.5	89.2
Lower middle income	59	50	−0.1	497	56,103	9.9	10.0	1.0	1.2	89.1	88.8
Upper middle income	29	25	0.1	193	12,741	7.5	8.0	0.9	1.0	91.5	90.9
Low & middle income	63	57	0.7	495	99,300	10.3	10.6	1.0	1.1	88.7	88.3
East Asia & Pacific	72	61	−0.1	565	15,886	12.1	13.3	2.2	2.7	85.7	83.9
Europe & Central Asia	37	36	0.0	122	23,868	12.2	11.3	0.4	0.4	87.4	88.3
Latin America & Carib.	29	23	−0.1	210	20,057	6.7	7.4	0.9	1.0	92.4	91.6
Middle East & N. Africa	46	41	1.2	603	11,111	4.8	4.9	0.6	0.7	94.6	94.3
South Asia	75	72	1.5	559	4,781	42.7	42.5	1.7	2.2	55.6	55.2
Sub-Saharan Africa	72	64	1.6	352	23,596	5.9	6.8	0.8	0.9	93.2	92.3
High income	23	20	−0.2	202	31,030	12.1	11.6	0.5	0.5	87.4	87.9
Europe EMU	25	22	−0.5	138	2,436	27.1	26.0	4.7	4.5	68.2	69.4

a. Includes Luxembourg. b. Includes Taiwan, China.

About the data

Indicators of rural development are sparse, as few indicators are disaggregated between rural and urban areas (for some that are, see tables 2.5, 3.5, and 3.10). This table shows indicators of rural population and land use. Rural population is approximated as the midyear nonurban population.

The data in the table show that land use patterns are changing. They also indicate major differences in resource endowments and uses among countries.

True comparability of the data is limited, however, by variations in definitions, statistical methods, and the quality of data collection. Countries use different definitions of rural population and land use, for example. The Food and Agriculture Organization (FAO), the primary compiler of these data, occasionally adjusts its definitions of land use categories and sometimes revises earlier data. Because the data reflect changes in data reporting procedures as well as actual changes in land use, apparent trends should be interpreted with caution.

Satellite images show land use that differs from that given by ground-based measures in both area under cultivation and type of land use. Moreover, land use data in countries such as India are based on reporting systems that were designed for the collection of tax revenue. Because taxes on land are no longer a major source of government revenue, the quality and coverage of land use data (except for cropland) have declined. Data on forest area, aggregated in the category other, may be particularly unreliable because of differences in definitions and irregular surveys (see *About the data* for table 3.4).

Definitions

• **Rural population** is calculated as the difference between the total population and the urban population (see *Definitions* for tables 2.1 and 3.10). • **Rural population density** is the rural population divided by the arable land area. • **Land area** is a country's total area, excluding area under inland water bodies, national claims to the continental shelf, and exclusive economic zones. In most cases the definition of inland water bodies includes major rivers and lakes. (See table 1.1 for the total surface area of countries.) • **Land use** is broken into three categories. • **Arable land** includes land defined by the FAO as land under temporary crops (double-cropped areas are counted once), temporary meadows for mowing or for pasture, land under market or kitchen gardens, and land temporarily fallow. Land abandoned as a result of shifting cultivation is excluded. • **Permanent cropland** is land cultivated with crops that occupy the land for long periods and need not be replanted after each harvest, such as cocoa, coffee, and rubber. This category includes land under flowering shrubs, fruit trees, nut trees, and vines, but excludes land under trees grown for wood or timber. • **Other land** includes forest and woodland as well as logged-over areas to be forested in the near future. Also included are uncultivated land, grassland not used for pasture, wetlands, wastelands, and built-up areas—residential, recreational, and industrial lands and areas covered by roads and other fabricated infrastructure.

3.1a

All income groups and all regions are becoming less rural

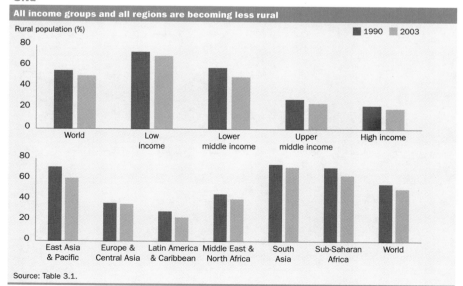

Rural population (%)

■ 1990 ■ 2003

Source: Table 3.1.

Data sources

The data on urban population shares used to estimate rural population come from the United Nations Population Division's *World Urbanization Prospects: The 2003 Revision*. The total population figures are World Bank estimates. The data on land area and land use are from the FAO's electronic files, which may contain more recent information than those published in its *Production Yearbook*. The FAO gathers these data from national agencies through annual questionnaires and by analyzing the results of national agricultural censuses.

	Arable land		Irrigated land		Land under cereal production		Fertilizer consumption		Agricultural machinery			
	hectares per capita		% of cropland		thousands of hectares		hundreds of grams per hectare of arable land		Tractors per 1,000 agricultural workers		Tractors per 100 sq. km of arable land	
	1989–91	2000–02	1989–91	2000–02	1989–91	2001–03	1989–91	2000–02	1989–91	2000–02	1989–91	2000–02
Afghanistan	0.45	0.29	31.2	29.6	..	..	63	19	0	0	1	1
Albania	0.18	0.18	58.9	48.6	295	162	1,378	420	13	11	195	139
Algeria	0.29	0.25	5.1	6.8	2,807	2,383	157	129	48	36	125	123
Angola	0.31	0.24	2.2	2.3	883	1,124	46	2	3	2	35	34
Argentina	0.89	0.93	5.2	4.5	8,557	10,474	56	244	184	205	94	89
Armenia	..	0.16	..	50.2	..	196	..	157	..	92	..	370
Australia	2.76	2.57	4.0	4.9	12,823	17,676	272	464	686	708	67	63
Austria	0.19	0.17	0.3	0.3	940	797	2,001	1,533	1,250	1,796	2,378	2,363
Azerbaijan	..	0.22	..	72.6	..	777	..	63	..	31	..	170
Bangladesh	0.08	0.06	31.0	52.0	11,083	11,582	1,048	1,730	0	0	6	7
Belarus	..	0.58	..	2.2	..	2,279	..	1,325	..	100	..	116
Belgium[a]	..	..	2.3	4.7	367	..	4,969	3,487	425	543	1,530	1,245
Benin	0.34	0.39	0.3	0.4	658	971	54	154	0	0	1	1
Bolivia	0.31	0.34	5.4	4.2	620	750	37	38	4	4	25	21
Bosnia and Herzegovina	..	0.25	..	0.3	..	337	..	356	..	321	..	289
Botswana	0.33	0.22	0.5	0.3	201	174	22	124	21	17	135	162
Brazil	0.34	0.34	4.6	4.4	20,101	18,614	653	1,201	47	62	142	138
Bulgaria	0.44	0.43	30.1	16.4	2,152	1,950	1,698	500	88	120	135	96
Burkina Faso	0.40	0.36	0.5	0.6	2,743	3,375	59	31	0	0	2	5
Burundi	0.17	0.14	5.5	5.5	218	211	32	33	0	0	2	2
Cambodia	0.39	0.29	6.3	7.1	1,860	2,068	9	0	0	1	3	7
Cameroon	0.51	0.39	0.3	0.5	755	810	38	75	0	0	1	1
Canada	1.65	1.47	1.6	1.7	21,446	17,071	468	550	1,496	1,921	164	160
Central African Republic	0.65	0.51	..	..	110	185	5	3	0	0	0	0
Chad	0.56	0.44	0.5	0.6	1,170	1,939	20	49	0	0	1	0
Chile	0.22	0.13	51.8	82.6	778	656	1,082	2,386	39	55	129	273
China	0.11	0.11	36.0	35.9	93,047	80,626	2,223	2,576	2	2	67	65
Hong Kong, China	..	..	..	..	..	..	..	..	..	..	..	..
Colombia	0.09	0.06	13.1	21.5	1,655	1,144	1,770	2,605	9	6	98	83
Congo, Dem. Rep.	0.18	0.13	0.1	0.1	1,840	2,023	11	7	0	0	4	4
Congo, Rep.	0.06	0.05	0.5	0.4	15	10	76	180	1	1	46	38
Costa Rica	0.09	0.06	15.0	20.6	89	57	4,256	6,455	21	22	248	311
Côte d'Ivoire	0.21	0.19	1.1	1.1	1,401	1,350	152	263	1	1	15	12
Croatia	..	0.33	..	0.3	..	709	..	1,303	..	18	..	20
Cuba	0.31	0.28	22.0	21.1	233	323	1,658	502	90	101	239	256
Czech Republic	..	0.30	..	0.7	..	1,584	..	1,186	..	209	..	310
Denmark	0.50	0.43	16.9	19.5	1,564	1,521	2,436	1,394	1,014	1,159	639	539
Dominican Republic	0.15	0.13	15.1	17.2	135	163	859	848	3	3	22	17
Ecuador	0.16	0.13	27.9	29.0	828	872	465	1,531	9	12	65	91
Egypt, Arab Rep.	0.04	0.04	100.0	100.0	2,280	2,696	4,181	4,473	7	11	250	309
El Salvador	0.11	0.10	4.9	5.0	428	351	1,392	1,054	5	4	62	53
Eritrea	..	0.12	..	4.7	..	325	..	134	..	0	..	9
Estonia	..	0.59	..	0.5	..	266	..	397	..	656	..	709
Ethiopia	..	0.16	..	1.7	..	7,160	..	145	..	0	..	3
Finland	0.46	0.42	2.8	2.9	1,144	1,182	1,904	1,353	1,116	1,425	1,059	886
France	0.32	0.31	10.3	13.3	9,244	9,069	3,217	2,221	1,057	1,475	799	685
Gabon	0.31	0.25	2.9	3.0	14	20	33	9	7	7	50	46
Gambia, The	0.20	0.18	0.5	0.8	92	141	64	33	0	0	2	2
Georgia	..	0.15	..	44.1	..	351	..	412	..	37	..	235
Germany	0.15	0.14	3.9	4.0	6,864	6,951	3,070	2,245	972	994	1,314	814
Ghana	0.18	0.20	0.2	0.2	1,066	1,477	36	60	1	1	15	9
Greece	0.28	0.25	30.3	37.3	1,473	1,288	2,307	1,580	225	323	752	917
Guatemala	0.15	0.12	6.6	6.8	726	664	999	1,477	3	2	32	32
Guinea	0.13	0.12	7.2	6.2	603	763	18	36	0	0	5	6
Guinea-Bissau	0.29	0.21	4.1	3.1	106	143	22	80	0	0	1	1
Haiti	0.12	0.10	6.8	6.8	408	445	32	181	0	0	3	2

	Arable land		Irrigated land		Land under cereal production		Fertilizer consumption		Agricultural machinery			
	hectares per capita		% of cropland		thousands of hectares		hundreds of grams per hectare of arable land		Tractors per 1,000 agricultural workers		Tractors per 100 sq. km of arable land	
	1989–91	2000–02	1989–91	2000–02	1989–91	2001–03	1989–91	2000–02	1989–91	2000–02	1989–91	2000–02
Honduras	0.30	0.16	4.1	5.6	475	387	191	1,193	6	7	31	49
Hungary	0.49	0.46	3.8	4.7	2,827	2,941	1,459	992	89	230	126	246
India	0.19	0.16	27.0	33.7	102,279	97,285	736	1,032	4	6	61	94
Indonesia	0.11	0.10	14.3	14.3	13,442	14,755	1,227	1,321	1	2	15	46
Iran, Islamic Rep.	0.29	0.23	41.1	45.1	9,503	8,396	760	921	39	38	136	163
Iraq	0.29	0.24	57.2	58.8	..	..	350	968	53	94	72	105
Ireland	0.30	0.29	..	..	306	294	6,609	5,308	895	989	1,624	1,431
Israel	0.07	0.05	47.0	45.8	111	90	2,876	2,610	370	355	795	725
Italy	0.16	0.15	21.9	24.3	4,481	4,196	2,135	1,819	682	1,287	1,593	1,974
Jamaica	0.05	0.07	11.3	8.8	2	1	2,079	1,258	11	12	252	177
Japan	0.04	0.03	54.3	54.7	2,469	1,998	3,865	3,066	441	779	4,306	4,562
Jordan	0.09	0.05	16.5	18.8	101	60	663	977	50	30	213	225
Kazakhstan	..	1.44	..	10.8	..	13,551	..	24	..	38	..	23
Kenya	0.18	0.15	1.2	1.7	1,845	1,941	258	320	1	1	24	27
Korea, Dem. Rep.	0.11	0.11	57.5	54.1	1,604	1,302	3,577	1,071	18	19	299	258
Korea, Rep.	0.05	0.04	63.7	60.4	1,427	1,156	4,888	4,294	12	88	215	1,176
Kuwait	0.00	0.01	60.0	85.6	0	2	417	747	8	7	222	77
Kyrgyz Republic	..	0.27	..	75.6	..	619	..	208	..	46	..	188
Lao PDR	0.19	0.17	15.7	18.0	643	826	18	95	1	1	11	12
Latvia	..	0.78	..	1.1	..	442	..	300	..	379	..	305
Lebanon	0.05	0.04	28.2	32.6	41	56	1,510	2,838	51	185	175	471
Lesotho	0.20	0.19	0.3	0.3	199	235	161	309	7	7	59	61
Liberia	0.16	0.12	0.4	0.5	179	123	25	0	1	0	8	9
Libya	0.42	0.34	20.2	21.9	418	343	445	349	228	381	179	219
Lithuania	..	0.84	..	0.2	..	897	..	579	..	490	..	349
Macedonia, FYR	..	0.28	..	9.1	..	198	..	502	..	473	..	960
Madagascar	0.23	0.18	30.1	30.9	1,308	1,417	32	31	1	1	11	12
Malawi	0.21	0.21	1.0	1.3	1,415	1,642	317	400	0	0	8	7
Malaysia	0.09	0.08	4.8	4.8	696	696	5,386	6,548	13	24	153	240
Mali	0.24	0.42	5.7	2.9	2,340	2,951	78	89	1	1	10	6
Mauritania	0.20	0.18	12.2	9.8	156	157	95	40	1	1	8	8
Mauritius	0.09	0.08	16.0	20.1	1	0	2,867	3,035	5	6	36	37
Mexico	0.29	0.25	21.6	23.1	10,014	10,504	716	727	35	38	124	131
Moldova	..	0.43	..	14.0	..	963	..	86	..	86	..	225
Mongolia	0.65	0.49	5.7	7.0	649	211	116	31	33	16	79	41
Morocco	0.36	0.29	13.5	14.1	5,545	5,217	369	440	10	11	45	56
Mozambique	0.24	0.22	2.8	2.5	1,561	2,008	10	53	1	1	17	14
Myanmar	0.24	0.21	10.0	18.6	5,154	7,069	84	146	1	1	13	10
Namibia	0.47	0.42	0.6	0.9	214	252	0	4	11	10	46	39
Nepal	0.13	0.13	41.0	35.4	3,013	3,318	322	251	1	0	19	15
Netherlands	0.06	0.06	61.0	59.9	192	226	6,506	4,286	583	621	2,074	1,642
New Zealand	0.73	0.39	7.3	8.5	161	143	1,525	5,704	456	450	301	507
Nicaragua	0.34	0.37	5.7	4.3	305	489	281	177	7	7	20	15
Niger	0.47	0.41	1.8	1.5	6,232	7,957	5	11	0	0	0	0
Nigeria	0.31	0.22	0.7	0.7	15,596	21,095	135	66	2	2	8	10
Norway	0.21	0.19	..	..	357	327	2,388	2,100	1,142	1,282	1,741	1,503
Oman	0.02	0.02	72.6	76.9	2	2	2,185	2,491	1	0	41	39
Pakistan	0.19	0.15	80.4	81.1	11,794	12,204	921	1,381	13	13	127	150
Panama	0.21	0.19	4.8	5.1	179	132	656	545	21	32	103	146
Papua New Guinea	0.05	0.04	..	..	2	3	671	556	1	1	60	55
Paraguay	0.51	0.55	3.0	2.2	447	689	92	319	25	23	71	56
Peru	0.16	0.14	30.5	27.8	802	1,141	320	759	5	4	37	36
Philippines	0.09	0.07	15.7	14.5	7,113	6,524	955	1,313	1	1	19	20
Poland	0.38	0.36	0.7	0.7	8,541	8,426	1,383	1,115	228	313	815	950
Portugal	0.24	0.19	20.2	24.0	832	486	1,152	1,062	153	269	563	849
Puerto Rico	0.02	0.01	34.5	47.6	1	0	..	..	..	..	..	..

	Arable land		Irrigated land		Land under cereal production		Fertilizer consumption		Agricultural machinery			
	hectares per capita		% of cropland		thousands of hectares		hundreds of grams per hectare of arable land		Tractors per 1,000 agricultural workers		Tractors per 100 sq. km of arable land	
	1989–91	2000–02	1989–91	2000–02	1989–91	2001–03	1989–91	2000–02	1989–91	2000–02	1989–91	2000–02
Romania	0.41	0.42	31.1	31.1	5,927	5,760	1,077	355	54	106	147	175
Russian Federation	..	0.86	..	3.7	..	40,911	..	121	..	87	..	56
Rwanda	0.12	0.13	0.3	0.4	250	306	20	48	0	0	1	1
Saudi Arabia	0.22	0.17	45.5	42.7	1,009	677	1,461	1,067	6	14	19	28
Senegal	0.32	0.25	3.6	2.9	1,211	1,230	58	140	0	0	2	3
Serbia and Montenegro	..	0.35	2.1	..	..	3,412	1,075	..	..	..	1,424	..
Sierra Leone	0.12	0.10	5.2	5.3	462	231	24	5	0	0	6	2
Singapore	0.00	0.00	..	..	..	..	54,333	25,920	11	22	620	650
Slovak Republic	..	..	..	..	..	..	..	..	..	..	..	..
Slovenia	..	0.09	..	1.5	..	101	..	4,239	..	..	..	..
Somalia	0.14	0.12	17.3	18.7	..	..	18	5	1	1	21	16
South Africa	0.38	0.33	9.0	9.5	6,175	4,465	573	558	75	43	108	49
Spain	0.40	0.33	16.8	20.3	7,756	6,586	1,282	1,605	390	725	481	684
Sri Lanka	0.05	0.05	27.1	33.1	810	864	2,127	2,862	2	2	75	107
Sudan	0.52	0.51	14.7	11.7	5,376	8,684	48	40	1	2	7	7
Swaziland	0.24	0.17	33.2	36.8	80	71	697	371	38	33	233	221
Sweden	0.33	0.30	4.0	4.3	1,235	1,152	1,148	1,010	836	1,131	604	613
Switzerland	0.06	0.06	6.1	5.7	210	168	4,297	2,272	567	718	2,874	2,723
Syrian Arab Republic	0.40	0.28	12.9	23.5	3,968	3,046	581	718	53	66	129	219
Tajikistan	..	0.15	..	68.0	..	379	..	175	..	27	..	241
Tanzania	0.14	0.12	3.3	3.3	2,990	2,870	378	31	1	1	19	19
Thailand	0.32	0.26	20.6	25.7	10,991	11,421	537	1,039	3	11	33	139
Togo	0.60	0.54	0.3	0.7	625	773	57	74	0	0	0	0
Trinidad and Tobago	0.06	0.06	3.3	3.3	6	2	833	631	50	55	355	360
Tunisia	0.36	0.29	6.7	7.7	1,372	807	328	372	31	37	86	125
Turkey	0.44	0.37	13.9	17.9	13,679	13,829	735	727	53	65	278	377
Turkmenistan	..	0.39	..	94.0	..	865	..	543	..	72	..	270
Uganda	0.29	0.21	0.1	0.1	1,078	1,411	1	14	1	1	9	9
Ukraine	..	0.66	..	7.0	..	12,907	..	154	..	108	..	116
United Arab Emirates	0.02	0.02	128.1	29.6	1	0	4,247	5,221	2	5	55	57
United Kingdom	0.12	0.10	2.4	2.9	3,677	3,106	3,553	3,147	829	970	762	868
United States	0.74	0.62	11.1	12.6	63,775	55,604	1,007	1,093	1,321	1,619	258	273
Uruguay	0.41	0.39	9.6	13.5	508	536	586	895	172	174	262	254
Uzbekistan	..	0.18	..	88.7	..	1,560	..	1,614	..	57	..	379
Venezuela, RB	0.14	0.10	13.4	17.2	819	869	1,579	1,157	55	62	169	193
Vietnam	0.08	0.08	44.8	34.8	6,549	8,301	1,183	3,157	1	6	51	250
West Bank and Gaza	..	..	..	..	..	..	..	..	..	..	..	..
Yemen, Rep.	0.12	0.08	22.4	30.4	781	595	134	95	3	2	40	43
Zambia	0.67	0.52	0.6	0.9	929	628	128	84	2	2	11	11
Zimbabwe	0.28	0.25	3.3	3.5	1,606	1,641	562	443	5	7	60	75
World	**0.27 w**	**0.23 w**	**17.8 w**	**19.7 w**	**695,097 s**	**665,131 s**	**999 w**	**986 w**	**22 w**	**20 w**	**191 w**	**190 w**
Low income	0.21	0.17	24.4	26.8	206,088	228,681	552	672	4	4	50	66
Middle income	0.25	0.23	18.1	19.7	345,990	304,868	1,104	1,051	13	12	132	130
Lower middle income	0.24	0.21	18.9	20.8	308,466	264,386	1,143	1,096	10	9	116	106
Upper middle income	0.36	0.32	13.0	13.4	37,524	40,482	880	808	93	119	231	258
Low & middle income	0.23	0.20	20.3	22.3	552,079	533,549	909	912	9	8	103	106
East Asia & Pacific	0.12	0.12	..	..	141,841	133,881	1,768	2,148	2	2	56	73
Europe & Central Asia	0.64	0.58	10.3	10.9	141,325	116,270	994	343	108	111	194	184
Latin America & Carib.	0.31	0.29	12.4	12.5	48,262	49,456	590	861	36	40	119	119
Middle East & N. Africa	0.23	0.18	33.5	38.4	27,826	24,278	702	855	22	25	107	136
South Asia	0.18	0.15	34.1	41.2	129,072	125,321	743	1,053	4	5	62	92
Sub-Saharan Africa	0.29	0.24	4.5	4.3	63,753	84,343	150	132	2	1	21	15
High income	0.43	0.38	10.9	12.2	143,018	131,582	1,248	1,205	642	918	433	436
Europe EMU	0.22	0.21	16.9	19.8	33,599	31,403	2,524	2,032	654	920	997	973

a. Includes Luxembourg.

About the data

Agricultural activities provide developing countries with food and revenue, but they also can degrade natural resources. Poor farming practices can cause soil erosion and loss of soil fertility. Efforts to increase productivity through the use of chemical fertilizers, pesticides, and intensive irrigation have environmental costs and health impacts. Excessive use of chemical fertilizers can alter the chemistry of soil. Pesticide poisoning is common in developing countries. And salinization of irrigated land diminishes soil fertility. Thus inappropriate use of inputs for agricultural production has far-reaching effects.

This table provides indicators of major inputs to agricultural production: land, fertilizer, and agricultural machinery. There is no single correct mix of inputs: appropriate levels and application rates vary by country and over time, depending on the type of crops, the climate and soils, and the production process used.

The data shown here and in table 3.3 are collected by the Food and Agriculture Organization (FAO) through annual questionnaires. The FAO tries to impose standard definitions and reporting methods, but exact consistency across countries and over time is not possible. Data on agricultural employment, in particular, should be used with caution. In many countries much agricultural employment is informal and unrecorded, including substantial work performed by women and children.

Fertilizer consumption measures the quantity of plant nutrients. Consumption is calculated as production plus imports minus exports. Because some chemical compounds used for fertilizers have other industrial applications, the consumption data may overstate the quantity available for crops.

To smooth annual fluctuations in agricultural activity, the indicators in the table have been averaged over three years.

Definitions

• **Arable land** includes land defined by the FAO as land under temporary crops (double-cropped areas are counted once), temporary meadows for mowing or for pasture, land under market or kitchen gardens, and land temporarily fallow. Land abandoned as a result of shifting cultivation is excluded. • **Irrigated land** refers to areas purposely provided with water, including land irrigated by controlled flooding. • **Cropland** refers to arable land and permanent cropland (see table 3.1). • **Land under cereal production** refers to harvested areas, although some countries report only sown or cultivated area. • **Fertilizer consumption** is the quantity of plant nutrients used per unit of arable land. Fertilizer products cover nitrogenous, potash, and phosphate fertilizers (including ground rock phosphate). Traditional nutrients—animal and plant manures—are not included. The time reference for fertilizer consumption is the crop year (July through June). • **Agricultural machinery** refers to wheel and crawler tractors (excluding garden tractors) in use in agriculture at the end of the calendar year specified or during the first quarter of the following year. • **Agricultural workers** refer to all economically active people engaged principally in agriculture, forestry, hunting, or fishing.

3.2a

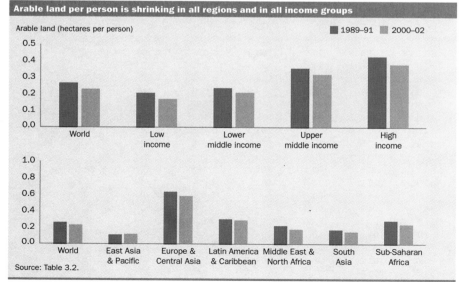

Arable land per person is shrinking in all regions and in all income groups

Source: Table 3.2.

Data sources

The data are from electronic files that the FAO makes available to the World Bank and that may contain more recent information than those published in the FAO's *Production Yearbook*.

3.3 Agricultural output and productivity

	Crop production index		Food production index		Livestock production index		Cereal yield		Agricultural productivity	
	1999–2001 = 100		1999–2001 = 100		1999–2001 = 100		kilograms per hectare		Agriculture value added per worker 2000 $	
	1992–94	2002–04	1992–94	2002–04	1992–94	2002–04	1992–94	2002–04	1989–91	2001–03
Afghanistan	..	..	..	..	..	..	..	..	..	..
Albania	..	..	..	..	..	..	2,465	3,143	770	1,354
Algeria	85.2	119.1	84.5	110.1	85.5	101.0	812	1,323	1,801	1,964
Angola	67.9	119.5	71.3	113.1	79.4	100.0	321	502	207	155
Argentina	68.7	106.0	75.9	101.8	92.5	97.1	2,907	3,212	6,507	9,272
Armenia	106.9	108.6	104.6	108.8	97.9	107.7	1,642	1,976	..	2,646
Australia	59.9	77.8	72.4	91.3	85.4	99.6	1,714	1,709	20,601	*26,957*
Austria	89.9	95.5	92.0	94.0	97.6	95.2	5,219	5,612	11,153	24,456
Azerbaijan	115.6	123.0	90.7	118.9	86.7	111.5	1,788	2,587	..	1,026
Bangladesh	74.8	103.9	74.1	103.6	80.3	102.3	2,583	3,410	239	309
Belarus	116.3	113.1	129.4	106.9	137.3	98.8	2,602	2,630	..	2,520
Belgium	87.4	103.9	98.4	99.9	98.7	99.3	6,563	8,504	19,687	38,431
Benin	66.0	111.0	67.8	108.3	92.3	105.7	930	1,060	360	582
Bolivia	68.2	114.7	72.6	111.5	77.5	108.0	1,466	1,880	662	739
Bosnia and Herzegovina	..	..	..	..	..	..	3,559	3,220	..	..
Botswana	100.7	112.9	113.6	105.9	115.4	104.8	248	212	570	408
Brazil	82.2	115.8	76.8	115.0	73.1	114.6	2,261	3,129	1,658	3,004
Bulgaria	113.1	102.9	114.5	102.2	116.3	96.6	2,756	3,026	2,434	6,310
Burkina Faso	76.5	127.4	79.4	115.3	76.4	106.3	865	988	140	163
Burundi	108.0	108.3	108.1	107.3	137.2	100.1	1,348	1,333	119	104
Cambodia	64.1	101.8	66.1	103.2	75.8	102.1	1,366	2,042	..	292
Cameroon	75.7	108.4	78.6	107.9	86.8	102.3	1,000	1,710	725	1,143
Canada	89.1	86.8	84.0	92.4	80.2	103.2	2,568	2,683	27,739	*36,702*
Central African Republic	76.6	100.0	76.0	105.5	77.4	113.1	935	1,047	291	408
Chad	68.7	108.3	73.8	109.1	84.1	104.3	659	713	164	220
Chile	85.9	106.7	82.8	105.4	78.6	104.8	4,304	5,239	4,775	6,177
China	75.0	108.0	68.4	110.5	61.2	112.3	4,481	4,984	242	365
Hong Kong, China	..	..	..	..	..	..	..	..	..	..
Colombia	98.2	105.2	87.2	103.0	84.1	102.0	2,521	3,475	3,315	2,900
Congo, Dem. Rep.	126.2	97.0	123.3	97.2	103.2	97.0	783	780	230	*196*
Congo, Rep.	83.3	104.0	82.2	105.3	79.6	110.2	752	780	319	329
Costa Rica	66.7	120.0	78.1	94.3	80.8	98.9	3,468	3,965	3,039	4,306
Côte d'Ivoire	73.5	92.2	75.4	96.4	78.1	117.6	921	1,138	610	804
Croatia	83.6	98.0	92.1	95.7	100.8	93.8	4,124	4,432	..	8,956
Cuba	82.5	112.6	84.7	108.1	99.1	91.2	1,625	3,167	..	..
Czech Republic	97.2	85.7	112.0	95.1	115.4	103.3	4,057	4,308	..	5,078
Denmark	94.2	96.0	96.7	100.8	93.9	103.2	5,174	6,003	18,564	36,320
Dominican Republic	114.9	110.9	104.6	108.2	85.5	106.8	3,826	4,722	2,273	4,076
Ecuador	91.2	97.2	80.7	107.3	70.5	115.3	1,933	2,204	1,969	1,441
Egypt, Arab Rep.	74.1	100.6	71.9	101.8	68.9	105.5	5,918	7,191	1,497	1,952
El Salvador	102.7	89.7	90.0	99.8	81.3	104.7	1,879	2,445	1,571	1,613
Eritrea	91.2	64.0	82.8	79.8	75.9	93.9	523	267	..	64
Estonia	113.4	94.6	160.7	102.1	166.6	105.3	1,687	2,184	..	3,372
Ethiopia	69.9	106.7	71.8	107.3	78.8	106.9	1,143	1,318	..	123
Finland	91.8	104.2	99.6	104.0	101.9	103.7	3,357	3,231	16,056	30,391
France	92.1	95.8	95.9	97.8	97.4	100.8	6,515	7,034	20,265	38,647
Gabon	86.0	101.5	88.3	100.9	88.4	99.9	1,805	1,641	1,571	1,696
Gambia, The	55.5	64.7	59.7	68.1	102.1	101.7	1,197	1,107	234	226
Georgia	119.7	94.7	100.9	104.3	77.8	109.1	1,927	2,049	..	1,374
Germany	83.7	90.1	91.8	94.8	96.8	100.6	5,625	6,324	10,963	22,127
Ghana	69.1	114.3	70.2	114.2	90.9	107.0	1,237	1,406	315	338
Greece	96.1	95.0	99.3	97.0	103.0	98.6	3,674	3,539	7,579	9,226
Guatemala	79.8	101.5	78.7	104.6	80.2	99.8	1,849	1,735	2,121	2,261
Guinea	80.5	104.4	79.9	107.7	68.5	111.1	1,133	1,406	171	225
Guinea-Bissau	73.1	101.6	76.0	101.6	86.4	102.3	1,423	1,138	224	247
Haiti	101.9	99.6	95.7	101.8	76.7	109.2	948	868	802	469

Agricultural output and productivity | **3.3**

	Crop production index		Food production index		Livestock production index		Cereal yield		Agricultural productivity	
	1999–2001 = 100		1999–2001 = 100		1999–2001 = 100		kilograms per hectare		Agriculture value added per worker 2000 $	
	1992–94	**2002–04**	**1992–94**	**2002–04**	**1992–94**	**2002–04**	**1992–94**	**2002–04**	**1989–91**	**2001–03**
Honduras	97.0	111.5	90.5	109.0	76.6	106.0	1,323	1,400	961	1,146
Hungary	89.1	88.5	93.5	96.0	101.7	103.9	3,567	4,250	3,456	4,114
India	84.0	97.0	80.8	100.1	75.2	107.2	2,075	2,313	341	402
Indonesia	87.8	106.3	89.4	107.2	100.4	113.6	3,866	4,229	479	538
Iran, Islamic Rep.	83.1	114.5	82.1	111.0	77.4	102.1	1,690	2,387	1,799	2,354
Iraq	..	..	..	..	..	..	..	..	..	..
Ireland	89.8	98.0	95.1	95.5	94.8	95.5	6,237	7,030	..	..
Israel	92.5	98.8	81.2	106.6	80.5	111.3	2,723	3,109	..	..
Italy	98.9	90.1	98.2	92.8	95.0	99.5	4,745	4,886	11,411	21,436
Jamaica	100.2	99.7	94.0	100.7	81.9	103.3	1,491	1,167	1,658	1,937
Japan	108.7	95.8	106.9	97.6	107.0	100.0	5,585	5,949	19,163	*25,339*
Jordan	109.0	144.3	98.5	135.1	92.8	98.9	1,462	1,073	1,456	960
Kazakhstan	123.0	114.7	136.7	107.5	174.9	105.7	1,056	1,057	..	1,385
Kenya	77.9	96.3	80.4	99.0	83.9	103.8	1,645	1,466	184	148
Korea, Dem. Rep.	..	..	..	..	..	..	5,487	3,310	..	..
Korea, Rep.	89.2	93.7	84.3	94.6	80.3	101.3	5,852	5,991	5,312	9,888
Kuwait	39.6	108.6	35.1	116.0	39.1	116.0	5,722	2,136	..	..
Kyrgyz Republic	60.8	106.7	71.8	103.6	102.6	102.6	2,349	2,767	..	931
Lao PDR	63.5	117.0	63.5	118.3	72.1	111.5	2,487	3,174	351	459
Latvia	126.9	119.0	188.2	108.7	220.3	97.9	1,752	2,290	..	2,385
Lebanon	115.2	95.7	106.3	100.8	68.3	116.3	2,107	2,486	..	43,100
Lesotho	74.1	103.3	95.2	101.4	125.8	100.0	801	963	503	506
Liberia	..	..	..	..	..	..	1,037	917	..	..
Libya	81.4	93.5	79.4	101.7	76.0	101.8	705	626	..	..
Lithuania	87.2	109.5	131.6	105.3	152.9	102.6	1,934	2,788	..	4,071
Macedonia, FYR	90.5	88.2	95.0	88.1	108.5	95.2	2,453	2,747	..	2,935
Madagascar	95.4	101.1	92.4	101.3	92.3	101.4	1,928	2,059	187	176
Malawi	57.7	79.5	49.3	81.3	85.3	101.8	956	1,135	76	121
Malaysia	79.8	109.7	78.4	110.4	97.2	110.8	2,996	3,275	3,694	4,571
Mali	75.6	102.2	81.7	102.4	85.1	110.8	773	822	203	228
Mauritania	85.6	93.6	82.3	105.6	81.2	107.5	793	959	244	278
Mauritius	107.3	100.7	100.4	103.8	82.2	117.8	4,135	4,854	3,718	5,034
Mexico	83.7	102.6	81.8	104.2	78.3	106.1	2,622	2,825	2,194	2,784
Moldova	147.1	107.2	149.7	107.0	168.3	100.0	2,981	2,659	..	726
Mongolia	171.5	112.7	83.1	100.6	81.3	99.6	812	676	1,003	694
Morocco	95.2	123.9	89.6	117.1	80.7	104.3	911	1,192	1,580	1,515
Mozambique	60.5	104.6	65.9	102.5	91.5	100.7	420	862	117	137
Myanmar	71.7	117.5	72.1	117.0	68.2	116.5	2,873	3,517	..	..
Namibia	70.3	107.5	108.2	94.7	115.3	91.0	277	410	792	1,003
Nepal	75.2	107.3	77.2	106.0	82.4	105.3	1,786	2,258	196	208
Netherlands	98.5	95.8	105.4	95.7	105.9	95.3	7,541	7,974	23,496	*38,085*
New Zealand	84.5	98.8	84.0	110.3	85.8	110.3	5,538	6,487	19,930	*26,526*
Nicaragua	73.9	106.5	73.9	114.5	73.4	119.9	1,733	1,792	1,167	1,934
Niger	74.2	112.7	78.6	110.6	86.2	103.0	313	415	174	172
Nigeria	79.4	103.6	79.5	103.8	82.8	105.5	1,150	1,058	576	836
Norway	115.3	101.8	105.7	98.6	102.3	97.1	3,496	3,901	19,055	30,854
Oman	69.2	88.9	66.9	90.3	75.2	92.0	2,168	2,318	..	..
Pakistan	79.9	100.4	76.8	105.9	75.2	109.2	1,893	2,332	563	690
Panama	111.7	101.9	97.5	104.2	80.2	104.8	1,901	2,447	2,320	3,470
Papua New Guinea	83.9	101.3	84.6	105.8	85.3	110.1	2,759	3,761	406	452
Paraguay	81.3	114.5	78.4	109.3	88.2	99.9	1,908	2,026	2,201	2,380
Peru	57.3	103.9	61.3	103.6	70.1	102.6	2,697	3,069	1,196	1,734
Philippines	87.2	107.6	81.5	111.6	67.4	121.5	2,209	2,825	910	1,013
Poland	101.3	91.5	99.2	102.7	99.3	104.4	2,573	3,131	..	1,358
Portugal	88.0	98.2	90.4	99.9	88.9	100.4	2,070	2,775	3,807	*5,444*
Puerto Rico	133.3	99.9	111.2	100.2	104.6	100.2	1,404	1,731	..	..

	Crop production index		Food production index		Livestock production index		Cereal yield		Agricultural productivity	
	1999–2001 = 100		1999–2001 = 100		1999–2001 = 100		kilograms per hectare		Agriculture value added per worker 2000 $	
	1992–94	2002–04	1992–94	2002–04	1992–94	2002–04	1992–94	2002–04	1989–91	2001–03
Romania	94.7	110.1	101.4	110.8	113.1	110.6	2,441	2,958	2,079	3,430
Russian Federation	114.8	114.1	122.5	113.1	142.7	107.8	1,612	1,891	..	2,204
Rwanda	86.6	117.8	85.4	117.0	76.8	105.5	1,150	1,001	179	225
Saudi Arabia	126.0	105.7	100.8	110.7	70.7	103.0	4,400	3,761	7,280	13,982
Senegal	72.3	73.6	74.1	78.8	83.9	98.2	792	944	270	260
Serbia and Montenegro	99.6	110.0	105.6	105.6	101.8	94.9	3,099	3,505	..	..
Sierra Leone	123.0	108.9	114.7	109.2	88.6	110.0	1,194	1,210	532	285
Singapore	116.1	100.0	215.2	66.2	212.4	71.3	..	..	25,523	32,915
Slovak Republic	..	..	..	..	..	..	..	..	..	..
Slovenia	101.0	98.2	86.6	105.6	83.2	109.1	4,150	4,927	..	30,306
Somalia	..	..	..	..	..	..	..	..	..	..
South Africa	81.4	100.6	85.4	105.7	93.8	109.8	1,901	2,676	1,890	2,238
Spain	81.6	104.3	83.4	103.8	80.5	107.6	2,342	3,395	8,740	14,852
Sri Lanka	89.4	98.4	91.2	99.6	87.9	107.2	2,961	3,305	696	737
Sudan	80.3	115.9	77.5	110.0	75.6	106.1	554	593	352	700
Swaziland	95.9	94.1	107.5	101.9	140.5	115.3	1,407	1,114	1,342	1,158
Sweden	94.0	103.0	96.3	100.4	97.2	97.5	4,003	4,882	20,416	30,469
Switzerland	112.2	93.5	104.3	99.9	103.3	101.9	6,137	6,005	..	..
Syrian Arab Republic	84.0	116.5	81.0	120.7	69.6	110.5	1,396	1,911	2,065	2,799
Tajikistan	118.6	128.7	129.9	126.5	183.7	132.3	1,012	1,977	..	412
Tanzania	88.1	102.6	87.2	104.0	87.7	109.0	1,162	1,476	246	283
Thailand	85.7	105.4	88.7	104.7	98.9	103.7	2,298	2,708	493	588
Togo	81.3	110.6	81.5	104.5	83.6	106.9	821	1,004	356	404
Trinidad and Tobago	116.8	91.9	91.0	121.5	75.0	141.7	3,496	2,688	1,623	2,397
Tunisia	91.7	93.4	84.9	94.7	66.7	98.6	1,208	1,422	2,144	2,438
Turkey	88.1	103.6	90.2	103.2	94.5	101.8	2,097	2,298	1,749	1,764
Turkmenistan	122.3	111.3	75.6	103.8	78.6	97.3	2,385	2,790	..	1,253
Uganda	81.4	107.4	82.5	108.7	86.1	116.8	1,522	1,651	187	230
Ukraine	127.4	112.8	134.9	108.4	155.5	107.2	2,952	2,542	..	1,442
United Arab Emirates	31.8	58.8	34.0	56.4	65.1	113.9	1,676	3,423	..	..
United Kingdom	102.5	100.5	106.4	99.0	106.1	98.5	6,435	7,082	21,655	25,609
United States	92.2	101.2	88.7	102.4	87.1	102.5	5,075	6,138	26,105	47,566
Uruguay	78.8	109.1	82.2	102.3	88.3	97.7	2,728	3,777	5,346	6,632
Uzbekistan	105.2	106.1	92.5	106.9	102.3	104.7	1,678	3,455	..	1,520
Venezuela, RB	79.5	93.1	77.3	99.6	79.5	103.2	2,817	3,242	5,016	6,126
Vietnam	67.2	114.9	70.3	116.0	64.7	120.2	3,344	4,484	212	290
West Bank and Gaza	..	..	..	..	..	..	..	..	..	..
Yemen, Rep.	83.0	99.5	79.1	105.9	73.7	112.9	1,104	871	361	504
Zambia	88.7	101.3	92.2	103.3	87.3	99.2	1,495	1,514	188	205
Zimbabwe	71.9	76.1	75.1	85.3	86.4	102.3	1,112	605	260	277
World	**84.3 w**	**105.1 w**	**83.6 w**	**105.8 w**	**83.9 w**	**106.7 w**	**2,793 w**	**3,163 w**	**772 w**	**776 w**
Low income	81.9	102.6	80.2	104.5	77.3	109.3	1,800	2,021	329	375
Middle income	82.2	109.6	80.3	110.0	79.3	110.4	2,782	3,249	550	719
Lower middle income	81.9	110.6	79.3	111.3	77.0	112.3	2,776	3,253	472	617
Upper middle income	84.4	102.2	86.1	102.2	89.8	101.5	2,828	3,222	3,440	3,970
Low & middle income	82.1	107.4	80.3	108.4	78.8	110.2	2,401	2,722	461	565
East Asia & Pacific	77.0	110.6	72.1	112.0	63.8	115.5	3,965	4,400	..	397
Europe & Central Asia	104.9	106.1	112.8	105.7	125.5	104.3	1,936	2,275	1,791	1,869
Latin America & Carib.	80.7	110.9	79.2	109.8	78.8	108.3	2,456	3,012	2,166	2,872
Middle East & N. Africa	86.2	111.0	82.1	110.1	74.4	106.3	1,898	2,398	1,825	2,238
South Asia	83.5	99.7	80.2	102.8	75.1	109.7	2,099	2,423	344	406
Sub-Saharan Africa	80.1	103.5	81.5	104.5	85.6	106.5	1,000	1,071	314	327
High income	90.9	97.9	91.0	99.7	91.7	101.2	4,383	4,939	..	..
Europe EMU	90.7	97.6	93.2	98.6	96.0	99.5	4,808	5,462	11,395	20,544

The agricultural production indexes in the table are prepared by the Food and Agriculture Organization (FAO). The FAO obtains data from official and semiofficial reports of crop yields, area under production, and livestock numbers. If data are not available, the FAO makes estimates. The indexes are calculated using the Laspeyres formula: production quantities of each commodity are weighted by average international commodity prices in the base period and summed for each year. Because the FAO's indexes are based on the concept of agriculture as a single enterprise, estimates of the amounts retained for seed and feed are subtracted from the production data to avoid double counting. The resulting aggregate represents production available for any use except as seed and feed. The FAO's indexes may differ from other sources because of differences in coverage, weights, concepts, time periods, calculation methods, and use of international prices.

To ease cross-country comparisons, the FAO uses international commodity prices to value production. These prices, expressed in international dollars (equivalent in purchasing power to the U.S. dollar), are derived using a Geary-Khamis formula applied to agricultural outputs (see Inter-Secretariat Working Group on National Accounts 1993, sections 16.93–96). This method assigns a single price to each commodity so that, for example, one metric ton of wheat has the same price regardless of where it was produced. The use of international prices eliminates fluctuations in the value of output due to transitory movements of nominal exchange rates unrelated to the purchasing power of the domestic currency.

Data on cereal yield may be affected by a variety of reporting and timing differences. The FAO allocates production data to the calendar year in which the bulk of the harvest took place. But most of a crop harvested near the end of a year will be used in the following year. Cereal crops harvested for hay or harvested green for food, feed, or silage, and those used for grazing, are generally excluded. But millet and sorghum, which are grown as feed for livestock and poultry in Europe and North America, are used as food in Africa, Asia, and countries of the former Soviet Union. So some cereal crops are excluded from the data for some countries and included elsewhere, depending on their use.

Agricultural productivity is measured by value added per unit of input. (For further discussion of the calculation of value added in national accounts, see *About the data* for tables 4.1 and 4.2.) Agricultural value added includes that from forestry and fishing. Thus interpretations of land productivity should be made with caution. To smooth annual fluctuations in agricultural activity, the indicators in the table have been averaged over three years.

• **Crop production index** shows agricultural production for each period relative to the base period 1999–2001. It includes all crops except fodder crops. The regional and income group aggregates for the FAO's production indexes are calculated from the underlying values in international dollars, normalized to the base period 1999–2001. The data in this table are three-year averages. • **Food production index** covers food crops that are considered edible and that contain nutrients. Coffee and tea are excluded because, although edible, they have no nutritive value. • **Livestock production index** includes meat and milk from all sources, dairy products such as cheese, and eggs, honey, raw silk, wool, and hides and skins. • **Cereal yield,** measured in kilograms per hectare of harvested land, includes wheat, rice, maize, barley, oats, rye, millet, sorghum, buckwheat, and mixed grains. Production data on cereals refer to crops harvested for dry grain only. Cereal crops harvested for hay or harvested green for food, feed, or silage, and those used for grazing, are excluded. • **Agricultural productivity** refers to the ratio of agricultural value added, measured in constant 2000 U.S. dollars, to the number of workers in agriculture.

3.3a

The 10 countries with the highest cereal yield in 2002–04—and the 10 with the lowest

Country	Kilograms per hectare	Country	Kilograms per hectare
Belgium	8,504	Botswana	212
Netherlands	7,974	Eritrea	267
Egypt, Arab Rep.	7,191	Namibia	410
United Kingdom	7,082	Niger	415
France	7,034	Angola	502
Ireland	7,030	Sudan	593
New Zealand	6,487	Zimbabwe	605
Germany	6,324	Libya	626
United States	6,138	Mongolia	676
Switzerland	6,005	Chad	713

Source: Table 3.3.

Data sources

The agricultural production indexes are prepared by the FAO and published annually in its *Production Yearbook*. The FAO makes these data and the data on cereal yield and agricultural employment available to the World Bank in electronic files that may contain more recent information than the published versions. For sources of data on agricultural value added, see *Data sources* for table 4.2.

3.4 Deforestation and biodiversity

	Forest area		Average annual deforestation[a]		Mammals		Birds		Higher plants[b]		Nationally protected areas	
	thousand sq. km 2000	% of total land area 2000	sq. km 1990–2000	% 1990–2000	Species 2002	Threatened species 2002	Species 2002	Threatened species 2002	Species 2002	Threatened species 2002	thousand sq. km 2003[c]	% of total land area 2003[c]
Afghanistan	14	2.1	..	..	119	13	181	11	4,000	1	2.0	0.3
Albania	10	36.2	78	0.8	68	3	193	3	3,031	0	1.0	3.8
Algeria	21	0.9	−266	−1.3	92	13	183	6	3,164	2	119.1	5.0
Angola	698	56.0	1,242	0.2	276	19	265	15	5,185	19	82.3	6.6
Argentina	346	12.7	2,851	0.8	320	34	362	39	9,372	42	180.6	6.6
Armenia	4	12.4	−42	−1.3	84	11	236	4	3,553	1	2.1	7.6
Australia	1,545	20.1	2,820	0.2	252	63	497	37	15,638	38	1,029.4	13.4
Austria	39	47.0	−77	−0.2	83	7	230	3	3,100	3	27.3	33.0
Azerbaijan	11	13.2	−130	−1.3	99	13	229	8	4,300	0	5.3	6.1
Bangladesh	13	10.2	−165	−1.3	125	23	166	23	5,000	12	1.0	0.8
Belarus	94	45.3	−2,562	−3.2	74	7	194	3	2,100	0	13.1	6.3
Belgium[d]	7	22.2	13	0.2	58	11	191	2	1,550	0	0.9	2.6
Benin	27	24.0	699	2.3	188	8	112	2	2,500	11	12.6	11.4
Bolivia	531	48.9	1,611	0.3	316	24	504	28	17,367	70	145.3	13.4
Bosnia and Herzegovina	23	44.4	0	0.0	72	10	205	3	..	1	0.3	0.5
Botswana	124	21.9	1,184	0.9	164	6	184	7	2,151	0	104.8	18.5
Brazil	5,439	64.3	23,093	0.4	394	81	686	114	56,215	..	566.6	6.7
Bulgaria	37	33.4	−204	−0.6	81	14	248	10	3,572	0	5.0	4.5
Burkina Faso	71	25.9	152	0.2	147	7	138	2	1,100	2	31.5	11.5
Burundi	1	3.7	147	9.0	107	6	145	7	2,500	2	1.5	5.7
Cambodia	93	52.9	561	0.6	123	24	183	19	..	29	32.7	18.5
Cameroon	239	51.3	2,218	0.9	409	40	165	15	8,260	155	20.9	4.5
Canada	2,446	26.5	0	0.0	193	14	310	8	3,270	1	1,023.5	11.1
Central African Republic	229	36.8	300	0.1	209	14	168	3	3,602	10	54.2	8.7
Chad	127	10.1	817	0.6	134	17	141	5	1,600	2	114.6	9.1
Chile	155	20.7	203	0.1	91	21	157	22	5,284	40	141.5	18.9
China	1,635	17.5	−18,063	−1.2	394	79	618	74	32,200	168	727.5	7.8
Hong Kong, China	..	..	..	..	..	1	..	11	..	..	..	0.5
Colombia	496	47.8	1,905	0.4	359	41	708	78	51,220	213	105.9	10.2
Congo, Dem. Rep.	1,352	59.6	5,324	0.4	200	15	130	3	6,000	33	113.4	5.0
Congo, Rep.	221	64.6	175	0.1	450	40	345	28	11,007	55	22.2	6.5
Costa Rica	20	38.5	158	0.8	205	14	279	13	12,119	109	11.7	23.0
Côte d'Ivoire	71	22.4	2,649	3.1	230	19	252	12	3,660	101	19.1	6.0
Croatia	18	31.9	−20	−0.1	76	9	224	4	4,288	0	4.2	7.5
Cuba	23	21.4	−277	−1.3	31	11	86	18	6,522	160	75.9	69.1
Czech Republic	26	34.1	−5	0.0	81	8	205	2	1,900	4	12.4	16.1
Denmark	5	10.7	−10	−0.2	43	5	196	1	1,450	3	14.4	34.0
Dominican Republic	14	28.4	0	0.0	20	5	79	15	5,657	29	25.1	51.9
Ecuador	106	38.1	1,372	1.2	302	33	640	62	19,362	197	50.7	18.3
Egypt, Arab Rep.	1	0.1	−20	−3.3	98	13	123	7	2,076	2	96.6	9.7
El Salvador	1	5.8	72	4.6	135	2	141	0	2,911	23	0.1	0.4
Eritrea	16	15.7	54	0.3	112	12	138	7	..	3	4.3	4.3
Estonia	21	48.6	−125	−0.6	65	4	204	3	1,630	0	5.0	11.8
Ethiopia	46	4.6	403	0.8	277	35	262	16	6,603	22	169.0	16.9
Finland	219	72.0	−80	0.0	60	5	243	3	1,102	1	28.3	9.3
France	153	27.9	−616	−0.4	93	18	283	5	4,630	2	73.2	13.3
Gabon	218	84.7	101	0.0	190	15	156	5	6,651	71	1.8	0.7
Gambia, The	5	48.1	−45	−1.0	117	3	154	2	974	3	0.2	2.3
Georgia	30	43.0	0	0.0	107	13	208	3	4,350	..	1.6	2.3
Germany	107	30.8	0	0.0	76	11	247	5	2,682	12	113.8	32.6
Ghana	63	27.8	1,200	1.7	222	14	206	8	3,725	115	12.7	5.6
Greece	36	27.9	−300	−0.9	95	13	255	7	4,992	2	4.6	3.6
Guatemala	29	26.3	537	1.7	250	6	221	6	8,681	77	21.7	20.0
Guinea	69	28.2	347	0.5	190	12	109	10	3,000	21	1.7	0.7
Guinea-Bissau	22	77.8	216	0.9	108	3	235	0	1,000	4	..	..
Haiti	1	3.2	70	5.7	20	4	62	14	5,242	27	0.1	0.4

Deforestation and biodiversity

	Forest area		Average annual deforestation[a]		Mammals		Birds		Higher plants[b]		Nationally protected areas	
	thousand sq. km 2000	% of total land area 2000	sq. km 1990–2000	% 1990–2000	Species 2002	Threatened species 2002	Species 2002	Threatened species 2002	Species 2002	Threatened species 2002	thousand sq. km 2003[c]	% of total land area 2003[c]
Honduras	54	48.1	589	1.0	173	10	232	5	5,680	108	7.2	6.4
Hungary	18	20.0	−72	−0.4	83	9	208	8	2,214	1	6.5	7.0
India	641	21.6	−381	−0.1	390	88	458	72	18,664	244	154.6	5.2
Indonesia	1,050	58.0	13,124	1.2	515	147	929	114	29,375	384	373.2	20.6
Iran, Islamic Rep.	73	4.5	0	0.0	140	22	293	13	8,000	1	78.5	4.8
Iraq	8	1.8	0	0.0	81	11	140	11	..	0	0.0	0.0
Ireland	7	9.6	−170	−3.0	25	5	143	1	950	1	1.2	1.7
Israel	1	6.1	−50	−4.9	116	14	162	12	2,317	0	3.3	15.8
Italy	100	34.0	−295	−0.3	90	14	250	5	5,599	3	23.2	7.9
Jamaica	3	30.0	54	1.5	24	5	75	12	3,308	206	..	..
Japan	241	66.1	−34	0.0	188	37	210	34	5,565	11	24.8	6.8
Jordan	1	1.0	0	0.0	71	10	117	8	2,100	0	3.0	3.4
Kazakhstan	121	4.5	−2,390	−2.2	178	16	379	15	6,000	1	72.9	2.7
Kenya	171	30.0	931	0.5	359	51	344	24	6,506	98	45.5	8.0
Korea, Dem. Rep.	82	68.2	0	0.0	..	13	150	19	2,898	3	3.1	2.6
Korea, Rep.	62	63.3	51	0.1	49	13	138	25	2,898	0	6.8	6.9
Kuwait	0	0.3	−2	−5.2	21	1	35	7	234	0	0.3	1.5
Kyrgyz Republic	10	5.2	−228	−2.6	83	7	168	4	4,500	1	28.9	15.0
Lao PDR	126	54.4	527	0.4	172	31	212	20	8,286	18	6.9	3.0
Latvia	29	47.1	−127	−0.4	83	4	216	3	1,153	0	8.3	13.4
Lebanon	0	3.5	1	0.3	57	5	116	7	3,000	0	0.1	0.5
Lesotho	0	0.5	0	0.0	33	3	123	7	1,591	0	0.1	0.2
Liberia	35	36.1	760	2.0	193	17	146	11	2,200	46	1.6	1.7
Libya	4	0.2	−47	−1.4	76	8	76	1	1,825	1	1.8	0.1
Lithuania	20	31.8	−48	−0.2	68	5	201	4	1,796	0	6.7	10.3
Macedonia, FYR	9	35.6	0	0.0	78	11	199	3	3,500	0	1.8	7.1
Madagascar	117	20.2	1,174	0.9	141	50	172	27	9,505	162	25.0	4.3
Malawi	26	27.2	707	2.4	195	8	219	11	3,765	14	10.5	11.2
Malaysia	193	58.7	2,369	1.2	300	50	254	37	15,500	681	18.7	5.7
Mali	132	10.8	993	0.7	137	13	191	4	1,741	6	45.1	3.7
Mauritania	3	0.3	98	2.7	61	10	172	2	1,100	0	17.4	1.7
Mauritius	0	7.9	1	0.6	..	3	..	9	..	..	0.2	7.8
Mexico	552	28.9	6,306	1.1	491	70	440	39	26,071	..	194.7	10.2
Moldova	3	9.9	−7	−0.2	68	6	175	5	1,752	0	0.5	1.4
Mongolia	106	6.8	600	0.5	133	14	274	16	2,823	0	180.1	11.5
Morocco	30	6.8	12	0.0	105	16	206	9	3,675	2	3.1	0.7
Mozambique	306	39.0	637	0.2	179	14	144	16	5,692	36	65.9	8.4
Myanmar	344	52.3	5,169	1.4	300	39	310	35	7,000	37	2.0	0.3
Namibia	80	9.8	734	0.9	250	15	201	11	3,174	5	112.0	13.6
Nepal	39	27.3	783	1.8	181	31	274	25	6,973	6	12.7	8.9
Netherlands	4	11.1	−10	−0.3	55	10	192	4	1,221	0	4.8	14.2
New Zealand	79	29.7	−390	−0.5	..	8	..	63	..	..	79.3	29.6
Nicaragua	33	27.0	1,172	3.0	200	6	215	5	7,590	39	21.6	17.8
Niger	13	1.0	617	3.7	131	11	125	3	1,460	2	97.5	7.7
Nigeria	135	14.8	3,984	2.6	274	27	286	9	4,715	119	30.1	3.3
Norway	89	29.0	−310	−0.4	54	10	241	2	1,715	2	20.9	6.8
Oman	0	0.0	0	0.0	56	9	109	10	1,204	6	43.3	14.0
Pakistan	24	3.1	394	1.5	188	19	237	17	4,950	2	37.8	4.9
Panama	29	38.6	519	1.6	218	20	302	16	9,915	193	16.2	21.7
Papua New Guinea	306	67.6	1,129	0.4	214	58	414	32	11,544	142	10.4	2.3
Paraguay	234	58.8	1,230	0.5	305	10	233	26	7,851	10	13.9	3.5
Peru	652	50.9	2,688	0.4	460	49	695	76	17,144	269	78.1	6.1
Philippines	58	19.4	887	1.4	153	50	404	67	8,931	193	17.0	5.7
Poland	90	29.7	−175	−0.2	84	15	233	4	2,450	4	37.7	12.4
Portugal	37	40.1	−570	−1.7	63	17	235	7	5,050	15	6.0	6.6
Puerto Rico	2	25.8	5	0.2	..	2	..	8	..	..	0.3	3.5

3.4 Deforestation and biodiversity

	Forest area		Average annual deforestation[a]		Mammals		Birds		Higher plants[b]		Nationally protected areas	
	thousand sq. km 2000	% of total land area 2000	sq. km 1990–2000	% 1990–2000	Species 2002	Threatened species 2002	Species 2002	Threatened species 2002	Species 2002	Threatened species 2002	thousand sq. km 2003[c]	% of total land area 2003[c]
Romania	64	28.0	−147	−0.2	84	17	257	8	3,400	1	10.8	4.7
Russian Federation	8,514	50.4	−1,353	0.0	269	45	528	38	11,400	7	1,317.3	7.8
Rwanda	3	12.4	150	3.9	151	9	200	9	2,288	3	1.5	6.2
Saudi Arabia	15	0.7	0	0.0	77	8	125	15	2,028	3	823.3	38.3
Senegal	62	32.2	450	0.7	192	12	175	4	2,086	7	22.3	11.6
Serbia and Montenegro	29	28.3	14	0.0	96	12	238	5	4,082	1	..	..
Sierra Leone	11	14.7	361	2.9	147	12	172	10	2,090	43	1.5	2.1
Singapore	0	3.0	0	0.0	85	3	142	7	2,282	54	0.0	4.9
Slovak Republic	22	..	−203	−1.0	85	9	199	4	3,124	2	11.0	..
Slovenia	11	55.0	−22	−0.2	75	9	201	1	3,200	0	1.2	6.0
Somalia	75	12.0	769	1.0	171	19	179	10	3,028	17	5.0	0.8
South Africa	89	7.3	80	0.1	247	42	304	28	23,420	45	67.2	5.5
Spain	144	28.8	−860	−0.6	82	24	281	7	5,050	14	42.5	8.5
Sri Lanka	19	30.0	348	1.6	88	22	126	14	3,314	280	8.7	13.5
Sudan	616	25.9	9,589	1.4	267	23	280	6	3,137	17	123.6	5.2
Swaziland	5	30.3	−58	−1.2	..	4	..	5	..	..	0.6	3.5
Sweden	271	65.9	−6	0.0	60	7	259	2	1,750	3	37.5	9.1
Switzerland	12	30.3	−43	−0.4	75	5	199	2	3,030	2	11.9	30.0
Syrian Arab Republic	5	2.5	0	0.0	63	4	145	8	3,000	0	..	..
Tajikistan	4	2.8	−20	−0.5	84	9	210	7	5,000	2	5.9	4.2
Tanzania	388	43.9	913	0.2	316	42	229	33	10,008	236	263.3	29.8
Thailand	148	28.9	1,124	0.7	265	37	285	37	11,625	78	71.0	13.9
Togo	5	9.4	209	3.4	196	9	117	0	3,085	9	4.3	7.9
Trinidad and Tobago	3	50.5	22	0.8	100	1	131	1	2,259	1	0.3	6.0
Tunisia	5	3.3	−11	−0.2	78	11	165	5	2,196	0	0.5	0.3
Turkey	102	13.3	−220	−0.2	116	17	278	11	8,650	3	12.3	1.6
Turkmenistan	38	8.0	0	0.0	103	13	204	6	..	0	19.7	4.2
Uganda	42	21.3	913	2.0	345	20	243	13	4,900	33	48.5	24.6
Ukraine	96	16.5	−310	−0.3	108	16	245	8	5,100	1	22.6	3.9
United Arab Emirates	3	3.8	−78	−2.8	25	3	34	8	..	0	0.0	0.0
United Kingdom	28	11.6	−170	−0.6	50	12	229	2	1,623	13	50.3	20.9
United States	2,260	24.7	−3,880	−0.2	428	37	508	55	19,473	..	2,372.2	25.9
Uruguay	13	7.4	−501	−5.0	81	6	115	11	2,278	1	0.5	0.3
Uzbekistan	20	4.8	−46	−0.2	97	9	203	9	4,800	1	8.3	2.0
Venezuela, RB	495	56.1	2,175	0.4	323	26	547	24	21,073	67	562.7	63.8
Vietnam	98	30.2	−516	−0.5	213	40	262	37	10,500	126	12.0	3.7
West Bank and Gaza	..	..	..	..	..	1	..	1	..	..	..	..
Yemen, Rep.	4	0.9	92	1.8	66	5	93	12	1,650	52	..	..
Zambia	312	42.0	8,509	2.4	233	12	252	11	4,747	8	237.1	31.9
Zimbabwe	190	49.2	3,199	1.5	270	12	229	10	4,440	14	46.8	12.1
World	**38,611 s**	**29.7 w**	**93,952 s**	**0.2 w**							**13,750.0 s**	**10.7 w**
Low income	7,939	26.1	60,183	0.7							2,285.5	7.7
Middle income	22,743	33.0	38,904	0.2							6,454.0	9.4
Lower middle income	20,316	36.2	23,971	0.1							4,271.0	7.7
Upper middle income	2,427	19.0	14,933	0.6							2,183.0	17.3
Low & middle income	30,682	30.9	99,087	0.3							8,739.5	8.9
East Asia & Pacific	4,284	27.0	7,025	0.2							1,454.8	9.2
Europe & Central Asia	9,463	39.6	−8,342	−0.1							1,610.2	6.8
Latin America & Carib.	9,552	47.6	46,701	0.5							2,237.8	11.2
Middle East & N. Africa	168	1.5	−239	−0.1							1,169.3	11.3
South Asia	780	16.3	979	0.1							228.6	4.8
Sub-Saharan Africa	6,435	27.3	52,963	0.8							2,038.8	8.7
High income	7,929	25.9	−5,135	−0.1							5,010.5	19.5
Europe EMU	853	35.0	−2,965	−0.4							324.9	13.5

a. Negative numbers indicate an increase in forest area. b. Flowering plants only. c. Data may refer to earlier years. They are the most recent reported by the World Conservation Monitoring Center in 2003. d. Includes Luxembourg.

About the data

The estimates of forest area are from the Food and Agriculture Organization's (FAO) *State of the World's Forests 2004,* which provides information on forest cover in 2000 and an estimate of forest cover in 1990. The current survey is the latest global forest assessment and the first to use a uniform global definition of forest. According to this assessment, the global rate of net deforestation has slowed to 9.5 million hectares a year, a rate 20 percent lower than that previously reported. No breakdown of forest cover between natural forest and plantation is shown in the table because of space limitations. (This breakdown is provided by the FAO only for developing countries.) For this reason the deforestation data in the table may underestimate the rate at which natural forest is disappearing in some countries.

Deforestation is a major cause of loss of biodiversity, and habitat conservation is vital for stemming this loss. Conservation efforts traditionally have focused on protected areas, which have grown substantially in recent decades. Measures of species richness are among the most straightforward ways to indicate the importance of an area for biodiversity. The number of small plants and animals is usually estimated by sampling plots. It is also important to know which aspects are under the most immediate threat. This, however, requires a large amount of data and time-consuming analysis. For this reason global analyses of the status of threatened species have been carried out for few groups of organisms. Only for birds has the status of all species been assessed. An estimated 45 percent of mammal species remain to be assessed. For plants the World Conservation Union's (IUCN) *1997 IUCN Red List of Threatened Plants* provides the first-ever comprehensive listing of threatened species on a global scale, the result of more than 20 years' work by botanists from around the world. Nearly 34,000 plant species, 12.5 percent of the total, are threatened with extinction.

The table shows information on protected areas, numbers of certain species, and numbers of those species under threat. The World Conservation Monitoring Centre (WCMC) compiles these data from a variety of sources. Because of differences in definitions and reporting practices, cross-country comparability is limited. Compounding these problems, available data cover different periods.

Nationally protected areas are areas of at least 1,000 hectares that fall into one of six management categories defined by the WCMC:

- Scientific reserves and strict nature reserves with limited public access.

- National parks of national or international significance (not materially affected by human activity).
- Natural monuments and natural landscapes with unique aspects.
- Managed nature reserves and wildlife sanctuaries.
- Protected landscapes and seascapes (which may include cultural landscapes).
- Areas managed mainly for the sustainable use of natural systems to ensure long-term protection and maintenance of biological diversity.

Designating land as a protected area does not necessarily mean that protection is in force. For small countries that may only have protected areas smaller than 1,000 hectares, this size limit in the definition will result in an underestimate of the extent and number of protected areas.

Threatened species are defined according to the IUCN's classification categories: endangered (in danger of extinction and unlikely to survive if causal factors continue operating), vulnerable (likely to move into the endangered category in the near future if causal factors continue operating), rare (not endangered or vulnerable but at risk), indeterminate (known to be endangered, vulnerable, or rare but not enough information is available to say which), out of danger (formerly included in one of the above categories but now considered relatively secure because appropriate conservation measures are in effect), and insufficiently known (suspected but not definitely known to belong to one of the above categories).

Figures on species are not necessarily comparable across countries because taxonomic concepts and coverage vary. And while the number of birds and mammals is fairly well known, it is difficult to make an accurate count of plants. Although the data in the table should be interpreted with caution, especially for numbers of threatened species (where knowledge is very incomplete), they do identify countries that are major sources of global biodiversity and show national commitments to habitat protection.

The dataset on protected areas is tentative and is being revised. Due to variations in consistency and methodology of collection, the quality of the data are highly variable across countries. Some countries update their information more frequently than others, some may have more accurate data on extent of coverage, and many underreport the number or extent of protected areas.

Definitions

- **Forest area** is land under natural or planted stands of trees, whether productive or not. • **Average annual deforestation** refers to the permanent conversion of natural forest area to other uses, including shifting cultivation, permanent agriculture, ranching, settlements, and infrastructure development. Deforested areas do not include areas logged but intended for regeneration or areas degraded by fuelwood gathering, acid precipitation, or forest fires. Negative numbers indicate an increase in forest area. • **Mammals** exclude whales and porpoises. • **Birds** are listed for countries included within their breeding or wintering ranges. • **Higher plants** refer to native vascular plant species. • **Threatened species** are the number of species classified by the IUCN as endangered, vulnerable, rare, indeterminate, out of danger, or insufficiently known. • **Nationally protected areas** are totally or partially protected areas of at least 1,000 hectares that are designated as scientific reserves with limited public access, national parks, natural monuments, nature reserves or wildlife sanctuaries, and protected landscapes and seascapes. The data do not include sites protected under local or provincial law. Total land area is used to calculate the percentage of total area protected (see table 3.1).

Data sources

The forestry data are from the FAO's *State of the World's Forests 2004.* The data on species are from the WCMC's electronic files and the IUCN's *2002 IUCN Red List of Threatened Animals* and *1997 IUCN Red List of Threatened Plants.* The data on protected areas are from the United Nations Environment Programme and WCMC.

	Renewable internal freshwater resources[a]		Annual freshwater withdrawals[b]					Access to improved water source			
	Flows billion cu. m	per capita cu. m	billion cu. m	% of internal resources	% for agriculture	% for industry	% for domestic	% of urban population		% of rural population	
	2003	**2003**	**1987–2003**	**1987–2003**	**1987–2003**	**1987–2003**	**1987–2003**	**1990**	**2002**	**1990**	**2002**
Afghanistan	55	1,912	26.1	47.5	99	0	1	..	19	..	11
Albania	27	8,520	1.4	5.2	71	0	29	99	99	95	95
Algeria	14	440	5.0	35.7	52	14	34	99	92	92	80
Angola	184	13,607	0.5	0.3	76	10	14	11	70	40	40
Argentina	276	7,506	28.6	10.4	75	9	16	97	97	73	..
Armenia	9	2,945	2.9	32.2	66	4	30	99	99	..	80
Australia	492	24,747	14.6	3.0	33	2	65	100	100	100	100
Austria	55	6,799	2.4	4.4	9	58	33	100	100	100	100
Azerbaijan	8	972	16.5	206.3	70	25	5	80	95	49	59
Bangladesh	105	761	14.6	13.9	86	2	12	83	82	68	72
Belarus	37	3,745	2.7	7.3	35	43	22	100	100	100	100
Belgium	12	1,157	..	..	..	..	..	100	100	..	..
Benin	10	1,488	0.1	1.0	67	10	23	71	79	54	60
Bolivia	304	34,490	1.2	0.4	87	3	10	91	95	48	68
Bosnia and Herzegovina	36	8,696	1.0	2.8	60	10	30	100	100	96	96
Botswana	3	1,742	0.1	3.3	48	20	32	100	100	88	90
Brazil	5,418	30,680	54.9	1.0	61	18	21	93	96	55	58
Bulgaria	21	2,684	13.9	66.2	22	75	3	100	100	100	100
Burkina Faso	13	1,074	0.4	3.1	81	0	19	63	82	35	44
Burundi	4	555	0.1	2.5	64	0	36	96	90	67	78
Cambodia	121	9,027	0.5	0.4	94	1	5	..	58	..	29
Cameroon	273	16,970	0.4	0.1	35	19	46	77	84	32	41
Canada	2,850	90,104	45.1	1.6	12	70	18	100	100	99	99
Central African Republic	141	36,332	0.1	0.1	74	5	21	70	93	35	61
Chad	15	1,748	0.2	1.3	82	2	16	45	40	13	32
Chile	884	56,042	20.3	2.3	84	11	5	98	100	49	59
China	2,812	2,183	525.5	18.7	78	18	5	100	92	59	68
Hong Kong, China	..	..	..	..	..	..	..	..	..	..	..
Colombia	2,112	47,371	8.9	0.4	37	4	59	98	99	78	71
Congo, Dem. Rep.	900	16,932	0.4	0.0	23	16	61	92	83	24	29
Congo, Rep.	222	59,086	0.0	0.0	11	27	62	..	72	..	17
Costa Rica	112	27,967	5.8	5.2	80	7	13	100	100	..	92
Côte d'Ivoire	77	4,574	0.7	0.9	67	11	22	74	98	66	74
Croatia	38	8,550	0.8	2.1	0	50	50	..	..	..	..
Cuba	38	3,355	5.2	13.7	51	0	49	95	95	..	78
Czech Republic	13	1,274	2.7	20.8	2	57	41	..	..	..	..
Denmark	6	1,114	1.2	20.0	43	27	30	100	100	100	100
Dominican Republic	21	2,403	8.3	39.5	89	0	11	97	98	72	85
Ecuador	432	33,210	17.0	3.9	82	6	12	81	92	54	77
Egypt, Arab Rep.	2	30	66.0	3,300.0	82	11	7	97	100	92	97
El Salvador	18	2,755	0.7	3.9	46	20	34	88	91	47	68
Eritrea	3	683	..	..	..	..	..	60	72	36	54
Estonia	13	9,608	0.2	1.5	5	39	56	..	..	..	..
Ethiopia	110	1,603	2.2	2.0	86	3	11	80	81	16	11
Finland	107	20,530	2.2	2.1	3	85	12	100	100	100	100
France	179	2,995	32.3	18.0	10	72	18	100	100	..	..
Gabon	164	121,984	0.1	0.1	6	22	72	95	95	..	47
Gambia, The	3	2,111	0.0	0.0	91	2	7	95	95	..	77
Georgia	58	11,315	3.5	6.0	59	20	21	..	90	..	61
Germany	107	1,296	46.3	43.3	20	69	11	100	100	100	100
Ghana	30	1,451	0.3	1.0	52	13	35	85	93	36	68
Greece	58	5,257	8.7	15.0	87	3	10	..	..	..	..
Guatemala	109	8,857	1.2	1.1	74	17	9	88	99	69	92
Guinea	226	28,575	0.7	0.3	87	3	10	70	78	32	38
Guinea-Bissau	16	10,744	0.0	0.0	36	4	60	..	79	..	49
Haiti	13	1,540	1.0	7.7	94	1	5	77	91	43	59

	Renewable internal freshwater resources[a]		Annual freshwater withdrawals[b]					Access to improved water source			
	Flows billion cu. m 2003	per capita cu. m 2003	billion cu. m 1987–2003	% of internal resources 1987–2003	% for agriculture 1987–2003	% for industry 1987–2003	% for domestic 1987–2003	% of urban population 1990	2002	% of rural population 1990	2002
Honduras	96	13,776	1.5	1.6	91	5	4	89	99	78	82
Hungary	6	592	6.8	113.3	36	55	9	100	100	98	98
India	1,261	1,185	500.0	39.7	92	3	5	88	96	61	82
Indonesia	2,838	13,220	74.3	2.6	93	1	6	92	89	62	69
Iran, Islamic Rep.	129	1,943	70.0	54.3	92	2	6	98	98	83	83
Iraq	35	1,417	42.8	122.3	92	5	3	97	97	50	50
Ireland	49	12,268	0.8	1.6	10	74	16	100	100	..	..
Israel	1	150	1.6	160.0	54	7	39	100	100	100	100
Italy	183	3,175	42.0	23.0	48	34	19	100	100	..	..
Jamaica	9	3,406	0.9	10.0	77	7	15	97	98	86	87
Japan	430	3,371	91.4	21.3	64	17	19	100	100	100	100
Jordan	1	188	1.0	100.0	75	3	22	100	91	91	91
Kazakhstan	75	5,041	33.7	44.9	81	17	2	96	96	72	72
Kenya	20	627	2.0	10.0	76	4	20	91	89	30	46
Korea, Dem. Rep.	67	2,963	14.2	21.2	73	16	11	100	100	100	100
Korea, Rep.	65	1,357	23.7	36.5	63	11	26	97	97	..	71
Kuwait	0	0	0.5		60	2	37	..	..	..	..
Kyrgyz Republic	46	9,105	10.1	22.0	94	3	3	98	98	..	66
Lao PDR	190	33,570	1.0	0.5	82	10	8	..	66	..	38
Latvia	17	7,324	0.3	1.8	13	32	55	..	..	..	..
Lebanon	5	1,112	1.3	26.0	68	6	27	100	100	100	100
Lesotho	5	2,789	0.1	2.0	56	22	22	..	88	..	74
Liberia	200	59,285	0.1	0.1	60	13	27	85	72	34	52
Libya	1	180	4.5	450.0	84	3	13	72	72	68	68
Lithuania	16	4,632	0.3	1.9	3	16	81	..	..	..	..
Macedonia, FYR	5	2,440	1.9	38.0	74	15	12	..	..	..	..
Madagascar	337	19,948	16.3	4.8	99	..	1	82	75	27	34
Malawi	16	1,460	0.9	5.6	86	3	10	90	96	34	62
Malaysia	580	23,411	12.7	2.2	77	13	11	96	96	..	94
Mali	60	5,150	1.4	2.3	97	1	2	50	76	29	35
Mauritania	0	0	1.6	..	92	2	6	19	63	57	45
Mauritius	..	..	..	..	..	..	..	100	100	100	100
Mexico	409	3,998	77.8	19.0	78	5	17	90	97	54	72
Moldova	1	236	3.0	300.0	26	65	9	97	97	..	88
Mongolia	35	14,115	0.4	1.1	53	27	20	87	87	30	30
Morocco	29	963	11.5	39.7	89	2	10	94	99	58	56
Mozambique	99	5,268	0.6	0.6	89	2	9	..	76	..	24
Myanmar	881	17,848	4.0	0.5	90	3	7	73	95	40	74
Namibia	6	2,978	0.2	3.3	68	3	29	99	98	43	72
Nepal	198	8,029	29.0	14.6	99	0	1	94	93	67	82
Netherlands	11	678	7.8	70.9	34	61	5	100	100	99	99
New Zealand	327	81,562	2.0	0.6	44	10	46	100	100	82	..
Nicaragua	190	34,672	1.3	0.7	84	2	14	92	93	42	65
Niger	4	340	0.5	12.5	82	2	16	62	80	35	36
Nigeria	221	1,620	3.6	1.6	54	15	31	78	72	33	49
Norway	382	83,735	2.0	0.5	8	72	20	100	100	100	100
Oman	1	385	1.2	120.0	94	2	5	81	81	72	72
Pakistan	52	350	155.6	299.2	97	2	2	95	95	78	87
Panama	147	49,262	1.6	1.1	70	2	28	99	99	..	79
Papua New Guinea	801	145,587	0.1	0.0	49	22	29	88	88	32	32
Paraguay	94	16,658	0.4	0.4	78	7	15	80	100	46	62
Peru	1,616	59,526	19.0	1.2	86	7	7	88	87	42	66
Philippines	479	5,877	55.4	11.6	88	4	8	93	90	82	77
Poland	54	1,414	12.3	22.8	11	76	13	100	100	..	..
Portugal	38	3,638	7.3	19.2	48	37	15	..	..	..	..
Puerto Rico	..	..	..	..	..	..	..	..	..	..	..

	Renewable internal freshwater resources[a]		Annual freshwater withdrawals[b]					Access to improved water source			
	Flows billion cu. m	per capita cu. m	billion cu. m	% of internal resources	% for agriculture	% for industry	% for domestic	% of urban population		% of rural population	
	2003	2003	1987–2003	1987–2003	1987–2003	1987–2003	1987–2003	1990	2002	1990	2002
Romania	42	1,932	26.0	61.9	59	33	8	..	91	..	16
Russian Federation	4,313	30,071	77.1	1.8	20	62	19	97	99	86	88
Rwanda	5	596	0.8	16.0	94	2	5	88	92	57	69
Saudi Arabia	2	89	17.0	850.0	90	1	9	97	97	63	..
Senegal	26	2,539	1.4	5.4	92	3	5	90	90	50	54
Serbia and Montenegro	44	5,429	13.0	29.5	8	86	6	99	99	86	86
Sierra Leone	160	29,982	0.4	0.3	89	4	7	..	75	..	46
Singapore	..	..	..	..	4	51	45	100	100	..	..
Slovak Republic	13	2,412	1.8	13.8	..	..	..	100	100	100	100
Slovenia	19	9,524	1.3	6.8	1	80	20	..	..	..	..
Somalia	6	623	0.8	13.3	97	0	3	..	32	..	27
South Africa	45	982	13.3	29.6	72	11	17	99	98	67	73
Spain	111	2,701	35.2	31.7	68	19	13	..	..	..	..
Sri Lanka	50	2,600	9.8	19.6	96	2	2	91	99	62	72
Sudan	30	894	17.8	59.3	94	1	4	85	78	57	64
Swaziland	..	..	..	..	..	..	..	..	87	..	42
Sweden	171	19,093	2.9	1.7	9	55	36	100	100	100	100
Switzerland	40	5,442	1.2	3.0	4	73	23	100	100	100	100
Syrian Arab Republic	7	403	12.0	171.4	90	2	8	94	94	64	64
Tajikistan	66	10,468	11.9	18.0	92	4	3	..	93	..	47
Tanzania	82	2,285	1.2	1.5	89	2	9	79	92	27	62
Thailand	210	3,386	33.1	15.8	91	4	5	87	95	78	80
Togo	12	2,468	0.1	0.8	25	13	62	81	80	37	36
Trinidad and Tobago	4	3,047	0.3	7.5	6	26	68	93	92	89	88
Tunisia	4	404	2.8	70.0	86	1	13	93	94	57	60
Turkey	227	3,210	35.5	15.6	73	12	16	92	96	65	87
Turkmenistan	1	206	23.8	2,380.0	98	1	1	..	93	..	54
Uganda	39	1,543	0.2	0.5	60	8	32	79	87	40	52
Ukraine	53	1,096	26.0	49.1	30	52	18	100	100	..	94
United Arab Emirates	0	49	2.1	1,050.0	67	9	24	..	..	..	..
United Kingdom	145	2,444	11.8	8.1	3	77	20	100	100	..	..
United States	2,800	9,628	467.3	16.7	42	45	13	100	100	100	100
Uruguay	59	17,455	0.7	1.2	91	3	6	98	98	..	93
Uzbekistan	16	625	58.1	363.1	94	2	4	97	97	84	84
Venezuela, RB	722	28,122	4.1	0.6	46	10	44	..	85	..	70
Vietnam	367	4,513	54.3	14.8	87	10	4	93	93	67	67
West Bank and Gaza	..	..	..	..	..	..	..	..	..	..	..
Yemen, Rep.	4	209	2.9	72.5	92	1	7	74	74	68	68
Zambia	80	7,690	1.7	2.1	77	7	16	86	90	27	36
Zimbabwe	14	1,069	1.2	8.6	79	7	14	99	100	69	74
World	**42,883 s**	**6,895 w**	**3,325 s**	**8 w**	**71 w**	**20 w**	**10 w**	**95 w**	**94 w**	**62 w**	**72 w**
Low income	8,278	3,583	947	11	92	3	5	86	89	56	70
Middle income	25,797	8,657	1,524	6	74	17	9	96	94	64	71
Lower middle income	22,242	8,397	1,323	6	74	18	8	97	94	63	71
Upper middle income	3,555	10,741	201	6	71	14	15	95	96	..	..
Low & middle income	34,075	6,441	2,471	7	81	12	7	93	93	60	70
East Asia & Pacific	9,455	5,103	776	8	81	14	5	97	92	61	69
Europe & Central Asia	5,255	11,128	387	7	57	33	10	97	98	..	80
Latin America & Carib.	13,428	25,245	263	2	74	9	18	93	96	58	69
Middle East & N. Africa	234	761	238	102	88	5	7	96	96	78	78
South Asia	1,816	1,275	735	40	94	3	4	89	93	63	80
Sub-Saharan Africa	3,887	5,546	73	2	85	6	10	81	82	37	46
High income	8,808	9,479	854	10	42	42	16	100	100	..	98
Europe EMU	910	2,970	185	21	38	47	15	100	100	..	..

a. River flows from other countries are not included because of data unreliability. b. Data are for most recent year available for 1987–2003 (see *Primary data documentation*).

About the data

The data on freshwater resources are based on estimates of runoff into rivers and recharge of groundwater. These estimates are based on different sources and refer to different years, so cross-country comparisons should be made with caution. Because the data are collected intermittently, they may hide significant variations in total renewable water resources from one year to the next. The data also fail to distinguish between seasonal and geographic variations in water availability within countries. Data for small countries and countries in arid and semiarid zones are less reliable than those for larger countries and countries with greater rainfall.

Caution is also needed in comparing data on annual freshwater withdrawals, which are subject to variations in collection and estimation methods. In addition, inflows and outflows are estimated at different times and at different levels of quality and precision, requiring caution in interpreting the data, particularly for water-short countries, notably in the Middle East.

The data on access to an improved water source measure the share of the population with reasonable and ready access to an adequate amount of safe water for domestic purposes. An improved source can be any form of collection or piping used to make water regularly available. While information on access to an improved water source is widely used, it is extremely subjective, and such terms as safe, improved, adequate, and reasonable may have very different meanings in different countries despite official World Health Organization (WHO) definitions (see *Definitions*). Even in high-income countries treated water may not always be safe to drink. While access to an improved water source is equated with connection to a public supply system, this does not take into account variations in the quality and cost (broadly defined) of the service once connected. Changes over time within countries may reflect changes in definitions or measurements. Thus cross-country comparisons must be made cautiously. The definition in this table and in table 2.15 differs from that used for the city-level data shown in table 3.11, which is more stringent.

3.5a

Agriculture uses more than 71 percent of freshwater globally

Share of annual freshwater withdrawals, most recent year available

World

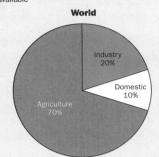

Industry 20%
Domestic 10%
Agriculture 70%

Low-income

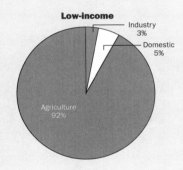

Industry 3%
Domestic 5%
Agriculture 92%

Middle-income

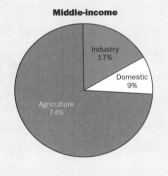

Industry 17%
Domestic 9%
Agriculture 74%

High-income

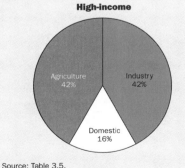

Agriculture 42%
Industry 42%
Domestic 16%

Source: Table 3.5.

Definitions

• **Renewable internal freshwater resources** refer to internal renewable resources (internal river flows and groundwater from rainfall) in the country. • Internal freshwater resources per capita are calculated using the World Bank's population estimates (see table 2.1). • **Annual freshwater withdrawals** refer to total water withdrawals, not counting evaporation losses from storage basins. Withdrawals also include water from desalination plants in countries where they are a significant source. Withdrawals can exceed 100 percent of total renewable resources where extraction from nonrenewable aquifers or desalination plants is considerable or where there is significant water reuse. Withdrawals for agriculture and industry are total withdrawals for irrigation and livestock production and for direct industrial use (including withdrawals for cooling thermoelectric plants). Withdrawals for domestic uses include drinking water, municipal use or supply, and use for public services, commercial establishments, and homes. • **Access to an improved water source** refers to the percentage of the population with reasonable access to an adequate amount of water from an improved source, such as a household connection, public standpipe, borehole, protected well or spring, or rainwater collection. Unimproved sources include vendors, tanker trucks, and unprotected wells and springs. Reasonable access is defined as the availability of at least 20 liters a person a day from a source within 1 kilometer of the dwelling.

Data sources

The data on freshwater resources and withdrawals are compiled by the World Resources Institute from various sources and published in *World Resources 2002–03* (produced in collaboration with the United Nations Environment Programme, United Nations Development Programme, and World Bank). These are supplemented by the Food and Agriculture Organization's AQUASTAT data. The data on access to an improved water source come from the WHO.

3.6 Water pollution

| | Emissions of organic water pollutants | | | | Industry shares of emissions of organic water pollutants | | | | | | | |
| | kilograms per day | | kilograms per worker per day | | Primary metals | Paper and pulp | Chemicals | Food and beverages | % of total Stone, ceramics, and glass | Textiles | Wood | Other |
	1990	2001[a]	1990	2001[a]	2001[a]	2001[a]	2001[a]	2001[a]	2001[a]	2001[a]	2001[a]	2001[a]
Afghanistan	..	..	..	..	..	..	..	..	..	..	..	..
Albania	34,785	6,512	0.14	0.29	14.3	0.9	5.5	73.5	0.3	5.0	0.0	0.4
Algeria	106,977	45,645	0.25	0.24	23.4	2.0	5.9	59.5	0.7	8.0	1.0	..
Angola	4,544	1,472	0.19	0.20	7.6	3.0	9.1	65.9	0.3	6.0	4.0	4.0
Argentina	186,686	149,455	0.20	0.23	4.9	7.2	4.2	71.1	0.0	7.0	1.0	4.6
Armenia	37,900	7,104	0.11	0.28	..	..	0.0	77.6	..	22.0	..	..
Australia	186,110	111,658	0.18	0.18	12.4	22.8	5.6	77.1	0.2	5.0	5.0	6.4
Austria	94,121	80,789	0.15	0.13	14.9	18.2	11.1	32.8	0.4	5.0	5.0	12.5
Azerbaijan	53,251	18,672	0.15	0.16	12.5	4.7	16.6	43.7	0.3	15.0	1.0	6.2
Bangladesh	171,087	273,082	0.17	0.14	1.8	6.8	2.5	23.2	0.1	64.0	1.0	0.7
Belarus	..	..	..	..	..	..	..	..	..	..	..	..
Belgium	117,978	102,460	0.16	0.17	13.7	18.0	12.0	40.4	0.2	6.0	2.0	7.6
Benin	..	..	..	..	..	..	..	..	..	..	..	..
Bolivia	8,404	12,759	0.24	0.25	0.9	20.5	6.6	61.4	0.3	7.0	2.0	1.4
Bosnia and Herzegovina	50,741	8,903	0.14	0.18	20.5	13.1	6.6	33.3	0.2	18.0	6.0	2.2
Botswana	4,509	3,543	0.19	0.25	1.7	6.7	5.4	77.9	0.2	10.0	3.0	2.5
Brazil	780,395	629,406	0.19	0.20	17.7	12.9	9.2	44.4	0.1	10.0	1.0	4.7
Bulgaria	149,381	90,976	0.11	0.17	7.9	7.2	8.2	46.8	0.2	22.0	2.0	5.7
Burkina Faso	..	2,598	..	0.22	3.5	1.1	5.4	73.8	0.1	4.0	10.0	2.2
Burundi	1,570	..	0.24	..	..	..	..	..	..	..	..	..
Cambodia	11,823	..	0.14	..	..	..	..	..	..	..	..	..
Cameroon	13,989	10,714	0.28	0.20	3.1	6.3	28.3	52.7	0.0	4.0	6.0	..
Canada	321,471	313,431	0.17	0.16	9.7	22.8	8.3	38.5	0.1	6.0	5.0	9.5
Central African Republic	998	670	0.18	0.17	0.0	..	4.0	62.0	0.0	14.0	20.0	..
Chad	..	..	..	..	..	..	..	..	..	..	..	..
Chile	66,783	72,850	0.22	0.24	6.9	11.3	8.9	62.7	0.1	5.0	3.0	2.1
China	7,038,131	6,088,663	0.14	0.14	20.4	10.9	14.8	28.1	0.5	15.0	1.0	9.2
Hong Kong, China	86,124	34,767	0.12	0.19	1.2	43.3	3.5	30.2	0.1	16.0	0.0	5.8
Colombia	93,253	93,879	0.19	0.21	3.1	16.2	9.7	53.2	0.2	14.0	1.0	2.6
Congo, Dem. Rep.	..	..	..	..	..	..	..	..	..	..	..	..
Congo, Rep.	..	..	..	..	..	..	..	..	..	..	..	..
Costa Rica	27,249	32,914	0.20	0.21	1.8	10.0	7.4	62.2	0.1	14.0	2.0	2.5
Côte d'Ivoire	..	12,401	..	0.24	..	5.5	7.1	71.9	0.0	9.0	6.0	..
Croatia	80,034	43,087	0.15	0.17	6.2	15.4	8.0	47.1	0.2	13.0	4.0	6.0
Cuba	..	..	..	..	..	..	..	..	..	..	..	..
Czech Republic	309,469	..	0.13	..	..	..	..	..	..	..	..	..
Denmark	91,871	83,591	0.18	0.17	4.4	29.1	7.9	44.2	0.2	2.0	3.0	9.3
Dominican Republic	..	..	..	..	..	..	..	..	..	..	..	..
Ecuador	25,567	32,266	0.23	0.27	2.3	10.8	6.2	71.8	0.1	6.0	1.0	1.7
Egypt, Arab Rep.	211,531	203,633	0.20	0.20	11.8	7.9	8.0	49.8	0.3	19.0	0.0	3.3
El Salvador	7,663	22,760	0.22	0.18	2.1	10.2	8.1	43.5	0.1	34.0	0.0	1.9
Eritrea	..	..	..	..	..	..	..	..	..	..	..	..
Estonia	..	..	..	..	..	..	..	..	..	..	..	..
Ethiopia	18,593	20,849	0.23	0.23	1.8	10.4	4.6	61.2	0.3	20.0	1.0	0.7
Finland	79,514	66,877	0.18	0.16	8.7	40.1	6.8	27.0	0.2	3.0	4.0	10.3
France	653,455	281,747	0.15	0.10	14.7	31.0	23.0	37.4	0.3	9.0	3.0	10.7
Gabon	2,018	1,886	0.25	0.26	0.0	6.0	4.9	79.7	0.1	1.0	7.0	1.3
Gambia, The	..	832	..	0.34	..	..	..	..	..	..	..	..
Georgia	..	..	..	..	..	..	..	..	..	..	..	..
Germany	835,019	1,020,145	0.12	0.14	9.0	20.9	11.3	38.7	0.2	3.0	2.0	15.0
Ghana	..	14,449	..	0.17	9.8	16.9	10.5	39.5	0.2	9.0	12.0	2.2
Greece	63,479	43,707	0.18	0.19	8.1	9.7	9.0	55.0	0.3	12.0	2.0	3.9
Guatemala	16,070	19,253	0.27	0.28	4.9	7.2	6.1	72.8	0.1	7.0	1.0	0.8
Guinea	..	..	..	..	..	..	..	..	..	..	..	..
Guinea-Bissau	..	..	..	..	..	..	..	..	..	..	..	..
Haiti	..	..	..	..	..	..	..	..	..	..	..	..

	Emissions of organic water pollutants				Industry shares of emissions of organic water pollutants							
	kilograms per day		kilograms per day per worker						% of total			
					Primary metals	Paper and pulp	Chemicals	Food and beverages	Stone, ceramics, and glass	Textiles	Wood	Other
	1990	2001[a]	1990	2001[a]	2001[a]	2001[a]	2001[a]	2001[a]	2001[a]	2001[a]	2001[a]	2001[a]
Honduras	17,824	34,036	0.23	0.20	1.1	7.8	3.9	55.5	0.1	27.0	4.0	0.6
Hungary	178,002	113,527	0.16	0.15	6.4	11.8	7.6	49.1	0.2	13.0	2.0	10.0
India	1,410,617	1,556,371	0.20	0.20	12.6	7.5	9.3	53.0	0.2	13.0	0.0	4.4
Indonesia	495,594	753,657	0.19	0.18	2.8	8.5	9.6	50.1	0.1	21.0	5.0	4.3
Iran, Islamic Rep.	102,689	140,775	0.16	0.16	17.4	7.0	10.7	43.6	0.6	13.0	1.0	6.7
Iraq	20,352	19,617	0.16	0.16	8.8	14.1	15.1	39.4	0.7	17.0	0.0	4.8
Ireland	34,610	49,144	0.18	0.15	1.3	14.2	11.4	56.4	0.2	3.0	2.0	11.4
Israel	46,359	39,824	0.16	0.14	3.2	8.2	7.7	54.5	0.1	10.0	2.0	14.2
Italy	358,084	495,973	0.13	0.12	9.3	16.8	10.8	30.1	0.3	16.0	4.0	12.6
Jamaica	18,736	17,507	0.29	0.29	6.9	7.2	3.8	70.8	0.1	10.0	1.0	0.1
Japan	1,556,648	1,279,287	0.14	0.15	7.0	21.9	9.0	43.2	0.2	5.0	2.0	11.7
Jordan	8,325	18,682	0.19	0.19	4.9	12.8	12.9	52.4	0.5	11.0	3.0	2.6
Kazakhstan	..	..	..	..	..	..	..	..	..	..	..	..
Kenya	42,588	53,029	0.23	0.25	4.1	11.9	5.7	70.0	0.1	8.0	2.0	2.3
Korea, Dem. Rep.	..	..	..	..	..	..	..	..	..	..	..	..
Korea, Rep.	369,193	309,517	0.12	0.12	11.4	18.2	12.9	26.0	0.2	14.0	1.0	16.3
Kuwait	9,052	11,412	0.16	0.17	2.5	16.4	10.6	49.4	0.4	12.0	3.0	5.7
Kyrgyz Republic	30,885	20,721	0.12	0.21	8.4	4.1	1.6	67.7	0.3	13.0	1.0	3.9
Lao PDR	..	..	..	..	..	..	..	..	..	..	..	..
Latvia	39,887	25,106	0.12	0.19	2.8	8.7	2.7	64.5	0.1	11.0	10.0	5.6
Lebanon	..	14,899	..	0.19	0.9	15.6	4.0	60.7	0.5	10.0	5.0	3.2
Lesotho	2,958	3,123	0.16	0.16	1.2	4.0	0.7	39.7	0.1	51.0	1.0	2.2
Liberia	..	..	..	..	..	..	..	..	..	..	..	..
Libya	..	..	..	..	..	..	..	..	..	..	..	..
Lithuania	53,818	37,539	0.13	0.18	1.2	11.3	5.1	54.8	0.2	18.0	6.0	3.5
Macedonia, FYR	32,419	23,490	0.18	0.18	11.7	9.6	6.2	45.0	0.1	21.0	2.0	4.5
Madagascar	..	..	..	..	..	..	..	..	..	..	..	..
Malawi	10,024	11,805	0.29	0.29	0.0	16.0	3.7	70.0	0.0	8.0	2.0	0.2
Malaysia	104,728	186,198	0.13	0.12	7.8	14.3	15.5	32.9	0.2	8.0	7.0	14.3
Mali	..	..	..	..	..	..	..	..	..	..	..	..
Mauritania	..	..	..	..	..	..	..	..	..	..	..	..
Mauritius	17,813	17,700	0.16	0.15	0.9	6.6	2.6	32.8	0.1	55.0	1.0	1.1
Mexico	174,266	296,093	0.18	0.20	7.8	12.5	10.4	55.6	0.2	7.0	1.0	5.5
Moldova	55,887	34,234	0.15	0.29	0.2	4.0	1.4	81.7	0.2	11.0	1.0	0.6
Mongolia	10,160	7,939	0.18	0.18	1.8	4.3	0.9	64.2	0.3	25.0	5.0	0.9
Morocco	41,710	88,779	0.14	0.18	0.7	7.0	6.4	54.4	0.4	27.0	1.0	3.2
Mozambique	20,414	10,230	0.27	0.31	1.1	7.1	2.7	81.2	0.1	6.0	1.0	0.8
Myanmar	7,663	5,681	0.17	0.14	47.6	5.0	14.9	16.1	1.1	3.0	11.0	1.3
Namibia	..	7,350	..	0.35	0.0	5.0	1.6	90.4	0.1	1.0	1.0	0.9
Nepal	20,894	26,550	0.13	0.14	1.5	8.1	3.9	43.3	1.2	39.0	2.0	1.0
Netherlands	136,686	124,182	0.18	0.18	7.3	26.7	11.3	43.0	0.2	2.0	1.0	8.7
New Zealand	50,243	46,099	0.22	0.22	3.2	21.7	5.2	57.3	0.1	5.0	4.0	3.5
Nicaragua	..	..	..	..	..	..	..	..	..	..	..	..
Niger	..	..	..	..	..	..	..	..	..	..	..	..
Nigeria	52,350	82,477	0.23	0.17	1.4	15.4	11.3	40.2	0.1	23.0	5.0	3.7
Norway	54,996	51,693	0.20	0.19	9.0	31.3	4.7	42.8	0.1	1.0	3.0	8.1
Oman	360	5,936	0.11	0.17	6.7	14.0	8.6	52.8	0.8	10.0	3.0	4.1
Pakistan	104,095	100,821	0.18	0.18	11.6	7.0	8.4	39.9	0.2	30.0	0.0	3.0
Panama	9,700	11,692	0.26	0.32	1.5	13.2	4.6	76.6	0.2	3.0	0.0	1.0
Papua New Guinea	..	..	..	..	..	..	..	..	..	..	..	..
Paraguay	3,250	..	0.28	..	..	..	..	..	..	..	..	..
Peru	56,144	52,644	0.20	0.21	8.1	13.5	8.9	52.8	0.2	12.0	2.0	2.5
Philippines	228,301	201,952	0.21	0.18	5.2	9.8	7.3	54.5	0.1	16.0	2.0	5.0
Poland	428,894	404,285	0.14	0.16	8.4	11.8	7.8	52.4	0.3	10.0	2.0	7.3
Portugal	147,873	131,200	0.15	0.14	3.6	15.3	4.8	36.9	0.4	27.0	6.0	5.9
Puerto Rico	19,026	15,367	0.15	0.14	1.9	14.9	21.9	34.4	0.2	15.0	1.0	10.7

3.6 Water pollution

	Emissions of organic water pollutants				Industry shares of emissions of organic water pollutants							
	kilograms per day		kilograms per day per worker		Primary metals	Paper and pulp	Chemicals	Food and beverages	Stone, ceramics, and glass	Textiles	Wood	Other
	1990	2001[a]	1990	2001[a]	2001[a]	2001[a]	2001[a]	2001[a]	2001[a]	2001[a]	2001[a]	2001[a]
Romania	413,864	38,395	0.12	0.07	17.1	17.6	9.0	5.1	0.3	29.0	13.0	9.6
Russian Federation	..	1,484,991	..	0.19	20.3	7.3	7.3	49.1	0.1	6.0	3.0	6.9
Rwanda	..	..	..	..	..	..	..	..	..	..	..	..
Saudi Arabia	24,436	24,436	0.14	0.14	4.4	15.9	21.1	45.1	1.0	4.0	2.0	6.5
Senegal	10,309	6,643	0.32	0.36	0.0	6.6	4.2	87.0	0.1	2.0	0.0	1.0
Serbia and Montenegro	137,795	98,696	0.15	0.16	9.9	11.8	8.2	47.4	0.0	13.0	2.0	7.7
Sierra Leone	..	4,170	..	0.32	..	9.6	3.0	82.3	0.1	2.0	2.0	..
Singapore	32,364	32,250	0.09	0.09	1.4	25.5	16.7	22.7	0.1	4.0	1.0	28.5
Slovak Republic	77,174	45,011	0.13	0.14	4.2	15.0	8.4	44.2	0.4	15.0	2.0	10.9
Slovenia	55,640	40,378	0.16	0.17	33.8	15.0	8.2	23.2	0.2	11.0	2.0	6.5
Somalia	..	..	..	..	..	..	..	..	..	..	..	..
South Africa	261,618	181,284	0.17	0.19	9.8	19.5	7.9	46.4	0.0	5.0	5.0	6.4
Spain	320,262	374,589	0.17	0.15	6.7	19.8	8.9	42.5	0.3	9.0	4.0	8.8
Sri Lanka	53,024	88,943	0.19	0.18	0.5	7.0	6.4	52.3	0.2	31.0	1.0	1.5
Sudan	..	..	..	..	..	..	..	..	..	..	..	..
Swaziland	6,586	2,009	0.33	0.23	..	79.8	0.3		0.2	17.0	2.0	..
Sweden	109,582	103,913	0.15	0.14	11.3	35.0	7.8	26.6	0.1	1.0	3.0	15.2
Switzerland	146,038	123,752	0.16	0.17	24.9	23.6	10.4	25.0	0.2	3.0	4.0	9.0
Syrian Arab Republic	21,702	15,115	0.22	0.20	4.1	1.5	3.9	69.8	0.9	19.0	0.0	0.7
Tajikistan	..	..	..	..	..	..	..	..	..	..	..	..
Tanzania	31,125	35,155	0.24	0.25	1.5	9.4	2.7	69.3	0.1	14.0	2.0	0.9
Thailand	291,552	355,819	0.17	0.16	6.1	5.3	5.3	42.2	0.2	35.0	1.0	4.8
Togo	..	..	..	..	..	..	..	..	..	..	..	..
Trinidad and Tobago	9,951	11,787	0.26	0.28	4.4	10.9	6.7	72.6	0.1	3.0	1.0	1.3
Tunisia	..	49,337	..	0.14	3.0	5.3	7.0	33.7	0.4	44.0	2.0	4.6
Turkey	177,264	159,225	0.18	0.18	13.5	8.6	8.7	49.5	0.3	12.0	2.0	5.4
Turkmenistan	..	..	..	..	..	..	..	..	..	..	..	..
Uganda	..	..	..	..	..	..	..	..	..	..	..	..
Ukraine	692,373	445,758	0.14	0.18	28.1	4.2	7.0	46.8	0.4	5.0	1.0	7.5
United Arab Emirates	..	..	..	..	..	..	..	..	..	..	..	..
United Kingdom	739,562	604,821	0.15	0.15	6.6	29.0	11.1	34.4	0.2	6.0	3.0	9.8
United States	2,565,226	1,968,196	0.15	0.12	10.5	11.0	13.8	38.4	0.2	7.0	4.0	15.1
Uruguay	38,661	16,362	0.23	0.28	1.2	7.2	6.7	75.9	0.1	8.0	1.0	1.8
Uzbekistan	..	..	..	..	..	..	..	..	..	..	..	..
Venezuela, RB	96,495	94,175	0.21	0.21	13.7	10.4	10.2	53.1	0.3	8.0	2.0	2.4
Vietnam	..	..	..	..	..	..	..	..	..	..	..	..
West Bank and Gaza	..	..	..	..	..	..	..	..	..	..	..	..
Yemen, Rep.	6,873	7,823	0.27	0.25	0.0	9.1	12.9	71.1	0.0	5.0	1.0	0.9
Zambia	15,880	11,433	0.23	0.22	3.4	10.8	7.3	63.6	0.0	9.0	3.0	2.8
Zimbabwe	37,149	26,810	0.20	0.19	5.2	10.2	7.9	54.2	0.0	16.0	3.0	3.5

Note: Industry shares may not sum to 100 percent because data may be from different years.
a. Data refer to any year from 1993 to 2001.

About the data

Emissions of organic pollutants from industrial activities are a major cause of degradation of water quality. Water quality and pollution levels are generally measured in terms of concentration or load—the rate of occurrence of a substance in an aqueous solution. Polluting substances include organic matter, metals, minerals, sediment, bacteria, and toxic chemicals. This table focuses on organic water pollution resulting from industrial activities. Because water pollution tends to be sensitive to local conditions, the national-level data in the table may not reflect the quality of water in specific locations.

The data in the table come from an international study of industrial emissions that may be the first to include data from developing countries (Hettige, Mani, and Wheeler 1998). These data were updated through 2001 by the World Bank's Development Research Group. Unlike estimates from earlier studies based on engineering or economic models, these estimates are based on actual measurements of plant-level water pollution. The focus is on organic water pollution caused by organic waste, measured in terms of biochemical oxygen demand (BOD), because the data for this indicator are the most plentiful and the most reliable for cross-country comparisons of emissions. BOD measures the strength of an organic waste by the amount of oxygen consumed in breaking it down. A sewage overload in natural waters exhausts the water's dissolved oxygen content. Wastewater treatment, by contrast, reduces BOD.

Data on water pollution are more readily available than other emissions data because most industrial pollution control programs start by regulating emissions of organic water pollutants. Such data are fairly reliable because sampling techniques for measuring water pollution are more widely understood and much less expensive than those for air pollution.

Hettige, Mani, and Wheeler (1998) used plant- and sector-level information on emissions and employment from 13 national environmental protection agencies and sector-level information on output and employment from the United Nations Industrial Development Organization (UNIDO). Their econometric analysis found that the ratio of BOD to employment in each industrial sector is about the same across countries. This finding allowed the authors to estimate BOD loads across countries and over time. The estimated BOD intensities per unit of employment were multiplied by sectoral employment numbers from UNIDO's industry database for 1980–98. The estimates of sectoral emissions were then totaled to get daily emissions of organic water pollutants in kilograms per day for each country and year. The data in the table were derived by updating these estimates through 2001.

Definitions

• **Emissions of organic water pollutants are** measured in terms of biochemical oxygen demand, which refers to the amount of oxygen that bacteria in water will consume in breaking down waste. This is a standard water treatment test for the presence of organic pollutants. Emissions per worker are total emissions divided by the number of industrial workers. • **Industry shares of emissions of organic water pollutants** refer to emissions from manufacturing activities as defined by two-digit divisions of the International Standard Industrial Classification (ISIC) revision 2: primary metals (ISIC division 37), paper and pulp (34), chemicals (35), food and beverages (31), stone, ceramics, and glass (36), textiles (32), wood (33), and other (38 and 39).

3.6a

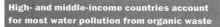

High- and middle-income countries account for most water pollution from organic waste

Emissions of organic water pollutants, 1998

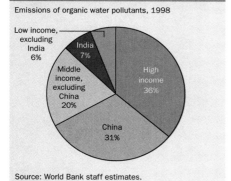

Low income, excluding India 6%
India 7%
Middle income, excluding China 20%
High income 36%
China 31%

Source: World Bank staff estimates.

Data sources

The data come from a 1998 study by Hemamala Hettige, Muthukumara Mani, and David Wheeler, "Industrial Pollution in Economic Development: Kuznets Revisited" (available at www.worldbank.org/nipr). These data were updated through 2001 by the World Bank's Development Research Group using the same methodology as the initial study. Sectoral employment numbers are from UNIDO's industry database.

3.7 | Energy production and use

	Total energy production		Energy use					Energy use per capita		
	thousands of metric tons of oil equivalent		Total thousands of metric tons of oil equivalent		Combustible renewables and waste % of total		average annual % growth	kg of oil equivalent		average annual % growth
	1990	**2002**	**1990**	**2002**	**1990**	**2002**	**1990–2002**	**1990**	**2002**	**1990–2002**
Afghanistan	..	..	..	..	..	..	..	..	..	..
Albania	2,449	771	2,662	1,944	13.6	6.9	−0.2	812	617	0.3
Algeria	104,507	150,292	23,874	30,845	0.1	0.2	1.8	954	985	−0.1
Angola	28,652	51,548	6,280	8,815	68.8	67.8	2.8	672	672	0.0
Argentina	48,456	81,692	46,110	56,297	3.7	5.3	2.3	1,428	1,543	1.3
Armenia	*263*	738	*4,298*	1,938	0.0	0.1	−2.6	*1,231*	632	−1.3
Australia	157,712	255,192	87,536	112,712	4.5	6.2	2.4	5,130	5,732	1.2
Austria	8,080	9,926	25,260	30,443	9.7	11.1	1.6	3,270	3,774	1.3
Azerbaijan	*18,150*	19,753	*16,675*	11,728	0.0	0.0	−3.5	*2,259*	1,435	−4.5
Bangladesh	10,747	16,747	12,815	21,004	53.6	37.5	4.4	116	155	2.6
Belarus	*4,103*	3,589	*39,703*	24,771	*1.5*	4.4	−3.3	*3,886*	2,496	−3.0
Belgium	12,490	13,164	48,685	56,887	1.4	1.6	1.6	4,884	5,505	1.3
Benin	1,774	1,546	1,678	2,231	93.2	69.3	2.6	356	340	−0.1
Bolivia	4,923	8,152	2,774	4,310	27.2	16.8	4.9	416	499	2.7
Bosnia and Herzegovina	*3,642*	3,318	*4,474*	4,324	*3.6*	4.2	5.8	..	1,052	..
Botswana	..	..	..	..	..	..	..	..	..	..
Brazil	97,616	161,737	133,531	190,664	30.9	24.3	3.4	902	1,093	2.0
Bulgaria	9,613	10,512	28,820	19,019	0.6	3.4	−2.5	3,306	2,417	−1.7
Burkina Faso	..	..	..	..	..	..	..	..	..	..
Burundi	..	..	..	..	..	..	..	..	..	..
Cambodia	..	..	..	..	..	..	..	..	..	..
Cameroon	12,090	12,004	5,031	6,569	75.9	79.2	2.4	431	417	−0.1
Canada	273,680	385,412	209,089	250,035	3.9	4.5	1.7	7,524	7,973	0.7
Central African Republic	..	..	..	..	..	..	..	..	..	..
Chad	..	..	..	..	..	..	..	..	..	..
Chile	7,640	8,783	13,629	24,708	19.6	17.4	5.7	1,040	1,585	4.2
China	902,689	1,220,812	879,923	1,228,574	22.8	17.7	2.8	775	960	1.7
Hong Kong, China	43	48	10,662	16,377	0.5	0.3	3.6	1,869	2,413	1.9
Colombia	48,479	72,275	25,048	27,397	23.2	18.0	0.9	716	625	−1.0
Congo, Dem. Rep.	12,019	16,134	11,903	15,402	84.0	93.6	2.2	319	299	−0.4
Congo, Rep.	9,005	13,199	1,056	923	69.4	67.3	−1.9	423	252	−5.0
Costa Rica	1,032	1,762	2,025	3,564	36.6	7.5	4.8	664	904	2.6
Côte d'Ivoire	3,382	6,528	4,408	6,555	72.1	66.0	3.7	374	397	0.9
Croatia	*4,346*	3,706	*6,714*	8,222	*3.8*	3.6	2.1	*1,502*	1,852	2.5
Cuba	6,271	6,480	16,524	14,197	33.7	17.1	0.0	1,555	1,262	−0.5
Czech Republic	38,474	30,668	47,379	41,725	*1.2*	2.0	−0.8	4,572	4,090	−0.7
Denmark	9,735	28,754	17,581	19,749	6.5	10.5	0.6	3,420	3,675	0.2
Dominican Republic	1,031	1,513	4,139	8,167	24.2	17.6	6.2	586	948	4.4
Ecuador	16,474	22,209	6,128	9,048	13.5	8.0	3.4	597	706	1.6
Egypt, Arab Rep.	54,869	59,766	31,895	52,393	3.3	2.6	4.3	608	789	2.3
El Salvador	1,722	2,367	2,535	4,299	48.2	33.1	4.3	496	670	2.3
Eritrea	..	..	..	..	..	..	..	..	..	..
Estonia	*4,118*	3,160	*6,271*	4,514	*2.9*	11.6	−2.2	*4,091*	3,324	−1.0
Ethiopia	14,158	18,445	15,151	19,934	92.8	91.7	2.5	296	297	0.2
Finland	12,081	16,089	29,171	35,622	15.6	19.9	1.8	5,851	6,852	1.4
France	111,439	134,379	227,276	265,881	4.9	4.2	1.2	4,006	4,470	0.8
Gabon	14,630	12,690	1,242	1,590	59.8	61.9	2.1	1,303	1,209	−0.6
Gambia, The	..	..	..	..	..	..	..	..	..	..
Georgia	*1,470*	1,325	*8,757*	2,559	*7.7*	25.2	−10.4	*1,611*	494	−10.0
Germany	186,159	134,771	356,221	346,352	1.3	2.6	0.0	4,485	4,198	−0.3
Ghana	4,392	5,974	5,337	8,344	73.1	66.4	4.0	349	411	1.5
Greece	9,200	10,232	22,181	29,025	4.0	3.6	2.5	2,183	2,637	1.8
Guatemala	3,390	5,408	4,478	7,384	67.9	52.8	4.7	512	616	2.0
Guinea	..	..	..	..	..	..	..	..	..	..
Guinea-Bissau	..	..	..	..	..	..	..	..	..	..
Haiti	1,253	1,515	1,585	2,081	76.5	71.6	3.2	245	251	1.0

	Total energy production		Energy use					Energy use per capita		
	thousands of metric tons of oil equivalent		Total thousands of metric tons of oil equivalent		Combustible renewables and waste % of total		average annual % growth	kg of oil equivalent		average annual % growth
	1990	2002	1990	2002	1990	2002	1990–2002	1990	2002	1990–2002
Honduras	1,694	1,618	2,416	3,426	62.0	41.1	2.7	496	504	−0.1
Hungary	14,325	10,834	28,553	25,449	1.3	1.6	−0.6	2,755	2,505	−0.4
India	334,056	438,797	365,377	538,305	48.1	38.7	3.4	430	513	1.6
Indonesia	161,308	240,908	94,836	156,086	39.3	27.4	4.1	532	737	2.7
Iran, Islamic Rep.	179,738	240,522	68,775	133,960	1.0	0.6	5.4	1,264	2,044	3.8
Iraq	106,715	105,414	20,841	28,996	0.1	0.1	4.1	1,153	1,199	1.6
Ireland	3,467	1,499	10,575	15,303	1.0	1.2	3.6	3,016	3,894	2.7
Israel	433	722	12,112	20,954	0.0	0.0	5.0	2,599	3,191	2.2
Italy	25,548	26,590	152,553	172,720	0.6	1.5	1.2	2,690	2,994	1.0
Jamaica	485	463	2,943	3,914	16.2	11.6	2.8	1,231	1,493	2.0
Japan	76,129	98,133	445,916	516,927	1.3	1.4	1.4	3,610	4,058	1.1
Jordan	162	261	3,499	5,359	0.1	0.1	3.6	1,104	1,036	−0.2
Kazakhstan	89,007	95,780	79,661	46,455	0.1	0.2	−5.5	4,823	3,123	−4.4
Kenya	10,272	12,877	12,479	15,324	78.4	80.1	2.1	534	489	−0.4
Korea, Dem. Rep.	28,725	18,358	32,874	19,537	2.9	5.2	−4.5	1,647	869	−5.4
Korea, Rep.	21,908	36,206	92,650	203,498	0.3	1.4	6.7	2,161	4,272	5.7
Kuwait	50,401	105,991	7,579	22,189	0.1	..	9.1	3,567	9,503	7.8
Kyrgyz Republic	1,818	1,204	5,066	2,536	0.1	0.2	−5.4	1,114	507	−6.4
Lao PDR	..	..	..	..	..	..	..	..	..	..
Latvia	794	1,870	5,979	4,266	8.1	30.1	−2.8	2,272	1,825	−1.6
Lebanon	143	192	2,309	5,369	4.5	2.4	7.1	635	1,209	5.3
Lesotho	..	..	..	..	..	..	..	..	..	..
Liberia	..	..	..	..	..	..	..	..	..	..
Libya	73,173	69,519	11,541	18,704	1.1	0.8	4.0	2,680	3,433	2.0
Lithuania	4,298	4,915	11,085	8,589	2.6	7.7	−2.1	2,996	2,476	−1.4
Macedonia, FYR	..	..	..	..	..	..	..	..	..	..
Madagascar	..	..	..	..	..	..	..	..	..	..
Malawi	..	..	..	..	..	..	..	..	..	..
Malaysia	48,727	80,243	22,455	51,753	9.5	4.8	6.7	1,234	2,129	4.1
Mali	..	..	..	..	..	..	..	..	..	..
Mauritania	..	..	..	..	..	..	..	..	..	..
Mauritius	..	..	..	..	..	..	..	..	..	..
Mexico	194,482	229,888	124,057	157,308	5.9	5.2	1.9	1,491	1,560	0.3
Moldova	58	66	6,884	2,993	0.5	2.0	−7.8	1,582	703	−7.6
Mongolia	..	..	..	..	..	..	..	..	..	..
Morocco	773	589	6,725	10,753	4.7	4.2	3.9	280	363	2.1
Mozambique	6,846	8,041	7,203	8,045	94.4	86.1	0.5	509	436	−1.8
Myanmar	10,651	15,825	10,683	12,578	84.4	76.7	1.6	264	258	0.0
Namibia	218	301	652	1,188	16.0	15.2	5.2	445	599	2.3
Nepal	5,501	7,618	5,806	8,515	93.4	87.2	3.4	320	353	0.9
Netherlands	60,316	59,924	66,491	77,923	1.1	1.7	1.1	4,447	4,827	0.5
New Zealand	12,153	14,876	13,914	18,013	4.9	6.9	2.4	4,035	4,573	1.3
Nicaragua	1,495	1,659	2,118	2,908	53.3	49.9	2.7	554	544	−0.2
Niger	..	..	..	..	..	..	..	..	..	..
Nigeria	150,453	192,660	70,905	95,675	79.8	79.1	2.3	737	718	−0.5
Norway	120,304	232,221	21,492	26,515	4.8	5.5	1.8	5,067	5,843	1.2
Oman	38,312	62,516	4,562	10,825	..	..	5.8	2,804	4,265	2.4
Pakistan	34,360	49,677	43,424	65,806	43.2	37.4	3.6	402	454	1.1
Panama	612	738	1,490	3,022	28.3	14.7	6.1	621	1,028	4.3
Papua New Guinea	..	..	..	..	..	..	..	..	..	..
Paraguay	4,578	6,293	3,083	3,905	72.3	55.0	2.5	743	709	0.1
Peru	10,596	9,234	9,952	12,024	26.9	18.8	2.3	461	450	0.5
Philippines	13,701	21,941	26,159	42,008	29.2	23.9	4.8	429	525	2.5
Poland	99,228	79,633	99,847	89,185	2.2	5.0	−0.9	2,619	2,333	−0.9
Portugal	3,393	3,643	17,746	26,392	14.0	10.7	3.6	1,793	2,546	3.3
Puerto Rico	..	..	..	..	..	..	..	..	..	..

	Total energy production		Energy use					Energy use per capita		
	thousands of metric tons of oil equivalent		Total thousands of metric tons of oil equivalent		Combustible renewables and waste % of total		average annual % growth	kg of oil equivalent		average annual % growth
	1990	2002	1990	2002	1990	2002	1990–2002	1990	2002	1990–2002
Romania	40,834	28,406	62,403	36,976	1.0	6.7	–3.6	2,689	1,696	–3.2
Russian Federation	1,118,707	1,034,519	774,823	617,843	1.6	1.1	–2.0	5,211	4,288	–1.7
Rwanda	..	..	..	..	..	..	..	..	..	..
Saudi Arabia	372,985	462,807	65,538	126,387	0.0	0.0	5.0	4,147	5,775	2.2
Senegal	1,362	1,807	2,238	3,192	60.6	56.6	3.4	305	319	0.6
Serbia and Montenegro	11,835	10,876	15,002	16,169	5.0	5.0	1.7	1,435	1,981	2.8
Sierra Leone	..	..	..	..	..	..	..	..	..	..
Singapore	..	64	13,357	25,307	..	..	4.5	4,384	6,078	1.7
Slovak Republic	5,273	6,650	21,426	18,546	0.8	1.7	–0.7	4,056	3,448	–0.9
Slovenia	2,765	3,379	5,008	6,951	5.3	6.7	3.0	2,508	3,486	3.0
Somalia	..	..	..	..	..	..	..	..	..	..
South Africa	114,534	146,506	91,229	113,458	11.4	11.2	1.9	2,592	2,502	–0.3
Spain	34,648	31,737	91,209	131,558	4.5	3.3	3.2	2,349	3,215	2.7
Sri Lanka	4,191	4,557	5,516	8,179	71.0	52.9	3.7	339	430	2.4
Sudan	8,775	25,013	10,627	15,850	81.8	79.8	3.7	426	483	1.3
Swaziland	..	..	..	..	..	..	..	..	..	..
Sweden	29,754	32,403	46,658	51,031	11.8	16.3	0.7	5,451	5,718	0.4
Switzerland	9,831	11,942	25,106	27,139	4.1	6.1	0.8	3,740	3,723	0.2
Syrian Arab Republic	22,570	36,706	11,928	18,054	0.0	0.0	3.3	984	1,063	0.4
Tajikistan	1,553	1,330	9,087	3,247	..	..	–7.3	1,631	518	–8.5
Tanzania	9,063	13,286	9,808	14,339	91.0	90.7	3.3	385	408	0.6
Thailand	26,496	45,303	43,860	83,339	33.4	16.4	5.2	789	1,353	4.4
Togo	778	1,081	1,001	1,540	77.7	70.2	4.4	290	324	1.5
Trinidad and Tobago	12,612	21,321	5,795	9,286	0.8	0.3	4.1	4,770	7,121	3.6
Tunisia	6,127	6,943	5,536	8,276	18.7	15.3	3.8	679	846	2.2
Turkey	25,857	24,432	53,005	75,418	13.6	8.0	3.6	944	1,083	1.7
Turkmenistan	48,822	53,645	11,314	16,606	..	..	3.3	2,914	3,465	1.2
Uganda	..	..	..	..	..	..	..	..	..	..
Ukraine	110,170	71,520	218,376	130,743	0.1	0.2	–4.8	4,187	2,684	–4.1
United Arab Emirates	109,446	142,148	17,839	36,072	0.2	0.0	5.9	10,061	9,609	–0.5
United Kingdom	207,007	257,541	212,176	226,508	0.3	1.0	0.6	3,686	3,824	0.4
United States	1,650,474	1,666,050	1,927,638	2,290,410	3.2	3.0	1.6	7,722	7,943	0.4
Uruguay	1,149	1,239	2,251	2,510	24.3	16.7	1.6	725	747	1.0
Uzbekistan	40,461	55,788	44,994	51,740	..	..	1.8	2,098	2,047	0.1
Venezuela, RB	148,854	210,150	43,918	54,006	1.2	1.0	2.1	2,224	2,141	0.0
Vietnam	24,711	53,439	24,324	42,645	77.7	54.5	4.9	367	530	3.2
West Bank and Gaza	..	..	..	..	..	..	..	..	..	..
Yemen, Rep.	9,384	22,235	2,708	4,107	2.8	1.9	2.8	228	221	–0.5
Zambia	4,923	6,226	5,470	6,549	73.4	81.3	1.4	703	639	–0.9
Zimbabwe	8,500	8,468	9,334	9,761	50.7	59.0	0.3	911	751	–1.7
World	**8,801,246 t**	**10,274,551 t**	**8,616,766 t**	**10,196,821 t**	**10.8 w**	**10.6 w**	**1.5 w**	**1,686 w**	**1,699 w**	**0.1 w**
Low income	846,065	1,145,938	799,880	1,080,050	54.9	49.4	2.6	463	493	0.6
Middle income	4,724,337	5,359,274	3,557,855	3,969,589	11.3	10.8	0.9	1,372	1,338	–0.2
Lower middle income	3,574,000	3,956,799	2,968,825	3,232,254	12.6	12.3	0.7	1,286	1,227	–0.4
Upper middle income	1,147,843	1,400,237	585,444	733,823	4.0	4.1	1.9	2,072	2,232	0.7
Low & middle income	5,567,198	6,493,223	4,348,016	5,030,378	18.6	18.4	1.2	1,020	990	–0.3
East Asia & Pacific	1,228,554	1,712,927	1,145,883	1,652,046	25.6	19.6	3.1	721	904	1.9
Europe & Central Asia	1,890,149	1,565,055	1,736,182	1,272,422	1.9	2.3	–2.7	3,725	2,697	–2.9
Latin America & Carib.	617,206	859,786	458,283	606,747	18.1	14.6	2.7	1,055	1,156	1.1
Middle East & N. Africa	978,411	1,229,008	262,130	458,221	1.4	1.0	4.5	1,107	1,504	2.4
South Asia	392,135	521,760	436,590	647,223	48.7	39.3	3.4	393	468	1.5
Sub-Saharan Africa	489,230	652,199	321,208	418,008	56.7	57.5	2.2	693	667	–0.3
High income	3,276,666	3,831,019	4,299,133	5,201,115	3.0	3.1	1.7	4,859	5,395	1.0
Europe EMU	466,852	442,010	1,050,939	1,192,147	3.1	3.7	1.2	3,583	3,895	0.8

Energy production and use | **3.7**

In developing countries growth in energy use is closely related to growth in the modern sectors—industry, motorized transport, and urban areas—but energy use also reflects climatic, geographic, and economic factors (such as the relative price of energy). Energy use has been growing rapidly in low- and middle-income countries, but high-income countries still use more than five times as much on a per capita basis.

Energy data are compiled by the International Energy Agency (IEA). IEA data for countries that are not members of the Organisation for Economic Co-operation and Development (OECD) are based on national energy data adjusted to conform to annual questionnaires completed by OECD member governments.

Total energy use refers to the use of domestic primary energy before transformation to other end-use fuels (such as electricity and refined petroleum products). It includes energy from combustible renewables and waste—solid biomass and animal products, gas and liquid from biomass, and industrial and municipal waste. Biomass is defined as any plant matter used directly as fuel or converted into fuel, heat, or electricity. (The data series published in *World Development Indicators 1998* and earlier editions did not include energy from combustible renewables and waste.) Data for combustible renewables and waste are often based on small surveys or other incomplete information. Thus the data give only a broad impression of developments and are not strictly comparable between countries. The IEA reports (see *Data sources*) include country notes that explain some of these differences. All forms of energy—primary energy and primary electricity—are converted into oil equivalents. To convert nuclear electricity into oil equivalents, a notional thermal efficiency of 33 percent is assumed; for hydroelectric power 100 percent efficiency is assumed.

3.7a

Ten of the top 15 energy producers are low-income countries . . .

Total energy production, 2002 (millions of metric tons of oil equivalent)

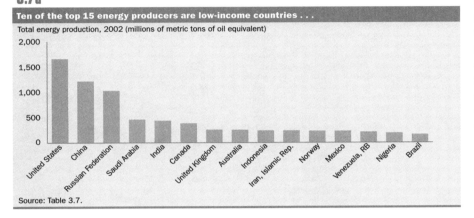

Source: Table 3.7.

3.7b

. . . but only 7 of the top 15 energy users are

Total energy use, 2002 (millions of metric tons of oil equivalent)

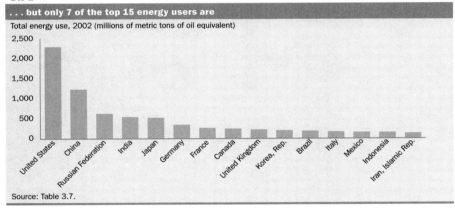

Source: Table 3.7.

3.7c

High-income countries have the highest energy use per capita

Energy use per capita, 2002 (thousands of kg of oil equivalent)

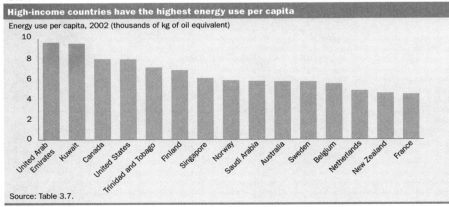

Source: Table 3.7.

• **Total energy production** refers to forms of primary energy—petroleum (crude oil, natural gas liquids, and oil from nonconventional sources), natural gas, solid fuels (coal, lignite, and other derived fuels), and combustible renewables and waste—and primary electricity, all converted into oil equivalents (see *About the data*). • **Energy use** refers to apparent consumption, which is equal to indigenous production plus imports and stock changes, minus exports and fuels supplied to ships and aircraft engaged in international transport (see *About the data*). • **Combustible renewables and waste** comprise solid biomass, liquid biomass, biogas, industrial waste, and municipal waste, measured as a percentage of total energy use.

3.8 Energy efficiency, dependency, and emissions

	GDP per unit of energy use		Net energy imports[a]		Carbon dioxide emissions					
	2000 PPP $ per kg oil equivalent		% of energy use		Total million metric tons		Per capita metric tons		kg per 2000 PPP $ of GDP	
	1990	2002	1990	2002	1990	2000	1990	2000	1990	2000
Afghanistan	..	..	..	..	2.6	0.9	0.1	0.0	..	..
Albania	3.9	6.7	8	60	7.3	2.9	2.2	0.9	0.7	0.2
Algeria	5.7	5.6	−338	−387	80.4	89.4	3.2	2.9	0.6	0.5
Angola	3.6	3.2	−356	−485	4.6	6.4	0.5	0.5	0.2	0.3
Argentina	6.2	6.9	−5	−45	109.7	138.2	3.4	3.9	0.4	0.3
Armenia	1.6	4.8	94	62	3.7	3.5	1.1	1.1	0.5	0.5
Australia	4.1	4.8	−80	−126	266.0	344.8	15.6	18.0	0.7	0.7
Austria	6.9	7.5	68	67	57.5	60.8	7.4	7.6	0.3	0.3
Azerbaijan	..	2.2	−9	−68	47.1	29.0	6.4	3.6	..	1.4
Bangladesh	10.1	10.5	16	20	15.4	29.3	0.1	0.2	0.1	0.1
Belarus	1.2	2.1	90	86	94.6	59.2	9.3	5.9	2.0	1.2
Belgium	4.6	4.8	74	77	100.5	102.2	10.1	10.0	0.5	0.4
Benin	2.3	3.0	−6	31	0.6	1.6	0.1	0.3	0.1	0.3
Bolivia	5.1	4.8	−77	−89	5.5	11.1	0.8	1.3	0.4	0.6
Bosnia and Herzegovina	..	5.3	19	23	4.7	19.3	..	4.8	..	0.9
Botswana	..	..	..	..	2.2	3.9	1.7	2.3	0.3	0.3
Brazil	7.2	6.8	27	15	202.6	307.5	1.4	1.8	0.2	0.2
Bulgaria	2.2	2.9	67	45	75.3	42.3	8.6	5.3	1.2	0.8
Burkina Faso	..	..	..	..	1.0	1.0	0.1	0.1	0.1	0.1
Burundi	..	..	..	..	0.2	0.2	0.0	0.0	0.0	0.1
Cambodia	..	..	..	..	0.5	0.5	0.0	0.0	..	0.0
Cameroon	4.8	4.7	−140	−83	1.5	6.5	0.1	0.4	0.1	0.2
Canada	3.1	3.6	−31	−54	428.8	435.9	15.4	14.2	0.7	0.5
Central African Republic	..	..	..	..	0.2	0.3	0.1	0.1	0.1	0.1
Chad	..	..	..	..	0.1	0.1	0.0	0.0	0.0	0.0
Chile	5.6	6.0	44	64	35.3	59.5	2.7	3.9	0.5	0.4
China	2.1	4.6	−3	1	2,401.7	2,790.5	2.1	2.2	1.3	0.6
Hong Kong, China	10.6	10.6	100	100	26.2	33.1	4.6	5.0	0.2	0.2
Colombia	8.3	9.8	−94	−164	55.9	58.5	1.6	1.4	0.3	0.2
Congo, Dem. Rep.	5.1	2.2	−1	−5	4.1	2.7	0.1	0.1	0.1	0.1
Congo, Rep.	2.3	3.7	−753	−1,330	2.0	1.8	0.8	0.5	0.8	0.5
Costa Rica	9.7	9.4	49	51	2.9	5.4	1.0	1.4	0.1	0.2
Côte d'Ivoire	4.9	3.7	23	0	11.9	10.5	1.0	0.7	0.6	0.4
Croatia	4.8	5.3	35	55	16.8	19.6	3.8	4.5	0.5	0.5
Cuba	..	..	62	54	32.0	30.9	3.0	2.8	..	..
Czech Republic	2.8	3.7	19	26	137.9	118.8	13.4	11.6	1.1	0.8
Denmark	7.1	8.1	45	−46	50.7	44.6	9.9	8.4	0.4	0.3
Dominican Republic	6.9	6.8	75	81	9.4	25.1	1.3	3.0	0.3	0.5
Ecuador	5.9	4.8	−169	−145	16.6	25.5	1.6	2.0	0.5	0.6
Egypt, Arab Rep.	4.8	4.6	−72	−14	75.4	142.2	1.4	2.2	0.5	0.6
El Salvador	7.3	7.1	32	45	2.6	6.7	0.5	1.1	0.1	0.2
Eritrea	..	..	..	..	..	0.6	..	0.1	..	0.2
Estonia	1.7	3.6	34	30	24.9	16.0	16.2	11.7	2.3	1.1
Ethiopia	2.1	2.4	7	7	3.0	5.6	0.1	0.1	0.1	0.1
Finland	3.8	3.7	59	55	52.9	53.4	10.6	10.3	0.5	0.4
France	5.5	5.8	51	49	357.5	362.4	6.3	6.2	0.3	0.2
Gabon	4.7	5.1	−1,078	−698	6.7	3.5	7.0	2.8	1.1	0.5
Gambia, The	..	..	..	..	0.2	0.3	0.2	0.2	0.1	0.1
Georgia	1.4	4.4	83	48	15.1	6.2	2.8	1.2	1.3	0.6
Germany	4.9	6.2	48	61	890.2	785.5	11.1	9.6	0.5	0.4
Ghana	4.7	5.0	18	28	3.5	5.9	0.2	0.3	0.1	0.2
Greece	6.4	6.8	59	65	72.2	89.6	7.1	8.2	0.5	0.5
Guatemala	6.8	6.4	24	27	5.1	9.9	0.6	0.9	0.2	0.2
Guinea	..	..	..	..	1.0	1.3	0.2	0.2	0.1	0.1
Guinea-Bissau	..	..	..	..	0.8	0.3	0.8	0.2	0.8	0.2
Haiti	10.1	6.6	21	27	1.0	1.4	0.2	0.2	0.1	0.1

Energy efficiency, dependency, and emissions | **3.8**

	GDP per unit of energy use		Net energy imports[a]		Carbon dioxide emissions					
	2000 PPP $ per kg oil equivalent		% of energy use		Total million metric tons		Per capita metric tons		kg per 2000 PPP $ of GDP	
	1990	2002	1990	2002	1990	2000	1990	2000	1990	2000
Honduras	5.1	5.0	30	53	2.6	4.8	0.5	0.7	0.2	0.3
Hungary	4.1	5.3	50	57	58.5	54.2	5.6	5.4	0.5	0.4
India	4.0	5.0	9	18	675.3	1,070.9	0.8	1.1	0.5	0.4
Indonesia	4.3	4.1	–70	–54	165.2	269.6	0.9	1.3	0.4	0.4
Iran, Islamic Rep.	3.6	3.1	–161	–80	212.4	310.3	3.9	4.9	0.8	0.9
Iraq	..	..	–412	–264	49.3	76.3	2.7	3.3	..	..
Ireland	5.1	9.1	67	90	29.8	42.2	8.5	11.1	0.6	0.4
Israel	6.1	6.0	96	97	34.6	63.1	7.4	10.0	0.5	0.5
Italy	8.1	8.5	83	85	398.9	428.2	7.0	7.4	0.3	0.3
Jamaica	3.1	2.5	84	88	8.0	10.8	3.3	4.2	0.9	1.1
Japan	6.4	6.4	83	81	1,070.7	1,184.5	8.7	9.3	0.4	0.4
Jordan	3.5	3.9	95	95	10.2	15.6	3.2	3.2	0.8	0.8
Kazakhstan	1.0	1.8	–12	–106	252.7	121.3	15.3	8.1	3.1	1.8
Kenya	2.1	2.0	18	16	5.8	9.4	0.2	0.3	0.2	0.3
Korea, Dem. Rep.	..	..	13	6	244.6	188.9	12.3	8.5	..	..
Korea, Rep.	4.3	3.9	76	82	241.2	427.0	5.6	9.1	0.6	0.6
Kuwait	..	1.7	–565	–378	42.2	47.9	19.9	21.9	..	1.4
Kyrgyz Republic	1.7	3.1	64	53	11.0	4.6	2.4	0.9	1.3	0.6
Lao PDR	..	..	..	..	0.2	0.4	0.1	0.1	0.1	0.1
Latvia	2.4	4.9	87	56	12.7	6.0	4.8	2.5	0.9	0.3
Lebanon	3.4	3.8	94	96	9.1	15.2	2.5	3.5	1.1	0.8
Lesotho	..	..	..	..	..	..	..	..	..	..
Liberia	..	..	..	..	0.5	0.4	0.2	0.1	..	..
Libya	..	..	–534	–272	37.8	57.1	8.8	10.9	..	..
Lithuania	2.8	4.0	61	43	21.4	11.9	5.8	3.4	0.7	0.4
Macedonia, FYR	..	..	..	..	10.6	11.2	5.5	5.5	0.8	0.8
Madagascar	..	..	..	..	0.9	2.3	0.1	0.1	0.1	0.2
Malawi	..	..	..	..	0.6	0.8	0.1	0.1	0.1	0.1
Malaysia	4.5	4.1	–117	–55	55.3	144.4	3.0	6.2	0.6	0.7
Mali	..	..	..	..	0.4	0.6	0.0	0.1	0.1	0.1
Mauritania	..	..	..	..	2.6	3.1	1.3	1.2	0.9	0.7
Mauritius	..	..	..	..	1.2	2.9	1.1	2.4	0.2	0.3
Mexico	5.1	5.6	–57	–46	305.4	424.0	3.7	4.3	0.5	0.5
Moldova	1.4	2.0	99	98	20.9	6.6	4.8	1.5	2.1	1.2
Mongolia	..	..	..	..	10.0	7.5	4.7	3.1	1.8	1.9
Morocco	12.0	10.1	89	95	23.5	36.5	1.0	1.3	0.3	0.4
Mozambique	1.2	2.3	5	0	1.0	1.2	0.1	0.1	0.1	0.1
Myanmar	..	..	0	–26	4.1	9.1	0.1	0.2	..	..
Namibia	12.3	10.2	67	75	0.0	1.8	0.0	1.0	0.0	0.2
Nepal	3.2	3.8	5	11	0.6	3.4	0.0	0.1	0.0	0.1
Netherlands	4.9	5.8	9	23	150.0	138.9	10.0	8.7	0.5	0.3
New Zealand	4.1	4.6	13	17	23.6	32.1	6.8	8.3	0.4	0.4
Nicaragua	5.3	5.7	29	43	2.6	3.7	0.7	0.7	0.2	0.2
Niger	..	..	..	..	1.1	1.2	0.1	0.1	0.2	0.1
Nigeria	1.2	1.3	–112	–101	88.7	36.1	0.9	0.3	1.0	0.3
Norway	5.2	6.1	–460	–776	31.7	49.9	7.5	11.1	0.3	0.3
Oman	4.1	3.0	–740	–478	11.5	19.8	7.1	8.2	0.6	0.7
Pakistan	3.9	4.3	21	25	67.9	104.8	0.6	0.8	0.4	0.4
Panama	7.3	5.9	59	76	3.1	6.3	1.3	2.2	0.3	0.4
Papua New Guinea	..	..	..	..	2.4	2.4	0.6	0.5	0.3	0.2
Paraguay	6.3	6.3	–48	–61	2.3	3.7	0.5	0.7	0.1	0.2
Peru	8.4	10.7	–6	23	21.7	29.5	1.0	1.1	0.3	0.2
Philippines	9.1	7.6	48	48	44.3	77.5	0.7	1.0	0.2	0.3
Poland	2.8	4.4	1	11	347.6	301.3	9.1	7.8	1.2	0.8
Portugal	7.5	6.9	81	86	42.3	59.8	4.3	5.8	0.3	0.3
Puerto Rico	..	..	..	..	11.8	8.7	3.3	2.3	0.2	0.1

3.8 Energy efficiency, dependency, and emissions

| | GDP per unit of energy use | | Net energy imports[a] | | Carbon dioxide emissions | | | | | |
| | 2000 PPP $ per kg oil equivalent | | % of energy use | | Total million metric tons | | Per capita metric tons | | kg per 2000 PPP $ of GDP | |
	1990	2002	1990	2002	1990	2000	1990	2000	1990	2000
Romania	2.4	3.8	35	23	155.1	86.3	6.7	3.8	1.0	0.7
Russian Federation	1.6	1.9	−44	−67	1,984.0	1,435.1	13.3	9.9	1.6	1.4
Rwanda	..	..			0.5	0.6	0.1	0.1	0.1	0.1
Saudi Arabia	2.8	2.1	−469	−266	177.9	374.3	11.3	18.1	1.0	1.4
Senegal	4.6	4.8	39	43	2.9	4.2	0.4	0.4	0.3	0.3
Serbia and Montenegro	..	..	21	33	..	39.5	..	3.7	..	..
Sierra Leone	..	..	..	..	0.3	0.6	0.1	0.1	0.1	0.2
Singapore	3.3	3.8	..	100	41.9	59.0	13.8	14.7	0.9	0.6
Slovak Republic	2.7	3.6	75	64	44.7	35.4	8.4	6.6	1.0	0.6
Slovenia	4.8	5.1	45	51	12.3	14.6	6.2	7.3	0.5	0.4
Somalia	..	..	..	..	0.0	..	0.0	..	..	..
South Africa	3.9	3.9	−26	−29	291.1	327.3	8.3	7.4	0.8	0.8
Spain	6.8	6.5	62	76	211.8	282.9	5.5	7.0	0.3	0.3
Sri Lanka	7.0	8.0	24	44	3.9	10.2	0.2	0.6	0.1	0.2
Sudan	2.7	3.6	17	−58	3.5	5.2	0.1	0.2	0.1	0.1
Swaziland	..	..	..	..	0.4	0.4	0.6	0.4	0.1	0.1
Sweden	3.9	4.4	36	37	48.5	46.9	5.7	5.3	0.3	0.2
Switzerland	7.7	7.8	61	56	42.7	39.1	6.4	5.4	0.2	0.2
Syrian Arab Republic	2.7	3.2	−89	−103	35.8	54.2	3.0	3.3	1.1	1.0
Tajikistan	0.9	1.8	83	59	20.6	4.0	3.7	0.6	2.5	0.8
Tanzania	1.4	1.4	8	7	2.3	4.3	0.1	0.1	0.2	0.2
Thailand	5.7	5.0	40	46	95.7	198.6	1.7	3.3	0.4	0.5
Togo	5.8	4.9	22	30	0.7	1.8	0.2	0.4	0.1	0.2
Trinidad and Tobago	1.5	1.3	−118	−130	16.9	26.4	13.9	20.5	2.0	2.3
Tunisia	6.7	7.7	−11	16	13.3	18.4	1.6	1.9	0.4	0.3
Turkey	5.6	5.7	51	68	143.8	221.6	2.6	3.3	0.5	0.5
Turkmenistan	1.7	1.4	−332	−223	28.0	34.6	7.2	7.5	1.5	2.0
Uganda	..	..	..	..	0.8	1.5	0.0	0.1	0.1	0.1
Ukraine	1.7	1.8	50	45	600.0	342.8	11.5	6.9	1.6	1.7
United Arab Emirates	2.6	..	−514	−294	60.9	58.9	34.3	18.1	1.3	1.6
United Kingdom	5.5	6.6	2	−14	569.3	567.8	9.9	9.6	0.5	0.4
United States	3.7	4.4	14	27	4,815.9	5,601.5	19.3	19.8	0.7	0.6
Uruguay	9.9	10.0	49	51	3.9	5.4	1.3	1.6	0.2	0.2
Uzbekistan	0.7	0.8	10	−8	113.3	118.6	5.3	4.8	3.4	3.2
Venezuela, RB	2.6	2.4	−239	−289	113.8	157.7	5.8	6.5	1.0	1.2
Vietnam	3.3	4.2	−2	−25	22.5	57.5	0.3	0.7	0.3	0.4
West Bank and Gaza	..	..	..	..	..	..	..	..	..	..
Yemen, Rep.	2.8	3.8	−247	−441	9.4	8.4	0.7	0.5	1.2	0.6
Zambia	1.4	1.3	10	5	2.4	1.8	0.3	0.2	0.3	0.2
Zimbabwe	3.0	3.0	9	13	16.6	14.8	1.6	1.2	0.6	0.5
World	**3.9 w**	**4.6 w**	**−2 w**	**−1 w**	**21,172.6 t**	**22,942.1 t**	**3.9 w**	**3.8 w**	**0.6 w**	**0.5 w**
Low income	3.5	4.1	−6	−6	1,419.3	1,764.4	0.8	0.8	0.4	0.4
Middle income	2.9	4.1	−33	−35	9,388.0	9,408.8	3.6	3.2	0.9	0.6
Lower middle income	2.8	4.1	−20	−22	7,811.9	7,397.3	3.4	2.9	1.0	0.6
Upper middle income	4.0	4.3	−96	−91	1,565.8	2,014.3	5.2	6.3	0.7	0.6
Low & middle income	3.0	4.1	−28	−29	10,805.5	11,173.2	2.4	2.2	0.8	0.6
East Asia & Pacific	2.6	4.6	−7	−4	3,051.6	3,752.7	1.9	2.1	1.0	0.5
Europe & Central Asia	2.1	2.5	−9	−23	4,845.2	3,144.8	10.2	6.7	1.3	1.1
Latin America & Carib.	5.9	6.1	−35	−42	964.0	1,359.2	2.2	2.7	0.4	0.4
Middle East & N. Africa	4.1	3.5	−273	−168	751.8	1,228.3	3.3	4.2	0.7	0.8
South Asia	4.2	5.1	10	19	765.9	1,220.3	0.7	0.9	0.4	0.4
Sub-Saharan Africa	2.8	2.8	−53	−56	473.4	480.5	0.9	0.7	0.5	0.4
High income	4.6	5.2	24	26	10,377.8	11,789.3	11.8	12.4	0.5	0.5
Europe EMU	5.7	6.4	56	63	2,349.7	2,414.6	6.9	7.9	0.3	0.3

a. A negative value indicates that a country is a net exporter.

The ratio of GDP to energy use provides a measure of energy efficiency. To produce comparable and consistent estimates of real GDP across countries relative to physical inputs to GDP—that is, units of energy use—GDP is converted to 2000 constant international dollars using purchasing power parity (PPP) rates. Differences in this ratio over time and across countries reflect in part structural changes in the economy, changes in the energy efficiency of particular sectors, and differences in fuel mixes.

Because commercial energy is widely traded, it is necessary to distinguish between its production and its use. Net energy imports show the extent to which an economy's use exceeds its domestic production. High-income countries are net energy importers; middle-income countries have been their main suppliers.

Carbon dioxide emissions, largely a by-product of energy production and use (see table 3.7), account for the largest share of greenhouse gases, which are associated with global warming. Anthropogenic carbon dioxide emissions result primarily from fossil fuel combustion and cement manufacturing. In combustion, different fossil fuels release different amounts of carbon dioxide for the same level of energy use. Burning oil releases about 50 percent more carbon dioxide than burning natural gas, and burning coal releases about twice as much. Cement manufacturing releases about half a metric ton of carbon dioxide for each metric ton of cement produced.

The Carbon Dioxide Information Analysis Center (CDIAC), sponsored by the U.S. Department of Energy, calculates annual anthropogenic emissions of carbon dioxide. These calculations are based on data on fossil fuel consumption (from the World Energy Data Set maintained by the United Nations Statistics Division) and data on world cement manufacturing (from the Cement Manufacturing Data Set maintained by the U.S. Bureau of Mines). Emissions

of carbon dioxide are often calculated and reported in terms of their content of elemental carbon. For this table these values were converted to the actual mass of carbon dioxide by multiplying the carbon mass by 3.664 (the ratio of the mass of carbon to that of carbon dioxide).

Although the estimates of global carbon dioxide emissions are probably within 10 percent of actual emissions (as calculated from global average fuel chemistry and use), country estimates may have larger error bounds. Trends estimated from a consistent time series tend to be more accurate than individual values. Each year the CDIAC recalculates the entire time series from 1950 to the present, incorporating its most recent findings and the latest corrections to its database. Estimates do not include fuels supplied to ships and aircraft engaged in international transport because of the difficulty of apportioning these fuels among the countries benefiting from that transport.

• **GDP per unit of energy use** is the PPP GDP per kilogram of oil equivalent of energy use. PPP GDP is gross domestic product converted to 1995 constant international dollars using purchasing power parity rates. An international dollar has the same purchasing power over GDP as a U.S. dollar has in the United States. • **Net energy imports** are estimated as energy use less production, both measured in oil equivalents. A negative value indicates that the country is a net exporter. • **Carbon dioxide emissions** are those stemming from the burning of fossil fuels and the manufacture of cement. They include carbon dioxide produced during consumption of solid, liquid, and gas fuels and gas flaring.

3.8a

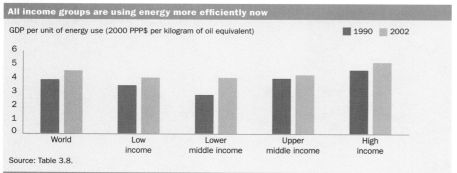

All income groups are using energy more efficiently now

GDP per unit of energy use (2000 PPP$ per kilogram of oil equivalent)   ■ 1990   ■ 2002

Source: Table 3.8.

Data sources

The underlying data on energy production and use are from electronic files of the International Energy Agency. The data on carbon dioxide emissions are from the CDIAC, Environmental Sciences Division, Oak Ridge National Laboratory, in the U.S. state of Tennessee.

3.9 Sources of electricity

	Electricity production		Access to electricity	Sources of electricity[a]								
									% of total			
	billion kwh		% of population	Hydropower		Coal		Oil		Gas		Nuclear power	
	1990	2002	2000	1990	2002	1990	2002	1990	2002	1990	2002	1990	2002
Afghanistan	..	..	6.0	..	..	..	..	..	..	..	..	..	..
Albania	3.2	3.7	..	89.1	95.3	..	..	10.9	4.7	..	..	..	..
Algeria	16.1	27.6	98.0	0.8	0.2	..	..	5.4	2.2	93.7	97.6	..	..
Angola	0.8	1.8	12.0	86.2	64.3	..	..	13.8	35.7	..	..	..	..
Argentina	51.0	84.5	94.6	35.6	42.5	1.3	1.4	9.7	1.8	39.0	45.9	14.3	6.9
Armenia	10.4	5.5	..	15.0	30.0	..	..	85.0	..	..	28.6	..	41.3
Australia	154.3	222.0	..	9.2	7.1	77.1	78.3	2.7	1.7	10.6	11.6	..	..
Austria	49.3	60.4	..	63.9	66.1	14.2	12.3	3.8	2.6	15.7	15.5	..	..
Azerbaijan	23.2	19.5	..	3.0	10.3	..	..	..	22.5	97.0	67.1	..	..
Bangladesh	7.7	18.4	32.5	11.4	6.0	..	..	4.3	8.5	84.3	85.5	..	..
Belarus	39.5	26.5	..	0.1	0.1	..	..	99.9	5.7	..	94.2	..	..
Belgium	70.3	80.9	..	0.4	0.4	28.2	15.6	1.9	1.2	7.7	22.1	60.8	58.5
Benin	0.0	0.1	22.0	..	3.2	..	..	100.0	96.8	..	..	..	..
Bolivia	2.1	4.2	60.4	55.3	53.1	..	..	5.3	17.5	37.6	27.3	..	..
Bosnia and Herzegovina	6.5	10.8	..	52.2	48.8	47.8	49.9	..	1.3	..	..	..	..
Botswana	..	..	22.0	..	..	..	..	..	..	..	..	..	..
Brazil	222.8	344.6	94.9	92.8	82.7	2.1	2.4	2.5	3.8	0.0	3.8	1.0	4.0
Bulgaria	42.1	42.2	..	4.5	5.2	35.4	41.2	4.7	2.0	20.6	3.6	34.8	48.0
Burkina Faso	..	..	13.0										
Burundi	..	..	..										
Cambodia	..	..	15.8	..	..	..	..	..	..	..	..	..	..
Cameroon	2.7	3.3	20.0	98.5	96.4	..	..	1.5	3.6	..	..	..	..
Canada	481.9	601.4	..	61.6	58.2	17.1	19.5	3.4	2.4	2.0	5.8	15.1	12.6
Central African Republic	..	..	..	..	..	..	..	..	..	..	..	..	..
Chad	..	..	..										
Chile	18.4	45.5	99.0	55.3	51.0	34.3	19.0	7.7	1.1	1.3	25.3	..	..
China	621.2	1,640.5	98.6	20.4	17.6	71.2	77.5	7.9	3.0	0.5	0.3	..	1.5
Hong Kong, China	28.9	34.3	..	..	..	98.3	63.8	1.7	0.4	..	35.8	..	..
Colombia	36.2	45.2	81.0	76.0	75.1	9.8	6.7	1.0	0.2	12.4	16.8	..	..
Congo, Dem. Rep.	5.6	5.9	6.7	99.6	99.7	..	..	0.4	0.3	..	..	..	..
Congo, Rep.	0.5	0.4	20.9	99.4	99.7	..	..	0.6	0.3	..	..	..	..
Costa Rica	3.5	7.5	95.7	97.5	79.2	..	..	2.5	1.6	..	..	..	..
Côte d'Ivoire	2.0	5.3	50.0	66.7	32.7	..	..	33.3	0.2	..	67.1	..	..
Croatia	8.9	12.2	..	48.8	43.9	..	17.3	35.8	18.2	15.4	20.7	..	..
Cuba	15.0	15.7	97.0	0.6	0.7	..	..	91.5	94.3	0.2	0.0	..	..
Czech Republic	62.6	76.0	..	2.3	3.3	71.8	66.8	4.8	0.5	1.0	3.9	20.1	24.7
Denmark	26.0	39.2	..	0.1	0.1	90.3	46.5	3.7	10.2	2.7	24.4	..	..
Dominican Republic	3.7	11.5	66.8	9.4	7.6	1.2	5.5	88.6	86.6	..	..	..	..
Ecuador	6.3	11.9	80.0	78.5	63.3	..	..	21.5	33.6	..	3.1	..	..
Egypt, Arab Rep.	42.3	86.1	93.8	23.5	16.3	..	..	36.9	7.5	39.6	76.0	..	..
El Salvador	2.2	4.1	70.8	73.5	27.8	..	..	6.9	47.5	..	..	..	..
Eritrea	..	..	17.0	..	..	..	..	..	..	..	..	..	..
Estonia	17.2	8.5	..	0.0	0.1	86.8	90.9	8.4	0.3	4.8	8.4	..	..
Ethiopia	1.2	2.0	4.7	88.4	98.9	..	..	11.6	1.0	..	..	..	..
Finland	54.4	74.9	..	20.0	14.4	33.0	26.3	3.1	0.8	8.6	15.1	35.3	29.8
France	416.7	554.8	..	12.8	10.9	8.5	4.5	2.1	0.8	0.7	4.2	75.4	78.7
Gabon	1.0	1.4	31.0	72.1	65.5	..	..	11.2	16.6	16.4	17.4	..	..
Gambia, The	..	..	..	..	..	..	..	..	..	..	..	..	..
Georgia	14.2	7.3	..	52.8	93.2	..	..	26.1	0.4	21.1	6.3	..	..
Germany	547.7	566.9	..	3.2	4.1	58.8	51.4	1.9	0.8	7.4	9.5	27.8	29.1
Ghana	5.7	7.3	45.0	100.0	69.0	..	..	..	31.0	..	..	..	..
Greece	34.8	53.9	..	5.1	5.2	72.4	64.1	22.3	16.0	0.3	13.1	..	..
Guatemala	2.3	6.2	66.7	76.0	27.5	..	15.7	9.0	43.1	..	..	..	..
Guinea	..	..	..	..	..	..	..	..	..	..	..	..	..
Guinea-Bissau	..	..	..	..	..	..	..	..	..	..	..	..	..
Haiti	0.6	0.6	34.0	76.5	47.6	..	..	20.6	52.4	..	..	..	..

	Electricity production (billion kwh)		Access to electricity (% of population)	Sources of electricity[a] (% of total)									
				Hydropower		Coal		Oil		Gas		Nuclear power	
	1990	2002	2000	1990	2002	1990	2002	1990	2002	1990	2002	1990	2002
Honduras	2.3	4.2	54.5	98.3	57.8	..	..	1.7	40.1	..	..	..	..
Hungary	28.4	36.2	..	0.6	0.5	30.5	25.1	4.8	5.9	15.7	29.7	48.3	38.6
India	289.4	596.5	43.0	24.8	10.7	65.3	70.1	4.3	4.7	3.4	10.5	2.1	3.3
Indonesia	33.3	108.2	53.4	20.2	9.2	31.5	39.7	42.7	23.3	2.3	22.1	..	..
Iran, Islamic Rep.	59.1	140.8	97.9	10.3	5.7	..	..	37.3	17.8	52.5	76.4	..	..
Iraq	24.0	31.2	95.0	10.8	2.0	..	..	89.2	98.0	..	..	..	..
Ireland	14.2	24.8	..	4.9	3.7	57.4	35.8	10.0	15.0	27.7	43.6	..	..
Israel	20.9	45.4	100.0	0.0	0.0	50.1	77.4	49.9	22.5	..	0.1	..	..
Italy	213.1	277.5	..	14.8	14.2	16.8	14.6	48.2	31.6	18.6	35.8	..	..
Jamaica	2.5	6.9	90.0	3.6	1.4	..	..	92.4	97.2	..	..	..	..
Japan	850.7	1,087.7	..	10.5	7.6	14.6	26.8	29.9	13.4	19.1	22.5	23.8	27.1
Jordan	3.6	8.1	95.0	0.3	0.7	..	..	87.8	90.9	11.9	8.4	..	..
Kazakhstan	87.4	58.3	..	8.4	15.2	..	69.9	91.6	4.2	..	10.6	0.6	..
Kenya	3.0	4.5	7.9	81.6	68.9	..	..	7.6	22.6	..	..	..	..
Korea, Dem. Rep.	27.7	19.8	20.0	56.3	53.7	40.1	41.2	3.6	5.1	..	..	..	..
Korea, Rep.	105.4	326.9	..	6.0	1.0	16.8	39.9	17.9	9.6	9.1	12.8	50.2	36.4
Kuwait	18.5	36.9	100.0	..	..	..	..	17.1	78.9	82.9	21.1	..	..
Kyrgyz Republic	13.4	11.9	..	67.3	90.5	..	4.8	32.7	..	..	4.8	..	..
Lao PDR	..	..	..	..	..	..	..	..	..	..	..	..	..
Latvia	6.6	4.0	..	67.7	62.0	..	1.0	32.3	3.4	..	33.1	..	..
Lebanon	1.5	9.7	95.0	33.3	7.0	..	..	66.7	93.0	..	..	..	..
Lesotho	..	..	5.0	..	..	..	..	..	..	..	..	..	..
Liberia	..	..	..	..	..	..	..	..	..	..	..	..	..
Libya	10.2	15.3	99.8	..	..	..	..	100.0	77.8	..	22.2	..	..
Lithuania	28.4	17.3	..	1.5	2.0	..	..	38.6	4.3	..	11.1	60.0	81.8
Macedonia, FYR	..	..	..	..	..	..	..	..	..	..	..	..	..
Madagascar	..	..	8.0	..	..	..	..	..	..	..	..	..	..
Malawi	..	..	5.0	..	..	..	..	..	..	..	..	..	..
Malaysia	23.0	74.2	96.9	17.3	7.1	4.8	6.0	55.9	9.3	22.0	77.5	..	..
Mali	..	..	..	..	..	..	..	..	..	..	..	..	..
Mauritania	..	..	..	..	..	..	..	..	..	..	..	..	..
Mauritius	..	..	100.0	..	..	..	..	..	..	..	..	..	..
Mexico	122.7	215.2	..	19.1	11.6	6.3	12.1	57.3	36.9	10.6	32.1	2.4	4.5
Moldova	15.5	3.2	..	1.7	3.7	32.3	3.8	26.6	0.7	39.5	91.8	..	..
Mongolia	..	..	90.0	..	..	..	..	..	..	..	..	..	..
Morocco	9.6	17.2	71.1	12.7	4.9	23.0	70.1	64.4	23.9	..	..	..	..
Mozambique	0.5	12.7	7.2	62.6	99.7	13.9	..	23.6	0.3	0.2	0.0	..	..
Myanmar	2.5	6.6	5.0	48.1	33.7	1.6	..	10.9	9.3	39.3	57.0	..	..
Namibia	1.4	1.5	34.0	95.2	96.8	1.5	0.4	3.3	2.8	..	..	..	..
Nepal	0.9	2.1	15.4	99.9	99.8	..	..	0.1	0.2	..	..	..	..
Netherlands	71.9	96.0	..	0.1	0.1	38.3	28.0	4.3	2.9	50.9	59.4	4.9	4.1
New Zealand	32.3	40.3	..	72.3	60.7	1.5	4.0	0.0	..	17.6	25.1	..	..
Nicaragua	1.4	2.7	48.0	28.8	11.4	..	..	39.8	78.8	..	..	..	..
Niger	..	..	..	..	..	..	..	..	..	..	..	..	..
Nigeria	13.5	15.3	40.0	32.6	46.2	0.1	..	13.7	9.8	53.7	44.0	..	..
Norway	121.6	130.1	..	99.6	99.3	0.2	0.2	0.0	0.0	..	0.2	..	..
Oman	4.5	10.3	94.0	..	..	..	..	18.4	18.0	81.6	82.0	..	..
Pakistan	37.7	75.7	52.9	44.9	29.5	0.1	0.3	20.6	32.2	33.6	35.7	0.8	2.3
Panama	2.7	5.3	76.1	83.2	64.3	..	..	14.7	35.4	..	..	..	..
Papua New Guinea	..	..	..	..	..	..	..	..	..	..	..	..	..
Paraguay	27.2	48.2	74.7	99.9	100.0	..	..	0.0	..	..	..	..	..
Peru	13.8	22.0	73.0	75.8	82.1	..	2.3	21.5	10.3	1.7	4.5	..	..
Philippines	25.2	48.5	87.4	24.0	14.5	7.7	33.3	46.7	13.0	..	18.1	..	..
Poland	134.4	142.5	..	1.1	1.6	97.5	94.5	1.2	1.7	0.1	1.5	..	..
Portugal	28.4	45.7	..	32.3	17.1	32.1	33.3	33.1	25.0	..	19.8	..	..
Puerto Rico	..	..	..	..	..	..	..	..	..	..	..	..	..

	Electricity production (billion kwh)		Access to electricity (% of population)	Sources of electricity[a] (% of total)									
				Hydropower		Coal		Oil		Gas		Nuclear power	
	1990	2002	2000	1990	2002	1990	2002	1990	2002	1990	2002	1990	2002
Romania	64.3	54.9	..	17.7	29.2	28.8	37.6	18.4	6.5	35.1	16.7	..	10.0
Russian Federation	1,082.2	889.3	..	15.4	18.2	5.2	19.2	68.0	3.1	..	43.3	10.8	15.9
Rwanda	..	..	..	..	..	..	..	..	..	..	..	..	..
Saudi Arabia	64.9	145.6	97.7	..	..	..	..	61.5	65.9	38.5	34.1	..	..
Senegal	0.9	1.5	30.1	..	..	..	..	98.0	100.0	2.0	0.1	..	..
Serbia and Montenegro	36.5	33.2	..	31.1	31.5	65.4	66.1	1.9	0.7	1.6	1.6	..	..
Sierra Leone	..	..	..	..	..	..	..	..	..	..	..	..	..
Singapore	15.7	35.4	100.0	..	..	..	..	100.0	39.6	..	58.3	..	..
Slovak Republic	23.4	32.2	..	8.0	16.4	32.2	17.3	3.4	2.2	4.9	7.8	51.4	55.7
Slovenia	12.1	14.7	..	28.2	23.2	36.2	36.1	2.5	0.4	0.2	2.0	32.9	37.6
Somalia	..	..	..	..	..	..	..	..	..	..	..	..	..
South Africa	165.4	218.4	66.1	0.6	1.3	94.3	93.1	..	..	..	..	5.1	5.5
Spain	151.2	242.7	..	16.8	9.5	40.1	34.0	5.7	11.8	1.0	13.3	35.9	26.0
Sri Lanka	3.2	7.0	62.0	99.8	38.7	..	..	0.2	61.2	..	..	..	..
Sudan	1.5	2.9	30.0	63.2	44.4	..	..	36.8	55.6	..	..	..	..
Swaziland	..	..	..	..	..	..	..	..	..	..	..	..	..
Sweden	146.0	146.0	..	49.7	45.6	1.2	2.6	0.8	2.0	0.3	0.4	46.7	46.3
Switzerland	54.6	64.9	..	54.6	54.2	0.1	..	0.5	0.1	0.6	1.4	43.3	41.9
Syrian Arab Republic	11.6	26.9	85.9	48.6	39.7	..	..	32.4	25.2	18.9	35.2	..	..
Tajikistan	18.1	15.2	..	90.9	97.7	..	..	9.1	..	6.7	2.3	..	..
Tanzania	1.6	3.0	10.5	95.1	91.4	..	3.5	4.9	5.1	..	..	..	..
Thailand	44.2	109.0	82.1	11.3	6.9	25.0	16.5	23.5	2.6	40.2	72.2	..	..
Togo	0.1	0.1	9.0	4.6	5.7	..	..	95.4	94.3	..	..	..	..
Trinidad and Tobago	3.6	6.1	99.0	..	..	..	..	0.1	0.0	99.0	99.5	..	..
Tunisia	5.8	11.8	94.6	0.8	0.6	..	..	35.5	10.2	63.7	89.0	..	..
Turkey	57.5	129.4	..	40.2	26.0	35.1	24.8	6.9	8.3	17.7	40.6	..	..
Turkmenistan	14.6	11.2	..	4.8	0.0	..	..	..	..	95.2	100.0	..	..
Uganda	..	..	3.7	..	..	..	..	..	..	..	..	..	..
Ukraine	298.8	173.7	..	3.6	5.6	27.6	17.2	14.9	0.7	28.4	31.6	25.5	44.9
United Arab Emirates	17.1	42.2	96.0	..	..	..	..	3.7	7.9	96.3	92.1	..	..
United Kingdom	317.8	384.5	..	1.6	1.2	65.0	32.8	10.9	1.8	1.6	39.6	20.7	22.9
United States	3,202.8	3,992.7	..	8.5	5.8	53.1	51.3	4.1	2.5	11.9	17.8	19.1	20.1
Uruguay	7.4	9.6	98.0	94.2	99.3	..	..	5.1	0.4	..	..	..	..
Uzbekistan	56.3	49.6	..	11.8	12.8	..	4.0	88.2	11.4	..	71.8	..	..
Venezuela, RB	59.3	87.4	94.0	62.3	66.2	..	..	11.5	11.6	26.2	22.2	..	..
Vietnam	8.7	35.8	75.8	61.8	50.8	23.1	13.6	15.0	12.3	0.1	23.3	..	..
West Bank and Gaza	..	..	..	..	..	..	..	..	..	..	..	..	..
Yemen, Rep.	1.7	3.8	50.0	..	..	..	..	100.0	100.0	..	..	..	..
Zambia	8.0	9.1	12.0	99.2	99.5	0.5	0.2	0.3	0.4	..	..	..	..
Zimbabwe	9.4	8.6	39.7	40.5	44.5	59.5	55.1	..	0.3	..	..	..	..
World	**11,708.5 s**	**16,014.1 s**	.. w	**18.1 w**	**16.2 w**	**37.9 w**	**39.1 w**	**11.2 w**	**7.1 w**	**13.9 w**	**19.1 w**	**17.2 w**	**16.6 w**
Low income	535.9	925.9	35.8	34.3	23.0	41.0	47.4	7.3	8.7	14.5	18.1	1.2	2.3
Middle income	3,817.1	5,519.5	90.4	21.2	21.8	34.4	39.2	15.8	9.2	20.3	21.9	7.5	6.9
Lower middle income	3,156.7	4,473.0	90.2	22.1	22.7	34.5	42.8	14.0	6.3	21.5	20.6	7.0	6.7
Upper middle income	660.5	1,046.5	..	17.3	17.8	34.0	23.9	24.3	21.8	14.4	27.6	9.6	7.7
Low & middle income	4,353.0	6,445.4	65.0	22.8	22.0	35.2	40.4	14.7	9.1	19.6	21.4	6.7	6.2
East Asia & Pacific	785.8	2,042.5	87.3	21.7	17.1	61.1	66.8	12.8	4.7	3.5	9.1	..	1.2
Europe & Central Asia	2,143.0	1,874.4	..	12.9	16.7	31.6	29.4	12.7	3.6	29.5	33.4	12.3	16.7
Latin America & Carib.	607.0	989.2	86.6	63.7	56.9	3.8	5.0	19.0	15.6	9.5	17.0	2.1	3.0
Middle East & N. Africa	254.9	534.5	90.4	10.3	6.6	0.9	2.3	50.5	38.3	38.4	52.8	..	..
South Asia	338.9	699.8	40.8	27.6	13.2	55.8	59.8	6.1	8.3	8.6	15.1	1.9	3.0
Sub-Saharan Africa	223.4	305.0	24.7	18.2	21.1	72.3	68.2	2.2	3.1	3.3	3.5	3.8	3.9
High income	7,355.4	9,568.7	..	15.3	12.2	39.6	38.2	9.2	5.8	10.6	17.6	23.3	23.6
Europe EMU	1,652.6	2,081.4	..	11.0	10.0	34.4	27.1	9.5	7.4	8.7	16.1	35.5	35.5

a. Shares may not sum to 100 percent because some sources of generated electricity are not shown.

About the data

Use of energy in general, and access to electricity in particular, are important in improving people's standard of living. But electricity generation also can damage the environment. Whether such damage occurs depends largely on how electricity is generated. For example, burning coal releases twice as much carbon dioxide—a major contributor to global warming—as does burning an equivalent amount of natural gas (see *About the data* for table 3.8). Nuclear energy does not generate carbon dioxide emissions, but it produces other dangerous waste products. The table provides information on electricity production by source. Shares may not sum to 100 percent because some sources of generated

electricity (such as wind, solar, and geothermal) are not shown.

The International Energy Agency (IEA) compiles data on energy inputs used to generate electricity. IEA data for countries that are not members of the Organisation for Economic Co-operation and Development (OECD) are based on national energy data adjusted to conform to annual questionnaires completed by OECD member governments. In addition, estimates are sometimes made to complete major aggregates from which key data are missing, and adjustments are made to compensate for differences in definitions.

The IEA makes these estimates in consultation with national statistical offices, oil companies, elec-

tricity utilities, and national energy experts. The IEA occasionally revises its time series to reflect political changes. Since 1990, for example, it has constructed energy statistics for countries of the former Soviet Union. In addition, energy statistics for other countries have undergone continuous changes in coverage or methodology as more detailed energy accounts have become available in recent years. Breaks in series are therefore unavoidable.

There is no single internationally accepted definition for access to electricity. The definition used here covers access at the household level—that is, the number of people who have electricity in their home. It includes commercially sold electricity, both on-grid and off-grid. For countries where access to electricity has been assessed through surveys by government agencies, the definition also includes self-generated electricity. The data do not capture unauthorized connections.

3.9a

Sources of electricity generation have shifted differently in different income groups

Sources of electricity generation, by income group (% of total production)

Source: Table 3.9.

Definitions

• **Electricity production** is measured at the terminals of all alternator sets in a station. In addition to hydropower, coal, oil, gas, and nuclear power generation, it covers generation by geothermal, solar, wind, and tide and wave energy as well as that from combustible renewables and waste. Production includes the output of electricity plants designed to produce electricity only, as well as that of combined heat and power plants. • **Access to electricity** refers to the number of people with access to electricity (both on-grid and off-grid) as a percentage of the total population (see table 2.1). • **Sources of electricity** refer to the inputs used to generate electricity: hydropower, coal, oil, gas, and nuclear power. • **Hydropower** refers to electricity produced by hydroelectric power plants. • **Oil** refers to crude oil and petroleum products. • **Gas** refers to natural gas but not to natural gas liquids. • **Nuclear power** refers to electricity produced by nuclear power plants.

Data sources

The data on electricity production are from the IEA's electronic files and its annual publications *Energy Statistics and Balances of Non-OECD Countries, Energy Statistics of OECD Countries,* and *Energy Balances of OECD Countries*. Data on access to electricity are from the IEA's *World Energy Outlook 2002: Energy and Poverty*.

	Urban population					Population in urban agglomerations of more than 1 million		Population in largest city		Access to improved sanitation facilities			
	millions		% of total population		average annual % growth	% of total population		% of urban population		% of urban population		% of rural population	
	1990	2003	1990	2003	1990–2003	1990	2005	1990	2005	1990	2002	1990	2002
Afghanistan	3.2	6.7	18	23	5.6	9	11	48	45	..	16	5	5
Albania	1.2	1.4	36	44	1.3	..	..	..	..	99	99	..	81
Algeria	12.9	18.7	51	59	2.9	8	10	15	17	99	99	76	82
Angola	2.6	4.9	28	36	4.9	17	20	62	52	62	56	19	16
Argentina	27.9	32.6	87	89	1.2	42	41	40	38	87	..	47	..
Armenia	2.4	2.1	67	67	–1.1	33	35	49	52	96	96	..	61
Australia	14.5	18.3	85	92	1.8	60	61	25	23	100	100	100	100
Austria	5.2	5.5	67	68	0.4	27	27	40	40	100	100	100	100
Azerbaijan	3.9	4.3	54	52	0.8	24	22	45	42	..	73	..	36
Bangladesh	21.8	37.0	20	27	4.1	9	13	30	31	71	75	11	39
Belarus	6.8	6.9	66	70	0.2	16	17	24	25	..	..	..	..
Belgium	9.6	10.1	97	98	0.4	..	..	10	10	..	..	..	..
Benin	1.6	3.0	34	45	4.7	..	..	..	..	31	58	1	12
Bolivia	3.7	5.6	56	64	3.2	25	31	29	26	49	58	13	23
Bosnia and Herzegovina	1.7	1.8	39	44	0.4	..	..	..	..	99	99	..	88
Botswana	0.5	0.9	42	50	3.6	..	..	..	..	61	57	21	25
Brazil	110.6	146.2	75	83	2.1	33	37	13	12	82	83	37	35
Bulgaria	5.8	5.3	66	68	–0.7	14	13	21	20	100	100	100	100
Burkina Faso	1.2	2.1	14	18	4.4	..	..	49	37	47	45	8	5
Burundi	0.3	0.7	6	10	5.7	..	..	..	..	42	47	44	35
Cambodia	1.2	2.5	13	19	5.6	6	8	..	..	..	53	..	8
Cameroon	4.7	8.2	40	51	4.3	16	22	21	22	43	63	7	33
Canada	21.3	25.1	77	79	1.3	34	37	18	20	100	100	99	99
Central African Republic	1.1	1.7	37	43	3.1	..	..	..	..	32	47	18	12
Chad	1.2	2.1	21	25	4.3	..	..	..	..	27	30	1	0
Chile	10.9	13.7	83	87	1.7	35	35	42	40	91	96	52	64
China	311.1	498.0	27	39	3.6	14	15	4	2	64	69	7	29
Hong Kong, China	5.7	6.8	100	100	1.4	100	100	100	100	..	..	..	..
Colombia	24.0	34.1	69	76	2.7	28	33	21	21	95	96	52	54
Congo, Dem. Rep.	..	..	..	..	..	9	10	..	..	56	43	3	23
Congo, Rep.	1.4	2.5	56	67	4.6	..	..	51	43	..	14	2	2
Costa Rica	1.6	2.4	54	61	3.0	..	..	45	45	..	89	97	97
Côte d'Ivoire	4.7	7.6	40	45	3.7	18	20	45	44	52	61	16	23
Croatia	2.6	2.6	54	59	0.1	..	..	..	..	..	..	..	..
Cuba	7.8	8.6	74	76	0.7	20	19	27	25	99	99	95	95
Czech Republic	7.7	7.6	75	75	–0.1	12	11	16	15	..	..	..	..
Denmark	4.4	4.6	85	85	0.4	26	20	31	24	..	..	..	..
Dominican Republic	4.1	5.9	58	67	2.7	22	21	37	31	60	67	33	43
Ecuador	5.7	8.4	55	64	3.0	26	29	28	27	73	80	36	59
Egypt, Arab Rep.	22.9	28.9	44	43	1.8	23	21	40	37	70	84	42	56
El Salvador	2.5	4.1	49	64	3.8	19	22	39	33	70	78	33	40
Eritrea	0.5	0.9	16	20	4.4	..	..	..	..	46	34	0	3
Estonia	1.1	0.9	71	70	–1.3	..	..	..	..	..	93	..	..
Ethiopia	6.5	11.4	13	17	4.3	3	4	28	23	14	19	2	4
Finland	3.1	3.1	61	59	0.0	17	21	28	36	100	100	100	100
France	42.0	45.3	74	76	0.6	23	23	22	22	..	..	..	..
Gabon	0.6	1.1	68	84	4.2	..	..	..	..	..	37	..	30
Gambia, The	0.2	0.5	25	33	5.3	..	..	..	..	..	72	..	46
Georgia	3.0	2.9	55	57	–0.3	22	21	41	36	96	96	..	69
Germany	67.8	72.7	85	88	0.5	40	41	9	9	..	..	..	..
Ghana	5.1	7.7	34	37	3.1	8	9	23	24	54	74	37	46
Greece	6.0	6.7	59	61	0.9	30	29	51	47	..	..	..	..
Guatemala	3.3	5.0	38	41	3.1	..	..	24	18	71	72	35	52
Guinea	1.3	2.3	23	29	4.1	15	18	65	60	27	25	13	6
Guinea-Bissau	0.2	0.5	24	34	5.7	..	..	..	..	..	57	..	23
Haiti	1.9	3.2	29	38	3.9	18	24	59	62	27	52	11	23

	Urban population					Population in urban agglomerations of more than 1 million		Population in largest city		Access to improved sanitation facilities			
	millions		% of total population		average annual % growth	% of total population		% of urban population		% of urban population		% of rural population	
	1990	2003	1990	2003	1990–2003	1990	2005	1990	2005	1990	2002	1990	2002
Honduras	2.0	3.9	42	56	4.9	..	..	35	25	77	89	31	52
Hungary	6.4	6.6	62	65	0.2	19	17	31	25	100	100	..	85
India	216.9	301.3	26	28	2.5	9	11	6	6	43	58	1	18
Indonesia	54.5	94.7	31	44	4.2	9	11	14	13	66	71	38	38
Iran, Islamic Rep.	30.6	43.9	56	66	2.8	22	22	21	16	86	86	78	78
Iraq	12.6	16.7	70	68	2.2	30	32	33	34	95	95	48	48
Ireland	2.0	2.4	57	60	1.4	..	..	46	42	..	..	..	..
Israel	4.2	6.2	90	92	2.9	48	58	43	47	100	100	..	..
Italy	37.8	38.9	67	67	0.2	23	20	12	10	..	..	..	..
Jamaica	1.2	1.5	51	58	1.6	..	..	..	..	85	90	64	68
Japan	95.6	101.1	77	79	0.4	42	44	34	35	100	100	100	100
Jordan	2.3	4.2	72	79	4.7	27	23	37	29	97	94	..	85
Kazakhstan	9.3	8.3	57	56	−0.9	7	7	12	13	87	87	52	52
Kenya	5.6	11.6	24	36	5.6	6	9	25	22	49	56	40	43
Korea, Dem. Rep.	11.7	13.8	58	61	1.3	15	20	21	23	..	58	..	60
Korea, Rep.	31.7	40.0	74	84	1.8	49	46	33	23	100	100	100	100
Kuwait	2.0	2.3	95	96	1.0	48	49	51	51	..	..	..	..
Kyrgyz Republic	1.7	1.7	38	34	0.3	..	..	38	47	..	75	..	51
Lao PDR	0.6	1.2	15	21	4.7	..	..	..	..	..	61	..	14
Latvia	1.9	1.4	70	60	−2.2	..	..	47	52	..	..	..	..
Lebanon	3.1	4.1	84	91	2.2	32	41	38	45	100	100	..	87
Lesotho	0.3	0.5	20	30	4.2	..	..	..	..	61	61	32	32
Liberia	1.0	1.6	42	47	3.3	..	..	..	..	59	49	24	7
Libya	3.5	4.9	82	88	2.6	35	36	43	41	97	97	96	96
Lithuania	2.5	2.4	68	69	−0.4	..	..	..	..	..	..	..	..
Macedonia, FYR	1.1	1.2	58	60	0.8	..	..	..	..	..	..	..	..
Madagascar	2.7	5.3	24	31	5.1	8	10	35	31	25	49	8	27
Malawi	1.0	1.7	12	16	4.4	..	..	..	..	52	66	34	42
Malaysia	9.1	14.7	50	59	3.7	6	5	12	9	94	..	98	98
Mali	2.0	3.8	24	32	4.8	9	11	37	34	50	59	32	38
Mauritania	0.9	1.8	44	62	5.2	..	..	..	..	31	64	26	9
Mauritius	0.4	0.5	41	42	1.4	..	..	..	..	100	100	99	99
Mexico	60.3	76.7	72	75	1.9	32	34	25	24	84	90	20	39
Moldova	2.0	1.8	47	42	−1.1	..	..	..	..	..	86	..	52
Mongolia	1.2	1.4	57	57	1.2	..	..	48	58	..	75	..	37
Morocco	11.6	17.3	48	57	3.0	21	24	23	21	87	83	28	31
Mozambique	3.0	6.7	21	36	6.2	5	7	26	18	..	51	14	14
Myanmar	10.0	14.4	25	29	2.8	7	8	29	27	39	96	15	63
Namibia	0.4	0.7	27	32	4.3	..	..	..	..	68	66	8	14
Nepal	1.6	3.2	9	13	5.2	..	..	..	..	62	68	7	20
Netherlands	13.3	14.6	89	90	0.7	14	14	8	8	100	100	100	100
New Zealand	2.9	3.5	85	86	1.3	25	28	30	32	..	..	88	..
Nicaragua	2.0	3.1	53	57	3.4	19	20	36	35	64	78	27	51
Niger	1.2	2.6	16	22	5.8	..	..	36	35	35	43	2	4
Nigeria	33.7	63.6	35	47	4.9	10	12	14	16	50	48	33	30
Norway	3.1	3.4	72	76	0.9	..	..	22	23	..	..	..	..
Oman	1.0	2.0	62	78	5.3	..	..	..	..	97	97	61	61
Pakistan	33.0	50.6	31	34	3.3	16	18	22	22	81	92	19	35
Panama	1.3	1.7	54	57	2.2	..	..	66	53	..	89	..	51
Papua New Guinea	0.6	1.0	15	18	4.0	..	..	..	..	67	67	41	41
Paraguay	2.0	3.3	49	58	3.7	22	29	46	50	71	94	46	58
Peru	14.9	20.1	69	74	2.3	27	29	39	39	68	72	15	33
Philippines	29.8	49.7	49	61	3.9	14	14	27	20	63	81	46	61
Poland	23.1	24.1	61	63	0.3	14	13	15	12	..	..	..	..
Portugal	4.6	7.1	47	68	3.3	30	31	40	27	..	..	..	..
Puerto Rico	2.5	3.0	71	76	1.3	44	59	61	77	..	..	..	..

	Urban population					Population in urban agglomerations of more than 1 million		Population in largest city		Access to improved sanitation facilities			
	millions		% of total population		average annual % growth	% of total population		% of urban population		% of urban population		% of rural population	
	1990	2003	1990	2003	1990–2003	1990	2005	1990	2005	1990	2002	1990	2002
Romania	12.4	12.1	54	56	−0.2	9	8	16	14	..	86	..	10
Russian Federation	108.7	104.6	73	73	−0.3	18	20	8	10	93	93	70	70
Rwanda	0.4	0.6	5	7	3.1	..	..	..	..	49	56	36	38
Saudi Arabia	12.4	19.7	78	88	3.6	31	45	19	26	100	100	..	..
Senegal	2.9	5.1	40	50	4.2	20	22	50	43	52	70	23	34
Serbia and Montenegro	5.4	4.2	51	52	−1.8	11	10	21	20	97	97	77	77
Sierra Leone	1.2	2.1	30	39	4.2	..	..	48	45	..	53	..	30
Singapore	3.0	4.3	100	100	2.6	99	99	99	99	100	100	..	..
Slovak Republic	3.0	3.1	56	58	0.4	..	..	..	..	100	100	100	100
Slovenia	1.0	1.0	50	49	−0.2	..	..	..	..	..	..	..	..
Somalia	1.7	2.8	24	29	3.6	11	12	44	41	..	47	..	14
South Africa	17.2	27.1	49	59	3.5	23	29	11	12	85	86	42	44
Spain	29.3	32.2	75	78	0.7	23	23	16	16	..	..	..	..
Sri Lanka	3.5	4.6	21	24	2.1	..	..	..	..	89	98	64	89
Sudan	6.6	13.0	27	39	5.2	9	13	36	31	53	50	26	24
Swaziland	0.2	0.3	24	27	3.9	..	..	..	..	..	78	..	44
Sweden	7.1	7.5	83	83	0.4	17	19	21	23	100	100	100	100
Switzerland	4.0	5.0	60	68	1.6	..	..	21	20	100	100	100	100
Syrian Arab Republic	5.9	9.1	49	53	3.3	27	27	26	26	97	97	56	56
Tajikistan	1.7	1.7	32	28	0.3	..	..	..	..	..	71	..	47
Tanzania	5.5	12.7	22	35	6.4	5	7	24	19	51	54	45	41
Thailand	10.4	12.7	19	20	1.5	11	11	57	51	95	97	74	100
Togo	1.0	1.7	29	35	4.2	..	..	..	..	71	71	24	15
Trinidad and Tobago	0.8	1.0	69	75	1.3	..	..	..	..	100	100	100	100
Tunisia	4.7	6.7	58	67	2.6	19	20	33	30	95	90	47	62
Turkey	34.4	47.4	61	67	2.5	22	26	19	20	96	94	67	62
Turkmenistan	1.7	2.2	45	45	2.2	..	..	..	..	..	77	..	50
Uganda	1.9	3.9	11	15	5.3	4	5	39	31	54	53	41	39
Ukraine	34.7	33.0	67	68	−0.4	14	15	7	8	100	100	97	97
United Arab Emirates	1.4	3.6	80	88	7.1	..	..	33	36	100	100	100	100
United Kingdom	51.3	53.2	89	90	0.3	24	23	15	14	..	..	..	..
United States	187.8	226.6	75	78	1.4	40	42	9	8	100	100	100	100
Uruguay	2.8	3.1	89	93	1.0	41	40	46	43	95	95	..	85
Uzbekistan	8.2	9.4	40	37	1.0	10	8	25	22	73	73	48	48
Venezuela, RB	16.6	22.5	84	88	2.3	31	34	17	14	..	71	..	48
Vietnam	13.4	20.7	20	25	3.3	13	13	30	23	46	84	16	26
West Bank and Gaza	..	..	..	..	..	..	..	..	..	..	..	..	..
Yemen, Rep.	2.7	4.9	23	26	4.6	6	8	25	30	59	76	11	14
Zambia	3.1	4.2	39	40	2.4	13	13	32	33	64	68	26	32
Zimbabwe	2.9	4.9	28	37	4.0	10	12	36	30	69	69	40	51
World	**2,263.3 s**	**3,015.7 s**	**44 w**	**49 w**	**2.2 w**	**.. w**	**.. w**	**17 w**	**16 w**	**77 w**	**79 w**	**21 w**	**35 w**
Low income	447.5	686.5	26	30	3.3	10	12	17	16	49	61	10	24
Middle income	1,148.1	1,570.8	44	53	2.4	..	..	16	15	79	81	25	41
Lower middle income	946.4	1,319.8	41	50	2.6	17	18	14	13	78	80	24	41
Upper middle income	201.8	251.1	71	75	1.7	..	..	27	26	89	..	..	..
Low & middle income	1,595.7	2,257.4	37	43	2.7	..	..	16	15	71	75	18	32
East Asia & Pacific	454.1	725.5	28	39	3.6	..	..	11	8	64	71	16	35
Europe & Central Asia	294.4	301.1	63	64	0.2	16	18	14	..	94	93	72	64
Latin America & Carib.	309.1	407.8	71	77	2.1	31	33	24	23	83	84	35	44
Middle East & N. Africa	126.6	181.8	54	59	2.8	22	24	27	27	88	90	52	56
South Asia	280.1	403.5	25	28	2.8	10	12	10	10	50	64	5	23
Sub-Saharan Africa	131.5	237.6	28	36	4.6	..	..	26	24	53	55	25	26
High income	667.6	758.3	77	80	1.0	..	..	19	19	..	..	..	..
Europe EMU	220.9	239.0	75	78	0.6	28	28	16	18	..	..	..	..

About the data

The population of a city or metropolitan area depends on the boundaries chosen. For example, in 1990 Beijing, China, contained 2.3 million people in 87 square kilometers of "inner city" and 5.4 million in 158 square kilometers of "core city." The population of "inner city and inner suburban districts" was 6.3 million, and that of "inner city, inner and outer suburban districts, and inner and outer counties" was 10.8 million. (For most countries the last definition is used.)

Estimates of the world's urban population would change significantly if China, India, and a few other populous nations were to change their definition of urban centers. According to China's State Statistical Bureau, by the end of 1996 urban residents accounted for about 43 percent of China's population, while in 1994 only 20 percent of the population was considered urban. In addition to the continuous migration of people from rural to urban areas, one of the main reasons for this shift was the rapid growth in the hundreds of towns reclassified as cities in

recent years. Because the estimates in the table are based on national definitions of what constitutes a city or metropolitan area, cross-country comparisons should be made with caution. To estimate urban populations, the United Nations' ratios of urban to total population were applied to the World Bank's estimates of total population (see table 2.1).

The urban population with access to improved sanitation facilities is defined as people with access to at least adequate excreta disposal facilities that can effectively prevent human, animal, and insect contact with excreta. The rural population with access is included to allow comparison of rural and urban access. This definition and the definition of urban areas vary, however, so comparisons between countries can be misleading.

Definitions

• **Urban population** is the midyear population of areas defined as urban in each country and reported to the United Nations (see *About the data*). • **Population in urban agglomerations of more than 1 million** is the percentage of a country's population living in metropolitan areas that in 2000 had a population of more than 1 million. • **Population in largest city** is the percentage of a country's urban population living in that country's largest metropolitan area. • **Access to improved sanitation facilities** refers to the percentage of the urban or rural population with access to at least adequate excreta disposal facilities (private or shared but not public) that can effectively prevent human, animal, and insect contact with excreta. Improved facilities range from simple but protected pit latrines to flush toilets with a sewerage connection. To be effective, facilities must be correctly constructed and properly maintained.

3.10a

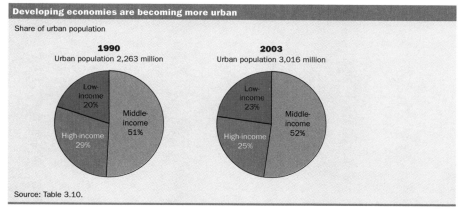

Developing economies are becoming more urban

Share of urban population

Source: Table 3.10.

3.10b

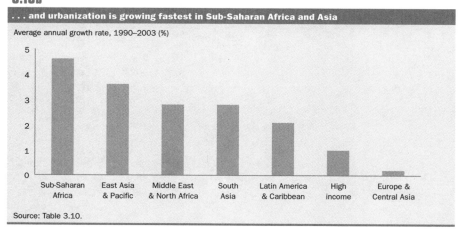

. . . and urbanization is growing fastest in Sub-Saharan Africa and Asia

Average annual growth rate, 1990–2003 (%)

Source: Table 3.10.

Data sources

The data on urban population and the population in urban agglomerations and in the largest city come from the United Nations Population Division's *World Urbanization Prospects: The 2003 Revision*. The total population figures are World Bank estimates. The data on access to sanitation in urban and rural areas are from the World Health Organization.

	City	Urban population	Secure tenure	House price to annual income ratio	Work trips by public trans-portation	Travel time to work	Households with access to services				Wastewater treated
							Potable water	Sewerage connection	Electricity	Telephone	
		thousands	% of population		%	minutes	%	%	%	%	%
		2005	1998	1998	1998	1998	1998	1998	1998	1998	1998
Algeria	Algiers	3,260	93.2	..	..	75	..	..	..	..	80
Argentina	Buenos Aires	13,349	92.1	5.10	59	42	100	98	100	70	..
	Córdoba	1,592	85.0	6.80	44	32	99	40	99	80	49
	Rosario	1,312	..	5.7	..	22	98	67	93	76	1
Armenia	Yerevan	1,066	100.0	4.0	84	30	98	98	100	88	36
Bangladesh	Chittagong	4,171	..	8.1	27	45	44	..	95	..	..
	Dhaka	12,560	..	16.7	9	45	60	22	90	7	..
	Sylhet	242[a]	..	6.0	10	50	29	0	93	40	..
	Tangail	152[a]	85.7	13.9	..	30	12	0	90	12	..
Barbados	Bridgetown	..	99.7	4.4	..	..	98	5	99	78	7
Belize	Belize City	55[a]	..	..	..	..	..	..	..	..	..
Bolivia	Santa Cruz de la Sierra	1,352	87.0	29.3	..	29	53	33	98	59	53
Bosnia and Herzegovina	Sarajevo	522[a]	..	..	100	12	95	90	100	..	..
Brazil	Belém	2,097	..	..	..	..	..	..	..	..	..
	Icapui	..	91.7	4.5	..	30	88	..	90	33	..
	Maranguape	..	..	..	30	20	73	..	..	..	..
	Porto Alegre	3,795	..	..	..	..	99	87	100	..	..
	Recife	3,527	..	12.5	46	35	89	41	100	29	33
	Rio de Janeiro	11,469	..	..	..	..	88	80	10	..	..
	Santo Andre	1,658[a]	80.3	23.4	43	40	98	95	100	79	..
Bulgaria	Bourgas	..	..	5.1	61	32	100	93	100	..	93
	Sofia	1,045	100.0	13.2	79	32	95	91	100	89	94
	Troyan	24[a]	100.0	3.7	44	22	99	82	100	45	..
	Veliko Tarnovo	..	100.0	5.4	46	30	98	98	100	96	50
Burkina Faso	Bobo-Dioulasso	..	100.0	..	..	..	24	..	29	6	..
	Koudougou	..	..	..	..	..	30	..	26	7	..
	Ouagadougou	870	100.0	..	2	..	30	..	47	11	19
Burundi	Bujumbura	373[a]	97.0	..	48	25	26	62	57	19	21
Cambodia	Phnom Penh	1,174	..	8.9	0	45	45	75	76	40	..
Cameroon	Douala	1,980	..	13.4	..	40	34	1	95	9	5
	Yaoundé	1,727	..	..	42	45	34	1	95	9	24
Canada	Hull	254[a]	100.0	..	16	..	100	100	100	100	100
Central African Republic	Bangui	..	94.0	..	66	60	31	..	18	11	0
Chad	N'Djamena	998[a]	..	..	35	..	42	0	13	6	21
Chile	Gran Concepción	..	..	..	57	35	100	91	95	69	6
	Santiago de Chile	5,623	..	..	60	38	100	99	99	73	3
	Tome	..	..	..	..	..	92	52	98	58	57
	Valparaiso	851[a]	91.8	..	55	..	98	92	97	63	100
	Viña del mar	851[a]	92.7	..	..	..	97	97	98	65	93
Colombia	Armenia	..	94.1	5.0	42	60	90	50	99	97	..
	Marinilla	170[a]	94.5	8.5	18	15	98	93	100	65	..
	Medellin	2,901[a]	..	..	38	35	100	99	100	87	..
Congo	Brazzaville	1,153	87.9	..	55	20	56	0	52	18	..
Côte d'Ivoire	Abidjan	3,516	..	14.5	..	45	26	15	41	5	45
Croatia	Zagreb	2,497[a]	96.5	7.8	56	31	98	97	100	94	..
Cuba	Baracoa	..	96.2	..	..	..	83	3	93	32	..
	Camaguey	..	84.7	..	2	60	72	47	97	..	..
	Cienfuegos	..	96.3	4.0	..	80	100	73	100	9	2
	Ciudad Habana	..	..	8.5	58	83	100	85	100	14	..
	Pinar Del Rio	..	96.4	..	..	80	97	48	100	..	..
	Santa Clara	..	98.8	..	7	48	95	42	100	43	..
Czech Republic	Brno	..	..	..	50	25	100	96	100	69	100
	Prague	1,164	99.3	..	55	22	99	100	100	100	..
Dem. Rep. of Congo	Kinshasa	5,717	94.9	..	72	57	72	0	66	1	..
Dominican Republic	Santiago de los Caballeros	691[a]	..	..	..	30	75	80	..	71	80
Ecuador	Ambato	286[a]	..	..	..	..	90	81	91	87	..

	City	Urban population	Secure tenure	House price to annual income ratio	Work trips by public transportation	Travel time to work	Households with access to services				Wastewater treated
							Potable water	Sewerage connection	Electricity	Telephone	
		thousands	% of population		%	minutes	%	%	%	%	%
		2005	**1998**	**1998**	**1998**	**1998**	**1998**	**1998**	**1998**	**1998**	**1998**
Ecuador	Cuenca	..	91.0	4.6	..	25	97	92	97	48	82
	Guayaquil	2,387	45.8	3.4	89	45	70	42	..	44	9
	Manta	126[a]	..	..	..	30	70	52	98	40	..
	Puyo	40[a]	..	2.1	..	15	80	30	90	60	..
	Quito	1,514	93.8	2.4	..	33	85	70	96	55	..
	Tena	..	..	6.3	..	5	80	60	..	..	..
El Salvador	San Salvador	1,472	90.5	3.5	..	..	82	80	98	70	..
Estonia	Riik	..	99.5	..	..	..	92	90	98	55	..
	Tallin	397[a]	98.8	6.4	..	35	98	98	100	86	10
Gabon	Libreville	523[a]	..	..	80	30	55	0	95	45	44
Gambia	Banjul	50[a]	91.8	11.4	55	22	23	12	24	..	..
Georgia	Tbilisi	1,042	100.0	9.4	..	..	..	98	100	58	..
Ghana	Accra	1,970	..	14.0	54	21	..	..	..	..	..
	Kumasi	862	77.7	13.7	51	21	65	..	95	51	..
Guatemala	Quetzaltenango	333[a]	..	4.3	..	15	60	55	80	40	..
Guinea	Conakry	1,465	..	..	26	45	30	32	54	6	..
Indonesia	Jakarta	13,194	95.5	14.6	..	..	50	65	99	..	16
	Semarang	816	80.2	..	..	..	34	..	85	..	..
	Surabaya	2,735	97.6	3.4	18	35	41	56	89	71	..
Iraq	Baghdad	5,911	..	..	..	..	..	..	..	..	..
Italy	Aversa	..	..	..	..	..	..	..	..	..	90
Jamaica	Kingston	655[a]	..	..	..	..	97	..	88	..	20
	Montego Bay	..	..	..	..	..	78	..	86	..	15
Jordan	Amman	1,292	97.3	6.1	21	25	98	81	99	62	54
Kenya	Kisumu	134[a]	97.3	8.5	43	24	38	31	49	..	65
	Mombasa	..	..	..	47	20	..	..	..	..	50
	Nairobi	2,819	..	..	71	57	89	..	..	..	52
Korea, Rep	Hanam	124[a]	..	3.7	..	..	81	68	100	100	81
	Pusan	3,527	100.0	4.0	39	42	98	69	100	100	69
	Seoul	9,592	98.6	5.7	71	60	100	99	100	..	99
Kuwait	Kuwait City	1,225	..	6.5	21	10	100	98	100	98	..
Kyrgyz Republic	Bishkek	829	94.8	..	95	35	30	23	100	20	15
Lao	Vientiane	562[a]	92.2	23.2	2	27	87	..	100	87	20
Latvia	Riga	719	97.4	15.6	..	..	95	93	100	70	..
Lebanon	Sin El Fil	..	..	8.3	50	10	80	30	98	80	..
Liberia	Monrovia	651[a]	57.6	28.0	80	60	..	..	..	..	..
Libya	Tripoli	2,093	..	0.8	18	20	97	90	99	6	40
Lithuania	Vilnius	578[a]	100.0	20.0	52	37	89	89	100	77	54
Madagascar	Antananarivo	1,808	..	..	..	..	..	..	..	..	..
Malawi	Lilongwe	765[a]	..	..	27	5	65	12	50	10	..
Malaysia	Penang	..	..	7.2	55	40	99	..	100	98	20
Mauritania	Nouakchott	881[a]	89.9	5.4	45	50	..	..	..	..	..
Mexico	Ciudad Juárez	1,469	..	..	24	23	89	77	96	45	..
Moldova	Chisinau	..	..	..	80	23	100	95	100	83	71
Mongolia	Ulaanbaatar	842	51.6	7.8	80	30	60	60	100	90	96
Morocco	Casablanca	3,743	..	..	..	30	83	93	91	..	..
	Rabat	1,859	..	..	40	20	93	97	52	..	..
Myanmar	Yangon	4,082	..	8.3	69	45	78	81	85	17	..
Nicaragua	Leon	..	98.8	..	..	15	78	..	84	21	..
Niger	Niamey	997	87.4	..	..	30	33	0	51	4	..
Nigeria	Ibadan	2,375	85.8	..	46	45	26	12	41	..	..
	Lagos	11,136	93.0	..	48	60	..	..	41	..	..
Oman	Muscat	887[a]	..	..	..	20	80	90	89	53	..
Panama	Colón	132[a]	..	14.2	..	15	..	..	..	..	..
Paraguay	Asunción	1,750	90.2	10.7	..	25	46	8	86	17	..
Peru	Cajamarca	..	90.0	3.9	..	20	86	69	81	38	62

3.11 | Urban environment

City		Urban population thousands 2005	Secure tenure % of population 1998	House price to annual income ratio 1998	Work trips by public trans-portation % 1998	Travel time to work minutes 1998	Households with access to services				Wastewater treated % 1998
							Potable water % 1998	Sewerage connection % 1998	Electricity % 1998	Telephone % 1998	
Peru	Huanuco	747[a]	..	30.0	..	20	57	28	80	32	..
	Huaras	54[a]	..	6.7	..	15	..	..	71	..	..
	Iquitos	347[a]	97.3	5.6	25	10	73	60	82	62	..
	Lima	8,180	80.6	10.4	82	..	75	71	99	..	4
	Tacna	..	..	4.0	..	25	65	58	74	16	64
	Tumbes	..	..	..	..	20	60	35	80	25	..
Philippines	Cebu	2,189[a]	95.0	13.3	..	35	41	92	80	25	..
Poland	Bydgoszcz	..	60.5	4.3	35	18	95	87	100	85	28
	Gdansk	851	..	4.4	56	20	99	94	100	56	100
	Katowice	2,914	27.8	1.7	29	36	99	94	100	75	67
	Poznan	..	65.5	5.8	51	25	95	96	100	86	78
Qatar	Doha	391	..	..	..	..	..	..	..	..	..
Russian Federation	Astrakhan	..	100.0	5.0	66	35	81	79	100	51	92
	Belgorod	..	100.0	4.0	..	25	90	89	100	51	96
	Kostroma	..	100.0	6.9	68	20	88	84	100	46	96
	Moscow	10,672	100.0	5.1	85	62	100	100	100	102	98
	Nizhny Novgorod	1,458[a]	100.0	6.9	79	35	98	98	100	64	98
	Novomoscowsk	..	100.0	4.2	61	25	99	93	100	62	97
	Omsk	1,132	99.7	3.9	86	43	87	87	100	41	89
	Pushkin	..	100.0	9.6	60	15	99	99	100	89	100
	Surgut	..	100.0	4.5	81	57	98	98	100	50	93
	Veliky Novgorod	..	100.0	3.4	75	30	97	97	100	51	95
Rwanda	Kigali	358[a]	..	11.4	32	45	36	20	57	6	20
Samoa	Apia	34[a]	..	10.0	..	..	60	0	98	96	..
Serbia and Montenegro	Belgrad	4,372	96.5	13.5	72	40	95	86	100	86	20
Singapore	Singapore	273[a]	100.0	3.1	53	30	100	100	100	100	100
Slovenia	Ljubljana	5,145	98.9	7.8	20	30	100	100	100	97	98
Spain	Madrid	..	..	..	16	32	..	..	..	..	100
	Pamplona	13[a]	..	..	..	..	100	..	100	..	79
Sweden	Amal	1,729	..	2.9	..	..	100	100	100	..	100
	Stockholm	104[a]	..	6.0	48	28	100	100	100	..	100
	Umea	170[a]	..	5.3	..	16	100	100	100	..	100
Switzerland	Basel	2,317	..	12.3	..	..	100	100	100	99	100
Syria	Damascus	6,604	..	10.3	33	40	98	71	95	10	3
Thailand	Bangkok	499[a]	77.2	8.8	28	60	99	100	100	60	..
	Chiang Mai	663[a]	96.5	6.8	5	30	95	60	100	75	70
Togo	Lomé	..	64.0	..	40	30	..	70	51	18	..
Trinidad and Tobago	Port of Spain	2,063	78.6	..	44	..	..	..	..	..	..
Tunisia	Tunis	3,594	..	5.0	..	..	75	47	95	27	83
Turkey	Ankara	65[a]	91.3	4.5	..	32	97	98	100	..	80
Uganda	Entebbe	92[a]	74.0	10.4	65	20	48	13	42	0	30
	Jinja	1,353	82.0	15.4	49	12	65	43	55	5	30
Uruguay	Montevideo	367[a]	88.0	5.6	60	45	98	79	100	75	34
West Bank and Gaza	Gaza	1,200[a]	87.3	5.4	..	..	85	38	99	38	..
Yemen	Aden	1,621	..	..	78	20	..	..	96	..	30
	Sana'a	1,116	..	..	78	20	30	9	96	..	30
Zimbabwe	Bulawayo	900[a]	99.4	..	75	15	100	100	98	..	80
	Chegutu	..	51.5	3.4	20	22	100	68	9	3	69
	Gweru	..	94.0	..	..	15	100	100	90	61	95
	Harare	1,528	99.9	..	32	45	100	100	88	42	..
	Mutare	149[a]	..	..	70	20	88	88	74	4	100

a. Data are for 2000 and are from the United Nations Population Division's *World Urbanization Prospects: The 2003 Revision.*

About the data

Despite the importance of cities and urban agglomerations as home to almost half the world's people, data on many aspects of urban life are sparse. The available data have been scattered among international agencies with different mandates, and compiling comparable data has been difficult. Even within cities it is difficult to assemble an integrated data set. Urban areas are often spread across many jurisdictions with no single agency responsible for collecting and reporting data for the entire area. Adding to the difficulties of data collection are gaps and overlaps in the data collection and reporting responsibilities of different administrative units. Creating a comprehensive, comparable international data set is further complicated by differences in the definition of an urban area and by uneven data quality.

The United Nations Global Plan of Action calls for monitoring the changing role of the world's cities and human settlements. The international agency with the mandate to assemble information on urban areas is the United Nations Centre for Human Settlements (UNCHS, or Habitat). Its Urban Indicators Programme is intended to provide data for monitoring and evaluating the performance of urban areas and for developing government policies and strategies. These data are collected through questionnaires completed by city officials in more than a hundred countries.

The table shows selected indicators for more than 160 cities from the UNCHS data set. A few more indicators are included on the *World Development Indicators* CD-ROM. The selection of cities in the UNCHS database does not reflect population weights or the economic importance of cities and is therefore biased toward smaller cities. Moreover, it is based on demand for participation in the Urban Indicators Programme. As a result, the database excludes a large number of major cities. The table reflects this bias as well as the criterion of data availability for the indicators shown.

The data should be used with care. Because different data collection methods and definitions may have been used, comparisons can be misleading. In addition, the definitions used here for access to potable water and urban population are more stringent than those used for tables 3.5 and 3.10 (see *Definitions*).

Definitions

• **Urban population** refers to the population of the urban agglomeration, a contiguous inhabited territory without regard to administrative boundaries. • **Secure tenure** refers to the percentage of the population protected from involuntary removal from land or residence—including subtenancy, residence in social housing, and residences owned, purchased, or privately rented—except through due legal process. • **House price to annual income ratio** is the average house price divided by the average household income. • **Work trips by public transportation** are the percentage of trips to work made by bus or minibus, tram, or train. Buses or minibuses are road vehicles other than cars taking passengers on a farepaying basis. Other means of transport commonly used in developing countries, such as taxi, ferry, rickshaw, or animal, are not included. • **Travel time to work** is the average time in minutes, for all modes, for a one-way trip to work. Train and bus times include average walking and waiting times, and car times include parking and walking to the workplace. • **Households with access to services** are the percentage of households in formal settlements with access to potable water and connections to sewerage, electricity, and telephone service. Households with access to potable water are those with access to safe or potable drinking water within 200 meters of the dwelling. • **Potable water** is water that is free from contamination and safe to drink without further treatment. • **Wastewater treated** is the percentage of all wastewater undergoing some form of treatment.

3.11a

The use of public transportation for work trips varied widely across cities in 1998

Country	City	Share of total work trips (%)	Country	City	Share of total work trips (%)
Lao PDR	Vientiane	2	Kyrgyz Republic	Bishkek	95
Spain	Madrid	16	Russian Federation	Moscow	85
Canada	Hull	16	Armenia	Yerevan	84
Libya	Tripoli	18	Peru	Lima	82
Slovenia	Ljubljana	20	Gabon	Libreville	80
Kuwait	Kuwait City	21	Liberia	Monrovia	80
Jordan	Amman	21	Mongolia	Ulaanbaatar	80
Mexico	Ciudad Juarez	24	Moldova	Chisinau	80
Guinea	Conakry	26	Bulgaria	Sofia	79
Malawi	Lilongwe	27	Yemen, Rep.	Aden	78

Source: Table 3.11.

Data sources

The data are from the Global Urban Indicators database of the UNCHS and the United Nations Population Division's *World Urbanization Prospects: The 2003 Revision*.

3.12 Traffic and congestion

	Motor vehicles				Passenger cars		Two-wheelers		Road traffic		Fuel prices	
	per 1,000 people		per kilometer of road		per 1,000 people		per 1,000 people		million vehicle kilometers		$ per liter	
											Super	Diesel
	1990	2002[a]	1990	2002	1990	2002	1990	2002	1990	2002	2004	2004
Afghanistan	..	..	..	..	..	..	..	..	..	..	0.53	0.58
Albania	11	66	3	11	2	43	3	1	..	29	1.23	1.02
Algeria	..	..	..	..	..	..	..	..	..	..	0.32	0.15
Angola	19	..	..	..	14	..	..	..	..	..	0.39	0.29
Argentina	181	181	27	37	134	140	1	..	43,119	27,458	0.63	0.49
Armenia	5	..	2	..	1	..	..	..	..	258	0.68	0.56
Australia	530	..	11	..	450	..	18	18	138,501	..	0.85	0.83
Austria	421	534	30	22	387	494	71	74	..	..	1.32	1.19
Azerbaijan	52	52	7	17	36	43	5	1	..	..	0.41	0.18
Bangladesh	1	1	0	..	0	0	1	1	..	..	0.59	0.34
Belarus	61	..	13	..	59	156	..	53	10,026	4,046	0.62	0.44
Belgium	423	518	30	36	385	464	14	30	..	156,633	1.50	1.07
Benin	3	..	2	..	2	..	34	..	..	..	0.77	0.72
Bolivia	41	..	6	..	25	..	9	0	1,139	..	0.54	0.40
Bosnia and Herzegovina	114	..	24	..	101	..	..	..	..	..	0.97	0.97
Botswana	18	69	3	11	10	30	..	1	..	..	0.66	0.61
Brazil	88	..	8	..	..	..	..	28	..	..	0.84	0.49
Bulgaria	163	326	39	69	146	287	55	0	..	213	0.92	0.89
Burkina Faso	4	..	3	..	2	..	9	..	..	..	1.18	0.94
Burundi	..	..	..	..	..	..	..	..	..	..	1.04	1.08
Cambodia	1	380	0	49	0	312	9	134	314	7,210	0.79	0.61
Cameroon	10	..	3	..	6	..	..	..	..	..	0.95	0.83
Canada	605	582	20	20	468	559	12	0	..	73,500	0.68	0.68
Central African Republic	1	..	0	..	1	..	0	..	1,494	..	1.29	1.14
Chad	2	..	0	..	1	..	0	..	..	..	1.17	1.01
Chile	81	133	13	25	52	87	2	2	..	..	0.85	0.64
China	5	12	4	11	1	7	3	26	..	840,960	0.48	0.43
Hong Kong, China	66	77	253	279	42	57	4	5	8,192	10,781	1.54	1.00
Colombia	..	51	..	19	..	43	8	12	50,945	41,587	0.72	0.36
Congo, Dem. Rep.	..	..	..	..	..	..	..	..	..	..	0.92	0.81
Congo, Rep.	18	..	3	..	12	..	..	..	..	..	0.87	0.59
Costa Rica	87	..	7	..	55	..	14	22	..	572,038	0.78	0.56
Côte d'Ivoire	24	..	6	..	15	..	..	..	..	..	1.14	0.95
Croatia	..	311	..	49	..	280	..	19	..	16,609	1.24	1.13
Cuba	37	..	16	..	18	..	19	..	..	..	0.95	0.55
Czech Republic	246	325	46	26	228	356	113	74	..	7,753	1.08	1.07
Denmark	368	425	27	32	320	360	9	15	36,304	46,302	1.51	1.35
Dominican Republic	75	..	48	..	21	..	..	..	..	..	0.85	0.61
Ecuador	35	49	8	14	31	44	2	2	10,306	17,528	0.54	0.27
Egypt, Arab Rep.	29	..	33	..	21	..	6	..	..	..	0.28	0.10
El Salvador	33	..	14	..	17	..	0	..	2,002	4,244	0.65	0.58
Eritrea	1	..	1	..	1	..	..	..	..	..	0.80	0.40
Estonia	211	359	22	9	154	296	66	5	..	6,843	0.94	0.94
Ethiopia	1	2	2	4	1	1	0	0	..	1,642	0.60	0.42
Finland	441	481	29	32	386	419	12	43	39,750	48,750	1.54	1.21
France	494	592	32	39	405	491	55	..	422,000	544,400	1.42	1.25
Gabon	32	..	4	..	19	..	..	..	..	..	0.90	0.69
Gambia, The	13	..	5	..	6	..	..	..	..	..	0.75	0.73
Georgia	107	72	27	16	89	56	5	1	4,620	..	0.73	0.67
Germany	405	..	53	..	386	516	18	56	446,000	589,500	1.46	1.29
Ghana	..	..	..	..	..	..	..	..	..	15,320	0.49	0.43
Greece	248	..	22	..	171	254	120	220	..	79,377	1.14	1.23
Guatemala	..	52	..	119	..	1	..	12	..	4,547	0.68	0.63
Guinea	4	..	1	..	2	..	..	..	..	..	0.75	0.69
Guinea-Bissau	7	..	2	..	4	..	..	..	..	..	0.00	0.00
Haiti	..	..	..	..	..	..	..	..	..	..	0.88	0.60

	Motor vehicles				Passenger cars		Two-wheelers		Road traffic		Fuel prices	
	per 1,000 people		per kilometer of road		per 1,000 people		per 1,000 people		million vehicle kilometers		$ per liter	
											Super	Diesel
	1990	2002[a]	1990	2002	1990	2002	1990	2002	1990	2002	2004	2004
Honduras	22	60	10	28	..	51	..	14	3,288	..	0.81	0.66
Hungary	212	302	21	19	188	259	16	0	22,898	23,260	1.30	1.22
India	4	9	2	..	2	6	15	0	..	..	0.87	0.62
Indonesia	16	..	10	..	7	..	34	59	..	..	0.27	0.18
Iran, Islamic Rep.	34	..	14	..	25	..	36	..	..	..	0.09	0.02
Iraq	14	..	6	..	1	..	..	..	..	..	0.03	0.01
Ireland	270	408	10	..	227	349	6	8	24,205	33,915	1.29	1.29
Israel	210	283	74	111	174	230	8	12	18,212	37,293	1.05	0.80
Italy	529	606	99	74	476	542	45	125	344,726	67,916	1.53	1.31
Jamaica	..	..	..	..	..	..	..	..	..	..	0.63	0.57
Japan	469	581	52	63	283	428	146	106	628,581	790,820	1.26	0.95
Jordan	60	..	26	..	..	..	0	..	1,098	526,677	0.61	0.19
Kazakhstan	76	89	8	16	50	72	..	5	18,248	3,824	0.52	0.38
Kenya	12	11	5	4	10	8	1	1	5,170	..	0.92	0.76
Korea, Dem. Rep.	..	..	..	..	..	..	..	..	..	..	0.78	0.61
Korea, Rep.	79	292	60	120	48	205	32	59	30,464	67,266	1.35	0.95
Kuwait	..	..	..	..	..	..	..	..	..	4,450	0.24	0.24
Kyrgyz Republic	44	..	10	..	44	38	..	4	5,220	1,917	0.48	0.43
Lao PDR	9	..	3	..	6	..	18	..	..	..	0.71	0.63
Latvia	135	314	6	12	106	266	76	10	3,932	..	0.94	0.90
Lebanon	321	..	183	..	300	..	13	..	..	..	0.71	0.43
Lesotho	11	..	4	..	3	..	..	..	..	..	0.73	0.68
Liberia	14	..	4	..	7	..	..	..	..	..	0.75	0.77
Libya	..	..	..	..	..	..	..	..	..	..	0.09	0.08
Lithuania	160	373	12	17	133	346	52	6	..	1,345	1.03	1.02
Macedonia, FYR	132	..	30	..	121	..	1	..	3,102	..	1.17	0.92
Madagascar	6	..	2	..	4	..	..	..	41,500	..	1.05	0.79
Malawi	4	..	4	..	2	..	..	..	..	..	0.95	0.88
Malaysia	124	..	26	79	101	..	167	238	..	..	0.37	0.22
Mali	3	..	2	..	2	..	..	..	..	..	1.16	0.90
Mauritania	10	..	3	..	7	..	..	..	..	..	0.80	0.59
Mauritius	59	117	35	69	44	86	54	104	..	78	0.74	0.56
Mexico	119	159	41	44	82	107	3	..	55,095	..	0.59	0.45
Moldova	53	92	17	26	48	74	45	22	..	691	0.45	0.31
Mongolia	21	41	1	2	6	26	22	10	340	2,093	0.61	0.67
Morocco	37	54	15	27	28	44	1	1	..	17,370	1.10	0.70
Mozambique	4	..	2	..	3	..	..	..	1,889	..	0.88	0.79
Myanmar	..	..	..	..	..	..	..	..	..	..	0.12	0.10
Namibia	71	82	1	2	39	38	1	1,877	1,896	2,317	0.68	0.65
Nepal	..	..	..	..	..	..	..	..	..	..	0.72	0.49
Netherlands	405	428	58	58	368	384	44	25	90,150	109,955	1.62	1.23
New Zealand	524	731	19	..	436	613	24	21	..	35,200	0.77	0.41
Nicaragua	19	37	5	10	10	16	3	5	108	441	0.69	0.64
Niger	6	..	4	..	5	..	..	..	178	..	1.02	0.91
Nigeria	30	..	21	..	12	..	5	..	..	..	0.39	0.45
Norway	458	520	22	26	380	417	48	61	..	33,482	1.61	1.44
Oman	130	..	9	..	83	..	3	..	..	..	0.31	0.26
Pakistan	6	8	4	..	4	7	8	11	..	234,515	0.62	0.41
Panama	75	..	18	..	60	..	2	..	..	..	0.54	0.48
Papua New Guinea	..	..	..	..	..	..	..	..	..	..	0.94	0.64
Paraguay	..	..	..	..	..	..	..	..	..	..	0.62	0.51
Peru	..	46	..	15	..	30	..	9	..	64	1.12	0.76
Philippines	10	34	4	13	7	9	6	18	6,189	9,548	0.52	0.34
Poland	168	307	18	32	138	259	36	21	59,608	138,100	1.20	1.09
Portugal	222	459	34	..	162	426	5	55	28,623	47,943	1.38	1.08
Puerto Rico	..	..	..	..	..	..	..	..	..	278,699	0.51	0.52

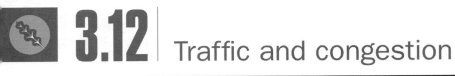

3.12 | Traffic and congestion

	Motor vehicles				Passenger cars		Two-wheelers		Road traffic		Fuel prices	
	per 1,000 people		per kilometer of road		per 1,000 people		per 1,000 people		million vehicle kilometers		$ per liter	
											Super	Diesel
	1990	2002ª	1990	2002	1990	2002	1990	2002	1990	2002	2004	2004
Romania	72	168	11	19	56	144	13	12	23,907	42,684	0.96	0.91
Russian Federation	87	176	14	48	65	132	..	43	..	59,522	0.55	0.45
Rwanda	2	..	1	..	1	..	..	..	..	..	0.98	0.99
Saudi Arabia	165	..	19	..	98	..	0	..	..	..	0.24	0.10
Senegal	11	14	6	2	8	11	0	0	..	4,013	1.10	0.90
Serbia and Montenegro	137	..	31	..	133	..	3	..	..	1,428	0.74	0.66
Sierra Leone	10	..	4	..	7	..	2	0	996	..	0.76	0.89
Singapore	130	..	142	..	89	..	40	..	..	..	0.89	0.55
Slovak Republic	194	279	57	35	163	247	61	9	..	534	1.17	1.19
Slovenia	306	481	42	47	289	438	8	25	5,620	9,744	1.12	1.11
Somalia	2	..	1	..	1	..	..	..	..	..	0.35	0.29
South Africa	139	..	26	..	97	94	8	4	..	..	0.81	0.80
Spain	360	539	43	33	309	441	79	80	100,981	224,370	1.21	1.10
Sri Lanka	21	34	4	..	7	..	24	49	3,468	15,630	0.72	0.41
Sudan	9	..	22	..	8	..	..	..	..	..	0.47	0.29
Swaziland	66	86	18	21	35	41	3	0	..	..	0.76	0.73
Sweden	464	500	29	21	426	452	11	34	61,040	72,000	1.51	1.37
Switzerland	491	549	46	56	449	507	114	102	48,660	59,007	1.29	1.37
Syrian Arab Republic	26	29	10	..	10	9	..	6	..	..	0.46	0.13
Tajikistan	3	..	1	..	0	..	..	..	..	1,730	0.67	0.59
Tanzania	5	..	2	..	1	..	..	..	..	..	0.93	0.87
Thailand	46	..	36	..	14	..	86	..	45,769	..	0.54	0.37
Togo	24	..	11	..	16	..	8	..	..	..	0.85	0.83
Trinidad and Tobago	..	..	..	..	..	..	..	..	..	..	0.35	0.24
Tunisia	48	79	19	..	23	53	..	1	..	19,231	0.68	0.39
Turkey	50	90	8	18	34	66	10	15	27,041	51,664	1.44	1.12
Turkmenistan	..	..	..	..	..	..	..	..	..	..	0.02	0.01
Uganda	2	..	..	..	1	..	0	3	..	..	1.02	0.88
Ukraine	63	135	20	..	63	108	..	0	59,500	12,190	0.55	0.44
United Arab Emirates	121	..	52	..	97	..	..	..	..	..	0.28	0.28
United Kingdom	400	391	64	62	341	384	14	3	399,000	462,400	1.56	1.60
United States	758	779	30	34	573	..	17	0	2,527,441	4,462,811	0.54	0.57
Uruguay	138	..	45	..	122	..	74	..	..	..	1.13	0.71
Uzbekistan	..	..	..	..	..	..	..	..	..	..	0.35	0.30
Venezuela, RB	..	..	..	..	..	..	..	..	..	..	0.04	0.02
Vietnam	..	..	..	..	..	..	45	..	..	..	0.48	0.32
West Bank and Gaza	..	..	..	..	..	..	..	..	..	..	1.17	0.70
Yemen, Rep.	34	..	8	..	14	..	..	..	8,681	..	0.19	0.09
Zambia	14	..	3	..	8	..	..	..	..	..	1.10	0.98
Zimbabwe	..	..	..	..	..	..	..	..	..	..	0.61	0.65
World	**118 w**	**135 w**			**91 w**	**105 w**					**0.78 m**	**0.64 m**
Low income	5	..			3	..					0.78	0.65
Middle income	38	56			25	42					0.68	0.55
Lower middle income	25	39			13	28					0.68	0.49
Upper middle income	149	196			114	153					0.76	0.58
Low & middle income	26	36			16	27					0.74	0.61
East Asia & Pacific	9	17			4	10					0.53	0.40
Europe & Central Asia	97	172			79	138					0.94	0.90
Latin America & Carib.	100	..			..	..					0.69	0.56
Middle East & N. Africa	48	..			31	..					0.31	0.14
South Asia	4	10			2	6					0.67	0.45
Sub-Saharan Africa	21	..			14	..					0.85	0.77
High income	505	601			396	436					1.29	1.10
Europe EMU	429	..			379	483					1.42	1.23

a. Data are for 2002 or most recent year available.

About the data

Traffic congestion in urban areas constrains economic productivity, damages people's health, and degrades the quality of their lives. The particulate air pollution emitted by motor vehicles—the dust and soot in exhaust—is proving to be far more damaging to human health than was once believed. (For information on particulate matter and other air pollutants, see table 3.13.)

In recent years ownership of passenger cars has increased, and the expansion of economic activity has led to the transport by road of more goods and services over greater distances (see table 5.9). These developments have increased demand for roads and vehicles, adding to urban congestion, air pollution, health hazards, traffic accidents, and injuries.

Congestion, the most visible cost of expanding vehicle ownership, is reflected in the indicators in the table. Other relevant indicators—such as average vehicle speed in major cities or the cost of traffic congestion, which takes a heavy toll on economic productivity—are not included because data are incomplete or difficult to compare. The data in the table—except for those on fuel prices—are compiled by the International Road Federation (IRF) through questionnaires sent to national organizations. The IRF uses a hierarchy of sources to gather as much information as possible. The primary sources are national road associations. Where such an association lacks data or does not respond, other agencies are contacted, including road directorates, ministries of transport or public works, and central statistical offices. As a result, the compiled data are of uneven quality. The coverage of each indicator may differ across countries because of differences in definitions. Comparability also is limited when time-series data are reported. Moreover, the data do not capture the quality or age of vehicles or the condition or width of roads. Thus comparisons over time and between countries should be made with caution.

The data on fuel prices are compiled by the German Agency for Technical Cooperation (GTZ) from its global network of regional offices and representatives as well as other sources, including the Allgemeiner Deutscher Automobil Club (for Europe) and a project of the Latin American Energy Organization (OLADE, for Latin America). Local prices have been converted to U.S. dollars using the exchange rate on the survey date as listed in the international monetary table of the *Financial Times*. For countries with multiple exchange rates the market, parallel, or black market rate was used rather than the official exchange rate.

Definitions

• **Motor vehicles** include cars, buses, and freight vehicles but not two-wheelers. Population figures refer to the midyear population in the year for which data are available. Roads refer to motorways, highways, main or national roads, and secondary or regional roads. A motorway is a road specially designed and built for motor traffic that separates the traffic flowing in opposite directions. • **Passenger cars** refer to road motor vehicles, other than two-wheelers, intended for the carriage of passengers and designed to seat no more than nine people (including the driver). • **Two-wheelers** refer to mopeds and motorcycles. • **Road traffic** is the number of vehicles multiplied by the average distances they travel. • **Fuel prices** refer to the pump prices of the most widely sold grade of gasoline and of diesel fuel. Prices have been converted from the local currency to U.S. dollars (see *About the data*).

3.12a

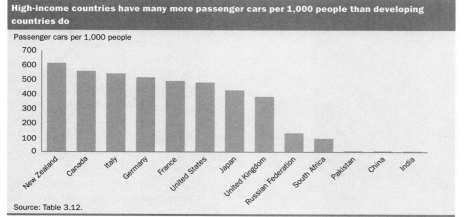

High-income countries have many more passenger cars per 1,000 people than developing countries do

Passenger cars per 1,000 people

Source: Table 3.12.

Data sources

The data on vehicles and traffic are from the IRF's electronic files and its annual *World Road Statistics*. The data on fuel prices are from the GTZ's electronic files.

City		City population	Particulate matter	Sulfur dioxide	Nitrogen dioxide
		thousands **2005**	micrograms per cubic meter **1999**	micrograms per cubic meter **1995–2001[a]**	micrograms per cubic meter **1995–2001[a]**
Argentina	Cordoba City	1,592	52	..	97
Australia	Melbourne	3,663	15	..	30
	Perth	1,484	15	5	19
	Sydney	4,388	22	28	81
Austria	Vienna	2,190	39	14	42
Belgium	Brussels	1,027	31	20	48
Brazil	Rio de Janeiro	11,469	40	129	..
	Sao Paulo	18,333	46	43	83
Bulgaria	Sofia	1,045	83	39	122
Canada	Montreal	3,511	22	10	42
	Toronto	5,060	26	17	43
	Vancouver	2,125	15	14	37
Chile	Santiago	5,623	73	29	81
China	Anshan	1,459	99	115	88
	Beijing	10,849	106	90	122
	Changchun	3,093	88	21	64
	Chengdu	3,478	103	77	74
	Chongqing	4,975	147	340	70
	Dalian	2,709	60	61	100
	Guangzhu	976	74	57	136
	Guiyang	2,467	84	424	53
	Harbin	2,898	91	23	30
	Jinan	2,654	112	132	45
	Kunming	1,748	84	19	33
	Lanzhou	1,788	109	102	104
	Liupanshui	2,118	70	102	..
	Nanchang	1,742	94	69	29
	Pinxiang	1,563	80	75	..
	Quingdao	2,431	..	190	64
	Shanghai	12,665	87	53	73
	Shenyang	4,916	120	99	73
	Taiyuan	2,516	105	211	55
	Tianjin	9,346	149	82	50
	Urumqi	1,467[b]	61	60	70
	Wuhan	6,003	94	40	43
	Zhengzhou	2,250	116	63	95
	Zibo	2,775	88	198	43
Colombia	Bogota	5,442[b]	33	..	..
Croatia	Zagreb	908[b]	39	31	..
Cuba	Havana	2,192	28	1	5
Czech Republic	Prague	1,164	27	14	33
Denmark	Copenhagen	1,091	24	7	54
Ecuador	Guayaquil	2,387	26	15	..
	Quito	1,514	34	22	..
Egypt, Arab Rep.	Cairo	11,146	178	69	..
Finland	Helsinki	1,103	22	4	35
France	Paris	9,854	15	14	57
Germany	Berlin	3,328	25	18	26
	Frankfurt	668[b]	22	11	45
	Munich	2,318	22	8	53
Ghana	Accra	1,970	31	..	..
Greece	Athens	3,238	50	34	64
Hungary	Budapest	1,670	26	39	51
Iceland	Reykjavik	164[b]	21	5	42
India	Ahmedabad	5,171	104	30	21
	Bangalore	6,532	56	..	..

About the data

In many towns and cities exposure to air pollution is the main environmental threat to human health. Long-term exposure to high levels of soot and small particles in the air contributes to a wide range of health effects, including respiratory diseases, lung cancer, and heart disease. Particulate pollution, on its own or in combination with sulfur dioxide, leads to an enormous burden of ill health.

Emissions of sulfur dioxide and nitrogen oxides lead to the deposition of acid rain and other acidic compounds over long distances. Acid deposition changes the chemical balance of soils and can lead to the leaching of trace minerals and nutrients critical to trees and plants.

Where coal is the primary fuel for power plants, steel mills, industrial boilers, and domestic heating, the result is usually high levels of urban air pollution—especially particulates and sometimes sulfur dioxide—and, if the sulfur content of the coal is high, widespread acid deposition. Where coal is not an important primary fuel or is used in plants with effective dust control, the worst emissions of air pollutants stem from the combustion of petroleum products.

The data on sulfur dioxide and nitrogen dioxide concentrations are based on reports from urban monitoring sites. Annual means (measured in micrograms per cubic meter) are average concentrations observed at these sites. Coverage is not comprehensive because not all cities have monitoring systems.

The data on concentrations of particulate matter are estimates, for selected cities, of average annual concentrations in residential areas away from air pollution "hotspots," such as industrial districts and transport corridors. The data have been extracted from a complete set of estimates developed by the World Bank's Development Research Group and Environment Department in a study of annual ambient concentrations of particulate matter in world cities with populations exceeding 100,000 (Pandey and others 2003).

Pollutant concentrations are sensitive to local conditions, and even in the same city different monitoring sites may register different concentrations. Thus these data should be considered only a general indication of air quality in each city, and cross-country comparisons should be made with caution. The current World Health Organization (WHO) air quality guidelines for annual mean concentrations are 50 micrograms per cubic meter for sulfur dioxide and 40 micrograms for nitrogen dioxide. The WHO has set no guidelines for particulate matter concentrations below which there are no appreciable health effects.

City		City population	Particulate matter	Sulfur dioxide	Nitrogen dioxide
		thousands **2005**	micrograms per cubic meter **1999**	micrograms per cubic meter **1995–2001**[a]	micrograms per cubic meter **1995–2001**[a]
India	Calcutta	14,299	153	49	34
	Chennai	6,915	..	15	17
	Delhi	15,334	187	24	41
	Hyderabad	6,146	51	12	17
	Kanpur	3,040	136	15	14
	Lucknow	2,589	136	26	25
	Mumbai	18,336	79	33	39
	Nagpur	2,359	69	6	13
	Pune	4,485	58		
Indonesia	Jakarta	13,194	103	..	..
Iran, Islamic Rep.	Tehran	7,352	71	209	..
Ireland	Dublin	1,033	23	20	..
Italy	Milan	4,007	36	31	248
	Rome	2,628	35	..	..
	Torino	969[b]	53	..	..
Japan	Osaka	2,626[b]	39	19	63
	Tokyo	35,327	43	18	68
	Yokohama	3,366[b]	32	100	13
Kenya	Nairobi	2,819	49	..	..
Korea, Rep	Pusan	3,527	43	60	51
	Seoul	9,592	45	44	60
	Taegu	2,510	49	81	62
Malaysia	Kuala Lumpur	1,392	24	24	..
Mexico	Mexico City	19,013	69	74	130
Netherlands	Amsterdam	1,157	37	10	58
New Zealand	Auckland	1,152	15	3	20
Norway	Oslo	808	23	8	43
Philippines	Manila	10,432[b]	60	33	..
Poland	Lodz	944	45	21	43
	Warsaw	2,204	49	16	32
Portugal	Lisbon	1,977	30	8	52
Romania	Bucharest	1,764	25	10	71
Russian Federation	Moscow	10,672	27	109	..
	Omsk	1,132	28	20	34
Singapore	Singapore	4,372	41	20	30
Slovak Republic	Bratislava	456[b]	22	21	27
South Africa	Capetown	3,103	15	21	72
	Durban	2,643	29	31	..
	Johannesburg	3,288	30	19	31
Spain	Barcelona	4,424	43	11	43
	Madrid	5,145	37	24	66
Sweden	Stockholm	1,729	15	3	20
Switzerland	Zurich	984	24	11	39
Thailand	Bangkok	6,604	82	11	23
Turkey	Ankara	3,594	53	55	46
	Istanbul	9,760[b]	62	120	..
Ukraine	Kiev	2,623	45	14	51
United Kingdom	Birmingham	2,215	17	9	45
	London	7,615	23	25	77
	Manchester	2,193	19	26	49
United States	Chicago	8,711	27	14	57
	Los Angeles	12,146	38	9	74
	New York	18,498	23	26	79
Venezuela, RB	Caracas	3,276	18	33	57

a. Data are for the most recent year available. b. Data are for 2000.

Definitions

• **City population** is the number of residents of the city or metropolitan area as defined by national authorities and reported to the United Nations. • **Particulate matter** refers to fine suspended particulates less than 10 microns in diameter that are capable of penetrating deep into the respiratory tract and causing significant health damage. The state of a country's technology and pollution controls is an important determinant of particulate matter concentrations. • **Sulfur dioxide** is an air pollutant produced when fossil fuels containing sulfur are burned. It contributes to acid rain and can damage human health, particularly that of the young and the elderly. • **Nitrogen dioxide** is a poisonous, pungent gas formed when nitric oxide combines with hydrocarbons and sunlight, producing a photochemical reaction. These conditions occur in both natural and anthropogenic activities. Nitrogen dioxide is emitted by bacteria, motor vehicles, industrial activities, nitrogenous fertilizers, combustion of fuels and biomass, and aerobic decomposition of organic matter in soils and oceans.

Data sources

City population data are from the United Nations Population Division. The data on sulfur dioxide and nitrogen dioxide concentrations are from the WHO's Healthy Cities Air Management Information System and the World Resources Institute, which relies on various national sources as well as, among others, the Organisation for Economic Co-operation and Development's (OECD) *OECD Environmental Data Compendium 1999*, the U.S. Environmental Protection Agency's *National Air Quality and Emissions Trends Report 1995*, the Aerometric Information Retrieval System (AIRS) Executive International database, and the United Nations Centre for Human Settlements' (UNCHS) Urban Indicators database. The data on particulate matter concentrations are from a recent World Bank study by Kiran D. Pandey, Kathrine Bolt, Uwe Deichman, Kirk Hamilton, Bart Ostro, and David Wheeler, "The Human Cost of Air Pollution: New Estimates for Developing Countries" (2003).

3.14 | Government commitment

	Environ-mental strategies or action plans	Biodiversity assessments, strategies, or action plans	Participation in treaties					
			Climate change[b]	Ozone layer	CFC control	Law of the Sea[c]	Biological diversity[b]	Kyoto Protocol
Afghanistan	..	..	2002	2004	2004	..	2002	..
Albania	1993	..	1995	1999	1999	2003[f]	1994[f]	..
Algeria	2001	..	1994	1992	1992	1996	1995	..
Angola	..	..	2000	2000	2000	1994	1998	..
Argentina	1992	..	1994	1990	1990	1995	1994	2001
Armenia	..	..	1994	1999	1999	2002[f]	1993[d]	2003[f]
Australia	1992	1994	1994	1987	1989	1994	1993	..
Austria	..	..	1994	1987	1989	1995	1994	2002
Azerbaijan	1998	..	1995	1996	1996	..	2000[e]	2000[f]
Bangladesh	1991	1990	1994	1990	1990	2001	1994	2001[f]
Belarus	..	..	2000	1986	1988	..	1993	..
Belgium	..	..	1996	1988	1988	1998	1996	2002
Benin	1993	..	1994	1993	1993	1997	1994	2002[f]
Bolivia	1994	1988	1995	1994	1994	1995	1994	1999
Bosnia and Herzegovina	..	..	2000	1992	1992	1994[g]	2002[f]	..
Botswana	1990	1991	1994	1991	1991	1994	1995	2003[f]
Brazil	..	1988	1994	1990	1990	1994	1994	2002
Bulgaria	..	1994	1995	1990	1990	1996	1996	2002
Burkina Faso	1993	..	1994	1989	1989	..	1993	..
Burundi	1994	1989	1997	1997	1997	..	1997	2001[f]
Cambodia	1999	..	1996	2001	2001	..	1995[f]	2002[f]
Cameroon	..	1989	1995	1989	1989	1994	1994	2002[f]
Canada	1990	1994	1994	1986	1988	2003	1992	2002
Central African Republic	..	..	1995	1993	1993	..	1995	..
Chad	1990	..	1994	1989	1994	..	1994	..
Chile	..	1993	1995	1990	1990	1997	1994	2002
China	1994	1994	1994	1989	1991	1996	1993	2002[e]
Hong Kong, China	..	..	..	..	..	..	..	..
Colombia	1998	1988	1995	1990	1993	..	1994	2001[f]
Congo, Dem. Rep.	..	1990	1995	1994	1994	1995	1996	..
Congo, Rep.	..	1990	1997	1994	1994	..	1994	..
Costa Rica	1990	1992	1994	1991	1991	1994	1994	2002
Côte d'Ivoire	1994	1991	1995	1993	1993	1994	1994	..
Croatia	2001	2000	1996	1991	1991	1994[g]	1996	..
Cuba	..	..	1994	1992	1992	1994	1994	2002
Czech Republic	1994	..	1994	1993	1993	1996	1993[e]	2001[e]
Denmark	1994	..	1994	1988	1988	2004	1993	2002
Dominican Republic	..	1995	1999	1993	1993	..	1996	2002[f]
Ecuador	1993	1995	1994	1990	1990	..	1993	2000
Egypt, Arab Rep.	1992	1988	1995	1988	1988	1994	1994	..
El Salvador	1994	1988	1996	1992	1992	..	1994	1998
Eritrea	1995	..	1995	..	..	..	1996[f]	..
Estonia	1998	..	1994	1996	1996	..	1994	2002
Ethiopia	1994	1991	1994	1994	1994	..	1994	..
Finland	1995	..	1994	1986	1988	1996	1994[d]	2002
France	1990	..	1994	1987	1988	1996	1994	2002[e]
Gabon	..	1990	1998	1994	1994	1998	1997	..
Gambia, The	1992	1989	1994	1990	1990	1994	1994	2001[f]
Georgia	1998	..	1994	1996	1996	1996[f]	1994[f]	1999[f]
Germany	..	..	1994	1988	1988	1994[f]	1993	2002
Ghana	1992	1988	1995	1989	1989	1994	1994	2003[f]
Greece	..	..	1994	1988	1988	1995	1994	2002
Guatemala	1994	1988	1996	1987	1989	1997	1995	1999
Guinea	1994	1988	1994	1992	1992	1994	1993	2000[f]
Guinea-Bissau	1993	1991	1996	2002	2002	1994	1995	..
Haiti	1999	..	1996	2000	2000	1996	1996	..

3.14a

The Kyoto Protocol on climate change

The Kyoto Protocol was adopted at the third conference of the parties to the United Nations Framework Convention on Climate Change, held in Kyoto, Japan, in December 1997 and was open for signature from March 1998 onward.

At the heart of the protocol are its legally binding greenhouse gas emissions targets for industrial and transition economies (known as "Annex I Parties"), which accounted for at least 55 percent of carbon dioxide emissions in 1990. The emissions targets amount to an aggregate reduction of greenhouse gas emissions by all Annex I Parties of at least 5 percent from 1990 levels during the commitment period, 2008–12. All Annex I Parties have individual emissions targets, which were decided in Kyoto after intensive negotiation and are listed in the protocol's Annex B.

The protocol's rules focus on:
- Commitments, including legally binding emissions targets and general commitments.
- Implementation, including domestic steps and three novel implementing mechanisms.
- Minimization of impacts on developing countries, including use of an Adaptation Fund.
- Accounting, reporting, and review, including in-depth review of national reporting.
- Compliance, including a Compliance Committee to assess and deal with problem cases.

In addition to emissions targets for Annex I Parties, the Kyoto Protocol also contains a set of general commitments that apply to all parties, such as:
- Improving the quality of emissions data.
- Mounting national mitigation and adaptation programs.
- Promoting environmentally friendly technology transfer.
- Cooperating in scientific research and international climate observation networks.
- Supporting education, training, public awareness, and capacity building initiatives.

The Protocol is subject to ratification, acceptance, approval, or accession by Parties to the Convention, which bind the parties to the protocol's commitments, once the protocol comes into force.

The table contains the latest information on dates of signature and ratification from the Secretary-General of the United Nations, the depository of the Kyoto Protocol. The dates are those of the receipt of the instrument of ratification, acceptance, approval, or accession. With a total of 141 countries accounting for at least 55 percent of global greenhouse gas emissions, the Kyoto Protocol finally came into force and became a legally binding treaty on February 16, 2005.

	Environmental strategies or action plans	Biodiversity assessments, strategies, or action plans	Participation in treaties					
			Climate change[b]	Ozone layer	CFC control	Law of the Sea[c]	Biological diversity[b]	Kyoto Protocol
Honduras	1993	..	1996	1993	1993	1994	1995	2000
Hungary	1995	..	1994	1988	1989	2002	1994	2002[f]
India	1993	1994	1994	1991	1992	1995	1994	2002[f]
Indonesia	1993	1993	1994	1992	1992	1994	1994	2004
Iran, Islamic Rep.	..	..	1996	1990	1990	..	1996	..
Iraq	..	..	..	..	..	1994	..	..
Ireland	..	..	1994	1988	1988	1996	1996	2002
Israel	..	..	1996	1992	1992	..	1995	2004
Italy	..	..	1994	1988	1988	1995	1994	2002
Jamaica	1994	..	1995	1993	1993	1994	1995	1999[f]
Japan	..	..	1994	1988	1988	1996	1993[d]	2002[d]
Jordan	1991	..	1994	1989	1989	1995[f]	1993	2003[f]
Kazakhstan	..	..	1995	1998	1998	..	1994	..
Kenya	1994	1992	1994	1988	1988	1994	1994	..
Korea, Dem. Rep.	..	..	1995	1995	1995	..	1994[e]	..
Korea, Rep.	..	..	1994	1992	1992	1996	1994	2002
Kuwait	..	..	1995	1992	1992	1994	2002	..
Kyrgyz Republic	1995	..	2000	2000	2000	..	1996[e]	2003[f]
Lao PDR	1995	..	1995	1998	1998	1998	1996[e]	2003[f]
Latvia	..	..	1995	1995	1995	..	1995	2002
Lebanon	..	..	1995	1993	1993	1995	1994	..
Lesotho	1989	..	1995	1994	1994	..	1995	2000[f]
Liberia	..	..	2003	1996	1996	..	2000	2002[f]
Libya	..	..	1999	1990	1990	..	2001	..
Lithuania	..	..	1995	1995	1995	2003[f]	1996	2003
Macedonia, FYR	..	..	1998	1994	1994	1994[g]	1997[f]	2004[f]
Madagascar	1988	1991	1999	1996	1996	2001	1996	2003[f]
Malawi	1994	..	1994	1991	1991	..	1994	2001[f]
Malaysia	1991	1988	1994	1989	1989	1996	1994	2002
Mali	..	1989	1995	1994	1994	1994	1995	2002
Mauritania	1988	..	1994	1994	1994	1996	1996	..
Mauritius	1990	..	1994	1992	1992	1994	1992	2001[f]
Mexico	..	1988	1994	1987	1988	1994	1993	2000
Moldova	2002	..	1995	1996	1996	..	1995	2003[f]
Mongolia	1995	..	1994	1996	1996	1996	1993	1999[f]
Morocco	..	1988	1996	1995	1995	..	1995	2002[f]
Mozambique	1994	..	1995	1994	1994	1997	1995	2005[f]
Myanmar	..	1989	1995	1993	1993	1996	1995	2003[f]
Namibia	1992	..	1995	1993	1993	1994	1997	2003[f]
Nepal	1993	..	1994	1994	1994	1998	1993	..
Netherlands	1994	..	1994	1988	1988	1996	1994[d]	2002[f]
New Zealand	1994	..	1994	1987	1988	1996	1993	2002
Nicaragua	1994	..	1996	1993	1993	2000	1995	1999
Niger	..	1991	1995	1992	1992	..	1995	2004
Nigeria	1990	1992	1994	1988	1988	1994	1994	..
Norway	..	1994	1994	1986	1988	1996	1993	2002
Oman	..	..	1995	1999	1999	1994	1995	2005[f]
Pakistan	1994	1991	1994	1992	1992	1997	1994	..
Panama	1990	..	1995	1989	1989	1996	1995	1999
Papua New Guinea	1992	1993	1994	1992	1992	1997	1993	2002
Paraguay	..	..	1994	1992	1992	1994	1994	1999
Peru	..	1988	1994	1989	1993	..	1993	2002
Philippines	1989	1989	1994	1991	1991	1994	1993	2003
Poland	1993	1991	1994	1990	1990	1998	1996	2002
Portugal	1995	..	1994	1988	1988	1997	1993	2002[e]
Puerto Rico	..	..	..	..	..	..	..	..

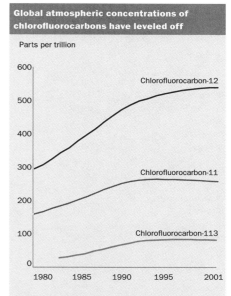

3.14b

Global atmospheric concentrations of chlorofluorocarbons have leveled off

Parts per trillion

Chlorofluorocarbon-12

Chlorofluorocarbon-11

Chlorofluorocarbon-113

Note: Chlorofluorocarbon-11, chlorofluorocarbon-12, and chlorofluorocarbon-113 are potent depletors of stratospheric ozone.
Source: World Resources Institute and others 2002.

	Environmental strategies or action plans	Biodiversity assessments, strategies, or action plans	Participation in treaties					
			Climate change[b]	Ozone layer	CFC control	Law of the Sea[c]	Biological diversity[b]	Kyoto Protocol
Romania	1995	..	1994	1993	1993	1996	1994	2001
Russian Federation	1999	1994	1995	1986	1988	1997	1995	2004
Rwanda	1991	..	1998	2001	2001	..	1996	2004[f]
Saudi Arabia	..	..	1995	1993	1993	1996	2001[e]	2005[f]
Senegal	1984	1991	1995	1993	1993	1994	1994	2001[f]
Serbia and Montenegro	..	..	2001	1992	1992	2001[g]	2002	..
Sierra Leone	1994	..	1995	2001	2001	1994	1994[e]	..
Singapore	1993	1995	1997	1989	1989	1994	1995	..
Slovak Republic	..	..	1994	1993	1993	1996	1994[e]	2002
Slovenia	1994	..	1996	1992	1992	1995[g]	1996	2002
Somalia			..	2001	2001	1994	..	..
South Africa	1993	..	1997	1990	1990	1997	1995	2002[f]
Spain	..	..	1994	1988	1988	1997	1995	2002
Sri Lanka	1994	1991	1994	1989	1989	1994	1994	2002[f]
Sudan	..	..	1994	1993	1993	1994	1995	2004
Swaziland			1997	1992	1992	..	1994	..
Sweden	..	..	1994	1986	1988	1996	1993	2002
Switzerland	..	..	1994	1987	1988	..	1994	2003
Syrian Arab Republic	1999	..	1996	1989	1989	..	1996	..
Tajikistan	..	..	1998	1996	1998	..	1997[e]	..
Tanzania	1994	1988	1996	1993	1993	1994	1996	2002[f]
Thailand	..	..	1995	1989	1989	..	2004	2002
Togo	1991	..	1995	1991	1991	1994	1995[d]	2004[f]
Trinidad and Tobago	..	..	1994	1989	1989	1994	1996	1999
Tunisia	1994	1988	1994	1989	1989	1994	1993	2003[f]
Turkey	1998	..	2004	1991	1991	..	1997	..
Turkmenistan	..	..	1995	1993	1993	..	1996[e]	1999
Uganda	1994	1988	1994	1988	1988	1994	1993	2002[f]
Ukraine	1999	..	1997	1986	1988	1999	1995	2004
United Arab Emirates	..	..	1996	1989	1989	..	2000	2005[f]
United Kingdom	1995	1994	1994	1987	1988	1997[f]	1994	2002
United States	1995	1995	1994	1986	1988	..	..	..
Uruguay	..	..	1994	1989	1991	1994	1993	2001
Uzbekistan	..	..	1994	1993	1993	..	1995[e]	1999
Venezuela, RB	..	..	1995	1988	1989	..	1994	..
Vietnam	..	1993	1995	1994	1994	1994	1994	2002
West Bank and Gaza	..	..	..	..	..	..	..	..
Yemen, Rep.	1996	1992	1996	1996	1996	1994	1996	2004[f]
Zambia	1994	..	1994	1990	1990	1994	1993	..
Zimbabwe	1987	..	1994	1992	1992	1994	1994	..

a. Ratification of the treaty. b. The years shown refer to the year the treaty entered into force in that country. c. Convention became effective November 16, 1994. d. Acceptance. e. Approval. f. Accession. g. Succession.

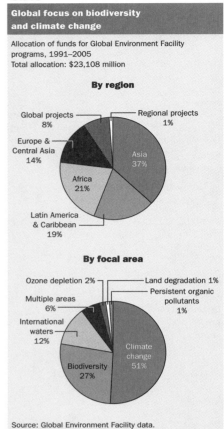

3.14c

Global focus on biodiversity and climate change

Allocation of funds for Global Environment Facility programs, 1991–2005
Total allocation: $23,108 million

By region

- Global projects 8%
- Regional projects 1%
- Asia 37%
- Europe & Central Asia 14%
- Africa 21%
- Latin America & Caribbean 19%

By focal area

- Ozone depletion 2%
- Land degradation 1%
- Multiple areas 6%
- Persistent organic pollutants 1%
- International waters 12%
- Climate change 51%
- Biodiversity 27%

Source: Global Environment Facility data.

National environmental strategies and participation in international treaties on environmental issues provide some evidence of government commitment to sound environmental management. But the signing of these treaties does not always imply ratification, nor does it guarantee that governments will comply with treaty obligations.

In many countries efforts to halt environmental degradation have failed, primarily because governments have neglected to make this issue a priority, a reflection of competing claims on scarce resources. To address this problem, many countries are preparing national environmental strategies—some focusing narrowly on environmental issues, and others integrating environmental, economic, and social concerns. Among such initiatives are conservation strategies and environmental action plans. Some countries have also prepared country environmental profiles and biodiversity strategies and profiles.

National conservation strategies—promoted by the World Conservation Union (IUCN)—provide a comprehensive, cross-sectoral analysis of conservation and resource management issues to help integrate environmental concerns with the development process. Such strategies discuss current and future needs, institutional capabilities, prevailing technical conditions, and the status of natural resources in a country.

National environmental action plans, supported by the World Bank and other development agencies, describe a country's main environmental concerns, identify the principal causes of environmental problems, and formulate policies and actions to deal with them (box 3.14a). These plans are a continuing process in which governments develop comprehensive environmental policies, recommend specific actions, and outline the investment strategies, legislation, and institutional arrangements required to implement them.

Biodiversity profiles—prepared by the World Conservation Monitoring Centre and the IUCN—provide basic background on species diversity, protected areas, major ecosystems and habitat types, and legislative and administrative support. In an effort to establish a scientific baseline for measuring progress in biodiversity conservation, the United Nations Environment Programme (UNEP) coordinates global biodiversity assessments.

To address global issues, many governments have also signed international treaties and agreements launched in the wake of the 1972 United Nations Conference on Human Environment in Stockholm and the 1992 United Nations Conference on Environment and Development (the Earth Summit) in Rio de Janeiro, which produced Agenda 21—an array of actions to address environmental challenges:

- The Framework Convention on Climate Change aims to stabilize atmospheric concentrations of greenhouse gases at levels that will prevent human activities from interfering dangerously with the global climate.
- The Vienna Convention for the Protection of the Ozone Layer aims to protect human health and the environment by promoting research on the effects of changes in the ozone layer and on alternative substances (such as substitutes for chlorofluorocarbons) and technologies, monitoring the ozone layer, and taking measures to control the activities that produce adverse effects.
- The Montreal Protocol for Chlorofluorocarbon Control requires that countries help protect the earth from excessive ultraviolet radiation by cutting chlorofluorocarbon consumption by 20 percent over their 1986 level by 1994 and by 50 percent over their 1986 level by 1999, with allowances for increases in consumption by developing countries.
- The United Nations Convention on the Law of the Sea, which became effective in November 1994, establishes a comprehensive legal regime for seas and oceans, establishes rules for environmental standards and enforcement provisions, and develops international rules and national legislation to prevent and control marine pollution.
- The Convention on Biological Diversity promotes conservation of biodiversity through scientific and technological cooperation among countries, access to financial and genetic resources, and transfer of ecologically sound technologies.

But 10 years after Rio the World Summit on Sustainable Development in Johannesburg recognized that many of the proposed actions have yet to materialize. To help developing countries comply with their obligations under these agreements, the Global Environment Facility (GEF) was created to focus on global improvement in biodiversity, climate change, international waters, and ozone layer depletion. The UNEP, United Nations Development Programme (UNDP), and the World Bank manage the GEF according to the policies of its governing body of country representatives. The World Bank is responsible for the GEF Trust Fund and is chair of the GEF.

- **Environmental strategies and action plans** provide a comprehensive, cross-sectoral analysis of conservation and resource management issues to help integrate environmental concerns with the development process. They include national conservation strategies, national environmental action plans, national environmental management strategies, and national sustainable development strategies. The year shown for a country refers to the year in which a strategy or action plan was adopted. • **Biodiversity assessments, strategies, and action plans** include biodiversity profiles (see *About the data*). • **Participation in treaties** covers five international treaties (see *About the data*). • **Climate change** refers to the Framework Convention on Climate Change (signed in New York in 1992). • **Ozone layer** refers to the Vienna Convention for the Protection of the Ozone Layer (signed in 1985). • **CFC control** refers to the Montreal Protocol for Chlorofluorocarbon Control (formally, the Protocol on Substances That Deplete the Ozone Layer, signed in 1987). • **Law of the Sea** refers to the United Nations Convention on the Law of the Sea (signed in Montego Bay, Jamaica, in 1982). • **Biological diversity** refers to the Convention on Biological Diversity (signed at the Earth Summit in Rio de Janeiro in 1992). The year shown for a country refers to the year in which a treaty entered into force in that country. • **Kyoto Protocol** refers to the protocol on climate change adopted at the third conference of the parties to the United Nations Framework Convention on Climate Change, held in Kyoto, Japan, in December 1997 (for more details see box 3.14a).

Data sources

The data are from the Secretariat of the United Nations Framework Convention on Climate Change, the Ozone Secretariat of the UNEP, the World Resources Institute, the UNEP, the U.S. National Aeronautics and Space Administration's Socioeconomic Data and Applications Center, and Center for International Earth Science Information Network.

	Gross national savings	Consumption of fixed capital	Net national savings	Education expenditure	Energy depletion	Mineral depletion	Net forest depletion	Carbon dioxide damage	Particulate emission damage	Adjusted net savings
	% of GNI 2003	% of GNI 2003	% of GNI 2003	% of GNI 2003	% of GNI 2003	% of GNI 2003	% of GNI 2003	% of GNI 2003	% of GNI 2003	% of GNI 2003
Afghanistan	..	..	..	..	..	..	..	..	..	..
Albania	18.2	9.6	8.6	2.8	0.9	0.0	0.0	0.3	0.1	10.2
Algeria	43.1	11.0	32.1	4.5	37.5	0.1	0.1	1.2	0.7	−2.9
Angola	22.2	11.0	11.2	4.4	43.6	0.0	0.0	0.5	..	−28.5[a]
Argentina	21.9	11.3	10.6	3.2	6.3	0.1	0.0	0.6	1.6	5.2
Armenia	17.2	8.6	8.6	1.8	0.0	0.1	0.0	1.1	2.0	7.3
Australia	19.7	16.1	3.6	4.5	1.3	1.4	0.0	0.5	0.1	4.9
Austria	22.7	14.5	8.2	5.6	0.1	0.0	0.0	0.2	0.2	13.3
Azerbaijan	22.2	15.0	7.2	3.0	45.4	0.0	0.0	5.0	1.0	−41.2
Bangladesh	28.4	5.8	22.6	1.3	2.0	0.0	0.8	0.4	0.3	20.5
Belarus	21.2	9.3	12.0	5.4	2.0	0.0	0.0	3.0	0.0	12.4
Belgium	24.0	14.4	9.6	3.0	0.0	0.0	0.0	0.2	0.2	12.2
Benin	4.8	8.2	−3.4	2.7	0.0	0.0	1.1	0.3	0.3	−2.4
Bolivia	12.0	9.2	2.8	4.8	8.7	0.9	0.0	1.2	0.7	−3.8
Bosnia and Herzegovina	10.3	9.3	1.0	..	0.1	0.0	0.0	2.0	0.4	..
Botswana	35.6	11.8	23.8	5.6	0.0	0.3	0.0	0.4	..	28.7[a]
Brazil	19.1	10.8	8.4	3.9	3.1	1.1	0.0	0.4	0.2	7.4
Bulgaria	13.3	10.5	2.8	3.0	0.1	0.4	0.0	1.8	2.1	1.3
Burkina Faso	6.6	7.6	−1.0	2.4	0.0	0.0	1.0	0.2	0.5	−0.2
Burundi	22.4	5.9	16.5	4.1	0.0	0.1	14.0	0.3	0.1	6.2
Cambodia	21.0	7.8	13.3	2.0	0.0	0.0	0.9	0.1	0.1	14.2
Cameroon	11.9	9.2	2.7	2.3	5.2	0.0	0.0	0.5	0.7	−1.4
Canada	20.5	13.0	7.5	6.9	4.7	0.1	0.0	0.4	0.2	9.0
Central African Republic	11.6	7.5	4.2	1.6	0.0	0.0	0.0	0.1	0.4	5.2
Chad	11.9	8.3	3.7	1.4	0.0	0.0	0.0	0.0	..	5.1[a]
Chile	24.5	10.1	14.4	3.8	0.4	5.9	0.0	0.6	1.0	10.3
China	47.9	9.2	38.7	2.0	2.9	0.2	0.0	2.2	1.0	34.5
Hong Kong, China	34.3	12.5	21.8	2.8	0.0	0.0	0.0	0.2	0.0	24.5
Colombia	14.6	10.2	4.4	3.1	7.7	0.3	0.0	0.6	0.1	−1.1
Congo, Dem. Rep.	..	6.6	..	0.9	2.2	0.0	0.0	0.3	0.0	..
Congo, Rep.	29.8	11.9	17.9	5.9	49.3	0.2	0.0	0.6	..	−26.3[a]
Costa Rica	15.3	6.0	9.3	4.9	0.0	0.0	0.3	0.3	0.3	13.4
Côte d'Ivoire	14.8	9.2	5.6	4.5	2.6	0.0	0.6	0.4	0.6	5.8
Croatia	22.2	12.0	10.2	..	1.1	0.0	0.0	0.6	0.3	..
Cuba	..	..	..	6.1	..	..	..	..	..	..
Czech Republic	22.4	12.5	9.9	4.0	0.1	0.0	0.0	0.9	0.1	12.8
Denmark	23.5	15.2	8.3	7.9	0.7	0.0	0.0	0.2	0.1	15.2
Dominican Republic	29.4	5.5	23.9	2.3	0.0	0.5	0.0	1.1	0.2	24.3
Ecuador	25.1	10.6	14.5	3.2	15.1	0.0	0.0	0.6	0.1	1.9
Egypt, Arab Rep.	20.1	9.3	10.9	4.4	7.7	0.1	0.2	1.1	1.4	4.8
El Salvador	16.4	9.8	6.6	2.4	0.0	0.0	0.5	0.3	0.2	8.0
Eritrea	3.0	5.6	−2.5	1.4	0.0	0.0	0.0	0.4	0.5	−2.0
Estonia	19.2	14.6	4.6	6.3	0.6	0.0	0.0	1.8	0.2	8.3
Ethiopia	18.4	5.9	12.5	4.0	0.0	0.1	12.6	0.5	0.3	2.9
Finland	24.5	16.2	8.2	7.0	0.0	0.0	0.0	0.3	0.1	14.8
France	20.0	12.7	7.3	5.2	0.0	0.0	0.0	0.2	0.0	12.3
Gabon	36.4	12.8	23.5	2.7	24.5	0.0	0.0	0.5	0.1	1.1
Gambia, The	8.8	7.8	1.0	3.4	0.0	0.0	0.6	0.5	0.7	2.5
Georgia	14.8	16.1	−1.3	4.3	0.4	0.0	0.0	1.0	2.5	−1.0
Germany	20.3	14.9	5.4	4.2	0.1	0.0	0.0	0.2	0.1	9.3
Ghana	..	7.2	..	2.8	0.0	1.1	2.3	0.6	0.2	..
Greece	20.3	8.8	11.5	3.1	0.1	0.1	0.0	0.4	0.7	13.5
Guatemala	13.9	10.1	3.8	1.6	0.9	0.0	0.9	0.3	0.2	3.1
Guinea	10.3	8.0	2.3	2.0	0.0	1.4	1.7	0.3	0.6	0.2
Guinea-Bissau	−5.7	6.9	−12.6	..	0.0	0.0	0.0	0.6	..	..
Haiti	..	1.8	..	1.5	0.0	0.0	0.0	1.3	0.3	0.2

Toward a broader measure of savings

	Gross national savings	Consumption of fixed capital	Net national savings	Education expenditure	Energy depletion	Mineral depletion	Net forest depletion	Carbon dioxide damage	Particulate emission damage	Adjusted net savings
	% of GNI 2003	% of GNI 2003	% of GNI 2003	% of GNI 2003	% of GNI 2003	% of GNI 2003	% of GNI 2003	% of GNI 2003	% of GNI 2003	% of GNI 2003
Honduras	23.6	5.6	18.0	3.5	0.0	0.1	0.0	0.5	0.2	20.8
Hungary	17.7	12.4	5.3	5.0	0.5	0.0	0.0	0.6	0.4	8.9
India	24.8	9.6	15.1	3.9	2.4	0.3	0.9	1.5	0.7	13.2
Indonesia	18.8	5.4	13.4	1.3	8.8	1.3	0.0	0.8	0.5	3.3
Iran, Islamic Rep.	42.7	10.0	32.8	4.6	33.2	0.1	0.0	1.7	0.7	1.7
Iraq	..	..	..	..	..	..	..	..	..	..
Ireland	26.4	12.6	13.8	5.7	0.0	0.1	0.0	0.3	0.1	19.0
Israel	14.2	14.7	−0.5	6.8	0.0	0.1	0.0	0.4	0.0	5.8
Italy	18.7	13.7	5.0	4.4	0.1	0.0	0.0	0.2	0.2	8.9
Jamaica	20.0	11.4	8.6	6.0	0.0	1.1	0.0	0.9	0.3	12.2
Japan	26.7	15.9	10.8	3.2	0.0	0.0	0.0	0.2	0.4	13.5
Jordan	28.1	10.6	17.5	4.4	0.4	1.0	0.0	1.2	0.7	18.6
Kazakhstan	28.1	10.5	17.5	4.4	38.9	0.6	0.0	4.1	0.4	−22.1
Kenya	13.1	8.0	5.1	6.1	0.0	0.0	0.6	0.4	0.2	9.9
Korea, Dem. Rep.	..	..	..	..	..	..	..	..	..	..
Korea, Rep.	31.5	12.4	19.2	3.0	0.0	0.0	0.0	0.5	0.8	20.9
Kuwait	24.8	7.2	17.6	5.0	50.8	0.0	0.0	0.7	2.0	−30.9
Kyrgyz Republic	15.1	8.0	7.1	3.2	1.2	0.0	0.0	2.3	0.2	6.5
Lao PDR	19.1	7.8	11.3	1.8	0.0	0.0	0.0	0.2	0.2	12.8
Latvia	20.5	10.8	9.7	5.1	0.0	0.0	0.0	0.6	0.3	13.8
Lebanon	−7.9	11.4	−18.4	2.5	0.0	0.0	0.0	0.6	0.6	−18.1
Lesotho	−2.4	6.9	−9.3	7.3	0.0	0.0	1.7	..	0.4	..
Liberia	0.6	7.4	−6.7	..	0.0	0.3	5.3	1.0	0.0	..
Libya	..	..	..	..	..	..	..	..	..	..
Lithuania	15.8	10.3	5.5	5.2	0.0	0.0	0.0	0.7	0.7	9.3
Macedonia, FYR	17.6	10.2	7.4	4.9	0.0	0.0	0.0	1.7	0.3	10.3
Madagascar	12.0	7.6	4.4	1.7	0.0	0.0	0.0	0.2	0.2	5.6
Malawi	−6.5	6.7	−13.2	4.4	0.0	0.0	2.3	0.3	0.2	−11.6
Malaysia	36.3	11.6	24.8	5.3	12.1	0.0	0.0	1.0	0.1	17.0
Mali	15.6	8.0	7.6	2.1	0.0	0.0	0.0	0.1	0.5	9.2
Mauritania	8.7	7.4	1.3	3.7	0.0	18.8	0.8	2.1	..	..
Mauritius	26.3	10.9	15.4	3.3	0.0	0.0	0.0	0.3	..	18.3[a]
Mexico	18.7	10.5	8.2	5.1	6.2	0.1	0.0	0.5	0.5	6.0
Moldova	17.0	6.8	10.1	3.5	0.0	0.0	0.0	2.8	0.5	10.3
Mongolia	18.1	10.9	7.1	5.7	0.0	2.4	0.0	4.6	0.5	5.3
Morocco	27.9	9.7	18.2	4.8	0.0	0.3	0.1	0.6	0.2	21.8
Mozambique	12.6	7.4	5.2	3.8	0.0	0.0	0.0	0.3	0.4	8.3
Myanmar	..	..	..	0.9	..	..	..	..	..	..
Namibia	31.5	12.3	19.3	7.4	0.0	0.3	0.0	0.3	0.2	25.9
Nepal	31.6	2.4	29.2	3.2	0.0	0.0	4.2	0.4	0.1	27.7
Netherlands	23.3	15.2	8.1	4.9	0.7	0.0	0.0	0.2	0.4	11.7
New Zealand	21.9	10.8	11.1	6.9	0.9	0.1	0.0	0.3	0.0	16.6
Nicaragua	21.6	8.8	12.7	3.7	0.0	0.1	1.0	0.6	0.0	14.7
Niger	4.6	7.1	−2.5	2.3	0.0	0.0	3.1	0.3	0.4	−4.1
Nigeria	20.3	9.2	11.1	0.9	42.1	0.0	0.0	0.5	0.8	−31.4
Norway	30.3	15.9	14.4	6.1	6.9	0.0	0.0	0.2	0.1	13.3
Oman	..	..	..	3.7	..	..	..	..	..	..
Pakistan	22.7	7.8	14.9	2.3	3.7	0.0	0.9	0.9	1.0	10.7
Panama	24.0	8.0	15.9	4.3	0.0	0.0	0.0	0.4	0.3	19.5
Papua New Guinea	..	9.6	..	..	13.5	8.3	0.0	0.6	0.0	..
Paraguay	8.2	9.1	−0.9	3.9	0.0	0.0	0.0	0.4	0.4	2.2
Peru	18.1	10.4	7.6	2.6	1.1	1.5	0.0	0.3	0.6	6.6
Philippines	22.8	8.0	14.8	2.8	0.2	0.2	0.2	0.7	0.4	16.0
Poland	17.1	11.4	5.7	5.1	0.5	0.1	0.0	1.2	0.7	8.3
Portugal	..	15.3	..	5.7	0.0	0.0	0.0	0.3	0.4	..
Puerto Rico	..	..	..	..	..	..	..	..	..	..

	Gross national savings	Consumption of fixed capital	Net national savings	Education expenditure	Energy depletion	Mineral depletion	Net forest depletion	Carbon dioxide damage	Particulate emission damage	Adjusted net savings
	% of GNI 2003	% of GNI 2003	% of GNI 2003	% of GNI 2003	% of GNI 2003	% of GNI 2003	% of GNI 2003	% of GNI 2003	% of GNI 2003	% of GNI 2003
Romania	18.5	10.5	8.1	3.6	3.2	0.0	0.0	1.2	0.2	7.1
Russian Federation	29.8	10.8	19.0	3.5	29.6	0.3	0.0	2.8	0.6	−10.7
Rwanda	11.7	6.7	5.0	3.5	0.0	0.0	3.3	0.3	0.0	4.8
Saudi Arabia	35.3	10.0	25.3	7.2	49.2	0.0	0.0	1.1	1.0	−18.8
Senegal	13.9	8.5	5.4	3.7	0.0	0.1	0.3	0.5	..	8.2[a]
Serbia and Montenegro	−6.5	10.4	−16.9	..	1.0	0.1	0.0	1.6	0.2	..
Sierra Leone	1.6	6.7	−5.1	3.9	0.0	0.0	5.5	0.4	0.4	−7.6
Singapore	44.8	14.4	30.4	2.3	0.0	0.0	0.0	0.5	0.4	31.8
Slovak Republic	24.2	11.4	12.8	4.0	0.1	0.0	0.0	0.9	0.1	15.7
Slovenia	25.5	12.6	12.9	5.3	0.0	0.0	0.0	0.4	0.2	17.7
Somalia	..	..	..	..	..	..	..	..	..	..
South Africa	16.3	13.3	3.0	7.6	1.1	0.9	0.2	1.5	0.2	6.6
Spain	23.3	12.9	10.4	4.3	0.0	0.0	0.0	0.2	0.4	14.0
Sri Lanka	21.7	5.2	16.5	2.9	0.0	0.0	0.6	0.3	0.3	18.1
Sudan	22.4	8.9	13.5	0.9	0.0	0.0	0.0	0.2	0.6	13.6
Swaziland	14.2	9.4	4.8	5.1	0.0	0.0	0.0	0.2	0.1	9.7
Sweden	23.1	13.9	9.2	7.7	0.0	0.1	0.0	0.1	0.0	16.7
Switzerland	..	14.9	..	4.9	0.0	0.0	0.0	0.1	0.2	..
Syrian Arab Republic	28.0	9.7	18.3	3.5	33.1	0.1	0.0	1.7	0.8	−13.9
Tajikistan	−7.6	7.6	−15.2	2.0	0.2	0.0	0.0	3.4	0.2	−17.0
Tanzania	9.4	7.4	2.0	2.4	0.0	0.5	0.0	0.3	0.2	3.4
Thailand	31.1	15.0	16.2	3.6	2.0	0.0	0.3	1.0	0.4	16.1
Togo	2.0	7.9	−5.9	4.2	0.0	0.7	3.3	0.9	0.3	−6.9
Trinidad and Tobago	25.9	12.2	13.7	3.9	38.5	0.0	0.0	2.0	0.0	−22.8
Tunisia	22.9	10.0	12.9	6.4	3.7	0.4	0.1	0.6	0.3	14.1
Turkey	19.2	7.0	12.3	3.3	0.2	0.0	0.0	0.6	1.2	13.5
Turkmenistan	..	9.4	..	..	..	0.0	0.0	7.4	0.3	..
Uganda	17.6	7.3	10.3	1.9	0.0	0.0	5.9	0.2	0.0	6.2
Ukraine	26.6	19.0	7.5	6.4	6.4	0.0	0.0	5.9	1.0	0.6
United Arab Emirates	..	..	..	..	..	..	..	..	0.0	..
United Kingdom	14.3	11.4	2.9	5.3	0.9	0.0	0.0	0.2	0.1	7.0
United States	13.5	11.8	1.6	4.8	1.2	0.0	0.0	0.4	0.3	4.7
Uruguay	13.0	11.0	2.0	2.4	0.0	0.0	0.3	0.3	1.9	1.9
Uzbekistan	23.4	7.8	15.6	9.4	61.0	0.0	0.0	9.1	0.6	−45.7
Venezuela, RB	22.1	7.4	14.6	4.3	37.2	0.4	0.0	1.0	0.0	−19.6
Vietnam	27.1	8.0	19.1	2.8	8.1	0.0	0.7	1.0	0.4	11.6
West Bank and Gaza	−22.8	8.1	−31.0	..	0.0	0.0	0.0	..	..	..
Yemen, Rep.	19.2	8.9	10.3	..	37.6	0.0	0.0	1.2	0.5	..
Zambia	15.9	8.1	7.8	2.0	0.0	1.2	0.0	0.4	..	8.2[a]
Zimbabwe	..	..	..	6.9	..	..	..	..	0.5	..
World	**20.8 w**	**12.6 w**	**8.2 w**	**4.4 w**	**2.3 w**	**0.1 w**	**0.0 w**	**0.5 w**	**0.3 w**	**9.4 w**
Low income	23.1	8.9	14.2	3.4	5.8	0.3	0.9	1.2	0.6	8.7
Middle income	27.9	10.1	17.8	3.7	9.0	0.4	0.0	1.4	0.7	10.1
Lower middle income	30.7	9.8	20.9	3.2	7.9	0.4	0.0	1.6	0.7	13.4
Upper middle income	22.1	10.7	11.4	5.0	11.4	0.3	0.0	0.8	0.6	3.3
Low & middle income	27.2	9.9	17.3	3.7	8.5	0.4	0.2	1.3	0.6	10.0
East Asia & Pacific	41.8	9.2	32.6	2.3	3.9	0.3	0.1	1.8	0.8	28.1
Europe & Central Asia	21.9	10.7	11.2	4.1	11.2	0.1	0.0	1.9	0.6	1.5
Latin America & Carib.	19.5	10.3	9.2	4.2	6.4	0.7	0.0	0.5	0.5	5.3
Middle East & N. Africa	31.2	10.0	21.3	5.5	30.7	0.1	0.1	1.2	0.8	−6.2
South Asia	24.9	9.0	15.9	3.5	2.4	0.3	0.9	1.4	0.7	13.8
Sub-Saharan Africa	16.9	10.6	6.3	4.7	8.0	0.5	0.6	0.9	0.4	0.7
High income	19.3	13.2	6.1	4.6	0.8	0.0	0.0	0.3	0.3	9.3
Europe EMU	21.3	13.9	7.5	4.6	0.1	0.0	0.0	0.2	0.2	11.6

Note: The cutoff date for data in the table is February 2005; later revisions are not captured in this table.
a. Adjusted net savings do not include particulate emission damage.

Adjusted net savings measure the change in value of a specified set of assets, excluding capital gains. If a country's net savings are positive and the accounting includes a sufficiently broad range of assets, economic theory suggests that the present value of social welfare is increasing. Conversely, persistently negative adjusted net savings indicate that an economy is on an unsustainable path.

The table provides a test to check the extent to which today's rents from a number of natural resources and changes in human capital are balanced by net savings, that is, this generation's bequest to future generations.

Adjusted net savings are derived from standard national accounting measures of gross national savings by making four adjustments. First, estimates of capital consumption of produced assets are deducted to obtain net national savings. Second, current public expenditures on education are added to net national savings (in standard national accounting these expenditures are treated as consumption). Third, estimates of the depletion of a variety of natural resources are deducted to reflect the decline in asset values associated with their extraction and harvest. And fourth, deductions are made for damages from carbon dioxide and particulate emissions.

The exercise treats public education expenditures as an addition to savings effort. The adjustment made to savings goes in the right direction. However, because of the wide variability in the effectiveness of government education expenditures, these figures cannot be construed as the value of investments in human capital. The reader should bear in mind that current expenditure of $1 on education does not necessarily yield $1 of human capital. The calculation should also consider private education expenditure, but data are not available for a large number of countries.

While extensive, the accounting of natural resource depletion and pollution costs still has some gaps. Key estimates missing on the resource side include the value of fossil water extracted from aquifers, net depletion of fish stocks, and depletion and degradation of soils. Important pollutants affecting human health and economic assets are excluded because no internationally comparable data are widely available on damage from ground-level ozone or from sulfur oxides.

Estimates of resource depletion are based on the calculation of unit resource rents. An economic rent represents an excess return to a given factor of production—in this case the returns from resource extraction or harvest are higher than the normal rate of return on capital. Natural resources give rise to rents because they are not produced; in contrast, for produced goods and services competitive forces will expand supply until economic profits are driven to zero. For each type of resource and each country, unit resource rents are derived by taking the difference between world prices and the average unit extraction or harvest costs (including a "normal" return on capital). Unit rents are then multiplied by the physical quantity extracted or harvested in order to arrive at a depletion figure. This figure is one of a range of depletion estimates that are possible, depending on the assumptions made about future quantities, prices, and costs, and there is reason to believe that it is at the high end of the range. World prices are used in order to reflect the social opportunity cost of depleting minerals and energy. Researchers should keep this in mind when using the depletion estimates. In general, the data on energy and mineral depletion should not be considered a substitute for energy and mineral gross domestic product.

A positive net depletion figure for forest resources implies that the harvest rate exceeds the rate of natural growth; this is not the same as deforestation, which represents a change in land use (see *Definitions* for table 3.4). In principle, there should be an addition to savings in countries where growth exceeds harvest, but empirical estimates suggest that most of this net growth is in forested areas that cannot be exploited economically at present. Because the depletion estimates reflect only timber values, they ignore all the external and nontimber benefits associated with standing forests.

Pollution damage from emissions of carbon dioxide is calculated as the marginal social cost per unit multiplied by the increase in the stock of carbon dioxide. The unit damage figure represents the present value of global damage to economic assets and to human welfare over the time the unit of pollution remains in the atmosphere.

Pollution damage from particulate emissions is estimated by valuing the human health effects from exposure to particulate matter less than 10 microns in diameter. The estimates are calculated as willingness to pay to avoid mortality attributable to particulate emissions (in particular, mortality relating to cardiopulmonary disease in adults, lung cancer in adults, and acute respiratory infections in children).

For a detailed methodological note see www.worldbank.org/data.

• **Gross national savings** are calculated as the difference between gross national income and public and private consumption, plus net current transfers. • **Consumption of fixed capital** represents the replacement value of capital used up in the process of production. • **Net national savings** are equal to gross national savings less the value of consumption of fixed capital. • **Education expenditure** refers to public current operating expenditures in education, including wages and salaries and excluding capital investments in buildings and equipment. • **Energy depletion** is equal to the product of unit resource rents and the physical quantities of energy extracted. It covers coal, crude oil, and natural gas. • **Mineral depletion** is equal to the product of unit resource rents and the physical quantities of minerals extracted. It refers to tin, gold, lead, zinc, iron, copper, nickel, silver, bauxite, and phosphate. • **Net forest depletion** is calculated as the product of unit resource rents and the excess of roundwood harvest over natural growth. • **Carbon dioxide emissions damage** is estimated to be $20 per ton of carbon (the unit damage in 1995 U.S. dollars) times the number of tons of carbon emitted. • **Particulate emissions damage** is calculated as the willingness to pay to avoid mortality attributable to particulate emissions. • **Adjusted net savings** are equal to net national savings plus education expenditure and minus energy depletion, mineral depletion, net forest depletion, and carbon dioxide and particulate emissions damage.

Data sources

Gross national savings are derived from the World Bank's national accounts data files, described in the *Economy* section. Consumption of fixed capital is from the United Nations Statistics Division's *National Accounts Statistics: Main Aggregates and Detailed Tables, 1997,* extrapolated to 2003. The education expenditure data are from the United Nations Statistics Division's *Statistical Yearbook 1997* and from the UNESCO Institute for Statistics online database. Missing data are estimated. The wide range of data sources and estimation methods used to arrive at resource depletion estimates are described in a World Bank working paper, "Estimating National Wealth" (Kunte and others 1998). The unit damage figure for carbon dioxide emissions is from Fankhauser (1995). The estimates of damage from particulate emissions are from Pandey and others (2003). The conceptual underpinnings of the savings measure appear in Hamilton and Clemens (1999).

4 | ECONOMY

Changes in the size and structure of national economies and the effects of these changes on the global economy are the topic of the tables in this section. The indicators in this section include measures of macroeconomic performance (GDP, consumption, investment, and international trade) and of stability (central government budgets, prices, the money supply, the balance of payments, and external debt). Other important economic indicators appear throughout the book, especially in the *States and markets* section (credit, investment, financial markets, tax policies, exchange rates) and the *Global links* section (trade and tariffs, foreign investment, and aid flows).

Economy recovery continues

Stronger performance by high-income economies in 2003 helped the world economy continue its recovery. The world economy grew 2.8 percent, an increase of 1 percentage point over 2002 but below the peak of 4 percent in 2000. The world's recorded output—and income—grew by almost $4 trillion in nominal terms. The low-income economies, boosted by an unprecedented 8.6 percent growth in India, registered the fastest growth, followed by lower middle-income economies. The upper middle-income economies grew by 3.3 percent, reversing the previous year's negative growth trend. The better performance was due to above-average growth in Argentina, Latvia, Lithuania, Malaysia, Poland, and Saudi Arabia. High-income economies grew by 2.2 percent (figure 4a).

Long-term growth trends

Economic growth in the past decade was fastest in the developing economies of East Asia and Pacific (averaging 6.7 percent a year) and South Asia (5.5 percent). Leading this growth were China and India, each accounting for more than 70 percent of its region's output. The two regions continued to do well in 2003, with East Asia registering 8.1 percent growth and South Asia recording 7.5 percent growth.

The transition economies of Europe and Central Asia continued their strong recovery, growing at an impressive 5.8 percent in 2003, after an average of 3.3 percent in 2000–02. Several countries of the former Soviet Union—such as Armenia, Azerbaijan, Tajikistan, and Turkmenistan—registered growth of more than 10 percent, buoyed by increased exports of natural gas and petroleum products. Russia also did well with growth of 7.3 percent in 2003, an increase from 4.7 percent in 2002, but still below the 10 percent in 2000.

In Latin America and the Caribbean and the Middle East and North Africa growth was faster in the 1990s than in the 1980s. But growth in Latin America decelerated sharply in 2001 and turned negative in 2002. The economies of Argentina, Uruguay, and Venezuela experienced large negative growth in 2002, while growth decelerated in Brazil and Mexico in 2001 and 2002. Better performance in 2003 by Argentina, Mexico, and Uruguay resulted in positive growth for the region, although growth in Brazil turned negative, and Venezuela, yet to recover, saw its GDP fall by 9.4 percent. The Middle East and North Africa region saw its growth rate more than double over 2002, due to about 7 percent growth in Algeria, Iran, and Saudi Arabia. The heavily indebted poor countries, many in Sub-Saharan Africa, registered 4.2 percent growth in 2003. Nigeria (10.7 percent) and Sudan (6 percent) had above average performance. As a result, Sub-Saharan Africa continued to improve its performance over earlier periods, with 3.9 percent growth.

With two decades of high growth, the total GDP of East Asia and Pacific nearly reached that of Latin America and the Caribbean (figure 4b). By contrast GDP in the Europe and Central Asia region, almost equal to that of East Asia and Pacific in 1992, is now only half the GDP of East Asia and Pacific after a decade of stagnant economic performance. With steady growth, South Asia's GDP has almost caught up with that of the Middle East and North Africa, but GDP per capita lags far behind in this populous region.

Growth paths

Most developing economies are following familiar growth paths, with agriculture giving way first to manufacturing and later to services as the main source of income. But some, such as Jordan and Panama, have moved directly from agriculture to service-based economies. For most economies services have been the fastest growing sector. In 1990–2003 the service sector grew by 3.8 percent a year in developing and transition economies and by 3.1 percent in high-income economies.

4b

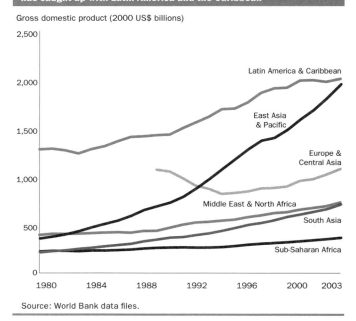

With more than two decades of rapid growth East Asia and Pacific has caught up with Latin America and the Caribbean

Gross domestic product (2000 US$ billions)

Source: World Bank data files.

4a

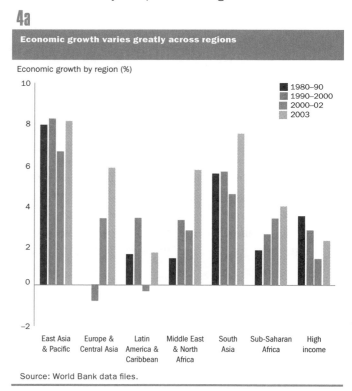

Economic growth varies greatly across regions

Economic growth by region (%)

Source: World Bank data files.

Among developing regions South Asia had the fastest growth in services in the 1990s, at 7 percent a year, and Europe and Central Asia the slowest, at 1.7 percent (table 4.1).

Services in developing economies generated slightly more than half of GDP in 2003, compared with 71 percent in high-income economies (table 4.2). But in East Asia and Pacific services produced only 36 percent of GDP, and from 1990 to 2003 growth in manufacturing, at 10 percent a year, outpaced growth in services, at 6.8 percent. This trend reflects the rapid growth of manufacturing in China (11.7 percent a year), which also had rapid expansion in services (8.8 percent a year).

The contribution of trade

Global trade (exports plus imports) grew by 6.3 percent in 2003, recovering from the low 3.6 percent in 2002. Trade in high-income economies, which account for more than 75 percent of global trade, grew by only 2.3 percent in 2002, after recovering from the decline in 2001. But trade in the low-income economies increased by 12.3 percent in 2003, and in the middle-income economies by 11.2 percent.

Trade in merchandise—primary commodities and manufactured goods—continues to dominate. In 2003 merchandise accounted for 81 percent of all exports of goods and commercial services, and manufactured goods for 77 percent of merchandise exports (tables 4.5 and 4.7). Exporters of primary nonfuel commodities saw their trade volumes increase, but a continuing decline in their terms of trade left them with less income (table 4.4). The economies of Sub-Saharan Africa were hit particularly hard.

The structure of trade in services is also changing. Transport services are being replaced in importance by travel, insurance and financial services, and computer, information, and other services. In the 1990s high-income countries were the main exporters of financial services. Now, many developing countries are emerging as exporters of these new services along with computer, information, and business services (table 4.7).

With expanding trade, and favorable current account balances, some exporting countries are accumulating large international reserves. The large trade deficit of the United States ($531 billion) and the efforts by many Asian exporters with large current account surpluses to prevent their currencies from appreciating against the dollar have resulted in large accumulations of international reserves in Asia. Workers' remittances, growing steadily in countries like India, also contributed to favorable current account balances and higher reserves. India has the seventh largest reserves, ahead of most high-income countries. Japan has the largest reserves, followed by China. Of the 10 economies with the largest reserves, seven are in Asia (table 4.15 and table 4c).

Steady trends in consumption, investment, and saving

Most of the world's output goes to final consumption by households (including individuals) and governments. The share of final consumption in world output has remained fairly constant over time, averaging about 80 percent in 1990–2003 (table 4.9). Growth of per capita household consumption expenditure provides an important indicator of the potential for reducing poverty. In 1990–2003 per capita consumption grew by 5.7 percent a year in East Asia and Pacific but by only 0.2 percent in Sub-Saharan Africa, 1.7 percent in Europe and Central Asia, and 2.7 percent in South Asia (table 4.10).

Output that is not consumed goes to exports (less imports) and gross capital formation (investment). Investment is financed out of domestic and foreign savings. High-income

countries consume a larger share of their output than do developing countries. So, some high-income countries, like the United States and United Kingdom, with low savings rates have to rely more on foreign savings to finance their investment.

In 2003 the global savings rate averaged 21 percent of total output. But global averages disguise large differences between countries. Savings rates are consistently lower in Sub-Saharan Africa. And they tend to be volatile in countries dependent on commodity exports. Gross domestic savings in the Middle East and North Africa rose from 20 percent of GDP in 1990 to 32 percent in 2003, buoyed by higher oil prices. The highest savings rate was in East Asia and Pacific, where gross domestic savings averaged above 35 percent during most of the past decade and reached 41 percent in 2003 (table 4.9).

Between 1990 and 2003 the rate of gross capital formation increased by about 7.9 percent a year in East Asia and Pacific and 6.4 percent in South Asia, but declined by 4 percent in Europe and Central Asia. East Asia and Pacific continued to have the highest investment rate in the world, at 38 percent of GDP in 2003. By contrast, investment averaged only 19 percent of GDP in Sub-Saharan Africa. Developing countries invested a larger proportion of their GDP (25 percent) than did high-income countries, which as a group saved and invested only about 20 percent of GDP (tables 4.9 and 4.10).

Greater monetary and fiscal stability

Governments, because of their size, have a large effect on economic performance. High taxes and subsidies can distort economic behavior; when governments finance large fiscal deficits by growth of the money supply, the likelihood of inflation increases. As governments have adopted policies leading to greater fiscal stability, inflation rates and interest rates have tended to decline. In 2003, 32 countries had double-digit inflation measured by the GDP deflator, down from nearly 50 in 2000 when the highest inflation rate was 516 percent (Democratic Republic of Congo, table 4.14 and table 4d).

The central governments of developing countries have had larger cash deficits than have high-income countries. Central governments of South Asian economies had expenses averaging 16 percent of GDP in 2003 and revenues (mainly from taxes on goods and services) averaging 12 percent of GDP, leaving a cash deficit of about 4 percent of GDP after taking grants into account (table 4.11).

Government expenses are mostly for the purchase of goods and services (including the wages and salaries of public employees) and for subsidies and current transfers to private and public enterprises and local governments. The rest go to interest payments and other expenses. In 2003 subsidies and other transfers accounted for 61 percent of government spending in high-income economies and 55 percent in Europe and Central Asia, but only 11 percent in the Middle East and North Africa (table 4.12).

4c

The 10 largest holders of foreign exchange reserves in 2003	Total reserves	
	$ millions	Months of imports
Japan	673,554	17
China	416,199	11
Taiwan, China	212,315	17
United States	184,024	1
Korea, Rep.	155,472	8
Hong Kong, China	118,388	5
India	103,737	12
Germany	96,835	1
Singapore	95,746	7
Russian Federation	78,409	7

Source: World Bank and IMF data files.

4d

Countries with more than 10 percent inflation in 2003 (%)

Country	Inflation rate
Angola	92
Venezuela, RB	37
Gambia, The	31
Belarus	29
Ghana	29
Dominican Republic	27
Haiti	25
Uzbekistan	24
Romania	23
Nigeria	21
Turkey	21
Zambia	20
Paraguay	18
Uruguay	18
Lao PDR	17
Iran, Islamic Rep.	16
Eritrea	15
Tonga	15
Ethiopia	14
Moldova	14
Russian Federation	14
Brazil	13
Congo, Dem. Rep.	13
Jamaica	13
Mozambique	13
Burundi	12
Guinea	12
Argentina	11
Kenya	11
Malawi	11
Tajikistan	10
Uganda	10

Source: World Bank data files.

The sources of government revenue have been changing. Taxes on international trade declined between 1995 and 2003. Taxes on income, profits, and capital gains and taxes on goods and services increased during the same period. High-income economies depended more on income taxes (28 percent) compared with low- and middle-income economies, which derived 32 percent of their revenue from taxes on goods and services and 8 percent from taxes on trade (table 4.13).

External debt continues to increase

In 2003 the external debt of low- and middle-income economies increased by $220 billion in nominal terms, about 9 percent of their total debt stock in 2002 (table 4.16). But the external debt burden measured as the ratio of external debt to gross national income continued to decline for all income groups (except upper middle-income economies) and regional groups (except Latin America and the Caribbean). The total debt burden declined significantly for the Sub-Saharan African countries, down 11 percentage points to 58 percent in 2003. The upper middle-income economies saw an increase of 2 percentage points to 36 percent—Latin America and the Caribbean saw an increase of 1 percentage point to 47 percent.

The debt servicing burden declined overall for developing countries by 1 percentage point in 2003. The largest improvement was for Sub-Saharan Africa, with a decline of 3 percentage points to 8 percent of the value of exports of goods and services, income, and workers' remittances. South Asia saw an increase of 2 percentage points to 16 percent, and Latin America and the Caribbean an increase of 1 percentage point to 31 percent.

Data on the economy—some changes in reporting methods

Most of the indicators in this section remain the same as last year. But there have been some changes in reporting methods. For the national accounts the reference year for the constant price has been changed from 1995 to 2000 in keeping with the recommended practice in estimating and reporting national accounts data. Because rescaling changes the implicit weights used in forming regional and income group aggregates, aggregate growth rates in this year's *World Development Indicators* are not comparable to those from earlier editions using different base years (for details see *About the data* for table 4.1). Readers interested in comparable aggregates over a long time period should consult the *World Development Indicators 2005* CD-ROM or *WDI Online*, which contains the revised aggregates by region and income. Government finance data in tables 4.11 through 4.13 are now reported on an accrual basis, as recommended by the International Monetary Fund's (IMF) *Government Finance Manual 2001*. Where data on an accrual basis are not available, the cash basis data have been recast into the new framework by IMF staff (see tables 4.11 through 4.13 for details on the changes).

The last major revision of the System of National Accounts, completed in 1993, introduced important changes in the concepts and methods used to measure the economy. The revised accounting structure includes the partitioning of the accounts and further integration of the balance sheets. New balancing items have been created. The scope of transactions to be included, such as illegal activities and nonmonetary flows, has been expanded. Government capital formation has been extended to include expenditures by the military on structures and equipment. And there is new treatment for write-offs of bad debts. Also noteworthy is the harmonization with the balance of payments. By 2004, 84 countries and territories, with 56 percent of world population and 92 percent of world GDP, had implemented the 1993 System of National Accounts, most of them high-income economies or transition economies of Eastern Europe and the former Soviet Union, which replaced accounts based on material product with the 1993 system.

Even as work continues on introducing the 1993 System of National Accounts in many small and poor economies still using earlier and nonstandard versions, a major review of the 1993 system is getting under way. As the global economy grows, the transactions that must be recorded in the national accounts grow in kind and complexity. For example, the treatment of financial derivatives, agreements to repurchase securities, and employee stock options are up for review. Long-standing issues, such as the capitalization of military expenditures and the inclusion of a return to capital in the estimated value of nonmarket outputs, are also on the agenda.

In 2003 the United Nations Statistical Commission called for a review of the 1993 System of National Accounts, stopping short of calling for fundamental changes. The commission was concerned that such a review could widen the statistical divide between countries and compromise international comparability. Moreover, comparability with other macroeconomic frameworks such as the balance of payments (whose revision is running in parallel) and government finance statistics should be maintained and improved. Where feasible, the latest developments in international business accounting standards should be taken into account.

The discussion of issues has to be brought to a conclusion in a spirit of consensus, with broad involvement by all countries. The review process will focus on a limited number of carefully selected issues, while conserving the conceptual framework and most of the recommendations of the 1993 System of National Accounts. So implementation of the 1993 version should proceed in all countries and regions while the updating of the well-specified issues is in progress. The update (1993 System of National Accounts, Rev. 1) is expected to be ready by 2008.

4.a

	Gross domestic product		Exports of goods and services		Imports of goods and services		GDP deflator		Current account balance		Total reserves[a]	
	average annual % growth		average annual % growth		average annual % growth		% growth		% of GDP		$ millions	months of import coverage
	2003	2004	2003	2004	2003	2004	2003	2004	2003	2004	2004	2004
Algeria	6.8	5.9	8.6	7.4	1.6	9.6	8.2	6.0	..	12.8	..	..
Argentina	8.8	7.0	6.0	3.5	37.6	45.4	10.7	6.1	6.0	1.0	..	..
Armenia	13.9	10.1	28.2	12.2	23.5	5.2	4.6	6.0	−6.8	−5.2	575	3.7
Azerbaijan	11.2	10.2	−4.4	12.1	43.5	25.8	4.0	6.4	−28.3	−30.4	1,075	2.2
Bangladesh	5.3	5.5	6.9	6.5	7.4	7.2	4.5	4.9	0.4	0.3	3,027	3.0
Bolivia	2.5	3.8	10.1	8.8	−2.7	−0.9	5.1	4.0	0.5	3.0	1,041	5.2
Bosnia and Herzegovina	2.7	4.7	10.4	7.3	8.0	12.3	1.2	1.1	−29.2	−20.1	1,886	4.6
Botswana	5.4	3.8	0.7	−4.7	−5.4	10.0	3.6	5.0	..	9.5	5,975	19.5
Brazil	−0.2	5.2	7.9	19.6	−1.9	20.3	12.8	7.2	0.8	1.9	52,900	..
Bulgaria	4.3	5.2	8.0	13.0	14.8	15.3	2.1	5.1	−8.4	−8.6	7,627	5.4
Cameroon	4.7	5.0	3.8	1.7	−2.6	4.1	0.9	2.1	..	−8.4	119	0.3
Chile	3.3	5.9	11.4	11.6	9.3	−0.2	4.4	2.5	−0.8	−1.9	16,016	7.7
China	9.3	9.5	26.8	27.0	24.8	25.5	2.2	6.3	3.2	2.6	609,900	11.7
Colombia	3.9	4.0	5.0	6.6	4.8	9.3	8.2	4.4	−1.5	−2.2	10,209	5.2
Congo, Dem. Rep.	5.6	6.3	..	..	..	..	13.3	5.0	..	−6.8	209	0.9
Congo, Rep.	2.7	4.0	−4.0	14.7	17.5	11.3	−4.0	8.5	−0.1	1.2	53	0.2
Costa Rica	6.5	3.8	12.5	−4.8	1.7	−3.3	7.8	9.7	−5.5	−5.3	1,451	1.8
Côte d'Ivoire	−3.8	1.8	−0.9	−0.7	−1.3	2.3	1.8	2.3	2.6	0.9	..	..
Croatia	4.3	3.7	10.1	5.8	10.9	3.5	3.2	3.1	−7.2	−6.0	8,971	5.6
Ecuador	2.7	5.5	3.2	12.4	0.8	−2.6	9.0	1.4	−1.7	2.8	1,245	1.6
Egypt, Arab Rep.	3.2	4.3	14.0	5.9	0.2	1.1	3.8	6.9	4.5	2.9	..	..
El Salvador	1.8	2.0	3.8	−0.4	4.8	−5.4	2.1	3.2	−4.9	−5.4	1,975	3.3
Estonia	5.1	5.5	5.7	6.6	11.0	−3.5	2.4	2.5	−13.2	−8.6	1,692	2.4
Gabon	2.8	2.0	3.2	3.3	3.3	3.8	−1.2	−5.8	..	6.2	..	..
Ghana	5.2	5.8	2.7	3.8	7.7	11.3	28.7	14.1	3.3	0.3	1,732	3.8
India	8.6	6.9	7.0	13.1	11.1	19.2	3.2	7.0	1.4	0.0	141,176	14.1
Indonesia	4.1	5.1	4.0	8.5	2.0	24.9	6.5	7.1	3.6	2.0	36,310	9.6
Iran, Islamic Rep.	6.6	6.5	11.2	7.4	8.0	5.0	16.5	17.1	1.5	−0.1	23,875	6.0
Jamaica	2.3	2.7	15.0	3.8	7.7	2.3	12.5	11.2	−9.3	−13.0	1,319	2.5
Jordan	3.2	5.2	4.1	6.7	6.6	6.8	1.9	0.2	9.8	1.8	3,906	6.2
Kazakhstan	9.2	9.4	5.9	4.2	−6.3	15.1	7.9	9.9	−0.1	−1.0	9,277	5.8
Kenya	1.8	2.4	9.9	4.6	8.0	16.1	11.4	−1.6	0.5	−1.4	1,550	3.8
Latvia	7.5	8.0	4.3	6.9	13.1	3.3	−1.1	6.0	−8.3	−12.0	..	..
Lesotho	3.3	3.0	−1.8	−2.9	−4.6	−2.2	7.3	6.0	..	−7.7	443	4.3
Lithuania	9.0	6.5	6.0	11.7	8.8	12.1	1.3	1.5	−7.0	−6.6	3,040	2.8

continues on page 196

4.b

Key macroeconomic indicators

	Nominal exchange rate			Real effective exchange rate		Money and quasi money		Gross domestic credit		Real interest rate		Short-term debt[a]
	local currency units per $	% change		2000 = 100		annual % growth		annual % growth		%		% of exports
	2004	2003	2004	2003	2004	2003	2004	2003	2004	2003	2004	2003
Algeria	72.6	−8.9	0.0	85.3	85.1	16.0	..	−2.4	..	−0.2	5.6	..
Argentina	3.0	−12.5	1.9	..	..	29.6	18.9	−2.3	5.3	7.6	2.6	62.2
Armenia	485.8	−3.2	−14.2	77.2	81.9	10.4	25.5	−9.6	49.0	15.5	11.8	1.3
Azerbaijan	4,903.0	0.6	−0.4	..	..	30.8	56.0	27.1	30.0	11.0	15.2	6.5
Bangladesh	60.7	1.5	3.3	..	..	13.1	..	5.0	..	11.0	..	5.5
Bolivia	8.1	4.5	2.8	86.1	79.0	13.9	2.2	0.6	−2.2	11.9	6.9	5.7
Bosnia and Herzegovina	1.4	−17.0	−7.3	..	..	9.5	22.3	20.7	14.4	9.6	6.1	3.4
Botswana	4.3	−18.7	−3.6	..	..	15.5	..	−64.9	..	12.3	6.2	0.8
Brazil	2.7	−18.2	−8.1	..	..	4.4	17.7	8.0	9.9	48.2	41.8	22.0
Bulgaria	1.4	−17.8	−7.3	115.6	121.3	20.2	20.8	33.9	32.4	6.6	2.5	24.3
Cameroon	481.6	−17.0	−7.3	112.3	112.5	1.3	6.8	7.3	3.6	16.9	..	..
Chile	559.8	−15.9	−6.6	78.5	82.6	8.1	11.9	3.1	14.2	1.7	−0.9	27.8
China	8.3	0.0	0.0	96.7	95.5	19.7	13.9	19.6	9.4	3.0	1.5	14.5
Colombia	2,412.1	−2.9	−13.3	82.0	90.9	10.3	11.5	10.3	8.7	6.4	6.4	18.5
Congo, Dem. Rep.	..	−3.3	..	35.1	30.0	32.3	..	798.1	..	..	..	..
Congo, Rep.	481.6	−17.0	−7.3	..	..	−2.4	11.6	10.7	7.2	23.0	..	68.5
Costa Rica	458.6	10.5	9.6	94.2	90.6	16.7	33.8	21.1	26.4	16.5	4.0	18.8
Côte d'Ivoire	481.6	−17.0	−7.3	115.8	117.3	−6.1	4.4	−10.9	−5.2	..	..	13.6
Croatia	5.6	−14.4	−7.9	103.4	104.3	10.7	8.4	12.3	11.6	8.1	..	26.4
Ecuador	25,000.0	0.0	0.0	153.4	145.6	18.9	19.6	0.1	15.9	3.8	4.1	20.5
Egypt, Arab Rep.	6.1	36.7	−0.4	..	..	21.3	14.3	13.3	9.7	9.4	0.9	16.1
El Salvador	8.8	0.0	0.0	..	..	2.3	1.6	9.8	8.5	..	..	28.2
Estonia	11.5	−16.9	−7.6	..	..	10.9	13.0	28.7	31.4	3.0	−1.4	34.4
Gabon	481.6	−17.0	−7.3	107.8	105.6	−1.2	5.7	−5.1	−12.8	19.4	..	..
Ghana	9,054.3	4.9	2.3	101.4	106.1	34.2	..	9.7	..	..	..	21.3
India	43.6	−5.0	−4.4	..	..	13.0	..	9.5	..	7.5	..	4.2
Indonesia	9,290.0	−5.3	9.7	..	..	8.1	5.9	3.9	9.4	9.8	3.0	32.2
Iran, Islamic Rep.	8,793.0	4.0	6.3	124.1	120.2	24.5	..	30.3	..	..	..	7.4
Jamaica	61.5	19.2	1.5	..	..	10.5	12.7	64.4	−11.3	5.6	2.8	19.6
Jordan	0.7	0.0	0.0	..	..	16.6	11.5	5.8	18.2	7.3	3.6	10.5
Kazakhstan	130.0	−6.7	−9.9	..	..	29.5	38.9	24.9	65.8	..	..	18.5
Kenya	77.3	−1.2	1.6	..	..	11.9	15.0	8.6	12.3	4.7	4.2	25.6
Latvia	0.5	−8.9	−4.6	..	..	22.1	26.9	39.9	41.2	6.5	1.5	111.4
Lesotho	5.6	−23.1	−15.2	104.3	82.4	6.0	8.6	−52.3	−183.0	8.1	..	0.5
Lithuania	2.5	−16.6	−8.2	..	..	18.2	20.5	42.4	43.8	4.4	0.6	35.7

continues on page 197

Recent economic performance

	Gross domestic product		Exports of goods and services		Imports of goods and services		GDP deflator		Current account balance		Total reservesᵃ	
	average annual % growth		average annual % growth		average annual % growth		% growth		% of GDP		$ millions	months of import coverage
	2003	2004	2003	2004	2003	2004	2003	2004	2003	2004	2004	2004
Macedonia, FYR	3.2	2.5	8.5	1.6	1.9	6.3	1.8	2.0	−6.0	−7.3	938	4.0
Malawi	4.4	3.6	−0.6	4.2	−16.6	1.2	11.2	12.8	−11.8	−15.9	..	..
Malaysia	5.3	7.0	6.3	14.6	5.0	17.0	3.5	4.0	12.9	13.6	55,998	5.4
Mauritius	3.2	5.0	−6.4	3.0	−3.0	3.7	5.6	5.0	2.3	2.3	1,518	5.6
Mexico	1.3	4.4	1.1	3.7	−1.0	3.7	6.5	6.1	−1.4	−1.3	61,496	..
Moldova	6.3	6.0	20.6	11.2	31.2	9.3	13.9	11.9	−7.2	−7.2	321	1.9
Morocco	5.2	3.3	0.6	2.6	7.4	5.8	0.0	2.4	3.6	2.9	..	..
Nicaragua	2.3	3.7	8.1	1.9	3.2	2.5	5.6	6.0	−19.1	−16.0	524	2.9
Nigeria	10.7	4.1	32.4	−0.7	10.8	−3.0	21.0	21.4	..	0.9	..	..
Pakistan	5.1	6.0	28.4	−3.3	11.2	0.1	4.6	6.8	4.3	0.8	11,271	6.6
Panama	4.1	5.0	−0.8	10.8	−3.8	6.8	1.4	1.3	−3.4	−2.0	1,131	1.3
Paraguay	2.6	2.1	13.2	4.9	15.4	5.5	18.3	7.5	2.4	1.3	1,080	4.4
Peru	3.8	4.2	5.9	9.5	3.3	2.7	0.0	3.7	−1.8	−0.5	11,292	9.2
Philippines	4.5	3.9	3.3	4.4	10.3	2.0	3.7	3.5	4.2	1.8	16,719	3.8
Poland	3.7	5.4	13.0	24.3	7.9	16.7	0.7	2.9	−2.2	−1.5	43,251	4.5
Romania	4.9	8.1	7.1	16.2	13.6	20.2	23.2	9.8	−5.8	−5.8	10,878	4.3
Russian Federation	7.3	7.0	13.7	2.5	19.5	9.8	14.4	12.5	8.3	8.2	106,000	9.5
Senegal	6.5	6.0	0.5	5.4	−1.6	5.6	0.9	1.9	−6.7	−6.2	855	3.3
Serbia and Montenegro	3.0	4.4	1.8	18.7	7.2	9.6	6.4	8.7	−10.2	−9.6	3,599	4.2
Slovak Republic	4.2	5.3	22.6	11.3	13.8	12.0	2.6	5.1	−0.9	−2.9	14,933	5.1
South Africa	1.9	3.7	−0.5	3.7	9.7	3.7	5.9	5.0	−0.9	−1.8	9,469	2.1
Sri Lanka	5.9	6.0	4.8	4.5	10.4	6.0	5.0	6.0	−0.7	−2.3	2,104	2.8
Swaziland	2.2	1.7	−6.0	1.1	−4.0	1.3	9.0	7.9	−4.5	−6.4	252	1.6
Syrian Arab Republic	2.5	3.6	5.8	−3.5	5.4	3.4	5.1	−0.1	3.5	2.3	4,290	6.5
Thailand	6.9	6.4	7.0	..	7.7	..	2.0	..	5.6	..	..	..
Trinidad and Tobago	13.2	6.2	10.1	14.3	−0.8	25.4	5.6	12.5	12.9	6.7	2,741	5.0
Tunisia	5.6	5.3	0.3	4.0	0.1	3.1	2.2	3.4	−2.9	−2.6	..	..
Turkey	5.8	8.0	16.0	28.6	27.1	34.9	21.3	9.8	−3.3	−5.3	37,639	4.1
Uganda	4.7	5.9	8.0	6.2	−2.3	3.7	10.1	5.5	−5.0	−11.3	1,112	6.5
Ukraine	9.4	12.0	10.3	12.0	16.4	12.1	6.9	12.0	5.8	9.7	11,000	3.7
Uruguay	2.5	9.0	4.1	18.0	1.6	26.1	17.9	7.0	0.5	1.1	2,233	6.5
Venezuela, RB	−9.4	9.0	−12.3	9.0	−19.6	23.4	36.8	25.0	13.5	12.9	26,147	13.3
Zambia	5.1	3.5	10.1	12.6	4.8	6.6	20.1	20.9	..	−11.0	173	0.9

Note: Data for 2004 are the latest preliminary estimates, and may differ from those in earlier World Bank publications.

a. International reserves including gold valued at London gold price.

Source: World Bank staff estimates.

4.b

Key macroeconomic indicators

	Nominal exchange rate			Real effective exchange rate		Money and quasi money		Gross domestic credit		Real interest rate		Short-term debt[a]
	local currency units per $	% change		2000 = 100		annual % growth		annual % growth		%		% of exports
	2004	2003	2004	2003	2004	2003	2004	2003	2004	2003	2004	2003
Macedonia, FYR	46.4	−16.3	−9.1	100.0	97.3	14.2	..	16.8	..	14.0	..	2.9
Malawi	108.9	24.6	1.3	79.7	82.6	27.5	26.6	21.2	25.7	33.9	18.2	15.5
Malaysia	3.8	0.0	0.0	97.1	92.3	9.3	18.2	11.0	12.3	2.7	−0.1	7.2
Mauritius	28.2	−10.6	8.1	..	..	10.9	13.0	11.1	18.4	14.6	10.9	47.5
Mexico	11.3	9.0	0.3	..	..	7.2	17.5	6.1	14.8	0.4	1.1	4.7
Moldova	12.5	−4.4	−5.7	87.7	97.3	30.4	39.8	24.3	25.8	4.8	7.2	35.4
Morocco	8.2	−13.9	−6.1	94.3	93.8	8.7	8.0	5.2	8.0	12.6	..	6.9
Nicaragua	16.3	6.0	5.0	87.1	82.8	12.6	..	8.4	..	9.4	3.7	34.1
Nigeria	132.4	8.0	−3.0	104.5	103.7	24.1	9.1	32.7	−0.1	−0.3	3.3	..
Pakistan	59.1	−2.3	3.3	92.6	90.2	17.5	17.0	9.4	23.9	..	..	6.6
Panama	1.0	0.0	0.0	..	..	4.8	9.2	1.6	10.0	8.4	5.1	5.2
Paraguay	6,250.0	−13.9	2.2	71.1	73.1	7.6	14.7	−24.5	2.2	26.7	11.7	17.7
Peru	3.3	−1.5	−5.2	92.6	90.2	−2.4	1.7	−7.7	−8.4	..	9.0	21.4
Philippines	56.3	4.7	1.3	85.9	82.7	3.6	7.0	6.9	8.0	5.6	1.6	13.3
Poland	3.4	−2.6	−15.6	98.9	104.2	5.7	..	8.1	..	6.6	..	25.6
Romania	29,067.0	−2.7	−10.8	105.3	110.0	23.3	33.6	50.4	32.9	..	..	6.5
Russian Federation	27.7	−7.3	−5.8	127.0	136.8	38.5	33.7	26.5	5.0	−1.3	−8.8	18.9
Senegal	481.6	−17.0	−7.3	..	..	14.6	20.5	7.1	4.7	..	..	6.7
Serbia and Montenegro	..	..	..	..	..	..	..	..	..	..	..	40.5
Slovak Republic	28.5	−17.6	−13.6	98.0	96.8	9.7	3.9	−5.7	6.7	5.7	..	30.7
South Africa	5.6	−23.1	−15.2	98.0	112.3	12.5	15.3	22.9	5.3	8.5	2.8	15.3
Sri Lanka	104.6	0.0	8.1	..	..	15.3	17.9	7.3	22.4	5.1	0.9	5.8
Swaziland	5.6	−23.1	−15.2	..	..	14.1	8.9	128.7	40.8	5.1	−2.3	3.2
Syrian Arab Republic	11.2	0.0	0.0	..	..	7.8	..	16.2	..	..	..	70.4
Thailand	39.1	−8.3	−1.3	..	..	6.6	5.4	2.7	7.4	3.8	2.1	11.3
Trinidad and Tobago	6.3	0.0	−0.4	104.9	101.3	−0.7	..	−3.8	..	5.3	3.3	14.8
Tunisia	1.2	−9.4	−0.7	93.3	88.5	6.4	10.3	5.4	11.0	..	..	6.6
Turkey	1,473,698.0	−15.0	−0.6	..	..	14.2	26.1	17.9	26.7	..	..	31.4
Uganda	1,738.6	4.5	−10.2	80.3	87.8	17.9	13.0	−5.8	−3.4	8.0	7.6	12.6
Ukraine	5.3	0.0	−0.5	86.6	81.4	46.9	46.1	39.6	30.7	10.3	3.4	4.2
Uruguay	26.4	7.7	−10.1	60.3	63.1	12.5	1.2	−8.0	−9.5	..	..	43.5
Venezuela, RB	1,918.0	14.0	20.0	68.8	67.0	57.6	47.2	−14.5	60.3	−8.5	−21.0	14.8
Zambia	4,771.3	7.2	2.7	101.3	111.9	17.9	35.1	3.3	11.8	17.1	6.1	9.1

Note: Data for 2004 are preliminary and may not cover the entire year.

a. More recent data on short-term debt are available on a Web site maintained by the Bank for International Settlements, the International Monetary Fund, the Organisation for Economic Co-operation and Development, and the World Bank: www.oecd.org/dac/debt.

Source: International Monetary Fund, *International Financial Statistics;* World Bank, Debtor Reporting System.

4.1 Growth of output

	Gross domestic product		Agriculture		Industry		Manufacturing		Services	
	average annual % growth		average annual % growth		average annual % growth		average annual % growth		average annual % growth	
	1980–90	1990–2003	1980–90	1990–2003	1980–90	1990–2003	1980–90	1990–2003	1980–90	1990–2003
Afghanistan	..	..	..	..	..	..	..	..	..	..
Albania[a]	1.5	4.6	1.9	3.6	2.1	2.0	..	..	–0.4	7.4
Algeria[a]	2.7	2.4	4.1	3.9	2.6	2.2	4.1	–1.7	3.0	2.6
Angola	3.4	3.2	0.5	2.3	6.3	5.5	–11.1	2.3	1.4	–0.8
Argentina[a]	–0.7	2.3	0.7	2.8	–1.3	1.5	–0.8	0.7	0.0	2.4
Armenia[a]	..	1.5	..	1.7	..	–2.3	..	–0.8	..	–1.1
Australia	3.4	3.8	3.2	2.7	3.1	2.9	1.9	2.2	3.7	4.2
Austria	2.3	2.1	1.4	3.4	1.8	2.6	2.5	2.9	2.8	1.9
Azerbaijan[a]	..	–1.5	..	1.6	..	3.5	..	..	..	1.5
Bangladesh	3.7	4.9	2.1	3.1	6.0	7.1	5.2	6.8	3.8	4.7
Belarus[a]	..	0.6	..	–2.3	..	1.1	..	2.1	..	1.4
Belgium	2.1	2.1	2.3	2.1	2.3	1.7	..	2.3	1.8	2.0
Benin	2.5	5.0	5.1	5.6	3.4	4.7	5.1	6.0	0.7	4.5
Bolivia	–0.2	3.5	1.5	2.7	–2.2	3.4	–1.1	3.3	–0.4	3.9
Bosnia and Herzegovina	..	..	..	..	..	..	..	..	..	..
Botswana[a]	11.0	5.2	2.5	–1.0	11.3	4.4	11.4	3.8	15.4	7.2
Brazil[a]	2.7	2.6	2.8	3.6	2.0	2.1	1.6	1.6	3.3	2.7
Bulgaria[a]	3.4	–0.2	–2.1	2.9	5.2	–2.5	..	..	4.7	–2.7
Burkina Faso[a]	3.6	4.2	3.1	3.6	3.8	2.8	2.0	1.5	3.8	5.0
Burundi[a]	4.4	–1.5	3.1	–0.4	4.5	–2.6	5.7	–8.0	5.6	–1.0
Cambodia	..	6.5	..	3.1	..	14.7	..	17.4	..	5.7
Cameroon[a]	3.4	2.7	2.2	5.7	5.9	1.4	5.0	3.3	2.1	0.8
Canada[a]	3.2	3.3	2.3	0.5	2.9	3.2	3.8	4.4	3.2	3.3
Central African Republic[a]	1.4	1.8	1.6	4.0	1.4	1.7	5.0	1.0	1.0	–2.9
Chad[a]	6.1	3.1	2.3	4.1	8.1	5.4	..	..	6.7	2.1
Chile	4.2	5.6	5.9	2.2	3.5	5.1	3.4	3.6	2.9	4.9
China	10.3	9.6	5.9	3.5	11.1	12.3	10.8	11.7	13.5	8.8
Hong Kong, China[a]	6.8	3.7	..	..	..	..	..	..	..	..
Colombia[a]	3.7	2.3	2.9	–1.4	5.0	1.2	3.5	–1.4	3.1	3.7
Congo, Dem. Rep.[a]	1.6	–3.9	2.5	0.3	0.9	–6.8	1.6	..	2.0	–10.4
Congo, Rep.	3.3	1.8	3.4	1.6	5.2	2.8	6.8	0.4	2.2	1.0
Costa Rica[a]	3.0	4.8	3.1	3.5	2.8	5.4	3.0	5.6	3.3	4.6
Côte d'Ivoire	0.7	2.4	0.3	3.1	4.4	3.0	3.0	2.2	–0.1	1.9
Croatia[a]	..	1.7	..	–2.0	..	–0.4	..	–0.8	..	3.0
Cuba	..	3.9	..	3.5	..	5.0	..	4.7	..	3.2
Czech Republic[a]	..	1.4	..	3.6	..	–0.1	..	..	..	2.3
Denmark[a]	2.0	2.3	2.6	2.0	2.0	2.2	1.3	2.0	1.9	2.4
Dominican Republic	3.1	5.8	–1.0	3.9	3.0	6.1	2.3	4.2	4.2	6.0
Ecuador	2.1	2.0	4.5	0.1	1.3	1.2	0.1	1.1	1.8	2.9
Egypt, Arab Rep.[a]	5.4	4.5	2.7	3.2	3.3	4.5	..	6.5	7.8	4.6
El Salvador	0.2	4.0	–1.1	0.9	0.2	4.8	–0.1	4.9	0.7	4.5
Eritrea[a]	..	3.7	..	–1.8	..	10.3	..	7.6	..	4.0
Estonia[a]	2.2	2.1	..	–2.3	..	0.5	..	7.7	..	3.8
Ethiopia[a]	2.2	4.3	0.6	1.7	3.1	4.1	2.7	4.1	4.5	6.6
Finland[a]	3.3	2.8	–1.4	1.7	3.2	3.9	3.5	5.8	3.7	2.6
France	2.4	1.9	1.3	1.3	1.4	1.6	1.3	2.6	3.0	2.2
Gabon	0.9	2.3	1.2	0.0	1.5	2.4	1.8	0.6	0.1	2.6
Gambia, The[a]	3.6	3.2	0.9	3.5	4.7	2.4	7.8	1.4	2.7	4.0
Georgia[a]	0.4	–3.1	..	–0.2	..	8.2	..	2.4	..	12.1
Germany	2.3	1.5	1.6	1.5	1.4	–0.2	..	0.1	3.0	2.5
Ghana	3.0	4.3	1.0	3.6	3.3	3.3	3.9	–0.9	5.7	5.3
Greece[a]	0.9	2.7	–0.1	–0.3	1.2	2.2	..	2.5	0.8	3.1
Guatemala	0.8	3.8	1.2	2.6	–0.2	3.7	0.0	2.5	0.9	4.4
Guinea[a]	..	4.2	..	4.6	..	4.7	..	4.3	..	3.3
Guinea-Bissau[a]	4.0	0.4	4.7	3.1	2.2	–1.5	..	–0.9	3.5	0.1
Haiti	–0.2	–0.8	–0.1	–4.2	–1.7	–1.5	–1.7	–7.9	0.9	0.7

Growth of output | 4.1

	Gross domestic product		Agriculture		Industry		Manufacturing		Services	
	average annual % growth		average annual % growth		average annual % growth		average annual % growth		average annual % growth	
	1980–90	1990–2003	1980–90	1990–2003	1980–90	1990–2003	1980–90	1990–2003	1980–90	1990–2003
Honduras[a]	2.7	3.0	2.7	2.3	3.3	3.5	3.7	4.1	2.5	3.7
Hungary[a]	1.3	2.4	1.7	−1.2	0.2	4.2	..	7.3	2.1	2.0
India[a]	5.7	5.9	3.1	2.7	6.9	6.0	7.4	6.5	6.9	7.9
Indonesia	6.1	3.5	3.6	1.9	7.3	4.2	12.8	5.5	6.5	3.3
Iran, Islamic Rep.[a]	1.7	3.7	4.5	3.3	3.3	−0.7	4.5	5.8	−1.0	7.5
Iraq[a]	−6.8	..	..	..	..	..	..	..	..	..
Ireland[a]	3.2	7.7	..	..	..	..	..	..	..	..
Israel[a]	3.5	4.3	..	..	..	..	..	..	..	..
Italy	2.5	1.6	−0.5	0.8	1.8	1.1	2.1	1.2	2.9	1.8
Jamaica	2.0	0.8	0.9	−0.2	2.4	−0.6	2.7	−1.9	1.6	1.8
Japan	3.9	1.2	1.0	−2.8	3.9	−0.1	4.7	0.7	4.1	2.0
Jordan[a]	2.5	4.6	6.8	−2.0	1.7	4.9	0.5	5.6	2.3	4.7
Kazakhstan[a]	..	−0.6	..	−4.5	..	−3.7	..	6.2	..	0.9
Kenya[a]	4.2	1.8	3.3	1.2	3.9	1.5	4.9	1.7	4.9	2.8
Korea, Dem. Rep.	..	..	..	..	..	..	..	..	..	..
Korea, Rep.	9.0	5.5	2.7	1.0	11.5	5.9	12.9	7.4	8.7	5.7
Kuwait	1.3	2.9	14.7	..	1.0	..	2.3	..	2.1	..
Kyrgyz Republic[a]	..	−1.4	..	2.8	..	−6.3	..	−11.7	..	−2.2
Lao PDR[a]	3.7	6.3	3.5	4.8	6.1	10.7	8.9	11.1	3.3	6.5
Latvia[a]	3.2	1.0	2.1	−2.6	4.6	−3.8	4.4	−3.2	3.2	4.9
Lebanon[a]	..	4.6	..	1.7	..	−0.4	..	−1.7	..	2.7
Lesotho[a]	4.5	3.4	2.8	1.9	5.9	4.7	9.8	5.9	4.0	3.6
Liberia[a]	−7.0	7.0	..	..	..	..	..	..	..	..
Libya[a]	−7.0	..	..	..	..	..	..	..	..	..
Lithuania[a]	..	−0.1	..	−0.4	..	5.1	..	7.2	..	5.5
Macedonia, FYR[a]	..	−0.1	..	−0.5	..	−1.5	..	−3.2	..	1.3
Madagascar[a]	1.1	2.1	2.5	1.8	0.9	2.1	2.1	2.2	0.3	2.4
Malawi[a]	2.5	3.0	2.0	6.6	2.9	0.4	3.6	−1.5	3.3	2.0
Malaysia	5.3	5.9	3.4	0.8	6.8	7.1	9.3	7.9	4.9	6.2
Mali[a]	0.8	4.9	3.3	2.9	4.3	7.6	6.8	−2.3	1.9	3.4
Mauritania[a]	1.8	4.4	1.7	3.3	4.9	2.4	−2.1	−1.1	0.4	6.1
Mauritius[a]	6.0	5.2	2.6	0.3	9.2	5.3	10.4	5.0	5.1	6.2
Mexico	1.1	3.0	0.8	1.9	1.1	3.2	1.5	3.7	1.4	2.9
Moldova[a]	2.8	−5.9	..	−7.2	..	−7.9	..	0.5	..	1.1
Mongolia	5.4	−1.3	1.4	−3.0	6.6	−0.7	..	1.6	8.4	−3.9
Morocco	4.2	2.7	6.7	0.9	3.0	3.3	4.1	2.9	4.2	3.0
Mozambique[a]	−0.1	7.0	6.6	5.2	−4.5	13.9	..	18.1	9.1	3.6
Myanmar	0.6	7.4	0.5	5.7	0.5	10.5	−0.2	7.9	0.8	7.2
Namibia[a]	1.3	3.7	1.9	2.9	0.0	2.4	3.7	3.0	3.6	4.2
Nepal[a]	4.6	4.6	4.0	2.8	8.8	6.0	9.3	6.7	3.9	5.5
Netherlands	2.4	2.7	3.3	1.7	1.7	1.6	2.6	2.1	2.5	3.3
New Zealand	1.9	3.2	4.1	2.7	1.0	2.2	..	2.1	1.2	3.7
Nicaragua	−1.9	3.7	−2.2	4.8	−2.3	3.9	−3.2	3.8	−1.5	3.1
Niger	−0.1	2.8	1.7	3.2	−1.7	2.3	−2.7	3.0	−0.7	2.6
Nigeria[a]	1.6	2.7	3.3	3.6	−1.1	1.3	0.7	2.2	3.7	3.4
Norway	3.0	3.5	0.1	1.4	4.0	2.9	0.2	1.4	2.5	3.9
Oman	8.4	4.3	7.9	..	10.3	..	20.6	..	5.9	..
Pakistan[a]	6.3	3.6	4.0	3.7	7.7	3.9	8.1	4.2	6.8	4.3
Panama[a]	0.5	4.2	2.5	3.7	−1.3	3.9	0.4	0.8	0.7	4.3
Papua New Guinea	1.9	2.8	1.8	2.5	1.9	3.1	0.1	3.4	2.0	0.9
Paraguay	2.5	1.7	3.6	2.5	0.3	2.2	4.0	0.5	3.1	1.0
Peru	−0.1	3.9	3.0	5.2	0.1	3.8	−0.2	3.2	−0.4	3.7
Philippines	1.0	3.5	1.0	2.1	−0.9	3.5	0.2	3.1	2.8	4.3
Poland[a]	..	4.2	..	1.1	..	5.2	..	7.7	..	4.1
Portugal	3.2	2.6	1.5	0.0	3.4	2.9	..	2.5	2.6	2.3
Puerto Rico	4.0	4.3	1.8	..	3.6	..	3.6	..	4.6	..

	Gross domestic product		Agriculture		Industry		Manufacturing		Services	
	average annual % growth		average annual % growth		average annual % growth		average annual % growth		average annual % growth	
	1980–90	1990–2003	1980–90	1990–2003	1980–90	1990–2003	1980–90	1990–2003	1980–90	1990–2003
Romania[a]	1.3	0.1	1.9	−1.1	−1.0	0.1	..	..	..	1.2
Russian Federation[a]	..	−1.8	..	−1.7	..	−3.2	..	..	..	0.0
Rwanda[a]	2.2	2.3	0.5	4.8	2.5	−0.1	2.6	−2.8	3.6	1.1
Saudi Arabia	−1.3	2.1	12.5	1.6	−3.8	1.7	6.2	5.3	0.6	2.5
Senegal	3.1	4.0	2.8	1.9	4.3	5.4	4.6	4.7	2.8	4.2
Serbia and Montenegro[a]	..	1.4	..	..	..	..	..	..	..	..
Sierra Leone	0.5	−3.2	3.1	−2.8	1.7	−3.2	..	..	−0.9	−2.2
Singapore	6.7	6.3	−5.3	−3.1	5.2	6.7	6.6	6.5	7.6	6.5
Slovak Republic	2.0	2.5	..	2.6	..	2.0	..	5.5	..	5.2
Slovenia[a]	..	3.1	..	−0.9	..	2.6	..	2.7	..	3.4
Somalia[a]	2.1	..	3.3	..	1.0	..	−1.7	..	0.9	..
South Africa[a]	1.0	2.3	2.9	1.1	0.7	1.4	1.1	1.7	2.4	2.9
Spain[a]	3.1	2.8	3.1	0.7	2.8	2.6	..	3.6	3.3	2.9
Sri Lanka[a]	4.0	4.7	2.2	1.5	4.6	5.8	6.3	6.6	4.7	5.3
Sudan[a]	2.3	5.7	1.8	9.1	1.6	6.2	4.8	2.1	4.5	3.2
Swaziland[a]	6.9	3.1	2.1	0.7	12.8	3.3	16.9	2.5	4.8	3.7
Sweden	2.5	2.3	1.6	0.1	2.8	4.0	..	7.7	2.5	2.0
Switzerland	2.0	1.2	..	..	..	..	..	..	..	..
Syrian Arab Republic	1.5	4.3	−0.6	4.2	6.6	8.1	..	8.9	1.6	2.8
Tajikistan[a]	2.0	−5.3	−2.8	−2.2	5.5	−5.3	5.6	−4.7	3.4	−1.1
Tanzania[b]	..	3.7	..	3.5	..	4.6	..	3.7	..	3.5
Thailand	7.6	3.7	3.9	1.7	9.8	4.9	9.5	6.0	7.3	3.0
Togo[a]	1.7	3.1	5.6	3.4	1.1	2.3	1.7	3.8	−0.3	3.4
Trinidad and Tobago	−3.3	3.8	2.4	2.6	−4.3	5.3	−5.0	5.9	−3.0	3.2
Tunisia[a]	3.3	4.6	2.8	2.0	3.1	4.6	3.7	5.3	3.5	5.3
Turkey[a]	5.3	3.1	1.2	1.0	7.7	3.0	7.9	3.8	4.5	3.3
Turkmenistan[a]	..	0.9	..	0.2	..	1.6	..	..	..	0.8
Uganda[a]	2.9	6.8	2.1	3.9	5.0	11.0	3.9	12.3	2.8	8.0
Ukraine[a]	..	−5.3	..	−3.3	..	−7.7	..	..	..	−4.9
United Arab Emirates[a]	−2.1	4.2	9.6	..	−4.2	..	3.1	..	3.6	..
United Kingdom	3.2	2.7	2.1	−0.2	3.1	1.1	..	..	3.1	3.4
United States	3.6	3.3	3.2	3.8	3.0	3.4	..	3.9	3.3	3.6
Uruguay[a]	0.5	1.5	0.1	1.6	−0.2	−0.5	0.4	−1.6	1.0	2.5
Uzbekistan[a]	..	1.2	..	1.5	..	−1.5	..	..	..	2.3
Venezuela, RB	1.1	0.5	3.4	0.8	2.0	0.6	1.4	−1.2	0.5	0.3
Vietnam	4.6	7.5	2.8	4.2	4.4	11.3	1.9	11.2	7.1	6.9
West Bank and Gaza[a]	..	−2.0	..	−4.7	..	−8.3	..	−2.3	..	1.2
Yemen, Rep.	..	5.8	..	5.6	..	6.0	..	2.7	..	5.7
Zambia	1.0	1.4	3.6	3.3	1.0	−2.0	4.1	1.9	−0.2	3.2
Zimbabwe[a]	3.6	1.1	3.1	2.9	3.2	−1.1	2.8	−2.0	3.0	2.0
World	**3.3 w**	**2.8 w**	**2.7 w**	**1.9 w**	**3.0 w**	**2.3 w**	**.. w**	**3.2 w**	**3.4 w**	**3.2 w**
Low income	4.4	4.7	2.8	3.0	4.6	5.0	6.1	5.6	5.1	5.9
Middle income	2.8	3.5	3.6	2.2	2.6	4.2	4.0	6.1	3.1	3.5
Lower middle income	4.2	3.9	3.8	2.3	4.6	4.9	5.4	7.1	4.7	3.9
Upper middle income	0.7	2.8	2.7	1.6	−0.2	2.7	1.6	3.7	1.1	3.0
Low & middle income	3.0	3.7	3.4	2.4	2.8	4.3	4.2	6.0	3.3	3.8
East Asia & Pacific	7.9	7.6	4.9	3.1	8.6	10.0	9.5	10.0	9.3	6.8
Europe & Central Asia	..	0.6	..	−0.4	..	−0.9	..	..	..	1.7
Latin America & Carib.	1.5	2.7	2.0	2.2	1.2	2.4	1.2	2.0	1.7	2.8
Middle East & N. Africa	1.3	3.2	4.8	2.7	−0.6	2.0	..	4.8	2.1	4.0
South Asia	5.5	5.4	3.1	2.8	6.9	5.9	7.3	6.2	6.4	7.0
Sub-Saharan Africa	1.7	2.8	2.3	3.3	1.2	2.3	1.9	2.0	2.6	2.9
High income	3.4	2.6	1.8	1.2	3.0	1.9	..	2.5	3.4	3.1
Europe EMU	2.4	2.0	1.1	1.1	1.7	1.1	..	1.6	2.9	2.4

a. Components are at basic prices. b. Data cover mainland Tanzania only.

About the data

An economy's growth is measured by the change in the volume of its output or in the real incomes of persons resident in the economy. The 1993 United Nations System of National Accounts (1993 SNA) offers three plausible indicators from which to calculate growth: the volume of gross domestic product (GDP), real gross domestic income, and real gross national income. The volume of GDP is the sum of value added, measured at constant prices, by households, government, and the industries operating in the economy. This year's edition of *World Development Indicators* continues to follow the practice of past editions, measuring the growth of the economy by the change in GDP measured at constant prices.

Each industry's contribution to growth in the economy's output is measured by growth in the industry's value added. In principle, value added in constant prices can be estimated by measuring the quantity of goods and services produced in a period, valuing them at an agreed set of base year prices, and subtracting the cost of intermediate inputs, also in constant prices. This double-deflation method, recommended by the 1993 SNA and its predecessors, requires detailed information on the structure of prices of inputs and outputs.

In many industries, however, value added is extrapolated from the base year using single volume indexes of outputs or, more rarely, inputs. Particularly in the services industries, including most of government, value added in constant prices is often imputed from labor inputs, such as real wages or the number of employees. In the absence of well-defined measures of output, measuring the growth of services remains difficult.

Moreover, technical progress can lead to improvements in production processes and in the quality of goods and services that, if not properly accounted for, can distort measures of value added and thus of growth. When inputs are used to estimate output, as is the case for nonmarket services, unmeasured technical progress leads to underestimates of the volume of output. Similarly, unmeasured changes in the quality of goods and services produced lead to underestimates of the value of output and value added. The result can be underestimates of growth and productivity improvement and overestimates of inflation. These issues are highly complex, and only a few high-income countries have attempted to introduce any GDP adjustments for these factors.

Informal economic activities pose a particular measurement problem, especially in developing countries, where much economic activity may go unrecorded.

Obtaining a complete picture of the economy requires estimating household outputs produced for home use, sales in informal markets, barter exchanges, and illicit or deliberately unreported activities. The consistency and completeness of such estimates depend on the skill and methods of the compiling statisticians and the resources available to them.

Rebasing national accounts

When countries rebase their national accounts, they update the weights assigned to various components to better reflect the current pattern of production or uses of output. The new base year should represent normal operation of the economy—that is, it should be a year without major shocks or distortions—but the choice of base year is often constrained by lack of data. Some developing countries have not rebased their national accounts for many years. Using an old base year can be misleading because implicit price and volume weights become progressively less relevant and useful.

To obtain comparable series of constant price data, the World Bank rescales GDP and value added by industrial origin to a common reference year. In this year's *World Development Indicators,* the reference year has been changed from 1995 to 2000. Because rescaling changes the implicit weights used in forming regional and income group aggregates, aggregate growth rates in this year's *World Development Indicators* are not comparable with those from earlier publications with different base years.

Rescaling may result in a discrepancy between the rescaled GDP and the sum of the rescaled components. Because allocating the discrepancy would cause distortions in the growth rates, the discrepancy is left unallocated. As a result, the weighted average of the growth rates of the components generally will not equal the GDP growth rate. The shift to a more recent reference year is to minimize the discrepancy in aggregate GDP and its components, particularly in recent years.

Growth rates of GDP and its components are calculated using constant price data in the local currency. Regional and income group growth rates are calculated after converting local currencies to constant price U.S. dollars using an exchange rate in the common reference year. The growth rates in the table are average annual compound growth rates. Methods of computing growth rates and the alternative conversion factor are described in *Statistical methods.*

Changes in the System of National Accounts

World Development Indicators adopted the terminology of the 1993 SNA in 2001. Although most countries continue to compile their national accounts according to the SNA version 3 (referred to as the 1968 SNA), more and more are adopting the 1993 SNA. Some low-income countries still use concepts from the even older 1953 SNA guidelines, including valuations such as factor cost, in describing major economic aggregates. Countries that use the 1993 SNA are identified in *Primary data documentation.*

Definitions

• **Gross domestic product** (GDP) at purchaser prices is the sum of gross value added by all resident producers in the economy plus any product taxes (less subsidies) not included in the valuation of output. It is calculated without deducting for depreciation of fabricated capital assets or for depletion and degradation of natural resources. Value added is the net output of an industry after adding up all outputs and subtracting intermediate inputs. The industrial origin of value added is determined by the International Standard Industrial Classification (ISIC) revision 3. • **Agriculture** corresponds to ISIC divisions 1–5 and includes forestry and fishing. • **Industry** covers mining, manufacturing (also reported separately), construction, electricity, water, and gas (ISIC divisions 10–45). • **Manufacturing** corresponds to industries belonging to ISIC divisions 15–37. • **Services** correspond to ISIC divisions 50–99. This sector is derived as a residual (from GDP less agriculture and industry) and may not properly reflect the sum of services output, including banking and financial services. For some countries it includes product taxes (minus subsidies) and may also include statistical discrepancies.

Data sources

The national accounts data for most developing countries are collected from national statistical organizations and central banks by visiting and resident World Bank missions. The data for high-income economies come from data files of the Organisation for Economic Co-operation and Development (for information on the OECD's national accounts series, see its monthly *Main Economic Indicators*). The World Bank rescales constant price data to a common reference year. The complete national accounts time series is available on the *World Development Indicators 2005* CD-ROM. The United Nations Statistics Division publishes detailed national accounts for UN member countries in *National Accounts Statistics: Main Aggregates and Detailed Tables* and publishes updates in the *Monthly Bulletin of Statistics.*

4.2 Structure of output

	Gross domestic product		Agriculture		Industry		Manufacturing		Services	
	$ millions		% of GDP		% of GDP		% of GDP		% of GDP	
	1990	2003	1990	2003	1990	2003	1990	2003	1990	2003
Afghanistan	..	4,708	..	52	..	24	..	18	..	24
Albania[a]	2,102	6,124	36	25	48	19	..	10	16	56
Algeria[a]	62,045	66,530	11	10	48	55	11	7	40	35
Angola	10,260	13,189	18	9	41	65	5	4	41	27
Argentina[a]	141,352	129,596	8	11	36	35	27	24	56	54
Armenia[a]	2,257	2,805	17	24	52	39	33	22	31	37
Australia	310,581	522,378	4	3	29	26	14	12	67	71
Austria	161,688	253,126	4	2	34	32	23	22	62	66
Azerbaijan[a]	8,858	7,138	29	14	33	55	30	23	38	31
Bangladesh	30,129	51,914	30	22	21	26	13	16	48	52
Belarus[a]	17,370	17,493	24	10	47	30	39	23	29	60
Belgium	197,176	301,896	2	1	33	26	..	19	65	72
Benin	1,845	3,476	36	36	13	14	8	9	51	50
Bolivia	4,868	7,867	17	15	35	30	18	15	48	55
Bosnia and Herzegovina	..	6,973	..	15	..	32	..	15	..	53
Botswana[a]	3,791	7,530	5	2	57	45	5	4	39	52
Brazil[a]	461,952	492,338	8	6	39	19	25	11	53	75
Bulgaria[a]	20,726	19,860	17	12	49	31	..	19	34	58
Burkina Faso[a]	3,120	4,182	28	31	20	19	15	13	52	50
Burundi[a]	1,132	595	56	49	19	19	13	..	25	32
Cambodia	1,115	4,228	..	34	..	30	..	22	..	36
Cameroon[a]	11,152	12,491	25	44	29	17	15	9	46	39
Canada[a]	574,192	856,523	3	..	32	..	17	..	65	..
Central African Republic[a]	1,488	1,198	48	61	20	25	11	..	33	14
Chad[a]	1,739	2,608	29	46	18	13	14	12	53	41
Chile	30,323	72,415	9	9	41	34	20	16	50	57
China	354,644	1,417,000	27	15	42	52	33	39	31	33
Hong Kong, China[a]	75,433	156,679	0	0	25	12	17	5	74	88
Colombia[a]	40,274	78,651	17	12	38	29	21	14	45	58
Congo, Dem. Rep.[a]	9,348	5,671	30	58	28	19	11	4	42	23
Congo, Rep.	2,799	3,564	13	6	41	60	8	6	46	34
Costa Rica[a]	5,713	17,427	18	9	29	29	22	21	53	62
Côte d'Ivoire	10,796	13,734	32	26	23	19	21	11	44	55
Croatia[a]	24,778	28,797	10	8	34	30	28	19	56	62
Cuba	..	..	..	..	..	..	..	..	..	..
Czech Republic[a]	34,880	89,715	6	3	49	39	..	27	45	57
Denmark[a]	133,360	211,888	4	2	27	26	18	16	69	71
Dominican Republic	7,074	16,541	13	11	31	31	18	15	55	58
Ecuador	10,356	27,201	13	8	38	29	19	11	49	64
Egypt, Arab Rep.[a]	43,130	82,427	19	16	29	34	18	19	52	50
El Salvador	4,807	14,879	17	9	27	32	22	24	56	59
Eritrea[a]	477	751	31	14	12	25	8	11	57	61
Estonia[a]	5,010	9,082	17	4	50	28	42	18	34	67
Ethiopia[a]	8,609	6,652	49	42	13	11	8	..	38	47
Finland[a]	136,962	161,876	7	3	34	31	23	24	59	66
France	1,215,932	1,757,613	4	3	30	24	21	18	66	73
Gabon	5,952	6,057	7	8	43	62	6	5	50	30
Gambia, The[a]	317	395	29	30	13	15	7	5	58	55
Georgia[a]	7,738	3,988	32	20	33	25	24	19	35	54
Germany	1,671,335	2,403,160	2	1	39	29	28	23	59	69
Ghana	5,886	7,624	45	36	17	25	10	8	38	39
Greece[a]	84,073	172,203	11	7	28	24	..	12	61	69
Guatemala	7,650	24,730	26	22	20	19	15	13	54	58
Guinea[a]	2,818	3,630	24	25	33	36	5	4	43	39
Guinea-Bissau[a]	244	239	61	69	19	13	8	10	21	18
Haiti	2,864	2,921	..	28	..	17	..	..	..	55

Structure of output | 4.2

	Gross domestic product		Agriculture		Industry		Manufacturing		Services	
	$ millions		% of GDP		% of GDP		% of GDP		% of GDP	
	1990	2003	1990	2003	1990	2003	1990	2003	1990	2003
Honduras[a]	3,049	6,978	22	13	26	31	16	20	51	56
Hungary[a]	33,056	82,732	15	4	39	31	23	23	46	65
India[a]	316,937	600,637	31	22	28	27	17	16	41	51
Indonesia	114,426	208,312	19	17	39	44	21	25	41	40
Iran, Islamic Rep.[a]	120,404	137,144	24	11	29	41	12	13	48	48
Iraq[a]	48,657	..	..	..	..	..	..	..	..	..
Ireland[a]	47,299	153,719	9	3	35	42	28	32	56	55
Israel[a]	52,490	110,227	..	..	..	..	..	..	..	..
Italy	1,102,380	1,468,314	4	3	34	28	25	20	63	70
Jamaica	4,592	8,147	7	5	40	30	19	13	52	65
Japan	3,039,693	4,300,858	2	1	39	30	27	21	58	68
Jordan[a]	4,020	9,860	8	2	28	26	15	16	64	72
Kazakhstan[a]	26,933	29,749	27	8	45	38	9	16	29	54
Kenya[a]	8,551	14,376	29	16	19	20	12	14	52	65
Korea, Dem. Rep.	..	..	..	..	..	..	..	..	..	..
Korea, Rep.	263,775	605,331	..	3	..	35	..	23	..	62
Kuwait	18,428	41,748	1	..	52	..	12	..	47	..
Kyrgyz Republic[a]	2,674	1,909	34	39	36	23	28	8	30	38
Lao PDR[a]	866	2,122	61	49	15	26	10	19	24	25
Latvia[a]	7,447	11,073	22	5	46	24	34	15	32	71
Lebanon[a]	2,838	19,000	..	12	..	20	..	9	..	68
Lesotho[a]	615	1,139	24	17	33	44	14	20	43	40
Liberia[a]	384	442	..	..	..	..	..	..	..	..
Libya[a]	28,905	19,131	..	..	..	..	..	..	..	..
Lithuania[a]	10,506	18,215	27	7	31	34	21	21	42	59
Macedonia, FYR[a]	4,478	4,666	9	12	46	30	36	19	45	57
Madagascar[a]	3,081	5,474	29	29	13	15	11	14	59	55
Malawi[a]	1,881	1,714	45	38	29	15	19	10	26	47
Malaysia	44,024	103,737	15	10	42	49	24	31	43	42
Mali[a]	2,421	4,326	46	38	16	26	9	3	39	36
Mauritania[a]	1,020	1,093	30	19	29	30	10	9	42	51
Mauritius[a]	2,383	5,224	13	6	33	31	25	22	54	63
Mexico	262,710	626,080	8	4	28	26	21	18	64	70
Moldova[a]	3,549	1,964	43	23	33	25	..	18	24	53
Mongolia	..	1,274	17	28	30	15	..	5	52	57
Morocco	25,821	43,727	18	17	32	30	18	17	50	54
Mozambique[a]	2,463	4,321	37	26	18	31	10	15	44	43
Myanmar	..	..	57	..	11	..	8	..	32	..
Namibia[a]	2,350	4,271	12	11	38	26	14	12	50	64
Nepal[a]	3,628	5,851	52	41	16	22	6	8	32	38
Netherlands	294,761	511,502	4	3	31	26	19	15	65	72
New Zealand	43,618	79,572	7	..	28	..	19	..	65	..
Nicaragua	1,009	4,083	31	18	21	26	17	15	48	56
Niger	2,481	2,731	35	40	16	17	7	7	49	43
Nigeria[a]	28,472	58,390	33	26	41	49	6	4	26	24
Norway	116,108	220,854	4	1	36	38	13	11	61	61
Oman	10,535	20,309	3	..	58	..	4	..	39	..
Pakistan[a]	40,010	82,324	26	23	25	23	17	16	49	53
Panama[a]	5,313	12,887	9	7	15	16	9	8	76	76
Papua New Guinea	3,221	3,182	29	26	30	39	9	9	41	35
Paraguay	5,265	6,030	28	27	25	24	17	14	47	49
Peru	26,294	60,577	9	10	27	29	18	16	64	60
Philippines	44,331	80,574	22	14	34	32	25	23	44	53
Poland[a]	58,976	209,563	8	3	50	31	..	18	42	66
Portugal	71,462	147,899	9	4	32	29	22	18	60	68
Puerto Rico	30,604	67,897	1	1	42	43	40	40	57	56

	Gross domestic product		Agriculture		Industry		Manufacturing		Services	
	$ millions		% of GDP		% of GDP		% of GDP		% of GDP	
	1990	2003	1990	2003	1990	2003	1990	2003	1990	2003
Romania[a]	38,299	56,951	24	12	50	36	*34*	30	26	52
Russian Federation[a]	516,814	432,855	17	5	48	34	..	..	35	61
Rwanda[a]	2,584	1,637	33	42	25	22	18	11	43	36
Saudi Arabia	116,778	214,748	6	5	49	55	9	10	45	40
Senegal	5,699	6,496	20	17	19	21	13	13	61	62
Serbia and Montenegro[a]	..	20,729	..	..	..	..	..	..	..	..
Sierra Leone	650	793	32	53	13	31	5	5	55	16
Singapore	36,901	91,342	..	0	..	35	..	28	..	65
Slovak Republic	15,485	32,519	7	4	59	30	..	20	33	67
Slovenia[a]	17,382	27,749	*6*	*3*	*46*	*36*	*35*	*27*	*49*	*61*
Somalia[a]	917	..	65	..	..	..	5	..	..	..
South Africa[a]	112,014	159,886	5	4	40	31	24	19	55	65
Spain[a]	509,997	838,652	6	3	35	30	..	17	59	67
Sri Lanka[a]	8,032	18,237	26	19	26	26	15	16	48	55
Sudan[a]	13,167	17,793	..	*39*	..	*18*	..	*9*	..	*43*
Swaziland[a]	859	1,845	14	12	43	52	36	40	43	36
Sweden	240,153	301,606	3	2	32	28	..	*21*	64	70
Switzerland	235,808	320,118	..	..	..	..	..	..	..	..
Syrian Arab Republic	12,309	21,499	28	23	24	29	20	25	48	48
Tajikistan[a]	2,629	1,553	33	23	38	20	25	..	29	56
Tanzania[b]	4,259	10,297	46	45	18	16	9	7	36	39
Thailand	85,345	142,953	12	10	37	44	27	35	50	46
Togo[a]	1,628	1,759	34	41	23	22	10	9	44	37
Trinidad and Tobago	5,068	10,511	3	1	45	49	13	7	52	50
Tunisia[a]	12,291	25,037	16	12	30	28	17	18	54	60
Turkey[a]	150,642	240,376	18	13	30	22	20	13	52	65
Turkmenistan[a]	3,232	6,201	32	*25*	30	*44*	..	..	38	*30*
Uganda[a]	4,304	6,297	57	32	11	21	6	9	32	46
Ukraine[a]	81,456	49,537	26	14	45	40	*44*	25	30	46
United Arab Emirates[a]	34,132	*70,960*	2	..	64	..	8	..	35	..
United Kingdom	989,524	1,794,878	2	1	35	27	23	*17*	63	72
United States	5,757,200	10,948,547	2	*2*	28	*23*	19	*15*	70	*75*
Uruguay[a]	9,286	11,182	9	13	35	27	28	19	56	60
Uzbekistan[a]	13,361	9,949	33	35	33	22	..	9	34	43
Venezuela, RB	48,597	85,394	5	4	61	41	15	9	34	54
Vietnam	6,472	39,164	39	22	23	40	12	21	39	38
West Bank and Gaza[a]	..	3,454	..	6	..	12	..	10	..	82
Yemen, Rep.	4,828	10,831	24	15	27	40	9	5	49	45
Zambia	3,288	4,335	21	23	51	27	36	12	28	50
Zimbabwe[a]	8,784	*17,750*	16	*17*	33	*24*	23	*13*	50	*59*
World	**21,687,666 t**	**36,460,632 t**	**5 w**	***4 w***	**34 w**	***28* w**	**22 w**	***18* w**	**61 w**	***68* w**
Low income	619,349	1,103,018	32	24	26	27	15	14	41	49
Middle income	3,377,092	6,023,146	15	10	39	36	24	22	46	54
Lower middle income	2,466,994	4,167,974	19	11	39	37	26	25	43	52
Upper middle income	919,157	1,855,670	8	6	39	35	20	18	52	59
Low & middle income	3,997,613	7,124,879	18	12	37	35	22	21	45	53
East Asia & Pacific	665,990	2,032,633	25	14	40	49	30	36	35	36
Europe & Central Asia	1,109,272	1,402,515	16	8	43	31	..	18	41	61
Latin America & Carib.	1,102,889	1,740,625	9	7	36	27	*22*	16	55	66
Middle East & N. Africa	420,753	744,756	14	11	38	43	13	13	48	47
South Asia	401,029	765,083	31	22	27	26	17	16	43	51
Sub-Saharan Africa	298,376	439,287	19	17	34	31	17	14	47	52
High income	17,691,266	29,340,557	3	*2*	33	*27*	22	*18*	65	*71*
Europe EMU	5,504,146	8,196,456	4	2	34	28	*24*	20	62	70

a. Components are at basic prices. b. Data cover mainland Tanzania only.

An economy's gross domestic product (GDP) represents the sum of value added by all producers in that economy. Value added is the value of the gross output of producers less the value of intermediate goods and services consumed in production, before taking account of the consumption of fixed capital in the production process. Since 1968 the United Nations System of National Accounts has called for estimates of value added to be valued at either basic prices (excluding net taxes on products) or producer prices (including net taxes on products paid by producers but excluding sales or value added taxes). Both valuations exclude transport charges that are invoiced separately by producers. Some countries, however, report such data at purchaser prices—the prices at which final sales are made (including transport charges)—which may affect estimates of the distribution of output. Total GDP shown in the table and elsewhere in this book is measured at purchaser prices. Value added by industry is normally measured at basic prices. When value added is measured at producer prices, this is noted in *Primary data documentation*.

While GDP estimates based on the production approach are generally more reliable than estimates compiled from the income or expenditure side, different countries use different definitions, methods, and reporting standards. World Bank staff review the quality of national accounts data and sometimes make adjustments to improve consistency with international guidelines. Nevertheless, significant discrepancies remain between international standards and actual practice. Many statistical offices, especially those in developing countries, face severe limitations in the resources, time, training, and budgets required to produce reliable and comprehensive series of national accounts statistics.

Data problems in measuring output

Among the difficulties faced by compilers of national accounts is the extent of unreported economic activity in the informal or secondary economy. In developing countries a large share of agricultural output is either not exchanged (because it is consumed within the household) or not exchanged for money.

Agricultural production often must be estimated indirectly, using a combination of methods involving estimates of inputs, yields, and area under cultivation. This approach sometimes leads to crude approximations that can differ from the true values over time and across crops for reasons other than climatic conditions or farming techniques. Similarly, agricultural inputs that cannot easily be allocated to

specific outputs are frequently "netted out" using equally crude and ad hoc approximations. For further discussion of the measurement of agricultural production, see *About the data* for table 3.3.

Ideally, industrial output should be measured through regular censuses and surveys of firms. But in most developing countries such surveys are infrequent, so earlier survey results must be extrapolated using an appropriate indicator. The choice of sampling unit, which may be the enterprise (where responses may be based on financial records) or the establishment (where production units may be recorded separately), also affects the quality of the data. Moreover, much industrial production is organized in unincorporated or owner-operated ventures that are not captured by surveys aimed at the formal sector. Even in large industries, where regular surveys are more likely, evasion of excise and other taxes and nondisclosure of income lower the estimates of value added. Such problems become more acute as countries move from state control of industry to private enterprise, because new firms enter business and growing numbers of established firms fail to report. In accordance with the System of National Accounts, output should include all such unreported activity as well as the value of illegal activities and other unrecorded, informal, or small-scale operations. Data on these activities need to be collected using techniques other than conventional surveys of firms.

In industries dominated by large organizations and enterprises, such as public utilities, data on output, employment, and wages are usually readily available and reasonably reliable. But in the services industry the many self-employed workers and one-person businesses are sometimes difficult to locate, and they have little incentive to respond to surveys, let alone to report their full earnings. Compounding these problems are the many forms of economic activity that go unrecorded, including the work that women and children do for little or no pay. For further discussion of the problems of using national accounts data, see Srinivasan (1994) and Heston (1994).

Dollar conversion

To produce national accounts aggregates that are measured in the same standard monetary units, the value of output must be converted to a single common currency. The World Bank conventionally uses the U.S. dollar and applies the average official exchange rate reported by the International Monetary Fund for the year shown. An alternative conversion

factor is applied if the official exchange rate is judged to diverge by an exceptionally large margin from the rate effectively applied to transactions in foreign currencies and traded products.

Definitions

• **Gross domestic product** (GDP) at purchaser prices is the sum of gross value added by all resident producers in the economy plus any product taxes (less subsidies) not included in the valuation of output. It is calculated without deducting for depreciation of fabricated assets or for depletion and degradation of natural resources. Value added is the net output of an industry after adding up all outputs and subtracting intermediate inputs. The industrial origin of value added is determined by the International Standard Industrial Classification (ISIC) revision 3. • **Agriculture** corresponds to ISIC divisions 1–5 and includes forestry and fishing. • **Industry** covers mining, manufacturing (also reported separately), construction, electricity, water, and gas (ISIC divisions 10–45). • **Manufacturing** corresponds to industries belonging to ISIC divisions 15–37. • **Services** correspond to ISIC divisions 50–99. This sector is derived as a residual (from GDP less agriculture and industry) and may not properly reflect the sum of services output, including banking and financial services. For some countries it includes product taxes (minus subsidies) and may also include statistical discrepancies.

Data sources

The national accounts data for most developing countries are collected from national statistical organizations and central banks by visiting and resident World Bank missions. The data for high-income economies come from data files of the Organisation for Economic Co-operation and Development (for information on the OECD's national accounts series, see its monthly *Main Economic Indicators*). The complete national accounts time series is available on the *World Development Indicators 2005* CD-ROM. The United Nations Statistics Division publishes detailed national accounts for UN member countries in *National Accounts Statistics: Main Aggregates and Detailed Tables* and publishes updates in the *Monthly Bulletin of Statistics*.

4.3 Structure of manufacturing

	Manufacturing value added		Food, beverages, and tobacco		Textiles and clothing		Machinery and transport equipment		Chemicals		Other manufacturing[a]	
	$ millions		% of total		% of total		% of total		% of total		% of total	
	1990	2001	1990	2001	1990	2001	1990	2001	1990	2001	1990	2001
Afghanistan	..	..	..	..	..	..	..	..	..	..	..	..
Albania	..	390	24	..	33	..	..	..	..	..	44	..
Algeria	6,452	4,063	13	..	17	..	..	..	..	..	70	..
Angola	513	359	..	..	..	..	..	..	..	..	..	..
Argentina	37,868	43,242	20	28	10	6	13	12	12	..	46	54
Armenia	681	426	..	..	..	..	..	..	..	..	..	..
Australia	38,867	39,664	18	..	6	..	20	..	7	..	48	..
Austria	33,385	37,015	15	7	7	3	28	31	7	4	43	56
Azerbaijan	1,561	372	..	..	..	..	..	..	..	..	..	..
Bangladesh	3,839	7,087	24	22	38	33	7	16	17	10	15	19
Belarus	6,630	3,300	..	..	..	..	..	..	..	..	..	..
Belgium	..	39,291	17	19	7	6	..	..	13	16	62	59
Benin	145	218	..	..	..	..	..	..	..	..	..	..
Bolivia	826	1,060	28	31	5	4	1	1	3	3	63	60
Bosnia and Herzegovina	..	514	12	..	15	..	18	..	7	..	49	..
Botswana	181	235	51	20	12	5	..	..	..	..	36	75
Brazil	89,966	63,247	14	..	12	..	27	..	..	..	48	..
Bulgaria	..	2,108	22	..	9	..	19	..	5	..	45	..
Burkina Faso	460	331	..	..	..	..	..	..	..	..	..	..
Burundi	134	60	83	..	9	..	..	..	2	..	7	..
Cambodia	58	651	..	..	..	..	..	..	..	..	..	..
Cameroon	1,581	909	61	47	-13	15	1	1	5	4	46	32
Canada	91,671	130,613	15	13	6	4	26	31	10	8	44	43
Central African Republic	154	81	57	..	6	..	2	..	6	..	28	..
Chad	239	244	..	..	..	..	..	..	..	..	..	..
Chile	5,613	9,280	25	32	7	4	5	5	10	14	52	45
China	116,573	407,514	15	15	15	12	24	32	13	12	34	28
Hong Kong, China	12,639	8,145	8	9	36	19	21	30	2	4	33	38
Colombia	8,034	11,634	31	33	15	9	9	5	14	17	31	35
Congo, Dem. Rep.	1,029	200	..	..	..	..	..	..	..	..	..	..
Congo, Rep.	234	124	..	..	..	..	..	..	..	..	..	..
Costa Rica	1,107	3,243	47	47	8	6	7	5	9	11	30	31
Côte d'Ivoire	2,257	1,525	..	42	..	10	..	3	..	12	..	33
Croatia	6,475	3,475	22	..	15	..	20	..	8	..	36	..
Cuba	..	..	..	..	..	..	..	..	..	..	..	..
Czech Republic	..	15,334	..	..	..	..	..	..	..	..	..	..
Denmark	20,757	22,165	22	..	4	..	24	..	12	..	39	..
Dominican Republic	1,270	3,475	..	..	..	..	..	..	..	..	..	..
Ecuador	1,988	2,466	22	38	10	6	5	3	8	4	56	50
Egypt, Arab Rep.	7,296	17,727	19	..	15	..	9	..	14	..	43	..
El Salvador	1,044	3,162	36	29	14	28	4	3	24	16	23	24
Eritrea	35	67	..	..	..	..	..	..	..	..	..	..
Estonia	1,985	923	..	..	..	..	..	..	..	..	..	..
Ethiopia	624	..	62	55	21	12	1	4	2	5	14	24
Finland	27,531	26,504	13	1	4	6	24	..	8	3	52	90
France	228,270	217,535	13	..	6	..	31	..	9	..	41	..
Gabon	332	211	45	..	2	..	1	..	7	..	45	..
Gambia, The	18	19	..	..	..	..	..	..	..	..	..	..
Georgia	1,773	536	..	..	..	..	..	..	..	..	..	..
Germany	456,405	385,924	..	8	..	2	..	41	..	10	..	38
Ghana	575	478	..	..	..	..	..	..	..	..	..	..
Greece	..	12,646	22	25	20	12	12	14	10	10	36	39
Guatemala	1,151	2,728	..	..	..	..	..	..	..	..	..	..
Guinea	126	120	..	..	..	..	..	..	..	..	..	..
Guinea-Bissau	19	20	..	..	..	..	..	..	..	..	..	..
Haiti	..	272	51	..	9	..	..	..	..	..	40	..

Structure of manufacturing | 4.3

	Manufacturing value added ($ millions)		Food, beverages, and tobacco (% of total)		Textiles and clothing (% of total)		Machinery and transport equipment (% of total)		Chemicals (% of total)		Other manufacturing[a] (% of total)	
	1990	2001	1990	2001	1990	2001	1990	2001	1990	2001	1990	2001
Honduras	443	1,134	45	..	10	..	3	..	5	..	36	..
Hungary	6,613	10,372	14	15	9	6	26	37	12	10	39	32
India	48,808	67,144	12	13	15	13	25	19	14	21	34	34
Indonesia	23,643	36,343	27	22	15	13	12	23	9	12	37	30
Iran, Islamic Rep.	14,503	15,009	12	10	20	6	20	23	8	19	40	43
Iraq	..	..	20	..	16	..	4	..	11	..	49	..
Ireland	11,982	28,969	27	16	4	1	29	31	16	36	24	16
Israel	..	..	14	9	9	5	32	33	9	2	37	51
Italy	247,917	203,248	8	9	13	13	34	27	7	8	37	44
Jamaica	853	1,049	41	..	5	..	..	..	..	..	54	..
Japan	810,232	865,810	9	12	5	3	40	38	10	11	37	36
Jordan	520	1,176	28	30	7	7	4	5	15	18	47	41
Kazakhstan	1,941	3,630	..	..	..	..	..	..	..	..	..	..
Kenya	864	1,234	38	48	10	8	10	9	9	8	33	28
Korea, Dem. Rep.	..	..	..	..	..	..	..	..	..	..	..	..
Korea, Rep.	64,604	117,576	11	8	12	8	32	45	9	9	36	30
Kuwait	2,142	..	4	7	3	4	2	4	3	2	88	83
Kyrgyz Republic	706	148	..	..	..	..	..	..	..	..	..	..
Lao PDR	85	310	..	..	..	..	..	..	..	..	..	..
Latvia	2,474	1,009	..	27	..	11	..	9	..	4	..	49
Lebanon	..	1,572	..	..	..	..	..	..	..	..	..	..
Lesotho	71	122	..	..	..	..	..	..	..	..	..	..
Liberia	..	34	..	..	..	..	..	..	..	..	..	..
Libya	..	..	..	..	..	..	..	..	..	..	..	..
Lithuania	2,164	2,192	..	..	..	..	..	..	..	..	..	..
Macedonia, FYR	1,411	582	20	..	26	..	14	..	9	..	31	..
Madagascar	314	520	..	..	..	..	..	..	..	..	..	..
Malawi	313	177	38	44	10	8	1	5	18	16	33	28
Malaysia	10,665	26,772	13	8	6	4	31	41	11	8	39	39
Mali	200	75	..	..	..	..	..	..	..	..	..	..
Mauritania	94	81	..	..	..	..	..	..	..	..	..	..
Mauritius	491	933	30	31	46	48	2	2	4	5	17	15
Mexico	49,992	110,382	22	25	5	4	24	27	18	15	32	28
Moldova	..	235	..	..	..	..	..	..	..	..	..	..
Mongolia	..	61	33	..	37	..	1	..	1	..	27	..
Morocco	4,753	5,739	22	36	17	16	8	8	12	13	41	27
Mozambique	230	476	..	..	..	..	..	..	..	..	..	..
Myanmar	..	..	..	..	..	..	..	..	..	..	..	..
Namibia	292	302	..	..	..	..	..	..	..	..	..	..
Nepal	209	483	37	..	31	..	1	..	5	..	25	..
Netherlands	52,330	53,769	21	1	3	5	25	..	16	..	35	95
New Zealand	7,574	8,186	28	..	8	..	13	..	7	..	44	..
Nicaragua	170	582	..	..	..	..	..	..	..	..	..	..
Niger	163	128	37	20	29	9	..	..	..	..	34	71
Nigeria	1,562	1,811	15	..	46	..	13	..	4	..	22	..
Norway	13,450	16,473	18	17	2	1	25	24	9	8	46	49
Oman	396	..	..	9	..	2	..	3	..	3	..	84
Pakistan	6,184	10,445	24	..	27	..	9	..	15	..	25	..
Panama	502	1,034	51	58	8	5	2	..	8	7	31	29
Papua New Guinea	289	254	..	..	..	..	..	..	..	..	..	..
Paraguay	883	964	55	..	16	..	..	..	..	..	29	..
Peru	3,926	7,762	23	..	11	..	8	..	9	..	49	..
Philippines	11,008	16,308	39	33	11	9	13	15	12	13	26	29
Poland	..	28,825	21	6	9	14	26	8	7	..	37	72
Portugal	13,630	17,332	15	13	21	18	13	19	6	5	45	45
Puerto Rico	12,126	27,099	16	8	5	2	18	18	44	61	17	12

4.3 Structure of manufacturing

	Manufacturing value added $ millions		Food, beverages, and tobacco % of total		Textiles and clothing % of total		Machinery and transport equipment % of total		Chemicals % of total		Other manufacturing[a] % of total	
	1990	2001	1990	2001	1990	2001	1990	2001	1990	2001	1990	2001
Romania	*9,152*	6,064	19	..	18	..	14	..	4	..	45	..
Russian Federation	..	..	..	19	..	2	..	23	..	5	..	49
Rwanda	473	200	..	..	..	..	..	..	..	..	..	..
Saudi Arabia	10,049	18,480	..	..	..	..	..	..	..	..	..	..
Senegal	747	601	60	*44*	3	*5*	5	*3*	9	*26*	23	*21*
Serbia and Montenegro	..	..	..	33	..	8	..	14	..	10	..	35
Sierra Leone	31	34	..	..	..	..	..	..	..	..	..	..
Singapore	..	20,399	4	3	3	1	53	59	10	16	29	21
Slovak Republic	..	4,631	..	*9*	..	7	..	*19*	..	5	..	*60*
Slovenia	5,190	4,693	12	10	15	10	16	14	9	11	48	55
Somalia	41	..	..	..	..	..	..	..	..	..	..	..
South Africa	24,043	19,320	14	*11*	8	*4*	18	*17*	9	*10*	50	*58*
Spain	..	96,059	18	*14*	8	7	25	*23*	10	*10*	39	*47*
Sri Lanka	1,077	2,220	51	*39*	24	*31*	4	*6*	4	4	17	*21*
Sudan	..	1,361	..	..	..	..	..	..	..	..	..	..
Swaziland	250	324	69	..	8	..	1	..	*0*	..	22	..
Sweden	..	40,381	10	7	2	*1*	32	*39*	9	*11*	47	*42*
Switzerland	..	..	10	*9*	4	*3*	34	*27*	..	..	53	*60*
Syrian Arab Republic	2,508	4,862	35	*27*	29	*24*	..	..	..	..	36	*49*
Tajikistan	653	250	..	..	..	..	..	..	..	..	..	..
Tanzania[b]	361	644	51	*45*	3	*0*	6	*5*	11	*7*	28	*43*
Thailand	23,217	38,619	24	..	30	..	19	..	2	..	26	..
Togo	162	118	..	..	..	..	..	..	..	..	..	..
Trinidad and Tobago	681	654	30	..	3	..	3	..	19	..	44	..
Tunisia	2,075	3,693	19	16	20	34	5	10	4	9	52	31
Turkey	26,882	19,686	16	3	15	0	16	..	10	..	43	96
Turkmenistan	..	491	..	..	..	..	..	..	..	..	..	..
Uganda	230	497	..	..	..	..	..	..	..	..	..	..
Ukraine	*32,977*	6,625	..	..	..	..	..	..	..	..	..	..
United Arab Emirates	2,643	..	..	..	..	..	..	..	..	..	..	..
United Kingdom	206,719	220,429	13	..	5	..	32	..	11	..	38	..
United States	1,040,600	1,423,000	12	..	5	..	31	..	12	..	40	..
Uruguay	2,597	3,025	31	*37*	18	*12*	9	*3*	10	*8*	32	*39*
Uzbekistan	..	890	..	..	..	..	..	..	..	..	..	..
Venezuela, RB	7,152	11,480	17	*22*	5	*2*	5	*10*	9	*11*	64	*76*
Vietnam	793	6,466	..	..	..	..	..	..	..	..	..	..
West Bank and Gaza	..	489	..	..	..	..	..	..	..	..	..	..
Yemen, Rep.	449	503	..	..	..	..	..	..	..	..	..	..
Zambia	1,048	358	44	..	11	..	7	..	9	..	29	..
Zimbabwe	1,799	1,115	28	..	19	..	9	..	6	..	38	..
World	**4,412,838 t**	**5,404,374 t**										
Low income	84,536	113,824										
Middle income	634,890	1,099,974										
Lower middle income	464,789	799,637										
Upper middle income	174,699	300,542										
Low & middle income	725,616	1,213,957										
East Asia & Pacific	187,470	536,083										
Europe & Central Asia	..	..										
Latin America & Carib.	204,582	285,233										
Middle East & N. Africa	47,258	80,632										
South Asia	60,476	87,909										
Sub-Saharan Africa	43,345	36,630										
High income	3,673,504	4,192,708										
Europe EMU	*1,216,519*	1,120,404										

a. Includes unallocated data. b. Data cover mainland Tanzania only.

About the data

The data on the distribution of manufacturing value added by industry are provided by the United Nations Industrial Development Organization (UNIDO). UNIDO obtains data on manufacturing value added from a variety of national and international sources, including the United Nations Statistics Division, the World Bank, the Organisation for Economic Co-operation and Development, and the International Monetary Fund. To improve comparability over time and across countries, UNIDO supplements these data with information from industrial censuses, statistics supplied by national and international organizations, unpublished data that it collects in the field, and estimates by the UNIDO Secretariat. Nevertheless, coverage may be less than complete, particularly for the informal sector. To the extent that direct information on inputs and outputs is not available, estimates may be used, which may result in errors in industry totals. Moreover, countries use different reference periods (calendar or fiscal year) and valuation methods (basic, producer, or purchaser prices) to estimate value added. (See also *About the data* for table 4.2.)

The data on manufacturing value added in U.S. dollars are from the World Bank's national accounts files. These figures may differ from those used by UNIDO to calculate the shares of value added by industry, in part because of differences in exchange rates. Thus estimates of value added in a particular industry calculated by applying the shares to total manufacturing value added will not match those from UNIDO sources.

The classification of manufacturing industries in the table accords with the United Nations International Standard Industrial Classification (ISIC) revision 2. First published in 1948, the ISIC has its roots in the work of the League of Nations Committee of Statistical Experts. The committee's efforts, interrupted by the Second World War, were taken up by the United Nations Statistical Commission, which at its first session appointed a committee on industrial classification. The latest revision, ISIC revision 3, was completed in 1989, and many countries have now switched to it. But revision 2 is still widely used for compiling cross-country data. Concordances matching ISIC categories to national systems of classification and to related systems such as the Standard International Trade Classification (SITC) are readily available.

In establishing a classification system, compilers must define both the types of activities to be described and the organizational units whose activities are to be reported. There are many possibilities, and the choices made affect how the resulting statistics can be interpreted and how useful they are in analyzing economic behavior. The ISIC emphasizes commonalities in the production process and is explicitly not intended to measure outputs (for which there is a newly developed Central Product Classification). Nevertheless, the ISIC views an activity as defined by "a process resulting in a homogeneous set of products" (United Nations 1990 [ISIC, series M, no. 4, rev. 3], p. 9).

Firms typically use a multitude of processes to produce a final product. For example, an automobile manufacturer engages in forging, welding, and painting as well as advertising, accounting, and many other service activities. In some cases the processes may be carried out by different technical units within the larger enterprise, but collecting data at such a detailed level is not practical. Nor would it be useful to record production data at the very highest level of a large, multiplant, multiproduct firm. The ISIC has therefore adopted as the definition of an establishment "an enterprise or part of an enterprise which independently engages in one, or predominantly one, kind of economic activity at or from one location...for which data are available..." (United Nations 1990, p. 25). By design, this definition matches the reporting unit required for the production accounts of the UN System of National Accounts.

Definitions

• **Manufacturing value added** is the sum of gross output less the value of intermediate inputs used in production for industries classified in ISIC major division 3. • **Food, beverages, and tobacco** correspond to ISIC division 31. • **Textiles and clothing** correspond to ISIC division 32. • **Machinery and transport equipment** correspond to ISIC groups 382–84. • **Chemicals** correspond to ISIC groups 351 and 352. • **Other manufacturing** covers wood and related products (ISIC division 33), paper and related products (ISIC division 34), petroleum and related products (ISIC groups 353–56), basic metals and mineral products (ISIC divisions 36 and 37), fabricated metal products and professional goods (ISIC groups 381 and 385), and other industries (ISIC group 390). When data for textiles and clothing, machinery and transport equipment, or chemicals are shown in the table as not available, they are included in "other manufacturing."

Data sources

The data on value added in manufacturing in U.S. dollars are from the World Bank's national accounts files. The data used to calculate shares of value added by industry are provided to the World Bank in electronic files by UNIDO. The most recent published source is UNIDO's *International Yearbook of Industrial Statistics 2004*. The ISIC system is described in the United Nations' *International Standard Industrial Classification of All Economic Activities, Third Revision* (1990). The discussion of the ISIC draws on Jacob Ryten's paper "Fifty Years of ISIC: Historical Origins and Future Perspectives" (1998).

4.3a

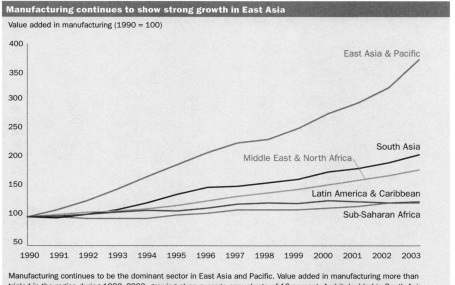

Manufacturing continues to show strong growth in East Asia

Value added in manufacturing (1990 = 100)

Manufacturing continues to be the dominant sector in East Asia and Pacific. Value added in manufacturing more than tripled in the region during 1990–2003, growing at an average annual rate of 10 percent. And it doubled in South Asia over the same period, with an average annual growth of 6.2 percent.

Source: World Bank data files.

	Export volume		Import volume		Export value		Import value		Net barter terms of trade	
	average annual % growth		average annual % growth		average annual % growth		average annual % growth		2000 = 100	
	1980–90	1990–2002	1980–90	1990–2002	1980–90	1990–2002	1980–90	1990–2002	1990	2002
Afghanistan	..	..	..	..	..	..	..	..	..	..
Albania[a]	..	..	..	..	..	12.9	..	16.5	..	..
Algeria	3.4	3.5	−8.0	1.9	−4.4	4.7	−2.7	1.1	74	90
Angola	9.1	5.4	−2.0	9.0	15.7	7.1	3.7	8.5	94	125
Argentina	2.0	7.4	−9.6	9.0	2.1	8.3	−6.5	8.0	64	99
Armenia[a]	..	..	..	..	..	−3.7	..	1.4	..	..
Australia[a]	6.3	6.8	6.0	8.5	6.6	4.5	6.4	5.1	116	106
Austria[a]	6.6	..	5.7	..	10.2	5.2	8.7	3.6	..	..
Azerbaijan[a]	..	..	..	..	..	1.7	..	1.7	..	..
Bangladesh	8.8	26.5	3.4	17.0	7.8	15.7	3.6	10.3	111	100
Belarus[a]	..	..	..	..	..	12.8	..	12.7	..	..
Belgium[a]	..	5.6	..	5.2	..	4.5	..	4.8	..	101
Benin	11.6	0.8	−10.0	6.3	18.7	2.4	−5.0	7.0	107	102
Bolivia	3.2	3.5	−1.2	7.3	−1.9	4.3	−0.3	7.3	102	98
Bosnia and Herzegovina	..	..	..	..	..	..	..	..	..	..
Botswana	14.7	4.5	9.5	3.2	18.4	3.8	9.0	1.3	98	101
Brazil	6.2	5.8	0.8	12.7	5.0	5.6	−2.0	9.4	66	97
Bulgaria[a]	..	..	..	..	−12.3	2.6	−14.0	6.0	100	..
Burkina Faso	−0.4	11.3	3.7	4.4	7.8	10.0	4.3	3.7	119	110
Burundi	3.4	10.1	1.0	7.2	2.5	−7.0	2.2	−5.9	128	82
Cambodia	..	..	..	..	..	..	..	..	..	..
Cameroon	8.1	2.1	4.8	7.0	2.5	0.3	0.1	3.4	81	100
Canada[a]	6.4	8.0	7.4	8.0	6.8	7.2	7.9	6.4	97	97
Central African Republic	0.2	16.9	4.2	2.6	3.5	2.4	7.9	−0.9	238	106
Chad	8.7	−0.2	11.0	10.4	9.4	1.5	12.7	9.3	112	165
Chile	9.1	10.0	−3.1	8.2	8.3	7.6	2.8	7.7	114	93
China[†]	13.9	14.1	11.8	13.6	12.9	14.1	13.1	13.4	102	102
Hong Kong, China	15.3	7.4	13.8	7.7	16.7	6.7	14.9	7.0	100	102
Colombia	7.9	4.0	−2.2	6.8	7.9	6.0	−0.1	7.3	81	93
Congo, Dem. Rep.	9.6	2.3	12.1	8.0	2.7	−5.2	3.1	−1.6	86	110
Congo, Rep.	7.4	5.6	0.8	1.8	2.0	7.7	2.7	0.7	63	95
Costa Rica	3.6	11.6	5.0	13.3	4.7	13.1	4.5	12.2	75	97
Côte d'Ivoire	2.6	4.5	−2.1	−1.1	1.7	5.3	−1.5	2.0	143	118
Croatia[a]	..	..	..	..	..	1.7	..	7.8	..	..
Cuba	..	..	..	..	..	..	..	..	..	..
Czech Republic[a]	..	..	..	..	..	10.2	..	9.9	..	..
Denmark[a]	4.1	5.4	3.1	5.5	9.0	3.2	6.8	3.3	102	101
Dominican Republic	−0.9	2.9	0.9	11.8	−2.1	3.4	3.2	11.7	96	101
Ecuador	7.1	5.1	−1.8	7.2	−0.4	5.5	−1.3	8.4	114	95
Egypt, Arab Rep.	13.4	1.4	8.1	0.8	7.3	1.8	12.5	3.2	101	98
El Salvador	−4.6	3.0	4.6	7.1	−4.7	7.9	2.6	10.0	84	96
Eritrea	..	−9.0	..	4.0	..	−10.5	..	2.5	99	99
Estonia[a]	..	..	..	..	..	15.2	..	16.4	..	..
Ethiopia	−1.0	10.5	4.0	7.6	−1.0	8.7	4.0	7.9	121	84
Finland[a]	2.3	9.3	4.4	4.3	7.4	6.4	6.9	4.2	111	96
France[a]	3.6	4.9	3.7	4.2	7.5	3.6	6.5	3.1	103	110
Gabon	2.5	2.1	−3.5	1.8	−3.8	0.6	1.1	1.7	157	142
Gambia, The	2.4	−12.5	−6.0	−1.0	6.8	−13.8	2.5	−2.4	100	100
Georgia	..	..	..	..	..	..	..	..	..	..
Germany[a, b]	4.5	5.9	4.9	4.3	9.2	3.8	7.1	3.0	110	104
Ghana	−17.2	6.2	−19.3	6.6	−2.7	7.0	0.5	6.2	100	112
Greece[a]	5.0	9.1	6.4	9.2	5.8	1.8	6.6	4.0	100	100
Guatemala	−1.1	7.3	0.0	10.4	−2.1	7.6	0.6	10.8	115	97
Guinea	..	6.4	..	1.4	..	1.6	..	−1.8	122	100
Guinea-Bissau	−1.9	13.1	−0.3	−6.5	4.1	12.2	5.2	−4.7	146	105
Haiti	−0.3	11.6	−4.7	12.4	−1.3	11.3	−2.8	13.3	132	100
[†]Data for Taiwan, China	26.2	1.6	30.4	3.4	16.6	5.8	18.5	6.4	97	117

Growth of merchandise trade | 4.4

	Export volume		Import volume		Export value		Import value		Net barter terms of trade	
	average annual % growth		average annual % growth		average annual % growth		average annual % growth		2000 = 100	
	1980–90	1990–2002	1980–90	1990–2002	1980–90	1990–2002	1980–90	1990–2002	1990	2002
Honduras	4.1	2.7	1.5	11.8	1.5	5.7	0.7	12.4	78	95
Hungary[a]	3.4	11.2	1.3	11.9	1.6	12.9	0.1	13.1	111	100
India	4.2	11.3	4.5	11.7	7.2	9.1	4.2	9.3	86	88
Indonesia	8.1	7.4	0.2	1.6	–0.9	6.9	1.8	1.1	95	100
Iran, Islamic Rep.	..	..	..	..	..	..	..	..	..	..
Iraq	..	..	..	..	..	..	..	..	..	..
Ireland[a]	9.3	14.5	4.8	10.5	12.8	12.9	7.0	9.7	106	102
Israel[a]	6.9	9.1	5.8	7.6	8.3	9.8	5.9	6.8	89	98
Italy[a]	4.3	4.0	5.3	3.9	8.7	3.9	6.9	3.2	94	103
Jamaica	..	..	..	..	..	..	..	..	..	..
Japan[a]	5.1	2.3	6.6	4.9	8.9	2.9	5.1	3.8	105	101
Jordan	7.7	6.1	1.2	3.8	6.1	7.3	–1.8	5.1	94	97
Kazakhstan[a]	..	..	..	..	..	12.2	..	6.2	..	..
Kenya	1.7	3.5	2.4	5.9	–1.1	5.3	1.8	5.2	70	98
Korea, Dem. Rep.	..	..	..	..	..	..	..	..	..	..
Korea, Rep.	12.5	14.9	11.8	9.1	15.1	8.4	12.0	6.2	134	95
Kuwait	..	..	..	..	..	..	..	..	..	..
Kyrgyz Republic[a]	..	..	..	..	..	3.8	..	3.7	..	..
Lao PDR[a]	..	..	..	..	11.0	11.1	6.6	8.1	..	..
Latvia[a]	..	7.4	..	..	..	10.4	..	16.2	..	..
Lebanon	..	..	..	..	..	..	..	..	..	..
Lesotho	7.0	15.8	4.0	2.1	3.7	12.9	3.4	–0.5	100	100
Liberia	..	..	..	..	..	..	..	..	..	..
Libya	..	..	..	..	..	..	..	..	..	..
Lithuania[a]	..	..	..	..	..	9.4	..	12.5	..	..
Macedonia, FYR[a]	..	..	..	..	..	1.0	..	4.2	..	..
Madagascar	–2.3	2.9	–6.2	4.3	–1.0	7.5	–4.3	4.9	81	114
Malawi	2.4	2.5	–0.1	–1.3	2.0	0.7	3.2	0.0	148	99
Malaysia	4.7	12.1	8.3	9.0	8.8	10.0	7.7	7.6	103	98
Mali	4.4	11.1	3.0	3.4	6.2	7.6	2.7	2.1	135	100
Mauritania	3.9	2.6	–3.0	4.6	8.0	–2.8	–2.0	0.0	97	88
Mauritius	11.5	3.3	11.5	3.6	14.3	3.2	12.9	2.8	93	98
Mexico	16.0	13.8	0.8	12.4	5.7	14.4	6.4	12.9	102	100
Moldova[a]	..	..	..	..	..	0.7	..	2.6	..	..
Mongolia	..	..	..	..	..	..	..	..	..	..
Morocco	5.5	6.6	3.2	7.1	6.2	6.6	3.7	5.0	85	107
Mozambique	–9.6	18.4	–2.7	2.4	–9.5	12.8	0.2	2.6	175	101
Myanmar	–8.2	16.0	–18.2	13.0	–7.3	15.9	–5.2	21.4	252	140
Namibia[a]	..	1.9	..	7.3	..	–0.2	..	3.3	93	99
Nepal[a]	..	..	..	..	8.1	9.5	6.9	7.2	..	..
Netherlands[a]	4.5	6.5	4.5	6.1	4.6	4.9	4.4	4.5	99	96
New Zealand[a]	3.5	4.4	4.3	5.4	6.2	3.4	5.4	4.5	100	100
Nicaragua	–4.8	9.7	–3.5	8.4	–5.8	8.7	–3.1	10.3	155	90
Niger	–5.1	3.1	–5.2	–2.1	–5.4	0.0	–3.5	0.7	165	100
Nigeria	–4.4	1.5	–21.4	2.6	–8.4	3.3	–15.6	3.0	89	91
Norway[a]	4.2	6.0	3.5	7.0	5.3	5.5	6.2	3.2	67	91
Oman	11.2	3.8	..	..	–2.3	8.1	..	..	..	..
Pakistan	8.0	3.6	2.7	1.8	8.0	4.0	3.0	2.4	109	95
Panama	–0.5	5.6	–6.8	5.5	–0.4	8.1	–3.6	6.3	69	99
Papua New Guinea	–0.6	–9.9	..	..	4.9	0.7	..	..	..	..
Paraguay	12.7	1.5	10.3	2.2	11.6	2.5	4.2	3.4	103	100
Peru	2.7	9.6	–2.0	8.3	–1.6	8.1	1.3	8.2	114	99
Philippines	20.1	13.3	20.5	9.7	4.3	15.9	2.9	10.0	87	104
Poland[a]	4.8	10.0	1.5	16.1	1.4	10.1	–3.2	15.5	92	105
Portugal[a]	11.9	0.1	15.1	0.0	15.1	4.4	10.3	4.3	104	106
Puerto Rico	..	..	..	..	..	..	..	..	..	..

	Export volume		Import volume		Export value		Import value		Net barter terms of trade	
	average annual % growth		average annual % growth		average annual % growth		average annual % growth		2000 = 100	
	1980–90	1990–2002	1980–90	1990–2002	1980–90	1990–2002	1980–90	1990–2002	1990	2002
Romania[a]	..	..	..	..	–4.0	9.2	–3.8	8.0	..	..
Russian Federation[a]	..	..	..	..	..	8.5	..	2.7	..	..
Rwanda	2.6	–3.3	1.7	0.1	–0.9	–2.0	2.7	–1.8	40	69
Saudi Arabia	–8.9	2.0	..	..	–13.4	3.9	..	..	..	..
Senegal	1.3	9.8	0.4	4.8	3.5	3.6	1.3	4.5	172	96
Serbia and Montenegro	..	..	..	..	..	..	..	..	..	..
Sierra Leone	–2.1	–41.2	–3.0	–12.1	–2.4	–19.5	–8.7	0.6	24	164
Singapore	12.3	9.9	8.7	6.3	10.0	7.7	8.1	5.7	116	94
Slovak Republic[a]	..	..	..	..	..	9.9	..	10.6	..	..
Slovenia[a]	..	..	..	..	..	7.2	..	7.7	..	..
Somalia	..	..	..	..	..	..	..	..	..	..
South Africa[a, c]	1.7	4.5	–0.9	6.4	0.8	2.2	–1.3	4.4	104	103
Spain[a]	2.7	10.3	9.1	9.0	10.8	7.5	10.6	6.0	100	107
Sri Lanka	4.6	6.4	1.6	9.1	5.1	8.9	2.1	10.6	82	100
Sudan	–5.0	14.0	–10.4	9.1	–2.5	16.1	–8.1	10.5	100	119
Swaziland	7.6	4.9	2.4	3.7	4.8	5.0	–0.4	3.9	100	100
Sweden[a]	4.4	8.1	5.0	5.8	8.0	4.3	6.7	3.3	108	95
Switzerland[a]	3.7	..	4.3	..	9.5	2.6	8.8	1.9	..	..
Syrian Arab Republic	19.6	3.4	..	..	2.5	3.2	..	..	..	..
Tajikistan	..	..	..	..	..	..	..	..	..	..
Tanzania	..	6.5	..	1.0	..	7.2	..	0.9	107	131
Thailand	13.6	9.1	11.0	2.3	14.3	8.9	12.6	4.4	119	90
Togo	–1.3	7.1	0.7	4.2	1.1	5.3	2.0	3.7	133	104
Trinidad and Tobago	..	..	..	..	..	..	..	..	..	..
Tunisia	2.9	5.8	1.7	5.0	3.4	5.8	2.6	5.0	109	104
Turkey	18.9	10.9	15.6	9.1	14.2	8.7	9.2	8.1	109	98
Turkmenistan	..	..	..	..	..	..	..	..	..	..
Uganda	–13.4	15.7	–7.0	17.1	–8.3	11.0	3.6	15.6	146	87
Ukraine[a]	..	..	..	..	..	7.2	..	6.0	..	..
United Arab Emirates	..	..	..	..	..	..	..	..	..	..
United Kingdom[a]	..	..	..	..	5.9	4.3	8.5	4.7	101	102
United States[a]	3.6	5.5	7.2	8.5	5.7	5.8	8.2	8.6	101	104
Uruguay	4.4	4.3	–0.6	6.0	4.4	2.7	–1.2	5.4	116	100
Uzbekistan	..	..	..	..	..	..	..	..	..	..
Venezuela, RB	3.5	4.2	–4.1	4.2	–4.3	5.3	–3.3	4.2	90	89
Vietnam	..	..	..	..	..	..	..	..	..	..
West Bank and Gaza	..	..	..	..	..	..	..	..	..	..
Yemen, Rep.[a]	..	..	–7.3	4.7	..	..	0.6	0.9	..	..
Zambia	–0.5	6.0	2.0	4.6	0.9	–1.2	0.0	2.7	207	93
Zimbabwe	3.8	7.2	3.4	7.3	2.5	1.2	–0.5	1.1	98	101

a. Data are from the International Monetary Fund's *International Financial Statistics* database. b. Data prior to 1990 refer to the Federal Republic of Germany before unification. c. Data refer to the South African Customs Union (Botswana, Lesotho, Namibia, South Africa, and Swaziland).

Growth of merchandise trade | 4.4

About the data

Data on international trade in goods are available from each country's balance of payments and customs records. While the balance of payments focuses on the financial transactions that accompany trade, customs data record the direction of trade and the physical quantities and value of goods entering or leaving the customs area. Customs data may differ from data recorded in the balance of payments because of differences in valuation and the time of recording. The 1993 System of National Accounts and the fifth edition of the International Monetary Fund's (IMF) *Balance of Payments Manual* (1993) attempted to reconcile the definitions and reporting standards for international trade statistics, but differences in sources, timing, and national practices limit comparability. Real growth rates derived from trade volume indexes and terms of trade based on unit price indexes may therefore differ from those derived from national accounts aggregates.

Trade in goods, or merchandise trade, includes all goods that add to or subtract from an economy's material resources. Thus the total supply of goods in an economy is made up of gross output plus imports less exports (currency in circulation, titles of ownership, and securities are excluded, but nonmonetary gold is included). Trade data are collected on the basis of a country's customs area, which in most cases is the same as its geographic area. Goods provided as part of foreign aid are included, but goods destined for extraterritorial agencies (such as embassies) are not.

Collecting and tabulating trade statistics are difficult. Some developing countries lack the capacity to report timely data; this is a problem especially for countries that are landlocked and those whose territorial boundaries are porous. As a result, it is necessary to estimate their trade from the data reported by their partners. (For further discussion of the use of partner country reports, see *About the data* for table 6.2.) Countries that belong to common customs unions may need to collect data through direct inquiry of companies. In some cases economic or political concerns may lead national authorities to suppress or misrepresent data on certain trade flows, such as oil, military equipment, or the exports of a dominant producer. In other cases reported trade data may be distorted by deliberate under- or over-invoicing to effect capital transfers or avoid taxes. And in some regions smuggling and black market trading result in unreported trade flows.

By international agreement customs data are reported to the United Nations Statistics Division,

which maintains the Commodity Trade (COMTRADE) database. The United Nations Conference on Trade and Development (UNCTAD) compiles a variety of international trade statistics, including price and volume indexes, based on the COMTRADE data. The IMF and the World Trade Organization also compile data on trade prices and volumes. The growth rates and terms of trade for low- and middle-income economies shown in the table were calculated from index numbers compiled by UNCTAD. Volume measures for high-income economies were derived by deflating the value of trade using deflators from the IMF's *International Financial Statistics*. In some cases price and volume indexes from different sources may vary significantly as a result of differences in estimation procedures. All indexes are rescaled to a 2000 base year. Terms of trade were computed from the same indicators.

The terms of trade measures the relative prices of a country's exports and imports. There are a number of ways to calculate terms of trade. The most common is the net barter (or commodity) terms of trade, constructed as the ratio of the export price index to the import price index. When a country's net barter terms of trade increase, its exports are becoming more valuable or its imports cheaper.

Definitions

• **Export and import volumes** are average annual growth rates calculated for low- and middle-income economies from UNCTAD's quantum index series and for high-income economies from export and import data deflated by the IMF's trade price deflators. • **Export and import values** are average annual growth rates calculated from UNCTAD's value indexes or from current values of merchandise exports and imports. • **Net barter terms of trade** are calculated as the ratio of the export price index to the corresponding import price index measured relative to the base year 2000.

Data sources

The main source of trade data for developing countries is UNCTAD's annual *Handbook of International Trade and Development Statistics*. The IMF's *International Financial Statistics* includes data on the export and import values and deflators for high-income and selected developing economies.

	Merchandise exports $ millions		Food % of total		Agricultural raw materials % of total		Fuels % of total		Ores and metals % of total		Manufactures % of total	
	1990	2003	1990	2003	1990	2003	1990	2003	1990	2003	1990	2003
Afghanistan	235	135	..	25	..	41	..	..	..	..	..	11
Albania	230	453	..	6	..	5	..	1	..	4	..	84
Algeria	12,930	24,639	0	0	0	0	96	97	0	0	3	2
Angola	3,910	8,790	0	..	0	..	93	..	6	..	0	..
Argentina	12,353	29,350	56	50	4	2	8	17	2	3	29	27
Armenia	..	678	..	14	..	1	..	2	..	21	..	62
Australia	39,752	71,544	22	19	10	5	21	21	20	16	24	30
Austria	41,265	96,187	3	6	4	2	1	3	3	2	88	78
Azerbaijan	..	2,592	..	5	..	2	..	86	..	1	..	6
Bangladesh	1,671	6,942	14	8	7	2	1	1	..	0	77	89
Belarus	..	9,964	..	8	..	4	..	22	..	1	..	62
Belgium[a]	117,703	268,637	..	9	..	1	..	5	..	2	..	80
Benin	288	541	15	33	56	59	15	0	0	0	13	8
Bolivia	926	1,573	19	31	8	2	25	31	44	19	5	17
Bosnia and Herzegovina	276	1,373	..	..	..	..	..	..	..	..	..	..
Botswana	1,784	2,866	..	3	..	0	..	0	..	5	..	91
Brazil	31,414	73,084	28	29	3	4	2	5	14	8	52	52
Bulgaria	5,030	7,534	..	10	..	2	..	6	..	10	..	66
Burkina Faso	152	315	..	20	..	62	..	0	..	0	..	17
Burundi	75	38	..	93	..	2	..	..	..	3	..	2
Cambodia	86	1,690	..	63	..	36	..	0	..	0	..	1
Cameroon	2,002	2,375	20	20	14	20	50	49	7	4	9	7
Canada	127,629	272,739	9	7	9	5	10	16	9	4	59	61
Central African Republic	120	130	..	1	..	25	..	0	..	37	..	37
Chad	188	260	..	..	..	..	..	..	..	..	..	..
Chile	8,372	21,046	24	28	9	9	1	2	55	42	11	16
China[†]	62,091	437,899	13	4	3	1	8	3	2	2	72	91
Hong Kong, China[b]	82,390	228,654	3	2	0	1	0	1	1	2	95	93
Colombia	6,766	12,671	33	18	4	6	37	39	0	1	25	36
Congo, Dem. Rep.	2,326	815	..	..	..	..	..	..	..	16	..	10
Congo, Rep.	981	3,055	..	..	..	..	..	..	..	..	..	..
Costa Rica	1,448	6,101	58	30	5	3	1	0	1	1	27	66
Côte d'Ivoire	3,072	5,844	..	56	..	9	..	13	..	0	..	20
Croatia	4,597	6,162	13	12	6	4	9	10	5	2	68	72
Cuba	5,100	1,500	..	59	..	0	..	1	..	29	..	10
Czech Republic	12,170	48,740	..	3	..	2	..	3	..	2	..	90
Denmark	36,870	67,377	27	19	3	3	3	7	1	1	60	66
Dominican Republic	2,170	5,439	21	41	0	2	0	16	0	2	78	34
Ecuador	2,714	6,039	44	42	1	6	52	40	0	0	2	12
Egypt, Arab Rep.	3,477	6,161	10	9	10	7	29	44	9	3	42	31
El Salvador	582	3,136	57	34	1	1	2	5	3	3	38	57
Eritrea	16	56	..	..	..	..	..	..	..	..	..	..
Estonia	..	5,597	..	11	..	8	..	4	..	3	..	74
Ethiopia	298	535	..	62	..	26	..	0	..	1	..	11
Finland	26,571	52,953	2	2	10	6	1	4	4	3	83	84
France	216,588	386,699	16	12	2	1	2	3	3	2	77	81
Gabon	2,204	2,540	..	..	..	..	..	..	..	..	..	..
Gambia, The	31	13	..	100	..	0	..	..	..	0	..	..
Georgia	..	444	..	36	..	3	..	5	..	25	..	31
Germany	421,100	748,320	5	4	1	1	1	2	3	2	89	84
Ghana	897	2,498	51	45	15	11	9	11	17	14	8	16
Greece	8,105	13,199	30	22	3	3	7	7	7	8	54	58
Guatemala	1,163	2,635	67	47	6	4	2	8	0	0	24	40
Guinea	671	824	..	2	..	1	..	0	..	72	..	25
Guinea-Bissau	19	69	..	..	..	..	..	..	..	..	..	..
Haiti	160	347	14	..	1	..	0	..	0	..	85	..
[†]Data for Taiwan, China	67,245	150,289	4	1	2	1	1	2	1	1	93	94

Structure of merchandise exports

	Merchandise exports ($ millions)		Food (% of total)		Agricultural raw materials (% of total)		Fuels (% of total)		Ores and metals (% of total)		Manufactures (% of total)	
	1990	2003	1990	2003	1990	2003	1990	2003	1990	2003	1990	2003
Honduras	831	1,332	82	58	4	15	1	0	4	5	9	21
Hungary	10,000	42,532	23	7	3	1	3	2	6	2	63	87
India	17,969	55,982	16	11	4	1	3	6	5	4	71	77
Indonesia	25,675	60,955	11	11	5	5	44	26	4	6	35	52
Iran, Islamic Rep.	19,305	36,230	..	4	..	0	..	88	..	1	..	8
Iraq	12,380	12,680	..	..	..	..	..	..	..	..	..	..
Ireland	23,743	92,723	22	8	2	0	1	0	1	0	70	86
Israel	12,080	31,577	8	5	3	1	1	0	2	1	87	93
Italy	170,304	292,052	6	7	1	1	2	2	1	1	88	87
Jamaica	1,158	1,195	19	23	0	0	1	3	10	10	69	64
Japan	287,581	471,817	1	1	1	1	0	0	1	1	96	93
Jordan	1,064	3,082	11	15	0	0	0	0	38	16	51	69
Kazakhstan	..	12,900	..	6	..	1	..	62	..	13	..	18
Kenya	1,031	2,411	49	43	6	11	13	19	3	3	29	24
Korea, Dem. Rep.	1,857	1,066	..	..	..	..	..	..	..	..	..	..
Korea, Rep.	65,016	193,817	3	1	1	1	1	4	1	1	94	93
Kuwait	7,042	19,371	1	0	0	0	93	92	0	0	6	7
Kyrgyz Republic	..	582	..	16	..	17	..	21	..	6	..	39
Lao PDR	79	378	..	..	..	..	..	..	..	..	..	..
Latvia	..	2,893	..	9	..	25	..	1	..	4	..	60
Lebanon	494	1,524	..	19	..	2	..	0	..	10	..	68
Lesotho	62	477	..	..	..	..	..	..	..	..	..	..
Liberia	868	230	..	..	..	..	..	..	..	..	..	..
Libya	13,225	14,950	0	..	0	..	94	..	0	..	5	..
Lithuania	..	7,234	..	12	..	4	..	19	..	2	..	63
Macedonia, FYR	1,199	1,351	..	17	..	1	..	5	..	5	..	72
Madagascar	319	655	73	55	4	4	1	0	8	1	14	38
Malawi	417	463	93	86	2	2	0	0	0	0	5	12
Malaysia	29,452	99,369	12	9	14	2	18	10	2	1	54	77
Mali	359	930	36	17	62	42	..	0	0	1	2	40
Mauritania	469	420	..	8	..	2	..	1	..	68	..	21
Mauritius	1,194	1,939	32	25	1	0	1	0	0	0	66	74
Mexico	40,711	165,396	12	6	2	1	38	11	6	1	43	81
Moldova	..	791	..	59	..	5	..	1	..	3	..	32
Mongolia	661	516	..	3	..	13	..	3	..	43	..	38
Morocco	4,265	8,729	26	21	3	2	4	1	15	7	52	69
Mozambique	126	880	..	23	..	4	..	10	..	55	..	8
Myanmar	325	2,600	51	..	36	..	0	..	2	..	10	..
Namibia	1,085	1,290	..	48	..	1	..	1	..	7	..	41
Nepal	204	662	13	..	3	..	..	..	0	..	83	..
Netherlands	131,775	294,051	20	17	4	4	10	6	3	2	59	71
New Zealand	9,394	16,496	47	49	18	12	4	1	6	4	23	29
Nicaragua	330	605	77	83	14	2	0	1	1	1	8	13
Niger	282	339	..	30	..	4	..	2	..	55	..	8
Nigeria	13,596	20,255	1	..	1	..	97	..	0	..	1	..
Norway	34,047	67,480	7	6	2	1	48	61	10	7	33	21
Oman	5,508	11,669	1	5	0	0	92	80	1	1	5	14
Pakistan	5,615	11,930	9	10	10	2	1	2	0	0	79	85
Panama	340	864	75	85	1	1	0	1	1	2	21	11
Papua New Guinea	1,177	2,174	22	21	9	3	0	22	58	49	10	6
Paraguay	959	1,289	52	77	38	9	0	0	0	0	10	14
Peru	3,230	8,954	21	27	3	3	10	10	47	38	18	22
Philippines	8,117	36,502	19	6	2	1	2	2	8	2	38	90
Poland	14,320	53,537	13	8	3	2	11	4	9	4	59	81
Portugal	16,417	31,369	7	8	6	2	3	2	3	2	80	86
Puerto Rico	..	..	..	..	..	..	..	..	..	..	..	..

	Merchandise exports $ millions		Food % of total		Agricultural raw materials % of total		Fuels % of total		Ores and metals % of total		Manufactures % of total	
	1990	2003	1990	2003	1990	2003	1990	2003	1990	2003	1990	2003
Romania	4,960	17,619	1	3	3	3	18	6	4	4	73	83
Russian Federation	..	134,377	..	2	..	3	..	53	..	7	..	21
Rwanda	110	60	..	52	..	7	..	7	..	23	..	10
Saudi Arabia	44,417	88,500	1	1	0	0	92	89	0	0	7	10
Senegal	761	1,331	53	37	3	3	12	20	9	3	23	34
Serbia and Montenegro	2,929	2,537	7	..	4	..	2	..	7	..	79	..
Sierra Leone	138	92	..	92	..	1	..	..	..	0	..	7
Singapore[b]	52,730	144,127	5	2	3	0	18	8	2	1	72	85
Slovak Republic	6,355	21,960	..	3	..	2	..	5	..	2	..	88
Slovenia	6,681	12,767	7	3	2	1	3	1	3	4	86	90
Somalia	150	202	..	..	..	..	..	..	..	..	..	..
South Africa[c]	23,549	36,482	7	10	3	3	6	10	9	19	36	58
Spain	55,642	151,682	15	15	2	1	5	3	2	2	75	77
Sri Lanka	1,912	5,125	34	21	6	2	1	0	2	2	54	74
Sudan	374	2,360	61	18	38	6	..	72	0	0	1	3
Swaziland	556	905	..	15	..	8	..	1	..	0	..	76
Sweden	57,540	101,245	2	3	7	5	3	3	3	2	83	81
Switzerland	63,784	99,390	3	3	1	0	0	0	3	3	94	93
Syrian Arab Republic	4,212	5,480	14	14	4	3	45	71	1	1	36	11
Tajikistan	..	798	..	..	..	..	..	..	..	..	..	..
Tanzania	331	1,222	..	59	..	12	..	2	..	9	..	18
Thailand	23,068	80,522	29	14	5	5	1	2	1	1	63	75
Togo	268	440	23	15	21	17	0	0	45	9	9	58
Trinidad and Tobago	1,960	4,565	5	6	0	0	67	60	1	0	27	33
Tunisia	3,526	8,027	11	8	1	1	17	9	2	1	69	81
Turkey	12,959	46,576	22	10	3	1	2	2	4	2	68	84
Turkmenistan	..	3,620	..	..	..	..	..	..	..	..	..	..
Uganda	152	562	..	67	..	23	..	0	..	0	..	9
Ukraine	..	23,080	..	13	..	2	..	9	..	8	..	67
United Arab Emirates	23,544	65,835	8	1	1	0	5	92	39	4	46	4
United Kingdom	185,172	304,596	7	6	1	1	8	8	3	2	79	78
United States	393,592	723,805	11	9	4	3	3	2	3	2	74	80
Uruguay	1,693	2,198	40	53	21	11	0	2	0	1	39	34
Uzbekistan	..	3,260	..	..	..	..	..	..	..	..	..	..
Venezuela, RB	17,497	23,650	2	1	0	0	80	82	7	4	10	13
Vietnam	2,404	20,176	..	25	..	2	..	21	..	1	..	50
West Bank and Gaza	..	..	..	..	..	..	..	..	..	..	..	..
Yemen, Rep.	692	3,802	75	..	10	..	8	..	7	..	1	..
Zambia	1,309	940	..	10	..	3	..	2	..	72	..	14
Zimbabwe	1,726	1,170	44	26	7	12	1	1	16	22	31	38
World	**3,505,243 t**	**7,578,698 t**	**10 w**	**8 w**	**3 w**	**2 w**	**9 w**	**7 w**	**4 w**	**3 w**	**72 w**	**77 w**
Low income	75,155	178,890	17	21	3	4	26	10	4	4	50	60
Middle income	591,019	1,817,552	16	10	4	2	25	17	5	4	48	65
Lower middle income	356,447	1,151,327	18	10	4	2	14	19	5	4	56	62
Upper middle income	232,649	666,283	14	11	4	2	38	14	6	3	37	69
Low & middle income	667,368	1,996,437	16	11	4	2	24	17	5	4	48	65
East Asia & Pacific	155,942	744,808	15	8	6	2	13	6	3	2	60	81
Europe & Central Asia[d]	..	459,184	..	6	..	3	..	22	..	4	..	60
Latin America & Carib.	143,271	374,551	23	19	3	2	28	18	10	6	36	55
Middle East & N. Africa	125,938	226,309	4	4	1	1	76	73	3	2	17	19
South Asia	27,728	81,009	16	11	5	1	2	5	4	3	71	78
Sub-Saharan Africa	68,416	110,571	..	..	..	..	..	..	..	..	..	..
High income	2,837,237	5,579,666	9	7	3	2	5	5	3	2	79	80
Europe EMU	1,245,697	2,460,430	11	9	2	2	3	3	2	2	80	81

Note: Components may not sum to 100 percent because of unclassified trade.

a. Includes Luxembourg. b. Includes re-exports. c. Data on total merchandise exports for 1990 refer to the South African Customs Union (Botswana, Lesotho, Namibia, South Africa, and Swaziland); those for 2003 refer to South Africa only. Data on export commodity shares refer to the South African Customs Union. d. Data for 2003 include the intratrade of the Baltic states and the Commonwealth of Independent States.

Structure of merchandise exports

About the data

Data on merchandise trade come from customs reports of goods movement into or out of an economy or from reports of the financial transactions related to merchandise trade recorded in the balance of payments. Because of differences in timing and definitions, estimates of trade flows from customs reports are likely to differ from those based on the balance of payments. Moreover, several international agencies process trade data, each making estimates to correct for unreported or misreported data, and this leads to other differences in the available data.

The most detailed source of data on international trade in goods is the Commodity Trade (COMTRADE) database maintained by the United Nations Statistics Division. In addition, the International Monetary Fund (IMF) collects customs-based data on exports and imports of goods. The value of exports is recorded as the cost of the goods delivered to the frontier of the exporting country for shipment—the free on board (f.o.b.) value. Many countries report trade data in U.S. dollars. When countries report in local currency, the United Nations Statistics Division applies the average official exchange rate for the period shown.

Countries may report trade according to the general or special system of trade (see *Primary data documentation*). Under the general system exports comprise outward-moving goods that are (a) goods wholly or partly produced in the country; (b) foreign goods, neither transformed nor declared for domestic consumption in the country, that move outward from customs storage; and (c) goods previously included as imports for domestic consumption but subsequently exported without transformation. Under the special system exports comprise categories a and c. In some compilations categories b and c

are classified as re-exports. Because of differences in reporting practices, data on exports may not be fully comparable across economies.

The data on total exports of goods (merchandise) in this table come from the World Trade Organization (WTO). The WTO uses two main sources, national statistical offices and the IMF's *International Financial Statistics*. It supplements these with the COMTRADE database and publications or databases of regional organizations, specialized agencies, and economic groups (such as the Commonwealth of Independent States, the Economic Commission for Latin America and the Caribbean, Eurostat, the Food and Agriculture Organization, the Organisation for Economic Co-operation and Development, and the Organization of Petroleum Exporting Countries). It also consults private sources, such as country reports of the Economist Intelligence Unit and press clippings. In recent years country Web sites and direct contacts through email have helped to improve the collection of up-to-date statistics for many countries, reducing the proportion of estimated figures. The WTO database now covers most of the major traders in Africa, Asia, and Latin America, which together with the high-income countries account for nearly 90 percent of total world trade. There has also been a remarkable improvement in the availability of recent, reliable, and standardized figures for countries in Europe and Central Asia.

The shares of exports by major commodity group were estimated by World Bank staff from the COMTRADE database. The values of total exports reported here have not been fully reconciled with the estimates of exports of goods and services from the national accounts (shown in table 4.9) or those from the balance of payments (table 4.15).

The classification of commodity groups is based on the Standard International Trade Classification (SITC) revision 1. Most countries now report using later revisions of the SITC or the Harmonized System. Concordance tables are used to convert data reported in one system of nomenclature to another. The conversion process may introduce some errors of classification, but conversions from later to early systems are generally reliable. Shares may not sum to 100 percent because of unclassified trade.

Definitions

• **Merchandise exports** are the f.o.b. value of goods provided to the rest of the world, valued in U.S. dollars. • **Food** corresponds to the commodities in SITC sections 0 (food and live animals), 1 (beverages and tobacco), and 4 (animal and vegetable oils and fats) and SITC division 22 (oil seeds, oil nuts, and oil kernels). • **Agricultural raw materials** correspond to SITC section 2 (crude materials except fuels) excluding divisions 22, 27 (crude fertilizers and minerals excluding coal, petroleum, and precious stones), and 28 (metalliferous ores and scrap). • **Fuels** correspond to SITC section 3 (mineral fuels). • **Ores and metals** correspond to the commodities in SITC divisions 27, 28, and 68 (nonferrous metals). • **Manufactures** correspond to the commodities in SITC sections 5 (chemicals), 6 (basic manufactures), 7 (machinery and transport equipment), and 8 (miscellaneous manufactured goods), excluding division 68.

4.5a

Some developing country regions are increasing their share of merchandise exports

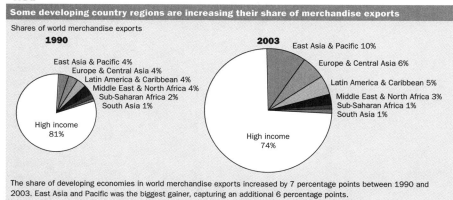

The share of developing economies in world merchandise exports increased by 7 percentage points between 1990 and 2003. East Asia and Pacific was the biggest gainer, capturing an additional 6 percentage points.

Source: World Trade Organization data files.

Data sources

The WTO publishes data on world trade in its *Annual Report*. The IMF publishes estimates of total exports of goods in its *International Financial Statistics* and *Direction of Trade Statistics*, as does the United Nations Statistics Division in its *Monthly Bulletin of Statistics*. And the United Nations Conference on Trade and Development (UNCTAD) publishes data on the structure of exports and imports in its *Handbook of International Trade and Development Statistics*. Tariff line records of exports and imports are compiled in the United Nations Statistics Division's COMTRADE database.

4.6 Structure of merchandise imports

	Merchandise imports $ millions		Food % of total		Agricultural raw materials % of total		Fuels % of total		Ores and metals % of total		Manufactures % of total	
	1990	2003	1990	2003	1990	2003	1990	2003	1990	2003	1990	2003
Afghanistan	936	1,190	..	6	..	1	..	5	..	0	..	29
Albania	380	1,864	..	20	..	1	..	9	..	2	..	69
Algeria	9,780	13,008	24	22	5	2	1	1	2	1	68	73
Angola	1,578	4,130	..	..	..	..	..	..	..	..	..	..
Argentina	4,076	13,813	4	5	4	2	8	5	6	3	78	84
Armenia	..	1,269	..	18	..	1	..	15	..	3	..	63
Australia	41,985	89,086	5	5	2	1	6	8	1	1	84	84
Austria	49,146	98,015	5	6	3	2	6	8	4	3	81	75
Azerbaijan	..	2,626	..	12	..	1	..	11	..	2	..	74
Bangladesh	3,618	9,476	19	20	5	7	16	8	3	2	56	63
Belarus	..	11,505	..	10	..	2	..	26	..	4	..	51
Belgium[a]	119,702	251,659	..	9	..	1	..	9	..	3	..	77
Benin	265	758	38	24	4	5	1	17	1	1	56	52
Bolivia	687	1,613	12	13	2	1	1	7	1	1	85	77
Bosnia and Herzegovina	360	4,460	..	..	..	..	..	..	..	..	..	..
Botswana	1,946	2,450	..	14	..	1	..	7	..	2	..	72
Brazil	22,524	50,665	9	7	3	2	27	16	5	3	56	72
Bulgaria	5,100	10,890	8	5	3	2	36	4	4	5	49	68
Burkina Faso	536	855	..	21	..	1	..	17	..	1	..	60
Burundi	231	157	..	11	..	2	..	13	..	2	..	71
Cambodia	164	1,715	..	6	..	1	..	7	..	1	..	84
Cameroon	1,400	2,200	19	19	0	2	2	12	1	1	78	66
Canada	123,244	245,021	6	6	2	1	6	6	3	2	81	82
Central African Republic	154	115	..	23	..	5	..	11	..	4	..	56
Chad	285	852	..	..	..	..	..	..	..	..	..	..
Chile	7,742	19,413	4	8	2	1	16	19	1	1	75	70
China[†]	53,345	413,062	9	4	6	4	2	7	3	5	80	80
Hong Kong, China	84,725	233,194	8	4	2	1	2	2	2	2	85	91
Colombia	5,590	13,892	7	11	4	2	6	2	3	2	77	81
Congo, Dem. Rep.	1,739	1,750	..	..	..	..	..	..	..	1	..	63
Congo, Rep.	621	1,200	..	..	..	..	..	..	..	..	..	..
Costa Rica	1,990	7,643	8	8	2	1	10	8	2	1	66	82
Côte d'Ivoire	2,097	4,500	..	22	..	1	..	17	..	1	..	48
Croatia	4,500	14,136	12	8	4	2	10	11	4	2	64	77
Cuba	4,600	4,660	..	18	..	1	..	20	..	1	..	60
Czech Republic	12,880	51,088	..	5	..	2	..	7	..	3	..	83
Denmark	33,333	57,792	12	12	3	3	7	5	2	2	73	77
Dominican Republic	3,006	7,883	..	12	..	2	..	23	..	1	..	62
Ecuador	1,861	6,534	9	9	3	2	2	4	2	1	84	84
Egypt, Arab Rep.	12,412	10,893	32	25	7	5	3	5	2	2	56	49
El Salvador	1,263	5,763	14	18	3	2	15	14	4	1	63	64
Eritrea	351	670	..	..	..	..	..	..	..	..	..	..
Estonia	..	7,930	..	11	..	3	..	6	..	2	..	78
Ethiopia	1,081	2,015	..	21	..	1	..	12	..	2	..	64
Finland	27,001	42,011	5	6	2	3	12	12	4	6	76	71
France	234,436	390,528	10	9	3	2	10	10	4	2	74	77
Gabon	918	1,076	..	..	..	..	..	..	..	..	..	..
Gambia, The	188	185	..	28	..	0	..	4	..	0	..	63
Georgia	..	1,058	..	18	..	0	..	18	..	1	..	63
Germany	355,686	601,691	10	7	3	2	8	9	4	3	72	71
Ghana	1,205	3,250	11	20	1	2	17	9	0	2	70	68
Greece	19,777	43,671	15	12	3	1	8	14	3	2	70	71
Guatemala	1,649	6,722	10	13	2	1	17	14	2	1	69	71
Guinea	723	820	..	23	..	1	..	22	..	1	..	53
Guinea-Bissau	86	140	..	..	..	..	..	..	..	..	..	..
Haiti	332	1,188	..	..	..	..	..	..	..	..	..	..
[†]Data for Taiwan, China	54,782	127,360	7	4	5	2	11	10	6	5	69	77

	Merchandise imports ($ millions)		Food (% of total)		Agricultural raw materials (% of total)		Fuels (% of total)		Ores and metals (% of total)		Manufactures (% of total)	
	1990	2003	1990	2003	1990	2003	1990	2003	1990	2003	1990	2003
Honduras	935	3,276	10	22	1	1	16	20	1	1	71	55
Hungary	10,340	47,602	8	3	4	1	14	6	4	2	70	86
India	23,580	70,707	3	6	4	3	27	32	8	4	51	54
Indonesia	21,837	32,551	5	11	5	5	9	24	4	3	77	56
Iran, Islamic Rep.	20,322	25,530	..	11	..	2	..	6	..	2	..	79
Iraq	7,660	7,910	..	..	..	..	..	..	..	..	..	..
Ireland	20,669	53,386	11	8	2	1	6	4	2	1	76	79
Israel	16,793	36,282	8	6	2	1	9	11	3	2	77	80
Italy	181,968	290,811	12	9	6	3	11	9	5	4	64	69
Jamaica	1,928	3,630	15	15	1	1	20	18	1	1	61	63
Japan	235,368	382,930	15	12	7	2	25	21	9	5	44	58
Jordan	2,600	5,653	26	18	2	2	18	17	1	2	51	60
Kazakhstan	..	8,327	..	8	..	1	..	11	..	2	..	78
Kenya	2,223	3,725	9	12	3	2	20	23	2	1	66	61
Korea, Dem. Rep.	2,930	2,049	..	..	..	..	..	..	..	..	..	..
Korea, Rep.	69,844	178,827	6	6	8	3	16	22	7	6	63	64
Kuwait	3,972	10,794	17	15	1	1	1	1	2	2	79	75
Kyrgyz Republic	..	717	..	13	..	2	..	25	..	3	..	57
Lao PDR	185	524	..	..	..	..	..	..	..	..	..	..
Latvia	..	5,242	..	12	..	3	..	9	..	2	..	74
Lebanon	2,529	7,171	..	18	..	2	..	16	..	2	..	62
Lesotho	672	1,021	..	..	..	..	..	..	..	..	..	..
Liberia	570	560	..	..	..	..	..	..	..	..	..	..
Libya	5,336	5,125	23	..	2	..	0	..	1	..	74	..
Lithuania	..	9,843	..	8	..	2	..	17	..	2	..	69
Macedonia, FYR	1,206	2,241	..	14	..	2	..	14	..	2	..	49
Madagascar	651	1,190	11	16	1	0	17	10	1	0	69	72
Malawi	575	702	9	17	1	1	11	12	1	1	78	69
Malaysia	29,258	81,948	7	5	1	1	5	6	4	3	82	83
Mali	602	1,251	26	16	1	1	19	22	1	1	53	67
Mauritania	388	500	..	..	..	..	..	..	..	..	..	..
Mauritius	1,618	2,381	12	17	3	2	8	11	1	1	76	69
Mexico	43,548	178,503	15	7	4	2	4	3	3	2	75	86
Moldova	..	1,399	..	14	..	4	..	21	..	1	..	61
Mongolia	924	787	..	14	..	1	..	20	..	1	..	65
Morocco	6,922	14,150	10	11	6	3	17	16	6	3	61	67
Mozambique	878	1,365	..	14	..	1	..	16	..	0	..	47
Myanmar	270	2,600	13	..	1	..	5	..	0	..	81	..
Namibia	1,163	1,975	..	15	..	1	..	10	..	4	..	69
Nepal	672	1,754	15	..	7	..	9	..	2	..	67	..
Netherlands	126,098	262,816	13	11	2	2	10	11	3	3	71	73
New Zealand	9,501	18,554	7	8	1	1	8	9	3	2	81	79
Nicaragua	638	1,887	19	15	1	0	19	16	1	0	59	66
Niger	388	551	..	34	..	4	..	17	..	1	..	44
Nigeria	5,627	10,890	6	..	1	..	0	..	2	..	67	..
Norway	27,231	39,486	6	8	2	2	4	4	6	5	82	80
Oman	2,681	6,572	19	17	1	1	4	3	1	5	69	71
Pakistan	7,411	13,038	17	10	4	6	21	22	4	3	54	59
Panama	1,539	3,050	12	14	1	1	16	12	1	1	70	72
Papua New Guinea	1,193	1,297	18	16	0	1	7	13	1	0	73	69
Paraguay	1,352	2,079	8	12	0	1	14	17	1	1	77	69
Peru	2,634	8,470	24	13	2	2	12	17	1	1	61	67
Philippines	13,042	39,502	10	7	2	1	15	10	3	2	53	80
Poland	11,570	68,004	8	5	3	2	22	9	4	3	63	80
Portugal	25,263	45,080	12	13	4	2	11	10	2	2	71	73
Puerto Rico	..	..	..	..	..	..	..	..	..	..	..	..

4.6 Structure of merchandise imports

	Merchandise imports $ millions		Food % of total		Agricultural raw materials % of total		Fuels % of total		Ores and metals % of total		Manufactures % of total	
	1990	2003	1990	2003	1990	2003	1990	2003	1990	2003	1990	2003
Romania	7,600	24,003	12	7	4	1	38	11	6	2	39	78
Russian Federation	..	74,231	..	19	..	1	..	2	..	2	..	66
Rwanda	288	240	..	12	..	4	..	16	..	2	..	67
Saudi Arabia	24,069	36,250	15	16	1	1	0	0	3	3	81	79
Senegal	1,219	2,364	29	30	2	2	16	19	2	3	51	47
Serbia and Montenegro	4,634	7,510	12	..	5	..	17	..	3	..	63	..
Sierra Leone	149	303	..	23	..	8	..	40	..	1	..	29
Singapore	60,774	127,934	6	3	2	0	16	14	2	1	73	80
Slovak Republic	6,670	22,481	..	5	..	2	..	12	..	3	..	79
Slovenia	6,142	13,851	9	6	4	3	11	8	4	4	67	79
Somalia	95	180	..	..	..	..	..	..	..	..	..	..
South Africa[b]	18,399	41,084	8	5	2	1	1	12	1	2	75	70
Spain	87,715	200,996	11	10	3	2	12	10	4	3	71	75
Sri Lanka	2,688	6,672	19	14	2	1	13	14	1	2	65	68
Sudan	618	2,670	13	19	1	1	20	5	0	1	66	74
Swaziland	663	1,030	..	20	..	2	..	2	..	1	..	72
Sweden	54,264	82,693	6	8	2	2	9	9	3	3	79	75
Switzerland	69,681	95,204	6	6	2	1	5	4	3	4	84	84
Syrian Arab Republic	2,400	4,960	31	19	2	4	3	4	1	3	62	70
Tajikistan	..	881	..	..	..	..	..	..	..	..	..	..
Tanzania	1,027	2,193	..	13	..	2	..	19	..	1	..	66
Thailand	33,045	75,809	5	5	5	3	9	12	4	3	75	76
Togo	581	568	22	17	1	1	8	19	1	2	67	61
Trinidad and Tobago	1,109	3,650	19	9	1	1	11	28	6	2	62	60
Tunisia	5,513	10,910	11	9	4	3	9	7	4	3	72	78
Turkey	22,302	69,340	8	4	4	4	21	13	5	6	61	68
Turkmenistan	..	2,515	..	..	..	..	..	..	..	..	..	..
Uganda	288	1,252	..	16	..	2	..	14	..	1	..	67
Ukraine	..	23,021	..	6	..	1	..	39	..	3	..	48
United Arab Emirates	11,199	36,000	14	11	1	1	3	1	4	2	77	86
United Kingdom	222,977	390,774	10	9	3	2	6	4	4	2	75	79
United States	516,987	1,303,050	6	5	2	1	13	13	3	2	73	76
Uruguay	1,343	2,190	7	13	4	5	18	22	2	2	69	59
Uzbekistan	..	2,570	..	..	..	..	..	..	..	..	..	..
Venezuela, RB	7,335	9,306	11	17	4	2	3	2	4	2	77	77
Vietnam	2,752	24,863	..	6	..	3	..	11	..	3	..	76
West Bank and Gaza	..	..	..	..	..	..	..	..	..	..	..	..
Yemen, Rep.	1,571	3,390	27	..	1	..	40	..	1	..	31	..
Zambia	1,220	1,503	..	14	..	2	..	7	..	2	..	75
Zimbabwe	1,847	2,935	4	11	3	2	16	8	2	2	73	76
World	**3,584,865 t**	**7,758,249 t**	**9 w**	**8 w**	**3 w**	**2 w**	**11 w**	**10 w**	**4 w**	**3 w**	**71 w**	**75 w**
Low income	83,571	203,046	..	9	..	3	..	25	..	3	..	59
Middle income	534,054	1,682,692	10	8	4	2	9	8	3	3	72	76
Lower middle income	354,079	1,072,097	10	8	5	3	11	10	3	4	70	73
Upper middle income	181,010	610,862	11	8	3	1	8	6	3	2	75	82
Low & middle income	619,290	1,885,737	10	8	4	2	10	10	4	3	71	75
East Asia & Pacific	160,531	678,826	8	5	5	3	6	9	3	4	77	78
Europe & Central Asia[c]	164,871	476,753	..	8	..	2	..	9	..	3	..	74
Latin America & Carib.	120,374	360,236	12	8	3	2	10	8	3	2	71	80
Middle East & N. Africa	105,965	154,681	20	17	3	2	4	5	3	2	70	70
South Asia	39,124	103,508	8	8	4	4	24	28	6	4	53	56
Sub-Saharan Africa	57,582	111,478	..	12	..	2	..	14	..	2	..	67
High income	2,954,445	5,870,228	9	7	3	2	11	10	4	3	72	75
Europe EMU	1,262,075	2,307,381	11	9	3	2	9	9	4	3	72	73

Note: Components may not sum to 100 percent because of unclassified trade.
a. Includes Luxembourg. b. Data on total merchandise imports for 1990 refer to the South African Customs Union (Botswana, Lesotho, Namibia, South Africa, and Swaziland); those for 2003 refer to South Africa only. Data on import commodity shares refer to the South African Customs Union. c. Data for 2003 include the intratrade of the Baltic states and the Commonwealth of Independent States.

About the data

Data on imports of goods are derived from the same sources as data on exports. In principle, world exports and imports should be identical. Similarly, exports from an economy should equal the sum of imports by the rest of the world from that economy. But differences in timing and definitions result in discrepancies in reported values at all levels. For further discussion of indicators of merchandise trade, see *About the data* for tables 4.4 and 4.5.

The value of imports is generally recorded as the cost of the goods when purchased by the importer plus the cost of transport and insurance to the frontier of the importing country—the cost, insurance, and freight (c.i.f.) value, corresponding to the landed cost at the point of entry of foreign goods into the country. A few countries, including Australia, Canada, and the United States, collect import data on a free on board (f.o.b.) basis and adjust them for freight and insurance costs. Many countries collect and report trade data in U.S. dollars. When countries report in local currency, the United Nations Statistics Division applies the average official exchange rate for the period shown.

Countries may report trade according to the general or special system of trade (see *Primary data documentation*). Under the general system imports include goods imported for domestic consumption and imports into bonded warehouses and free trade zones. Under the special system imports comprise goods imported for domestic consumption (including transformation and repair) and withdrawals for domestic consumption from bonded warehouses and free trade zones. Goods transported through a country en route to another are excluded.

The data on total imports of goods (merchandise) in this table come from the World Trade Organization (WTO). For further discussion of the WTO's sources and methodology, see *About the data* for table 4.5. The shares of imports by major commodity group were estimated by World Bank staff from the United Nations Statistics Division's Commodity Trade (COMTRADE) database. The values of total imports reported here have not been fully reconciled with the estimates of imports of goods and services from the national accounts (shown in table 4.9) or those from the balance of payments (table 4.15).

The classification of commodity groups is based on the Standard International Trade Classification (SITC) revision 1. Most countries now report using later revisions of the SITC or the Harmonized System. Concordance tables are used to convert data reported in one system of nomenclature to another. The conversion process may introduce some errors of classification, but conversions from later to early systems are generally reliable. Shares may not sum to 100 percent because of unclassified trade.

Definitions

- **Merchandise imports** are the c.i.f. value of goods purchased from the rest of the world valued in U.S. dollars. • **Food** corresponds to the commodities in SITC sections 0 (food and live animals), 1 (beverages and tobacco), and 4 (animal and vegetable oils and fats) and SITC division 22 (oil seeds, oil nuts, and oil kernels). • **Agricultural raw materials** correspond to SITC section 2 (crude materials except fuels) excluding divisions 22, 27 (crude fertilizers and minerals excluding coal, petroleum, and precious stones), and 28 (metalliferous ores and scrap). • **Fuels** correspond to SITC section 3 (mineral fuels). • **Ores and metals** correspond to the commodities in SITC divisions 27, 28, and 68 (nonferrous metals). • **Manufactures** correspond to the commodities in SITC sections 5 (chemicals), 6 (basic manufactures), 7 (machinery and transport equipment), and 8 (miscellaneous manufactured goods), excluding division 68.

4.6a

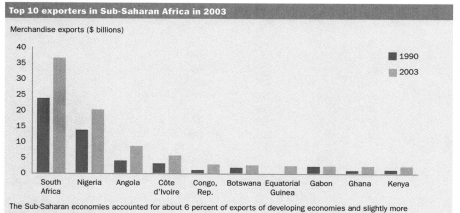

Top 10 exporters in Sub-Saharan Africa in 2003

Merchandise exports ($ billions)

Legend: 1990, 2003

Countries: South Africa, Nigeria, Angola, Côte d'Ivoire, Congo, Rep., Botswana, Equatorial Guinea, Gabon, Ghana, Kenya

The Sub-Saharan economies accounted for about 6 percent of exports of developing economies and slightly more than 1 percent of world exports.

Note: No data are available for Equatorial Guinea for 1990.

Source: World Trade Organization data files.

Data sources

The WTO publishes data on world trade in its *Annual Report.* The International Monetary Fund (IMF) publishes estimates of total imports of goods in its *International Financial Statistics* and *Direction of Trade Statistics,* as does the United Nations Statistics Division in its *Monthly Bulletin of Statistics.* And the United Nations Conference on Trade and Development (UNCTAD) publishes data on the structure of exports and imports in its *Handbook of International Trade and Development Statistics.* Tariff line records of exports and imports are compiled in the United Nations Statistics Division's COMTRADE database.

4.7 Structure of service exports

	Commercial service exports ($ millions)		Transport (% of commercial services)		Travel (% of commercial services)		Insurance and financial services (% of commercial services)		Computer, information, communications, and other commercial services (% of commercial services)	
	1990	2003	1990	2003	1990	2003	1990	2003	1990	2003
Afghanistan	..	..	..	..	..	..	..	..	..	..
Albania	32	695	20.0	9.9	11.1	75.2	2.2	3.4	66.7	11.5
Algeria	479	..	41.7	..	13.4	..	5.9	..	39.0	..
Angola	65	207	48.8	8.1	20.6	17.9	4.6	..	26.1	74.0
Argentina	2,264	3,909	51.1	22.2	39.9	53.6	0.0	0.0	9.0	24.1
Armenia	..	199	..	36.6	..	36.5	..	4.5	..	22.4
Australia	9,833	20,622	35.5	23.2	43.2	50.0	4.2	5.3	17.2	21.6
Austria	22,755	42,352	6.4	17.5	59.0	33.0	2.9	6.5	31.7	43.1
Azerbaijan	..	392	..	50.6	..	14.7	..	1.2	..	33.5
Bangladesh	296	398	12.9	18.1	6.4	14.3	0.1	8.1	80.6	59.5
Belarus	..	1,481	..	58.1	..	18.0	..	0.2	..	23.7
Belgiumª	26,646	48,970	27.5	20.8	14.0	15.5	18.2	27.8	40.3	35.9
Benin	109	133	33.4	14.7	50.2	63.4	6.9	2.3	9.5	19.6
Bolivia	133	283	35.8	30.3	43.6	39.2	10.0	17.5	10.6	13.0
Bosnia and Herzegovina	..	619	..	6.6	..	59.6	..	6.6	..	27.1
Botswana	183	439	20.4	12.6	64.1	72.7	8.2	2.1	7.3	12.6
Brazil	3,706	9,591	36.4	19.2	37.3	25.8	3.1	5.1	23.2	49.9
Bulgaria	837	3,123	27.5	30.1	38.2	53.1	3.1	1.2	31.2	15.6
Burkina Faso	34	32	37.1	14.6	34.1	61.6	..	0.4	28.9	23.4
Burundi	7	2	38.7	31.6	51.4	32.2	1.6	0.6	8.3	35.6
Cambodia	50	518	..	16.0	..	75.0	..	..	..	8.9
Cameroon	369	..	42.6	..	14.4	..	9.4	..	33.6	..
Canada	18,350	41,945	23.0	17.6	34.7	25.2	..	10.2	42.3	47.0
Central African Republic	17	..	50.9	..	16.0	..	18.8	..	14.3	..
Chad	23	..	18.4	..	34.1	..	0.2	..	47.3	..
Chile	1,786	4,728	40.0	56.5	29.8	18.2	4.9	3.4	25.3	21.8
China	5,748	46,375	47.1	17.0	30.2	37.5	3.9	1.0	18.7	44.4
Hong Kong, China	..	45,203	..	30.5	..	15.1	..	8.3	..	46.1
Colombia	1,548	1,810	31.3	34.4	26.2	48.0	17.1	2.0	25.5	15.6
Congo, Dem. Rep.	..	..	..	..	..	..	..	..	..	..
Congo, Rep.	65	79	53.9	3.6	12.9	25.1	..	0.7	33.1	70.6
Costa Rica	583	1,996	16.3	12.4	48.9	64.8	1.5	0.2	34.8	22.6
Côte d'Ivoire	425	601	62.4	19.4	12.1	14.0	8.3	..	17.2	66.6
Croatia	..	8,621	..	9.1	..	74.0	..	0.8	..	16.1
Cuba	..	..	..	..	..	..	..	..	..	..
Czech Republic	..	7,754	..	27.8	..	46.0	..	2.3	..	24.0
Denmark	12,731	31,672	32.5	44.3	26.2	16.6	2.3	..	39.0	39.1
Dominican Republic	1,086	3,368	5.6	2.8	66.8	92.4	0.2	..	27.3	4.8
Ecuador	508	830	47.6	34.3	37.0	49.0	9.3	0.2	6.1	16.5
Egypt, Arab Rep.	4,812	10,837	50.1	30.4	22.9	42.3	1.0	1.1	26.1	26.2
El Salvador	301	782	26.2	43.0	25.2	28.9	7.5	7.8	41.1	20.3
Eritrea	73	..	85.7	..	1.0	..	..	..	13.3	..
Estonia	200	2,199	74.7	44.8	13.7	30.7	0.1	1.4	11.5	23.1
Ethiopia	261	588	80.6	50.7	2.1	19.4	0.7	1.0	16.6	28.9
Finland	4,562	7,806	38.4	25.6	25.8	23.9	0.1	1.1	35.6	49.4
France	74,948	98,930	21.7	22.3	27.0	37.4	14.8	3.3	36.4	37.0
Gabon	214	..	33.4	..	1.4	..	5.7	..	59.4	..
Gambia, The	53	..	8.8	..	87.9	..	0.1	..	3.3	..
Georgia	..	403	..	49.2	..	36.5	..	4.9	..	9.4
Germany	50,561	115,597	29.2	24.9	28.3	19.9	1.0	9.3	41.5	45.9
Ghana	79	612	49.2	20.3	5.6	67.7	2.7	1.1	42.6	10.9
Greece	6,514	24,204	4.9	44.8	39.7	44.5	0.1	1.2	55.2	9.6
Guatemala	313	954	7.4	8.8	37.6	65.0	1.9	6.7	53.0	19.4
Guinea	91	55	14.2	12.1	32.6	0.1	0.1	0.6	53.1	87.2
Guinea-Bissau	4	6	5.4	1.9	..	35.8	..	10.3	94.6	52.1
Haiti	43	116	19.8	..	78.9	80.2	1.3	..	0.0	19.8

Structure of service exports | **4.7**

	Commercial service exports		Transport		Travel		Insurance and financial services		Computer, information, communications, and other commercial services	
	$ millions		% of commercial services		% of commercial services		% of commercial services		% of commercial services	
	1990	2003	1990	2003	1990	2003	1990	2003	1990	2003
Honduras	121	516	35.1	10.9	24.0	65.3	12.9	3.5	28.0	20.2
Hungary	2,677	7,894	1.6	12.9	36.8	43.6	0.2	2.9	61.4	40.7
India	4,610	25,043	20.8	*10.9*	33.8	*12.5*	2.7	*1.5*	42.7	*75.1*
Indonesia	2,488	5,143	2.8	16.6	86.5	78.5	..	0.1	10.7	4.8
Iran, Islamic Rep.	343	..	10.5	..	8.2	..	6.4	..	74.9	..
Iraq	..	..	..	..	..	..	..	..	..	..
Ireland	3,286	37,732	31.1	5.3	44.4	10.2	..	23.8	24.5	60.7
Israel	4,546	12,227	30.8	21.2	30.7	16.7	-0.2	0.1	38.8	62.0
Italy	48,579	70,052	21.0	14.3	33.9	44.6	5.5	2.9	39.6	38.2
Jamaica	976	2,097	18.0	22.4	77.0	64.6	1.4	1.6	3.6	11.3
Japan	41,384	75,933	*40.4*	34.9	*7.9*	11.7	*-0.4*	5.1	*52.1*	48.4
Jordan	1,430	1,461	26.0	20.7	35.7	55.7	..	..	38.3	23.5
Kazakhstan	..	1,622	..	49.8	..	34.8	..	1.0	..	14.5
Kenya	774	832	32.0	54.6	60.2	40.8	0.7	1.3	7.1	3.3
Korea, Dem. Rep.	..	..	..	..	..	..	..	..	..	..
Korea, Rep.	9,155	31,502	34.7	54.0	34.5	16.7	0.1	2.4	30.7	26.9
Kuwait	1,054	1,584	87.5	86.2	12.5	7.4	..	5.3	0.0	1.1
Kyrgyz Republic	..	134	..	31.4	..	35.7	..	1.4	..	31.5
Lao PDR	11	*127*	74.8	*18.0*	24.3	*82.0*	0.9	..	..	..
Latvia	*290*	1,496	*94.9*	59.6	*2.5*	14.8	*0.0*	6.9	*2.6*	18.6
Lebanon	..	..	..	..	..	..	..	..	..	..
Lesotho	34	*31*	14.1	*1.3*	51.2	*64.0*	..	*0.0*	34.7	*34.7*
Liberia	..	..	..	..	..	..	..	..	..	..
Libya	83	..	83.8	..	7.7	..	..	..	8.5	..
Lithuania	..	1,864	..	50.0	..	34.2	..	0.4	..	15.4
Macedonia, FYR	..	306	..	30.2	..	18.5	..	1.7	..	49.5
Madagascar	129	202	32.1	28.5	31.3	37.5	0.3	1.7	36.3	32.3
Malawi	37	*49*	46.1	*32.7*	42.6	*67.3*	0.1	..	11.2	*0.0*
Malaysia	3,769	13,459	31.8	20.6	44.7	43.8	0.1	2.5	23.5	33.1
Mali	71	*150*	31.0	*14.0*	54.3	*69.5*	4.9	*2.8*	9.8	*13.7*
Mauritania	14	..	35.3	..	64.7	..	..	..	0.0	..
Mauritius	478	1,274	32.9	26.3	51.1	54.7	0.1	1.7	15.8	17.3
Mexico	7,222	12,572	12.4	8.9	76.5	75.2	4.6	9.2	6.5	6.7
Moldova	..	231	..	54.8	..	25.1	..	1.5	..	18.6
Mongolia	48	*179*	41.8	*21.8*	10.4	*72.7*	4.6	*0.8*	43.2	*4.7*
Morocco	1,871	5,126	9.6	17.8	68.4	62.8	0.8	1.5	21.2	17.9
Mozambique	103	300	61.3	30.1	..	32.5	..	1.5	38.7	35.8
Myanmar	94	277	10.3	29.0	20.9	20.9	0.5	..	68.3	50.1
Namibia	106	344	..	..	81.0	96.5	5.9	0.0	13.1	3.5
Nepal	166	302	3.6	11.9	65.6	65.9	..	0.2	30.8	22.0
Netherlands	28,478	63,074	45.4	32.2	14.6	14.7	0.8	2.6	39.2	50.5
New Zealand	2,415	6,370	43.4	21.1	42.7	62.4	-0.3	1.0	14.2	15.6
Nicaragua	34	213	19.2	15.9	35.5	70.7	..	1.1	45.3	12.4
Niger	22	..	5.2	..	59.5	..	13.5	..	21.8	..
Nigeria	965	..	3.9	..	2.5	..	0.3	..	93.3	..
Norway	12,452	21,465	68.7	57.4	12.6	11.7	0.4	4.2	18.3	26.7
Oman	68	457	15.3	47.8	84.7	47.8	..	1.1	0.0	3.2
Pakistan	1,218	1,475	59.3	56.7	12.0	8.1	1.4	2.3	27.3	32.8
Panama	907	2,520	64.9	55.9	18.9	23.2	3.8	12.4	12.4	8.5
Papua New Guinea	198	*285*	11.2	*7.5*	12.0	*1.8*	0.5	*1.8*	76.3	*88.9*
Paraguay	404	558	18.3	15.0	21.1	11.4	..	4.6	60.5	68.9
Peru	714	1,560	43.4	19.0	30.4	59.2	11.2	5.7	15.0	16.2
Philippines	2,897	2,954	8.5	19.7	16.1	49.6	0.5	3.8	74.9	27.0
Poland	3,200	11,170	57.3	35.8	11.2	36.4	4.0	3.4	27.6	24.4
Portugal	5,054	11,703	15.6	19.8	70.4	59.3	0.7	2.1	13.3	18.8
Puerto Rico	..	..	..	..	..	..	..	..	..	..

	Commercial service exports		Transport		Travel		Insurance and financial services		Computer, information, communications, and other commercial services	
	$ millions		% of commercial services		% of commercial services		% of commercial services		% of commercial services	
	1990	2003	1990	2003	1990	2003	1990	2003	1990	2003
Romania	610	3,000	50.5	40.2	17.4	15.0	5.6	3.3	26.6	41.6
Russian Federation	..	15,889	..	38.5	..	28.3	..	2.0	..	31.1
Rwanda	31	48	56.1	25.7	32.8	65.3	1.0	..	10.0	9.0
Saudi Arabia	3,031	5,720	..	..	..	..	..	..	..	..
Senegal	356	389	19.1	9.6	42.7	48.7	0.5	1.6	37.6	40.0
Serbia and Montenegro	..	..	..	..	..	..	..	..	..	..
Sierra Leone	45	66	9.7	4.6	76.2	90.7	0.1	0.2	14.1	4.5
Singapore	12,719	30,613	17.5	38.5	36.6	13.1	0.7	8.7	45.3	39.7
Slovak Republic	..	3,270	..	43.2	..	26.4	..	2.3	..	28.0
Slovenia	1,219	2,787	22.6	27.7	55.0	48.2	1.2	1.0	21.2	23.2
Somalia	..	..	..	..	..	..	..	..	..	..
South Africa	3,290	6,414	21.6	19.7	55.8	66.6	10.8	5.0	11.9	8.7
Spain	27,649	76,252	17.2	15.0	67.2	54.8	4.3	4.3	11.3	26.0
Sri Lanka	425	1,386	39.7	40.5	30.2	30.6	4.2	3.5	25.9	25.4
Sudan	134	31	14.1	29.2	15.7	56.3	0.5	2.7	69.7	11.9
Swaziland	102	113	24.5	9.4	29.2	23.3	..	..	46.3	67.3
Sweden	13,453	30,337	35.8	21.4	21.7	17.5	9.1	5.3	33.5	55.8
Switzerland	18,325	33,229	16.3	11.4	40.4	28.1	23.7	35.9	19.6	24.7
Syrian Arab Republic	740	1,181	29.7	16.8	43.3	65.5	..	1.9	27.0	15.8
Tajikistan	..	66	..	74.2	..	2.3	..	2.6	..	20.8
Tanzania	131	609	19.9	10.1	36.4	71.8	0.5	3.9	43.1	14.3
Thailand	6,292	15,694	21.1	22.3	68.7	50.1	0.2	0.9	10.0	26.8
Togo	114	72	26.9	27.9	50.7	18.4	13.7	6.4	8.6	47.3
Trinidad and Tobago	322	598	50.7	33.9	29.4	40.5	..	16.7	19.9	9.0
Tunisia	1,575	2,842	23.0	25.6	64.8	55.7	1.5	2.6	10.7	16.1
Turkey	7,882	18,989	11.7	11.5	40.9	69.5	1.7	2.6	47.4	16.3
Turkmenistan	..	..	..	..	..	..	..	..	..	..
Uganda	..	284	..	14.0	..	66.4	..	6.0	..	13.7
Ukraine	..	5,013	..	70.1	..	18.7	..	0.7	..	10.6
United Arab Emirates	..	..	..	..	..	..	..	..	..	..
United Kingdom	53,830	145,749	25.2	14.5	29.0	15.6	16.4	22.6	29.4	47.3
United States	132,880	287,694	28.1	16.5	37.9	29.2	3.5	7.8	30.5	46.4
Uruguay	460	751	36.9	38.5	51.8	45.9	1.0	8.6	10.3	7.0
Uzbekistan	..	..	..	..	..	..	..	..	..	..
Venezuela, RB	1,121	784	40.9	39.3	44.2	41.2	0.2	0.3	14.7	19.3
Vietnam	..	2,948	..	..	..	..	..	..	..	..
West Bank and Gaza	..	..	..	..	..	..	..	..	..	..
Yemen, Rep.	82	244	27.2	21.2	48.8	56.8	..	..	24.0	21.9
Zambia	94	..	68.9	..	13.5	..	4.1	..	13.4	..
Zimbabwe	253	..	44.3	..	25.3	..	1.2	..	29.2	..
World	**749,408 s**	**1,729,132 s**	**26.6 w**	**22.5 w**	**35.2 w**	**30.2 w**	**6.6 w**	**8.7 w**	**32.1 w**	**38.8 w**
Low income	11,742	32,671	29.2	16.3	28.4	19.7	2.5	1.8	40.3	62.4
Middle income	82,300	268,567	27.0	24.1	45.4	46.9	3.2	2.6	25.0	26.5
Lower middle income	52,413	174,809	25.9	23.4	44.1	46.1	3.6	2.0	27.3	28.5
Upper middle income	29,888	93,758	29.0	25.5	47.9	48.3	2.7	3.8	20.5	22.4
Low & middle income	94,042	301,238	27.3	24.4	43.2	46.6	3.1	2.6	27.0	26.5
East Asia & Pacific	22,049	84,513	26.1	18.7	48.5	44.0	1.3	1.3	24.2	36.1
Europe & Central Asia	15,237	96,431	21.9	29.8	32.8	44.3	1.7	2.3	44.0	23.6
Latin America & Carib.	25,940	51,495	27.9	21.9	51.6	51.8	4.5	5.9	16.2	20.9
Middle East & N. Africa	14,513	27,869	33.8	25.8	38.6	51.2	..	1.4	26.5	21.7
South Asia	6,816	29,033	27.9	14.8	30.1	14.4	2.4	1.6	39.7	69.2
Sub-Saharan Africa	9,487	11,897	28.4	25.2	40.1	57.4	5.8	3.5	26.8	15.1
High income	655,366	1,427,894	26.5	22.1	33.8	26.7	7.1	10.0	32.9	41.7
Europe EMU	299,031	572,936	23.9	20.8	33.3	31.9	7.2	8.5	35.6	38.8

a. Includes Luxembourg.

About the data

Balance of payments statistics, the main source of information on international trade in services, have many weaknesses. Some large economies—such as the former Soviet Union—did not report data on trade in services until recently. Disaggregation of important components may be limited, and it varies significantly across countries. There are inconsistencies in the methods used to report items. And the recording of major flows as net items is common (for example, insurance transactions are often recorded as premiums less claims). These factors contribute to a downward bias in the value of the service trade reported in the balance of payments.

Efforts are being made to improve the coverage, quality, and consistency of these data. Eurostat and the Organisation for Economic Co-operation and Development, for example, are working together to improve the collection of statistics on trade in services in member countries. In addition, the International Monetary Fund (IMF) has implemented the new classification of trade in services introduced in the fifth edition of its *Balance of Payments Manual* (1993).

Still, difficulties in capturing all the dimensions of international trade in services mean that the record is likely to remain incomplete. Cross-border intrafirm service transactions, which are usually not captured in the balance of payments, have increased in recent years. One example of such transactions is transnational corporations' use of mainframe computers around the clock for data processing, exploiting time zone differences between their home country and the host countries of their affiliates. Another important dimension of service trade not captured by conventional balance of payments statistics is

establishment trade—sales in the host country by foreign affiliates. By contrast, cross-border intrafirm transactions in merchandise may be reported as exports or imports in the balance of payments.

The data on exports of services in this table and on imports of services in table 4.8, unlike those in editions before 2000, include only commercial services and exclude the category "government services not included elsewhere." The data are compiled by the IMF based on returns from national sources. Data on total trade in goods and services from the IMF's Balance of Payments database are shown in table 4.15.

Definitions

• **Commercial service exports** are total service exports minus exports of government services not included elsewhere. International transactions in services are defined by the IMF's *Balance of Payments Manual* (1993) as the economic output of intangible commodities that may be produced, transferred, and consumed at the same time. Definitions may vary among reporting economies. • **Transport** covers all transport services (sea, air, land, internal waterway, space, and pipeline) performed by residents of one economy for those of another and involving the carriage of passengers, movement of goods (freight), rental of carriers with crew, and related support and auxiliary services. Excluded are freight insurance, which is included in insurance services; goods procured in ports by nonresident carriers and repairs of transport equipment, which are included in goods; repairs of harbors, railway facilities, and airfield facilities, which are included in construction services; and rental of carriers without crew, which is included in other services. • **Travel** covers goods and services acquired from an economy by travelers in that economy for their own use during visits of less than one year for business or personal purposes. Travel services include the goods and services consumed by travelers, such as meals, lodging, and transport (within the economy visited), including car rental. • **Insurance and financial services** cover freight insurance on goods exported and other direct insurance such as life insurance, financial intermediation services such as commissions, foreign exchange transactions, and brokerage services; and auxiliary services such as financial market operational and regulatory services. • **Computer, information, communications, and other commercial services** include such activities as international telecommunications and postal and courier services; computer data; news-related service transactions between residents and nonresidents; construction services; royalties and license fees; miscellaneous business, professional, and technical services; and personal, cultural, and recreational services.

4.7a

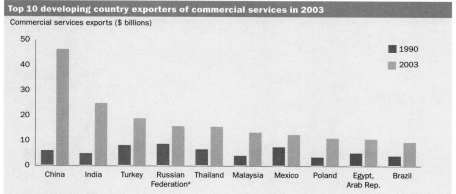

Top 10 developing country exporters of commercial services in 2003

Commercial services exports ($ billions)

■ 1990
■ 2003

China, India, Turkey, Russian Federation[a], Thailand, Malaysia, Mexico, Poland, Egypt, Arab Rep., Brazil

The top 10 developing country exporters accounted for almost 60 percent of developing country commercial service exports and 10 percent of world commercial service exports in 2003.

a. Data for 1994 are used in place of data for 1990.
Source: International Monetary Fund data files and staff estimates.

Data sources

The data on exports of commercial services are from the IMF. The IMF publishes balance of payments data in its *International Financial Statistics* and *Balance of Payments Statistics Yearbook*.

	Commercial service imports		Transport		Travel		Insurance and financial services		Computer, information, communications, and other commercial services	
	$ millions		% of commercial services		% of commercial services		% of commercial services		% of commercial services	
	1990	**2003**	**1990**	**2003**	**1990**	**2003**	**1990**	**2003**	**1990**	**2003**
Afghanistan	..	..	..	..	..	..	..	..	..	..
Albania	29	734	26.3	21.3	*1.4*	66.6	2.9	3.6	70.8	8.5
Algeria	1,155	..	58.1	..	12.9	..	9.8	..	19.2	..
Angola	1,288	*3,197*	38.3	*14.9*	3.0	*0.6*	2.6	*4.0*	56.1	80.5
Argentina	2,876	5,300	32.6	22.2	40.7	48.6	*1.7*	5.5	26.7	23.8
Armenia	..	264	..	57.4	..	25.4	..	6.2	..	10.9
Australia	13,388	21,033	33.9	34.0	31.5	34.9	4.8	4.5	29.8	26.6
Austria	14,104	41,298	8.4	11.2	54.9	28.5	4.6	6.2	32.1	54.1
Azerbaijan	..	2,027	..	9.4	..	5.5	..	1.2	..	83.9
Bangladesh	554	1,606	71.1	75.7	14.1	10.3	6.6	7.6	8.3	6.5
Belarus	..	914	..	20.9	..	53.9	..	0.8	..	24.4
Belgium[a]	25,924	*42,856*	23.3	*19.5*	21.1	*24.7*	14.7	*19.1*	40.8	36.7
Benin	113	*186*	46.9	*67.9*	12.8	*9.3*	5.7	*10.2*	34.6	12.6
Bolivia	291	461	61.7	34.8	20.6	21.1	10.0	23.7	7.6	20.5
Bosnia and Herzegovina	..	340	..	48.6	..	36.6	..	9.1	..	5.8
Botswana	371	*508*	57.5	*42.0*	15.0	*36.2*	5.5	*3.4*	22.0	18.4
Brazil	6,733	14,540	44.4	24.8	22.4	15.6	2.7	9.0	30.5	50.7
Bulgaria	600	2,541	40.5	45.1	31.5	29.5	4.5	3.8	23.5	21.6
Burkina Faso	196	*135*	64.7	*65.1*	16.6	*16.1*	5.1	*14.7*	13.6	4.2
Burundi	59	38	62.6	52.6	29.0	38.3	6.3	4.1	2.2	5.0
Cambodia	*64*	386	24.5	60.5	..	9.4	..	5.0	75.5	25.1
Cameroon	1,018	..	45.3	..	27.5	..	7.2	..	20.1	..
Canada	27,479	50,015	21.1	20.3	39.8	26.5	..	13.6	39.2	39.5
Central African Republic	166	..	49.7	..	30.6	..	8.9	..	10.7	..
Chad	223	..	45.1	..	31.2	..	4.4	..	19.2	..
Chile	1,982	5,429	47.4	45.7	21.5	14.1	3.3	11.6	27.9	28.5
China	4,113	54,852	78.9	33.2	11.4	27.7	2.3	8.7	7.4	30.3
Hong Kong, China	..	25,185	..	*26.6*	..	*50.1*	..	*4.8*	..	18.5
Colombia	1,683	3,322	34.9	37.9	27.0	30.9	13.7	12.0	24.4	19.2
Congo, Dem. Rep.	..	..	..	..	..	..	..	..	..	..
Congo, Rep.	748	537	18.4	12.6	15.2	9.8	1.6	8.1	64.9	69.6
Costa Rica	540	1,175	41.2	38.6	28.8	30.1	6.0	5.6	24.0	25.7
Côte d'Ivoire	1,518	1,606	32.1	43.8	11.1	20.9	4.7	..	52.0	35.3
Croatia	..	2,948	..	17.1	..	22.8	..	6.3	..	53.8
Cuba	..	..	..	..	..	..	..	..	..	..
Czech Republic	..	7,240	..	16.6	..	26.7	..	9.7	..	47.0
Denmark	10,106	28,254	38.3	42.6	36.5	23.6	1.6	..	23.6	33.9
Dominican Republic	435	1,178	40.0	59.8	33.1	22.1	4.1	10.1	22.8	8.0
Ecuador	755	1,540	41.6	42.8	23.2	23.0	8.1	6.3	27.2	27.9
Egypt, Arab Rep.	3,327	6,038	44.0	33.3	3.9	21.9	4.6	7.4	47.5	37.4
El Salvador	296	978	45.9	49.7	20.5	16.3	12.0	12.8	21.5	21.2
Eritrea	..	..	..	..	..	..	..	..	..	..
Estonia	*123*	1,361	*76.3*	37.8	*15.4*	23.6	*0.3*	1.6	8.0	36.9
Ethiopia	348	695	76.5	59.5	3.3	7.1	3.4	6.2	16.8	27.1
Finland	7,432	10,217	26.1	30.2	37.2	23.8	1.8	1.0	34.8	45.0
France	59,560	83,716	29.4	25.9	20.7	28.2	19.2	5.4	30.7	40.6
Gabon	984	..	23.2	..	13.9	..	5.3	..	57.6	..
Gambia, The	35	..	65.1	..	23.1	..	9.0	..	2.8	..
Georgia	..	347	..	38.2	..	37.5	..	8.0	..	16.2
Germany	83,338	171,722	20.6	21.5	46.8	37.6	1.0	3.4	31.6	37.5
Ghana	226	734	55.1	44.5	5.9	18.8	11.2	4.9	27.8	31.8
Greece	2,756	10,731	34.0	52.0	39.5	22.7	5.4	5.4	21.0	19.9
Guatemala	363	1,086	41.0	51.7	27.4	28.7	3.4	13.1	28.2	6.5
Guinea	243	188	57.5	28.9	12.2	13.8	5.5	10.0	24.8	47.3
Guinea-Bissau	17	*27*	54.5	*57.4*	19.8	*19.0*	5.6	*1.2*	20.0	22.4
Haiti	71	244	47.9	97.5	52.1	..	..	..	..	2.5

Structure of service imports | 4.8

	Commercial service imports		Transport		Travel		Insurance and financial services		Computer, information, communications, and other commercial services	
	$ millions		% of commercial services		% of commercial services		% of commercial services		% of commercial services	
	1990	2003	1990	2003	1990	2003	1990	2003	1990	2003
Honduras	213	639	45.4	52.0	17.6	21.7	15.0	..	22.0	26.3
Hungary	2,264	8,043	8.8	17.3	25.9	25.2	1.0	6.0	64.3	51.5
India	5,943	21,593	57.5	*34.1*	6.6	*13.2*	5.8	*3.7*	30.1	48.9
Indonesia	5,898	17,171	47.4	28.1	14.2	18.0	4.0	1.7	34.5	52.2
Iran, Islamic Rep.	3,703	..	47.3	..	9.2	..	10.8	..	32.8	..
Iraq	..	..	..	..	..	..	..	..	..	..
Ireland	5,145	52,237	24.3	3.7	22.6	9.1	1.9	10.6	51.2	76.6
Israel	4,825	11,730	39.6	38.7	29.7	21.7	4.4	3.7	26.2	35.8
Italy	46,602	73,318	23.7	21.8	22.1	28.1	10.4	3.5	43.8	46.5
Jamaica	667	1,527	47.9	44.5	17.0	16.5	6.7	6.8	28.4	32.1
Japan	84,281	110,262	*30.8*	31.0	*27.9*	26.3	*2.1*	5.2	39.3	37.5
Jordan	1,118	1,564	52.0	49.5	30.1	24.1	5.2	7.3	12.7	19.0
Kazakhstan	..	3,984	..	21.0	..	16.8	..	3.3	..	59.0
Kenya	598	568	66.2	44.0	6.4	22.4	8.9	11.4	18.5	22.2
Korea, Dem. Rep.	..	..	..	..	..	..	..	..	..	..
Korea, Rep.	10,050	39,861	39.8	33.8	27.5	25.1	0.3	1.3	32.4	39.8
Kuwait	2,805	5,476	31.9	36.5	65.5	61.2	1.2	1.6	1.4	0.7
Kyrgyz Republic	..	145	..	36.9	..	11.4	..	13.0	..	38.7
Lao PDR	25	5	73.0	*99.0*	13.3	*1.0*	6.3	..	20.6	..
Latvia	*120*	926	*82.3*	32.5	*10.9*	35.4	*4.8*	8.2	2.1	23.9
Lebanon	..	..	..	..	..	..	..	..	..	..
Lesotho	48	*45*	67.9	*68.0*	24.7	*30.7*	5.6	*1.1*	1.7	0.1
Liberia	..	..	..	..	..	..	..	..	..	..
Libya	926	..	41.9	..	45.7	..	4.1	..	8.3	..
Lithuania	..	1,215	..	41.9	..	38.7	..	1.3	..	18.0
Macedonia, FYR	..	323	..	41.8	..	14.8	..	4.2	..	39.1
Madagascar	172	405	43.5	58.4	23.4	15.7	3.5	3.6	29.5	22.2
Malawi	268	*222*	81.8	*50.1*	5.9	*35.2*	8.7	*0.0*	3.7	14.7
Malaysia	5,394	17,323	46.9	36.1	26.9	16.4	..	3.4	26.2	44.0
Mali	352	*380*	57.4	*60.6*	15.8	*9.5*	1.9	*5.8*	24.9	24.1
Mauritania	126	..	76.9	..	18.3	..	3.1	..	1.7	..
Mauritius	407	876	51.6	45.7	23.0	24.7	5.5	5.3	19.9	24.3
Mexico	10,063	17,671	25.0	10.9	54.9	35.4	6.2	41.1	14.0	12.6
Moldova	..	264	..	37.8	..	36.8	..	2.6	..	22.7
Mongolia	155	*260*	56.2	*38.3*	0.8	*45.8*	6.3	*2.7*	36.8	13.2
Morocco	940	2,350	58.3	48.0	19.9	23.3	6.0	2.4	15.9	26.3
Mozambique	206	528	57.7	28.4	..	26.5	4.3	4.2	38.1	40.8
Myanmar	73	339	35.4	65.0	22.6	9.4	2.5	..	39.5	25.6
Namibia	341	242	46.9	25.2	17.9	30.6	6.8	9.5	28.5	34.7
Nepal	159	256	40.8	44.5	28.5	31.6	3.2	6.7	27.5	17.2
Netherlands	28,995	65,176	37.7	23.3	25.4	22.4	1.0	4.5	35.9	49.8
New Zealand	3,251	5,546	40.6	35.3	29.5	32.1	2.5	3.8	27.5	28.8
Nicaragua	73	349	70.7	55.3	20.1	21.5	7.9	3.7	1.4	19.4
Niger	209	..	68.3	..	10.4	..	4.3	..	17.1	..
Nigeria	1,901	..	33.6	..	30.3	..	3.1	..	32.9	..
Norway	12,247	19,784	44.6	35.9	30.0	33.4	1.7	4.0	23.6	26.8
Oman	719	2,059	36.6	39.8	6.5	28.0	4.1	5.6	52.8	26.6
Pakistan	1,863	3,104	67.0	51.1	23.1	29.8	1.3	4.7	8.6	14.4
Panama	666	1,244	66.6	49.0	14.8	16.7	10.2	19.2	8.4	15.1
Papua New Guinea	393	*662*	35.6	*26.1*	12.8	*5.8*	4.0	*7.3*	47.6	60.8
Paraguay	361	316	61.6	57.1	19.8	21.2	11.4	15.8	7.3	5.9
Peru	1,070	2,484	43.5	39.4	27.6	24.9	10.9	11.0	18.0	24.7
Philippines	1,721	4,171	56.9	53.6	6.4	15.2	3.4	8.6	33.2	22.6
Poland	2,847	10,526	52.4	21.8	14.9	26.6	1.0	6.6	31.8	44.9
Portugal	3,772	7,760	48.4	32.6	23.0	34.8	5.1	4.5	23.5	28.1
Puerto Rico	..	..	..	..	..	..	..	..	..	..

4.8 Structure of service imports

	Commercial service imports		Transport		Travel		Insurance and financial services		Computer, information, communications, and other commercial services	
	$ millions		% of commercial services		% of commercial services		% of commercial services		% of commercial services	
	1990	2003	1990	2003	1990	2003	1990	2003	1990	2003
Romania	787	2,913	65.5	38.9	13.1	16.4	7.3	7.1	14.1	37.6
Russian Federation	..	26,487	..	11.7	..	48.6	..	4.1	..	35.5
Rwanda	94	124	69.0	71.9	23.7	19.2	0.0	..	7.3	8.9
Saudi Arabia	12,694	7,861	18.1	34.9	..	..	2.2	3.9	79.7	61.2
Senegal	368	457	60.1	55.7	12.4	9.5	8.8	11.2	18.7	23.6
Serbia and Montenegro	..	..	..	..	..	..	..	..	..	..
Sierra Leone	67	89	29.5	40.7	32.7	41.9	4.8	7.9	33.0	9.5
Singapore	8,575	29,412	41.0	45.7	21.0	16.7	9.1	7.4	29.0	30.2
Slovak Republic	..	3,012	..	29.8	..	19.0	..	8.7	..	42.4
Slovenia	1,034	2,165	42.5	21.9	27.3	34.9	2.5	2.3	27.8	40.8
Somalia	..	..	..	..	..	..	..	..	..	..
South Africa	3,593	7,348	40.2	46.0	31.5	33.4	11.6	8.8	16.7	11.8
Spain	15,197	45,615	30.8	24.5	28.0	18.2	6.3	7.4	34.9	49.9
Sri Lanka	620	1,646	64.2	58.4	11.9	16.9	6.8	5.8	17.1	18.8
Sudan	202	805	31.9	84.8	25.4	14.8	4.9	0.0	37.8	0.4
Swaziland	171	134	6.1	15.4	20.6	24.6	..	8.7	73.4	51.2
Sweden	16,959	28,647	23.2	16.1	37.1	29.0	7.9	3.3	31.7	51.7
Switzerland	11,093	19,135	33.7	25.4	53.0	39.0	1.4	4.9	12.0	30.6
Syrian Arab Republic	702	1,697	54.5	47.9	35.5	41.2	4.4	1.9	5.7	8.9
Tajikistan	..	120	..	79.3	..	1.8	..	7.5	..	11.4
Tanzania	288	647	58.0	27.3	7.9	52.2	6.2	4.8	27.9	15.7
Thailand	6,160	17,999	58.0	47.1	23.3	16.2	5.5	6.3	13.2	30.4
Togo	217	147	56.9	70.2	18.4	3.4	9.1	13.3	15.5	13.0
Trinidad and Tobago	460	340	51.7	34.5	26.6	54.7	9.9	0.1	11.9	10.7
Tunisia	682	1,510	51.4	50.7	26.2	19.9	7.3	7.3	15.0	22.1
Turkey	2,794	7,769	32.2	34.8	18.6	27.2	9.6	12.8	49.2	25.1
Turkmenistan	..	..	..	..	..	..	..	..	..	..
Uganda	195	494	58.3	42.6	..	..	6.5	9.3	35.2	48.1
Ukraine	..	3,192	..	17.9	..	24.7	..	20.1	..	37.3
United Arab Emirates	..	..	..	..	..	..	..	..	..	..
United Kingdom	44,713	118,318	33.2	23.7	41.0	40.4	2.4	5.9	23.4	29.9
United States	97,950	228,535	36.3	28.8	38.9	26.1	4.5	13.5	20.4	31.6
Uruguay	363	582	48.2	48.4	30.7	29.0	1.5	5.5	19.6	17.1
Uzbekistan	..	..	..	..	..	..	..	..	..	..
Venezuela, RB	2,390	3,226	33.5	38.5	42.8	26.6	4.3	8.9	19.4	26.0
Vietnam	..	3,698	..	..	..	..	..	..	..	..
West Bank and Gaza	..	..	..	..	..	..	..	..	..	..
Yemen, Rep.	639	947	27.6	48.8	9.9	8.1	5.4	8.5	57.1	34.6
Zambia	370	..	76.8	..	14.6	..	5.3	..	3.3	..
Zimbabwe	460	..	51.8	..	14.4	..	3.4	..	30.4	..
World	**778,681 s**	**1,686,079 s**	**31.9 w**	**26.7 w**	**32.7 w**	**28.0 w**	**6.0 w**	**7.8 w**	**30.4 w**	**37.9 w**
Low income	22,415	36,040	51.2	39.3	14.2	13.8	4.8	4.5	30.1	42.8
Middle income	98,472	295,890	41.0	30.6	25.2	26.7	5.2	9.1	32.5	34.4
Lower middle income	51,851	197,252	50.0	32.5	18.6	26.7	6.1	7.3	25.6	33.5
Upper middle income	46,621	98,638	30.9	26.6	35.3	26.5	4.0	12.6	40.1	36.3
Low & middle income	120,887	331,930	42.9	31.6	23.0	26.3	5.1	8.9	32.0	33.9
East Asia & Pacific	24,308	112,290	56.0	36.1	18.2	22.0	4.1	6.4	22.6	35.5
Europe & Central Asia	9,321	87,634	36.0	21.1	19.6	32.4	2.1	6.6	43.0	39.9
Latin America & Carib.	33,098	64,306	37.3	28.8	35.7	26.5	6.1	18.6	21.4	26.4
Middle East & N. Africa	26,605	24,025	33.3	39.6	..	24.1	4.7	5.3	54.1	38.9
South Asia	9,176	28,325	60.4	40.0	11.3	13.4	4.9	4.2	23.4	42.4
Sub-Saharan Africa	18,379	15,350	44.1	46.2	19.6	26.4	6.3	7.5	30.5	21.6
High income	657,794	1,354,149	29.5	25.5	34.6	28.3	6.1	7.5	30.3	39.0
Europe EMU	292,825	578,250	25.4	20.6	31.6	27.3	8.0	6.5	35.0	45.5

a. Includes Luxembourg.

Structure of service imports | 4.8

About the data

Trade in services differs from trade in goods because services are produced and consumed at the same time. Thus services to a traveler may be consumed in the producing country (for example, use of a hotel room) but are classified as imports of the traveler's country. In other cases services may be supplied from a remote location; for example, insurance services may be supplied from one location and consumed in another. For further discussion of the problems of measuring trade in services, see *About the data* for table 4.7.

The data on exports of services in table 4.7 and on imports of services in this table, unlike those in editions before 2000, include only commercial services and exclude the category "government services not included elsewhere." The data are compiled by the International Monetary Fund (IMF) based on returns from national sources.

Definitions

• **Commercial service imports** are total service imports minus imports of government services not included elsewhere. International transactions in services are defined by the IMF's *Balance of Payments Manual* (1993) as the economic output of intangible commodities that may be produced, transferred, and consumed at the same time. Definitions may vary among reporting economies. • **Transport** covers all transport services (sea, air, land, internal waterway, space, and pipeline) performed by residents of one economy for those of another and involving the carriage of passengers, movement of goods (freight), rental of carriers with crew, and related support and auxiliary services. Excluded are freight insurance, which is included in insurance services; goods procured in ports by nonresident carriers and repairs of transport equipment, which are included in goods; repairs of harbors, railway facilities, and airfield facilities, which are included in construction services; and rental of carriers without crew, which is included in other services. • **Travel** covers goods and services acquired from an economy by travelers in that economy for their own use during visits of less than one year for business or personal purposes. Travel services include the goods and services consumed by travelers, such as meals, lodging, and transport (within the economy visited), including car rental. • **Insurance and financial services** cover freight insurance on goods imported and other direct insurance such as life insurance, financial intermediation services such as commissions, foreign exchange transactions, and brokerage services; and auxiliary services such as financial market operational and regulatory services. • **Computer, information, communications, and other commercial services** include such activities as international telecommunications, and postal and courier services; computer data; news-related service transactions between residents and nonresidents; construction services; royalties and license fees; miscellaneous business, professional, and technical services; and personal, cultural, and recreational services.

4.8a

The mix of commercial service imports is changing

Commercial service imports by developing economies (% of total)

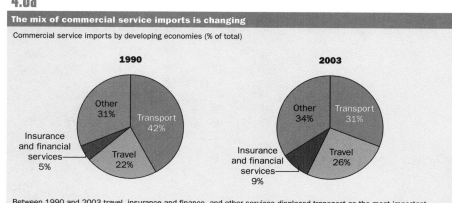

Between 1990 and 2003 travel, insurance and finance, and other services displaced transport as the most important categories of service imports for developing economies.

Source: International Monetary Fund data files.

Data sources

The data on imports of commercial services are from the IMF. The IMF publishes balance of payments data in its *International Financial Statistics* and *Balance of Payments Statistics Yearbook*.

4.9 Structure of demand

	Household final consumption expenditure		General government final consumption expenditure		Gross capital formation		Exports of goods and services		Imports of goods and services		Gross domestic savings	
	% of GDP		% of GDP		% of GDP		% of GDP		% of GDP		% of GDP	
	1990	2003	1990	2003	1990	2003	1990	2003	1990	2003	1990	2003
Afghanistan	..	108	..	9	..	16	..	57	..	89	..	−16
Albania	61	89	19	8	29	25	15	19	23	42	21	2
Algeria	57	41	16	14	29	30	23	39	25	24	27	45
Angola	36	63	34	..ᵃ	12	32	39	71	21	67	30	37
Argentina	77	63	3	11	14	15	10	25	5	14	20	26
Armenia	46	83	18	10	47	25	35	32	46	50	36	7
Australia	59	60	19	18	22	25	17	20	17	22	22	22
Austria	55	57	19	19	25	23	40	52	38	50	26	25
Azerbaijan	51	63	18	12	27	49	44	43	39	67	31	25
Bangladesh	86	77	4	5	17	23	6	14	14	20	10	18
Belarus	47	58	24	21	27	24	46	66	44	70	29	20
Belgium	55	55	20	23	22	20	71	82	69	80	24	22
Benin	87	81	11	14	14	18	14	14	26	27	2	5
Bolivia	77	74	12	17	13	11	23	24	24	25	11	10
Bosnia and Herzegovina	..	92	..	22	..	20	..	25	..	59	..	−14
Botswana	33	26	24	35	37	27	55	44	50	34	43	38
Brazil	59	59	19	19	20	18	8	17	7	13	21	22
Bulgaria	60	69	18	19	26	22	33	53	37	63	22	12
Burkina Faso	82	83	13	13	18	19	11	9	24	23	5	4
Burundi	95	87	11	9	15	15	8	7	28	18	−5	4
Cambodia	91	81	7	6	8	22	6	62	13	71	2	13
Cameroon	67	71	13	12	18	17	20	26	17	25	21	17
Canada	56	56	23	19	21	20	26	42	26	37	21	25
Central African Republic	86	75	15	13	12	18	15	24	28	31	−1	12
Chad	88	71	10	8	16	53	13	21	28	53	2	21
Chile	62	61	10	12	25	24	35	36	31	33	28	27
China	50	40	12	13	35	44	18	34	14	32	38	47
Hong Kong, China	57	57	7	11	28	23	132	170	124	161	35	32
Colombia	66	65	9	21	19	15	21	21	15	22	24	14
Congo, Dem. Rep.	79	92	12	4	9	7	30	19	29	22	9	4
Congo, Rep.	62	36	14	17	16	23	54	78	46	53	24	47
Costa Rica	61	67	18	15	27	20	35	47	41	49	21	18
Côte d'Ivoire	72	69	17	8	7	10	32	47	27	34	11	23
Croatia	74	59	24	21	10	30	78	47	86	57	2	21
Cuba	..	..	..	..	..	..	..	..	..	..	..	..
Czech Republic	49	51	23	24	25	28	45	63	43	65	28	25
Denmark	49	47	26	26	20	20	36	43	31	37	25	26
Dominican Republic	80	72	4	7	25	23	34	52	44	54	15	21
Ecuador	67	68	11	9	21	28	33	24	32	29	22	23
Egypt, Arab Rep.	73	72	11	13	29	17	20	22	33	24	16	15
El Salvador	89	89	10	11	14	16	19	27	31	43	1	0
Eritrea	104	111	22	52	8	22	11	14	45	99	−26	−63
Estonia	62	58	16	19	30	31	60	75	54	83	22	23
Ethiopia	74	75	18	24	12	20	8	17	12	37	7	1
Finland	51	52	22	22	29	18	23	37	24	30	27	26
France	55	55	22	24	23	19	21	26	22	25	22	21
Gabon	50	55	13	..ᵃ	22	24	46	62	31	41	37	45
Gambia, The	76	74	14	11	22	19	60	41	72	45	11	15
Georgia	65	81	10	9	31	24	40	32	46	46	25	10
Germany	57	59	20	19	24	18	25	36	25	32	24	22
Ghana	85	77	9	12	14	23	17	40	26	52	5	11
Greece	72	67	15	15	23	26	18	20	28	28	13	18
Guatemala	84	90	7	5	14	17	21	16	25	28	10	5
Guinea	73	85	9	7	18	10	31	22	31	25	18	7
Guinea-Bissau	87	88	10	13	30	13	10	30	37	44	3	−1
Haiti	81	99	8	..ᵃ	13	25	18	13	20	37	11	1

Structure of demand | 4.9

	Household final consumption expenditure		General government final consumption expenditure		Gross capital formation		Exports of goods and services		Imports of goods and services		Gross domestic savings	
	% of GDP		% of GDP		% of GDP		% of GDP		% of GDP		% of GDP	
	1990	2003	1990	2003	1990	2003	1990	2003	1990	2003	1990	2003
Honduras	66	74	14	14	23	29	36	36	40	54	20	12
Hungary	61	67	11	11	25	24	31	65	29	68	28	22
India	66	65	12	13	24	24	7	14	9	16	23	22
Indonesia	59	69	9	9	31	16	25	31	24	26	32	22
Iran, Islamic Rep.	62	43	11	14	29	41	22	25	24	23	27	43
Iraq	..	..	..	..	..	..	..	..	..	..	..	..
Ireland	58	44	16	15	21	22	57	94	52	75	26	41
Israel	56	60	30	31	25	16	35	37	45	44	14	9
Italy	58	60	20	19	22	20	20	25	20	25	22	20
Jamaica	65	73	13	15	26	30	48	41	52	59	22	11
Japan	53	57	13	18	33	24	10	12	9	10	34	26
Jordan	74	80	25	23	32	23	62	45	93	70	1	–3
Kazakhstan	52	56	18	11	32	27	74	50	75	44	30	33
Kenya	67	74	19	18	20	13	26	25	31	29	14	8
Korea, Dem. Rep.	..	..	..	..	..	..	..	..	..	..	..	..
Korea, Rep.	55	55	10	13	36	29	28	38	29	36	35	32
Kuwait	57	56	39	26	18	9	45	48	58	40	4	18
Kyrgyz Republic	71	71	25	17	24	16	29	38	50	42	4	12
Lao PDR	..	75	9	5	..	20	11	25	25	25	..	21
Latvia	53	62	9	18	40	31	48	47	49	57	39	21
Lebanon	140	96	25	13	18	17	18	13	100	39	–64	–9
Lesotho	138	106	14	18	53	30	17	41	122	95	–52	–24
Liberia	..	..	..	..	..	..	..	..	..	..	..	..
Libya	48	58	24	17	19	14	40	48	31	36	27	26
Lithuania	57	64	19	20	33	21	52	54	61	60	24	15
Macedonia, FYR	72	85	19	12	19	22	26	35	36	53	9	3
Madagascar	86	83	8	9	17	18	17	21	28	32	6	8
Malawi	72	85	15	20	23	8	24	27	33	41	13	–5
Malaysia	52	44	14	14	32	21	75	114	72	93	34	42
Mali	80	71	14	10	23	23	17	26	34	31	6	19
Mauritania	69	78	26	19	20	45	46	34	61	75	5	3
Mauritius	64	62	13	13	31	23	64	60	71	57	23	25
Mexico	70	69	8	13	23	20	19	28	20	30	22	18
Moldova	77	95	..a	18	25	22	49	54	51	88	23	–12
Mongolia	58	63	32	19	38	31	24	68	53	80	9	18
Morocco	65	59	15	21	25	24	26	32	32	36	19	20
Mozambique	92	77	14	11	22	28	8	23	36	39	–6	11
Myanmar	89	..	..a	..	13	15	3	..	5	..	11	..
Namibia	51	56	31	29	34	23	52	39	67	47	18	15
Nepal	84	76	9	10	18	26	11	17	22	29	7	14
Netherlands	50	50	23	25	23	21	54	63	51	58	27	26
New Zealand	61	60	19	18	20	21	27	32	27	31	20	23
Nicaragua	59	73	43	16	19	38	25	24	46	51	–2	11
Niger	84	84	15	11	8	14	15	16	22	25	1	5
Nigeria	56	45	15	23	15	23	43	50	29	41	29	32
Norway	49	46	21	23	23	18	40	41	34	28	30	31
Oman	27	43	38	23	13	13	53	57	31	35	35	34
Pakistan	74	73	15	12	19	15	16	20	23	20	11	16
Panama	57	63	18	11	17	26	87	59	79	58	25	27
Papua New Guinea	59	..	25	..	24	..	41	..	49	..	16	..
Paraguay	77	88	6	7	23	20	33	32	39	47	17	5
Peru	74	71	8	10	16	19	16	18	14	18	18	19
Philippines	72	72	10	11	24	19	28	48	33	51	18	16
Poland	48	70	19	16	26	19	29	21	22	26	33	14
Portugal	63	61	16	21	28	25	33	30	39	38	21	18
Puerto Rico	65	..	14	..	17	..	77	81	101	100	21	..

	Household final consumption expenditure		General government final consumption expenditure		Gross capital formation		Exports of goods and services		Imports of goods and services		Gross domestic savings	
	% of GDP		% of GDP		% of GDP		% of GDP		% of GDP		% of GDP	
	1990	2003	1990	2003	1990	2003	1990	2003	1990	2003	1990	2003
Romania	66	76	13	9	30	21	17	33	26	39	21	15
Russian Federation	49	53	21	16	30	20	18	32	18	21	30	31
Rwanda	84	85	10	14	15	20	6	9	14	28	6	1
Saudi Arabia	47	33	29	25	15	19	41	47	32	24	24	42
Senegal	76	77	15	15	14	20	25	28	30	40	9	8
Serbia and Montenegro	..	86	..	19	..	18	..	22	..	45	..	–5
Sierra Leone	83	92	8	19	10	16	22	22	24	49	9	–12
Singapore	47	41	10	12	36	13	..	..	36	80	43	47
Slovak Republic	54	55	22	21	33	25	27	78	36	80	24	24
Slovenia	*55*	53	*19*	22	*17*	25	*84*	60	*74*	60	*26*	25
Somalia	112	..	..ᵃ	..	16	..	10	..	38	..	–12	..
South Africa	57	62	20	19	17	17	24	28	19	26	23	19
Spain	60	58	17	18	27	26	16	28	20	30	23	24
Sri Lanka	76	76	10	8	23	22	29	36	38	42	14	16
Sudan	..	75	..	..ᵃ	..	21	..	16	..	12	..	25
Swaziland	61	66	19	25	20	19	77	84	76	94	20	9
Sweden	49	49	27	28	24	16	30	44	29	37	24	23
Switzerland	57	*61*	11	*12*	31	*20*	36	*44*	34	*37*	32	*27*
Syrian Arab Republic	69	58	14	11	17	24	28	40	28	33	17	31
Tajikistan	74	91	9	9	25	19	28	60	35	79	17	0
Tanzaniaᵇ	81	79	18	11	26	19	13	18	37	27	1	10
Thailand	57	57	9	11	41	25	34	66	42	59	34	32
Togo	71	85	14	10	27	19	33	34	45	47	15	5
Trinidad and Tobago	59	62	12	10	13	19	45	50	29	41	29	28
Tunisia	58	62	16	17	32	25	44	43	51	47	25	21
Turkey	69	67	11	14	24	23	13	28	18	31	20	20
Turkmenistan	49	*55*	23	*13*	40	*27*	..	*41*	..	*42*	28	*32*
Uganda	92	78	8	15	13	21	7	12	19	26	1	7
Ukraine	57	60	17	16	27	19	28	53	29	48	26	24
United Arab Emirates	39	..	16	..	20	..	65	..	40	..	45	..
United Kingdom	63	66	20	21	20	16	24	25	27	28	18	13
United States	67	*71*	17	*15*	18	*18*	10	*10*	11	*14*	16	*14*
Uruguay	70	73	12	12	12	13	24	26	18	23	18	15
Uzbekistan	61	57	25	19	32	17	29	37	48	30	13	24
Venezuela, RB	62	68	8	7	10	9	39	31	20	15	29	25
Vietnam	84	66	12	7	13	35	36	60	45	68	3	27
West Bank and Gaza	..	84	..	53	..	3	..	10	..	49	..	–37
Yemen, Rep.	74	74	17	14	15	17	14	31	20	36	9	12
Zambia	64	67	19	15	17	26	36	21	37	28	17	19
Zimbabwe	63	*72*	19	*17*	17	*8*	23	*24*	23	*22*	17	*11*
World	**60 w**	**62 w**	**17 w**	**17 w**	**23 w**	**21 w**	**19 w**	**24 w**	**19 w**	**24 w**	**23 w**	**21 w**
Low income	70	67	13	13	21	23	13	21	17	24	18	20
Middle income	59	57	14	15	26	25	22	33	21	30	27	28
Lower middle income	58	55	14	15	28	28	19	31	19	29	28	30
Upper middle income	63	62	13	15	21	19	29	37	25	32	24	24
Low & middle income	61	58	14	14	25	25	21	31	20	29	25	27
East Asia & Pacific	53	47	12	12	34	38	23	42	22	39	35	41
Europe & Central Asia	56	62	17	16	27	22	24	35	24	35	26	22
Latin America & Carib.	67	65	12	15	19	18	17	24	15	21	22	21
Middle East & N. Africa	60	50	20	18	23	25	31	34	33	27	20	32
South Asia	69	67	11	12	23	23	9	16	12	18	20	21
Sub-Saharan Africa	64	65	18	18	17	19	27	32	26	33	19	18
High income	60	*63*	17	*18*	23	*20*	19	*22*	19	*23*	23	*20*
Europe EMU	57	59	20	21	24	20	27	33	28	31	23	22

a. Data on general government final consumption expenditure are not available separately; they are included in household final consumption expenditure. b. Data cover mainland Tanzania only.

Gross domestic product (GDP) from the expenditure side is made up of household final consumption expenditure, general government final consumption expenditure, gross capital formation (private and public investment in fixed assets, changes in inventories, and net acquisitions of valuables), and net exports (exports minus imports) of goods and services. Such expenditures are recorded in purchaser prices and include net taxes on products.

Because policymakers have tended to focus on fostering the growth of output, and because data on production are easier to collect than data on spending, many countries generate their primary estimate of GDP using the production approach. Moreover, many countries do not estimate all the separate components of national expenditures but instead derive some of the main aggregates indirectly using GDP (based on the production approach) as the control total.

Household final consumption expenditure (private consumption in the 1968 System of National Accounts, or SNA) is often estimated as a residual, by subtracting from GDP all other known expenditures. The resulting aggregate may incorporate fairly large discrepancies. When household consumption is calculated separately, many of the estimates are based on household surveys, which tend to be one-year studies with limited coverage. Thus the estimates quickly become outdated and must be supplemented by estimates using price- and quantity-based statistical procedures. Complicating the issue, in many developing countries the distinction between cash outlays for personal business and those for household use may be blurred. *World Development Indicators* includes in household consumption the expenditures of nonprofit institutions serving households.

General government final consumption expenditure (general government consumption in the 1968 SNA) includes expenditures on goods and services for individual consumption as well as those on services for collective consumption. Defense expenditures, including those on capital outlays (with certain exceptions), are treated as current spending.

Gross capital formation (gross domestic investment in the 1968 SNA) consists of outlays on additions to the economy's fixed assets plus net changes in the level of inventories. It is generally obtained from reports by industry of acquisition and distinguishes only the broad categories of capital formation. The 1993 SNA recognizes a third category of capital formation: net acquisitions of valuables. Included in gross capital formation under the

1993 SNA guidelines are capital outlays on defense establishments that may be used by the general public, such as schools, airfields, and hospitals, and intangibles such as computer software and mineral exploration outlays. Data on capital formation may be estimated from direct surveys of enterprises and administrative records or based on the commodity flow method using data from production, trade, and construction activities. The quality of data on fixed capital formation by government depends on the quality of government accounting systems (which tend to be weak in developing countries). Measures of fixed capital formation by households and corporations—particularly capital outlays by small, unincorporated enterprises—are usually unreliable.

Estimates of changes in inventories are rarely complete but usually include the most important activities or commodities. In some countries these estimates are derived as a composite residual along with household final consumption expenditure. According to national accounts conventions, adjustments should be made for appreciation of the value of inventory holdings due to price changes, but this is not always done. In highly inflationary economies this element can be substantial.

Data on exports and imports are compiled from customs reports and balance of payments data. Although the data from the payments side provide reasonably reliable records of cross-border transactions, they may not adhere strictly to the appropriate definitions of valuation and timing used in the balance of payments or correspond to the change-of-ownership criterion. This issue has assumed greater significance with the increasing globalization of international business. Neither customs nor balance of payments data usually capture the illegal transactions that occur in many countries. Goods carried by travelers across borders in legal but unreported shuttle trade may further distort trade statistics.

Domestic savings, a concept used by the World Bank, represent the difference between GDP and total consumption. Domestic savings also satisfy the fundamental identity: exports minus imports equal domestic savings minus capital formation. Domestic savings differ from savings as defined in the national accounts; the SNA concept of savings represents the difference between disposable income and consumption. For further discussion of the problems in compiling national accounts, see Srinivasan (1994), Heston (1994), and Ruggles (1994). For a classic analysis of the reliability of foreign trade and national income statistics, see Morgenstern (1963).

• **Household final consumption expenditure** is the market value of all goods and services, including durable products (such as cars, washing machines, and home computers), purchased by households. It excludes purchases of dwellings but includes imputed rent for owner-occupied dwellings. It also includes payments and fees to governments to obtain permits and licenses. *World Development Indicators* includes in household consumption expenditure the expenditures of nonprofit institutions serving households, even when reported separately by the country. In practice, household consumption expenditure may include any statistical discrepancy in the use of resources relative to the supply of resources. • **General government final consumption expenditure** includes all government current expenditures for purchases of goods and services (including compensation of employees). It also includes most expenditures on national defense and security but excludes government military expenditures that potentially have wider public use and are part of government capital formation. • **Gross capital formation** consists of outlays on additions to the fixed assets of the economy, net changes in the level of inventories, and net acquisitions of valuables. Fixed assets include land improvements (fences, ditches, drains, and so on); plant, machinery, and equipment purchases; and the construction of roads, railways, and the like, including schools, offices, hospitals, private residential dwellings, and commercial and industrial buildings. Inventories are stocks of goods held by firms to meet temporary or unexpected fluctuations in production or sales, and "work in progress." • **Exports** and **imports of goods and services** represent the value of all goods and other market services provided to, or received from, the rest of the world. They include the value of merchandise, freight, insurance, transport, travel, royalties, license fees, and other services, such as communication, construction, financial, information, business, personal, and government services. They exclude labor and property income (factor services in the 1968 SNA) as well as transfer payments. • **Gross domestic savings** are calculated as GDP less total consumption.

The national accounts indicators for most developing countries are collected from national statistical organizations and central banks by visiting and resident World Bank missions. The data for high-income economies come from Organisation for Economic Co-operation and Development data files (see the OECD's *National Accounts of OECD Countries, Detailed Tables 1970–2002*, volumes 1 and 2). The United Nations Statistics Division publishes detailed national accounts for UN member countries in *National Accounts Statistics: Main Aggregates and Detailed Tables* and updates in the *Monthly Bulletin of Statistics*.

4.10 Growth of consumption and investment

	Household final consumption expenditure						General government final consumption expenditure		Gross capital formation	
	$ millions		average annual % growth		per capita average annual % growth		average annual % growth		average annual % growth	
	1990	2003	1980–90	1990–2003	1980–90	1990–2003	1980–90	1990–2003	1980–90	1990–2003
Afghanistan	..	4,310	..	..	..	..	..	..	..	..
Albania	1,271	3,894	..	5.5	..	6.0	..	2.2	–0.3	22.3
Algeria	35,265	27,373	1.5	0.7	–1.4	–1.1	0.7	3.3	–1.8	0.9
Angola	3,674	..	–0.1	..	..	..	6.7	..	–5.1	..
Argentina	109,038	81,198	..	0.1	..	–0.8	..	1.0	–5.2	1.6
Armenia	1,097	2,346	..	1.8	..	3.1	..	–0.5	..	3.0
Australia	182,442	245,914	2.9	3.6	1.4	2.4	3.8	2.7	3.4	6.2
Austria	89,787	144,159	2.4	2.3	2.2	2.0	1.4	1.4	2.4	2.1
Azerbaijan	4,658	4,510	..	5.4	..	4.4	..	–0.5	..	35.0
Bangladesh	24,988	39,682	2.7	2.9	0.2	1.1	2.7	5.4	7.2	8.9
Belarus	8,223	10,422	..	3.0	..	3.3	1.1	0.0	..	–4.0
Belgium	109,154	165,383	2.0	1.8	1.9	1.6	1.1	1.8	3.2	2.2
Benin	1,602	2,802	1.9	4.1	–1.2	1.3	0.5	6.3	–5.3	12.7
Bolivia	3,741	5,796	1.2	3.3	–1.0	1.1	–3.8	3.4	0.8	3.6
Bosnia and Herzegovina	..	6,398	..	..	..	..	..	..	..	..
Botswana	1,260	2,028	6.3	3.0	2.7	0.6	14.9	7.6	7.6	3.5
Brazil[a]	273,952	291,568	1.2	3.4	–0.7	2.0	7.3	0.6	3.3	2.2
Bulgaria	12,401	13,720	3.1	–0.4	3.2	0.4	5.1	–4.6	2.2	6.6
Burkina Faso	2,284	3,398	2.6	3.8	0.1	1.3	6.2	–0.4	8.6	7.9
Burundi	1,070	519	3.4	–1.7	0.5	–3.7	3.2	–1.6	6.9	1.2
Cambodia[a]	1,016	3,405	..	4.4	..	1.9	..	8.0	..	12.7
Cameroon	7,423	8,860	3.6	4.1	0.6	1.6	6.8	3.3	–2.6	3.0
Canada	322,557	407,967	3.1	2.8	1.9	1.8	2.4	0.8	5.1	4.5
Central African Republic[a]	1,274	917	1.5	..	..	..	–1.7	..	10.0	..
Chad[a]	1,538	1,353	2.9	2.4	0.2	–0.7	17.0	–0.1	22.0	20.0
Chile	18,759	43,943	2.0	5.8	0.3	4.3	0.4	3.9	6.4	5.4
China	174,249	631,629	8.8	8.5	7.2	7.4	9.8	8.9	10.8	10.9
Hong Kong, China	43,364	89,963	6.6	3.0	5.2	1.4	5.3	3.2	3.6	4.4
Colombia	26,357	50,795	2.6	1.8	0.5	–0.1	4.2	8.1	1.4	0.9
Congo, Dem. Rep.[a]	7,398	5,109	3.4	–2.9	0.4	–5.4	0.0	–15.9	–5.1	0.3
Congo, Rep.[a]	1,746	1,268	2.3	2.2	–0.9	–1.0	4.3	–1.0	–11.6	3.3
Costa Rica[a]	3,502	11,715	3.6	4.2	0.6	2.0	1.1	1.9	4.6	5.7
Côte d'Ivoire	7,766	9,464	1.5	2.7	–2.1	–0.1	–0.1	1.5	–10.4	6.0
Croatia	13,527	16,914	..	3.4	..	3.9	..	–0.4	..	7.5
Cuba	..	..	..	..	..	..	..	..	..	..
Czech Republic	17,195	45,590	..	2.8	..	2.9	..	0.4	..	4.4
Denmark	65,429	100,329	1.4	1.7	1.4	1.3	0.9	2.2	4.7	5.3
Dominican Republic[a]	5,689	11,982	3.9	4.1	1.7	2.4	–3.2	12.8	4.5	8.5
Ecuador[a]	6,988	18,473	1.1	2.3	–1.5	0.5	–0.7	–0.7	–1.3	1.9
Egypt, Arab Rep.	30,933	59,548	4.6	4.2	2.0	2.2	3.1	2.6	0.0	5.2
El Salvador	4,273	13,308	0.8	4.5	–0.2	2.6	0.1	2.6	2.2	5.5
Eritrea	496	835	..	–3.9	..	–6.3	..	15.5	..	8.2
Estonia	3,019	5,142	..	2.5	..	3.7	..	4.0	..	3.6
Ethiopia	6,382	5,002	0.7	5.1	–2.4	2.7	4.1	10.7	4.7	6.5
Finland	68,686	84,554	3.7	2.1	3.3	1.8	3.2	1.2	3.3	2.0
France	672,982	976,151	2.2	1.6	1.7	1.3	2.6	2.0	3.3	2.0
Gabon[a]	2,961	..	1.5	2.2	–1.6	–0.4	–0.6	3.6	–5.7	2.9
Gambia, The	240	293	–2.4	3.8	–5.9	0.5	1.7	1.2	0.0	2.6
Georgia	5,231	3,124	..	4.5	..	5.0	..	3.1	..	–6.0
Germany	950,060	1,408,217	2.3	1.5	2.2	1.3	1.5	1.5	1.6	0.5
Ghana	5,016	6,167	2.8	1.7	–0.6	–0.7	2.4	4.6	3.3	1.3
Greece	60,163	114,602	2.0	2.4	1.5	1.7	1.1	1.7	–0.7	5.5
Guatemala[a]	6,398	22,251	1.1	4.0	–1.4	1.3	2.6	5.3	–1.8	5.9
Guinea	2,068	3,092	..	3.7	..	1.2	..	5.1	..	2.6
Guinea-Bissau	212	210	0.8	2.3	–1.9	–0.6	7.2	1.7	12.9	–8.6
Haiti	2,332	2,668	0.9	..	..	..	–4.4	..	–0.6	6.6

Growth of consumption and investment

	Household final consumption expenditure						General government final consumption expenditure		Gross capital formation	
	$ millions		average annual % growth		per capita average annual % growth		average annual % growth		average annual % growth	
	1990	2003	1980–90	1990–2003	1980–90	1990–2003	1980–90	1990–2003	1980–90	1990–2003
Honduras[a]	2,026	5,132	2.7	3.1	−0.5	0.3	3.3	4.0	2.9	4.9
Hungary	20,290	56,298	1.3	1.6	1.7	1.8	1.9	1.5	−0.9	7.8
India	215,762	384,285	4.2	4.9	2.0	3.1	7.3	6.1	6.2	6.9
Indonesia	65,010	136,602	5.3	5.4	3.4	3.9	4.6	1.5	7.7	−2.0
Iran, Islamic Rep.	74,476	60,362	2.8	3.5	−0.6	1.9	−5.0	3.9	−2.5	4.8
Iraq	..	..	..	..	..	..	..	..	..	..
Ireland	27,956	*54,839*	2.2	*5.6*	1.9	*4.7*	−0.3	*5.3*	−0.6	*9.5*
Israel	32,112	64,861	..	*3.9*	..	*1.4*	..	*3.0*	..	*−2.1*
Italy	634,161	887,337	2.9	1.6	2.8	1.5	2.9	0.6	2.9	−0.2
Jamaica	2,980	5,982	..	*7.4*	..	*6.5*	..	*4.9*	..	*1.1*
Japan	1,617,984	2,447,796	3.7	1.4	3.1	1.1	3.3	3.1	5.3	−0.5
Jordan	2,978	7,650	1.9	5.1	−1.9	1.4	1.9	3.9	−1.9	0.4
Kazakhstan[a]	*12,856*	16,825	..	−4.3	..	−3.4	..	−3.6	..	−9.4
Kenya	5,320	10,603	4.6	2.1	1.1	−0.3	2.6	7.1	0.4	2.0
Korea, Dem. Rep.	..	..	..	..	..	..	..	..	..	..
Korea, Rep.	134,180	325,947	8.0	4.7	6.8	3.8	5.8	4.4	12.5	3.1
Kuwait	10,459	20,698	−1.4	..	..	..	2.2	..	−4.5	..
Kyrgyz Republic	1,906	1,358	..	−3.7	..	−4.7	..	−5.6	..	−2.0
Lao PDR	..	1,583	..	..	..	..	..	..	..	..
Latvia	3,923	6,980	2.3	0.3	1.8	1.5	5.0	3.5	3.4	−4.5
Lebanon	3,961	18,269	..	2.3	..	0.6	..	5.8	..	2.8
Lesotho	855	1,086	1.3	−0.8	−0.8	−1.8	3.6	5.8	5.0	0.8
Liberia	..	420	..	..	..	..	..	..	..	..
Libya	13,999	*10,970*	..	..	..	..	..	..	..	..
Lithuania[a]	5,967	11,791	..	*5.4*	..	*6.1*	..	*1.6*	..	*9.3*
Macedonia, FYR	3,021	3,458	..	2.1	..	1.5	..	1.2	..	2.2
Madagascar	2,663	4,544	−0.7	2.4	−3.4	−0.6	0.5	1.3	4.9	4.9
Malawi	1,345	1,455	1.5	4.4	−1.7	2.3	6.3	−0.5	−2.8	−12.6
Malaysia	22,806	45,359	3.3	4.9	0.4	2.4	2.7	6.0	3.1	2.9
Mali	1,943	2,796	0.6	3.1	−1.9	0.6	7.9	5.5	3.6	4.6
Mauritania	705	852	1.4	4.1	−0.9	1.4	−3.8	2.7	6.9	9.3
Mauritius	1,519	3,231	6.2	4.7	5.3	3.5	3.3	4.9	10.3	3.8
Mexico	182,791	433,059	1.1	2.8	−1.0	1.2	2.4	1.6	−3.3	4.1
Moldova[a]	*1,780*	1,857	..	8.7	..	9.0	..	−7.5	..	−10.2
Mongolia[a]	..	894	..	..	..	..	..	..	..	..
Morocco	16,833	28,599	4.3	2.9	2.0	1.1	2.1	3.7	1.2	4.3
Mozambique[a]	3,179	3,338	−1.6	2.6	−3.1	0.3	−1.1	5.1	3.8	13.6
Myanmar	..	..	0.6	*3.9*	..	..	..	..	−4.1	*15.3*
Namibia	1,204	2,381	1.3	4.1	−1.9	1.3	3.7	3.0	−3.2	6.8
Nepal	3,028	4,572	..	..	..	..	..	..	..	..
Netherlands	146,162	*208,629*	1.4	*2.8*	0.9	*2.2*	2.9	*2.2*	3.1	*2.9*
New Zealand	26,632	*35,679*	2.1	*3.2*	1.2	*2.0*	1.6	*2.6*	2.9	*5.2*
Nicaragua[a]	592	2,993	−3.6	3.7	−6.2	0.9	3.4	2.5	−4.8	11.3
Niger	2,079	2,286	0.0	*1.8*	..	..	4.4	0.8	−7.1	*4.0*
Nigeria	15,816	26,238	−2.6	*3.7*	..	..	−3.5	8.4	−8.5	10.1
Norway	57,047	101,962	2.2	3.4	1.9	2.8	2.4	2.9	1.0	3.9
Oman	2,810	*8,752*	..	..	..	..	..	..	25.5	..
Pakistan	29,512	60,573	4.3	4.0	1.6	1.5	10.3	1.3	5.8	1.6
Panama[a]	3,022	8,065	3.8	4.9	1.7	3.2	1.2	2.3	−9.4	8.6
Papua New Guinea	1,902	..	0.4	*5.6*	..	..	−0.1	2.7	−0.9	*0.5*
Paraguay	4,063	5,290	2.4	2.8	−0.5	0.4	1.5	3.7	−0.8	−2.0
Peru[a]	19,376	43,004	0.7	3.5	−1.5	1.7	−0.9	4.2	−3.8	4.2
Philippines	31,566	55,180	2.6	3.7	0.2	1.4	0.6	2.9	−2.1	3.6
Poland[a]	28,281	136,490	..	4.7	..	4.7	..	2.8	..	7.6
Portugal	44,676	*74,270*	2.5	*2.8*	2.4	*2.4*	5.0	*3.0*	3.1	*5.0*
Puerto Rico	19,827	..	3.5	..	..	..	5.1	..	6.9	..

	$ millions		Household final consumption expenditure average annual % growth		per capita average annual % growth		General government final consumption expenditure average annual % growth		Gross capital formation average annual % growth	
	1990	2003	1980–90	1990–2003	1980–90	1990–2003	1980–90	1990–2003	1980–90	1990–2003
Romania[a]	25,232	40,319	..	2.2	..	2.6	..	0.8	..	–1.7
Russian Federation	252,561	219,034	..	0.9	..	1.2	..	–1.1	..	–11.5
Rwanda[a]	2,162	1,417	1.2	2.5	–1.8	0.8	5.2	1.9	4.3	2.9
Saudi Arabia	54,508	71,161	..	..	..	..	..	..	..	..
Senegal	4,353	5,026	2.1	3.2	–0.8	0.5	3.3	4.7	5.2	8.0
Serbia and Montenegro	..	18,273								
Sierra Leone	546	759	–2.7	–4.2	–4.7	–6.3	–4.7	4.5	–1.1	–0.7
Singapore	17,018	39,406	5.8	5.4	3.9	2.6	6.6	8.7	3.1	2.5
Slovak Republic	8,350	18,151	..	4.1	..	4.0	..	2.9	..	5.1
Slovenia	9,246	15,103	..	3.4	..	3.4	..	3.2	..	9.4
Somalia	..	..	1.3	..	..	..	7.0	..	–2.6	..
South Africa	64,251	99,157	2.4	2.8	–0.2	0.6	3.5	0.9	–5.3	3.3
Spain	306,970	485,777	2.6	2.6	2.3	2.1	4.9	3.1	5.9	3.5
Sri Lanka[a]	6,143	13,923	4.0	4.8	2.9	3.4	7.3	9.9	0.6	5.3
Sudan	..	..	0.0	..	–2.5	..	–0.5	..	–1.8	11.3
Swaziland[a]	524	1,212	5.6	3.0	2.4	0.0	1.4	3.9	–0.4	1.6
Sweden	116,602	147,763	2.2	1.7	2.0	1.4	1.6	0.7	4.7	1.8
Switzerland	134,460	167,221	1.6	1.3	1.1	0.7	3.1	1.0	3.8	1.4
Syrian Arab Republic	8,458	13,883	3.6	2.3	0.2	–0.5	–3.6	0.2	–5.3	2.1
Tajikistan	1,940	1,357	..	–1.4	..	–2.7	..	–15.9	–4.3	–10.8
Tanzania[b]	3,526	7,939	..	1.8	..	–0.9	..	6.9	..	1.0
Thailand	48,270	81,009	5.9	3.4	4.1	2.6	4.2	4.3	9.5	–3.5
Togo	1,158	1,492	4.7	3.9	1.3	1.0	–1.2	0.0	2.7	1.8
Trinidad and Tobago	2,975	6,491	–6.2	2.9	–7.3	2.3	0.2	1.4	–13.5	8.2
Tunisia	7,152	15,615	2.9	4.5	0.3	3.0	3.8	4.2	–1.8	3.7
Turkey	103,324	160,079	..	2.5	..	0.7	..	4.0	..	2.5
Turkmenistan	1,616	3,343	..	..	..	..	..	..	..	..
Uganda	4,002	4,923	2.6	6.0	–0.6	3.1	2.0	6.7	8.0	7.4
Ukraine	46,497	28,074	..	–3.6	..	–3.0	..	–2.4	..	–11.1
United Arab Emirates	12,726	..	4.6	..	..	..	–3.9	..	–8.7	..
United Kingdom	619,757	1,174,962	4.0	3.1	3.8	2.9	0.8	1.3	6.4	4.3
United States	3,839,900	7,385,300	3.9	3.7	3.0	2.4	3.4	1.1	4.0	6.2
Uruguay[a]	6,525	8,151	0.7	2.4	0.1	1.7	1.8	1.0	–6.6	1.1
Uzbekistan	8,204	5,452	..	..	..	..	..	..	..	0.7
Venezuela, RB	30,178	57,867	1.3	0.1	–1.4	–1.9	2.0	0.5	–5.3	–0.8
Vietnam	5,485	25,364	..	5.2	..	3.7	..	3.6	..	16.5
West Bank and Gaza	..	2,842	..	–1.8	..	–5.9	..	11.9	..	–26.7
Yemen, Rep.	3,561	7,983	..	3.9	..	0.6	..	2.5	..	6.7
Zambia	2,078	2,889	1.8	–2.6	–1.3	–4.7	–3.4	–5.5	–4.3	7.6
Zimbabwe	5,543	12,866	3.7	0.4	0.0	–1.5	4.7	–2.9	3.6	–5.2
World	**12,900,484 t**	**20,187,351 t**	**3.4 w**	**2.9 w**	**1.6 w**	**1.5 w**	**3.0 w**	**1.9 w**	**3.8 w**	**2.8 w**
Low income	431,487	728,384	3.5	4.2	1.1	2.1	5.8	4.3	4.5	6.2
Middle income	1,964,270	3,417,501	2.8	3.6	1.0	2.4	..	2.8	1.6	2.9
Lower middle income	1,408,178	2,298,206	3.6	4.1	1.9	3.0	5.2	3.2	3.6	2.6
Upper middle income	562,110	1,118,075	..	2.6	..	1.3	..	2.0	–2.7	4.1
Low & middle income	2,394,782	4,140,471	2.9	3.7	0.9	2.1	4.6	3.0	1.9	3.3
East Asia & Pacific	357,312	998,714	6.8	6.9	5.1	5.7	6.9	7.3	8.8	7.9
Europe & Central Asia	608,577	841,200	..	1.8	..	1.7	..	0.6	..	–4.0
Latin America & Carib.	724,961	1,145,676	1.2	2.7	–0.7	1.1	4.7	1.5	–0.9	3.0
Middle East & N. Africa	238,714	366,798	..	..	..	..	..	..	..	..
South Asia	281,604	506,957	4.0	4.6	1.8	2.7	7.5	5.6	6.0	6.4
Sub-Saharan Africa	189,561	278,645	2.2	2.7	–0.7	0.2	3.0	1.4	–3.3	3.5
High income	10,506,412	16,461,709	3.5	2.8	2.8	2.0	2.8	1.7	4.1	2.7
Europe EMU	3,116,520	4,695,028	2.4	1.9	2.1	1.5	2.4	1.7	2.6	1.6

a. Household final consumption expenditure includes statistical discrepancy. b. Data cover mainland Tanzania only.

Measures of growth in consumption and capital formation are subject to two kinds of inaccuracy. The first stems from the difficulty of measuring expenditures at current price levels, as described in *About the data* for table 4.9. The second arises in deflating current price data to measure volume growth, where results depend on the relevance and reliability of the price indexes and weights used. Measuring price changes is more difficult for investment goods than for consumption goods because of the one-time nature of many investments and because the rate of technological progress in capital goods makes capturing change in quality difficult. (An example is computers—prices have fallen as quality has improved.) Several countries estimate capital formation from the supply side, identifying capital goods entering an economy directly from detailed production and international trade statistics. This means that the price indexes used in deflating production and international trade, reflecting delivered or offered prices, will determine the deflator for capital formation expenditures on the demand side.

The data in the table on household final consumption expenditure (private consumption in the 1968 System of National Accounts), in current U.S. dollars, are converted from national currencies using official exchange rates or an alternative conversion factor as noted in *Primary data documentation*. (For a discussion of alternative conversion factors, see *Statistical methods*.) Growth rates of household final consumption expenditure, household final consumption expenditure per capita, general government final consumption expenditure, and gross capital formation are estimated using constant price data. (Consumption and capital formation as shares of GDP are shown in table 4.9.)

To obtain government consumption in constant prices, countries may deflate current values by applying a wage (price) index or extrapolate from the change in government employment. Neither technique captures improvements in productivity or changes in the quality of government services. Deflators for household consumption are usually calculated on the basis of the consumer price index. Many countries estimate household consumption as a residual that includes statistical discrepancies associated with the estimation of other expenditure items, including changes in inventories; thus these estimates lack detailed breakdowns of household consumption expenditures.

- **Household final consumption expenditure** is the market value of all goods and services, including durable products (such as cars, washing machines, and home computers), purchased by households. It excludes purchases of dwellings but includes imputed rent for owner-occupied dwellings. It also includes payments and fees to governments to obtain permits and licenses. *World Development Indicators* includes in household consumption expenditure the expenditures of nonprofit institutions serving households, even when reported separately by the country. In practice, household consumption expenditure may include any statistical discrepancy in the use of resources relative to the supply of resources. • **General government final consumption expenditure** includes all government current expenditures for purchases of goods and services (including compensation of employees). It also includes most expenditures on national defense and security but excludes government military expenditures that potentially have wider public use and are part of government capital formation. • **Gross capital formation** consists of outlays on additions to the fixed assets of the economy, net changes in the level of inventories, and net acquisitions of valuables. Fixed assets include land improvements (fences, ditches, drains, and so on); plant, machinery, and equipment purchases; and the construction of roads, railways, and the like, including schools, offices, hospitals, private residential dwellings, and commercial and industrial buildings. Inventories are stocks of goods held by firms to meet temporary or unexpected fluctuations in production or sales, and "work in progress."

4.10a

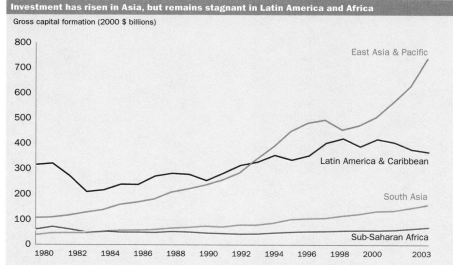

Investment has risen in Asia, but remains stagnant in Latin America and Africa

Gross capital formation (2000 $ billions)

A seven-fold increase in investment in East Asia has resulted in rapid growth of GDP and GDP per capita. Starting from a lower level, South Asia has experienced a four-fold increase in investment. On the other hand investment is almost stagnant in Sub-Saharan Africa and Latin America and the Caribbean.

Source: World Bank data files.

Data sources

The national accounts indicators for most developing countries are collected from national statistical organizations and central banks by visiting and resident World Bank missions. Data for high-income economies come from data files of the Organisation for Economic Co-operation and Development (see the OECD's *National Accounts of OECD Countries, Detailed Tables, 1970–2002*, volumes 1 and 2). The United Nations Statistics Division publishes detailed national accounts for UN member countries in *National Accounts Statistics: Main Aggregates and Detailed Tables* and updates in the *Monthly Bulletin of Statistics*.

	Revenue[a]		Expense		Cash surplus or deficit		Net incurrence of liabilities				Debt and interest payments	
	% of GDP		% of GDP		% of GDP		Domestic % of GDP		Foreign % of GDP		Total debt % of GDP	Interest % of revenue
	1995	2003	1995	2003	1995	2003	1995	2003	1995	2003	2003	2003
Afghanistan	..	..	..	..	..	..	..	..	..	..	..	..
Albania[b]	21.2	..	25.6	..	−8.9	..	7.4	..	2.1	..	..	..
Algeria[b]	30.2	36.0	24.2	24.6	−1.3	1.2	−7.4	1.8	8.6	−1.7	48.1	8.6
Angola	..	..	..	..	..	..	..	..	..	..	..	..
Argentina	..	13.7	..	19.4	..	−5.8	..	3.3	..	2.0	..	49.0
Armenia[b]	..	17.7	..	16.4	..	−0.7	..	0.1	..	2.4	40.5	3.4
Australia	..	26.5	..	25.7	..	0.8	1.7	..	0.7	..	24.7	4.8
Austria	37.8	39.1	40.9	40.5	−2.9	−1.0	..	2.5	..	..	..	8.7
Azerbaijan[b]	18.0	..	19.8	..	−3.1	..	..	..	..	..	..	..
Bangladesh[b]	..	10.1	..	9.1	..	−0.1	..	1.6	..	1.0	36.2	16.7
Belarus[b]	30.0	26.6	28.7	24.7	−2.7	1.1	2.2	0.6	0.4	−0.1	12.3	2.0
Belgium	43.5	43.1	45.0	43.2	−1.2	0.0	..	−4.3	..	3.8	..	12.8
Benin	..	..	..	..	..	..	..	..	..	..	..	..
Bolivia	..	19.3	..	29.0	..	−7.8	..	4.2	..	4.7	96.5	11.1
Bosnia and Herzegovina	..	..	..	..	..	..	..	..	..	..	..	..
Botswana[b]	40.5	..	30.3	..	4.9	..	0.2	..	−0.4	..	..	..
Brazil[b]	23.5	..	23.9	..	0.0	..	..	..	..	..	..	..
Bulgaria[b]	35.5	35.4	39.4	34.0	−5.1	0.2	..	..	..	..	..	5.8
Burkina Faso	..	..	..	..	..	..	..	..	..	..	..	..
Burundi[b]	19.3	..	23.6	..	−4.7	..	3.0	..	4.0	..	..	..
Cambodia	..	..	..	..	..	..	..	..	..	..	..	..
Cameroon	..	..	..	..	..	..	..	..	..	..	..	..
Canada[b]	20.6	20.0	24.6	18.4	−4.4	1.4	5.0	0.1	0.0	0.1	56.4	8.8
Central African Republic	..	..	..	..	..	..	..	..	..	..	..	..
Chad	..	..	..	..	..	..	..	..	..	..	..	..
Chile	..	21.2	..	18.4	..	−0.5	..	−0.9	..	1.0	15.7	5.5
China	5.7	8.9	..	..	..	..	1.4	4.6	..	0.1	..	..
Hong Kong, China	..	15.3	..	21.8	..	−7.0	..	1.6	..	..	28.3	0.0
Colombia	..	18.8	..	22.9	..	−4.6	..	5.4	..	2.6	21.1	28.1
Congo, Dem. Rep.[b]	5.3	7.9	8.2	8.3	0.0	−0.1	0.0	..	..	..	..	9.3
Congo, Rep.[b]	23.6	31.9	29.8	28.1	−8.2	−5.2	..	..	..	..	..	26.3
Costa Rica[b]	20.3	22.7	21.3	23.4	−2.1	−1.6	..	..	−0.8	1.4	38.3	18.9
Côte d'Ivoire	20.1	17.0	..	..	..	..	−1.2	−1.1	3.8	0.2	102.6	18.9
Croatia[b]	43.1	39.5	42.5	43.3	−1.3	−4.8	−2.7	1.3	0.8	1.4	..	5.0
Cuba	..	..	..	..	..	..	..	..	..	..	..	..
Czech Republic	..	33.2	..	38.2	..	−5.0	..	3.2	..	0.6	19.4	2.1
Denmark	39.4	37.6	38.5	35.6	1.5	2.0	..	−0.7	..	..	44.2	8.6
Dominican Republic[b]	16.0	17.3	10.2	14.7	0.8	−0.2	0.0	..	−1.0	..	..	6.6
Ecuador	..	..	..	..	..	..	..	..	..	..	..	..
Egypt, Arab Rep.[b]	34.8	..	28.1	..	3.4	..	..	..	..	..	..	..
El Salvador	..	15.4	..	15.4	..	−2.5	..	−0.7	..	2.3	51.5	11.2
Eritrea	..	..	..	..	..	..	..	..	..	..	..	..
Estonia[b]	32.8	28.1	31.9	26.7	0.6	0.9	−0.2	0.0	0.9	−0.1	2.5	0.6
Ethiopia[b]	17.1	..	16.8	..	−4.4	..	2.6	..	3.7	..	..	..
Finland	40.2	39.0	39.0	36.8	1.6	2.9	..	−0.6	..	3.8	45.9	4.8
France	44.0	43.9	47.1	48.1	−3.0	−4.3	..	0.5	..	1.0	..	6.0
Gabon	..	..	..	..	..	..	..	..	..	..	..	..
Gambia, The	..	..	..	..	..	..	..	..	..	..	..	..
Georgia[b]	12.2	10.3	15.4	10.7	−4.3	−0.9	2.2	0.6	2.4	1.1	53.7	18.1
Germany	30.7	30.2	33.3	32.8	−2.2	−2.1	−0.6	..	3.2	..	..	6.2
Ghana	..	..	..	..	..	..	..	..	..	..	..	..
Greece	45.4	46.5	45.6	45.3	−2.6	−1.1	..	..	..	..	..	17.7
Guatemala[b]	8.4	10.9	7.6	12.7	−0.5	−2.3	..	1.5	0.4	1.5	18.4	10.2
Guinea	..	..	..	..	..	..	−0.1	..	..	..	..	..
Guinea-Bissau	..	..	..	..	..	..	..	..	..	..	..	..
Haiti	..	..	..	..	..	..	..	..	..	..	..	..

	Revenue[a]		Expense		Cash surplus or deficit		Net incurrence of liabilities				Debt and interest payments	
	% of GDP		% of GDP		% of GDP		Domestic % of GDP		Foreign % of GDP		Total debt % of GDP	Interest % of revenue
	1995	2003	1995	2003	1995	2003	1995	2003	1995	2003	2003	2003
Honduras	..	..	..	..	..	..	..	..	..	..	..	..
Hungary	..	37.3	..	41.8	..	−6.2	..	0.3	..	5.4	58.5	10.9
India[b]	12.3	11.6	14.5	16.1	−2.2	−4.3	5.2	5.4	0.0	0.1	64.5	37.1
Indonesia[b]	17.7	21.0	9.7	..	3.0	..	−0.6	..	−0.4	..	..	..
Iran, Islamic Rep.[b]	23.0	29.7	15.1	20.0	1.1	1.6	..	1.6	0.1	−2.0	..	0.7
Iraq	..	..	..	..	..	..	..	..	..	..	..	..
Ireland[b]	25.4	..	28.6	..	−2.0	..	..	..	..	..	..	..
Israel	..	44.4	..	52.4	..	−4.1	4.9	..	0.1	..	98.3	10.6
Italy	38.9	38.1	41.7	39.6	−2.9	−0.5	..	..	..	..	..	16.6
Jamaica[b]	..	32.5	33.4	41.8	..	−9.8	..	..	..	..	147.5	59.2
Japan	..	..	..	..	..	..	..	..	..	..	..	..
Jordan[b]	28.2	24.0	26.1	30.5	0.9	−0.3	−2.5	2.0	6.1	−3.9	91.9	7.2
Kazakhstan[b]	14.0	14.4	18.7	14.4	−1.8	−0.6	0.8	1.1	2.8	0.2	13.7	4.9
Kenya[b]	26.0	24.4	25.8	23.7	−0.8	2.6	5.3	0.1	0.0	1.6	..	11.2
Korea, Dem. Rep.	..	..	..	..	..	..	..	..	..	..	..	..
Korea, Rep.[b]	17.8	22.8	14.3	18.6	2.4	2.9	−0.3	−2.3	−0.1	−0.1	..	5.1
Kuwait	37.7	..	47.5	..	−13.9	..	..	..	..	..	..	..
Kyrgyz Republic[b]	16.7	16.1	25.6	15.8	−10.8	−0.8	..	..	..	..	99.3	8.4
Lao PDR	..	..	..	..	..	..	..	..	..	..	..	..
Latvia[b]	25.8	26.3	28.3	27.5	−2.7	−1.3	2.4	1.7	1.5	−0.7	13.8	2.7
Lebanon	..	19.6	..	29.7	..	−13.3	..	−12.6	..	27.1	..	81.1
Lesotho[b]	49.8	39.9	34.4	35.1	5.1	0.6	0.0	..	6.2	..	..	6.0
Liberia	..	..	..	..	..	..	..	..	..	..	..	..
Libya	..	..	..	..	..	..	..	..	..	..	..	..
Lithuania	..	28.1	..	28.8	..	−2.0	..	−0.2	..	1.0	20.8	4.4
Macedonia, FYR	..	..	..	..	..	..	..	..	..	..	..	..
Madagascar	..	8.0	..	9.4	..	−4.4	..	1.5	..	3.2	96.8	12.6
Malawi	..	..	..	..	..	..	..	..	..	..	..	..
Malaysia[b]	24.4	23.7	17.2	20.1	2.4	−4.3	..	..	..	−0.8	..	10.5
Mali	..	..	..	..	..	..	..	..	..	..	..	..
Mauritania	..	..	..	..	..	..	..	..	..	..	..	..
Mauritius[b]	21.6	21.8	19.9	21.3	−1.3	−3.4	3.1	8.6	−0.6	0.1	48.7	13.5
Mexico[b]	15.3	14.7	15.0	15.4	−0.6	−1.2	..	..	5.5	−0.7	23.2	14.0
Moldova[b]	28.4	27.0	38.4	22.5	−6.3	2.0	3.0	1.6	2.7	−2.7	53.2	7.9
Mongolia	..	37.9	..	30.8	..	−0.5	..	11.3	..	−6.8	119.8	3.1
Morocco[b]	27.7	..	28.6	..	−4.5	..	5.7	..	−0.7	..	..	..
Mozambique	..	..	..	..	..	..	..	..	..	..	..	..
Myanmar	6.4	4.7	..	..	..	..	..	..	..	..	..	..
Namibia[b]	31.7	32.7	..	30.0	..	−1.0	..	−27.3	..	−0.1	..	8.0
Nepal	10.5	11.6	..	..	..	..	0.6	1.1	2.5	0.8	66.8	10.8
Netherlands	..	40.6	..	43.2	..	−3.0	..	3.4	3.3	..	53.6	5.9
New Zealand	..	36.8	..	33.3	..	3.1	..	1.4	..	0.2	50.5	4.9
Nicaragua[b]	15.0	20.9	16.3	21.3	0.6	−1.1	..	..	..	..	..	14.7
Niger	..	..	..	..	..	..	..	..	..	..	..	..
Nigeria	..	..	..	..	..	..	..	..	..	..	..	..
Norway	..	47.6	..	38.4	..	9.0	..	1.8	..	5.5	28.6	2.7
Oman[b]	31.7	27.0	36.9	26.9	−10.1	−2.8	−0.2	3.0	0.0	−2.1	19.9	4.5
Pakistan[b]	17.2	14.6	19.1	17.0	−5.3	−2.9	..	..	..	..	74.7	33.9
Panama[b]	26.1	25.6	22.0	23.2	1.5	0.9	..	..	..	..	..	19.3
Papua New Guinea[b]	23.9	23.8	25.8	23.4	−0.5	−2.4	1.5	5.2	−0.7	−2.3	73.9	19.9
Paraguay[b]	15.3	15.2	13.0	13.4	0.1	−0.6	..	−0.4	..	1.4	..	7.9
Peru[b]	16.9	16.2	16.0	16.8	−2.1	−1.8	..	0.5	..	1.6	..	12.7
Philippines[b]	17.7	14.4	..	17.4	..	−3.9	−0.5	3.0	−0.7	3.5	70.8	38.5
Poland[b]	35.8	29.5	36.7	34.5	−1.9	−5.7	1.4	5.0	1.0	0.3	43.2	10.6
Portugal	37.1	37.7	39.7	41.5	−3.1	−4.0	−3.7	2.5	4.3	2.9	..	8.1
Puerto Rico	..	..	..	..	..	..	..	..	..	..	..	..

4.11 Central government finances

	Revenue[a] % of GDP		Expense % of GDP		Cash surplus or deficit % of GDP		Net incurrence of liabilities Domestic % of GDP		Foreign % of GDP		Debt and interest payments Total debt % of GDP	Interest % of revenue
	1995	2003	1995	2003	1995	2003	1995	2003	1995	2003	2003	2003
Romania[b]	29.5	26.7	30.1	28.4	−2.2	−3.6	3.0	..	0.9	..	..	11.4
Russian Federation	..	27.4	..	22.9	..	2.2	..	−0.6	..	−2.2	41.3	6.0
Rwanda	..	..	..	..	..	..	..	..	..	..	..	..
Saudi Arabia	..	..	..	..	..	..	..	..	..	..	..	..
Senegal[b]	16.6	17.8	..	15.4	..	−2.2	..	1.4	..	1.6	72.8	4.6
Serbia and Montenegro[b]	..	35.5	..	39.5	..	−2.9	..	..	..	..	..	2.6
Sierra Leone	8.8	..	..	..	..	..	0.2	..	..	..	..	..
Singapore[b]	26.8	22.2	12.5	16.9	19.9	4.8	10.3	6.5	0.0	..	111.5	1.3
Slovak Republic	..	35.3	..	37.0	..	−3.3	..	2.9	..	−0.2	46.7	7.0
Slovenia[b]	37.2	43.4	35.7	43.6	−0.2	−1.3	−0.4	1.0	0.3	−0.2	26.8	3.7
Somalia	..	..	..	..	..	..	..	..	..	..	..	..
South Africa[b]	25.0	27.0	29.7	28.9	−5.5	−2.5	5.2	3.1	0.3	−0.2	39.1	14.2
Spain	30.1	27.9	34.1	31.6	−2.7	0.3	3.5	1.3	399.2	..	..	7.4
Sri Lanka[b]	20.4	16.4	26.0	22.9	−7.6	−7.6	5.2	7.0	3.2	0.1	105.5	43.6
Sudan[b]	7.0	..	6.6	..	−0.4	..	0.3	..	..	..	..	..
Swaziland[b]	..	28.1	..	24.3	..	−0.9	..	..	..	..	28.7	1.9
Sweden	40.7	37.7	39.3	37.2	2.2	0.3	..	−1.3	..	0.5	62.5	7.4
Switzerland[b]	22.7	18.8	25.8	18.9	−0.6	0.3	−0.5	−0.8	..	..	25.3	4.5
Syrian Arab Republic[b]	22.9	..	..	..	..	..	..	..	..	..	..	..
Tajikistan[b]	9.3	11.4	11.4	9.6	−3.3	−0.2	0.1	−0.2	2.3	0.2	80.9	4.8
Tanzania	..	..	..	..	..	..	..	..	..	..	..	..
Thailand	..	19.5	..	15.4	..	2.0	..	0.8	..	−0.6	28.8	5.8
Togo	..	..	..	..	..	..	..	..	..	..	..	..
Trinidad and Tobago[b]	27.2	..	25.3	..	−0.1	..	2.8	..	2.6	..	..	..
Tunisia[b]	30.1	29.4	28.4	27.9	−2.5	−2.4	0.9	0.7	2.9	2.5	60.3	9.5
Turkey[b]	17.9	..	21.0	..	−4.1	..	5.5	..	..	..	..	..
Turkmenistan	..	..	..	..	..	..	..	..	..	..	..	..
Uganda[b]	10.7	12.2	..	20.1	..	−4.6	..	1.5	..	4.6	39.3	7.3
Ukraine[b]	..	29.2	..	29.0	..	0.3	..	0.4	..	−0.4	33.5	4.0
United Arab Emirates[b]	10.5	..	9.7	..	0.5	..	..	..	..	..	..	..
United Kingdom	37.3	36.0	37.2	39.7	0.3	−3.7	−0.3	3.6	0.0	0.0	48.9	5.6
United States	..	17.4	..	21.0	..	−3.7	..	1.1	..	2.7	36.9	11.2
Uruguay[b]	27.6	25.2	27.1	30.2	−1.2	−4.7	..	..	..	..	..	9.2
Uzbekistan	..	..	..	..	..	..	..	..	..	..	..	..
Venezuela, RB[b]	16.4	23.5	17.9	24.6	−2.2	−4.0	1.1	6.1	0.1	0.2	..	19.5
Vietnam	22.5	19.1	..	..	..	..	1.2	..	−0.7	..	..	4.1
West Bank and Gaza	..	..	..	..	..	..	..	..	..	..	..	..
Yemen, Rep.[b]	17.3	..	19.1	..	−3.9	..	..	..	..	..	..	..
Zambia[b]	20.0	..	21.4	..	−3.1	..	..	..	16.2	..	..	..
Zimbabwe[b]	26.7	..	32.1	..	−5.4	..	−1.4	..	1.6	..	..	..
World	.. w	25.8 w	.. w	.. w	.. w	.. w	.. m	.. m	.. m	.. m	.. m	.. m
Low income	14.0	12.0	15.8	15.7	−2.5	−3.8	..	..	..	..	..	..
Middle income	17.7	..	..	..	..	..	..	..	..	..	..	10.6
Lower middle income	16.4	..	..	..	..	..	..	..	..	..	..	9.1
Upper middle income	..	..	..	..	..	..	..	..	..	0.6	..	9.4
Low & middle income	17.2	..	..	..	..	..	..	..	..	..	..	..
East Asia & Pacific	8.9	11.4	..	..	..	..	..	..	..	..	..	..
Europe & Central Asia	..	..	..	..	..	..	..	..	..	..	43.6	7.5
Latin America & Carib.	19.8	..	19.7	..	−0.4	..	..	..	..	..	..	12.7
Middle East & N. Africa	..	..	..	..	..	..	..	..	..	..	..	..
South Asia	13.2	11.8	15.4	15.6	−2.7	−3.8	3.8	1.6	1.1	0.8	57.8	25.3
Sub-Saharan Africa	..	..	..	..	..	..	..	..	..	..	..	..
High income	..	25.7	..	27.7	..	−1.9	..	1.3	..	..	..	6.2
Europe EMU	36.7	35.9	39.3	38.2	−2.3	−1.8	..	0.0	..	..	..	6.2

a. Excluding grants. b. Data were reported on a cash basis and have been adjusted to the accrual framework.

Central government finances | 4.11

About the data

Tables 4.11–4.13 present an overview of the size and role of central governments relative to national economies. For the first time the data in these tables are based on the concepts and recommendations of the second edition of the International Monetary Fund's (IMF) *Government Finance Statistics Manual 2001*. Previous editions of *World Development Indicators* used data derived on the basis of 1986 manual. The 2001 manual, which is harmonized with the 1993 System of National Accounts, recommends an accrual accounting method instead of the cash-based method of the 1986 manual. The new manual focuses on all economic events affecting assets, liabilities, revenues, and expenses, instead of only those represented by cash transactions. The new manual takes all stocks into account, so that the stock data at the end of an accounting period is equal to stock data at the beginning of the period plus the flows during the period. The 1986 manual considered only the debt stock data. Further, the new manual does not distinguish between current and capital revenue or expenditures unlike the 1986 manual. The new manual also introduces the concept of nonfinancial and financial assets. Countries are still following the previous manual, however. The IMF has reclassified historical *Government Finance Statistics Yearbook* data to conform to the format of the 2001 manual. Because of differences in reporting, the reclassified data understate both revenue and expense.

Government Finance Statistics Manual 2001 describes the economic functions of a government as the provision of goods and services to the community on a nonmarket basis for collective or individual consumption, and the redistribution of income and wealth through transfer payments. The activities of government are financed mainly by taxation and other transfers of income, though other forms of financing such as borrowing for temporary periods can also be used. The definition of government excludes public corporations

and quasi corporations (such as the central bank).

Units of government meeting this definition exist at many levels, from local administrative units to the highest level of national government, but inadequate statistical coverage precludes the presentation of subnational data. Although data for general government are available for a few countries under the 2001 manual, only data for the central government are shown for all the countries to minimize disparities. However, cross-country comparisons are potentially misleading due to different accounting concepts of central government.

Central government can refer to one of two accounting concepts: consolidated or budgetary. For most countries central government finance data have been consolidated into one account, but for others only budgetary central government accounts are available. Countries reporting budgetary data are noted in *Primary data documentation*. Because budgetary accounts do not necessarily include all central government units (such as extrabudgetary accounts and social security funds), the picture they provide of central government activities is usually incomplete.

Data on government revenues and expenditures are collected by the IMF through questionnaires distributed to member governments and by the Organisation for Economic Co-operation and Development. Despite the IMF's efforts to systematize and standardize the collection of public finance data, statistics on public finance are often incomplete, untimely, and not comparable across countries.

Government finance statistics are reported in local currency. The indicators here are shown as percentages of GDP. Many countries report government finance data by fiscal year; see *Primary data documentation* for information on fiscal year end by country. For further discussion of government finance statistics, see *About the data* for tables 4.12 and 4.13.

Definitions

- **Revenue** is cash receipts from taxes, social contributions, and other revenues such as fines, fees, rent, and income from property or sales. Grants are also considered as revenue but are excluded here
- **Expense** is cash payments for operating activities of the government in providing goods and services. It includes compensation of employees (such as wages and salaries), interest and subsidies, grants, social benefits, and other expenses such as rent and dividends. • **Cash surplus or deficit** is revenue (including grants) minus expense, minus net acquisition of nonfinancial assets. In the earlier version nonfinancial assets were included under revenue and expenditure in gross terms. This cash surplus or deficit is closest to the earlier overall budget balance (still missing is lending minus repayments, which are brought in below as a financing item under net acquisition of financial assets). • **Net incurrence of government liabilities** includes **foreign financing** (obtained from nonresidents) and **domestic financing** (obtained from residents), or the means by which a government provides financial resources to cover a budget deficit or allocates financial resources arising from a budget surplus. The net incurrence of liabilities should be offset by the net acquisition of financial assets (a third financing item) The difference between the cash surplus or deficit and the three financing items is the net change in the stock of cash • **Debt** is the entire stock of direct government fixed-term contractual obligations to others outstanding on a particular date. It includes domestic and foreign liabilities such as currency and money deposits, securities other than shares, and loans. It is the gross amount of government liabilities reduced by the amount of equity and financial derivatives held by the government. Because debt is a stock rather than a flow, it is measured as of a given date, usually the last day of the fiscal year.
- **Interest payments** include interest payments on government debt—including long-term bonds, long-term loans, and other debt instruments—to domestic and foreign residents.

Data sources

The data on central government finances are from the IMF's *Government Finance Statistics Yearbook, 2004* and IMF data files. Each country's accounts are reported using the system of common definitions and classifications in the IMF's *Government Finance Statistics Manual 2001*. See these sources for complete and authoritative explanations of concepts, definitions, and data sources.

4.11a

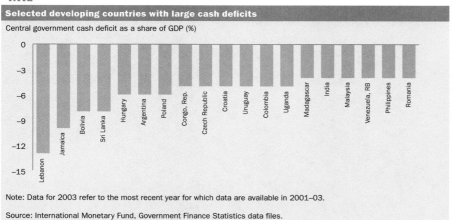

Selected developing countries with large cash deficits

Central government cash deficit as a share of GDP (%)

Note: Data for 2003 refer to the most recent year for which data are available in 2001–03.

Source: International Monetary Fund, Government Finance Statistics data files.

	Goods and services		Compensation of employees		Interest payments		Subsidies, grants, and other social benefits		Other expense	
	% of expense		% of expense		% of expense		% of expense		% of expense	
	1995	**2003**	**1995**	**2003**	**1995**	**2003**	**1995**	**2003**	**1995**	**2003**
Afghanistan	..	..	..	..	..	..	..	..	..	..
Albania[a]	18	..	14	..	9	..	59	..	0	..
Algeria[a]	6	6	39	32	13	12	34	50	8	..
Angola	..	..	..	..	..	..	..	..	..	..
Argentina	..	4	..	10	..	35	..	47	..	5
Armenia[a]	..	53	..	5	..	4	..	34	..	4
Australia	..	10	..	10	..	5	..	69	..	6
Austria	7	6	13	13	8	8	65	68	7	5
Azerbaijan[a]	49	..	10	..	0	..	41	..	0	..
Bangladesh[a]	..	16	..	25	..	21	..	29	..	9
Belarus[a]	39	12	5	14	1	2	55	69	0	3
Belgium	2	3	7	7	15	13	71	74	4	4
Benin	..	..	..	..	..	..	..	..	..	..
Bolivia	..	17	..	24	..	9	..	45	..	5
Bosnia and Herzegovina	..	..	..	..	..	..	..	..	..	..
Botswana[a]	32	..	30	..	2	..	36	..	..	..
Brazil[a]	9	..	12	..	14	..	66	..	..	..
Bulgaria[a]	18	23	7	12	37	6	38	57	..	2
Burkina Faso	..	..	..	..	..	..	..	..	..	..
Burundi[a]	20	..	30	..	6	..	14	..	16	..
Cambodia	..	..	..	..	..	..	..	..	..	..
Cameroon	..	..	..	..	..	..	..	..	..	..
Canada[a]	8	8	10	11	18	10	64	65	..	7
Central African Republic	..	..	..	..	..	..	..	..	..	..
Chad	..	..	..	..	..	..	..	..	..	..
Chile	..	10	..	23	..	6	..	61	..	..
China	..	..	..	..	..	..	..	..	..	..
Hong Kong, China	..	23	..	26	..	0	..	26	..	26
Colombia	..	10	..	21	..	23	..	1	..	..
Congo, Dem. Rep.[a]	37	24	58	24	1	9	2	4	..	..
Congo, Rep.[a]	7	27	35	22	47	30	10	20	..	0
Costa Rica[a]	12	13	38	43	20	18	26	21	4	5
Côte d'Ivoire	..	..	..	..	..	..	..	..	..	..
Croatia[a]	35	20	27	25	3	5	32	47	3	3
Cuba	..	..	..	..	..	..	..	..	..	..
Czech Republic	..	7	..	9	..	2	..	59	..	24
Denmark	8	9	13	13	13	9	62	61	4	7
Dominican Republic[a]	16	15	41	49	9	8	19	15	6	13
Ecuador	..	..	..	..	..	..	..	..	..	..
Egypt, Arab Rep.[a]	18	..	22	..	26	..	6	..	..	..
El Salvador	..	15	..	48	..	11	..	4	..	22
Eritrea	..	..	..	..	..	..	..	..	..	..
Estonia[a]	33	32	14	10	1	1	46	58	0	0
Ethiopia[a]	35	..	40	..	15	..	18	..	0	..
Finland	10	10	10	10	9	5	63	68	8	7
France	7	7	23	22	6	6	58	60	5	5
Gabon	..	..	..	..	..	..	..	..	..	..
Gambia, The	..	..	..	..	..	..	..	..	..	..
Georgia[a]	52	18	11	14	10	18	26	49	..	..
Germany	4	4	6	5	7	6	80	81	3	4
Ghana	..	..	..	..	..	..	..	..	..	..
Greece	10	10	24	24	20	19	40	41	6	7
Guatemala[a]	15	14	50	27	12	9	18	20	6	30
Guinea	..	..	..	..	..	..	..	..	..	..
Guinea-Bissau	..	..	..	..	..	..	..	..	..	..
Haiti	..	..	..	..	..	..	..	..	..	..

Central government expenses | 4.12

	Goods and services		Compensation of employees		Interest payments		Subsidies, grants, and other social benefits		Other expense	
	% of expense		% of expense		% of expense		% of expense		% of expense	
	1995	2003	1995	2003	1995	2003	1995	2003	1995	2003
Honduras	..	..	..	..	..	..	..	..	..	..
Hungary	..	8	..	14	..	10	..	60	..	8
India[a]	14	13	10	9	27	27	33	29	0	1
Indonesia[a]	21	..	20	..	16	..	41	..	2	..
Iran, Islamic Rep.[a]	21	12	56	45	0	1	..	30	..	11
Iraq	..	..	..	..	..	..	..	..	..	..
Ireland[a]	5	..	13	..	15	..	63	..	4	..
Israel	..	23	..	27	..	10	..	31	..	9
Italy	4	5	15	16	19	16	57	59	5	5
Jamaica[a]	22	13	24	32	32	46	1	2	21	8
Japan	..	..	..	..	..	..	..	..	..	..
Jordan[a]	7	6	67	67	11	8	12	12	4	7
Kazakhstan[a]	..	26	..	8	3	5	58	51	..	10
Kenya[a]	19	30	31	51	29	13	..	4	0	2
Korea, Dem. Rep.	..	..	..	..	..	..	..	..	..	..
Korea, Rep.[a]	16	12	15	11	3	6	63	56	3	15
Kuwait[a]	33	..	31	..	5	..	24	..	7	..
Kyrgyz Republic[a]	32	34	36	41	5	9	27	17	..	..
Lao PDR	..	..	..	..	..	..	..	..	..	..
Latvia[a]	20	13	20	16	3	3	56	48	0	20
Lebanon	..	3	..	33	..	53	..	9	..	2
Lesotho[a]	32	32	45	37	5	7	..	4	..	..
Liberia	..	..	..	..	..	..	..	..	..	..
Libya	..	..	..	..	..	..	..	..	..	..
Lithuania	..	15	..	18	..	4	..	55	..	7
Macedonia, FYR	..	..	..	..	..	..	..	..	..	..
Madagascar	..	18	..	49	..	13	..	10	..	10
Malawi	..	..	..	..	..	..	..	..	..	..
Malaysia[a]	23	26	34	30	17	12	27	31	1	1
Mali	..	..	..	..	..	..	..	..	..	..
Mauritania	..	..	..	..	..	..	..	..	..	..
Mauritius[a]	12	13	45	38	12	14	28	33	2	3
Mexico[a]	9	8	19	17	19	13	..	2	..	..
Moldova[a]	10	8	8	20	11	9	71	52	1	10
Mongolia	..	36	..	30	..	4	..	31	..	0
Morocco[a]	17	..	39	..	21	..	19	..	4	..
Mozambique	..	..	..	..	..	..	..	..	..	..
Myanmar	..	..	..	..	..	..	..	..	..	..
Namibia[a]	..	29	..	50	..	9	..	11	..	..
Nepal	..	..	..	..	..	..	..	..	..	..
Netherlands	..	7	..	8	..	6	..	76	..	3
New Zealand	..	31	..	29	..	5	..	31	..	4
Nicaragua[a]	16	16	23	30	15	18	34	34	13	2
Niger	..	..	..	..	..	..	..	..	..	..
Nigeria	..	..	..	..	..	..	..	..	..	..
Norway	..	11	..	16	..	3	..	65	..	4
Oman[a]	55	54	30	32	7	5	8	10	0	0
Pakistan[a]	..	22	..	4	28	31	2	43	..	..
Panama[a]	16	16	45	37	8	21	30	25	1	1
Papua New Guinea[a]	19	35	36	28	20	21	26	16	..	..
Paraguay[a]	12	8	51	52	5	9	31	30	0	0
Peru[a]	22	21	19	22	21	12	38	44	0	1
Philippines[a]	..	26	..	31	..	24	..	..	..	..
Poland[a]	12	8	15	11	11	9	61	69	0	3
Portugal	7	8	30	32	10	7	41	44	11	10
Puerto Rico	..	..	..	..	..	..	..	..	..	..

	Goods and services		Compensation of employees		Interest payments		Subsidies, grants, and other social benefits		Other expense	
	% of expense		% of expense		% of expense		% of expense		% of expense	
	1995	2003	1995	2003	1995	2003	1995	2003	1995	2003
Romania[a]	15	20	21	15	4	11	51	49	8	6
Russian Federation	..	19	..	18	..	7	..	55	..	1
Rwanda	..	..	..	..	..	..	..	..	..	..
Saudi Arabia	..	..	..	..	..	..	..	..	..	..
Senegal[a]	..	25	..	34	..	6	..	34	..	..
Serbia and Montenegro[a]	..	10	..	14	..	2	..	68	..	6
Sierra Leone	..	..	..	..	..	..	..	..	..	..
Singapore[a]	38	34	39	31	8	2	15	33	..	..
Slovak Republic	..	12	..	13	..	7	..	63	..	5
Slovenia[a]	19	20	21	27	3	4	55	47	3	3
Somalia	..	..	..	..	..	..	..	..	..	..
South Africa[a]	9	13	16	15	18	13	6	56	3	3
Spain	5	6	18	16	11	8	59	65	7	4
Sri Lanka[a]	23	14	20	25	22	32	24	22	10	7
Sudan[a]	44	..	38	..	8	..	10	..	..	..
Swaziland[a]	..	26	..	45	..	2	..	27	..	..
Sweden	11	12	9	10	13	8	62	64	5	6
Switzerland[a]	24	9	6	6	4	5	66	78	0	3
Syrian Arab Republic[a]	..	..	..	..	..	..	..	..	..	..
Tajikistan[a]	47	36	8	17	12	6	33	42	..	0
Tanzania	..	..	..	..	..	..	..	..	..	..
Thailand	..	26	..	36	..	7	..	25	..	6
Togo	..	..	..	..	..	..	..	..	..	..
Trinidad and Tobago[a]	20	..	36	..	20	..	24	..	..	..
Tunisia[a]	7	8	37	41	13	10	36	..	7	..
Turkey[a]	8	..	32	..	13	..	31	..	4	..
Turkmenistan	..	..	..	..	..	..	..	..	..	..
Uganda[a]	..	50	..	11	..	7	..	32	..	..
Ukraine[a]	..	13	..	17	..	4	..	64	..	1
United Arab Emirates[a]	50	..	37	..	..	..	..	..	..	..
United Kingdom	22	18	7	14	9	5	53	54	9	10
United States	..	15	..	13	..	9	..	62	..	2
Uruguay[a]	13	11	17	16	6	8	64	64	0	0
Uzbekistan	..	..	..	..	..	..	..	..	..	..
Venezuela, RB[a]	6	8	22	19	27	19	..	53	2	2
Vietnam	..	..	..	..	..	..	..	..	..	..
West Bank and Gaza	..	..	..	..	..	..	..	..	..	..
Yemen, Rep.[a]	8	..	67	..	16	..	8	..	..	..
Zambia[a]	32	..	35	..	16	..	19	..	0	..
Zimbabwe[a]	16	..	34	..	31	..	19	..	..	..
World	**18** m	**14** m	**32** m	**24** m	**11** m	**9** m	**38** m	**34** m	**..** m	**..** m
Low income	..	..	..	..	..	..	..	..	..	..
Middle income	18	13	30	23	12	9	29	39	2	4
Lower middle income	18	16	26	24	12	9	31	30	2	..
Upper middle income	18	13	31	19	11	10	28	53	1	3
Low & middle income	18	17	32	25	12	11	30	32	..	..
East Asia & Pacific	..	..	..	..	..	..	..	..	..	..
Europe & Central Asia	19	15	17	14	4	6	49	55	2	8
Latin America & Carib.	16	13	37	29	13	13	25	26	1	5
Middle East & N. Africa	13	6	39	41	13	11	12	10	4	..
South Asia	32	22	23	24	22	21	15	29	4	2
Sub-Saharan Africa	..	..	..	..	..	..	..	..	..	..
High income	10	12	23	16	9	6	53	60	5	6
Europe EMU	7	7	15	10	9	6	59	68	6	5

Note: Components may not sum to 100 percent due to missing data.
a. Data were reported on a cash basis and have been adjusted to the accrual framework.

Central government expenses | 4.12

The term "expense" has replaced "expenditure" in this table in accordance with use in the IMF's *Government Finance Statistics Manual 2001*. Government expenses include all nonrepayable payments, whether current or capital, requited or unrequited. Total central government expense as presented in the International Monetary Fund's (IMF) *Government Finance Statistics Yearbook* is comparable to the concept used in the 1993 System of National Accounts (SNA).

Expenses can be measured either by function (health, defense, education) or by economic type (interest payments, wages and salaries, purchases of goods and services). Functional data are often incomplete, and coverage varies by country because functional responsibilities stretch across levels of government for which no data are available. Defense expenses, usually the central government's responsibility, are shown in table 5.8. For more information on education expenses, see table 2.10; for more on health expenses, see table 2.14.

The classification of expenses by economic type in this table shows whether the government produces goods and services and distributes them, purchases the goods and services from a third party and distributes them, or transfers cash to households to make the purchases directly. When the government produces and provides goods and services, the cost is reflected in compensation of employees, use of goods and services, and consumption of fixed capital. Purchases from a third party and cash transfers to households are shown as subsidies, grants, other social benefits, and other expenses. The economic

classification can be problematic. For example, the distinction between current and capital expense may be arbitrary, and subsidies to public corporations or banks may be disguised as capital financing. Subsidies may also be hidden in special contractual pricing for goods and services.

For further discussion of government finance statistics, see *About the data* for tables 4.11 and 4.13.

• **Goods and services** include all government payments in exchange for goods and services used for the production of market and nonmarket goods and services. Own-account capital formation is excluded. • **Compensation of employees** consists of all payments in cash, as well as in kind (such as food and housing), to employees in return for services rendered, and government contributions to social insurance schemes such as social security and pensions that provide benefits to employees. • **Interest payments** are payments made to nonresidents, to residents, and to other general government units for the use of borrowed money. (Repayment of principal is shown as a financing item, and commission charges are shown as purchases of services.) • **Subsidies, grants, and other social benefits** include all unrequited, nonrepayable transfers on current account to private and public enterprises; grants to foreign governments, international organizations, and other government units; and social security, social assistance benefis, and employer social benefits in cash and in kind • **Other expense** is spending on dividends, rent, and other miscellaneous expenses, including provision for consumption of fixed capital.

4.12a

Interest payments are a large part of government expenditure for some developing economies

Central government interest payments as share of total expense (%)

Note: Data for 2003 refer to the most recent year for which data are available in 2001–03. No data are available for Lebanon, Argentina, Colombia, and Bangladesh for 1995.

Source: International Monetary Fund, Government Finance Statistics data files.

The data on central government expenses are from the IMF's *Government Finance Statistics Yearbook, 2004* and IMF data files. Each country's accounts are reported using the system of common definitions and classifications in the IMF's *Government Finance Statistics Manual 2001*. See these sources for complete and authoritative explanations of concepts, definitions, and data sources.

Central government revenues

	Taxes on income, profits, and capital gains		Taxes on goods and services		Taxes on international trade		Other taxes		Social contributions		Grants and other revenue	
	% of revenue		% of revenue		% of revenue		% of revenue		% of revenue		% of revenue	
	1995	2003	1995	2003	1995	2003	1995	2003	1995	2003	1995	2003
Afghanistan	..	..	..	..	..	..	..	..	..	..	..	..
Albania[a]	8	..	39	..	14	..	1	..	15	..	22	..
Algeria[a]	65	66	10	9	18	13	1	1	..	..	5	11
Angola	..	..	..	..	..	..	..	..	..	..	..	..
Argentina	..	13	..	28	..	14	..	13	..	20	..	11
Armenia[a]	..	10	..	43	..	3	..	10	..	13	..	20
Australia	..	62	..	25	..	3	..	1	..	..	..	9
Austria	24	25	24	25	0	0	4	4	42	40	6	7
Azerbaijan[a]	31	..	34	..	33	..	2	..	..	..	0	..
Bangladesh[a]	..	11	..	32	..	25	..	3	..	..	..	28
Belarus[a]	16	7	33	36	6	8	11	3	31	41	3	6
Belgium	37	38	23	23	..	..	2	1	35	36	3	3
Benin	..	..	..	..	..	..	..	..	..	..	..	..
Bolivia	..	6	..	39	..	3	..	9	..	10	..	33
Bosnia and Herzegovina	..	..	..	..	..	..	..	..	..	..	..	..
Botswana[a]	21	..	4	..	15	..	0	..	..	..	59	..
Brazil[a]	17	..	23	..	3	..	5	..	37	..	17	..
Bulgaria[a]	17	12	28	39	8	2	3	0	21	29	23	18
Burkina Faso	..	..	..	..	..	..	..	..	..	..	..	..
Burundi[a]	14	..	30	..	20	..	1	..	5	..	30	..
Cambodia	..	..	..	..	..	..	..	..	..	..	..	..
Cameroon	..	..	..	..	..	..	..	..	..	..	..	..
Canada[a]	50	52	17	17	2	1	..	..	22	24	10	6
Central African Republic	..	..	..	..	..	..	..	..	..	..	..	..
Chad	..	..	..	..	..	..	..	..	..	..	..	..
Chile	..	21	..	49	..	3	..	4	..	7	..	17
China	9	11	61	65	7	9	0	3	..	..	22	12
Hong Kong, China	..	38	..	13	..	0	..	10	..	0	..	39
Colombia	..	36	..	29	..	5	..	4	..	0	..	..
Congo, Dem. Rep.[a]	21	25	12	24	21	27	5	1	..	..	41	23
Congo, Rep.[a]	6	..	21	20	18	6	1	0	..	3	54	71
Costa Rica[a]	11	15	32	38	15	5	1	2	28	32	12	8
Côte d'Ivoire	15	20	14	21	58	41	3	4	5	8	5	6
Croatia[a]	11	8	42	46	9	6	1	1	33	33	4	5
Cuba	..	..	..	..	..	..	..	..	..	..	..	..
Czech Republic	..	20	..	26	..	1	..	1	..	45	..	6
Denmark	34	35	40	42	..	..	7	2	5	6	14	16
Dominican Republic[a]	16	21	34	35	36	32	1	2	4	4	9	6
Ecuador	..	..	..	..	..	..	..	..	..	..	..	..
Egypt, Arab Rep.[a]	17	..	13	..	10	..	10	..	10	..	41	..
El Salvador	..	22	..	43	..	8	..	1	..	15	..	13
Eritrea	..	..	..	..	..	..	..	..	..	..	..	..
Estonia[a]	19	13	39	41	0	0	0	..	31	35	10	11
Ethiopia[a]	19	..	13	..	27	..	3	..	1	..	36	..
Finland	21	21	34	35	0	0	2	2	32	31	12	11
France	23	23	26	24	0	0	3	4	40	42	7	7
Gabon	..	..	..	..	..	..	..	..	..	..	..	..
Gambia, The	..	..	..	..	..	..	..	..	..	..	..	..
Georgia[a]	7	3	48	54	10	7	..	..	13	24	22	12
Germany	17	16	19	22	..	..	..	..	60	58	5	4
Ghana	..	..	..	..	..	..	..	..	..	..	..	..
Greece	20	21	30	29	0	0	3	4	30	29	16	17
Guatemala[a]	19	26	46	56	23	11	3	1	2	2	6	4
Guinea	..	..	..	..	..	..	..	..	..	..	..	..
Guinea-Bissau	..	..	..	..	..	..	..	..	..	..	..	..
Haiti	..	..	..	..	..	..	..	..	..	..	..	..

	Taxes on income, profits, and capital gains		Taxes on goods and services		Taxes on international trade		Other taxes		Social contributions		Grants and other revenue	
	% of revenue		% of revenue		% of revenue		% of revenue		% of revenue		% of revenue	
	1995	2003	1995	2003	1995	2003	1995	2003	1995	2003	1995	2003
Honduras	..	..	..	..	..	..	..	..	..	..	..	..
Hungary	..	19	..	36	..	2	..	2	..	33	..	8
India[a]	23	30	28	33	24	15	0	0	0	0	25	22
Indonesia[a]	46	*31*	33	*25*	4	*3*	1	*3*	6	*2*	9	*36*
Iran, Islamic Rep.[a]	12	10	5	2	9	10	1	1	6	12	66	66
Iraq	..	..	..	..	..	..	..	..	..	..	..	..
Ireland[a]	38	..	35	..	..	..	3	..	14	..	10	..
Israel	..	28	..	28	..	1	..	5	..	16	..	22
Italy	*33*	35	23	23	..	..	6	5	33	33	5	4
Jamaica[a]	..	30	..	34	..	9	..	7	..	7	..	0
Japan	..	..	..	..	..	..	..	..	..	..	..	..
Jordan[a]	10	8	23	28	22	10	9	9	..	1	36	43
Kazakhstan[a]	*11*	39	*28*	41	*3*	6	*5*	0	48	..	*6*	14
Kenya[a]	34	*25*	36	*40*	15	*17*	1	*0*	0	*0*	14	*17*
Korea, Dem. Rep.	..	..	..	..	..	..	..	..	..	..	..	..
Korea, Rep.[a]	31	*25*	32	*31*	7	*4*	10	*7*	8	*15*	12	*18*
Kuwait[a]	1	..	0	..	2	..	0	..	..	..	97	..
Kyrgyz Republic[a]	26	*16*	56	*55*	5	*2*	1	*0*	..	..	11	*26*
Lao PDR	..	..	..	..	..	..	..	..	..	..	..	..
Latvia[a]	7	12	41	39	3	1	0	0	35	33	13	15
Lebanon	..	*11*	..	*44*	..	*11*	..	*12*	..	*1*	..	*21*
Lesotho[a]	15	24	12	17	49	39	1	0	..	..	24	20
Liberia	..	..	..	..	..	..	..	..	..	..	..	..
Libya	..	..	..	..	..	..	..	..	..	..	..	..
Lithuania	..	20	..	39	..	1	..	0	..	30	..	9
Macedonia, FYR	..	..	..	..	..	..	..	..	..	..	..	..
Madagascar	..	*18*	..	*24*	..	*36*	..	*1*	..	..	..	*20*
Malawi	..	..	..	..	..	..	..	..	..	..	..	..
Malaysia[a]	37	47	26	21	12	6	5	0	1	..	19	26
Mali	..	..	..	..	..	..	..	..	..	..	..	..
Mauritania	..	..	..	..	..	..	..	..	..	..	..	..
Mauritius[a]	12	12	25	43	34	20	6	5	6	4	16	17
Mexico[a]	27	*34*	54	*62*	4	*4*	2	*1*	14	*10*	16	*10*
Moldova[a]	*6*	3	*38*	46	*5*	6	*1*	0	38	27	2	18
Mongolia	..	16	..	35	..	6	..	0	..	16	..	27
Morocco[a]	20	..	40	..	15	..	3	..	9	..	13	..
Mozambique	..	..	..	..	..	..	..	..	..	..	..	..
Myanmar	20	*16*	26	*22*	12	*2*	..	..	..	..	42	*60*
Namibia[a]	27	*43*	32	*21*	28	*25*	2	*1*	..	*1*	11	*9*
Nepal	10	11	33	31	26	23	4	4	..	..	27	30
Netherlands	..	24	..	28	..	1	..	3	..	37	..	7
New Zealand	..	52	..	29	..	3	..	0	..	0	..	16
Nicaragua[a]	8	15	46	40	6	4	0	0	10	16	29	25
Niger	..	..	..	..	..	..	..	..	..	..	..	..
Nigeria	..	..	..	..	..	..	..	..	..	..	..	..
Norway	..	29	..	27	..	0	..	1	..	21	..	22
Oman[a]	21	*21*	1	*1*	3	*3*	2	*2*	..	..	74	*73*
Pakistan[a]	18	19	27	32	24	9	7	9	..	..	24	31
Panama[a]	20	*15*	..	*9*	..	*9*	3	*4*	16	*20*	34	*44*
Papua New Guinea[a]	40	*50*	8	*13*	27	*26*	2	*3*	0	*0*	23	*8*
Paraguay[a]	15	10	36	38	18	11	4	2	6	6	22	33
Peru[a]	17	24	49	54	10	7	5	3	9	7	12	14
Philippines[a]	33	39	26	26	29	17	4	4	..	..	8	15
Poland[a]	28	*17*	28	*39*	8	*2*	1	*1*	26	*32*	10	*9*
Portugal	*23*	24	32	32	*0*	0	2	2	29	31	*14*	*11*
Puerto Rico	..	..	..	..	..	..	..	..	..	..	..	..

	Taxes on income, profits, and capital gains		Taxes on goods and services		Taxes on international trade		Other taxes		Social contributions		Grants and other revenue	
	% of revenue		% of revenue		% of revenue		% of revenue		% of revenue		% of revenue	
	1995	2003	1995	2003	1995	2003	1995	2003	1995	2003	1995	2003
Romania[a]	29	10	24	30	6	3	3	1	27	41	11	15
Russian Federation	..	5	..	31	..	12	..	0	..	30	..	21
Rwanda	..	..	..	..	..	..	..	..	..	..	..	..
Saudi Arabia	..	..	..	..	..	..	..	..	..	..	..	..
Senegal[a]	17	20	19	30	36	33	2	4	..	..	26	13
Serbia and Montenegro[a]	..	13	..	39	..	7	..	4	..	29	..	9
Sierra Leone	15	..	34	..	39	..	0	..	..	..	12	..
Singapore[a]	26	31	20	19	1	2	15	8	..	..	38	40
Slovak Republic	..	17	..	29	..	1	..	0	..	40	..	13
Slovenia[a]	13	13	33	31	9	1	0	3	42	36	3	15
Somalia	..	..	..	..	..	..	..	..	..	..	..	..
South Africa[a]	50	52	35	34	4	2	3	4	2	2	6	5
Spain	26	24	23	15	0	0	0	0	40	40	10	21
Sri Lanka[a]	12	14	49	56	17	12	4	1	1	1	18	16
Sudan[a]	17	..	41	..	27	..	1	..	..	..	14	..
Swaziland[a]	..	24	..	13	..	50	..	4	..	..	..	9
Sweden	15	4	26	34	..	..	12	12	35	40	13	10
Switzerland[a]	11	16	21	32	1	1	2	4	49	40	17	8
Syrian Arab Republic[a]	23	..	37	..	13	..	8	..	0	..	19	..
Tajikistan[a]	6	3	63	53	12	16	0	1	13	18	5	9
Tanzania	..	..	..	..	..	..	..	..	..	..	..	..
Thailand	..	29	..	40	..	10	..	0	..	4	..	17
Togo	..	..	..	..	..	..	..	..	..	..	..	..
Trinidad and Tobago[a]	50	..	26	..	6	..	1	..	2	..	15	..
Tunisia[a]	16	23	20	35	28	8	4	4	15	19	17	12
Turkey[a]	31	..	39	..	4	..	3	..	..	..	23	..
Turkmenistan	..	..	..	..	..	..	..	..	..	..	..	..
Uganda[a]	10	13	45	28	7	19	2	0	..	..	37	40
Ukraine[a]	..	12	..	30	..	4	..	0	..	35	..	20
United Arab Emirates[a]	..	..	15	..	..	..	..	..	1	..	84	..
United Kingdom	39	36	31	32	..	..	6	6	19	21	5	4
United States	..	51	..	4	..	1	..	1	..	40	..	3
Uruguay[a]	10	15	32	37	4	3	10	8	31	23	8	11
Uzbekistan	..	..	..	..	..	..	..	..	..	..	..	..
Venezuela, RB[a]	38	13	33	23	9	4	0	8	4	2	19	50
Vietnam	16	26	28	35	25	19	12	2	..	..	19	17
West Bank and Gaza	..	..	..	..	..	..	..	..	..	..	..	..
Yemen, Rep.[a]	17	..	10	..	18	..	3	..	..	..	51	..
Zambia[a]	27	..	22	..	36	..	0	..	0	..	15	..
Zimbabwe[a]	36	..	22	..	17	..	3	..	2	..	19	..
World	**19 m**	**20 m**	**28 m**	**29 m**	**15 m**	**6 m**	**2 m**	**2 m**	**.. m**	**.. m**	**19 m**	**17 m**
Low income	18	16	24	28	22	16	1	..	..	..	24	27
Middle income	19	19	32	38	13	7	2	2	10	15	16	15
Lower middle income	17	17	33	38	16	8	3	2	8	8	15	16
Upper middle income	19	19	28	36	9	3	1	2	16	30	16	13
Low & middle income	18	16	28	32	17	8	2	1	..	..	19	19
East Asia & Pacific	32	..	28	..	23	..	2	..	..	..	19	..
Europe & Central Asia	19	12	39	39	6	2	1	0	29	30	11	14
Latin America & Carib.	17	21	34	39	10	6	2	3	8	7	13	14
Middle East & N. Africa	17	11	13	29	15	11	3	4	9	..	36	21
South Asia	11	14	28	31	24	19	2	2	..	..	26	31
Sub-Saharan Africa	19	..	22	..	27	..	1	..	..	..	19	..
High income	23	28	26	25	1	1	4	3	30	26	13	12
Europe EMU	23	23	24	28	0	0	3	3	35	37	7	7

Note: Components may not sum to 100 percent due to missing data or adjustment to tax revenue.
a. Data were reported on a cash basis and have been adjusted to the accrual framework.

The International Monetary Fund (IMF) classifies government revenues as taxes, grants, and property income. Taxes are classified by the base on which the tax is levied, grants by the source, and property income by type (for example, interest, dividends, or rent). The most important source of revenue is taxes. Grants are unrequited, nonrepayable, noncompulsory receipts from other government units and foreign governments or from international organizations. Transactions are generally recorded on an accrual basis.

The IMF's *Manual on Government Finance Statistics* (2001) describes taxes as compulsory, unrequited payments made to governments by individuals, businesses, or institutions. Taxes are classified in six major groups by the base on which the tax is levied: income, profits, and capital gains; payroll and workforce; property; goods and services; international trade and transactions; and other taxes. However, the distinctions are not always clear. Taxes levied on the income and profits of individuals and corporations are classified as direct taxes, and taxes and duties levied on goods and services are classified as indirect taxes. This distinction may be a useful simplification, but it has no particular analytical significance except with respect to the capacity to fix tax rates. Direct taxes tend to be progressive, whereas indirect taxes are proportional.

Social security taxes do not reflect compulsory payments made by employers to provident funds or other agencies with a like purpose. Similarly, expenditures from such funds are not reflected in government expenditure (see table 4.12).

For further discussion of taxes and tax policies, see *About the data* for table 5.6. For further discussion of government revenues and expenditures, see About the data for tables 4.11 and 4.12.

• **Taxes on income, profits, and capital gains** are levied on the actual or presumptive net income of individuals, on the profits of corporations and enterprises, and on capital gains, whether realized or not, on land, securities, and other assets. Intragovernmental payments are eliminated in consolidation. • **Taxes on goods and services** include general sales and turnover or value added taxes, selective excises on goods, selective taxes on services, taxes on the use of goods or property, taxes on extraction and production of minerals, and profits of fiscal monopolies. • **Taxes on international trade** include import duties, export duties, profits of export or import monopolies, exchange profits, and exchange taxes. • **Other taxes** include employer payroll or labor taxes, taxes on property, and taxes not allocable to other categories, such as penalties for late payment or nonpayment of taxes. • **Social contributions** include social security contributions by employees, employers, and self-employed individuals, and other contributions whose source cannot be determined. They also include actual or imputed contributions to social insurance schemes operated by governments. • **Grants and other revenue** include grants from other foreign governments, international organizations, and other government units; interest; dividends; rent; requited, nonrepayable receipts for public purposes (such as fines, administrative fees, and entrepreneurial income from government ownership of property); and voluntary, unrequited, nonrepayable receipts other than grants.

4.13a

Taxes on income, profit, and capital gains as a share of revenue, 2001–03 (%)

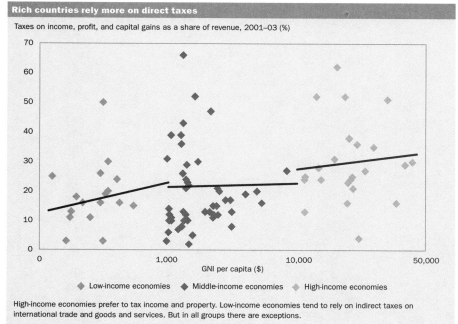

◆ Low-income economies   ◆ Middle-income economies   ◆ High-income economies

High-income economies prefer to tax income and property. Low-income economies tend to rely on indirect taxes on international trade and goods and services. But in all groups there are exceptions.

Source: International Monetary Fund, Government Finance Statistics data files.

The data on central government revenues are from the IMF's *Government Finance Statistics Yearbook, 2004* and IMF data files. Each country's accounts are reported using the system of common definitions and classifications in the IMF's *Manual on Government Finance Statistics* (2001). The IMF receives additional information from the Organisation for Economic Co-operation and Development on the tax revenues of some of its members. See the IMF sources for complete and authoritative explanations of concepts, definitions, and data sources.

4.14 Monetary indicators and prices

	Money and quasi money		Claims on private sector		Claims on governments and other public entities		GDP implicit deflator		Consumer price index		Food price index	
	M2 annual % growth		Annual growth % of M2		Annual growth % of M2		average annual % growth		average annual % growth		average annual % growth	
	1990	2003	1990	2003	1990	2003	1980–90	1990–2003	1980–90	1990–2003	1980–90	1990–2003
Afghanistan	..	..	..	..	..	..	..	..	..	..	21.6	..
Albania	..	7.6	..	2.9	..	5.3	−0.4	26.9	..	19.2	..	22.1
Algeria	11.4	16.0	12.2	1.0	3.2	−2.5	8.3	14.7	9.1	12.7	9.7	13.4
Angola	..	64.6	..	28.8	..	7.1	5.9	518.4	..	501.6	..	..
Argentina	1,113.3	29.6	1,444.7	−8.4	1,573.2	−6.8	391.1	4.9	390.6	7.2	486.5	6.8
Armenia	..	10.4	..	1.4	..	−6.9	..	119.9	..	36.9	..	65.2
Australia	12.8	13.3	13.8	19.9	−2.2	−3.2	7.2	1.8	7.9	2.4	7.4	3.0
Austria[a]	..	..	..	..	..	..	3.3	1.8	3.2	2.1	2.7	1.6
Azerbaijan	..	30.8	..	17.6	..	−2.4	..	65.6	..	109.1	..	91.1
Bangladesh	10.4	13.1	9.2	6.9	−0.2	−2.1	9.8	3.8	..	5.0	10.8	4.7
Belarus	..	56.8	..	49.9	..	32.9	..	252.5	..	185.8	2.4	117.1
Belgium[a]	..	..	..	..	..	..	4.1	1.8	4.2	1.9	4.0	1.3
Benin	28.6	−11.3	−1.3	14.3	12.4	3.3	1.7	7.0	..	6.5	−3.5	7.6
Bolivia	52.8	13.9	40.8	−0.1	18.0	1.0	326.9	7.1	322.5	7.0	321.8	6.2
Bosnia and Herzegovina	..	9.5	..	15.9	..	0.2	..	3.5	..	..	..	..
Botswana	−14.0	15.5	12.6	7.0	−51.9	60.5	13.6	8.6	10.0	9.6	10.1	9.4
Brazil	1,289.2	4.4	1,566.4	11.7	3,093.6	3.2	284.0	118.8	285.6	114.0	314.0	−13.7
Bulgaria	51.7	20.2	37.5	22.2	80.2	−3.4	1.8	75.1	6.3	83.8	1.8	79.8
Burkina Faso	−0.5	19.0	3.6	11.5	−1.5	2.9	3.3	4.7	3.4	4.6	0.7	4.6
Burundi	9.6	15.8	15.4	10.4	−6.9	4.8	4.4	12.0	7.1	14.6	6.1	..
Cambodia	..	14.9	..	9.6	..	−0.4	..	3.4	..	4.3	..	4.0
Cameroon	−1.7	1.3	0.9	4.8	−3.0	1.3	5.6	4.3	8.7	5.5	..	3.9
Canada	7.8	7.0	9.2	5.6	0.6	1.8	4.6	1.5	5.3	1.8	4.6	1.7
Central African Republic	−3.7	−8.0	−1.6	−0.3	2.3	5.7	7.9	3.9	3.2	4.4	2.0	4.6
Chad	−2.4	−3.1	1.3	5.6	−17.3	4.9	1.4	6.7	0.6	7.2	−5.3	6.8
Chile	24.2	8.1	21.7	9.0	16.3	−4.1	20.7	7.0	20.6	7.2	20.7	6.2
China	28.9	19.7	26.5	15.9	1.5	0.2	5.7	4.9	..	6.0	8.8	11.3
Hong Kong, China	8.5	6.3	7.9	−1.8	−1.0	1.2	7.8	1.8	7.0	3.5	6.3	3.5
Colombia	33.0	10.3	107.1	6.4	23.9	4.8	24.7	17.8	22.7	17.0	24.6	15.6
Congo, Dem. Rep.	195.4	32.3	18.0	6.9	429.7	23.3	62.9	617.0	57.1	691.7	..	..
Congo, Rep.	18.5	−2.4	5.1	4.9	−12.6	3.7	0.5	7.9	0.9	7.3	4.3	7.2
Costa Rica	27.5	16.7	7.3	14.6	8.2	4.5	23.6	14.9	23.0	14.1	16.0	5.1
Côte d'Ivoire	−2.6	−6.1	−3.9	−5.1	−3.0	−2.5	2.8	7.3	5.4	6.0	6.6	..
Croatia	..	10.7	..	11.8	..	0.2	..	53.0	304.1	52.8	124.6	50.4
Cuba	..	..	..	..	..	..	..	..	..	..	..	..
Czech Republic	..	7.4	..	3.5	..	8.9	..	9.1	..	6.1	..	−0.3
Denmark	6.5	6.0	3.0	17.8	−3.1	1.1	5.8	2.0	5.6	2.2	4.8	2.1
Dominican Republic	42.5	63.1	19.1	28.6	1.1	−2.3	21.6	9.2	22.4	8.7	25.4	7.4
Ecuador	50.3	18.9	9.3	5.0	−26.5	−8.8	−5.4	3.9	35.8	37.7	40.7	36.9
Egypt, Arab Rep.	28.7	21.3	6.3	5.4	25.3	10.2	13.7	7.0	17.4	7.0	22.0	6.2
El Salvador	−17.5	2.3	−24.2	7.8	10.2	4.0	16.3	5.8	19.6	6.6	21.5	7.2
Eritrea	..	15.1	..	4.0	..	8.6	..	10.1	..	..	..	..
Estonia	76.5	10.9	27.6	22.6	−6.8	2.2	2.3	35.5	..	..	..	−20.2
Ethiopia	19.9	12.4	0.3	3.0	21.8	9.1	3.6	5.3	4.0	4.0	3.8	−3.8
Finland[a]	..	..	..	..	..	..	6.8	2.0	6.2	1.6	5.8	0.0
France[a]	..	..	..	..	..	..	5.8	1.5	5.8	1.6	5.7	1.6
Gabon	3.3	−1.2	0.7	−5.9	−20.6	0.9	1.8	5.1	5.1	4.6	4.9	3.8
Gambia, The	8.4	35.3	7.8	13.9	−35.4	0.2	17.9	6.1	20.0	4.0	20.3	3.7
Georgia	..	22.8	..	16.3	..	7.9	1.9	185.6	..	17.7	..	14.3
Germany[a]	..	..	..	..	..	..	2.7	1.6	..	1.8	..	0.7
Ghana	13.3	34.2	4.9	13.0	9.9	1.9	42.1	26.4	39.1	27.0	33.1	23.8
Greece[a]	..	..	..	..	..	..	19.3	7.5	18.7	7.2	18.0	6.4
Guatemala	25.8	15.0	15.0	5.1	0.5	−2.1	14.6	9.3	14.0	9.1	22.1	9.0
Guinea	−17.4	33.2	13.1	5.7	2.9	31.0	..	5.5	..	..	..	..
Guinea-Bissau	574.6	14.4	90.5	−1.8	460.7	−4.0	57.4	22.8	..	24.6	..	..
Haiti	2.5	39.0	−0.6	9.3	0.4	9.3	7.3	19.2	5.2	19.7	4.1	..

	Money and quasi money M2 annual % growth		Claims on private sector Annual growth % of M2		Claims on governments and other public entities Annual growth % of M2		GDP implicit deflator average annual % growth		Consumer price index average annual % growth		Food price index average annual % growth	
	1990	2003	1990	2003	1990	2003	1980–90	1990–2003	1980–90	1990–2003	1980–90	1990–2003
Honduras	21.4	15.8	13.0	12.4	−10.5	3.3	5.7	16.2	6.3	16.4	5.2	15.6
Hungary	29.2	12.4	23.0	25.2	69.7	−3.0	8.9	16.4	9.6	16.9	9.5	15.8
India	15.1	13.0	5.9	5.0	10.5	4.1	8.2	6.8	8.6	7.9	8.8	7.4
Indonesia	44.6	8.1	66.9	8.4	−6.7	−4.1	8.5	15.3	8.3	13.9	8.7	16.1
Iran, Islamic Rep.	18.0	24.5	14.7	25.2	5.8	3.7	14.4	24.6	18.2	22.8	16.2	23.3
Iraq	..	..	..	..	..	..	10.3	..	..	..	10.9	..
Ireland[a]	..	..	..	..	..	..	6.6	3.8	6.8	2.7	6.0	3.0
Israel	19.4	−0.1	18.5	−3.4	4.9	−1.2	101.1	8.2	101.7	7.7	102.4	6.9
Italy[a]	..	..	..	..	..	..	10.0	3.4	9.1	3.3	8.2	2.8
Jamaica	21.5	10.5	12.5	11.5	−16.0	24.0	19.9	18.9	15.1	18.3	16.1	17.1
Japan	8.2	1.8	9.7	−3.3	1.5	7.8	2.0	−0.5	1.7	0.4	1.5	0.2
Jordan	8.3	16.6	4.7	2.1	1.0	2.3	4.3	2.5	5.7	3.0	4.7	3.1
Kazakhstan	..	29.5	..	43.4	..	−27.6	..	120.2	..	38.8	..	89.8
Kenya	20.1	11.9	8.0	2.0	21.5	4.5	9.1	12.3	11.2	12.6	10.0	8.8
Korea, Dem. Rep.	..	..	..	..	..	..	..	..	..	..	..	..
Korea, Rep.	17.2	6.7	36.1	10.7	−1.2	0.9	6.5	4.8	4.9	4.5	5.0	4.8
Kuwait	−100.0	7.8	−89.7	15.2	−23.0	−1.9	−2.8	2.6	2.9	1.9	1.6	1.5
Kyrgyz Republic	..	33.4	..	7.8	..	0.6	..	72.1	..	16.5	..	39.7
Lao PDR	7.8	20.1	3.6	−0.9	7.0	1.2	37.6	28.7	..	29.7	..	..
Latvia	..	22.1	..	36.0	..	6.4	0.0	31.5	..	19.0	..	16.0
Lebanon	55.1	13.0	27.6	−0.1	18.5	4.6	..	12.2	..	..	..	19.8
Lesotho	8.4	6.0	6.8	−26.2	−14.9	6.8	12.1	9.6	13.6	9.0	13.5	9.8
Liberia	−100.0	1.5	−39.8	−1.7	−271.0	−331.2	2.9	51.2	..	..	3.7	..
Libya	19.0	7.8	2.0	4.5	15.0	−29.7	1.2	..	7.5	3.5	..	..
Lithuania	..	18.2	..	28.6	..	−4.0	..	45.8	..	19.3	2.7	39.5
Macedonia, FYR	..	14.2	..	9.5	..	−0.2	..	48.8	..	7.1	..	..
Madagascar	4.5	8.8	23.8	2.7	−14.8	5.1	17.1	16.0	16.6	15.8	15.7	15.7
Malawi	11.1	27.5	15.5	8.7	−12.9	9.2	15.1	31.1	16.9	31.0	16.4	31.4
Malaysia	10.6	9.3	20.8	5.7	−1.2	4.1	1.7	3.4	2.6	3.1	2.2	4.3
Mali	−4.9	22.7	0.1	11.4	−13.4	−7.3	4.5	6.0	..	4.3	2.7	4.4
Mauritania	11.5	10.5	20.2	18.7	1.5	−15.8	8.4	5.5	7.1	5.6	..	6.3
Mauritius	21.2	10.9	14.0	3.8	0.8	5.2	9.4	5.9	6.9	6.5	7.8	8.3
Mexico	83.8	7.2	48.4	2.3	9.4	4.0	71.5	16.5	73.8	16.7	73.1	16.3
Moldova	358.0	30.4	53.3	25.8	469.1	−2.6	..	78.9	..	17.8	..	110.5
Mongolia	31.6	49.6	40.2	44.3	29.8	28.5	−1.6	40.5	..	29.5	..	..
Morocco	21.5	8.7	44.2	5.1	−4.9	−0.2	7.1	2.3	7.0	3.1	6.7	2.9
Mozambique	37.2	18.3	22.0	1.9	−5.1	−2.2	38.3	24.8	..	24.8	24.4	..
Myanmar	37.7	1.4	12.8	−17.2	24.2	23.3	12.2	24.6	11.5	25.9	11.9	27.8
Namibia	30.3	20.7	15.4	30.3	−4.2	9.5	13.7	10.1	12.6	9.4	13.9	9.0
Nepal	18.5	12.9	5.7	..	7.3	−2.0	11.1	6.9	10.2	7.4	10.5	7.9
Netherlands[a]	..	..	..	..	..	..	1.5	2.3	2.0	2.6	1.3	1.3
New Zealand	12.5	10.6	4.2	12.0	−1.6	−0.1	10.5	1.8	11.0	1.9	9.8	1.8
Nicaragua	7,677.8	12.6	4,932.9	16.6	..	3.0	422.3	29.1	535.7	22.3	69.2	20.3
Niger	−4.1	−13.2	−5.1	5.3	1.4	7.5	1.9	5.2	0.7	5.0	−1.5	5.7
Nigeria	32.7	24.1	7.8	15.7	27.1	11.6	16.7	24.2	18.9	26.0	22.5	24.1
Norway	5.6	3.4	5.0	10.4	−0.6	−5.4	5.4	3.2	7.4	2.3	7.8	1.7
Oman	10.0	2.5	9.6	1.7	−10.9	−0.5	−3.6	2.0	..	0.2	0.9	0.1
Pakistan	11.6	17.5	5.9	11.9	7.7	−4.2	6.7	8.6	6.3	8.1	6.6	8.2
Panama	36.6	4.8	0.8	−1.4	−25.7	3.3	1.9	2.8	1.4	1.1	1.5	0.7
Papua New Guinea	4.3	−0.4	−0.9	−0.7	8.8	−4.6	5.3	7.6	5.6	10.3	4.6	9.6
Paraguay	54.4	7.6	32.0	−15.8	−9.2	−2.9	24.4	11.4	21.7	11.8	24.9	10.5
Peru	6,384.9	−2.4	2,123.7	−3.3	2,129.5	−2.1	..	..	246.1	18.5	221.8	18.7
Philippines	22.4	3.6	15.6	0.6	3.4	5.5	14.9	7.7	13.4	7.3	14.1	6.7
Poland	160.1	5.7	158.7	4.5	−20.6	2.3	..	17.7	50.9	19.1	52.4	16.1
Portugal[a]	..	..	..	..	..	..	17.9	4.9	17.1	4.0	16.7	3.4
Puerto Rico	..	..	..	..	..	..	3.5	3.1	..	..	2.7	10.1

	Money and quasi money		Claims on private sector		Claims on governments and other public entities		GDP implicit deflator		Consumer price index		Food price index	
	M2 annual % growth		Annual growth % of M2		Annual growth % of M2		average annual % growth		average annual % growth		average annual % growth	
	1990	2003	1990	2003	1990	2003	1980–90	1990–2003	1980–90	1990–2003	1980–90	1990–2003
Romania	26.4	23.3	..	14.4	0.0	−5.0	*1.5*	78.1	..	78.7	4.3	64.2
Russian Federation	..	38.5	..	30.0	..	−3.9	..	106.4	..	*66.6*	..	*91.9*
Rwanda	5.6	15.4	−10.0	8.4	26.8	13.3	4.0	10.6	3.9	*12.3*	6.4	11.9
Saudi Arabia	4.6	8.5	−4.5	5.9	4.2	9.5	−3.8	1.9	−0.8	0.5	−0.2	0.5
Senegal	−4.8	14.6	−8.4	10.0	−5.3	−4.2	6.5	3.8	6.2	4.3	5.3	4.7
Serbia and Montenegro	..	..	..	..	..	..	..	52.9	..	..	..	7.1
Sierra Leone	74.0	21.9	4.9	9.7	228.7	13.4	60.3	24.7	72.4	22.4	71.0	..
Singapore	20.0	8.1	13.7	5.1	−4.9	1.9	2.0	0.6	1.6	1.3	1.0	1.4
Slovak Republic	..	9.7	..	−6.5	..	−15.5	*1.8*	9.3	..	*8.1*	1.6	14.2
Slovenia	*123.0*	6.2	*96.1*	10.8	*−10.4*	3.3	..	*9.6*	..	10.3	129.5	19.4
Somalia	..	..	..	..	..	..	49.7	..	..	..	*37.4*	..
South Africa	11.4	12.5	13.7	31.3	1.8	−2.8	15.5	9.0	14.8	8.0	15.2	9.3
Spain[a]	..	..	..	..	..	..	9.3	3.8	9.0	3.5	9.3	3.2
Sri Lanka	19.9	15.3	16.2	12.0	4.4	−2.8	11.0	9.0	10.9	9.7	11.0	10.1
Sudan	48.8	30.3	12.6	18.0	29.4	6.1	38.4	48.1	37.6	*63.6*	40.3	..
Swaziland	0.6	14.1	20.5	21.4	−13.1	13.1	10.3	12.2	14.4	9.2	13.3	11.7
Sweden	0.8	4.1	13.4	10.2	−12.1	−7.6	7.3	1.9	7.0	1.7	8.2	0.1
Switzerland	0.8	8.4	11.7	4.1	1.0	0.4	3.4	*0.9*	2.9	1.3	3.1	0.8
Syrian Arab Republic	26.1	7.8	3.4	3.0	11.4	2.5	15.3	6.6	23.2	*4.9*	25.0	3.5
Tajikistan	..	40.9	..	13.7	..	−30.1	*2.5*	147.0	..	..	..	*477.3*
Tanzania	41.9	16.6	22.6	12.0	80.6	−12.3	..	17.6	31.0	16.2	32.0	17.3
Thailand	26.7	6.6	30.0	5.6	−4.0	−1.9	3.9	3.4	3.5	4.1	2.7	4.6
Togo	9.5	5.9	1.8	16.7	6.9	−8.1	4.8	5.4	2.5	6.6	1.1	1.3
Trinidad and Tobago	6.2	−0.7	2.7	1.6	−1.9	−7.2	5.0	4.9	10.7	5.2	14.6	*12.5*
Tunisia	7.6	6.4	5.9	7.0	1.8	−0.6	7.4	4.0	*7.4*	3.9	8.3	4.1
Turkey	53.2	14.2	42.9	12.4	0.4	8.3	45.3	68.7	44.9	72.4	18.3	33.8
Turkmenistan	..	*23.8*	..	3.4	..	*−10.3*	..	226.6	..	..	..	..
Uganda	60.2	17.9	0.0	6.7	−0.9	−11.1	*113.8*	8.8	102.5	7.9	..	*8.5*
Ukraine	..	46.9	..	39.3	..	−1.9	..	155.0	..	*85.8*	2.0	83.7
United Arab Emirates	−8.2	15.5	1.3	11.3	−4.8	4.8	0.8	*2.8*	..	..	..	..
United Kingdom	10.5	9.7	13.1	12.1	1.9	−0.7	5.8	2.7	5.8	2.7	4.5	1.7
United States	4.9	2.1	−0.4	5.4	1.4	−0.2	3.8	*1.9*	4.2	2.6	3.9	2.4
Uruguay	118.5	12.5	56.2	−17.6	25.8	7.6	62.7	23.9	61.1	25.5	62.0	*25.1*
Uzbekistan	..	..	..	..	..	..	..	162.4	..	..	..	..
Venezuela, RB	64.9	57.6	17.6	5.7	45.3	−18.8	19.3	39.6	20.9	41.1	35.1	38.1
Vietnam	..	33.1	..	23.1	..	4.3	*222.2*	11.6	..	*2.8*	..	..
West Bank and Gaza	..	..	..	..	..	..	..	8.9	..	..	..	..
Yemen, Rep.	*11.3*	19.7	*1.4*	4.4	*10.2*	11.3	..	18.6	..	20.8	*2.6*	..
Zambia	47.9	17.9	22.8	10.1	195.2	−3.3	42.2	41.8	*72.5*	*48.4*	42.8	45.4
Zimbabwe	15.1	430.0	13.5	345.5	5.0	123.3	11.6	*32.3*	13.8	*36.1*	15.1	48.6

Note: The inconsistencies in the growth rates of the GDP deflator and consumer and food price indexes are mainly due to uneven coverage of the time period.
a. As members of the European Monetary Union, these countries share a single currency, the euro.

Money and the financial accounts that record the supply of money lie at the heart of a country's financial system. There are several commonly used definitions of the money supply. The narrowest, M1, encompasses currency held by the public and demand deposits with banks. M2 includes M1 plus time and savings deposits with banks that require a notice for withdrawal. M3 includes M2 as well as various money market instruments, such as certificates of deposit issued by banks, bank deposits denominated in foreign currency, and deposits with financial institutions other than banks. However defined, money is a liability of the banking system, distinguished from other bank liabilities by the special role it plays as a medium of exchange, a unit of account, and a store of value.

The banking system's assets include its net foreign assets and net domestic credit. Net domestic credit includes credit extended to the private sector and general government and credit extended to the nonfinancial public sector in the form of investments in short- and long-term government securities and loans to state enterprises; liabilities to the public and private sectors in the form of deposits with the banking system are netted out. Net domestic credit also includes credit to banking and nonbank financial institutions.

Domestic credit is the main vehicle through which changes in the money supply are regulated, with central bank lending to the government often playing the most important role. The central bank can regulate lending to the private sector in several ways—for example, by adjusting the cost of the refinancing facilities it provides to banks, by changing market interest rates through open market operations, or by controlling the availability of credit through changes in the reserve requirements imposed on banks and ceilings on the credit provided by banks to the private sector.

Monetary accounts are derived from the balance sheets of financial institutions—the central bank, commercial banks, and nonbank financial intermediaries. Although these balance sheets are usually reliable, they are subject to errors of classification, valuation, and timing and to differences in accounting practices. For example, whether interest income is recorded on an accrual or a cash basis can make a substantial difference, as can the treatment of non-performing assets. Valuation errors typically arise with respect to foreign exchange transactions, particularly in countries with flexible exchange rates or in those that have undergone a currency devaluation

during the reporting period. The valuation of financial derivatives and the net liabilities of the banking system can also be difficult. The quality of commercial bank reporting also may be adversely affected by delays in reports from bank branches, especially in countries where branch accounts are not computerized. Thus the data in the balance sheets of commercial banks may be based on preliminary estimates subject to constant revision. This problem is likely to be even more serious for nonbank financial intermediaries.

Controlling inflation is one of the primary goals of monetary policy and is intimately linked to the growth in money supply. Inflation is measured by the rate of increase in a price index, but actual price change can also be negative. Which index is used depends on which set of prices in the economy is being examined. The GDP deflator reflects changes in prices for total gross domestic product. The most general measure of the overall price level, it takes into account changes in government consumption, capital formation (including inventory appreciation), international trade, and the main component, household final consumption expenditure. The GDP deflator is usually derived implicitly as the ratio of current to constant price GDP, resulting in a Paasche index. It is defective as a general measure of inflation for use in policy because of the long lags in deriving estimates and because it is often only an annual measure.

Consumer price indexes are more current and produced more frequently. They are also constructed explicitly, based on surveys of the cost of a defined basket of consumer goods and services. Nevertheless, consumer price indexes should be interpreted with caution. The definition of a household, the basket of goods chosen, and the geographic (urban or rural) and income group coverage of consumer price surveys can all vary widely across countries. In addition, the weights are derived from household expenditure surveys, which, for budgetary reasons, tend to be conducted infrequently in developing countries, leading to poor comparability over time. Although useful for measuring consumer price inflation within a country, consumer price indexes are of less value in making comparisons across countries. Food price indexes, like consumer price indexes, should be interpreted with caution because of the high variability across countries in the items covered.

The least-squares method is used to calculate the growth rates of the GDP implicit deflator, consumer price index, and food price index.

• **Money and quasi money** comprise the sum of currency outside banks, demand deposits other than those of the central government, and the time, savings, and foreign currency deposits of resident sectors other than the central government. This definition of the money supply, often called M2, corresponds to lines 34 and 35 in the International Monetary Fund's (IMF) *International Financial Statistics* (IFS). The change in money supply is measured as the difference in end-of-year totals relative to M2 in the preceding year. • **Claims on private sector** (IFS line 32d) include gross credit from the financial system to individuals, enterprises, nonfinancial public entities not included under net domestic credit, and financial institutions not included elsewhere. • **Claims on governments and other public entities** (IFS line 32an + 32b + 32bx + 32c) usually comprise direct credit for specific purposes, such as financing the government budget deficit; loans to state enterprises; advances against future credit authorizations; and purchases of treasury bills and bonds, net of deposits by the public sector. Public sector deposits with the banking system also include sinking funds for the service of debt and temporary deposits of government revenues. • **GDP implicit deflator** measures the average annual rate of price change in the economy as a whole for the periods shown. • **Consumer price index** reflects changes in the cost to the average consumer of acquiring a basket of goods and services that may be fixed or may change at specified intervals, such as yearly. The Laspeyres formula is generally used. • **Food price index** is a subindex of the consumer price index.

The monetary, financial, and consumer price index data are published by the IMF in its monthly *International Financial Statistics* and annual *International Financial Statistics Yearbook*. The IMF collects data on the financial systems of its member countries. The World Bank receives data from the IMF in electronic files that may contain more recent revisions than the published sources. The GDP deflator data are from the World Bank's national accounts files. The food price index data are from the United Nations Statistics Division's *Statistical Yearbook* and *Monthly Bulletin of Statistics*. The discussion of monetary indicators draws from an IMF publication by Marcello Caiola, *A Manual for Country Economists* (1995). Also see the IMF's *Monetary and Financial Statistics Manual* (2000) for guidelines for the presentation of monetary and financial statistics.

Balance of payments current account

	Goods and services				Net income		Net current transfers		Current account balance		Total reserves[a]	
	$ millions				$ millions		$ millions		$ millions		$ millions	
	Exports		Imports									
	1990	2003	1990	2003	1990	2003	1990	2003	1990	2003	1990	2003
Afghanistan	..	..	..	..	..	..	..	..	..	..	638	..
Albania	354	1,167	485	2,586	–2	170	15	842	–118	–407	..	1,038
Algeria	13,462	..	10,106		–2,268	..	333	..	1,420	..	2,703	35,455
Angola	3,992	8,955	3,385	7,653	–765	–1,832	–77	135	–236	–150	..	634
Argentina	14,800	33,555	6,846	18,649	–4,400	–7,669	998	601	4,552	7,838	6,222	14,157
Armenia	..	903	..	1,406	..	93	..	218	..	–191	1	510
Australia	49,843	91,682	53,056	107,350	–13,176	–14,550	439	–160	–15,950	–30,377	19,319	33,258
Austria	63,694	132,672	61,580	129,870	–942	–1,836	–6	–2,330	1,166	–1,363	17,228	12,729
Azerbaijan	..	3,057	..	4,770	..	–442	..	134	..	–2,021	..	821
Bangladesh	2,064	7,907	3,960	11,060	–116	–223	1,613	3,558	–398	183	660	2,625
Belarus	..	11,577	..	12,263	..	–36	..	195	..	–527	..	595
Belgium[b]	138,605	213,811	135,098	203,106	2,316	2,907	–2,197	–4,220	3,627	9,392	23,789[c]	14,449[c]
Benin	364	521	454	745	–25	–13	97	163	–18	–75	69	510
Bolivia	977	1,872	1,086	1,976	–249	–301	159	441	–199	36	511	1,097
Bosnia and Herzegovina	..	2,059	..	5,745	..	249	..	1,398	..	–2,038	..	1,796
Botswana	2,005	3,470	1,987	2,842	–106	–294	69	212	–19	170	3,331	5,340
Brazil	35,170	83,552	28,184	63,851	–11,608	–18,552	799	2,867	–3,823	4,016	9,200	49,297
Bulgaria	6,950	10,609	8,027	12,487	–758	–489	125	692	–1,710	–1,676	670	6,826
Burkina Faso	349	408	758	945	0	–30	332	118	–77	–449	305	435
Burundi	89	43	318	175	–15	–17	174	124	–69	–25	112	67
Cambodia	314	2,572	507	2,990	–21	–183	120	475	–93	–125	..	982
Cameroon	2,508	..	2,475	..	–558	..	–26	..	–551	..	37	652
Canada	149,538	328,729	149,118	294,943	–19,388	–16,738	–796	221	–19,764	17,268	23,530	36,268
Central African Republic	220	..	410	..	–22	..	123	..	–89	..	123	137
Chad	271	..	488	..	–21	..	192	..	–46	..	132	192
Chile	10,221	25,851	9,166	23,602	–1,737	–3,280	198	438	–485	–594	6,784	15,843
China[†]	57,374	485,003	46,706	448,924	1,055	–7,838	274	17,634	11,997	45,875	34,476	416,199
Hong Kong, China	..	269,860	..	255,621	..	4,384	..	–1,889	..	16,734	24,656	118,388
Colombia	8,679	15,572	6,858	16,642	–2,305	–3,447	1,026	3,334	542	–1,191	4,869	10,920
Congo, Dem. Rep.	..	..	..	..	..	..	..	..	..	..	261	..
Congo, Rep.	1,488	1,546	1,282	995	–460	–546	3	–8	–251	–3	10	39
Costa Rica	1,963	8,152	2,346	8,483	–233	–849	192	213	–424	–967	525	1,837
Côte d'Ivoire	3,503	6,557	3,445	5,048	–1,091	–687	–181	–469	–1,214	353	21	2,230
Croatia	..	14,929	..	17,196	..	–1,213	..	1,396	..	–2,085	167	8,191
Cuba	..	..	..	..	..	..	..	..	..	..	..	..
Czech Republic	..	56,526	..	58,561	..	–4,166	..	541	..	–5,661	..	26,955
Denmark	48,902	96,210	41,415	83,094	–5,708	–2,616	–408	–3,536	1,372	6,963	11,226	37,998
Dominican Republic	1,832	8,875	2,233	9,099	–249	–1,244	371	2,336	–280	867	69	261
Ecuador	3,262	7,095	2,519	7,858	–1,210	–1,465	107	1,772	–360	–455	1,009	1,165
Egypt, Arab Rep.	9,895	20,060	14,091	19,662	–1,022	–253	7,545	3,599	2,327	3,743	3,620	14,604
El Salvador	973	3,987	1,624	6,429	–132	–408	631	2,117	–152	–734	595	2,139
Eritrea	..	81	..	555	..	–5	450	350	188	–128	..	25
Estonia	664	6,837	711	7,566	–13	–577	97	106	36	–1,199	198	1,377
Ethiopia	597	1,265	1,271	2,636	–69	–24	449	1,196	–294	–199	55	956
Finland	31,180	60,409	33,456	50,219	–3,735	–2,353	–952	–1,008	–6,962	6,829	10,415	11,173
France	285,389	461,601	283,238	445,625	–3,896	7,595	–8,199	–19,187	–9,944	4,384	68,291	70,762
Gabon	2,730	..	1,812	..	–617	..	–134	..	168	..	279	202
Gambia, The	168	..	192	..	–11	..	59	..	23	..	55	107
Georgia	..	1,273	..	1,855	..	34	..	177	..	–371	..	191
Germany	473,670	876,097	427,621	774,854	20,593	–13,849	–21,954	–32,529	44,688	54,866	104,547	96,835
Ghana	983	3,192	1,506	4,180	–111	–157	411	1,399	–223	255	309	1,470
Greece	13,018	36,864	19,564	49,437	–1,709	–2,924	4,718	4,272	–3,537	–11,225	4,721	5,801
Guatemala	1,568	4,107	1,812	7,302	–196	–318	227	2,462	–213	–1,051	362	2,925
Guinea	829	743	953	952	–149	–112	70	135	–203	–185	80	171
Guinea-Bissau	26	71	88	86	–22	–10	39	33	–45	–1	18	164
Haiti	318	469	515	1,375	–18	–14	193	907	–22	–13	10	63
[†]Data for Taiwan, China	74,172	166,575	67,015	144,631	4,362	9,559	–596	–2,719	10,923	28,784	77,653	212,315

Balance of payments current account

	Goods and services (Exports)		Goods and services (Imports)		Net income		Net current transfers		Current account balance		Total reserves[a]	
	$ millions				$ millions		$ millions		$ millions		$ millions	
	Exports		Imports									
	1990	2003	1990	2003	1990	2003	1990	2003	1990	2003	1990	2003
Honduras	1,032	2,654	1,127	3,719	−237	−183	280	968	−51	−279	47	1,439
Hungary	12,035	51,203	11,017	54,766	−1,427	−4,455	787	653	379	−7,364	1,185	12,780
India	22,911	90,568	29,527	96,590	−3,257	−4,703	2,837	18,885	−7,036	8,160	5,637	103,737
Indonesia	29,295	68,547	27,511	56,663	−5,190	−6,217	418	1,869	−2,988	7,534	8,657	36,256
Iran, Islamic Rep.	19,741	40,254	22,292	39,320	378	2,195	2,500	−1,065	327	2,063	..	..
Iraq	..	..	..	..	..	..	..	..	..	..	..	..
Ireland	26,786	127,578	24,576	104,077	−4,955	−26,142	2,384	536	−361	−2,105	5,362	4,152
Israel	17,312	42,365	20,228	44,287	−1,981	−4,358	5,060	6,378	163	98	6,598	26,315
Italy	219,971	364,339	218,573	357,465	−14,712	−19,318	−3,164	−8,112	−16,479	−20,556	88,595	63,257
Jamaica	2,217	3,517	2,390	4,896	−430	−571	291	1,189	−312	−761	168	1,195
Japan	323,692	526,740	297,306	454,252	22,492	71,240	−4,800	−7,512	44,078	136,215	87,828	673,554
Jordan	2,511	4,575	3,569	6,841	−214	122	1,045	3,107	−227	963	1,139	5,366
Kazakhstan	..	15,040	..	13,170	..	−1,744	..	−165	..	−39	..	4,962
Kenya	2,228	3,565	2,705	4,226	−418	−88	368	816	−527	68	236	1,482
Korea, Dem. Rep.	..	..	..	..	..	..	..	..	..	..	..	..
Korea, Rep.	73,297	230,339	76,373	215,789	−88	595	1,150	−2,825	−2,014	12,321	14,916	155,472
Kuwait	8,268	22,875	7,169	16,254	7,738	3,325	−4,951	−2,379	3,886	7,567	2,929	8,636
Kyrgyz Republic	..	745	..	821	..	−62	..	112	..	−26	..	399
Lao PDR	102	482	212	503	−1	−49	56	..	−55	−82	8	257
Latvia	1,090	4,685	997	6,112	2	−21	96	531	191	−917	..	1,536
Lebanon	511	3,687	2,836	7,426	622	−788	1,818	1,144	115	−3,382	4,210	16,367
Lesotho	100	509	754	1,006	433	216	286	121	65	−119	72	460
Liberia	..	96	..	145	..	−64	..	80	..	−34	..	8
Libya	11,468	..	8,960	..	174	..	−481	..	2,201	..	7,225	21,513
Lithuania	..	9,536	..	10,626	..	−482	..	294	..	−1,278	107	3,450
Macedonia, FYR	..	1,685	..	2,539	..	−32	..	608	..	−279	..	935
Madagascar	471	1,126	809	1,654	−161	−79	234	299	−265	−309	92	414
Malawi	443	457	549	637	−80	−43	99	21	−86	−203	142	132
Malaysia	32,665	118,577	31,765	96,820	−1,872	−5,928	102	−2,447	−870	13,381	10,659	45,003
Mali	420	990	830	1,213	−37	−240	225	146	−221	−149	198	909
Mauritania	471	..	520	..	−46	..	86	..	−10	..	59	420
Mauritius	1,722	3,219	1,916	3,123	−23	−30	97	56	−119	122	761	1,603
Mexico	48,805	177,635	51,915	188,787	−8,316	−11,641	3,975	13,858	−7,451	−8,936	10,217	59,027
Moldova	..	1,057	..	1,719	..	215	..	305	..	−142	..	302
Mongolia	493	816	1,096	1,081	−44	−11	7	138	−640	−105	23	243
Morocco	6,239	14,250	7,783	15,978	−988	−792	2,336	4,102	−196	1,582	2,338	14,147
Mozambique	229	1,184	996	1,776	−97	−166	448	242	−415	−516	232	1,009
Myanmar[d]	319	2,810	603	2,288	−192	−602	39	129	−436	50	410	647
Namibia	1,220	1,621	1,584	1,975	37	226	354	465	28	337	50	325
Nepal	422	1,066	834	1,947	14	−20	109	1,072	−289	171	354	1,286
Netherlands	159,304	317,413	147,652	291,954	−620	−1,244	−2,943	−7,813	8,089	16,403	34,401	21,441
New Zealand	11,683	23,277	11,699	22,866	−1,576	−3,896	138	145	−1,453	−3,339	4,129	4,878
Nicaragua	392	1,298	682	2,393	−217	−203	202	519	−305	−780	166	508
Niger	533	..	728	..	−54	..	14	..	−236	..	226	114
Nigeria	14,550	..	6,909	..	−2,738	..	85	..	4,988	..	4,129	7,415
Norway	47,078	90,739	38,910	60,741	−2,700	1,288	−1,476	−2,960	3,992	28,326	15,788	37,712
Oman	5,577	12,127	3,342	8,145	−254	−863	−874	−1,672	1,106	1,446	1,784	3,594
Pakistan	6,835	14,837	10,205	15,272	−1,084	−2,225	2,794	6,233	−1,661	3,573	1,046	11,816
Panama	4,438	7,601	4,193	7,464	−255	−820	219	241	209	−442	344	1,011
Papua New Guinea	1,381	2,458	1,509	1,817	−103	−458	156	13	−76	286	427	520
Paraguay	2,514	2,850	2,169	2,869	2	0	43	165	390	146	675	983
Peru	4,120	10,664	4,087	10,864	−1,733	−2,082	281	1,221	−1,419	−1,061	1,891	10,242
Philippines	11,430	37,812	13,967	40,292	−872	5,215	714	612	−2,695	3,347	2,036	16,886
Poland	19,037	72,181	15,095	77,379	−3,386	−3,639	2,511	4,234	3,067	−4,603	4,674	33,959
Portugal	21,554	44,623	27,146	54,049	−96	−2,418	5,507	3,408	−181	−8,437	20,579	12,813
Puerto Rico	..	..	..	..	..	..	..	..	..	..	..	..

4.15 | Balance of payments current account

	Goods and services				Net income		Net current transfers		Current account balance		Total reserves[a]	
	Exports		Imports		$ millions		$ millions		$ millions		$ millions	
	1990	2003	1990	2003	1990	2003	1990	2003	1990	2003	1990	2003
Romania	6,380	20,646	9,901	25,113	161	−705	106	1,861	−3,254	−3,311	1,374	9,449
Russian Federation	..	151,959	..	102,558	..	−13,171	..	−385	..	35,845	..	78,409
Rwanda	143	143	354	465	−16	−24	143	153	−85	−192	44	215
Saudi Arabia	47,445	100,715	43,939	54,713	7,979	−1,285	−15,637	−14,903	−4,152	29,815	13,437	24,538
Senegal	1,453	1,854	1,840	2,726	−129	−20	153	459	−363	−433	22	795
Serbia and Montenegro	..	3,970	..	8,675	..	−237	..	2,821	..	−2,121	..	..
Sierra Leone	210	177	215	404	−71	−15	7	163	−69	−80	5	67
Singapore	67,489	188,515	64,953	158,059	1,006	−1,126	−421	−1,144	3,122	28,187	27,748	95,746
Slovak Republic	..	25,241	..	25,649	..	−119	..	245	..	−282	..	12,149
Slovenia	7,900	15,709	6,930	15,727	−38	−188	46	108	978	−99	112	8,598
Somalia	..	..	..	..	..	..	..	..	..	..	..	..
South Africa	27,742	45,304	21,016	42,556	−4,271	−3,385	−321	−819	2,134	−1,456	2,583	8,154
Spain	83,595	236,426	100,870	248,427	−3,533	−11,919	2,799	244	−18,009	−23,676	57,238	26,809
Sri Lanka	2,293	6,541	2,965	7,714	−167	−192	541	1,234	−298	−131	447	2,265
Sudan	499	2,579	877	3,366	−136	−869	141	718	−372	−939	11	848
Swaziland	658	1,500	768	1,682	59	47	102	52	51	−83	216	278
Sweden	70,560	132,733	70,490	111,918	−4,473	297	−1,936	1,732	−6,339	22,844	20,324	22,169
Switzerland	97,033	150,391	96,389	127,757	7,878	26,663	−2,398	−5,166	6,124	44,131	61,284	69,563
Syrian Arab Republic	5,030	7,093	2,955	6,236	−401	−857	88	752	1,762	752	..	..
Tajikistan	185	782	238	1,033	0	−89	..	299	−53	−41	..	118
Tanzania	538	1,691	1,474	2,679	−185	−12	562	29	−559	−971	193	2,038
Thailand	29,229	93,882	35,870	85,078	−853	−1,792	213	941	−7,281	7,953	14,258	42,162
Togo	663	673	847	901	−32	−9	132	91	−84	−140	358	182
Trinidad and Tobago	2,289	5,877	1,427	4,230	−397	−362	−6	66	459	1,351	513	2,477
Tunisia	5,203	10,964	6,039	11,909	−455	−1,093	828	1,307	−463	−730	867	3,036
Turkey	21,042	70,292	25,524	73,797	−2,508	−5,427	4,365	1,027	−2,625	−7,905	7,626	35,549
Turkmenistan	1,238	3,725	857	3,243	0	−81	66	42	447	444	..	..
Uganda	178	858	686	1,765	−48	−176	293	766	−263	−316	44	1,080
Ukraine	..	28,953	..	27,665	..	−581	..	2,184	..	2,891	469	6,938
United Arab Emirates	..	..	..	..	..	..	..	..	..	..	4,891	15,088
United Kingdom	239,226	457,090	264,090	506,919	−5,154	35,771	−8,794	−14,587	−38,811	−28,645	43,146	46,052
United States	535,260	1,020,503	616,120	1,517,010	28,560	33,281	−26,660	−67,439	−78,960		173,094	184,024
Uruguay	2,158	3,051	1,659	2,707	−321	−364	8	72	186	52	1,446	2,087
Uzbekistan	..	3,775	..	3,096	−11	−116	2	319	−236	882	..	..
Venezuela, RB	18,806	27,732	9,451	13,828	−774	−2,387	−302	7	8,279	11,524	12,733	20,821
Vietnam	..	23,358	..	26,839	..	−853	..	1,921	..	−604	..	6,224
West Bank and Gaza	..	..	..	..	..	..	..	..	..	..	..	..
Yemen, Rep.	1,490	4,252	2,170	4,561	−372	−909	1,790	1,367	739	149	441	5,008
Zambia	1,360	1,327	1,897	1,948	−437	−91	380	..	−594	..	201	248
Zimbabwe	2,012	..	2,001	..	−263	..	112	..	−140	..	295	132
World	**4,299,355 t**	**9,272,788 t**	**4,313,730 t**	**9,230,166 t**								
Low income	88,118	241,166	105,757	257,272								
Middle income	664,641	2,138,308	621,046	1,954,183								
Lower middle income	388,908	1,345,995	383,680	1,243,368								
Upper middle income	273,405	792,750	237,198	711,454								
Low & middle income	753,769	2,377,574	727,891	2,209,363								
East Asia & Pacific	167,124	838,017	165,466	765,621								
Europe & Central Asia	..	574,412	..	562,394								
Latin America & Carib.	169,543	440,607	145,473	412,559								
Middle East & N. Africa	131,008	263,526	134,516	200,983								
South Asia	34,799	121,654	47,773	133,383								
Sub-Saharan Africa	77,723	135,481	71,959	134,433								
High income	3,538,257	6,893,753	3,570,269	7,019,221								
Europe EMU	1,537,105	2,970,780	1,496,703	2,794,473								

a. International reserves including gold valued at London gold price. b. Includes Luxembourg. c. Excludes Luxembourg. d. Data are for fiscal years.

Balance of payments current account

About the data

The balance of payments records an economy's transactions with the rest of the world. Balance of payments accounts are divided into two groups: the current account, which records transactions in goods, services, income, and current transfers, and the capital and financial account, which records capital transfers, acquisition or disposal of nonproduced, nonfinancial assets, and transactions in financial assets and liabilities. The table presents data from the current account with the addition of gross international reserves.

The balance of payments is a double-entry accounting system that shows all flows of goods and services into and out of an economy; all transfers that are the counterpart of real resources or financial claims provided to or by the rest of the world without a quid pro quo, such as donations and grants; and all changes in residents' claims on and liabilities to nonresidents that arise from economic transactions. All transactions are recorded twice—once as a credit and once as a debit. In principle the net balance should be zero, but in practice the accounts often do not balance. In these cases a balancing item, net errors and omissions, is included.

Discrepancies may arise in the balance of payments because there is no single source for balance of payments data and therefore no way to ensure that the data are fully consistent. Sources include customs data, monetary accounts of the banking system, external debt records, information provided by enterprises, surveys to estimate service transactions, and foreign exchange records. Differences in collection methods—such as in timing, definitions of residence and ownership, and the exchange rate used to value transactions—contribute to net errors and omissions. In addition, smuggling and other illegal or quasi-legal transactions may be unrecorded or misrecorded. For further discussion of issues relating to the recording of data on trade in goods and services, see About the data for tables 4.4–4.8.

The concepts and definitions underlying the data in the table are based on the fifth edition of the International Monetary Fund's (IMF) Balance of Payments Manual (1993). The fifth edition redefined as capital transfers some transactions previously included in the current account, such as debt forgiveness, migrants' capital transfers, and foreign aid to acquire capital goods. Thus the current account balance now reflects more accurately net current transfer receipts in addition to transactions in goods, services (previously nonfactor services), and income (previously factor income). Many countries maintain their data collection systems according to the fourth edition. Where necessary, the IMF converts data reported in such systems to conform to the fifth edition (see Primary data documentation). Values are in U.S. dollars converted at market exchange rates.

The data in this table come from the IMF's Balance of Payments and International Financial Statistics databases, supplemented by estimates by World Bank staff for countries for which the IMF does not collect balance of payments statistics. In addition, World Bank staff make estimates of missing data for up to three years prior to the current year.

Definitions

• **Exports and imports of goods and services** comprise all transactions between residents of an economy and the rest of the world involving a change in ownership of general merchandise, goods sent for processing and repairs, nonmonetary gold, and services. • **Net income** refers to receipts and payments of employee compensation for nonresident workers, and investment income (receipts and payments on direct investment, portfolio investment, and other investments and receipts on reserve assets). Income derived from the use of intangible assets is recorded under business services. • **Net current transfers** are recorded in the balance of payments whenever an economy provides or receives goods, services, income, or financial items without a quid pro quo. All transfers not considered to be capital are current. • **Current account balance** is the sum of net exports of goods and services, net income, and net current transfers. • **Total reserves** comprise holdings of monetary gold, special drawing rights, reserves of IMF members held by the IMF, and holdings of foreign exchange under the control of monetary authorities. The gold component of these reserves is valued at year-end (31 December) London prices ($385.00 an ounce in 1990, and $417.25 an ounce in 2003).

4.15a

The 15 economies with the largest current account surplus and the 15 with the largest deficit—in 2002

Country	$ billons	% of GDP	Country	$ billons	% of GDP
Japan	136	3.2	United States	−531	4.8
Germany	55	2.3	Australia	−30	5.8
China	46	3.2	United Kingdom	−30	1.7
Switzerland	44	13.6	Spain	−24	2.8
Russian Federation	36	8.3	Italy	−21	1.4
Saudi Arabia	30	13.8	Greece	−11	6.5
Taiwan, China	29	10.2	Mexico	−9	1.4
Norway	28	12.8	Portugal	−8	5.7
Singapore	28	30.9	Turkey	−8	3.3
Sweden	23	7.6	Hungary	−7	8.9
Canada	17	2.0	Czech Republic	−6	6.3
Hong Kong, China	17	10.7	Poland	−5	2.2
Netherlands	16	3.2	Lebanon	−3	17.8
Malaysia	13	12.9	New Zealand	−3	4.2
Korea, Rep.	12	2.0	Romania	−3	5.8

Source: International Monetary Fund, Balance of Payments data files.

Data sources

More information about the design and compilation of the balance of payments can be found in the IMF's Balance of Payments Manual, fifth edition (1993), Balance of Payments Textbook (1996a), and Balance of Payments Compilation Guide (1995). The balance of payments data are published in the IMF's Balance of Payments Statistics Yearbook and International Financial Statistics. The World Bank exchanges data with the IMF through electronic files that in most cases are more timely and cover a longer period than the published sources. The IMF's International Financial Statistics and Balance of Payments databases are available on CD-ROM.

	Total external debt		Long-term debt		Public and publicly guaranteed debt				Private nonguaranteed external debt		Use of IMF credit	
							IBRD loans and IDA credits					
	$ millions		$ millions		Total		$ millions		$ millions		$ millions	
	1990	2003	1990	2003	1990	2003	1990	2003	1990	2003	1990	2003
Afghanistan	5,086	..	5,046	..	5,046	..	0	..	0	..	0	..
Albania	..	1,482	..	1,242	..	1,230	..	583	..	12	..	90
Algeria	28,149	23,386	26,688	22,253	26,688	21,741	1,208	1,056	0	512	670	988
Angola	8,594	9,698	7,605	8,576	7,605	8,576	0	292	0	0	0	0
Argentina	62,233	166,207	48,676	127,687	46,876	99,300	2,609	7,508	1,800	28,387	3,083	15,523
Armenia	..	1,127	..	899	..	875	..	669	..	24	..	215
Australia	..	..	..	..	..	..	..	..	..	..	..	..
Austria	..	..	..	..	..	..	..	..	..	..	..	..
Azerbaijan	..	1,680	..	1,208	..	1,132	..	422	..	76	..	259
Bangladesh	12,439	18,778	11,658	18,088	11,658	18,088	4,159	8,069	0	0	626	74
Belarus	..	2,692	..	691	..	678	..	84	..	13	..	26
Belgium	..	..	..	..	..	..	..	..	..	..	..	..
Benin	1,292	1,828	1,218	1,726	1,218	1,726	326	730	0	0	18	73
Bolivia	4,275	5,684	3,864	5,289	3,687	4,258	587	1,571	177	1,031	257	279
Bosnia and Herzegovina	..	2,920	..	2,674	..	2,629	..	1,223	..	45	..	134
Botswana	553	514	547	485	547	485	169	13	0	0	0	0
Brazil	119,965	235,431	94,429	187,514	87,758	94,985	8,427	8,588	6,671	92,529	1,821	28,317
Bulgaria	..	13,289	..	9,439	..	7,749	..	1,266	..	1,690	..	1,188
Burkina Faso	834	1,844	750	1,652	750	1,652	282	861	0	0	0	125
Burundi	907	1,310	851	1,234	851	1,234	398	732	0	0	43	29
Cambodia	1,845	3,139	1,683	2,814	1,683	2,814	0	400	0	0	27	104
Cameroon	6,657	9,189	5,577	8,497	5,347	7,882	871	1,090	230	615	121	347
Canada	..	..	..	..	..	..	..	..	..	..	..	..
Central African Republic	698	1,328	624	917	624	917	265	453	0	0	37	36
Chad	528	1,499	468	1,371	468	1,371	186	804	0	0	31	106
Chile	19,226	43,231	14,687	35,727	10,425	8,053	1,874	427	4,263	27,674	1,156	0
China	55,301	193,567	45,515	120,600	45,515	85,570	5,881	20,971	0	35,030	469	0
Hong Kong, China	..	..	..	..	..	..	..	..	..	..	..	..
Colombia	17,222	32,979	15,784	29,423	14,671	22,816	3,874	3,246	1,113	6,607	0	0
Congo, Dem. Rep.	10,259	11,170	8,994	10,077	8,994	10,077	1,161	1,771	0	0	521	703
Congo, Rep.	4,947	5,516	4,200	4,426	4,200	4,426	239	238	0	0	11	28
Costa Rica	3,756	5,424	3,367	3,797	3,063	3,622	412	81	304	175	11	0
Côte d'Ivoire	17,251	12,187	13,223	10,844	10,665	9,701	1,920	2,267	2,558	1,144	431	425
Croatia	..	23,452	..	19,174	..	10,062	..	777	..	9,112	..	0
Cuba	..	..	..	..	..	..	..	..	..	..	..	..
Czech Republic	..	34,630	..	20,654	..	8,558	..	66	..	12,096	..	0
Denmark	..	..	..	..	..	..	..	..	..	..	..	..
Dominican Republic	4,372	6,291	3,518	5,077	3,419	5,077	258	362	99	0	72	130
Ecuador	12,107	16,864	10,029	14,702	9,865	11,371	848	906	164	3,331	265	390
Egypt, Arab Rep.	33,017	31,383	28,439	27,581	27,439	27,266	2,401	1,925	1,000	316	125	0
El Salvador	2,149	7,080	1,938	5,321	1,913	5,213	164	386	26	108	0	0
Eritrea	..	635	..	605	..	605	..	301	..	0	..	0
Estonia	..	6,972	..	4,530	..	560	..	49	..	3,970	..	0
Ethiopia	8,630	7,151	8,479	6,906	8,479	6,906	851	3,179	0	0	6	157
Finland	..	..	..	..	..	..	..	..	..	..	..	..
France	..	..	..	..	..	..	..	..	..	..	..	..
Gabon	3,983	3,792	3,150	3,395	3,150	3,395	69	49	0	0	140	59
Gambia, The	369	629	308	561	308	561	102	220	0	0	45	35
Georgia	..	1,935	..	1,608	..	1,564	..	583	..	44	..	289
Germany	..	..	..	..	..	..	..	..	..	..	..	..
Ghana	3,837	7,957	2,772	6,805	2,740	6,804	1,423	3,954	33	1	745	453
Greece	..	..	..	..	..	..	..	..	..	..	..	..
Guatemala	3,080	4,981	2,605	3,724	2,478	3,639	293	428	127	86	67	0
Guinea	2,476	3,457	2,253	3,154	2,253	3,154	420	1,212	0	0	52	136
Guinea-Bissau	692	745	630	712	630	712	146	267	0	0	5	21
Haiti	910	1,308	772	1,173	772	1,173	324	518	0	0	38	18

	Total external debt		Long-term debt		Public and publicly guaranteed debt				Private nonguaranteed external debt		Use of IMF credit	
					\$ millions							
					Total		IBRD loans and IDA credits					
	\$ millions		\$ millions						\$ millions		\$ millions	
	1990	2003	1990	2003	1990	2003	1990	2003	1990	2003	1990	2003
Honduras	3,718	5,641	3,487	5,005	3,420	4,595	635	1,228	66	411	32	172
Hungary	21,202	45,785	17,931	36,769	17,931	14,751	1,512	253	0	22,017	330	0
India	83,628	113,467	72,462	108,731	70,974	92,822	20,996	26,760	1,488	15,909	2,623	0
Indonesia	69,872	134,389	58,242	101,205	47,982	73,412	10,385	10,659	10,261	27,793	494	10,276
Iran, Islamic Rep.	9,020	11,601	1,797	8,397	1,797	8,209	86	350	0	188	0	0
Iraq	..	..	..	..	..	..	..	..	..	..	..	..
Ireland	..	..	..	..	..	..	..	..	..	..	..	..
Israel	..	..	..	..	..	..	..	..	..	..	..	..
Italy	..	..	..	..	..	..	..	..	..	..	..	..
Jamaica	4,746	5,584	4,043	4,593	4,009	4,516	672	476	34	77	357	9
Japan	..	..	..	..	..	..	..	..	..	..	..	..
Jordan	8,333	8,337	7,202	7,173	7,202	7,173	593	1,067	0	0	94	421
Kazakhstan	..	22,835	..	20,002	..	3,546	..	1,265	..	16,457	..	0
Kenya	7,055	6,766	5,639	5,728	4,759	5,704	2,056	2,742	880	24	482	112
Korea, Dem. Rep.	..	..	..	..	..	..	..	..	..	..	..	..
Korea, Rep.	..	..	..	..	..	..	..	..	..	..	..	..
Kuwait	..	..	..	..	..	..	..	..	..	..	..	..
Kyrgyz Republic	..	2,021	..	1,780	..	1,588	..	530	..	192	..	202
Lao PDR	1,768	2,846	1,758	2,801	1,758	2,801	131	560	0	0	8	44
Latvia	..	8,803	..	3,166	..	1,238	..	185	..	1,928	..	6
Lebanon	1,779	18,598	358	15,474	358	14,778	34	362	0	696	0	0
Lesotho	396	706	378	676	378	676	112	266	0	0	15	27
Liberia	1,849	2,568	1,116	1,127	1,116	1,127	248	260	0	0	322	332
Libya	..	..	..	..	..	..	..	..	..	..	..	..
Lithuania	..	8,342	..	4,793	..	2,107	..	280	..	2,687	..	45
Macedonia, FYR	..	1,837	..	1,713	..	1,438	..	531	..	275	..	68
Madagascar	3,704	4,958	3,335	4,622	3,335	4,622	797	1,975	0	0	144	172
Malawi	1,558	3,134	1,385	2,960	1,382	2,960	854	1,959	3	0	115	102
Malaysia	15,328	49,074	13,422	40,249	11,592	25,517	1,102	708	1,830	14,732	0	0
Mali	2,468	3,129	2,337	2,910	2,337	2,910	498	1,322	0	0	69	169
Mauritania	2,113	2,360	1,806	2,084	1,806	2,084	264	634	0	0	70	104
Mauritius	984	2,550	910	1,000	762	928	195	97	148	72	22	0
Mexico	104,442	140,004	81,809	130,826	75,974	77,473	11,030	10,717	5,835	53,353	6,551	0
Moldova	..	1,901	..	1,218	..	848	..	365	..	369	..	143
Mongolia	..	1,472	..	1,138	..	1,138	..	227	..	..	..	50
Morocco	25,017	18,795	23,860	17,542	23,660	15,224	3,138	2,741	200	2,318	750	0
Mozambique	4,650	4,930	4,231	4,381	4,211	2,992	268	1,232	19	1,389	74	209
Myanmar	4,695	7,318	4,466	5,857	4,466	5,857	716	762	0	0	0	0
Namibia	..	..	..	..	..	..	..	..	..	..	..	..
Nepal	1,640	3,253	1,572	3,176	1,572	3,176	668	1,388	0	0	44	11
Netherlands	..	..	..	..	..	..	..	..	..	..	..	..
New Zealand	..	..	..	..	..	..	..	..	..	..	..	..
Nicaragua	10,745	6,915	8,313	6,107	8,313	5,898	299	998	0	209	0	213
Niger	1,726	2,116	1,487	1,945	1,226	1,900	461	1,007	261	46	85	131
Nigeria	33,439	34,963	31,935	31,563	31,545	31,563	3,321	1,988	391	0	0	0
Norway	..	..	..	..	..	..	..	..	..	..	..	..
Oman	2,736	3,886	2,400	2,642	2,400	1,480	52	0	0	1,161	0	0
Pakistan	20,663	36,345	16,643	32,992	16,506	31,373	3,922	8,564	138	1,619	836	2,108
Panama	6,506	8,770	3,855	8,286	3,855	6,563	462	270	0	1,723	272	45
Papua New Guinea	2,594	2,463	2,461	2,231	1,523	1,504	349	355	938	727	61	122
Paraguay	2,105	3,210	1,732	2,658	1,713	2,224	320	280	19	434	0	0
Peru	20,064	29,857	13,959	27,193	13,629	22,072	1,188	2,789	330	5,121	755	139
Philippines	30,580	62,663	25,241	55,287	24,040	36,221	4,044	3,660	1,201	19,066	912	1,197
Poland	49,364	95,219	39,261	75,719	39,261	34,964	55	2,453	0	40,755	509	0
Portugal	..	..	..	..	..	..	..	..	..	..	..	..
Puerto Rico	..	..	..	..	..	..	..	..	..	..	..	..

	Total external debt		Long-term debt		Public and publicly guaranteed debt				Private nonguaranteed external debt		Use of IMF credit	
					Total		IBRD loans and IDA credits					
	$ millions		$ millions		$ millions				$ millions		$ millions	
	1990	2003	1990	2003	1990	2003	1990	2003	1990	2003	1990	2003
Romania	1,140	21,280	230	19,320	223	11,730	0	2,296	7	7,590	0	595
Russian Federation	..	175,257	..	139,386	..	98,264	..	6,289	..	41,121	..	5,069
Rwanda	712	1,540	664	1,418	664	1,418	340	909	0	0	0	92
Saudi Arabia	..	..	..	..	..	..	..	..	..	..	..	..
Senegal	3,739	4,419	3,003	4,023	2,943	3,983	835	1,806	60	40	314	240
Serbia and Montenegro[a]	..	14,885	..	11,227	..	9,680	..	2,889	..	1,548	..	917
Sierra Leone	1,196	1,612	940	1,420	940	1,420	92	542	0	0	108	169
Singapore	..	..	..	..	..	..	..	..	..	..	..	..
Slovak Republic	..	18,379	..	10,344	..	4,508	..	293	..	5,836	..	0
Slovenia	..	..	..	..	..	..	..	..	..	..	..	..
Somalia	2,370	2,838	1,926	1,936	1,926	1,936	419	431	0	0	159	166
South Africa	..	27,807	..	20,448	..	9,120	0	16	..	11,328	0	0
Spain	..	..	..	..	..	..	..	..	..	..	..	..
Sri Lanka	5,863	10,238	5,049	9,374	4,947	9,106	946	2,054	102	268	410	393
Sudan	14,762	17,496	9,651	10,066	9,155	9,570	1,048	1,262	496	496	956	599
Swaziland	243	400	238	346	238	346	44	19	0	0	0	0
Sweden	..	..	..	..	..	..	..	..	..	..	..	..
Switzerland	..	..	..	..	..	..	..	..	..	..	..	..
Syrian Arab Republic	17,259	21,566	15,108	15,848	15,108	15,848	523	30	0	0	0	0
Tajikistan	..	1,166	..	984	..	926	..	228	..	59	..	100
Tanzania	6,454	7,516	5,794	6,248	5,782	6,233	1,493	3,477	12	16	140	437
Thailand	28,095	51,793	19,771	40,889	12,460	17,764	2,530	2,178	7,311	23,125	1	0
Togo	1,281	1,707	1,081	1,489	1,081	1,489	398	686	0	0	87	42
Trinidad and Tobago	2,512	2,751	2,055	1,861	1,782	1,751	41	85	273	110	329	0
Tunisia	7,688	15,502	6,878	14,690	6,660	13,134	1,406	1,812	218	1,556	176	0
Turkey	49,424	145,662	39,924	98,558	38,870	64,758	6,429	5,297	1,054	33,799	0	24,092
Turkmenistan	..	..	..	..	..	..	..	30	..	..	..	0
Uganda	2,583	4,553	2,160	4,168	2,160	4,168	969	3,061	0	0	282	236
Ukraine	..	16,309	..	13,243	..	8,893	..	2,271	..	4,350	..	1,836
United Arab Emirates	..	..	..	..	..	..	..	..	..	..	..	..
United Kingdom	..	..	..	..	..	..	..	..	..	..	..	..
United States	..	..	..	..	..	..	..	..	..	..	..	..
Uruguay	4,415	11,764	3,114	7,903	3,045	7,430	359	722	69	473	101	2,416
Uzbekistan	..	5,006	..	4,742	..	4,250	..	299	..	492	..	43
Venezuela, RB	33,171	34,851	28,159	30,506	24,509	24,491	974	485	3,650	6,016	3,012	0
Vietnam	23,270	15,817	21,378	14,189	21,378	14,189	59	2,472	0	0	112	339
West Bank and Gaza	..	..	..	..	..	..	..	..	..	..	..	..
Yemen, Rep.	6,352	5,377	5,160	4,747	5,160	4,747	602	1,568	0	0	0	401
Zambia	6,916	6,425	4,554	5,439	4,552	5,043	813	2,409	2	396	949	859
Zimbabwe	3,279	4,445	2,681	3,425	2,496	3,367	449	946	185	58	7	302
World	.. s	.. s	.. s	.. s	.. s	.. s	.. s	.. s	.. s	.. s	.. s	.. s
Low income	341,580	424,472	293,109	379,860	285,416	356,039	56,677	101,676	7,692	23,821	10,823	11,149
Middle income[b]	995,453	2,129,666	806,118	1,665,355	753,803	1,094,050	80,643	121,202	52,315	571,305	23,828	95,716
Lower middle income	653,470	1,392,764	535,787	1,076,964	501,654	738,632	59,612	95,160	34,132	338,332	8,305	77,611
Upper middle income[b]	341,983	736,902	270,331	588,391	252,149	355,418	21,030	26,043	18,182	232,973	15,523	18,105
Low & middle income[b]	1,337,033	2,554,138	1,099,227	2,045,215	1,039,220	1,450,089	137,319	222,879	60,007	595,126	34,652	106,865
East Asia & Pacific	234,081	525,535	194,622	387,943	172,986	267,440	25,306	43,087	21,635	120,503	2,085	12,131
Europe & Central Asia	217,224	675,998	176,378	505,912	171,457	299,311	10,429	31,477	4,921	206,601	1,305	35,315
Latin America & Carib.	444,900	779,632	352,971	648,564	327,942	420,708	35,877	42,461	25,029	227,856	18,298	47,758
Middle East & N. Africa	139,555	158,827	118,044	136,713	116,626	129,966	10,074	11,023	1,418	6,747	1,815	1,831
South Asia	124,396	182,785	107,527	173,031	105,800	155,235	30,717	46,942	1,727	17,796	4,537	2,586
Sub-Saharan Africa	176,878	231,360	149,684	193,052	144,408	177,429	24,916	47,890	5,276	15,623	6,612	7,244
High income												
Europe EMU												

a. Data for 1990 refer to the former Socialist Federal Republic of Yugoslavia. Data for 2003 are estimates and reflect borrowings by the former Socialist Federal Republic of Yugoslavia that are not yet allocated to the successor republics. b. Includes data for Gibraltar not included in other tables.

Data on the external debt of developing countries are gathered by the World Bank through its Debtor Reporting System. World Bank staff calculate the indebtedness of these countries using loan-by-loan reports submitted by them on long-term public and publicly guaranteed borrowing, along with information on short-term debt collected by the countries or collected from creditors through the reporting systems of the Bank for International Settlements and the Organisation for Economic Co-operation and Development. These data are supplemented by information on loans and credits from major multilateral banks, loan statements from official lending agencies in major creditor countries, and estimates by World Bank and International Monetary Fund (IMF) staff. In addition, the table includes data on private nonguaranteed debt for 80 countries either reported to the World Bank or estimated by its staff.

The coverage, quality, and timeliness of debt data vary across countries. Coverage varies for both debt instruments and borrowers. With the widening spectrum of debt instruments and investors and the expansion of private nonguaranteed borrowing, comprehensive coverage of long-term external debt becomes more complex. Reporting countries differ in their capacity to monitor debt, especially private nonguaranteed debt. Even data on public and publicly guaranteed debt are affected by coverage and accuracy in reporting—again because of monitoring capacity and sometimes because of unwillingness to provide information. A key part often underreported is military debt.

Because debt data are normally reported in the currency of repayment, they have to be converted into U.S. dollars to produce summary tables. Stock figures (amount of debt outstanding) are converted using end-of-period exchange rates, as published in the IMF's *International Financial Statistics* (line ae). Flow figures are converted at annual average exchange rates (line rf). Projected debt service is converted using end-of-period exchange rates. Debt repayable in multiple currencies, goods, or services and debt with a provision for maintenance of the value of the currency of repayment are shown at book value.

Because flow data are converted at annual average exchange rates and stock data at end-of-period exchange rates, year-to-year changes in debt outstanding and disbursed are sometimes not equal to net flows (disbursements less principal repayments); similarly, changes in debt outstanding, including undisbursed debt, differ from commitments less repayments. Discrepancies are particularly significant when exchange rates have moved sharply during the year. Cancellations and reschedulings of other liabilities into long-term public debt also contribute to the differences.

Variations in reporting rescheduled debt also affect cross-country comparability. For example, rescheduling under the auspices of the Paris Club of official creditors may be subject to lags between the completion of the general rescheduling agreement and the completion of the specific, bilateral agreements that define the terms of the rescheduled debt. Other areas of inconsistency include country treatment of arrears and of nonresident national deposits denominated in foreign currency.

• **Total external debt** is debt owed to nonresidents repayable in foreign currency, goods, or services. It is the sum of public, publicly guaranteed, and private nonguaranteed long-term debt, use of IMF credit, and short-term debt. Short-term debt includes all debt having an original maturity of one year or less and interest in arrears on long-term debt. • **Long-term debt** is debt that has an original or extended maturity of more than one year. It has three components: public, publicly guaranteed, and private nonguaranteed debt. • **Public and publicly guaranteed debt** comprises the long-term external obligations of public debtors, including the national government and political subdivisions (or an agency of either) and autonomous public bodies, and the external obligations of private debtors that are guaranteed for repayment by a public entity. • **IBRD loans and IDA credits** are extended by the World Bank. The International Bank for Reconstruction and Development (IBRD) lends at market rates. The International Development Association (IDA) provides credits at concessional rates. • **Private nonguaranteed external debt** consists of the long-term external obligations of private debtors that are not guaranteed for repayment by a public entity. • **Use of IMF credit** denotes repurchase obligations to the IMF for all uses of IMF resources (excluding those resulting from drawings on the reserve tranche). These obligations, shown for the end of the year specified, comprise purchases outstanding under the credit tranches (including enlarged access resources) and all special facilities (the buffer stock, compensatory financing, extended fund, and oil facilities), trust fund loans, and operations under the structural adjustment and enhanced structural adjustment facilities.

4.16a

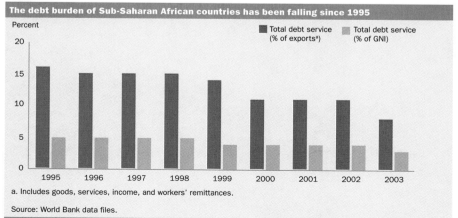

The debt burden of Sub-Saharan African countries has been falling since 1995

Percent

Legend:
- Total debt service (% of exports[a])
- Total debt service (% of GNI)

a. Includes goods, services, income, and workers' remittances.

Source: World Bank data files.

The main sources of external debt information are reports to the World Bank through its Debtor Reporting System from member countries that have received IBRD loans or IDA credits. Additional information has been drawn from the files of the World Bank and the IMF. Summary tables of the external debt of developing countries are published annually in the World Bank's *Global Development Finance* and on its *Global Development Finance* CD-ROM.

External debt management

	Indebtedness classification[a]	Present value of debt		Public and publicly guaranteed debt service				Multilateral debt service		Short-term debt	
		% of GNI	% of exports of goods, services, and income	% of GNI		% of exports of goods, services, and income		% of public and publicly guaranteed		% of total debt	
	2003	2003	2003	1990	2003	1990	2003	1990	2003	1990	2003
Afghanistan	..	..	..	..	..	..	..	3.9	..	0.8	..
Albania	L	20	90	..	0.6	..	2.9	..	49.6	..	10.1
Algeria	L	40	..	14.3	5.9	63.3	..	5.0	20.6	2.8	0.6
Angola	S	102	117	3.4	12.4	7.1	14.8	2.2	0.7	11.5	11.6
Argentina	S	117	533	3.6	5.3	28.9	17.7	16.2	96.8	16.8	13.8
Armenia	L	29	86	..	2.3	..	6.1	..	38.3	..	1.2
Australia	..	..	..	..	..	..	..	..	..	..	..
Austria	..	..	..	..	..	..	..	..	..	..	..
Azerbaijan	L	23	49	..	1.6	..	3.4	..	19.1	..	12.7
Bangladesh	L	25	176	1.6	1.1	23.3	7.3	22.8	59.3	1.3	3.3
Belarus	L	18	27	..	0.9	..	1.4	..	27.1	..	73.4
Belgium	..	..	..	..	..	..	..	..	..	..	..
Benin	M	28[b]	..[b]	1.8	1.4	8.6	..	95.7	51.9	4.3	1.6
Bolivia	M	38[b]	166[b]	5.9	3.6	27.6	13.8	67.6	91.0	3.6	2.0
Bosnia and Herzegovina	L	37	108	..	1.4	..	4.2	..	61.5	..	3.9
Botswana	L	8	13	2.9	0.7	4.3	1.3	61.3	68.5	1.0	5.6
Brazil	S	54	330	1.3	4.3	15.7	23.4	43.5	23.1	19.8	8.3
Bulgaria	S	86	152	..	3.6	..	6.4	..	31.8	..	20.0
Burkina Faso	M	19[b]	202[b]	0.9	1.1	7.7	11.0	73.0	68.1	10.1	3.7
Burundi	S	150	2,182	3.6	4.9	40.7	62.9	51.1	85.3	1.5	3.6
Cambodia	M	70	112	2.6	0.3	..	0.4	..	67.9	7.3	7.1
Cameroon	M	53[b]	..[b]	3.0	2.7	12.6	..	43.5	31.5	14.4	3.8
Canada	..	..	..	..	..	..	..	..	..	..	..
Central African Republic	S	155	..	1.1	0.0	7.5	..	50.0	..	5.4	28.2
Chad	S	45[b]	..[b]	0.4	1.4	2.4	..	72.3	61.3	5.6	1.5
Chile	M	67	178	5.6	2.1	15.1	5.5	35.7	17.8	17.6	17.4
China	L	15	48	1.6	1.0	9.7	2.8	7.6	37.9	16.8	37.7
Hong Kong, China	..	..	..	..	..	..	..	..	..	..	..
Colombia	M	47	232	8.2	7.4	34.5	34.6	32.2	28.8	8.4	10.8
Congo, Dem. Rep.	S	150	..	1.6	2.6	..	..	49.6	66.8	7.2	3.5
Congo, Rep.	S	368	404	20.4	1.9	31.6	3.3	12.7	90.3	14.9	19.3
Costa Rica	L	36	77	7.9	4.5	20.7	8.9	36.1	31.0	10.0	30.0
Côte d'Ivoire	S	90	176	5.7	2.3	14.7	4.5	77.5	48.0	20.8	7.5
Croatia	S	102	193	..	4.4	..	7.9	..	9.4	..	18.2
Cuba	..	..	..	..	..	..	..	..	..	..	..
Czech Republic	L	48	69	..	2.1	..	3.0	..	14.0	..	40.4
Denmark	..	..	..	..	..	..	..	..	..	..	..
Dominican Republic	L	33	71	2.1	4.3	7.2	7.1	50.3	22.5	17.9	17.2
Ecuador	S	82	296	9.6	5.3	26.6	19.1	34.8	38.5	15.0	10.5
Egypt, Arab Rep.	L	31	152	5.9	2.7	23.2	11.0	18.7	28.7	13.5	12.1
El Salvador	M	55	198	3.7	3.2	17.7	11.7	60.2	49.9	9.8	24.8
Eritrea	S	47	333	..	1.2	..	13.0	..	56.0	..	4.6
Estonia	S	101	119	..	0.7	..	0.8	..	15.8	..	35.0
Ethiopia	M	24[b]	138[b]	2.3	1.2	33.1	6.2	14.5	65.3	1.7	1.2
Finland	..	..	..	..	..	..	..	..	..	..	..
France	..	..	..	..	..	..	..	..	..	..	..
Gabon	S	89	..	1.9	6.8	3.8	..	32.6	30.8	17.4	8.9
Gambia, The	S	90[b]	..[b]	10.4	5.2	17.9	..	25.4	46.9	4.3	5.2
Georgia	L	43	129	..	2.4	..	6.6	..	22.1	..	2.0
Germany	..	..	..	..	..	..	..	..	..	..	..
Ghana	L	38[b]	87[b]	3.3	2.7	20.1	6.4	30.7	30.5	8.3	8.8
Greece	..	..	..	..	..	..	..	..	..	..	..
Guatemala	L	21	115	2.2	1.7	10.4	9.8	36.8	56.4	13.3	25.2
Guinea	S	59[b]	238[b]	5.6	3.2	17.7	15.1	22.1	52.5	6.9	4.8
Guinea-Bissau	S	246[b]	736[b]	2.4	4.3	21.8	13.7	70.2	32.3	8.2	1.6
Haiti	L	29	214	0.5	1.2	4.4	7.6	69.2	94.6	11.1	8.9

External debt management | 4.17

	Indebtedness classification[a]	Present value of debt		Public and publicly guaranteed debt service				Multilateral debt service		Short-term debt	
		% of GNI	% of exports of goods, services, and income	% of GNI		% of exports of goods, services, and income		% of public and publicly guaranteed		% of total debt	
	2003	2003	2003	1990	2003	1990	2003	1990	2003	1990	2003
Honduras	M	54	134	10.8	2.7	29.1	6.8	90.7	84.0	5.4	8.2
Hungary	M	71	99	11.9	4.6	30.4	6.8	8.0	16.2	13.9	19.7
India	L	19	123	1.9	2.9	25.6	18.1	22.5	26.0	10.2	4.2
Indonesia	S	82	204	6.8	3.7	24.9	10.6	22.5	38.4	15.9	17.0
Iran, Islamic Rep.	L	8	30	0.2	1.1	1.3	3.5	30.4	6.6	80.1	27.6
Iraq	..	..	..	..	..	..	..	..	..	..	..
Ireland	..	..	..	..	..	..	..	..	..	..	..
Israel	..	..	..	..	..	..	..	..	..	..	..
Italy	..	..	..	..	..	..	..	..	..	..	..
Jamaica	M	80	172	11.6	10.4	20.7	20.9	38.6	23.8	7.3	17.6
Japan	..	..	..	..	..	..	..	..	..	..	..
Jordan	S	84	164	14.5	10.6	21.4	20.4	26.8	23.8	12.4	8.9
Kazakhstan	S	95	184	..	1.6	..	3.0	..	40.7	..	12.4
Kenya	M	43	162	6.3	3.5	22.7	13.9	44.7	28.6	13.2	13.7
Korea, Dem. Rep.	..	..	..	..	..	..	..	..	..	..	..
Korea, Rep.	..	..	..	..	..	..	..	..	..	..	..
Kuwait	..	..	..	..	..	..	..	..	..	..	..
Kyrgyz Republic	S	98	241	..	1.3	..	3.2	..	94.6	..	1.9
Lao PDR	S	91	356	1.0	1.9	8.0	8.4	53.6	66.8	0.1	0.0
Latvia	S	92	204	..	1.7	..	3.8	..	78.9	..	64.0
Lebanon	S	110	603	1.1	15.8	3.2	73.2	27.8	4.3	79.9	16.8
Lesotho	L	47	81	2.2	4.7	4.1	8.5	44.7	60.6	0.7	0.6
Liberia	S	646	1,942	..	..	..	..	100.0	..	22.2	43.2
Libya	..	..	..	..	..	..	..	..	..	..	..
Lithuania	M	58	106	..	5.8	..	10.5	..	7.9	..	42.0
Macedonia, FYR	L	40	103	..	2.8	..	7.4	..	37.3	..	3.0
Madagascar	M	31[b]	138[b]	5.2	1.2	31.9	5.7	23.7	57.6	6.1	3.3
Malawi	S	108[b]	394[b]	5.5	1.6	22.4	5.7	38.2	96.2	3.7	2.3
Malaysia	M	56	45	8.7	5.8	10.6	4.7	9.9	4.0	12.4	18.0
Mali	L	42[b]	..[b]	1.8	1.3	9.7	1.3	54.3	72.8	2.5	1.6
Mauritania	M	73[b]	..[b]	10.9	3.8	24.8	..	73.8	58.0	11.2	7.3
Mauritius	M	52	81	3.4	2.9	4.5	4.7	51.6	24.8	5.3	60.8
Mexico	L	25	88	3.1	3.3	15.1	11.3	26.0	15.3	15.4	6.6
Moldova	M	95	161	..	2.9	..	4.8	..	71.5	..	28.4
Mongolia	M	95	149	..	22.2	..	33.4	..	2.6	..	19.4
Morocco	L	47	136	5.9	8.7	23.1	25.7	39.8	41.0	1.6	6.7
Mozambique	L	38[b]	121[b]	2.2	1.3	17.2	4.2	30.6	48.2	7.4	6.9
Myanmar	S	..	192	..	..	17.7	3.8	43.6	2.3	4.9	20.0
Namibia	..	..	..	..	..	..	..	..	..	..	..
Nepal	L	38	193	1.5	1.9	12.1	9.7	36.8	67.5	1.5	2.0
Netherlands	..	..	..	..	..	..	..	..	..	..	..
New Zealand	..	..	..	..	..	..	..	..	..	..	..
Nicaragua	L	40	129	1.0	3.4	2.4	10.3	21.1	25.0	22.6	8.6
Niger	M	26[b]	..[b]	0.7	0.7	3.1	..	71.3	81.4	8.9	1.9
Nigeria	M	76	..	12.8	3.3	22.3	..	15.5	29.9	4.5	9.7
Norway	..	..	..	..	..	..	..	..	..	..	..
Oman	L	..	32	6.9	..	12.0	5.3	5.1	14.6	12.3	32.0
Pakistan	M	41	234	3.3	2.4	19.8	12.7	40.3	59.0	15.4	3.4
Panama	S	93	124	2.8	6.3	2.5	9.1	90.7	22.2	36.6	5.0
Papua New Guinea	M	80	106	8.7	6.3	18.2	7.0	23.0	42.2	2.8	4.5
Paraguay	M	51	112	5.6	3.3	11.5	6.6	35.9	67.9	17.7	17.2
Peru	S	60	335	0.7	3.7	4.1	19.8	28.8	36.2	26.7	8.5
Philippines	M	80	147	6.6	6.6	22.2	12.4	28.7	15.5	14.5	9.9
Poland	M	48	150	1.5	2.4	4.3	6.5	9.2	9.2	19.4	20.5
Portugal	..	..	..	..	..	..	..	..	..	..	..
Puerto Rico	..	..	..	..	..	..	..	..	..	..	..

	Indebtedness classification[a]	Present value of debt		Public and publicly guaranteed debt service				Multilateral debt service		Short-term debt	
		% of GNI	% of exports of goods, services, and income	% of GNI		% of exports of goods, services, and income		% of public and publicly guaranteed		% of total debt	
	2003	2003	2003	1990	2003	1990	2003	1990	2003	1990	2003
Romania	L	46	126	..	3.7	..	9.8	..	23.7	79.8	6.4
Russian Federation	M	52	135	..	2.7	..	7.1	..	8.1	..	17.6
Rwanda	S	57[b]	632[b]	0.6	1.1	10.2	12.8	60.7	47.6	6.6	1.9
Saudi Arabia	..	..	..	..	..	..	..	..	..	..	..
Senegal	L	36[b]	114[b]	3.8	3.0	13.8	9.6	39.8	35.7	11.3	3.5
Serbia and Montenegro	S	83	392	..	3.3	..	16.9	..	32.7	..	18.4
Sierra Leone	S	118[b]	697[b]	2.8	3.0	7.8	12.7	26.1	35.7	12.4	1.4
Singapore	..	..	..	..	..	..	..	..	..	..	..
Slovak Republic	M	70	90	..	5.5	..	6.9	..	6.8	..	43.7
Slovenia	..	..	..	..	..	..	..	..	..	..	..
Somalia	S	..	..	0.8	..	..	..	100.0	..	12.0	25.9
South Africa	L	23	69	..	1.3	..	4.3	..	0.7	..	26.5
Spain	..	..	..	..	..	..	..	..	..	..	..
Sri Lanka	M	51	133	3.6	2.7	11.9	7.2	13.8	22.0	6.9	4.6
Sudan	S	120	799	0.2	0.0	4.5	0.3	100.0	100.0	28.1	39.0
Swaziland	L	26	28	5.0	1.4	5.6	1.6	73.0	68.8	1.9	13.4
Sweden	..	..	..	..	..	..	..	..	..	..	..
Switzerland	..	..	..	..	..	..	..	..	..	..	..
Syrian Arab Republic	S	111	271	9.3	1.1	20.3	3.0	3.5	35.1	12.5	26.5
Tajikistan	S	77	127	..	3.0	..	5.7	..	31.2	..	7.0
Tanzania	L	22[b, c]	132[b, c]	3.4	0.7	25.1	4.1	52.7	64.4	8.1	11.1
Thailand	M	41	59	3.9	5.2	10.4	7.6	22.1	9.8	29.6	21.1
Togo	S	91	233	3.8	0.0	8.6	0.0	40.8	100.0	8.8	10.3
Trinidad and Tobago	L	34	59	7.3	2.1	14.6	3.6	4.7	47.5	5.1	32.3
Tunisia	M	75	155	10.3	6.3	23.0	13.7	26.0	47.3	8.3	5.2
Turkey	S	81	251	4.3	5.2	29.6	17.1	23.3	8.1	19.2	15.8
Turkmenistan	M	..	..	..	..	..	..	..	..	..	..
Uganda	M	33[b]	241[b]	2.0	0.9	47.1	6.4	37.4	86.3	5.4	3.3
Ukraine	L	37	64	..	2.8	..	4.7	..	22.0	..	7.5
United Arab Emirates	..	..	..	..	..	..	..	..	..	..	..
United Kingdom	..	..	..	..	..	..	..	..	..	..	..
United States	..	..	..	..	..	..	..	..	..	..	..
Uruguay	S	90	353	7.9	5.9	29.4	19.2	16.2	52.0	27.2	12.3
Uzbekistan	M	47	142	..	7.4	..	19.0	..	10.9	..	4.4
Venezuela, RB	M	42	139	8.8	9.0	19.4	25.3	1.6	9.3	6.0	12.5
Vietnam	L	39	67	2.4	1.8	..	3.0	3.4	5.5	7.7	8.2
West Bank and Gaza	..	..	..	..	..	..	..	..	..	..	..
Yemen, Rep.	L	40	95	2.3	1.5	7.1	3.4	51.0	56.1	18.8	4.3
Zambia	S	121	372	5.7	6.3	12.7	18.9	41.6	17.8	20.4	2.0
Zimbabwe	S	..	..	4.3	..	18.2	..	24.0	24.0	18.0	16.2
World				.. w	.. w	.. w	.. w	.. w	.. w	.. w	.. w
Low income				2.9	2.7	20.0	12.6	26.7	29.3	11.0	7.9
Middle income				3.5	3.2	15.0	8.4	19.5	22.9	16.6	17.3
Lower middle income				3.3	2.8	18.0	8.1	21.4	23.4	16.7	17.1
Upper middle income				3.9	4.0	11.6	8.9	15.8	21.8	16.4	17.7
Low & middle income				3.4	3.1	15.6	8.7	20.6	23.7	15.2	15.7
East Asia & Pacific				3.6	2.1	13.7	4.8	17.5	24.5	16.0	23.9
Europe & Central Asia				..	3.3	18.3	7.6	17.1	12.2	18.2	19.9
Latin America & Carib.				3.0	4.3	17.6	15.6	26.5	28.6	16.5	10.7
Middle East & N. Africa				4.2	..	12.5	..	10.8	24.8	14.1	12.8
South Asia				2.1	2.7	23.1	16.1	25.0	30.1	9.9	3.9
Sub-Saharan Africa				..	2.2	15.3	6.1	30.0	23.2	11.6	13.4
High income											
Europe EMU											

a. S = severely indebted, M = moderately indebted, L = less indebted. b. Data are from debt sustainability analyses undertaken as part of the Heavily Indebted Poor Countries (HIPC) Initiative. Present value estimates for these countries are for public and publicly guaranteed debt only. c. Data refer to mainland Tanzania only.

About the data

The indicators in the table measure the relative burden on developing countries of servicing external debt. The present value of external debt provides a measure of future debt service obligations that can be compared with the current value of such indicators as gross national income (GNI) and exports of goods and services. The table shows the present value of total debt service both as a percentage of GNI in 2003 and as a percentage of exports in 2003. The ratios compare total debt service obligations with the size of the economy and its ability to obtain foreign exchange through exports. The ratios shown here may differ from those published elsewhere because estimates of exports and GNI have been revised to incorporate data available as of February 1, 2005. Exports refer to exports of goods, services, and income. Workers' remittances are not included here, though they are included with income receipts in other World Bank publications such as *Global Development Finance*.

The present value of external debt is calculated by discounting the debt service (interest plus amortization) due on long-term external debt over the life of existing loans. Short-term debt is included at its face value. The data on debt are in U.S. dollars converted at official exchange rates (see *About the data* for table 4.16). The discount rate applied to long-term debt is determined by the currency of repayment of the loan and is based on reference rates for commercial interest established by the Organisation for Economic Co-operation and Development. Loans from the International Bank for Reconstruction and Development (IBRD) and credits from the International Development Association (IDA) are discounted using a special drawing rights (SDR) reference rate,

as are obligations to the International Monetary Fund (IMF). When the discount rate is greater than the interest rate of the loan, the present value is less than the nominal sum of future debt service obligations.

The ratios in the table are used to assess the sustainability of a country's debt service obligations, but there are no absolute rules that determine what values are too high. Empirical analysis of the experience of developing countries and their debt service performance has shown that debt service difficulties become increasingly likely when the ratio of the present value of debt to exports reaches 200 percent. Still, what constitutes a sustainable debt burden varies from one country to another. Countries with fast-growing economies and exports are likely to be able to sustain higher debt levels.

The World Bank classifies countries by their level of indebtedness for the purpose of developing debt management strategies. The most severely indebted countries may be eligible for debt relief under special programs, such as the HIPC Debt Initiative. Indebted countries may also apply to the Paris and London Clubs for renegotiation of obligations to public and private creditors. In 2003, countries with a present value of debt service greater than 220 percent of exports or 80 percent of GNI were classified as severely indebted, countries that were not severely indebted but whose present value of debt service exceeded 132 percent of exports or 48 percent of GNI were classified as moderately indebted, and countries that did not fall into either group were classified as less indebted.

Definitions

• **Indebtedness classification** refers to assessment on a three-point scale: severely indebted (S), moderately indebted (M), and less indebted (L). • **Present value of debt** is the sum of short-term external debt plus the discounted sum of total debt service payments due on public, publicly guaranteed, and private nonguaranteed long-term external debt over the life of existing loans. • **Public and publicly guaranteed debt service** is the sum of principal repayments and interest actually paid in foreign currency, goods, or services on long-term obligations of public debtors and long-term private obligations guaranteed by a public entity. • **Multilateral debt service** is the repayment of principal and interest to the World Bank, regional development banks, and other multilateral and intergovernmental agencies. • **Short-term debt** includes all debt having an original maturity of one year or less and interest in arrears on long-term debt. • **Exports of goods, services, and income** refer to international transactions involving a change in ownership of general merchandise, goods sent for processing and repairs, nonmonetary gold, services, receipts of employee compensation for nonresident workers, and investment income.

4.17a

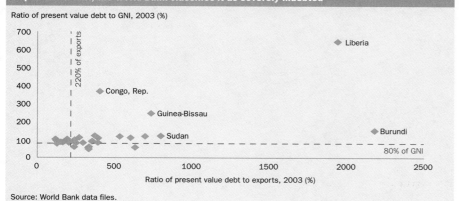

When the present value of a country's external debt exceeds 220 percent of exports or 80 percent of GNI, the World Bank classifies it as severely indebted

Ratio of present value debt to GNI, 2003 (%)

Ratio of present value debt to exports, 2003 (%)

Source: World Bank data files.

Data sources

The main sources of external debt information are reports to the World Bank through its Debtor Reporting System from member countries that have received IBRD loans or IDA credits. Additional information has been drawn from the files of the World Bank and the IMF. The data on GNI and exports of goods and services are from the World Bank's national accounts files and the IMF's Balance of Payments database. Summary tables of the external debt of developing countries are published annually in the World Bank's *Global Development Finance* and on its *Global Development Finance* CD-ROM.

5 | STATES AND MARKETS

The state in the twenty-first century plays many roles. It ensures law and order. It delivers essential services, such as education and health. It creates the preconditions for markets to function effectively by maintaining macroeconomic stability, establishing sound regulations, providing basic infrastructure, and protecting individuals and investors from arbitrary state actions. And it balances diverse interests to solve common problems.

Successful development requires that states complement markets, not substitute for them. States that foster a good investment climate—an environment that provides opportunities and incentives for firms, from microenterprises to multinationals, to invest productively, create jobs, and expand—are managing better in the global economy. Government institutions can support the development of markets in many ways—by providing information, encouraging competition, and enforcing contracts. By leveling the playing field, governments create opportunities for poor people to participate in markets and improve their standards of living, giving them hope for a better future for their children.

How do governments get the balance right between society's interests and firms' incentives to invest? First, they restrain corruption by public officials, firms, and other interest groups. Second, they establish credibility by maintaining economic and political stability and preventing arbitrary behavior by the key agencies of the state. Third, they foster public trust and legitimacy through open and participatory policymaking, transparency, and equity. Fourth, they establish policies that reflect current conditions and continue to adapt to changing economic and business conditions.

This section covers a broad range of indicators showing how effective and accountable government and an energetic private initiative create a sound investment climate. Its 12 tables cover three cross-cutting development themes: private sector development (including improving the investment climate), public sector policies, and infrastructure, information, and telecommunications.

Creating the conditions for private sector development and improving the investment and business climates

A good investment climate plays a central role in growth and poverty reduction by ensuring that contracts are enforced, markets function, basic infrastructure is provided, and people (especially poor people) are empowered to participate and manage better in the global economy. Although every country confronts different constraints, the main elements to get right are security and stability, regulation and taxation, finance, infrastructure, and labor markets. Governments that focus on creating a good climate for finance and infrastructure through sound regulation and private participation help to improve productivity and growth. Governments can also foster a better workforce by making education more inclusive, increasing equity in the workforce, and helping workers cope with labor mobility.

During the past few years the World Bank, in partnership with local chambers of commerce or business associations, government statistics agencies, and a government partner, pioneered new measures of the investment climate derived from surveys of firms. The core survey has two parts. The main part deals with characteristics of the business and investment climate and is administered to the firm's management or owners. It seeks business owners' opinions on the business environment and their motivations for business decisions. The second part focuses on productivity measures, collecting information on the availability of physical infrastructure, the structure and functioning of factor and product markets, interbusiness relations and networking, industrial regulation, law and order, tax and customs administration, and other aspects of governance (table 5.2). The investment climate surveys measure specific constraints facing firms and relate them to measures of firm performance, growth, and investment. Some of the challenges of this new data initiative for measuring the investment climate are presented in box 5b.

What are some of the major findings from these surveys? Although each country confronts different constraints, investment climate surveys show that firms in developing countries rate policy uncertainty as their major concern. Other important concerns are macroeconomic stability, tax rates and regulation, and tax administration.

The annual *Doing Business* reports, produced by the World Bank–sponsored Doing Business Project, also shed light on the investment climate. These reports investigate the scope and manner of regulations that enhance business activity and those that constrain it. Quantitative indicators cover obstacles faced by an entrepreneur performing standardized tasks such as starting a business, hiring and firing workers, obtaining business licenses, getting credit, registering property, protecting investors, enforcing contracts, and closing down a business (table 5.3).

The main findings in *Doing Business in 2005*, the second in a series, are:
- *Businesses face much larger regulatory burdens in poor countries than in rich countries.* They face three times the administrative costs and nearly twice as many bureaucratic procedures and delays, and they have fewer than half the protections of property rights of rich countries.
- *Heavy regulation and weak property rights exclude the poor from doing business.* In poor countries 40 percent of the economy is informal. Women, young, and low-skilled workers are hurt the most.
- *The payoffs from reform appear large.* A hypothetical improvement on all aspects of the Doing Business Indicators to reach the level of the top quartile of countries is associated with an estimated 1.4–2.2 percentage points more in annual economic growth.

Public sector policies and institutions can improve service delivery—and private sector business activities

Improving people's standard of living by ensuring access to essential services such as health, education, safety, water, sanitation, and electricity is widely viewed as government's responsibility. An efficient and accountable public sector has institutions that are responsive to citizens, provide information, deliver services efficiently and equitably, and help to enforce people's rights. Making services work better, especially for poor people who often do not get their fair share of public spending on services, is a challenge that can be met by governments, citizens, and private service providers working together.

Good governance—sound management of a country's economic and social resources, and strong institutions that support, regulate, and stabilize markets and ensure fair treatment of all citizens—strengthens the investment climate. Government functions and policies affect many areas of social and economic life: health and education, natural resources and environmental protection, fiscal and monetary stability, and flows of trade. Data related to these topics are presented in the respective sections. This section provides data on key public sector activities: tax policies, exchange rates, and defense expenditures (tables 5.6–5.8).

Taxes are the main source of revenue for most governments. They are levied mainly on income, profits, capital gains, goods and services, and exports and imports. (Grants and other revenue are also important in some economies; see table 4.13.) A comparison of tax levels across countries provides an overview of the fiscal obligations and incentives facing the private sector. Central government tax revenues range from 2–3 percent of GDP in Myanmar to almost 30 percent in Israel and the United Kingdom (table 5.6).

The level and progressivity of taxes on personal and corporate income influence incentives to work and invest. Marginal tax rates on individual income range from 0 percent to 50 percent or more. Most marginal tax rates on corporate income are in the 20–30 percent range (table 5.6).

Policy uncertainty dominates the investment climate concerns of firms

Constraints in the investment climate, based on rankings by country, 2002–04

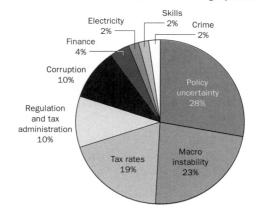

Source: World Bank 2005b.

Infrastructure is central to growth, poverty reduction, and achievement of the Millennium Development Goals

Improved infrastructure such as roads, rails, power, telecommunications, water supply, and sanitation systems are important elements in the investment climate and are crucial for economic growth, competitiveness, poverty reduction, and achievement of the Millennium Development Goals (tables 1.2–1.4 and *World view*). New ways of providing infrastructure are expanding services to poor people. For example, private firms participating in infrastructure contribute capital and know-how and improve access to basic infrastructure services. In developing countries private firms invest mainly in the communications and energy sectors. Although investment in projects with private participation plays a role in delivering improved access and quality of infrastructure services, public investment (with accompanying policy reform) will likely be the main driver of increased service delivery going forward (table 5.1).

Quality infrastructure services such as safe water and sanitation systems are essential for sustaining life and maintaining health (tables 2.15 and 3.5). A good transportation network and reliable power are needed for businesses to operate efficiently and remain globally competitive. And good transportation and schooling advance gender equality and the empowerment of women (tables 1.5, 3.7, 3.8, and 5.9). But many people in developing countries, especially in rural areas, lack access to good quality services at affordable prices.

New information and communications technologies are helping people everywhere improve their quality of life by creating, using, and sharing information and knowledge (tables 5.10 and 5.11).

Assessing the impact of reforms in infrastructure sectors requires better data, including data reflecting the impact on people's lives. Because there are no international agencies that specialize in infrastructure, definitions, methods, and data collection efforts for infrastructure have been fragmented. World Bank staff are compiling an infrastructure database from several sources and covering several policy dimensions: access, affordability, quality, efficiency, and fiscal sustainability. This effort complements the World Bank's drive toward managing for results and recognition of the need for good quality statistical data and for continuing support for statistical capacity building. The World Bank's Results Measurement System for assessing development progress in member countries of the International Development Association includes infrastructure indicators such as the share of population with sustainable access to an improved water source, fixed lines and mobile telephones per 1,000 inhabitants, access of rural population to an all-season road, and the household electrification rate.

5b

Data initiative

Challenges in measuring the investment climate

The main challenges in developing investment climate data include:

- *Multidimensional nature of the concept being measured.* Reducing details to those that contribute to a single measure may miss important insights and hide the degree of variation within a country.

- *Some dimensions are inherently difficult to measure.* Certain investment climate constraints are relatively easy to identify and measure, such as the reliability of the power supply or the time to register a business. But others are sensitive issues, such as corruption, and can lead to underreporting. Other dimensions that are difficult to quantify are competitive pressures and policy-related risks.

- *Differences in perspective across firms and activities.* The same dimension of the investment climate can affect firms or activities in different ways. Deficiencies in port and customs infrastructure can be a major impediment to firms engaged in exporting but have only limited effects on other firms. Some firms may benefit from government-mandated monopolies, while other firms lose by being denied the opportunity to compete or by paying higher prices for products from the protected industry. Taxes levied to improve public services or to meet other social goals and regulations to safeguard the environment or consumers can affect the ability of some firms to compete fairly. Thus both objective and perception-based opinions from firms can vary by type of respondent, but taken together both types of measures help to capture the range of perspectives and evaluations of constraints.

- *Differences across locations within countries.* Investment climate conditions may vary considerably in different locations. This is most obviously the case in large countries with federal structures, where subnational governments may differ in their policies and behavior. But it also true with more centralized governments, where there are often important differences within the country in matters like infrastructure provision and enforcement of national laws and regulations.

- *Experience on the ground does not always reflect formal policies.* In some countries the gap between the formal statement of policy and its implementation is substantial. Variations in the degree of discretion officials have, the resources made available, and the political will to enforce regulations can have a big impact. The distinction can be important in determining the priorities and expected benefits of reform initiatives.

In grappling with these issues, objective and perception-based data can each make a contribution. Objective measures have advantages of allowing more precise and consistent benchmarking of conditions. But for some factors subjective indicators may be the only effective way to gauge differences across locations or types of firms. Because investment decisions ultimately depend on subjective judgments, measures that reflect firm perceptions add additional insight.

Additional information on the investment climate is available in World Bank (2005a) and World Bank (2005b). Their datasets are available at http://econ.worldbank.org/wdr/wdr2005, http://lresearch.worldbank.org/ics, and http://rru.worldbank.org/DoingBusiness.

Source: World Bank 2005b.

	Domestic credit to private sector		Foreign direct investment		Investment in infrastructure projects with private participation[a]							
									$ millions			
	% of GDP		% of GDP		Telecommunications		Energy		Transport		Water and sanitation	
	1990	2003	1990	2003	1990–95	1996–2003	1990–95	1996–2003	1990–95	1996–2003	1990–95	1996–2003
Afghanistan	..	..	..	0.0	..	70.0	..	..	..	..	..	..
Albania	..	7.8	0.0	2.9	..	283.2	..	8.0	..	..	..	..
Algeria	44.4	11.4	0.0	1.0	..	1,164.5	2,300.0	..	..	..	..	..
Angola	..	5.5	-3.3	10.7	..	75.3	..	..	..	..	..	..
Argentina	15.6	10.8	1.3	0.8	11,907.0	12,228.4	12,057.1	13,930.4	6,112.0	8,385.5	5,166.0	3,071.5
Armenia	40.4	6.0	0.0	4.3	..	468.4	..	37.0	..	50.0	..	..
Australia	61.6	99.0	2.6	1.3	..	..	..	..	..	..	..	..
Austria	91.6	105.2	0.4	2.9	..	..	..	..	..	..	..	..
Azerbaijan	10.8	6.7	0.0	46.0	14.0	245.6	..	375.2	..	..	..	..
Bangladesh	16.7	28.8	0.0	0.2	146.0	1,049.4	..	1,056.4	..	..	..	..
Belarus	..	12.0	0.0	1.0	10.0	416.3	..	500.0	..	..	..	..
Belgium	37.0	76.2	4.1	32.4	..	..	..	..	..	..	..	..
Benin	20.3	14.5	3.4	1.5	..	90.4	..	..	..	..	..	..
Bolivia	24.0	49.0	0.6	2.1	38.0	808.9	252.4	2,718.2	..	185.3	..	682.0
Bosnia and Herzegovina	..	42.0	..	5.5	..	..	..	..	..	..	..	..
Botswana	9.4	18.3	2.5	1.1	..	80.0	..	..	..	..	..	..
Brazil	38.9	34.6	0.2	2.1	..	76,339.0	613.6	56,058.4	1,317.4	19,251.2	156.3	3,362.2
Bulgaria	82.8	27.6	0.0	7.1	64.0	949.6	..	697.6	..	..	..	152.0
Burkina Faso	16.8	14.0	0.0	0.3	..	36.6	..	5.6	..	..	..	..
Burundi	13.7	28.1	0.1	0.0	0.5	15.6	..	..	..	..	..	..
Cambodia	..	7.9	0.0	2.1	31.6	155.7	..	123.2	120.0	72.2	..	..
Cameroon	26.7	10.2	-1.0	1.7	..	266.1	..	91.9	30.8	95.0	..	..
Canada	75.9	81.3	1.3	0.7	..	..	..	..	..	..	..	..
Central African Republic	7.2	5.9	0.0	0.3	1.1	..	..	..	..	..	0.7	..
Chad	7.3	4.4	0.5	32.1	..	13.0	..	..	..	..	..	..
Chile	47.2	63.3	2.2	4.1	148.9	1,631.8	2,260.0	6,687.3	539.9	6,727.6	67.5	3,940.1
China	87.7	147.2	1.0	3.8	..	13,325.0	6,113.5	16,202.6	6,219.8	16,768.8	104.0	2,436.4
Hong Kong, China	163.7	150.6	..	8.6	..	..	..	..	..	..	..	..
Colombia	30.8	23.4	1.2	2.2	1,551.2	1,704.9	1,813.2	5,762.2	1,008.8	1,608.2	..	330.0
Congo, Dem. Rep.	1.8	0.9	-0.2	2.8	..	369.7	..	..	..	..	..	..
Congo, Rep.	15.7	3.6	0.8	5.6	4.6	111.9	..	325.0	..	..	..	..
Costa Rica	15.8	31.3	2.8	3.3	..	..	76.3	243.1	..	161.0	..	..
Côte d'Ivoire	36.5	13.6	0.4	1.3	..	827.4	147.2	223.0	..	178.0	..	..
Croatia	..	54.3	0.0	6.9	..	1,761.5	..	375.6	..	672.2	..	298.7
Cuba	..	..	..	..	371.0	60.0	..	165.0	..	..	..	600.0
Czech Republic	..	32.4	0.0	2.8	876.0	9,605.1	356.0	4,809.4	263.7	126.7	36.5	314.6
Denmark	52.2	152.1	0.8	0.6	..	..	..	..	..	..	..	..
Dominican Republic	27.5	41.1	1.9	1.9	10.0	433.2	372.5	1,936.3	..	833.9	..	..
Ecuador	13.6	19.9	1.2	5.7	51.2	728.8	..	310.0	12.5	886.8	..	550.0
Egypt, Arab Rep.	30.6	61.5	1.7	0.3	..	3,247.4	..	1,378.0	..	1,057.2	6.0	..
El Salvador	17.2	41.2	0.0	0.6	..	910.7	106.0	879.2	..	..	..	..
Eritrea	..	33.9	0.0	2.9	..	40.0	..	..	..	..	..	..
Estonia	20.2	33.2	0.0	9.8	211.7	733.5	..	26.5	..	299.4	..	81.0
Ethiopia	19.5	26.1	0.1	0.9	..	..	..	..	..	..	..	..
Finland	86.6	64.2	0.6	2.1	..	..	..	..	..	..	..	..
France	96.1	90.2	1.1	2.7	..	..	..	..	..	..	..	..
Gabon	13.0	10.8	1.2	0.9	..	35.0	..	624.8	..	46.7	..	..
Gambia, The	11.0	16.7	0.0	15.2	..	6.6	..	..	..	..	..	..
Georgia	..	8.7	0.0	8.5	21.6	134.3	..	172.0	..	..	..	..
Germany	90.6	117.3	0.2	0.5	..	..	..	..	..	..	..	..
Ghana	4.9	11.8	0.3	1.8	25.0	460.4	..	383.8	..	10.0	..	..
Greece	36.3	72.5	1.2	0.4	..	..	..	..	..	..	..	..
Guatemala	14.2	19.1	0.6	0.5	20.0	1,673.3	134.8	1,298.4	..	33.8	..	..
Guinea	3.5	4.0	0.6	2.2	45.0	75.3	36.4	..	..	..	..	..
Guinea-Bissau	22.0	1.9	0.8	0.9	..	..	23.2	..	..	..	..	..
Haiti	12.6	17.9	0.0	0.3	..	19.5	4.7	..	..	..	..	..

Private sector development

| | Domestic credit to private sector | | Foreign direct investment | | Investment in infrastructure projects with private participation[a] | | | | | | | |
| | % of GDP | | % of GDP | | Telecommunications | | Energy | | Transport | | Water and sanitation | |
	1990	2003	1990	2003	1990–95	1996–2003	1990–95	1996–2003	1990–95	1996–2003	1990–95	1996–2003
Honduras	31.1	40.6	1.4	2.8	..	71.1	95.3	86.8	..	130.5	..	220.0
Hungary	46.6	43.0	0.9	3.0	3,510.9	8,513.4	2,156.7	1,916.0	1,004.0	135.0	10.9	167.6
India	25.2	32.0	0.1	0.7	779.5	16,996.9	2,974.7	9,713.5	126.9	2,300.0	..	216.0
Indonesia	46.9	24.2	1.0	-0.3	3,549.0	10,481.0	3,202.5	7,534.7	1,204.9	2,314.6	3.8	919.5
Iran, Islamic Rep.	32.5	35.3	-0.3	0.1	5.0	28.0	..	..	..	..	..	..
Iraq	..	..	0.0	..	..	..	..	..	..	..	..	..
Ireland	47.6	117.6	1.3	17.3								
Israel	57.6	92.2	0.3	3.3								
Italy	56.5	85.8	0.6	1.1								
Jamaica	36.1	17.6	3.0	8.8	..	494.0	289.0	201.0	30.0	390.0	..	..
Japan	196.0	102.4	0.1	0.1								
Jordan	72.3	71.7	0.9	3.8	43.0	967.9	..	..	..	182.0	..	169.0
Kazakhstan	..	22.9	0.0	7.0	30.0	2,027.0	..	2,125.0	..	..	..	40.0
Kenya	32.8	21.3	0.7	0.6	..	507.0	..	171.5	..	53.4	..	..
Korea, Dem. Rep.	..	..										
Korea, Rep.	62.8	103.8	0.3	0.5								
Kuwait	52.1	79.8	0.0	-0.2								
Kyrgyz Republic	..	4.8	0.0	2.4	..	94.0	..	..	..	..	..	..
Lao PDR	1.0	6.5	0.7	0.9	..	185.5	..	535.5	..	100.0	..	..
Latvia	..	34.6	0.0	2.7	230.0	1,473.3	..	177.1	..	75.0	..	..
Lebanon	79.4	83.1	0.2	1.9	100.0	573.8	..	..	..	150.0	..	..
Lesotho	15.8	5.9	2.8	3.7	..	33.5	..	..	..	..	..	..
Liberia	30.9	4.0	0.0	0.0								
Libya	31.0	18.0	0.5	-0.4								
Lithuania	..	20.6	0.0	1.0	74.2	1,584.0	..	284.5	..	..	..	..
Macedonia, FYR	..	19.6	0.0	2.0	..	670.2	..	..	..	..	..	..
Madagascar	16.9	8.8	0.7	0.2	5.0	10.1	..	..	..	20.3	..	..
Malawi	10.9	7.7	1.2	1.3	8.0	25.5	..	..	..	6.0	..	..
Malaysia	108.5	141.3	5.3	2.4	2,630.0	3,590.8	6,909.5	4,210.0	4,657.6	9,605.1	3,986.7	1,105.5
Mali	12.8	19.2	0.2	3.0	..	42.7	0.1	747.0	..	..	..	..
Mauritania	43.5	31.7	0.7	19.6	..	99.6	..	..	..	..	..	..
Mauritius	35.6	59.3	1.7	1.2	..	365.6	..	109.3	..	42.6	..	..
Mexico	17.5	18.5	1.0	1.7	18,031.0	19,974.0	1.0	7,659.1	7,910.3	5,534.2	312.1	331.5
Moldova	5.9	20.6	0.0	3.0	..	84.6	..	85.3	..	..	..	..
Mongolia	19.0	30.3	..	10.3	13.1	20.4	..	..	..	..	..	..
Morocco	34.0	56.0	0.6	5.2	..	3,643.0	2,300.0	5,868.9	..	..	..	1,000.0
Mozambique	17.6	2.2	0.4	7.8	..	44.0	..	1,200.0	..	959.7	..	0.6
Myanmar	4.7	12.1	..	..	4.0	..	394.0	..	..	50.0	..	..
Namibia	22.6	52.8	1.3	3.1	18.0	4.0	..	5.0	..	450.0	..	..
Nepal	12.8	..	0.0	0.3	..	45.6	131.4	137.2	..	..	..	..
Netherlands	79.9	154.0	3.6	3.1								
New Zealand	76.0	118.6	4.0	3.1								
Nicaragua	112.6	26.4	0.0	4.9	9.9	162.2	..	347.4	..	104.0	..	..
Niger	12.3	5.2	1.6	1.1	..	52.7	..	..	..	..	..	4.9
Nigeria	9.4	15.7	2.1	2.1	..	2,797.7	..	259.0	..	22.8	..	..
Norway	81.7	89.6	0.9	0.9								
Oman	22.9	38.6	1.4	0.1	..	..	204.5	1,001.3	..	551.3	..	..
Pakistan	27.7	25.7	0.6	0.6	602.0	500.0	3,417.3	2,519.7	299.6	148.7	..	..
Panama	46.7	92.1	2.6	6.1	..	1,429.2	..	1,064.9	409.9	806.0	..	25.0
Papua New Guinea	28.6	12.1	4.8	3.2	..	..	..	65.0	..	..	..	175.0
Paraguay	15.8	15.5	1.5	1.5	48.1	204.4	..	..	..	58.0	..	..
Peru	11.8	20.8	0.2	2.3	2,568.7	5,511.4	1,207.8	4,085.7	6.6	325.8	..	56.0
Philippines	22.3	34.6	1.2	0.4	1,279.0	7,232.1	6,820.9	7,393.1	300.0	2,124.5	..	5,867.7
Poland	21.1	29.0	0.2	2.0	479.0	13,788.2	145.0	2,760.6	3.1	826.9	..	22.1
Portugal	49.1	148.1	3.7	0.7								
Puerto Rico	..	..	..									

	Domestic credit to private sector		Foreign direct investment		Investment in infrastructure projects with private participation[a]							
									$ millions			
					Telecommunications		Energy		Transport		Water and sanitation	
	% of GDP		% of GDP									
	1990	2003	1990	2003	1990–95	1996–2003	1990–95	1996–2003	1990–95	1996–2003	1990–95	1996–2003
Romania	..	9.5	0.0	3.2	5.0	4,058.7	..	100.0	..	23.4	..	1,134.0
Russian Federation	..	20.9	0.0	1.8	861.1	9,884.2	1,100.0	2,295.3	..	515.4	..	128.0
Rwanda	6.9	11.0	0.3	0.3	..	15.6	..	..	..	..	..	..
Saudi Arabia	54.7	55.4	1.6	0.0	..	4,080.0	..	..	..	245.0	..	52.0
Senegal	26.5	20.8	1.0	1.2	..	606.0	..	124.0	..	..	..	6.3
Serbia and Montenegro	..	..		6.6	..	2,120.6	..	..	..	..	..	..
Sierra Leone	3.2	5.0	5.0	0.4	..	23.5	..	..	..	..	..	..
Singapore	96.8	116.2	15.1	12.5	..	..	..	..	..	..	..	..
Slovak Republic	..	32.6	0.0	1.8	118.6	2,394.4	..	3,323.6	..	..	..	..
Slovenia	34.9	41.5	0.9	1.2	..	..	..	..	..	..	..	..
Somalia	..	..	0.6	..	..	2.0	..	..	..	..	..	..
South Africa	81.0	142.1	-0.1	0.5	1,072.8	11,535.6	3.0	1,244.3	..	1,891.1	..	212.5
Spain	80.2	119.3	2.7	3.0	..	..	..	..	..	..	..	..
Sri Lanka	19.6	29.9	0.5	1.3	43.6	1,139.6	21.7	286.6	..	240.0	..	..
Sudan	4.8	6.0	0.0	7.6	..	6.0	..	..	..	..	..	..
Swaziland	21.3	16.9	3.5	2.4	..	33.6	..	..	..	..	..	..
Sweden	127.4	104.1	0.8	1.1	..	..	..	..	..	..	..	..
Switzerland	162.6	159.4	2.4	5.5	..	..	..	..	..	..	..	..
Syrian Arab Republic	7.5	10.1	0.6	0.7	..	130.0	..	..	..	..	..	..
Tajikistan	..	14.0	0.0	2.0	..	1.0	..	..	..	..	..	..
Tanzania	13.9	7.6	0.0	2.4	30.1	383.0	6.0	490.0	..	23.0	..	4.8
Thailand	83.4	102.9	2.9	1.4	4,814.0	5,086.2	2,059.6	8,214.0	2,395.9	591.4	153.0	347.5
Togo	22.6	16.3	1.1	1.1	..	5.0	..	..	..	..	..	..
Trinidad and Tobago	44.7	39.0	2.2	5.9	47.0	146.7	..	207.0	..	..	..	120.0
Tunisia	66.2	66.6	0.6	2.2	..	277.0	627.0	265.0	..	..	..	..
Turkey	16.7	16.3	0.5	0.6	190.3	8,216.2	2,478.0	5,167.2	..	724.8	..	942.0
Turkmenistan	..	1.9	0.0	1.6	..	..	..	..	..	..	..	..
Uganda	4.0	6.9	0.0	3.1	8.8	288.1	..	11.3	..	..	..	..
Ukraine	2.6	24.6	0.0	2.9	110.6	2,094.1	..	160.0	..	..	..	..
United Arab Emirates	37.4	55.9	..	..	..	..	..	..	..	..	..	..
United Kingdom	115.8	148.4	3.4	1.2	..	..	..	..	..	..	..	..
United States	148.4	238.7	0.8	0.4	..	..	..	..	..	..	..	..
Uruguay	32.4	44.6	0.0	2.5	19.0	61.4	86.0	330.0	96.0	280.2	10.0	351.0
Uzbekistan	..	..	0.0	0.7	2.5	370.5	..	..	..	..	..	..
Venezuela, RB	25.4	8.6	0.9	3.0	4,603.3	6,709.3	..	133.0	100.0	268.0	..	44.0
Vietnam	2.5	49.0	2.8	3.7	128.0	295.0	..	2,627.5	10.0	115.0	..	212.8
West Bank and Gaza	..	..	..	..	65.0	410.6	..	150.0	..	..	..	9.5
Yemen, Rep.	6.1	6.9	-2.7	-0.8	25.0	340.0	..	..	..	190.0	..	..
Zambia	8.9	6.7	6.2	2.3	..	56.9	..	289.4	..	..	..	..
Zimbabwe	23.0	37.0	-0.1	0.1	..	54.0	..	603.0	18.0	85.0	..	..
World	**112.9 w**	**139.1 w**	**0.9 w**	**1.5 w**	.. s	.. s	.. s	.. s	.. s	.. s	.. s	.. s
Low income	22.3	27.0	0.3	1.5	1,869.7	27,841.5	7,135.0	22,146.1	605.3	4,555.1	0.7	620.4
Middle income	43.0	64.2	0.7	2.4	59,958.9	270,230.7	56,297.4	183,850.8	33,592.4	85,662.7	10,012.8	29,153.0
Lower middle income	50.1	76.6	0.4	2.4	16,965.3	179,446.3	31,910.8	133,926.0	12,495.9	50,686.7	423.1	19,158.3
Upper middle income	27.4	36.6	1.2	2.3	42,993.6	90,784.4	24,386.6	49,924.8	21,096.5	34,976.0	9,589.7	9,994.7
Low & middle income	39.3	58.6	0.6	2.3	61,828.6	298,072.2	63,432.4	205,996.9	34,197.7	90,217.8	10,013.5	29,773.4
East Asia & Pacific	74.0	123.6	1.6	3.0	12,481.7	40,521.3	25,500.0	46,905.6	14,908.2	31,741.6	4,247.5	11,064.4
Europe & Central Asia	..	24.2	0.1	2.5	6,809.5	71,971.9	6,235.7	25,395.9	1,270.8	3,448.8	47.4	3,280.0
Latin America & Carib.	28.4	25.7	0.8	2.1	39,489.4	131,395.3	19,504.2	104,204.7	17,543.4	46,007.6	5,711.9	13,753.4
Middle East & N. Africa	39.5	46.4	0.6	0.9	238.0	14,862.2	5,431.5	8,663.2	..	2,425.5	6.0	1,230.5
South Asia	24.6	31.0	0.1	0.7	1,571.1	19,801.5	6,545.1	13,713.4	426.5	2,688.7	..	216.0
Sub-Saharan Africa	42.4	63.7	0.3	2.5	1,238.9	19,520.0	215.9	7,114.1	48.8	3,905.6	0.7	229.1
High income	125.8	158.3	1.0	1.4	..	..	..	..	..	..	..	..
Europe EMU	79.8	105.0	1.1	3.1	..	..	..	..	..	..	..	..

a. Data refer to total for the period shown.

About the data

Private sector development and investment—that is, tapping private sector initiative and investment for socially useful purposes—are critical for poverty reduction. In parallel with public sector efforts, private investment, especially in competitive markets, has tremendous potential to contribute to growth. Private markets serve as the engine of productivity growth, creating productive jobs and higher incomes. And with government playing a complementary role of regulation, funding, and provision of services, private initiative and investment can help provide the basic services and conditions that empower the poor—by improving health, education, and infrastructure.

Credit is an important link in the money transmission process; it finances production, consumption, and capital formation, which in turn affect the level of economic activity. The data on domestic credit to the private sector are taken from the banking survey of the International Monetary Fund's (IMF) International Financial Statistics or, when data are unavailable, from its monetary survey. The monetary survey includes monetary authorities (the central bank), deposit money banks, and other banking institutions, such as finance companies, development banks, and savings and loan institutions. In some cases credit to the private sector may include credit to state-owned or partially state-owned enterprises.

The statistics on foreign direct investment are based on balance of payments data reported by the IMF, supplemented by data on net foreign direct investment reported by the Organisation for Economic Co-operation and Development and official national sources. (For a detailed discussion of data

on foreign direct investment, see About the data for table 6.7).

Private participation in infrastructure has made important contributions to easing fiscal constraints, improving the efficiency of infrastructure services, and extending their delivery to poor people. The privatization trend in infrastructure that began in the 1970s and 1980s took off in the 1990s, peaking in 1997. Developing countries have been at the head of this wave, pioneering better approaches to providing infrastructure services and reaping the benefits of greater competition and customer focus. In 1990–2003 more than 130 developing countries introduced private participation in at least one infrastructure sector, awarding more than 2,500 projects attracting investment commitments of $890 billion. In 2003 more than 100 new infrastructure projects with private participation, valued at about $50 billion, were implemented.

The data on investment in infrastructure projects with private participation refer to all investment (public and private) in projects in which a private company assumes operating risk during the operating period or assumes development and operating risk during the contract period. Foreign state-owned companies are considered private entities for the purposes of this measure. The data are from the World Bank's Private Participation in Infrastructure (PPI) Project Database, which tracks more than 2,500 projects, newly owned or managed by private companies, that reached financial closure in low- and middle-income economies in 1990–2003. For more information, see http://ppi.worldbank.org/.

Definitions

• **Domestic credit to private sector** refers to financial resources provided to the private sector—such as through loans, purchases of nonequity securities, and trade credits and other accounts receivable—that establish a claim for repayment. For some countries these claims include credit to public enterprises. • **Foreign direct investment** is net inflows of investment to acquire a lasting management interest (10 percent or more of voting stock) in an enterprise operating in an economy other than that of the investor. It is the sum of equity capital, reinvestment of earnings, other long-term capital, and short-term capital as shown in the balance of payments. • **Investment in infrastructure projects with private participation** covers infrastructure projects in telecommunications, energy (electricity and natural gas transmission and distribution), transport, and water and sanitation that have reached financial closure and directly or indirectly serve the public. Incinerators, movable assets, stand-alone solid waste projects, and small projects such as windmills are excluded. The types of projects included are operation and management contracts, operation and management contracts with major capital expenditure, greenfield projects (in which a private entity or a public-private joint venture builds and operates a new facility), and divestiture.

5.1a

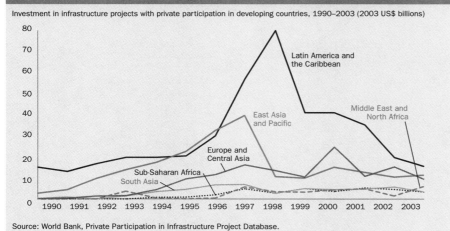

Latin America and the Caribbean still has the highest investment levels, but activity has declined for the fifth consecutive year

Investment in infrastructure projects with private participation in developing countries, 1990–2003 (2003 US$ billions)

Source: World Bank, Private Participation in Infrastructure Project Database.

Data sources

The data on domestic credit are from the IMF's *International Financial Statistics*. The data on foreign direct investment are based on estimates compiled by the IMF in its *Balance of Payments Statistics Yearbook*, supplemented by World Bank staff estimates. The data on investment in infrastructure projects with private participation are from the World Bank's Private Participation in Infrastructure (PPI) Project Database (http://ppi.worldbank.org).

	Survey year	Policy uncertainty Major constraint %	Corruption Major constraint %	Courts Major constraint %	Lack confidence courts uphold property rights %	Crime Major constraint %	Regulation and tax administration Tax rates as a major constraint %	Time dealing with officials % of management time	Average time to clear customs days	Finance Major constraint %	Electricity Major constraint %	Labor — Major constraint % Skills	Labor — Major constraint % Regulation
Afghanistan		..	..	..	..	..	..	..	..	..	..	..	..
Albania	2002	48.5	47.5	32.9	50.6	21.2	37.1	13.6	2.4	20.1	57.1	13.2	7.3
Algeria	2003	..	35.2	..	27.3	..	44.8	..	21.6	51.3	11.5	25.5	12.9
Angola		..	..	..	..	..	..	..	..	..	..	..	..
Argentina		..	..	..	..	..	..	..	..	..	..	..	..
Armenia	2002	32.0	13.5	8.2	44.1	3.6	35.5	7.4	3.7	25.9	15.8	6.0	1.8
Australia		..	..	..	..	..	..	..	..	..	..	..	..
Austria		..	..	..	..	..	..	..	..	..	..	..	..
Azerbaijan	2002	6.7	19.5	4.4	31.0	2.6	18.8	7.3	2.6	12.3	20.2	4.5	1.3
Bangladesh	2002	45.4	57.9	..	83.0	39.4	35.8	4.6	11.5	45.7	73.2	19.8	10.8
Belarus	2002	59.0	17.9	11.2	48.1	12.3	47.0	11.0	2.4	30.1	2.8	8.4	9.3
Belgium		..	..	..	..	..	..	..	..	..	..	..	..
Benin		..	..	..	..	..	..	..	..	..	..	..	..
Bolivia	2001	..	..	..	..	..	..	..	9.3	..	..	..	..
Bosnia and Herzegovina	2002	40.5	34.8	22.6	38.0	18.7	26.9	11.8	3.6	27.9	5.6	5.7	9.1
Botswana		..	..	..	..	..	..	..	..	..	..	..	..
Brazil	2003	75.9	67.2	32.8	39.6	52.2	84.5	9.4	13.8	71.7	20.3	39.6	56.9
Bulgaria	2002	59.5	25.4	17.9	50.6	18.8	33.1	8.5	4.2	40.3	8.0	10.2	7.8
Burkina Faso		..	..	..	..	..	..	..	..	..	..	..	..
Burundi		..	..	..	..	..	..	..	..	..	..	..	..
Cambodia	2003	40.1	55.9	31.4	61.0	41.7	18.6	14.6	..	9.9	12.7	6.6	5.9
Cameroon		..	..	..	..	..	..	..	..	..	..	..	..
Canada		..	..	..	..	..	..	..	..	..	..	..	..
Central African Republic		..	..	..	..	..	..	..	..	..	..	..	..
Chad		..	..	..	..	..	..	..	..	..	..	..	..
Chile		..	..	..	..	..	..	..	..	..	..	..	..
China	2002/03	32.9	27.3	..	17.5	20.0	36.8	19.0	7.9	22.3	29.7	30.7	20.7
Hong Kong, China		..	..	..	..	..	..	..	..	..	..	..	..
Colombia		..	..	..	..	..	..	..	..	..	..	..	..
Congo, Dem. Rep.		..	..	..	..	..	..	..	..	..	..	..	..
Congo, Rep.		..	..	..	..	..	..	..	..	..	..	..	..
Costa Rica		..	..	..	..	..	..	..	..	..	..	..	..
Côte d'Ivoire		..	..	..	..	..	..	..	..	..	..	..	..
Croatia	2002	35.9	22.5	27.6	33.3	8.5	27.8	9.0	3.8	21.6	1.1	8.7	5.4
Cuba		..	..	..	..	..	..	..	..	..	..	..	..
Czech Republic	2002	20.2	12.5	11.1	47.1	14.3	25.6	5.5	4.4	23.1	5.3	9.1	3.5
Denmark		..	..	..	..	..	..	..	..	..	..	..	..
Dominican Republic		..	..	..	..	..	..	..	..	..	..	..	..
Ecuador	2003	60.7	49.2	34.1	70.8	27.8	38.1	17.7	16.4	42.2	28.3	22.3	14.1
Egypt, Arab Rep.		..	..	..	..	..	..	..	..	..	..	..	..
El Salvador		..	..	..	..	..	..	..	..	..	..	..	..
Eritrea	2002	31.5	2.7	..	..	1.3	31.1	5.9	9.1	53.7	38.2	41.0	5.2
Estonia	2002	12.0	5.4	4.8	28.6	6.5	16.7	6.2	1.6	8.4	10.1	23.8	4.2
Ethiopia	2002	39.3	39.0	..	..	9.5	73.6	5.7	13.5	40.2	42.5	17.9	4.6
Finland		..	..	..	..	..	..	..	..	..	..	..	..
France		..	..	..	..	..	..	..	..	..	..	..	..
Gabon		..	..	..	..	..	..	..	..	..	..	..	..
Gambia, The		..	..	..	..	..	..	..	..	..	..	..	..
Georgia	2002	44.3	35.1	11.2	59.0	19.0	30.5	14.7	3.2	14.2	22.4	8.6	4.0
Germany		..	..	..	..	..	..	..	..	..	..	..	..
Ghana		..	..	..	..	..	..	..	..	..	..	..	..
Greece		..	..	..	..	..	..	..	..	..	..	..	..
Guatemala	2003	66.4	80.9	36.7	71.3	80.4	56.5	17.4	9.4	38.7	26.6	31.4	16.7
Guinea		..	..	..	..	..	..	..	..	..	..	..	..
Guinea-Bissau		..	..	..	..	..	..	..	..	..	..	..	..
Haiti		..	..	..	..	..	..	..	..	..	..	..	..

	Survey year	Policy uncertainty Major constraint %	Corruption Major constraint %	Courts Major constraint %	Lack confidence courts uphold property rights %	Crime Major constraint %	Regulation and tax administration Tax rates as a major constraint %	Time dealing with officials % of management time	Average time to clear customs days	Finance Major constraint %	Electricity Major constraint %	Labor Major constraint % Skills	Regulation
Honduras	2003	47.0	62.8	21.8	56.1	60.9	35.6	14.2	5.1	55.4	36.4	26.4	14.2
Hungary	2002	21.1	8.8	4.5	40.3	4.9	30.2	8.7	4.3	20.2	1.2	12.5	7.3
India	2003	20.9	37.4	..	29.4	15.6	27.9	15.3	6.7	19.2	28.9	12.5	16.7
Indonesia	2004	48.2	41.5	24.7	40.8	22.0	29.5	14.6	5.8	23.0	22.3	18.9	25.9
Iran, Islamic Rep.		..	..	..	..	..	..	..	..	..	..	..	..
Iraq		..	..	..	..	..	..	..	..	..	..	..	..
Ireland		..	..	..	..	..	..	..	..	..	..	..	..
Israel		..	..	..	..	..	..	..	..	..	..	..	..
Italy		..	..	..	..	..	..	..	..	..	..	..	..
Jamaica		..	..	..	..	..	..	..	..	..	..	..	..
Japan		..	..	..	..	..	..	..	..	..	..	..	..
Jordan		..	..	..	..	..	..	..	..	..	..	..	..
Kazakhstan	2002	18.5	14.2	4.0	48.5	8.4	13.8	14.6	5.3	14.1	3.6	6.3	0.8
Kenya	2003	51.5	73.8	..	51.3	69.8	68.2	13.8	8.9	58.3	48.1	27.6	22.5
Korea, Dem. Rep.		..	..	..	..	..	..	..	..	..	..	..	..
Korea, Rep.		..	..	..	..	..	..	..	..	..	..	..	..
Kuwait		..	..	..	..	..	..	..	..	..	..	..	..
Kyrgyz Republic	2002/03	34.7	31.4	15.7	66.3	18.5	32.5	13.2	3.3	27.7	4.7	7.7	4.5
Lao PDR		..	..	..	..	..	..	..	..	..	..	..	..
Latvia	2002	27.4	11.7	3.2	49.1	6.4	27.3	10.7	1.2	7.7	4.0	15.5	4.1
Lebanon		..	..	..	..	..	..	..	..	..	..	..	..
Lesotho		..	..	..	..	..	..	..	..	..	..	..	..
Liberia		..	..	..	..	..	..	..	..	..	..	..	..
Libya		..	..	..	..	..	..	..	..	..	..	..	..
Lithuania	2002	33.5	15.6	12.0	59.5	16.2	36.5	10.0	2.4	7.0	4.5	7.5	8.5
Macedonia, FYR	2002	37.3	31.2	27.1	50.6	20.4	21.0	13.5	4.9	16.6	5.4	3.7	4.6
Madagascar		..	..	..	..	..	..	..	..	..	..	..	..
Malawi		..	..	..	..	..	..	..	..	..	..	..	..
Malaysia	2003	22.4	14.5	..	19.1	11.4	21.7	10.2	3.7	17.8	14.8	25.0	14.5
Mali		..	..	..	..	..	..	..	..	..	..	..	..
Mauritania		..	..	..	..	..	..	..	..	..	..	..	..
Mauritius		..	..	..	..	..	..	..	..	..	..	..	..
Mexico		..	..	..	..	..	..	..	..	..	..	..	..
Moldova	2002/03	57.0	40.2	19.8	72.1	26.5	54.9	7.1	2.1	39.6	5.4	11.0	5.2
Mongolia		..	..	..	..	..	..	..	..	..	..	..	..
Morocco	2001	..	..	..	..	..	..	..	2.7	..	..	..	..
Mozambique		..	..	..	..	..	..	..	..	..	..	..	..
Myanmar		..	..	..	..	..	..	..	..	..	..	..	..
Namibia		..	..	..	..	..	..	..	..	..	..	..	..
Nepal		..	..	..	..	..	..	..	..	..	..	..	..
Netherlands		..	..	..	..	..	..	..	..	..	..	..	..
New Zealand		..	..	..	..	..	..	..	..	..	..	..	..
Nicaragua	2003	58.2	65.7	33.3	60.4	39.2	34.7	17.3	5.8	57.6	34.7	17.0	6.9
Niger		..	..	..	..	..	..	..	..	..	..	..	..
Nigeria	2001	..	..	..	..	36.3	..	..	17.8	..	97.4	..	..
Norway		..	..	..	..	..	..	..	..	..	..	..	..
Oman		..	..	..	..	..	..	..	..	..	..	..	..
Pakistan	2002	40.1	40.4	..	62.6	21.5	45.6	10.6	17.1	40.1	39.2	12.8	15.0
Panama		..	..	..	..	..	..	..	..	..	..	..	..
Papua New Guinea		..	..	..	..	..	..	..	..	..	..	..	..
Paraguay		..	..	..	..	..	..	..	..	..	..	..	..
Peru	2002	71.1	59.6	..	34.7	51.6	..	..	7.9	55.8	11.1	12.5	..
Philippines	2003	29.5	35.2	..	33.8	26.5	30.4	11.0	2.8	18.2	33.4	11.9	24.7
Poland	2002/03	59.1	27.6	27.0	46.2	24.9	64.7	12.3	3.1	42.6	5.8	12.2	25.2
Portugal		..	..	..	..	..	..	..	..	..	..	..	..
Puerto Rico		..	..	..	..	..	..	..	..	..	..	..	..

	Survey year	Policy uncertainty — Major constraint %	Corruption — Major constraint %	Courts — Major constraint %	Courts — Lack confidence courts uphold property rights %	Crime — Major constraint %	Regulation and tax administration — Tax rates as a major constraint %	Time dealing with officials % of management time	Average time to clear customs days	Finance — Major constraint %	Electricity — Major constraint %	Labor — Major constraint % Skills	Labor — Major constraint % Regulation
Romania	2002	43.3	34.9	20.9	45.8	19.8	51.6	10.7	1.4	32.3	9.5	10.8	8.1
Russian Federation	2002	31.5	13.7	9.5	65.3	12.4	24.6	14.1	6.9	17.0	4.6	9.9	3.3
Rwanda		..	..	..	..	..	..	..	..	..	..	..	..
Saudi Arabia		..	..	..	..	..	..	..	..	..	..	..	..
Senegal	2004	31.3	39.9	13.3	40.5	15.4	50.8	13.8	6.5	60.0	30.7	18.5	16.3
Serbia and Montenegro	2002	47.8	16.3	13.8	28.6	8.9	35.3	15.1	5.5	28.3	6.2	11.9	6.9
Sierra Leone		..	..	..	..	..	..	..	..	..	..	..	..
Singapore		..	..	..	..	..	..	..	..	..	..	..	..
Slovak Republic	2002	44.6	27.5	25.3	53.9	15.4	31.7	9.5	2.2	30.1	3.0	9.7	7.4
Slovenia	2002	11.8	6.1	8.0	45.6	3.3	11.2	7.7	3.1	11.2	0.5	4.3	2.7
Somalia		..	..	..	..	..	..	..	..	..	..	..	..
South Africa		..	..	..	..	..	..	..	..	..	..	..	..
Spain		..	..	..	..	..	..	..	..	..	..	..	..
Sri Lanka		..	..	..	..	..	..	..	..	..	..	..	..
Sudan		..	..	..	..	..	..	..	..	..	..	..	..
Swaziland		..	..	..	..	..	..	..	..	..	..	..	..
Sweden		..	..	..	..	..	..	..	..	..	..	..	..
Switzerland		..	..	..	..	..	..	..	..	..	..	..	..
Syrian Arab Republic		..	..	..	..	..	..	..	..	..	..	..	..
Tajikistan	2002/03	24.4	21.0	9.1	48.2	3.0	26.2	8.3	9.6	20.1	17.1	2.4	2.3
Tanzania	2003	31.5	51.1	20.0	55.1	25.5	73.4	16.2	17.5	53.0	58.9	25.0	12.1
Thailand		..	..	..	..	..	..	..	..	..	..	..	..
Togo		..	..	..	..	..	..	..	..	..	..	..	..
Trinidad and Tobago		..	..	..	..	..	..	..	..	..	..	..	..
Tunisia		..	..	..	..	..	..	..	..	..	..	..	..
Turkey	2002	53.8	23.7	11.9	33.0	12.9	38.1	8.0	3.7	23.2	17.3	12.8	8.7
Turkmenistan		..	..	..	..	..	..	..	..	..	..	..	..
Uganda	2003	27.6	38.2	..	30.1	26.8	48.3	5.0	..	52.8	44.5	30.8	10.8
Ukraine	2002	46.9	27.8	15.3	49.0	19.6	39.6	15.4	5.8	29.1	5.9	13.0	5.8
United Arab Emirates		..	..	..	..	..	..	..	..	..	..	..	..
United Kingdom		..	..	..	..	..	..	..	..	..	..	..	..
United States		..	..	..	..	..	..	..	..	..	..	..	..
Uruguay		..	..	..	..	..	..	..	..	..	..	..	..
Uzbekistan	2002/03	27.2	8.7	7.6	25.4	7.0	19.9	12.1	6.0	20.6	4.8	4.9	1.7
Venezuela, RB		..	..	..	..	..	..	..	..	..	..	..	..
Vietnam		..	..	..	..	..	..	..	..	..	..	..	..
West Bank and Gaza		..	..	..	..	..	..	..	..	..	..	..	..
Yemen, Rep.		..	..	..	..	..	..	..	..	..	..	..	..
Zambia	2003	57.0	46.4	38.6	36.0	48.8	57.5	14.1	4.8	67.7	39.6	35.7	16.9
Zimbabwe		..	..	..	..	..	..	..	..	..	..	..	..

Note: Data are based on enterprise surveys conducted by the World Bank and its partners during 2001–04. While averages are reported, there are significant variations across firms.

About the data

This year the table includes recently available data from World Bank–sponsored Investment Climate Surveys covering more than 26,000 firms in 53 developing countries for 2001–03. The new data provide fresh insights into how investment climates vary around the world.

A good investment climate requires government policies that provide an environment in which firms and entrepreneurs can invest productively, create jobs, and contribute to growth and poverty reduction. The goal is an investment climate that benefits society as a whole, not just firms.

Governments face four primary challenges in improving the investment climate and getting the balance right between society's interests and firms' incentives to invest. One is establishing credibility by maintaining economic and political stability and restraining arbitrary behavior by the key agencies of the state. Two is restraining corruption by public officials, firms, and other interest groups. Three is fostering public trust and legitimacy through participatory policymaking, transparency, and equity. Four is ensuring that government policies realistically reflect current conditions and adapt to changing economic and business conditions.

Firms evaluating alternative investment options, governments interested in improving the investment climate, and economists seeking to understand how different factors influence economic performance have all grappled with defining and measuring the investment climate. The World Bank, working with client governments and others, recently pioneered new indicators of the investment climate. The Investment Climate Surveys measure specific constraints facing firms and relate them to indicators of firm performance, growth, and investment.

The investment climate indicators in the table cover eight dimensions of the investment climate. Firms in developing countries rate *policy uncertainty* as their dominant concern among investment climate constraints. It measures the credibility of governments and their policies and their ability to deliver what they promise. *Corruption*—the exploitation of public office for private gain—harms the investment climate in several ways. It can distort policymaking, undermine the credibility of government, act as a tax on entrepreneurial activities, and divert resources from public coffers. Better *courts* reduce the risks firms face, making investment more attractive. The importance of courts grows as the number of large and complex long-term transactions increases. Robbery, fraud, and other *crimes* against property

and people undermine the investment climate and stifle entrepreneurial activity. For example, in Latin America, more than half of surveyed firms considered crime to be a serious obstacle to doing business.

Most countries have room to improve *regulation and taxation* without compromising broader social interests. The investment climate is harmed when governments impose unnecessary costs by increasing uncertainty and risk and by erecting unjustified barriers to competition. Improvements in the tax system include broadening the tax base, simplifying tax structures, increasing the autonomy of tax agencies, and improving compliance through computerization. When *financial markets* work well, they connect firms to lenders and investors, allowing firms to seize business opportunities and expand their businesses. But too often government distortions introduced by state ownership or directed credit undermine financial sector development, productivity, and economic growth. Firms that have access to modern *infrastructure*— telecommunications, reliable electricity supplies, and efficient transportation—are more productive. Ill-considered *labor regulations* can discourage firms from creating more jobs, and while some employees may benefit, the unemployed, low-skilled, and those in the informal economy will not.

Whenever possible, Investment Climate Surveys draw from sampling frames from a well-defined universe of firms and follow a stratified random sampling methodology. At a minimum, both manufacturing and services sectors are included. In addition, because the distribution of establishments in most countries is overwhelmingly populated by small and medium-size enterprises, surveys generally oversample large establishments. The target unit for the surveys is the business establishment, rather than the firm. Sample sizes for most recent surveys range from 200 to 1,500 establishments. Note that unavoidable departures from the ideal sample design in some countries can affect comparability across countries. In a typical survey of about 500 firms, the sampling error is about ±4.5 percentage points.

The *World Development Report* survey of micro and informal firms was also conducted in 11 countries: Bangladesh, Brazil, Cambodia, Guatemala, India, Indonesia, Kenya, Pakistan, Senegal, Tanzania, and Uganda. The findings of these surveys are not reflected in table 5.2. For more information, see Hallward-Driemeier and Stone (2004). Additional information on the investment climate is available at: http://econ.worldbank.org/wdr/wdr2005 and http://iresearch.worldbank.org/ics.

Definitions

• **Policy uncertainty** measures the share of senior managers who ranked economic and regulatory policy uncertainty as a major or very severe constraint. • **Corruption** measures the share of senior managers who ranked corruption as a major or very severe constraint. • **Courts** measure the share of senior managers who ranked courts and dispute resolution systems as a major or very severe constraint. • **Lack confidence that courts uphold property rights** is the share of senior managers who do not agree with the statement: "I am confident that the judicial system will enforce my contractual and property rights in business disputes." • **Crime** measures the share of senior managers who ranked crime, theft, and disorder as a major or very severe constraint. • **Tax rates as a major constraint** measure the share of senior managers who ranked tax rates as a major or very severe constraint. • **Time dealing with officials** is the percentage of management time in a given week spent on requirements imposed by government regulations (taxes, customs, labor regulations, licensing and registration). • **Average time to clear customs** is the number of days to clear an imported good through customs. • **Finance** is the average of the shares of senior managers who ranked access to finance or cost of finance as a major or very severe constraint. • **Electricity** is the share of senior managers who ranked electricity as a major or severe constraint. • **Skills** are the share of senior managers who ranked skills of available workers as a major or severe constraint. • **Labor regulations** are the share of senior managers who ranked labor regulations as a major or severe constraint.

Data sources

All data are from the World Bank's Investment Climate Surveys (http://iresearch.worldbank.org/ics).

5.3 Business environment

	Starting a business		Registering property		Getting credit				Hiring and firing workers	Enforcing contracts		Protecting investors	Closing a business
					Index of borrower and lender legal rights 0 (less access) to 10 (more access)	borrowers per 1,000 adults			Rigidity of employment index 0 (less rigid) to 100 (more rigid)			Disclosure index 0 (less disclosure) to 10 (more disclosure)	Time to resolve insolvency years
	Number of start-up procedures January 2004	Time required days January 2004	Number of procedures January 2004	Time required days January 2004	January 2004	Public registry coverage January 2004	Private bureau coverage January 2004		January 2004	Number of procedures January 2004	Time required days January 2004	January 2004	January 2004
Afghanistan	..	..	..	..	..	..	..		..	..	..	..	..
Albania	11	47	7	47	9	0	0		30	39	390	3	4.0
Algeria	14	26	16	52	3	0	0		55	49	407	2	3.5
Angola	14	146	8	335	3	7	0		75	47	1,011	2	4.7
Argentina	15	32	5	44	3	201	733		51	33	520	5	2.8
Armenia	10	25	4	18	4	0	0		36	24	195	3	1.9
Australia	2	2	5	7	9	0	954		17	11	157	6	1.0
Austria	9	29	3	32	5	11	393		40	20	374	6	1.0
Azerbaijan	14	123	7	61	6	0	0		38	25	267	2	2.7
Bangladesh	8	35	..	..	..	7	0		24	29	365	3	4.0
Belarus	16	79	7	231	5	..	0		54	28	250	1	5.8
Belgium	4	34	2	132	7	533	0		20	27	112	4	0.9
Benin	8	32	3	50	4	2	0		61	49	570	1	3.1
Bolivia	15	59	7	92	3	96	0		40	47	591	2	1.8
Bosnia and Herzegovina	12	54	7	331	5	0	156		49	36	330	2	3.3
Botswana	11	108	4	69	9	0	309		20	26	154	5	2.2
Brazil	17	152	14	42	2	78	425		72	25	566	5	10.0
Bulgaria	10	32	9	19	6	13	0		28	34	440	2	3.3
Burkina Faso	13	135	8	107	4	2	0		90	41	458	..	4.0
Burundi	11	43	5	94	..	2	0		50	51	512	1	4.0
Cambodia	11	94	7	56	4	0	0		48	31	401	0	..
Cameroon	12	37	5	93	4	1	0		74	58	585	1	3.2
Canada	2	3	6	20	7	0	1,000		4	17	346	7	0.8
Central African Republic	10	14	3	69	3	1	0		76	45	660	..	4.8
Chad	19	75	6	44	3	0	0		80	52	526	..	10.0
Chile	9	27	6	31	4	290	220		19	28	305	6	5.6
China	12	41	3	32	2	4	0		30	25	241	4	2.4
Hong Kong, China	5	11	3	56	10	0	615		0	16	211	6	1.1
Colombia	14	43	7	23	4	0	300		51	37	363	2	3.0
Congo, Dem. Rep.	13	155	8	106	3	0	0		77	51	909	1	5.2
Congo, Rep.	8	67	6	103	3	1	0		86	47	560	3	3.0
Costa Rica	11	77	6	21	4	10	1,000		35	34	550	1	3.5
Côte d'Ivoire	11	58	7	340	2	2	0		69	25	525	2	2.2
Croatia	12	49	5	956	4	0	0		57	22	415	4	3.1
Cuba	..	..	..	..	..	..	..		..	..	..	..	..
Czech Republic	10	40	4	122	6	21	249		28	22	300	6	9.2
Denmark	4	4	6	42	7	0	71		17	15	83	5	3.4
Dominican Republic	10	78	7	107	4	..	294		40	29	580	1	3.5
Ecuador	14	92	12	21	3	124	0		51	41	388	1	4.3
Egypt, Arab Rep.	13	43	7	193	0	102	0		53	55	410	2	4.2
El Salvador	12	115	5	52	5	198	823		52	41	275	1	4.0
Eritrea	..	..	..	..	..	..	..		..	..	..	..	..
Estonia	6	72	4	65	..	0	95		44	25	150	4	3.0
Ethiopia	7	32	15	56	5	0	0		43	30	420	2	2.4
Finland	3	14	3	14	6	0	148		44	27	240	5	0.9
France	7	8	10	193	3	17	0		66	21	75	6	1.9
Gabon	..	..	..	..	..	..	..		..	..	..	..	..
Gambia, The	..	..	..	..	..	..	..		..	..	..	..	..
Georgia	9	25	8	39	7	0	0		49	18	375	5	3.2
Germany	9	45	4	41	8	6	856		55	26	184	5	1.2
Ghana	12	85	7	382	5	0	1		34	23	200	2	1.9
Greece	15	38	12	23	1	0	111		66	14	151	5	2.0
Guatemala	15	39	5	55	4	0	124		40	37	1,459	1	4.0
Guinea	13	49	6	104	2	0	0		59	44	306	4	3.8
Guinea-Bissau	..	..	..	..	..	..	..		..	..	..	..	..
Haiti	12	203	5	195	2	3	0		24	35	368	1	5.7

Business environment | 5.3

	Starting a business		Registering property		Getting credit			Hiring and firing workers	Enforcing contracts		Protecting investors	Closing a business
					Index of borrower and lender legal rights 0 (less access) to 10 (more access)	borrowers per 1,000 adults		Rigidity of employment index 0 (less rigid) to 100 (more rigid)			Disclosure index 0 (less disclosure) to 10 (more disclosure)	Time to resolve insolvency years
	Number of start-up procedures January 2004	Time required days January 2004	Number of procedures January 2004	Time required days January 2004	January 2004	Public registry coverage January 2004	Private bureau coverage January 2004	January 2004	Number of procedures January 2004	Time required days January 2004	January 2004	January 2004
Honduras	13	62	7	36	5	61	0	31	36	545	0	3.7
Hungary	6	52	4	79	5	0	33	40	21	365	5	2.0
India	11	89	6	67	4	0	0	48	40	425	4	10.0
Indonesia	12	151	6	33	5	4	0	57	34	570	4	6.0
Iran, Islamic Rep.	9	48	9	36	5	..	0	40	23	545	2	4.5
Iraq	..	..	..	..	..	..	..	..	..	..	..	..
Ireland	4	24	5	38	8	0	1,000	29	16	217	6	0.4
Israel	5	34	7	144	8	0	11	33	27	585	7	4.0
Italy	9	13	8	27	3	79	571	50	18	1,390	5	1.2
Jamaica	7	31	5	54	6	0	0	10	18	202	2	1.1
Japan	11	31	6	14	6	0	615	24	16	60	6	0.5
Jordan	11	36	8	22	6	5	0	34	43	342	3	4.3
Kazakhstan	9	25	8	52	5	0	0	27	41	400	5	3.3
Kenya	12	47	7	39	8	0	1	24	25	360	2	4.5
Korea, Dem. Rep.	..	..	..	..	..	..	..	..	..	..	..	..
Korea, Rep.	12	22	7	11	6	0	1,000	34	29	75	6	1.5
Kuwait	13	35	8	75	5	0	166	20	52	390	1	4.2
Kyrgyz Republic	8	21	7	15	8	0	0	38	46	492	3	3.5
Lao PDR	9	198	9	135	2	0	0	50	53	443	1	5.0
Latvia	7	18	10	62	8	6	0	49	23	189	5	1.1
Lebanon	6	46	8	25	4	31	0	28	39	721	1	4.0
Lesotho	9	92	6	101	..	0	0	27	49	285	4	2.6
Liberia	..	..	..	..	..	..	..	..	..	..	..	..
Libya	..	..	..	..	..	..	..	..	..	..	..	..
Lithuania	8	26	3	3	4	44	0	41	17	154	6	1.2
Macedonia, FYR	13	48	6	74	6	6	0	38	27	509	4	3.7
Madagascar	13	44	6	114	4	3	0	49	29	280	1	..
Malawi	10	35	6	118	..	0	0	21	16	277	2	2.6
Malaysia	9	30	4	143	8	339	676	3	31	300	5	2.3
Mali	13	42	5	44	3	1	0	66	28	340	..	3.6
Mauritania	11	82	4	49	7	2	0	70	28	410	..	8.0
Mauritius	..	..	..	..	..	..	..	..	..	..	..	..
Mexico	8	58	5	74	2	0	382	72	37	421	5	1.8
Moldova	10	30	5	81	6	0	0	54	37	280	3	2.8
Mongolia	8	20	4	10	5	23	0	37	26	314	3	4.0
Morocco	5	11	3	82	2	6	0	70	17	240	4	1.8
Mozambique	14	153	7	33	4	5	0	64	38	580	5	5.0
Myanmar	..	..	..	..	..	..	..	..	..	..	..	..
Namibia	10	85	9	28	..	0	353	33	31	270	1	1.0
Nepal	7	21	..	..	4	1	0	44	28	350	3	5.0
Netherlands	7	11	4	5	9	0	645	43	22	48	5	1.7
New Zealand	2	12	2	2	9	0	978	7	19	50	5	2.0
Nicaragua	9	45	7	65	4	62	0	51	18	155	1	2.2
Niger	11	27	5	49	4	1	0	90	33	330	1	5.0
Nigeria	10	44	21	274	8	0	0	44	23	730	6	1.5
Norway	4	23	1	1	6	0	1,000	30	14	87	5	0.9
Oman	9	34	4	16	3	0	0	35	41	455	1	7.0
Pakistan	11	24	5	49	4	2	3	49	46	395	4	2.8
Panama	7	19	7	44	6	0	530	63	45	355	1	2.0
Papua New Guinea	8	56	4	72	..	0	0	17	22	295	4	2.8
Paraguay	17	74	7	48	3	90	..	59	46	285	4	3.9
Peru	10	98	5	31	2	143	271	55	35	441	4	3.1
Philippines	11	50	8	33	5	0	34	41	25	380	6	5.6
Poland	10	31	6	204	2	0	380	34	41	1,000	4	1.4
Portugal	11	78	5	83	5	637	79	58	24	320	5	2.5
Puerto Rico	7	7	..	..	6	0	643	21	43	270	..	3.8

5.3 Business environment

	Starting a business		Registering property		Getting credit			Hiring and firing workers	Enforcing contracts		Protecting investors	Closing a business
					Index of borrower and lender legal rights 0 (less access) to 10 (more access)	borrowers per 1,000 adults		Rigidity of employment index 0 (less rigid) to 100 (more rigid)			Disclosure index 0 (less disclosure) to 10 (more disclosure)	Time to resolve insolvency years
	Number of start-up procedures January 2004	Time required days January 2004	Number of procedures January 2004	Time required days January 2004	January 2004	Public registry coverage January 2004	Private bureau coverage January 2004	January 2004	Number of procedures January 2004	Time required days January 2004	January 2004	January 2004
Romania	5	28	8	170	4	4	0	63	43	335	2	4.6
Russian Federation	9	36	6	37	3	0	0	27	29	330	3	1.5
Rwanda	9	21	5	354	5	1	0	76	29	395	0	..
Saudi Arabia	12	64	4	4	..	1	0	13	44	360	2	2.8
Senegal	9	57	6	114	3	3	0	64	36	485	1	3.0
Serbia and Montenegro	11	51	6	186	5	1	0	23	36	1,028	3	2.6
Sierra Leone	9	26	8	58	5	0	0	76	58	305	1	2.5
Singapore	7	8	3	9	10	0	335	0	23	69	5	0.8
Slovak Republic	9	52	5	22	9	6	0	10	27	565	6	4.7
Slovenia	10	61	6	391	6	25	0	53	25	1,003	4	3.6
Somalia	..	..	..	..	..	..	..	..	..	..	..	..
South Africa	9	38	6	20	6	0	636	52	26	277	6	2.0
Spain	6	108	3	25	5	394	65	69	23	169	7	1.0
Sri Lanka	8	50	8	63	3	0	19	40	17	440	4	2.2
Sudan	..	..	..	..	..	..	..	..	..	..	..	..
Swaziland	..	..	..	..	..	..	..	..	..	..	..	..
Sweden	3	16	1	2	6	0	980	43	23	208	6	2.0
Switzerland	6	20	4	16	6	0	233	17	22	170	5	4.6
Syrian Arab Republic	12	47	4	23	5	0	0	37	48	672	1	4.1
Tajikistan	..	..	..	..	..	..	..	..	..	..	..	..
Tanzania	13	35	12	61	5	0	0	65	21	242	1	3.0
Thailand	8	33	2	2	5	0	150	42	26	390	6	2.6
Togo	13	53	6	212	2	3	0	76	37	535	2	3.0
Trinidad and Tobago	..	..	..	..	..	..	..	..	..	..	..	..
Tunisia	9	14	5	57	4	93	0	54	14	27	6	1.3
Turkey	8	9	8	9	1	32	300	55	22	330	2	2.9
Turkmenistan	..	..	..	..	..	..	..	..	..	..	..	..
Uganda	17	36	8	48	5	0	0	7	15	209	2	2.1
Ukraine	15	34	9	93	6	0	0	64	28	269	3	2.6
United Arab Emirates	12	54	3	9	4	18	0	33	53	614	2	5.1
United Kingdom	6	18	2	21	10	0	1,000	20	14	288	7	1.0
United States	5	5	4	12	7	0	1,000	3	17	250	7	3.0
Uruguay	11	45	8	66	4	72	756	31	39	620	1	2.1
Uzbekistan	9	35	12	97	5	0	0	58	35	368	4	4.0
Venezuela, RB	13	116	8	34	4	286	0	56	41	445	1	4.0
Vietnam	11	56	5	78	4	8	0	51	37	404	1	5.5
West Bank and Gaza	..	..	..	..	..	..	..	..	..	..	..	..
Yemen, Rep.	12	63	6	21	2	12	0	37	37	360	..	3.0
Zambia	6	35	6	70	6	0	0	27	16	274	1	2.7
Zimbabwe	10	96	4	30	7	0	0	24	33	350	6	2.2
World	**10 u**	**50 u**	**6 u**	**80 u**	**5 u**	**31 u**	**167 u**	**41 u**	**31 u**	**381 u**	**3 u**	**3.3 u**
Low income	11	63	7	100	4	3	0	52	35	418	2	3.9
Middle income	10	51	7	80	5	33	137	38	31	401	3	3.4
Lower middle income	11	53	7	67	4	25	91	40	31	398	3	3.4
Upper middle income	9	46	5	108	5	51	247	34	31	408	4	3.4
Low & middle income	10	56	7	88	4	21	80	44	33	408	3	3.6
East Asia & Pacific	8	59	5	59	4	22	23	27	29	347	2	3.8
Europe & Central Asia	10	42	7	123	5	6	49	41	30	389	4	3.3
Latin America & Carib.	12	71	7	58	4	79	325	45	35	473	2	3.6
Middle East & N. Africa	10	39	7	48	3	25	0	41	37	413	2	3.7
South Asia	9	47	6	56	4	1	3	42	30	349	3	5.1
Sub-Saharan Africa	11	63	7	107	5	1	41	56	35	431	2	3.6
High income	7	27	5	50	6	68	499	32	23	280	5	2.0
Europe EMU	8	37	5	56	5	152	352	49	22	298	5	1.3

About the data

The table presents key indicators on the environment for doing business. The indicators, covering starting a business, registering property, getting credit, hiring and firing workers, enforcing contracts, protecting investors, and closing a business, identify regulations that enhance or constrain business investment, productivity, and growth. The data are from the World Bank's Doing Business database.

A vibrant private sector is central to promoting growth and expanding opportunities for poor people. But encouraging firms to invest, improve productivity, and create jobs requires a legal and regulatory environment that fosters access to credit, protection of property rights, and efficient judicial, taxation, and customs systems. The indicators in the table point to the administrative and regulatory reforms and institutions needed to create a favorable environment for doing business.

When entrepreneurs start a business, the first obstacles they face are the administrative and legal procedures required to register the new firm. Countries differ widely in how they regulate the entry of new businesses. In some countries the process is straightforward and affordable. But in others the procedures are so burdensome that entrepreneurs may opt to run their business informally. The data on starting a business cover the number of procedures and the time required.

Property registries were first developed to help raise tax revenue, and they have proven useful for entrepreneurs as well. Securing rights to land and buildings, a major source of wealth in most countries, strengthens incentives to invest and facilitates trade. More complex procedures to register property are associated with less perceived security of property rights, more informality, and more corruption. The data cover the number of procedures and time required to secure rights to property.

Lack of access to credit is one of the biggest barriers entrepreneurs face in starting and operating a business. Information on credit histories made available in credit registries is one way for creditors to assess risk and allocate credit more efficiently.

The index of legal rights of borrowers and lenders measures how well collateral and bankruptcy laws facilitate lending. It is based on research on collateral and insolvency laws supported by responses to a survey on secured transactions laws. It includes three aspects related to legal rights in bankruptcy and seven aspects found in collateral law. The indicators related to creditor rights in bankruptcy are based on the methodology of La Porta and others (1998). A public credit registry is a database owned by a public authority (usually the central bank or banking supervisory) that collects information on the standing of borrowers in the financial system and makes it available to financial institutions. A private credit bureau is a private firm or nonprofit organization that maintains a database on the standing of borrowers in the financial system. Its primary role is to facilitate exchange of information among banks and financial institutions. Coverage of public credit registries and private credit bureaus provides an indication of how many borrowers, as a share of the adult population, have information on their payment histories available in credit registries.

Every economy has a complex system of laws and institutions to protect the interests of workers and guarantee a minimum standard of living for its population. The rigidity of employment index focuses on the regulation of employment, specifically the hiring and firing of workers and the rigidity of working hours. This index is the average of three subindexes: a difficulty of hiring index, a rigidity of hours index, and a difficulty of firing index. All subindexes have several components and take values between 0 and 100, with higher values indicating more rigid regulation.

Contract enforcement is critical to enable businesses to engage with new borrowers or customers. Without good contract enforcement, trade and credit will be restricted to a small community of people who have developed relationships through repeated dealings or through the security of assets. The institution that enforces contracts between debtors and creditors, and suppliers and customers, is the court. The efficiency of contract enforcement is reflected in two indicators: the number of judicial procedures to resolve a dispute and the time required to enforce a commercial contract.

What companies must disclose to the public has a large impact on legal protection for investors. Both investors and entrepreneurs benefit greatly from this protection. The disclosure index is based on several measures of ownership disclosure that reduce expropriation and help investors.

Unviable businesses prevent assets and human capital from being allocated to more productive uses in new companies or in viable companies that are financially distressed. The time it takes to resolve an insolvency measures the average time to complete the procedures needed to close an insolvent business, as estimated by insolvency lawyers. Information is collected on the sequence of the bankruptcy procedures and whether any procedures can be carried out simultaneously. Delays due to legal derailment tactics used by parties to an insolvency, in particular extension of response periods or appeals, are taken into account.

For cross-country comparability, such standard characteristics of a company as size, ownership, location, legal status, and type of activities undertaken, are defined in all surveys. The data were collected through studies of laws and regulations in each country, surveys of regulators or private sector professionals, and cooperative arrangements with private consulting firms and business and law associations.

Definitions

• **Start-up procedures** are those required to start a business, including interactions to obtain necessary permits and licenses and to complete all inscriptions, verifications, and notifications to start operations. Data are for businesses with specific characteristics of ownership, size, and type of production. • **Time required to start a business** is the number of calendar days needed to complete the procedures to legally operate a business. If a procedure can be speeded up at additional cost, the fastest procedure, independent of cost, is chosen. • **Number of procedures to register property** is the number of procedures required for a businesses to secure rights to property • **Time required to register property** is the number of calendar days needed for businesses to secure rights to property • **Index of borrower and lender legal rights** measures the degree to which collateral and bankruptcy laws facilitate lending. It includes three aspects related to legal rights in bankruptcy and seven aspects found in collateral law. The index ranges from 0 to 10, with higher scores indicating that collateral and bankruptcy laws are better designed to expand access to credit. • **Public registry coverage** and **private bureau coverage** measure the number of borrowers per 1,000 adults with records contained in the public credit registry and any private credit bureaus. A score of 0 indicates that a public registry or private bureau does not operate in the country. The maximum score is 1,000. • **The rigidity of employment index** measures the regulation of employment, specifically the hiring and firing of workers and the rigidity of working hours. This index is the average of three subindexes: a difficulty of hiring index, a rigidity of hours index, and a difficulty of firing index. The index ranges from 0 to 100, with higher values indicating more rigid regulations. • **Number of procedures to enforce a contract** are the number of independent actions, mandated by law or courts, that demand interaction between the parties of a contract or between them and the judge or court officer. • **Time required to enforce a contract** is the number of calendar days from the filing of the lawsuit in court until the final determination and, in appropriate cases, payment. • **Disclosure index** measures the degree to which investors are protected through disclosure of ownership and financial information. The index ranges from 0 to 7, with higher values indicating more disclosure. • **Time to resolve insolvency** is the number of years from the filing for insolvency in court until the resolution of distressed assets.

Data sources

All data are from the World Bank's Doing Business project (http://rru.worldbank.org/DoingBusiness/).

	Market capitalization				Market liquidity		Turnover ratio		Listed domestic companies		S&P/IFC Investable index	
	$ millions		% of GDP		value traded as % of GDP		value of shares traded as % of market capitalization		number		% change in price index	
	1990	2004	1990	2003	1990	2003	1990	2004	1990	2004	2003	2004
Afghanistan	..	..	..	..	..	..	..	..	..	..	..	..
Albania	..	..	..	..	..	..	..	..	..	..	..	..
Algeria	..	..	..	..	..	..	..	..	..	..	..	..
Angola	..	..	..	..	..	..	..	..	..	..	..	..
Argentina	3,270	46,432	2.3	30.0	0.6	3.8	33.6	17.8	179	104	131.4	24.6
Armenia	..	28	..	1.0	..	..	..	3.9	..	213	..	..
Australia	109,000	585,475	35.1	112.1	12.9	70.8	31.6	76.5	1,089	1,405	..	..
Austria	11,500	54,528	7.1	21.5	11.5	4.3	110.3	25.1	97	86	..	..
Azerbaijan	..	..	..	..	..	..	..	..	..	..	..	..
Bangladesh	321	3,317	1.1	3.1	0.0	0.6	1.5	36.1	134	250	15.4[a]	104.3[a]
Belarus	..	..	..	..	..	..	..	..	..	..	..	..
Belgium	65,400	173,612	33.2	57.5	3.3	12.4	..	24.9	182	152	..	..
Benin	..	..	..	..	..	..	..	..	..	..	..	..
Bolivia	..	1,282	..	16.3	..	0.0	..	0.2	..	32	..	..
Bosnia and Herzegovina	..	..	..	..	..	..	..	..	..	..	..	..
Botswana	261	2,548	6.6	28.3	0.2	1.2	6.1	2.3	9	18	25.6[a]	21.1[a]
Brazil	16,400	330,347	3.6	47.6	1.2	12.3	23.6	34.8	581	357	105.4	33.7
Bulgaria	..	2,804	..	8.8	..	1.0	..	22.8	..	332	189.2[a]	82.7[a]
Burkina Faso	..	..	..	..	..	..	..	..	..	..	..	..
Burundi	..	..	..	..	..	..	..	..	..	..	..	..
Cambodia	..	..	..	..	..	..	..	..	..	..	..	..
Cameroon	..	..	..	..	..	..	..	..	..	..	..	..
Canada	242,000	893,950	42.1	104.4	12.4	54.6	26.7	63.7	1,144	3,578	..	..
Central African Republic	..	..	..	..	..	..	..	..	..	..	..	..
Chad	..	..	..	..	..	..	..	..	..	..	..	..
Chile	13,600	117,065	44.9	119.2	2.6	9.0	6.3	12.1	215	239	79.5	18.3
China	2,030	639,765	0.5	48.1	0.2	33.6	158.9	113.3	14	1,384	77.7	−2.1
Hong Kong, China	83,400	714,597	110.6	456.1	45.9	211.7	43.1	56.3	284	1,029	..	..
Colombia	1,420	25,223	3.5	18.1	0.2	0.5	5.6	7.7	80	114	27.3[a]	115.4[a]
Congo, Dem. Rep.	..	..	..	..	..	..	..	..	..	..	..	..
Congo, Rep.	..	..	..	..	..	..	..	..	..	..	..	..
Costa Rica	475	1,723	5.5	9.9	..	..	5.8	..	82	..	..	..
Côte d'Ivoire	549	2,083	5.1	12.0	0.2	0.2	3.4	2.7	23	39	27.4[a]	41.1[a]
Croatia	..	10,959	..	21.3	..	0.8	..	5.9	2	145	12.8[a]	−7.7[a]
Cuba	..	..	..	..	..	..	..	..	..	..	..	..
Czech Republic	..	30,863	..	19.7	..	9.8	..	78.5	..	54	54.4	76.3
Denmark	39,100	127,997	29.3	60.4	8.3	31.6	28.0	65.4	258	187	..	..
Dominican Republic	..	..	..	..	..	..	..	..	..	..	..	..
Ecuador	69	2,581	0.6	7.9	..	0.1	..	4.2	65	30	14.6[a]	46.7[a]
Egypt, Arab Rep.	1,760	38,516	4.1	32.8	0.3	4.0	..	17.3	573	792	79.3	126.4
El Salvador	..	3,286	..	22.1	..	0.1	..	0.3	..	34	..	..
Eritrea	..	..	..	..	..	..	..	..	..	..	..	..
Estonia	..	6,203	..	41.7	..	6.2	..	17.5	..	13	41.5[a]	70.5[a]
Ethiopia	..	..	..	..	..	..	..	..	..	..	..	..
Finland	22,700	170,283	16.6	105.2	2.9	101.0	..	105.8	73	142	..	..
France	314,000	1,355,643	25.8	77.1	9.6	56.6	..	85.7	578	723	..	..
Gabon	..	..	..	..	..	..	..	..	..	..	..	..
Gambia, The	..	..	..	..	..	..	..	..	..	..	..	..
Georgia	..	203	..	5.1	..	..	..	0.5	..	278	..	..
Germany	355,000	1,079,026	21.2	44.9	30.0	47.7	139.3	130.0	413	684	..	..
Ghana	76	2,644	1.2	18.7	..	0.6	..	3.2	13	29	65.4[a]	32.7[a]
Greece	15,200	106,845	18.1	62.0	4.7	22.4	36.3	44.0	145	339	−31.2	..
Guatemala	..	..	..	1.1	..	0.0	..	3.1	..	5	..	..
Guinea	..	..	..	..	..	..	..	..	..	..	..	..
Guinea-Bissau	..	..	..	..	..	..	..	..	..	..	..	..
Haiti	..	..	..	..	..	..	..	..	..	..	..	..

| | Market capitalization | | | | Market liquidity | | Turnover ratio | | Listed domestic companies | | S&P/IFC Investable index | |
| | \$ millions | | % of GDP | | value traded as % of GDP | | value of shares traded as % of market capitalization | | number | | % change in price index | |
	1990	2004	1990	2003	1990	2003	1990	2004	1990	2004	2003	2004
Honduras	40	..	1.3	..	..	..	..	..	26	..	..	..
Hungary	505	28,711	1.5	20.2	0.3	10.0	6.3	59.9	21	47	28.6	93.7
India	38,600	387,851	12.2	46.5	6.9	47.4	65.9	115.5	2,435	4,730	76.5	20.1
Indonesia	8,080	73,251	7.1	26.2	3.5	7.1	75.8	43.3	125	331	69.7	39.3
Iran, Islamic Rep.	34,300	34,444	..	25.1	..	3.9	30.4	21.7	97	370	..	..
Iraq	..	..	..	..	..	..	..	..	..	..	..	..
Ireland	..	85,070	..	55.3	..	28.6	..	60.7	..	55	..	..
Israel	3,320	95,505	6.3	68.7	10.5	37.7	95.8	55.6	216	571	59.5	13.4
Italy	149,000	614,842	13.5	41.9	3.9	45.2	26.8	121.5	220	271	..	..
Jamaica	911	14,415	19.8	104.3	0.7	3.1	3.4	4.2	44	38	−3.4[a]	107.4[a]
Japan	2,920,000	3,040,665	96.1	70.7	52.7	52.8	43.8	88.0	2,071	3,116	37.8[b]	12.5[b]
Jordan	2,000	18,383	49.7	111.2	10.1	26.4	20.0	36.3	105	192	65.4[a]	55.0[a]
Kazakhstan	..	2,425	..	8.2	..	1.4	..	22.0	..	41	..	..
Kenya	453	3,891	5.3	29.1	0.1	1.5	2.2	8.1	54	47	186.2[a]	−15.0[a]
Korea, Dem. Rep.	..	..	..	..	..	..	..	..	..	..	..	..
Korea, Rep.	111,000	428,649	42.1	54.5	28.8	112.8	61.3	174.0	669	1,573	33.3	25.7
Kuwait	..	..	..	..	..	..	..	..	..	..	..	..
Kyrgyz Republic	..	31	..	1.6	..	..	..	58.1	..	17	..	..
Lao PDR	..	..	..	..	..	..	..	..	..	..	..	..
Latvia	..	1,655	..	10.3	..	1.3	..	8.1	..	39	62.6[a]	49.8[a]
Lebanon	..	2,321	..	7.9	..	0.7	..	10.3	..	13	0.9	53.5[a]
Lesotho	..	..	..	..	..	..	..	..	..	..	..	..
Liberia	..	..	..	..	..	..	..	..	..	..	..	..
Libya	..	..	..	..	..	..	..	..	..	..	..	..
Lithuania	..	6,463	..	19.3	..	1.1	..	9.8	..	43	117.9[a]	56.2[a]
Macedonia, FYR	..	362	..	7.8	..	0.5	..	8.1	..	92	..	..
Madagascar	..	..	..	..	..	..	..	..	..	..	..	..
Malawi	..	..	..	9.2	..	1.3	..	13.8	..	8	..	..
Malaysia	48,600	190,011	110.4	162.3	24.7	48.3	24.6	33.4	282	962	25.5	12.7
Mali	..	..	..	..	..	..	..	..	..	..	..	..
Mauritania	..	..	..	113.3	..	..	..	..	..	..	..	..
Mauritius	268	2,379	11.2	37.4	0.3	1.9	1.9	4.4	13	41	43.7[a]	17.8[a]
Mexico	32,700	171,940	12.4	19.6	4.6	3.8	44.0	29.4	199	152	30.4	47.9
Moldova	..	507	..	25.8	..	1.8	..	7.7	..	23	..	..
Mongolia	..	42	..	3.3	..	..	..	2.2	..	402	..	..
Morocco	966	25,064	3.7	30.1	0.2	1.6	..	9.1	71	52	44.0	18.3
Mozambique	..	..	..	..	..	..	..	..	..	..	..	..
Myanmar	..	..	..	..	..	..	..	..	..	..	..	..
Namibia	21	442	0.7	7.2	..	0.0	..	4.8	3	13	37.1	36.7[a]
Nepal	..	..	..	..	..	..	..	..	..	73	..	..
Netherlands	120,000	488,647	40.7	95.5	13.6	90.6	29.0	104.1	260	183	..	..
New Zealand	8,840	33,052	20.3	41.5	4.4	13.2	17.3	38.3	171	157	..	..
Nicaragua	..	..	..	..	..	..	..	..	..	..	..	..
Niger	..	..	..	..	..	..	..	..	..	..	..	..
Nigeria	1,370	14,464	4.8	16.3	0.0	1.5	0.9	13.7	131	207	57.5[a]	23.9[a]
Norway	26,100	94,679	22.5	42.9	12.1	31.7	54.4	86.4	112	156	..	..
Oman	1,060	6,325	9.4	19.7	0.9	2.6	12.3	31.5	55	96	47.0	25.2[a]
Pakistan	2,850	29,002	7.1	20.1	0.6	80.9	8.7	322.5	487	661	50.4[a]	20.7[a]
Panama	226	3,075	3.4	23.9	0.0	0.3	0.9	1.5	13	25	..	..
Papua New Guinea	..	..	..	..	..	..	..	..	..	..	..	..
Paraguay	..	..	..	..	..	..	..	..	..	..	..	..
Peru	812	20,115	3.1	26.5	0.4	1.3	19.3	6.3	294	194	88.1	−0.7
Philippines	5,930	28,948	13.4	29.2	2.7	3.3	13.6	14.0	153	233	41.4	25.0
Poland	144	71,102	0.2	17.7	0.0	4.1	89.7	33.1	9	225	29.5	59.3
Portugal	9,200	58,285	12.9	39.4	2.4	14.5	16.9	42.4	181	59	..	..
Puerto Rico	..	..	..	..	..	..	..	..	..	..	..	..

5.4 Stock markets

	Market capitalization				Market liquidity		Turnover ratio		Listed domestic companies		S&P/IFC Investable index	
	\$ millions		% of GDP		value traded as % of GDP		value of shares traded as % of market capitalization		number		% change in price index	
	1990	2004	1990	2003	1990	2003	1990	2004	1990	2004	2003	2004
Romania	..	11,786	..	9.8	..	0.8	..	11.6	..	4,030	42.5[a]	99.3[a]
Russian Federation	244	267,957	0.0	53.3	..	18.7	..	53.0	13	215	68.5	12.8
Rwanda	..	..	..	..	..	..	..	..	..	..	..	..
Saudi Arabia	48,200	306,248	36.7	73.2	1.7	74.1	..	204.1	59	73	49.5[a]	83.6[a]
Senegal	..	..	..	..	..	..	..	..	..	..	..	..
Serbia and Montenegro	..	142	..	0.7	..	2.6	..	122.3	..	342	..	..
Sierra Leone	..	..	..	..	..	..	..	..	..	..	..	..
Singapore	34,300	145,117	93.0	158.9	55.0	96.2	..	71.1	150	475	..	..
Slovak Republic	..	4,410	..	8.5	..	2.0	..	19.8	..	258	57.2[a]	41.0[a]
Slovenia	..	9,677	..	25.7	..	2.6	..	14.6	24	140	42.1[a]	128.5[a]
Somalia	..	..	..	..	..	..	..	..	..	..	..	..
South Africa	138,000	455,536	123.2	167.5	7.3	64.3	..	47.4	732	403	37.6	341.0
Spain	111,000	726,243	21.8	86.6	8.0	111.5	..	157.5	427	3,191	..	..
Sri Lanka	917	3,657	11.4	14.9	0.5	4.2	5.8	18.4	175	245	35.6[a]	−59.2[a]
Sudan	..	..	..	..	..	..	..	..	..	..	..	..
Swaziland	17	172	2.0	9.3	..	0.6	..	0.0	1	5	..	..
Sweden	97,900	287,500	40.8	95.3	7.3	90.6	14.9	113.6	258	264	..	..
Switzerland	160,000	725,659	67.9	226.7	28.8	179.8	..	90.0	182	289	..	..
Syrian Arab Republic	..	..	..	..	..	..	..	..	..	..	..	..
Tajikistan	..	..	..	..	..	..	..	..	..	..	..	..
Tanzania	..	..	..	4.2	..	0.1	..	1.9	..	..	..	..
Thailand	23,900	115,099	28.0	83.0	26.8	67.6	92.6	95.3	214	439	147.2	7.4
Togo	..	..	..	..	..	..	..	..	..	..	..	..
Trinidad and Tobago	696	17,051	13.7	100.9	1.1	3.8	10.0	3.8	30	37	46.7[a]	36.8[a]
Tunisia	533	2,641	4.3	9.8	0.2	0.7	3.3	9.2	13	44	14.9[a]	4.2[a]
Turkey	19,100	98,299	12.7	28.4	3.9	41.4	42.5	182.3	110	296	113.2	167.8
Turkmenistan	..	..	..	..	..	..	..	..	..	..	..	..
Uganda	..	..	..	0.6	..	..	..	..	..	..	..	..
Ukraine	..	11,778	..	8.7	..	0.2	..	2.5	..	155	40.3[a]	170.3[a]
United Arab Emirates	..	..	..	11.4	..	0.0	..	3.4	..	..	..	..
United Kingdom	849,000	2,412,434	85.8	134.4	28.2	119.8	33.4	100.6	1,701	2,311	26.3[c]	15.3[c]
United States	3,060,000	14,266,266	53.2	130.3	30.4	142.0	53.4	122.8	6,599	5,295	26.4[d]	9.0[d]
Uruguay	..	170	..	1.5	..	0.0	..	0.4	36	11	..	..
Uzbekistan	..	14	..	0.1	..	..	..	108.7	..	478	..	..
Venezuela, RB	8,360	6,117	17.2	4.5	4.6	0.2	43.0	9.0	76	59	14.3[a]	−50.4[a]
Vietnam	..	..	..	..	..	..	..	..	..	..	..	..
West Bank and Gaza	..	6,292	..	182.1	..	1.7	..	1.7	..	27	..	..
Yemen, Rep.	..	..	..	..	..	..	..	..	..	..	..	..
Zambia	..	..	..	6.0	..	1.3	..	22.5	..	..	..	..
Zimbabwe	2,400	1,941	27.3	87.9	0.6	14.0	2.9	9.2	57	79	−74.8[a]	−26.7[a]
World	9,403,525 s	32,436,350 s	48.0 w	89.7 w	28.5 w	83.4 w	57.2 w	72.4 w	25,424 s	50,038 s		
Low income	46,543	319,611	10.5	37.3	5.0	42.5	48.2	130.5	3,321	7,988		
Middle income	328,522	2,534,088	19.4	44.5	5.1	21.6	..	60.9	4,370	14,456		
Lower middle income	220,746	1,838,275	14.8	47.3	8.5	24.5	..	70.8	3,271	11,866		
Upper middle income	107,776	695,813	29.6	38.4	6.1	15.3	50.3	21.2	1,099	2,590		
Low & middle income	375,065	2,853,699	18.8	43.5	5.2	24.3	..	72.4	7,691	22,444		
East Asia & Pacific	86,510	1,047,309	16.4	53.5	6.6	32.8	118.1	103.5	774	3,582		
Europe & Central Asia	19,100	403,420	2.2	29.7	..	15.7	..	37.9	110	7,776		
Latin America & Carib.	78,451	550,731	7.7	33.2	2.1	6.0	29.8	22.0	1,748	1,468		
Middle East & N. Africa	5,259	258,200	27.4	47.3	2.2	32.0	..	64.4	817	1,803		
South Asia	42,688	300,004	10.8	39.8	5.6	46.8	54.0	131.2	3,231	6,909		
Sub-Saharan Africa	143,057	294,034	52.3	105.9	..	31.7	..	39.3	1,011	906		
High income	9,028,460	29,582,653	51.6	100.1	31.4	96.8	59.4	110.1	17,733	27,594		
Europe EMU	1,183,500	4,950,359	21.7	60.4	14.2	55.3	..	107.5	2,630	5,929		

Note: Because aggregates for market capitalization are unavailable for 2004, those shown refer to 2003. a. Data refer to the S&P/IFC Global index. b. Data refer to the Nikkei 225 index. c. Data refer to the FT 100 index. d. Data refer to the S&P 500 index.

The development of an economy's financial markets is closely related to its overall development. Well functioning financial systems provide good and easily accessible information. That lowers transaction costs, which in turn improves resource allocation and boosts economic growth. Both banking systems and stock markets enhance growth, the main factor in poverty reduction. At low levels of economic development commercial banks tend to dominate the financial system, while at higher levels domestic stock markets tend to become more active and efficient relative to domestic banks.

Open economies with sound macroeconomic policies, good legal systems, and shareholder protection attract capital and therefore have larger financial markets. Recent research on stock market development shows that new communications technology and increased financial integration have resulted in more cross-border capital flows, a stronger presence of financial firms around the world, and the migration of stock exchange activities to international exchanges. Many firms in emerging markets now cross-list on international exchanges, which provides them with lower cost capital and more liquidity-traded shares. However, this also means that exchanges in emerging markets may not have enough financial activity to sustain them, putting pressure on them to rethink their operations.

The stock market indicators in the table include measures of size (market capitalization, number of listed domestic companies) and liquidity (value traded as a percentage of gross domestic product, value of shares traded as a percentage of market capitalization). The comparability of such indicators between countries may be limited by conceptual and statistical weaknesses, such as inaccurate reporting and differences in accounting standards. The percentage change in stock market prices in U.S. dollars, from the Standard & Poor's Investable (S&P/IFCI) and Global (S&P/IFCG) country indexes, is an important measure of overall performance. Regulatory and institutional factors that can affect investor confidence, such as entry and exit restrictions, the existence of a securities and exchange commission, and the quality of laws to protect investors, may influence the functioning of stock markets but are not included in the table.

Stock market size can be measured in a number of ways, and each may produce a different ranking of countries. Market capitalization shows the overall size of the stock market in U.S. dollars and as a percentage of GDP. The number of listed domestic companies is another measure of market size. Market size is positively correlated with the ability to mobilize capital and diversify risk.

Market liquidity, the ability to easily buy and sell securities, is measured by dividing the total value traded by GDP. This indicator complements the market capitalization ratio by showing whether market size is matched by trading. The turnover ratio—the value of shares traded as a percentage of market capitalization—is also a measure of liquidity as well as of transaction costs. (High turnover indicates low transaction costs.) The turnover ratio complements the ratio of value traded to GDP, because the turnover ratio is related to the size of the market and the value traded ratio to the size of the economy. A small, liquid market will have a high turnover ratio but a low value traded ratio. Liquidity is an important attribute of stock markets because, in theory, liquid markets improve the allocation of capital and enhance prospects for long-term economic growth. A more comprehensive measure of liquidity would include trading costs and the time and uncertainty in finding a counterpart in settling trades.

Standard & Poor's maintains a series of indexes for investors interested in investing in stock markets in developing countries. At the core of the Standard & Poor's family of emerging market indexes, the S&P/IFCG index is intended to represent the most active stocks in the markets it covers and to be the broadest possible indicator of market movements. The S&P/IFCI index, which applies the same calculation methodology as the S&P/IFCG index, is designed to measure the returns foreign portfolio investors might receive from investing in emerging market stocks that are legally and practically open to foreign portfolio investment.

Standard & Poor's Emerging Markets Data Base, the source for all the data in the table, provides regular updates on 55 emerging stock markets encompassing more than 2,613 stocks. The S&P/IFCG index includes 33 markets and 1,702 stocks, and the S&P/IFCI index covers 22 markets and 911 stocks. In addition, 289 companies from 20 "frontier" markets are covered. These indexes are widely used benchmarks for international portfolio management. See Standard & Poor's (2001b) for further information on the indexes.

Because markets included in Standard & Poor's emerging markets category vary widely in level of development, it is best to look at the entire category to identify the most significant market trends. And it is useful to remember that stock market trends may be distorted by currency conversions, especially when a currency has registered a significant devaluation.

About the data is based on Demirgüç-Kunt and Levine (1996a), Beck and Levine (2001), and Claessens, Klingebiel, and Schmukler (2002).

• **Market capitalization** (also known as market value) is the share price times the number of shares outstanding. • **Market liquidity** is the total value traded divided by GDP. Value traded is the total value of shares traded during the period. • **Turnover ratio** is the total value of shares traded during the period divided by the average market capitalization for the period. Average market capitalization is calculated as the average of the end-of-period values for the current period and the previous period. • **Listed domestic companies** are the domestically incorporated companies listed on the country's stock exchanges at the end of the year. This indicator does not include investment companies, mutual funds, or other collective investment vehicles. • **S&P/IFC Investable index price change** is the U.S. dollar price change in the stock markets covered by the S&P/IFCI country index, supplemented by the S&P/IFCG country index.

Data sources

The data on stock markets are from Standard & Poor's *Global Stock Markets Factbook 2004,* which draws on the Emerging Markets Data Base, supplemented by other data from Standard & Poor's. The firm collects data through an annual survey of the world's stock exchanges, supplemented by information provided by its network of correspondents and by Reuters. The GDP data are from the World Bank's national accounts data files.

	Domestic credit provided by banking sector		Liquid liabilities		Quasi-liquid liabilities		Ratio of bank liquid reserves to bank assets		Interest rate spread		Risk premium on lending	
	% of GDP		% of GDP		% of GDP		%		Lending minus deposit rate percentage points		Prime lending rate minus treasury bill rate percentage points	
	1990	2003	1990	2003	1990	2003	1990	2003	1990	2003	1990	2003
Afghanistan	..	..	..	..	..	..	..	..	..	..	..	..
Albania	..	44.1	..	60.1	..	40.7	..	10.3	2.1	5.9	..	5.5
Algeria	74.5	35.0	73.5	63.9	24.8	32.2	1.3	27.9	..	2.8	..	6.8
Angola	..	6.6	..	18.2	..	11.1	..	14.7	..	69.9	..	..
Argentina	32.4	50.6	11.5	30.1	7.1	18.7	7.4	16.2	..	9.0	..	..
Armenia	58.7	5.5	79.9	14.4	42.9	6.8	13.6	11.1	..	14.0	..	8.9
Australia	71.4	104.5	55.0	75.2	43.2	46.5	1.5	0.8	4.4	5.1	3.7	3.9
Austria	121.4	122.7	..	..	..	..	2.1	..	..	..	..	..
Azerbaijan	65.9	9.4	38.6	14.7	13.4	7.6	4.5	11.5	..	5.9	..	7.5
Bangladesh	23.9	38.4	23.4	40.2	16.8	31.1	12.8	8.8	4.0	8.2	..	..
Belarus	..	21.2	..	17.2	..	10.9	..	8.5	..	6.5	..	..
Belgium	73.1	112.2	..	..	..	..	0.2	..	6.9	5.2	3.4	4.7
Benin	22.4	9.8	26.7	22.0	5.9	7.3	29.3	16.8	9.0	..	..	..
Bolivia	30.7	60.0	24.5	53.3	18.0	44.0	18.8	6.0	18.0	6.3	..	7.7
Bosnia and Herzegovina	..	41.6	..	48.7	..	21.5	..	15.1	..	6.8	..	..
Botswana	−46.0	−9.3	21.9	29.5	13.6	21.9	11.0	4.4	1.8	6.3	..	..
Brazil	89.8	61.1	26.4	30.0	18.5	22.7	7.6	18.9	..	45.1	..	45.0
Bulgaria	118.5	29.8	74.5	48.7	56.2	25.4	6.7	9.3	13.0	5.9	8.6	6.0
Burkina Faso	12.1	13.7	18.8	19.4	6.6	7.6	12.7	12.4	9.0	..	..	..
Burundi	23.2	36.6	18.2	26.8	6.5	8.2	2.8	4.4	..	..	..	..
Cambodia	..	7.2	..	19.7	..	14.1	..	58.8	..	16.5	..	..
Cameroon	31.2	16.0	22.6	18.7	10.1	8.1	3.4	22.8	11.0	13.0	..	..
Canada	82.3	92.3	74.3	78.5	59.8	54.8	1.6	0.5	4.2	3.6	1.3	1.8
Central African Republic	12.9	14.7	15.3	13.9	1.8	1.6	2.8	3.7	11.0	13.0	..	..
Chad	11.5	11.4	14.6	12.1	0.6	0.7	3.3	15.1	11.0	13.0	..	..
Chile	73.0	70.6	40.8	38.2	32.8	28.3	3.6	4.7	8.5	3.4	..	..
China	90.0	177.9	79.2	190.6	41.4	116.9	15.7	12.2	0.7	3.3	..	..
Hong Kong, China	154.9	147.8	179.4	262.1	164.7	235.6	0.1	0.8	3.3	4.9	2.7	5.1
Colombia	35.9	35.2	29.8	32.0	19.3	20.9	27.4	6.4	8.8	7.4	..	..
Congo, Dem. Rep.	25.3	1.4	12.9	5.4	2.1	2.3	49.0	5.9	..	..	..	..
Congo, Rep.	29.1	12.8	22.0	13.7	6.1	2.4	2.0	31.4	11.0	13.0	..	..
Costa Rica	29.9	39.0	42.7	40.5	30.0	26.6	68.5	11.5	11.4	15.2	..	..
Côte d'Ivoire	44.5	18.9	28.8	28.1	10.9	7.8	2.1	11.3	9.0	..	..	..
Croatia	..	65.5	..	66.5	..	48.9	..	16.1	499.3	10.1	..	..
Cuba	..	..	..	..	..	..	..	..	..	..	..	..
Czech Republic	..	49.5	..	72.9	..	34.8	..	3.3	..	4.6	..	3.9
Denmark	63.0	161.9	59.0	52.9	29.4	19.3	1.1	0.7	6.2	4.7	..	..
Dominican Republic	31.5	44.0	28.6	48.9	13.3	34.8	31.2	27.1	15.2	10.9	..	..
Ecuador	15.5	19.7	21.1	21.7	11.8	14.4	19.0	3.3	−6.0	7.6	..	..
Egypt, Arab Rep.	106.8	117.2	87.9	106.6	60.7	84.1	17.1	25.1	7.0	5.3	..	6.6
El Salvador	23.6	50.5	26.0	42.0	16.7	33.9	27.3	13.1	3.2	..	..	..
Eritrea	..	148.2	..	169.5	..	103.0	..	23.6	..	..	..	..
Estonia	66.7	54.8	136.0	40.0	95.2	15.5	43.1	10.5	..	3.1	..	..
Ethiopia	55.4	62.4	42.1	59.4	12.2	26.8	23.9	15.1	6.0	4.7	3.0	6.7
Finland	83.0	69.5	54.4	..	..	..	4.1	..	4.1	3.3	..	..
France	104.4	107.2	..	..	..	..	1.0	..	6.1	3.9	0.4	4.3
Gabon	20.0	17.5	17.8	16.8	6.6	7.0	2.0	15.3	11.0	13.0	..	..
Gambia, The	3.4	25.3	20.7	43.5	8.8	19.6	8.8	13.7	15.2	11.3	..	..
Georgia	..	19.5	..	12.5	..	6.4	..	13.9	..	23.0	..	−12.0
Germany	104.4	142.9	68.8	..	..	..	3.2	..	4.5	7.0	3.5	6.7
Ghana	17.5	25.9	14.1	30.4	3.4	14.2	20.2	12.3	..	..	..	..
Greece	99.3	105.1	..	..	..	..	13.9	..	8.1	4.3	3.6	4.4
Guatemala	17.4	15.5	21.2	32.6	11.8	18.9	31.8	17.8	5.1	10.2	..	..
Guinea	6.1	15.2	0.8	15.2	0.8	2.9	6.2	17.0	0.2	..	..	..
Guinea-Bissau	77.5	12.8	68.9	71.2	4.4	0.4	10.8	22.2	13.1	..	..	..
Haiti	34.3	36.9	32.6	48.5	16.6	34.8	74.9	42.5	..	16.6	..	10.1

Financial depth and efficiency **5.5**

	Domestic credit provided by banking sector		Liquid liabilities		Quasi-liquid liabilities		Ratio of bank liquid reserves to bank assets		Interest rate spread		Risk premium on lending	
	% of GDP		% of GDP		% of GDP		%		Lending minus deposit rate percentage points		Prime lending rate minus treasury bill rate percentage points	
	1990	2003	1990	2003	1990	2003	1990	2003	1990	2003	1990	2003
Honduras	40.9	37.7	33.6	56.4	18.8	42.2	6.7	18.4	8.3	9.3	..	..
Hungary	105.5	58.3	43.8	48.0	19.0	28.4	11.2	3.6	4.1	−1.4	−1.4	1.4
India	51.5	57.3	43.1	63.9	28.1	45.7	14.8	5.3	..	..	..	..
Indonesia	45.5	55.7	40.4	53.4	29.1	41.1	4.2	12.0	3.3	6.3	..	..
Iran, Islamic Rep.	70.8	46.8	57.6	42.0	31.1	25.6	66.0	21.6	..	..	..	..
Iraq	..	..	..	..	..	..	..	..	..	..	..	..
Ireland	55.2	118.4	44.5	..	..	..	4.8	..	5.0	2.8	0.4	..
Israel	106.2	86.9	70.2	102.2	63.6	93.6	11.9	7.9	12.0	4.0	11.4	3.7
Italy	89.4	105.3	70.5	..	..	..	12.0	..	7.3	4.1	1.7	2.8
Jamaica	32.2	37.9	47.2	44.2	35.0	30.8	37.4	19.5	6.6	10.4	4.3	−7.1
Japan	260.7	157.3	183.2	135.8	156.0	62.8	1.6	4.5	3.4	1.8	..	..
Jordan	117.9	90.3	131.2	132.2	77.8	91.7	20.5	34.9	2.2	6.2	..	..
Kazakhstan	..	13.7	..	21.1	..	10.3	..	5.3	..	..	..	..
Kenya	52.9	40.6	43.3	41.5	29.3	23.7	9.9	6.8	5.1	12.4	4.0	13.1
Korea, Dem. Rep.	..	..	..	..	..	..	..	..	..	..	..	..
Korea, Rep.	62.9	105.6	52.3	89.3	43.7	80.2	6.3	2.7	0.0	2.0	..	..
Kuwait	243.0	106.0	..	83.6	..	62.6	1.2	1.3	0.0	3.0	0.0	..
Kyrgyz Republic	..	11.4	..	17.6	..	4.9	..	7.6	..	14.1	..	11.9
Lao PDR	5.1	10.1	7.2	18.8	3.1	15.1	3.4	29.5	2.5	23.9	..	5.6
Latvia	..	45.5	..	36.6	..	17.1	..	4.3	..	2.4	..	2.1
Lebanon	132.6	188.0	193.7	225.7	170.9	215.7	3.9	48.2	23.1	4.7	21.1	5.7
Lesotho	32.8	4.4	39.2	26.7	22.6	8.8	23.0	7.7	7.4	10.9	4.1	4.1
Liberia	319.5	196.1	..	11.2	..	1.7	67.3	45.8	0.0	11.8	..	..
Libya	104.1	50.3	68.1	41.3	13.7	9.0	26.4	30.9	1.5	4.0	1.5	1.5
Lithuania	..	23.7	..	31.5	..	12.6	..	11.3	..	4.6	..	3.2
Macedonia, FYR	..	17.9	..	31.5	..	20.7	..	9.0	..	8.0	..	..
Madagascar	26.2	18.0	17.8	23.4	5.3	6.1	8.5	15.5	5.3	12.8	..	12.3
Malawi	19.7	22.6	20.2	25.8	10.8	15.2	32.9	20.1	8.9	23.8	8.1	9.6
Malaysia	75.7	152.1	..	130.7	−21.3	103.9	5.9	3.3	3.1	3.2	2.7	3.5
Mali	13.7	16.3	20.5	30.4	5.5	6.9	50.8	21.7	9.0	..	..	..
Mauritania	54.7	−7.2	28.5	16.2	7.0	5.0	6.1	3.5	5.0	13.0	..	..
Mauritius	48.4	78.6	67.9	88.0	52.7	74.3	8.8	5.0	5.4	11.5	..	..
Mexico	36.3	38.5	22.4	29.1	16.0	19.1	3.2	7.4	..	3.8	..	0.7
Moldova	62.8	29.8	70.3	32.1	35.4	16.0	8.3	14.2	..	6.7	..	4.2
Mongolia	72.4	38.0	56.2	48.1	14.7	33.6	2.0	11.5	..	12.3	..	..
Morocco	60.1	84.5	61.0	92.3	18.4	20.9	11.3	11.0	0.5	8.8	..	..
Mozambique	15.6	11.0	26.5	32.0	5.2	18.1	61.5	17.4	..	12.5	..	9.4
Myanmar	32.8	35.1	27.9	33.5	7.8	13.1	286.7	25.5	2.1	5.5	..	..
Namibia	20.3	55.8	24.3	41.6	14.2	17.3	4.4	3.3	10.6	5.9	6.3	4.2
Nepal	28.9	..	32.2	37.7	18.5	37.7	12.7	19.8	2.5	2.9	6.5	2.7
Netherlands	103.4	166.9	..	..	..	..	0.3	..	8.4	0.5	..	..
New Zealand	80.6	118.6	77.0	90.8	65.5	75.0	0.8	0.5	4.4	4.7	2.2	4.6
Nicaragua	206.6	96.5	56.9	42.0	23.1	35.2	20.2	27.3	12.5	10.0	..	..
Niger	16.2	9.2	..	7.4	−11.5	2.8	42.9	23.5	9.0	..	..	..
Nigeria	23.7	23.4	23.6	26.3	10.3	10.1	11.9	18.1	5.5	6.5	6.9	5.9
Norway	89.0	94.6	59.5	56.0	26.8	8.2	0.5	2.5	4.5	2.6	..	..
Oman	16.6	40.3	28.9	35.4	19.3	25.5	6.9	3.2	1.4	5.9	..	..
Pakistan	50.9	35.8	39.8	48.6	10.0	19.8	8.9	8.7	..	..	..	..
Panama	52.7	88.0	41.1	76.4	33.0	65.1	..	..	3.6	5.9	..	..
Papua New Guinea	35.7	22.2	35.2	27.0	24.0	11.5	3.2	11.9	6.9	5.2	4.1	−5.3
Paraguay	14.9	18.8	22.3	32.4	13.7	22.6	31.0	38.1	8.1	34.2	..	..
Peru	20.2	20.8	24.8	29.8	11.8	19.6	22.0	26.9	2,335.0	10.4	..	..
Philippines	26.9	59.5	37.0	60.4	28.4	48.5	20.9	7.5	4.6	4.3	0.4	3.6
Poland	19.5	37.0	34.0	42.7	17.2	26.3	20.6	4.4	462.5	3.6	−5.0	..
Portugal	69.4	151.1	..	..	..	..	29.0	..	7.8	..	8.3	..
Puerto Rico	..	..	..	..	..	..	..	..	..	..	..	..

	Domestic credit provided by banking sector		Liquid liabilities		Quasi-liquid liabilities		Ratio of bank liquid reserves to bank assets		Interest rate spread		Risk premium on lending	
	% of GDP		% of GDP		% of GDP		%		Lending minus deposit rate percentage points		Prime lending rate minus treasury bill rate percentage points	
	1990	2003	1990	2003	1990	2003	1990	2003	1990	2003	1990	2003
Romania	79.7	15.9	60.4	24.4	32.7	18.7	1.2	62.1	..	..	..	..
Russian Federation	..	27.6	..	29.8	..	13.4	..	17.8	..	8.5	..	7.6
Rwanda	17.1	13.9	14.9	18.7	7.0	9.4	4.3	8.2	6.3	..	..	..
Saudi Arabia	52.7	70.3	42.9	51.5	19.6	23.7	5.6	5.5	..	..	..	..
Senegal	33.8	22.5	22.9	29.5	9.7	11.8	14.1	16.8	9.0	..	..	..
Serbia and Montenegro	..	..	..	..	..	..	..	..	..	..	..	..
Sierra Leone	36.3	47.3	18.1	24.7	3.6	8.9	64.1	6.8	12.0	11.6	5.0	4.3
Singapore	75.2	88.4	122.7	122.4	99.9	98.1	3.7	2.5	2.7	4.8	3.7	4.7
Slovak Republic	..	44.7	..	64.3	..	34.7	..	5.2	..	3.1	..	..
Slovenia	*36.8*	49.9	*34.2*	54.2	*25.8*	40.9	*2.7*	3.6	*142.0*	4.8	..	4.2
Somalia	..	..	..	..	..	..	..	..	..	..	..	..
South Africa	97.8	158.2	44.6	53.8	27.2	22.8	3.3	2.3	2.1	5.2	3.2	4.3
Spain	107.0	138.7	..	..	..	..	8.7	..	5.4	*1.8*	1.8	*1.0*
Sri Lanka	38.0	42.1	34.9	49.9	22.6	40.8	9.9	6.9	−6.4	4.3	−1.1	2.3
Sudan	20.4	11.9	20.1	15.8	2.9	5.9	79.5	19.8	..	..	..	..
Swaziland	7.7	11.5	29.0	21.4	20.3	13.9	21.5	6.6	5.8	7.0	3.4	4.0
Sweden	139.2	110.7	51.9	..	..	..	1.9	0.6	6.8	3.3	3.0	1.8
Switzerland	173.4	174.7	140.6	161.0	114.9	105.9	1.1	0.9	−0.9	3.1	−0.9	3.1
Syrian Arab Republic	56.6	30.1	54.7	82.6	10.5	24.2	46.0	10.0	5.0	*5.0*	..	..
Tajikistan	..	14.0	..	8.3	..	3.6	..	15.7	..	6.9	..	..
Tanzania	34.6	8.4	19.9	22.7	6.3	12.2	5.3	12.4	0.0	11.4	..	8.2
Thailand	91.1	113.0	74.9	112.4	66.0	97.8	3.1	4.9	2.2	4.6	..	..
Togo	21.3	18.0	..	24.3	−17.0	10.3	59.0	16.2	9.0	..	..	..
Trinidad and Tobago	58.5	38.3	54.6	46.8	42.7	35.1	13.5	12.5	6.9	8.3	5.4	6.5
Tunisia	62.5	71.7	..	59.1	−24.8	36.6	1.6	3.2	..	..	..	..
Turkey	19.5	53.9	24.1	43.6	16.4	37.8	16.4	7.9	..	..	..	..
Turkmenistan	..	*19.1*	..	*16.5*	..	*7.8*	..	*6.9*	..	..	..	..
Uganda	*17.8*	12.5	7.6	20.5	1.4	10.1	15.2	8.1	7.4	9.1	−2.3	2.1
Ukraine	*83.2*	32.7	*50.1*	35.8	*9.0*	15.6	*49.0*	8.9	..	10.9	..	..
United Arab Emirates	34.7	*47.6*	46.3	*66.6*	37.7	*48.6*	4.4	9.4	..	..	..	..
United Kingdom	121.0	150.4	..	..	..	..	0.5	0.3	2.2	..	0.7	0.1
United States	174.5	261.8	65.4	67.8	49.4	51.6	2.7	1.2	..	..	2.5	3.1
Uruguay	46.7	71.1	58.1	67.7	51.5	61.6	31.2	22.7	76.6	*37.4*	..	..
Uzbekistan	..	..	..	..	..	..	..	..	..	..	..	..
Venezuela, RB	37.4	10.3	38.8	22.3	29.4	8.4	21.9	31.9	7.7	8.0	..	..
Vietnam	*4.7*	52.5	*22.7*	62.4	*9.3*	36.5	*25.3*	8.1	..	2.9	..	3.7
West Bank and Gaza	..	..	..	..	..	..	..	..	..	..	..	..
Yemen, Rep.	60.6	4.8	55.1	39.5	10.4	22.0	121.2	21.4	..	5.0	..	5.1
Zambia	67.8	38.2	21.8	20.8	10.6	13.4	33.7	17.9	9.4	18.6	9.2	10.6
Zimbabwe	41.7	*58.7*	41.8	*61.3*	30.3	*24.8*	12.2	22.5	2.9	61.4	3.3	44.6
World	**139.0 w**	**162.1 w**	**83.2 w**	**85.4 w**	**.. w**	**55.1 w**	**10.3 m**	**11.3 m**	**5.5 m**	**6.3 m**	**.. m**	**.. m**
Low income	44.3	45.3	36.2	51.9	20.6	34.1	12.8	15.6	8.2	12.4	..	..
Middle income	64.3	85.3	42.2	81.4	24.7	51.5	13.5	10.8	5.0	6.3	..	..
Lower middle income	73.0	99.6	48.3	96.8	28.7	61.1	17.1	11.1	*5.3*	6.9	..	..
Upper middle income	45.5	53.5	29.0	46.9	16.0	30.2	9.9	7.4	6.2	4.7	..	..
Low & middle income	60.8	79.3	41.1	76.9	24.0	48.9	13.2	12.3	6.6	8.0	..	..
East Asia & Pacific	76.4	150.9	63.1	158.8	37.1	102.0	5.1	11.9	3.1	5.2	..	..
Europe & Central Asia	..	37.7	..	39.9	..	23.8	..	9.8	..	6.5	..	..
Latin America & Carib.	59.0	45.0	25.2	31.0	17.6	21.3	21.9	18.1	8.2	9.3	..	..
Middle East & N. Africa	70.4	69.9	59.0	68.4	26.9	40.0	14.2	21.5	2.2	5.2	..	..
South Asia	48.8	53.2	41.0	60.1	25.2	41.7	12.7	8.7	2.5	*7.3*	..	..
Sub-Saharan Africa	56.6	74.6	32.1	37.4	16.8	16.6	11.9	15.1	8.2	12.4	..	..
High income	153.1	181.9	92.8	*104.3*	..	74.8	2.0	1.2	4.5	3.9	2.4	*3.2*
Europe EMU	99.5	125.1	..	..	..	..	4.1	..	6.5	4.0	2.6	*3.6*

About the data

The organization and performance of financial activities in a country affect economic growth through their impact on how businesses raise and manage funds. These funds come from savings: savers accumulate claims on financial institutions, which pass the funds to their final users. But even if a country has savings, growth may not materialize—because the financial system may fail to direct the savings to where they can be invested most efficiently. Enabling it to do so requires established payments systems, the availability of price information, a way to manage uncertainty and control risk, and mechanisms to deal with problems of asymmetric information between parties to a financial transaction.

As an economy develops, the indirect lending by savers to investors becomes more efficient and gradually increases financial assets relative to gross domestic product (GDP). More specialized savings and financial institutions emerge and more financing instruments become available, spreading risks and reducing costs to liability holders. Securities markets mature, allowing savers to invest their resources directly in financial assets issued by firms. Financial systems vary widely across countries: banks, nonbank financial institutions, and stock markets are larger, more active, and more efficient in richer countries.

The ratio of domestic credit provided by the banking sector to GDP is used to measure the growth of the banking system because it reflects the extent to which savings are financial. In a few countries governments may hold international reserves as deposits in the banking system rather than in the central bank. Since the claims on the central government are a net item (claims on the central government minus central government deposits), this net figure may be negative, resulting in a negative figure for domestic credit provided by the banking sector.

Liquid liabilities are a general indicator of the size of financial intermediaries relative to the size of the economy, or an overall measure of financial sector development. Quasi-liquid liabilities are long-term deposits and assets—such as bonds, commercial paper, and certificates of deposit—that can be converted into currency or demand deposits, but at a cost. The ratio of bank liquid reserves to bank assets captures the banking system's liquidity. In countries whose banking system is liquid, adverse macroeconomic conditions should be less likely to lead to banking and financial crises. Data on domestic credit and liquid and quasi-liquid liabilities are cited on an end-of-year basis.

No less important than the size and structure of the financial sector is its efficiency, as indicated by the margin between the cost of mobilizing liabilities and the earnings on assets—or the interest rate spread. A narrowing of the interest rate spread reduces transaction costs, which lowers the overall cost of investment and is therefore crucial to economic growth. Interest rates reflect the responsiveness of financial institutions to competition and price incentives. The interest rate spread, also known as the intermediation margin, is a summary measure of a banking system's efficiency (although if governments set interest rates, the spreads become less reliable measures of efficiency). The risk premium on lending can be approximated by the spread between the lending rate to the private sector (line 60p in the International Monetary Fund's *International Financial Statistics,* or IFS) and the "risk free" treasury bill interest rate (IFS line 60c). A small spread indicates that the market considers its best corporate customers to be low risk. Interest rates are expressed as annual averages.

In some countries financial markets are distorted by restrictions on foreign investment, selective credit controls, and controls on deposit and lending rates. Interest rates may reflect the diversion of resources to finance the public sector deficit through statutory reserve requirements and direct borrowing from the banking system. And where state-owned banks dominate the financial sector, noncommercial considerations may unduly influence credit allocation. The indicators in the table provide quantitative assessments of each country's financial sector, but qualitative assessments of policies, laws, and regulations are needed to analyze overall financial conditions. Recent international financial crises highlight the risks of weak financial intermediation, poor corporate governance, and deficient government policies.

The accuracy of financial data depends on the quality of accounting systems, which are weak in some developing countries. Some indicators in the table are highly correlated, particularly the ratios of domestic credit, liquid liabilities, and quasi-liquid liabilities to GDP, because changes in liquid and quasi-liquid liabilities flow directly from changes in domestic credit. Moreover, the precise definition of the financial aggregates presented varies by country.

The indicators reported here do not capture the activities of the informal sector, which remains an important source of finance in developing economies. Personal credit or credit extended through community-based pooling of assets may be the only source of credit for small farmers, small businesses, and home-based producers. And in financially repressed economies the rationing of formal credit forces many borrowers and lenders to turn to the informal market, which is very expensive, or to self-financing and family savings.

Definitions

• **Domestic credit provided by banking sector** includes all credit to various sectors on a gross basis, with the exception of credit to the central government, which is net. The banking sector includes monetary authorities, deposit money banks, and other banking institutions for which data are available (including institutions that do not accept transferable deposits but do incur such liabilities as time and savings deposits). Examples of other banking institutions include savings and mortgage loan institutions and building and loan associations. • **Liquid liabilities** are also known as broad money, or M3. They include bank deposits of generally less than one year plus currency. Liquid liabilities are the sum of currency and deposits in the central bank (M0); plus transferable deposits and electronic currency (M1); plus time and savings deposits, foreign currency transferable deposits, certificates of deposit, and securities repurchase agreements (M2); plus travelers' checks, foreign currency time deposits, commercial paper, and shares of mutual funds or market funds held by residents. The ratio of liquid liabilities to GDP indicates the relative size of these readily available forms of money—money that the owners can use to buy goods and services without incurring any cost. • **Quasi-liquid liabilities** are the M3 money supply less M1. • **Ratio of bank liquid reserves to bank assets** is the ratio of domestic currency holdings and deposits with the monetary authorities to claims on other governments, nonfinancial public enterprises, the private sector, and other banking institutions. • **Interest rate spread** is the interest rate charged by banks on loans to prime customers minus the interest rate paid by commercial or similar banks for demand, time, or savings deposits. • **Risk premium on lending** is the interest rate charged by banks on loans to prime private sector customers minus the "risk free" treasury bill interest rate at which short-term government securities are issued or traded in the market. In some countries this spread may be negative, indicating that the market considers its best corporate clients to be lower risk than the government.

Data sources

The data on credit, liabilities, bank reserves, and interest rates are collected from central banks and finance ministries and reported in the print and electronic editions of the International Monetary Fund's *International Financial Statistics.*

	Tax revenue	Taxes on income, profits, and capital gains		Taxes on goods and services		Taxes on exports		Customs and other import duties		Highest marginal tax rate[a]		
	% of GDP	% of total taxes		% of value added in industry and services		% of tax revenue		% of tax revenue		%	Individual on income over $	Corporate %
	2003	1995	2003	1995	2003	1995	2003	1995	2003	2004	2004	2004
Afghanistan	..	..	..	..	..	..	..	..	..	..	..	..
Albania[b]	..	13.3	..	19.0	..	..	..	20.9	..	..	..	..
Algeria[b]	32.0	68.5	74.0	3.8	3.8	..	..	19.5	14.6	..	..	..
Angola	..	..	..	..	..	..	..	..	..	..	..	..
Argentina	9.4	..	19.5	..	4.6	..	16.1	..	4.2	35	41,667	35
Armenia[b]	14.0	..	15.1	..	13.0	..	..	..	4.7	..	..	..
Australia	24.1	..	67.6	..	7.4	..	..	..	2.9	47	46,538	30
Austria	21.0	..	47.1	..	11.0	..	..	..	0.0	50	64,052	34
Azerbaijan[b]	..	30.9	..	9.1	..	16.2	..	8.6	..	35	7,307	24
Bangladesh[b]	8.1	..	15.7	..	4.8	..	0.0	..	34.9	..	..	..
Belarus[b]	14.2	24.6	12.3	13.4	12.7	3.0	..	4.4	..	..	..	..
Belgium	26.7	..	60.8	..	11.5	..	..	..	..	50	30,210	33
Benin	..	..	..	..	..	..	..	..	..	..	..	..
Bolivia	13.3	..	11.1	..	12.2	..	..	..	5.7	13	..	25
Bosnia and Herzegovina	..	..	..	..	..	..	..	..	..	..	..	..
Botswana[b]	..	51.3	..	2.0	..	0.0	..	37.7	..	25	20,950	15
Brazil[b]	..	35.4	..	6.8	..	0.0	..	5.3	..	28	8,843	15
Bulgaria[b]	19.0	29.9	22.6	13.2	18.6	0.4	0.0	11.1	3.5	29	4,550	20
Burkina Faso	..	..	..	..	..	..	..	..	..	..	..	..
Burundi[b]	..	21.7	..	17.3	..	11.8	..	18.5	..	..	..	..
Cambodia	..	..	..	..	..	..	..	..	..	20	36,356	20
Cameroon[b]	..	31.5	..	4.4	..	4.5	..	23.9	..	..	..	..
Canada[b]	14.1	72.5	73.6	3.9	..	..	..	2.6	1.7	29	80,972	21
Central African Republic	..	..	..	..	..	..	..	..	..	..	..	..
Chad	..	..	..	..	..	..	..	..	..	..	..	..
Chile	16.2	..	27.1	..	13.7	..	..	..	..	40	6,127	17
China[b]	8.3	12.0	12.5	5.1	7.3	..	..	9.6	..	45	12,082	..
Hong Kong, China	9.3	..	61.8	..	2.0	..	..	..	0.6	17	13,462	18
Colombia	13.9	..	48.6	..	6.7	..	..	..	7.1	35	29,426	37
Congo, Dem. Rep.[b]	6.3	35.8	32.0	2.3	4.6	2.6	1.8	32.8	32.9	50	6,056	40
Congo, Rep.[b]	8.4	12.6	..	5.8	6.9	..	..	40.3	20.5	..	..	..
Costa Rica[b]	13.5	18.5	24.9	8.4	10.4	4.4	0.3	19.4	5.8	30	16,860	30
Côte d'Ivoire[b]	14.9	16.8	23.1	4.0	4.8	17.2	16.8	33.9	30.3	10	3,837	35
Croatia[b]	24.4	16.9	13.3	25.2	24.7	..	..	14.8	10.4	45	35,171	..
Cuba	..	..	..	..	..	..	..	..	..	..	..	..
Czech Republic	16.4	..	41.6	..	10.2	..	..	..	2.5	32	12,910	28
Denmark	30.1	..	44.4	..	18.9	..	..	..	..	59	51,162	30
Dominican Republic[b]	15.7	18.0	23.6	6.2	6.9	0.0	0.0	38.7	33.8	25	23,734	25
Ecuador[b]	..	56.5	..	..	..	0.4	..	11.8	..	25	57,600	25
Egypt, Arab Rep.[b]	..	33.8	..	6.0	..	..	..	20.5	..	..	..	..
El Salvador	11.3	..	29.7	..	0.8	..	..	..	10.7	..	..	..
Eritrea	..	..	..	..	..	..	..	..	..	..	..	..
Estonia[b]	15.5	32.8	24.2	16.0	13.9	..	..	0.7	0.2	26	1,354	35
Ethiopia[b]	..	31.0	..	6.3	..	5.2	..	29.2	..	..	..	..
Finland	23.0	..	36.7	..	16.7	..	..	..	0.0	34	68,517	29
France	22.6	..	45.5	..	12.2	..	..	..	0.0	48	60,673	33
Gabon	..	..	..	..	..	..	..	..	..	..	..	..
Gambia, The[b]	..	..	..	..	..	..	..	..	..	..	..	..
Georgia[b]	7.0	11.1	5.3	9.2	7.9	..	..	15.5	11.0	..	..	..
Germany	11.5	47.3	42.2	6.5	7.5	..	..	..	..	45	65,224	25
Ghana[b]	..	21.7	..	9.1	..	7.0	..	26.1	..	30	5,647	33
Greece	..	..	..	..	..	..	..	..	..	40	29,464	35
Guatemala[b]	10.3	20.8	27.6	5.1	8.0	0.0	0.0	24.6	11.7	31	35,853	31
Guinea[b]	..	..	..	..	..	..	..	..	..	..	..	..
Guinea-Bissau	..	..	..	..	..	..	..	..	..	..	..	..
Haiti	..	..	..	..	..	..	..	..	..	..	..	..

	Tax revenue	Taxes on income, profits, and capital gains		Taxes on goods and services		Taxes on exports		Customs and other import duties		Highest marginal tax rate[a]		
	% of GDP	% of total taxes		% of value added in industry and services		% of tax revenue		% of tax revenue		Individual		Corporate
										%	on income over $	%
	2003	1995	2003	1995	2003	1995	2003	1995	2003	2004	2004	2004
Honduras	..	..	..	..	..	..	..	..	..	25	27,778	25
Hungary	22.2	..	32.3	..	16.4	..	..	..	3.2	38	7,214	16
India[b]	9.1	29.9	38.0	5.4	5.5	0.1	0.1	31.6	19.6	30	3,283	36
Indonesia[b]	13.0	54.5	49.6	7.1	6.4	0.3	0.3	4.5	4.7	35	22,371	30
Iran, Islamic Rep.[b]	6.7	42.4	42.6	1.6	0.7	0.3	..	9.8	43.2	35	125,345	25
Iraq	..	..	..	..	..	..	..	..	..	..	..	..
Ireland[b]	..	49.6	..	11.3	..	..	..	..	..	42	35,443	13
Israel	29.9	..	45.8	..	..	..	..	..	0.9	49	90,040	36
Italy	..	..	..	..	..	..	..	..	..	45	88,608	33
Jamaica[b]	25.2	38.2	37.9	10.6	11.5	..	..	12.3	9.8	25	1,993	33
Japan[b]	..	62.9	..	3.0	..	..	..	1.7	..	37	167,395	30
Jordan[b]	18.8	15.6	14.8	9.1	11.0	..	..	32.6	15.9	..	..	..
Kazakhstan[b]	13.6	23.5	45.2	4.8	7.5	0.0	0.7	4.7	5.0	20	47,552	30
Kenya[b]	..	39.9	..	17.0	..	0.0	..	17.1	..	30	5,841	30
Korea, Dem. Rep.	..	..	..	..	..	..	..	..	..	..	..	..
Korea, Rep.[b]	15.4	39.3	37.2	6.1	7.3	..	..	8.2	6.2	36	66,644	27
Kuwait[b]	..	24.7	..	0.0	..	..	..	69.9	..	..	..	..
Kyrgyz Republic[b]	12.4	29.6	21.9	18.4	16.0	..	..	..	..	..	..	..
Lao PDR	..	..	..	..	..	..	..	..	..	..	..	..
Latvia[b]	14.3	14.2	21.9	13.2	12.6	..	..	5.4	2.1	..	..	15
Lebanon	15.1	..	14.2	..	11.0	..	..	..	14.3	..	..	..
Lesotho[b]	33.5	19.5	29.5	9.1	9.6	0.0	..	68.0	..	..	..	..
Liberia	..	..	..	..	..	..	..	..	..	..	..	..
Libya	..	..	..	..	..	..	..	..	..	..	..	..
Lithuania	17.4	..	33.9	..	13.4	..	..	..	1.5	..	..	15
Macedonia, FYR	..	..	..	..	..	..	..	..	..	..	..	..
Madagascar	7.7	..	22.9	..	3.6	..	..	..	32.1	..	..	..
Malawi	..	..	..	..	..	..	..	..	..	..	..	..
Malaysia[b]	17.6	46.3	63.9	7.2	5.6	2.4	1.9	12.9	5.6	28	65,789	28
Mali	..	..	..	..	..	..	..	..	..	..	..	..
Mauritania	..	..	..	..	..	..	..	..	..	..	..	..
Mauritius[b]	17.5	15.9	15.4	6.9	11.4	3.4	..	44.0	25.0	25	951	25
Mexico[b]	..	38.9	..	9.6	..	0.0	..	5.7	..	33	9,555	33
Moldova[b]	14.8	12.3	5.2	15.5	18.6	..	..	3.6	9.8	..	..	..
Mongolia	22.6	..	28.2	..	17.5	..	0.5	..	9.4	..	..	..
Morocco[b]	..	26.0	..	12.9	..	0.0	..	19.4	..	..	..	..
Mozambique	..	..	..	..	..	..	..	..	..	32	42,314	32
Myanmar[b]	2.3	34.4	40.5	4.2	..	..	..	20.7	4.7	..	..	..
Namibia[b]	29.6	30.2	47.6	13.1	8.5	..	0.0	..	27.9	35	29,851	35
Nepal[b]	9.4	14.0	15.7	7.5	7.5	1.7	2.1	33.9	31.6	..	..	..
Netherlands	22.8	..	43.3	..	13.1	..	..	..	..	52	63,777	35
New Zealand	30.8	..	62.4	..	..	..	..	..	1.8	39	39,242	33
Nicaragua[b]	15.3	13.7	26.0	11.7	12.5	..	..	10.6	6.7	..	..	..
Niger	..	..	..	..	..	..	..	..	..	..	..	..
Nigeria	..	..	..	..	..	..	..	..	..	..	..	..
Norway	27.5	..	50.8	..	15.0	..	..	..	0.4	..	..	28
Oman[b]	7.4	77.5	77.1	..	..	..	..	11.5	10.3	0	..	12
Pakistan[b]	10.9	24.3	27.5	7.1	7.1	..	..	31.4	13.2	35	11,746	41
Panama[b]	9.3	39.3	41.5	4.7	2.5	1.0	0.0	20.2	23.7	30	200,000	30
Papua New Guinea[b]	22.3	52.6	54.0	2.9	4.1	10.9	4.4	24.0	24.4	..	..	..
Paraguay[b]	9.5	20.2	17.0	7.4	8.1	..	..	24.9	18.1	0	..	30
Peru[b]	12.9	21.5	30.8	10.2	10.9	..	..	13.1	9.2	30	49,899	30
Philippines[b]	12.3	35.8	45.4	5.8	4.4	..	..	31.4	19.7	32	8,995	32
Poland[b]	17.4	42.8	29.0	12.3	13.6	..	..	12.0	2.8	40	19,211	19
Portugal	22.0	40.8	41.2	14.5	14.6	..	..	0.0	0.0	40	67,139	25
Puerto Rico	..	..	..	..	..	..	..	..	..	33	50,000	20

	Tax revenue	Taxes on income, profits, and capital gains		Taxes on goods and services		Taxes on exports		Customs and other import duties		Highest marginal tax rate[a]		
	% of GDP	% of total taxes		% of value added in industry and services		% of tax revenue		% of tax revenue		Individual %	on income over $	Corporate %
	2003	1995	2003	1995	2003	1995	2003	1995	2003	2004	2004	2004
Romania[b]	11.8	47.2	23.4	9.6	10.6	..	..	9.1	6.6	40	4,617	25
Russian Federation	13.2	..	9.5	..	10.1	..	16.8	..	9.0	13	..	24
Rwanda[b]	..	..	..	..	..	..	..	..	..	..	..	..
Saudi Arabia	..	..	..	..	..	..	..	..	..	0	..	0
Senegal[b]	17.0	22.9	22.8	5.0	7.4	..	..	..	..	..	..	..
Serbia and Montenegro[b]	22.8	..	21.0	..	..	..	..	..	10.8	..	..	..
Sierra Leone[b]	..	17.0	..	6.1	..	..	..	43.2	..	..	..	..
Singapore[b]	13.3	41.5	51.7	5.8	4.4	..	..	2.0	3.3	22	188,191	20
Slovak Republic	16.8	..	35.5	..	10.8	..	..	..	2.0	38	14,087	25
Slovenia[b]	21.6	23.2	27.1	15.3	16.4	..	..	15.9	2.8	50	..	25
Somalia	..	..	..	..	..	..	..	..	..	..	..	..
South Africa[b]	25.1	54.0	56.1	10.0	10.7	..	..	4.5	2.3	40	38,060	30
Spain	12.9	..	61.3	..	5.7	..	..	..	0.0	29	56,962	35
Sri Lanka[b]	14.0	14.5	17.0	15.6	13.4	0.0	..	20.6	12.8	30	8,083	30
Sudan[b]	..	..	..	..	..	..	..	..	..	..	..	..
Swaziland[b]	..	..	..	..	..	..	..	..	..	33	5,496	30
Sweden	19.0	..	8.6	..	15.1	..	..	..	..	25	59,756	28
Switzerland[b]	10.2	30.6	30.3	..	..	..	..	2.3	2.4	..	..	9
Syrian Arab Republic[b]	..	28.9	..	11.8	..	3.0	..	12.5	..	..	..	..
Tajikistan[b]	8.3	..	3.7	..	9.4	..	..	..	21.4	..	..	..
Tanzania	..	..	..	..	..	..	..	..	..	30	6,090	30
Thailand	15.4	..	36.4	..	8.7	..	0.3	..	12.0	37	101,420	30
Togo	..	..	..	..	..	..	..	..	..	..	..	..
Trinidad and Tobago[b]	..	60.2	..	7.3	..	..	..	6.9	..	30	7,937	30
Tunisia[b]	20.6	23.1	32.8	6.8	11.8	0.2	0.1	39.6	10.8	..	..	..
Turkey[b]	..	40.2	..	9.4	..	..	..	4.8	..	40	100,298	30
Turkmenistan	..	..	..	..	..	..	..	..	..	..	..	..
Uganda[b]	11.8	..	21.4	..	8.7	..	..	..	..	30	2,523	30
Ukraine[b]	14.0	..	26.1	..	12.0	..	0.0	..	7.5	13	..	25
United Arab Emirates[b]	..	..	..	..	..	..	..	..	..	..	..	..
United Kingdom	27.2	..	48.8	..	13.4	..	..	..	..	40	51,358	30
United States	9.9	..	89.8	..	0.7	..	..	..	2.0	35	319,100	35
Uruguay[b]	17.5	15.5	22.1	9.7	10.5	0.1	0.1	5.3	4.1	..	..	35
Uzbekistan	..	..	..	..	..	..	..	..	..	30	666	18
Venezuela, RB[b]	11.3	49.3	27.9	6.0	6.1	..	..	12.0	7.3	34	60,324	34
Vietnam[b]	16.4	19.4	32.0	8.8	9.0	..	..	30.9	22.8	..	..	28
West Bank and Gaza	..	..	..	..	..	..	..	..	..	..	..	..
Yemen, Rep.[b]	..	35.2	..	2.3	..	..	..	36.6	..	..	..	..
Zambia[b]	..	31.4	..	6.3	..	0.3	..	42.0	..	30	368	35
Zimbabwe[b]	..	46.2	..	8.8	..	..	..	18.8	..	45	26,249	30

a. These data are from PricewaterhouseCoopers' *Individual Taxes: Worldwide Summaries 2004–2005* and *Corporate Taxes: Worldwide Summaries 2004–2005*, copyright 2004 by PricewaterhouseCoopers by permission of John Wiley and Sons, Inc. b. Data were reported on a cash basis and have been adjusted to the accrual framework.

For the first time the data in this table are based on the concepts and recommendations of the second edition of the International Monetary Fund's (IMF) *Government Finance Statistics Manual 2001.* Previous editions of *World Development Indicators* used data derived on the basis of 1986 manual. The 2001 manual, which is harmonized with the 1993 System of National Accounts, recommends an accrual accounting method instead of the cash-based method of the 1986 manual. The new manual focuses on all economic events affecting assets, liabilities, revenues, and expenses, instead of only those represented by cash transactions. See *About the data* for tables 4.11 and 4.13 for more detailed information.

Taxes are the main source of revenue for many governments. The sources of tax revenue and the relative contributions of these sources are determined by government policy choices about where and how to impose taxes and by changes in the structure of the economy. Tax policy may reflect concerns about distributional effects, economic efficiency (including corrections for externalities), and the practical problems of administering a tax system. There is no ideal level of taxation. But taxes influence incentives and thus the behavior of economic actors and the economy's competitiveness.

Taxes are compulsory transfers to governments from individuals, businesses, and institutions. Certain compulsory transfers, such as fines, penalties, and most social security contributions, are excluded from tax revenue.

The level of taxation is typically measured by tax revenue as a share of gross domestic product (GDP). Comparing levels of taxation across countries provides a quick overview of the fiscal obligations and incentives facing the private sector. In this table tax data in local currencies are normalized by scaling values in the same units to ease cross-country comparisons. The table shows only central government data, which may significantly understate the total tax burden, particularly in countries where provincial and municipal governments are large or have considerable tax authority.

Low ratios of tax revenue to GDP may reflect weak administration and large-scale tax avoidance or evasion. Low ratios may also reflect the presence of a sizable parallel economy with unrecorded and undisclosed incomes. Tax revenue ratios tend to rise with income, with higher income countries relying on taxes to finance a much broader range of social services and social security than lower income countries are able to provide.

As economies develop, their capacity to tax residents' income, profits, and capital gains typically expands and other taxes become less important as a source of revenue. Thus the share of taxes on income, profits, and capital gains is one measure of an economy's (and tax system's) level of development. In the early stages of development governments tend to rely on other taxes because the administrative costs of collecting them are relatively low. The two main other categories of taxes are taxes on goods and services and taxes on international trade and transactions (including customs and other import duties). The table shows taxes on goods and services as a percentage of value added in industry and services.

Taxes on exports and customs and other import duties are shown separately because the burden they impose on the economy (and thus growth) is likely to be large. Taxes on exports, typically levied on primary (particularly agricultural) products, often take the place of taxes on income and profits, but they reduce the incentive to export and encourage a shift to other products. High customs and other import duties penalize consumers, create protective barriers—which promote higher priced output and inefficient production—and implicitly tax exports. By contrast, lower trade taxes enhance openness—to foreign competition, knowledge, technologies, and resources—energizing development in many ways. Seeing this pattern, some of the fastest growing economies have lowered import tariffs in recent years. In some countries, such as members of the European Union, most customs duties are collected by a supranational authority; these revenues are not reported in the individual countries' accounts.

The tax revenues collected by governments are the outcomes of systems that are often complex, containing many exceptions, exemptions, penalties, and other inducements that affect the incidence of taxes and thus influence the decisions of workers, managers, and entrepreneurs. A potentially important influence on both domestic and international investors is a tax system's progressivity, as reflected in the highest marginal tax rate levied at the national level on individual and corporate income. Figures for individual marginal tax rates generally refer to employment income. In some countries the highest marginal tax rate is also the basic or flat rate, and other surtaxes, deductions, and the like may apply. And in many countries several different corporate tax rates may be levied, depending on the type of business (mining, banking, insurance, agriculture, manufacturing), ownership (domestic or foreign), volume of sales, or whether surtaxes or exemptions are included. The corporate tax rates in the table are mainly general rates applied to domestic companies. For more detailed information, see the country's laws, regulations, and tax treaties.

Definitions

• **Tax revenue** refers to compulsory transfers to the central government for public purposes. Certain compulsory transfers such as fines, penalties, and most social security contributions are excluded. Refunds and corrections of erroneously collected tax revenue are treated as negative revenue. • **Taxes on income, profits, and capital gains** are levied on wages, salaries, tips, fees, commissions, and other compensation for labor services; interest, dividends, rent, and royalties; profits of businesses, estates, and trusts; and capital gains and losses. Social security contributions based on gross pay, payroll, or number of employees are not included, but taxable portions of social security, pension, and other retirement account distributions are included. • **Taxes on goods and services** are all taxes and duties levied on the production, extraction, sale, transfer, leasing, or delivery of goods and rendering of services, or on the use of goods or permission to use goods or perform activities. These include value added taxes, general sales taxes, turnover and other general taxes on goods and services, excise taxes, profits on fiscal monopolies, taxes on specific services, taxes on use of goods and on permission to use goods or perform activities, motor vehicle taxes, and other taxes such as on extraction of minerals, fossil fuels, and other exhaustible resources. • **Taxes on exports** are all levies on goods being transported out of the country or services being delivered to nonresidents by residents. Rebates on exported goods that are repayments of previously paid general consumption taxes, excise taxes, or import duties are deducted from the gross amounts receivable from these taxes, not from amounts receivable from export taxes. • **Customs and other import duties** are all levies collected on goods that are entering the country or services delivered by nonresidents to residents. They include levies imposed for revenue or protection purposes and determined on a specific or ad valorem basis as long as they are restricted to imported goods or services. • **Highest marginal tax rate** is the highest rate shown on the national level schedule of tax rates applied to the annual taxable income of individuals and corporations. Also presented are the income levels for individuals above which the highest marginal tax rates levied at the national level apply.

Data sources

The definitions used here are from the IMF *Government Finance Statistics Manual 2001.* The data on tax revenues are from print and electronic editions of the IMF's *Government Finance Statistics Yearbook.* The data on individual and corporate tax rates are from PricewaterhouseCoopers's *Individual Taxes: Worldwide Summaries 2004–2005* and *Corporate Taxes: Worldwide Summaries 2004–2005.*

5.7 Relative prices and exchange rates

	Exchange rate arrangements[a]		Official exchange rate	Purchasing power parity (PPP) conversion factor		Ratio of PPP conversion factor to official exchange rate	Real effective exchange rate	Interest rate		
	Classification 2003	Structure 2003	local currency units to $ 2003	local currency units to international $ 1990	2003	2003	Index 2000 = 100 2003	Deposit 2003	% Lending 2003	Real 2003
Afghanistan	MF	U	3,000.00	..	..	..	..	..	..	..
Albania	IF	U	121.86	2.0	51.4	0.4	..	8.4	14.3	10.0
Algeria	MF	U	77.39	5.0	26.5	0.3	85.3	5.3	8.0	−0.2
Angola	MF	U	74.61	0.0	31.0	0.4	..	26.2	96.1	2.0
Argentina	MF	U	2.90	0.3	0.8	0.3	..	10.2	19.1	7.6
Armenia	IF	U	578.76	0.0	144.7	0.3	77.2	6.9	20.8	15.5
Australia	IF	U	1.54	1.4	1.4	0.9	113.7	3.3	8.4	5.4
Austria	Euro	U	0.89	0.9	0.9	1.0	104.3	..	..	..
Azerbaijan	MF	U	4,910.73	..	1,177.0	0.2	..	9.5	15.5	11.0
Bangladesh	MF	U	58.15	9.5	12.3	0.2	..	7.8	16.0	11.0
Belarus	P	U	2,051.27	0.0	600.8	0.3	..	17.4	24.0	−3.7
Belgium	Euro	U	0.89	0.9	0.9	1.0	105.4	1.6	6.9	5.1
Benin	EA/Euro	U	581.20	159.8	269.7	0.5	..	3.5	..	..
Bolivia	P	U	7.66	1.3	2.6	0.3	86.1	11.4	17.7	11.9
Bosnia and Herzegovina	CB/Euro	U	1.73	..	0.5	0.3	..	4.0	10.9	9.6
Botswana	P	D	4.95	1.2	2.5	0.5	..	10.0	16.3	12.3
Brazil	IF	U	3.08	0.0	1.1	0.4	..	22.0	67.1	48.2
Bulgaria	CB/Euro	U	1.73	0.0	0.6	0.3	115.6	2.9	8.8	6.6
Burkina Faso	EA/Euro	U	581.20	135.4	170.9	0.3	..	3.5	..	..
Burundi	MF	U	1,082.62	49.3	138.1	0.1	65.5	..	18.2	5.9
Cambodia	M	D	3,973.33	..	604.8	0.2	..	2.0	18.5	15.9
Cameroon	EA/Euro	U	581.20	170.9	213.0	0.4	112.3	5.0	18.0	16.9
Canada	IF	U	1.40	1.3	1.2	0.9	106.7	1.1	4.7	3.3
Central African Republic	EA/Euro	U	581.20	135.1	164.8	0.3	114.4	5.0	18.0	14.5
Chad	EA/Euro	U	581.20	107.7	145.7	0.3	..	5.0	18.0	18.5
Chile	IF	U	691.43	148.7	308.9	0.4	78.5	2.7	6.2	1.7
China	P	U	8.28	1.3	1.8	0.2	96.7	2.0	5.3	3.0
Hong Kong, China	CB	U	7.79	6.4	6.6	0.8	..	0.1	5.0	10.7
Colombia	IF	U	2,877.65	119.8	757.5	0.3	82.0	7.8	15.2	6.4
Congo, Dem. Rep.	IF	U	405.34	0.0	62.1	0.2	35.1	..	66.8	31.5
Congo, Rep.	EA/Euro	U	581.20	385.8	571.6	1.0	..	5.0	18.0	23.0
Costa Rica	P	U	398.66	32.6	180.6	0.5	94.2	10.4	25.6	16.5
Côte d'Ivoire	EA/Euro	U	581.20	167.1	321.1	0.6	115.8	3.5	..	..
Croatia	MF	U	6.70	0.0	3.9	0.6	103.4	1.5	11.6	8.1
Cuba	..	..	..	..	..	..	..	..	..	..
Czech Republic	MF	U	28.21	8.2	15.2	0.5	114.2	1.3	5.9	4.2
Denmark	P	U	6.59	8.1	8.2	1.3	108.5	2.4	7.1	5.4
Dominican Republic	MF	U	30.83	2.6	8.6	0.3	74.8	20.5	31.4	3.1
Ecuador	EA/Other	U	1.00	0.4	0.6	0.6	153.4	5.5	13.1	3.8
Egypt, Arab Rep.	MF	U	5.85	0.8	1.6	0.3	..	8.2	13.5	9.4
El Salvador	EA/Other	U	8.75	2.4	4.2	0.5	..	..	..	..
Eritrea	P	D	13.88	1.1	2.8	0.2	..	..	..	..
Estonia	CB	U	13.86	0.1	6.9	0.5	..	2.4	5.5	3.0
Ethiopia	MF	U	8.60	0.7	1.2	0.1	..	3.4	8.0	−5.7
Finland	Euro	U	0.89	1.0	1.0	1.1	106.5	1.5	4.8	3.9
France	Euro	U	0.89	1.0	0.9	1.1	106.4	2.7	6.6	5.0
Gabon	EA/Euro	U	581.20	339.4	409.3	0.7	107.8	5.0	18.0	19.4
Gambia, The	MF	U	19.92	1.8	3.9	0.2	52.1	12.7	24.0	6.9
Georgia	MF	U	2.15	0.0	0.6	0.3	..	9.3	32.3	27.8
Germany	Euro	U	0.89	1.0	0.9	1.0	106.7	2.7	9.7	8.0
Ghana	MF	U	8,677.37	94.3	1,430.3	0.2	101.4	14.3	..	..
Greece	Euro	U	0.89	0.3	0.7	0.8	109.3	2.5	6.8	3.2
Guatemala	IF	U	7.94	1.4	3.8	0.5	..	4.8	15.0	8.7
Guinea	P	D	1,984.93	223.9	434.8	0.2	..	6.5	..	..
Guinea-Bissau	EA/Euro	U	581.20	10.9	131.0	0.2	..	3.5	..	..
Haiti	MF	U	42.37	1.1	8.0	0.2	..	14.0	30.6	4.1

	Exchange rate arrangements[a]		Official exchange rate	Purchasing power parity (PPP) conversion factor		Ratio of PPP conversion factor to official exchange rate	Real effective exchange rate	Interest rate		
			local currency units to $	local currency units to international $			Index 2000 = 100	Deposit	% Lending	Real
	Classification **2003**	Structure **2003**	**2003**	**1990**	**2003**	**2003**	**2003**	**2003**	**2003**	**2003**
Honduras	P	U	17.35	1.3	6.5	0.4	..	11.5	20.8	11.2
Hungary	P/Euro	U	224.31	22.1	125.7	0.6	121.7	11.0	9.6	1.6
India	MF	U	46.58	4.8	9.0	0.2	..	..	11.5	7.5
Indonesia	MF	U	8,577.13	639.3	2,476.2	0.3	..	10.6	16.9	9.8
Iran, Islamic Rep.	MF	U	8,193.89	179.5	2,419.8	0.3	124.1	..	..	..
Iraq	MF	U	*0.31*	..	..	..	..	..	..	..
Ireland	Euro	U	0.89	0.8	0.9	1.0	117.4	0.0	2.8	*−1.5*
Israel	P	U	4.55	1.8	3.7	0.8	83.2	6.6	10.6	10.5
Italy	Euro	U	0.89	0.7	0.8	0.9	109.3	0.9	5.0	2.0
Jamaica	MF	U	57.74	4.4	43.4	0.8	..	8.5	18.9	5.6
Japan	IF	U	115.93	187.9	139.8	1.2	81.4	0.0	1.8	4.4
Jordan	P	U	0.71	0.3	0.3	0.4	..	3.1	9.3	7.3
Kazakhstan	MF	U	149.58	0.0	44.8	0.3	..	..	..	..
Kenya	MF	U	75.94	9.0	33.0	0.4	..	4.1	16.6	4.7
Korea, Dem. Rep.	..	..	..	..	..	..	..	..	..	..
Korea, Rep.	IF	U	1,191.61	579.8	837.8	0.7	..	4.3	6.2	3.9
Kuwait	P	U	0.30	..	0.3	1.0	..	2.4	5.4	*3.0*
Kyrgyz Republic	MF	U	43.65	0.0	9.4	0.2	..	5.0	19.1	14.8
Lao PDR	MF	U	10,569.04	174.2	2,264.0	0.2	..	6.6	30.5	11.8
Latvia	P	U	0.57	0.0	0.3	0.5	..	3.0	5.4	6.5
Lebanon	P	U	1,507.50	305.4	1,255.2	0.8	..	8.7	13.4	12.0
Lesotho	P	U	7.56	1.0	1.9	0.2	104.3	5.2	16.0	8.1
Liberia	IF	U	59.38	..	..	..	..	5.3	17.1	44.2
Libya	P	U	1.29	..	..	..	..	3.0	7.0	..
Lithuania	CB	U	3.06	0.0	1.4	0.5	..	1.3	5.8	4.4
Macedonia, FYR	P	U	54.32	0.0	18.2	0.3	100.0	8.0	16.0	14.0
Madagascar	IF	U	6,191.64	513.4	2,479.6	0.4	..	11.5	24.3	20.9
Malawi	IF	U	97.43	1.4	25.3	0.3	79.7	25.1	48.9	33.9
Malaysia	P	U	3.80	1.5	1.7	0.4	97.1	3.1	6.3	2.7
Mali	EA/Euro	U	581.20	140.7	217.1	0.4	..	3.5	..	..
Mauritania	MF	U	263.03	36.2	57.2	0.2	..	8.0	21.0	18.9
Mauritius	MF	U	27.90	6.5	10.8	0.4	..	9.5	21.0	14.6
Mexico	IF	U	10.79	1.4	7.2	0.7	..	3.1	6.9	0.4
Moldova	MF	U	13.94	0.0	4.3	0.3	87.7	12.6	19.3	4.8
Mongolia	MF	U	1,146.54	2.2	318.5	0.3	..	14.0	26.3	20.6
Morocco	P	U	9.57	3.2	3.5	0.4	94.3	3.8	12.6	12.6
Mozambique	MF	U	23,782.27	319.4	4,896.8	0.2	..	12.1	24.7	10.7
Myanmar	MF	D	6.08	..	..	..	..	9.5	15.0	*−6.2*
Namibia	P	U	7.56	1.0	2.6	0.3	..	8.8	14.7	16.2
Nepal	P	U	76.14	6.8	13.0	0.2	..	*4.8*	*7.7*	*4.9*
Netherlands	Euro	U	0.89	0.9	1.0	1.1	111.6	2.5	3.0	*0.6*
New Zealand	IF	U	1.72	1.6	1.5	0.9	120.5	5.1	9.8	*9.5*
Nicaragua	P	U	15.10	0.0	3.4	0.2	87.1	5.6	15.5	9.4
Niger	EA/Euro	U	581.20	121.5	161.7	0.3	..	3.5	..	..
Nigeria	MF	M	129.22	3.7	52.7	0.4	104.5	14.2	20.7	*−0.3*
Norway	IF	U	7.08	8.0	9.1	1.3	110.2	2.1	4.7	2.4
Oman	P	U	0.38	0.3	*0.2*	0.6	..	2.4	8.2	*6.6*
Pakistan	MF	U	57.75	6.2	15.5	0.3	92.6	..	..	..
Panama	EA/Other	U	1.00	0.6	0.6	0.6	..	4.0	9.9	8.4
Papua New Guinea	IF	U	3.56	0.5	0.8	0.2	97.1	8.2	13.4	7.1
Paraguay	MF	U	6,424.34	405.4	1,468.3	0.2	71.1	15.8	50.0	26.7
Peru	MF	U	3.48	0.1	1.5	0.4	..	3.8	14.2	..
Philippines	IF	U	54.20	5.6	12.4	0.2	85.9	5.2	9.5	5.6
Poland	IF	U	3.89	0.2	1.9	0.5	98.9	3.7	7.3	6.6
Portugal	Euro	U	0.89	0.5	0.7	0.8	109.1	..	..	..
Puerto Rico	..	..	..	0.7	*0.7*	..	..	..	..	..

	Exchange rate arrangements[a]		Official exchange rate	Purchasing power parity (PPP) conversion factor		Ratio of PPP conversion factor to official exchange rate	Real effective exchange rate	Interest rate		
			local currency units to $	local currency units to international $			Index 2000 = 100	Deposit	% Lending	Real
	Classification **2003**	Structure **2003**	**2003**	**1990**	**2003**	**2003**	**2003**	**2003**	**2003**	**2003**
Romania	P	U	33,200.07	6.9	11,949.3	0.4	105.3	..	..	..
Russian Federation	MF	U	30.69	0.0	10.0	0.3	127.0	4.5	13.0	−1.3
Rwanda	MF	U	537.66	31.2	82.7	0.2	..	8.1	..	..
Saudi Arabia	P	U	3.74	2.9	2.7	0.7	89.1	1.6	..	..
Senegal	EA/Euro	U	581.20	185.1	223.3	0.4	..	3.5	..	..
Serbia and Montenegro	MF	U	..	..	..	..	..	..	..	..
Sierra Leone	IF	D	2,347.94	29.8	636.5	0.3	82.4	8.4	20.0	12.8
Singapore	MF	U	1.74	1.8	1.5	0.9	93.8	0.5	5.3	5.7
Slovak Republic	MF	U	36.77	5.8	16.4	0.4	98.0	5.3	8.5	5.7
Slovenia	P	U	207.11	*16.2*	150.4	0.7	..	5.9	10.8	9.8
Somalia	IF	D	..	..	..	..	..	..	..	..
South Africa	IF	U	7.56	1.0	2.6	0.3	98.0	9.8	15.0	8.5
Spain	Euro	U	0.89	0.6	0.8	0.9	109.5	*2.5*	*4.3*	*−0.1*
Sri Lanka	IF	U	96.52	10.2	24.2	0.3	..	6.0	10.3	5.1
Sudan	MF	U	260.98	0.7	72.5	0.3	..	..	..	..
Swaziland	P	U	7.56	0.8	2.7	0.4	..	7.6	14.6	5.1
Sweden	IF	U	8.09	9.6	10.2	1.3	99.8	1.5	4.8	2.5
Switzerland	IF	U	1.35	2.1	1.9	1.4	106.4	0.2	3.3	*2.9*
Syrian Arab Republic	P	M	11.23	10.2	17.3	1.5	..	*4.0*	*9.0*	*7.4*
Tajikistan	MF	U	3.06	0.0	0.7	0.2	..	9.7	16.6	6.1
Tanzania	IF	U	1,038.42	75.7	479.5	0.5	..	3.0	14.5	8.3
Thailand	MF	U	41.48	10.8	12.6	0.3	110.3	1.3	5.9	3.8
Togo	EA/Euro	U	581.20	93.9	124.0	0.2	110.3	3.5	..	..
Trinidad and Tobago	MF	U	6.30	3.1	4.7	0.7	104.9	2.9	11.2	5.3
Tunisia	P	U	1.29	0.4	0.5	0.4	93.3	..	..	..
Turkey	IF	U	1,500,885.25	1,629.0	751,242.0	0.5	..	37.7	..	..
Turkmenistan	P	D	*5,200.00*	0.0	2,048.9	*0.3*	..	..	..	..
Uganda	IF	U	1,963.72	110.7	322.0	0.2	80.3	9.8	18.9	8.0
Ukraine	P	U	5.33	0.0	1.0	0.2	86.6	7.0	17.9	10.3
United Arab Emirates	P	U	3.67	3.4	..	..	..	..	*8.1*	*13.5*
United Kingdom	IF	U	0.61	0.6	0.7	1.1	95.4	..	3.7	0.6
United States	IF	U	1.00	1.0	1.0	1.0	98.0	..	4.1	*3.1*
Uruguay	IF	U	28.21	0.6	11.3	0.4	60.3	*14.3*	*126.1*	90.5
Uzbekistan	MF	U	..	*0.0*	216.5	..	..	..	..	..
Venezuela, RB	P	U	1,606.96	24.4	1,087.8	0.7	68.8	17.2	25.2	−8.5
Vietnam	MF	U	15,509.58	641.1	2,990.5	0.2	..	6.6	9.5	3.9
West Bank and Gaza	..	..	..	..	..	..	..	..	..	..
Yemen, Rep.	IF	U	183.45	20.3	116.6	0.6	..	13.0	18.0	8.1
Zambia	MF	U	4,733.27	18.6	2,249.9	0.5	101.3	22.0	40.6	17.1
Zimbabwe	P	D	697.42	0.9	*16.4*	*0.3*	..	35.9	97.3	*−34.2*

a. Exchange rate arrangements are given for the end of the year in 2003. Exchange rate classifications include independent floating (IF), managed floating (MF), pegged (P), currency board (CB), and several exchange arrangements (EA): Euro that the currency is pegged to the Euro, and other that the currency of another country is used as legal tender. Exchange rate structures include dual exchange rates (D), multiple exchange rates (M), and unitary rate (U).

About the data

In a market-based economy the choices households, producers, and governments make about the allocation of resources are influenced by relative prices, including the real exchange rate, real wages, real interest rates, and a host of other prices in the economy. Relative prices also reflect, to a large extent, the choices of these agents. Thus relative prices convey vital information about the interaction of economic agents in an economy and with the rest of the world.

The exchange rate is the price of one currency in terms of another. Official exchange rates and exchange rate arrangements are established by governments. (Other exchange rates fully recognized by governments include market rates, which are determined largely by legal market forces, and for countries maintaining multiple exchange arrangements, principal rates, secondary rates, and tertiary rates.) Also see *Statistical methods* for information on alternative conversion factors used in the *Atlas* method of calculating gross national income (GNI) per capita in U.S. dollars.

The official or market exchange rate is often used to compare prices in different currencies. Since exchange rates reflect at best the relative prices of tradable goods, the volume of goods and services that a U.S. dollar buys in the United States may not correspond to what a U.S. dollar converted to another country's currency at the official exchange rate would buy in that country. Since identical volumes of goods and services in different countries correspond to different values (and vice versa) when official exchange rates are used, an alternative method of comparing prices across countries has been developed. In this method national currency estimates of GNI are converted to a common unit of account by using conversion factors that reflect equivalent purchasing power. Purchasing power parity (PPP) conversion factors are based on price and expenditure surveys conducted by the International Comparison Program and represent the conversion factors applied to equalize price levels across countries. See *About the data* for table 1.1 for further discussion of the PPP conversion factor.

The ratio of the PPP conversion factor to the official exchange rate (also referred to as the national price level) makes it possible to compare the cost of the bundle of goods that make up gross domestic product (GDP) across countries. These national price levels vary systematically, rising with GNI per capita.

Real effective exchange rates represent a nominal effective exchange rate index adjusted for relative movements in national price or cost indicators of the home country, selected countries, and the euro area. A nominal effective exchange rate index represents the ratio (expressed on the base 2000 = 100) of an index of a currency's period-average exchange rate to a weighted geometric average of exchange rates for currencies of selected countries and the euro area. For most high-income countries, weights are derived from trade in manufactured goods among industrial countries. The data are compiled from the nominal effective exchange rate index and a cost indicator of relative normalized unit labor costs in manufacturing. For selected other countries the nominal effective exchange rate index is based on each country's trade in both manufactured goods and primary products with its partner or competitor countries. For these countries the real effective exchange rate index is derived from the nominal index adjusted for relative changes in consumer prices. An increase in the real effective exchange rate represents an appreciation of the local currency. Because of conceptual and data limitations, changes in real effective exchange rates should be interpreted with caution.

Many interest rates coexist in an economy, reflecting competitive conditions, the terms governing loans and deposits, and differences in the position and status of creditors and debtors. In some economies interest rates are set by regulation or administrative fiat. In economies with imperfect markets, or where reported nominal rates are not indicative of effective rates, it may be difficult to obtain data on interest rates that reflect actual market transactions. Deposit and lending rates are collected by the International Monetary Fund (IMF) as representative interest rates offered by banks to resident customers. The terms and conditions attached to these rates differ by country, however, limiting their comparability. Real interest rates are calculated by adjusting nominal rates by an estimate of the inflation rate in the economy. A negative real interest rate indicates a loss in the purchasing power of the principal. The real interest rates in the table are calculated as $(i - P) / (1 + P)$, where i is the nominal interest rate and P is the inflation rate (as measured by the GDP deflator).

Definitions

• **Exchange rate arrangements** describe the arrangements furnished to the IMF by each member country under article IV, section 2(a) of the IMF's Articles of Agreement. • **Classification** indicates how the exchange rate is determined in the main market when there is more than one market: floating (managed or independent), pegged (conventional, within horizontal bands, crawling peg, or crawling band), currency board (implicit legislative commitment to exchange domestic currency for a specified foreign currency at a fixed exchange rate), and exchange arrangement (currency is pegged to the French franc, or another country's currency is used as legal tender). • **Structure** shows whether countries have a unitary exchange rate or dual or multiple rates. • **Official exchange rate** is the exchange rate determined by national authorities or the rate determined in the legally sanctioned exchange market. It is calculated as an annual average based on monthly averages (local currency units relative to the U.S. dollar). • **Purchasing power parity (PPP) conversion factor** is the number of units of a country's currency required to buy the same amount of goods and services in the domestic market as a U.S. dollar would buy in the United States. • **Ratio of PPP conversion factor to official exchange rate** is the result obtained by dividing the PPP conversion factor by the official exchange rate. • **Real effective exchange rate** is the nominal effective exchange rate (a measure of the value of a currency against a weighted average of several foreign currencies) divided by a price deflator or index of costs. • **Deposit interest rate** is the rate paid by commercial or similar banks for demand, time, or savings deposits. • **Lending interest rate** is the rate charged by banks on loans to prime customers. • **Real interest rate** is the lending interest rate adjusted for inflation as measured by the GDP deflator.

Data sources

The information on exchange rate arrangements is from the IMF's *Exchange Arrangements and Exchange Restrictions Annual Report, 2004*. The official and real effective exchange rates and deposit and lending rates are from the IMF's *International Financial Statistics*. PPP conversion factors are from the World Bank. The real interest rates are calculated using World Bank data on the GDP deflator.

5.8 Defense expenditures and arms transfers

	Military expenditures				Armed forces personnel				Arms transfers			
	% of GDP		% of central government expenditure		Total thousands		% of labor force		Exports		Imports	
									\$ millions 1990 prices			
	1995	2003	1995	2003	1995	2003	1995	2003	1995	2003	1995	2003
Afghanistan	..	..	..	..	383	130	4.3	1.1	0	0	0	17
Albania	2.1	1.2	8.2	..	87	22	5.6	1.4	..	..	21	1
Algeria	3.0	3.3	12.2	15.2	163	309	1.9	2.6	..	..	342	513
Angola	18.1	4.9	..	..	122	130	2.4	2.1	0	0	1	0
Argentina	1.7	1.1	..	6.2	99	103	0.7	0.7	3	0	67	127
Armenia	4.1	2.7	..	16.7	61	46	3.8	2.8	..	..	47	0
Australia	2.0	1.9	..	7.2	57	54	0.6	0.5	20	30	147	485
Austria	0.9	0.8	..	1.9	56	35	1.5	0.9	0	2	38	55
Azerbaijan	2.3	1.9	11.7	..	127	82	3.9	2.1	..	..	0	0
Bangladesh	1.4	1.2	..	12.8	171	189	0.3	0.3	..	..	121	0
Belarus	1.6	1.2	5.5	5.7	106	183	2.0	3.4	8	60	0	0
Belgium	1.6	1.3	..	3.0	47	41	1.1	1.0	297	6	16	27
Benin	..	..	..	..	7	7	0.3	0.2	..	..	0	6
Bolivia	1.9	1.7	..	6.0	64	69	2.1	1.9	..	..	0	0
Bosnia and Herzegovina	..	9.0	..	..	92	19	5.9	1.0	0	0	0	0
Botswana	3.5	4.0	11.4	..	9	11	1.3	1.4	..	..	7	0
Brazil	1.5	1.5	6.3	..	681	673	0.9	0.8	40	0	226	87
Bulgaria	2.6	2.6	6.6	7.6	136	85	3.2	2.1	2	18	0	2
Burkina Faso	1.5	1.3	..	..	10	15	0.2	0.3	..	..	0	0
Burundi	4.2	6.2	17.8	..	15	56	0.4	1.5	..	..	0	0
Cambodia	5.5	2.3	..	..	309	192	5.7	2.9	0	0	0	0
Cameroon	1.4	1.5	..	..	24	32	0.4	0.5	..	..	0	0
Canada	1.6	1.2	6.3	6.4	76	62	0.5	0.4	387	556	146	94
Central African Republic	1.2	1.1	..	..	5	4	0.3	0.2	..	..	0	0
Chad	1.4	1.5	..	..	35	35	1.1	0.9	0	0	1	0
Chile	3.3	3.5	..	18.9	130	114	2.3	1.7	0	0	464	156
China	1.8	2.3	..	..	4,130	3,750	0.6	0.5	845	404	419	2,548
Hong Kong, China	..	..	..	..	..	..	..	..	..	..	..	..
Colombia	2.6	4.0	..	17.4	233	305	1.5	1.5	..	..	37	48
Congo, Dem. Rep.	1.5	1.0	..	11.4	65	98	0.3	0.5	..	..	0	0
Congo, Rep.	..	1.4	..	..	17	12	1.4	0.8	..	..	0	0
Costa Rica	..	..	..	..	16	17	1.2	1.0	..	..	0	0
Côte d'Ivoire	0.8	1.6	..	..	15	..	0.3	..	..	..	2	22
Croatia	9.4	2.1	22.2	6.0	150	31	6.8	1.5	0	0	22	0
Cuba	..	..	..	..	124	73	2.4	1.3	..	..	0	0
Czech Republic	1.7	2.1	..	5.4	92	63	1.6	1.1	156	48	0	111
Denmark	1.7	1.6	..	4.4	33	23	1.1	0.8	0	3	127	7
Dominican Republic	..	..	..	..	40	40	1.2	1.0	..	..	0	76
Ecuador	2.4	2.4	..	..	57	60	1.4	1.1	..	..	10	0
Egypt, Arab Rep.	3.5	2.8	12.5	..	610	780	2.9	2.9	16	0	1,738	504
El Salvador	0.1	0.1	..	4.6	39	28	1.7	1.0	0	0	3	0
Eritrea	20.8	19.4	..	..	55	202	3.1	9.2	0	0	3	180
Estonia	1.0	1.8	3.0	5.9	6	8	0.7	1.1	0	0	19	16
Ethiopia	2.2	4.5	13.3	..	120	162	0.5	0.5	0	0	0	0
Finland	1.5	1.2	..	3.3	35	30	1.3	1.2	21	10	159	125
France	3.1	2.6	..	5.4	502	360	1.9	1.3	679	1,753	43	120
Gabon	..	..	..	..	10	7	1.8	1.1	..	..	0	0
Gambia, The	0.8	0.6	..	..	1	1	0.1	0.1	..	..	0	0
Georgia	2.2	1.1	8.2	10.0	14	29	0.5	1.1	0	0	0	0
Germany	1.7	1.5	4.9	4.4	365	285	0.9	0.7	1,456	1,549	175	69
Ghana	0.8	0.7	..	..	13	7	0.2	0.1	..	..	0	0
Greece	4.3	4.1	..	10.7	202	182	4.5	3.7	0	0	901	1,957
Guatemala	1.0	0.5	13.1	3.8	57	50	1.6	1.1	..	..	3	0
Guinea	1.2	2.9	..	..	19	12	0.6	0.3	..	..	0	0
Guinea-Bissau	0.9	3.1	..	..	9	14	1.7	2.1	..	..	0	0
Haiti	..	..	..	..	7	5	0.2	0.1	..	..	..	..

	Military expenditures				Armed forces personnel				Arms transfers			
	% of GDP		% of central government expenditure		Total thousands		% of labor force		$ millions 1990 prices			
									Exports		Imports	
	1995	2003	1995	2003	1995	2003	1995	2003	1995	2003	1995	2003
Honduras	..	0.8	..	..	24	18	1.2	0.7	..	..	0	0
Hungary	1.6	1.8	..	4.4	73	47	1.5	1.0	6	0	1	0
India	2.2	2.3	15.2	14.2	2,150	2,415	0.5	0.5	2	0	918	3,621
Indonesia	1.6	1.2	16.2	..	461	497	0.5	0.5	30	20	334	333
Iran, Islamic Rep.	2.3	4.5	15.2	22.5	763	580	4.1	2.4	2	0	290	323
Iraq	..	..	..	..	407	432	7.3	6.2	0	0	0	0
Ireland	1.0	0.6	3.6	..	13	10	0.9	0.6	0	0	0	2
Israel	8.3	8.7	..	17.7	178	175	7.8	6.0	116	212	280	318
Italy	1.8	1.9	..	5.3	585	454	2.3	1.8	265	277	238	348
Jamaica	..	..	..	..	4	3	0.3	0.2	..	..	0	0
Japan	0.9	1.0	..	..	252	252	0.4	0.4	16	0	782	210
Jordan	12.4	8.5	47.5	28.0	129	111	10.3	6.4	0	0	19	258
Kazakhstan	1.1	0.9	5.7	6.6	75	100	1.0	1.3	27	0	99	62
Kenya	1.6	1.7	7.1	7.7	29	29	0.2	0.2	..	..	0	0
Korea, Dem. Rep.	..	..	..	..	1,243	1,271	11.2	10.9	48	0	41	0
Korea, Rep.	2.8	2.4	19.4	13.3	641	691	2.9	2.8	25	36	1,630	299
Kuwait	13.9	12.5	29.3	..	22	22	3.2	2.1	0	0	657	21
Kyrgyz Republic	1.7	1.4	6.5	8.7	7	16	0.4	0.7	61	76	0	9
Lao PDR	2.9	2.1	..	..	137	129	6.0	4.5	..	..	0	0
Latvia	0.9	1.8	3.1	6.4	11	8	0.8	0.6	0	0	12	29
Lebanon	6.7	4.3	..	14.9	63	85	4.7	5.0	0	0	35	0
Lesotho	3.7	2.7	10.7	6.7	2	2	0.3	0.3	..	..	0	0
Liberia	..	7.5	..	..	21	15	2.2	1.1	..	..	0	0
Libya	4.1	2.4	..	..	81	77	5.3	4.0	0	23	0	0
Lithuania	0.5	1.9	..	6.7	9	27	0.5	1.5	0	0	4	0
Macedonia, FYR	3.0	2.8	..	..	18	20	2.0	2.1	..	..	0	0
Madagascar	0.9	1.4	..	13.9	29	22	0.4	0.3	..	..	..	..
Malawi	0.8	0.8	..	..	10	7	0.2	0.1	0	0	0	0
Malaysia	2.8	2.3	16.0	11.5	140	124	1.7	1.2	0	0	900	242
Mali	2.2	2.0	..	..	15	12	0.3	0.2	..	..	0	0
Mauritania	2.6	1.8	..	..	21	21	2.0	1.7	..	..	1	0
Mauritius	0.4	0.2	1.8	1.0	2	2	0.4	0.4	..	..	0	0
Mexico	0.6	0.5	3.8	3.3	189	204	0.5	0.5	..	..	43	43
Moldova	0.9	0.4	2.4	1.8	15	10	0.7	0.5	0	0	6	0
Mongolia	1.7	2.1	..	..	31	16	2.8	1.2	..	..	0	0
Morocco	4.6	4.2	16.1	..	238	246	2.4	2.0	..	..	30	0
Mozambique	2.5	2.4	..	..	12	8	0.1	0.1	..	..	0	0
Myanmar	3.7	2.3	..	..	371	595	1.6	2.2	..	..	216	31
Namibia	1.9	2.8	..	9.3	8	15	1.2	1.9	..	..	2	5
Nepal	0.9	1.5	..	..	63	103	0.6	0.9	..	..	1	5
Netherlands	1.9	1.6	..	3.7	78	60	1.1	0.8	367	268	34	132
New Zealand	1.4	1.0	..	3.1	10	9	0.6	0.4	0	0	4	71
Nicaragua	1.1	0.9	6.8	4.1	12	14	0.7	0.6	5	0	0	0
Niger	1.0	0.9	..	..	11	11	0.3	0.2	..	..	0	0
Nigeria	0.7	1.0	..	..	89	161	0.2	0.3	0	0	2	51
Norway	2.4	2.0	..	5.2	31	27	1.4	1.1	46	150	83	0
Oman	16.7	12.3	45.2	45.2	48	46	8.1	6.1	0	0	157	14
Pakistan	6.0	4.1	31.4	23.9	846	909	1.9	1.6	0	0	..	..
Panama	1.2	..	5.6	..	12	12	1.1	0.9	..	..	0	0
Papua New Guinea	1.2	0.9	4.7	2.9	4	3	0.2	0.1	..	..	0	0
Paraguay	..	0.7	..	5.5	28	33	1.6	1.5	..	..	0	4
Peru	2.0	1.5	13.6	8.7	178	177	2.1	1.7	0	0	32	0
Philippines	1.4	1.0	..	6.2	149	150	0.5	0.4	..	..	32	8
Poland	2.0	1.9	5.5	5.4	302	184	1.6	0.9	187	89	125	420
Portugal	2.5	2.1	5.7	5.1	104	93	2.1	1.7	0	0	18	68
Puerto Rico	..	..	..	..	..	..	..	..	..	..	..	..

	Military expenditures				Armed forces personnel				Arms transfers			
	% of GDP		% of central government expenditure		Total thousands		% of labor force		$ millions 1990 prices Exports		Imports	
	1995	2003	1995	2003	1995	2003	1995	2003	1995	2003	1995	2003
Romania	2.8	2.4	9.2	8.6	297	177	2.8	1.7	6	22	0	46
Russian Federation	4.4	4.3	..	18.8	1,800	1,370	2.3	1.7	3,133	6,980	40	0
Rwanda	4.4	3.0	..	..	47	61	1.6	1.3	..	..	0	0
Saudi Arabia	9.3	8.7	..	..	178	215	3.4	3.1	0	0	983	487
Senegal	1.8	1.4	..	9.7	17	19	0.5	0.4	..	..	2	0
Serbia and Montenegro	5.3	4.2	..	10.2	165	109	3.3	2.8	0	0	21	0
Sierra Leone	2.7	2.1	..	..	7	13	0.4	0.7	..	..	15	0
Singapore	4.4	5.2	35.1	30.3	66	169	3.7	8.0	0	0	240	121
Slovak Republic	3.2	1.8	..	4.9	51	22	1.8	0.7	114	0	220	0
Slovenia	1.7	1.5	4.7	3.5	13	11	1.3	1.1	..	..	18	14
Somalia	..	..	..	..	225	..	7.0	..	..	..	0	0
South Africa	2.2	1.7	7.3	5.8	277	56	1.7	0.3	18	23	38	13
Spain	1.5	1.2	..	3.8	282	224	1.7	1.2	65	124	357	97
Sri Lanka	5.3	2.5	20.3	13.6	236	241	3.2	2.7	..	..	49	8
Sudan	1.9	2.2	..	..	134	115	1.2	0.9	..	..	3	0
Swaziland	2.4	1.7	..	7.9	3	..	0.9	..	..	..	0	0
Sweden	2.3	1.7	..	4.9	100	63	2.1	1.3	185	186	70	23
Switzerland	1.3	1.0	5.2	5.6	31	28	0.8	0.7	77	35	93	41
Syrian Arab Republic	7.1	6.9	..	..	531	427	12.6	7.4	0	0	43	15
Tajikistan	1.0	1.3	..	12.2	18	7	0.8	0.3	..	..	0	0
Tanzania	1.5	1.5	..	..	36	28	0.2	0.2	..	..	0	0
Thailand	2.1	1.3	..	8.4	421	427	1.2	1.2	0	5	522	163
Togo	2.4	1.6	..	..	8	9	0.5	0.4	..	..	3	0
Trinidad and Tobago	..	..	..	..	7	3	1.3	0.4	..	..	0	0
Tunisia	1.9	1.6	6.7	5.8	59	47	1.8	1.1	..	..	59	0
Turkey	3.9	4.9	18.6	..	690	665	2.5	2.0	0	61	1,271	504
Turkmenistan	2.3	..	..	..	11	29	0.6	1.3	..	..	..	..
Uganda	2.2	2.5	..	12.3	52	62	0.5	0.5	..	..	39	19
Ukraine	3.1	2.9	..	9.6	519	403	2.0	1.6	218	234	..	..
United Arab Emirates	5.5	3.6	49.2	..	71	51	5.7	2.4	27	0	429	922
United Kingdom	3.0	2.4	..	6.0	233	213	0.8	0.7	1,122	525	135	555
United States	3.8	4.1	..	19.4	1,636	1,480	1.2	1.0	9,215	4,385	390	515
Uruguay	1.7	1.1	6.3	5.9	27	25	1.9	1.6	0	0	7	0
Uzbekistan	1.1	0.8	..	..	42	72	0.5	0.6	0	510	0	0
Venezuela, RB	1.5	1.3	8.7	5.4	80	105	0.9	1.0	0	0	0	0
Vietnam	..	..	..	..	622	524	1.7	1.2	..	..	270	7
West Bank and Gaza	..	..	..	..	..	..	..	..	..	..	1	0
Yemen, Rep.	7.0	7.0	36.4	..	70	137	1.5	2.4	..	..	120	30
Zambia	2.2	0.6	..	..	23	20	0.6	0.4	0	0	0	0
Zimbabwe	3.6	3.5	11.2	..	68	51	1.3	0.9	..	..	0	23
World	**2.5 w**	**2.6 w**	**.. w**	**10.8 w**	**30,182 t**	**28,161 t**	**1.1 w**	**0.9 w**				
Low income	2.6	2.3	17.3	14.8	7,891	8,189	0.9	0.8				
Middle income	2.5	2.5	..	..	16,113	14,497	1.2	0.9				
Lower middle income	2.4	2.7	..	..	14,328	12,955	1.1	0.9				
Upper middle income	2.8	2.3	..	..	1,785	1,542	1.4	1.1				
Low & middle income	2.5	2.5	..	..	24,004	22,686	1.1	0.9				
East Asia & Pacific	1.9	2.2	..	..	8,021	7,682	0.8	0.7				
Europe & Central Asia	3.4	3.2	..	11.1	4,971	3,835	2.2	1.6				
Latin America & Carib.	1.5	1.2	6.1	..	2,112	2,136	1.1	0.9				
Middle East & N. Africa	5.8	6.1	..	..	3,350	3,503	3.9	3.1				
South Asia	2.7	2.4	17.8	15.0	3,852	3,986	0.7	0.6				
Sub-Saharan Africa	2.3	1.8	..	..	1,698	1,544	0.7	0.5				
High income	2.4	2.6	..	10.7	6,178	5,476	1.3	1.1				
Europe EMU	2.0	1.8	..	4.5	2,270	1,775	1.7	1.3				

Note: Data for some countries are based on partial or uncertain data or rough estimates; see SIPRI (2004).

Defense expenditures and arms transfers | **5.8**

Although national defense is an important function of government and security from external threats contributes to economic development, high levels of defense spending burden the economy and may impede growth. Comparisons of defense spending between countries should take into account the many factors that influence perceptions of vulnerability and risk, including historical and cultural traditions, the length of borders that need defending, the quality of relations with neighbors, and the role of the armed forces in the body politic.

Data on military expenditures as a share of gross domestic product (GDP) are a rough indicator of the portion of national resources used for military activities and of the burden on the national economy. As an "input" measure, military spending is not directly related to the "output" of military activities, capabilities, or military security. Data on defense spending from governments are often incomplete and unreliable. Even in countries where the parliament vigilantly reviews government budgets and spending, defense spending and arms transfers often do not receive close scrutiny. For a detailed critique of the quality of such data, see Ball (1984) and Happe and Wakeman-Linn (1994).

This and the previous two editions of *World Development Indicators* use data on military expenditures and arms transfers from the Stockholm International Peace Research Institute (SIPRI). The data on military expenditures as a percentage of GDP are from SIPRI, and military expenditures as a percentage of central government expenditure are calculated from SIPRI data on military expenditures and International Monetary Fund (IMF) data on central government expenditures.

SIPRI's primary source of military expenditure data is official data provided by national governments. These data are derived from national budget documents, defense white papers, and other public documents from official government agencies, including governments' responses to questionnaires sent by SIPRI, the United Nations, or the Organization for Security and Co-operation in Europe. Secondary sources include international statistics, such as those of the North Atlantic Treaty Organization (NATO) and the IMF's *Government Finance Statistics Yearbook*. Other secondary sources include country reports of the Economist Intelligence Unit, country reports by IMF staff, and specialist journals and newspapers. Data on military expenditures presented in the table may therefore differ from national source data.

Lack of sufficiently detailed data makes it difficult to apply a common definition of military expenditure globally, so SIPRI has adopted a definition (derived from the NATO definition) as a guideline (see *Definitions*). This definition cannot be applied for all countries, however, since that would require much more detailed information than is available about what is included in military budgets and off-budget military expenditure items. In the many cases where SIPRI cannot make independent estimates, it uses the national data provided. Because of the differ-

ences in definitions and the difficulty in verifying the accuracy and completeness of data, the data on military spending are not strictly comparable across countries.

The data on armed forces are from the International Institute for Strategic Studies' *The Military Balance 2004–2005*. These data refer to military personnel on active duty, including paramilitary forces. Reserve forces, which are units that are not fully staffed or operational in peace time, are not included. These data also exclude civilians in the defense establishment and so are not consistent with the data on military spending on personnel. Moreover, because data exclude personnel not on active duty, they underestimate the share of the labor force working for the defense establishment. Because governments rarely report the size of their armed forces, such data typically come from intelligence sources.

The data on arms transfers are from SIPRI's Arms Transfers Project, which reports on international flows of conventional weapons. Data are collected from open sources, and since publicly available information is inadequate for tracking all weapons and other military equipment, SIPRI covers only what it terms *major conventional weapons.*

SIPRI's data on arms transfers cover sales of weapons, manufacturing licenses, aid, and gifts; therefore the term *arms transfers* rather than *arms trade* is used. The transferred weapons must be transferred voluntarily by the supplier, must have a military purpose, and must be destined for the armed forces, paramilitary forces, or intelligence agencies of another country. SIPRI data also cover weapons supplied to or from rebel forces in an armed conflict as well as arms deliveries for which neither the supplier nor the recipient can be identified with an acceptable degree of certainty; these data are available in SIPRI's database.

SIPRI's estimates of arms transfers, presented in 1990 constant price U.S. dollars, are designed as a trend-measuring device in which similar weapons have similar values, reflecting both the value and quality of weapons transferred. The trends presented in the tables are based on actual deliveries only. SIPRI cautions that these estimated values do not reflect financial value (payments for weapons transferred) for three reasons: reliable data on the value of the transfer are not available; even when the value of a transfer is known, it usually includes more than the actual conventional weapons such as spares, support systems, and training; and even when the value of the transfer is known, details of the financial arrangements such as credit and loan conditions and discounts are usually not known.

Given these measurement issues, SIPRI's method of estimating the transfer of military resources includes an evaluation of the technical parameters of the weapons. Weapons for which a price is not known are compared with the same weapons for which actual acquisition prices are available ("core weapons") or for the closest match. These weapons are assigned a value in an index that reflects their mili-

tary resource value in relation to the "core weapons." These matches are based on such characteristics as size, performance, and type of electronics, and adjustments are made for second-hand weapons. More information on SIPRI's estimation methods and sources of arms transfers is available at http://projects.sipri.se/armstrade/atmethods.html.

• **Military expenditures** data from SIPRI are derived from the NATO definition, which includes all current and capital expenditures on the armed forces, including peacekeeping forces; defense ministries and other government agencies engaged in defense projects; paramilitary forces, if these are judged to be trained and equipped for military operations; and military space activities. Such expenditures include military and civil personnel, including retirement pensions of military personnel and social services for personnel; operation and maintenance; procurement; military research and development; and military aid (in the military expenditures of the donor country). Excluded are civil defense and current expenditures for previous military activities, such as for veterans' benefits, demobilization, conversion, and destruction of weapons. This definition cannot be applied for all countries, however, since that would require much more detailed information than is available about what is included in military budgets and off-budget military expenditure items. (For example, military budgets might or might not cover civil defense, reserves and auxiliary forces, police and paramilitary forces, dual-purpose forces such as military and civilian police, military grants in kind, pensions for military personnel, and social security contributions paid by one part of government to another.) • **Armed forces personnel** are active duty military personnel, including paramilitary forces if the training, organization, equipment and control suggest they may be used to support or replace regular military forces. • **Arms transfers** cover the supply of military weapons through sales, aid, gifts, and those made through manufacturing licenses. Data cover major conventional weapons such as aircraft, armored vehicles, artillery, radar systems, missiles, and ships designed for military use. Excluded are transfers of other military equipment such as small arms and light weapons, trucks, small artillery, ammunition, support equipment, technology transfers, and other services. See *About the data* for more detail.

Data sources

The data on military expenditures and arms transfers are from SIPRI's *Yearbook 2004: Armaments, Disarmament and International Security*. The data on armed forces personnel are from the International Institute for Strategic Studies' *The Military Balance 2004–2005*.

5.9 Transport services

	Roads				Railways			Ports	Air		
	Total road network km 1997–2002[a]	Paved roads % 1997–2002[a]	Passengers carried passenger-km millions 1997–2002[a]	Goods hauled ton-km millions 1997–2002[a]	Rail lines total route-km 2000–03[a]	Passengers carried passenger-km millions 2000–03[a]	Goods hauled ton-km millions 2000–03[a]	Container traffic TEU thousands 2003	Aircraft departures thousands 2003	Passengers carried thousands 2003	Air freight ton-km millions 2003
Afghanistan	21,000	13.3	..	..	..	..	..	..	..	..	..
Albania	18,000	39.0	197	1,830	447	123	21	..	4	159	0
Algeria	104,000	68.9	..	..	3,572	954	2,246	311.1	44	3,293	19
Angola	51,429	10.4	166,045	..	2,761	..	..	..	5	198	57
Argentina	215,471	29.4	..	..	35,754	..	..	718.6	92	6,030	113
Armenia	8,431	96.8	1,716	75	711	47	344	..	4	367	5
Australia	811,603	38.7	..	..	41,286	12,100	158,100	4,769.1	530	41,386	1,355
Austria	200,000	100.0	..	16,100	5,693	8,415	17,644	..	128	6,903	431
Azerbaijan	28,030	92.4	9,603	5,534	2,122	584	6,980	..	9	684	67
Bangladesh	207,486	9.5	..	..	2,791	3,972	952	625.2	7	1,579	179
Belarus	79,990	86.7	9,090	7,945	5,512	14,349	34,169	..	6	234	1
Belgium	149,028	78.2	..	17,487	3,518	8,260	8,363	6,556.6	133	2,904	605
Benin	6,787	20.0	..	..	438	66	86	..	1	46	7
Bolivia	60,282	6.6	..	..	3,698	..	..	..	29	1,768	25
Bosnia and Herzegovina	21,846	52.3	..	..	1,032	53	293	..	5	73	1
Botswana	10,217	55.0	2,602	..	888	171	842	..	8	183	0
Brazil	1,724,929	5.5	..	..	30,403	..	..	4,333.4	487	32,372	1,478
Bulgaria	37,077	92.0	8,596	168	4,318	2,598	4,627	..	1	75	0
Burkina Faso	12,506	16.0	..	..	622	..	..	..	1	55	0
Burundi	..	..	..	..	..	..	..	..	..	..	..
Cambodia	12,323	16.2	201	412	603	45	92	..	4	116	3
Cameroon	34,300	12.5	..	..	1,016	308	1,186	..	10	315	20
Canada	1,408,800	..	..	87,522	49,422	..	323,600	3,631.1	1,036	35,884	1,496
Central African Republic	23,810	2.7	..	..	..	..	..	..	1	46	7
Chad	33,400	0.8	..	..	..	..	..	..	1	46	7
Chile	79,605	20.2	..	..	4,923	769	1,317	1,249.5	83	5,247	1,130
China	1,765,222	..	780,577	633,040	60,627	489,971	1,508,686	61,621.5[b]	946	86,041	5,651
Hong Kong, China	1,831	100.0	..	..	..	..	..	..	87	13,025	5,781
Colombia	112,988	14.4	..	31	3,154	..	..	995.2	172	9,143	646
Congo, Dem. Rep.	157,000	..	..	..	3,641	160	429	..	5	95	7
Congo, Rep.	12,800	9.7	..	..	1,026	76	307	..	5	52	0
Costa Rica	35,303	12.0	..	..	848	..	..	669.3	35	781	10
Côte d'Ivoire	50,400	9.7	..	..	639	148	606	612.6	1	46	7
Croatia	28,344	84.6	3,557	7,413	2,726	1,195	2,420	..	20	1,267	3
Cuba	60,858	49.0	..	..	4,382	..	..	..	9	611	41
Czech Republic	127,204	100.0	90,055	45,059	9,499	6,562	17,042	..	52	3,392	36
Denmark	71,847	100.0	61,258	11,810	2,273	5,528	1,867	638.7	91	5,886	171
Dominican Republic	12,600	49.4	..	..	1,743	..	..	480.7	..	..	..
Ecuador	43,197	18.9	7,769	4,646	966	..	..	515.6	13	1,123	8
Egypt, Arab Rep.	64,000	78.1	..	..	5,150	40,837	4,188	1,458.0	42	4,172	229
El Salvador	10,029	19.8	..	..	283	..	..	..	25	2,966	3
Eritrea	4,010	21.8	..	..	306	..	..	..	..	..	..
Estonia	55,944	24.8	2,330	4,387	967	177	9,330	..	8	395	2
Ethiopia	33,297	12.0	219,113	..	681	..	..	..	27	1,147	94
Finland	78,650	64.0	66,900	29,000	5,850	3,305	9,664	1,162.4	107	6,184	256
France	893,100	100.0	..	245,400	29,352	73,227	50,036	3,553.5	696	47,259	5,067
Gabon	8,464	9.9	..	..	731	63	1,834	..	8	386	54
Gambia, The	2,700	35.4	..	..	..	..	..	..	..	..	..
Georgia	20,229	93.5	4,987	543	1,565	401	5,065	..	2	124	2
Germany	230,735	..	76,186	226,982	35,868	69,848	73,971	10,504.8	845	72,693	7,298
Ghana	46,179	18.4	..	..	977	85	242	..	3	241	17
Greece	117,000	91.8	5,889	13,909	2,383	1,836	327	1,914.8	114	7,519	63
Guatemala	14,118	34.5	..	..	886	..	..	726.0	..	..	..
Guinea	30,500	16.5	..	..	837	..	..	..	..	..	..
Guinea-Bissau	4,400	10.3	..	..	..	..	..	..	..	..	..
Haiti	4,160	24.3	..	..	..	..	..	..	..	..	..

	Roads				Railways			Ports	Air		
	Total road network km 1997–2002[a]	Paved roads % 1997–2002[a]	Passengers carried passenger-km millions 1997–2002[a]	Goods hauled ton-km millions 1997–2002[a]	Rail lines total route-km 2000–03[a]	Passengers carried passenger-km millions 2000–03[a]	Goods hauled ton-km millions 2000–03[a]	Container traffic TEU thousands 2003	Aircraft departures thousands 2003	Passengers carried thousands 2003	Air freight ton-km millions 2003
Honduras	13,603	20.4	..	..	699	..	..	470.6	..	..	..
Hungary	159,568	43.9	13,300	11,200	7,729	7,548	7,703	..	35	2,369	28
India	3,315,231	57.3	..	958	63,140	493,489	333,228	3,916.1	264	19,456	580
Indonesia	368,362	58.0	..	..	6,458	16,381	4,474	4,560.4	156	12,221	424
Iran, Islamic Rep.	167,157	56.3	..	..	6,151	8,582	15,842	1,147.7	85	9,554	80
Iraq	45,550	84.3	..	..	2,339	570	1,682	..	..	..	..
Ireland	95,736	100.0	..	5,900	1,919	1,628	426	869.5	231	28,864	122
Israel	16,903	100.0	..	..	676	1,116	1,107	1,605.0	36	3,672	1,394
Italy	479,688	100.0	26,075	219,800	16,307	47,177	23,420	8,473.2	328	34,953	1,359
Jamaica	18,700	70.1	..	..	272	..	..	1,137.8	24	1,838	49
Japan	1,171,647	77.1	954,294	313,072	20,096	239,246	21,900	14,567.0	639	103,606	7,985
Jordan	7,301	100.0	..	..	292	..	522	..	15	1,353	190
Kazakhstan	82,980	93.9	19,928	6,962	13,597	10,449	133,088	..	20	1,010	21
Kenya	63,942	12.1	..	..	2,634	288	1,538	..	27	1,678	142
Korea, Dem. Rep.	31,200	6.4	..	..	5,214	..	..	..	1	75	2
Korea, Rep.	86,990	76.7	66,853	74,504	3,129	28,787	10,784	12,993.4	240	33,334	8,312
Kuwait	4,450	80.6	..	..	..	..	..	..	18	2,198	219
Kyrgyz Republic	18,500	91.1	5,081	875	417	50	331	..	5	206	5
Lao PDR	21,716	44.5	..	..	..	..	..	..	7	219	2
Latvia	60,472	94.6	2,361	6,160	2,269	744	15,020	..	10	340	1
Lebanon	7,300	84.9	..	..	401	..	..	299.4	11	935	75
Lesotho	5,940	18.3	..	..	..	..	..	..	..	..	..
Liberia	10,600	6.2	..	..	490	..	..	..	6	627	0
Libya	83,200	57.2	..	..	2,757	..	..	..	6	627	0
Lithuania	77,148	89.7	2,046	10,709	1,775	498	9,767	..	10	329	1
Macedonia, FYR	8,684	63.8	..	..	699	98	334	..	2	201	0
Madagascar	49,827	11.6	..	..	883	10	12	..	9	404	10
Malawi	28,400	18.5	..	..	797	..	..	..	5	109	1
Malaysia	65,877	77.9	..	..	1,636	1,123	1,106	10,072.1	152	15,214	2,176
Mali	15,100	12.1	..	..	733	196	189	..	1	46	7
Mauritania	7,660	11.3	..	..	717	..	..	..	2	116	0
Mauritius	2,000	98.0	..	..	..	..	..	381.5	15	1,035	195
Mexico	329,532	32.8	385,296	197,958	26,656	..	..	1,690.9	287	20,688	350
Moldova	12,719	86.3	1,298	1,152	1,120	355	2,715	..	4	179	1
Mongolia	49,250	3.5	761	134	1,810	1,073	6,452	..	7	295	8
Morocco	57,694	56.4	3	2,952	1,907	2,145	4,974	346.7	35	2,565	51
Mozambique	30,400	18.7	..	..	2,072	137	808	..	8	281	7
Myanmar	..	..	..	..	3,955	..	..	..	21	1,117	2
Namibia	42,237	12.8	47	145,044	2,382	..	..	..	6	266	46
Nepal	15,308	30.8	..	..	59	..	..	..	13	625	19
Netherlands	116,500	90.0	193,900	32,700	2,806	14,288	3,685	7,232.4	248	23,455	4,331
New Zealand	92,382	64.0	..	..	3,898	..	3,853	1,530.3	247	12,259	801
Nicaragua	18,712	11.4	..	..	6	..	..	..	..	..	..
Niger	10,100	7.9	..	..	..	..	..	..	1	46	7
Nigeria	194,394	30.9	..	..	3,505	..	..	..	9	520	10
Norway	91,852	77.5	55,330	13,287	4,077	2,477	2,668	..	249	12,779	175
Oman	32,800	30.0	..	..	..	..	..	2,246.8	28	2,777	190
Pakistan	257,683	59.0	209,959	111,323	7,791	20,782	4,572	878.9	45	4,477	351
Panama	11,643	34.6	..	..	355	..	..	1,605.1	26	1,264	20
Papua New Guinea	19,600	3.5	..	..	..	..	..	..	18	691	17
Paraguay	29,500	50.8	..	1	441	..	..	..	11	313	0
Peru	78,230	13.4	..	..	2,123	..	..	627.0	36	2,233	114
Philippines	202,124	9.5	..	..	429	123	..	3,468.8	56	6,467	274
Poland	364,697	68.3	30,997	74,403	20,223	17,310	46,560	261.4	73	3,252	71
Portugal	17,135	86.0	87,150	14,200	2,880	3,683	2,585	860.0	117	7,590	206
Puerto Rico	24,023	94.0	..	..	96	..	..	1,669.2	..	..	..

	Roads				Railways			Ports	Air		
	Total road network km	Paved roads %	Passengers carried passenger-km millions	Goods hauled ton-km millions	Rail lines total route-km	Passengers carried passenger-km millions	Goods hauled ton-km millions	Container traffic TEU thousands	Aircraft departures thousands	Passengers carried thousands	Air freight ton-km millions
	1997–2002[a]	1997–2002[a]	1997–2002[a]	1997–2002[a]	2000–03[a]	2000–03[a]	2000–03[a]	2003	2003	2003	2003
Romania	198,755	50.4	5,283	25,350	11,364	8,502	14,867	..	27	1,251	7
Russian Federation	537,289	67.4	164	139	85,542	152,900	1,510,200	946.6	351	22,723	1,113
Rwanda	12,000	8.3	..	..	..	..	..	..	..	..	..
Saudi Arabia	152,044	29.9	..	..	1,078	239	772	2,440.3	108	13,822	852
Senegal	14,576	29.3	..	..	906	138	371	..	2	130	0
Serbia and Montenegro	50,414	59.3	..	1,063	3,809	1,023	2,408	..	22	1,298	47
Sierra Leone	11,300	8.0	..	..	..	..	..	..	0	14	7
Singapore	3,130	100.0	..	..	..	..	..	18,441.0	64	14,737	6,683
Slovak Republic	42,970	87.3	33,234	22,347	3,657	2,682	10,679	..	7	208	0
Slovenia	20,250	100.0	1,143	4,611	1,229	749	3,078	..	16	758	4
Somalia	22,100	11.8	..	..	..	..	..	..	..	..	..
South Africa	275,971	20.9	..	..	20,041	12,873	105,719	1,942.3	147	9,481	891
Spain	664,852	99.0	411,379	114,011	13,856	20,733	13,781	7,364.8	519	42,507	876
Sri Lanka	97,286	81.0	21,067	..	1,449	..	..	1,959.4	13	1,958	238
Sudan	11,900	36.3	..	..	4,578	73	993	..	8	421	36
Swaziland	3,107	..	..	..	301	..	..	..	2	*89,500*	0
Sweden	213,237	78.6	95,800	39,609	9,857	6,621	12,002	858.3	184	11,586	253
Switzerland	71,212	..	94,750	24,500	3,223	12,835	9,732	..	189	10,589	1,248
Syrian Arab Republic	64,697	14.2	589	..	2,450	364	1,812	..	7	908	16
Tajikistan	27,767	..	..	..	617	41	1,087	..	7	413	7
Tanzania	88,200	4.2	..	..	4,460[c]	471[c]	1,350[c]	..	6	150	2
Thailand	57,403	98.5	..	..	4,071	..	..	4,410.0	94	16,623	1,764
Togo	7,520	31.6	..	..	568	..	..	..	1	*46*	7
Trinidad and Tobago	8,320	51.1	..	..	..	..	..	440.4	18	1,084	34
Tunisia	18,997	65.4	..	..	1,909	1,265	2,252	..	19	1,720	19
Turkey	354,421	41.6	163,327	150,912	8,671	5,204	7,169	2,773.9	104	10,701	379
Turkmenistan	24,000	81.2	..	..	2,523	1,118	6,437	..	25	1,412	14
Uganda	27,000	6.7	..	..	259	..	218	..	0	40	23
Ukraine	169,679	96.8	36,612	20,593	22,079	50,544	193,141	..	33	1,477	18
United Arab Emirates	1,088	100.0	..	..	..	..	..	6,955.8	70	11,384	2,686
United Kingdom	371,913	100.0	666,000	150,700	17,052	40,442	19,585	7,135.3	891	76,377	5,251
United States	6,378,254	58.8	..	1,534,430	141,961	..	2,200,123[d]	32,641.6	7,789[e]	588,997[e]	34,206[e]
Uruguay	8,983	90.0	..	..	2,993	..	..	*301.6*	7	464	23
Uzbekistan	81,600	87.3	..	..	4,126	2,163	18,428	..	22	1,466	71
Venezuela, RB	96,155	33.6	..	..	433	..	32	*924.1*	106	3,824	2
Vietnam	93,300	25.1	..	..	2,545	3,426	2,000	2,195.9	48	4,553	165
West Bank and Gaza	..	..	..	..	..	..	..	..	..	..	..
Yemen, Rep.	67,000	11.5	..	..	..	..	..	377.4	15	844	49
Zambia	91,440	22.0	..	..	1,273[c]	186[c]	554[c]	..	5	51	0
Zimbabwe	18,338	47.4	..	..	3,077	..	..	..	4	201	19
World	47.4 m	.. m	.. m	.. s	1,265 m	3,078 m	291,801 s	21,372 s	1,679,838 s	129,570 s	
Low income	13.3	..	..		160	707	..	637	42,573	1,902	
Middle income	54.0	..	..	458,110	1,123	5,020	115,089	4,447	340,444	19,413	
Lower middle income	53.0	7,291	..	332,569	1,265	4,974	93,575	3,159	252,690	14,025	
Upper middle income	72.3	..	..	946	7,703	*17,415*	1,289	87,754	5,388		
Low & middle income	30.8	..	..	592,154	577	2,123	122,439	5,084	383,016	21,315	
East Asia & Pacific	22.5	..	..	..	..	..	86,329	1,576	145,040	10,558	
Europe & Central Asia	89.7	5,283	7,413	219,116	1,118	7,169	..	867	55,604	1,899	
Latin America & Carib.	26.9	..	..	..	..	..	15,660	1,530	93,435	4,071	
Middle East & N. Africa	63.8	..	..	25,249	1,110	2,246	..	416	42,570	1,770	
South Asia	42.9	..	..	..	..	..	6,501	347	28,192	1,367	
Sub-Saharan Africa	13.3	..	..	..	143	554	..	348	18,174	1,651	
High income	94.8	..	19,504	..	8,260	10,784	169,362	16,289	1,296,821	108,255	
Europe EMU	99.5	76,186	32,700	120,432	8,415	9,664	48,492	3,507	281,684	24,960	

a. Data are for the latest year available in the period shown. b. Includes Hong Kong, China. c. Excludes Tazara railway. d. Refers to Class 1 railways only. e. Data cover only carriers designated by the U.S. Department of Transportation as major and national air carriers.

About the data

Transport infrastructure—highways, railways, ports and waterways, and airports and air traffic control systems—and the services that flow from it are crucial to the activities of households, producers, and governments. Because performance indicators vary significantly by transport mode and focus (whether physical infrastructure or the services flowing from that infrastructure), highly specialized and carefully specified indicators are required. The table provides selected indicators of the size, extent, and productivity of roads, railways, and air transport systems and of the volume of traffic in these modes and in ports.

Data for transport sectors are not always internationally comparable. Unlike for demographic statistics, national income accounts, and international trade data, the collection of infrastructure data has not been "internationalized." But data on roads are collected by the International Road Federation (IRF), and data on air transport by the International Civil Aviation Organization (ICAO).

National road associations are the primary source of IRF data. In countries without such an association or where it does not respond, IRF contacts other agencies, such as road directorates, ministries of transport or public works, or central statistical offices. As a result, there are differences in definitions, data collection methods, and quality of the compiled data. Moreover, the quality of transport service (reliability, transit time, and condition of goods delivered) is rarely measured, though it may be as important as quantity in assessing an economy's transport system. Several new initiatives are under way to improve data availability and consistency. The IRF is collaborating with national and international development agencies to improve the quality and coverage of road statistics. To improve measures of progress and performance, the World Bank is also working on better measures of access, affordability, efficiency, quality, and fiscal and institutional aspects of infrastructure.

Unlike the road sector, where qualified motor vehicle operators can operate anywhere on the network, railways are a restricted transport system with vehicles confined to a fixed guideway. Considering their cost and service characteristics, railways generally are best suited to carry—and can effectively compete for—bulk commodities and containerized freight for distances of 500–5,000 kilometers, and passengers for distances of 50–1,000 kilometers. Below these limits road transport tends to be more competitive, while above these limits air transport for passengers and freight or sea transport for freight tend to be more competitive. The railways indicators in the table focus on scale and output measures: route-kilometers, passenger-kilometers, and goods (freight) hauled in ton-kilometers.

Measures of port container traffic, much of it commodities of medium to high value added, give some indication of economic growth in a country. But when traffic is merely transshipment, much of the economic benefit goes to the terminal operator and ancillary services for ships and containers rather than to the country more broadly. In transshipment centers empty containers may account for as much as 40 percent of traffic.

The air transport data cover total (international and domestic) scheduled traffic carried by the air carriers registered in a country. Countries submit air transport data to ICAO on the basis of standard instructions and definitions issued by ICAO. In many cases, however, the data include estimates by ICAO for nonreporting carriers. Where possible, these estimates are based on previous submissions supplemented by information published by the air carriers, such as flight schedules.

The data cover the air traffic carried on scheduled services, but changes in air transport regulations in Europe have made it more difficult to classify traffic as scheduled or nonscheduled. Thus recent increases shown for some European countries may be due to changes in the classification of air traffic rather than to actual growth. For countries with few air carriers or only one, the addition or discontinuation of a home-based air carrier may cause significant changes in air traffic.

Definitions

• **Total road network** covers motorways, highways, main or national roads, secondary or regional roads, and all other roads in a country. • **Paved roads** are roads surfaced with crushed stone (macadam) and hydrocarbon binder or bituminized agents, with concrete, or with cobblestones. • **Passengers carried by road** are the number of passengers transported by road times kilometers traveled. • **Goods hauled by road** are the volume of goods transported by road vehicles, measured in metric tons times kilometers traveled. • **Rail lines** are the length of railway route available for train service, irrespective of the number of parallel tracks. • **Passengers carried by railway** are the number of passengers transported by rail times kilometers traveled. • **Goods hauled by railway** are the volume of goods transported by railway, measured in metric tons times kilometers traveled. • **Port container traffic** measures the flow of containers from land to sea transport modes and vice versa in twenty-foot-equivalent units (TEUs), a standard-size container. Data cover coastal shipping as well as international journeys. Transshipment traffic is counted as two lifts at the intermediate port (once to off-load and again as an outbound lift) and includes empty units. • **Aircraft departures** are domestic and international takeoffs of air carriers registered in the country. • **Air passengers carried** include both domestic and international passengers of air carriers registered in the country. • **Air freight** is the volume of freight, express, and diplomatic bags carried by air carriers registered in the country on each flight stage (operation of an aircraft from takeoff to its next landing), measured in metric tons times kilometers traveled.

Data sources

The data on roads are from the IRF's *World Road Statistics.* The data on railways are from a database maintained by the World Bank's Transport and Urban Development Department, Transport Division. The data on port container traffic are from Containerisation International's *Containerisation International Yearbook.* And the data on air transport are from the ICAO's *Civil Aviation Statistics of the World* and ICAO staff estimates.

5.9a

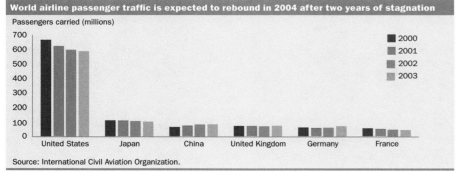

World airline passenger traffic is expected to rebound in 2004 after two years of stagnation

Passengers carried (millions)

Legend: 2000, 2001, 2002, 2003

Countries: United States, Japan, China, United Kingdom, Germany, France

Source: International Civil Aviation Organization.

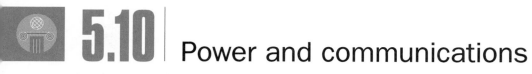

Power and communications

	Electric power		Telephone mainlines[a]							Mobile phones[a]	International communications[a]	
	Consumption per capita kwh	Transmission and distribution losses % of output	per 1,000 people	In largest city per 1,000 people	Waiting list thousands	Faults per 100 mainlines	per employee	Revenue per line $	Cost of local call $ per 3 minutes	per 1,000 people	Outgoing traffic minutes per subscriber	Cost of call to U.S. $ per 3 minutes
	2002	2002	2003	2002	2003	2003	2003	2003	2003	2003	2003	2003
Afghanistan	..	..	2	8	..	..	..	..	..	10	..	..
Albania	1,390	35	83	94	98.5	57.2	65	1,139	0.02	358	282	2.47
Algeria	662	16	69	124	727.0	6.0	105	192	0.04	46	111	..
Angola	109	14	7	21	240.3	..	38	..	0.09	9	404	1.34
Argentina	2,024	17	219	..	..	..	337	931	0.02	178	53	..
Armenia	1,113	26	148	224	60.8	52.9	98	142	0.02	30	66	0.00
Australia	9,663	7	542	..	0.0	8.0	216	1,377	0.19	719	215	0.68
Austria	6,838	5	481	..	0.0	5.4	228	1,459	0.19	879	371	..
Azerbaijan	1,878	20	114	299	55.4	45.2	106	108	0.10	128	45	5.55
Bangladesh	100	21	5	30	153.1	..	29	593	0.03	10	77	2.07
Belarus	2,657	13	311	397	292.8	24.8	115	72	0.01	113	87	2.25
Belgium	7,592	5	489	..	..	5.6	206	1,615	0.17	793	352	..
Benin	76	156	9	42	..	6.0	48	1,044	0.11	34	294	5.76
Bolivia	419	13	72	109	..	..	187	742	..	152	68	..
Bosnia and Herzegovina	1,633	17	245	502	..	..	130	247	0.02	274	106	3.02
Botswana	..	..	75	..	..	..	83	1,238	0.02	297	425	..
Brazil	1,776	17	223	311	200.0	1.7	400	546	0.03	264	21	..
Bulgaria	3,060	15	380	..	114.6	2.6	110	394	0.03	466	31	1.46
Burkina Faso	..	..	5	42	12.4	19.7	51	1,022	0.10	19	307	2.58
Burundi	..	..	3	..	4.7	..	27	718	0.07	9	127	3.71
Cambodia	..	..	3	19	..	..	37	515	0.03	35	147	..
Cameroon	161	23	7	..	..	..	50	..	0.06	66	208	..
Canada	15,613	8	629	..	0.0	..	237	1,040	0.00	417	0	..
Central African Republic	..	..	2	..	1.2	..	23	1,196	0.43	10	466	13.59
Chad	..	..	2	8	..	60.8	16	..	0.11	8	363	9.11
Chile	2,617	6	221	333	32.3	25.0	179	698	0.10	511	79	2.18
China	987	7	209	584	..	..	..	211	0.03	215	4	..
Hong Kong, China	5,612	12	559	580	0.0	1.3	184	1,700	0.00	1,079	1,156	2.62
Colombia	817	19	179	327	1,174.7	33.0	229	499	0.03	141	44	..
Congo, Dem. Rep.	43	4	0	..	..	..	..	..	..	19	..	..
Congo, Rep.	82	70	2	..	..	..	..	..	..	94	..	..
Costa Rica	1,611	10	251	..	15.8	4.2	213	351	0.02	111	125	..
Côte d'Ivoire	..	..	14	68	3.4	81.0	70	2,267	0.09	77	274	6.38
Croatia	2,855	17	417	..	0.0	12.0	171	679	0.10	584	198	..
Cuba	1,094	15	51	121	..	9.6	34	1,370	0.09	2	65	7.35
Czech Republic	4,982	6	360	666	27.3	6.8	159	1,103	0.15	965	95	0.83
Denmark	6,024	6	669	..	0.0	9.0	177	1,521	0.11	883	225	..
Dominican Republic	853	33	115	4	..	..	..	..	0.06	271	245	..
Ecuador	665	24	122	133	14.5	35.3	275	336	0.03	189	48	1.75
Egypt, Arab Rep.	1,073	13	127	264	99.5	1.0	164	321	0.02	84	35	2.57
El Salvador	595	13	116	..	38.2	..	168	903	0.07	176	243	1.23
Eritrea	..	..	9	43	46.2	51.1	60	458	0.03	0	127	3.55
Estonia	3,882	15	341	593	4.5	16.3	136	1,195	0.11	777	190	0.74
Ethiopia	25	10	6	60	146.1	100.0	53	295	0.02	1	36	7.05
Finland	15,326	4	492	..	0.0	..	147	1,944	0.16	910	172	1.06
France	6,606	6	566	..	0.0	..	232	938	0.15	696	139	..
Gabon	804	18	29	..	..	0.5	18	3,712	0.26	224	854	10.88
Gambia, The	..	..	28	97	10.6	..	34	760	0.03	73	352	3.46
Georgia	1,032	17	133	233	138.8	17.2	39	208	0.03	107	108	0.68
Germany	6,046	5	657	696	0.0	..	240	1,313	0.11	785	167	0.35
Ghana	297	24	13	83	154.8	67.4	57	460	0.03	36	213	1.13
Greece	4,231	7	454	731	1.7	13.6	208	1,312	0.09	902	173	0.67
Guatemala	361	22	71	..	..	..	236	593	0.08	131	172	..
Guinea	..	..	3	..	1.4	..	33	1,119	0.08	14	734	4.61
Guinea-Bissau	..	..	8	..	..	..	..	..	..	1	..	..
Haiti	36	51	17	..	..	..	28	..	..	38	..	..

Power and communications

	Electric power		Telephone mainlines[a]							Mobile phones[a]	International communications[a]	
	Consumption per capita kwh 2002	Transmission and distribution losses % of output 2002	per 1,000 people 2003	In largest city per 1,000 people 2002	Waiting list thousands 2003	Faults per 100 mainlines 2003	per employee 2003	Revenue per line $ 2003	Cost of local call $ per 3 minutes 2003	per 1,000 people 2003	Outgoing traffic minutes per subscriber 2003	Cost of call to U.S. $ per 3 minutes 2003
Honduras	537	23	48	..	342.2	3.6	62	1,210	0.06	49	..	2.85
Hungary	3,099	12	349	588	28.0	..	176	1,294	0.16	769	44	0.79
India	380	26	46	136	1,648.8	126.0	92	198	0.02	25	16	3.20
Indonesia	411	16	39	261	..	20.0	181	300	0.03	87	37	..
Iran, Islamic Rep.	1,677	16	220	381	1,654.8	..	316	118	0.01	51	23	1.95
Iraq	1,213	6	28	..	..	..	..	..	..	3	..	..
Ireland	5,555	8	491	..	..	6.0	133	2,081	0.17	880	441	..
Israel	5,857	3	458	..	..	..	249	1,228	0.02	961	385	..
Italy	4,901	7	484	..	..	..	..	1,288	0.11	1,018	169	..
Jamaica	2,406	9	170	..	168.6	39.7	192	1,050	0.02	535	310	..
Japan	7,718	5	472	554	0.0	..	526	2,805	0.07	679	37	..
Jordan	1,317	12	114	183	1.1	12.6	115	1,330	0.05	242	380	1.96
Kazakhstan	2,911	16	130	..	168.3	..	65	289	0.00	64	63	..
Kenya	120	21	10	77	134.0	..	17	1,563	0.07	50	75	4.36
Korea, Dem. Rep.	..	..	41	..	..	..	..	..	..	0	..	..
Korea, Rep.	6,171	6	538	632	0.0	1.0	249	958	0.03	701	45	1.74
Kuwait	10,888	5	198	46	0.0	4.0	66	1,778	0.00	578	503	1.48
Kyrgyz Republic	1,269	37	76	168	41.5	..	53	110	0.09	27	66	9.04
Lao PDR	..	..	12	65	..	..	50	448	0.06	20	104	6.37
Latvia	2,088	25	285	500	16.2	20.3	228	376	0.12	526	76	2.02
Lebanon	1,951	16	199	..	..	..	..	..	0.10	227	149	..
Lesotho	..	..	13	64	21.1	72.8	80	415	0.11	42	64	2.31
Liberia	..	..	2	..	..	..	..	..	..	1	868	..
Libya	2,250	20	136	..	..	..	..	..	..	23	68	..
Lithuania	1,938	8	239	427	1.3	16.3	217	804	0.16	630	43	2.31
Macedonia, FYR	..	..	271	..	..	..	143	406	0.01	177	116	..
Madagascar	2,204	..	4	9	1.8	26.6	105	1,614	0.07	17	147	7.41
Malawi	..	..	8	41	17.4	..	17	620	0.06	13	435	0.06
Malaysia	2,832	6	182	..	49.0	40.0	222	948	0.02	442	144	2.37
Mali	..	..	5	24	..	..	37	1,159	0.07	23	300	12.28
Mauritania	..	..	14	..	..	..	52	2,390	0.11	128	393	..
Mauritius	..	..	285	376	13.5	56.8	219	499	0.04	267	125	2.50
Mexico	1,660	15	158	156	..	1.9	139	1,134	0.16	291	134	3.04
Moldova	909	50	219	350	88.0	5.2	106	157	0.02	132	79	2.21
Mongolia	..	..	56	99	35.6	20.6	35	452	0.02	130	33	..
Morocco	475	7	40	..	..	..	94	1,612	0.17	243	226	1.63
Mozambique	341	8	5	..	12.7	70.0	39	1,533	0.08	23	274	..
Myanmar	108	19	7	32	102.6	155.0	46	86	0.06	1	26	0.36
Namibia	..	..	66	157	2.6	40.4	81	1,542	0.04	116	499	..
Nepal	64	20	16	315	319.5	88.1	78	257	0.01	2	102	..
Netherlands	6,179	4	614	..	..	..	..	1,313	0.11	768	260	..
New Zealand	8,832	10	448	..	0.0	..	357	1,757	0.00	648	313	..
Nicaragua	279	29	37	..	..	4.6	102	744	0.08	85	108	3.20
Niger	..	..	2	24	..	104.6	16	848	0.10	2	292	8.77
Nigeria	68	38	7	12	..	..	58	..	0.10	26	124	..
Norway	23,855	7	713	..	0.0	..	221	1,535	0.15	909	165	0.31
Oman	3,177	17	84	..	2.1	..	105	2,237	0.07	229	729	0.78
Pakistan	363	26	27	..	190.3	..	73	394	0.02	18	35	..
Panama	1,375	22	122	284	..	8.3	62	..	0.12	268	120	..
Papua New Guinea	..	..	12	115	..	..	..	..	0.08	3	402	..
Paraguay	842	3	46	91	..	3.4	25	1,069	0.09	299	104	0.82
Peru	723	10	67	..	33.0	..	372	888	0.08	106	82	..
Philippines	459	16	41	265	..	..	273	884	0.00	270	52	..
Poland	2,514	10	319	..	501.6	17.2	76	786	0.09	451	147	1.79
Portugal	4,000	8	411	..	..	10.1	278	1,842	0.13	898	124	0.93
Puerto Rico	..	..	346	..	..	..	261	1,583	..	316	..	..

	Electric power		Telephone mainlines[a]							Mobile phones[a]	International communications[a]	
	Consumption per capita kwh	Transmission and distribution losses % of output	per 1,000 people	In largest city per 1,000 people	Waiting list thousands	Faults per 100 mainlines	per employee	Revenue per line $	Cost of local call $ per 3 minutes	per 1,000 people	Outgoing traffic minutes per subscriber	Cost of call to U.S. $ per 3 minutes
	2002	2002	2003	2002	2003	2003	2003	2003	2003	2003	2003	2003
Romania	1,632	13	199	..	465.0	8.9	100	410	0.12	324	39	1.82
Russian Federation	4,291	12	242	..	5,809.6	..	..	209	..	249	34	..
Rwanda	..	..	3	..	..	..	61	934	0.09	16	245	..
Saudi Arabia	5,275	8	155	214	73.6	26.2	155	1,893	0.05	321	578	2.40
Senegal	135	7	22	71	9.8	17.3	152	852	0.20	56	294	1.81
Serbia and Montenegro	..	..	243	424	313.5	..	181	146	0.01	338	121	2.08
Sierra Leone	..	..	5	..	..	..	19	..	0.03	13	336	..
Singapore	7,039	9	450	471	0.0	99.2	221	1,738	0.02	852	1,020	..
Slovak Republic	4,222	3	241	665	7.0	27.0	106	604	0.12	684	134	0.79
Slovenia	5,907	5	407	..	0.5	22.5	227	839	0.07	871	106	0.52
Somalia	..	..	10	..	..	..	..	..	..	3	..	..
South Africa	3,860	8	107	..	..	48.2	116	1,102	0.15	364	117	0.58
Spain	5,048	8	434	..	..	..	209	2,198	0.07	909	183	..
Sri Lanka	297	18	49	299	257.7	99.6	72	379	0.03	73	58	2.33
Sudan	74	15	27	80	444.0	..	150	368	0.03	20	80	3.92
Swaziland	..	..	44	131	15.6	..	67	784	0.05	84	657	2.42
Sweden	14,742	8	736	..	..	..	304	1,189	0.11	980	..	0.32
Switzerland	7,381	6	744	..	0.0	..	231	1,799	0.15	843	481	..
Syrian Arab Republic	1,000	32	123	156	2,805.9	50.0	84	238	0.01	65	90	4.81
Tajikistan	2,236	15	37	133	5.9	144.0	48	37	0.01	7	47	6.95
Tanzania	62	23	4	23	8.0	24.0	46	1,471	0.12	25	73	5.28
Thailand	1,626	7	105	452	582.7	91.7	222	636	0.07	394	52	1.54
Togo	..	..	12	37	27.5	6.2	57	823	0.10	44	349	2.15
Trinidad and Tobago	4,330	5	250	..	..	..	100	958	0.04	278	218	2.22
Tunisia	1,019	11	118	99	108.7	29.0	143	451	0.02	192	164	2.28
Turkey	1,458	18	268	388	77.2	30.4	309	334	0.14	394	50	2.09
Turkmenistan	1,371	14	77	183	36.8	86.4	52	145	..	2	64	..
Uganda	..	..	2	..	..	..	23	5,002	0.21	30	125	3.51
Ukraine	2,229	19	216	..	2,158.7	..	86	211	..	136	36	..
United Arab Emirates	9,656	9	281	348	0.4	0.3	115	1,994	0.00	736	1,732	1.73
United Kingdom	5,618	8	591	..	0.0	11.0	148	2,087	0.18	841	258	..
United States	12,183	6	621	..	..	12.4	170	1,568	0.00	543	217	..
Uruguay	1,834	17	280	335	..	..	168	751	..	193	87	..
Uzbekistan	1,670	9	67	248	38.9	87.4	69	118	0.01	13	36	..
Venezuela, RB	2,472	25	111	..	..	2.0	192	864	0.02	273	104	..
Vietnam	374	14	54	..	..	..	49	366	0.02	34	17	..
West Bank and Gaza	..	..	87	..	0.7	97.0	188	353	0.05	133	132	0.15
Yemen, Rep.	152	15	28	95	704.8	..	100	266	0.02	35	81	4.10
Zambia	583	3	8	22	11.6	90.8	28	808	0.09	22	178	6.45
Zimbabwe	831	21	26	74	131.0	..	62	817	0.04	32	309	..
World	**2,225 w**	**9 w**	**183 w**	**294 w**	**.. w**	**.. m**	**113 m**	**831 m**	**0.05 m**	**223 w**	**123 m**	**2.63 m**
Low income	312	24	32	111	4,380.3	..	43	718	0.07	24	108	4.53
Middle income	1,422	12	178	386	..	25.0	141	579	0.04	225	93	2.37
Lower middle income	1,289	11	175	490	..	29.0	116	398	0.03	207	68	2.65
Upper middle income	2,496	12	199	..	..	17.1	165	881	0.09	395	129	2.18
Low & middle income	970	13	112	321	..	..	75	612	0.05	137	104	3.04
East Asia & Pacific	891	8	161	502	..	..	49	448	0.03	195	42	..
Europe & Central Asia	2,808	13	228	..	10,859.2	27.3	113	318	0.10	301	66	2.08
Latin America & Carib.	1,506	16	170	..	..	4.7	174	888	0.08	246	106	..
Middle East & N. Africa	1,412	13	135	..	6,099.3	..	140	1,128	0.05	102	132	1.96
South Asia	344	26	39	127	2,623.8	99.6	64	379	0.02	23	35	2.66
Sub-Saharan Africa	457	11	11	39	..	..	43	850	0.09	52	208	4.53
High income	8,693	6	560	..	..	..	224	1,351	0.10	708	214	..
Europe EMU	5,912	6	544	..	..	..	208	1,728	0.16	842	183	..

a. Data are from the International Telecommunication Union's (ITU) *World Telecommunication Development Report* database. Please cite the ITU for third-party use of these data.

The quality of an economy's infrastructure, including power and communications, is an important element in investment decisions for both domestic and foreign investors. Government effort alone is not enough to meet the need for investments in modern infrastructure; public-private partnerships, especially those involving local providers and financiers, are critical for lowering costs and delivering value for money. In telecommunications, competition in the marketplace, along with sound regulation, is lowering costs and improving the quality of and access to services around the globe.

An economy's production and consumption of electricity is a basic indicator of its size and level of development. Although a few countries export electric power, most production is for domestic consumption. Expanding the supply of electricity to meet the growing demand of increasingly urbanized and industrialized economies without incurring unacceptable social, economic, and environmental costs is one of the great challenges facing developing countries.

Data on electric power production and consumption are collected from national energy agencies by the International Energy Agency (IEA) and adjusted by the IEA to meet international definitions (for data on electricity production, see table 3.9). Electricity consumption is equivalent to production less power plants' own use and transmission, distribution, and transformation losses. It includes consumption by auxiliary stations, losses in transformers that are considered integral parts of those stations, and electricity produced by pumping installations. Where data are available, it covers electricity generated by primary sources of energy—coal, oil, gas, nuclear, hydro, geothermal, wind, tide and wave, and combustible renewables. Neither production nor consumption data capture the reliability of supplies, including breakdowns, load factors, and frequency of outages.

Over the past decade new financing and technology, along with privatization and liberalization, have spurred dramatic growth in telecommunications in many countries. The table presents some common performance indicators for telecommunications, including measures of supply and demand, service quality, productivity, economic and financial performance, and tariffs. The quality of data varies among reporting countries as a result of differences in regulations covering the provision of data.

Operators are the main source of telecommunications data, so information on subscribers is widely available for most countries. This gives a general idea of access, but a more precise measure is the penetration rate—the share of households with access to telecommunications. Also important are data on actual use of the telecommunications equipment. Ideally, statistics on telecommunications (and other information and communications technologies) should be compiled for all three measures: subscription/possession, access, and use.

Demand for telecommunications is often measured by the sum of telephone mainline subscribers and registered applicants for new connections. (A mainline is normally identified by a unique number that is the one billed.) In some countries the list of registered applicants does not reflect real current pending demand, which is often hidden or suppressed, reflecting an extremely short supply that has discouraged potential applicants from applying for telephone service. And in some countries the waiting list may overstate demand because applicants have placed their names on the list several times to improve their chances. The number of mainlines no longer reflects a telephone system's full capacity because mobile telephones—whose use has been expanding rapidly in most countries, rich and poor—provide an alternative point of access.

Telephone mainline faults refer to the number of reported faults per 100 main telephone lines. It is calculated by the total number of reported faults for the year divided by the number of telephone mainlines and multiplied by 100. The definition of fault varies among countries: some operators define faults as including malfunctioning customer equipment while others include only technical faults.

In addition to waiting list and mainline faults, the table includes two other measures of efficiency in telecommunications: mainlines per employee and revenue per mainline. Caution should be used in interpreting the estimates of mainlines per employee because firms often subcontract part of their work. The cross-country comparability of revenue per mainline may also be limited because, for example, some countries do not require telecommunications providers to submit financial information; the data usually do not include revenues from mobile phones or from radio, paging, and data services; and there are definitional and accounting differences among countries.

• **Electric power consumption** measures the production of power plants and combined heat and power plants less transmission, distribution, and transformation losses and own use by heat and power plants. • **Electric power transmission and distribution losses** are losses in transmission between sources of supply and points of distribution and in distribution to consumers, including pilferage. • **Telephone mainlines** are telephone lines connecting a subscriber to the telephone exchange equipment. Data are presented for the entire country and for the largest city. • **Waiting list** shows the number of applications for a connection to a mainline that have been held up by a lack of technical capacity. • **Telephone mainline faults** is the number of reported faults per 100 telephone mainlines. • **Telephone mainlines per employee** are calculated by dividing the number of mainlines by the number of telecommunications staff (with part-time staff converted to full-time equivalents) employed by enterprises providing public telecommunications services. • **Revenue per line** is the revenue received by firms per mainline for providing telecommunications services. • **Cost of local call** is the cost of a three-minute, peak rate, fixed-line call within the same exchange area using the subscriber's equipment (that is, not from a public phone). • **Mobile phones** refer to portable telephone subscribers to an automatic public mobile telephone service using cellular technology that provides access to the telephone exchange equipment, per 1,000 people. • **International telecommunications outgoing traffic** is the telephone traffic, measured in minutes per subscriber, that originates in the country and has a destination outside the country. • **Cost of call to U.S.** is the cost of a three-minute, peak rate, fixed line call from the country to the United States.

Data sources

The data on electricity consumption and losses are from the IEA's *Energy Statistics and Balances of Non-OECD Countries 2001–2002*, the IEA's *Energy Statistics of OECD Countries 2001–2002*, and the United Nations Statistics Division's *Energy Statistics Yearbook*. The telecommunications data are from the International Telecommunication Union's *World Telecommunication Development Report* database.

5.10a

Mobile phone access outpaced fixed-line access in some developing country regions in 2003

Subscribers per 1,000 people, 1995 and 2003

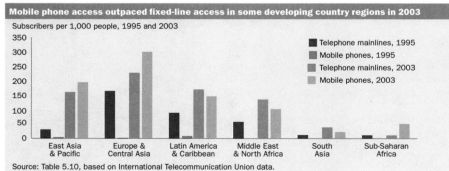

■ Telephone mainlines, 1995
■ Mobile phones, 1995
■ Telephone mainlines, 2003
■ Mobile phones, 2003

Source: Table 5.10, based on International Telecommunication Union data.

	Daily newspapers	Radios	Television[a]		Personal computers[a]	Internet				Information and communications technology expenditures	
			per 1,000 people				Total monthly price[a]				
						Users per 1,000 people[a]	20 hours of use $	% of monthly GNI per capita $	Secure servers number	% of GDP	per capita $
	per 1,000 people	per 1,000 people	Sets	Cable subscribers	per 1,000 people						
	2000	1997–2003[b]	2003	2003	2003	2003	2003	2003	2004	2003	2003
Afghanistan	5	114	14	0.0	..	1	..	..	1	..	..
Albania	35	260	318	2.3	11.7	10	29	24.8	2	..	..
Algeria	27	244	114	0.0	7.7	16	18	12.4	3	..	..
Angola	11	78	52	..	1.9	3	79	143.3	3	..	..
Argentina	40	697	326	162.9	82.0	112	13	3.9	386	5.7	200
Armenia	23	264	229	1.2	15.8	37	45	68.0	4	..	..
Australia	161	1,996	722	76.3	565.1	567	18	1.1	8,224	5.9	1,560
Austria	309	763	637	156.9	369.3	462	33	1.7	1,586	5.3	1,664
Azerbaijan	10	22	334	0.6	..	37	108	183.0	3	..	..
Bangladesh	9	49	59	27.0	7.8	2	20	66.8	3	2.7	10
Belarus	154	199	362	77.2	..	141	13	11.3	4	..	..
Belgium	153	793	541	377.7	318.1	386	29	1.5	946	5.5	1,601
Benin	5	445	12	..	3.7	10	46	146.5	..	..	..
Bolivia	99	671	..	7.4	22.8	32	22	29.8	16	5.8	52
Bosnia and Herzegovina	152	243	..	19.4	..	26	7	6.9	15	..	..
Botswana	25	150	44	..	40.7	35	27	10.9	1	..	..
Brazil	46	433	369	13.4	74.8	82	28	11.8	2,001	6.9	193
Bulgaria	173	543	..	133.5	51.9	206	12	8.3	46	3.9	100
Burkina Faso	1	433	12	0.0	2.1	4	45	247.5	2	..	..
Burundi	2	220	35	0.0	1.8	2	81	971.3	2	..	..
Cambodia	2	113	8	..	2.3	2	57	245.8	2	..	..
Cameroon	6	161	75	..	5.7	4	52	110.7	3	4.9	38
Canada	168	1,047	691	252.9	487.0	513	13	0.7	15,441	5.8	1,575
Central African Republic	2	80	6	..	2.0	1	175	807.9	..	..	..
Chad	0	233	2	..	1.7	2	69	375.6	..	..	..
Chile	98	759	523	57.4	119.3	272	22	6.1	274	6.7	306
China	59	339	350	75.0	27.6	63	10	13.0	293	5.3	58
Hong Kong, China	218	686	504	124.8	422.0	472	4	0.2	965	8.4	1,921
Colombia	26	548	319	..	49.3	53	19	12.2	159	9.0	159
Congo, Dem. Rep.	3	385	2	..	..	..	74	986.7	..	..	..
Congo, Rep.	6	109	13	..	4.3	4	121	207.8	..	..	..
Costa Rica	70	816	..	..	197.2	193	26	7.6	216	7.5	326
Côte d'Ivoire	16	185	61	0.0	9.3	14	67	132.1	3	..	..
Croatia	134	330	..	8.1	173.8	232	17	4.4	146	..	..
Cuba	54	185	251	..	31.8	11	58	32.2	1	..	..
Czech Republic	254	803	538	94.4	177.4	308	21	4.5	316	6.6	576
Denmark	283	1,400	859	236.7	576.8	513	18	0.7	1,724	5.7	2,224
Dominican Republic	28	181	..	..	..	64	33	17.1	33	..	..
Ecuador	98	422	252	13.9	31.1	46	32	26.3	38	3.7	76
Egypt, Arab Rep.	31	339	229	0.0	21.9	39	5	4.5	28	1.2	15
El Salvador	29	481	233	..	25.2	84	48	27.8	35	..	..
Eritrea	..	464	53	0.0	2.9	7	27	200.9	..	..	..
Estonia	192	1,136	507	117.0	440.4	444	14	3.9	113	..	..
Ethiopia	0	189	6	..	2.2	1	27	329.1	1	..	..
Finland	445	1,624	679	210.6	441.7	534	23	1.2	1,283	6.9	2,137
France	143	950	632	57.5	347.1	366	14	0.8	3,855	5.9	1,726
Gabon	29	488	308	11.5	22.4	26	122	46.9	6	..	..
Gambia, The	2	394	15	..	13.8	..	27	116.2	..	..	..
Georgia	5	568	357	12.4	31.6	31	26	48.4	11	..	..
Germany	291	570	675	250.8	484.7	473	14	0.7	13,847	5.7	1,647
Ghana	14	695	53	0.3	3.8	8	44	194.8	1	..	..
Greece	153	466	519	0.0	81.7	150	38	3.9	290	4.3	665
Guatemala	33	79	145	..	14.4	33	31	21.4	50	..	..
Guinea	..	52	47	0.0	5.5	5	63	185.2	..	..	..
Guinea-Bissau	5	178	36	..	..	15	105	840.7	..	..	..
Haiti	3	18	60	7.2	..	18	130	354.5	5	..	..

The information age

	Daily newspapers	Radios	Television[a]		Personal computers[a]	Internet				Information and communications technology expenditures	
			per 1,000 people				Total monthly price[a]				
						Users per 1,000 people[a]	20 hours of use	% of monthly GNI per capita	Secure servers number		per capita
	per 1,000 people	per 1,000 people	Sets	Cable subscribers	per 1,000 people					% of GDP	$
	2000	1997–2003[b]	2003	2003	2003	2003	2003	2003	2004	2003	2003
Honduras	55	411	119	21.6	13.6	25	41	52.9	31	4.5	45
Hungary	162	690	475	190.7	108.4	232	10	2.3	210	6.1	499
India	60	120	83	38.9	7.2	17	9	21.9	462	3.7	21
Indonesia	23	159	153	0.3	11.9	38	22	37.6	85	3.4	33
Iran, Islamic Rep.	28	281	173	..	90.5	72	6	4.2	13	2.2	46
Iraq	19	222	..	..	8.3	1	..	..	..	..	..
Ireland	148	695	694	134.0	420.8	317	28	1.4	1,245	3.9	1,491
Israel	290	526	330	1467.7	242.6	301	30	2.1	869	7.9	1,298
Italy	109	878	..	1.4	230.7	337	17	1.0	1,994	4.1	1,055
Jamaica	62	795	374	..	53.9	228	44	18.5	24	11.5	353
Japan	566	956	785	193.4	382.2	483	21	0.8	20,465	7.4	2,489
Jordan	74	372	177	..	44.7	81	26	18.0	21	8.8	164
Kazakhstan	..	411	338	6.6	..	16	34	27.4	6	..	..
Kenya	8	221	26	0.5	6.4	13	46	152.4	8	3.1	14
Korea, Dem. Rep.	208	154	160	0.0	..	..	..	..	..	..	..
Korea, Rep.	393	1,034	458	282.2	558.0	610	10	1.2	894	6.7	842
Kuwait	374	570	418	..	162.8	228	25	2.0	52	1.7	304
Kyrgyz Republic	15	110	49	3.6	12.7	38	15	62.1	2	..	..
Lao PDR	4	148	52	0.0	3.5	..	32	123.4	..	..	..
Latvia	138	700	859	176.8	188.0	404	58	20.0	80	..	..
Lebanon	63	182	357	29.9	80.5	117	37	11.1	29	..	..
Lesotho	9	61	35	..	..	10	43	110.7	..	..	..
Liberia	14	274	..	..	..	0	..	..	..	..	..
Libya	14	273	..	..	23.4	29	19	3.8	..	..	..
Lithuania	31	524	487	76.9	109.7	202	34	11.2	47	..	..
Macedonia, FYR	54	205	..	..	..	19	13.3	1	..	..	
Madagascar	5	216	25	..	4.9	4	67	336.7	1	..	..
Malawi	2	499	4	0.0	1.5	3	62	465.0	1	..	..
Malaysia	95	420	210	0.0	166.9	344	8	2.9	284	6.9	289
Mali	1	180	33	..	1.4	2	58	289.8	..	..	..
Mauritania	0	148	44	..	10.8	4	39	113.1	..	..	..
Mauritius	116	379	299	..	116.5	123	15	4.7	19	..	..
Mexico	94	330	282	24.3	82.0	118	23	4.6	634	3.1	191
Moldova	153	758	296	24.6	17.5	80	19	49.6	9	..	..
Mongolia	18	50	81	20.5	77.3	58	18	48.6	5	..	..
Morocco	30	243	167	..	19.9	33	25	25.5	17	5.6	82
Mozambique	3	44	14	..	4.5	3	51	290.2	1	..	..
Myanmar	9	66	7	..	5.6	1	43	180.9	2	..	..
Namibia	17	134	269	16.0	99.3	34	33	22.5	9	..	..
Nepal	12	39	8	..	3.7	3	13	70.3	8	..	..
Netherlands	279	980	648	401.4	466.6	522	24	1.2	3,779	6.4	2,009
New Zealand	202	991	574	7.1	413.8	526	13	1.1	1,733	10.0	1,984
Nicaragua	30	270	123	..	27.9	17	51	138.6	14	..	..
Niger	0	122	10	..	0.6	1	97	683.6	..	..	..
Nigeria	25	200	103	0.5	7.1	6	85	353.7	13	..	..
Norway	569	3,324	884	184.5	528.3	346	26	0.8	1,130	5.1	2,480
Oman	29	621	553	0.0	35.0	71	24	3.8	6	..	..
Pakistan	39	105	150	26.7	4.2	10	16	45.7	37	7.3	40
Panama	62	300	191	..	38.3	62	36	10.7	149	9.2	395
Papua New Guinea	14	86	23	4.2	58.7	14	20	45.3	1	..	..
Paraguay	43	188	..	21.3	34.6	20	36	37.3	9	..	..
Peru	23	269	172	16.6	43.0	104	33	19.2	129	6.9	153
Philippines	67	161	182	37.0	27.7	44	17	20.1	161	5.8	57
Poland	102	523	229	94.0	142.0	232	16	4.1	565	4.5	249
Portugal	102	299	413	128.2	134.4	194	21	2.3	458	4.2	601
Puerto Rico	126	761	339	91.2	..	175	..	..	116	..	..

5.11 The information age

	Daily newspapers	Radios	Television[a]		Personal computers[a]	Internet				Information and communications technology expenditures	
								Total monthly price[a]			
			per 1,000 people			Users per 1,000 people[a]	20 hours of use	% of monthly GNI per capita	Secure servers		
	per 1,000 people	per 1,000 people	Sets	Cable subscribers	per 1,000 people				number	% of GDP	per capita $
	2000	1997–2003[b]	2003	2003	2003	2003	2003	2003	2004	2003	2003
Romania	300	358	697	172.5	96.6	184	26	17.1	65	2.8	74
Russian Federation	105	418	..	43.6	88.7	..	10	5.6	297	3.7	111
Rwanda	1	85	..	..	..	3	67	348.3	..	..	..
Saudi Arabia	59	326	265	0.3	130.2	67	35	4.9	57	2.5	239
Senegal	5	126	78	0.1	21.2	22	41	103.7	3	7.4	47
Serbia and Montenegro	107	297	..	..	27.1	79	13	11.3	9	..	..
Sierra Leone	4	259	13	..	..	2	12	102.9	..	..	..
Singapore	273	672	303	84.5	622.0	509	11	0.6	981	10.5	2,254
Slovak Republic	14	965	409	127.3	180.4	256	21	6.3	63	5.3	319
Slovenia	168	405	366	160.3	300.6	376	25	3.1	130	..	..
Somalia	1	60	14	..	..	9	..	..	..	..	..
South Africa	26	336	177	0.0	72.6	68	33	15.4	909	8.0	281
Spain	98	330	564	24.3	196.0	239	21	1.7	2,837	3.8	773
Sri Lanka	29	215	117	0.3	13.2	12	15	21.5	30	5.7	54
Sudan	26	461	386	0.0	6.1	9	161	550.8	..	..	..
Swaziland	26	162	34	..	28.7	26	21	21.0	2	..	..
Sweden	410	2,811	965	246.0	621.3	573	22	1.1	2,354	7.0	2,365
Switzerland	372	1,002	552	376.2	708.7	351	22	0.7	2,821	7.2	3,150
Syrian Arab Republic	20	276	182	0.0	19.4	..	55	58.6	..	..	..
Tajikistan	20	141	357	0.1	..	1	54	362.3	..	..	..
Tanzania	4	406	45	0.2	5.7	7	117	501.4	1	..	..
Thailand	197	235	300	12.9	39.8	111	7	4.2	258	3.5	82
Togo	2	263	123	..	32.0	42	30	134.9	1	..	..
Trinidad and Tobago	123	534	345	..	79.5	106	13	2.5	15	..	..
Tunisia	19	158	207	..	40.5	64	17	10.4	19	5.2	132
Turkey	111	470	423	14.8	44.6	85	20	9.5	882	7.3	250
Turkmenistan	7	279	182	..	..	2	20	20.2	..	..	..
Uganda	3	122	18	0.3	4.0	5	97	464.4	2	..	..
Ukraine	175	889	..	38.6	19.0	19	17	26.0	53	7.1	73
United Arab Emirates	156	309	252	..	129.0	275	13	0.8	173	..	..
United Kingdom	326	1,445	950	57.2	405.7	423	24	1.1	21,034	7.3	2,223
United States	196	2,109	938	255.0	658.9	551	15	0.5	198,098	8.8	3,309
Uruguay	293	603	..	..	110.1	119	26	7.3	79	7.1	234
Uzbekistan	3	456	280	3.7	..	19	20	53.8	1	..	..
Venezuela, RB	206	292	186	32.4	60.9	60	19	5.7	114	5.2	173
Vietnam	6	109	197	..	9.8	43	20	55.4	10	..	..
West Bank and Gaza	..	..	148	..	36.2	40	25	32.8	..	..	..
Yemen, Rep.	15	65	308	..	7.4	..	31	75.3	1	..	..
Zambia	22	179	51	1.2	8.5	6	33	118.7	2	..	..
Zimbabwe	18	362	56	..	52.7	43	23	58.3	7	11.8	92
World	**76** w	**419** w	**275** w	**65.5** w	**100.8** w	**150** u	**37** u	**88.7** u	**322,041** s		
Low income	44	137	84	27.2	6.9	16	58	254.8	618		
Middle income	55	345	280	57.3	42.9	116	30	21.0	9,882		
Lower middle income	51	330	326	58.5	35.6	63	30	28.9	5,806		
Upper middle income	88	467	326	47.0	100.6	208	29	8.3	4,076		
Low & middle income	34	257	190	40.2	28.4	75	41	113.2	10,500		
East Asia & Pacific	60	287	317	70.1	26.3	68	31	66.1	1,139		
Europe & Central Asia	102	447	..	47.5	73.4	161	26	39.5	2,950		
Latin America & Carib.	61	411	289	33.5	67.4	106	33	30.0	4,657		
Middle East & N. Africa	33	277	200	..	38.2	48	31	29.9	194		
South Asia	59	112	84	37.3	6.8	10	30	58.6	541		
Sub-Saharan Africa	12	198	69	..	11.9	20	64	268.8	1,019		
High income	262	1,265	735	190.9	466.5	377	23	1.6	311,541		
Europe EMU	188	812	597	157.9	317.2	378	24	1.5	32,303		

a. Data are from the International Telecommunication Union's (ITU) *World Telecommunication Development Report* database. Please cite the ITU for third-party use of these data. b. Data are the latest year available in the period shown.

About the data

The digital and information revolution has changed the way the world learns, communicates, does business, and treats illnesses. New information and communications technologies offer vast opportunities for progress in all walks of life in all countries—opportunities for economic growth, improved health, better service delivery, learning through distance education, and social and cultural advances. This table presents indicators of the penetration of the information economy (newspapers, radios, televisions, personal computers, and Internet use) as well as some of the economics of the information age (Internet access charges, the number of secure servers, and spending on information and communications technology).

The data on the number of daily newspapers in circulation and radio receivers in use are from statistical surveys by the United Nations Educational, Scientific, and Cultural Organization (UNESCO). In some countries definitions, classifications, and methods of enumeration do not entirely conform to UNESCO standards. For example, newspaper circulation data should refer to the number of copies distributed, but in some cases the figures reported are the number of copies printed. In addition, many countries impose radio and television license fees to help pay for public broadcasting, discouraging radio and television owners from declaring ownership. Because of these and other data collection problems, estimates of the number of newspapers and radios vary widely in reliability and should be interpreted with caution.

The data for other electronic communications and information technology are from the International Telecommunication Union (ITU), the Internet Software Consortium, Netcraft, the World Information Technology and Services Alliance (WITSA), and Global Insights. The ITU collects data on television sets and cable television subscribers through annual questionnaires sent to national broadcasting authorities and industry associations. Some countries require that television sets be registered. To the extent that households do not register their televisions or do not register all of them, the data on licensed sets may understate the true number.

The estimates of personal computers are derived from an annual ITU questionnaire, supplemented by other sources. In many countries mainframe computers are used extensively. Since thousands of users can be connected to a single mainframe computer, the number of personal computers understates the total use of computers.

The data on Internet users are based on nationally reported data. Some countries derive these data from Internet surveys, but since survey questions and definitions differ across countries, the estimates may not be strictly comparable. For example, questions on the age of Internet users and frequency of use vary by country. Countries that do not have surveys generally derive their estimates from reported Internet service provider (ISP) subscriber counts, calculated by multiplying the number of subscribers by a selected multiplier. This method may undercount the actual number of people using the Internet, particularly in developing countries, where many commercial subscribers rent out computers connected to the Internet or pre-paid cards are used to access the Internet.

The total monthly Internet price is shown as the sum of monthly ISP charges and telephone usage charges and as a percentage of monthly GNI per capita. Data are generally derived from the prices listed by the largest ISP and incumbent telephone company. The number of secure servers, from the Netcraft Secure Server Survey, gives an indication of how many companies are conducting encrypted transactions over the Internet.

The data on information and communications technology expenditures cover the world's 70 largest buyers of such technology among countries and regions.

Ensuring universal access to information and communication technology is a goal of many countries, but not all countries regularly track accessibility. There is no common set of information and communication technology indicators and definitions, and data are often drawn from administrative records rather than from specific surveys. Access needs to be accurately measured in three major areas: individual, household, and community access.

Definitions

• **Daily newspapers** refer to those published at least four times a week and calculated as average circulation (or copies printed) per 1,000 people. • **Radios** refer to radio receivers in use for broadcasts to the general public. • **Television sets** refer to those in use. • **Cable television subscribers** are households that subscribe to a multichannel television service delivered by a fixed line connection. Some countries also report subscribers to pay-television using wireless technology or those cabled to community antenna systems. • **Personal computers** are self-contained computers designed for use by a single individual. • **Internet users** are people with access to the worldwide network. • **Total monthly price** refers to the sum of ISP and telephone usage charges for 20 hours of use and as a percentage of monthly GNI per capita. • **Secure servers** are servers using encryption technology in Internet transactions. • **Information and communications technology expenditures** include computer hardware (computers, storage devices, printers, and other peripherals); computer software (operating systems, programming tools, utilities, applications, and internal software development); computer services (information technology consulting, computer and network systems integration, web hosting, data processing services, and other services); and communications services (voice and data communications services) and wired and wireless communications equipment.

Data sources

The data on newspapers and radios are compiled by the UNESCO Institute for Statistics. The data on television sets, cable television subscribers, personal computers, Internet users, and Internet access charges are from the ITU and are reported in the ITU's *World Telecommunication Development Report* database. The data on information and communications technology expenditures are from *Digital Planet 2004: The Global Information Economy* by the World Information Technology and Services Alliance (WITSA), and Global Insight, Inc. The data on secure servers are from Netcraft (www.netcraft.com/).

5.11a

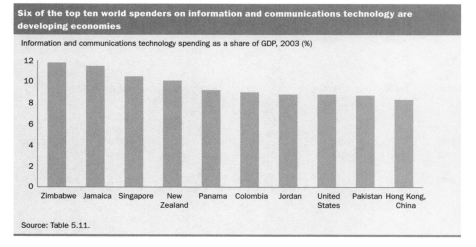

Six of the top ten world spenders on information and communications technology are developing economies

Information and communications technology spending as a share of GDP, 2003 (%)

Source: Table 5.11.

	Researchers in R&D	Technicians in R&D	Scientific and technical journal articles	Expenditures for R&D	High-technology exports		Royalty and license fees		Patent applications filed[a]		Trademark applications filed[b]	
	per million people	per million people		% of GDP	$ millions	% of manu-factured exports	Receipts $ millions	Payments $ millions	Residents	Non-residents	Residents	Non-residents
	1996–2002[c]	1996–2002[c]	2001	1996–2002[c]	2003	2003	2003	2003	2002	2002	2002	2002
Afghanistan	..	..	0	..	..	..	..	..	..	..	..	..
Albania	..	..	17	..	4	1	5	8	0	89,821	0	1,758
Algeria	..	..	225	..	12	2	..	..	42	88,839	1,313	3,088
Angola	..	..	3	..	..	..	4	0	..	..	..	..
Argentina	715	166	2,930	0.39	692	9	32	342	0	6,634	30,839	12,007
Armenia	1,606	147	152	0.25	5	1	..	..	204	89,361	388	2,084
Australia	3,446	..	14,788	1.54	2,760	14	394	1,268	10,823	96,434	26,831	17,113
Austria	2,346	993	4,526	2.19	9,283	13	155	1,117	3,313	250,719	7,272	9,996
Azerbaijan	1,248	197	68	0.30	8	5	..	0	0	89,337	144	2,051
Bangladesh	..	..	177	..	1	0	0	4	..	..	..	..
Belarus	1,870	207	528	0.62	223	4	1	6	908	89,686	1,730	4,548
Belgium	3,180	1,462	5,984	2.24	17,268	8	887	1,246	2,122	161,472	21,010[d]	10,695[d]
Benin	..	..	20	..	0	2	0	1	..	..	..	..
Bolivia	118	6	33	0.28	21	8	2	8	..	..	..	..
Bosnia and Herzegovina	..	..	9	..	..	..	..	..	0	89,872	0	3,283
Botswana	..	..	41	..	6	0	0	8	0	10	..	..
Brazil	324	129	7,205	1.04	4,505	12	108	1,228	6,521	95,225	81,036	13,218
Bulgaria	1,158	466	784	0.49	213	4	5	25	306	158,051	4,043	5,576
Burkina Faso	17	16	23	0.17	1	2	..	0	..	..	..	..
Burundi	..	..	3	..	0	22	0	0	..	..	20	132
Cambodia	..	..	5	..	..	..	..	6	..	..	333	1,305
Cameroon	..	..	75	..	3	2	..	..	..	..	..	..
Canada	3,487	1,105	22,626	1.91	23,129	14	2,555	4,821	5,934	102,418	17,068	19,664
Central African Republic	47	27	4	..	0	0	..	..	..	..	..	..
Chad	..	..	2	..	..	..	..	..	..	..	..	..
Chile	419	307	1,203	0.54	110	3	45	266	241	2,879	..	..
China	633	..	20,978	1.23	107,543	27	107	3,548	40,346	140,910	321,034	57,597
Hong Kong, China	1,568	226	1,817	0.60	1,845	13	196	491	112	9,018	5,903	14,543
Colombia	81	46	324	0.10	292	7	6	72	52	87,859	7,265	7,096
Congo, Dem. Rep.	..	..	6	..	..	..	..	..	..	..	..	..
Congo, Rep.	29	32	13	..	..	..	..	..	..	..	..	..
Costa Rica	533	..	92	0.39	1,700	45	0	64	0	89,225	..	..
Côte d'Ivoire	..	..	40	..	93	8	0	6	..	..	..	..
Croatia	1,920	444	710	1.12	543	12	35	130	444	89,877	843	5,600
Cuba	538	2,510	299	0.53	49	29	..	..	13	89,468	0	1,551
Czech Republic	1,467	792	2,622	1.22	5,800	13	50	176	608	158,592	8,114	9,756
Denmark	4,822	3,153	4,988	2.52	8,402	20	..	..	3,875	250,103	3,914	6,744
Dominican Republic	..	..	6	..	4	1	0	30	..	..	..	..
Ecuador	84	73	20	0.08	41	6	0	43	13	85,290	4,219	4,634
Egypt, Arab Rep.	..	..	1,548	0.19	9	0	121	165	627	798	0	2,496
El Salvador	47	..	0	0.01	39	5	0	22	..	..	..	..
Eritrea	..	..	2	..	..	..	..	..	..	..	..	..
Estonia	2,253	386	339	0.75	528	13	5	14	33	157,901	1,017	5,213
Ethiopia	..	..	93	..	0	0	0	0	3	4	..	..
Finland	7,431	3,471	5,098	3.46	10,485	24	502	615	2,941	248,668	2,830	6,095
France	3,134	..	31,317	2.26	56,336	19	3,941	2,436	21,959	160,056	58,035	12,774
Gabon	..	..	20	..	..	..	..	..	..	..	..	..
Gambia, The	..	..	17	..	..	..	..	..	0	177,146	..	..
Georgia	2,317	241	110	0.29	34	24	6	10	202	89,881	202	2,438
Germany	3,222	1,435	43,623	2.53	102,869	16	4,262	5,242	80,661	230,066	53,817	12,827
Ghana	..	..	90	..	5	3	0	0	0	177,371	..	..
Greece	1,357	406	3,329	0.65	962	12	18	335	614	162,387	5,290	6,075
Guatemala	..	..	14	..	78	7	0	0	0	0	3,048	5,040
Guinea	286	104	2	..	0	0	0	1	..	..	..	..
Guinea-Bissau	..	..	6	..	..	..	..	0	..	..	..	..
Haiti	..	..	1	..	..	..	0	0	..	..	..	..

	Researchers in R&D	Technicians in R&D	Scientific and technical journal articles	Expenditures for R&D	High-technology exports		Royalty and license fees		Patent applications filed[a]		Trademark applications filed[b]	
	per million people	per million people		% of GDP	$ millions	% of manu-factured exports	Receipts $ millions	Payments $ millions	Residents	Non-residents	Residents	Non-residents
	1996–2002c	1996–2002c	2001	1996–2002c	2003	2003	2003	2003	2002	2002	2002	2002
Honduras	74	261	*11*	0.05	*0*	0	0	12	7	161	..	..
Hungary	1,473	486	2,479	1.02	9,631	26	313	440	962	91,497	4,316	9,546
India	120	102	11,076	0.85	2,292	5	*29*	*356*	220	91,704	..	..
Indonesia	..	..	207	..	4,580	14	..	..	0	90,922	..	..
Iran, Islamic Rep.	484	391	995	..	51	2	..	..	0	0	*9,858*	1,224
Iraq	..	..	21	..	..	..	..	..	..	..	..	..
Ireland	2,315	686	1,665	1.13	27,578	34	206	16,160	1,255	162,170	1,167	4,577
Israel	1,570	518	6,487	5.08	5,322	18	425	435	2,323	94,961	2,842	4,827
Italy	1,156	1,346	22,313	1.11	20,027	8	525	1,698	4,086	159,865	0	9,385
Jamaica	..	..	*44*	..	*1*	0	12	11	15	54	663	1,433
Japan	5,085	..	57,420	3.12	105,454	24	12,271	11,003	371,495	115,411	100,645	16,827
Jordan	1,977	728	240	..	28	2	..	..	..	..	..	..
Kazakhstan	744	305	116	0.32	200	9	0	20	2	89,421	1,809	2,902
Kenya	..	..	230	..	23	4	12	39	0	177,559	0	1,166
Korea, Dem. Rep.	..	..	1	..	..	..	..	..	0	88,052	0	1,913
Korea, Rep.	2,979	..	11,037	2.53	57,161	32	1,325	3,597	76,860	126,836	90,014	17,862
Kuwait	73	180	257	0.20	*11*	1	0	0	..	..	..	..
Kyrgyz Republic	413	51	10	0.20	2	2	2	3	123	89,357	67	1,850
Lao PDR	..	..	2	..	..	..	..	..	..	..	25	656
Latvia	1,476	282	157	0.42	76	4	4	10	8	140,637	1,262	5,699
Lebanon	..	..	202	..	17	2	..	..	0	*104*	..	..
Lesotho	42	26	1	..	..	..	*11*	0	0	177,309	0	774
Liberia	..	..	1	..	..	..	..	..	0	89,507	0	760
Libya	361	493	*19*	..	..	..	..	..	..	..	..	..
Lithuania	1,824	430	272	0.67	211	5	1	18	91	140,674	1,540	5,602
Macedonia, FYR	500	69	74	0.26	13	1	2	7	42	140,588	411	3,541
Madagascar	15	47	..	0.12	1	0	1	13	4	89,526	162	293
Malawi	..	..	*36*	..	1	1	*0*	*0*	0	177,315	138	440
Malaysia	294	57	494	0.69	47,042	58	20	782	..	..	..	..
Mali	..	..	*11*	..	2	8	*0*	1	..	..	..	..
Mauritania	..	..	2	..	..	..	..	..	..	..	..	..
Mauritius	..	..	*16*	0.29	72	5	0	2	..	..	..	..
Mexico	259	184	3,209	0.39	28,734	21	84	608	627	94,116	40,141	18,509
Moldova	171	201	77	0.87	7	3	1	3	240	89,396	1,391	2,690
Mongolia	710	72	*8*	0.28	0	0	*0*	..	121	89,864	255	3,260
Morocco	..	..	469	..	680	11	26	29	0	89,300	0	2,849
Mozambique	..	..	*14*	..	*2*	3	15	1	0	176,319	0	931
Myanmar	..	..	*10*	..	..	..	0	0	..	..	..	..
Namibia	..	..	*13*	..	15	3	0	4	..	..	..	..
Nepal	62	145	*39*	0.66	..	..	..	..	..	..	..	..
Netherlands	2,826	1,424	12,602	1.89	49,546	31	1,885	2,829	7,496	158,485	..	..
New Zealand	2,593	..	2,903	1.16	471	10	118	436	2,137	91,240	8,818	11,276
Nicaragua	73	33	*8*	0.08	3	4	0	0	..	..	..	..
Niger	..	..	21	..	1	3	..	..	..	..	..	..
Nigeria	..	..	332	..	..	..	..	..	..	..	..	..
Norway	4,442	1,524	3,252	1.67	2,662	19	195	394	504	90,712	0	6,981
Oman	..	..	96	..	26	2	..	..	0	75,825	..	..
Pakistan	88	14	282	0.22	120	1	8	36	0	*1,168*	5,342	1,560
Panama	95	213	*37*	0.38	1	1	0	42	7	*153*	..	..
Papua New Guinea	..	..	*36*	..	47	39	..	..	..	..	..	..
Paraguay	83	118	*4*	0.10	10	6	193	2	..	..	..	..
Peru	225	1	93	0.10	27	2	2	65	..	..	*6,940*	6,983
Philippines	..	..	158	..	23,942	74	2	273	0	81,697	..	..
Poland	1,469	296	5,686	0.59	1,334	3	28	745	2,324	92,176	12,355	11,607
Portugal	1,745	283	2,142	0.93	2,340	9	36	283	185	251,752	6,929	7,829
Puerto Rico	..	..	..	..	..	..	..	..	..	..	..	..

	Researchers in R&D	Technicians in R&D	Scientific and technical journal articles	Expenditures for R&D	High-technology exports		Royalty and license fees		Patent applications filed[a]		Trademark applications filed[b]	
	per million people	per million people		% of GDP	$ millions	% of manu-factured exports	Receipts $ millions	Payments $ millions	Residents	Non-residents	Residents	Non-residents
	1996–2002c	1996–2002c	2001	1996–2002c	2003	2003	2002	2002	2002	2002	2002	2002
Romania	910	289	997	0.38	530	4	3	80	1,486	141,294	6,026	6,485
Russian Federation	3,415	2,315	15,846	1.25	5,327	19	174	711	24,049	96,315	29,279	14,215
Rwanda	..	..	4	..	1	25	0	0	..	..	..	..
Saudi Arabia	..	..	580	..	24	0	0	0	61	552	..	..
Senegal	..	..	62	..	36	9	0	3	..	..	..	..
Serbia and Montenegro	1,330	568	547	0.00	..	..	..	..	507	90,893	0	4,758
Sierra Leone	..	..	3	..	1	31	0	0	0	177,366	0	787
Singapore	4,352	381	2,603	2.15	71,421	59	197	3,334	511	93,748	3,344	20,282
Slovak Republic	1,707	564	955	0.58	716	4	50	91	276	157,652	2,350	7,742
Slovenia	2,364	1,599	876	1.53	719	6	11	90	332	136,912	1,086	6,612
Somalia	..	..	0	..	..	..	..	..	..	..	..	..
South Africa	192	74	2,327	0.67	908	5	49	266	184	90,471	..	..
Spain	2,036	742	15,570	1.03	8,889	7	539	2,505	4,330	251,260	66,471	12,460
Sri Lanka	197	48	76	0.18	19	1	..	..	0	89,759	..	..
Sudan	..	..	43	..	4	7	..	..	2	177,336	0	795
Swaziland	..	..	6	..	4	1	0	46	0	88,379	0	828
Sweden	5,171	..	10,314	4.27	12,717	15	2,336	1,277	9,443	246,886	0	5,976
Switzerland	3,594	2,315	8,107	2.57	20,472	22	..	..	7,977	246,451	0	10,592
Syrian Arab Republic	29	24	55	0.18	5	1	..	10	0	30	0	0
Tajikistan	..	..	20	..	..	..	1	0	40	89,352	0	1,522
Tanzania	..	..	87	..	3	2	0	0	0	176,850	0	16
Thailand	289	116	727	0.24	18,203	30	7	1,268	1,117	4,548	..	..
Togo	..	..	11	..	2	1	0	0	..	..	..	..
Trinidad and Tobago	347	886	37	0.10	25	2	..	..	2	89,901	340	1,317
Tunisia	1,013	34	344	0.63	244	4	18	6	0	72,604	..	..
Turkey	345	..	4,098	0.66	815	2	0	167	550	250,492	28,209	7,611
Turkmenistan	..	..	0	..	..	..	..	..	0	89,333	0	1,648
Uganda	25	15	91	0.81	1	8	4	4	0	177,305	0	14
Ukraine	1,749	456	2,256	1.16	572	5	14	292	37	90,563	0	5,285
United Arab Emirates	..	..	159	..	17	2	..	..	0	89,666	..	..
United Kingdom	2,691	..	47,660	1.88	64,511	26	10,245	7,382	33,671	251,239	51,399	17,135
United States	4,526	..	200,870	2.66	160,212	31	48,227	20,049	198,339	183,398	181,693	30,944
Uruguay	370	51	155	0.24	16	2	0	10	44	572	5,863	9,514
Uzbekistan	..	..	204	..	..	..	..	..	717	89,902	756	2,166
Venezuela, RB	222	..	535	0.44	130	4	0	183	56	2,292	..	..
Vietnam	..	..	158	..	145	2	..	..	2	90,135	0	1,929
West Bank and Gaza	..	..	..	..	..	..	..	..	..	..	..	..
Yemen, Rep.	..	..	10	..	..	..	..	..	..	..	..	..
Zambia	47	16	26	0.01	2	2	..	..	0	157,720	0	554
Zimbabwe	..	..	113	..	21	3	..	..	0	177,483	1	17
World	.. w	.. w	648,500 s	2.36 w	1,043,222 s	18 w	92,116 s	99,946 s	936,630 s	12,882,065 s	1,316,564 s	604,897
Low income	..	..	13,147	..	..	4	44	111	1,469	3,003,874	8,489	26,165
Middle income	806	..	84,507	0.75	198,304	21	1,570	12,353	81,554	4,790,264	589,487	258,839
Lower middle income	820	..	61,791	0.85	103,213	20	902	8,404	76,113	2,876,674	480,507	155,982
Upper middle income	705	275	22,716	0.51	88,846	22	668	3,948	5,441	1,913,590	108,980	102,857
Low & middle income	..	..	97,654	0.72	..	20	1,614	12,464	83,023	7,794,138	597,976	285,004
East Asia & Pacific	627	..	22,722	1.11	..	33	136	5,877	40,469	581,580	321,648	66,765
Europe & Central Asia	1,952	1,190	39,077	0.90	26,221	12	700	2,956	34,159	3,071,921	106,252	137,176
Latin America & Carib.	..	..	16,045	0.58	36,799	14	518	3,050	7,255	1,166,254	163,101	62,928
Middle East & N. Africa	..	..	4,699	..	993	2	164	210	730	327,948	1,313	8,433
South Asia	120	102	11,611	0.75	..	4	14	40	220	181,463	5,342	2,242
Sub-Saharan Africa	..	..	3,500	..	..	..	81	330	190	2,464,972	320	7,460
High income	3,575	..	550,846	2.54	834,168	18	90,502	87,482	853,607	5,087,927	718,588	319,893
Europe EMU	2,511	1,266	148,169	2.20	306,581	14	12,188	33,325	129,155	2,448,271	222,821	92,713

Note: The original information on patent and trademark applications was provided by the World Intellectual Property Organization (WIPO). The International Bureau of WIPO assumes no responsibility with respect to the transformation of these data.

a. Other patent applications filed in 2002 include those filed under the auspices of the African Regional Industrial Property Organization (3 by residents, 88,378 by nonresidents), European Patent Office (67,677 by residents, 97,737 by nonresidents), and the Eurasian Patent Organization (549 by residents, 88,857 by nonresidents). b. Other trademark applications filed in 2002 include those filed under the auspices of the Office for Harmonization in the Internal Market (29,345 by residents, 15,669 by nonresidents). c. Data are for the latest year available. d. Includes Luxembourg and the Netherlands.

About the data

The best opportunities to improve living standards, including new ways of reducing poverty, will come from science and technology. Science, advancing rapidly in virtually all fields—particularly in biotechnology—is playing a growing economic role: countries able to access, generate, and apply relevant scientific knowledge will have a competitive edge over those that cannot. And there is greater appreciation of the need for high-quality scientific input into public policy issues such as regional and global environmental concerns. Technological innovation, often fueled by government-led research and development (R&D), has been the driving force for industrial growth around the world.

Science and technology cover a range of issues too complex and too broad to be quantified by any single set of indicators, but those in the table shed light on countries' "technological base"—the availability of skilled human resources, the number of scientific and technical articles published, the competitive edge countries enjoy in high-technology exports, sales and purchases of technology through royalties and licenses, and the number of patent and trademark applications filed.

The United Nations Educational, Scientific, and Cultural Organization (UNESCO) Institute for Statistics collects data on researchers, technicians, and R&D expenditure from countries and territories around the world through questionnaires and special surveys, supplemented by information from other international sources. Data for researchers and technicians are normally calculated in terms of full-time equivalents.

R&D expenditures are all expenditures for R&D performed within a country, including both capital expenditures and current costs (annual wages, salaries, and associated costs of researchers, technicians, and supporting staff and noncapital purchases of materials, supplies, and R&D equipment such as utilities, books, journals, reference materials, subscriptions to libraries and scientific societies, and materials for laboratories).

The information does not reflect the quality of training and education, which varies widely. Similarly, R&D expenditures are no guarantee of progress; governments need to pay close attention to the practices that make R&D expenditures effective.

Article counts are from a set of journals classified and covered by the Institute for Scientific Information's Science Citation Index (SCI) and the Social Sciences Citation Index (SSCI). Article counts are based on fractional assignments; for example, an article with two authors from different countries is counted as half an article for each country (see *Definitions* for the fields covered). The SCI and SSCI databases cover the core set of scientific journals but may exclude some of regional or local importance. They may also reflect some bias toward English-language journals.

The method used for determining a country's high-technology exports was developed by the Organisation for Economic Co-operation and Development in collaboration with Eurostat. Termed the "product approach" to distinguish it from a "sectoral approach," the method is based on the calculation of R&D intensity (R&D expenditure divided by total sales) for groups of products from six countries (Germany, Italy, Japan, the Netherlands, Sweden, and the United States). Because industrial sectors characterized by a few high-technology products may also produce many low-technology products, the product approach is more appropriate for analyzing international trade than is the sectoral approach. To construct a list of high-technology manufactured products (services are excluded), the R&D intensity was calculated for products classified at the three-digit level of the Standard International Trade Classification revision 3. The final list was determined at the four- and five-digit levels. At these levels, since no R&D data were available, final selection was based on patent data and expert opinion. This method takes only R&D intensity into account. Other characteristics of high technology are also important, such as know-how, scientific and technical personnel, and technology embodied in patents; considering these characteristics would result in a different list. (See Hatzichronoglou 1997 for further details.) Moreover, the R&D for high-technology exports may not have occurred in the reporting country.

Most countries have adopted systems that protect patentable inventions. Most patent legislation requires that an idea, to be protected by law (patentable), be new in the sense that it has not already been published or publicly used; nonobvious (involve an inventive step) in the sense that it would not have occurred to any specialist in the industrial field had such a specialist been asked to find a solution to the problem; and capable of industrial application in the sense that it can be industrially manufactured or used. Information on patent applications filed is shown separately for residents and nonresidents.

A trademark provides protection to its owner by ensuring the exclusive right to use it to identify goods or services or to authorize another to use it in return for payment. The period of protection varies, but a trademark can be renewed indefinitely by paying additional fees. The trademark system helps consumers identify and purchase a product or service whose nature and quality, indicated by its unique trademark, meet their needs.

Definitions

• **Researchers in R&D** are professionals engaged in the conception or creation of new knowledge, products, processes, methods, or systems and in the management of the projects concerned. Postgraduate PhD students (ISCED97 level 6) engaged in R&D are included. • **Technicians in R&D** and equivalent staff are people whose main tasks require technical knowledge and experience in engineering, physical and life sciences (technicians), or social sciences and humanities (equivalent staff). They participate in R&D by performing scientific and technical tasks involving the application of concepts and operational methods, normally under the supervision of researchers. • **Scientific and technical journal articles** refer to published scientific and engineering articles in physics, biology, chemistry, mathematics, clinical medicine, biomedical research, engineering and technology, and earth and space sciences. • **Expenditures for R&D** are current and capital expenditures on creative work undertaken systematically to increase knowledge, including knowledge of humanity, culture, and society, and the use of knowledge for new applications. *R&D* covers basic research, applied research, and experimental development. • **High-technology exports** are products with high R&D intensity, as in aerospace, computers, pharmaceuticals, and scientific instruments. • **Royalty and license fees** are payments and receipts between residents and nonresidents for the authorized use of intangible, nonproduced, nonfinancial assets and proprietary rights (patents, copyrights, trademarks, franchises, industrial processes) and for the use, through licensing agreements, of produced originals of prototypes (films, manuscripts). • **Patent applications filed** are those filed with a national patent office for exclusive rights to an invention—a product or process that provides a new way of doing something or a new technical solution to a problem. A patent protects the invention for the patent owner for a set period, generally 20 years. • **Trademark applications filed** are applications to register a trademark with a national or regional trademark office. Trademarks are distinctive signs identifying goods or services as produced or provided by a specific person or enterprise. Trademarks protect owners of the mark by ensuring exclusive right to use it to identify goods or services or to authorize its use in return for payment.

Data sources

The data on researchers, technicians, and expenditures in R&D are from the UNESCO Institute for Statistics. The data on journal articles are from the National Science Foundation's *Science and Engineering Indicators 2004*. The data on high-technology exports are from the United Nations Statistics Division's Commodity Trade (COMTRADE) database. The data on royalty and license fees are from the International Monetary Fund's *Balance of Payments Statistics Yearbook,* and the data on patents and trademarks are from the World Intellectual Property Organization's *Industrial Property Statistics.*

6 | GLOBAL LINKS

In an integrated global economy goods and services move more freely between countries. Financial markets are more efficiently linked. And there is more international movement of people. Cheaper and faster transportation, new information and technological innovation, trade liberalization, better economic management—all have contributed to greater integration.

Over the past decade integration has come to dominate discussions of the global economy. This section of *World Development Indicators* looks at measures that help track changes in the movements of goods, financial flows, and people. With more open policies and stronger investment climates, many developing countries are now participating more in financial and trading markets and benefiting from global integration. All regions are growing faster than in the 1990s. The global economy slowed in 2001, but by 2003 the recovery in developing countries appears to have preceded rather than followed recovery in high-income countries. In 2003 growth of developing countries outpaced that of high-income economies.

Movement of goods

Trade spurs economic growth by encouraging specialization in line with a country's comparative advantage while increasing consumer choice. And it has reached unprecedented levels in the last decade. Since the economic downturn following the financial crisis in East Asia, the rapid expansion of trade has continued, while investment flows have lagged behind. The annual growth of world trade (the sum of imports plus exports) averaged more than 6 percent in 2003, while developing country trade grew 11 percent. World trade in goods as a share of world GDP increased from 33 percent in 1990 to 42 percent in 2003. The change for developing countries was dramatic: an increase of 21 percentage points, compared with 6 percentage points in high-income economies. China's continuing expansion into the global marketplace drove trade in East Asia and Pacific from 47 percent of GDP in 1990 to 71 percent in 2003. In 2003 China alone made up 5 percent of world trade and 20 percent of developing country trade (table 6.1).

Success is based not only on how much is being traded but also on what is traded. In 1980 merchandise exports from developing countries were mainly primary products. But in the past 15 years the largest increase in merchandise exports from developing countries has come from manufactured goods. The share of manufactured goods in the imports of high-income Organisation for Economic Co-operation and Development (OECD) economies from low-income economies increased from 41 percent in 1993 to 53 percent in 2003 and from middle-income economies from 51 percent to 67 percent (table 6.3).

Despite more than 50 years of trade and tariff negotiations, trade barriers continue to impede global trade. Tariff and nontariff barriers have declined through successive rounds of multilateral trade negotiations, but the reductions have been larger for manufactured and processed primary products than for agricultural goods and natural resources. With more than half the population of most developing countries living in rural areas, reducing agricultural protection is important for reducing poverty. In the 1990s developing countries lowered their average agricultural tariff rates from 30 percent to 18 percent. Tariffs are even lower in industrial countries, but the average tariffs imposed by industrial countries on agricultural products, when they can be measured, are two to four times higher than the tariffs on manufactured products. Average tariffs on imports from developing countries declined between 1993 and 2003, yet tariffs on food exported from low-income countries to high-income OECD countries increased (table 6.3). The continuing expansion of global markets depends, in part, on further trade liberalization under the Doha Round.

Financial flows

The growing importance of international private capital flows shows greater integration of financial markets. The ratio of gross (two-way) capital flows to GDP increased in low- and middle-income countries from 6 percent in 1990 to 13 percent by 2003 (figure 6a). East Asia and Pacific, the Middle East and North Africa, and South Asia experienced the greatest increases. But the average for developing countries is still half that of high-income countries (table 6.1).

As financial openness has spread across the world, global flows of foreign direct investment have more than doubled relative to GDP. For developing countries, foreign direct investment has been the largest source of external funding. In 2003 China received 9 percent of total net (inward) foreign

direct investment flows and 35 percent of developing country flows. But worldwide flows remain far below their peak in 2000. In high-income countries net flows of foreign direct investment hit $1.1 trillion in 2000 but declined to $421 billion in 2003, the lowest since 1997. Developing countries experienced a similar downturn, with flows falling to $152 billion in 2003, down from $182 billion in 1999 (table 6.7).

Countries that have difficulty tapping financial markets must rely largely on aid flows to fund development programs. Members of the OECD Development Assistance Committee, the largest group of official donors, provided official development assistance (ODA) totaling a record $69 billion in 2003, up from $58 billion in 2002 (table 6.9). Inflation and exchange rate movements, notably the weakening of the dollar, accounted for some of the increase. But aid flows in 2003 were their highest ever, in both nominal and real terms. The war on terrorism is one reason. Between 2001 and 2003 total net aid to Afghanistan increased from $408 million to $1.5 billion. Aid to Iraq increased from $116 million in 2002 to $2.3 billion in 2003 (table 6.10).

Even so, aid flows have not kept up with the economic growth of DAC members or with the needs of the poorest countries. As a share of donor gross national income (GNI) ODA declined sharply, from 0.33 percent in 1992 to 0.22 percent in 2001. Since then, there has been an upward trend: to 0.25 percent in 2003. Yet only five countries have reached the United Nations ODA target of 0.7 percent of GNI: Denmark, Luxembourg, the Netherlands, Norway, and Sweden. Sweden and Norway are striving for 1 percent, Sweden by 2006 and Norway between 2006 and 2009. Six other countries intend to reach the 0.7 percent target before 2015: Ireland, Belgium, Finland, France, Spain, and the United Kingdom. If donor countries follow through on their promises at the United Nations International Conference on Financing for Development, in Monterrey, Mexico, in 2002, aid is expected to rise to about $88 billion in 2006.

Movement of people

Migration is another key element of integration. In regions with poor institutions and high transport costs, wages may be low, and the free movement of goods and capital will not bring those wages into line with wages in good locations. The benefits of migration to the sending region include higher wages for those who remain behind. In addition, migrants send a large volume of remittances back to family members. In 2003 the flow of remittances to developing countries from migrants and emigrants working and living abroad was $116.6 billion (figure 6b). India received 18 times as much in remittances from its workers overseas as it received in foreign aid. Brazil received almost 10 times as much. Not all remittances go from high-income to developing countries. Flows also take place between developing countries. (Box 6c provides additional information on measuring remittances.)

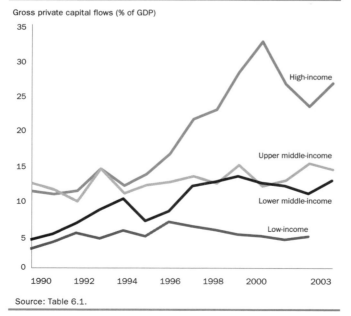

6a

Average gross capital flows to developing countries are half those to high-income countries

Gross private capital flows (% of GDP)

High-income

Upper middle-income

Lower middle-income

Low-income

Source: Table 6.1.

6b

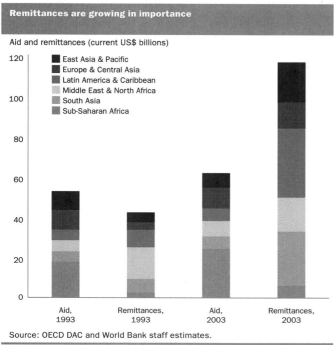

Aid and remittances (current US$ billions)

Legend:
- East Asia & Pacific
- Europe & Central Asia
- Latin America & Caribbean
- Middle East & North Africa
- South Asia
- Sub-Saharan Africa

Source: OECD DAC and World Bank staff estimates.

This year, table 6.13, "Movement of people," includes data on net migration flows, migration stocks, refugees, and remittances for developing and high-income countries. Monitoring and measuring the international movement of people are impeded by poor data availability, quality, and comparability. Illegal migration is especially difficult to capture accurately. In recognition of the importance of the temporary and permanent movement of people, the incomes they earn, and the funds they return to their home countries, efforts are under way to improve measurements of migration and remittance flows.

In 2000 some 175 million people, 3 percent of the world's population, lived in a country of which they were not a citizen or in which they were not born. In developing countries the foreign population stock almost doubled, from 44 million in 1960 to 86 million in 2000. In high-income countries the migration stock increased from 29 million to 89 million during the same period. The net outflow of people from developing countries to high-income economies has grown considerably. During 1960–65 developing countries sent 2.8 million people to high-income countries. During 1995–2000 the number increased to 13.6 million. The greatest numbers came from East Asia and Pacific, Latin America and the Caribbean, and South Asia. In addition to trade and investment, migration can also be important for global integration.

6c

Data initiative

Improving data on remittance flows

Remittances—transfers of resources from individuals in one country to individuals in another—are an important source of private funds in developing countries. Unlike foreign investment, which goes to a limited number of well-established economies, or the volatile earnings from trade, remittances tend to be stable, thus helping to cushion domestic economic shocks. And they are of direct benefit to the individuals and households that receive them.

Aggregate estimates of remittance flows are compiled and reported by countries as components in the balance of payments framework. For many developed countries remittances are relatively small compared with other components, so they do not receive close attention in data collection and compilation. Further, the balance of payments framework does not require a breakdown by origin and destination, which is important for understanding the major remittance pathways. Further, personal remittances are not reported as a specific component in the balance of payments, although an approximation can be obtained by aggregating relevant items (notably workers' remittances and compensation of employees).

There are also technical problems in collecting remittance data for the balance of payments. One relates to weak data from the source. Reports from banks or money transfer companies often lack the details required to distinguish remittances from other kinds of transfers, and many remittances are made using informal nonbanking mechanisms, such as the *havala* markets. Another difficulty is that the balance of payments framework requires that migrants be classified either as residents or nonresidents based on a one-year residency rule, which is often difficult to apply in practice. Some countries have developed

model-based estimation methods, which use the size of the foreign-born labor force and its propensity to remit, but these methods require good demographic and labor statistics and information on remittances from household surveys.

More detailed studies of remittance mechanisms, motives, and impacts require detailed information from household surveys. Some surveys in developing countries have included modules to collect data on migration and remittances, particularly from households that receive remittances from abroad. Surveys of remittance senders are less common, and the methodology is less well developed. The problems in surveying remittance senders are similar to those in surveying migrant groups. Households containing migrants may be relatively scarce and unevenly distributed, and some migrants are undocumented, so devising representative sampling schemes is difficult. Migrants may also be reluctant to accurately disclose amounts remitted and the remittance methods they use.

Because of these problems and the importance of remittances for development, countries and international agencies are working together to improve statistics on remittances and migration. A new initiative launched by the World Bank and the International Monetary Fund, in collaboration with the United Nations, aims to provide a practical definition of remittances for the collection of aggregate statistics. It also plans to draw on the knowledge and experiences of countries to develop guidelines for cost-effective data collection and estimation. In addition, the World Bank will develop guidance and questionnaire modules for conducting household surveys of remittance senders and receivers.

6.1 Integration with the global economy

	Trade in goods				Ratio of commercial service exports to merchandise exports		Growth in real trade less growth in real GDP	Gross private capital flows		Gross foreign direct investment	
	% of GDP		% of goods GDP		%		percentage points	% of GDP		% of GDP	
	1990	**2003**	**1990**	**2003**	**1990**	**2003**	**1990–2003**	**1990**	**2003**	**1990**	**2003**
Afghanistan	..	28.1	..	..	..	..	..	..	..	..	..
Albania	29.0	37.8	34.5	81.7	13.7	153.3	13.1	18.0	5.8	..	2.9
Algeria	36.6	56.6	55.0	83.9	3.7	..	0.0	2.6	..	0.0	..
Angola	53.5	98.0	91.0	133.5	1.7	*2.8*	..	10.1	*32.2*	3.3	*16.4*
Argentina	11.6	33.3	27.0	68.0	18.3	13.3	4.5	8.2	21.6	1.3	4.0
Armenia	..	69.4	..	105.1	..	29.4	–9.1	..	11.7	..	4.3
Australia	26.3	30.7	68.7	*96.1*	24.7	28.8	3.2	9.3	22.6	3.7	5.4
Austria	55.9	76.7	140.5	210.5	55.1	44.0	4.2	9.8	34.4	1.5	5.7
Azerbaijan	..	73.1	..	..	..	15.1	14.8	..	85.4	..	79.3
Bangladesh	17.6	31.6	..	..	17.7	5.7	4.6	0.9	2.5	0.0	0.2
Belarus	..	122.7	..	227.5	..	14.9	–2.8	..	3.9	..	1.0
Belgium	120.4	172.3	321.0	529.2	22.6	*24.5*	2.4	5.1	85.8	5.1	18.6
Benin	30.0	37.4	60.8	74.7	38.0	*35.7*	–2.6	10.7	*11.4*	3.7	*3.9*
Bolivia	33.1	40.5	61.5	83.8	14.3	18.0	1.3	3.1	12.4	0.7	2.2
Bosnia and Herzegovina	..	83.7	..	..	..	45.1	–3.7	..	19.7	..	5.5
Botswana	98.4	70.6	..	..	10.3	*18.9*	–1.7	9.0	*20.3*	4.4	*8.3*
Brazil	11.7	25.1	..	..	11.8	13.1	4.7	1.9	6.7	0.4	2.1
Bulgaria	48.9	92.8	70.8	190.3	16.6	41.5	6.6	39.2	16.2	0.0	7.3
Burkina Faso	22.0	28.0	43.3	52.8	22.1	*13.8*	–2.0	1.0	*4.2*	..	*0.4*
Burundi	27.0	32.7	35.1	..	8.7	5.9	7.1	3.7	6.2	0.1	0.0
Cambodia	22.4	80.5	33.6	121.7	*18.8*	30.7	10.7	*3.2*	11.3	*1.7*	2.8
Cameroon	30.5	36.6	..	..	18.4	..	2.2	15.5	..	1.1	..
Canada	43.7	60.4	115.1	..	14.4	15.4	3.7	8.1	13.1	2.7	3.4
Central African Republic	18.4	20.4	26.4	23.5	14.5	..	..	2.2	..	0.5	..
Chad	27.2	42.6	54.9	71.2	12.5	..	3.8	5.6	..	..	..
Chile	53.1	55.9	100.5	105.9	21.3	22.5	2.8	15.0	23.9	2.2	7.4
China	32.5	60.1	..	..	9.3	10.6	..	2.5	14.3	1.2	4.5
Hong Kong, China	221.5	294.8	772.3	1,985.2	..	19.8	3.5	..	76.4	..	27.7
Colombia	30.7	33.8	..	..	22.9	14.3	2.9	3.1	12.6	1.3	3.4
Congo, Dem. Rep.	43.5	45.2	74.5	*59.3*	..	..	6.5	..	..	..	..
Congo, Rep.	57.2	119.4	107.0	180.2	6.7	2.6	2.7	6.6	11.7	..	6.5
Costa Rica	60.2	78.9	..	..	40.3	32.7	3.4	7.0	10.6	2.9	4.3
Côte d'Ivoire	47.9	75.3	86.0	168.2	13.8	10.3	0.1	3.5	6.4	0.4	1.3
Croatia	*88.8*	70.5	*164.8*	142.7	..	139.9	4.2	..	33.6	..	7.4
Cuba	..	..	..	..	..	..	..	..	..	..	..
Czech Republic	*83.6*	111.3	..	229.3	..	15.9	8.7	..	19.6	..	3.2
Denmark	52.6	59.1	144.1	166.0	34.5	47.0	3.4	15.1	36.9	2.0	9.3
Dominican Republic	73.2	80.5	163.2	192.4	50.1	61.9	3.9	5.0	19.8	1.9	2.1
Ecuador	44.2	46.2	..	..	18.7	13.7	1.9	11.0	11.1	1.2	5.7
Egypt, Arab Rep.	36.8	20.7	72.9	*36.3*	138.4	175.9	–2.4	6.8	8.6	1.7	0.3
El Salvador	38.4	59.8	87.6	147.2	51.7	24.9	6.5	2.0	13.4	0.8	1.8
Eritrea	*76.9*	96.7	*132.9*	200.0	*454.4*	..	–1.1	*53.0*	..	..	..
Estonia	..	148.9	..	378.2	..	39.3	8.1	*4.0*	42.9	*2.2*	14.1
Ethiopia	16.0	38.3	25.5	63.8	87.4	109.8	2.9	1.6	3.1	..	..
Finland	39.1	58.7	85.6	143.4	17.4	14.7	4.8	17.4	43.6	3.6	13.4
France	37.1	44.2	101.6	137.7	34.6	25.6	3.8	20.6	23.4	3.9	6.0
Gabon	52.5	59.7	97.7	..	9.7	..	–1.6	18.0	..	8.4	..
Gambia, The	69.1	50.1	134.4	96.7	170.6	..	–2.8	0.9	..	..	..
Georgia	..	37.7	..	76.4	..	90.8	11.8	..	11.1	..	8.6
Germany	46.5	56.2	108.8	161.3	12.0	15.4	4.0	9.8	19.5	1.8	4.2
Ghana	35.7	75.4	58.0	124.3	8.8	24.5	3.7	2.9	3.7	0.3	1.8
Greece	33.2	33.0	83.5	93.7	80.4	183.4	3.8	3.9	22.9	1.2	1.1
Guatemala	36.8	37.8	..	..	26.9	36.2	2.9	2.9	16.5	0.6	0.9
Guinea	49.5	45.3	85.5	70.8	13.6	6.7	–1.2	3.9	4.1	0.6	2.2
Guinea-Bissau	43.0	87.6	53.3	106.0	19.4	*11.6*	4.0	23.0	*12.9*	..	*2.3*
Haiti	17.2	52.5	..	..	26.7	33.4	–1.3	1.1	3.9	0.3	0.3

	Trade in goods				Ratio of commercial service exports to merchandise exports		Growth in real trade less growth in real GDP	Gross private capital flows		Gross foreign direct investment	
	% of GDP		% of goods GDP		%		percentage points	% of GDP		% of GDP	
	1990	2003	1990	2003	1990	2003	1990–2003	1990	2003	1990	2003
Honduras	57.9	66.0	106.4	128.3	14.5	38.8	−0.3	7.2	6.4	1.4	2.8
Hungary	61.5	108.9	102.4	256.8	26.8	18.6	8.8	4.6	28.1	..	10.2
India	13.1	21.1	..	..	25.7	44.7	6.9	0.8	3.1	..	0.8
Indonesia	41.5	44.9	68.1	74.6	9.7	8.4	0.6	4.1	4.0	1.0	1.7
Iran, Islamic Rep.	32.9	45.0	61.8	86.5	1.8	..	−8.4	2.6	..	..	..
Iraq	41.2	..	..	..	..	..	..	..	..	..	..
Ireland	93.9	95.0	186.8	225.8	13.8	40.7	6.8	22.2	328.1	2.2	59.5
Israel	55.0	61.6	..	..	37.6	38.7	0.9	6.5	13.4	0.7	5.1
Italy	32.0	39.7	83.3	118.0	28.5	24.0	3.0	10.6	17.8	1.3	2.8
Jamaica	67.2	59.2	162.2	159.7	84.2	175.5	−1.6	8.4	48.3	3.0	10.3
Japan	17.2	19.9	44.2	69.3	14.4	16.1	2.7	5.4	17.1	1.7	1.0
Jordan	91.1	88.6	205.2	247.7	134.4	47.4	−2.2	6.3	13.2	1.7	3.8
Kazakhstan	..	71.4	..	143.2	..	12.6	−2.8	..	32.7	..	9.3
Kenya	38.1	42.7	68.3	100.1	75.0	34.5	1.8	3.6	6.1	0.7	0.6
Korea, Dem. Rep.	..	..	..	..	..	..	..	..	..	..	..
Korea, Rep.	51.1	61.6	92.1	124.3	14.1	16.3	6.2	5.3	8.1	0.7	1.2
Kuwait	59.8	72.3	112.9	..	15.0	8.2	..	19.3	49.6	1.3	12.1
Kyrgyz Republic	..	68.1	..	104.6	..	23.0	−2.3	..	11.8	..	2.4
Lao PDR	30.5	42.5	40.2	56.9	13.5	38.2	..	3.7	1.4	0.7	1.4
Latvia	..	73.5	..	209.9	..	51.7	5.5	2.2	28.7	0.7	3.8
Lebanon	106.5	45.8	..	..	..	..	−2.2	..	..	..	..
Lesotho	119.3	131.5	188.8	201.8	54.9	8.4	−0.6	9.6	11.2	2.8	11.0
Liberia	374.1	178.7	..	..	..	..	..	..	..	..	..
Libya	64.2	85.2	..	..	0.6	..	..	7.3	..	0.9	..
Lithuania	..	93.8	..	213.5	..	25.8	8.5	..	15.6	..	3.8
Macedonia, FYR	103.8	77.0	167.6	151.5	..	22.7	5.1	..	8.6	..	2.0
Madagascar	31.5	33.7	53.7	51.4	40.5	30.8	2.8	1.8	1.1	0.7	0.2
Malawi	52.7	68.0	70.6	118.7	8.8	12.1	−2.2	3.2	3.2	..	0.3
Malaysia	133.4	174.8	232.3	325.1	12.8	13.5	3.0	10.3	22.6	5.3	5.8
Mali	39.7	50.4	63.4	69.9	19.7	16.9	2.2	2.0	27.9	0.2	12.4
Mauritania	84.1	84.1	134.0	154.6	3.0	..	−4.1	48.8	..	0.7	..
Mauritius	118.0	82.7	219.8	185.9	40.0	65.7	−0.2	8.0	7.5	1.7	1.3
Mexico	32.1	54.9	78.9	154.7	17.7	7.6	8.6	9.2	5.4	1.0	2.0
Moldova	..	111.5	..	203.3	..	29.2	11.9	..	15.3	..	3.0
Mongolia	..	102.2	..	174.5	7.3	39.7	..	..	13.7	..	7.0
Morocco	43.3	52.3	86.5	112.7	43.9	58.7	2.5	5.5	9.3	0.6	5.3
Mozambique	40.8	52.0	68.9	97.9	81.7	34.1	0.0	0.4	11.3	0.4	7.8
Myanmar	..	..	..	..	29.0	10.7	..	..	..	..	..
Namibia	95.6	76.4	195.3	182.2	9.7	26.7	0.1	16.5	27.5	5.0	6.9
Nepal	24.1	41.3	..	..	81.5	45.6	..	3.5	11.6	..	0.3
Netherlands	87.5	108.9	229.1	335.2	21.6	21.5	3.7	29.8	64.5	8.3	10.4
New Zealand	43.3	44.0	121.0	..	25.7	38.6	2.2	17.8	9.6	11.5	5.6
Nicaragua	95.9	61.0	183.0	122.4	10.4	35.3	5.7	9.0	5.6	..	4.9
Niger	27.0	32.6	49.9	55.1	7.8	..	..	2.8	..	1.6	..
Nigeria	67.5	53.3	90.8	69.8	7.1	..	1.5	5.9	..	2.1	..
Norway	52.8	48.4	126.6	111.5	36.6	31.8	1.4	11.9	24.7	2.1	3.3
Oman	77.7	84.6	127.4	..	1.2	3.9	..	3.8	2.9	1.4	0.1
Pakistan	32.6	30.3	..	..	21.7	12.4	−0.9	4.2	2.8	0.6	0.7
Panama	35.4	30.4	..	..	266.7	291.7	−4.5	106.6	28.5	2.6	6.3
Papua New Guinea	73.6	109.1	123.9	157.1	16.8	15.7	..	5.7	14.4	4.8	2.0
Paraguay	43.9	55.9	82.8	108.5	42.1	43.3	−2.9	5.4	12.5	1.5	2.6
Peru	22.3	28.8	..	..	22.1	17.4	3.3	3.2	7.4	0.2	2.4
Philippines	47.7	94.3	84.7	201.4	35.7	8.1	2.7	4.4	39.9	1.2	0.6
Poland	43.9	58.0	75.2	138.9	22.3	20.9	7.8	11.0	11.3	0.2	2.5
Portugal	58.3	51.7	140.8	143.7	30.8	37.3	3.6	11.4	53.7	3.9	3.8
Puerto Rico	..	..	..	..	..	..	−0.5	..	..	..	..

	Trade in goods				Ratio of commercial service exports to merchandise exports		Growth in real trade less growth in real GDP	Gross private capital flows		Gross foreign direct investment	
	% of GDP		% of goods GDP		%		percentage points	% of GDP		% of GDP	
	1990	2003	1990	2003	1990	2003	1990–2003	1990	2003	1990	2003
Romania	32.8	73.1	45.2	*117.7*	12.3	17.0	8.7	2.9	8.2	0.0	3.3
Russian Federation	..	48.2	..	103.6	..	11.8	3.0	..	19.6	..	5.0
Rwanda	15.4	18.3	26.9	28.9	28.0	*84.9*	0.2	2.8	*0.9*	0.3	*0.2*
Saudi Arabia	58.6	58.1	107.5	97.3	6.8	6.5	..	8.8	16.7	1.6	0.3
Senegal	34.7	56.9	90.0	149.9	46.8	*36.5*	−0.9	4.8	*7.9*	1.3	*2.7*
Serbia and Montenegro	..	48.5	..	..	..	..	..	..	..	..	..
Sierra Leone	44.2	49.8	..	..	32.8	71.8	−5.5	11.0	0.4	5.0	0.4
Singapore	307.6	297.8	..	887.2	24.1	21.2	..	54.2	99.4	20.6	18.6
Slovak Republic	*110.8*	136.7	*192.1*	409.3	..	14.9	6.8	..	15.5	..	4.3
Slovenia	*102.4*	95.9	*197.7*	211.8	*18.3*	21.8	1.6	*3.4*	18.9	*0.9*	4.8
Somalia	26.7	..	33.2	..	..	..	..	..	..	..	..
South Africa	37.4ᵃ	48.5ᵃ	73.6ᵃ	119.3ᵃ	14.0	17.6	3.0	2.2	6.1	0.2	1.0
Spain	28.1	42.1	70.6	116.7	49.7	50.3	6.0	11.4	38.9	3.4	7.0
Sri Lanka	57.3	64.7	..	..	22.2	27.1	2.5	13.1	2.4	0.5	1.4
Sudan	7.5	28.3	..	*50.1*	35.9	1.3	5.6	0.3	10.5	..	7.6
Swaziland	141.8	104.9	230.1	139.9	18.3	*12.1*	1.2	10.9	*19.9*	5.1	*8.6*
Sweden	46.6	61.0	118.5	167.1	23.4	30.0	4.3	33.9	33.2	7.0	9.7
Switzerland	56.6	60.8	..	..	28.7	33.4	3.1	28.1	41.5	4.7	9.4
Syrian Arab Republic	53.7	48.6	102.4	*94.4*	17.6	21.6	3.9	18.0	6.4	..	5.0
Tajikistan	..	108.1	..	177.8	..	8.3	5.8	..	6.4	..	2.0
Tanzania	31.9	33.2	47.8	51.4	39.5	*69.6*	−0.7	0.2	*3.3*	..	2.5
Thailand	65.7	109.4	132.2	204.2	27.3	19.5	2.8	13.5	11.0	3.0	1.7
Togo	52.1	57.3	92.6	91.0	42.6	*16.9*	−1.5	9.6	*13.0*	1.1	*4.6*
Trinidad and Tobago	60.6	78.2	123.9	159.1	16.4	*15.4*	3.9	11.4	*19.7*	3.1	*10.4*
Tunisia	73.5	75.6	161.6	188.2	44.7	35.4	0.2	9.5	5.3	0.6	2.2
Turkey	23.4	48.2	44.5	105.3	60.8	40.8	6.8	4.3	6.8	0.5	0.9
Turkmenistan	..	98.9	..	156.7	..	..	3.6	..	..	..	..
Uganda	10.2	28.8	..	..	..	50.6	3.1	1.1	6.7	..	3.1
Ukraine	..	93.1	..	178.7	..	21.7	3.7	..	14.2	..	2.9
United Arab Emirates	101.8	*119.4*	159.6	..	..	..	..	..	..	..	..
United Kingdom	41.2	38.7	102.6	116.4	29.1	47.8	3.5	35.3	71.4	7.4	8.6
United States	15.8	18.5	44.7	*66.2*	33.8	39.7	4.4	5.6	11.4	2.8	3.0
Uruguay	32.7	39.2	85.0	111.3	27.2	34.2	2.3	12.7	49.3	..	2.5
Uzbekistan	..	58.6	..	94.9	..	..	−1.6	..	..	..	..
Venezuela, RB	51.1	38.6	74.7	83.9	6.4	3.3	2.4	49.9	12.9	1.7	4.4
Vietnam	79.7	115.0	129.7	..	..	*17.8*	15.0	..	*5.8*	..	*4.0*
West Bank and Gaza	..	..	..	..	..	..	−3.1	..	..	..	..
Yemen, Rep.	46.9	66.4	90.0	*97.1*	11.8	6.4	2.2	16.2	3.2	2.7	2.9
Zambia	76.9	56.4	102.3	103.5	7.2	..	1.3	64.7	..	6.2	..
Zimbabwe	40.7	*20.1*	74.5	..	14.7	..	4.8	1.7	..	0.1	..
World	**32.5 w**	**41.5 w**	**80.7 w**	**152.1 w**	**21.4 w**	**22.8 w**		**10.3 w**	**24.2 w**	**2.7 w**	**4.9 w**
Low income	24.6	34.9	..	..	15.6	18.3		2.8	*4.6*	0.4	*1.5*
Middle income	35.5	58.3	*82.3*	140.4	13.9	14.8		6.7	13.2	1.0	3.4
Lower middle income	31.3	53.8	..	..	14.7	15.2		4.1	12.7	0.8	3.5
Upper middle income	45.0	68.4	85.9	159.2	12.8	14.1		12.2	14.2	1.5	3.3
Low & middle income	33.6	54.7	*84.4*	138.0	14.1	15.1		6.0	12.8	0.9	3.3
East Asia & Pacific	47.0	70.5	..	..	14.1	11.3		5.0	14.4	1.7	3.9
Europe & Central Asia	..	66.7	..	147.7	..	21.0		..	16.5	..	4.4
Latin America & Carib.	23.2	42.2	*65.7*	133.1	18.1	13.7		8.0	9.9	0.9	2.8
Middle East & N. Africa	46.6	50.4	84.0	101.4	11.5	12.3		6.0	12.6	0.8	1.3
South Asia	16.5	24.1	..	..	24.6	35.8		1.4	*3.4*	0.1	*0.8*
Sub-Saharan Africa	42.4	52.7	77.4	108.7	13.9	10.8		5.1	6.7	1.0	1.9
High income	32.3	38.3	80.8	*156.4*	23.1	25.6		11.1	26.6	3.0	5.2
Europe EMU	44.9	..	112.6	..	24.0	23.3		14.1	..	2.9	..

a. Data refer to the South African Customs Union (Botswana, Lesotho, Namibia, South Africa, and Swaziland).

Integration with the global economy | 6.1

The growing integration of societies and economies has helped reduce poverty in many countries. Between 1990 and 2001 the number of people living on less than $1 a day declined by about 118 million. Although global integration is a powerful force in reducing poverty, more needs to be done. All countries have a stake in helping developing countries integrate with the global economy and gain better access to rich country markets.

One indication of increasing global economic integration is the growing importance of trade in the world economy. Another is the increased size and importance of private capital flows to developing countries that have liberalized their financial markets. This table presents standardized measures of the size of trade and capital flows relative to gross domestic product (GDP). The numerators are based on gross flows that capture the two-way flow of goods and capital. In conventional balance of payments accounting exports are recorded as a credit and imports as a debit. And in the financial account inward investment is a credit and outward investment a debit. Thus net flows, the sum of credits and debits, represent a balance in which many transactions are canceled out. Gross flows are a better measure of integration because they show the total value of financial transactions during a given period.

Trade in goods (exports and imports) is shown relative to both total GDP and goods GDP (GDP less services such as storage, transport, communications, retail trade, business services, public administration,

restaurants and hotels, and social, community, and personal services). As a result of the growing share of services in GDP, trade as a share of total GDP appears to be declining for some economies. Comparing merchandise trade with GDP after deducting value added in services thus provides a better measure of its relative size than does comparing it with total GDP, although this neglects the growing service component of most goods output.

Trade in services (such as transport, travel, finance, insurance, royalties, construction, communications, and cultural services) is an increasingly important element of global integration. The ratio of commercial service exports to merchandise exports highlights the growing importance of the service sector in world trade. The difference between the growth of real trade in goods and services and the growth of GDP helps to identify economies that have integrated with the global economy by liberalizing trade, lowering barriers to foreign investment, and harnessing their abundant labor to gain a competitive advantage in labor-intensive manufactures and services.

Trade and capital flows are converted to U.S. dollars at the International Monetary Fund's average official exchange rate for the year shown. An alternative conversion factor is applied if the official exchange rate diverges by an exceptionally large margin from the rate effectively applied to transactions in foreign currencies and traded products.

• **Trade in goods as a share of GDP** is the sum of merchandise exports and imports divided by the value of GDP, all in current U.S. dollars. • **Trade in goods as a share of goods GDP** is the sum of merchandise exports and imports divided by the value of GDP after subtracting value added in services, all in current U.S. dollars. • **Ratio of commercial service exports to merchandise exports** is total service exports minus exports of government services not included elsewhere over the free on board (f.o.b.) value of goods provided to the rest of the world, all in current U.S. dollars. • **Growth in real trade less growth in real GDP** is the difference between annual growth in trade of goods and services and annual growth in GDP. Growth rates are calculated using constant price series taken from national accounts and are expressed as a percentage. • **Gross private capital flows** are the sum of the absolute values of direct, portfolio, and other investment inflows and outflows recorded in the balance of payments financial account, excluding changes in the assets and liabilities of monetary authorities and general government. The indicator is calculated as a ratio to GDP in U.S. dollars. • **Gross foreign direct investment** is the sum of the absolute values of inflows and outflows of foreign direct investment recorded in the balance of payments financial account. It includes equity capital, reinvestment of earnings, other long-term capital, and short-term capital. This indicator differs from the standard measure of foreign direct investment, which captures only inward investment (see table 6.7). The indicator is calculated as a ratio to GDP in U.S. dollars.

6.1a

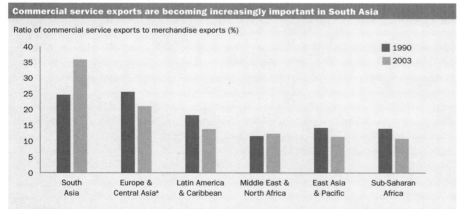

Commercial service exports are becoming increasingly important in South Asia

Ratio of commercial service exports to merchandise exports (%)

■ 1990
■ 2003

South Asia · Europe & Central Asiaᵃ · Latin America & Caribbean · Middle East & North Africa · East Asia & Pacific · Sub-Saharan Africa

Merchandise still makes up approximately 80 percent of global exports, but commercial service exports are rising in importance in South Asia. In India the ratio of commercial service exports to merchandise exports increased from 26 percent in 1990 to 45 percent in 2003.

a. Data are for 1994 and 2003.

Source: World Trade Organization and IMF.

The data on merchandise trade are from the World Trade Organization. The data on GDP come from the World Bank's national accounts files, converted from national currencies to U.S. dollars using the official exchange rate, supplemented by an alternative conversion factor if the official exchange rate is judged to diverge by an exceptionally large margin from the rate effectively applied to transactions in foreign currencies and traded products. Data on commercial service exports are from the International Monetary Fund's (IMF) Balance of Payments database. The data on real trade and GDP growth come from the World Bank's national accounts files. Gross private capital flows and foreign direct investment were calculated using the IMF's Balance of Payments database.

6.2 Direction and growth of merchandise trade

High-income importers

% of world trade

Source of exports	European Union	Japan	United States	Other industrial	All industrial	Other high income	All high income
High-income economies	30.8	2.5	10.2	5.7	49.3	6.6	56.0
Industrial economies	29.5	1.7	8.7	5.4	45.4	5.0	50.4
European Union	24.5	0.6	3.5	2.2	30.8	1.8	32.6
Japan	1.0		1.6	0.3	2.9	1.6	4.6
United States	2.1	0.7		2.7	5.5	1.2	6.7
Other industrial economies	1.9	0.4	3.6	0.3	6.1	0.4	6.5
Other high-income economies	1.3	0.8	1.5	0.3	3.9	1.6	5.5
Low- and middle-income economies	7.1	2.0	6.3	0.9	16.3	3.9	20.3
East Asia & Pacific	1.6	1.5	2.1	0.4	5.5	2.7	8.3
Europe & Central Asia	3.1	0.0	0.2	0.2	3.7	0.3	3.9
Latin America & Caribbean	0.6	0.1	3.0	0.1	3.9	0.2	4.0
Middle East & N. Africa	0.9	0.3	0.4	0.1	1.8	0.4	2.2
South Asia	0.3	0.0	0.2	0.0	0.6	0.2	0.8
Sub-Saharan Africa	0.5	0.1	0.3	0.1	0.9	0.1	1.0
World	38.0	4.6	16.5	6.7	65.7	10.6	76.2

Low- and middle-income importers

% of world trade

Source of exports	East Asia & Pacific	Europe & Central Asia	Latin America & Caribbean	Middle East & N. Africa	South Asia	Sub-Saharan Africa	All low- & middle-income	World
High-income economies	6.3	4.0	3.2	1.5	0.7	0.9	16.5	72.5
Industrial economies	3.6	3.8	3.1	1.3	0.5	0.8	13.1	63.5
European Union	1.0	3.5	0.7	1.0	0.3	0.6	7.1	39.6
Japan	1.4	0.1	0.2	0.1	0.1	0.1	2.0	6.5
United States	0.8	0.1	2.0	0.1	0.1	0.1	3.3	10.0
Other industrial economies	0.3	0.1	0.1	0.1	0.1	0.0	0.8	7.3
Other high-income economies	2.7	0.2	0.1	0.1	0.2	0.1	3.4	8.9
Low- and middle-income economies	2.0	2.3	1.1	0.6	0.5	0.7	7.3	27.5
East Asia & Pacific	1.1	0.3	0.2	0.2	0.2	0.4	2.4	10.6
Europe & Central Asia	0.2	1.7	0.0	0.2	0.1	0.0	2.2	6.2
Latin America & Caribbean	0.2	0.1	0.8	0.1	0.0	0.0	1.2	5.2
Middle East & N. Africa	0.3	0.1	0.0	0.1	0.1	0.1	0.7	2.9
South Asia	0.1	0.0	0.0	0.1	0.1	0.0	0.3	1.2
Sub-Saharan Africa	0.1	0.0	0.0	0.0	0.1	0.2	0.5	1.5
World	8.3	6.3	4.3	2.1	1.2	1.6	23.8	100.0

Direction and growth of merchandise trade

Nominal growth of trade, 1993–2003

High-income importers

annual % growth

Source of exports	European Union	Japan	United States	Other industrial	All industrial	Other high income	All high income
High-income economies	7.3	3.2	6.0	5.3	6.5	4.8	6.3
Industrial economies	7.4	2.4	6.5	5.3	6.8	4.2	6.5
European Union	8.3	5.1	9.6	6.2	8.2	6.2	8.1
Japan	1.8		0.9	1.4	1.3	3.1	1.9
United States	3.9	0.8		5.2	4.0	3.3	3.9
Other industrial economies	5.6	1.7	7.5	5.9	6.4	3.7	6.2
Other high-income economies	4.7	5.0	3.2	4.3	4.1	7.1	4.9
Low- and middle-income economies	10.9	8.0	11.6	11.8	10.8	11.2	10.9
East Asia & Pacific	13.1	9.3	12.8	13.1	11.9	11.5	11.7
Europe & Central Asia	14.2	2.9	13.7	14.9	14.0	14.5	14.0
Latin America & Caribbean	5.2	1.9	11.4	7.7	9.5	8.9	9.5
Middle East & N. Africa	6.1	6.8	10.2	8.8	7.2	7.7	7.3
South Asia	7.8	–1.0	10.1	7.7	7.9	11.9	8.8
Sub-Saharan Africa	10.3	15.7	8.7	13.6	10.2	22.0	10.8
World	7.9	5.0	7.7	6.0	7.4	6.8	7.3

Low- and middle-income importers

annual % growth

Source of exports	East Asia & Pacific	Europe & Central Asia	Latin America & Caribbean	Middle East & N. Africa	South Asia	Sub-Saharan Africa	All low- & middle-income	World
High-income economies	8.5	11.9	5.5	3.2	6.8	4.8	7.6	6.6
Industrial economies	7.8	12.0	5.7	3.2	6.5	4.8	7.4	6.7
European Union	8.2	13.2	5.6	4.9	8.3	6.4	9.2	8.3
Japan	7.2	5.5	–0.4	–0.4	1.1	–3.9	4.8	2.7
United States	8.5	0.6	6.8	–2.5	4.5	3.7	5.9	4.5
Other industrial economies	7.4	11.9	4.1	2.8	9.0	6.5	6.8	6.3
Other high-income economies	9.6	10.9	1.9	4.1	7.5	4.6	8.6	6.2
Low- and middle-income economies	16.6	14.0	8.1	9.2	13.1	15.1	13.0	11.4
East Asia & Pacific	17.3	14.9	15.9	11.3	16.1	16.7	16.0	12.6
Europe & Central Asia	9.2	15.0	10.1	8.8	13.0	12.6	13.5	13.8
Latin America & Caribbean	16.6	11.7	6.6	8.0	16.6	11.9	8.5	9.3
Middle East & N. Africa	20.5	6.8	3.9	8.2	2.3	12.5	10.5	8.0
South Asia	16.7	4.1	14.7	8.6	15.7	16.8	12.4	9.7
Sub-Saharan Africa	26.8	22.6	13.6	8.2	16.0	14.0	16.5	12.2
World	10.0	12.6	6.1	4.7	8.9	8.3	9.0	7.7

The table provides estimates of the flow of trade in goods between groups of economies. The data are from the International Monetary Fund's (IMF) Direction of Trade database. All high-income countries and 22 of the 156 developing countries report trade on a timely basis, covering about 80 percent of trade for recent years. Trade by less timely reporters and by countries that do not report is estimated using reports of trading partner countries. Because the largest exporting and importing countries are reliable reporters, a large portion of the missing trade flows can be estimated from partner reports. Partner country data may introduce discrepancies due to smuggling, confidentiality, different exchange rates, overreporting of transit trade, inclusion or exclusion of freight rates, and different points of valuation and times of recording.

In addition, estimates of trade within the European Union (EU) have been significantly affected by changes in reporting methods following the creation of a customs union. The current system for collecting data on trade between EU members—Intrastat, introduced in 1993—has less exhaustive coverage than the previous customs-based system and has resulted in some problems of asymmetry (estimated imports are about 5 percent less than exports). Despite these issues, only a small portion of world trade is estimated to be omitted from the IMF's *Direction of Trade Statistics Yearbook* and Direction of Trade database.

Most countries report their trade data in national currencies, which are converted into U.S. dollars using the IMF's published period average exchange rates (series rf or rh, monthly averages of the market or official rates) for the reporting country or, if those are not available, monthly average rates in New York. Because imports are reported at cost, insurance, and freight (c.i.f.) valuations, and exports at free on board (f.o.b.) valuations, the IMF adjusts country reports of import values by dividing them by 1.10 to estimate equivalent export values. This approximation is more or less accurate, depending on the set of partners and the items traded. Other factors affecting the accuracy of trade data include lags in reporting, recording differences across countries, and whether the country reports trade according to the general or special system of trade. (For further discussion of the measurement of exports and imports, see *About the data* for tables 4.5 and 4.6.)

The regional trade flows shown in the table were calculated from current price values. The growth rates are presented in nominal terms; that is, they include the effects of changes in both volumes and prices.

• **Merchandise trade** includes all trade in goods; trade in services is excluded. • **High-income economies** are those classified as such by the World Bank (see inside front cover). • **Industrial economies** are those classified as such in the IMF's *Direction of Trade Statistics Yearbook*. They include the countries of the European Union, Japan, the United States, and the other industrial economies listed below. • **European Union** comprises Austria, Belgium, Denmark, Finland, France, Germany, Greece, Ireland, Italy, Luxembourg, the Netherlands, Portugal, Spain, Sweden, and the United Kingdom. • **Other industrial economies** include Australia, Canada, Iceland, New Zealand, Norway, and Switzerland. • **Other high-income economies** include Aruba, the Bahamas, Bahrain, Bermuda, Brunei, Cyprus, Faeroe Islands, French Polynesia, Greenland, Guam, Hong Kong (China), Israel, the Republic of Korea, Kuwait, Macao (China), Malta, Netherlands Antilles, New Caledonia, Qatar, Singapore, Slovenia, Taiwan (China), and the United Arab Emirates. • **Low- and middle-income regional groupings** are based on World Bank classifications and may differ from those used by other organizations.

6.2a

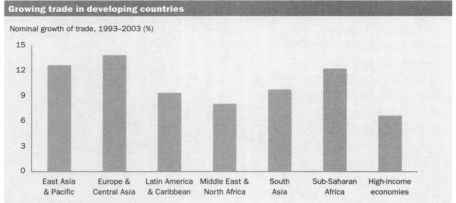

Nominal growth of trade, 1993–2003 (%)

Between 1993 and 2003 exports from developing countries to the world grew faster (in nominal terms) than exports from high-income economies. Europe and Central Asia had the highest growth rate, followed by East Asia and Pacific and Sub-Saharan Africa.

Source: IMF Direction of Trade database.

Intercountry trade flows are published in the IMF's *Direction of Trade Statistics Yearbook* and Direction of Trade Statistics Quarterly; the data in the table were calculated using the IMF's Direction of Trade database.

OCED trade with low- and middle-income economies | 6.3

Exports to low-income economies

	High-income OECD countries		European Union		Japan		United States	
	1993	2003	1993	2003	1993	2003	1993	2003
Total ($ billions)	**52.0**	**83.8**	**27.8**	**46.0**	**8.6**	**8.9**	**7.0**	**12.3**
% of total								
Food	9.2	8.8	9.9	9.8	0.8	0.5	20.1	13.4
Cereals	3.8	2.7	2.6	2.4	0.3	0.2	15.3	7.8
Agricultural raw materials	2.2	2.5	1.4	1.5	1.5	1.5	3.6	6.0
Ores and nonferrous metals	1.5	2.4	1.4	2.3	0.4	1.2	1.5	1.3
Fuels	3.1	2.8	2.8	2.4	0.7	0.9	2.2	1.4
Crude petroleum	0.0	0.0	0.0	0.0	0.0	0.0	0.0	0.0
Petroleum products	2.3	1.8	2.7	2.3	0.5	0.4	2.1	1.3
Manufactured goods	81.9	79.5	82.8	80.7	96.0	92.4	69.4	71.7
Chemical products	10.9	11.2	12.8	12.0	4.7	6.8	11.8	12.0
Iron and steel	4.1	3.3	4.4	2.8	6.0	9.9	1.0	1.2
Mach. and transport equip.	47.0	43.3	41.5	39.4	74.2	60.3	47.9	46.6
Furniture	0.3	0.4	0.4	0.5	0.2	0.2	0.2	0.3
Textiles	3.2	3.9	2.4	2.0	3.6	5.0	4.1	7.0
Footwear	0.2	0.1	0.3	0.2	0.0	0.0	0.1	0.1
Other	16.2	17.3	20.9	24.0	7.2	10.3	4.4	4.4
Miscellaneous goods	2.1	4.0	1.6	3.3	0.6	3.5	3.2	6.1

Imports from low-income economies

	High-income OECD countries		European Union		Japan		United States	
Total ($ billions)	**56.2**	**120.4**	**27.8**	**54.5**	**6.4**	**8.7**	**17.4**	**46.6**
% of total								
Food	15.9	13.8	20.9	18.7	21.9	20.7	6.8	7.3
Cereals	0.3	0.3	0.4	0.4	0.3	0.2	0.2	0.2
Agricultural raw materials	5.9	2.8	7.1	4.6	12.8	2.3	1.2	0.7
Ores and nonferrous metals	5.9	3.0	5.4	3.9	17.6	10.2	1.9	0.4
Fuels	29.8	27.5	19.3	16.6	15.2	25.1	50.6	38.2
Crude petroleum	27.8	24.7	18.4	14.5	12.0	21.2	47.5	35.0
Petroleum products	1.8	1.7	0.8	0.5	2.5	2.7	3.1	2.5
Manufactured goods	41.9	52.4	46.8	55.5	30.9	41.1	39.1	52.8
Chemical products	1.9	3.2	2.2	3.2	0.8	2.7	1.4	2.8
Iron and steel	0.9	1.0	0.5	1.0	2.5	1.1	0.9	0.8
Mach. and transport equip.	2.0	4.5	2.8	5.3	0.3	9.9	1.2	2.7
Furniture	0.1	1.2	0.2	1.2	0.1	1.9	0.1	1.0
Textiles	22.5	26.9	24.8	26.1	16.8	12.8	21.4	31.7
Footwear	0.8	3.5	1.1	5.9	0.1	2.5	0.5	1.0
Other	13.7	12.2	15.3	12.7	10.1	10.3	13.6	12.7
Miscellaneous goods	0.6	0.6	0.4	0.6	1.6	0.6	0.5	0.6

Simple applied tariff rates on imports from low-income economies (%)

	High-income OECD countries		European Union		Japan		United States	
Food	3.2	4.1	3.0	1.3	6.7	5.4	1.2	3.1
Cereals	5.5	3.2	15.0	0.6	9.0	10.3	1.0	0.9
Agricultural raw materials	0.6	1.3	0.3	0.1	0.3	0.3	0.2	0.4
Ores and nonferrous metals	0.6	0.7	0.1	0.4	0.2	0.1	0.2	0.2
Fuels	1.4	0.9	0.3	0.0	1.0	0.2	2.6	0.5
Crude petroleum	0.9	1.0	0.0	0.0	0.0	0.0	..	0.0
Petroleum products	2.0	1.3	0.6	0.0	2.0	0.5	2.6	1.0
Manufactured goods	4.1	3.4	0.5	0.8	2.6	2.3	5.6	5.0
Chemical products	2.0	1.6	0.5	0.4	0.8	0.2	2.0	0.8
Iron and steel	2.6	1.2	0.8	0.0	0.6	0.2	4.7	0.7
Mach. and transport equip.	1.1	0.9	0.2	0.1	0.0	0.0	0.6	0.3
Furniture	3.1	1.9	0.1	0.0	0.0	0.0	0.8	1.0
Textiles	8.3	7.6	1.1	2.6	5.3	5.2	11.8	10.6
Footwear	10.0	7.8	1.3	2.4	13.3	10.7	14.3	9.3
Other	5.1	4.3	0.6	1.2	3.1	3.2	6.8	6.3
Miscellaneous goods	0.8	0.5	0.6	0.3	0.0	0.0	1.7	0.1
Average	**3.7**	**3.3**	**0.8**	**0.8**	**2.9**	**2.5**	**4.8**	**4.5**

Exports to middle-income economies

	High-income OECD countries		European Union		Japan		United States	
	1993	2003	1993	2003	1993	2003	1993	2003
Total ($ billions)	442.7	896.8	195.0	447.5	79.8	132.1	121.3	201.4
% of total								
Food	8.2	5.9	9.3	5.2	0.4	0.3	10.8	10.2
Cereals	2.7	1.3	2.2	0.9	0.1	0.0	4.8	2.9
Agricultural raw materials	1.9	2.0	1.3	1.4	0.8	1.0	2.6	3.5
Ores and nonferrous metals	1.7	2.2	1.6	1.7	1.0	2.0	1.6	2.1
Fuels	2.0	2.0	1.8	1.3	0.8	0.5	2.5	3.0
Crude petroleum	0.2	0.1	0.2	0.0	0.0	0.0	0.0	0.0
Petroleum products	1.5	1.5	1.5	1.1	0.8	0.5	1.8	2.5
Manufactured goods	83.5	84.0	84.3	86.9	96.1	92.7	78.1	76.7
Chemical products	10.0	12.1	12.0	13.0	5.3	8.1	9.3	11.3
Iron and steel	4.2	3.2	4.0	3.0	8.7	6.4	1.1	1.1
Mach. and transport equip.	50.1	48.9	47.3	48.1	66.7	63.2	50.0	45.6
Furniture	0.7	0.6	0.8	0.9	0.2	0.2	0.9	0.5
Textiles	4.9	4.9	5.4	5.6	2.9	2.7	4.1	4.8
Footwear	0.3	0.2	0.5	0.3	0.0	0.0	0.1	0.1
Other	13.4	14.0	14.3	16.0	12.2	12.1	12.6	13.3
Miscellaneous goods	2.6	3.7	1.7	3.5	0.9	3.4	4.5	4.5

Imports from middle-income economies

	High-income OECD countries		European Union		Japan		United States	
Total ($ billions)	475.3	1,343.5	194.1	529.9	76.7	168.0	161.7	511.8
% of total								
Food	12.7	7.4	14.7	8.8	15.3	9.5	9.2	5.2
Cereals	0.4	0.4	0.2	0.3	0.7	0.4	0.2	0.2
Agricultural raw materials	3.6	1.7	3.8	2.3	6.8	2.2	1.6	1.0
Ores and nonferrous metals	5.4	3.6	6.1	4.0	8.9	6.1	2.9	1.7
Fuels	25.3	18.7	27.4	18.8	33.3	24.0	17.9	16.1
Crude petroleum	17.2	13.2	18.1	12.8	20.9	14.7	13.3	12.8
Petroleum products	3.9	2.7	4.2	3.2	2.8	1.7	4.0	2.5
Manufactured goods	51.4	67.0	46.4	65.1	34.9	57.1	66.4	73.6
Chemical products	3.3	3.3	4.1	3.7	2.5	2.9	2.3	2.7
Iron and steel	1.7	1.7	1.6	2.3	1.9	0.9	1.4	1.2
Mach. and transport equip.	15.5	30.5	10.9	28.3	6.4	24.6	25.8	35.5
Furniture	1.3	2.7	1.4	2.4	1.1	1.6	1.5	3.4
Textiles	13.5	10.5	14.6	11.1	11.4	11.7	13.8	10.0
Footwear	2.7	1.8	1.8	1.4	1.1	1.3	4.9	2.6
Other	13.4	16.4	12.0	16.0	10.4	14.2	16.7	18.1
Miscellaneous goods	1.6	1.5	1.7	1.0	0.9	1.1	2.1	2.4

Simple applied tariff rates on imports from middle-income economies (%)

	High-income OECD countries		European Union		Japan		United States	
Food	6.1	4.5	9.2	3.3	9.4	7.7	1.6	3.2
Cereals	6.8	5.6	19.6	1.3	14.9	12.1	1.3	1.0
Agricultural raw materials	1.1	1.2	1.0	0.2	0.4	0.4	0.5	0.5
Ores and nonferrous metals	1.4	0.7	1.3	0.3	0.3	0.1	0.8	0.4
Fuels	1.4	0.9	1.0	0.0	0.8	0.5	1.1	1.1
Crude petroleum	1.1	0.8	0.0	0.0	0.0	0.0	0.0	0.0
Petroleum products	2.2	1.2	1.5	0.0	1.6	0.9	1.7	1.8
Manufactured goods	4.9	3.2	2.6	0.7	1.8	2.3	4.6	3.0
Chemical products	3.3	1.6	3.1	0.2	0.8	0.3	2.3	1.0
Iron and steel	3.6	1.4	3.2	1.5	0.7	0.3	4.1	0.5
Mach. and transport equip.	2.8	1.1	1.6	0.1	0.0	0.0	1.2	0.3
Furniture	4.2	2.2	1.5	0.0	0.0	0.0	0.8	0.3
Textiles	9.8	8.3	4.5	2.3	5.0	7.2	11.5	9.1
Footwear	12.2	9.1	4.4	2.4	16.2	18.5	14.0	8.8
Other	5.9	4.2	3.0	1.0	2.5	3.5	6.0	4.3
Miscellaneous goods	1.8	0.7	2.1	0.4	0.0	0.0	1.3	0.3
Average	**4.8**	**3.2**	**3.1**	**0.9**	**2.7**	**2.7**	**4.1**	**2.9**

Developing countries are becoming increasingly important in the global trading system. Since the early 1990s trade between high-income members of the Organisation for Economic Co-operation and Development (OECD) and low- and middle-income economies has grown faster than trade between OECD members. The increased trade benefits consumers and producers. But as the World Trade Organization's (WTO) Ministerial Conference in Doha, Qatar, in October 2001 showed, achieving a more pro-development outcome from trade remains a major challenge. Meeting this challenge will require strengthening international consultation. Negotiations after the Doha meetings have been launched on services, agriculture, manufactures, WTO rules, the environment, dispute settlement, intellectual property rights protection, and disciplines on regional integration. These negotiations are scheduled to be concluded in 2005.

Trade flows between high-income OECD members and low- and middle-income economies reflect the changing mix of exports to and imports from developing economies. While food and primary commodities have continued to fall as a share of OECD imports, the share of manufactures in goods imports from both low- and middle-income countries has grown. Moreover, trade between developing countries has grown substantially over the past decade. This growth has resulted from many factors, including developing countries' increasing share of world output and the liberalization of their trade.

Yet trade barriers remain high. This year, the table includes information about tariff rates by selected product groups. Applied tariff rates are the tariffs in effect for partners in preferential trade agreements such as the North American Free Trade Agreement. When these are unavailable, most favored nation rates are used. The difference between most favored nation and applied rates can be substantial. Simple averages of applied rates are shown because they are generally a better indicator of tariff protection.

The data come from the United Nations Conference on Trade and Development (UNCTAD). Partner country reports by high-income OECD countries were used for both exports and imports. Exports are recorded free on board (f.o.b.); imports include insurance and freight charges (c.i.f.). Because of differences in sources of data, timing, and treatment of missing data, the data in this table may not be fully comparable with those used to calculate the direction of trade statistics in table 6.2 or the aggregate flows in tables 4.4–4.6. Data are classified using the Harmonized System of trade at the six- or eight-digit level. Tariff line data were matched to Standard International Trade Classification (SITC) revision 1 codes to define commodity groups. For further discussion of merchandise trade statistics, see *About the data* for tables 4.4–4.6 and 6.2, and for information about tariff barriers, see table 6.6.

The product groups in the table are defined in accordance with the SITC revision 1: food (0, 1, 22, and 4) and cereals (04); agricultural raw materials (2 excluding 22, 27, and 28); ores and nonferrous metals (27, 28, and 68); fuels (3), crude petroleum (331), and petroleum products (332); manufactured goods (5–8 excluding 68), chemical products (5), iron and steel (67), machinery and transport equipment (7), furniture (82), textiles (65 and 84), footwear (85), and other manufactured goods (6 and 8 excluding 65, 67, 68, 82, 84, and 85); and miscellaneous goods (9). • **Exports** are all merchandise exports by high-income OECD countries to low-income and middle-income economies as recorded in the United Nations Statistics Division's COMTRADE database. • **Imports** are all merchandise imports by high-income OECD countries from low-income and middle-income economies as recorded in the United Nations Statistics Division's COMTRADE database. • **High-income OECD countries** in 2003 were Australia, Austria, Belgium, Canada, Denmark, Finland, France, Germany, Greece, Iceland, Ireland, Italy, Japan, the Republic of Korea, Luxembourg, the Netherlands, New Zealand, Norway, Portugal, Spain, Sweden, Switzerland, the United Kingdom, and the United States. • **European Union** comprises Austria, Belgium, Denmark, Finland, France, Germany, Greece, Ireland, Italy, Luxembourg, the Netherlands, Portugal, Spain, Sweden, and the United Kingdom. • **Simple applied tariff rate** is the unweighted average of effectively applied rates or most favored nation rates for all products subject to tariffs calculated for all traded goods.

6.3a

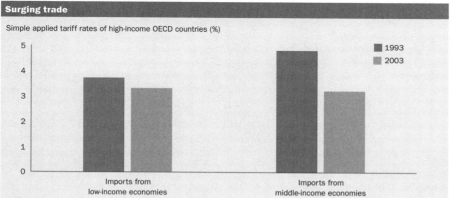

Simple applied tariff rates of high-income OECD countries (%)

Imports from developing economies by high-income OECD countries have doubled over the past 10 years. Tariff rates have fallen, but the decline has been greater for imports from middle-income economies.

Source: United Nations Statistics Division, COMTRADE database; United Nations Conference on Trade and Development, TRAINS database.

Trade values are from United Nations Statistics Division's COMTRADE database. Tariff data are from UNCTAD's TRAINS database and are calculated by World Bank staff using the World Integrated Trade Solution (WITS) system.

	1970	1980	1990	1995	1998	1999	2000	2001	2002	2003	2004
World Bank commodity price index											
(1990 = 100)											
Nonenergy commodities	156	159	100	104	99	89	89	84	89	91	102
Agriculture	163	175	100	112	108	93	90	84	93	95	99
Beverages	203	230	100	129	141	108	91	76	91	87	89
Food	166	177	100	100	105	88	87	91	97	96	105
Raw materials	130	133	100	116	88	89	93	81	89	98	101
Fertilizers	108	164	100	88	123	115	109	105	108	106	120
Metals and minerals	144	120	100	87	76	74	85	80	78	82	107
Petroleum	19	204	100	64	57	80	127	113	117	126	157
Steel products[a]	111	100	100	91	75	69	79	71	73	79	115
MUV G-5 index	28	79	100	117	100	99	97	94	93	100	105
Commodity prices											
(1990 prices)											
Agricultural raw materials											
Cotton (cents/kg)	225	260	182	182	145	118	134	112	109	140	130
Logs, Cameroon ($/cu. m)[a]	153	319	344	290	287	271	283	282	..	..	..
Logs, Malaysian ($/cu. m)	154	248	177	218	163	188	195	169	175	187	187
Rubber (cents/kg)	145	181	86	135	72	63	69	61	82	108	124
Sawnwood, Malaysian ($/cu. m)	625	503	533	632	486	605	612	510	565	551	553
Tobacco ($/mt)	3,836	2,887	3,392	2,258	3,349	3,064	3,063	3,185	2,947	2,645	2,608
Beverages (cents/kg)											
Cocoa	240	330	127	122	168	114	93	113	191	175	147
Coffee, robustas	330	411	118	237	183	150	94	64	71	81	75
Coffee, Arabica	409	440	197	285	299	231	198	146	146	141	169
Tea, avg., 3 auctions	298	211	206	127	205	185	193	169	162	152	160
Energy											
Coal, Australian ($/mt)	..	50	40	34	29	26	27	34	29	28	52
Coal, U.S. ($/mt)	..	55	42	33	35	33	34	48	43	..	..
Natural gas, Europe ($/mmbtu)	..	4	3	2	2	2	4	4	3	4	4
Natural gas, U.S. ($/mmbtu)	0.59	1.97	1.70	1.47	2.09	2.28	4.43	4.19	3.60	5.49	5.60
Petroleum ($/bbl)	4.31	46.78	22.88	14.67	13.12	18.20	29.05	25.82	26.76	28.89	35.86

About the data

Primary commodities—raw or partially processed materials that will be transformed into finished goods—are often the most significant exports of developing countries, and revenues obtained from them have an important effect on living standards. Price data for primary commodities are collected from a variety of sources, including trade journals, international study groups, government market surveys, newspaper and wire service reports, and commodity exchange spot and near-term forward prices.

This table is based on frequently updated price reports. When possible, the prices received by

exporters are used; if export prices are unavailable, the prices paid by importers are used. Annual price series are generally simple averages based on higher frequency data. The constant price series in the table is deflated using the manufactures unit value (MUV) index for the G-5 countries (see below).

The commodity price indexes are calculated as Laspeyres index numbers, in which the fixed weights are the 1987–89 export values for low- and middle-income economies, rebased to 1990. Each index represents a fixed basket of primary commodity exports. The nonenergy commodity price index contains 37 price series for 31 nonenergy commodities.

Separate indexes are compiled for petroleum and for steel products, which are not included in the nonenergy commodity price index.

The MUV index is a composite index of prices for manufactured exports from the five major (G-5) industrial countries (France, Germany, Japan, the United Kingdom, and the United States) to low- and middle-income economies, valued in U.S. dollars. The index covers products in groups 5–8 of the Standard International Trade Classification (SITC) revision 1. To construct the MUV G-5 index, unit value indexes for each country are combined using weights determined by each country's export share.

	1970	1980	1990	1995	1998	1999	2000	2001	2002	2003	2004
Commodity prices (continued)											
(1990 prices)											
Fertilizers ($/mt)											
Phosphate rock	39	59	41	30	43	44	45	44	43	38	39
TSP	152	229	132	128	174	156	142	135	143	149	177
Food											
Fats and oils ($/mt)											
Coconut oil	1,417	855	337	572	660	742	463	337	452	467	628
Groundnut oil	1,350	1,090	964	846	913	793	734	721	738	1,243	1,102
Palm oil	927	740	290	536	674	439	319	303	419	443	448
Soybeans	417	376	247	221	244	203	218	208	228	264	291
Soybean meal	367	332	200	168	171	153	195	192	188	211	229
Soybean oil	1,021	758	447	534	628	430	348	375	488	554	585
Grains ($/mt)											
Sorghum	185	164	104	102	98	85	91	101	109	106	104
Maize	208	159	109	105	102	91	91	95	107	105	106
Rice	450	521	271	274	305	250	208	183	206	198	226
Wheat	196	219	136	151	127	113	117	134	159	146	149
Other food											
Bananas ($/mt)	590	481	541	380	491	376	436	618	568	375	499
Beef (cents/kg)	465	350	256	163	173	186	199	226	226	198	239
Oranges ($/mt)	599	496	531	454	444	434	374	631	606	681	817
Sugar, EU domestic (cents/kg)	40	62	58	59	60	60	57	56	59	60	64
Sugar, U.S. domestic (cents/kg)	59	84	51	43	49	47	44	50	50	47	43
Sugar, world (cents/kg)	29	80	28	25	20	14	19	20	16	16	15
Metals and minerals											
Aluminum ($/mt)	1,982	1,847	1,639	1,542	1,363	1,371	1,594	1,531	1,449	1,431	1,631
Copper ($/mt)	5,038	2,768	2,662	2,508	1,660	1,584	1,866	1,673	1,674	1,778	2,724
Iron ore (cents/dmtu)	35	36	33	24	31	28	30	32	31	32	36
Lead (cents/kg)	108	115	81	54	53	51	47	50	49	51	84
Nickel ($/mt)	10,148	8,270	8,864	7,028	4,647	6,055	8,888	6,303	7,271	9,626	13,139
Tin (cents/kg)	1,310	2,128	609	531	556	544	559	475	436	489	809
Zinc (cents/kg)	105	97	151	88	103	108	116	94	84	83	100

a. Series not included in the nonenergy index.

Definitions

• **Nonenergy commodity price index** covers the 31 nonenergy primary commodities that make up the agriculture, fertilizer, and metals and minerals indexes. • **Agriculture** includes beverages, food, and agricultural raw material. • **Beverages** include cocoa, coffee, and tea. • **Food** includes rice, wheat, maize, sorghum, soybeans, soybean oil, soybean meal, palm oil, coconut oil, groundnut oil, bananas, beef, oranges, and sugar. • **Agricultural raw materials** include cotton, timber (logs and sawnwood), natural rubber, and tobacco. • **Fertilizers** include phosphate rock and triple superphosphate (TSP). • **Metals and minerals** include aluminum, copper, iron ore, lead,

nickel, tin, and zinc. • **Petroleum price index** refers to the average spot price of Brent, Dubai, and West Texas Intermediate crude oils, equally weighted. • **Steel products price index** is the composite price index for eight steel products based on quotations free on board (f.o.b.) Japan excluding shipments to China and the United States, weighted by product shares of apparent combined consumption (volume of deliveries) for Germany, Japan, and the United States. • **MUV G-5 index** is the manufactures unit value index for G-5 country exports to low- and middle-income economies. • **Commodity prices**—for definitions and sources, see "Commodity Price Data" (also

known as the "Pink Sheet") at the Global Prospects Web site (http://www.worldbank.org/prospects).

Data sources

Commodity price data and the G-5 MUV index are compiled by the World Bank's Development Prospects Group. Monthly updates of commodity prices are available on the Web at http://www.worldbank.org/prospects.

6.5 Regional trade blocs

					$ millions					
	1970	1980	1990	1995	1998	1999	2000	2001	2002	2003
High-income and low- and middle-income economies										
APEC[a]	58,633	357,697	901,560	1,688,708	1,734,386	1,896,213	2,262,091	2,070,709	2,168,713	2,419,912
CEFTA	1,157	7,766	4,235	12,118	14,234	13,226	15,123	17,054	19,180	25,309
CIS	..	..	..	29,943	27,037	20,842	27,043	22,240	28,007	36,439
EMFTA	65,442	404,328	867,042	1,118,848	1,341,891	1,522,340	1,548,725	1,526,375	1,620,295	1,938,877
FTAA	33,924	167,719	300,700	525,346	682,067	734,848	859,330	814,028	791,110	833,829
European Union	76,451	456,857	981,260	1,259,699	1,223,801	1,396,574	1,409,464	1,398,298	1,480,493	1,768,984
NAFTA	22,078	102,218	226,273	394,472	521,649	581,161	676,440	639,138	626,985	651,213
Latin America and the Caribbean										
ACS	758	4,892	5,398	11,049	12,505	11,199	16,060	14,966	15,263	16,766
Andean Group	97	1,161	1,312	4,812	5,408	3,929	5,116	5,461	5,070	4,781
CACM	287	1,174	667	1,594	2,010	2,175	2,377	2,376	2,379	2,542
CARICOM	52	576	448	867	1,020	1,136	1,050	1,202	1,221	1,500
Central American Group of Four	176	692	399	1,026	1,230	1,369	1,543	1,524	1,542	1,648
Group of Three	59	706	1,046	3,460	3,921	2,912	3,721	4,178	3,657	3,363
LAIA (ALADI)	1,263	10,981	12,331	35,299	42,959	34,785	42,717	40,633	35,644	39,839
MERCOSUR	451	3,424	4,127	14,199	20,352	15,313	17,829	15,156	10,228	12,732
OECS	..	8	29	39	36	37	38	40	43	54
Middle East and Asia										
Arab Common Market	110	671	911	1,368	978	951	1,312	1,728	1,997	1,797
ASEAN	1,456	13,350	28,648	81,911	72,352	80,415	101,848	89,478	95,864	104,872
Bangkok Agreement	132	1,464	4,476	12,066	12,851	14,463	16,844	16,733	18,299	21,733
EAEG	9,197	98,532	281,067	634,606	549,010	612,415	772,426	698,552	779,390	940,963
ECO	63	15,891	1,243	4,746	4,031	3,903	4,518	4,498	5,016	7,539
GAFTA	543	9,441	13,313	13,129	13,548	13,752	16,238	17,537	19,238	21,497
GCC	156	4,632	6,906	6,832	7,358	7,306	7,958	8,103	8,899	9,287
SAARC	99	664	863	2,024	2,466	2,180	2,593	2,827	2,998	4,773
UMA	60	109	958	1,109	881	919	1,094	1,136	1,187	1,352
Sub-Saharan Africa										
CEMAC	22	75	139	120	153	127	102	120	123	159
CEPGL	3	2	7	8	8	9	10	11	13	15
COMESA	434	646	1,026	1,471	1,641	1,478	1,695	1,684	1,913	2,638
Cross Border Initiative	209	447	613	1,002	1,156	964	1,059	843	1,008	1,443
EAC	142	211	230	530	555	438	485	453	479	573
ECCAS	162	89	163	163	198	179	196	217	194	235
ECOWAS	86	692	1,557	1,936	2,350	2,364	2,835	2,371	3,229	3,073
Indian Ocean Commission	23	39	73	127	95	91	107	136	107	179
MRU	1	7	0	1	2	4	5	4	5	6
SADC	483	617	1,630	3,373	3,865	4,224	4,453	3,933	4,027	5,159
UDEAC	22	75	139	120	152	126	101	119	120	157
UEMOA	52	460	621	560	752	805	741	775	857	1,043

Note: Regional bloc memberships are as follows: **Asia Pacific Economic Cooperation (APEC)**, Australia, Brunei Darussalam, Canada, Chile, China, Hong Kong (China), Indonesia, Japan, the Republic of Korea, Malaysia, Mexico, New Zealand, Papua New Guinea, Peru, the Philippines, the Russian Federation, Singapore, Taiwan (China), Thailand, the United States, and Vietnam; **Central European Free Trade Area (CEFTA)**, Bulgaria, the Czech Republic, Hungary, Poland, Romania, the Slovak Republic, and Slovenia; **Commonwealth of Independent States (CIS)**: Azerbaijan, Armenia, Belarus, Georgia, Moldova, Kazakhstan, Russian Federation, Ukraine, Uzbekistan, Tajikistan, and Kyrgyz Republic; **Euro-Mediterranean Free Trade Area (EMFTA)**: EU, Algeria, Cyprus, Egypt, Israel, Jordan, Lebanon, Malta, Morocco, Syrian Arab Republic, Tunisia, Turkey, and West Bank and Gaza; **Free Trade Areas of Americas (FTAA)**: Antigua and Barbuda, Argentina, Bahamas, Barbados, Belize, Bolivia, Brazil, Canada, Chile, Colombia, Costa Rica, Dominica, Dominican Republic, Ecuador, El Salvador, Grenada, Guatemala, Guyana, Haiti, Honduras, Jamaica, Mexico, Nicaragua, Panama, Paraguay, Peru, Republica Bolivariana de Venezuela, St. Kitts and Nevis, St. Lucia, St. Vincent and the Grenadines, Suriname, Trinidad and Tobago, United States, and Uruguay; **European Union (EU; formerly European Economic Community and European Community)**, Austria, Belgium, Denmark, Finland, France, Germany, Greece, Ireland, Italy, Luxembourg, the Netherlands, Portugal, Spain, Sweden, and the United Kingdom; **North American Free Trade Area (NAFTA)**, Canada, Mexico, and the United States; **Association of Caribbean States (ACS)**, Antigua and Barbuda, the Bahamas, Barbados, Belize, Colombia, Costa Rica, Cuba, Dominica, the Dominican Republic, El Salvador, Grenada, Guatemala, Guyana, Haiti, Jamaica, Mexico, Nicaragua, Panama, St. Kitts and Nevis, St. Lucia, St. Vincent and the Grenadines, Suriname, Trinidad and Tobago, and República Bolivariana de Venezuela; **Andean Group**, Bolivia, Colombia, Ecuador, Peru, and República Bolivariana de Venezuela; **Central American Common Market (CACM)**, Costa Rica, El Salvador, Guatemala, Honduras, and Nicaragua; **Caribbean Community and Common Market (CARICOM)**, Antigua and Barbuda, the Bahamas (part of the Caribbean Community but not of the Common Market), Barbados, Belize, Dominica, Grenada, Guyana, Jamaica, Montserrat, St. Kitts and Nevis, St. Lucia, St. Vincent and the Grenadines, Suriname, and Trinidad and Tobago; **Central American Group of Four**, El Salvador, Guatemala, Honduras, and Nicaragua; **Group of Three**, Colombia, Mexico, and República Bolivariana de Venezuela; **Latin American Integration Association (LAIA; formerly Latin American Free Trade Area)**, Argentina, Bolivia, Brazil, Chile, Colombia, Ecuador, Mexico, Paraguay, Peru, Uruguay, and República Bolivariana de Venezuela; **Southern Cone Common Market (MERCOSUR)**, Argentina, Brazil, Paraguay, and Uruguay; **Organization of Eastern Caribbean States (OECS)**, Antigua and Barbuda, Dominica, Grenada, Montserrat, St. Kitts and Nevis, St. Lucia, and St. Vincent and the Grenadines; **Economic and Monetary Community of Central Africa (CEMAC)**, Cameroon, the Central African Republic, Chad, the Republic of Congo, Equatorial Guinea, Gabon, and São Tomé and

a. No preferential trade agreement.

Merchandise exports within bloc

					% of total bloc exports					
	1970	1980	1990	1995	1998	1999	2000	2001	2002	2003
High-income and low- and middle-income economies										
APEC	57.8	57.9	68.3	71.8	69.7	71.8	73.1	72.6	73.4	72.5
CEFTA	12.9	14.8	9.9	14.6	13.0	12.1	12.2	12.4	12.2	12.5
CIS	..	..	..	27.6	26.6	20.7	19.2	18.2	18.8	19.6
EMFTA	53.9	56.0	60.8	58.4	60.0	65.8	64.6	63.3	63.2	63.8
FTAA	45.0	43.4	46.6	52.5	58.1	59.7	60.8	60.6	60.9	60.1
European Union	59.5	60.8	65.9	62.4	56.8	62.9	61.6	60.8	60.6	61.1
NAFTA	36.0	33.6	41.4	46.2	51.7	54.6	55.7	55.5	56.7	56.1
Latin America and the Caribbean										
ACS	9.6	8.7	8.4	8.5	7.2	5.6	6.5	6.5	6.5	6.7
Andean Group	1.8	3.8	4.1	12.0	12.8	8.8	8.5	10.3	9.5	7.8
CACM	26.1	24.4	15.3	21.8	15.8	13.6	13.2	13.9	13.4	13.0
CARICOM	4.2	5.3	8.1	12.1	17.3	16.9	14.6	13.9	13.0	12.4
Central American Group of Four	20.1	18.1	13.7	22.2	17.1	14.6	12.8	12.6	12.3	12.3
Group of Three	1.1	1.8	2.0	3.2	2.6	1.7	1.7	2.1	1.8	1.6
LAIA (ALADI)	9.9	13.7	10.8	17.1	16.7	12.7	12.7	12.8	11.1	11.2
MERCOSUR	9.4	11.6	8.9	20.3	25.0	20.6	20.0	17.1	11.5	11.9
OECS	..	9.1	8.1	12.6	12.0	13.1	10.0	5.2	3.7	6.8
Middle East and Asia										
Arab Common Market	2.3	2.4	2.7	6.7	4.8	3.3	2.9	4.4	5.1	4.1
ASEAN	22.9	18.7	19.8	25.4	21.9	22.4	23.9	23.2	23.7	23.0
Bangkok Agreement	2.7	3.7	3.7	5.0	5.0	5.1	5.1	5.5	5.6	5.7
EAEG	28.9	35.6	39.7	47.9	42.0	43.8	46.6	46.6	48.2	49.4
ECO	1.5	73.2	3.2	7.9	6.8	5.8	5.7	5.6	5.9	6.8
GAFTA	6.5	5.0	10.3	9.9	11.0	8.9	7.3	8.4	9.2	8.5
GCC	2.9	3.0	8.0	6.8	8.0	6.7	4.9	5.3	5.8	4.9
SAARC	3.2	5.2	3.2	4.4	4.8	4.0	4.1	4.3	4.2	5.6
UMA	1.4	0.3	2.9	3.8	3.3	2.5	2.3	2.6	2.7	2.4
Sub-Saharan Africa										
CEMAC	4.8	1.6	2.3	2.1	2.3	1.7	1.0	1.3	1.4	1.4
CEPGL	0.4	0.1	0.5	0.5	0.6	0.8	0.8	0.8	0.8	1.1
COMESA	9.6	6.4	7.1	8.2	9.5	8.1	6.3	7.1	6.7	8.0
Cross Border Initiative	9.3	8.8	10.3	11.9	13.9	12.1	10.5	8.8	10.0	12.4
EAC	16.9	10.2	13.4	17.4	19.0	14.4	16.1	13.8	13.4	14.1
ECCAS	9.6	1.4	1.4	1.5	1.8	1.3	1.1	1.3	1.1	1.1
ECOWAS	2.9	10.1	7.9	9.0	10.7	10.4	7.9	8.5	10.9	8.4
Indian Ocean Commission	8.4	3.9	4.1	6.0	4.7	4.8	4.4	5.7	4.4	6.1
MRU	0.2	0.8	0.0	0.1	0.1	0.4	0.4	0.3	0.2	0.3
SADC	8.0	2.0	4.8	8.7	10.4	11.9	12.0	9.7	8.8	9.4
UDEAC	4.9	1.6	2.3	2.1	2.3	1.7	1.0	1.3	1.4	1.4
UEMOA	6.5	9.6	13.0	10.3	11.0	13.1	13.1	12.7	12.2	13.0

Principe; **Economic Community of the Countries of the Great Lakes (CEPGL)**, Burundi, the Democratic Republic of Congo, and Rwanda; **Common Market for Eastern and Southern Africa (COMESA)**, Angola, Burundi, Comoros, the Democratic Republic of Congo, Djibouti, the Arab Republic of Egypt, Eritrea, Ethiopia, Kenya, Madagascar, Malawi, Mauritius, Namibia, Rwanda, Seychelles, Sudan, Swaziland, Uganda, Tanzania, Zambia, and Zimbabwe; **Cross-Border Initiative**, Burundi, Comoros, Kenya, Madagascar, Malawi, Mauritius, Namibia, Rwanda, Seychelles, Swaziland, Tanzania, Uganda, Zambia, and Zimbabwe; **East African Community (EAC)**: Kenya, Tanzania, and Uganda; **Economic Community of Central African States (ECCAS)**, Angola, Burundi, Cameroon, the Central African Republic, Chad, the Democratic Republic of the Congo, the Republic of Congo, Equatorial Guinea, Gabon, Rwanda, and São Tomé and Principe; **Economic Community of West African States (ECOWAS)**, Benin, Burkina Faso, Cape Verde, Côte d'Ivoire, the Gambia, Ghana, Guinea, Guinea-Bissau, Liberia, Mali, Mauritania, Niger, Nigeria, Senegal, Sierra Leone, and Togo; **Indian Ocean Commission**, Comoros, Madagascar, Mauritius, Reunion, and Seychelles; **Mano River Union (MRU)**, Guinea, Liberia, and Sierra Leone; **Southern African Development Community (SADC; formerly Southern African Development Coordination Conference)**, Angola, Botswana, the Democratic Republic of the Congo, Lesotho, Malawi, Mauritius, Mozambique, Namibia, Seychelles, South Africa, Swaziland, Tanzania, Zambia, and Zimbabwe; **Central African Customs and Economic Union (UDEAC; formerly Union Douanière et Economique de l'Afrique Centrale)**, Cameroon, the Central African Republic, Chad, the Republic of Congo, Equatorial Guinea, and Gabon; **West African Economic and Monetary Union (UEMOA)**, Benin, Burkina Faso, Côte d'Ivoire, Guinea-Bissau, Mali, Niger, Senegal, and Togo; **Arab Common Market**, the Arab Republic of Egypt, Iraq, Jordan, Libya, Mauritania, the Syrian Arab Republic, and the Republic of Yemen; **Association of South-East Asian Nations (ASEAN)**, Brunei, Cambodia, Indonesia, the Lao People's Democratic Republic, Malaysia, Myanmar, the Philippines, Singapore, Thailand, and Vietnam; **Bangkok Agreement**, Bangladesh, India, the Republic of Korea, the Lao People's Democratic Republic, the Philippines, Sri Lanka, and Thailand; **East Asian Economic Caucus (EAEC)**, Brunei, China, Hong Kong (China), Indonesia, Japan, the Republic of Korea, Malaysia, the Philippines, Singapore, Taiwan (China), and Thailand; **Economic Cooperation Organization (ECO)**, Afghanistan, Azerbaijan, the Islamic Republic of Iran, Kazakhstan, the Kyrgyz Republic, Pakistan, Tajikistan, Turkey, Turkmenistan, and Uzbekistan; **Greater Arab Free Trade Area (GAFTA)**: Bahrain, Egypt, Iraq, Jordan, Kuwait, Lebanon, Libya, Morocco, Oman, Qatar, Saudi Arabia, Somalia, Sudan, Syria, Tunisia, United Arab Emirates, West Bank and Gaza, and Yemen; **Gulf Cooperation Council (GCC)**, Bahrain, Kuwait, Oman, Qatar, Saudi Arabia, and the United Arab Emirates; **South Asian Association for Regional Cooperation (SAARC)**, Bangladesh, Bhutan, India, Maldives, Nepal, Pakistan, and Sri Lanka; and **Arab Maghreb Union (UMA)**, Algeria, Libya, Mauritania, Morocco, and Tunisia.

6.5 Regional trade blocs

	% of world exports									
	1970	1980	1990	1995	1998	1999	2000	2001	2002	2003
High-income and low- and middle-income economies										
APEC	36.0	33.7	39.0	46.3	46.1	46.6	48.5	46.5	45.9	44.5
CEFTA	3.2	2.9	1.3	1.6	2.0	1.9	2.0	2.2	2.4	2.7
CIS	..	..	..	2.1	1.9	1.8	2.2	2.0	2.3	2.5
EMFTA	43.0	39.4	42.2	37.7	41.4	40.8	37.6	39.2	39.8	40.6
FTAA	26.7	21.1	19.1	19.7	21.8	21.7	22.2	21.9	20.2	18.5
European Union	45.6	41.0	44.0	39.7	39.9	39.2	35.9	37.5	38.0	38.7
NAFTA	21.7	16.6	16.2	16.8	18.7	18.8	19.0	18.7	17.2	15.5
Latin America and the Caribbean										
ACS	2.8	3.1	1.9	2.6	3.2	3.5	3.9	3.8	3.6	3.3
Andean Group	1.9	1.7	0.9	0.8	0.8	0.8	0.9	0.9	0.8	0.8
CACM	0.4	0.3	0.1	0.1	0.2	0.3	0.3	0.3	0.3	0.3
CARICOM	0.4	0.6	0.2	0.1	0.1	0.1	0.1	0.1	0.1	0.2
Central American Group of Four	0.3	0.2	0.1	0.1	0.1	0.2	0.2	0.2	0.2	0.2
Group of Three	1.8	2.1	1.5	2.1	2.8	3.0	3.3	3.2	3.1	2.8
LAIA (ALADI)	4.5	4.4	3.4	4.1	4.8	4.8	5.3	5.2	5.0	4.7
MERCOSUR	1.7	1.6	1.4	1.4	1.5	1.3	1.4	1.4	1.4	1.4
OECS	0.0	0.0	0.0	0.0	0.0	0.0	0.0	0.0	0.0	0.0
Sub-Saharan Africa										
CEMAC	0.2	0.3	0.2	0.1	0.1	0.1	0.2	0.2	0.1	0.2
CEPGL	0.3	0.1	0.0	0.0	0.0	0.0	0.0	0.0	0.0	0.0
COMESA	1.6	0.6	0.4	0.4	0.3	0.3	0.4	0.4	0.4	0.4
Cross Border Initiative	0.8	0.3	0.2	0.2	0.2	0.1	0.2	0.2	0.2	0.2
EAC	0.3	0.1	0.1	0.1	0.1	0.1	0.0	0.1	0.1	0.1
ECCAS	0.6	0.3	0.3	0.2	0.2	0.2	0.3	0.3	0.3	0.3
ECOWAS	1.1	0.4	0.6	0.4	0.4	0.4	0.6	0.5	0.5	0.5
Indian Ocean Commission	0.1	0.1	0.1	0.0	0.0	0.0	0.0	0.0	0.0	0.0
MRU	0.1	0.0	0.1	0.0	0.0	0.0	0.0	0.0	0.0	0.0
SADC	2.2	1.6	1.0	0.8	0.7	0.6	0.6	0.7	0.7	0.7
UDEAC	0.2	0.3	0.2	0.1	0.1	0.1	0.2	0.2	0.1	0.2
UEMOA	0.3	0.3	0.1	0.1	0.1	0.1	0.1	0.1	0.1	0.1
Middle East and Asia										
Arab Common Market	1.7	1.5	1.0	0.4	0.4	0.5	0.7	0.6	0.6	0.6
ASEAN	2.3	3.9	4.3	6.4	6.1	6.3	6.7	6.3	6.3	6.1
Bangkok Agreement	1.8	2.2	3.6	4.8	4.8	5.0	5.2	4.9	5.1	5.1
EAEG	11.3	15.1	20.9	26.1	24.2	24.7	26.0	24.4	25.1	25.4
ECO	1.5	1.2	1.1	1.2	1.1	1.2	1.3	1.3	1.3	1.5
GAFTA	3.0	10.3	3.8	2.6	2.3	2.7	3.5	3.4	3.3	3.4
GCC	1.9	8.5	2.5	2.0	1.7	1.9	2.6	2.5	2.4	2.5
SAARC	1.1	0.7	0.8	0.9	0.9	1.0	1.0	1.1	1.1	1.1
UMA	1.5	2.3	1.0	0.6	0.5	0.6	0.7	0.7	0.7	0.8

About the data

Trade blocs are groups of countries that have established special preferential arrangements governing trade between members. Although in some cases the preferences—such as lower tariff duties or exemptions from quantitative restrictions—may be no greater than those available to other trading partners, such arrangements are intended to encourage exports by bloc members to one another—sometimes called intratrade.

Most countries are members of a regional trade bloc, and more than a third of the world's trade takes place within such arrangements. While trade blocs vary widely in structure, they all have the same main objective: to reduce trade barriers between member countries. But effective integration requires more than reducing tariffs and quotas. Economic gains from competition and scale may not be achieved unless other barriers that divide markets and impede the free flow of goods, services, and investments are lifted. For example, many regional trade blocs retain contingent protections or restrictions on intrabloc trade. These include antidumping, countervailing duties, and "emergency protection" to address balance of payments problems or to protect an industry from surges in imports. Other barriers include differing product standards, discrimination in public procurement, and cumbersome and costly border formalities.

Membership in a regional trade bloc may reduce the frictional costs of trade, increase the credibility of reform initiatives, and strengthen security among partners. But making it work effectively is a challenge for any government. All sectors of an economy may be affected, and some sectors may expand while others contract, so it is important to weigh the potential costs and benefits that membership may bring.

The table shows the value of merchandise intratrade for important regional trade blocs (service exports are excluded) as well as the size of intratrade relative to each bloc's total exports of goods and the share of the bloc's total exports in world exports. Although the Asia Pacific Economic Cooperation (APEC) has no preferential arrangements, it is included in the table because of the volume of trade between its members.

The data on country exports are drawn from the International Monetary Fund's (IMF) Direction of Trade database and should be broadly consistent with those from other sources, such as the United Nations Statistics Division's Commodity Trade (COMTRADE) database. However, trade flows between many developing countries, particularly in Africa,

are not well recorded. Thus the value of intratrade for certain groups may be understated. Data on trade between developing and high-income countries are generally complete.

Membership in the trade blocs shown is based on the most recent information available, from the World Bank Policy Research Report *Trade Blocs* (2000a), from the World Bank's *Global Economic Prospects 2005*, and from consultation with the World Bank's international trade unit. Although bloc exports have been calculated back to 1970 on the basis of current membership, most of the blocs came into existence in later years and their membership may have changed over time. For this reason, and because systems of preferences also change over time, intratrade in earlier years may not have been affected by the same preferences as in recent years. In addition, some countries belong to more than one trade bloc, so shares of world exports exceed 100 percent. Exports of blocs include all commodity trade, which may include items not specified in trade bloc agreements. Differences from previously published estimates may be due to changes in bloc membership or to revisions in the underlying data.

Definitions

• **Merchandise exports within bloc** are the sum of merchandise exports by members of a trade bloc to other members of the bloc. They are shown both in U.S. dollars and as a percentage of total merchandise exports by the bloc. • **Total merchandise exports by bloc** as a share of world exports are the ratio of the bloc's total merchandise exports (within the bloc and to the rest of the world) to total merchandise exports by all economies in the world.

Data sources

Data on merchandise trade flows are published in the IMF's *Direction of Trade Statistics Yearbook* and *Direction of Trade Statistics Quarterly;* the data in the table were calculated using the IMF's Direction of Trade database. The United Nations Conference on Trade and Development (UNCTAD) publishes data on intratrade in its *Handbook of International Trade and Development Statistics.* The information on trade bloc membership is from the World Bank Policy Research Report *Trade Blocs* (2000a), the World Bank's *Global Economic Prospects 2005,* and the World Bank's international trade unit.

	Year	Binding coverage	Simple mean bound rate	All products % Simple mean tariff	All products % Weighted mean tariff	Share of lines with international peaks	Share of lines with specific rates	Ad valorem equivalent of nontariff barriers[a]	Primary products % Simple mean tariff	Primary products % Weighted mean tariff	Manufactured products % Simple mean tariff	Manufactured products % Weighted mean tariff
Albania	1997	..	..	17.0	14.4	56.0	0.0	..	15.7	12.8	17.2	15.2
	2001	100.0	7.0	11.7	11.3	38.0	0.0	0.6	12.1	10.6	11.6	11.6
Algeria	1993	..	..	21.9	15.4	45.8	0.0	..	22.5	8.9	21.7	18.7
	2003	..	..	18.4	12.0	41.2	0.0	1.1	18.5	10.5	18.3	12.5
Angola	2002	100.0	59.2	8.2	8.5	15.9	1.7	..	11.5	14.7	7.5	5.8
Argentina	1992	..	..	14.2	12.7	31.0	0.0	..	8.1	5.8	14.7	13.6
	2004[b]	100.0	31.9	11.9	6.3	36.6	0.0	4.7	8.8	2.5	12.1	7.0
Armenia	2001	100.0	8.5	3.3	2.2	0.0	0.0	..	6.4	3.3	2.9	1.3
Australia	1991[b]	..	..	12.8	9.3	30.6	1.5	..	3.0	1.7	14.1	10.5
	2004[b]	97.1	10.0	5.1	3.8	5.9	2.9	0.6	1.4	0.7	5.6	4.4
Azerbaijan	2002	..	..	10.1	6.2	0.1	6.3	..	11.9	4.8	9.9	7.0
Bangladesh	1989	..	..	106.5	88.4	98.2	1.3	..	79.8	53.6	109.0	109.9
	2004	15.1	161.8	16.5	15.9	44.5	0.0	1.7	16.4	13.1	16.5	17.4
Belarus	1996	..	..	12.2	8.9	30.8	0.0	..	9.4	6.5	12.6	10.5
	2002	..	..	11.5	8.9	17.6	2.2	0.0	11.1	7.1	11.6	10.4
Benin	2001	..	..	14.3	12.7	55.0	0.0	..	15.5	12.9	14.1	12.4
	2004	39.1	28.6	14.3	12.7	55.9	0.0	..	15.4	12.9	14.1	12.5
Bolivia	1993	..	..	9.8	9.4	0.0	0.0	..	10.0	10.0	9.7	9.3
	2004[b]	100.0	40.0	7.7	5.3	0.0	0.0	0.8	7.8	5.1	7.7	5.3
Bosnia and Herzegovina	2001[b]	..	..	5.2	4.9	0.0	0.0	..	3.5	5.3	5.4	4.7
Botswana	2001[b]	89.0	17.3	6.4	1.0	19.3	1.9	..	3.2	0.3	6.8	1.1
Brazil	1989	..	..	43.0	31.9	92.2	0.5	..	31.5	18.6	44.0	37.1
	2004[b]	100.0	31.4	13.2	8.0	38.0	0.0	2.4	9.1	2.0	13.6	10.2
Bulgaria	2001	..	..	8.7	5.6	20.9	1.4	..	16.0	10.2	7.8	4.3
	2004[b]	100.0	24.2	10.3	9.6	24.9	2.4	..	15.2	10.7	9.8	9.3
Burkina Faso	1993	..	..	25.6	21.4	74.2	0.0	..	27.5	23.1	25.4	20.3
	2004	38.9	42.2	13.8	11.4	53.1	0.0	..	14.0	11.3	13.8	11.5
Burundi	2002	20.9	67.6	19.6	14.5	31.8	0.7	..	21.8	10.5	19.3	16.7
Cambodia	2001[b]	..	..	17.0	15.8	31.6	0.0	..	20.5	18.6	16.4	14.6
Cameroon	1994	..	..	19.2	13.8	53.1	0.0	..	23.5	14.7	18.7	13.5
	2002	12.5	79.9	18.3	15.1	50.7	0.0	0.1	21.5	19.1	17.9	14.2
Canada	1989[b]	..	..	9.7	6.1	14.6	3.4	..	4.2	2.6	10.5	6.6
	2003[b]	99.7	5.0	3.9	0.9	6.5	3.6	1.5	1.9	0.4	4.2	1.0
Central African Republic	1995[b]	..	..	17.0	13.6	50.4	0.4	..	18.8	16.0	16.7	13.0
	2002	62.6	36.2	18.9	17.9	54.0	0.0	..	22.6	23.3	18.2	15.4
Chad	1995[b]	..	..	15.7	14.5	42.0	0.0	..	18.8	15.9	15.1	13.2
	2002	12.7	79.9	17.1	14.0	44.9	0.0	..	21.4	24.5	16.7	13.0
Chile	1992[b]	..	..	11.0	11.0	0.0	0.0	..	11.0	11.0	11.0	10.9
	2004[b]	100.0	25.1	4.8	3.7	0.0	0.0	1.0	4.4	1.9	4.9	4.4
China	1992	..	..	40.4	32.1	77.6	0.0	..	36.1	14.1	40.6	35.6
	2004	100.0	10.0	9.8	6.0	16.0	0.0	1.5	10.0	5.6	9.7	6.0
Colombia	1991	..	..	6.0	6.5	1.6	0.0	..	7.0	7.5	5.8	6.0
	2004[b]	100.0	42.8	11.7	9.6	20.5	0.0	3.4	11.3	9.9	11.7	9.4
Congo, Dem. Rep.	2003	100.0	96.1	13.2	12.6	43.7	0.5	..	14.7	12.1	13.0	12.9
Congo, Rep.	1994	..	..	20.9	17.7	62.0	0.0	..	24.1	20.8	20.4	16.1
	2002	15.2	27.5	19.6	17.8	56.2	0.0	..	23.8	22.1	18.9	16.3
Costa Rica	1995[b]	..	..	10.2	8.6	29.4	0.1	..	12.9	10.6	9.9	8.0
	2004[b]	100.0	42.9	6.3	3.8	0.8	0.0	0.2	9.0	5.8	5.9	3.4
Côte d'Ivoire	1993	..	..	24.5	22.2	76.3	0.0	..	26.5	21.6	24.1	22.5
	2004	33.0	11.1	12.9	10.7	46.3	0.0	2.0	14.9	11.5	12.6	10.1
Croatia	2001	..	..	7.8	4.6	18.7	0.1	..	7.4	4.0	7.8	4.7
	2004	100.0	5.8	4.2	3.3	5.6	3.4	..	6.4	4.0	3.8	3.1
Cuba	1993[b]	..	..	13.9	10.8	31.5	0.0	..	12.1	7.2	14.0	12.9
	2004[b]	31.0	21.3	10.7	9.9	11.7	0.0	..	11.1	8.7	10.5	10.4
Czech Republic	1996	..	..	6.4	5.8	5.3	0.0	..	5.8	4.1	6.5	6.2
	2003	100.0	5.0	5.1	4.4	4.7	0.0	1.1	5.5	4.1	5.0	4.3
Dominican Republic	1997	..	..	15.6	13.1	34.4	0.0	..	18.4	10.9	15.1	14.3
	2004	100.0	34.9	9.8	8.8	30.3	0.3	..	12.8	7.1	9.4	9.5
Ecuador	1993	..	..	9.4	8.2	20.4	0.0	..	9.1	6.4	9.3	8.3
	2004[b]	99.9	21.8	11.9	9.0	22.4	0.0	..	10.9	6.6	11.9	9.5
Egypt, Arab Rep.	1995	..	..	24.4	16.7	53.1	1.2	..	26.0	7.7	24.1	22.2
	2002	98.9	37.1	19.1	13.7	46.9	6.8	0.1	18.3	7.7	19.1	16.7
El Salvador	1995	..	..	10.2	9.1	27.3	0.0	..	12.8	10.2	9.8	8.7
	2004[b]	100.0	36.6	6.0	4.3	8.8	0.0	6.9	6.9	3.7	5.8	4.5
Estonia	1995	..	..	0.1	0.4	0.1	0.0	..	0.0	0.0	0.1	0.5
	2003	100.0	8.6	0.9	0.9	5.2	0.0	..	8.0	4.0	0.0	0.0
Ethiopia	1995	..	..	32.3	17.5	70.7	0.2	..	36.0	18.3	32.0	17.2
	2002	..	..	20.8	13.5	57.0	0.2	0.0	22.6	6.7	20.6	15.7
European Union	1988[b]	..	..	3.1	3.7	4.0	12.5	..	5.8	2.7	2.5	4.3
	2003[b]	100.0	3.9	1.4	1.3	1.9	10.6	1.5	2.2	0.9	1.2	1.4
Gabon	1995	..	..	20.6	16.4	61.3	0.0	..	24.4	20.4	19.9	15.2
	2002	100.0	21.4	20.2	14.9	59.8	0.0	0.2	24.0	20.3	19.5	13.1
Georgia	1999	..	..	9.9	10.1	0.0	1.0	..	11.9	12.0	9.5	8.3
	2004	100.0	7.1	7.1	8.7	4.8	1.8	..	12.0	12.7	6.3	6.3
Ghana	1993	..	..	14.4	9.8	40.5	0.0	..	19.4	13.3	13.8	9.2
	2004	14.3	92.1	12.3	14.8	40.0	0.3	0.1	18.0	27.3	11.5	9.6
Guatemala	1995	..	..	9.9	8.7	25.3	0.0	..	12.6	10.2	9.4	8.0
	2004[b]	34.9	36.4	5.4	4.9	1.3	0.0	0.0	7.4	5.1	5.2	4.8

	Year	Binding coverage	Simple mean bound rate	All products %					Primary products %		Manufactured products %	
				Simple mean tariff	Weighted mean tariff	Share of lines with international peaks	Share of lines with specific rates	Ad valorem equivalent of nontariff barriers[a]	Simple mean tariff	Weighted mean tariff	Simple mean tariff	Weighted mean tariff
Guinea-Bissau	2001	..	..	14.0	14.2	54.3	0.0	..	16.9	18.6	13.4	12.4
	2004	97.7	48.7	14.1	13.6	56.1	0.0	..	16.6	14.6	13.6	12.9
Honduras	1995	..	..	9.7	8.9	25.2	0.0	..	13.1	12.9	9.2	7.6
	2004[b]	100.0	32.5	4.3	7.8	0.5	0.0	0.0	5.6	6.8	4.1	8.0
Hungary	1991[b]	..	..	12.4	10.1	19.0	0.0	..	13.4	5.5	12.1	11.7
	2002	96.2	9.8	8.9	7.9	10.9	0.0	1.0	17.9	6.7	7.7	8.0
India	1990	..	..	79.0	56.1	97.0	0.9	..	69.8	34.1	79.9	70.8
	2004[b]	73.8	46.1	28.3	28.0	92.4	0.0	3.2	30.0	36.9	27.9	25.3
Indonesia	1989	..	..	19.2	13.0	50.3	0.3	..	18.2	5.9	19.2	15.1
	2003[b]	96.6	37.5	6.4	5.2	3.5	0.2	0.5	8.0	3.1	6.1	5.8
Iran, Islamic Rep.	2000	..	..	37.5	22.7	65.0	0.0	..	23.9	6.6	38.2	28.6
	2004	..	..	17.8	14.8	42.1	0.5	..	14.3	13.6	18.0	15.0
Israel	1993[b]	76.3	18.8	7.9	4.2	15.2	0.0	..	4.6	2.5	8.2	4.3
Jamaica	1996	..	..	21.2	17.9	44.0	41.2	..	23.7	14.2	20.7	20.9
	2003	100.0	49.8	9.5	9.8	37.6	0.4	..	15.6	11.0	8.6	9.3
Japan	1988[b]	..	..	4.2	3.6	8.5	12.9	..	8.3	4.4	3.5	2.7
	2004[b]	99.6	2.7	2.9	2.4	8.1	2.8	1.6	5.3	3.9	2.4	1.6
Jordan	2000	..	..	24.0	18.9	63.5	0.4	..	28.0	16.9	23.4	19.8
	2003	100.0	16.2	14.5	11.4	41.0	0.2	10.2	20.2	11.9	13.6	11.0
Kazakhstan	1996	..	..	10.0	8.4	26.5	0.0	..	10.6	8.2	9.7	8.5
Kenya	1994[b]	..	..	32.0	21.4	87.1	1.2	..	32.3	16.7	31.9	23.3
	2004	14.0	95.1	17.2	10.3	41.8	0.1	0.3	21.2	10.8	16.7	10.0
Korea, Rep.	1988	..	..	18.6	14.0	72.8	10.3	..	19.3	8.3	18.6	17.0
	2002	94.4	15.5	9.5	10.0	5.3	0.5	0.0	20.9	19.0	7.8	5.0
Kuwait	2002	100.0	100.0	3.5	3.9	0.1	1.4	..	1.5	3.7	4.0	4.0
Kyrgyz Republic	1995	..	..	0.0	0.0	0.0	19.8	..	0.0	0.0	0.0	0.0
	2003	99.9	7.4	4.3	4.3	0.1	2.1	..	6.6	6.1	3.9	2.9
Lao PDR	2000	..	..	9.3	13.5	11.3	2.0	..	15.6	14.7	8.6	12.6
	2001[b]	..	..	9.5	13.5	12.2	0.0	..	15.9	17.3	8.8	11.8
Latvia	1996	..	..	3.8	2.2	2.2	0.0	..	6.5	1.5	3.3	2.6
	2001	100.0	12.7	3.4	2.6	2.9	0.0	0.4	8.1	5.5	2.7	1.5
Lebanon	1999	..	..	14.4	12.3	29.7	0.1	..	13.1	11.2	14.4	12.8
	2002[b]	..	..	7.5	6.3	13.0	0.4	..	14.8	6.1	6.4	6.4
Libya	1996	..	..	23.0	21.3	58.3	1.4	..	24.9	9.6	22.5	25.6
	2002	..	..	20.0	25.2	46.6	2.0	..	19.2	15.0	19.9	28.6
Lithuania	1995[b]	..	..	3.1	2.6	6.9	0.0	..	6.2	3.7	2.6	1.8
	2003[b]	100.0	9.2	1.3	0.6	3.1	0.0	..	3.3	1.2	1.0	0.4
Macedonia, FYR	2001[b]	..	..	10.2	9.3	29.4	0.0	..	12.0	10.6	9.9	8.4
	2004	..	..	10.9	8.1	28.3	3.0	..	12.3	8.5	10.7	7.8
Madagascar	1995	..	..	7.6	5.2	5.9	0.0	..	6.3	2.9	7.6	6.3
	2001	29.7	27.4	5.4	3.6	4.7	0.0	0.6	5.8	1.7	5.3	4.6
Malawi	1994	..	..	31.6	22.3	87.0	0.0	..	29.1	12.9	31.9	26.6
	2001[b]	29.7	75.5	13.3	10.2	41.8	0.0	..	12.7	9.0	13.4	10.7
Malaysia	1988[b]	..	..	14.5	9.7	46.1	7.2	..	10.9	4.6	14.9	10.8
	2003[b]	83.7	14.0	7.3	4.2	21.1	1.0	1.7	4.5	2.1	7.8	4.6
Mali	1995	..	..	16.3	10.3	41.6	0.0	..	19.3	13.4	16.0	8.5
	2004	40.7	29.3	13.1	10.6	47.7	0.0	..	15.7	11.5	12.7	10.3
Mauritania	2001	39.4	19.6	12.0	11.2	45.1	0.0	..	12.8	9.3	11.8	12.4
Mauritius	1995[b]	..	..	36.2	23.8	64.7	0.0	..	26.0	25.9	37.2	22.9
	2002	18.0	94.0	25.4	13.0	42.2	0.1	0.0	20.0	9.9	25.8	14.4
Mexico	1991	..	..	14.5	11.9	20.7	0.0	..	13.4	8.3	14.6	13.0
	2004[b]	100.0	34.7	16.8	13.8	43.6	0.0	1.8	17.0	20.3	16.7	12.8
Moldova	1996	..	..	6.0	1.9	22.9	0.7	..	11.3	1.5	4.7	2.3
	2001	..	..	5.1	2.8	0.1	0.7	..	8.9	2.6	4.5	2.9
Morocco	1993	..	..	64.4	45.4	96.8	0.1	..	55.0	30.2	65.0	55.2
	2003	100.0	41.2	28.9	24.9	75.8	0.0	0.5	33.7	25.4	28.4	24.6
Mozambique	1994	..	..	5.0	5.0	0.0	0.0	..	5.0	5.0	5.0	5.0
	2003[b]	100.0	99.6	12.9	9.9	37.8	0.0	..	15.8	9.9	12.3	9.9
Myanmar	2001[b]	..	..	4.7	4.8	3.7	0.0	..	8.0	5.1	4.3	4.7
	2003[b]	16.5	82.8	4.8	3.9	3.9	0.0	..	8.7	4.9	4.1	3.4
Namibia	2001[b]	88.9	17.4	6.5	0.5	19.1	2.9	..	5.4	0.4	6.6	0.6
Nepal	1993[b]	..	..	21.8	17.5	59.2	1.0	..	11.8	9.3	22.9	21.0
	2004	..	..	14.5	15.6	20.4	1.4	..	15.4	14.0	14.2	15.6
New Zealand	1992	..	..	10.2	8.5	36.0	2.8	..	5.5	4.0	10.7	9.4
	2004[b]	99.9	9.7	3.8	2.9	7.5	6.1	2.2	1.7	0.5	4.1	3.5
Nicaragua	1995[b]	..	..	7.5	5.6	20.4	0.0	..	7.7	7.1	7.4	4.6
	2004[b]	100.0	41.7	5.4	3.7	0.7	0.0	..	7.6	4.0	5.1	3.6
Niger	2001	..	..	14.4	12.9	55.8	0.0	..	15.1	12.9	14.3	12.8
	2004	96.8	44.6	12.9	13.7	49.0	0.0	..	15.5	15.9	12.6	12.9
Nigeria	1988	..	..	26.0	23.8	62.9	0.4	..	33.4	32.3	25.3	21.4
	2002	19.3	118.0	26.7	16.9	54.7	1.0	0.4	40.1	20.6	24.9	15.5
Norway	1988[b]	..	..	1.9	0.7	5.0	7.9	..	0.6	0.2	2.1	0.8
	2003[b]	100.0	2.7	0.5	0.4	0.5	5.6	0.3	1.6	1.4	0.4	0.2
Oman	1992	..	..	5.5	7.5	1.5	0.0	..	7.2	14.2	5.1	5.4
	2002	100.0	13.8	8.0	13.6	0.7	2.6	0.9	9.5	31.6	7.6	6.5
Pakistan	1995[b]	..	..	50.1	44.4	90.1	5.1	..	40.5	36.1	51.3	49.2
	2004	44.8	52.2	15.9	13.0	49.7	0.1	..	13.9	8.9	16.1	15.7

	Year	Binding coverage	Simple mean bound rate	All products % Simple mean tariff	Weighted mean tariff	Share of lines with international peaks	Share of lines with specific rates	Ad valorem equivalent of nontariff barriers[a]	Primary products % Simple mean tariff	Weighted mean tariff	Manufactured products % Simple mean tariff	Weighted mean tariff
Panama	1997	..	..	12.5	10.6	36.4	0.4	..	17.9	9.6	11.8	11.0
	2001	..	..	8.1	6.9	1.1	0.2	..	11.4	5.9	7.7	7.4
Papua New Guinea	1997	..	..	21.1	15.3	36.3	2.1	..	36.4	18.7	18.9	13.1
	2004	100.0	31.6	6.4	2.2	26.2	0.7	..	15.4	3.3	5.1	1.7
Paraguay	1991	..	..	15.7	11.9	41.8	0.0	..	14.1	3.6	15.7	14.5
	2004[b]	100.0	33.6	6.7	5.2	20.1	0.0	1.7	5.1	1.9	6.9	6.1
Peru	1993	..	..	18.1	16.4	25.4	0.0	..	18.3	15.8	18.0	16.6
	2004[b]	100.0	30.1	9.8	8.9	10.8	0.0	1.7	11.3	9.7	9.6	8.4
Philippines	1988	..	..	28.3	22.4	77.1	0.1	..	29.9	18.5	27.9	23.4
	2003	66.8	25.3	4.5	2.6	1.6	0.0	0.4	5.7	5.0	4.2	2.0
Poland	1991	..	..	12.3	10.4	24.8	0.0	..	12.2	8.2	12.2	11.2
	2003[b]	96.2	11.3	3.4	1.7	6.4	7.4	1.2	10.9	3.7	2.4	1.2
Romania	1991	..	..	19.2	11.9	55.7	0.0	..	20.0	8.1	18.9	17.9
	2001[b]	100.0	40.4	11.4	8.3	28.7	0.0	2.5	17.8	11.4	10.5	7.3
Russian Federation	1993	..	..	8.4	6.3	3.2	0.0	..	3.1	3.9	9.5	7.4
	2002	..	..	10.4	8.7	8.4	19.0	..	9.7	8.2	10.5	8.9
Rwanda	1993	..	..	40.4	25.3	65.1	1.9	..	60.7	24.9	37.4	25.5
	2003[b]	100.0	89.1	8.7	6.6	11.6	0.0	1.4	12.2	6.4	8.3	6.6
Saudi Arabia	1994	..	..	12.3	10.9	10.2	0.1	..	12.0	9.1	12.4	11.5
	2004	..	..	6.6	7.3	10.9	0.3	0.9	5.9	10.5	6.7	6.6
Senegal	2001	..	..	13.9	9.4	53.0	0.0	..	14.5	8.3	13.8	10.4
	2004	100.0	30.0	13.9	9.2	53.5	0.0	0.0	14.8	8.1	13.8	10.5
Serbia and Montenegro	2001[b]	..	..	9.0	5.8	26.3	0.0	..	10.2	6.0	8.8	5.7
	2002	..	..	10.4	7.9	23.0	0.0	..	13.1	7.6	10.0	7.9
Singapore	1989	..	..	0.4	1.1	0.3	1.6	..	0.2	2.5	0.4	0.6
	2003[b]	69.8	6.9	0.0	0.0	0.0	0.2	0.5	0.0	0.0	0.0	0.0
Slovak Republic	2002	100.0	5.0	22.2	21.2	51.3	0.0	..	19.3	12.8	22.5	23.6
Slovenia	1999	..	..	11.5	11.4	20.8	3.1	..	9.5	7.5	11.7	12.1
	2003[b]	100.0	23.3	4.3	1.6	11.3	1.6	0.6	6.5	3.3	4.0	1.1
South Africa	1988[c]	..	..	11.5	12.0	32.3	18.8	..	4.8	3.6	11.8	12.3
	2001[b]	88.9	17.4	9.4	5.6	32.5	2.2	0.5	7.5	3.9	9.5	5.8
Sri Lanka	1990	..	..	27.4	27.0	51.7	1.4	..	32.4	32.3	26.6	24.2
	2004[b]	36.8	29.2	10.2	6.8	24.1	0.7	0.0	15.4	9.2	9.6	5.7
Sudan	1996[b]	..	..	5.0	3.7	8.3	0.0	..	12.0	3.3	4.4	3.9
	2002	..	..	21.5	19.6	44.9	0.0	..	28.8	24.0	20.8	18.9
Swaziland	2001	88.9	17.4	3.5	0.6	12.1	1.3	..	1.7	0.1	3.8	0.9
Sweden	1988[b]	..	..	1.7	1.0	1.7	0.9	..	0.9	0.6	1.8	1.1
	1989	..	..	5.4	4.3	3.6	2.2	..	1.4	1.0	6.0	5.0
Switzerland[d]	1990	..	..	..	..	..	53.3	..	..	..	..	..
	2001	99.8	1.7	3.2	1.5	..	37.7	1.2	15.0	9.5	1.1	0.2
Syrian Arab Republic	2002	..	..	14.7	15.5	23.2	0.1	..	14.4	11.7	14.5	16.6
Tajikistan	2002	..	..	8.0	7.1	9.5	2.1	..	9.9	6.7	7.8	7.5
Tanzania	1993	..	..	16.0	15.6	43.3	0.0	..	22.7	19.9	15.3	15.0
	2003[b]	13.4	120.0	15.2	8.2	42.3	0.0	0.0	16.7	7.4	15.0	8.7
Thailand	1989	..	..	38.5	33.0	72.8	22.0	..	30.0	24.3	39.0	35.0
	2003[b]	75.0	19.2	14.0	8.3	48.0	0.8	0.3	16.4	4.4	13.5	9.3
Togo	2001	..	..	14.3	10.9	52.9	0.0	..	14.7	10.5	14.2	11.2
	2004	13.2	80.0	13.6	14.0	51.9	0.0	..	16.3	13.6	13.2	14.2
Trinidad and Tobago	1991[b]	..	..	19.0	13.4	40.5	0.0	..	25.6	10.1	17.9	15.7
	2003	100.0	55.7	10.1	4.9	38.0	0.0	0.2	15.1	4.0	9.4	5.5
Tunisia	1990	..	..	28.1	25.8	97.0	0.0	..	25.1	17.4	28.3	28.4
	2004	57.8	57.7	25.6	23.2	65.7	0.0	0.8	36.8	21.8	24.5	23.5
Turkey	1993[b]	..	..	7.3	6.1	5.9	0.0	..	6.3	7.9	7.4	5.3
	2003[b]	50.0	28.6	2.6	2.0	4.5	1.2	0.2	11.6	3.5	1.7	1.5
Turkmenistan	1998	..	..	0.0	0.0	0.0	0.0	..	0.0	0.0	0.0	0.0
	2002	..	..	5.3	2.9	14.8	2.9	..	16.0	13.2	3.7	1.1
Uganda	1994[b]	..	..	17.0	13.6	52.8	0.0	..	19.3	17.4	16.7	12.3
	2004[b]	14.9	73.5	7.3	5.5	0.0	0.0	0.1	9.6	5.7	7.0	5.3
Ukraine	1995	..	..	7.6	3.4	10.5	0.0	..	8.9	2.7	7.3	4.3
	2002	..	..	7.9	3.9	11.4	10.2	0.0	7.1	1.5	7.9	6.4
United States	1989[b]	..	..	5.1	3.8	8.0	12.7	..	2.5	2.0	5.5	4.0
	2004[b]	100.0	3.0	3.2	1.8	4.0	6.8	1.6	2.7	1.1	3.3	1.9
Uruguay	1992	..	..	7.1	5.8	0.0	0.0	..	7.9	5.8	7.0	5.8
	2004[b]	100.0	31.7	11.4	4.3	36.2	0.0	1.9	7.2	1.8	11.7	6.1
Uzbekistan	2001	..	..	10.6	5.9	27.2	0.0	..	10.8	4.6	10.7	6.2
Venezuela, RB	1992	..	..	17.2	16.4	47.4	1.0	..	16.3	14.7	17.1	16.5
	2004[b]	99.9	36.8	12.6	11.0	23.1	0.0	1.4	12.7	11.8	12.5	10.7
Vietnam	1994	..	..	14.8	20.6	32.6	1.0	..	20.9	46.7	13.9	13.1
	2004[b]	..	..	13.7	13.7	33.9	0.2	..	18.1	16.7	12.9	12.5
Yemen, Rep.	2000	..	..	13.0	11.7	11.4	0.0	..	14.3	9.8	12.8	12.9
Zambia	1993	..	..	25.9	17.9	90.9	0.0	..	30.0	12.4	25.2	20.0
	2003[b]	15.9	105.6	14.2	9.4	34.6	0.0	0.2	14.1	9.8	14.2	9.2
Zimbabwe	1996[b]	..	..	40.8	38.5	94.2	1.5	..	34.2	35.6	41.2	38.8
	2002	20.8	88.6	16.7	18.9	38.1	6.0	..	19.6	24.3	16.2	17.1

a. Ad valorem equivalents of nontariff barriers are calculated for 2000 only. b. Rates are either partially or fully recorded applied rates. All other simple and weighted tariff rates are most favored nation rates. c. Data for 1988 refer to South African Customs Union (Botswana, Lesotho, Namibia, South Africa, and Swaziland). d. Data for Switzerland include all specific rates converted to their ad valorem equivalents.

Poor people in developing countries work primarily in agriculture and labor-intensive manufactures, sectors that confront the greatest trade barriers. Removing barriers to merchandise trade could increase growth by about 0.9 percent a year in these countries—even more if trade in services (retailing, business, financial, and telecommunications services) were also liberalized.

In general, tariffs in high-income countries on imports from developing countries, though low, are four times those collected from other high-income countries. But protection is also an issue for developing countries, which maintain high tariffs on agricultural commodities, labor-intensive manufactures, and other products and services. In some developing regions new trade policies could make the difference between achieving important Millennium Development Goals—reducing poverty, lowering maternal and child mortality rates, improving educational attainment—and falling far short.

Countries use a combination of tariff and nontariff measures to regulate imports. The most common form of tariff is an ad valorem duty, based on the value of the import, but tariffs may also be levied on a specific, or per unit, basis or may combine ad valorem and specific rates. Tariffs may be used to raise fiscal revenues or to protect domestic industries from foreign competition—or both. Nontariff barriers, which limit the quantity of imports of a particular good, include quotas, prohibitions, licensing schemes, export restraint arrangements, and health and quarantine measures.

Nontariff barriers are generally considered less desirable than tariffs because changes in an exporting country's efficiency and costs no longer result in changes in market share in the importing country. Further, the quotas or licenses that regulate trade become very valuable, and resources are often wasted in attempts to acquire these assets. A high percentage of products subject to nontariff barriers suggests a protectionist trade regime, but the frequency of nontariff barriers does not measure how much they restrict trade. Moreover, a wide range of domestic policies and regulations (such as health regulations) may act as nontariff barriers.

Estimates of ad valorem equivalents of nontariff barriers are given at the six-digit level of the Harmonized System, which provides the simple averages of core nontariff barriers, including quantity control measures such as nonautomatic licensing, quotas, prohibitions, and export restraint arrangements but excluding tariff-quotas and enterprise-specific restrictions; financial measures, which include advance payment requirements, multiple exchange rates, and restrictive official foreign exchange allocation and exclude regulations on terms of payment, transfer delays, and queuing; and price control measures, which affect the cost of imports based on differences between domestic prices and foreign prices. They include administrative price fixing, voluntary export price restraints, variable charges, anti-dumping measures, and countervailing measures.

Countries typically maintain a hierarchy of trade preferences applicable to specific trading partners. The tariff rates used in calculating the indicators in the table are most favored nation rates unless they are specified as applied rates. Effectively applied rates are those in effect for partners in preferential trade agreements such as the North American Free Trade Agreement. The difference between most favored nation and applied rates can be substantial. As more countries report their free trade agreements, suspensions of tariffs, or other special preferences, *World Development Indicators* will include their effectively applied rates.

Three measures of average tariffs are shown: the simple and the weighted mean rates and simple bound rates. The most favored nation or applied rates are calculated using all traded items, while bound rates are based on all products in a country's tariff schedule. Weighted mean tariffs are weighted by the value of the country's trade with each trading partner. Simple averages are often a better indicator of tariff protection than weighted averages, which are biased downward because higher tariffs discourage trade and reduce the weights applied to these tariffs. Bound rates have resulted from trade negotiations that are incorporated into a country's schedule of concessions and are thus enforceable. If a contracting party raises a tariff to a higher level than its bound rate, beneficiaries of the earlier binding have a right to receive compensation, usually as reduced tariffs on other products they export to the country. If the beneficiaries are not compensated, they may retaliate by raising their own tariffs against an equivalent value of the original country's exports. Specific duties (not expressed as a proportion of declared value) are not included in the table, except for Switzerland. Work is under way to complete the estimations for ad valorem equivalents of specific duties for all countries.

Some countries set fairly uniform tariff rates across all imports. Others are more selective, setting high tariffs to protect favored domestic industries. The standard deviation of tariffs is a measure of the dispersion of tariff rates around their mean value. Highly dispersed rates increase the costs of protection substantially. But these nominal tariff rates tell only part of the story. The effective rate of protection—the degree to which the value added in an industry is protected—may exceed the nominal rate if the tariff system systematically differentiates among imports of raw materials, intermediate products, and finished goods.

Two other measures of tariff coverage are shown: the share of tariff lines with international peaks (those for which ad valorem tariff rates exceed 15 percent) and the share of tariff lines with specific duties (those not covered by ad valorem rates). Some countries—for example, Switzerland—apply only specific duties.

The indicators were calculated from data supplied by the United Nations Conference on Trade and Development (UNCTAD) and the World Trade Organization (WTO). Data are classified using the Harmonized System of trade at the six- or eight-digit level. Tariff line data were matched to Standard International Trade Classification (SITC) revision 2 codes to define commodity groups and import weights. Import weights were calculated using the United Nations Statistics Division's Commodity Trade (COMTRADE) database. Data are shown only for the first and last year for which complete data are available. To conserve space, data for the European Union are shown instead of data for individual members.

• **Primary products** are commodities classified in SITC revision 2 sections 0–4 plus division 68 (nonferrous metals). • **Manufactured products** are commodities classified in SITC revision 2 sections 5–8 excluding division 68. • **Binding coverage** is the percentage of product lines with an agreed bound rate. • **Simple mean bound rate** is the unweighted average of all the lines in the tariff schedule in which bound rates have been set. • **Simple mean tariff** is the unweighted average of effectively applied rates or most favored nation rates for all products subject to tariffs calculated for all traded goods. • **Weighted mean tariff** is the average of effectively applied rates or most favored nation rates weighted by the product import shares corresponding to each partner country. • **Share of lines with international peaks** is the share of lines in the tariff schedule with tariff rates that exceed 15 percent. • **Share of lines with specific rates** is the share of lines in the tariff schedule that are set on a per unit basis or that combine ad valorem and per unit rates. • **Ad valorem equivalent of nontariff barriers** are the simple average of core nontariff barriers transformed into a price effect using import demand elasticities; they are calculated for traded products only.

All indicators in the table were calculated by World Bank staff using the World Integrated Trade Solution (WITS) system. Tariff data were provided by UNCTAD and the WTO. Data on global imports come from the United Nations Statistics Division's COMTRADE database.

	Net private capital flows		Foreign direct investment		Portfolio investment flows				Bank and trade-related lending	
					Bonds		Equity			
	$ millions		$ millions		$ millions				$ millions	
	1990	2003	1990	2003	1990	2003	1990	2003	1990	2003
Afghanistan	0	..	0	..	0	..	0	..	0	..
Albania	..	176	0	178	..	0	0	0	..	−3
Algeria	−424	593	0	634	−16	0	0	0	−409	−41
Angola	235	1,903	−335	1,415	0	0	0	0	570	488
Argentina	−216	1,169	1,836	1,020	−857	−18	0	65	−1,195	100
Armenia	..	115	0	121	..	0	0	0	..	−6
Australia	..	..	8,111	6,851	..	..	..	..	..	..
Austria	..	..	653	7,276	..	..	..	..	..	..
Azerbaijan	..	3,235	0	3,285	..	0	0	0	..	−50
Bangladesh	59	86	3	102	0	0	0	2	55	−18
Belarus	..	127	0	172	..	0	0	3	..	−48
Belgium	..	..	8,047[a]	125,060	..	..	..	..	..	..
Benin	62	51	62	51	0	0	0	0	0	0
Bolivia	3	295	27	167	0	0	0	0	−24	128
Bosnia and Herzegovina	..	400	0	382	..	0	0	0	..	18
Botswana	77	84	96	86	0	0	0	0	−19	−2
Brazil	666	13,432	989	10,144	129	8,339	103	2,973	−555	−8,023
Bulgaria	..	1,655	0	1,419	..	−50	0	−26	..	311
Burkina Faso	0	11	0	11	0	0	0	0	−1	0
Burundi	−5	8	1	0	0	0	0	0	−6	8
Cambodia	0	87	0	87	0	0	0	0	0	0
Cameroon	−124	154	−113	215	0	0	0	0	−12	−61
Canada	..	..	7,581	6,273	..	..	..	..	..	..
Central African Republic	0	4	1	4	0	0	0	0	−1	0
Chad	9	837	9	837	0	0	0	0	−1	0
Chile	2,216	3,844	661	2,982	−7	3,328	367	312	1,194	−2,778
China	8,107	59,455	3,487	53,505	−48	675	0	7,729	4,668	−2,454
Hong Kong, China	..	..	..	13,538	..	..	..	..	..	..
Colombia	345	−1,185	500	1,746	−4	−569	0	−52	−151	−2,310
Congo, Dem. Rep.	−27	187	−15	158	0	0	0	0	−12	29
Congo, Rep.	−77	201	23	201	0	0	0	0	−100	0
Costa Rica	22	842	163	577	−42	204	0	0	−99	61
Côte d'Ivoire	57	69	48	180	−1	0	0	4	10	−115
Croatia	..	8,031	0	1,998	..	480	0	15	..	5,538
Cuba	789	..	1	..	0	..	0	..	788	..
Czech Republic	..	5,342	0	2,514	..	−91	0	1,104	..	1,815
Denmark	..	..	1,132	1,185	..	..	..	..	..	..
Dominican Republic	129	1,112	133	310	0	580	0	0	−3	222
Ecuador	184	2,143	126	1,555	0	0	0	9	58	579
Egypt, Arab Rep.	668	−361	734	237	−1	0	0	37	−65	−635
El Salvador	7	406	2	89	0	349	0	0	6	−32
Eritrea	..	22	0	22	..	0	0	0	..	0
Estonia	..	2,170	0	891	..	73	0	108	..	1,099
Ethiopia	−45	54	12	60	0	0	0	0	−57	−6
Finland	..	..	812	3,436	..	..	..	..	..	..
France	..	..	13,183	47,753	..	..	..	..	..	..
Gabon	103	−20	74	53	0	0	0	0	29	−73
Gambia, The	−8	60	0	60	0	0	0	0	−8	0
Georgia	..	320	0	338	..	0	0	0	..	−18
Germany	..	..	3,005	11,267	..	..	..	..	..	..
Ghana	−5	−166	15	137	0	−250	0	0	−20	−53
Greece	..	..	1,005	717	..	..	..	..	..	..
Guatemala	44	68	48	116	−11	−32	0	0	7	−16
Guinea	−1	79	18	79	0	0	0	0	−19	0
Guinea-Bissau	2	2	2	2	0	0	0	0	0	0
Haiti	0	8	0	8	0	0	0	0	0	0

	Net private capital flows $ millions		Foreign direct investment $ millions		Portfolio investment flows $ millions Bonds		Equity		Bank and trade-related lending $ millions	
	1990	2003	1990	2003	1990	2003	1990	2003	1990	2003
Honduras	75	140	44	198	0	0	0	0	32	−58
Hungary	−147	5,149	311	2,506	921	−1,066	0	266	−1,379	3,442
India	1,842	10,651	237	4,269	147	−2,944	0	8,237	1,458	1,089
Indonesia	2,923	−3,685	1,093	−597	26	600	0	1,130	1,804	−4,819
Iran, Islamic Rep.	−392	1,151	−362	120	0	0	0	0	−30	1,031
Iraq	−1,740	..	0	..	0	..	0	..	−1,740	..
Ireland	..	..	627	26,599	..	..	..	..	..	..
Israel	..	..	151	3,672	..	..	..	..	..	..
Italy	..	..	6,411	16,538	..	..	..	..	..	..
Jamaica	92	513	138	721	0	−176	0	0	−46	−32
Japan	..	..	1,777	6,238	..	..	..	..	..	..
Jordan	252	−161	38	376	0	−467	0	−58	214	−12
Kazakhstan	..	5,674	0	2,088	..	725	0	64	..	2,797
Kenya	122	195	57	82	0	0	0	1	65	113
Korea, Dem. Rep.	17	..	0	..	0	..	0	..	17	..
Korea, Rep.	..	..	788	3,222	..	..	..	..	..	..
Kuwait	..	..	0	−67	..	..	..	..	..	..
Kyrgyz Republic	..	−12	0	46	..	0	0	0	..	−58
Lao PDR	6	19	6	19	0	0	0	0	0	0
Latvia	..	570	0	300	..	0	0	39	..	231
Lebanon	13	394	6	358	0	108	0	3	6	−75
Lesotho	17	36	17	42	0	0	0	0	0	−6
Liberia	0	0	0	0	0	0	0	0	0	0
Libya	165	..	159	..	0	..	0	..	6	..
Lithuania	..	−141	0	179	..	−741	0	4	..	417
Macedonia, FYR	..	90	0	95	..	0	0	1	..	−5
Madagascar	7	13	22	13	0	0	0	0	−15	0
Malawi	26	23	23	23	0	0	1	0	2	0
Malaysia	476	2,207	2,332	2,473	−1,239	841	0	1,340	−617	−2,447
Mali	5	129	6	129	0	0	0	0	−1	0
Mauritania	5	218	7	214	0	0	0	0	−1	4
Mauritius	86	88	41	63	0	0	0	8	45	18
Mexico	9,600	9,541	2,549	10,783	661	−1,233	1,995	−123	4,396	113
Moldova	..	84	0	58	..	−2	0	1	..	26
Mongolia	..	131	0	132	..	0	0	0	..	0
Morocco	483	2,395	165	2,279	0	416	0	8	318	−307
Mozambique	35	313	9	337	0	0	0	0	26	−24
Myanmar	155	98	163	134	0	0	0	0	−8	−35
Namibia	30	..	30	..	0	..	0	..	0	..
Nepal	−14	14	0	15	0	0	0	0	−14	0
Netherlands	..	..	10,676	15,695	..	..	..	..	..	..
New Zealand	..	..	1,735	2,438	..	..	..	..	..	..
Nicaragua	20	230	0	201	0	0	0	0	20	28
Niger	51	23	41	31	0	0	0	0	10	−8
Nigeria	467	952	588	1,200	0	0	0	0	−121	−248
Norway	..	..	1,003	2,055	..	..	..	..	..	..
Oman	−257	−557	142	138	0	0	0	96	−400	−791
Pakistan	182	132	245	534	0	−120	0	−26	−63	−256
Panama	129	1,077	136	792	−2	133	−1	0	−4	153
Papua New Guinea	204	2	155	101	0	0	0	0	49	−99
Paraguay	68	121	77	91	0	0	0	0	−9	30
Peru	59	2,562	41	1,377	0	1,206	0	1	18	−22
Philippines	639	1,350	530	319	395	1,684	0	457	−286	−1,111
Poland	71	7,118	89	4,123	0	3,592	0	−837	−18	240
Portugal	..	..	2,610	969	..	..	..	..	..	..
Puerto Rico	..	..	..	..	..	..	..	..	..	..

6.7 Global private financial flows

	Net private capital flows ($ millions)		Foreign direct investment ($ millions)		Portfolio investment flows ($ millions)				Bank and trade-related lending ($ millions)	
					Bonds		Equity			
	1990	2003	1990	2003	1990	2003	1990	2003	1990	2003
Romania	4	3,880	0	1,844	0	792	0	69	4	1,175
Russian Federation	..	15,784	0	7,958	..	4,422	0	413	..	2,992
Rwanda	6	5	8	5	0	0	0	0	−2	0
Saudi Arabia	1,947	..	1,864	..	−50	..	0	..	133	..
Senegal	43	79	57	78	0	0	1	0	−15	1
Serbia and Montenegro	..	1,462	0	1,360	..	0	0	0	..	102
Sierra Leone	36	3	32	3	0	0	0	0	4	−1
Singapore	..	..	5,575	11,409	..	..	..	..	..	..
Slovak Republic	..	1,525	0	571	..	−125	0	59	..	1,019
Slovenia	..	..	..	337	..	..	..	..	..	..
Somalia	6	1	6	1	0	0	0	0	0	0
South Africa	..	4,148	−76	820	..	4,809	389	685	..	−2,166
Spain	..	..	13,984	25,513	..	..	..	..	..	..
Sri Lanka	54	236	43	229	0	0	0	−14	10	21
Sudan	0	1,349	0	1,349	0	0	0	0	0	0
Swaziland	26	44	30	44	0	0	−2	0	−2	0
Sweden	..	..	1,982	3,268	..	..	..	..	..	..
Switzerland	..	..	5,545	17,547	..	..	..	..	..	..
Syrian Arab Republic	63	146	72	150	0	0	0	0	−9	−4
Tajikistan	..	6	0	32	..	0	0	0	..	−26
Tanzania	5	264	0	248	0	0	0	0	5	16
Thailand	4,370	1,155	2,444	1,949	−87	−1,829	440	1,194	1,574	−159
Togo	23	20	18	20	0	0	4	0	0	0
Trinidad and Tobago	−68	616	109	616	−52	0	0	0	−126	0
Tunisia	−116	1,326	76	541	−60	632	5	14	−137	138
Turkey	1,836	2,849	684	1,562	597	1,137	89	1,009	466	−858
Turkmenistan	..	..	0	100	..	..	0	0	..	..
Uganda	16	202	0	194	0	0	0	1	16	7
Ukraine	..	1,550	0	1,424	..	446	0	−1,705	..	1,385
United Arab Emirates	..	..	..	..	..	..	..	..	..	..
United Kingdom	..	..	33,504	20,696	..	..	..	..	..	..
United States	..	..	48,490	39,889	..	..	..	..	..	..
Uruguay	−192	37	0	275	−16	−82	0	0	−176	−156
Uzbekistan	..	79	0	70	..	0	0	0	..	9
Venezuela, RB	−126	3,539	451	2,520	345	706	0	97	−922	216
Vietnam	180	1,192	180	1,450	0	0	0	0	0	−258
West Bank and Gaza	..	..	..	..	..	..	..	..	..	..
Yemen, Rep.	30	−89	−131	−89	0	0	0	0	161	0
Zambia	194	91	203	100	0	0	0	0	−9	−10
Zimbabwe	85	−5	−12	20	−30	0	0	0	127	−25
World	.. s	.. s	192,682 s	572,774 s	.. s	.. s	.. s	.. s	.. s	.. s
Low income	3,920	21,541	1,693	16,128	116	−3,316	7	8,219	2,104	510
Middle income	38,103	177,903	20,380	135,648	966	29,932	3,383	16,593	13,374	−4,270
Lower middle income	25,208	124,703	11,208	99,552	1,296	23,687	1,022	13,942	11,682	−12,478
Upper middle income	12,894	53,200	9,172	36,096	−330	6,245	2,361	2,651	1,692	8,208
Low & middle income	42,022	199,444	22,073	151,776	1,082	26,616	3,390	24,812	15,478	−3,760
East Asia & Pacific	17,180	62,049	10,512	59,612	−952	1,972	440	11,850	7,180	−11,385
Europe & Central Asia	7,347	67,110	1,084	35,614	1,893	9,592	89	588	4,281	21,315
Latin America & Carib.	13,195	41,087	8,192	36,533	101	12,869	2,464	3,376	2,439	−11,690
Middle East & N. Africa	319	4,848	741	4,756	−76	688	5	100	−350	−696
South Asia	2,129	11,143	536	5,163	147	−3,064	1	8,199	1,446	846
Sub-Saharan Africa	1,851	13,208	1,008	10,099	−31	4,559	393	698	482	−2,149
High income	..	..	170,610	420,998	..	..	..	..	..	..
Europe EMU	..	..	52,966	280,824	..	..	..	..	..	..

a. Includes Luxembourg.

About the data

The data on foreign direct investment are based on balance of payments data reported by the International Monetary Fund (IMF), supplemented by data on net foreign direct investment reported by the Organisation for Economic Co-operation and Development (OECD) and official national sources.

The internationally accepted definition of foreign direct investment is provided in the fifth edition of the IMF's *Balance of Payments Manual* (1993). Under this definition foreign direct investment has three components: equity investment, reinvested earnings, and short- and long-term intercompany loans between parent firms and foreign affiliates. But many countries fail to report reinvested earnings, and the definition of long-term loans differs among countries. Foreign direct investment, as distinguished from other kinds of international investment, is made to establish a lasting interest in or effective management control over an enterprise in another country. As a guideline, the IMF suggests that investments should account for at least 10 percent of voting stock to be counted as foreign direct investment. In practice, many countries set a higher threshold.

The OECD has also published a definition, in consultation with the IMF, Eurostat, and the United Nations. Because of the multiplicity of sources and differences in definitions and reporting methods, there may be more than one estimate of foreign direct investment for a country and data may not be comparable across countries.

Foreign direct investment data do not give a complete picture of international investment in an economy. Balance of payments data on foreign direct investment do not include capital raised locally, which has become an important source of financing for investment projects in some developing countries. In addition, foreign direct investment data capture only cross-border investment flows involving equity participation and thus omit nonequity cross-border transactions such as intrafirm flows of goods and services. For a detailed discussion of the data issues, see the World Bank's *World Debt Tables 1993–94* (volume 1, chapter 3).

Portfolio flow data are compiled from several market and official sources, including Euromoney databases and publications; Micropal; Lipper Analytical Services; published reports of private investment houses, central banks, national securities and exchange commissions, and national stock exchanges; and the World Bank's Debtor Reporting System.

Gross statistics on international bond and equity issues are produced by aggregating individual transactions reported by market sources. Transactions of public and publicly guaranteed bonds are reported through the Debtor Reporting System by World Bank member economies that have received either loans from the International Bank for Reconstruction and Development or credits from the International Development Association. Information on private nonguaranteed bonds is collected from market sources, because official national sources reporting to the Debtor Reporting System are not asked to report the breakdown between private nonguaranteed bonds and private nonguaranteed loans. Information on transactions by nonresidents in local equity markets is gathered from national authorities, investment positions of mutual funds, and market sources.

The volume of portfolio investment reported by the World Bank generally differs from that reported by other sources because of differences in the sources, in the classification of economies, and in the method used to adjust and disaggregate reported information. Differences in reporting arise particularly for foreign investments in local equity markets because clarity, adequate disaggregation, and comprehensive and periodic reporting are lacking in many developing economies. By contrast, capital flows through international debt and equity instruments are well recorded, and for these the differences in reporting lie primarily in the classification of economies, the exchange rates used, whether particular installments of the transactions are included, and the treatment of certain offshore issuances.

Definitions

• **Net private capital flows** consist of private debt and nondebt flows. Private debt flows include commercial bank lending, bonds, and other private credits, as well as foreign direct investment and portfolio equity investment. • **Foreign direct investment** is net inflows of investment to acquire a lasting management interest (10 percent or more of voting stock) in an enterprise operating in an economy other than that of the investor. It is the sum of equity capital, reinvestment of earnings, other long-term capital, and short-term capital, as shown in the balance of payments. • **Portfolio investment flows** are net and include non-debt-creating portfolio equity flows (the sum of country funds, depository receipts, and direct purchases of shares by foreign investors) and portfolio debt flows (bond issues purchased by foreign investors). • **Bank and trade-related lending** covers commercial bank lending and other private credits.

6.7a

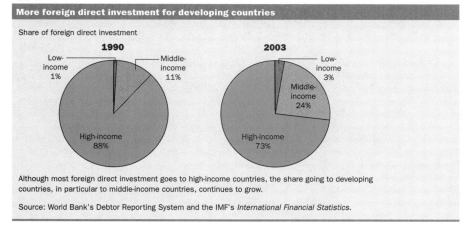

More foreign direct investment for developing countries

Share of foreign direct investment

1990
Low-income 1%
Middle-income 11%
High-income 88%

2003
Low-income 3%
Middle-income 24%
High-income 73%

Although most foreign direct investment goes to high-income countries, the share going to developing countries, in particular to middle-income countries, continues to grow.

Source: World Bank's Debtor Reporting System and the IMF's *International Financial Statistics*.

Data sources

The data are compiled from a variety of public and private sources, including the World Bank's Debtor Reporting System, the IMF's *International Financial Statistics* and Balance of Payments databases, and other sources mentioned in *About the data*. These data are also published in the World Bank's *Global Development Finance 2005*.

Net flows to part I countries

$ millions	Official development assistance				Other official flows	Private flows					Net grants by NGOs	Total net flows
	Total 2003	Bilateral grants 2003	Bilateral loans 2003	Contributions to multilateral institutions 2003	2003	Total 2003	Foreign direct investment 2003	Bilateral portfolio investment 2003	Multilateral portfolio investment 2003	Private export credits 2003	2003	2003
Australia	1,219	975	..	244	80	1,374	239	1,135	..	..	337	3,010
Austria	505	266	−37	276	44	824	765	..	..	59	71	1,445
Belgium	1,853	1,496	−27	385	955	−1,752	..	−33	..	−1,719	165	1,221
Canada	2,031	1,681	−333	683	−358	2,711	2,626	82	..	3	566	4,949
Denmark	1,748	1,144	−113	717	41	106	106	..	..	..	..	1,896
Finland	558	300	8	250	7	−622	78	−403	..	−297	13	−44
France	7,253	5,725	−511	2,040	2,806	−3,123	681	−1,460	..	−2,345	..	6,936
Germany	6,784	4,737	−678	2,724	−3,564	−519	1,237	−1,539	−465	249	1,008	3,709
Greece	362	228	..	134	..	33	33	..	..	..	8	403
Ireland	504	352	..	152	..	1,547	..	1,547	..	..	283	2,334
Italy	2,433	1,126	−65	1,372	−285	2,044	505	−106	..	1,644	27	4,218
Japan	8,880	4,443	1,891	2,545	−2,149	−731	7,016	−11,760	371	3,643	335	6,335
Luxembourg	194	150	..	44	..	..	..	..	..	..	7	201
Netherlands	3,981	3,084	−133	1,030	119	7,766	3,837	3,376	651	−98	300	12,167
New Zealand	165	129	..	36	3	21	21	..	..	..	18	208
Norway	2,042	1,455	7	580	0	1,264	1,199	0	..	65	..	3,306
Portugal	320	183	−1	137	−2	823	680	..	..	143	4	1,145
Spain	1,961	938	213	810	73	4,633	4,737	..	..	−104	..	6,667
Sweden	2,400	1,753	26	621	−15	−1,153	−337	0	..	−816	23	1,255
Switzerland	1,299	929	16	355	0	2,104	2,051	..	−1	54	280	3,684
United Kingdom	6,282	3,576	285	2,421	50	−1,016	−3,111	2,774	..	−679	389	5,705
United States	16,254	16,294	−1,701	1,661	1,068	14,147	14,298	−224	78	−6	6,326	37,795
Total	**69,029**	**50,965**	**−1,153**	**19,217**	**−1,127**	**30,481**	**36,660**	**−6,611**	**635**	**−203**	**10,162**	**108,545**

Net flows to part II countries

$ millions	Official aid				Other official flows	Private flows				Net grants by NGOs	Total net flows
	Total 2003	Bilateral grants 2003	Bilateral loans 2003	Contributions to multilateral institutions 2003	2003	Total 2003	Foreign direct investment 2003	Bilateral portfolio investment 2003	Private export credits 2003	2003	2003
Australia	9	2	..	7	..	−1,582	1,219	−2,801	..	..	−1,573
Austria	245	162	0	84	−1	3,585	3,585	..	..	13	3,841
Belgium	163	14	14	134	−34	..	..	..	..	..	129
Canada	102	102	0	..	−41	3,422	3,172	250	..	..	3,483
Denmark	202	96	19	86	32	635	635	..	..	..	868
Finland	82	39	1	42	1	297	487	−168	−22	1	381
France	2,027	1,388	42	597	−109	8,906	1,740	8,005	−840	..	10,823
Germany	1,181	460	−75	796	−877	4,536	593	4,330	−387	100	4,940
Greece	81	21	..	60	..	464	464	..	..	..	546
Ireland	1	1	..	..	..	..	..	..	..	..	1
Italy	497	20	−5	481	−61	559	325	−26	261	0	995
Japan	−219	123	−422	79	−1,120	−2,641	1,955	−6,700	2,104	..	−3,980
Luxembourg	6	4	..	2	..	..	..	..	..	..	6
Netherlands	248	167	−19	100	..	..	..	..	..	..	248
New Zealand	1	1	..	0	..	..	..	..	..	..	1
Norway	50	48	..	2	1	409	416	..	−6	..	460
Portugal	51	0	..	51	−4	10	3	..	7	..	57
Spain	5	10	−5	..	..	1,439	1,439	..	..	..	1,445
Sweden	127	105	..	22	−20	627	577	0	49	..	733
Switzerland	77	64	2	11	1	1,147	1,160	..	−13	11	1,237
United Kingdom	698	73	0	626	..	14,943	5,425	9,489	29	5	15,646
United States	1,471	1,566	−165	70	−278	36,898	16,404	20,124	371	4,254	42,345
Total	**7,106**	**4,467**	**−611**	**3,250**	**−2,512**	**73,654**	**39,599**	**32,502**	**1,553**	**4,385**	**82,633**

Note: Data may not sum to totals because of gaps in reporting.

About the data

The high-income members of the Development Assistance Committee (DAC) of the Organisation for Economic Co-operation and Development (OECD) are the main source of official external finance for developing countries. This table shows the flow of official and private financial resources from DAC members to official and private recipients in developing and transition economies.

DAC exists to help its members coordinate their development assistance and to encourage the expansion and improve the effectiveness of the aggregate resources flowing to recipient economies. In this capacity DAC monitors the flow of all financial resources, but its main concern is official development assistance (ODA). DAC has three criteria for ODA: It is undertaken by the official sector. It promotes the economic development and welfare of developing countries as a main objective. And it is provided on concessional terms, with a grant element of at least 25 percent on loans (calculated at a rate of discount of 10 percent).

This definition excludes nonconcessional flows from official creditors, which are classified as "other official flows," and military aid, which is not recorded in DAC statistics. The definition includes food aid, capital projects, emergency relief, technical cooperation, and postconflict peacekeeping efforts. Also included are contributions to multilateral institutions, such as the United Nations and its specialized agencies, and concessional funding to the multilateral development banks. In 1999, to avoid double counting extrabudgetary expenditures reported by DAC

countries and flows reported by the United Nations, all United Nations agencies revised their data to include only regular budgetary expenditures since 1990 (except for the World Food Programme and the United Nations High Commissioner for Refugees, which revised their data from 1996 onward).

DAC maintains a list of countries and territories that are aid recipients. Part I of the list comprises developing countries and territories considered by DAC members to be eligible for ODA. Part II comprises economies in transition: more advanced countries of Central and Eastern Europe, the countries of the former Soviet Union, and certain advanced developing countries and territories. Flows to these recipients that meet the criteria for ODA are termed official aid.

The data in the table were compiled from replies by DAC member countries to questionnaires issued by the DAC Secretariat. Net flows of ODA, official aid, and other official resources are defined as gross disbursements of grants and loans minus repayments of principal on earlier loans. Because the data are based on donor country reports, they do not provide a complete picture of the resources received by developing and transition economies, for two reasons. First, flows from DAC members are only part of the aggregate resource flows to these economies. Second, the data that record contributions to multilateral institutions measure the flow of resources made available to those institutions by DAC members, not the flow of resources from those institutions to developing and transition economies.

Definitions

• **Official development assistance** comprises grants and loans (net of repayments of principal) that meet the DAC definition of ODA and are made to countries and territories in part I of the DAC list of aid recipients.
• **Official aid** comprises grants and loans (net of repayments) that meet the criteria for ODA and are made to countries and territories in part II of the DAC list of aid recipients. • **Bilateral grants** are transfers of money or in kind for which no repayment is required.
• **Bilateral loans** are loans extended by governments or official agencies that have a grant element of at least 25 percent (calculated at a rate of discount of 10 percent). • **Contributions to multilateral institutions** are concessional funding received by multilateral institutions from DAC members in the form of grants or capital subscriptions. • **Other official flows** are transactions by the official sector whose main objective is other than development or whose grant element is less than 25 percent. • **Private flows** consist of flows at market terms financed from private sector resources in donor countries. They include changes in holdings of private long-term assets by residents of the reporting country. • **Foreign direct investment** is investment by residents of DAC member countries to acquire a lasting management interest (at least 10 percent of voting stock) in an enterprise operating in the recipient country. The data reflect changes in the net worth of subsidiaries in recipient countries whose parent company is in the DAC source country. • **Bilateral portfolio investment** covers bank lending and the purchase of bonds, shares, and real estate by residents of DAC member countries in recipient countries. • **Multilateral portfolio investment** records the transactions of private banks and nonbanks in DAC member countries in the securities issued by multilateral institutions. • **Private export credits** are loans extended to recipient countries by the private sector in DAC member countries to promote trade; they may be supported by an official guarantee. • **Net grants by NGOs** are private grants by nongovernmental organizations, net of subsidies from the official sector. • **Total net flows** comprise ODA or official aid flows, other official flows, private flows, and net grants by NGOs.

6.8a

Who were the largest donors in 2003?

Official development assistance as share of total

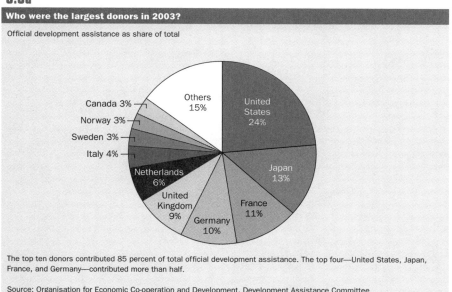

The top ten donors contributed 85 percent of total official development assistance. The top four—United States, Japan, France, and Germany—contributed more than half.

Source: Organisation for Economic Co-operation and Development, Development Assistance Committee.

Data sources

The data on financial flows are compiled by DAC and published in its annual statistical report, *Geographical Distribution of Financial Flows to Aid Recipients*, and its annual *Development Cooperation Report*. Data are available electronically on the OECD's *International Development Statistics* CD-ROM and to registered users at http://www.oecd.org/dataoecd/50/17/5037721.htm.

Net official development assistance / Untied aid[a]

	$ millions 1998	$ millions 2003	% of GNI 1998	% of GNI 2003	average annual % change in volume[b] 1997–98 to 2002–03	Per capita of donor country[b] $ 1998	Per capita of donor country[b] $ 2003	% of general government disbursement 1998	% of general government disbursement 2003	% of bilateral ODA commitments 1998	% of bilateral ODA commitments 2003
Australia	960	1,219	0.27	0.25	2.0	49	50	0.72	0.66	92.8	67.2
Austria	459	505	0.22	0.20	1.9	51	51	0.40	0.39	68.6	51.4
Belgium	883	1,853	0.35	0.60	11.7	78	145	0.70	1.19	50.0	99.1
Canada	1,707	2,031	0.30	0.24	0.4	58	55	0.62	0.58	34.5	52.6
Denmark	1,704	1,748	0.99	0.84	0.1	295	265	1.72	1.47	81.4	71.5
Finland	396	558	0.31	0.35	5.6	70	89	0.58	0.68	78.6	85.8
France	5,742	7,253	0.40	0.41	1.4	87	100	0.74	0.76	66.8	93.1
Germany	5,581	6,784	0.26	0.28	1.8	59	68	0.53	0.58	86.5	94.6
Greece	179	362	0.15	0.21	11.8	16	26	0.31	0.44	..	93.8
Ireland	199	504	0.30	0.39	15.8	54	103	0.65	0.96	..	100.0
Italy	2,278	2,433	0.20	0.17	5.6	37	34	0.38	0.34	63.9	..
Japan	10,640	8,880	0.27	0.20	–1.2	82	66	0.75	0.55	93.6	96.1
Luxembourg	112	194	0.65	0.81	9.8	241	354	1.41	1.57	94.0	..
Netherlands	3,042	3,981	0.80	0.80	2.4	189	199	1.64	1.59	85.9	..
New Zealand	130	165	0.27	0.23	1.2	32	32	0.56	0.56	..	81.4
Norway	1,321	2,042	0.89	0.92	3.1	350	388	1.77	1.90	89.8	99.9
Portugal	259	320	0.24	0.22	2.8	26	25	0.52	0.45	82.6	93.7
Spain	1,376	1,961	0.24	0.23	5.2	34	37	0.57	0.59	26.6	55.8
Sweden	1,573	2,400	0.72	0.79	7.2	153	218	1.04	1.36	79.3	93.6
Switzerland	898	1,299	0.32	0.39	3.4	122	154	0.92	1.15	71.7	96.4
United Kingdom	3,864	6,282	0.27	0.34	7.4	65	95	0.68	0.82	79.6	100.0
United States	8,786	16,254	0.10	0.15	11.6	35	55	0.29	0.41	..	..
Total or average	**52,087**	**69,029**	**0.23**	**0.25**	**4.4**	**60**	**70**	**0.57**	**0.61**	**81.4**	**92.0**

Net official aid

	$ millions 1998	$ millions 2003	% of GNI 1998	% of GNI 2003	average annual % change in volume[b] 1997–98 to 2002–03	Per capita of donor country[b] $ 1998	Per capita of donor country[b] $ 2003
Australia	1	9	0.00	0.00	77.6	0	0
Austria	191	245	0.09	0.10	3.7	21	25
Belgium	68	163	0.03	0.05	14.9	6	13
Canada	157	102	0.03	0.01	–9.0	5	3
Denmark	118	202	0.07	0.10	7.6	21	31
Finland	82	82	0.07	0.05	–0.5	14	13
France	823	2,027	0.06	0.11	20.3	13	28
Germany	654	1,181	0.03	0.05	8.9	7	12
Greece	15	81	0.01	0.05	29.2	1	6
Ireland	0	1	0.00	0.00	108.7	0	0
Italy	243	497	0.02	0.03	–2.1	4	7
Japan	132	–219	0.00	–0.01	–188.2	1	–2
Luxembourg	3	6	0.02	0.03	26.8	6	11
Netherlands	130	248	0.03	0.05	25.2	8	12
New Zealand	0	1	0.00	0.00	83.8	0	0
Norway	52	50	0.03	0.02	–6.2	14	10
Portugal	22	51	0.02	0.04	13.5	2	4
Spain	5	5	0.00	0.00	15.8	0	0
Sweden	105	127	0.05	0.04	–0.3	10	12
Switzerland	76	77	0.03	0.02	–1.9	10	9
United Kingdom	435	698	0.03	0.04	7.5	7	11
United States	2,726	1,471	0.03	0.01	–7.8	11	5
Total or average	**6,040**	**7,106**	**0.03**	**0.03**	**1.9**	**7**	**7**

a. Excluding administrative costs and technical cooperation. b. At 2002 exchange rates and prices.

About the data

Effective aid supports institutional development and policy reforms, which are at the heart of successful development. To be effective, especially in reducing global poverty, aid requires partnerships among recipient countries, aid agencies, and donor countries. It also requires improvements in economic policies and institutions. Where traditional methods of nurturing such reforms have failed, aid agencies need to find alternative approaches and new opportunities.

As part of its work, the Development Assistance Committee (DAC) of the Organisation for Economic Co-operation and Development (OECD) assesses the aid performance of member countries relative to the size of their economies. As measured here, aid comprises bilateral disbursements of concessional financing to recipient countries plus the provision by donor governments of concessional financing to multilateral institutions. Volume amounts, at constant prices and exchange rates, are used to measure the change in real resources provided over time. Aid flows to part I recipients—official development assistance (ODA)—are tabulated separately from those to part II recipients—official aid (see *About the data* for table 6.8 for more information on the distinction between the two types of aid flows).

Measures of aid flows from the perspective of donors differ from aid receipts from the perspective of recipients for two main reasons. First, aid flows include expenditure items about which recipients may have no precise information, such as development-oriented research, stipends and tuition costs for aid-financed students in donor countries, or payment of experts hired by donor countries. Second, donors record their concessional funding (usually grants) to multilateral agencies when they make payments, while the agencies make funds available to recipients with a time lag and in many cases in the form of soft loans where donors' grants have been used to reduce the interest burden over the life of the loan.

Aid as a share of gross national income (GNI), aid per capita, and ODA as a share of the general government disbursements of the donor are calculated by the OECD. The denominators used in calculating these ratios may differ from corresponding values elsewhere in this book because of differences in timing or definitions.

DAC members have progressively introduced the new United Nations System of National Accounts (adopted in 1993), which replaced gross national product (GNP) with GNI. Because GNI includes items not included in GNP, ratios of ODA to GNI are slightly smaller than the previously reported ratios of ODA to GNP.

The proportion of untied aid is reported here because tying arrangements may prevent recipients from obtaining the best value for their money and so reduce the value of the aid received. Tying arrangements require recipients to purchase goods and services from the donor country or from a specified group of countries. They may be justified on the grounds that they prevent a recipient from misappropriating or mismanaging aid receipts, but they may also be motivated by a desire to benefit suppliers in the donor country. The same volume of aid may have different purchasing power depending on the relative costs of suppliers in countries to which the aid is tied and the degree to which each recipient's aid basket is untied.

Definitions

• **Net official development assistance** (ODA) and **net official aid** record the actual international transfer by the donor of financial resources or of goods or services valued at the cost to the donor, less any repayments of loan principal during the same period. Data are shown at current prices and dollar exchange rates. • **Aid as a percentage of GNI** shows the donor's contributions of ODA or official aid as a share of its gross national income. • **Average annual percentage change in volume** and **aid per capita of donor country** are calculated using 2002 exchange rates and prices. • **Aid as a percentage of general government disbursements** shows the donor's contributions of ODA as a share of public spending. • **Untied aid** is the share of ODA that is not subject to restrictions by donors on procurement sources.

6.9a

Official development assistance from non-DAC donors ($ millions)

Donor	1999	2000	2001	2002	2003
OECD members (non-DAC)					
Czech Republic	15	16	26	45	91
Hungary	..	..	..	..	21
Iceland	8	9	10	13	18
Korea, Rep.	317	212	265	279	366
Poland	20	29	36	14	27
Slovak Republic	7	6	8	7	15
Turkey	120	82	64	73	67
Arab countries					
Kuwait	147	165	73	20	133
Saudi Arabia	185	295	490	2,478	2,391
United Arab Emirates	92	150	127	156	188
Other donors					
Israel[a]	114	164	76	114	92
Other donors[b]	0	1	2	3	4
Total	**1,026**	**1,128**	**1,178**	**3,201**	**3,411**

Note: China also provides aid, but does not disclose the amount.

a. These figures include $66.8 million in 2000, $50.1 million in 2001, $87.8 million in 2002, and $68.8 million in 2003 for first-year sustenance expenses for people arriving from developing countries (many of which are experiencing civil war or severe unrest) or people who have left their country for humanitarian or political reasons. b. Includes Estonia, Latvia, and Lithuania.

Source: Organisation for Economic Co-operation and Development.

Data sources

The data on financial flows are compiled by DAC and published in its annual statistical report, *Geographical Distribution of Financial Flows to Aid Recipients,* and its annual *Development Cooperation Report.* Data are available electronically on the OECD's *International Development Statistics* CD-ROM and to registered users at http://www.oecd.org/dataoecd/50/17/5037721.htm.

	Net official development assistance or official aid		Aid per capita		Aid dependency ratios							
					Aid as % of GNI		Aid as % of gross capital formation		Aid as % of imports of goods and services		Aid as % of central government expenditure	
	$ millions		$									
	1998	2003	1998	2003	1998	2003	1998	2003	1998	2003	1998	2003
Afghanistan	154	1,533	6	..	..	..	..	..	..	..	..	..
Albania	269	342	87	108	9.5	5.4	60.0	22.0	28.3	13.1	35.0	..
Algeria	421	232	14	7	0.9	0.4	3.1	1.2	..	..	3.7	..
Angola	335	499	29	37	6.4	4.6	14.6	11.8	5.9	5.2	..	..
Argentina	84	109	2	3	0.0	0.1	0.1	0.6	0.2	0.4	..	..
Armenia	194	247	61	81	9.9	8.5	53.6	35.7	18.4	16.7	..	53.7
Australia												
Austria												
Azerbaijan	120	297	15	36	2.7	4.4	8.1	8.5	4.9	5.6	14.4	..
Bangladesh	1,158	1,393	9	10	2.5	2.5	12.1	11.5	14.2	12.3	..	29.7
Belarus	39	32	4	3	0.3	0.2	1.0	0.8	0.5	0.3	1.0	..
Belgium												
Benin	205	294	35	44	8.8	8.5	51.7	46.5	25.5	..	..	..
Bolivia	629	930	79	105	7.5	12.3	31.3	106.3	25.3	39.6	..	40.8
Bosnia and Herzegovina	905	539	240	130	19.6	7.4	58.8	38.8	22.1	9.2	..	..
Botswana	106	30	66	17	2.1	0.4	6.4	1.5	3.5	0.9	..	..
Brazil	335	296	2	2	0.0	0.1	0.2	0.3	0.3	0.3	0.2	..
Bulgaria	239	414	29	53	1.9	2.1	11.1	9.6	3.6	3.1	6.3	6.1
Burkina Faso	400	451	37	37	14.3	10.8	52.7	57.6	..	45.5	..	..
Burundi	67	224	10	31	7.7	39.0	87.5	246.1	38.0	115.8	34.1	..
Cambodia	337	508	28	38	11.1	12.5	91.9	54.1	22.6	15.8	..	..
Cameroon	499	884	35	55	6.1	7.5	32.7	41.7	..	..	..	..
Canada												
Central African Republic	120	50	33	13	11.7	4.2	84.6	23.0	..	..	..	..
Chad	168	247	23	29	9.7	10.6	47.7	17.2	..	..	..	..
Chile	107	76	7	5	0.1	0.1	0.5	0.4	0.4	0.3	..	0.6
China	2,456	1,325	2	1	0.3	0.1	0.7	0.2	1.3	0.3	..	..
Hong Kong, China	7	5	1	1	0.0	0.0	0.0	0.0	0.0	0.0	..	..
Colombia	169	802	4	18	0.2	1.1	0.9	6.7	0.8	3.9	..	4.5
Congo, Dem. Rep.	125	5,381	3	101	2.2	99.9	112.2	695.0	..	..	18.6	..
Congo, Rep.	66	70	20	19	4.4	2.6	12.6	8.6	3.8	4.5	8.8	..
Costa Rica	30	28	8	7	0.2	0.2	1.0	0.8	0.4	0.3	1.0	0.7
Côte d'Ivoire	967	252	64	15	8.0	1.9	56.7	18.4	18.3	4.3	..	..
Croatia	39	121	9	27	0.2	0.4	0.8	1.4	0.4	0.6	0.4	..
Cuba	80	70	7	6	..	..	..	..	..	..	..	..
Czech Republic	449	263	44	26	0.8	0.3	2.6	1.1	1.2	0.4	..	0.8
Denmark												
Dominican Republic	121	69	15	8	0.8	0.5	3.3	1.8	1.2	0.6	5.7	..
Ecuador	179	176	15	14	0.8	0.7	3.0	2.3	2.2	1.9	..	..
Egypt, Arab Rep.	1,955	894	32	13	2.3	1.1	11.3	6.3	8.8	4.4	..	..
El Salvador	181	192	30	29	1.5	1.3	8.6	7.9	3.8	2.7	..	73.1
Eritrea	167	307	43	70	19.2	34.2	69.4	182.5	23.8	54.6	..	..
Estonia	91	85	66	62	1.7	1.0	5.4	3.0	1.8	1.0	5.7	..
Ethiopia	660	1,504	11	22	10.2	22.8	59.1	110.6	35.1	56.1	54.6	..
Finland												
France												
Gabon	45	–11	37	–8	1.1	–0.2	2.6	–0.7	1.6	..	..	..
Gambia, The	39	60	32	42	9.7	16.2	50.4	78.7	..	..	..	..
Georgia	209	220	39	43	5.5	5.5	27.6	22.6	15.0	11.0	40.3	51.5
Germany												
Ghana	702	907	37	44	9.6	12.2	40.7	51.3	18.4	20.8	..	..
Greece												
Guatemala	233	247	22	20	1.2	1.0	6.9	6.0	4.4	3.2	12.8	7.9
Guinea	359	238	51	30	10.4	6.6	47.7	66.0	33.0	22.1	..	..
Guinea-Bissau	96	145	74	98	49.8	63.6	409.5	468.1	..	149.0	..	..
Haiti	407	200	53	24	10.8	6.9	42.0	22.0	38.7	14.4	..	..

Aid dependency

	Net official development assistance or official aid		Aid per capita		Aid dependency ratios							
	$ millions		$		Aid as % of GNI		Aid as % of gross capital formation		Aid as % of imports of goods and services		Aid as % of central government expenditure	
	1998	2003	1998	2003	1998	2003	1998	2003	1998	2003	1998	2003
Honduras	320	389	52	56	6.3	5.7	20.2	19.1	10.4	9.8	..	..
Hungary	240	248	24	25	0.5	0.3	1.8	1.2	0.7	0.4	..	0.7
India	1,610	942	2	1	0.4	0.2	1.8	0.7	2.5	0.9	2.6	1.0
Indonesia	1,266	1,743	6	8	1.4	0.9	7.9	5.2	2.3	2.7	9.9	..
Iran, Islamic Rep.	165	133	3	2	0.2	0.1	0.6	0.2	0.9	0.3	0.4	0.5
Iraq	116	2,265	5	92	..	..	..	..	..	..	..	..
Ireland												
Israel	1,066	440	179	66	1.1	0.4	4.6	2.4	2.5	0.9	..	..
Italy												
Jamaica	19	3	8	1	0.3	0.0	1.0	0.1	0.4	0.1	0.7	0.1
Japan												
Jordan	411	1,234	89	233	5.3	12.6	23.8	55.2	7.3	17.1	18.2	41.1
Kazakhstan	223	268	14	18	1.0	1.0	6.4	3.4	2.7	1.8	6.0	6.3
Kenya	415	483	14	15	3.6	3.4	20.8	26.0	10.5	11.1	..	..
Korea, Dem. Rep.	109	167	5	7	..	..	..	..	..	..	..	..
Korea, Rep.	−50	−458	−1	−10	0.0	−0.1	−0.1	−0.3	0.0	−0.2	−0.1	..
Kuwait	6	4	3	2	0.0	0.0	0.1	0.1	0.0	0.0	0.0	..
Kyrgyz Republic	240	198	50	39	15.3	10.7	94.2	64.0	23.4	22.3	72.0	..
Lao PDR	276	299	55	53	22.1	14.3	88.0	69.2	42.9	54.2	..	..
Latvia	98	114	41	49	1.5	1.0	6.1	3.6	2.4	1.7	4.7	3.7
Lebanon	241	228	57	51	1.4	1.3	5.1	7.2	3.3	2.7	..	..
Lesotho	61	79	36	44	5.4	5.7	14.6	23.3	5.9	7.6	..	19.8
Liberia	72	107	24	32	22.4	28.3	..	278.0	..	51.1	..	..
Libya	7	10	1	2	..	..	0.2	..	0.1	..	..	..
Lithuania	134	372	38	108	1.2	2.1	4.7	9.3	2.0	3.3	..	7.1
Macedonia, FYR	105	234	52	114	3.0	5.0	13.2	23.1	5.0	8.9	..	..
Madagascar	481	539	33	32	13.1	10.0	87.1	55.1	39.1	30.8	..	..
Malawi	435	498	44	45	25.6	29.8	186.0	358.0	61.2	72.7	..	..
Malaysia	208	109	9	4	0.3	0.1	1.1	0.5	0.3	0.1	1.7	0.5
Mali	347	528	34	45	13.6	12.7	64.0	52.1	36.8	34.8	..	..
Mauritania	165	243	66	85	17.1	20.9	87.1	49.5	32.6	..	..	..
Mauritius	42	−15	36	−12	1.0	−0.3	3.6	−1.3	1.5	−0.5	5.1	−1.3
Mexico	44	103	0	1	0.0	0.0	0.0	0.1	0.0	0.1	0.1	..
Moldova	40	117	9	28	2.3	5.1	9.0	27.4	3.0	6.4	7.0	26.5
Mongolia	204	247	86	100	21.0	19.7	59.5	51.0	29.9	22.3	..	63.0
Morocco	530	523	19	17	1.5	1.2	6.7	5.0	4.2	3.1	5.4	..
Mozambique	1,040	1,033	61	55	28.4	25.1	110.9	85.7	78.8	51.7	..	..
Myanmar	72	126	2	3	..	..	..	..	2.5	4.3	..	..
Namibia	181	146	102	73	5.2	3.2	20.7	15.0	8.7	7.2	..	..
Nepal	402	467	18	19	8.3	8.0	33.3	30.9	27.5	23.2	..	..
Netherlands												
New Zealand												
Nicaragua	603	833	125	152	17.8	21.0	54.4	54.3	30.3	32.0	97.0	95.8
Niger	292	453	29	39	14.2	16.7	124.7	117.0	..	..	..	..
Nigeria	204	318	2	2	0.7	0.6	2.6	2.4	1.3	..	..	..
Norway												
Oman	44	45	19	17	0.3	..	1.3	..	0.6	0.5	1.0	..
Pakistan	1,053	1,068	8	7	1.7	1.3	9.6	7.8	7.3	6.0	9.2	7.5
Panama	22	30	8	10	0.2	0.3	0.7	0.9	0.2	0.3	1.0	..
Papua New Guinea	362	221	74	40	10.0	8.1	53.3	46.3	16.8	9.6	39.9	..
Paraguay	77	51	15	9	0.9	0.8	3.9	4.2	1.6	1.7	6.5	6.2
Peru	503	500	20	18	0.9	0.9	3.8	4.4	4.0	3.8	5.8	4.9
Philippines	618	737	8	9	0.9	0.9	4.7	4.9	1.5	1.7	..	..
Poland	876	1,191	23	31	0.5	0.6	2.1	3.0	1.6	1.4	1.5	..
Portugal												
Puerto Rico												

6.10 Aid dependency

	Net official development assistance or official aid $ millions		Aid per capita $		Aid dependency ratios							
					Aid as % of GNI		Aid as % of gross capital formation		Aid as % of imports of goods and services		Aid as % of central government expenditure	
	1998	2003	1998	2003	1998	2003	1998	2003	1998	2003	1998	2003
Romania	367	601	16	28	0.9	1.1	4.9	4.3	2.7	2.3	2.7	..
Russian Federation	1,078	1,255	7	9	0.4	0.3	2.7	1.4	1.2	1.0	..	1.3
Rwanda	350	332	48	39	17.7	20.0	118.8	100.3	79.8	67.3	..	..
Saudi Arabia	25	22	1	1	0.0	0.0	0.1	0.1	0.1	0.0	..	..
Senegal	501	450	55	44	10.9	7.0	54.5	34.5	26.5	15.6	..	..
Serbia and Montenegro	108	1,317	10	163	..	6.4	7.0	41.4	2.0	14.7	..	..
Sierra Leone	106	297	22	56	16.3	39.0	322.8	315.6	68.5	70.6	..	..
Singapore	2	7	0	2	0.0	0.0	0.0	0.1	0.0	0.0	0.0	..
Slovak Republic	155	160	29	30	0.7	0.5	2.1	1.9	1.0	0.6	..	1.3
Slovenia	42	66	21	33	0.2	0.2	0.8	0.9	0.4	0.4	0.6	0.5
Somalia	80	175	10	18	..	..	..	..	..	..	..	..
South Africa	514	625	12	14	0.4	0.4	2.3	2.3	1.4	1.3	1.3	1.4
Spain												
Sri Lanka	425	672	24	35	2.7	3.7	10.7	16.5	6.0	8.3	12.4	..
Sudan	209	621	7	19	2.0	3.8	10.6	17.0	10.8	14.6	27.5	..
Swaziland	35	27	35	24	2.6	1.4	11.4	7.6	2.4	1.5	..	..
Sweden												
Switzerland												
Syrian Arab Republic	155	160	10	9	1.1	0.8	4.7	3.2	2.7	2.2	..	..
Tajikistan	161	144	26	23	12.7	9.9	78.9	51.4	19.5	12.8	107.1	..
Tanzania	1,000	1,669	31	47	12.1	16.3	86.2	87.0	40.2	60.0	..	..
Thailand	704	−966	12	−16	0.7	−0.7	3.1	−2.7	1.3	−1.1	..	−4.4
Togo	128	45	30	9	8.4	2.6	49.2	13.5	16.7	4.6	..	..
Trinidad and Tobago	14	−2	11	−2	0.2	0.0	0.7	−0.1	0.4	0.0	..	..
Tunisia	150	306	16	31	0.8	1.3	2.8	4.9	1.5	2.3	2.8	4.4
Turkey	29	166	0	2	0.0	0.1	0.1	0.3	0.0	0.2	0.0	..
Turkmenistan	24	27	5	6	0.9	0.4	2.0	1.7	1.2	0.8	..	..
Uganda	647	959	29	38	9.9	15.6	61.0	73.7	33.1	48.8	..	..
Ukraine	465	323	9	7	1.1	0.7	5.3	3.2	2.3	1.1	..	..
United Arab Emirates	4	5	1	1	0.0	..	0.0	..	..	..	0.1	..
United Kingdom												
United States												
Uruguay	25	17	8	5	0.1	0.2	0.7	1.1	0.5	0.5	0.4	..
Uzbekistan	158	194	7	8	1.1	2.0	5.1	9.8	4.4	6.0	..	..
Venezuela, RB	42	82	2	3	0.0	0.1	0.2	1.0	0.2	0.5	0.2	0.4
Vietnam	1,177	1,769	15	22	4.4	4.5	14.9	12.9	8.2	6.3	..	..
West Bank and Gaza	607	972	222	289	12.0	25.3	36.4	1,123.3	..	..	..	..
Yemen, Rep.	370	243	22	13	6.0	2.4	18.2	13.1	10.9	4.4	19.8	..
Zambia	349	560	37	54	11.5	13.4	65.7	49.4	23.1	26.5	50.3	..
Zimbabwe	261	186	21	14	4.9	..	26.6	..	..	..	..	..
World	**58,299 s**	**77,453 s**	**10 w**	**12 w**	**0.2 w**	**0.2 w**	**0.9 w**	**.. w**	**0.7 w**	**0.7 w**	**.. w**	**.. w**
Low income	21,199	32,128	10	14	2.7	3.0	12.9	13.1	11.1	11.4	..	..
Middle income	22,875	26,455	8	9	0.5	0.4	1.8	1.7	1.5	1.2	..	..
Lower middle income	18,663	21,783	7	8	0.6	0.5	2.1	1.8	2.1	1.6	..	..
Upper middle income	3,588	3,779	11	11	0.2	0.2	1.0	1.0	0.6	0.5	..	..
Low & middle income	56,167	76,184	11	14	1.0	1.1	4.0	4.2	3.3	3.1	..	..
East Asia & Pacific	8,436	7,131	5	4	0.6	0.4	1.9	0.9	1.9	0.9	..	..
Europe & Central Asia	8,880	10,465	19	22	0.9	0.8	4.1	3.3	2.2	1.7	..	..
Latin America & Carib.	5,562	6,151	11	12	0.3	0.4	1.3	1.9	1.2	1.3	..	..
Middle East & N. Africa	5,356	7,629	19	24	0.9	1.0	4.0	4.2	3.3	3.5	..	..
South Asia	4,883	6,171	4	4	0.9	0.8	4.2	3.6	5.1	4.2	..	..
Sub-Saharan Africa	14,528	24,146	23	34	4.7	6.0	23.9	29.5	12.4	15.9	..	..
High income												
Europe EMU												

Note: Regional aggregates include data for economies not specified elsewhere. World and income group totals include aid not allocated by country or region.

About the data

Ratios of aid to gross national income (GNI), gross capital formation, imports, and government spending provide a measure of the recipient country's dependency on aid. But care must be taken in drawing policy conclusions. For foreign policy reasons some countries have traditionally received large amounts of aid. Thus aid dependency ratios may reveal as much about a donor's interest as they do about a recipient's needs. Ratios in Sub-Saharan Africa are generally much higher than those in other regions, and they increased in the 1980s. These high ratios are due only in part to aid flows. Many African countries saw severe erosion in their terms of trade in the 1980s, which, along with weak policies, contributed to falling incomes, imports, and investment. Thus the increase in aid dependency ratios reflects events affecting both the numerator and the denominator.

As defined here, aid includes official development assistance (ODA) and official aid (see *About the data* for table 6.8). The data cover loans and grants from Development Assistance Committee (DAC) member countries, multilateral organizations, and non-DAC donors. They do not reflect aid given by recipient countries to other developing countries. As a result, some countries that are net donors (such as Saudi Arabia) are shown in the table as aid recipients (see table 6.9a).

The data in the table do not distinguish among different types of aid (program, project, or food aid; emergency assistance; postconflict peacekeeping assistance; or technical cooperation), each of which may have very different effects on the economy. Expenditures on technical cooperation do not always directly benefit the economy to the extent that they defray costs incurred outside the country on the salaries and benefits of technical experts and the overhead costs of firms supplying technical services.

In 1999, to avoid double counting extrabudgetary expenditures reported by DAC countries and flows reported by the United Nations, all United Nations agencies revised their data since 1990 to include only regular budgetary expenditures (except for the World Food Programme and the United Nations High Commissioner for Refugees, which revised their data from 1996 onward). These revisions have affected net ODA and official aid and, as a result, aid per capita and aid dependency ratios.

Because the table relies on information from donors, it is not consistent with information recorded by recipients in the balance of payments, which often excludes all or some technical assistance—particularly payments to expatriates made directly by the donor. Similarly, grant commodity aid may not always be recorded in trade data or in the balance of payments. Moreover, DAC statistics exclude purely military aid.

The nominal values used here may overstate the real value of aid to the recipient. Changes in international prices and in exchange rates can reduce the purchasing power of aid. The practice of tying aid, still prevalent though declining in importance, also tends to reduce its purchasing power (see *About the data* for table 6.9).

The values for population, GNI, gross capital formation, imports of goods and services, and central government expenditure used in computing the ratios are taken from World Bank and International Monetary Fund (IMF) databases. The aggregates also refer to World Bank definitions. Therefore the ratios shown may differ somewhat from those computed and published by the Organisation for Economic Co-operation and Development (OECD). Aid not allocated by country or region—including administrative costs, research on development issues, and aid to nongovernmental organizations—is included in the world total. Thus regional and income group totals do not sum to the world total.

Definitions

• **Net official development assistance** consists of disbursements of loans made on concessional terms (net of repayments of principal) and grants by official agencies of the members of DAC, by multilateral institutions, and by non-DAC countries to promote economic development and welfare in countries and territories in part I of the DAC list of aid recipients. It includes loans with a grant element of at least 25 percent (calculated at a rate of discount of 10 percent). • **Net official aid** refers to aid flows (net of repayments) from official donors to countries and territories in part II of the DAC list of aid recipients: more advanced countries of Central and Eastern Europe, the countries of the former Soviet Union, and certain advanced developing countries and territories. Official aid is provided under terms and conditions similar to those for ODA. • **Aid per capita** includes both ODA and official aid. • **Aid dependency ratios** are calculated using values in U.S. dollars converted at official exchange rates. For definitions of GNI, gross capital formation, imports of goods and services, and central government expenditure, see *Definitions* for tables 1.1, 4.9, and 4.12.

6.10a

New directions for aid

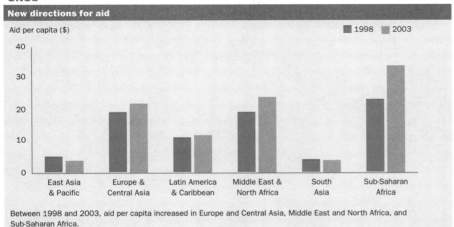

Aid per capita ($)   ■ 1998 ■ 2003

Between 1998 and 2003, aid per capita increased in Europe and Central Asia, Middle East and North Africa, and Sub-Saharan Africa.

Source: Organisation for Economic Co-operation and Development, Development Assistance Committee.

Data sources

The data on financial flows are compiled by DAC and published in its annual statistical report, *Geographical Distribution of Financial Flows to Aid Recipients,* and in its annual *Development Cooperation Report.* Data are available in electronic format on the OECD's *International Development Statistics* CD-ROM and to registered users at http://www.oecd.org/dataoecd/50/17/5037721. htm. The data on population, GNI, gross capital formation, imports of goods and services, and central government expenditure are from World Bank and IMF databases.

	Total $ millions	United States	France	Japan	Germany	United Kingdom	Netherlands	Sweden	Norway	Belgium	Canada	Other DAC donors $ millions
	2003	**2003**	**2003**	**2003**	**2003**	**2003**	**2003**	**2003**	**2003**	**2003**	**2003**	**2003**
Afghanistan	1,199.7	485.8	12.5	134.4	82.1	98.6	77.4	41.9	68.8	3.1	73.1	122.1
Albania	230.3	40.0	3.5	10.7	21.1	4.5	12.7	5.4	6.0	0.0	1.7	124.7
Algeria	168.8	3.2	125.0	0.1	0.1	0.8	1.5	1.4	3.4	4.2	1.9	27.1
Angola	372.2	152.9	14.3	33.1	13.5	13.8	21.1	14.0	24.2	2.8	5.6	77.0
Argentina	98.2	10.4	10.5	11.6	16.9	..	0.2	0.3	0.4	0.4	2.6	45.1
Armenia	127.4	74.2	3.0	7.0	13.9	3.2	9.9	1.6	3.4	..	0.9	10.3
Australia												
Austria												
Azerbaijan	158.5	49.3	1.3	79.8	13.6	0.3	3.9	0.3	5.4	..	1.1	3.6
Bangladesh	694.9	56.6	7.2	115.3	32.4	260.5	57.4	35.1	12.2	1.3	38.4	78.8
Belarus	20.1	−0.2	3.8	0.2	8.5	0.1	1.8	2.3	0.1	..	0.1	3.5
Belgium												
Benin	196.1	32.5	36.8	6.3	31.3	21.1	19.8	0.2	0.2	10.6	5.6	31.9
Bolivia	552.7	248.3	11.6	32.3	43.8	13.1	50.1	23.5	3.8	14.2	12.1	99.9
Bosnia and Herzegovina	331.2	68.7	2.1	54.0	21.8	12.6	25.2	35.4	21.6	0.7	7.3	81.9
Botswana	27.4	13.3	1.2	1.3	4.1	1.1	0.6	0.6	1.5	0.3	1.1	2.3
Brazil	184.3	−56.1	31.0	92.2	49.2	13.5	13.5	2.1	3.9	3.8	8.1	23.0
Bulgaria	226.1	44.6	19.8	25.2	89.6	3.9	6.0	0.2	0.8	0.2	2.1	33.8
Burkina Faso	265.7	14.1	66.0	10.6	28.8	0.1	39.4	10.7	0.2	12.5	11.4	71.9
Burundi	121.2	49.0	4.4	0.1	4.8	3.5	12.7	5.2	12.2	15.9	5.1	8.4
Cambodia	319.2	51.2	25.8	125.9	22.0	15.0	7.2	18.7	2.5	5.3	9.0	36.6
Cameroon	755.8	16.9	290.6	10.8	349.2	18.0	10.9	5.3	1.9	26.7	20.4	5.3
Canada												
Central African Republic	32.4	0.3	23.9	1.7	4.3	..	0.6	0.1	0.2	0.0	0.5	0.5
Chad	95.5	8.0	57.3	0.3	15.1	1.6	1.6	0.3	0.1	0.6	0.3	10.4
Chile	61.4	−3.0	12.9	7.1	31.0	0.4	1.3	0.8	0.6	3.5	2.8	4.1
China	1,139.5	25.6	74.3	759.7	152.2	47.4	16.8	6.1	11.9	−2.3	28.4	19.3
Hong Kong, China	5.0	0.5	0.8	2.0	0.0	..	1.0	..	..	0.1	..	0.6
Colombia	767.1	670.9	14.8	−7.2	19.3	2.8	12.3	8.6	9.3	1.6	5.7	29.0
Congo, Dem. Rep.	5,009.5	1,415.5	1,274.0	0.6	541.6	22.7	220.6	171.0	17.1	789.6	74.5	482.5
Congo, Rep.	33.9	4.8	18.1	0.1	0.9	4.0	2.7	3.0	0.7	0.5	0.2	−1.0
Costa Rica	31.0	−21.0	5.8	−4.2	8.6	19.3	6.9	1.4	..	0.4	3.0	10.8
Côte d'Ivoire	281.2	62.6	116.5	2.4	54.4	2.1	14.9	2.8	0.9	4.7	13.9	6.1
Croatia	80.3	46.0	3.2	1.0	−3.0	1.7	2.8	7.0	14.2	0.2	1.5	5.8
Cuba	59.3	10.2	3.1	5.8	4.7	−2.4	3.5	2.6	1.7	2.6	7.6	20.0
Czech Republic	43.2	1.6	9.7	1.8	18.5	0.5	1.7	0.1	0.2	0.6	0.7	8.0
Denmark												
Dominican Republic	60.4	−6.3	3.5	30.6	7.5	0.2	1.5	0.1	0.5	0.2	1.3	21.4
Ecuador	173.6	72.6	5.3	7.3	16.8	0.4	10.8	1.1	2.7	12.6	5.4	38.7
Egypt, Arab Rep.	775.1	441.8	100.0	21.7	98.4	3.5	9.6	0.9	0.7	−1.2	11.5	88.3
El Salvador	170.4	72.9	2.7	21.4	12.4	2.4	6.4	5.5	1.1	1.1	5.4	39.1
Eritrea	185.5	91.7	1.4	11.7	5.8	4.4	8.3	2.4	21.6	3.4	2.6	32.3
Estonia	22.9	0.6	1.4	0.4	3.7	0.1	0.2	2.7	0.5	0.1	0.7	12.5
Ethiopia	1,033.3	567.8	15.6	56.5	47.6	62.9	57.2	28.6	37.2	8.0	38.0	113.9
Finland												
France												
Gabon	−41.2	3.5	−48.9	1.8	0.7	..	0.2	..	..	0.1	1.2	0.2
Gambia, The	19.7	3.8	0.4	8.9	2.1	0.9	0.4	0.3	0.3	0.3	0.7	1.7
Georgia	163.9	75.0	2.6	16.4	31.7	3.4	5.0	2.4	5.0	0.4	3.0	19.1
Germany												
Ghana	478.7	83.9	18.2	29.8	46.8	131.3	65.8	0.4	0.6	0.2	20.6	81.2
Greece												
Guatemala	216.0	67.9	1.7	37.4	19.0	0.2	17.0	11.8	12.4	3.0	9.7	36.0
Guinea	134.6	44.4	29.6	20.8	16.9	2.1	4.2	0.9	3.4	1.2	8.9	2.2
Guinea-Bissau	97.6	2.4	3.6	0.1	0.3	..	5.1	2.3	0.1	1.7	0.3	81.7
Haiti	153.2	94.7	19.5	4.7	3.2	0.3	4.5	0.4	2.0	2.4	15.8	5.6

	Total $ millions	United States	France	Japan	Germany	Ten major DAC donors $ millions United Kingdom	Netherlands	Sweden	Norway	Belgium	Canada	Other DAC donors $ millions
	2003	**2003**	**2003**	**2003**	**2003**	**2003**	**2003**	**2003**	**2003**	**2003**	**2003**	**2003**
Honduras	235.5	70.1	1.2	32.0	17.1	5.2	6.5	13.5	1.6	0.6	12.7	75.0
Hungary	54.5	1.5	9.6	6.6	22.1	0.7	1.1	0.4	0.4	0.4	0.6	11.2
India	384.3	36.0	−15.4	325.8	3.5	329.9	43.1	18.4	8.1	3.8	−281.5	−87.5
Indonesia	1,550.7	210.9	57.0	1,141.8	−91.1	7.4	76.9	5.9	6.6	1.4	21.6	112.3
Iran, Islamic Rep.	102.1	0.5	9.5	11.3	38.8	1.1	7.7	0.4	9.7	4.4	0.9	17.9
Iraq	2,095.0	1,549.3	12.1	3.1	35.9	180.0	73.3	12.1	58.7	−0.2	47.9	122.7
Ireland												
Israel	437.8	462.5	6.4	0.7	−36.8	..	1.1	..	..	0.1	0.0	3.8
Italy												
Jamaica	1.1	1.2	−0.6	−11.4	−2.7	8.5	−2.3	0.4	0.5	2.1	8.6	−3.1
Japan												
Jordan	1,092.2	948.4	2.3	48.3	50.4	3.9	0.4	1.3	1.5	0.9	3.3	31.5
Kazakhstan	228.0	47.8	1.7	136.3	16.4	1.9	2.5	0.5	1.5	..	0.8	18.6
Kenya	320.3	111.2	20.5	−6.6	35.4	79.4	7.7	25.6	10.3	6.4	8.0	22.5
Korea, Dem. Rep.	114.8	42.9	−0.4	..	7.2	37.2	0.8	4.9	4.4	..	5.0	12.8
Korea, Rep.	−459.8	−44.4	13.9	−438.6	8.1	..	0.1	..	..	..	..	1.0
Kuwait	1.7	..	1.5	0.1	0.1	..	..	..	..	..	..	0.0
Kyrgyz Republic	112.6	40.1	0.7	31.2	14.8	7.1	4.8	1.0	3.1	..	0.4	9.5
Lao PDR	188.8	6.8	18.5	86.0	15.9	0.3	0.9	22.7	4.1	4.1	1.7	28.0
Latvia	34.8	1.5	3.5	1.2	5.8	0.1	0.8	6.6	0.7	0.0	0.8	13.8
Lebanon	118.8	29.6	46.8	13.5	8.9	0.3	0.6	1.1	6.0	..	2.1	9.9
Lesotho	32.9	2.7	−0.8	4.0	6.2	5.1	0.1	0.0	0.3	..	0.7	14.5
Liberia	70.3	30.2	1.3	..	−3.2	7.6	9.0	5.1	9.0	0.2	1.8	9.3
Libya	5.4	..	2.2	0.3	2.4	..	..	..	..	..	..	0.5
Lithuania	36.3	−1.6	2.7	2.5	9.8	0.1	0.9	8.8	0.6	0.1	0.4	11.9
Macedonia, FYR	179.3	69.8	2.0	4.8	26.7	2.2	31.5	6.0	11.5	..	1.2	23.6
Madagascar	224.9	43.2	128.1	9.7	16.4	5.1	0.6	0.2	6.2	1.3	1.8	12.4
Malawi	313.7	59.5	2.8	31.4	29.4	111.1	7.3	13.9	28.2	2.0	16.7	11.4
Malaysia	104.5	2.6	−3.5	79.2	6.3	0.5	0.1	0.0	1.4	0.1	0.5	17.4
Mali	271.9	56.0	69.9	14.1	23.5	0.2	42.6	11.5	7.5	4.5	25.2	17.0
Mauritania	136.1	27.7	45.5	23.9	10.3	1.6	0.6	1.1	0.8	1.4	2.2	21.0
Mauritius	−17.7	0.2	−20.5	2.9	−0.4	−1.2	0.0	0.0	..	0.4	0.3	0.6
Mexico	73.6	57.5	5.3	11.3	22.7	−3.6	0.0	0.5	0.1	0.4	5.0	−25.4
Moldova	80.4	41.7	2.7	4.3	5.5	5.3	4.9	4.6	2.3	0.0	0.5	8.6
Mongolia	148.0	16.1	1.8	67.3	29.9	−0.3	5.4	10.6	2.5	0.0	1.2	13.5
Morocco	335.6	−9.8	205.0	64.8	15.7	..	1.8	0.7	0.4	10.0	4.7	42.3
Mozambique	696.5	135.4	16.6	35.3	37.9	63.4	46.7	56.5	54.1	8.7	26.7	215.2
Myanmar	83.4	5.6	1.2	43.1	2.4	11.1	0.6	2.2	5.1	..	1.4	10.7
Namibia	110.3	29.2	2.9	0.8	31.8	2.9	2.9	9.8	3.8	1.8	0.6	23.7
Nepal	320.4	37.8	−0.9	60.6	63.1	53.1	9.9	1.2	20.2	1.9	6.1	67.4
Netherlands												
New Zealand												
Nicaragua	521.8	69.6	26.3	24.4	128.6	2.7	22.3	35.9	12.7	1.9	8.5	188.9
Niger	244.5	16.1	155.9	13.7	14.9	0.4	3.7	0.1	1.9	10.6	6.8	20.5
Nigeria	199.8	98.7	8.0	6.4	10.3	42.6	7.0	1.3	4.5	0.7	12.4	8.0
Norway												
Oman	10.5	−5.6	0.7	2.7	0.1	..	..	..	..	12.5	..	0.2
Pakistan	536.3	102.3	11.7	266.2	−4.7	112.1	6.9	1.6	10.0	0.1	13.3	16.9
Panama	31.3	10.5	0.7	8.4	1.8	0.1	0.2	..	..	0.1	1.1	8.5
Papua New Guinea	218.8	..	0.3	−3.1	2.5	..	1.0	0.1	0.2	..	0.4	217.6
Paraguay	55.4	12.2	0.9	20.2	4.9	−0.4	1.4	1.3	0.7	0.0	1.6	12.6
Peru	447.7	204.4	9.0	104.9	24.3	2.7	15.7	3.5	9.0	6.5	11.1	56.8
Philippines	703.8	55.3	−5.7	528.8	27.8	0.6	16.3	2.2	1.9	4.4	15.6	56.7
Poland	439.5	0.9	203.9	−3.6	64.0	0.5	2.5	3.9	1.0	0.8	61.0	104.6
Portugal												
Puerto Rico												

	Total $ millions	Ten major DAC donors ($ millions)										Other DAC donors $ millions
		United States	France	Japan	Germany	United Kingdom	Netherlands	Sweden	Norway	Belgium	Canada	
	2003	2003	2003	2003	2003	2003	2003	2003	2003	2003	2003	2003
Romania	239.9	40.9	30.9	70.9	46.5	8.5	6.1	0.8	0.5	1.0	2.4	31.4
Russian Federation	993.9	643.8	34.6	4.9	82.6	37.9	11.1	40.3	30.5	0.1	17.0	91.3
Rwanda	213.4	52.6	7.9	0.7	13.9	42.9	23.0	13.1	8.0	20.7	10.8	19.9
Saudi Arabia	9.9	0.1	4.6	4.4	0.9	..	..	..	0.1	−0.2	..	0.1
Senegal	314.4	48.1	119.5	28.7	20.5	0.7	12.8	0.3	1.3	15.0	17.6	50.0
Serbia and Montenegro	852.7	209.7	207.9	12.1	116.8	13.7	25.3	34.9	43.8	4.0	10.5	174.1
Sierra Leone	208.3	58.8	1.4	3.7	12.4	54.9	20.6	3.8	5.2	8.0	2.8	36.7
Singapore	7.0	..	2.2	2.0	2.2	0.1	..	..	..	..	..	0.5
Slovak Republic	49.7	3.9	4.9	11.1	9.4	2.6	1.8	0.1	0.5	0.3	1.2	14.0
Slovenia	2.7	0.6	1.4	0.2	−2.4	..	..	0.1	0.0	..	0.1	2.7
Somalia	113.6	33.8	0.8	..	2.6	3.5	10.3	6.6	40.0	..	1.0	15.0
South Africa	477.1	106.2	20.2	17.6	41.2	122.9	29.4	23.8	15.6	13.3	13.1	73.9
Spain												
Sri Lanka	271.0	−8.6	−1.3	172.3	16.3	9.3	21.5	13.5	28.6	0.1	5.8	13.5
Sudan	332.0	175.4	4.0	1.5	15.5	33.0	21.0	12.7	33.3	0.2	6.3	29.2
Swaziland	12.7	1.0	0.0	5.0	−2.1	1.4	0.2	0.1	0.4	..	0.4	6.3
Sweden												
Switzerland												
Syrian Arab Republic	28.8	0.1	20.0	−6.6	−0.6	0.0	5.3	0.8	2.0	0.2	0.0	7.8
Tajikistan	80.3	47.1	0.2	4.8	4.7	1.1	1.1	1.8	1.9	..	2.5	15.3
Tanzania	965.6	75.2	1.6	74.5	98.5	285.5	95.7	66.2	67.4	8.8	34.3	158.0
Thailand	−984.4	27.1	−4.1	−1,002.2	−13.0	−27.8	5.6	4.8	−1.4	−0.2	3.1	23.8
Togo	46.3	5.5	21.2	0.3	11.8	0.4	1.5	0.2	0.3	1.1	1.8	2.2
Trinidad and Tobago	5.1	0.2	1.1	2.2	0.3	0.3	..	..	..	..	1.0	0.1
Tunisia	207.7	−17.2	107.6	85.5	11.7	..	−3.4	0.6	0.1	1.1	1.9	19.9
Turkey	19.5	−43.4	8.2	1.0	−11.4	−1.9	5.0	1.5	7.3	−4.1	−2.7	59.9
Turkmenistan	16.7	6.5	0.4	6.8	1.0	0.7	0.1	..	0.1	..	0.4	0.9
Uganda	587.3	174.0	4.7	9.5	26.7	104.7	57.7	32.9	38.4	6.6	6.7	125.3
Ukraine	216.9	104.9	8.1	1.8	41.5	11.7	2.8	7.3	0.2	0.0	15.0	23.6
United Arab Emirates	4.9	0.2	3.4	0.2	1.1	0.1	..	..	..	..	..	0.0
United Kingdom												
United States												
Uruguay	7.7	−1.9	2.0	2.1	2.2	..	0.0	0.2	..	0.1	1.3	1.7
Uzbekistan	167.5	68.4	2.3	63.2	19.0	0.6	1.1	0.1	1.1	..	0.5	11.1
Venezuela, RB	64.2	12.0	6.4	3.5	2.9	0.1	0.1	0.0	0.2	0.5	2.1	36.3
Vietnam	967.7	33.7	99.0	484.2	61.7	34.6	38.8	20.9	11.5	11.7	23.2	148.4
West Bank and Gaza	490.8	194.1	22.2	4.5	35.3	31.1	13.1	35.2	53.5	..	8.8	93.0
Yemen, Rep.	126.2	22.7	4.1	24.5	33.0	2.9	28.4	0.3	0.3	0.1	0.5	9.4
Zambia	591.7	63.6	2.1	28.3	233.2	65.9	34.8	20.0	35.6	3.3	17.5	87.4
Zimbabwe	160.7	35.0	5.2	5.0	11.6	58.9	6.7	10.1	6.9	2.8	7.1	11.6
World	53,667.8 s	15,995.0 s	6,643.3 s	6,036.0 s	4,445.0 s	3,933.8 s	3,098.7 s	1,884.8 s	1,510.2 s	1,496.7 s	1,450.0 s	7,174.5 s
Low income	21,865.0	5,136.5	2,822.9	2,348.3	2,329.8	2,214.7	1,217.1	757.0	660.7	1,018.6	342.9	3,016.7
Middle income	18,365.3	6,846.5	1,855.2	2,964.2	1,480.0	627.6	613.1	385.3	446.9	119.7	442.8	2,584.3
Lower middle income	16,034.0	6,527.9	1,247.2	2,744.2	1,187.7	542.8	572.4	332.5	382.3	90.3	328.5	2,078.2
Upper middle income	1,654.4	177.4	438.8	199.3	239.2	83.5	22.6	34.6	28.4	21.0	94.5	315.3
Low & middle income	52,564.1	15,551.9	5,643.2	6,468.7	4,464.1	3,933.4	2,999.4	1,884.7	1,509.7	1,496.2	1,449.9	7,163.0
East Asia & Pacific	5,294.9	685.3	373.2	2,380.3	228.6	113.3	173.7	104.6	57.8	26.7	120.7	1,030.8
Europe & Central Asia	5,492.8	1,683.1	654.0	572.7	694.5	128.5	185.2	207.9	188.9	15.1	131.4	1,031.7
Latin America & Carib.	4,590.4	1,798.0	213.2	463.9	473.3	153.4	195.0	139.4	75.0	67.9	175.9	835.6
Middle East & N. Africa	5,704.7	3,183.3	735.1	286.4	336.1	223.9	138.7	57.2	137.3	31.7	85.9	489.2
South Asia	3,467.4	711.0	13.9	1,097.0	194.2	863.8	221.8	112.2	149.2	10.2	−143.8	237.9
Sub-Saharan Africa	17,566.1	4,638.5	2,992.3	523.4	1,931.8	1,486.2	1,016.9	678.5	576.3	1,039.2	495.6	2,187.5
High income												
Europe EMU												

Note: Regional aggregates include data for economies not specified elsewhere. World and income group totals include aid not allocated by country or region.

About the data

The data in the table show net bilateral aid to low- and middle-income economies from members of the Development Assistance Committee (DAC) of the Organisation for Economic Co-operation and Development (OECD). The DAC compilation of the data includes aid to some countries and territories not shown in the table and aid to unspecified economies that is recorded only at the regional or global level. Aid to countries and territories not shown in the table has been assigned to regional totals based on the World Bank's regional classification system. Aid to unspecified economies has been included in regional totals and, when possible, in income group totals. Aid not allocated by country or region—including administrative costs, research on development issues, and

aid to nongovernmental organizations—is included in the world total; thus regional and income group totals do not sum to the world total.

In 1999 all United Nations agencies revised their data since 1990 to include only regular budgetary expenditures (except for the World Food Programme and the United Nations High Commissioner for Refugees, which revised their data from 1996 onward). They did so to avoid double counting extrabudgetary expenditures reported by DAC countries and flows reported by the United Nations.

The data in the table are based on donor country reports of bilateral programs, which may differ from reports by recipient countries. Recipients may lack access to information on such aid expenditures as

development-oriented research, stipends and tuition costs for aid-financed students in donor countries, and payment of experts hired by donor countries. Moreover, a full accounting would include donor country contributions to multilateral institutions, the flow of resources from multilateral institutions to recipient countries, and flows from countries that are not members of DAC.

The expenditures that countries report as official development assistance (ODA) have changed. For example, some DAC members have reported as ODA the aid provided to refugees during the first 12 months of their stay within the donor's borders.

Some of the aid recipients shown in the table are also aid donors. See table 6.9a for a summary of ODA from non-DAC countries.

Definitions

• **Net aid** comprises net bilateral official development assistance to part I recipients and net bilateral official aid to part II recipients (see *About the data* for table 6.8). • **Other DAC donors** are Australia, Austria, Denmark, Finland, Greece, Ireland, Italy, Luxembourg, New Zealand, Portugal, Spain, and Switzerland.

6.11a

The flow of aid from DAC members reflects global events and priorities

Total bilateral aid, 2003

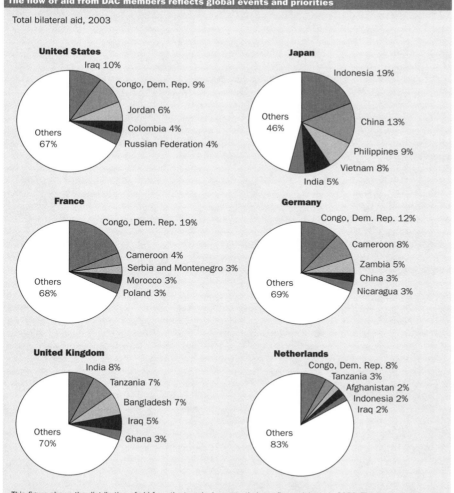

This figure shows the distribution of aid from the top six donors to their top five recipients in 2003. The Democratic Republic of Congo and Iraq appeared for the first time among the largest recipients.

Source: Organisation for Economic Co-operation and Development, Development Assistance Committee.

Data sources

Data on financial flows are compiled by DAC and published in its annual statistical report, *Geographical Distribution of Financial Flows to Aid Recipients,* and its annual *Development Cooperation Report.* Data are available electronically on the OECD's *International Development Statistics* CD-ROM and to registered users at www.oecd.org/dataoecd/50/17/5037721.htm.

6.12 | Net financial flows from multilateral institutions

	International financial institutions							United Nations					Total
							$ millions						
	World Bank		IMF		Regional development banks					$ millions			
	IDA	IBRD	Conces-sional	Non-concessional	Conces-sional	Non-concessional	Others	UNDP	UNFPA	UNICEF	WFP	Others	$ millions
	2003	2003	2003	2003	2003	2003	2003	2003	2003	2003	2003	2003	2003
Afghanistan	..	..	..	..	..	..	..	0.6	6.0	14.5	1.5	9.0	31.7
Albania	59.4	0.0	1.7	0.0	0.0	10.9	26.0	1.6	0.3	0.7	2.3	2.3	105.1
Algeria	0.0	−151.9	0.0	−438.8	0.0	51.2	115.8	1.0	0.8	1.2	3.6	6.0	−411.1
Angola	1.3	0.0	0.0	0.0	−0.1	−2.4	4.3	3.8	2.0	10.3	28.1	10.5	57.8
Argentina	0.0	−1,005.2	0.0	−141.7	0.0	299.8	0.0	0.2	0.2	0.3	..	4.7	−841.7
Armenia	77.4	−0.5	11.5	−9.8	0.0	−7.6	−3.3	0.8	0.4	0.7	1.1	3.3	73.9
Australia													
Austria													
Azerbaijan	74.7	0.0	20.5	−63.3	0.0	−4.7	7.4	2.5	0.6	0.9	1.9	3.0	43.3
Bangladesh	394.7	−6.3	66.0	−69.4	94.4	20.5	22.0	15.9	22.3	10.9	16.1	12.0	599.0
Belarus	0.0	−14.3	0.0	−32.7	0.0	−13.9	−6.9	0.4	0.2	0.7	..	1.2	−65.3
Belgium													
Benin	23.5	0.0	−0.5	0.0	9.5	−0.4	8.6	5.0	1.7	1.8	2.5	2.8	54.5
Bolivia	136.4	0.0	−19.0	90.0	176.4	−61.9	281.8	1.8	2.2	1.2	2.6	2.6	614.2
Bosnia and Herzegovina	48.2	−24.1	0.0	−17.2	0.0	−1.3	32.6	1.6	0.4	0.6	..	13.4	54.1
Botswana	−0.5	−3.0	0.0	0.0	−1.8	−5.8	−8.4	0.5	1.7	1.3	..	3.6	−12.5
Brazil	0.0	−342.0	0.0	5,227.1	0.0	−779.6	4.0	1.0	0.7	1.1	..	105.7	4,217.9
Bulgaria	0.0	134.6	0.0	38.3	0.0	−6.0	18.8	0.7	0.2	..	..	2.3	188.9
Burkina Faso	52.3	0.0	1.4	0.0	34.2	−0.2	5.5	5.9	1.7	5.5	4.2	4.0	114.5
Burundi	26.9	0.0	0.0	13.5	−0.9	−0.6	−2.1	6.0	1.2	4.0	6.8	9.9	64.6
Cambodia	62.6	0.0	−0.1	−1.5	58.2	0.0	6.2	4.2	3.8	3.3	3.1	4.5	144.3
Cameroon	29.2	−0.1	10.9	0.0	9.5	−13.5	11.0	2.1	2.4	2.6	2.0	4.2	60.2
Canada													
Central African Republic	0.0	0.0	0.0	0.0	0.0	0.0	0.0	2.2	2.2	1.8	2.1	4.5	12.7
Chad	92.0	21.6	−6.1	0.0	11.1	0.0	−3.8	5.2	1.9	2.9	4.3	2.7	131.8
Chile	−0.7	−135.2	0.0	0.0	−2.1	80.1	−0.3	0.2	0.1	0.6	..	1.9	−55.4
China	−6.3	−837.4	0.0	0.0	0.0	−1,347.8	49.7	8.6	4.9	12.0	10.8	11.8	−2,093.7
Hong Kong, China	..	..	..	..	..	..	..	..	..	..	..	..	..
Colombia	−0.7	775.5	0.0	0.0	−13.9	1,249.9	159.2	1.1	0.4	0.9	0.6	8.0	2,181.1
Congo, Dem. Rep.	147.4	0.0	74.7	0.0	−4.0	0.0	−0.9	8.9	3.2	17.5	11.5	26.7	284.9
Congo, Rep.	21.5	−6.4	−3.9	−3.8	−0.2	−13.4	−1.4	1.9	0.7	1.9	0.2	8.4	5.5
Costa Rica	−0.2	−11.6	0.0	0.0	−12.5	7.8	159.6	0.4	0.3	0.6	..	2.4	146.8
Côte d'Ivoire	43.7	−82.1	−105.0	0.0	0.4	0.6	−4.6	4.4	1.1	4.7	1.9	10.4	−124.5
Croatia	0.0	112.6	0.0	0.0	0.0	54.7	75.4	0.2	..	0.2	..	7.8	250.9
Cuba	..	..	..	..	..	..	..	0.6	0.5	0.7	2.3	2.3	6.4
Czech Republic	0.0	−134.9	0.0	0.0	0.0	−1.2	333.2	0.1	..	..	..	1.5	198.7
Denmark													
Dominican Republic	−0.7	−1.2	0.0	94.7	−18.3	120.9	2.1	0.3	0.6	0.8	0.4	1.2	200.9
Ecuador	−1.1	59.3	0.0	49.8	−25.1	42.2	129.6	0.0	1.3	0.9	1.9	4.4	263.2
Egypt, Arab Rep.	−3.9	−48.0	0.0	0.0	9.7	−48.9	81.5	1.2	1.9	2.5	3.9	7.7	7.6
El Salvador	−0.8	1.0	0.0	0.0	−21.9	42.8	61.4	0.4	0.9	0.6	0.1	1.6	86.1
Eritrea	58.5	0.0	0.0	0.0	10.0	0.0	1.0	3.3	1.6	1.9	3.4	16.4	96.0
Estonia	0.0	1.9	0.0	0.0	0.0	0.0	1.8	0.1	0.0	..	0.1	0.7	4.6
Ethiopia	195.5	0.0	6.2	0.0	13.6	−3.4	10.6	10.7	4.5	14.6	15.2	23.2	290.6
Finland													
France													
Gabon	0.0	−3.2	0.0	−14.1	−0.2	−49.4	1.4	0.1	0.2	0.7	..	4.8	−59.8
Gambia, The	10.4	0.0	0.0	0.0	16.3	0.0	3.1	2.3	0.5	0.7	1.2	2.6	37.0
Georgia	43.5	0.0	−31.1	−16.2	0.0	−6.2	1.1	1.5	0.4	0.8	0.5	4.5	−1.2
Germany													
Ghana	190.3	−1.9	71.5	0.0	62.8	4.3	−12.2	3.6	4.0	3.6	1.1	5.9	332.8
Greece													
Guatemala	0.0	27.1	0.0	0.0	−15.5	12.6	−0.2	0.6	10.3	0.8	2.5	1.3	39.6
Guinea	26.3	0.0	−12.6	0.0	13.0	1.9	−27.5	1.0	1.0	3.1	3.3	23.6	33.0
Guinea-Bissau	11.6	0.0	−2.6	−2.2	7.4	0.0	−1.3	2.4	0.4	1.0	1.2	2.1	20.0
Haiti	0.0	0.0	−4.2	−10.4	15.1	0.0	−0.2	3.0	1.5	2.6	6.0	2.0	15.5

Net financial flows from multilateral institutions

6.12

	International financial institutions ($ millions)							United Nations ($ millions)					Total
	World Bank		IMF		Regional development banks								
	IDA	IBRD	Concessional	Non-concessional	Concessional	Non-concessional	Others	UNDP	UNFPA	UNICEF	WFP	Others	$ millions
	2003	2003	2003	2003	2003	2003	2003	2003	2003	2003	2003	2003	2003
Honduras	35.8	−20.6	−7.6	−33.2	69.3	−21.6	1.3	0.8	1.7	1.1	1.9	2.1	31.1
Hungary	0.0	−280.5	0.0	0.0	0.0	−173.9	36.1	0.2	..	..	..	2.5	−415.6
India	242.8	−1,089.2	0.0	0.0	0.0	−866.9	−25.9	19.5	6.8	26.3	2.5	26.3	−1,657.7
Indonesia	63.8	−950.0	0.0	555.3	36.4	−38.1	−33.8	5.9	4.5	5.6	0.0	16.4	−334.0
Iran, Islamic Rep.	0.0	−49.3	0.0	0.0	0.0	0.0	−1.6	0.8	2.3	2.3	1.2	17.8	−26.6
Iraq	..	..	..	..	..	..	..	1.6	0.4	3.9	0.5	18.5	24.9
Ireland													
Israel	..	..	..	..	..	..	..	..	..	..	..	0.2	..
Italy													
Jamaica	0.0	−31.4	0.0	−16.0	−5.2	−22.9	9.4	0.5	0.1	0.7	..	1.5	−63.5
Japan													
Jordan	−2.6	−30.0	0.0	−99.9	0.0	0.0	−26.4	0.5	0.3	0.7	1.3	91.9	−64.1
Kazakhstan	0.0	−4.1	0.0	0.0	0.0	41.9	−8.8	0.6	0.5	1.0	..	1.7	32.9
Kenya	74.3	−7.7	15.3	0.0	−2.7	−8.7	−41.3	6.3	2.2	6.8	11.6	28.7	84.8
Korea, Dem. Rep.	..	..	..	..	..	..	..	1.6	0.6	2.5	3.2	3.1	11.0
Korea, Rep.	..	..	..	..	..	..	..	−0.1	..	..	..	2.1	..
Kuwait	..	..	..	..	..	..	..	..	..	..	..	0.3	..
Kyrgyz Republic	31.9	0.0	3.1	−5.6	25.7	−10.7	5.0	1.6	0.6	1.0	..	1.7	54.3
Lao PDR	41.7	0.0	−2.7	0.0	47.3	0.0	−1.1	2.1	1.2	1.5	2.1	2.0	94.1
Latvia	0.0	−106.1	0.0	−10.7	0.0	0.2	46.0	0.3	0.1	..	..	0.3	−70.0
Lebanon	0.0	22.7	0.0	0.0	0.0	0.0	569.7	0.5	0.5	0.7	..	55.2	649.3
Lesotho	11.6	−18.6	2.4	0.0	0.6	−1.6	−1.4	0.6	0.4	1.2	2.4	1.6	−0.8
Liberia	0.0	0.0	0.0	0.0	0.0	0.0	0.0	1.0	0.6	5.4	6.5	8.2	21.7
Libya	..	..	..	..	..	..	..	..	..	..	..	4.5	..
Lithuania	0.0	−20.0	0.0	−82.6	0.0	3.3	15.8	0.3	0.1	..	..	0.4	−82.8
Macedonia, FYR	32.9	18.2	−6.4	1.4	0.0	−3.7	11.3	1.2	..	0.6	0.1	5.1	60.7
Madagascar	186.0	0.0	12.3	0.0	11.0	−1.6	−0.9	4.9	2.1	4.7	4.7	4.1	227.3
Malawi	46.8	−1.7	1.4	0.0	23.3	−0.2	0.0	4.6	3.2	5.0	4.2	3.8	90.3
Malaysia	0.0	−10.7	0.0	0.0	0.0	−57.6	−2.3	0.4	0.2	0.5	..	2.3	−67.2
Mali	90.3	0.0	−0.2	0.0	41.3	0.0	15.5	3.8	2.0	5.1	3.8	3.8	165.4
Mauritania	40.8	0.0	−6.8	0.0	14.6	18.7	27.4	2.1	1.4	1.2	8.6	3.3	111.4
Mauritius	−0.6	−12.7	0.0	0.0	−0.1	−6.7	−0.4	0.2	0.1	0.5	..	1.2	−18.6
Mexico	0.0	−79.8	0.0	0.0	0.0	224.6	0.1	0.7	2.5	0.7	..	8.1	156.9
Moldova	15.7	−9.1	0.0	−22.1	0.0	−10.2	−11.1	1.0	0.2	0.7	..	2.2	−32.8
Mongolia	27.9	0.0	2.8	0.0	38.3	0.0	4.6	1.0	1.5	0.9	..	2.9	79.9
Morocco	−1.4	−162.9	0.0	0.0	0.7	−467.7	92.5	0.9	2.1	1.4	0.4	3.7	−530.4
Mozambique	153.8	0.0	3.1	0.0	27.4	−1.2	9.1	8.9	9.0	7.8	8.8	6.6	233.4
Myanmar	0.0	0.0	0.0	0.0	0.0	0.0	−1.4	5.8	1.7	7.2	1.1	8.8	23.1
Namibia	..	..	..	..	..	..	..	0.1	0.8	0.8	1.2	7.1	10.0
Nepal	79.3	0.0	6.9	0.0	−11.4	0.0	−2.8	5.4	2.8	4.2	6.3	12.6	103.3
Netherlands													
New Zealand													
Nicaragua	112.2	0.0	23.9	0.0	91.4	−1.2	2.9	2.3	2.1	0.7	1.7	1.7	237.7
Niger	71.8	0.0	18.4	0.0	34.5	0.0	5.7	5.7	3.1	6.6	1.9	3.9	151.6
Nigeria	46.1	−202.7	0.0	0.0	0.4	−14.0	0.0	4.8	6.6	21.3	..	17.0	−120.4
Norway													
Oman	0.0	0.0	0.0	0.0	0.0	0.0	−46.5	..	0.0	0.5	..	1.7	−44.3
Pakistan	29.4	−240.9	390.5	−497.7	28.9	155.9	−101.5	7.4	4.9	12.7	11.3	30.8	−168.4
Panama	0.0	−18.8	0.0	−9.3	−10.7	50.4	−0.4	0.4	0.4	0.6	..	3.4	16.0
Papua New Guinea	−3.6	−14.9	0.0	−5.2	−1.9	−3.4	−4.1	0.9	0.4	1.1	..	2.0	−28.7
Paraguay	−1.6	22.9	0.0	0.0	−16.2	41.2	−2.3	0.3	0.7	0.8	..	0.7	46.5
Peru	0.0	180.4	0.0	−112.3	−9.9	−63.9	147.9	0.7	1.6	0.9	1.9	9.7	156.9
Philippines	−6.2	−136.9	0.0	−607.6	−9.3	6.9	6.2	2.0	3.7	2.6	..	4.4	−734.1
Poland	0.0	−209.2	0.0	0.0	0.0	0.0	0.0	0.5	0.1	..	..	1.0	−207.7
Portugal													
Puerto Rico													

	International financial institutions ($ millions)							United Nations ($ millions)					Total ($ millions)
	World Bank		IMF		Regional development banks								
	IDA	IBRD	Concessional	Non-concessional	Concessional	Non-concessional	Others	UNDP	UNFPA	UNICEF	WFP	Others	
	2003	2003	2003	2003	2003	2003	2003	2003	2003	2003	2003	2003	2003
Romania	0.0	−13.8	0.0	119.9	2.8	−47.4	315.0	0.5	0.5	0.7	..	1.9	380.1
Russian Federation	0.0	−486.0	0.0	−1,896.9	0.0	82.3	0.0	0.3	0.7	1.0	1.1	13.7	−2,283.7
Rwanda	23.6	0.0	−0.9	0.0	6.9	0.0	−3.0	3.5	2.0	3.0	6.7	8.2	49.9
Saudi Arabia	..	..	..	..	..	..	..	0.1	0.0	0.0	..	12.1	..
Senegal	94.5	0.0	−27.1	0.0	10.1	−0.8	38.4	2.8	1.7	2.3	3.5	4.2	129.5
Serbia and Montenegro	95.1	0.0	0.0	0.0	0.0	0.0	80.2	1.1	1.0	0.5	..	1.1	179.0
Sierra Leone	24.3	0.0	18.2	0.0	6.8	0.0	4.6	3.8	1.4	3.9	5.3	30.6	98.7
Singapore	..	..	..	..	..	..	..	..	..	..	..	0.1	..
Slovak Republic	0.0	56.4	0.0	0.0	0.0	−1.4	−7.3	0.3	..	..	..	1.1	49.1
Slovenia	..	..	..	..	..	..	..	0.3	..	..	..	0.7	..
Somalia	0.0	0.0	0.0	0.0	0.0	0.0	0.0	4.3	0.6	5.1	2.1	9.3	21.4
South Africa	0.0	3.1	0.0	0.0	0.0	65.8	0.0	2.2	0.6	1.1	..	7.4	80.2
Spain													
Sri Lanka	165.9	−1.8	22.4	28.9	124.0	33.9	12.8	3.2	−0.2	1.1	1.8	10.5	402.5
Sudan	−2.8	0.0	0.0	−26.2	0.0	−0.9	0.0	4.3	1.7	5.3	5.9	21.0	8.3
Swaziland	−0.3	5.8	0.0	0.0	−0.4	−4.9	−0.9	0.5	0.4	0.8	0.9	2.2	4.0
Sweden													
Switzerland													
Syrian Arab Republic	−1.5	−7.5	0.0	0.0	0.0	0.0	−47.4	1.2	1.7	0.9	1.0	66.5	14.9
Tajikistan	13.3	0.0	−0.2	−3.9	14.7	0.3	−0.8	1.9	0.7	1.9	0.4	1.9	30.3
Tanzania	387.4	−2.6	17.6	0.0	47.6	0.0	−1.8	6.8	4.5	8.0	7.3	28.2	503.1
Thailand	−3.4	−250.4	0.0	−402.2	−3.0	−172.6	−13.4	0.5	0.6	0.9	..	10.1	−832.8
Togo	−0.1	0.0	−13.7	0.0	0.0	0.0	3.4	2.7	1.1	1.7	..	1.8	−3.0
Trinidad and Tobago	0.0	−1.9	0.0	0.0	−0.1	−15.6	33.7	0.1	0.0	..	..	1.4	17.7
Tunisia	−2.1	45.8	0.0	0.0	0.0	53.2	131.4	0.3	0.5	0.7	..	1.8	231.6
Turkey	−5.9	−220.2	0.0	−46.0	0.0	0.0	−36.2	0.9	0.9	0.9	..	5.4	−300.3
Turkmenistan	0.0	−1.6	0.0	0.0	0.0	0.0	..	0.8	0.5	1.0	0.1	0.8	1.6
Uganda	244.4	0.0	−19.1	0.0	15.6	7.8	23.9	4.5	6.2	5.4	19.6	17.4	325.7
Ukraine	0.0	−34.9	0.0	−202.2	0.0	61.1	−41.6	1.7	0.5	1.2	..	3.5	−210.8
United Arab Emirates	..	..	..	..	..	..	..	−0.6	..	..	..	0.4	0.4
United Kingdom													
United States													
Uruguay	0.0	19.2	0.0	429.6	−2.4	273.9	26.2	0.1	0.2	0.6	..	1.1	748.4
Uzbekistan	0.2	2.8	0.0	−23.3	3.3	29.5	0.0	1.4	0.6	1.8	..	1.6	18.1
Venezuela, RB	0.0	−186.9	0.0	0.0	0.0	−121.9	192.8	0.4	0.7	0.7	..	4.4	−109.8
Vietnam	565.2	0.0	−67.6	−5.6	182.4	−1.8	2.4	0.5	5.3	4.1	..	5.5	690.2
West Bank and Gaza	..	..	..	..	..	..	..	2.3	1.6	2.8	1.7	264.5	272.9
Yemen, Rep.	66.1	0.0	−12.3	−6.8	0.0	0.0	11.0	4.6	2.2	3.5	9.2	7.1	84.6
Zambia	74.3	−7.2	−70.7	0.0	11.0	−2.5	−16.8	2.5	1.5	3.6	2.7	14.5	12.9
Zimbabwe	0.0	−0.1	−4.5	0.0	0.0	0.9	−2.8	2.6	1.1	2.0	4.9	5.1	9.1
World	.. s	.. s	.. s	.. s	.. s	.. s	.. s	301.7 s	273.0 s	634.0 s	355.8 s	1,996.7 s	.. s
Low income	4,190.3	−1,667.1	385.1	−670.4	1,022.2	−719.4	−44.8	234.6	151.4	289.4	268.3	525.5	3,965.2
Middle income	865.4	−4,550.1	3.0	2,660.4	294.9	−595.3	2,395.6	66.9	66.9	76.8	51.2	960.7	2,296.3
Lower middle income	864.3	−2,551.7	−4.4	2,489.1	326.2	−1,177.7	1,530.0	60.1	56.0	67.5	51.1	767.7	2,478.3
Upper middle income	1.1	−1,998.3	7.4	171.2	−31.3	582.4	865.6	6.7	7.6	8.8	0.1	131.7	−247.1
Low & middle income	5,055.8	−6,217.2	388.2	1,990.0	1,317.2	−1,314.8	2,350.8	301.6	273.0	634.0	355.4	1,989.8	7,123.8
East Asia & Pacific	745.6	−2,202.4	−67.5	−466.8	351.8	−1,610.8	1.6	36.5	31.3	46.8	20.4	83.6	−3,030.0
Europe & Central Asia	486.3	−1,232.8	−0.9	−1,993.1	46.6	23.7	872.2	24.0	9.3	17.8	7.6	117.2	−1,622.2
Latin America & Carib.	301.4	−743.0	0.8	5,568.3	231.6	1,373.9	1,213.0	17.7	32.0	21.3	22.0	211.4	8,250.4
Middle East & N. Africa	79.6	−381.2	−12.3	−547.3	9.2	−412.3	317.0	15.2	16.9	22.3	23.6	606.9	−262.4
South Asia	921.2	−1,338.2	485.8	−538.2	242.7	−656.6	−88.2	53.9	43.8	71.1	43.2	104.7	−654.8
Sub-Saharan Africa	2,521.7	−319.5	−17.7	−32.9	435.4	−32.7	35.3	154.2	95.6	192.8	202.9	514.5	3,749.5
High income													
Europe EMU													

Note: The aggregates for the United Nations and total net financial flows include amounts for economies not specified elsewhere.

Net financial flows from multilateral institutions

6.12

GLOBAL LINKS

About the data

The table shows concessional and nonconcessional financial flows from the major multilateral institutions—the World Bank, the International Monetary Fund (IMF), regional development banks, United Nations agencies, and regional groups such as the Commission of the European Communities. Much of the data comes from the World Bank's Debtor Reporting System.

The multilateral development banks fund their nonconcessional lending operations primarily by selling low-interest, highly rated bonds (the World Bank, for example, has an AAA rating) backed by prudent lending and financial policies and the strong financial support of their members. These funds are then on-lent at slightly higher interest rates and with relatively long maturities (15–20 years) to developing countries. Lending terms vary with market conditions and the policies of the banks.

Concessional flows from bilateral donors are defined by the Development Assistance Committee (DAC) of the Organisation for Economic Co-operation and Development (OECD) as financial flows containing a grant element of at least 25 percent. The grant element of loans is evaluated assuming a nominal market interest rate of 10 percent. The grant element is nil for a loan carrying a 10 percent interest rate, and it is 100 percent for a grant, which requires no repayment. Concessional flows from multilateral development agencies are credits provided through their concessional lending facilities. The cost of these loans is reduced through subsidies provided by donors or drawn from other resources available to the agencies. Grants provided by multilateral agencies are not included in the net flows.

All concessional lending by the World Bank is carried out by the International Development Association (IDA). Eligibility for IDA resources is based on gross national income (GNI) per capita; countries must also meet performance standards assessed by World Bank staff. Since July 1, 2004, the GNI per capita cutoff has been set at $765, measured in 2003 using the *World Bank Atlas* method (see *Users guide*). In exceptional circumstances IDA extends eligibility temporarily to countries that are above the cutoff and are undertaking major adjustment efforts but are not creditworthy for lending by the International Bank for Reconstruction and Development (IBRD). An exception has also been made for small island economies. Lending by the International Finance Corporation is not included in this table.

The IMF makes concessional funds available through its Poverty Reduction and Growth Facility, which replaced the Enhanced Structural Adjustment Facility in 1999, and through the IMF Trust Fund. Eligibility is based principally on a country's per capita income and eligibility under IDA, the World Bank's concessional window.

Regional development banks also maintain concessional windows for funds. Loans from the major regional development banks—the African Development Bank, Asian Development Bank, and Inter-American Development Bank—are recorded in the table according to each institution's classification.

In 1999 all United Nations agencies revised their data since 1990 to include only regular budgetary expenditures (except for the World Food Programme and the United Nations High Commissioner for Refugees, which revised their data from 1996 onward). They did so to avoid double counting extrabudgetary expenditures reported by DAC countries and flows reported by the United Nations.

Definitions

• **Net financial flows** in this table are disbursements of public or publicly guaranteed loans and credits, less repayments of principal. • **IDA** is the International Development Association, the concessional loan window of the World Bank. • **IBRD** is the International Bank for Reconstruction and Development, the founding and largest member of the World Bank Group. • **IMF** is the International Monetary Fund. Its nonconcessional lending consists of the credit it provides to its members, mainly to meet their balance of payments needs. It provides concessional assistance through the Poverty Reduction and Growth Facility and the IMF Trust Fund. • **Regional development banks** include the African Development Bank, in Tunis, Tunisia, which lends to all of Africa, including North Africa; the Asian Development Bank, in Manila, Philippines, which serves countries in South and Central Asia and East Asia and Pacific; the European Bank for Reconstruction and Development, in London, United Kingdom, which serves countries in Europe and Central Asia; the European Development Fund, in Brussels, Belgium, which serves countries in Africa, the Caribbean, and the Pacific; and the Inter-American Development Bank, in Washington, D.C., which is the principal development bank of the Americas. Concessional financial flows cover disbursements made through concessional lending facilities. Nonconcessional financial flows cover all other disbursements. • **Others** is a residual category in the World Bank's Debtor Reporting System. It includes such institutions as the Caribbean Development Bank and the European Investment Bank. • **United Nations** includes the United Nations Development Programme (UNDP), United Nations Population Fund (UNFPA), United Nations Children's Fund (UNICEF), World Food Programme (WFP), and other United Nations agencies, such as the United Nations High Commissioner for Refugees, United Nations Relief and Works Agency for Palestine Refugees in the Near East, and United Nations Regular Programme for Technical Assistance.

Data sources

The data on net financial flows from international financial institutions come from the World Bank's Debtor Reporting System. These data are published in the World Bank's *Global Development Finance 2005* and electronically as *GDF Online*. The data on aid from United Nations agencies come from the DAC annual *Development Cooperation Report*. Data are available in electronic format on the OECD's *International Development Statistics* CD-ROM and to registered users at http://www.oecd.org/dataoecd/50/17/5037721.htm.

6.12a

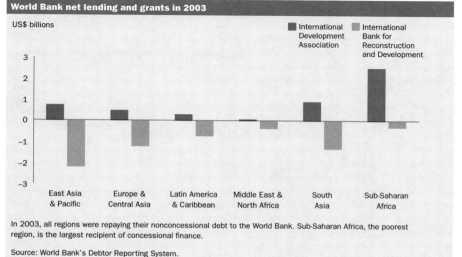

World Bank net lending and grants in 2003

US$ billions

Legend: ■ International Development Association ▨ International Bank for Reconstruction and Development

(Chart showing values by region: East Asia & Pacific, Europe & Central Asia, Latin America & Caribbean, Middle East & North Africa, South Asia, Sub-Saharan Africa)

In 2003, all regions were repaying their nonconcessional debt to the World Bank. Sub-Saharan Africa, the poorest region, is the largest recipient of concessional finance.

Source: World Bank's Debtor Reporting System.

Movement of people

	Net migration		Migration stock				Refugees				Workers' remittances and compensation of employees, received	
	thousands		thousands		% of population		By country of origin thousands		By country of asylum thousands		$ millions	
	1990–95	1995–2000	1990	2000	1990	2000	1994	2003	1994	2003	1990	2003
Afghanistan	3,313	−397	28	36	0.2	0.1	2,731.2	2,136.0	19.1	0.0	..	..
Albania	−423	−267	12	12	0.4	0.4	5.0	10.4	3.0	0.0	..	889
Algeria	−58	−185	274	250	1.1	0.8	20.7	11.7	219.1	169.0	352	1,090
Angola	143	−120	34	46	0.4	0.4	282.6	329.6	10.7	13.4	..	..
Argentina	50	−100	1,662	1,419	5.1	4.0	0.5	0.8	11.9	2.6	..	253
Armenia	−500	−225	571	300	16.1	9.6	201.8	13.2	304.0	239.3	..	168
Australia	390	510	3,984	4,705	23.3	24.5	0.0	0.0	57.6	56.3	2,370	2,259
Austria	262	45	473	756	6.1	9.4	0.1	0.1	40.7	16.1	635	2,294
Azerbaijan	−116	−128	361	148	5.0	1.8	299.1	253.3	231.6	0.3	..	171
Bangladesh	−260	−300	882	988	0.8	0.8	56.2	5.6	116.2	19.8	779	3,191
Belarus	15	14	1,271	1,284	12.5	12.8	0.0	7.8	1.8	0.6	..	162
Belgium	85	99	899	879	9.0	8.6	0.0	0.0	19.5	12.6	3,583	3,933
Benin	105	−29	75	101	1.6	1.6	0.1	0.3	70.4	5.0	101	84
Bolivia	−100	−100	60	61	0.9	0.7	0.2	0.3	0.7	0.5	5	126
Bosnia and Herzegovina	−1,000	350	56	96	1.3	2.4	776.1	300.0	..	22.5	..	1,178
Botswana	−7	−7	27	52	2.2	3.1	0.0	0.0	0.5	2.8	86	27
Brazil	−184	−130	809	546	0.5	0.3	0.0	0.4	2.2	3.2	573	2,821
Bulgaria	−309	−50	22	101	0.2	1.3	4.7	2.6	1.1	4.1	..	67
Burkina Faso	−128	−121	438	1,124	4.9	10.0	0.1	0.9	50.0	0.5	140	50
Burundi	−250	−400	333	77	6.1	1.1	389.7	531.6	300.3	41.0	..	..
Cambodia	194	100	38	211	0.4	1.7	8.5	31.4	0.0	0.1	..	138
Cameroon	−5	0	174	150	1.5	1.0	0.2	6.2	44.0	58.6	23	11
Canada	643	733	4,319	5,826	15.5	18.9	0.0	0.1	186.6	133.1	..	..
Central African Republic	37	11	56	59	1.9	1.6	0.3	35.4	47.8	44.8	..	..
Chad	20	99	17	41	0.3	0.5	212.0	52.3	0.1	146.4	..	..
Chile	90	60	108	153	0.8	1.0	15.5	1.6	0.2	0.5	..	13
China	−1,281	−1,950	380	513	0.0	0.0	113.9	132.4	287.1	299.4	124	4,625
Hong Kong, China	300	300	2,218	2,701	38.9	40.5	0.3	0.0	1.7	1.9	..	1
Colombia	−200	−200	102	115	0.3	0.3	1.4	38.0	0.3	0.2	495	3,076
Congo, Dem. Rep.	1,208	−1,410	938	739	2.5	1.5	73.3	453.5	1,724.4	234.0	..	..
Congo, Rep.	14	42	108	197	4.3	5.7	0.0	29.0	15.5	91.4	..	1
Costa Rica	62	128	418	311	13.7	8.2	0.2	0.1	24.6	13.5	12	321
Côte d'Ivoire	200	150	1,953	2,336	16.5	14.8	0.1	33.6	360.1	76.0	44	141
Croatia	153	−150	483	425	10.1	9.7	76.3	230.2	183.6	4.4	..	1,069
Cuba	−100	−100	100	82	0.9	0.7	23.3	16.1	2.0	0.8	..	..
Czech Republic	38	52	146	236	1.4	2.3	4.7	6.7	1.2	1.5	..	500
Denmark	58	84	220	304	4.3	5.7	0.0	0.0	49.6	69.9	..	941
Dominican Republic	−220	−180	103	136	1.5	1.6	0.0	0.1	1.3	..	315	2,325
Ecuador	−50	−300	78	82	0.8	0.7	0.2	0.7	0.2	6.4	51	1,545
Egypt, Arab Rep.	−600	−500	176	169	0.3	0.3	0.5	5.7	7.2	88.8	4,284	2,961
El Salvador	−57	−38	47	24	0.9	0.4	30.7	5.7	0.2	0.3	366	2,122
Eritrea	−359	−9	12	13	0.4	0.3	422.4	124.1	0.7	3.9	..	..
Estonia	−117	−46	405	365	25.8	26.7	0.3	1.0	..	0.0	..	40
Ethiopia	888	−77	1,153	660	2.3	1.0	226.4	62.7	348.1	130.3	5	46
Finland	43	20	61	134	1.2	2.6	..	0.0	9.5	10.8	63	642
France	424	219	5,907	6,277	10.4	10.7	0.0	0.1	195.3	130.8	4,035	11,418
Gabon	20	14	128	250	13.4	19.8	0.0	0.0	0.6	14.0	..	4
Gambia, The	45	45	118	185	12.7	14.1	0.0	0.8	2.2	7.5	10	40
Georgia	−560	−350	365	219	6.7	4.2	5.1	12.5	..	3.9	..	246
Germany	2,688	1,134	5,236	7,349	6.6	8.9	0.5	0.7	1,354.6	960.4	4,876	5,693
Ghana	40	−51	507	614	3.3	3.1	14.3	15.9	113.7	44.0	6	65
Greece	470	300	370	534	3.6	4.9	0.1	0.3	7.8	2.8	1,817	1,564
Guatemala	−360	−390	264	43	3.0	0.4	49.6	6.7	4.7	0.7	119	2,147
Guinea	350	−227	407	741	7.1	10.0	0.1	3.9	553.2	184.3	..	111
Guinea-Bissau	20	−11	14	19	1.4	1.4	5.0	1.0	23.9	7.6	1	18
Haiti	−105	−105	19	26	0.3	0.3	9.8	7.6	..	..	61	811

	Net migration		Migration stock				Refugees				Workers' remittances and compensation of employees, received	
							By country of origin thousands		By country of asylum thousands		$ millions	
	thousands		thousands		% of population							
	1990–95	1995–2000	1990	2000	1990	2000	1994	2003	1994	2003	1990	2003
Honduras	−40	−20	277	44	5.7	0.7	1.2	0.6	0.1	0.0	63	867
Hungary	101	100	348	296	3.4	3.0	4.5	3.4	2.9	7.0	..	295
India	−1,407	−1,400	7,393	6,271	0.9	0.6	3.3	13.7	258.3	164.8	2,384	17,406
Indonesia	−725	−900	466	397	0.3	0.2	8.7	16.2	0.1	0.2	166	1,489
Iran, Islamic Rep.	−1,512	−456	3,809	2,321	7.0	3.6	121.3	132.5	2,236.4	984.9	..	340
Iraq	170	139	84	147	0.5	0.6	749.8	368.6	119.6	134.2	..	..
Ireland	−1	89	230	310	6.6	8.1	0.0	0.0	0.4	6.0	286	337
Israel	484	276	1,633	2,256	35.0	35.9	0.9	0.6	..	4.2	812	299
Italy	573	600	1,346	1,634	2.4	2.8	0.2	0.2	73.1	12.8	5,075	2,137
Jamaica	−100	−100	17	13	0.7	0.5	0.0	0.3	0.0	..	229	1,398
Japan	248	280	877	1,620	0.7	1.3	0.0	0.0	5.9	2.3	..	1,078
Jordan[a]	495	35	1,147	1,945	36.2	39.8	0.4	1.2	0.6	1.2	499	2,201
Kazakhstan	−1,509	−1,320	3,777	3,028	23.1	20.1	0.0	6.6	5.0	15.8	..	147
Kenya	222	−21	146	327	0.6	1.1	8.8	3.2	252.4	237.5	139	494
Korea, Dem. Rep.	0	0	34	37	0.2	0.2	0.0	0.3	..	..	..	..
Korea, Rep.	−115	−80	572	597	1.3	1.3	0.0	0.2	..	0.0	1,037	824
Kuwait	−626	347	1,560	1,108	73.4	50.6	0.8	0.6	30.0	1.5	..	..
Kyrgyz Republic	−273	−27	677	572	15.3	11.6	0.0	3.1	21.2	5.6	..	108
Lao PDR	−10	−7	14	16	0.3	0.3	54.9	10.4	..	..	11	1
Latvia	−174	−56	681	613	25.5	25.8	0.1	3.2	..	0.0	..	171
Lebanon[a]	178	−30	533	634	14.7	14.6	15.7	24.9	1.4	2.5	1,818	2,700
Lesotho	−84	−36	7	6	0.4	0.3	..	0.0	0.1	..	428	184
Liberia	−283	555	81	160	3.3	5.1	797.8	353.4	120.2	34.0	..	..
Libya	10	10	457	570	10.6	10.9	0.7	1.6	2.0	11.9	..	..
Lithuania	−100	−109	371	339	10.0	9.7	0.1	1.5	..	0.4	..	115
Macedonia, FYR	−27	−5	25	33	1.3	1.6	0.4	6.0	14.9	0.2	..	171
Madagascar	−6	−3	58	61	0.5	0.4	0.0	0.1	0.1	..	8	16
Malawi	−835	−50	1,157	280	13.6	2.7	0.1	0.1	90.2	3.2	..	1
Malaysia	230	390	1,014	1,392	5.6	6.0	0.1	0.2	5.3	7.4	325	987
Mali	−260	−284	60	48	0.7	0.4	172.9	0.5	15.8	10.0	107	138
Mauritania	−15	10	94	63	4.6	2.4	68.0	30.5	82.2	0.5	14	2
Mauritius	−7	−2	9	8	0.8	0.7	0.0	0.1	..	..	..	215
Mexico	−1,800	−2,000	701	521	0.8	0.5	0.3	1.7	47.4	6.1	3,098	14,595
Moldova	−121	−70	579	474	13.3	11.1	0.5	11.2	..	0.1	..	465
Mongolia	−60	−90	7	8	0.3	0.3	0.0	0.3	..	..	..	56
Morocco	−300	−300	41	26	0.2	0.1	0.2	1.3	0.3	2.1	2,006	3,614
Mozambique	650	75	122	366	0.9	2.1	234.5	0.1	0.3	0.3	70	69
Myanmar	−126	60	100	113	0.2	0.2	204.5	151.4	..	..	6	78
Namibia	3	20	119	143	8.5	7.5	0.1	1.3	1.1	19.8	13	13
Nepal	−101	−99	413	619	2.3	2.7	0.0	1.2	103.3	123.7	..	785
Netherlands	190	161	1,192	1,576	8.0	9.9	0.1	0.3	62.2	140.9	709	767
New Zealand	79	20	529	850	15.4	22.0	..	0.0	3.7	5.8	762	1,199
Nicaragua	−110	−155	41	27	1.1	0.5	28.6	4.0	0.3	0.3	..	439
Niger	5	−6	114	119	1.5	1.1	22.0	0.7	15.1	0.3	14	8
Nigeria	−96	−95	447	751	0.5	0.6	0.6	24.4	6.0	9.2	10	1,677
Norway	42	67	185	299	4.4	6.6	0.0	0.0	44.6	46.1	158	322
Oman	25	−40	450	682	27.7	28.3	0.0	0.0	..	..	39	39
Pakistan	−2,611	−41	6,556	4,243	6.1	3.1	4.4	24.4	1,055.4	1,124.3	2,006	3,964
Panama	8	11	62	82	2.6	2.9	0.5	0.0	1.0	1.5	110	85
Papua New Guinea	0	0	33	23	0.8	0.4	..	0.0	8.5	7.5	5	6
Paraguay	−25	−25	183	203	4.4	3.8	0.1	0.0	0.1	0.0	34	222
Peru	−450	−350	56	46	0.3	0.2	4.3	5.6	0.7	0.7	87	860
Philippines	−900	−900	163	160	0.3	0.2	0.4	0.4	0.7	0.1	1,465	7,880
Poland	−77	−71	1,709	2,088	4.5	5.4	35.9	15.2	0.4	1.8	..	2,314
Portugal	−7	175	136	233	1.4	2.3	0.0	0.1	0.3	0.4	4,479	3,024
Puerto Rico	−4	−1	322	383	9.1	10.0	0.0	..	..	..	..	..

	Net migration (thousands)		Migration stock (thousands)		% of population		Refugees By country of origin (thousands)		By country of asylum (thousands)		Workers' remittances and compensation of employees, received ($ millions)	
	1990–95	1995–2000	1990	2000	1990	2000	1994	2003	1994	2003	1990	2003
Romania	−529	−350	143	94	0.6	0.4	22.3	8.4	1.2	2.0	..	124
Russian Federation	1,858	2,300	11,689	13,259	7.9	9.1	251.4	96.4	..	9.9	..	1,453
Rwanda	−1,714	1,977	73	89	1.0	1.2	2,257.6	75.3	6.0	36.6	3	7
Saudi Arabia	−325	75	4,220	5,255	26.7	25.4	0.2	0.2	18.0	240.8	..	..
Senegal	−100	−100	293	284	4.0	3.0	25.6	8.4	73.0	20.7	142	344
Serbia and Montenegro	200	−100	132	626	1.3	5.9	55.0	296.6	450.7	291.4	..	1,397
Sierra Leone	−380	−110	112	47	2.8	0.9	275.3	70.6	15.9	61.2	..	26
Singapore	250	368	727	1,352	23.9	33.6	0.0	0.0	0.0	0.0	..	..
Slovak Republic	9	9	16	32	0.3	0.6	0.0	0.7	0.2	0.4	..	425
Slovenia	38	8	25	51	1.3	2.6	14.8	0.6	29.2	2.1	..	255
Somalia	−1,083	−214	634	22	8.9	0.3	631.4	402.3	0.4	0.4	..	..
South Africa	1,125	364	1,225	1,303	3.5	3.0	1.5	0.3	91.9	26.6	136	436
Spain	500	676	766	1,259	2.0	3.1	0.0	0.1	5.4	5.9	2,186	6,068
Sri Lanka	−182	−160	461	397	2.8	2.1	114.5	122.0	0.0	0.0	401	1,438
Sudan	−158	−207	1,261	780	5.1	2.5	405.1	606.2	727.2	138.2	62	1,224
Swaziland	−38	−12	73	42	9.4	4.0	0.0	0.0	0.6	0.7	113	62
Sweden	151	60	781	993	9.1	11.2	0.0	0.0	200.8	112.2	153	578
Switzerland	80	80	1,376	1,801	20.5	25.1	0.0	0.0	75.3	50.1	924	1,709
Syrian Arab Republic[a]	−30	−30	711	903	5.9	5.6	7.1	20.3	40.3	3.7	664	618
Tajikistan	−313	−345	446	330	8.4	5.3	57.1	58.9	0.7	3.3	..	146
Tanzania	591	−206	574	893	2.3	2.6	0.1	0.7	883.3	649.8	..	7
Thailand	−88	−88	386	353	0.7	0.6	0.1	0.3	100.8	119.1	973	1,601
Togo	−122	128	162	179	4.7	3.9	167.9	10.6	12.4	12.4	27	103
Trinidad and Tobago	−24	−20	51	41	4.2	3.2	0.0	0.0	..	..	3	79
Tunisia	−22	−20	38	38	0.5	0.4	0.2	2.6	0.0	0.1	551	1,250
Turkey	71	135	1,150	1,503	2.0	2.2	28.9	185.7	24.9	2.5	3,246	729
Turkmenistan	50	−50	320	223	8.7	4.8	0.0	0.8	15.4	13.5	..	..
Uganda	135	−66	550	529	3.2	2.3	31.5	35.3	286.5	230.9	..	295
Ukraine	598	−700	7,097	6,947	13.7	14.0	0.9	94.2	5.2	2.9	..	330
United Arab Emirates	340	567	1,556	1,922	87.7	59.2	..	0.0	0.4	0.2	..	..
United Kingdom	381	574	3,753	4,029	6.5	6.8	0.1	0.2	85.2	276.5	2,099	5,029
United States	5,200	6,200	23,251	34,988	9.3	12.4	0.4	0.4	631.1	452.6	1,170	3,031
Uruguay	−20	−16	98	89	3.2	2.7	0.4	0.1	0.1	0.1	..	32
Uzbekistan	−340	−400	1,714	1,367	8.4	5.5	29.1	7.4	8.0	44.7	..	..
Venezuela, RB	40	40	1,024	1,006	5.2	4.1	0.4	0.6	2.2	0.1	1	21
Vietnam	−270	−200	28	22	0.0	0.0	539.1	363.2	5.0	15.4	..	2,700
West Bank and Gaza[a]	−5	11	1,181	1,665	59.9	56.1	82.6	427.9	..	..	..	692
Yemen, Rep.	650	−50	107	248	0.9	1.4	0.2	1.6	48.3	61.9	1,498	1,270
Zambia	−7	86	323	377	4.2	3.8	0.0	0.1	141.1	226.7	..	..
Zimbabwe	−182	−125	804	656	7.8	5.2	0.0	7.2	2.2	12.7	1	..
World	..[b]	..[b]	153,662 s	174,467 s	2.9 w	2.9 w	15,733.7[c,d] s	9,680.3[c,d] s	15,733.7[d] s	9,680.3[d] s	68,776 s	173,103 s
Low income	−3,448	−4,542	32,562	28,814	1.8	1.3	10,556.9	6,246.6	8,039.9	4,344.3	8,115	36,741
Middle income	−9,835	−9,494	55,183	57,116	2.1	2.0	3,159.7	2,909.3	4,522.8	2,818.9	23,228	79,866
Lower middle income	−8,185	−7,726	39,933	40,121	1.7	1.5	3,003.1	2,615.2	4,210.6	2,498.6	17,494	55,385
Upper middle income	−1,650	−1,768	15,250	16,995	5.4	5.3	156.6	294.1	312.2	320.3	5,734	24,481
Low & middle income	−13,283	−14,036	87,745	85,930	2.0	1.7	13,716.6	9,155.9	12,562.6	7,163.2	31,343	116,607
East Asia & Pacific	−3,072	−3,859	2,732	3,330	0.2	0.2	930.5	707.9	407.4	449.1	3,177	19,714
Europe & Central Asia	−3,398	−1,858	34,564	35,011	7.4	7.4	1,859.2	1,636.9	1,277.1	678.2	3,246	12,880
Latin America & Carib.	−3,776	−4,156	6,390	5,167	1.5	1.0	168.1	91.1	109.0	38.3	5,775	34,425
Middle East & N. Africa	−1,355	−1,321	13,286	14,880	5.6	5.1	1,017.6	1,000.5	2,726.5	1,728.1	11,711	16,775
South Asia	−1,368	−2,401	15,744	12,565	1.4	0.9	3,012.8	2,406.9	1,552.4	1,432.6	5,572	26,787
Sub-Saharan Africa	−314	−439	15,029	14,977	2.9	2.3	6,728.5	3,312.6	6,490.2	2,836.9	1,862	6,026
High income	13,254	14,029	65,917	88,536	7.6	9.5	18.4	4.9	3,171.1	2,517.1	37,433	56,496
Europe EMU	5,247	3,538	16,730	21,104	5.7	6.9	0.9	1.8	1,768.9	1,300.8	27,744	38,707

a. Palestinian refugees under the mandate of the United Nations Relief and Works Agency for Palestine Refugees are not included in statistics from the United Nations Office of the High Commissioner for Refugees (UNHCR). b. World totals computed by the UN sum to zero, but because the aggregates shown here refer to World Bank definitions, regional and income group totals do not equal zero. c. World totals come from UNHCR. Thus regional and income group totals do not add up to the world total. d. World totals include refugees without a specified country or region, which are classified by UNHCR in the category "various."

Movement of people, most often through migration, is a significant part of integration. Migrants contribute to the economies of both their host country and their country of origin. Yet reliable statistics on migration are difficult to collect and are often incomplete, making international comparisons a challenge.

The data used to estimate the international migrant stock at a particular point in time are obtained mainly from population censuses. The estimates are derived from the data on foreign-born population – those who have residence in one country but whose place of birth is another. When data on the foreign-born population are not available, data on foreign population are used as estimates.

After the breakup of the Soviet Union in 1991, people living in one of the newly independent countries who were born in another of the countries were classified as international migrants. Estimates of migration stock in the newly independent states from 1990 on are based on the 1989 census of the Soviet Union.

For countries with information on the international migration stock for at least two points in time, interpolation or extrapolation was used to estimate the international migrant stock on July 1 of the reference years. For countries with only one observation, estimates for the reference years were derived using rates of change in the migrant stock in the years preceding or following the single observation available. A model was used to estimate migration for countries that had no data.

Registration, together with other sources—including estimates and surveys—are the main sources of refugee data. Yet there are difficulties in collecting accurate statistics. Although refugees are often registered individually, the accuracy of registrations varies greatly. Many refugees may not be aware of the need to register or may choose not to do so. And administrative records tend to overestimate the actual number of refugees because it is easier to register than to de-register. Palestinian refugees under the mandate of the United Nations Relief and Works Agency for Palestinian Refugees are not included in United Nations Office of the High Commissioner for Refugees (UNHCR) statistics.

Workers' remittances and compensation of employees are World Bank staff estimates based on data from the International Monetary Fund's (IMF) *Balance of Payments Yearbook*. Migrants' transfers are also included. The IMF data are supplemented by World Bank staff estimates for missing data for countries where workers' remittances are important.

The items that constitute workers' remittances and compensation of employees are taken from the IMF *Balance of Payments Manual* (fifth edition). These are workers' remittances, compensation of employees, and migrants' transfers. Workers' remittances are classified as current private transfers from migrant workers who are residents of the host country to recipients in their country of origin. They include only transfers made by workers who have been living in the host country for more than a year, irrespective of their immigration status. Compensation of employees is the income of migrants who have lived in the host country for less than a year. Migrants' transfers are defined as the net worth of migrants who are expected to remain in the host country for more than one year that is transferred from one country to another at the time of migration.

The distinction between these three items is not always consistent in the data reported by countries to the IMF. In some cases, countries compile data on the basis of the citizenship of migrant workers rather than their residency status. Some countries also report remittances entirely as workers' remittances or compensation of employees. Following the fifth edition of the *Balance of Payments Manual* in 1993, migrants' transfers are considered a capital transaction but in previous editions they were regarded as current transfers. For these reasons the figures presented in the table take all three items into account.

• **Net migration** is the net average annual number of migrants during the period, that is, the annual number of immigrants less the annual number of emigrants, including both citizens and noncitizens. Data shown in the table are five-year estimates.
• **Migration stock** is the number of people born in a country other than that in which they live. It also includes refugees. • **Refugees** are people who are recognized as refugees under the 1951 Convention Relating to the Status of Refugees or its 1967 Protocol, the 1969 Organization of African Unity Convention Governing the Specific Aspects of Refugee Problems in Africa, people recognized as refugees in accordance with the UNHCR statute, people granted a refugee-like humanitarian status, and people provided with temporary protection. Asylum seekers are people who have applied for asylum or refugee status and who have not yet received a decision or who are otherwise registered as asylum seekers.
• **Country of asylum** is the country where an asylum claim was filed. • **Country of origin** generally refers to the nationality or country of citizenship of a claimant. • **Workers' remittances and compensation of employees, received** comprise current transfers by migrant workers and wages and salaries earned by nonresident workers.

Data sources

Data on net migration come from the United Nations Population Division's *World Population Prospects: The 2004 Revision*. Data on migration stock come from the United Nations Population Division's *Trends in Total Migrant Stock: The 2003 Revision*. Refugee data are from the United Nations High Commissioner for Refugees' *Statistical Yearbook 2003*. Remittances data are World Bank staff estimates based on IMF balance of payments data.

	International tourism				International tourism receipts				International tourism expenditures			
	thousands				$ millions		% of exports		$ millions		% of imports	
	Inbound tourists		Outbound tourists									
	1995	2003	1995	2003	1995	2003	1995	2003	1995	2003	1995	2003
Afghanistan	..	..	..	..	..	..	..	..	1	..	..	..
Albania	40	*34*	12	..	70	537	23.2	46.0	19	507	2.3	19.6
Algeria	520	1,166	1,090	1,254	32	161	..	..	186	*248*	..	..
Angola	9	107	3	..	10	71	0.3	0.8	113	*52*	3.2	*0.7*
Argentina	2,289	3,374	3,815	3,346	2,550	2,397	10.2	7.1	4,013	3,080	15.4	16.5
Armenia	12	206	..	169	14	90	4.7	10.0	12	97	1.7	6.9
Australia	3,726	4,354	2,519	3,388	11,658	14,528	16.8	15.8	7,074	10,136	9.5	9.4
Austria	17,173	19,078	*3,713*	5,060	14,529	16,247	16.2	12.2	11,686	12,650	12.7	9.7
Azerbaijan	93	*834*	432	*1,141*	87	70	11.1	2.3	165	120	12.8	2.5
Bangladesh	156	*207*	830	*1,075*	..	59	..	0.7	*251*	404	*3.4*	3.7
Belarus	161	*61*	626	*1,386*	28	339	0.5	2.9	101	530	1.8	4.3
Belgium	5,560	6,690	*5,645*	7,268	..	8,758	..	..	..	13,196	..	..
Benin	138	*72*	..	..	..	86	..	16.4	48	*48*	5.4	*6.4*
Bolivia	284	352	249	672	92	176	7.5	9.4	72	136	4.6	6.9
Bosnia and Herzegovina	*115*	165	..	..	..	258	..	12.5	..	98	..	1.7
Botswana	521	975	..	..	176	..	7.3	..	153	..	7.5	..
Brazil	1,991	*3,783*	2,600	*1,861*	1,085	2,673	2.1	3.2	3,982	2,874	6.3	4.5
Bulgaria	3,466	4,048	3,524	3,403	662	2,106	9.8	19.9	312	1,065	4.8	8.5
Burkina Faso	124	163	..	..	..	25	..	9.6	..	35	..	5.4
Burundi	34	*36*	36	*35*	2	1	1.9	2.8	..	..	..	..
Cambodia	220	701	31	..	71	441	7.3	17.1	22	60	1.6	2.0
Cameroon	100	*226*	..	..	75	..	3.7	..	140	..	8.7	..
Canada	16,932	17,534	18,206	17,739	9,176	12,213	4.2	3.7	12,658	16,222	6.3	5.5
Central African Republic	26	..	..	..	4	*3*	..	..	43	*29*	..	..
Chad	19	21	..	*39*	43	25	..	..	38	*80*	..	..
Chile	1,540	1,614	1,070	2,100	1,186	1,362	6.1	5.3	934	1,044	5.1	4.4
China	20,034	32,970	4,520	20,222	*12,626*	18,707	*6.1*	3.9	*9,220*	16,716	*5.6*	3.7
Hong Kong, China	10,200	15,537	3,023	*4,709*	..	9,623	..	3.6	..	..	..	..
Colombia	1,399	*541*	1,057	*1,241*	887	1,114	7.2	7.2	1,162	1,313	7.3	7.9
Congo, Dem. Rep.	35	35	..	..	..	..	..	..	..	..	..	..
Congo, Rep.	37	*28*	..	..	15	*26*	1.1	*1.0*	69	*85*	5.1	*5.3*
Costa Rica	785	*1,113*	273	*364*	763	1,424	17.1	17.5	336	434	7.1	5.1
Côte d'Ivoire	188	..	..	..	103	*56*	2.4	*1.0*	312	*490*	8.2	*12.2*
Croatia	1,485	7,409	..	..	..	6,579	..	44.1	..	709	..	4.1
Cuba	742	*1,656*	72	*111*	963	*1,633*	..	..	..	..	..	..
Czech Republic	3,381	5,076	44,873	36,074	..	4,069	..	7.2	..	2,177	..	3.7
Denmark	2,124	2,016	*5,035*	5,564	..	..	..	..	..	..	..	..
Dominican Republic	1,776	3,282	168	321	..	..	..	..	267	396	4.4	4.4
Ecuador	440	761	271	613	315	408	6.1	5.8	331	500	5.8	6.4
Egypt, Arab Rep.	2,871	5,746	2,683	3,644	2,954	4,704	22.3	23.4	1,371	1,465	8.0	7.5
El Salvador	235	857	348	940	152	514	7.5	12.9	99	241	2.7	3.7
Eritrea	315	80	..	..	58	*73*	..	55.9	..	..	..	..
Estonia	530	1,462	1,764	2,075	452	886	17.6	13.0	121	412	4.2	5.4
Ethiopia	103	*156*	120	..	177	*261*	23.1	*24.5*	30	55	2.1	*2.7*
Finland	1,779	2,601	5,147	5,585	2,383	2,654	5.0	4.4	2,853	2,902	7.6	5.8
France	60,033	75,048	18,686	17,426	31,295	..	8.6	..	20,699	..	6.2	..
Gabon	125	222	..	236	94	..	3.2	..	182	..	10.3	..
Gambia, The	45	*79*	..	..	*67*	..	*30.5*	..	16	..	6.9	..
Georgia	85	*298*	228	*317*	*75*	172	*13.1*	13.5	*171*	172	*12.1*	9.3
Germany	14,847	18,399	*55,800*	74,600	24,052	31,641	4.0	3.6	66,981	73,652	11.3	9.5
Ghana	286	*483*	..	..	30	441	1.9	13.8	74	216	3.5	5.2
Greece	10,130	*14,180*	..	..	4,182	10,842	26.9	29.4	1,495	2,439	6.0	4.9
Guatemala	563	880	333	658	216	646	7.7	15.7	167	373	4.5	5.1
Guinea	*12*	44	..	..	1	*8*	0.1	*1.0*	29	36	2.9	3.8
Guinea-Bissau	..	8	..	..	..	..	..	..	6	*10*	6.7	*11.6*
Haiti	145	*142*	..	..	..	..	..	..	..	..	..	..

	International tourism				International tourism receipts				International tourism expenditures			
	thousands											
	Inbound tourists		Outbound tourists		$ millions		% of exports		$ millions		% of imports	
	1995	2003	1995	2003	1995	2003	1995	2003	1995	2003	1995	2003
Honduras	271	610	149	277	85	341	5.2	12.8	99	217	5.3	5.8
Hungary	2,878	2,948	13,083	14,283	2,938	3,498	14.9	6.8	1,500	2,133	7.5	3.9
India	2,124	2,384	3,056	4,205	..	..	..	..	..	..	..	..
Indonesia	4,324	4,467	1,782	..	..	4,461	..	6.5	..	4,427	..	7.8
Iran, Islamic Rep.	489	1,585	1,000	2,921	205	..	1.1	..	247	..	1.6	..
Iraq	61	127	..	..	..	..	..	..	..	..	..	..
Ireland	4,818	6,774	2,547	4,634	2,698	5,265	5.5	4.1	..	4,832	..	4.6
Israel	2,215	1,063	2,259	3,299	3,491	2,379	12.7	5.6	2,626	3,342	7.4	7.5
Italy	31,052	39,604	18,173	26,817	30,426	32,566	10.3	8.9	17,219	23,724	6.9	6.6
Jamaica	1,147	1,350	..	..	1,199	1,621	35.3	46.1	173	269	4.6	5.5
Japan	3,345	5,212	15,298	13,296	4,894	11,475	1.0	2.2	46,966	36,506	11.2	8.0
Jordan	1,074	1,573	1,128	1,533	973	1,019	28.0	22.3	719	573	14.7	8.4
Kazakhstan	..	2,410	523	2,374	155	638	2.6	4.2	296	783	4.9	5.9
Kenya	896	927	..	..	590	611	20.0	17.1	183	183	5.2	4.6
Korea, Dem. Rep.	..	..	..	..	..	..	..	..	..	..	..	..
Korea, Rep.	3,753	4,754	3,819	7,086	6,670	6,903	4.5	3.0	6,947	10,901	4.5	5.1
Kuwait	72	73	..	..	309	328	2.2	1.4	2,513	3,752	19.9	23.1
Kyrgyz Republic	36	140	42	45	..	65	..	8.7	7	30	0.7	3.7
Lao PDR	60	196	..	..	52	..	12.8	..	34	..	4.5	..
Latvia	539	971	1,812	2,286	37	271	1.8	5.8	62	365	2.8	6.0
Lebanon	450	1,016	..	..	710	956	56.1	33.1	..	..	..	..
Lesotho	87	124	..	..	29	..	14.6	..	17	16	1.6	2.0
Liberia	..	..	..	..	..	..	..	..	..	..	..	..
Libya	56	142	484	..	4	..	0.1	..	98	..	1.7	..
Lithuania	650	1,491	1,925	3,502	102	700	3.2	7.3	107	476	2.7	4.5
Macedonia, FYR	147	158	..	..	35	65	2.7	3.9	30	71	1.7	2.8
Madagascar	75	139	39	..	106	61	14.2	8.6	79	109	8.0	10.9
Malawi	192	421	..	..	21	43	4.5	9.4	53	48	8.0	7.5
Malaysia	7,469	10,577	20,642	36,248	5,044	8,084	6.1	7.5	2,722	3,330	3.1	3.6
Mali	42	70	..	..	26	105	4.9	10.1	74	62	7.5	5.6
Mauritania	..	..	..	..	..	..	..	..	30	..	5.9	..
Mauritius	422	702	107	161	616	960	26.2	29.8	184	236	7.5	7.6
Mexico	20,241	18,665	8,450	11,044	6,847	10,153	7.7	5.7	3,587	7,252	4.4	3.8
Moldova	32	21	71	67	71	83	8.0	7.9	73	116	7.3	6.7
Mongolia	108	201	..	..	33	154	6.5	18.9	22	114	4.2	10.6
Morocco	2,602	4,552	1,317	1,694	1,469	3,802	16.2	26.7	356	845	3.2	5.3
Mozambique	..	943	..	..	..	106	..	9.0	..	141	..	7.9
Myanmar	117	206	..	..	169	68	12.9	2.4	38	36	1.5	1.6
Namibia	399	695	..	..	..	..	..	..	..	..	..	..
Nepal	363	338	100	258	232	232	22.5	21.8	167	119	10.3	6.1
Netherlands	6,574	9,181	12,320	16,760	10,611	11,745	4.4	4.5	13,151	14,201	6.1	5.8
New Zealand	1,409	2,104	920	1,374	..	..	..	..	..	..	..	..
Nicaragua	281	526	255	562	51	155	7.7	11.9	56	139	4.9	5.8
Niger	35	58	10	..	15	28	4.7	..	21	16	4.6	..
Nigeria	656	887	..	..	54	263	0.4	..	938	..	7.3	..
Norway	2,880	3,146	590	..	2,730	3,082	4.9	3.4	4,481	6,746	9.6	11.1
Oman	279	817	..	2,060	..	372	..	3.1	..	751	..	9.2
Pakistan	378	479	..	..	582	618	5.7	4.2	654	1,162	4.6	7.6
Panama	345	566	185	227	372	809	4.9	10.6	181	290	2.3	3.9
Papua New Guinea	42	56	51	92	..	..	..	..	..	..	..	..
Paraguay	438	268	427	141	162	81	3.4	2.8	173	115	3.3	4.0
Peru	444	931	508	889	521	959	7.9	9.0	428	878	4.5	8.1
Philippines	1,760	1,907	1,615	1,803	1,141	1,549	4.3	4.1	551	985	1.7	2.4
Poland	19,215	13,720	36,387	38,730	6,927	4,733	19.4	6.6	5,865	3,002	17.3	3.9
Portugal	9,511	11,707	..	..	5,646	7,886	17.5	17.7	2,539	3,253	6.4	6.0
Puerto Rico	3,131	3,238	1,237	1,272	1,828	2,677	..	..	833	985	..	..

	International tourism				International tourism receipts				International tourism expenditures			
	thousands				$ millions		% of exports		$ millions		% of imports	
	Inbound tourists		Outbound tourists									
	1995	2003	1995	2003	1995	2003	1995	2003	1995	2003	1995	2003
Romania	2,757	3,204	5,737	5,757	689	523	7.3	2.5	749	572	6.6	2.3
Russian Federation	10,290	7,943	21,329	20,343	..	5,879	..	3.9	..	13,427	..	13.1
Rwanda	..	113	..	..	4	29	5.4	18.2	13	33	3.5	7.6
Saudi Arabia	3,325	7,332	..	4,104	..	3,420	..	4.4	..	4,165	..	7.6
Senegal	280	354	..	..	168	210	11.2	13.8	154	112	8.5	5.4
Serbia and Montenegro	228	481	..	..	42	77	1.6	2.4	..	..	..	..
Sierra Leone	38	37	6	13	..	..	..	..	51	38	19.4	9.3
Singapore	6,422	5,705	2,867	4,221	..	..	..	..	..	..	..	..
Slovak Republic	903	1,387	218	408	630	876	5.7	3.5	338	662	3.2	2.6
Slovenia	732	1,373	..	2,114	1,128	1,427	10.9	9.1	605	809	5.6	5.1
Somalia	..	..	..	..	..	..	..	..	..	..	..	..
South Africa	4,488	6,505	2,520	3,794	2,654	5,232	7.7	11.5	2,415	3,232	7.2	7.6
Spain	34,920	52,478	3,648	4,094	27,510	45,967	20.6	19.4	5,768	10,544	4.3	4.2
Sri Lanka	403	501	504	561	367	692	7.9	10.6	279	462	4.7	6.0
Sudan	29	52	195	..	..	..	..	..	..	..	..	..
Swaziland	300	256	..	..	54	31	5.3	2.9	45	34	3.5	2.9
Sweden	2,310	7,627	10,127	12,579	4,390	6,548	4.6	4.9	6,816	9,375	8.4	8.4
Switzerland	6,946	6,530	11,148	11,427	11,354	11,344	9.2	7.5	9,478	9,448	8.7	7.4
Syrian Arab Republic	815	2,788	1,746	3,932	..	..	..	..	..	..	..	..
Tajikistan	..	4	..	3	..	7	..	0.9	..	..	..	..
Tanzania	285	552	157	..	343	441	28.4	28.1	424	361	21.6	16.2
Thailand	6,952	10,082	1,820	2,152	9,257	10,422	13.2	11.1	4,791	4,046	5.8	4.8
Togo	53	61	..	..	..	16	..	3.1	40	26	6.0	3.6
Trinidad and Tobago	260	384	261	..	232	402	8.3	8.8	91	208	4.3	5.1
Tunisia	4,120	5,114	1,778	2,274	1,838	1,935	23.0	17.6	294	355	3.3	3.0
Turkey	7,083	13,341	3,981	5,928	..	..	..	..	..	..	..	..
Turkmenistan	218	..	21	..	13	..	0.7	..	74	..	4.1	..
Uganda	160	305	148	387	..	221	..	25.8	..	..	..	..
Ukraine	3,716	6,326	6,552	9,270	448	1,204	2.2	4.2	405	953	1.9	3.4
United Arab Emirates	2,315	5,871	..	..	632	1,439	..	..	..	3,959	..	..
United Kingdom	23,537	24,785	41,345	61,453	27,624	30,656	8.6	6.7	30,749	58,602	9.4	11.6
United States	43,318	40,356	50,835	54,206	93,700	99,816	11.8	9.8	60,924	80,621	6.8	5.3
Uruguay	2,022	1,420	562	495	725	406	20.7	13.3	332	236	9.3	8.7
Uzbekistan	92	231	246	400	15	48	0.4	1.3	..	..	..	..
Venezuela, RB	700	337	534	832	995	368	4.8	1.3	1,852	1,311	11.0	9.5
Vietnam	1,351	1,599	..	..	..	..	..	..	..	..	..	..
West Bank and Gaza	..	40	..	..	104	4	..	..	..	..	..	..
Yemen, Rep.	61	76	..	..	..	..	..	..	..	134	..	2.9
Zambia	163	578	..	..	47	149	6.1	11.2	83	..	6.2	..
Zimbabwe	1,363	2,068	256	..	145	44	..	..	106	..	..	..
World	537,987 t	681,723 t	631,322 t	802,249 t	479,583 t	605,706 t	7.9 w	6.8 w	465,309 t	588,155 t	7.9 w	6.9 w
Low income	11,818	16,746	..	..	..	..	..	..	..	..	..	..
Middle income	165,808	222,163	230,625	283,702	113,563	140,496	8.3	6.6	75,272	92,637	5.6	5.7
Lower middle income	91,106	136,111	78,314	109,376	63,265	81,293	7.7	6.2	43,425	64,552	5.6	5.7
Upper middle income	75,002	85,988	155,940	165,809	42,523	60,296	9.3	7.5	28,281	28,308	6.9	5.5
Low & middle income	180,340	242,640	273,333	345,985	123,497	153,921	8.1	6.6	86,118	104,632	5.7	5.6
East Asia & Pacific	44,254	64,926	36,006	66,158	34,517	44,012	7.1	5.2	21,014	28,468	4.9	4.2
Europe & Central Asia	59,808	75,701	152,346	156,807	..	..	..	6.8	..	..	..	6.8
Latin America & Carib.	39,818	45,316	21,948	27,381	20,571	29,236	7.1	6.2	18,735	21,780	6.5	5.8
Middle East & N. Africa	17,774	32,268	14,364	19,072	..	..	..	11.0	..	..	..	7.1
South Asia	3,819	4,333	5,151	6,994	..	..	..	..	..	..	..	..
Sub-Saharan Africa	12,582	19,438	..	..	6,316	11,844	6.8	11.7	6,723	7,026	7.0	6.6
High income	352,217	432,522	307,111	387,248	371,251	452,724	7.7	6.9	387,342	482,664	8.2	7.4
Europe EMU	197,165	256,521	137,605	175,177	..	227,354	8.2	8.1	169,911	203,727	8.2	7.7

About the data

Tourism is defined as the activities of people traveling to and staying in places outside their usual environment for no more than one year for leisure, business, and other purposes not related to an activity remunerated from within the place visited. The social and economic phenomenon of tourism has grown substantially over the past quarter century.

Past descriptions of tourism focused on the characteristics of visitors, such as the purpose of their visit and the conditions in which they traveled and stayed. Now, there is a growing awareness of the direct, indirect, and induced effects of tourism on employment, value added, personal income, government income, and the like.

Statistical information on tourism is based mainly on data on arrivals and overnight stays along with balance of payments information. But these data do not completely capture the economic phenomenon of tourism or give governments, businesses, and citizens the information needed for effective public policies and efficient business operations. Credible data are needed on the scale and significance of tourism. Information on the role tourism plays in national economies throughout the world is particularly deficient. Although the World Tourism Organization reports that progress has been made in harmonizing definitions and measurement units, differences in national practices still prevent full international comparability.

The data in the table are from the World Tourism Organization, a specialized agency of the United Nations. The data on international inbound and outbound tourists refer to the number of arrivals and departures of visitors within the reference period, not to the number of people traveling. Thus a person who makes several trips to a country during a given period is counted each time as a new arrival. International visitors include tourists (overnight visitors), same-day visitors, cruise passengers, and crew members.

The World Tourism Organization is improving its coverage of tourism expenditure data. It is now using balance of payments data from the International Monetary Fund (IMF), supplemented by data received from individual countries. The new data, shown in the table, now include travel and passenger transport items as defined in the IMF's *Balance of Payments Manual.*

Regional and income group aggregates are based on the World Bank's classification of countries and differ from those in the World Tourism Organization's publications. Countries not shown in the table but for which data are available are included in the regional and income group totals. World totals are no longer calculated by the World Tourism Organization. The aggregates in the table are calculated using the World Bank's weighted aggregation methodology (see *Statistical methods*) and differ from aggregates provided by the World Tourism Organization.

Definitions

• **International inbound tourists** (overnight visitors) are the number of tourists who travel to a country other than that in which they have their usual residence, but outside their usual environment, for a period not exceeding 12 months and whose main purpose in visiting is other than an activity remunerated from within the country visited. • **International outbound tourists** are the number of departures that people make from their country of usual residence to any other country for any purpose other than a remunerated activity in the country visited. • **International tourism receipts** are expenditures by international inbound visitors, including payments to national carriers for international transport. These receipts include any other prepayment made for goods or services received in the destination country. They also may include receipts from same-day visitors, except in cases where these are important enough to justify separate classification. Their share in exports is calculated as a ratio to exports of goods and services (for definition of exports of goods and services see *Definitions* for table 4.9). • **International tourism expenditures** are expenditures of international outbound visitors in other countries, including payments to foreign carriers for international transport. These expenditures may include those by residents traveling abroad as same-day visitors, except in cases where these are important enough to justify separate classification. Their share in imports is calculated as a ratio to imports of goods and services (for definition of imports of goods and services see *Definitions* for table 4.9).

6.14a

Tourism from developing countries is on the rise

International tourism departures (millions)

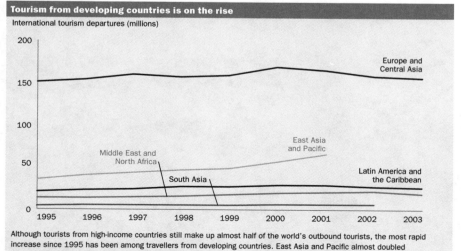

Although tourists from high-income countries still make up almost half of the world's outbound tourists, the most rapid increase since 1995 has been among travellers from developing countries. East Asia and Pacific almost doubled its number of outbound tourists between 1995 and 2001.

Source: World Tourism Organization.

Data sources

The visitor and expenditure data are available in the World Tourism Organization's *Yearbook of Tourism Statistics* and *Compendium of Tourism Statistics 2005.* The data in the table were updated from electronic files provided by the World Tourism Organization. The data on exports and imports are from the IMF's *International Financial Statistics* and World Bank staff estimates.

PRIMARY DATA DOCUMENTATION

The World Bank is not a primary data collection agency for most areas other than living standards surveys and debt. As a major user of socioeconomic data, however, the World Bank places particular emphasis on data documentation to inform users of data in economic analysis and policymaking. The tables in this section provide information on the sources, treatment, and currentness of the principal demographic, economic, and environmental indicators in the World Development Indicators.

Differences in the methods and conventions used by the primary data collectors—usually national statistical agencies, central banks, and customs services—may give rise to significant discrepancies over time both within countries and across them. Delays in reporting data and the use of old surveys as the base for current estimates may severely compromise the quality of national data.

Although data quality is improving in some countries, many developing countries lack the resources to train and maintain the skilled staff and obtain the equipment needed to measure and report demographic, economic, and environmental trends in an accurate and timely way. The World Bank recognizes the need for reliable data to measure living standards, track and evaluate economic trends, and plan and monitor development projects. Thus, working with bilateral and other multilateral agencies, it continues to fund and participate in technical assistance projects to improve statistical organization and basic data methods, collection, and dissemination.

The World Bank is working at several levels to meet the challenge of improving the quality of the data that it collates and disseminates. At the country level the World Bank is carrying out technical assistance, training, and survey activities—with a view to strengthening national capacity—in the following areas:

- Poverty assessments in most borrower member countries.
- Living standards measurement and other household and farm surveys with country partner statistical agencies.
- National accounts and inflation.
- Price and expenditure surveys for the International Comparison Program.
- Projects to improve statistics in the countries of the former Soviet Union.
- External debt management.
- Environmental and economic accounting.

PRIMARY DATA DOCUMENTATION

	National currency	Fiscal year end	Reporting period	Base year	SNA price valuation	Alternative conversion factor[a]	PPP survey year	Balance of Payments Manual in use	External debt	System of trade	Accounting concept	IMF data dissemination standard
Afghanistan	Afghan afghani	Mar. 20	FY	2002	VAB							
Albania	Albanian lek	Dec. 31	CY	1990[b]	VAB		1996	BPM5	Actual	G	C	G
Algeria	Algerian dinar	Dec. 31	CY	1980	VAB			BPM5	Actual	S	B	
Angola	Angolan kwanza	Dec. 31	CY	1997	VAP	1991–96		BPM4	Preliminary	S		G
Argentina	Argentine peso	Dec. 31	CY	1993	VAB	1971–84	1996	BPM5	Preliminary	S	C	S*
Armenia	Armenian dram	Dec. 31	CY	1996[b,c]	VAB	1990–95	2000	BPM5	Actual	S	C	S*
Australia	Australian dollar	Jun. 30	FY	2000[b,c]	VAB		2000	BPM5		G	C	S*
Austria	Euro	Dec. 31	CY	2000[b]	VAB		2000	BPM5		S	C	S*
Azerbaijan	Azeri manat	Dec. 31	CY	2003[b,c]	VAB	1992–95	2000	BPM5	Preliminary	G	C	G
Bangladesh	Bangladesh taka	Jun. 30	FY	1996	VAB	1960–03	1996	BPM5	Actual	G	C	G
Belarus	Belarussian rubel	Dec. 31	CY	1990[b,c]	VAB	1990–95	2000	BPM5	Actual	G	C	S*
Belgium	Euro	Dec. 31	CY	2000[b]	VAB		2000	BPM5		S	C	S*
Benin	CFA franc	Dec. 31	CY	1985	VAP	1992	1996	BPM5	Actual	S		G
Bolivia	Boliviano	Dec. 31	CY	1990[b]	VAB	1960–85	1996	BPM5	Actual	S	C	G
Bosnia and Herzegovina	Convertible mark	Dec. 31	CY	1996[c]	VAB			BPM5	Actual			
Botswana	Botswana pula	Jun. 30	FY	1994	VAB		1996	BPM5	Actual	G	B	G
Brazil	Brazilian real	Dec. 31	CY	1995	VAB		1996	BPM5	Preliminary	S	C	S*
Bulgaria	Bulgarian lev	Dec. 31	CY	2002[b,c]	VAB	1978–89, 1991–92	2000	BPM5	Actual	G	C	S*
Burkina Faso	CFA franc	Dec. 31	CY	1990	VAP	1992–93		BPM4	Actual	G	C	G
Burundi	Burundi franc	Dec. 31	CY	1980	VAB			BPM5	Actual	G	C	
Cambodia	Cambodian riel	Dec. 31	CY	2000	VAB			BPM5	Actual	G		G
Cameroon	CFA franc	Dec. 31	CY	1990	VAB	1965–01	1996	BPM5	Actual	S	B	G
Canada	Canadian dollar	Mar. 31	CY	2000[b]	VAB		2000	BPM5		G	C	S*
Central African Republic	CFA franc	Dec. 31	CY	1987	VAB			BPM4	Actual	S		G
Chad	CFA franc	Dec. 31	CY	1995	VAB			BPM5	Actual	S	C	G
Chile	Chilean peso	Dec. 31	CY	1986	VAB		1996	BPM5	Actual	S	C	S*
China	Chinese yuan	Dec. 31	CY	1990	VAP	1978–93	1986	BPM5	Preliminary	S	B	G
Hong Kong, China	Hong Kong dollar	Dec. 31	CY	2000	VAB		1996	BPM5		G	C	S*
Colombia	Colombian peso	Dec. 31	CY	1994	VAB	1992–94	1993	BPM5	Actual	S	B	S*
Congo, Dem. Rep.	Congo Franc	Dec. 31	CY	1987	VAB	1999–2001		BPM5	Actual	S	C	G
Congo, Rep.	CFA Franc	Dec. 31	CY	1978	VAP		1996	BPM5	Estimate	S	C	G
Costa Rica	Costa Rican colon	Dec. 31	CY	1991[b]	VAB			BPM5	Actual	S	C	S*
Côte d'Ivoire	CFA franc	Dec. 31	CY	1996	VAP		1996	BPM5	Estimate	S	C	G
Croatia	Croatian kuna	Dec. 31	CY	1997[b]	VAB		2000	BPM5	Actual	G	C	S*
Cuba	Cuban peso	Dec. 31	CY	1984	VAP					G		
Czech Republic	Czech koruna	Dec. 31	CY	1995[b]	VAB		2000	BPM5	Preliminary	G	C	S*
Denmark	Danish krone	Dec. 31	CY	2000[b]	VAB		2000	BPM5		G	C	S*
Dominican Republic	Dominican peso	Dec. 31	CY	1990	VAP			BPM5	Actual	G	C	
Ecuador	Ecuadorian sucre	Dec. 31	CY	2000	VAP	`	1996	BPM5	Preliminary	S	B	S*
Egypt, Arab Rep.	Egyptian pound	Jun. 30	FY	1992	VAB	1965–91	1996	BPM5	Actual	S	C	S*
El Salvador	Salvadoran colone	Dec. 31	CY	1990	VAP	1982–90		BPM5	Actual	S	C	S*
Eritrea	Eritrean Nakfa	Dec. 31	CY	1992	VAB			BPM4	Actual			
Estonia	Estonian kroon	Dec. 31	CY	2000[b]	VAB	1991–95	2000	BPM5	Actual	G	C	S*
Ethiopia	Ethiopian birr	Jul. 7	FY	1981	VAB	1965–03		BPM5	Preliminary	G	B	G
Finland	Euro	Dec. 31	CY	2000[b]	VAB		2000	BPM5		G	C	S*
France	Euro	Dec. 31	CY	2000[b,c]	VAB		2000	BPM5		S	C	S*
Gabon	CFA franc	Dec. 31	CY	1991	VAP	1993	1996	BPM5	Actual	S	B	G
Gambia, The	Gambian dalasi	Jun. 30	CY	1987	VAB			BPM5	Actual	G	B	G
Georgia	Georgian lari	Dec. 31	CY	1994[b,c]	VAB	1990–95	2000	BPM5	Actual	G	C	
Germany	Euro	Dec. 31	CY	2000[b]	VAB		2000	BPM5		S	C	S*
Ghana	Ghanaian cedi	Dec. 31	CY	1975	VAP	1973–87		BPM5	Preliminary	G	B	
Greece	Euro	Dec. 31	CY	2000[b,c]	VAB		2000	BPM5	Estimate	S	C	S*
Guatemala	Guatemalan quetzal	Dec. 31	CY	1958	VAP		1980	BPM5	Actual	S	B	G
Guinea	Guinean franc	Dec. 31	CY	1996	VAB		1996	BPM5	Estimate	S	B	G
Guinea-Bissau	CFA franc	Dec. 31	CY	1986	VAB	1970–86		BPM5	Estimate	G		G
Haiti	Haitian gourde	Sep. 30	FY	1976	VAB	1991		BPM5	Actual	G		

PRIMARY DATA DOCUMENTATION

	Latest population census (including registration-based censuses)	Latest demographic, education, or health household survey	Source of most recent income and expenditure data	Vital registration complete	Latest agricultural census	Latest industrial data	Latest trade data	Latest water withdrawal data
Afghanistan	1979	MICS, 2000					1977	1987
Albania	2001	MICS, 2000	LSMS, 2002	Yes	1995	1990	2003	1995
Algeria	1998	MICS, 2000	HLSS, 1995		1973	1996	2003	1995
Angola	1970	MICS, 2000			1964–65		1991	1987
Argentina	2001		EPH, 2001	Yes	1988	1999	2003	1995
Armenia	2001	DHS, 2000	LSMS, 1998	Yes			2003	1994
Australia	2001			Yes	1990	1992	2003	1985
Austria	2001			Yes	1990	2000	2003	1991
Azerbaijan	1999	MICS, 2000	HBS, 2001	Yes			2003	1995
Bangladesh	2001	Special, 2001	HES. 2000		1976	1997	2003	1990
Belarus	1999		IES, 2000	Yes	1994		2003	1990
Belgium	2001			Yes	1990	1997	2003	..
Benin	2002	DHS, 2001			1992–93	1981	2002	1994
Bolivia	2001	DHS, 2003	EH, 1999		1997		2003	1987
Bosnia and Herzegovina	1991	MICS, 2000	LSMS, 2001	Yes	1991		2003	1995
Botswana	2001	MICS, 2000	HIES, 1993-94		1993	2000	2001	1992
Brazil	2000	DHS, 1996	PNAD, 2001		1996	1995	2003	1992
Bulgaria	2001		LSMS, 2001	Yes		1996	2003	1988
Burkina Faso	1996	DHS, 2003	Priority survey, 1998		1993		2002	1992
Burundi	1990	MICS, 2000	Priority survey, 1998			1991	2002	1987
Cambodia	1998	DHS, 2000	SES, 1997				1972	1987
Cameroon	1987	DHS, 2004	Priority survey, 2001		1972–73	1999	2003	1987
Canada	2001			Yes	1991	2002	2003	1991
Central African Republic	1988	MICS, 2000	EPI, 1993			1993	2003	1987
Chad	1993	MICS, 2000					1995	1987
Chile	2002		CASEN, 2000	Yes	1997	2002	2003	1987
China	2000	Population, 1995	HHS (Rural/Urban), 2001		1996	2001	2003	1993
Hong Kong, China	2001			Yes		2001		
Colombia	1993	DHS, 2000	ECV, 1999		1988	2002	2003	1996
Congo, Dem. Rep.	1984	MICS, 2000			1990		1986	1990
Congo, Rep.	1996				1986	1988	1995	1987
Costa Rica	2000	CDC, 1993	EHPM, 2000	Yes	1973	2002	2003	1997
Cote d'Ivoire	1998	MICS, 2000	LSMS, 2002		1974–75	1997	2003	1987
Croatia	2001		HBS, 2001	Yes		1992	2003	1996
Cuba	2002	MICS, 2000		Yes		1989	2001	1995
Czech Republic	2001	CDC, 1993	Microcensus 1996/97	Yes	..		2003	1991
Denmark	2001			Yes	1989	2002	2003	1990
Dominican Republic	2002	DHS, 2002	ENFT, 1998		1971	2002	2001	1994
Ecuador	2001	CDC, 1999	LSMS, 1998		1997	2002	2003	1997
Egypt, Arab Rep.	1996	SPA, 2002	HECS, 2000	Yes	1989–90	1996	2003	1996
El Salvador	1992	CDC, 1994	EHPM, 2000	Yes	1970–71	1998	2003	1992
Eritrea	1984	DHS, 2002					2002	
Estonia	2000		HIE, 1998	Yes	1994		2003	1995
Ethiopia	1994	DHS, 2000	ICES, 2000		1988–89	2001	2003	1987
Finland	2000			Yes	1990	2002	2003	1991
France	1999			Yes	1988	2002	2003	1999
Gabon	1993	DHS, 2000			1974–75	1995	2003	1987
Gambia, The	2003	MICS, 2000	HHS, 1998			1993	2002	1982
Georgia, Rep.	2002	MICS, 2000	SGH, 2001	Yes			2003	1990
Germany	1995			Yes	1993	2000	2003	1991
Ghana	2000	SPA, 2002, DHS, 2003	LSMS, 1998/1999		1984	2002	2002	1997
Greece	2001			Yes	1993	2002	2003	1980
Guatemala	2002	DHS, 1998-99	LSMS, 2000, ENCOVI, 2000	Yes	1979	1988	2003	1992
Guinea	1996	DHS, 1999	LSMS, 1994		1996		2002	1987
Guinea-Bissau	1991	MICS, 2000	IES, 1993		1988		1995	1991
Haiti	2003	DHS, 2000			1971	1996	1997	1991

	National currency	Fiscal year end	Reporting period	Base year	SNA price valuation	Alternative conversion factor[a]	PPP survey year	Balance of Payments Manual in use	External debt	System of trade	Accounting concept	IMF data dissemination standard
Honduras	Honduran lempira	Dec. 31	CY	1978	VAB	1988–89		BPM5	Actual	S		
Hungary	Hungarian forint	Dec. 31	CY	2000[b]	VAB		2000	BPM5	Actual	S	C	S*
India	Indian rupee	Mar. 31	FY	1993	VAB	1960–03		BPM5	Actual	G	C	S*
Indonesia	Indonesian rupiah	Mar. 31	CY	1993	VAP		1996	BPM5	Actual	S	C	S*
Iran, Islamic Rep.	Iranian rial	Mar. 20	FY	1982	VAB	1980–90	1996	BPM5	Actual	G	C	
Iraq	Iraqi dinar	Dec. 31	CY	1969	VAB					S		
Ireland	Euro	Dec. 31	CY	2000[b]	VAB		2000	BPM5		G	C	S*
Israel	Israeli new shekel	Dec. 31	CY	2000[b]	VAP		2000	BPM5		S	C	S*
Italy	Euro	Dec. 31	CY	2000[b]	VAB		2000	BPM5		S	C	S*
Jamaica	Jamaica dollar	Dec. 31	CY	1996	VAP		1996	BPM5	Actual	G	C	G
Japan	Japanese yen	Mar. 31	CY	2000	VAB		2000	BPM5		G	C	S*
Jordan	Jordan dinar	Dec. 31	CY	1994	VAB		1996	BPM5	Actual	G	B	G
Kazakhstan	Kazakh tenge	Dec. 31	CY	1995[b,c]	VAB	1987–95	2000	BPM5	Actual	G	C	S*
Kenya	Kenya shilling	Jun. 30	CY	1982	VAB		1996	BPM5	Actual	G	B	G
Korea, Dem. Rep.	Democratic Republic of Korea won	Dec. 31	CY	..	..			BPM5				
Korea, Rep.	Korean won	Dec. 31	CY	2000[b]	VAP		2000	BPM5	Actual	S	C	S*
Kuwait	Kuwaiti dinar	Jun. 30	CY	1984	VAP			BPM5		S	C	G
Kyrgyz Republic	Kyrgyz som	Dec. 31	CY	1995[b,c]	VAB	1990–95	2000	BPM5	Actual	G	B	S*
Lao PDR	Lao kip	Dec. 31	CY	1990	VAB		1993	BPM5	Preliminary	G		
Latvia	Latvian lat	Dec. 31	CY	2000[b]	VAB	1991–95	1996	BPM5	Actual	S	C	S*
Lebanon	Lebanese pound	Dec. 31	CY	1994	VAB			BPM4	Actual	G	B	G
Lesotho	Lesotho loti	Mar. 31	CY	1995	VAB			BPM5	Actual	G	C	G
Libya	Libyan dinar	Dec. 31	CY	1975	VAB	1986		BPM5		G		
Liberia	Liberian dollar	Dec. 31	CY	1992	VAB				Estimate			
Lithuania	Lithuanian litas	Dec. 31	CY	2000[b]	VAB	1990–95	2000	BPM5	Actual	G	C	S*
Macedonia, FYR	Macedonian denar	Dec. 31	CY	1997[b]	VAB		2000	BPM5	Actual	G		G
Madagascar	Malagasy franc	Dec. 31	CY	1984	VAB		1996	BPM5	Preliminary	S	C	G
Malawi	Malawi kwacha	Mar. 31	CY	1994	VAB		1996	BPM5	Estimate	G	B	G
Malaysia	Malaysian ringgit	Dec. 31	CY	1987	VAP		1993	BPM5	Actual	G	C	S*
Mali	CFA franc	Dec. 31	CY	1987	VAB		1996	BPM4	Actual	G		G
Mauritania	Mauritanian ouguiya	Dec. 31	CY	1985	VAB			BPM4	Actual	G		G
Mauritius	Mauritian rupee	Jun. 30	FY	1998	VAB		1996	BPM5	Actual	G	C	G
Mexico	Mexican new peso	Dec. 31	CY	1993[b]	VAB		2000	BPM5	Actual	G	C	S*
Moldova	Moldovan leu	Dec. 31	CY	1996	VAB	1987–95	2000	BPM5	Actual	G	C	G
Mongolia	Mongolian tugrik	Dec. 31	CY	1995	VAP		2000	BPM5	Actual	S	C	G
Morocco	Moroccan dirham	Dec. 31	CY	1980	VAP		1996	BPM5	Actual	S	C	
Mozambique	Mozambican metical	Dec. 31	CY	1995	VAB	1992–95		BPM5	Preliminary	S		G
Myanmar	Myanmar kyat	Mar. 31	FY	1985	VAP			BPM5	Estimate	G	C	
Namibia	Namibia dollar	Mar. 31	CY	1995	VAB			BPM5	Estimate		B	G
Nepal	Nepalese rupee	Jul. 14	FY	1995	VAB	1966–03	1996	BPM5	Actual	S	C	G
Netherlands	Euro	Dec. 31	CY	2000[b,c]	VAB		2000	BPM5		S	C	S*
New Zealand	New Zealand dollar	Mar. 31	FY	2000	VAB		2000	BPM5		G	C	
Nicaragua	Nicaraguan gold cordoba	Dec. 31	CY	1998	VAP	1965–93		BPM5	Actual	S	C	G
Niger	CFA franc	Dec. 31	CY	1987	VAP	1993		BPM5	Preliminary	S		G
Nigeria	Nigerian naira	Dec. 31	CY	1987	VAB	1971–98	1996	BPM5	Actual	G		G
Norway	Norwegian krone	Dec. 31	CY	2000[b,c]	VAB		2000	BPM5		G	C	S*
Oman	Rial Omani	Dec. 31	CY	1978	VAP		1996	BPM5	Actual	G	B	G
Pakistan	Pakistan rupee	Jun. 30	FY	2000	VAB	1972–03	1996	BPM5	Preliminary	G	C	G
Panama	Panamanian balboa	Dec. 31	CY	1996[c]	VAP		1996	BPM5	Actual	S	C	G
Papua New Guinea	Papua New Guinea kina	Dec. 31	CY	1983	VAP	1989		BPM5	Actual	G	B	
Paraguay	Paraguayan guarani	Dec. 31	CY	1982	VAP	1982–88		BPM5	Actual	S	B	G
Peru	Peruvian new sol	Dec. 31	CY	1994	VAB	1985–91	1996	BPM5	Actual	S	C	S*
Philippines	Philippine peso	Dec. 31	CY	1985	VAP		1996	BPM5	Actual	G	B	S*
Poland	Polish zloty	Dec. 31	CY	2002[b,c]	VAB		2000	BPM5	Actual	S	C	S*
Portugal	Euro	Dec. 31	CY	2000[b]	VAB		2000	BPM5		S	C	S*
Puerto Rico	U.S. dollar	Jun. 30	FY	1954	VAP					G		

PRIMARY DATA DOCUMENTATION

	Latest population census (including registration-based censuses)	Latest demographic, education, or health household survey	Source of most recent income and expenditure data	Vital registration complete	Latest agricultural census	Latest industrial data	Latest trade data	Latest water withdrawal data
Honduras	2001	CDC, 1994	EPHPM, 1999		1993	2002	2003	1992
Hungary	2001		FBS, 2002	Yes	1994	2002	2003	1991
India	2001	Benckmark, 1998-2002	LSMS, 1999/00		1986	2002	2003	1990
Indonesia	2000	DHS, 2002, Special, 2002	SUSENAS, 2002		1993	2001	2003	1990
Iran, Islamic Republic	1996	Demographic, 1995	SECH, 1998	Yes	1988	2002	2003	1993
Iraq	1997	MICS, 2000			1981	1992	1976	1990
Ireland	2002			Yes	1991	2002	2003	1980
Israel	1995			Yes	1983	2002	2003	1997
Italy	2001			Yes	1990	2000	2003	1998
Jamaica	2001	CDC, 1997, MICS, 2000	LSMS, 2000	Yes	1979	2002	2002	1993
Japan	2000			Yes	1990	2002	2003	1992
Jordan	1994	DHS, 2002	HIES, 1997		1997	2002	2003	1993
Kazakhstan	1999	DHS, 1999	HBS, 2003	Yes			2003	1993
Kenya	1999	DHS, 2003	WMS II, 1997		1981	2002	2003	1990
Korea, Dem. Rep.	1993	MICS, 2000						1987
Korea, Rep.	2000			Yes	1991	2002	2003	1994
Kuwait	1995	FHS, 1996		Yes	1970	1999	2001	1994
Kyrgyz Rep.	1999	DHS, 1997	HBS, 2002	Yes			2003	1994
Lao PDR	1995	MICS, 2000	ECS I, 1997		1999		1974	1987
Latvia, Rep.	2000		HBS, 1998	Yes	1994	2001	2003	1994
Lebanon	1970	MICS, 2000			1999		2003	1996
Lesotho	2001	MICS, 2000	HBS, 1995		1989–90	1985	2002	1987
Libya	1995	MICS, 2000			1987		1998	1999
Liberia	1984						1984	1987
Lithuania	2001		LSMS, 2000	Yes	1994		2003	1995
Macedonia, FYR	2002		HBS, 1998	Yes	1994	1996	2003	1996
Madagascar	1993	MICS, 2000, DHS, 2003	Priority survey, 2001		1984	1988	2003	1984
Malawi	1998	EdData, 2002	HHS, 1997/98		1992–93	1998	2003	1994
Malaysia	2000		HIBAS, 1997	Yes		2000	2003	1995
Mali	1998	DHS, 2001	EMCES, 1994		1978		2001	1987
Mauritania	2000	Special, 2003	LSMS, 2000		1985		1996	1985
Mauritius	2000	CDC, 1991		Yes		1997	2003	..
Mexico	2000	Population, 1995	ENIGH, 2000	Yes	1991	2000	2003	1998
Moldova	1989	MICS, 2000	HBS, 2001				2003	1992
Mongolia	2000	MICS, 2000	LSMS/Integrated Survey, 1998	Yes		1995	2003	1993
Morocco	1994	DHS, 2003	LSMS, 1998/99		1997	2000	2003	1998
Mozambique	1997	Interim, 2003	NHS, 96/97				2002	1992
Myanmar	1983	MICS, 2000			1993		1992	1987
Namibia	2001	DHS, 2000	NHIES, 1993		1995	1994	2003	1991
Nepal	2001	DHS, 2001	LSMS, 1996		1992	1996	2003	1994
Netherlands	2002			Yes	1989	2002	2003	1991
New Zealand	2001			Yes	1990	2002	2003	1991
Nicaragua	1995	DHS, 2001	LSMS, 2001		1963	2002	2003	1998
Niger	2001	MICS, 2000	LSMS, 1995		1980	1998	2003	1988
Nigeria	1991	DHS, 2003	NCS, 1996/97		1960	1996	2003	1987
Norway	2001			Yes	1989	2002	2003	1985
Oman	2003	FHS, 1995			1979	2001	2003	1991
Pakistan	1998	RHS, 2000-01	PIHS, 1998/99		1990	2002	2003	1991
Panama	2000	LSMS, 1997	EH, 2000		1990	2002	2003	1990
Papua New Guinea	2000	DHS, 1996	HGS, 1996			2002	2003	1987
Paraguay	2002	CDC, 1998	EPH, 2000		1991	2002	2003	1987
Peru	1993	DHS, 2000	ENAHO, 2000		1994	1996	2003	1992
Philippines	2000	DHS, 2003	FIES, 2000	Yes	1991	2002	2003	1995
Poland	2002		HBS, 2001	Yes	1990	2002	2003	1991
Portugal	2001			Yes	1989	2002	2003	1990
Puerto Rico	2000			Yes	1987	2001		

	National currency	Fiscal year end	Reporting period	Base year	SNA price valuation	Alternative conversion factor[a]	PPP survey year	Balance of Payments Manual in use	External debt	System of trade	Government finance Accounting concept	IMF data dissemination standard
Romania	Romanian leu	Dec. 31	CY	1998c	VAB	1987–89, 1992	2000	BPM5	Preliminary	S	C	G
Russian Federation	Russian ruble	Dec. 31	CY	2000b,c	VAB	1987–95	2000	BPM5	Preliminary	G	C	S*
Rwanda	Rwanda franc	Dec. 31	CY	1995	VAP			BPM5	Estimate	G		
Saudi Arabia	Saudi Arabian riyal	Dec. 31	CY	1999	VAP			BPM4	Estimate	G		
Senegal	CFA franc	Dec. 31	CY	1987	VAP		1996	BPM5	Preliminary	S	B	G
Serbia and Montenegro	Yugoslav new dinar	Dec. 31	CY	1994	VAB				Preliminary		C	
Sierra Leone	Sierra Leonean leone	Jun. 30	CY	1990	VAB	1971–79, 1987	1996	BPM5	Actual	G	B	G
Singapore	Singapore dollar	Mar. 31	CY	1995	VAB		1996	BPM5		G	C	S*
Slovak Republic	Slovak koruna	Dec. 31	CY	1995b	VAP		2000	BPM5	Actual	G	C	S*
Slovenia	Slovenian tolar	Dec. 31	CY	2000b	VAB		2000	BPM5	Actual	S	C	S*
Somalia	Somali shilling	Dec. 31	CY	1985	VAB	1977–90			Estimate			
South Africa	South African rand	Mar. 31	CY	1995	VAB			BPM5	Preliminary	S	C	S*
Spain	Euro	Dec. 31	CY	2000b	VAB		2000	BPM5		S	C	S*
Sri Lanka	Sri Lankan rupee	Dec. 31	CY	1996	VAB		1996	BPM5	Actual	G	B	G
Sudan	Sudanese dinar	Dec. 31	CY	1982	VAB	1970–95		BPM5	Estimate	G	B	G
Swaziland	Lilangeni	Jun. 30	FY	1985	VAB				Actual		B	G
Sweden	Swedish krona	Jun. 30	CY	2000c	VAB		2000	BPM5		G	C	S*
Switzerland	Swiss franc	Dec. 31	CY	2000	VAB		2000	BPM5	Estimate	S	C	S*
Syrian Arab Republic	Syrian pound	Dec. 31	CY	1995	VAP	1970–03	1996	BPM5	Estimate	S	C	
Tajikistan	Tajik somoni	Dec. 31	CY	1985b	VAB	1990–95	2000	BPM5	Preliminary	G		G
Tanzania	Tanzania shilling	Dec. 31	CY	1992	VAB		1996	BPM5	Preliminary	S		G
Thailand	Thai baht	Sep. 30	CY	1988	VAP		1996	BPM5	Preliminary	G	C	S*
Togo	CFA franc	Dec. 31	CY	1978	VAP		1993	BPM5	Estimate	S		G
Trinidad and Tobago	Trinidad and Tobago dollar	Dec. 31	CY	2000	VAP		1996	BPM5	Actual	S	C	G
Tunisia	Tunisian dinar	Dec. 31	CY	1990	VAP		1996	BPM5	Actual	G	C	S*
Turkey	Turkish lira	Dec. 31	CY	1987	VAB		2000	BPM5	Actual	S	B	S*
Turkmenistan	Turkmen manat	Dec. 31	CY	1987b	VAB	1987–95	2000	BPM5		G		
Uganda	Uganda shilling	Jun. 30	FY	1998	VAB	1980–99		BPM5	Actual	G	B	G
Ukraine	Ukrainian hryvnia	Dec. 31	CY	1990b,c	VAB	1990–95	2000	BPM5	Actual	G	C	S*
United Arab Emirates	U.A.E. dirham	Dec. 31	CY	1985	VAB		1993	BPM4		G	C	
United Kingdom	Pound sterling	Dec. 31	CY	2000b	VAB		2000	BPM5		G	C	S*
United States	U.S. dollar	Sep. 30	CY	2000c	VAB		2000	BPM5		G	C	S*
Uruguay	Uruguayan peso	Dec. 31	CY	1983	VAP		1996	BPM5	Actual	S	C	
Uzbekistan	Uzbek sum	Dec. 31	CY	1997c	VAB	1990–95	2000	BPM5	Actual	G		
Venezuela, RB	Venezuelan bolivar	Dec. 31	CY	1984	VAB		1996	BPM5	Actual	G	C	G
Vietnam	Vietnamese dong	Dec. 31	CY	1994	VAP	1991	1996	BPM4	Preliminary	G	B	G
West Bank and Gaza	Israeli new shekel	Dec. 31	CY	1998	VAB		1993					
Yemen, Rep.	Yemen rial	Dec. 31	CY	1990	VAP	1991–96	1996	BPM5	Actual	G	B	G
Zambia	Zambian kwacha	Dec. 31	CY	1994	VAB	1990–92	1996	BPM5	Estimate	G	B	G
Zimbabwe	Zimbabwe dollar	Jun. 30	CY	1990	VAB	1991, 1998	1996	BPM5	Actual	G	C	G

Note: For explanation of the abbreviations used in the table see notes following the table.
a. World Bank estimates including adjustments for fiscal year reporting. b. Country uses the 1993 System of National Accounts methodology. c. Original chained constant price data are rescaled.

	Latest population census (including registration-based censuses)	Latest demographic, education, or health household survey	Source of most recent income and expenditure data	Vital registration complete	Latest agricultural census	Latest industrial data	Latest trade data	Latest water withdrawal data
Romania	2002	CDC, 1999	LSMS, 2002	Yes		1993	2003	1994
Russian Federation	2002	LSMS, 1992	LMS, Round 9, 2002	Yes	1994–95	2001	2003	1994
Rwanda	2002	SPA, 2001	LSMS, 1999/2000		1984	1986	2003	1993
Saudi Arabia	1992	Demographic, 1999			1983		2003	1992
Senegal	2002	DHS, 2004	ESASM 1995		1960	2001	2003	1987
Serbia and Montenegro	2002	MICS, 2000		Yes				
Sierra Leone	1985	MICS,2000	SHEHEA, 1989-90		1985	1993	2002	1987
Singapore	2000	General household, 1995		Yes		2002	2003	1975
Slovak Republic	2001		Microcensus, 1996	Yes		1994	2003	1991
Slovenia	2002		HBS, 1998	Yes	1991	2001	2003	1996
Somalia	1987	MICS, 2000					1982	1987
South Africa	2001	DHS, 1998	IES, 2000			2002	2003	1990
Spain	2001			Yes	1989	2002	2003	1997
Sri Lanka	2001	DHS, 1993	SES, 1999/00	Yes	1982	2000	2003	1990
Sudan	1993	MICS, 2000					2002	1995
Swaziland	1997	MICS, 2000	SHIES, 1994/95			1995	2002	..
Sweden	1990			Yes	1981	2002	2003	1991
Switzerland	2000			Yes	1990	1997	2003	1991
Syrian Arab Republic	1994	MICS, 2000			1981	1998	2003	1995
Tajikistan	2000	MICS, 2000	LSMS, 2003	Yes	1994		2000	1994
Tanzania	2002	AIS, 2003	LSMS, 1993		1995	1999	2003	1994
Thailand	2000	DHS, 1987	SES, 2000		1993	1994	2003	1990
Togo	1981	MICS, 2000			1996		2003	1987
Trinidad and Tobago	2000	MICS, 2000	LSMS, 1992	Yes	1982	1995	2003	1997
Tunisia	1994	MICS, 2000			1961	2002	2003	1996
Turkey	2000	DHS, 1998	LSMS, 2000		1991	2002	2003	1997
Turkmenistan	1995	DHS,2000	LSMS, 1998	Yes			2000	1994
Uganda	2002	AIS, 2004	NIHS II, 1999		1991	2002	2003	1970
Ukraine	2001	MICS, 2000	HIES, 1999	Yes			2002	1992
United Arab Emirates	1995				1998	1981	2001	1995
United Kingdom	2001			Yes	1993	2002	2003	1991
United States	2000	Current population, 1997		Yes	1997	2002	2003	1990
Uruguay	1996		ECH, 2000	Yes	1990	1997	2003	1965
Uzbekistan	1989	Special, 2002	FBS, 2000	Yes				1994
Venezuela, R.B.	2001	MICS, 2000	EHM, 1998	Yes	1997–98	2002	2003	1970
Vietnam	1999	MICS, 2000, DHS 2002	LSMS, 1997/98		1994		2002	1990
West Bank and Gaza	1997	Demographic, 1995			1971			
Yemen, Rep.	1994	DHS, 1997	HBS, 1998		1982–85		2000	1990
Zambia	2000	EdData, 2002	LCMS II, 1998		1990	1994	2002	1994
Zimbabwe	2002	DHS, 1999	ICES, 1995/96		1960	1996	2002	1987

• **Fiscal year end** is the date of the end of the fiscal year for the central government. Fiscal years for other levels of government and the reporting years for statistical surveys may differ, but if a country is designated as a fiscal year reporter in the following column, the date shown is the end of its national accounts reporting period. • **Reporting period** for national accounts and balance of payments data is designated as either calendar year basis (CY) or fiscal year basis (FY). Most economies report their national accounts and balance of payments data using calendar years, but some use fiscal years that straddle two calendar years. In *World Development Indicators* fiscal year data are assigned to the calendar year that contains the larger share of the fiscal year. If a country's fiscal year ends before June 30, the data are shown in the first year of the fiscal period; if the fiscal year ends on or after June 30, the data are shown in the second year of the period. Balance of payments data are shown by calendar year and so are not comparable to the national accounts data of the countries that report their national accounts on a fiscal year basis. • **Base year** is the year used as the base period for constant price calculations in the country's national accounts. Price indexes derived from national accounts aggregates, such as the GDP deflator, express the price level relative to prices in the base year. Constant price data reported in *World Development Indicators* are rescaled to a common 2000 reference year. See *About the data* for table 4.1 for further discussion. • **SNA price valuation** shows whether value added in the national accounts is reported at basic prices (VAB) or at producer prices (VAP). Producer prices include the value of taxes paid by producers and thus tend to overstate the actual value added in production. See *About the data* for tables 4.1 and 4.2 for further discussion of national accounts valuation. • **Alternative conversion factor** identifies the countries and years for which a World Bank–estimated conversion factor has been used in place of the official (line rf in the International Monetary Fund's *International Financial Statistics*) exchange rate. Estimates also include adjustments to correspond to the fiscal years in which national accounts data have been reported. See *Statistical methods* for further discussion of the use of alternative conversion factors. • **PPP survey year** refers to the latest available survey year for the International Comparison Program's estimates of purchasing power parities (PPPs). • **Balance of Payments Manual in use** refers to the classification system used for compiling and reporting data on balance of payments items in table 4.15. BPM4 refers to the fourth

edition of the International Monetary Fund's (IMF) *Balance of Payments Manual* (1977), and BPM5 to the fifth edition (1993). Since 1995 the IMF has adjusted all balance of payments data to BPM5 conventions, but some countries continue to report using the older system. • **External debt** shows debt reporting status for 2003 data. *Actual* indicates that data are as reported, *preliminary* that data are preliminary and include an element of staff estimation, and *estimate* that data are staff estimates. • **System of trade** refers to the general trade system (G) or the special trade system (S). For imports under the general trade system both goods entering directly for domestic consumption and goods entered into customs storage are recorded as imports at the time of their first arrival; under the special trade system goods are recorded as imports when declared for domestic consumption whether at time of entry or on withdrawal from customs storage. Exports under the general system comprise outward-moving goods: (a) national goods wholly or partly produced in the country; (b) foreign goods, neither transformed nor declared for domestic consumption in the country, that move outward from customs storage; and (c) nationalized goods that have been declared from domestic consumption and move outward without having been transformed. Under the special system of trade, exports comprise categories (a) and (c). In some compilations categories (b) and (c) are classified as re-exports. Direct transit trade, consisting of goods entering or leaving for transport purposes only, is excluded from both import and export statistics. See *About the data* for tables 4.5 and 4.6 for further discussion. • **Government finance accounting concept** describes the accounting basis for reporting central government financial data. For most countries government finance data have been consolidated (C) into one set of accounts capturing all the central government's fiscal activities. Budgetary central government accounts (B) exclude some central government units. See *About the data* for tables 4.11, 4.12, and 4.13 for further details. • **IMF data dissemination standard** shows the countries that subscribe to the IMF's Special Data Dissemination Standard (SDDS) or the General Data Dissemination System (GDDS). *S* refers to countries that subscribe to the SDDS; *S** indicates subscribers that have posted data on the Dissemination Standards Bulletin Board web site [dsbb.imf.org]; while *G* refers to countries that subscribe to the GDDS. The SDDS was established by the IMF for member countries that have or that might seek access to international capital markets to guide them in providing their economic

and financial data to the public. The GDDS helps them disseminate comprehensive, timely, accessible, and reliable economic, financial, and socio-demographic statistics. IMF member countries voluntarily elect to participate in either the SDDS or the GDDS. Both the GDDS and the SDDS are expected to enhance the availability of timely and comprehensive data and therefore contribute to the pursuit of sound macroeconomic policies; the SDDS is also expected to contribute to the improved functioning of financial markets. • **Latest population census** shows the most recent year in which a census was conducted and at least preliminary results have been released. • **Latest demographic, education, or health household survey** gives information on the household surveys used in compiling the demographic, education, and health data presented in section 2. CDC is Centers for Disease Control and Prevention, DHS is Demographic and Health Survey, FHS is Family Health Survey, LSMS is Living Standards Management Study, MICS is the Multiple Indicator Cluster Survey, RHS is Reproductive Health Survey, and SPA is Service Provision Assessment. • **Source of most recent income and expenditure data** shows household surveys that collect income and expenditure data. HBS is Household Budget Survey, ICES is Income, Consumption and Expenditure Survey, IES is Income and Expenditure Survey, LSMS is Living Standards Measurement Study, and SES is Socio Economic Survey. • **Vital registration complete** identifies countries judged to have complete registries of vital (birth and death) statistics by the United Nations Department of Economic and Social Information and Policy Analysis, Statistical Division, and reported in *Population and Vital Statistics Reports*. Countries with complete vital statistics registries may have more accurate and more timely demographic indicators. • **Latest agricultural census** shows the most recent year in which an agricultural census was conducted and reported to the Food and Agriculture Organization. • **Latest industrial data** refer to the most recent year for which manufacturing value added data at the three-digit level of the International Standard Industrial Classification (revision 2 or revision 3) are available in the United Nations Industrial Development Organization database. • **Latest trade data** show the most recent year for which structure of merchandise trade data from the United Nations Statistical Division's Commodity Trade (COMTRADE) database are available. • **Latest water withdrawal data** refer to the most recent year for which data have been compiled from a variety of sources. See *About the data* for table 3.5 for more information.

ABBREVIATIONS

Technical terms

AIDS	acquired immune deficiency syndrome
ARI	acute respitory infections
BOD	biochemical oxygen demand
CFC	chlorofluorocarbon
c.i.f.	cost, insurance, and freight
COMTRADE	United Nations Statistics Division's Commodity Trade database
CO$_2$	carbon dioxide
cu. m	cubic meter
DHS	Demographic and Health Survey
DMTU	dry metric ton unit
DOTS	directly observed treatment, short-course (strategy)
DPT	diphtheria, pertussis, and tetanus
DRS	World Bank's Debtor Reporting System
ESAF	Enhanced Structural Adjustment Facility
f.o.b.	free on board
GDP	gross domestic product
GEMS	Global Environment Monitoring System
GIS	geographic information system
GNI	gross national income (formerly referred to as gross national product)
ha	hectare
HIPC	heavily indebted poor country
HIV	human immunodeficiency virus
ICD	International Classification of Diseases
ICSE	International Classification of Status in Employment
ICT	information and communications technology
ISCED	International Standard Classification of Education
ISIC	International Standard Industrial Classification
ISP	Internet service provider
kg	kilogram
km	kilometer
kwh	kilowatt-hour
LIBOR	London interbank offered rate
LSMS	Living Standards Measurement Study
M1	narrow money (currency and demand deposits)
M2	money plus quasi money
M3	broad money or liquid liabilities
MICS	Multiple Indicator Cluster Survey
mmbtu	millions of British thermal units
mt	metric ton
MUV	manufactures unit value
NEAP	national environmental action plan
NGO	nongovernmental organization
NO$_2$	nitrogen dioxide
ODA	official development assistance
ORS	oral rehydration salts
PC	personal computer
PM10	particulate matter smaller than 10 microns
PPI	private participation in infrastructure
PPP	purchasing power parity
R&D	research and development
SDR	special drawing right
SITC	Standard International Trade Classification
SNA	System of National Accounts
SO$_2$	sulfur dioxide
sq. km	square kilometer
SSCI	Social Sciences Citation Indexes
STD	sexually transmitted disease
TB	tuberculosis
TEU	twenty-foot equivalent unit
TFP	total factor productivity
ton-km	metric ton-kilometers
TSP	total suspended particulates
TU	traffic unit
WITS	World Integrated Trade Solution

Organizations

ADB	Asian Development Bank
AfDB	African Development Bank
APEC	Asia Pacific Economic Cooperation
CDC	Centers for Disease Control and Prevention
CDIAC	Carbon Dioxide Information Analysis Center
CEC	Commission of the European Community
DAC	Development Assistance Committee of the OECD
EBRD	European Bank for Reconstruction and Development
EDF	European Development Fund
EFTA	European Free Trade Area
EIB	European Investment Bank
EMU	European Monetary Union
EU	European Union
Eurostat	Statistical Office of the European Communities
FAO	Food and Agriculture Organization
G-8	G-7 plus Russian Federation
GEF	Global Environment Facility
GTZ	Germany Technical Cooperation
IBRD	International Bank for Reconstruction and Development
ICAO	International Civil Aviation Organization
ICP	International Comparison Program
ICSID	International Centre for Settlement of Investment Disputes
IDA	International Development Association
IDB	Inter-American Development Bank
IDF	International Diabetes Federation
IEA	International Energy Agency
IFC	International Finance Corporation
IFS	International Financial Statistics
ILO	International Labour Organization
IMF	International Monetary Fund
IRF	International Road Federation
ITU	International Telecommunication Union
IUCN	World Conservation Union
MIGA	Multilateral Investment Guarantee Agency
NAFTA	North American Free Trade Agreement
NATO	North Atlantic Treaty Organization
NSF	National Science Foundation
OECD	Organisation for Economic Co-operation and Development
PARIS21	Partnership in Statistics for Development in the 21st Century
SCI	Institute for Scientific Information's Science Citation Index
SIPRI	Stockholm International Peace Research Institute
S&P	Standard & Poor's
UIP	Urban Indicators Programme
UIS	UNESCO Institute for Statistics
UN	United Nations
UNAIDS	Joint United Nations Programme on HIV/AIDS
UNCED	United Nations Conference on Environment and Development
UNCHS	United Nations Centre for Human Settlements (Habitat)
UNCTAD	United Nations Conference on Trade and Development
UNDP	United Nations Development Programme
UNECE	United Nations Economic Commission for Europe
UNEP	United Nations Environment Programme
UNESCO	United Nations Educational, Scientific, and Cultural Organization
UNFPA	United Nations Population Fund
UN-HABITAT	United Nations Human Settlements Program
UNHCR	United Nations High Commissioner for Refugees
UNICEF	United Nations Children's Fund
UNIDO	United Nations Industrial Development Organization
UNRISD	United Nations Research Institute for Social Development
UNSD	United Nations Statistics Division
USAID	U.S. Agency for International Development
WCMC	World Conservation Monitoring Centre
WFP	World Food Programme
WHO	World Health Organization
WIPO	World Intellectual Property Organization
WITSA	World Information Technology and Services Alliance
WTO	World Trade Organization
WWF	World Wildlife Fund

STATISTICAL METHODS

This section describes some of the statistical procedures used in preparing the World Development Indicators. It covers the methods employed for calculating regional and income group aggregates and for calculating growth rates, and it describes the World Bank's Atlas method for deriving the conversion factor used to estimate gross national income (GNI) and GNI per capita in U.S. dollars. Other statistical procedures and calculations are described in the About the data sections following each table.

Aggregation rules

Aggregates based on the World Bank's regional and income classifications of economies appear at the end of most tables. The countries included in these classifications are shown on the flaps on the front and back covers of the book. Most tables also include aggregates for the member countries of the European Monetary Union (EMU). Members of the EMU on 1 January 2004 were Austria, Belgium, Finland, France, Germany, Greece, Ireland, Italy, Luxembourg, the Netherlands, Portugal, and Spain. Other classifications, such as the European Union and regional trade blocs, are documented in About the data for the tables in which they appear.

Because of missing data, aggregates for groups of economies should be treated as approximations of unknown totals or average values. Regional and income group aggregates are based on the largest available set of data, including values for the 152 economies shown in the main tables, other economies shown in table 1.6, and Taiwan, China. The aggregation rules are intended to yield estimates for a consistent set of economies from one period to the next and for all indicators. Small differences between sums of subgroup aggregates and overall totals and averages may occur because of the approximations used. In addition, compilation errors and data reporting practices may cause discrepancies in theoretically identical aggregates such as world exports and world imports.

Five methods of aggregation are used in *World Development Indicators:*

- For group and world totals denoted in the tables by a *t,* missing data are imputed based on the relationship of the sum of available data to the total in the year of the previous estimate. The imputation process works forward and backward from 1995. Missing values in 1995 are imputed using one of several proxy variables for which complete data are available in that year. The imputed value is calculated so that it (or its proxy) bears the same relationship to the total of available data. Imputed values are usually not calculated if missing data account for more than a third of the total in the benchmark year. The variables used as proxies are GNI in U.S. dollars, total population, exports and imports of goods and services in U.S. dollars, and value added in agriculture, industry, manufacturing, and services in U.S. dollars.
- Aggregates marked by an *s* are sums of available data. Missing values are not imputed. Sums are not computed if more than a third of the observations in the series or a proxy for the series are missing in a given year.
- Aggregates of ratios are denoted by a *w* when calculated as weighted averages of the ratios (using the value of the denominator or, in some cases, another

indicator as a weight) and denoted by a *u* when calculated as unweighted averages. The aggregate ratios are based on available data, including data for economies not shown in the main tables. Missing values are assumed to have the same average value as the available data. No aggregate is calculated if missing data account for more than a third of the value of weights in the benchmark year. In a few cases the aggregate ratio may be computed as the ratio of group totals after imputing values for missing data according to the above rules for computing totals.

- Aggregate growth rates are denoted by a *w* when calculated as a weighted average of growth rates. In a few cases growth rates may be computed from time series of group totals. Growth rates are not calculated if more than half the observations in a period are missing. For further discussion of methods of computing growth rates see below.
- Aggregates denoted by an *m* are medians of the values shown in the table. No value is shown if more than half the observations for countries with a population of more than 1 million are missing.

Exceptions to the rules occur throughout the book. Depending on the judgment of World Bank analysts, the aggregates may be based on as little as 50 percent of the available data. In other cases, where missing or excluded values are judged to be small or irrelevant, aggregates are based only on the data shown in the tables.

Growth rates

Growth rates are calculated as annual averages and represented as percentages. Except where noted, growth rates of values are computed from constant price series. Three principal methods are used to calculate growth rates: least squares, exponential endpoint, and geometric endpoint. Rates of change from one period to the next are calculated as proportional changes from the earlier period.

Least-squares growth rate. Least-squares growth rates are used wherever there is a sufficiently long time series to permit a reliable calculation. No growth rate is calculated if more than half the observations in a period are missing. The least-squares growth rate, r, is estimated by fitting a linear regression trend line to the logarithmic annual values of the variable in the relevant period. The regression equation takes the form

$$\ln X_t = a + bt,$$

which is equivalent to the logarithmic transformation of the compound growth equation,

$$X_t = X_o (1 + r)^t.$$

In this equation X is the variable, t is time, and $a = \ln X_o$ and $b = \ln (1 + r)$ are parameters to be estimated. If b^* is the least-squares estimate of $b,$ then the average annual growth rate, *r*, is obtained as [exp(*b**) − 1] and is multiplied by 100 for expression as a percentage. The calculated growth rate is an average rate that is representative of the available observations over the entire period. It does not necessarily match the actual growth rate between any two periods.

Exponential growth rate. The growth rate between two points in time for certain demographic indicators, notably labor force and population, is calculated from the equation

$$r = \ln(p_n/p_0)/n,$$

where p_n and p_0 are the last and first observations in the period, *n* is the number of years in the period, and ln is the natural logarithm operator. This growth rate is based on a model of continuous, exponential growth between two points in time. It does not take into account the intermediate values of the series. Nor does it correspond to the annual rate of change measured at a one-year interval, which is given by $(p_n − p_{n-1})/p_{n-1}$.

Geometric growth rate. The geometric growth rate is applicable to compound growth over discrete periods, such as the payment and reinvestment of interest or dividends. Although continuous growth, as modeled by the exponential growth rate, may be more realistic, most economic phenomena are measured only at intervals, in which case the compound growth model is appropriate. The average growth rate over *n* periods is calculated as

$$r = \exp[\ln(p_n/p_0)/n] − 1.$$

Like the exponential growth rate, it does not take into account intermediate values of the series.

World Bank *Atlas* method

In calculating GNI and GNI per capita in U.S. dollars for certain operational purposes, the World Bank uses the *Atlas* conversion factor. The purpose of the *Atlas* conversion factor is to reduce the impact of exchange rate fluctuations in the cross-country comparison of national incomes.

The *Atlas* conversion factor for any year is the average of a country's exchange rate (or alternative conversion factor) for that year and its exchange rates for the two preceding years, adjusted for the difference between the rate of inflation in the country and that in Japan, the United Kingdom, the United States, and the Euro Zone. A country's inflation rate is measured by the change in its GDP deflator.

The inflation rate for Japan, the United Kingdom, the United States, and the Euro Zone, representing international inflation, is measured by the change in the SDR deflator. (Special drawing rights, or SDRs, are the International Monetary Fund's unit of account.) The SDR deflator is calculated as a weighted average of these countries' GDP deflators in SDR terms, the weights being the amount of each country's currency in one SDR unit. Weights vary over time because both the composition of the SDR and the relative exchange rates for each currency change. The SDR deflator is calculated in SDR terms first and then converted to U.S. dollars using the SDR to dollar *Atlas* conversion factor. The *Atlas* conversion factor is then applied to a country's GNI. The resulting GNI in U.S. dollars is divided by the midyear population to derive GNI per capita.

When official exchange rates are deemed to be unreliable or unrepresentative of the effective exchange rate during a period, an alternative estimate of the exchange rate is used in the *Atlas* formula (see below).

The following formulas describe the calculation of the *Atlas* conversion factor for year *t*:

$$e_t^* = \frac{1}{3}\left[e_{t-2}\left(\frac{p_t}{p_{t-2}} \Big/ \frac{p_t^{S\$}}{p_{t-2}^{S\$}} \right) + e_{t-1}\left(\frac{p_t}{p_{t-1}} \Big/ \frac{p_t^{S\$}}{p_{t-1}^{S\$}} \right) + e_t \right]$$

and the calculation of GNI per capita in U.S. dollars for year *t*:

$$Y_t^\$ = (Y_t/N_t)/e_t^*,$$

where e_t^* is the *Atlas* conversion factor (national currency to the U.S. dollar) for year *t*, e_t is the average annual exchange rate (national currency to the U.S. dollar) for year *t*, p_t is the GDP deflator for year *t*, $p_t^{S\$}$ is the SDR deflator in U.S. dollar terms for year *t*, $Y_t^\$$ is the *Atlas* GNI per capita in U.S. dollars in year *t*, Y_t is current GNI (local currency) for year *t*, and N_t is the midyear population for year *t*.

Alternative conversion factors

The World Bank systematically assesses the appropriateness of official exchange rates as conversion factors. An alternative conversion factor is used when the official exchange rate is judged to diverge by an exceptionally large margin from the rate effectively applied to domestic transactions of foreign currencies and traded products. This applies to only a small number of countries, as shown in *Primary data documentation*. Alternative conversion factors are used in the *Atlas* methodology and elsewhere in *World Development Indicators* as single-year conversion factors.

CREDITS

Credits

This book draws on a wide range of World Bank reports and numerous external sources, listed in the bibliography following this section. Many people inside and outside the World Bank helped in writing and producing *World Development Indicators*. The team would like to particularly acknowledge the help and encouragement of François Bourguignon, Senior Vice President and Chief Economist of the World Bank, and Shaida Badiee, Director, Development Data Group. The team is also grateful to those who provided valuable comments on the entire book. The poverty estimates were prepared by Shaohua Chen of the World Bank's Poverty Monitoring Group with help from Prem Sangraula and Johan Mistiaen. This note identifies those who made specific contributions. Numerous others, too many to acknowledge here, helped in many ways for which the team is extremely grateful.

1. World view

The introduction to section 1 was prepared by Eric Swanson with help from Amy Heyman, Johan Mistiaen, Sulekha Patel, and Saeed Ordoubadi. Valuable inputs came from Peter Ghys and Elizabeth Zaniewski at UNAIDS. Stimulating discussions with members of the UN Interagency and Expert Group on the MDGs are gratefully acknowledged. K. M. Vijayalakshmi prepared table 1.1. Yonas Biru prepared the estimates of gross national income in purchasing power parity terms. Tables 1.2, 1.3, and 1.5 were prepared by Vivienne Wang. Table 1.4 was prepared by Amy Heyman. The team is grateful to Joaquin Montes, Guy Karsenty, and Jurgen Richtering of the World Trade Organization for providing the trade indicators; Valeries Gaveeau at OECD for data on ODA; and to Luca Bandiera, Sona Varma, Dorte Domeland-Narvaez for reviewing the data on HIPC countries in table 1.4. Mariea Estela Rivero-Fuentes provided inputs to table 1.5.

2. People

Section 2 was prepared by Sulekha Patel and Vivienne Wang, in partnership with the World Bank's Human Development Network and the Development Research Group in the Development Economics Vice Presidency. Masako Hiraga and Mehdi Akhlaghi provided invaluable assistance in data and table preparation. Maria Estela Rivero-Fuentes wrote the introduction, with input from Sulekha Patel and Sarwar Lateef. The poverty estimates were prepared by Shaohua Chen of the World Bank's Poverty Monitoring Group with help from Prem Sangraula and Johan Mistiaen. Contributions were provided by Eduard Bos and Emi Suzuki (population, health, and nutrition); Montserrat Pallares-Miralles (vulnerability and security); Raymond Muhula, Laura Gregory, and Lianqin Wang (education); Lucia Fort and Maria Estela Rivero-Fuentes (gender) and Eldaw Abdalla Suliman (social indicators of poverty). Comments and suggestions at various stages of production came from Eric Swanson.

3. Environment

Section 3 was prepared by M. H. Saeed Ordoubadi and Mayhar Eshragh-Tabary in partnership with the World Bank's Environmentally and Socially Sustainable Development Network and in collaboration with the World Bank's Development Research Group and Transportation, Water, and Urban Development Department.

Important contributions were made by Christian Layke, Daniel Prager, and Robin White of the World Resources Institute, Ricardo Quercioli of the International Energy Agency, Edward Gillin of the Food and Agriculture Organization, Laura Battlebury of the World Conservation Monitoring Centre, Gerhard Metchies of GTZ, and Christine Auclair, Moses Ayiemba, Bildad Kagai, Guenter Karl, Pauline Maingi, and Markanley Rai of the Urban Indicators Programme, United Nations Centre for Human Settlements. Mehdi Akhlaghi managed the databases for this section. The World Bank's Environment Department and Rural Development Department devoted substantial staff resources to the book, for which the team is very grateful. M. H. Saeed Ordoubadi wrote the introduction to the section with valuable comments and input from Sarwar Lateef, Eric Swanson, Christine Kessides, Solly Angel and Micah Perlin and Bruce Ross-Larson, who also edited the text. Other contributions were made by Mahyar Eshragh-Tabary, Augusto Clavijo, Solly Angel and Micah Perlin (urban housing conditions); Susmita Dasgupta, Craig Meisner, Kiran Pandey, and David Wheeler (air and water pollution); and Giovanni Ruta and Kirk Hamilton (adjusted savings). Valuable comments and contributions were also provided by Deepak Kataria, Paul Wade, Rashid Aziz, Waqar Haider and Penelope J. Brook.

4. Economy

Section 4 was prepared by K. M. Vijayalakshmi in close collaboration with the Macroeconomic Data Team of the World Bank's Development Data Group, led by Soong Sup Lee. Eric Swanson and K. M. Vijayalakshmi wrote the introduction with valuable suggestions from Sarwar Lateef and Barbro Hexeberg. Contributions to the section were provided by Azita Amjadi (trade) and Ibrahim Levent (external debt). The national accounts data for low- and middle-income economies were gathered from the World Bank's regional staff through the annual Unified Survey. Maja Bresslauer, Victor Gabor, Sun Jung Park, and Soong Sup Lee worked on updating, estimating, and validating the databases for national accounts. The national accounts data for OECD countries were processed by Mehdi Akhlaghi. The team is grateful to Guy Karsenty and Andreas Maurer of the World Trade Organization and Sanja Blazevic, Arunas Butkevicius, and Lydia Lancia Conte of the United Nations Conference on Trade and Development, for providing data on trade in goods; to Tetsuo Yamada for help in obtaining the United Nations Industrial Development Organization database.

5. States and markets

Section 5 was prepared by David Cieslikowski in partnership with the World Bank's Private Sector Department, the Infrastructure Network, its Poverty Reduction and Economic Management Network, the International Finance Corporation, and external partners. Raymond Muhula, Murat Omur, and Juan Carlos Rodriguez provided invaluable assistance in data and table preparation. David Cieslikowski wrote the introduction to the section with valuable comments from Stephen Knack, Barbara Lee, Sarwar Lateef, and Eric Swanson. Other contributors include Ada Karina Izaguirre and Kathy Khuu (privatization and infrastructure projects); Mary Hallward-Driemeier (Investment climate) Simeon Djankov and Caralee McLeish (Business environment); Alka Banerjee and Isilay Cabuk (Standard & Poor's Global stock market indexes); Yonas Biru (purchasing power parity conversion factors); Esperanza Magpantay of the International Telecommunication Union (communications and information); Paul Amos, Marc Juhel, and Peter Roberts, (transport); Jane Degerlund of Containerisation International (ports); Ernesto Fernandez Polcuch of the United Nations Educational, Scientific and Cultural Organization Institute for Statistics (culture, research and development, researchers and technicians); Anders Halvorsen of the World Information Technology and Services Alliance; Terrence Taylor of the International Institute for Strategic Studies (military personnel); Bjorn Hagelin and Petter Stålenheim of the Stockholm International Peace Research Institute (military expenditures and arms transfers); and Lise McLeod of the World Intellectual Property Organization (patents data).

6. Global links
Section 6 was prepared by Amy Heyman in partnership with the World Bank's Development Research Group (trade) and external partners. Amy Heyman wrote the introduction in collaboration with Eric Swanson and Neil Fantom (remittances). Sarwar Lateef provided helpful comments. Substantial input came from Azita Amjadi, Jerzy Rozanski (tariffs), and Ibrahim Levent (financial data). Other contributors include Aaditya Matoo and Francis Ng (trade); Betty Dow (commodity prices); Eduard Bos, Bela Hovy and Christian Oxenball (UNHCR), Keiko Osaki, Thomas Buettner, and Francois Pelletier (UN Population Division), Cecile Thoreau (OECD) (migration); Brian Hammond, Yasmin Ahmad and Elena Bernaldo (OECD) (aid); Antonio Massieu and Teresa Ciller (World Tourism Organization) (tourism). Mehdi Akhlaghi provided valuable technical assistance.

Other parts
Preparation of the maps on the inside covers was coordinated by Jeff Lecksell of the World Bank's Map Design Unit. *Users guide* was prepared by David Cieslikowski. *Statistical methods* was written by Eric Swanson. *Primary data documentation* was coordinated by K. M. Vijayalakshmi, who served as database administrator. Estela Zamora assisted in updating the *Primary data documentation* table. Mehdi Akhlaghi was responsible for database updates and aggregation. *Acronyms and abbreviations* was prepared by Amy Heyman. *Partners* was prepared by Priya Pandya. The index was collated by Richard Fix and Gonca Okur.

Database management
Database management was coordinated by Mehdi Akhlaghi with the cross-team participation of Development Data Group staff to create an integrated World Development Indicators database. This database was used to generate the tables for World Development Indicators and related products such as *WDI Online, The Little Data Book, The Little Green Data Book,* and the *World Development Indicators* CD-ROM.

Design, production, and editing
Richard Fix, with the assistance of Gonca Okur, coordinated all stages of production with Communications Development Incorporated. Communications Development Incorporated provided overall design direction, editing, and layout, led by Meta de Coquereaumont and Bruce Ross-Larson. The editing and production team consisted of Joseph Costello, Christopher Trott, Timothy Walker, and Elaine Wilson. Communications Development's London partner, Grundy & Northedge, provided art direction and design. Staff from External Affairs oversaw printing and dissemination of the book.

Client services
The Development Data Group's Client Services Team (Azita Amjadi, Richard Fix, Gonca Okur, Priya Pandya, and William Prince) contributed to the design and planning of *World Development Indicators* and helped coordinate work with the Office of the Publisher.

Administrative assistance and office technology support
Estela Zamora provided administrative assistance and assisted in updating the databases. Jean-Pierre Djomalieu, Gytis Kanchas, Nacer Megherbi, and Shahin Outadi provided information technology support.

Publishing and dissemination
The Office of the Publisher, under the direction of Dirk Koehler, provided valuable assistance throughout the production process. Randi Park coordinated printing and supervised marketing and distribution. Chris Neal of the Development Economics Vice President's office and Carl Hanlon of External Affairs managed the communications strategy.

World Development Indicators CD-ROM
Programming and testing were carried out by Reza Farivari and his team: Azita Amjadi, Ying Chi, Ramgopal Erabelly, Nacer Megherbi, Gonca Okur, Shahin Outadi, and William Prince. Masako Hiraga produced the social indicators tables. William Prince coordinated user interface design and overall production and provided quality assurance. Photo credits: Curt Carnemark, Francis Dobbs, Julio Etchart, Tran Thi Hoa, Edwin Huffman, Anvar Ilyasov, Michael Mertaugh, Shehzad Noorani, Tomas Sennett, and Ray Witlin (World Bank). The interactive text was produced by Intermax, Inc.

WDI Online
Design, programming, and testing were carried out by Reza Farivari and his team: Mehdi Akhlaghi, Azita Amjadi, Saurabh Gupta, Gonca Okur, and Shahin Outadi. William Prince coordinated production and provided quality assurance. Cybele Arnaud and Triinu Tombak of the Office of the Publisher were responsible for implementation of *WDI Online* and management of the subscription service.

Client feedback
The team is grateful to the many people who have taken the time to provide comment on its publications. Their feedback and suggestions have helped improve this year's edition.

BIBLIOGRAPHY

AbouZahr, Carla. 2003. "Global Burden of Maternal Death and Disability." *British Medical Bulletin* 67 (December): 1–11.

AbouZahr, Carla, and Tessa Wardlaw. 2003. "Maternal Mortality in 2000: Estimates developed by WHO, UNICEF, and UNFPA."

Ahmad, Sultan. 1992. "Regression Estimates of Per Capita GDP Based on Purchasing Power Parities." Policy Research Working Paper 956. World Bank, International Economics Department, Washington, D.C.

———. 1994. "Improving Inter-Spatial and Inter-Temporal Comparability of National Accounts." *Journal of Development Economics* 44: 5375.

Alderman, Harold, Peter F. Orazem and Elizabeth Paterno. 2001. "School Quality, School Cost and the Public/Private School Choices of Low-Income Households in Pakistan." *Journal of Human Resources.* Vol. 36, pp. 304–326.

Ball, Nicole. 1984. "Measuring Third World Security Expenditure: A Research Note." *World Development* 12(2): 15764.

Barro, Robert J. 1991. "Economic Growth in a Cross-Section of Countries." *Quarterly Journal of Economics* 106(2): 40744.

Beck, Thorsten, and Ross Levine. 2001. "Stock Markets, Banks, and Growth: Correlation or Causality?" Policy Research Working Paper 2670. World Bank, Development Research Group, Washington, D.C.

Behrman, Jere R., and Mark R. Rosenzweig. 1994. "Caveat Emptor: Cross-Country Data on Education and the Labor Force." *Journal of Development Economics* 44: 14771.

Bhalla, Surjit. 2002. *Imagine There Is No Country: Poverty, Inequality, and Growth in the Era of Globalization.* Washington, D.C.: Institute for International Economics.

Bilsborrow, R.E., Graeme Hugo, A.S. Oberai and Hania Zlotnik. 1997. *International Migration Statistics.* Geneva: International Labour Office.

Bloom, David E., and Jeffrey G. Williamson. 1998. "Demographic Transitions and Economic Miracles in Emerging Asia." *World Bank Economic Review* 12(3): 41955.

Brown, Lester R., and others. 1999. *Vital Signs 1999: The Environmental Trends That Are Shaping Our Future.* New York and London: W. W. Norton for Worldwatch Institute.

Brown, Lester R., Christopher Flavin, Hilary F. French, and others. 1998. *State of the World 1998.* Washington, D.C.: Worldwatch Institute.

Brown, Lester R., Michael Renner, Christopher Flavin, and others. 1998. *Vital Signs 1998.* Washington, D.C.: Worldwatch Institute.

Bulatao, Rodolfo. 1998. *The Value of Family Planning Programs in Developing Countries.* Santa Monica, Calif.: Rand.

Caiola, Marcello. 1995. *A Manual for Country Economists.* Training Series 1, vol. 1. Washington, D.C.: International Monetary Fund.

Carr, Dara. 2004. "Improving the Health of the World's Poorest People." Health Bulletin No. 1. Population Reference Bureau, Washington, D.C.

Centro Latinoamericano de Demografia. *Boletín Demografico.* (various years). Santiago.

Chaudhury, Nazmul, Jeffrey S. Hammer, Michael Kremer, Karthik Muralidharan, and F. Halsey Rogers. 2004. "Teacher and Health Care Provider Absenteeism: A Multi-Country Study." World Bank, Washington, D.C.

Chen, Shaohua, and Martin Ravallion. 2004. "How Have the World's Poorest Fared Since the 1980s?" *World Bank Research Observer* 19(2): 141–69. World Bank, Development Research Group, Washington, D.C.

Collier, Paul, and David Dollar. 1999. "Aid Allocation and Poverty Reduction." Policy Research Working Paper 2041. World Bank, Development Research Group, Washington, D.C.

———. 2001. "Can the World Cut Poverty in Half? How Policy Reform and Effective Aid Can Meet the International Development Goals." Policy Research Working Paper 2403. World Bank, Development Research Group, Washington, D.C.

Commission of the European Communities, International Monetary Fund, Organisation for Economic Co-operation and Development, United Nations, and World Bank. 2002. *System of Environmental and Economic Accounts: SEEA 2000.* New York.

Containerisation International. 2005. *Containerisation International Yearbook 2005.* London.

Corrao, Marlo Ann, G. Emmanuel Guindon, Namita Sharma, and Donna Fakhrabadi Shokoohi, eds. 2000. *Tobacco Control Country Profiles.* Atlanta: American Cancer Society.

Deaton, Angus. 2002. "Counting the World's Poor: Problems and Possible Solutions." *World Bank Research Observer* 16(2): 12547.

Demirgüç-Kunt, Asli, and Enrica Detragiache. 1997. "The Determinants of Banking Crises: Evidence from Developed and Developing Countries." Working paper. World Bank and International Monetary Fund, Washington, D.C.

Demirgüç-Kunt, Asli, and Ross Levine. 1996a. "Stock Market Development and Financial Intermediaries: Stylized Facts." *World Bank Economic Review* 10(2): 291321.

———. 1996b. "Stock Markets, Corporate Finance, and Economic Growth: An Overview." *World Bank Economic Review* 10(2): 22339.

———. 1999. "Bank-Based and Market-Based Financial Systems: Cross-Country Comparisons." Policy Research Working Paper 2143. World Bank, Development Research Group, Washington, D.C.

de Onis, Mercedes, and Monika Blossner. 2000. "The WHO Global Database on Child Growth and Malnutrition: Methodology and Applications." *International Journal of Epidemiology* 32: 51826.

Development Committee. September 22, 2003. SecM2003-0370: "Supporting Sound Policies with Adequate and Appropriate Financing: Implementing the Monterrey Consensus at the Country Level."

DKT International. 1998. *1997 Contraceptive Social Marketing Statistics.* Washington, D.C.

Doyle, John J., and Gabrielle J. Persley, eds. 1996. *Enabling the Safe Use of Biotechnology: Principles and Practice.* Environmentally Sustainable Development Studies and Monographs Series, no. 10. Washington, D.C.: World Bank.

Drucker, Peter F. 1994. "The Age of Social Transformation." *Atlantic Monthly* 274 (November).

Easterly, William. 2000. "Growth Implosions, Debt Explosions, and My Aunt Marilyn: Do Growth Slowdowns Cause Public Debt Crises?" Policy Research Working Paper 2531. World Bank, Development Research Group, Washington, D.C.

Eurostat (Statistical Office of the European Communities). Various years. *Demographic Statistics.* Luxembourg.

———. Various years. *Statistical Yearbook.* Luxembourg.

Evenson, Robert E., and Carl E. Pray. 1994. "Measuring Food Production (with Reference to South Asia)." *Journal of Development Economics* 44: 17397.

Faiz, Asif, Christopher S. Weaver, and Michael P. Walsh. 1996. *Air Pollution from Motor Vehicles: Standards and Technologies for Controlling Emissions.* Washington, D.C.: World Bank.

Fankhauser, Samuel. 1995. *Valuing Climate Change: The Economics of the Greenhouse.* London: Earthscan.

FAO (Food and Agriculture Organization). 1986. "Inter-Country Comparisons of Agricultural Production Aggregates." Economic and Social Development Paper 61. Rome.

———. 1996. *Food Aid in Figures 1994.* Vol. 12. Rome.

———. 2003. *State of the World's Forests 2003.* Rome.

———. Various years. *Fertilizer Yearbook.* FAO Statistics Series. Rome.

———. Various years. *Production Yearbook.* FAO Statistics Series. Rome.

———. Various years. *The State of Food Insecurity in the World.* Rome.

———. Various years. *Trade Yearbook.* FAO Statistics Series. Rome.

Frankel, Jeffrey. 1993. "Quantifying International Capital Mobility in the 1990s." In Jeffrey Frankel, ed., *On Exchange Rates.* Cambridge, Mass.: MIT Press.

Frankhauser, Pierre. 1994. «Fractales, tissus urbains et reseaux de transport.» *Revue d'economie politique* 104: 43555.

Fredricksen, Birger. 1993. *Statistics of Education in Developing Countries: An Introduction to Their Collection and Analysis.* Paris: UNESCO.

Gallup, John L., and Jeffrey D. Sachs. 1998. "The Economic Burden of Malaria." Harvard Institute for International Development, Cambridge, Mass.

Gannon, Colin, and Zmarak Shalizi. 1995. "The Use of Sectoral and Project Performance Indicators in Bank-Financed Transport Operations." TWU Discussion Paper 21. World Bank, Transportation, Water, and Urban Development Department, Washington, D.C.

Gardner, Robert. 1998. "Education." Demographic and Health Surveys, Comparative Study 29. Macro International, Calverton, Md.

Gardner-Outlaw, Tom, and Robert Engelman. 1997. "Sustaining Water, Easing Scarcity: A Second Update." Population Action International, Washington, D.C.

Goldfinger, Charles. 1994. *L'utile et le futile: L'économie de l'immatériel.* Paris: Editions Odile Jacob.

GTZ (German Agency for Technical Cooperation). 2004. *Fuel Prices and Taxation.* Eschborn, Germany.

Gupta, Sanjeev, Hamid Davoodi, and Erwin Tiongson. 2000. "Corruption and the Provision of Health Care and Education Services." IMF Working Paper 00/116. International Monetary Fund, Washington, D.C.

Gupta, Sanjeev, Brian Hammond, and Eric Swanson. 2000. "Setting the Goals." *OECD Observer* (223): 1517.

Gwatkin, Davidson, and Michel Guillot. 2000. "The Burden of Disease among the Global Poor." Health, Nutrition, and Population Series. World Bank, Washington, D.C.

Habyarimana, James, Jishnu Das, Stefan Dercon, and Pramila Krishnan. 2003. "Sense and Absence: Absenteeism and Learning in Zambian Schools." World Bank, Washington, D.C.

Hamilton, Kirk, and Michael Clemens. 1999. "Genuine Savings Rates in Developing Countries." *World Bank Economic Review* 13(2): 33356.

Hanushek, Eric. 2002. *The Long-Run Importance of School Quality.* NBER Working Paper 9071. Cambridge, Mass.: National Bureau of Economic Research.

Happe, Nancy, and John Wakeman-Linn. 1994. "Military Expenditures and Arms Trade: Alternative Data Sources." IMF Working Paper 94/69. International Monetary Fund, Policy Development and Review Department, Washington, D.C.

Harrison, Ann. 1995. "Factor Markets and Trade Policy Reform." World Bank, Washington, D.C.

Hatzichronoglou, Thomas. 1997. "Revision of the High-Technology Sector and Product Classification." STI Working Paper 1997/2. OECD Directorate for Science, Technology, and Industry, Paris.

Heck, W. W. 1989. "Assessment of Crop Losses from Air Pollutants in the U.S." In J. J. McKenzie and M. T. El Ashry, eds., *Air Pollution's Toll on Forests and Crops.* New Haven, Conn.: Yale University Press.

Heston, Alan. 1994. "A Brief Review of Some Problems in Using National Accounts Data in Level of Output Comparisons and Growth Studies." *Journal of Development Economics* 44: 2952.

Hettige, Hemamala, Muthukumara Mani, and David Wheeler. 1998. "Industrial Pollution in Economic Development: Kuznets Revisited." Policy Research Working Paper 1876. World Bank, Development Research Group, Washington, D.C.

IEA (International Energy Agency). 2002. *World Energy Outlook: Energy and Poverty.* Paris.

———. Various years. *Energy Balances of OECD Countries.* Paris.

BIBLIOGRAPHY

————. Various years. *Energy Statistics and Balances of Non-OECD Countries.* Paris.

————. Various years. *Energy Statistics of OECD Countries.* Paris.

IFPRI (International Food Policy Research Institute). 1999. *Soil Degradation: A Threat to Developing-Country Food Security by 2020.* Washington, D.C.

ILO (International Labour Organization). Various years. *Key Indicators of the Labour Market.* Geneva: International Labour Office.

————. Various years. *Yearbook of Labour Statistics.* Geneva: International Labour Office.

IMF (International Monetary Fund). 1977. *Balance of Payments Manual.* 4th ed. Washington, D.C.

————. 1993. *Balance of Payments Manual.* 5th ed. Washington, D.C.

————. 1995. *Balance of Payments Compilation Guide.* Washington, D.C.

————. 1996a. *Balance of Payments Textbook.* Washington, D.C.

————. 2000. *Monetary and Financial Statistics Manual.* Washington, D.C.

————. 2001. *Government Finance Statistics Manual.* Washington, D.C.

————. 2004. *Annual Report on Exchange Arrangements and Exchange Restrictions, 2004.* Washington, D.C.

————. Various issues. *Direction of Trade Statistics.* Quarterly. Washington, D.C.

————. Various issues. *International Financial Statistics.* Monthly. Washington, D.C.

————. Various years. *Balance of Payments Statistics Yearbook.* Parts 1 and 2. Washington, D.C.

————. Various years. *Direction of Trade Statistics Yearbook.* Washington, D.C.

————. Various years. *Government Finance Statistics Yearbook.* Washington, D.C.

————. Various years. *International Financial Statistics Yearbook.* Washington, D.C.

IMF (International Monetary Fund), OECD (Organisation for Economic Co-operation and Development), United Nations, and World Bank. 2000. *A Better World for All: Progress towards the International Development Goals.* Washington, D.C.

International Civil Aviation Organization. *Civil Aviation Statistics of the World database.* Montreal.

International Institute for Strategic Studies. 2004. *The Military Balance 2004–2005.* London: Oxford University Press.

International Road Federation. 2004. *World Road Statistics 2004.* Geneva.

International Working Group of External Debt Compilers (Bank for International Settlements, International Monetary Fund, Organisation for Economic Co-operation and Development, and World Bank). 1987. *External Debt Definitions.* Washington, D.C.

Inter-Secretariat Working Group on National Accounts (Commission of the European Communities, International Monetary Fund, Organisation for Economic Co-operation and Development, United Nations, and World Bank). 1993. *System of National Accounts.* Brussels, Luxembourg, New York, and Washington, D.C.

IPCC (Intergovernmental Panel on Climate Change). 2001. *Climate Change 2001.* Cambridge: Cambridge University Press.

ITU (International Telecommunication Union). 2004. *World Telecommunication Indicators Database.* Geneva.

IUCN (World Conservation Union). 1998. *1997 IUCN Red List of Threatened Plants.* Gland, Switzerland.

————. 2000. *2000 IUCN Red List of Threatened Animals.* Gland, Switzerland.

Journal of Development Economics. 1994. Special issue on Database for Development Analysis. Edited by T. N. Srinivasan. Vol. 44, no. 1.

Knetter, Michael. 1994. *Why Are Retail Prices in Japan So High? Evidence from German Export Prices.* NBER Working Paper 4894. Cambridge, Mass.: National Bureau of Economic Research.

Kunte, Arundhati, Kirk Hamilton, John Dixon, and Michael Clemens. 1998. "Estimating National Wealth: Methodology and Results." Environmental Economics Series, no. 57. World Bank, Environment Department, Washington, D.C.

Lanjouw, Jean O., and Peter Lanjouw. 2001. "The Rural Non-Farm Sector: Issues and Evidence from Developing Countries." *Agricultural Economics* 26: 123.

La Porta, Rafael, Florencio Lopez-de-Silanes, Andrei Shleifer, and Robert W. Vishny. 1998. "Law and Finance." *Journal of Political Economy* 106(6): 1113–55.

Lanjouw, Peter, and Gershon Feder. 2001. *Rural Nonfarm Activities and Rural Development: From Experience toward Strategy.* Rural Strategy Discussion Paper 4. Washington, D.C.: World Bank.

Lewis, Karen K. 1995. "Puzzles in International Financial Markets." In Gene Grossman and Kenneth Rogoff, eds., *Handbook of International Economics.* Vol. 3. Amsterdam: North Holland.

Lewis, Stephen R., Jr. 1989. "Primary Exporting Countries." In Hollis Chenery and T. N. Srinivasan, eds., *Handbook of Development Economics.* Vol. 2. Amsterdam: North Holland.

Lovei, Magdolna. 1997. "Toward Effective Pollution Management." *Environment Matters* (fall): 5253.

Lucas, R. E. 1988. "On the Mechanics of Economic Development." *Journal of Monetary Economics* 22: 322.

Mani, Muthukumara, and David Wheeler. 1997. "In Search of Pollution Havens? Dirty Industry in the World Economy, 1960–95." World Bank, Policy Research Department, Washington, D.C.

McCarthy, F. Desmond, and Holger Wolf. 2001. "Comparative Life Expectancy in Africa." Policy Research Working Paper 2668. World Bank, Development Research Group, Washington, D.C.

Midgley, Peter. 1994. *Urban Transport in Asia: An Operational Agenda for the 1990s.* World Bank Technical Paper 224. Washington, D.C.

Morgenstern, Oskar. 1963. *On the Accuracy of Economic Observations.* Princeton, N.J.: Princeton University Press.

Morisset, Jacques. 2000. "Foreign Direct Investment in Africa: Policies Also Matter." Policy Research Working Paper 2481. World Bank, Washington, D.C.

National Science Foundation. 2004. *Science and Engineering Indicators 2004.* Arlington, Va.

Netcraft. 2004. *Netcraft Secure Server Survey.* [http://www.netcraft.com/].

NRI (National Research Institute) and World Bank. 2003. "Public Expenditure and Service Delivery in Papua New Guinea: Draft." Washington, D.C.

Obstfeldt, Maurice. 1995. "International Capital Mobility in the 1990s." In P. B. Kenen, ed., *Understanding Interdependence: The Macroeconomics of the Open Economy.* Princeton, N.J.: Princeton University Press.

Obstfeldt, Maurice, and Kenneth Rogoff. 1996. *Foundations of International Macroeconomics.* Cambridge, Mass.: MIT Press.

OECD (Organisation for Economic Co-operation and Development). 1985. *Measuring Health Care 1960–1983: Expenditure, Costs, Performance.* Paris.

———. 1996. *Trade, Employment, and Labour Standards: A Study of Core Workers' Rights and International Trade.* Paris.

———. 1997. *Employment Outlook.* Paris.

———. 2003. *Agricultural Policies in OECD Countries: Monitoring and Evaluation 2003.* Paris

———. Various issues. *Main Economic Indicators.* Monthly. Paris.

———. Various years. *International Development Statistics.* CD-ROM. Paris.

———. Various years. *National Accounts.* Vol. 1, *Main Aggregates.* Paris.

———. Various years. *National Accounts.* Vol. 2, *Detailed Tables.* Paris.

———. Various years. *Trends in International Migration: Continuous Reporting System on Migration.* Paris.

Organisation for Economic Co-operation and Development (OECD), Development Assistance Committee. Various years. *Development Cooperation.* Paris.

———. Various years. *Geographical Distribution of Financial Flows to Aid Recipients: Disbursements, Commitments, Country Indicators.* Paris.

O'Meara, Molly. 1999. "Reinventing Cities for People and the Planet." Worldwatch Paper 147. Worldwatch Institute, Washington, D.C.

Palacios, Robert, and Montserrat Pallares-Miralles. 2000. "International Patterns of Pension Provision." Social Protection Discussion Paper 0009. World Bank, Human Development Network, Washington, D.C.

Pandey, Kiran Dev, Katharine Bolt, Uwe Deichmann, Kirk Hamilton, Bart Ostro, and David Wheeler. 2003. "The Human Cost of Air Pollution: New Estimates for Developing Countries." World Bank, Development Research Group and Environment Department, Washington, D.C.

Pearce, David, and Giles Atkinson. 1993. "Capital Theory and the Measurement of Sustainable Development: An Indicator of Weak Sustainability." *Ecological Economics* 8: 10308.

Pilling, David. 1999. "In Sickness and in Wealth." *Financial Times,* 22 October.

Plucknett, Donald L. 1991. "Saving Lives through Agricultural Research." *Issues in Agriculture* (World Bank, Consultative Group on International Agricultural Research, Washington, D.C.) 16.

PricewaterhouseCoopers. 2004a. *Corporate Taxes 2004–2005: Worldwide Summaries.* New York.

———. 2004b. *Individual Taxes 2004–2005: Worldwide Summaries.* New York.

Rama, Martin, and Raquel Artecona. 2002. "A Database of Labor Market Indicators across Countries." World Bank, Development Research Group, Washington, D.C.

Ravallion, Martin, and Shaohua Chen. 1996. "What Can New Survey Data Tell Us about the Recent Changes in Living Standards in Developing and Transitional Economies?" World Bank, Policy Research Department, Washington, D.C.

Rodrik, Dani. 1996. "Labor Standards in International Trade: Do They Matter and What Do We Do About Them?" Overseas Development Council, Washington, D.C.

Romer, P. M. 1986. "Increasing Returns and Long-Run Growth." *Journal of Political Economy* 94: 100237.

Ruggles, Robert. 1994. "Issues Relating to the UN System of National Accounts and Developing Countries." *Journal of Development Economics* 44(1): 87102.

Ryten, Jacob. 1998. "Fifty Years of ISIC: Historical Origins and Future Perspectives." ECA/STAT.AC. 63/22. United Nations Statistics Division, New York.

Sala-i-Martin, Xavier. 2002. *The Disturbing 'Rise' in Global Income Inequality.* NBER Working Paper 8904. Cambridge, Mass.: National Bureau of Economic Research.

Shiklovanov, Igor. 1993. "World Fresh Water Resources." In Peter H. Gleick, ed., *Water in Crisis: A Guide to Fresh Water Resources.* New York: Oxford University Press.

Smith, Lisa and Laurence Haddad. 2000. *Overcoming Child Malnutrition in Developing Countries: Past Achievements and Future Choices.* International Food Policy Research Institute. Washington, D.C.

SIPRI (Stockholm International Peace Research Institute). 2004. *SIPRI Yearbook 2004: Armaments, Disarmament, and International Security.* Oxford: Oxford University Press.

Srinivasan, T. N. 1994. "Database for Development Analysis: An Overview." *Journal of Development Economics* 44(1): 328.

Standard & Poor's. 2000. *The S&P Emerging Market Indices Methodology, Definitions, and Practices.* New York.

———. 2004. *Global Stock Markets Factbook 2004.* New York.

Taylor, Alan M. 1996a. *International Capital Mobility in History: Purchasing Power Parity in the Long Run.* NBER Working Paper 5742. Cambridge, Mass.: National Bureau of Economic Research.

———. 1996b. *International Capital Mobility in History: The Saving-Investment Relationship.* NBER Working Paper 5743. Cambridge, Mass.: National Bureau of Economic Research.

UNACC/SCN (United Nations Administrative Committee on Co-ordination, Subcommittee on Nutrition). Various years. *Update on the Nutrition Situation.* Geneva.

BIBLIOGRAPHY

UNAIDS (Joint United Nations Programme on HIV/AIDS) and WHO (World Health Organization). 2004. *2004 Report on the Global AIDS Epidemic.* Geneva.

UNCTAD (United Nations Conference on Trade and Development). 2003. *The Least Developed Countries Report.* Geneva.

————. Various years. *Handbook of International Trade and Development Statistics.* Geneva.

UNEP (United Nations Environment Programme). 1991. *Urban Air Pollution.* Nairobi.

UNESCO (United Nations Educational, Scientific, and Cultural Organization). 1997. *International Standard Classification of Education.* Paris

UNESCO (United Nations Educational, Scientific, and Cultural Organization) Institute for Statistics. 2003. *Global Education Digest 2003.* Paris.

UNFCC (United Nations Framework Convention on Climate Change). 2005. *Kyoto Protocol.*

UN-HABITAT (United Nations Human Settlements Programme). 2003. *Global Report on Human Settlements.* Nairobi.

UNICEF (United Nations Children's Fund). (various years). *The State of the World's Children.* New York: Oxford University Press.

UNIDO (United Nations Industrial Development Organization). Various years. *International Yearbook of Industrial Statistics.* Vienna.

United Nations. 1947. *Measurement of National Income and the Construction of Social Accounts.* New York.

————. 1968. *A System of National Accounts: Studies and Methods.* Series F, no. 2, rev. 3. New York.

————. 1990. *International Standard Industrial Classification of All Economic Activities, Third Revision.* Statistical Papers Series M, no. 4, rev. 3. New York.

————. 1992. *Handbook of the International Comparison Programme.* Studies in Methods Series F, no. 62. New York.

————. 1993. *SNA Handbook on Integrated Environmental and Economic Accounting.* Statistical Office of the United Nations. Series F, no. 61. New York.

————. 1999. *Integrated Environmental and Economic Accounting: An Operational Manual.* Studies in Methods Series F, no. 78. New York.

————. 2000. *We the Peoples: The Role of the United Nations in the 21st Century.* New York.

————. 2004. *Trends in Total Migrant Stock: The 2003 Revision* (POP/DB/MIG/Rev.2003). Department of Economic and Social Affairs. New York.

United Nations Economic and Social Commission for Western Asia. 1997. *Purchasing Power Parities: Volume and Price Level Comparisons for the Middle East, 1993.* E/ESCWA/STAT/1997/2. Amman.

United Nations High Commissioner for Refugees. 2005. *Statistical Yearbook 2003* (forthcoming). Geneva.

United Nations Millennium Project. 2005. *Taking Action: Achieving Gender Equality and Empowering Women.* Task Force on Education and Gender Equality. London: Earthscan.

United Nations Population Division. 2002. *International Migration Report 2002.* New York.

————. 2003. *World Population Prospects: The 2004 Revision.* POP/DB/WPP/Rev. 2004/1/F10. Department of Economic and Social Affairs, New York.

————. 2004. *World Urbanization Prospects: The 2003 Revision.* New York.

————. Various years. *Levels and Trends of Contraceptive Use.* New York.

United Nations Statistics Division. 1985. *National Accounts Statistics: Compendium of Income Distribution Statistics.* New York.

————. Various issues. *Monthly Bulletin of Statistics.* New York.

————. Various years. *Energy Statistics Yearbook.* New York.

————. Various years. *International Trade Statistics Yearbook.* New York.

————. Various years. *National Accounts Statistics: Main Aggregates and Detailed Tables.* Parts 1 and 2. New York.

————. Various years. *National Income Accounts.* New York.

————. Various years. *Population and Vital Statistics Report.* New York.

————. Various years. *Statistical Yearbook.* New York.

U.S. Environmental Protection Agency. 1995. *National Air Quality and Emissions Trends Report 1995.* Washington, D.C.

Walsh, Michael P. 1994. "Motor Vehicle Pollution Control: An Increasingly Critical Issue for Developing Countries." World Bank, Washington, D.C.

Watson, Robert, John A. Dixon, Steven P. Hamburg, Anthony C. Janetos, and Richard H. Moss. 1998. *Protecting Our Planet, Securing Our Future: Linkages Among Global Environmental Issues and Human Needs.* A joint publication of the United Nations Environment Programme, U.S. National Aeronautics and Space Administration, and World Bank, Nairobi and Washington, D.C.

WCMC (World Conservation Monitoring Centre). 1992. *Global Biodiversity: Status of the Earth's Living Resources.* London: Chapman and Hall.

————. 1994. *Biodiversity Data Sourcebook.* Cambridge: World Conservation Press.

WHO (World Health Organization). 1983. *International Classification of Diseases.* 10th rev. Geneva.

————. 1997. *Coverage of Maternity Care.* Geneva.

————. 2002. *The Tobacco Atlas.* Geneva.

————. 2004a. *Beyond the Numbers: Reviewing Maternal Deaths and Complications to Make Pregnancy Safer.* Geneva.

————. 2004b. *Tobacco Control Country Profiles 2003.* Geneva.

————. 2004c. *World Report on Road Traffic Injury Prevention.* Geneva.

————. Various years. *Global Tuberculosis Control Report.* Geneva.

————. Various years. *World Health Report.* Geneva.

WHO (World Health Organization) and UNICEF (United Nations Children's Fund). 2003. *The Africa Malaria Report 2003.* Geneva.

WITSA (World Information Technology and Services Alliance). 2004. *Digital Planet 2004: The Global Information Economy.* Based on research by Global Insights. Vienna, Va.

Wolf, Holger C. 1997. *Patterns of Intra- and Inter-State Trade*. NBER Working Paper 5939. Cambridge, Mass.: National Bureau of Economic Research.

World Bank. 1990. *World Development Report 1990: Poverty*. New York: Oxford University Press.

———. 1992. *World Development Report 1992: Development and the Environment*. New York: Oxford University Press.

———. 1995. "China's GDP in U.S. Dollars, Based on Purchasing Power Parity." Policy Research Working Paper 1415. Washington, D.C.

———. 1996a. *Environment Matters* (summer). Environment Department, Washington, D.C.

———. 1996b. *Livable Cities for the 21st Century*. A Directions in Development book. Washington, D.C.

———. 1996c. *National Environmental Strategies: Learning from Experience*. Environment Department, Washington, D.C.

———. 1997a. *Can the Environment Wait? Priorities for East Asia*. Washington, D.C.

———. 1997b. *Expanding the Measure of Wealth: Indicators of Environmentally Sustainable Development*. Environmentally Sustainable Development Studies and Monographs Series, no. 17. Washington, D.C.

———. 1997c. *Rural Development: From Vision to Action*. Environmentally Sustainable Development Studies and Monographs Series, no. 12. Washington, D.C.

———. 1999a. *Fuel for Thought: Environmental Strategy for the Energy Sector*. Environment Department, Energy, Mining, and Telecommunications Department, and International Finance Corporation, Washington, D.C.

———. 1999b. *Greening Industry: New Roles for Communities, Markets, and Governments*. A World Bank Policy Research Report. New York: Oxford University Press.

———. 2000a. *Trade Blocs*. A World Bank Policy Research Report. New York: Oxford University Press.

———. 2000b. *World Development Report 2000/2001: Attacking Poverty*. New York: Oxford University Press.

———. 2002a. *A Case for Aid: Building a Consensus for Development Assistance*. Washington, D.C.

———. 2002b. *The Environment and the Millennium Development Goals*. Washington, D.C.

———. 2002c. *Financial Impact of the HIPC Initiative: First 24 Country Cases*. [http://www.worldbank.org/hipc].

———. 2002d. *Globalization, Growth, and Poverty: Building an Inclusive World Economy*. A World Bank Policy Research Report. New York: Oxford University Press.

———. 2002e. *Private Sector Development Strategy: Directions for the World Bank Group*. Private Sector Development Network, Washington, D.C.

———. 2002f. *World Development Report 2002: Building Institutions for Markets*. New York: Oxford University Press.

———. 2003a. "The Millennium Development Goals for Health: Rising to the Challenges." World Bank, Washington, D.C.

———. 2003b. *World Bank Atlas*. Washington, D.C.

———. 2003c. *World Development Report 2004: Making Services Work for the Poor*. New York: Oxford University Press.

———. 2004a. *Measuring Results: Improving National Statistics in IDA Countries*. International Development Association, Washington, D.C. (http://siteresources.worldbank.org/IDA/Resources/MeasuringResultsStatistics.pdf).

———. 2004b. *Partnerships in Development: Progress in the Fight against Poverty*. Washington, D.C.

———. 2004c. Private Participation in Infrastructure Project Database. (http://ppi.worldbank.org/).

———. 2004d. *World Bank Atlas*. Washington, D.C.

———. 2004e. *World Development Report 2005: A Better Investment Climate for Everyone*. New York: Oxford University Press.

———. 2005a. *Doing Business in 2005: Removing Obstacles to Growth* . Washington, D.C.: Copublication of the World Bank, the International Finance Corporation, and Oxford University Press.

———. 2005b. *World Development Report 2005: A Better Investment Climate for Everyone*. New York: Oxford University Press.

———. Various issues. *Global Commodity Markets*. Quarterly. Washington, D.C.

———. Various years. *Global Development Finance*. Washington, D.C. (Also available on CD-ROM.)

———. Various years. *Global Economic Prospects and the Developing Countries*. Washington, D.C.

———. Various years. *World Development Indicators*. Washington, D.C.

World Energy Council. 1995. *Global Energy Perspectives to 2050 and Beyond*. London.

World Intellectual Property Organization. 2004. *Industrial Property Statistics*. Publication A. Geneva.

World Resources Institute, UNEP (United Nations Environment Programme), UNDP (United Nations Development Programme), and World Bank. Various years. *World Resources: A Guide to the Global Environment*. New York: Oxford University Press.

World Tourism Organization. 2002a. *Compendium of Tourism Statistics 2002*. Madrid.

———. 2002b. *Yearbook of Tourism Statistics*. Vols. 1 and 2. Madrid.

WTO (World Trade Organization). Various years. *Annual Report*. Geneva.

INDEX OF INDICATORS

References are to table numbers.

INDEX OF INDICATORS

F

INDEX OF INDICATORS

H

I

INDEX OF INDICATORS

L

Labor force

Land area

Land use

Life expectancy at birth

Liquidity

Literacy

M

Malnutrition, in children under five

Mammals

Management time dealing with officials

Manufacturing

Market access to high-income countries

Merchandise

Migration

INDEX OF INDICATORS

INDEX OF INDICATORS

INDEX OF INDICATORS